Fourth Edition

INVESTMENTS

William F. Sharpe

Stanford University and Sharpe–Tint, Inc.

Gordon J. Alexander

University of Minnesota

PRENTICE HALL, Englewood Cliffs, New Jersey 07632

Library of Congress Cataloging-in-Publication Data

Sharpe, William F.
    Investments / William F. Sharpe, Gordon J. Alexander.—4th ed.
        p.   cm.
    ISBN 0–13–504382–4
    1. Investments.   2. Investment analysis.   I. Alexander, Gordon
J., 1947– .   II. Title.
HG4521.S48   1990
332.6—dc20
                                                            89–23158
                                                            CIP

Editorial/production supervision: Denise Gannon
Interior design: Jayne Conte and Maureen Eide
Cover design: Maureen Eide
Manufacturing buyer: Mary Ann Gloriande

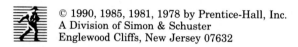 © 1990, 1985, 1981, 1978 by Prentice-Hall, Inc.
A Division of Simon & Schuster
Englewood Cliffs, New Jersey 07632

Printed in the United States of America

10 9 8 7 6 5 4 3 2

ISBN   0-13-504382-4

Prentice-Hall International (UK) Limited, *London*
Prentice-Hall of Australia Pty. Limited, *Sydney*
Prentice-Hall Canada Inc., *Toronto*
Prentice-Hall Hispanoamericana, S.A., *Mexico*
Prentice-Hall of India Private Limited, *New Delhi*
Prentice-Hall of Japan, Inc., *Tokyo*
Simon & Schuster Asia Pte. Ltd., *Singapore*
Editora Prentice-Hall do Brasil, Ltda., *Rio de Janeiro*

To Kathy
WFS

To my parents
GJA

BRIEF CONTENTS

CONTENTS

9 FACTOR MODELS AND ARBITRAGE PRICING THEORY 241

10 TAXES 268

18 OPTIONS 533

PREFACE

Not too many years ago, investments textbooks were devoted to discussions of the art of security analysis and the institutional features of how security markets functioned. Readers were introduced to the mysteries of accounting, some of the details of major industries, and various rules of thumb for selecting "good" and "bad" securities. Security markets were discussed in terms of the mechanics of how organized exchanges and over-the-counter markets functioned. However, a framework for understanding why security prices were at certain levels and why they changed over time was typically not provided.

Harry Markowitz published seminal articles and a book on portfolio theory in the 1950s. His work provided a way to methodically deal with security risk and return. Subsequently, the original Capital Asset Pricing Model was developed by one of the present authors (WFS), along with John Lintner and Jan Mossin, in the 1960s. Later, in the 1970s, Fischer Black and Myron Scholes published articles on the pricing of options. Most recently, Stephen Ross has published articles that develop the Arbitrage Pricing Theory, which provides additional insights into asset pricing. With this array of theories, it is now possible to approach the field of investments in a rigorous manner.

Unlike many fields, investments is blessed with a wealth of quantitative data that allow theories to be subjected to empirical tests. Early investigations suggested that the theories conformed reasonably well with reality. A few deviations were found, but they were accommodated by extending the basic theories. In general, it was felt that security markets were efficient, meaning that security prices seemed to fully reflect all publicly available information and that only luck or inside information would allow an investor to make abnormally high returns.

However, recent empirical work has cast some doubt on these early views. In particular, the statistical tests have been found to be relatively weak, meaning they may have been unable to identify important disparities between theory and reality. Furthermore, systematic "anomalies" have been

found that seem to be inconsistent with the theories. In addition, some scholars now believe that stock prices have been more volatile (with Black Monday and Terrible Tuesday, October 19–20, 1987, being prime examples) than any existing theory would suggest. Indeed, there is a view held in some quarters that investors tend to overreact to news, particularly bad news, which often causes market prices to deviate from "fair" values.

In reaction to these findings, investigators have turned their attention to developing more rigorous tests. For example, some have focused on identifying the factors that determine security returns. Others have attempted to determine if these findings can be reconciled with extended versions of certain theories. In summary, the field of investments is still in the midst of a revolution that began with Markowitz.

This book is intended to provide the reader with an understanding of the investment environment and process. The investment environment includes the kinds of marketable securities that exist and where and how they are bought and sold. The investment process is concerned with certain decisions an investor has to make. These decisions concern how much to invest in each security and when to make these investments. Thus, the book contains discussions of stocks, bonds, and other securities such as options and futures. Furthermore, the theories of Markowitz, Sharpe, Lintner, Mossin, Black, Scholes, and Ross are presented.

Some people will wonder how *Investments* compares with the recently published *Fundamentals of Investments* that we have also written. Both books are intended to be comprehensive, covering the major features and theories of investing in the current economy, while avoiding excessive detail. Furthermore, both books contain a glossary of terms that have been introduced earlier, and both books have supplements that include an instructor's manual and software.

However, the books are dissimilar in two significant ways. First, they are organized differently. *Investments* is written in an integrated fashion, while *Fundamentals* is more modular in design.

Second, *Investments* is somewhat more theoretical and technical than *Fundamentals*. For example, *Investments* discusses extended versions of the CAPM in Chapter 8, testing of asset pricing theories in Chapter 9, federal estate and gift taxation in Chapter 10, factor models of stock returns in Chapter 15, the binomial option pricing model in Chapter 18, and additional methods of evaluating portfolio performance in Chapter 23. These topics are either not discussed or discussed in less detail in *Fundamentals*.

Consequently, *Investments* is intended primarily for MBA students while *Fundamentals* is designed to appeal to both advanced undergraduates and MBAs. Readers of either book are expected to have some basic knowledge of economics, statistics, and accounting.

This edition of *Investments* differs in two significant ways from the previous edition. First, the coverage has been expanded. The part of the book devoted to asset pricing models has an additional chapter, thereby allowing for more in-depth presentation of the portfolio selection problem as well as the solutions that were developed by Markowitz and Tobin. Furthermore,

the chapter on bond prices and yields has been divided into two chapters so as to provide a more extensive discussion of bond analysis and portfolio management.

Besides adding these two new chapters, the discussions in some of the other chapters have been expanded. For example, there is an increased discussion of margin purchasing and short selling in Chapter 2, term structure in Chapter 4, empirical regularities in Chapter 15, dividend discount models in Chapter 16, put options in Chapter 18, and risk tolerance in Chapter 22.

The second major change between this edition and the previous one has to do with updating the coverage. Besides updating the figures and tables, the current edition discusses, for example, the National Market System of NASDAQ in Chapter 2, the Tax Reform Act of 1986 in Chapter 10, coupon stripping by the Treasury Department in Chapter 12, Americus trust securities in Chapter 15, the triple-witching hour in Chapter 19, and American Depository Receipts in Chapter 24.

Many people have provided us with assistance in preparing this book, and we would like to acknowledge their help. Accordingly, we would like to thank Seth Anderson, Jeffrey Born, James Conley, Thomas Eyssell, Joseph Finnerty, Robert Jennings, Linda Kramer, Jaroslaw Komarynsky, K. C. Ma, S. Maheswaren, Carl McGowan, Ronald Melicher, Tom Nohel, Thomas O'Brien, Sailesh Ramamurtie, Anthony Sanders, Arlene Spiegel, Leonard Washko, and J. Kenton Zumwalt for their help at various stages in preparing this book for publication. Special appreciation is due to Jeffrey Bailey for his comments on the manuscript and preparation of the end-of-chapter questions and problems and the glossary. We are also especially grateful for the efforts of six people at Prentice Hall: finance editor, Scott Barr; copy editor, Linda Thompson; production editor, Denise Gannon; designers, Jayne Conte and Maureen Eide; and marketing manager, Gary June.

We learned a lot by writing this book, and hope that you will learn a lot by reading it. While we believe that the book is free of errors of any sort, experience tells us that this might not be the case. Thus, we encourage anybody with constructive comments to send them to us.

WFS
GJA

ABOUT THE AUTHORS

GORDON J. ALEXANDER

Gordon J. Alexander is presently the IDS Professor of Finance at the University of Minnesota. Dr. Alexander has published articles in the *Journal of Finance, Journal of Financial Economics, Journal of Financial and Quantitative Analysis, Journal of Banking and Finance, Financial Management*, and the *Journal of Portfolio Management*. In addition, he is currently an Associate Editor for the *Journal of Financial and Quantitative Analysis*, as well as the Book Review Editor of the *Journal of Finance*. Dr. Alexander received his Ph.D. in Finance, M.A. in Mathematics, and M.B.A. from the University of Michigan, and his B.S. in Business Administration from the State University of New York at Buffalo.

WILLIAM F. SHARPE

William F. Sharpe is currently Timken Professor of Finance at the Stanford University Graduate School of Business. Dr. Sharpe has published articles in a number of professional journals, including *Management Science, Journal of Business, Journal of Finance, Journal of Financial Economics, Journal of Financial and Quantitative Analysis*, and the *Journal of Portfolio Management*. Dr. Sharpe is a past President of the American Finance Association, and founder of Sharpe-Tint, Inc., an investment management firm specializing in asset allocation. He received his A.B., M.A., and Ph.D. degrees in Economics from the University of California at Los Angeles.

Chapter 1

INTRODUCTION

This book is about investing in marketable securities. Accordingly, it focuses on the investment environment and process. The *investment environment* encompasses the kinds of marketable securities that exist and where and how they are bought and sold. The *investment process* is concerned with how an investor should proceed in making decisions about marketable securities in which to invest, how extensive the investments should be, and when the investments should be made. Before discussing the investment environment and process in more detail, the term *investment* will be described.

Investment, in its broadest sense, means the sacrifice of certain present value for (possibly uncertain) future value. Two different attributes are generally involved: time and risk. The sacrifice takes place in the present and is certain. The reward comes later, if at all, and the magnitude is generally uncertain. In some cases the element of time predominates (for example, government bonds). In other cases risk is the dominant attribute (for example, call options on common stocks). In yet others, both time and risk are important (for example, shares of common stock).

A distinction is often made between investment and *savings*. Savings is defined as foregone consumption; investment is restricted to "real" investment of the sort that increases national output in the future. Although this definition may prove useful in other contexts, it is not especially helpful here. However, it is useful to make a distinction between real and financial investments.

Real investments generally involve some kind of tangible asset, such as land, machinery, or factories. *Financial investments* involve contracts written on pieces of paper, such as stocks and bonds. In primitive economies most investment is of the real variety. However, in a modern economy, much investment is of the financial variety. Highly developed institutions for financial investment greatly facilitate real investment. By and large, the two forms of investment are complementary, not competitive.

The financing of an apartment house provides a good example. Apartments are sufficiently tangible ("bricks and mortar") to be considered real investment. But from where do the resources come to pay for the land and the construction of the apartments? Some may come from direct investment— for example, a wealthy doctor who wants to build an apartment house may

1

use some of his or her money to finance the project. The rest of the resources may be provided by a mortgage. In essence, someone loans money to the doctor, with repayment promised in fixed amounts on a specified schedule over many years. In the typical case the "someone" is not a person but an institution acting as a financial intermediary. Thus, the doctor has made a real investment in the apartment house, and the institution has made a financial investment in the doctor.

As a second example, consider what happens when General Motors finds itself in need of money to pay for plant construction. This real investment may be financed by the sale of new common stock in the *primary market* for securities. The common stock itself represents a financial investment to the purchasers, who may subsequently trade these shares in the *secondary market* (for example, on the New York Stock Exchange). Although transactions in the secondary market do not generate money for General Motors, the fact that such a market exists makes the common stock more attractive and thus facilitates real investment. Investors would pay less for new shares of common stock if there were no subsequent way to sell them quickly and inexpensively.

These examples have introduced the three main elements of the investment environment—*securities* (also known as financial investments or financial assets), *security markets* (also known as financial markets), and *financial intermediaries* (also known as financial institutions). They are discussed in more detail next.

1.1 THE INVESTMENT ENVIRONMENT

☐ 1.1.1 Securities

When someone borrows money from a pawnbroker, he or she must leave some item of value as *security*. Failure to repay the loan (plus interest) means that the pawnbroker can sell the pawned item to recover the amount of the loan (plus interest) and perhaps make a profit. The terms of the agreement are recorded via pawn tickets. When a college student borrows money to buy a car, the lender usually holds formal title to the car until the loan is repaid. In the event of default, the lender can repossess the car and attempt to sell it to recover his or her costs. In this case the official certificate of title, issued by the state, serves as the security for the loan.

When someone borrows money for a vacation, he or she may simply sign a piece of paper promising repayment with interest. The loan is unsecured in the sense that there is no collateral, meaning no specific asset has been promised to the lender in the event of default. In such a situation, the lender would have to take the borrower to court to try to recover the amount of the loan. Only a piece of paper, called a *promissory note*, stands as evidence of such a loan.

When a firm borrows money, it may or may not offer collateral. For example, some loans may be secured (backed) with specific pieces of property (buildings, equipment, and so on). Such loans are recorded by means of

mortgage bonds, which indicate the terms of repayment and the particular assets pledged to the lender in the event of default. However, it is much more common for a corporation simply to pledge all its assets, perhaps with some provision for the manner in which the division will take place in the event of default. Such a promise is known as a *debenture bond*.

Finally, a firm may promise a right to share in the firm's profits in return for an investor's funds. Nothing is pledged, and no irrevocable promises are made. The firm simply pays whatever its directors deem reasonable from time to time. However, to protect against serious malfeasance, the investor is given the right to participate in the determination of who will be members of the board of directors. His or her property right is represented by a share of common stock, which can be sold to someone else who will then be able to exercise that right. The holder of common stock is said to be an owner of the corporation and can, in theory, exercise control over its operation through the board of directors.

In general, only a piece of paper represents the investor's rights to certain prospects or property and the conditions under which he or she may exercise those rights. This piece of paper, serving as evidence of property rights, is called a *security*. It and with it, all its rights and conditions, may be transferred to another investor. Thus, everything from a pawn ticket to a share of GM common stock is a security. Hereafter the term *security* will be used to refer to *a legal representation of the right to receive prospective future benefits under stated conditions*. The task of *security analysis* is to identify mispriced securities by determining these prospective future benefits, the conditions under which they will be received, and the likelihood of such conditions.

By and large the focus here is on securities that may be easily and efficiently transferred from one owner to another. Thus, the concern is with stocks and bonds rather than with pawn tickets, although much of the material in this book applies to all three types of instruments.

Figure 1.1 and Table 1.1 show the year-by-year results obtained from investing in four types of securities over the 61-year period from 1926 through 1986. In each case the percentage change in a hypothetical investor's wealth from the beginning to the end of the year is shown. This amount, known as the *rate of return* (or simply the return), is calculated as follows:

$$\text{Return} = \frac{\text{end-of-period wealth} - \text{beginning-of-period wealth}}{\text{beginning-of-period wealth}} \quad \text{(1.1)}$$

In calculating the return on a security, it can be assumed that the investor purchased one unit (for example, one bond or one share of common stock) of the security at the beginning of the period. The cost of such an investment would be the value entered in the denominator of equation (1.1). Then, the value in the numerator is the answer to a simple question—how much better (or worse) off is the investor at the end of the period if, hypothetically speaking, this investment had been made at the beginning of the period?

For example, assume that Widget Corporation's common stock was selling for $40 per share at the beginning of 1987 and for $45 at the end of

Annual Returns, 1926–1986

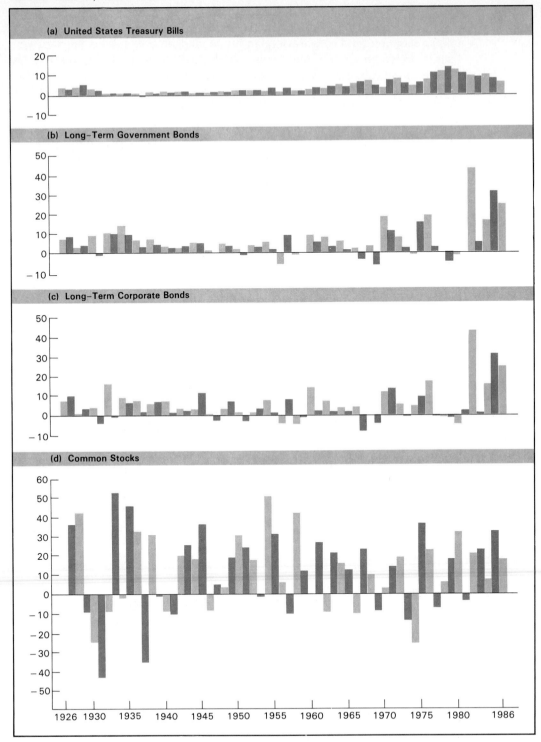

FIGURE 1–1
Annual returns, 1926–1986.

SOURCE: Roger Ibbotson and Rex A. Sinquefield, *Stocks, Bonds, Bills, and Inflation: 1926–1982* (Charlottesville, Va; Financial Analysts Research Foundation, 1983); Ibbotson Associates, *1987 Yearbook* (Chicago: 1987).

TABLE 1.1

Annual Returns: Stocks, Bonds, and Treasury Bills
and Changes in the Consumer Price Index.

		TOTAL RETURNS			
Year	Treasury Bills	Long-Term Government Bonds	Long-Term Corporate Bonds	Stocks	Change in the Consumer Price Index
1926	3.27%	7.77%	7.37%	11.62%	−1.49%
1927	3.12	8.93	7.44	37.49	−2.08
1928	3.24	.10	2.84	43.61	−.97
1929	4.75	3.42	3.27	−8.42	.19
1930	2.41	4.66	7.98	−24.90	−6.03
1931	1.07	−5.31	−1.85	−43.34	−9.52
1932	.96	16.84	10.82	−8.19	−10.30
1933	.30	.08	10.38	53.99	.51
1934	.16	10.02	13.84	−1.44	2.03
1935	.17	4.98	9.61	47.67	2.99
1936	.18	7.51	6.74	33.92	1.21
1937	.31	.23	2.75	−35.03	3.10
1938	−.02	5.53	6.13	31.12	−2.78
1939	.02	5.94	3.97	−.41	−.48
1940	.00	6.09	3.39	−9.78	.96
1941	.06	.93	2.73	−11.59	9.72
1942	.27	3.22	2.60	20.34	9.29
1943	.35	2.08	2.83	25.90	3.16
1944	.33	2.81	4.73	19.75	2.11
1945	.33	10.73	4.08	36.44	2.25
1946	.35	−.10	1.72	−8.07	18.17
1947	.50	−2.63	−2.34	5.71	9.01
1948	.81	3.40	4.14	5.50	2.71
1949	1.10	6.45	3.31	18.79	−1.80
1950	1.20	.06	2.12	31.71	5.79
1951	1.49	−3.94	−2.69	24.02	5.87
1952	1.66	1.16	3.52	18.37	.88
1953	1.82	3.63	3.41	−.99	.62
1954	.86	7.19	5.39	52.62	−.50
1955	1.57	−1.30	.48	31.56	.37
1956	2.46	−5.59	−6.81	6.56	2.86
1957	3.14	7.45	8.71	−10.78	3.02
1958	1.54	−6.10	−2.22	43.36	1.76
1959	2.95	−2.26	−.97	11.95	1.50
1960	2.66	13.78	9.07	.47	1.48
1961	2.13	.97	4.82	26.89	.67
1962	2.73	6.89	7.95	−8.73	1.22
1963	3.12	1.21	2.19	22.80	1.65
1964	3.54	3.51	4.77	16.48	1.19
1965	3.93	.71	−.46	12.45	1.92
1966	4.76	3.65	.20	−10.06	3.35
1967	4.21	−9.19	−4.95	23.98	3.04
1968	5.21	−.26	2.57	11.06	4.72
1969	6.58	−5.08	−8.09	−8.50	6.11
1970	6.53	12.10	18.37	4.01	5.49
1971	4.39	13.23	11.01	14.31	3.36
1972	3.84	5.68	7.26	18.98	3.41
1973	6.93	−1.11	1.14	−14.66	8.80
1974	8.00	4.35	−3.06	−26.47	12.20
1975	5.80	9.19	14.64	37.20	7.01
1976	5.08	16.75	18.65	23.84	4.81
1977	5.12	−.67	1.71	−7.18	6.77

5

TABLE 1.1 (*Continued*)

		TOTAL RETURNS			
Year	Treasury Bills	Long-Term Government Bonds	Long-Term Corporate Bonds	Stocks	Change in the Consumer Price Index
1978	7.18	−1.16	−.07	6.56	9.03
1979	10.38	−1.22	−4.18	18.44	13.31
1980	11.24	−3.95	−2.62	32.42	12.40
1981	14.71	1.85	−.96	−4.91	8.94
1982	10.54	40.35	43.79	21.41	3.87
1983	8.80	.68	4.70	22.51	3.80
1984	9.85	15.43	16.39	6.27	3.95
1985	7.72	30.97	30.90	32.16	3.77
1986	6.17	24.44	19.85	18.47	1.13
Average:	3.51	4.71	5.33	12.12	3.14
Std. dev.:	3.34	8.48	8.44	21.04	4.84

SOURCE: Roger G. Ibbotson and Rex A. Sinquefield, *Stocks, Bonds, Bills and Inflation, 1926–1982* (Charlottesville, Va.: Financial Analysts Research Foundation, 1983); Ibbotson Associates, *1987 Yearbook* (Chicago: 1987).

1987 and paid dividends of $3 per share during the year. The 1987 return on Widget would then be calculated as [($45 + $3) − $40]/$40 = .20, or 20%.[1]

Treasury Bills

The first type of security listed in Figure 1.1 involves loaning money on a short-term basis to the U.S. Treasury Department.[2] Such a loan carries little (if any) risk that payment will not be made as promised. Moreover, while the rate of return varies from period to period, at the beginning of any single period it is known with certainty. The return on these investments, known as Treasury bills, ranged from a high of 14.71% per year (in 1981) to a low of virtually zero (in 1940), with an average value of 3.51% during the entire 61-year period.

The second and third types of securities shown in Figure 1.1 involve the purchase of bonds and thus also involve loaning money. Each type of bond represents a fairly long-term commitment on the part of the issuer (that is, the borrower) to the investor (that is, the lender). This commitment is to make cash payments each year (the coupon amount) up to some point in time (the maturity date), when a single final cash payment (the principal)

---

[1] Generally, any cash received during the period is treated as if it were received at the end of the period. However, as will be shown in Chapter 5, assuming it is received at the end of the period typically understates the actual return. For example, if the dividends on Widget were received at midyear, the investor could have put them in a bank savings account and earned, for example, 5% interest on them for the rest of the year. This interest then would have amounted to .05 × $3.00 = $.15, resulting in the annual return being equal to [($45 + $3 + $.15) − $40]/$40 = .20375, or 20.375%.

[2] For more details on this security as well as the others, see Roger G. Ibbotson and Rex A. Sinquefield, *Stocks, Bonds, Bills and Inflation, 1926–1982* (Charlottesville, Va.: Financial Analysts Research Foundation, 1983), 7–12.

will also be made. The amount for which such bonds can be bought and sold varies from time to time. Thus, while coupon payments are easily predicted, the end-of-period selling price of the security is quite uncertain at the beginning of the period, making it difficult to predict the return in advance.

Long-Term Bonds

The second type of security (long-term government bonds, also known as Treasury bonds) involves 20-year loans to the U.S. Treasury Department. The third type of security (long-term corporate bonds), simply called corporate bonds, involves 20-year loans to high-quality U.S. corporations. To date, both types of bonds had their highest annual return in 1982, reaching 40.35% for government bonds and 43.79% for corporate bonds. However, the lowest annual return was reached in different years. For government bonds, the lowest return occurred in 1967 (-9.19%) whereas the lowest return for corporate bonds was reached in 1969 (-8.09%). Note that on average, government bonds had a higher return than Treasury bills (4.71% > 3.51%) and corporate bonds had a higher return than government bonds (5.33% > 4.71%). Thus, whereas the second and third types of securities have considerable variability, on average they provide somewhat larger returns than Treasury bills.

Common Stocks

The fourth and final type of security involves the purchase of a group of common stocks, each of which represents a commitment on the part of a corporation to pay periodically whatever its board of directors deems appropriate as a cash dividend. Although the amount of cash dividends to be paid in a year is subject to some uncertainty, it is relatively predictable. However, the amount for which a stock can be bought or sold varies considerably from time to time, making the annual return highly unpredictable. Figure 1.1 shows the return from a portfolio of stocks (currently 500 different firms) selected by Standard & Poor's Corporation to represent the average performance of common stocks. Returns ranged from an exhilarating 53.99% in 1933 to a depressing -43.34% in 1931 and averaged 12.12% per year over the entire period. Such investments can provide substantial returns, being even larger on the average than the returns provided by corporate bonds. However, they also have substantial variability, being even more volatile than either type of long-term bond.

Table 1.1 provides year-by-year annual returns for the four types of securities shown in Figure 1.1. The table also includes the annual percentage change in the Consumer Price Index as an indicator of variations in the cost of living. Average annual returns are shown at the bottom of the table. Below these values are the values of the standard deviations of annual returns, which serve as measures of the variability of the returns on the respective securities.[3] The historical record revealed in Figure 1.1 and Table 1.1 illus-

---

[3] Standard deviation was calculated as being equal to the square root of $\Sigma_{t=1}^{61} (r_t - \bar{r})^2/60$, where r_t is the return for year t ($t = 1$ corresponds to 1926, $t = 2$ to 1927, and so on) and $\bar{r}$ is the average return over the 61-year period. A larger standard deviation means a greater amount of dispersion in the 61 returns and hence indicates more risk.

trates a general principle: *When sensible investment strategies are compared with one another, risk and return tend to go together*. That is, securities that have higher average returns tend to have greater amounts of risk.

It is important to note that historical variability is not necessarily an indication of prospective risk. The former deals with the record over some past period; the latter has to do with uncertainty about the future. The pattern of returns on Treasury bills provides one example. Although the values have varied from period to period, in any given period the amount to be earned is known in advance and is thus riskless. On the other hand, the annual return on a common stock is very difficult to predict. For such an investment, variability in the past may provide a fairly good measure of the uncertainty surrounding the future return.

To see how difficult it is to predict common stock returns, cover the portion on Table 1.1 from 1941 on and then try to guess the return in 1941. Having done this, uncover the value for 1941 and try to guess the return for 1942. Proceed in this manner a year at a time, keeping track of your overall predictive accuracy. Unless you are very clever or very lucky, you will conclude that the past pattern of stock returns provides little help in predicting next year's return. It will be seen that this is a characteristic of an *efficient market*—that is, a market where security prices reflect information immediately. At this stage, it is enough to indicate that the past variability of stock returns can be taken as a rough approximation of future risk.

Is one of these four types of securities obviously "the best"? No. To oversimplify, the right security or combination of securities depends on the ultimate beneficiary's situation and preferences for return relative to his or her distaste for risk. There may be right or wrong securities for a particular person or purpose. But it would be surprising indeed to find a security that is clearly wrong for everyone and every purpose. Such situations are simply not present in an efficient market.

☐ 1.1.2 Security Markets

Security markets exist in order to bring together buyers and sellers of securities, meaning they are mechanisms that exist in order to facilitate the exchange of financial assets. There are many ways in which they can be analyzed. One way has already been mentioned—primary and secondary financial markets. Here the key distinction was whether or not the securities were being offered for sale by the issuer. Interestingly, the primary market itself can be subdivided into seasoned and unseasoned new issues. A *seasoned* new issue refers to the offering of an additional amount of an already existing security, whereas an *unseasoned* new issue involves the initial offering of a security to the public. Unseasoned new issues are often referred to as initial public offerings, or ipo's.

Another way of distinguishing security markets involves the life span of financial assets. *Money markets* typically involve financial assets that have a life span of one year or less, whereas *capital markets* typically involve

financial assets that have a life span greater than one year. Thus, Treasury bills are traded in a money market, and Treasury bonds are traded in a capital market.

☐ 1.1.3 Financial Intermediaries

Financial intermediaries, also known as financial institutions, are organizations that issue financial claims against themselves (meaning that they sell financial assets representing claims on themselves in return for cash) and use the proceeds from this issuance to purchase primarily the financial assets of others. Since financial claims simply represent the right-hand side of the balance sheet for an organization, the key distinction between financial intermediaries and other types of organizations involves what is on the left-hand side of the balance sheet.

For example, a typical commercial bank issues financial claims against itself in the form of debt (for example, checking and savings accounts) and equity, but then again so does a typical manufacturing firm. However, looking at the assets held by a commercial bank reveals that most of the bank's money is invested in loans to individuals and corporations as well as in U.S. government securities such as Treasury bills, whereas the typical manufacturing firm has its money invested mostly in land, buildings, machinery, and inventory. Thus, the bank has invested primarily in financial assets, whereas the manufacturing firm has invested primarily in real assets. Accordingly, banks are classified as financial intermediaries and manufacturing firms are not. Other types of financial intermediaries include savings and loan associations, savings banks, credit unions, life insurance companies, mutual funds, and pension funds.

Having made this introduction to the investment environment, the investment process is introduced next.

1.2 THE INVESTMENT PROCESS

As previously mentioned, the investment process describes how an investor should go about making decisions about marketable securities in which to invest, how extensive the investment should be, and when the investment should be made. A five-step procedure for making these decisions forms the basis of the investment process:

1. Set investment policy.
2. Perform security analysis.
3. Construct a portfolio.
4. Revise the portfolio.
5. Evaluate the performance of the portfolio.

□ 1.2.1 Investment Policy

The first step, setting *investment policy*, involves first determining the investor's objectives and the amount of his or her investable wealth. Since there is a positive relationship between risk and return for sensible investment strategies, it is not appropriate for an investor to say that his or her objective is to make a lot of money. What is appropriate for an investor in this situation is to state that the objective is to attempt to make a lot of money while recognizing there is some chance that large losses may be incurred. Thus, investment objectives should be stated in terms of both risk and return.

This first step of the investment process concludes with identification of the potential categories of financial assets for consideration in the ultimate portfolio. This identification will be based on, among other things, the investment objectives, amount of investable wealth, and tax status of the investor. For example, as shall be seen later, it does not usually make sense for individual investors to purchase preferred stock or for tax-exempt investors (such as pension funds) to invest in tax-exempt securities like municipal bonds.

□ 1.2.2 Security Analysis

The second step of the investment process, performing *security analysis*, involves examining a number of individual securities (or groups of securities) within the broad categories of financial assets previously identified. One purpose in conducting such examinations is to identify those securities that currently appear to be mispriced. There are a wide variety of approaches to security analysis. However, most of these approaches fall into one of two classifications. The first classification is known as *technical analysis*; those who utilize this approach to security analysis are known as technical analysts. The second classification is known as *fundamental analysis*; those who utilize it are known as fundamental analysts. In discussing these two approaches to security analysis, the focus at first is on common stocks. Later they are discussed in terms of other types of financial assets.

In its simplest form, technical analysis involves the study of stock market prices in an attempt to predict future price movements for the common stock of a particular firm. Initially, past prices are examined in order to identify recurring trends or patterns in price movements. Then, more recent stock prices are analyzed in order to identify emerging trends or patterns that are similar to past ones. This matching of emerging trends or patterns with past ones is done in the belief that these trends or patterns repeat themselves; thus, by identifying an emerging trend or pattern, the analyst will (allegedly) be able to predict future price movements for that particular stock.

Fundamental analysis begins with the assertion that the "true" (or "intrinsic") value of any financial asset is equal to the present value of all cash flows that the owner of the asset expects to receive. Accordingly, the fundamental stock analyst will attempt to forecast the timing and size of

these cash flows and then will convert them to their equivalent present value by using an appropriate discount factor and dividend discount model. What this means is that the analyst must attempt to forecast the stream of dividends that a particular stock will provide in the future, which is equivalent to forecasting the firm's earnings per share and payout ratios. Once the true value of the common stock of a particular firm has been determined, it is compared to the current market price of the common stock in order to see if the stock is fairly priced or not. Stocks that have a true value less than their current market price are known as *overvalued*, or *overpriced*, stocks, whereas those that have a true value greater than their current market price are known as *undervalued*, or *underpriced*, stocks. The magnitude of the difference between the true value and current market price is also important information, since the strength of the analyst's conviction that a given stock is mispriced will depend, in part, on it. Fundamental analysts believe that notable cases of mispricing will be corrected by the market in the future, meaning that prices of undervalued stocks will show unusual appreciation and prices of overvalued stocks will show unusual depreciation.

☐ 1.2.3 Portfolio Construction

The third step of the investment process, *portfolio construction*, involves identifying those specific assets in which to invest as well as determining the proportions of the investor's wealth to put in each one. Here the issues of selectivity, timing, and diversification need to be addressed by the investor. *Selectivity*, also known as microforecasting, refers to security analysis and thus focuses on forecasting price movements of individual securities. *Timing*, also known as macroforecasting, involves the forecasting of price movements of common stocks in general relative to fixed-income securities, such as corporate bonds. *Diversification* involves constructing the investor's portfolio in a manner such that risk is minimized, subject to certain restrictions.

☐ 1.2.4 Portfolio Revision

The fourth step of the investment process, *portfolio revision*, concerns the periodic repetition of the previous three steps. That is, over time the investor may change his or her investment objectives, which, in turn, means that the currently held portfolio may no longer be optimal. Instead, perhaps a new portfolio should be formed by selling certain securities that are currently held and purchasing certain other ones that are not currently held. Another motivation for revising a given portfolio is that over time the prices of securities change, meaning that some securities that initially were not attractive may become attractive and others that were attractive at one time may no longer be so. Thus, the investor may want to add the former to his or her portfolio while simultaneously deleting the latter. Such a decision will depend upon, among other things, the size of the transactions costs

incurred in making these changes as well as the magnitude of the perceived improvement in the investment outlook for the revised portfolio.

☐ 1.2.5 Portfolio Performance Evaluation

The fifth step of the investment process, *portfolio performance evaluation*, involves periodically determining how the portfolio performed in terms not only of the return earned but also the risk experienced by the investor. Thus, appropriate measures of return and risk as well as relevant standards (or *benchmarks*) are needed.

1.3 ASSET OWNERSHIP

Who owns securities in the United States? According to the most recent New York Stock Exchange survey, approximately 47 million U.S. residents directly owned shares of common stock in 1985. However, many more residents had indirect ownership of stocks through financial intermediaries such as pension plans. Table 1.2 shows the percent of the adult population in the United States that directly owned common stock. After increasing through 1970, there was a decline over the next ten years, followed by another increase to a current level that is comparable to 1970. Table 1.3 provides some demographics of stockholders from the NYSE 1985 survey. It suggests that the typical stockholder has an above-average income, at least some college education, and is (or was) a white-collar worker.

Table 1.4 shows the financial assets and liabilities of U.S. households. Note that the three largest assets are time and savings deposits, pension funds, and direct ownership of common stocks of corporations. The largest

TABLE 1.2
Stockholders of Public Corporations, 1952–1985.

YEAR	STOCKHOLDERS AS A PERCENT OF THE U.S. ADULT POPULATION
1952	6%
1956	8
1959	13
1962	17
1965	17
1970	25
1975	17
1980	19
1981	19
1983	25
1985	25

SOURCE: The New York Stock Exchange Fact Book, various issues.

TABLE 1.3

Demographics of Stockholders of Public Corporations, 1985.

Age:	
Under 21 years	4.8%
21 to 34 years	23.6
35 to 44 years	23.3
45 to 54 years	16.8
55 to 64 years	17.5
65 years and older	14.0
	100.0%
Household income:	
Under $5,000	N/A
$ 5,000 to $ 9,999	5.0%
$10,000 to $14,999	2.8
$15,000 to $24,999	16.5
$25,000 to $49,999	49.5
$50,000 and over	26.2
	100.0%
Education:	
3 years high school or less	5.7%
4 years high school	17.8
1 to 3 years college	31.6
4 years college or more	44.9
	100.0%
Occupation:	
Professional and technical	22.5%
Managers and proprietors	19.5
Clerical and sales	14.6
Craftsmen and foremen	6.5
Operatives and laborers	5.4
Service workers	3.2
Farmers and farm laborers	.9
Homemakers, retired persons, and nonemployed adults	27.4
	100.0%

SOURCE: *New York Stock Exchange Fact Book 1988*, pp. 62–63.

liability involves home mortgages. Although some mortgages are held as assets by other individuals (as shown in the table), most are held by banks and savings and loan companies, who obtain them by lending money provided by individuals (reflected in the table by the first two assets listed).

Although the difference between assets and liabilities in Table 1.4 is large, the net worth of households is actually much larger than the indicated $5165 billion. This is so because nonfinancial assets, such as cars and household furnishings, have not been taken into consideration in this table.

1.4 THE INVESTMENT INDUSTRY

Government statisticians group a number of related occupations into an industry called Finance, Insurance, and Real Estate. Table 1.5 shows the number of people employed in such occupations in recent years. As can be seen, the absolute and relative size of the industry has been increasing. In

TABLE 1.4

Financial Assets and Liabilities of U.S. Households, 1985.

CATEGORY	VALUE[a]
Assets:	
Checkable deposits and currency	$ 418.9
Time and savings deposits	2050.0
Money market fund shares	207.5
Value of life insurance policies	253.8
Value of pension funds	1705.9
Investment company shares	293.6
Other corporate shares	1549.4
U.S. government securities	448.4
State and local government obligations	312.0
Corporate and foreign bonds	74.7
Mortgages	155.3
Miscellaneous	154.6
Total assets	$7624.1
Liabilities:	
Mortgages	$1497.1
Consumer credit	673.1
Other loans	288.9
Total liabilities	$2459.1
Financial assets less liabilities	$5165.0

[a] In billions of dollars.
SOURCE: *Statistical Abstract of the United States, 1987*, p. 476.

1985 approximately 1 out of every 16 nonagricultural workers dealt with investments, broadly defined. Some provide advice (and are thus known as *investment advisors*), some are in sales, some arrange transfers of property or securities from one investor to another, others manage investors' funds

TABLE 1.5

Number of Employees: Finance, Insurance, and Real Estate.

EMPLOYER	NUMBER OF EMPLOYEES (thousands)					
	1960	1965	1970	1975	1980	1985
Banking	673	792	1044	1274	1571	1713
Credit agencies, other than banks	261	327	360	432	570	752
Security and commodity brokerages and services	114	129	205	170	227	353
Insurance carriers	832	893	1030	1085	1224	1282
Insurance agents, brokers, and services	196	233	288	339	452	549
Real estate	517	569	661	748	981	1130
Other finance, insurance, and real estate	76	80	57	117	135	175
Total	2669	3023	3645	4165	5160	5953
Employees in this industry as a percent of total employees in nonagricultural industries	4.92%	4.97%	5.14%	5.41%	5.71%	6.10%

SOURCE: U.S. Bureau of the Census, *Statistical Abstract of the United States* (Washington, D.C.), various editions.

(and are known as *professional money managers*), and still others handle the record keeping in this most abstract and paper-oriented of industries.

1.5 SUMMARY

Because this book is about investing, it focuses on the investment environment and process. In particular, elements of the investment environment, such as securities, markets, and financial intermediaries, are defined and examples are presented. One important concept introduced in this chapter is the notion of an efficient market, defined as a market where security prices reflect information immediately. Thus, in a market that is efficient, securities will be fairly priced, implying that security analysis will not enable investors to make abnormally high returns.

The investment process can be thought of as the method an investor uses to make decisions about marketable securities in which to invest, how extensive the investments should be, and when the investment should be made. A five-step procedure for conducting this process was then presented. One method of performing all five steps that is discussed in later chapters involves the use of modern portfolio theory (MPT).

Although the investment industry is of relatively modest importance relative to total employment figures, this part of the economy has a profound impact on virtually everyone's life. A clear understanding of the investment environment and process is valuable not only for the 1 in 16 who work in the industry but also for the 15 who do not. Although most people obtain the majority of their income in the form of salary and wages, income from investments is important to nearly everyone, particularly those who have retired. Accordingly, this book is intended to provide an understanding of the investment environment and process for people with either a professional or a personal interest.

QUESTIONS AND PROBLEMS

1. Why don't secondary security markets generate capital for the issuers of securities traded in those markets?

2. At the end of 1988, Ray Fisher decided to take $30,000 in savings out of the bank and invest it in a portfolio of stocks and bonds; $10,000 was placed into common stocks and $20,000 into corporate bonds. A year later, at the end of 1989, Ray's stock and bond holdings were worth $13,000 and $16,000, respectively. During 1989, $500 in cash dividends was received on the stocks and $2000 in coupon interest payments was received on the bonds. (This stock and bond income was not reinvested in his portfolio.)

   a. What was the return on Ray's stock portfolio during 1989?

   b. What was the return on Ray's bond portfolio during 1989?

   c. What was the return on Ray's total portfolio during 1989?

3. Does it seem reasonable that higher return securities historically have exhibited higher risk? Why?

4. Examining Table 1.1, one can find many years in which Treasury bills produced returns greater than common stocks. How can you reconcile this fact with the statements made in the text citing a positive relationship between risk and return?

5. Again referring to Table 1.1, in terms of total returns, what was the worst single calendar year for common stock investors? What was the worst year in the 1970s? Compare these two years in terms of return in "constant dollars" (that is, purchasing power). Does this comparison show that the stock market slump of the 1970s was not as disastrous as the "crash" associated with the Great Depression? Explain.

6. Describe how life insurance companies, mutual funds, and pension plans each act as financial intermediaries.

7. Why does it not make sense to establish an investment objective of "making a lot of money"?

8. Distinguish between technical and fundamental security analysis.

Chapter 2

SECURITIES AND MARKETS

When a security is sold, many people are likely to be involved. Although it is possible for two investors to trade with each other directly, the usual transaction employs the services provided by brokers, dealers, and markets.

A *broker* acts as an agent for an investor and is compensated via commission. Many individual investors deal with brokers in large retail or "wire" houses—firms with many offices that are connected by private wires with their own headquarters and, through the headquarters, with major markets. The people in these brokerage firms with prime responsibility for individual investors are termed *account executives*, or *registered representatives*.

Institutional investors, such as commercial banks and pension funds, deal with these large retail brokerage firms and also with smaller firms that maintain only one or two offices and specialize in institutional business. Two other types of brokerage firms are *regional brokerage firms* and *discount brokers*. The former concentrate on transactions within a geographic area, meaning the securities being traded have a special following in that area of the country. This may be because the issuers of the securities are located in that area. Discount brokers provide "bare-bones" services at low cost, meaning they provide fewer services than full-service brokerage firms such as Merrill Lynch and Shearson Lehman Hutton. Investors who simply want to have their orders executed and do not seek advice can reduce the commission they pay up to 50% by using a discount broker.

An account executive's compensation is typically determined in large part by the *commissions* paid by his or her customers—an amount that is directly related to the amount of turnover (that is, trading) in an investor's account. This provides some temptation to recommend frequent changes in investors' holdings. Furthermore, since the commission rates on various types of investments differ, there is some temptation to recommend changes in those types of investments with the highest rates. In the long run, account executives who encourage excessive turnover (or "churning") will often lose customers and may even be subjected to lawsuits. Nonetheless, such behavior may be advantageous for them in the short run.

It is a simple matter to open an account with a brokerage firm: simply appear at (or call) the local office. An account executive is assigned to you and helps you fill out some forms. After the initial forms have been signed, everything else can be done by mail or telephone. Transactions are posted

to your account as they are to a bank account. For example, you can deposit money, purchase securities using money from the account, and add the proceeds from security sales to the account. Brokers exist (and charge fees) to make security transactions as simple as possible. All that the investor has to do is to provide the broker with what is referred to here as *order specifications*.

In discussing order specifications, it will be assumed that the investor's order involves common stock. In this situation the investor must specify

1. The name of the firm,
2. Whether the order is to buy or sell shares,
3. The size of the order,
4. How long the order is to be outstanding, and
5. What type of order is to be used.

The last three specifications are discussed next in more detail.

2.1   ORDER SIZE

In buying or selling common stock, the investor places an order involving either a round lot, an odd lot, or both. Generally, a *round lot* means that the order is for 100 shares or a multiple of 100 shares.[1] *Odd lot* orders generally are for 1 to 99 shares. Orders that are for more than 100 shares but are not multiples of 100 are viewed as a mixture of round and odd lots. Thus an order for 259 shares is viewed as an order for two round lots and an odd lot of 59 shares.

2.2   TIME LIMIT

The investor must specify a time limit on his or her order, meaning the time within which the broker should attempt to fill the order. For *day orders*, the broker will attempt to fill the order only during the day in which it was entered. If the order is not filled by the end of the day, then it is canceled. If a time limit is not specified by the investor, the broker will treat an order as a day order. Week and month orders expire at the end of the calendar week and month, respectively, during which they were entered, provided they have not been filled by then.

Open orders, also known as *good-till-canceled*, or GTC, orders, remain in effect until they are either filled or canceled by the investor. However, during the time period before the order has been filled, the broker may periodically ask the investor to confirm the order. In contrast to GTC orders are *fill-or-kill orders*, also known as FOK orders. These orders are canceled immediately if the broker is unable to execute them.

---

[1] Occasionally, a round lot is for less than 100 shares. When this happens, it is usually for stocks that are either high-priced or traded infrequently.

Discretionary orders allow the broker to set the specifications for the order. The broker may have virtually complete discretion, in which case he or she decides on all the order specifications, or limited discretion, in which case he or she decides only on the price and timing of the order.

2.3 TYPES OF ORDERS

☐ 2.3.1 Market Orders

By far the most common type of order is the *market order*. Here the broker is instructed to buy or sell a stated number of shares immediately. In this situation the broker is obligated to act on a "best-efforts" basis to get the best possible price (as low as possible for a purchase order, as high as possible for a sell order) at the time the order is placed. Consequently, when placing a market order the investor can be fairly certain that the order will be executed but is uncertain of the price. However, there is generally fairly good information available beforehand concerning the likely price at which such an order will be executed. Not surprisingly, market orders are day orders.

☐ 2.3.2 Limit Orders

A second type of order is a *limit order*. Here, a *limit price* is specified by the investor when the order is placed with the broker. If the order is to purchase shares, then the broker is to execute the order only at a price that is less than or equal to the limit price. If the order is to sell shares, then the broker is to execute the order only at a price that is greater than or equal to the limit price. Thus, for limit orders to purchase shares the investor specifies a ceiling on the price, and for limit orders to sell shares the investor specifies a floor on the price. In contrast to a market order, an investor using a limit order may not be certain that the order will be executed.

For example, assume that the common stock of the ABC Corporation is currently selling for $25 a share. An investor placing a limit order to sell 100 shares of ABC with a limit price of $30 per share and a time limit of one day is not likely to have his or her order executed, since this price is notably above the current price of $25. Only if today's price becomes much more favorable (meaning in this case that the stock price rise by at least $5 per share) will the limit order be executed.

☐ 2.3.3 Stop Orders

Two special kinds of orders are stop orders (also known as stop-loss orders) and stop limit orders. For a *stop order* the investor must specify what is known as a *stop price*. If it is a sell order, the stop price must be below the market price at the time the order is placed; conversely, if it is a buy order, the stop price must be above the market price at the time the order is placed.

If someone else later trades the stock at a price that reaches or passes the stop price, then the stop order becomes, in effect, a market order. Hence, a stop order can be viewed as a conditional market order.

Continuing with the ABC Corporation example, a stop-sell order at $20 would not be executed until a trade involving others had taken place at a price of $20 or lower. Conversely, a stop-buy order at $30 would not be executed until a trade involving others had taken place at a price of $30 or more. If the price did not fall to $20, then the stop-sell order would not be executed. Similarly, if the price did not rise to $30, the stop-buy order would not be executed. In contrast, a limit order to sell at $20 or a limit order to buy at $30 would be executed immediately, since the current market price is $25.

One potential use of stop orders is to "lock in" paper profits. For example, assume an investor had purchased ABC stock at $10 per share two years ago, and thus has paper profits of $25 − $10 = $15 per share. Entering a stop-sell order at $20 per share means that the investor will be sure of making roughly $20 − $10 = $10 per share if the stock falls in price to $20 or less. If, instead of falling, the stock price rises, then the investor's stop-sell order is ignored and the investor's paper profits increase in size. Thus, the stop-sell order will provide the investor with a degree of profit protection.[2]

One of the dangers of stop orders is that the actual price at which the order is executed may be some distance from the stop price. This can occur if the stock price moves very rapidly in a given direction. For example, ABC may have an industrial accident that results in a spate of lawsuits and causes the stock price to fall very rapidly to $12 per share. In this situation a stop-sell order at $20 may be executed at $16, for example, instead of near the stop price of $20.

☐ 2.3.4 Stop-Limit Orders

The *stop-limit order* is a type of order that is designed to overcome the uncertainty of the execution price associated with a stop order. With a stop-limit order the investor specifies not one but two prices—a stop price and a limit price. What happens is that once someone trades the stock at a price that reaches or passes the stop price, then a limit order is created at the limit price. Hence, a stop-limit order can be viewed as a conditional limit order.

Continuing with the example, the investor could place a stop-limit order to sell ABC stock where the stop price is $20 and the limit price is $19. In effect, a limit order to sell ABC stock at a price of $19 or higher would be activated for the investor only if others trade ABC at a price of $20 or less. Conversely, the investor could enter a stop-limit order to buy ABC stock where the stop price is $30 and the limit price is $31. This means that a

---

[2] Stop-buy orders can be used to lock in paper profits for what are known as short sales, which are discussed later in this chapter.

limit order to buy ABC stock at a price of $31 or lower would be activated for the investor only if others trade ABC at a price of $30 or more.

Note that if the stop price is reached, execution is assured for a stop order but not for a stop-limit order. Continuing with the ABC example, the industrial accident may cause the stock price to fall to $12 so rapidly that the stop-limit order to sell (where the stop price was $20 and the limit price was $19) might not have been executed, whereas the stop order (where the stop price was $20) would have been executed at $16.

2.4 MARGIN ACCOUNTS

A *cash account* with a brokerage firm is like a regular checking account: Deposits (cash and the proceeds from selling securities) must cover withdrawals (cash and the costs of purchasing securities). A *margin account* is like a checking account that has overdraft privileges: Within limits, if more money is needed than is in the account, a loan is automatically made by the broker.[3]

When opening a margin account with a brokerage firm, an investor must sign a *hypothecation agreement*. This agreement grants the brokerage firm the right to pledge the investor's securities as collateral for bank loans, provided the securities were purchased using a margin account. Most brokerage firms also expect investors to allow them to lend their securities to others who wish to "sell them short," a procedure that is described later in this chapter.

In order to facilitate either the pledging or lending of securities, brokerage firms request that securities purchased through a margin account be held in *street name*.[4] This means that the owner of the security, as far as the original issuer is concerned, is the brokerage firm—that is, the registered owner is the brokerage firm. As a result, in the case of common stock the issuer will send all dividends, annual reports, and voting rights to the brokerage firm, not to the investor. However, the brokerage firm will act merely as a conduit in this situation and simply forward these items to the investor.[5] Accordingly, holding a security in street name will not result in the investor being treated in a substantively different manner from holding the security in his or her own name.[6]

With a margin account, an investor then may undertake certain types

---

[3] There are other types of accounts; it should be noted that an investor may have more than one type of account with a brokerage firm.

[4] Investors with cash accounts may voluntarily elect to have their securities held in street name. Reasons offered for doing so include reduced risk of theft and improved record keeping (typically the brokerage firm will send monthly statements detailing the investor's holdings).

[5] It is possible that the investor will not receive the voting rights if the stock has been loaned to a short seller. This is discussed later in the chapter.

[6] The investor whose securities are held in street name may be concerned about what would happen if the brokerage firm were to go bankrupt. If this were to happen, the Securities Investor Protection Corporation (SIPC), a government-chartered firm that insures investors' account against brokerage firm failure, would step in and cover the investors' losses up to $500,000. Some brokerage firms have gone further and purchased private insurance in addition to the insurance offered by SIPC.

of transactions that are not allowed with a cash account. These transactions are known as margin purchases and short sales, which are discussed next.

☐ 2.4.1 Margin Purchases

With a cash account, an investor who purchases a security must pay the entire cost of the purchase with cash. However, with a margin account the investor must come up with cash for only a percentage of the cost and can borrow the rest from the broker.[7] The amount borrowed from the broker as a result of such a *margin purchase* is referred to as the investor's *debit balance*. The interest charged on loans advanced by a broker for a margin purchase is usually calculated by adding a service charge (for example, 1%) to the broker's *call money rate*. In turn, the call money rate is the rate paid by the broker to a bank that loaned the broker the cash that ultimately went to the investor to pay for part of the purchase.

For example the bank may loan money to the broker at a rate of 10% and then the broker may loan this money to the investor at a rate of 11%. Note that the call money rate (10% in this example) can change over time and with it the interest rate that investors are charged.

The securities purchased by the investor serve as collateral on the loan made by the broker. In turn, the broker uses these securities as collateral on the loan made by the bank. Thus, the broker is, in a sense, acting as a go-between in the lending process, facilitating a loan from the bank to the investor.

Initial Margin Requirement

The minimum percentage of the purchase price that must come from the investor's own funds is known as the *initial margin requirement*. Regulations T, U, and G, prescribed in accordance with the Securities Exchange Act of 1934, give the Federal Reserve Board the responsibility for setting this percentage when either common stocks or convertible bonds are being purchased.[8] However, exchanges (where the purchase orders are filled) are allowed to set a percentage higher than the one set by the Federal Reserve Board, and brokers are allowed to set it even higher. Thus, hypothetically, the Federal Reserve Board could set the initial margin requirement at 50%, the New York Stock Exchange would then make it 55%, and the broker could ultimately make it 60%. As can be seen in Table 2.1, the initial margin

---

[7] With either a cash or a margin account, the investor usually has up to five business days after an order is executed to provide the broker with the necessary cash. Accordingly, the fifth business day after execution is known as the settlement date. For margin purchases, the loan value of certain other securities can be used instead of cash as a down payment, in which case these securities must be provided by the settlement date. Sellers of securities must also provide their brokers with their securities by the settlement date. If requested, an investor may be able to get an extension to the settlement date.

[8] Regulation T covers credit extended by brokers and dealers, Regulation U covers credit extended by banks, and Regulation G covers credit extended by anyone other than brokers, dealers, or banks. All common stocks and convertible bonds that are listed on a national securities exchange (for example, the New York Stock Exchange, the American Stock Exchange, or the National Market System of NASDAQ) can be purchased on margin. Furthermore, four times a year the Federal Reserve Board publishes a roster of other securities that can purchased on margin. The determination of which firms are put on this roster is based on factors such as the number of shareholders and firm size.

TABLE 2.1

Initial Margin Requirements of the Federal Reserve Board.

PERIOD		INITIAL MARGIN REQUIREMENTS		
Beginning Date	Ending Date	Margin Stocks	Short Sales	Convertible Bonds
Oct. 1, 1934	Jan. 31, 1936	25–45%	(a)	(b)
Feb. 1, 1936	Mar. 31, 1936	25–55%	(a)	(b)
April 1, 1936	Oct. 31, 1937	55%	(a)	(b)
Nov. 1, 1937	Feb. 4, 1945	40%	50%	(b)
Feb. 5, 1945	Jul. 4, 1945	50%	50%	(b)
Jul. 5, 1945	Jan. 20, 1946	75%	75%	(b)
Jan. 21, 1946	Jan. 31, 1947	100%	100%	(b)
Feb. 1, 1947	Mar. 29, 1949	75%	75%	(b)
Mar. 30, 1949	Jan. 16, 1951	50%	50%	(b)
Jan. 17, 1951	Feb. 19, 1953	75%	75%	(b)
Feb. 20, 1953	Jan. 3, 1955	50%	50%	(b)
Jan. 4, 1955	Apr. 22, 1955	60%	60%	(b)
Apr. 23, 1955	Jan. 15, 1958	70%	70%	(b)
Jan. 16, 1958	Aug. 4, 1958	50%	50%	(b)
Aug. 5, 1958	Oct. 15, 1958	70%	70%	(b)
Oct. 16, 1958	Jul. 27, 1960	90%	90%	(b)
Jul. 28, 1960	Jul. 9, 1962	70%	70%	(b)
Jul. 10, 1962	Nov. 5, 1963	50%	50%	(b)
Nov. 6, 1963	Mar. 10, 1968	70%	70%	(b)
Mar. 11, 1968	Jun. 7, 1968	70%	70%	50%
Jun. 8, 1968	May 5, 1970	80%	80%	60%
May 6, 1970	Dec. 5, 1971	65%	65%	50%
Dec. 6, 1971	Nov. 23, 1972	55%	55%	50%
Nov. 24, 1972	Jan. 2, 1974	65%	65%	50%
Jan. 3, 1974	Present	50%	50%	50%

[a] Requirement was the margin "customarily required" by the broker.
[b] Initial margin requirements for convertible bonds were not adopted by the Federal Reserve Board until March 11, 1968.
SOURCE: *Federal Reserve Bulletin*, various issues.

requirement since 1934 as set by the Federal Reserve Board has ranged from 40% to 100%. In 1988 it was 50%.[9]

Consider, as an example, an investor who purchases on margin 100 shares of Widget Corporation for $50 per share. With a margin requirement of 60%, the investor must pay the broker .6 × 100 shares × $50 per share = $3000. The remainder of the purchase price, (1 − .6) × 100 shares × $50 per share = $2000, is funded by a loan from the broker to the investor.[10]

Actual Margin

The *actual margin* in the account of an investor who has purchased stocks can be calculated daily as

---

[9] Initial margin requirements on nonconvertible bonds are set in a similar fashion, except that the Federal Reserve Board is not involved. Typically, the investor wishing to purchase nonconvertible bonds on margin will face a much lower initial margin requirement (for example, 10% for purchases of U.S. Treasury securities).

[10] Generally, at the end of each month the interest on the loan will be calculated and added to the amount of the loan appearing on the right-hand side of the investor's balance sheet. For ease of exposition, this fact is ignored in the examples given here.

$$\text{Actual margin} = \frac{\text{market value of assets} - \text{loan}}{\text{market value of assets}}. \qquad (2.1)$$

This daily calculation of the actual margin in an investor's account is known as having the account *marked to the market*. Upon examination of equation (2.1), it can be seen that at the time of the margin purchase, the actual margin and initial margin are the same. However, subsequent to the purchase, the actual margin can be either greater than or less than the initial margin. In this example, if widget stock fell to $25 per share, then the actual margin would drop to $500/$2,500 = 20%.

Keep in mind that the 100 shares of Widget are being kept as collateral on the loan of $2000 to the investor. If the price of Widget drops further, the broker may become nervous, since an additional sudden price decline could bring the value of the collateral below the amount of the loan. For example, if the price dropped to $15 per share, the broker would have collateral worth $15 × 100 shares = $1500, whereas the amount of the loan is $2000. If the investor skipped town, the broker would still have to make good on the bank loan of $2000 but would only have $1500 worth of the investor's assets to seize in order to pay off the loan. This means that the broker would have to bear the $500 difference and hope to track down the investor and recoup this amount at a later date.

Maintenance Margin

To prevent such an occurrence, brokers require that investors keep the actual margin in their accounts at or above a certain percentage. This percentage is known as *maintenance margin* and is set by the exchanges, not the Federal Reserve Board, with the brokers given the right to set it even higher. As of 1988, the New York Stock Exchange had set this percentage for common stock and convertible bond purchases at 25%.

If an account falls below the maintenance margin requirement, the account is said to be *undermargined*. Accordingly, the broker will issue a *margin call*, requesting the investor to either (1) deposit cash or securities into the account, (2) pay off part of the loan, or (3) sell some securities currently held in the account and use the proceeds to pay off part of the loan. Any of these actions will raise the numerator or lower the denominator on the right-hand side of equation (2.1), thereby increasing the actual margin.[11] If the investor does not act (or cannot be reached), then in accordance with the terms of the account, the broker will sell securities from the account to restore the actual margin to (at least) the maintenance margin requirement.

If, instead of falling, the stock price rises, then the investor can take part of the increase out of the account in the form of cash, since the actual margin in the account will have risen above the initial margin requirement.[12] In this situation the account is said to be *unrestricted*, or *overmargined*.

---

[11] The broker may ask the investor immediately (in some cases within five business days, in other cases even sooner) to bring the actual margin up to a level corresponding to the maintenance margin requirement or to a level that is even higher, ranging up to the initial margin requirement.

[12] Alternatively, the cash could be used as part of the initial margin requirement on an additional margin purchase by the investor. In fact, if it was large enough, it could be used to meet the entire requirement.

Having discussed the cases where the stock price of the shares purchased on margin either (1) fell to such a degree that the actual margin was below the maintenance margin requirement, meaning the account was undermargined, or (2) increased, resulting in the actual margin being above the initial margin requirement and the account being unrestricted, there remains one case left to consider. This case involves the situation where the stock price falls but not by enough to make the actual margin drop below the maintenance margin requirement. That is, the actual margin in the account is below the initial margin requirement but above the maintenance margin requirement. In this situation, no action by the investor is necessary. However, the account will be *restricted*, meaning that any transaction having the effect of decreasing the actual margin further (such as withdrawing cash) will not be allowed.

The use of margin purchases allows the investor to engage in *financial leverage*. That is, by using debt to fund part of the purchase price, the investor can increase the expected rate of return of the investment. However, there is a mitigating factor in the use of margin, and that is the effect on the risk of the investment.

Consider Widget again. If the investor believes the stock will rise by $15 per share over the next year, the expected rate of return on the cash purchase of 100 shares of Widget will be ($15 × 100 shares)/($50 × 100 shares) = 30%, assuming that no cash dividends are paid and the purchase price is $50 per share. A margin purchase, on the other hand, would have an expected return of [($15 × 100 shares) − (.11 × $2000)]/$3,000 = ($1500 − $220)/$3000 = 42.7%, where the interest rate on margin loans is 11% and the initial margin requirement is 60%. Thus, the investor has increased the expected rate of return from 30% to 42.7% by the use of margin.

However, what will happen to the rate of return if the stock falls by $10 per share? In this case the investor who made a cash purchase will have a rate of return equal to (−$10 × 100 shares)/($50 × 100 shares) = −20%. The margin purchaser, on the other hand, will have a rate of return equal to [(−$10 × 100) − (.11 × $2000)]/$3,000 = (−$1,000 − $220)/$3000 = −40.7%. Thus, the margin purchaser will experience a much larger loss than the cash purchaser for a given dollar decline in the price of the stock.

Margin purchases are usually made in the expectation that the stock price will rise in the near future, meaning that the investor thinks the stock's current price is too low. If an investor thinks that a given stock is not too low but too high, then the investor may engage in what is known as a short sale, which is discussed next.

□ 2.4.2 Short Sales

An old adage from Wall Street is to "buy low, sell high." Most investors hope to do just that by buying securities first and selling them later.[13] However, with a *short sale* this process is reversed: The investor sells a security first

---

[13] After purchasing a security, an investor is said to have established a long position in the security.

and buys it back later. In this case the old adage about investors aspirations might be reworded as "sell high, buy low."

Short sales are accomplished by borrowing stock certificates for use in the initial trade and then repaying the loan with certificates obtained in a later trade. Note that the loan here involves certificates, not dollars and cents (although it is true that the certificates at any point in time have a certain monetary value). This means the borrower must repay the lender by returning certificates, not dollars and cents (although it is true that an equivalent monetary value, determined on the date the loan is repaid, can be remitted instead). It also means that there are no interest payments to be made by the borrower.

Rules Governing Short Sales

Any order for a short sale must be identified as such. The Securities and Exchange Commission has ruled that short sales may not be made when the market price for the security is falling, on the assumption that the short seller could exacerbate the situation, cause a panic, and profit therefrom—an assumption inappropriate for an efficient market with astute, alert traders. The precise rule is that a short sale must be made on an *up-tick* (for a price higher than that of the previous trade) or on a *zero-plus tick* (for a price equal to that of the previous trade but higher than that of the last trade at a different price).[14]

Within five business days after a short sale has been made, the short-seller's broker must borrow and deliver the appropriate securities to the purchaser. The borrowed securities may come from the inventory of securities owned by the brokerage firm itself or from the inventory of another brokerage firm. However, they are more likely to come from the inventory of securities held in street name by the brokerage firm for investors that have margin accounts with the firm. The life of the loan is indefinite, meaning there is no time limit on it.[15] If the lender wants to sell the securities, then the short seller will not have to repay the loan if the brokerage firm can borrow shares elsewhere, thereby transferring the loan from one source to another. However, if the brokerage firm cannot find a place to borrow the shares, then the short seller will have to repay the loan immediately. Interestingly, the identities of the borrower and lender are known only to the brokerage firm—that is, the lender does not know who the borrower is and the borrower does not know who the lender is.

An Example

An example of a short sale is indicated in Figure 2.1. At the start of the day, Mr. Lane owns 100 shares of the XYZ Company, which are being held for

---

[14] The tick rule is not applicable in the over-the-counter (OTC) market, suggesting that short selling can be done at any time in that market. (The OTC market is discussed later.)

[15] The New York Stock Exchange, the American Stock Exchange, and NASDAQ publish monthly lists of the *short interest* in their stocks (short interest refers to the number of shares of a given company that have been sold short where, as of a given date, the loan remains outstanding). To be on the NYSE or AMEX list, either the total short interest must be equal to or greater than 100,000 shares or the change in the short interest from the previous month must be equal to or greater than 50,000 shares. The respective figures for NASDAQ are 50,000 and 25,000.

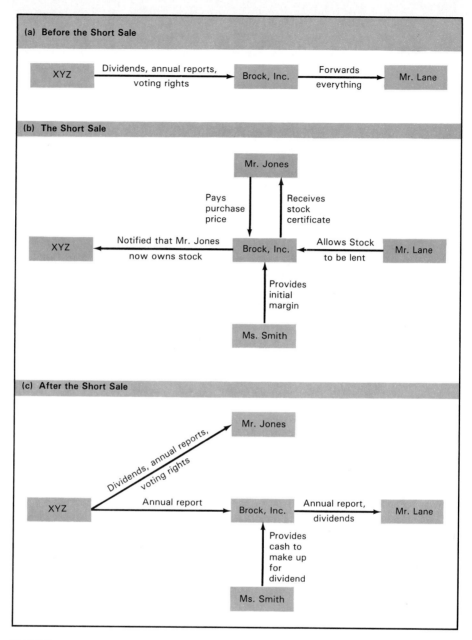

FIGURE 2–1
Short selling of common stock.

him in street name by Brock, Inc., his broker. During this particular day, Ms. Smith places an order with her broker at Brock to short sell 100 shares of XYZ (Mr. Lane believes the price of XYZ stock is going to rise in the near future, whereas Ms. Smith believes it is going to fall). In this situation, Brock takes the 100 shares of XYZ that they are holding in street name for Mr.

Lane and sells them for Ms. Smith to some other investor, in this case Mr. Jones. At this point XYZ will receive notice that the ownership of 100 shares of its stock has changed hands, going from Brock (remember that Mr. Lane held his stock in street name) to Mr. Jones. At some later date, Ms. Smith will tell her broker at Brock to purchase 100 shares of XYZ (perhaps from a Ms. Poole) and use these shares to pay off her debt to Mr. Lane. At this point, XYZ will receive another notice that the ownership of 100 shares has changed hands, going from Ms. Poole to Brock, restoring Brock to their original position.

What happens when XYZ declares and subsequently pays a cash dividend to its stockholders? *Before the short sale*, Brock would receive a check for cash dividends on 100 shares of stock. After depositing this check in their own account at a bank, Brock would write a check for an identical amount and give it to Mr. Lane. Thus, neither Brock or Mr. Lane has been worse off by having his shares held in street name. *After the short sale*, XYZ will see that the owner of those 100 shares is not Brock any more but is now Mr. Jones. Thus, XYZ will now mail the dividend check to Mr. Jones, not Brock. However, Mr. Lane will still be expecting his dividend check from Brock. Indeed, if there was a risk that he would not receive it, he would not have agreed to have his securities held in street name. Brock would like to mail him a check for the same amount of dividends that Mr. Jones received from XYZ—that is, for the amount of dividends Mr. Lane would have received from XYZ had he held his stock in his own name. If Brock does this, then they will be losing an amount of cash equal to the amount of the dividends paid. In order to prevent themselves from experiencing this loss, they make Ms. Smith, the short seller, give them a check for an equivalent amount!

Consider all the parties involved in the short sale now. Mr. Lane is content, since he has received his dividend check from his broker. Brock is content, since their net cash outflow is still zero, just as it was before the short sale. Mr. Jones is content, since he received his dividend check directly from XYZ. What about Ms. Smith? She should not be upset with having to reimburse Brock for the dividend check given by them to Mr. Lane, since the price of XYZ's common stock can be expected to fall by an amount roughly equal to the amount of the cash dividend, thereby reducing the dollar value of her loan from Brock by an equivalent amount.

What about annual reports and voting rights? Before the short sale, these were sent to Brock, who then forwarded them to Mr. Lane. After the short sale, Brock no longer received them, so what happened? Annual reports are easily procured by brokerage firms free of charge, so Brock probably got copies of them from XYZ and mailed a copy to Mr. Lane. However, voting rights are different. These are limited to the registered stockholders (in this case, Mr. Jones) and cannot be replicated in the manner of cash dividends by Ms. Smith, the short seller. Thus, when voting rights are issued, the brokerage firm (Brock, Inc.) will try to find voting rights to give to Mr. Lane (perhaps Brock owns shares or manages a portfolio that owns shares of XYZ and will give these voting rights to Mr. Lane). Unless he is insistent, however, there is a chance he will not get his voting rights once his shares have been

borrowed and used in a short sale. In all other matters, he will be treated just as if he were holding the shares of XYZ in his own name.

As previously mentioned, a short sale involves a loan. Thus, there is a risk that the borrower (in the example, Ms. Smith) will not repay the loan. In this situation the broker would be left without the 100 shares that the short seller, Ms. Smith, owes him or her. Either the brokerage firm, Brock, is going to lose money or else the lender, Mr. Lane, is going to lose money. To prevent this from happening, the cash proceeds from the short sale, paid by Mr. Jones, are not given to the short seller, Ms. Smith. Instead, they are held in her account with Brock until she repays her loan. Unfortunately this will not assure the brokerage firm that the loan will be repaid.

In the example, assume the 100 shares of XYZ were sold at a price of $100 per share. In this case, the proceeds from the short sale of $10,000 are held in Ms. Smith's account, but she is prohibited from withdrawing it until the loan is repaid. Now imagine that at some date after the short sale, XYZ stock rises by $20 per share. In this situation, Ms. Smith owes Brock 100 shares of XYZ with a current market value of 100 shares × $120 per share = $12,000 but has only $10,000 in her account. If she skips town, Brock will have collateral of $10,000 (in cash) but a loan of $12,000, resulting in a loss of $2000. However, Brock can use margin requirements to protect itself from experiencing losses from short sellers who do not repay their loans. In this example, Ms. Smith must not only leave the short-sale proceeds with her broker, but she must also give her broker initial margin applied to the amount of the short sale.[16] Assuming the initial margin requirement is 60%, she must give her broker .6 × $10,000 = $6000 cash.

In this example, XYZ stock would have to rise in value to a price above $160 per share in order for Brock to be in jeopardy of not being repaid. Thus, initial margin provides the brokerage firm with a certain degree of protection. However, this protection is not complete, since it is not unheard of for stocks to rise in value by more than 60%. It is maintenance margin that protects the brokerage firm from losing money in such situations. In order to examine the use of maintenance margin in short sales, the actual margin in a short sale is defined as:

$$\text{Actual margin} = \frac{\text{market value of assets} - \text{loan}}{\text{loan}} \qquad (2.2)$$

The numerator in equation (2.2) is identical to the numerator for calculating actual margin for margin purchases in equation (2.1). However, the denominator is different. For short sales it is equal to the current dollar value of the loan, whereas for margin purchases it is equal to the current market value of the assets held in the account.

In this example, if XYZ stock rises to $130 per share, the actual margin in Ms. Smith's account will be $\{[(\$100 \times 100) \times (1 + .6)] - (\$130 \times 100)\}/(\$130 \times 100) = 23\%$. Assuming the maintenance margin requirement is

---

[16] Table 2.1 presents the initial margin requirement for short sales; note that it has been set at the same level as for margin purchases of common stocks in the postwar period.

30%, the account is undermargined, and Ms. Smith will receive a margin call. Just as in margin calls on margin purchases, she will be asked to put up more margin, meaning she will be asked to add cash or securities to her account.

If, instead of rising, the stock price falls, then the short seller can take a bit more than the drop in the price out of the account in the form of cash, since in this case the actual margin has risen above the initial margin requirement and the account is thus unrestricted.[17]

Having discussed the cases for short sales where the stock price either (1) fell and the account was thereby unrestricted or (2) went up to such a degree that the maintenance margin requirement was violated and the account was thereby undermargined, there is one more case left to be considered. This is the case where the stock price goes up but not to such a degree that the maintenance margin requirement is violated. In this case, the initial margin requirement has been violated, which means that the account is restricted. Here, *restricted* has a meaning similar to its meaning for margin purchases. That is, any transaction that has the effect of further decreasing the actual margin in the account will be prohibited.

An interesting question is, What happens to the cash in the short seller's account? When the loan is repaid, the short seller will have access to the cash (actually, the cash is usually used to repay the loan). Before the loan is repaid, however, it may be that the short seller can earn interest on the portion of the cash balance that represents margin (some brokerage firms will accept certain securities, such as Treasury bills, in lieu of cash for meeting margin requirements). In regard to the cash proceeds from the short sale, sometimes the securities may be lent only on the payment of a premium by the short seller, meaning the short seller not only does not earn interest on the cash proceeds but must pay a fee for the loan. At other times the lender may pay the short seller interest on the cash proceeds. Usually, however, securities are loaned "flat"—the brokerage firm keeps the cash proceeds from the short sale and enjoys the use of this money, and neither the short seller nor the investor who lent the securities receives any direct compensation. In this case, the brokerage firm makes money not only from the commission paid by the short seller but also on the cash proceeds from the sale (they may, for example, earn interest by purchasing Treasury bills with these proceeds).

☐ **2.4.3 Aggregation**

An investor with a margin account may purchase several different securities on margin or may short sell several different securities. Alternatively, he or she may purchase some on margin and short sell others. The determination of whether an account is undermargined, restricted, or overmargined depends on the total activity in the account. For example, if one stock is undermargined and another is overmargined, then the overmargined stock can

---

[17] Alternatively, the short seller could short sell a second security and not have to put up all (or perhaps any) of the initial margin.

be used to offset the undermargined stock, provided it is overmargined to a sufficiently large degree. How these multiple transactions are aggregated in one account in order to see if the account is undermargined, restricted, or overmargined on any given day is shown next.

In the case of multiple margin purchases, aggregation is straightforward. The investor's balance sheet is restated by recalculating the market value of all the stocks held using current market prices. Here the current market price of any particular security usually means the price at which the last trade was made in the market involving that security on the previous day. Next, the total amount of the investor's liabilities is carried over from the previous day, since the amounts of the margin loans do not change from day to day. In turn, this allows equation (2.1) to be used in order to recalculate the actual margin in the account.

In a similar manner, the actual margin of an investor who has short sold more than one stock can be determined. In this case, however, it is not the assets that are reevaluated every day as the account is marked to the market. Instead, it is the liabilities that are reevaluated based on current market prices, since the short seller's liabilities are shares whose market value is changing every day. Once the dollar values of the liabilities are recalculated, the actual margin in the account can be determined using equation (2.2).

The situation where the investor has purchased some stocks, perhaps on margin, and has short sold others is more complicated than either of the situations just described. This is because the equation used to calculate actual margin for margin purchases, equation (2.1), and the equation used to calculate actual margin for short sales, equation (2.2), are different. This can be seen by simply noting what is in the denominator in each equation. For margin purchases, the market value of the assets appears in the denominator. However, for short sales, the market value of the loan appears in the denominator. If both kind of transactions appear in the same account, neither equation can be used to calculate the overall actual margin in the account. However, the account can be analyzed in terms of the dollar amount of assets that are necessary for the account to meet the maintenance margin requirement. This can be illustrated with an example.

Consider an investor who short sells 100 shares of Widget on July 1 at $50 per share and purchases 100 shares of XYZ on margin at $100 per share on July 15. Here the initial margin and maintenance margin requirements are 60% and 30%, respectively. Furthermore, assume Widget and XYZ are selling for $60 and $80 per share on July 31. In this situation, the broker will require the investor to have assets of sufficient value to protect the short sale loan of Widget stock and the cash loan to purchase XYZ on margin. In general, the amount required as collateral against a short sale is equal to the current market value of the shorted stock times the quantity of 1 plus the maintenance margin requirement. For the short sale loan of Widget stock, this amounts to $6000 × (1 + .3) = $7800, where .3 corresponds to the maintenance margin requirement.

The amount required as collateral against a margin purchase is, in general, equal to the dollar value of the margin loan divided by the quantity

of 1 minus the maintenance margin requirement. For the cash loan to purchase XYZ, this amounts to $4000/(1 − .3) = $5714.

The total amount required in this example is thus $7800 + $5714 = $13,514. Since the assets in the account are currently worth $16,000, the investor will not receive a margin call. To see if the account is restricted, the previous calculations are repeated using the initial margin requirement of 60% instead of the maintenance margin requirement of 30%. For the Widget stock loan, the amount required for the account to be unrestricted is $6000 × (1 + .6) = $9600. The corresponding amount for the XYZ loan is $4000/(1 − .6) = $10,000. Summing these amounts gives a total of $9600 + $10,000 = $19,600, indicating this account is restricted.

2.5   CALL AND CONTINUOUS SECURITY MARKETS

☐ 2.5.1   Call Markets

A *security market* can be defined as a mechanism for bringing together buyers and sellers of financial assets in order to facilitate trading. Security markets are *secondary* (as opposed to primary) markets, since the financial assets traded on them were issued at some previous point in time. In *call markets*, trading is allowed only at certain specified times. In such a market, when a security is called, those individuals that are interested in either buying or selling it are physically brought together.[18] Then there may be an explicit *auction*, in which prices are called out until the quantity demanded is as close as possible to the quantity supplied (this procedure is used by the Paris Bourse for major stocks). Alternatively, orders may be left with a clerk, and periodically an official of the exchange sets a price that allows the maximum number of shares from the previously accumulated orders to be traded (this procedure is used by the Paris Bourse for less-active stocks).

☐ 2.5.2   Continuous Markets

In *continuous markets*, trades may occur at any time. Although only investors are needed for such a market to operate, it generally would not be very effective without intermediaries also being present. In a continuous market without intermediaries, an investor who wants to buy or sell a security quickly might have either to spend a great deal of money searching for a good offer or to run the risk of accepting a poor one. Since orders from investors arrive more or less randomly, prices in such a market would vary considerably, depending on the flow of buy orders relative to the flow of sell orders. However, anyone willing to take temporary positions in securities could potentially make a profit by ironing out these transitory variations in supply and demand. This is the role of intermediaries known as dealers (also known as market-makers) and specialists. In the pursuit of personal gain, they

---

[18] Enough time is allowed to elapse between calls (for example, an hour or more) so that a substantial number of orders to buy and sell will accumulate.

generally reduce fluctuations in security prices that are unrelated to changes in value and, in doing so, provide *liquidity* for investors. Here, liquidity refers to the ability of investors to convert securities into cash at a price that is similar to the price of the previous trade, assuming no new information has arrived since the previous trade.

Security markets for common stocks (as well as certain other securities) in the United States typically involve dealers or specialists. This chapter provides a detailed description of how these markets function and the role played by dealers and specialists. Although the focus is on markets for common stocks, many of the features of such markets are applicable to the markets for other types of financial assets (such as bonds). *Organized exchanges*, which are central physical locations where trading is done under a set of rules and regulations, are discussed first. Examples of such exchanges for common stocks are the New York Stock Exchange, American Stock Exchange, and various regional exchanges.

2.6 MAJOR MARKETS IN THE UNITED STATES

☐ 2.6.1 The New York Stock Exchange

The New York Stock Exchange (NYSE) is a corporation that has 1366 full members. It has a charter and a set of rules and regulations that govern its operation and the activities of its members. A 27-person board of directors that is elected by the membership supervises the exchange. Twelve of the directors are members and 12 are not members; the latter are known as "public directors." The remaining three directors are a full-time chairman, an executive vice-chairman, and a president.

In order to become a member, a *seat* (comparable to a membership card) must be purchased from a current member.[19] By holding a seat, the member has the privilege of being able to execute trades using the facilities provided by the exchange. Since most trades of common stocks, in both dollar value and number of shares, take place on the NYSE, this privilege is valuable.[20] Not surprisingly, many brokerage firms are members, meaning that either an officer (if the brokerage firm is a corporation), a general partner (if the brokerage firm is a partnership), or an employee of the firm is a member. Indeed, many brokerage firms have more than one member. A brokerage firm with one or more NYSE memberships is often referred to as a *member firm* (or *member corporation*, or *member organization*).

A stock that is available for trading on the NYSE is known as a *listed*

---

[19] The applicant for membership must also pass a written examination, be sponsored by two current members of the exchange, and be approved by the board. Recently, the NYSE began allowing members to lease their seats to individuals acceptable to the exchange; as of the end of 1987, there were 503 leased seats. In addition to the 1366 full memberships, in 1987 there were 120 individuals who held special memberships; in return for an annual fee, these members are granted access to the trading floor. For an extensive discussion of the NYSE and other equity markets, see Robert A. Schwartz, *Equity Markets* (New York: Harper & Row, 1988).

[20] During 1987, trading volume on the NYSE averaged, on a daily basis, 188.9 million shares, worth in excess of $7 billion. The American Stock Exchange, the second largest organized exchange, had comparable daily values of less than one-tenth these amounts.

security. In order for a company's stock to be listed, the company must apply to the NYSE. The initial application is usually informal and confidential. If approved, the company then makes a formal application that is publicly known. Given an earlier approval on the informal application, approval at this stage is almost certain. The criteria used by the NYSE in approving an application are "(1) the degree of national interest in the company, (2) its relative position and stability in the industry, and (3) whether it is engaged in an expanding industry, with prospects of at least maintaining its relative position." [21] The specific requirements are displayed in Table 2.2. Companies that are approved for listing must agree to pay a nominal annual fee and provide certain information to the public. After listing, if trading interest in a security declines substantially, it may be *delisted* by the exchange, meaning that it is no longer available for trading on the NYSE. (Delistings also occur when a listed company is acquired by another company or is merged into another company.) At other times there may be a *trading halt*, meaning that there is a temporary suspension of trading in that security. Table 2.2 shows various criteria that are used by the NYSE to determine whether or not to delist a stock. Companies may apply for listing on more than one exchange, and under certain conditions an exchange may set up unlisted trading privileges for transactions in a stock already listed on another exchange.

An interesting example of securities that are dually listed involves certain foreign companies that are listed on a major exchange in their home country as well as on a U.S. exchange. In some cases the stock itself is traded in the United States (most dually listed Canadian stocks are traded in this manner). In other cases, what is traded in the United States is not the foreign company's stock but what is known as *American depository receipts* (ADRs). ADRs are financial assets that are issued by U.S. banks and represent indirect ownership of a certain number of shares of a specific foreign company that are held on deposit in a bank in the company's home country. The U.S. bank that has created the ADRs sees to it that the U.S. investor receives, in U.S. dollars, all cash dividends that the company pays. In addition, anything else that is received by the bank, such as annual reports, is forwarded to the investor. In return for providing these services, the bank charges the investor a small fee.[22]

New York Stock Exchange Members

Members in the NYSE fall into one of four categories, depending on the type of trading activity in which they engage. These categories are commission brokers, floor brokers, floor traders, and specialists. Of the 1366 members on the NYSE, roughly 700 are commission brokers, 400 are specialists, 225 are floor brokers, and 41 are floor traders. The trading activities of members in these categories are as follows:

1. *Commission brokers*. These members take orders that the public has placed with brokerage firms and see to it that they are executed on the

---

[21] New York Stock Exchange, *Fact Book 1988*, p. 22.

[22] ADRs are discussed in more detail in Chapter 24.

TABLE 2.2

New York Stock Exchange Criteria for Listing
and Delisting a Security.

(a) INITIAL LISTING REQUIREMENTS OF THE NYSE [a]

1. Either (a) the pretax income for the most recent year must be at least $2,500,000 and the pretax income over each of the preceding two years must be at least $2,000,000 or (b) the pretax income over the most recent three years must be at least $6,500,000 in total with a minimum of $4,500,000 in the most recent year.
2. Net tangible assets must be worth at least $18,000,000.
3. There must be at least 1,100,000 shares outstanding that are publicly held, and these shares must have an aggregate market value of at least $18,000,000 (this amount is subject to periodic adjustment based on market conditions).
4. There must be either (a) at least 2000 stockholders who each own a minimum of 100 shares or (b) at least 2200 stockholders with the monthly trading volume averaging at least 100,000 shares over the most recent six months.

(b) NYSE CONDITIONS FOR DELISTING A SECURITY [b]

1. The number of stockholders that each own at least 100 shares falls below 1200.
2. The number of shares that are publicly held falls below 600,000.
3. The aggregate market value of publicly-held shares falls below $5,000,000 (this amount is subject to periodic adjustment based on market conditions).

[a] Generally, *all* these requirements must be met for initial listing.
[b] Normally a security will be considered for delisting if *any one* of these conditions occur. However, under certain circumstances a security may be delisted even though none of the conditions occur.
SOURCE: Adapted from the New York Stock Exchange *Fact Book 1988*.

exchange; the brokerage firms that they work for are paid commissions by the customers for their services.

2. *Floor brokers*. These members assist commission brokers when there are too many orders flowing into the market for the commission brokers to handle alone. For their assistance, they receive part of the commission paid by the customer to the commission broker. (Sometimes both floor brokers, as defined here, and commission brokers are lumped together and called floor brokers.)

3. *Floor traders*. These members trade solely for themselves and are prohibited by exchange rules from handling public orders; they hope to make money by taking advantage of perceived trading imbalances that result in temporary mispricing, thereby allowing them to buy low and sell high. These members are also known as registered competitive market makers, competitive traders, or registered traders.

4. *Specialists*. These members perform two roles. First, any limit order that the commission broker cannot execute immediately because the current market price is not at or better than the specified limit price is left with the specialist for possible execution in the future. If this order is subsequently executed, the specialist is paid part of the customer's commission. The specialist keeps these orders in what is known as the *limit order book* or *specialist's book*. Stop and stop-limit orders are also left with the specialist, who then enters them in the specialist's

book. In this capacity, the specialist is acting as a broker (that is, agent) for the customer's broker and can be thought of as a "broker's broker."

Second, the specialist acts as a *dealer* in certain stocks (in particular, for the same stocks in which he or she acts as a broker). This means that the specialist buys and sells certain stocks for his or her own account and is allowed to seek a profit in doing so. However, in acting as a dealer, the NYSE requires the specialist to maintain a "fair and orderly market" in those stocks in which he or she is registered as a specialist. Thus, the NYSE expects the specialist to buy or sell shares from his or her own account when there is a temporary imbalance between the number of buy and sell orders (in doing so, specialists are allowed to short sell their assigned stocks). Even though the NYSE monitors the trading activities of the specialists, this requirement is so ill-defined that it is difficult, if not impossible, to enforce.

As might be inferred from the preceding discussion, specialists are at the center of the trading activity on the NYSE. Each stock that is listed on the NYSE has a specialist assigned to it.[23] In only a few instances are two (or more) specialists assigned to the same stock. Since there are over 1600 common stocks listed on the NYSE and only 400 specialists, this suggests that each specialist is assigned more than one stock, and indeed this is the case. All orders involving a given stock must be taken physically to a *trading post*, a spot on the floor of the NYSE where the specialist for that stock stands at all times during the hours the NYSE is open.[24] It is here that an order is either executed or left with the specialist.

Placing a Market Order

The operation of the New York Stock Exchange is best described by an example. Mr. B asks his broker for the current price of General Motors shares. The broker punches a few buttons on a televisionlike quotation machine and finds that the current *bid* and *asked* prices on the NYSE are as favorable as the prices available on any other market, being equal to 61 and $61\frac{1}{4}$, respectively. In addition, the quotation machine indicates that these bid and asked prices are good for orders of at least 100 and 500 shares, respectively. This means that the NYSE specialist is willing to buy at least 100 shares of GM at a price of $61 (the bid price) and is willing to sell at least 500 shares of GM at $61.25 (the asked price).[25] After being given this information, Mr. B instructs his broker to "buy 300 at market," meaning he wishes to place a market order with his broker for 300 shares of GM.

---

[23] The assignment is made by the board of directors and also includes any preferred stock or warrants that the company has listed on the exchange. In 1987 there were 1647 companies listed on the NYSE, with 2244 issues being traded, meaning there were almost 600 different issues of preferred stocks and warrants being traded on the NYSE. Bonds are also listed on the NYSE but are traded in an entirely different manner that does not involve the use of specialists; in 1987 there were 885 issuers that had 3346 issues of bonds listed on the NYSE.

[24] The NYSE is currently open from 9:30 A.M. until 4:00 P.M. However, the NYSE is considering extending its hours of operation in order to overlap with the London and Tokyo stock markets.

[25] As a matter of NYSE policy, only the specialist is allowed to see the contents of the limit order book. Accordingly, these orders may represent either orders for the specialist's own account or public orders on the limit order book.

At this point the broker transmits the order to his or her firm's New York headquarters, where the order is subsequently relayed to the brokerage firm's booth on the exchange floor. Upon receiving the order, the firm's commission broker goes to the trading post for GM.

The existence of a standing order to buy at 61 means that no one else is prepared to sell at a lower price, and the existence of a standing order to sell at $61\frac{1}{4}$ means that no higher price need be paid. This leaves only the spread between the two prices for possible negotiation. If Mr. B is lucky, another broker (for example, one with a market order to sell 300 shares for Ms. S) will "take" the order at a price "between the quotes" (here, at $61\frac{1}{8}$). Information will be exchanged between the two brokers and the sale will be made. Figure 2.2 illustrates the procedure used to fill Mr. B's order.

If the gap between the quoted bid and asked prices is wide enough, an auction may occur among various commission brokers, with sales made at one or more prices between the specialist's quoted values. Ths auction is known as a *double* (or two-way) *auction*, since both buyers and sellers are participating in the bidding process.

What if no response had been forthcoming from the floor when Mr. B's order arrived? In such a case, the specialist would "take the other side," selling 300 shares to Mr. B's broker at a price of $61.25 per share. The actual seller might be the specialist or another investor whose limit order is being executed by the specialist.

If the bid-ask spread on a stock is no larger than the standard unit in which prices are quoted (typically $\frac{1}{8}$ of a point, or 12.5¢), market orders are generally executed directly by the specialist. This is because there is no spread for possible negotiation. In the previous example, if the specialist had quoted bid and asked prices of 61 and $61\frac{1}{8}$, then there is no incentive for Mr. B's commission broker to try to obtain a better price for the purchase order than $61\frac{1}{8}$, since any seller could obtain a price of 61 from the specialist. That is, to entice someone other than the specialist to sell GM to Mr. B, his commission broker would have to offer a better price than 61, since this is the price the seller could obtain from the specialist. Given that the next highest price is $61\frac{1}{8}$ and that the specialist is willing to trade at that price, Mr. B's commission broker will deal with the specialist rather than the "crowd."

Placing a Limit Order

So far, the discussion has been concerned with what would happen to a market order that was placed by Mr. B. What if Mr. B had placed a limit order instead of a market order? There are two situations that can occur with a limit order. First, the limit price may be within the bid and asked prices of the specialist. Second, the limit price may be outside these prices.

In the first situation, where the specialist is quoting prices of 61 and $61\frac{1}{4}$, assume Mr. B has placed a limit order with his broker to buy 300 shares of GM at a price of $61\frac{1}{8}$ or better. When this order is carried to the trading post, it is possible that it will be executed by the commission broker for the limit price of $61\frac{1}{8}$, since someone in the crowd may be willing to take the other side of the transaction. After all, anyone with a sell order can

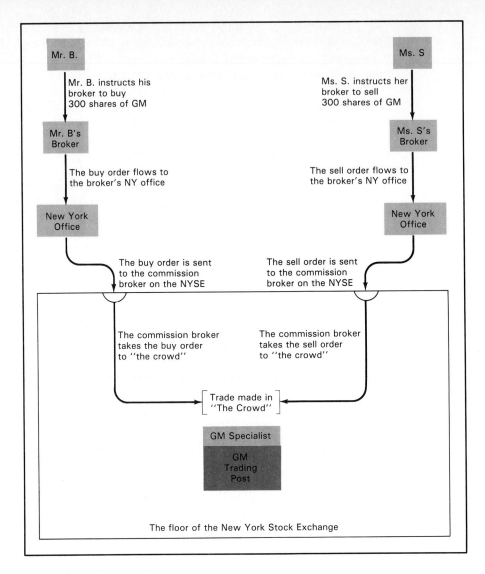

FIGURE 2–2
Order flow for a NYSE-listed security.

transact with the specialist at the specialist's price of 61. To these people, the limit price of $61\frac{1}{8}$ looks more attractive, since it represents a higher selling price to them. Thus, they would prefer doing business with Mr. B's commission broker rather than with the specialist.

In the second situation, assume Mr. B has placed a limit order to buy 300 shares of GM with a limit price of 60. When this order is carried to the trading post, the commission broker will not even attempt to fill it, since the limit price is outside the specialist's current bid and asked prices. That is, since anyone with a sell order can deal with the specialist at a price of

61, there is no chance that anyone will want to sell to Mr. B for the lower limit price of 60. Thus, the order will be given to the specialist to be entered in the specialist's book for possible execution in the future. Limit orders in the book are executed in order of price. For example, all purchase orders with limit prices of $60\frac{1}{2}$ will be executed (if at all) before Mr. B's order is executed. If there are several limit orders in the book at the same price, they are executed in order of arrival (that is, first in, first out).

It may not be possible to fill an entire order at a single price. For example, a broker with a market order to buy 500 shares might obtain 300 shares at $61\frac{1}{8}$ and have to pay $61\frac{1}{4}$ for the remaining 200. Similarly, a limit order to buy 500 shares at $61\frac{1}{8}$ or better might result in the purchase of 300 shares at $61\frac{1}{8}$ and the entry of a limit order in the specialist's book for the other 200 shares.

Large and Small Orders

The NYSE has developed special procedures to handle both routine small orders and exceptionally large orders. Small orders, generally defined as orders involving 2099 or fewer shares, can be handled with a procedure known as the *super designated order turnaround* system (or SuperDOT, known earlier as DOT). In order to use SuperDOT, the member firm must be a participating subscriber. With this system, the New York office of the customer's brokerage firm can send the order directly to the specialist, whereupon it will be executed immediately (if possible), with a confirmation of the execution sent immediately to the brokerage firm.[26]

Exceptionally large orders are generally defined as orders involving 10,000 or more shares and are known as *blocks*. Typically, these orders are placed by institutional customers and may be handled in a variety of ways. One way of handling a block order is to take it directly to the specialist and negotiate a price for it. However, if the block is large enough, it is quite likely that the specialist will lower the bid price (for sell orders) or raise the asked price (for buy orders) by a substantial amount. This will occur because of the risks involved, since specialists are prohibited by the exchange from soliciting offsetting orders from the public and, thus, do not know how easily they can obtain an offsetting order. Even with these disadvantages, this procedure is used on occasion, generally for relatively small blocks, and is referred to as a *specialist block purchase* or *specialist block sale*, depending on whether the institution is selling or buying shares.[27]

Larger blocks can be handled by use of an *exchange distribution* (for sell orders) or *exchange acquisition* (for buy orders). Here, a brokerage firm

---

[26] For odd-lot orders, the brokerage firm may execute the order internally (meaning it sells shares from its own inventory or adds shares to its inventory, depending on whether the customer is buying or selling) or may use SuperDOT. There are special features of SuperDOT that are used to execute opening orders—that is, orders that are received up to the time the NYSE opens in the morning.

[27] One alternative for the institution that is thinking of placing the block order is to sequentially place many small orders. However, institutions generally do not want to do this, since it means that their block order will not be executed with due speed.

attempts to execute the order by finding enough offsetting orders from its customers. The block seller or buyer pays all brokerage costs, and the trade price is within the current bid and asked prices as quoted by the specialist. A similar procedure, known as a *special offering* (for sell orders) or *special bid* (for buy orders), involves letting all brokerage firms solicit offsetting orders from their customers.

Another way of selling blocks is to have a *secondary distribution*, where the shares are sold off the exchange after the close of trading in a manner similar to the sale of new issues of common stock. The exchange must give approval for such distributions and usually does so if it appears that the block could not be absorbed easily in normal trading on the exchange. Accordingly, secondary distributions generally involve the sale of exceptionally large blocks (they are discussed in more detail later in the chapter).

Although all these ways of handling block orders are used at one time or another, most block orders are handled in what is known as the *upstairs dealer market*. By using *block houses*, which are set up to deal with large orders, institutions have been able to get better prices for their orders. This occurs because the block houses, when informed by an institution that it wants to place a block order, will proceed to line up trading partners (including itself) to take the other side of the order. After this is done the block house will attempt to reach a mutually acceptable price with the original institution. Assuming such a price is reached (if not, the institution can take the order to a different block house), the order will be "crossed" on the floor of the exchange, meaning that the specialist is given the opportunity to fill any limit orders that are in the specialist's book at the block's selling price.[28] However, there is a limit on the number of shares (1000 shares or 5% of the size of the block, whichever is greater) that can be taken by the specialist to fill these limit orders.

For example, suppose the PF Pension Fund informs a block house that it wishes to sell 20,000 shares of GM common stock. The block house then finds three institutional investors that want to buy, say, 5000 shares apiece; the block house decides that it too will buy 5000 shares of GM stock from PF. Noting that the buyers have said that they would be willing to pay $70 per share, the block house subsequently informs PF that it will buy the 20,000 shares for $69.75 each, less a commission of $8000. Assuming PF accepts the deal, the block house now becomes the owner of the shares but must first cross them on the NYSE, since the block house is a member of the exchange. In this example, assume that when the block is crossed at $69.75, the specialist buys 500 shares at this price for a limit order that is in his or her book. After the cross, the block house gives 5000 shares to each of the institutional buyers in exchange for $350,000 (5,000 shares × $70 per share) and hopes that the remaining 4500 shares that it now owns can be sold in the near future at a favorable price. Needless to say, the possibility of not being able to sell them at a favorable price is one of the risks involved in being a block house.

---

[28] The order must be crossed on an exchange where the stock is listed, provided the block house is a member of that exchange.

Table 2.3 shows the total trading volume of securities listed on each of the active stock exchanges in the United States in 1986. Not surprisingly, the New York Stock Exchange dominates the list. Second in importance is the American Stock Exchange (AMEX), which lists shares of somewhat smaller companies of national interest (a few of which are also listed on the New York Stock Exchange). All others are termed *regional exchanges*, since historically each served as the sole location for trading securities primarily of interest to investors in its region. However, the major regional exchanges now depend to a substantial extent on transactions in securities that are also listed on a national exchange. Interestingly, the regional exchanges are currently larger, in aggregate, than the AMEX. Major regional exchanges currently in existence include the Boston, Cincinnati, Midwest, Pacific, and Philadelphia exchanges.

Other stock exchanges use procedures similar to those of the New York Stock Exchange. The role of specialists and the extent of automation may differ slightly, but the approach is basically the same.

Options exchanges and futures exchanges utilize some procedures that differ significantly from those employed by stock exchanges. Futures exchanges often have daily price limits instead of having specialists with directions to maintain fair and orderly markets. The Chicago Board Options Exchange separates the two functions of the specialist; an *order book official*

TABLE 2.3

Trading Volumes of the Stock Exchanges.

(a) 1986 TRADING VOLUME.

Market	Shares [a]		Dollars [a]	
	Annual	Daily	Annual	Daily
NYSE	35,680	141.0	$1,374,350	$5,432.2
AMEX	2,979	11.8	44,453	175.7
Regionals	6,088	24.1	200,770	793.6
NASDAQ	28,737	113.6	378,216	1,494.9
Third market	1,326	5.2	48,649	192.3

(b) FIVE-YEAR COMPARISONS.

Year	NYSE			NASDAQ		
	Companies	Issues	Daily Share Volume [a]	Companies	Issues	Daily Share Volume [a]
1986	1,573	2,257	141.0	4,417	5,189	113.6
1985	1,540	2,298	109.2	4,136	4,784	82.1
1984	1,543	2,319	91.2	4,097	4,723	59.9
1983	1,550	2,325	85.3	3,901	4,467	62.9
1982	1,526	2,225	65.1	3,264	3,664	33.3

[a] In millions.
SOURCE: Adapted from the New York Stock Exchange *Fact Book 1987* and the NASDAQ *1987 Fact Book*.

is charged with the maintenance of the book of limit orders, with one or more registered *market-makers* assigned the role of dealer. These exchanges are discussed in more detail in Chapters 18 and 19.

□ **2.6.3   The Over-the-Counter Market**

In the early days of the United States, banks acted as the primary dealers for stocks and bonds, and investors literally bought and sold securities over the counter at the banks. Transactions are more impersonal now, but the designation remains in use for transactions that are executed not on an original exchange but, instead, involve the use of a dealer. Most bonds are sold over the counter, as are the securities of small (and some not-so-small) companies.

The over-the-counter (OTC) market for stocks is highly automated. In 1971 the *National Association of Securities Dealers* (NASD), which serves as a self-regulating agency for its members, put into operation the *National Association of Security Dealers Automated Quotations* system (NASDAQ). This nationwide communications network allows brokers to know instantly the terms offered currently by all major dealers in securities covered by the system.

Dealers who subscribe to Level III of NASDAQ are given terminals with which to enter bid and asked prices for any stock in which they "make a market." Such dealers must be prepared to execute trades for at least one normal unit of trading (usually 100 shares) at the prices quoted. As soon as a bid or asked price is entered for a security, it is placed in a central computer file and may be seen by other subscribers (including other dealers) on their own terminals. When new quotations are entered, they replace the dealer's former prices.

When there is competition among dealers, those who are not well informed either price themselves out of the market by having too wide a bid-ask spread or go out of business after incurring heavy losses. In the first situation, nobody does business with such a dealer, since there are better prices available with other dealers. The second situation occurs when the dealer accumulates a large inventory at too high a price or disposes of inventory at too low a price, thus, doing the opposite of buying low and selling high. In general, the interests of investors are best served by a market in which dealers with unlimited access to all sources of information compete with one another, thereby leading to narrow bid-ask spreads around the "intrinsic" value of the security.

Most brokerage firms subscribe to Level II of NASDAQ for their trading rooms, obtaining terminals that can display the current quotations on any security in the system. All bid and asked quotations are displayed, with the dealer offering each quotation being identified so that orders can be routed to the dealer with the best price.[29] Imagine how difficult it would be to get

---

[29] Generally the order will be a market order, since there is no limit order book in the over-the-counter market. Limit orders will be handled (if at all) in an informal manner by the broker, who will periodically check to see if the order can be executed without violating the limit price; stop and stop limit orders are not allowed in the OTC market.

the best price for a customer in the absence of such a terminal (as was the case before NASDAQ existed). A broker would have to contact dealers one by one to try to find the best price; after determining what appears to be the best price, the broker would then contact that dealer again. However, when this dealer is contacted, it may turn out that the price has gone up or down in the meantime and that the previously quoted price may no longer be the best one.

Level I of NASDAQ is used by individual account executives to get a feel for the market. It shows the highest bid and the lowest asked price for each security.

NASDAQ classifies stocks with larger trading volumes (which also meet certain other requirements) as belonging to the *national market system* (NASDAQ/NMS). Every transaction made by a dealer for such a stock is reported directly, providing up-to-date detailed trading information to NASDAQ users. Furthermore, any stock included in NASDAQ/NMS is automatically eligible for margin purchases and short sales. For the less-active issues, dealers report only the total transactions at the close of each day, and only certain ones are eligible for margin purchases and short sales (four times each year, the Federal Reserve Board determines which ones are eligible).

As its name indicates, NASDAQ is primarily a quotation system. Actual transactions are made via direct negotiation between broker and dealer.[30] The price paid by a customer buying shares is likely to be higher than the amount paid by the broker to procure the shares, with the difference being known as a *markup*. When selling shares, the customer receives a price less than that received by the broker, with the difference being known as a *markdown*. (In both cases, the customer may also be charged a commission.) The size of these markups and markdowns is usually less than 5% of the price paid or received; brokers are periodically examined by the Securities and Exchange Commission to see that these markups and markdowns are reasonable.

To be included in NASDAQ, a security must have at least two registered market-makers (that is, dealers) and a minimum number of publicly held shares; moreover, the issuing firm must meet stated capital and asset requirements. As shown in Table 2.3, 5189 issues were included in the system at the end of 1986.[31] Although this total is more than double the total for the NYSE, trading volume is less than that of the NYSE, especially when measured in dollars.

The NASDAQ system covers only a portion of the outstanding OTC stocks and no bonds. Brokers with orders to buy or sell other OTC securities rely on quotations that are published daily, known as *pink sheets*, and less formal communication networks to obtain "best execution" for their clients.

---

[30] Trades involving up to 1000 shares of any NASDAQ/NMS security (for non-NMS securities, the limit is 500 shares) are handled by a computer system known as the *Small-Order Execution System* (SOES).

[31] Of this total, 266 were foreign securities consisting of 88 ADRs and 178 non-ADRs; 119 of the 178 non-ADRs were Canadian issues.

Until the 1970s, the New York Stock Exchange required its member firms to trade all NYSE-listed stocks at the Exchange and to charge fixed commissions. For large institutions this was expensive. In particular, the existence of a required minimum commission rate created a serious problem, since it exceeded the marginal cost of arranging large trades. Brokerage firms that were not members of the exchange faced no restrictions on the commissions they could charge and thus could compete effectively for large trades in NYSE-listed stocks. Such transactions were said to take place in the *third market*. More generally, the term third market now refers to the trading of any exchange-listed security in the OTC market. The existence of such a market is enhanced today by the fact that their trading hours are not fixed (unlike exchanges) and that they can continue to trade securities even when trading is halted on an exchange. As can be seen in Table 2.3, on the average 5.2 million shares were traded in the third market during each day of 1986.

Until 1976, NYSE member firms were prohibited by Rule 394 from either acting as dealers in the third market or executing orders involving NYSE-listed securities for their customers in the third market. In 1976, Rule 394 was replaced by Rule 390, which permits the execution of these orders in the third market but still prohibits member firms from acting as dealers in the third market. However, the Securities and Exchange Commission has issued a rule that permits member firms to act as dealers in securities that became listed on the NYSE after April 26, 1979. Controversy still exists over Rule 390, as some people argue that it should be abolished completely to spur competition between the NYSE and the OTC market, whereas others argue that having all orders funneled to the NYSE will lead to the most competitive marketplace possible.

Many institutions have dispensed with brokers and exchanges altogether for transactions in exchange-listed stocks and other securities. Trades of this type, where the buyer and seller deal directly with each other, are sometimes said to take place in the *fourth market*. In the United States, some of these transactions are facilitated by an automated computer-communications system called *Instinet*, which automatically provides quotations and execution.[32] A subscriber can enter a limit order in the computerized "book," where it can be seen by other subscribers, who can, in turn, signal their desire to take it. Whenever two orders are matched, the system automatically records the transaction and sets up the paperwork for its completion. Subscribers can also use the system to find likely partners for a trade and then conduct negotiations by telephone. A similar system, called Ariel, is used in the United Kingdom.

---

[32] The use of an intermediary such as a computer system makes it difficult to categorize such trades. Some people refer to the market where trades involving a "matchmaker" take place as the 3.5 market. The term fourth market is then used only when referring to the market where no matchmaker is involved.

2.7 INFORMATION-MOTIVATED AND LIQUIDITY-MOTIVATED TRADERS

There are two major reasons for security transactions. An investor may believe that a security has become mispriced—meaning that its value is outside the current bid and asked prices. One who feels this way believes that he or she has information not known to (or understood by) the market in general and may be termed an *information-motivated* trader. On the other hand, an investor may simply want to sell some securities to buy a new car, or buy some securities with recently inherited money, or the like. Such a person may be called *liquidity-motivated*: in making security transactions, he or she does not presume that others in the market have evaluated the prospects for the security incorrectly.

Dealers can make money by trading with liquidity-motivated traders or with inept information-motivated traders. But, on the average, they can only lose money by trading with clever information-motivated traders. The larger a dealer's bid-ask spread, the less business he or she will do; but whatever the spread, when a clever information-motivated investor makes a trade, the dealer may expect to lose. In the absence of unwise investors, the very existence of a dealer depends on investors' desires for liquidity. A dealer must select a bid-ask spread wide enough to limit the number of trades with customers possessing superior information, but narrow enough to attract an adequate number of liquidity-motivated transactions.

A dealer can take either a passive or an active role. For example, a bid-ask spread can be established and a tentative price set. As orders come in and are filled, the dealer's inventory (position) will vary and may even become negative when promises to deliver securities exceed promises to accept delivery. But any clear trend suggests that the price should be altered. In effect, a *passive dealer* lets the market indicate the appropriate price.

An *active dealer* tries to get as much information as possible and to alter bid and ask prices in advance to keep the flow of orders more in balance. The better a dealer's information, the smaller the bid-ask spread required to make a profit.

When there is competition among dealers, those who are not well informed either price themselves out of the market by requiring too high a bid-ask spread or go out of business after incurring heavy losses. In general, the interests of investors are best served by a market in which dealers with unlimited access to all sources of information compete with one another.

2.8 PRICES AS INFORMATION SOURCES

The usual description of a market assumes that every trader wishes to purchase or sell a known quantity at each possible price. All the traders come together, and in one way or another a price is found that clears the

market—that is, makes the quantity demanded as close as possible to the quantity supplied.

This may or may not be an adequate description of the markets for consumer goods, but it is clearly inadequate when describing security markets. The value of any capital asset depends on future prospects that are almost always uncertain. Any information that bears on such prospects may lead to a revised estimate of value. The fact that a knowledgeable trader is willing to buy or sell some quantity of a security at a particular price is likely to be information of just this sort. Offers to trade may thus affect other offers. Prices may both clear markets and convey information.

The dual role of prices has a number of implications. For example, it behooves the liquidity-motivated trader to publicize his or her motives and thereby avoid an adverse effect on the market. Thus an institution purchasing securities for a pension fund that intends simply to hold a representative cross section of securities should make it clear that it does not consider the securities underpriced. On the other hand, any firm trying to buy or sell a large number of shares that it considers mispriced should try to conceal either its motives, its identity, or both (and many do try). Such attempts may be ineffective, however, as those asked to take the other side of such trades try to find out exactly what is going on (and many do find out).

Since offers may affect other offers, the way in which a market functions can affect the prices at which trades are made. And different markets function in different ways. For example, the New York Stock Exchange specialist's "books" contain information on both the prices and the quantities specified in standing orders, but only the lowest ask price and the highest bid price and the quantities associated with each are revealed to the general market. In the over-the-counter market, dealers publicly announce bid and ask prices that are firm for small quantities, but they negotiate prices for larger quantities.

The extent to which standing orders are made public may thus affect (1) the prices at which such orders are executed, (2) the extent to which investors will place them with brokers, and (3) the extent to which brokers will place them in a central "book," where they can be seen by others.

Some investors depend almost entirely on price for information about value. This raises the possibility that a clever trader could make money by placing orders to trigger foolish responses from such investors. While this may occur in isolated instances, it is limited by the presence of informed traders who use external information sources to assess value. Given a large-enough number of people who study fundamental aspects, it is possible for most investors to assume that market price reflects value.

2.9 THE CENTRAL MARKET

The Securities Acts Amendments of 1975 mandated that the U.S. Securities and Exchange Commission should move as rapidly as possible toward the implementation of a truly nationwide competitive central security market:

☐ The linking of all markets for qualified securities through communication and data processing facilities will foster efficiency, enhance competition, increase the information available to brokers, dealers, and investors, facilitate the off-setting of investors' orders, and contribute to best execution of such orders.[33]

Implementation of these objectives has proceeded in steps. In 1975, a *Consolidated Tape* began to report trades in stocks listed on the New York and American Stock Exchanges that took place on the two exchanges, on major regional exchanges, in the OTC market using the NASDAQ system, and in the fourth market using the Instinet system. Since 1976, this information has been used to produce the *composite stock price tables* published in the daily press.

The second step involved the setting of commissions charged to investors by brokerage firms that are members of the NYSE. Prior to 1975, investors found the same commission being charged by all NYSE member firms for a given order. This was due to the fact that the NYSE required its members to charge a fixed commission. However, as a result of the Securities Acts Amendments of 1975, this system of fixed commissions was abolished and all brokerage firms were free to set their commissions at whatever level they desired.

The next step involved quotations. To obtain the best possible terms for a client, a broker must know the prices currently available on all major markets. To facilitate this, the Securities and Exchange Commission instructed stock exchanges to make their quotations available for use in a *consolidated quotation system* (CQS). With the implementation of this system in 1978, bid and asked prices were made more accessible to those subscribing to quotation services. Increasingly, a broker is able to rely on electronic equipment to determine the best available terms for a trade, thus avoiding the need for extensive shopping around.

In 1978, the *Intermarket Trading System* (ITS) was inaugurated. This electronic communications network links seven exchanges (the NYSE, AMEX, Boston, Cincinnati, Midwest, Pacific, and Philadelphia exchanges) and certain over-the-counter security dealers, enabling brokers, dealers, and specialists at various locations to interact with one another. ITS display monitors provide the bid and asked prices quoted by market-makers (these quotes are obtained from CQS), and the system allows the broker to route orders electronically to where the best price exists at that moment. However, the market-maker providing the best price may withdraw it on receipt of an order. Another drawback is that brokers are not required to route orders to the market-maker providing the best price. At the end of 1987, 1537 exchange-listed stocks were included on the system, and daily trading volume averaged 8.6 million shares.

The final step in the process has not been implemented. It involves the establishment of a single centralized limit order book (CLOB), with associated procedures for linking markets electronically and the setting of rules concerning its use and disclosure. In implementing this step, many issues

---

[33] From *Securities Acts Amendments of 1975*, Section 11A.

must be settled: Should there be specialists, and if so, how should they operate? What requirements (if any) should be imposed on market-makers? Who should operate the central market system?

There are many long-entrenched and powerful institutions in the securities industry. The eventual nature of the central market will undoubtedly depend in part on the relative political power of the various vested interests. But the goals seem relatively clear, and on balance, the changes are likely to benefit investors.

2.10   CLEARING PROCEDURES

Most securities are sold the standard way, which requires delivery of certificates within 5 business days. On rare occasions, a sale may be made as a cash transaction, requiring delivery the same day, or as a seller's option, giving the seller the choice of any delivery day within a specified period (typically, no more than 60 days). On other occasions, extensions to the 5-day time limit are granted.

It would be extremely inefficient if every security transaction had to end with a physical transfer of stock certificates from the seller to the buyer. A brokerage firm might sell 500 shares of American Telephone & Telegraph (AT&T) stock for one client, Mr. S, and later that day buy 500 shares for Ms. B, another client. Mr. S's 500 shares could be delivered to his buyer, and Ms. B's shares could be obtained by accepting delivery from her seller. However, it would be much easier to transfer Mr. S's shares to Ms. B and instruct B's seller to deliver 500 shares directly to S's buyer. This would be especially helpful if the brokerage firm's clients, Mr. S and Ms. B, held their securities in street name. Then, the 500 shares they traded would not have to be physically moved and their ownership would not have to be changed on the books of AT&T.

□ 2.10.1   Clearinghouses

The process can be facilitated even more by a *clearinghouse*, the members of which are brokerage firms, banks, and other financial institutions. Records of transactions made by members during a day are sent there. At the end of the day, both sides of the trades are verified for consistency; then all transactions are netted out. Each member receives a list of the net amounts of securities to be delivered or received along with the net amount of money to be paid or collected. Every day, each member settles with the clearinghouse instead of with various other firms.

A centralized clearinghouse, operated by the National Securities Clearing Corporation, handles trades made on the New York and American stock exchanges and in the over-the-counter market. Some regional exchanges also maintain clearinghouses. Not all exchange members join such organizations; some choose to use the services of other members. Some banks belong in

order to facilitate delivery of securities which, for example, serve as collateral for call loans.

By holding securities in street name and using clearinghouses, brokers can reduce the costs of transfer operations. But even more can be done: Certificates can be immobilized almost completely. The *Depository Trust Company* (DTC) accomplishes this by maintaining computerized records of the securities "owned" by its member firms (brokers, banks, and so on). Members' stock certificates are credited to their accounts at the DTC, but the certificates are transferred to the DTC on the books of the issuing corporation and remain registered in its name unless a member subsequently withdraws them. Whenever possible, one member will "deliver" securities to another by initiating a simple bookkeeping entry in which one account is credited and the other debited for the shares involved. Dividends paid on securities held by the DTC are simply credited to members' accounts based on their holdings and may be subsequently withdrawn in cash.

The Securities Acts Amendments of 1975 instruct the Securities and Exchange Commission to develop a central system of this sort to eliminate the movement of stock certificates and possibly eliminate stock certificates entirely. Eventually, when cash dividends are to be paid by a corporation, instead of writing checks, its computers may transfer money directly using other computers that are in touch with still other computers in banks, brokerage firms, and other financial institutions. Moreover, the central market system may be integrated with the central clearing system so that agreement of two parties to the terms of a transaction will automatically bring about the transfer of ownership required to complete the trade.

2.11 INSURANCE

In the late 1960s, many brokerage firms were confronted with an unexpectedly large volume of transactions. Unfortunately, at that time computerized systems were unable to handle the workload. This gave rise to back-office problems and resulted in a rash of *fails to deliver*—situations in which a seller's broker did not deliver certificates to a buyer's broker on or before the required settlement date.

Worse yet, several brokerage firms subsequently failed, and some of their clients discovered for the first time that certificates in their accounts were not physically available. Such events led to serious concern about the desirability of any procedure that kept certificates out of the hands of investors. To avoid erosion of investor confidence, member firms of the New York Stock Exchange spent substantial sums to cover the losses of failed firms or to merge them with successful firms. But such remedies were only temporary; insurance provided a more permanent solution.

Securities Investor Protection Corporation. The Securities Investor Protection Act of 1970 established the *Securities Investor Protection Corporation* (SIPC), a quasi-governmental agency that insures the accounts of clients of all brokers and members of exchanges registered with the Securities

and Exchange Commission against loss due to a brokerage firm's failure. Each account is insured up to a stated amount ($500,000 per customer in 1988). The cost of the insurance is supposed to be borne by the covered broker and members through premiums; should this amount be insufficient, SIPC can borrow up to $1 billion from the U.S. Treasury. A number of brokerage firms have gone farther, arranging for additional coverage from private insurance companies.

2.12 COMMISSIONS

□ 2.12.1 Fixed Commissions

In the 1770s, people interested in buying and selling stocks and bonds met under a buttonwood tree at 68 Wall Street in New York City. In May 1792, a group of brokers pledged "not to buy or sell from this day for any person whatsoever, any kind of public stock at a less rate than one quarter per cent commission on the specie value, and that we will give preference to each other in our negotiations." [34] A visitor to the New York Stock Exchange in the early 1970s could see this "buttonwood agreement" publicly displayed. This was not surprising, since the Exchange is a lineal descendant of the group that met under the buttonwood tree. And, until 1968, the Exchange required its member brokers to charge fixed minimum commissions for stocks, with no "rebates, returns, discounts or allowances in 'any shape or manner,' direct or indirect." [35] The terms had changed, but the principle established 180 years earlier remained in effect.

In the United States, most cartels designed to limit competition by fixing prices are illegal. But this one was exempted from prosecution under the antitrust laws. Before 1934 the Exchange was, in essence, considered a private club for its members. This changed with passage of the Securities and Exchange Act of 1934, which required most exchanges to be registered with the Securities and Exchange Commission (SEC). The SEC, in turn, encouraged exchanges to "self-regulate" their activities, including the setting of minimum commissions.

□ 2.12.2 Competitive Commissions

As mentioned earlier in this chapter, the system of fixed commissions was finally terminated by the Securities Act Amendments of 1975 (but only after repeated challenges by the NYSE). Since May 1, 1975 (known in the trade as *May Day*), brokers have been free to set commissions at any desired rate or to negotiate with customers concerning the fees charged for particular trades. The former procedure is more commonly employed in "retail" trades

---

[34] See Wilford J. Eiteman, Charles A. Dice, and David K. Eiteman, *The Stock Market* (New York: McGraw-Hill, 1969), 19.

[35] Ibid, 138.

executed for small investors, whereas the latter is used more often when handling large trades involving institutional investors and others.

In the era of fixed commissions, brokerage firms did not compete with one another over commissions. However, those brokerage firms that belonged to the New York Stock Exchange competed with one another in a different manner—namely, by offering a panoply of ancillary services to customers. Large institutions were provided with security analysis, performance measurement services, and the like in return for *soft dollars*—brokerage commissions ostensibly paid for having a brokerage firm execute their trades and indirectly designated as payment for services rendered. It appears that for every $3 in commissions received on large trades, brokerage firms were willing to spend up to roughly $2 to provide ancillary services to the customers. Thus, it follows that it cost brokerage firms roughly $1 per $3 of commission received just to execute a large trade for a customer. Apparently, up to two-thirds of the fixed commission rate ($2 out of $3) on such large orders was pure (marginal) profit.

Experience after May Day provided confirmation. Rates for large trades fell substantially. So did those charged for small trades by firms offering only bare-bones brokerage services. On the other hand, broad-line firms that provided extensive services to small investors for no additional fee continued to charge commissions similar to those specified in the earlier fixed schedules. In succeeding years, as costs have risen, charges for smaller transactions have increased, whereas those for large trades have not.

During the 1960s and 1970s, a number of procedures were used to subvert the fixed commission rates. In particular, the third and fourth markets expanded their operations while regional exchanges invented ways to serve as conduits to return a portion of the fixed commissions to institutional investors.

No legal restriction gave the New York Stock Exchange its monopoly power in the first instance. Instead, the situation has been attributed to the natural monopoly arising from economies of scale in bringing together many people (either physically or via modern communication technology) to trade with one another. The potential profits from such a monopoly are limited by the advantages it confers. The increasing institutionalization of security holdings and progress in communications and computer technology have diminished the advantages associated with a centralized physical exchange. Thus, the removal of legal protection for this particular type of price fixing may only have accelerated a trend already under way.

Increased competition among brokerage firms has resulted in a wide range of alternatives for investors. Following May Day, some firms *unbundled*—meaning they priced their services separately from their pricing of order execution. Other firms *went discount*, meaning they dropped almost all ancillary services and cut commissions accordingly. Still others bundled new services into comprehensive packages. Some of these approaches have not stood the test of time, but just as mail-order firms, discount houses, department stores, and expensive boutiques coexist in retail trade, many different combinations are viable in the brokerage industry.

Figure 2.3 shows typical commission rates charged by retail brokerage

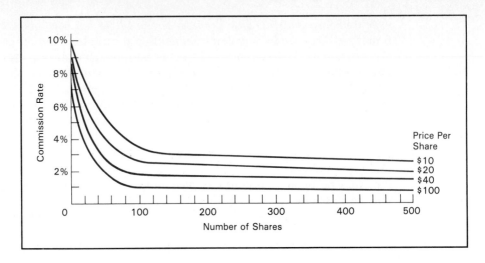

FIGURE 2–3
Typical commission rates for selected transactions; dollar commission as a percentage of the value of the order.

firms for small to medium-sized trades. These rates are representative of those charged by full-time retail brokers that provide offices with quotation boards, research reports, account executives available for advice and information, and the like. The rates also apply to trades made by customers whose volume of business is small. Discount firms with little but execution capability typically charge 30% to 70% less. As in any other competitive industry, it behooves the customer to decide what is worth paying for and then to shop around to obtain the best possible price.

2.13   TRANSACTION COSTS

☐ 2.13.1   The Bid-Ask Spread

Commission costs are only a portion of the total cost associated with buying or selling a security. Consider a "round-trip" transaction, in which a stock is purchased and then sold during a period in which no new information causes investors collectively to reassess the value of the stock (more concretely, the bid and asked prices quoted by dealers do not change). The stock will typically be purchased at the dealers' asked price and sold at the bid price, which is lower. The *bid-ask spread* thus constitutes a portion of the round-trip transaction costs.

According to one study, the spread between the bid and asked prices for a typical stock is approximately $.30 per share for the securities of large, actively traded companies. This amounts to less than 1% of the price per share for most stocks of this type—a reasonably small amount to pay for the ability to buy or sell in a hurry.

TABLE 2.4
Bid-Ask Spreads and Round-Trip Transaction Costs.

(a) COMMON STOCK BID-ASK SPREADS: SMALL ORDERS.

CAPITALIZATION

Sector	From (millions)	To (millions)	Number of Issues	Percent of U.S. Market	Average Price	Average Spread	Spread Price
1 (small)	$ 0	$ 10	1,009	.36%	$ 4.58	$.30	6.55%
2	10	25	754	.89	10.30	.42	4.07
3	25	50	613	1.59	15.16	.46	3.03
4	50	75	362	1.60	18.27	.34	1.86
5	75	100	202	1.27	21.85	.32	1.46
6	100	500	956	15.65	28.31	.32	1.13
7	500	1,000	238	12.29	35.43	.27	.76
8	1,000	1,500	102	8.87	44.34	.29	.65
9 (large)	1,500	99,999	180	57.48	52.40	.27	.52

(b) PERCENTAGE ROUND-TRIP TRANSACTION COSTS, COMMON STOCK.

CAPITALIZATION

Sector	Dollar Value of Block ($ thousands)								
	5	25	250	500	1,000	2,500	5,000	10,000	20,000
1 (small)	17.3%	27.3%	43.8%						
2	8.9	12.0	23.8	34.4%					
3	5.0	7.6	18.8	25.9	30.0%				
4	4.3	5.8	9.6	16.9	25.4	31.5%			
5	2.8	3.9	5.9	8.1	11.5	15.7	25.7%		
6	1.8	2.1	3.2	4.4	5.6	7.9	11.0	16.2%	
7	1.9	2.0	3.1	4.0	5.6	7.7	10.4	14.3	20.2%
8	1.9	1.9	2.7	3.3	4.6	6.2	8.9	13.6	18.1
9 (large)	1.1	1.2	1.3	1.7	2.1	2.8	4.1	5.9	8.0

SOURCE: Thomas F. Loeb, "Trading Cost: The Critical Link Between Investment Information and Results," *Financial Analysis Journal* 39, no. 3 (May/June 1983):41–2.

However, not all securities enjoy this type of liquidity. Shares of smaller firms tend to sell at lower prices but at similar bid-ask spreads. As a result, the percentage transaction cost is considerably larger. This is shown in part (a) of Table 2.4. Stocks were assigned to sectors based on each firm's *market capitalization*, which is equal to the market value of the firm's outstanding equity. For example, if the total market value of the common stock of a company was less than $10 million, it was considered to be in sector 1 (the smallest capitalization sector), and if the market value was greater than $1.5 billion, the company was included in sector 9 (the largest capitalization sector). As the table shows, the larger the capitalization, the greater was the average price per share. Note also that the average spread in dollars was actually greater for the smallest capitalization stocks than for the largest. Most importantly, however, the ratio of the average spread to the average price fell continuously from 6.55% for the smallest sector to .52% for the

largest sector. This means that the larger the capitalization of the firm, the greater the liquidity will be for that investment.

☐ 2.13.2 Price Impact

Brokerage commissions and bid-ask spreads represent transaction costs for small orders (typically 100 shares). For larger-sized orders, the possibility of *price impacts* must be considered. Consider purchase orders. Due to the law of supply and demand, the larger the size of the order, the more likely the investor's purchase price will be higher. Furthermore, the more rapidly the order is to be completed and the more knowledgeable the individual or organization placing the order, the higher is the purchase price charged by the dealer.

Part (b) of Table 2.4 provides estimates of average costs for transactions in the "upstairs dealer" market. All three sources of costs are included: bid-ask spreads, brokerage commissions, and price impacts. The figures refer to the total cost for a round-trip—a purchase followed by a sale—and reveal that for any capitalization sector, larger block sizes are associated with larger percentage transaction costs. The figures also reveal that for any given dollar-size block, larger capitalization sectors are associated with smaller percentage transaction costs (a similar observation can be made upon examination of panel (a)).

Part (a) of Figure 2.4 plots the percentage transaction costs for blocks of $25,000 each, which corresponds to the values in the third column from the left in part (b) of Table 2.4. Values range from over 27% (for small capitalization stocks) to 1.2% (for large capitalization stocks).

Part (b) of Figure 2.4 shows the relationship between order size and transaction cost for each of the three largest capitalization sectors, which correspond to the last three rows of part (b) of Table 2.4. The figure shows that the impact of a very large order on price can be substantial, and the impact is greater for smaller capitalizations.

2.14 INVESTMENT BANKING

The discussion so far has focused on secondary markets for securities, where securities that were initially issued at some previous point in time are subsequently traded. The focus now shifts to the *primary market* for securities, which is the name given to the markets where the initial issuance itself takes place. Some issuers deal directly with purchasers in this market, but many rely on *investment bankers*, who serve as intermediaries between issuers and the ultimate purchasers of their securities.[36]

---

[36] For more on investment banking, see Chapter 17 of Stephen A. Ross and Randolph W. Westerfield, *Corporate Finance* (St. Louis, Mo.: Times Mirror/Moseby College Publishing, 1988), Chapter 15 of Richard A. Brealey and Stewart C. Myers, *Principles of Corporate Finance* (New York: McGraw-Hill, 1988), and the January/February 1986 issue of the *Journal of Financial Economics*, which contains papers presented at a symposium of investment banking.

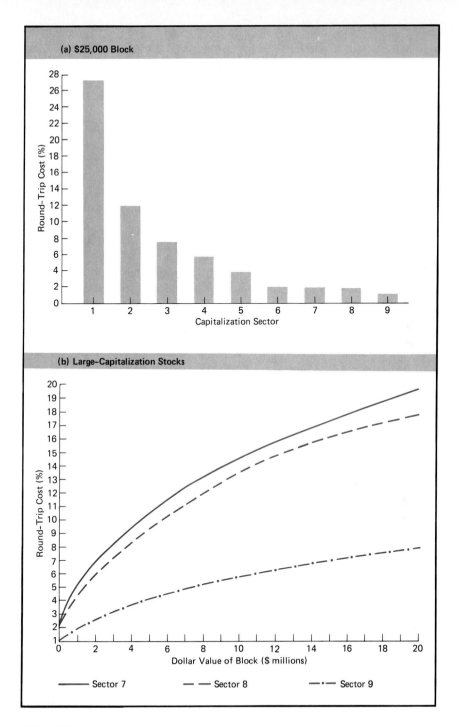

FIGURE 2–4
Round-trip transaction costs.

Investment banking services are typically performed by brokerage firms and, to a limited extent, by commercial banks. In some instances, only a few large institutional investors are solicited, and the entire issue is sold to one or more of them. Such *private placements* are frequently used for bond issues. As long as relatively few potential buyers are contacted (say, less than 25), requirements for detailed disclosure, public notice, and so on may be waived, considerably reducing the cost of floating an issue. Such placements are often announced after the fact, via advertisements in the financial press.

When public sale is contemplated, much more must be done. Many firms may serve as intermediaries in the process. One, acting as the "lead" investment banker, will put together a syndicate (or purchase group) and a selling group. The *syndicate* includes firms that purchase the securities from the issuing corporation and are thus said to *underwrite* the offering. The *selling group* includes firms that contact potential buyers and do the actual selling, usually on a commission basis.

The process begins with discussions between the issuing corporation and one or more investment bankers. Some issuers utilize *competitive bidding* and then select the investment banker offering the best overall terms. This procedure is used for many government bond issues and is required by law for securities issued by firms in certain regulated industries. However, many corporations maintain a continuing relationship with a single investment banker and negotiate the terms of each new offering with that firm. The investment banker is likely to be heavily involved in the planning of an offering, the terms involved, the amount to be offered, and so on, serving, in effect, as a financial consultant to the corporation.

Once the basic characteristics of an offering have been established, a *registration statement* is filed with the Securities and Exchange Commission and a preliminary *prospectus* disclosing material relevant to the prospective buyer is issued. (This prospectus is often referred to as a *red herring*, since it has a disclaimer printed in red ink across the first page that informs reader that it is not an offer to sell.) The actual price of the security is not included in the preliminary prospectus, and no final sales may be made until the registration becomes effective and a final prospectus issued, indicating the offer price at which the stock will be sold. The final prospectus may be issued as soon as, in the opinion of the Securities and Exchange Commission, there has been adequate disclosure and a reasonable waiting period has passed (usually 20 days). The SEC, however, does not take a position regarding the investment merits of an offering or the reasonableness of the price.

A security issue may be completely underwritten by an investment banker and the other members of the syndicate. If it is, the issuing corporation receives the public offering price less a stated percentage spread (although underwriters will occasionally be compensated with some combination of shares and warrants, perhaps in addition to a smaller spread). The underwriters, in turn, sell the securities at the public offering price (or less) and may take some of the securities themselves. Underwriters who provide this sort of *firm commitment* bear all the risk, since the public may not be willing to buy the entire issue.

Not all agreements are of this type. In the case of a *rights offering*

(where the current stockholders are given the opportunity to buy the new shares first), an underwriter may agree to purchase at a fixed price all securities not taken by current stockholders. This is termed a *standby agreement*. In the case of a nonrights offering (where the shares are offered to the general public first), members of an investment banking group may serve as agents instead of dealers, agreeing only to handle an offering on a *best-efforts* basis.

During the period when new securities remain unsold, the investment banker is allowed to attempt to "stabilize" the price of the security in the secondary market by standing ready to make purchases at a particular price. Such *pegging* may continue for up to ten days after the official offering date. There is a limit to the amount that can be purchased in this manner, usually stated in the agreement under which the underwriting syndicate is formed, since the members typically share the cost of such transactions. If there is to be any pegging, a statement to that effect must be included in the prospectus.

In any security transaction, there may be explicit and implicit costs. In a primary distribution, the explicit cost is the underwriting spread and the implicit cost is any difference between the public offering price and the price that might have been obtained otherwise. The spread provides the investment banker with compensation for selling the issue and bearing the risk that the issue may not be completely sold to the public, thereby leaving them with ownership of the unsold shares. The lower the public offering price, the smaller the risk that the issue will not be sold quickly at that price. If an issue is substantially underpriced, the investment banking syndicate can be assured that the securities will sell rapidly, requiring little or no support in the secondary market. Since many corporations deal with only one investment banker and since the larger investment banking firms rely on one another for inclusion in syndicates, it has been alleged that issuers pay too much in spreads, given the prices at which their securities are offered. In other words, the returns to underwriting are alleged to be overly large relative to the risks involved, owing to ignorance on the part of issuers or the existence of an informal cartel among investment bankers.

☐ 2.14.1 Underpricing of Ipo's

Whether or not returns to underwriting are overly large, a number of *initial public offerings* (ipo's) do appear to have been underpriced. Ipo's are the first offerings of shares of a company to the public and are sometimes referred to as *unseasoned offerings*. The abnormal returns for a sample of ipo's are shown in Figure 2.5. Each one of the first 60 months after the initial offering is shown on the horizontal axis, and the corresponding average abnormal return, meaning the average return over and above that of stocks of equal risk, is shown on the vertical axis. The leftmost point indicates the average abnormal return obtained by an investor who purchased such a stock at its offering price and sold it for the bid price at the end of the month during which it was offered. The average abnormal return was substantial: 11.4%.

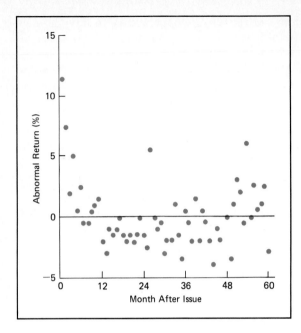

FIGURE 2–5
Average abnormal returns: 112 common stock initial public offerings, 1960–1969.

SOURCE: Roger G. Ibbotson, "Price Performance of Common Stock New Issues," *Journal of Financial Economics* 2, no. 3 (September 1975): 252.

The remaining points show the average abnormal returns that could have been obtained by an investor who purchased the security in the secondary market at the beginning of the month indicated and then sold it in the secondary market at the end of that particular month. Some of these post-offering abnormal returns were positive, but only one was significantly different from zero. Moreover, none was large enough to overcome the transaction costs associated with trades on the secondary market.

On the average, offerings of these unseasoned securities appear to have been underpriced. Investors able to purchase a cross-section of such shares at their offering prices might thus expect better performance than those holding other securities of equal risk. It is not surprising that such offerings are often rationed by the members of the selling group to "favored" customers. It is "not uncommon for underwriters to receive, prior to the effective date, 'public indication of interest' for five times the number of shares available." [37] Unfavored customers are presumably allowed to buy only the new issues that are not substantially underpriced. And since costs may be incurred in becoming a favored customer, it is not clear that even such an investor obtains abnormally large returns overall.

Whereas the return obtained by the purchaser of a new issue may be substantial on the average, the amount may be very good or very bad in any particular instance, as Figure 2.6 shows. Although the odds may be in the purchaser's favor, a single investment of this type is far from a sure bet.

---

[37] Securities and Exchange Commission, *Report of Special Study on Security Markets*, 1973.

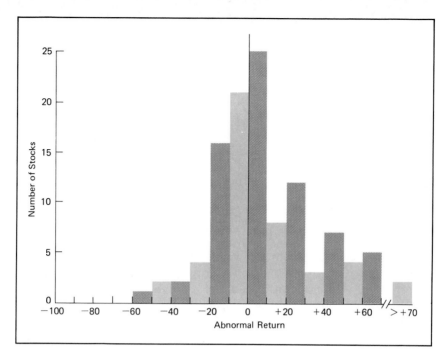

FIGURE 2–6
Average abnormal returns from offering price to bid price at the end of the offering month, 112 common stock initial public Offerings, 1960–1969.

SOURCE: Roger G. Ibbotson, "Price Performance of Common Stock New Issues," *Journal of Financial Economics* 2, no. 3 (September 1975): 248.

☐ 2.14.2 Seasoned Offerings

Interestingly, the announcement of a seasoned stock offering seems to result in a decline of roughly 2% to 4% in the firm's stock price. This could be because managers tend to issue stock when they think it is overpriced in the marketplace. Thus, the announcement of the offering causes investors to revise downward their assessment of the value of the stock, leading to a price decline.[38]

☐ 2.14.3 Shelf Registration

A relatively recent change in regulations has made it possible for large corporations to foster greater competition among underwriters. Starting in 1982, the Securities and Exchange Commission allowed firms to register

---

[38] See Stewart C. Myers and Nicholas S. Majluf, "Corporate Financing and Investment Decisions When Firms have Information That Investors Do Not Have," *Journal of Financial Economics* 13, no. 2 (June 1984):187–221, and Wayne H. Mikkelson and M. Megan Partch, "Valuation Effects of Security Offerings and the Issuance Process," *Journal of Financial Economics* 15, no. 1/2 (January/February 1986):31–60.

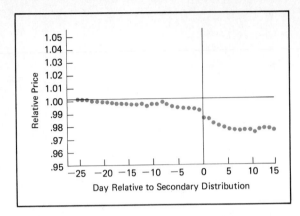

FIGURE 2–7
Prices for 345 secondary distributions, 1961–1965.

SOURCE: Myron S. Scholes, "The Market for Securities: Substitution versus Price Pressure and the Effects of Information on the Share Prices." *Journal of Business* 45, no. 2 (April 1972): 193.

securities in advance of issuance under Rule 415. With such a *shelf registration*, securities may be sold up to two years later. With securities "on the shelf," the corporation can require investment bankers to bid competitively, simply refusing to sell shares if desirable bids are not forthcoming. Thus, one purpose of the SEC in allowing shelf registration was to reduce the costs of issuing securities, and the evidence seems to suggest that indeed such costs have been reduced.[39]

☐ **2.14.4   SECONDARY DISTRIBUTIONS**

As mentioned earlier, an individual or institution wishing to sell a large block of stock can do so through a secondary distribution. An investment banking group buys the block from the seller and then offers the shares to the public; typically, the shares are first offered after normal trading hours at the day's closing price. The buyer often pays no commission, and the original seller receives the total proceeds less an underwriting spread.

The Securities and Exchange Commission requires that a secondary distribution be registered, with public announcement and disclosure and a 20-day waiting period if the original seller has a "control relationship" with the issuer of the securities. Otherwise, the distribution may be unregistered.

The impact of the sale of a large block on the market price of the stock provides information on the resiliency of the capital market. Figure 2.7 shows that the average price (adjusted for market changes) for 345 secondary distributions, with the price 25 days prior to the distribution taken as 1.0. On the average, a secondary distribution leads to a 2% to 3% decline in price. Since there is no evidence of a subsequent price rebound, this decline is most likely due to the information contained in the fact that someone has decided to sell. Additional analysis of these results, as shown in Table 2.5, supports the assertion. The size of the decline was related to the identity of the seller—

---

[39] See Sanjai Bhagat, M. Wayne Marr, and G. Rodney Thompson, "The Rule 415 Experiment: Equity Markets," *Journal of Finance* 40, no. 5 (December 1985):1385–1401.

TABLE 2.5

Average Price Decline Versus Type of Seller: 345 Secondary Distributions, 1961–1965.

TYPE OF SELLER	PERCENTAGE CHANGE IN ADJUSTED PRICE FROM TEN DAYS BEFORE THE DISTRIBUTION TO TEN DAYS AFTER THE DISTRIBUTION
Corporations and officers	2.9%
Investment companies and mutual funds	2.5
Individuals	1.1
Estates	.7
Banks and insurance companies	.3

SOURCE: Myron S. Scholes, "The Market for Securities: Substitution Versus Price Pressure and the Effects of Information on Share Prices," *Journal of Business* 45, no. 2 (April 1972): 202.

being the greatest for sellers likely to be information-motivated and smallest for sellers likely to be liquidity-motivated.[40]

2.15 REGULATION OF SECURITY MARKETS

Directly or indirectly, security markets in the United States are regulated under both federal and state laws. The Securities Act of 1933 was the first major legislation at the federal level. Sometimes called the *truth-in-securities* law, it requires registration of new issues and disclosure of relevant information by the issuer. Furthermore, the act prohibits misrepresentation and fraud in security sales. The Securities Exchange Act of 1934 extended the principles of the earlier act to cover secondary markets and required national exchanges, brokers, and dealers to be registered.

Since 1934, both acts (and subsequent amendments to them, such as the Securities Acts Amendments of 1975 that was discussed earlier in the chapter) have been administered by the Securities and Exchange Commission. The SEC is run by five commissioners appointed by the President and confirmed by the Senate; each commissioner is appointed for a five-year term. The commissioners are aided by a large permanent staff of lawyers, accountants, economists, and others.

The SEC is the prime administrative agency for a number of other pieces of federal legislation. The Public Utility Holding Company Act of 1935 brought such corporations under the SEC's jurisdiction. The Bankruptcy Act of 1938 specified that the SEC should advise the court in the reorganization of a firm under bankruptcy proceedings whenever there is a substantial public interest in the firm's securities. The Maloney Act of 1938 extended the SEC's jurisdiction to include the over-the-counter market. The Trust Indenture Act of 1939 gave the SEC power to ensure that bond indenture

---

[40] A more recent study has confirmed these findings; see Wayne H. Mikkelson and M. Megan Partch, "Stock Price Effects and Costs of Secondary Distributions," *Journal of Financial Economics* 14, no. 2 (June 1985):165–94.

trustees (individuals who represent bondholders in dealing with bond issuers) were free from any conflicts of interest. The Investment Company Act of 1940 extended disclosure and registration requirements to investment companies (these are companies that use their funds primarily to purchase securities issued by the U.S. government, state governments, other companies, and so on). The Investment Advisers Act of 1940 required the registration of those individuals who provide others with advice about security transactions; advisors were also required to disclose any potential conflicts of interest. As mentioned earlier, the Securities Investor Protection Act of 1970 provided for the coverage of losses by investors in the event of failure of a brokerage firm by establishing the Securities Investor Protection Corporation.

Federal securities legislation relies heavily on the principle of *self-regulation*. The SEC has delegated its power to control trading practices for listed securities to the registered exchanges. However, the SEC has retained the power to alter or supplement any of the resulting rules or regulations. The SEC's power to control trading in over-the-counter securities has similarly been delegated to the National Association of Securities Dealers (NASD), a private association of brokers and dealers in OTC securities. In practice, the SEC staff usually discusses proposed changes with both the NASD and the registered exchanges in advance. Consequently, few rules are formally altered or rejected.

An important piece of legislation that makes security markets in the United States different from those in many other countries is the Banking Act of 1933, also known as the Glass-Steagall Act. This act prohibited commercial banks from engaging in investment banking activities, since it was felt that there was an inherent conflict of interest in allowing banks to engage in both types of activities. Because of this act, banks have not played as prominent a role in security markets in the United States as elsewhere. Recently, however, their role has increased, as the federal government has taken action to spur competition among various types of financial institutions. Two key pieces of legislation were the Depository Institutions Deregulation and Monetary Control Act of 1980 and the Depository Institution Act of 1982. Many banks now offer security brokerage services, retirement funds, and the like via subsidiaries of their holding companies. Furthermore, long-standing limitations on rates paid on deposits and checking accounts were removed. As a result, the line between commercial banking and investment banking is becoming more blurred every day.

Initially, security regulation in the United States was the province of state governments. Beginning in 1911, blue-sky laws were passed by states to prevent "speculative schemes which have no more basis than so many feet of blue sky." [41] Although such statutes vary substantially from state to state, most of them outlaw fraud in security sales and require the registration of certain securities as well as brokers and dealers (and, in some cases, investment advisers). Some order has been created by the passage in many

---

[41] See *Hall* v. *Geiger-Jones Co.*, 242 U.S. 539 (1917).

states of all or part of the Uniform Securities Acts proposed by the National Conference of Commissions on Uniform State Laws in 1956.

Securities that are traded across state lines, as well as the brokers, dealers, and exchanges involved in such trading, typically fall under the purview of federal legislation. However, a considerable domain still comes under the exclusive jurisdiction of the states. Moreover, federal legislation only supplements state legislation; it does not supplant it. Some argue that the investor is overprotected as a result. Others suggest that the regulatory agencies (especially those that rely on self-regulation by powerful industry organizations) in fact protect the members of the regulated industry against competition, thereby damaging the interests of their customers instead of protecting them. Both positions undoubtedly contain some elements of truth.

2.16 SUMMARY

This chapter has been devoted to describing the mechanics of buying and selling securities along with the operations of security markets. Although the primary focus has been on common stocks, most of the material is also applicable to other securities, such as corporate bonds, treasury securities, and preferred stocks. Investors face a large number of decisions when buying or selling a security, even if they know which issue they are going to trade. These decisions have been called order specifications here, and they concern such things as how big the order should be, how long the order is to be outstanding, and what type of order to place.

Investors may open up a cash account or a margin account with a brokerage firm. With the former, all transactions involve the use of cash. With the latter, loans will be involved if the investor makes either margin purchases or short sales. In the case of margin purchases, part of the purchase price is paid for by a loan of cash; in the case of short sales, a loan of securities is made. In both of these situations the investor is hoping to buy low, sell high. In the case of the margin purchase the buy occurs first, and the sell occurs second. With a short sale, the order is reversed in that the sell occurs first and the buy occurs second. Financial leverage is involved in both types of transaction in that a given percentage move in the price of the security involved will result in a percentage move of even greater magnitude in the position of the investor. Thus, margin purchases and short sales not only increase an investor's expected return but also increase the investor's risk in regard to the particular security involved.

The major secondary markets for trading common stocks in the United States include organized exchanges such as the New York Stock Exchange and the American Stock Exchange. In these markets, trading is centered around the activities of specialists. Each one of these individuals is given the responsibility of maintaining a fair and orderly market in certain assigned stocks. In carrying out their responsibilities, specialists act both as brokers, executing orders, and dealers, quoting bid and asked prices at which they are willing to buy or sell their assigned stocks.

Another kind of secondary market is the over-the-counter market, where individuals act as dealers in a manner similar to specialists. However, unlike specialists, OTC dealers face competition from others who are dealers in the same stocks. Much of the trading in the OTC market is currently done through a computerized system known as NASDAQ.

Trading in listed securities may take place outside the various exchanges. When such trading takes place in the OTC market, the trade is often said to have taken place in the third market. Alternatively, when such trading involves direct contact between the buyer and seller, it is said to take place in the fourth market.

The primary market for securities was also discussed in this chapter. This market involves the initial issuance of securities. Although some issuers deal directly with purchasers, most issuers hire investment bankers to assist them in the sale of the securities.

Regulation of the security markets in the United States involves both federal and state law. The most prominent regulator is the Securities and Exchange Commission, a federal agency that is run by five commissioners. The SEC has delegated to the various exchanges and National Association of Security Dealers the power to control trading practices that involve their facilities. However, the SEC retains the power to alter or supplement any of the resulting rules and regulations. This method of regulation is often known as *self-regulation*. Whether it is the best method is an issue that is open to much debate.

QUESTIONS AND PROBLEMS

1. Discuss the advantages and disadvantages to the investor of the following:
   a. Market order
   b. Limit order
   c. Stop order

2. Buck Ewing opened a margin account at a local brokerage firm. Buck's initial investment was to purchase 100 shares of Dover Corporation on margin at $40 per share. Buck borrowed $2000 from a broker to complete the purchase.
   a. At the time of the purchase, what was the actual margin in Buck's account?
   b. If Dover stock subsequently rises in price to $60 per share, what is the actual margin in Buck's account?
   c. If Dover stock subsequently falls in price to $35 per share, what is the actual margin in Buck's account?

3. Helena Company's stock is currently selling for $15 per share. The initial margin requirement is 55% and the maintenance margin requirement is 35%. Cap Anson buys 100 shares of Helena stock on margin. To what price must the stock fall for Cap to receive a margin call?

4. Lizzie Arlington has deposited $15,000 in a margin account with a brokerage firm. If the initial margin requirement is 60%, what is the maximum dollar amount of stock that Lizzie can purchase on margin?

5. Ed Delahanty purchased 500 shares of Niagara Corporation stock on margin at the end of 1988 for $30 per share. The initial margin requirement was 55%. Ed paid 13% interest on the margin loan and never faced a margin call. Niagara paid dividends of $1.00 per share during 1989.

   a. At the end of 1989, if Ed sold the Niagara stock for $35 per share, what would his rate of return be for the year?

   b. At the end of 1989, if Ed sold the Niagara stock for $25 per share, what would his rate of return be for the year?

   c. Recalculate your answers to parts (a) and (b) assuming that Ed made the Niagara stock purchase for cash instead of on margin.

6. Through a margin account, Candy Cummings sells short 200 shares of Madison Inc. stock for $50 per share. The initial margin requirement is 45%.

   a. If Madison stock subsequently rises to $60 per share, what is the actual margin in Candy's account?

   b. If Madison stock subsequently falls to $40 per share, what is the actual margin in Candy's account?

7. Austin Corporation stock currently sells for $60 per share. The initial margin requirement is 50% and the maintenance margin requirement is 40%. If Willie Keeler sells short 300 shares of Austin stock, to what price can the stock rise before Willie receives a margin call?

8. Eddie Gaedel is an inveterate short seller. Is it true that Eddie's potential losses are infinite? Why? Conversely, is it true that the maximum return that Eddie can earn on his investment is 100%? Why?

9. On May 1, Ivy Olson sold short 100 shares of Topeka Associates stock at $25 per share and bought on margin 200 shares of Columbus Company stock for $40 per share. The initial margin requirement was 50%. In June 30, Topeka stock sold for $36 per share and Columbus stock sold for $45 per share.

   a. Prepare a balance sheet showing the aggregate financial position in Ivy's margin account as of June 30.

   b. Determine whether Ivy's account is restricted as of June 30.

10. What are ADRs? Why are they attractive to U.S. investors seeking to make investments in foreign corporations?

11. Differentiate between the role of a specialist on the NYSE and the role of a dealer on the OTC market.

12. Olympia Company is listed on the NYSE. Gabby Hartnett, the specialist handling Olympia stock, is currently bidding $25\frac{3}{8}$ and asking $25\frac{5}{8}$. What would be the likely outcomes of the following trading orders?

   a. Through a broker, Eppa Rixey places a market order to buy 100 shares of Olympia stock. No other broker from the crowd takes the order.

   b. Through a broker, Eppa places a limit order to sell 100 shares of Olympia stock at 26.

   c. Through a broker, Eppa places a limit order to buy 100 shares of Olympia stock at $25\frac{1}{2}$. Another broker offers to sell 100 shares at $25\frac{1}{2}$.

13. Because specialists such as Chick Gandil are charged with maintaining a "fair and orderly" market, at times they will be required to sell when others are buying and buy when others are selling. How can Chick earn a profit when required to act in such a manner?

14. What are some of the major steps that have been taken toward the ultimate emergence of a truly nationwide security market?

15. Transaction costs can be thought of as being derived from three sources. Identify and describe those sources.

16. Why are liquid and continuous secondary security markets important to the effective functioning of primary security markets?

Chapter **3**

INVESTMENT VALUE

AND MARKET PRICE

Payments provided by securities may differ in both timing and riskiness. Thus, a security analyst must estimate when and under what conditions payments will be received (and, of course, the size of such payments). This typically requires detailed analysis of the firm involved, the industry or industries in which the firm operates, and the economy as a whole.

Once such estimates have been made, the overall investment value of the security must be determined. This generally requires conversion of uncertain future values to certain present values. The current prices of other securities can often be utilized in this process. If it is possible to obtain a similar set of payments in some other way, the market price of doing so provides a benchmark for the investment value of the security being analyzed, since an investor would neither want to pay more than this for the security nor sell it for less. In some cases, however, equivalent alternatives may not exist, or the mere act of buying or selling the security in question in the quantities being considered might substantially affect the price. Under these conditions, the preferences of the investor may have to be utilized explicitly in the process of estimating the security's investment value.

Later chapters discuss in detail the manner in which estimated future payments can be used to determine investment value. Methods for estimating the payments and finding equivalent alternatives will be discussed after the characteristics of the securities have been introduced. In this chapter, some general principles of investment value are presented, leaving procedures designed for specific types of securities for later.

3.1 SECURITY PRICE DETERMINATION

Although there are over one billion shares of American Telephone & Telegraph common stock outstanding, on an average day less than 2 million shares will be traded. What determines the prices at which such trades take place? A simple (and correct) answer is demand and supply. A more fundamental (and also correct) answer is investors' estimates of AT&T's future

67

earnings and dividends, since such estimates greatly influence demand and supply. Before dealing with such influences, it is useful to examine the role of demand and supply in the determination of security prices.

As shown in the preceding chapter, securities are traded by many people in many different ways. Whereas the forces that determine prices are similar in all markets, they are slightly more obvious in markets using periodic "calls"; one such market, mentioned in Chapter 2, is the Paris Bourse.

☐ 3.1.1 The Demand-to-Buy Schedule

At a designated time, all brokers holding orders to buy or sell a given stock for customers gather at a specified location on the floor of the exchange. Some of the orders are market orders. For example, Mr. A may have instructed his broker to buy 100 shares of Michelin at the lowest possible price, whatever it is. His personal *demand-to-buy schedule* at that time is shown in Figure 3.1(a): He wishes to buy 100 shares no matter what the price. Although this schedule captures the contractual nature of Mr. A's market order at a specific point in time, Mr. A undoubtedly has a good idea that his ultimate purchase price will be near the price for which orders were executed just before he placed his order. Thus, his true demand schedule might be sloping downward from the upper-left portion to the lower-right portion of the graph. This is shown by the dashed line in the figure. It indicates his desire to buy more shares if the price is lower. However, to simplify his own tasks as well as his broker's tasks, he has estimated that the price for which his order will be ultimately executed will be in the range at which he would choose to hold 100 shares. In the example shown here, this price is 945 francs per share.

Other customers may place limit orders with their brokers. Thus, Ms. B may have instructed her broker to buy 200 shares of Michelin at the lowest possible price if and only if that price is less than or equal to 940 francs per share. Her demand schedule is shown in Figure 3.1(b).

Some customers may give their broker two or more orders for the same security. Thus, Mr. C may wish to buy 100 shares of Michelin at a price of 955 or less, plus an additional 100 shares if the price is at or below 945. To do this, Mr. C places a limit order for 100 shares at 955 and a second limit order for 100 shares at 945. Figure 3.1(c) portrays his demand schedule.

If one could look at all the brokers' books and aggregate all the orders to buy Michelin (both market and limit orders), it would be possible to determine how many shares would be bought at every possible price. Assuming that only Mr. A, Ms. B, and Mr. C have placed buy orders, the resulting aggregate demand-to-buy schedule would look like line *DD* in Figure 3.1(d). Note that at lower prices more shares would be demanded.

☐ 3.1.2 The Supply-to-Sell Schedule

Brokers will also hold market orders to sell shares of Michelin. For example, Ms. X may have placed a market order to sell 100 shares of Michelin at the highest possible price. Figure 3.2(a) displays her *supply-to-sell schedule*. As

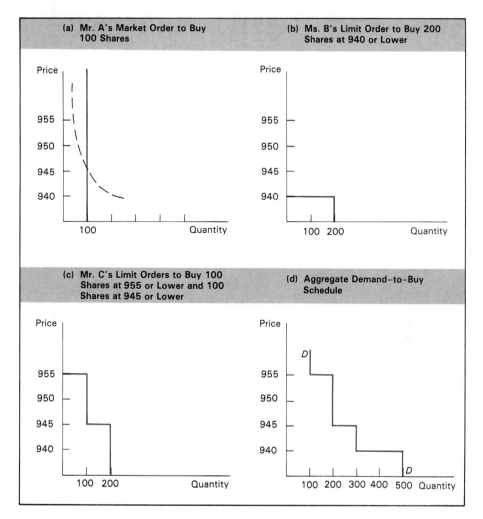

FIGURE 3–1
Individual investors' demand-to-buy
schedules.

with market orders to buy, customers generally place such orders on the supposition that the actual price will be in the range in which their true desire to sell the stated number of shares would lie. Thus, Ms. X's actual supply schedule might appear more like the dashed line in Figure 3.2(a), indicating her willingness to sell more shares at higher prices.

Customers may also place limit orders to sell shares of Michelin. For example, Mr. Y may have placed a limit order to sell 100 shares at a price of 940 or higher, and Ms. Z may have placed a limit order to sell 100 shares at a price of 945 or higher. Panels (b) and (c) of Figure 3.2 illustrate these two supply-to-sell schedules.

As with the buy orders, if one could look at all the brokers' books and

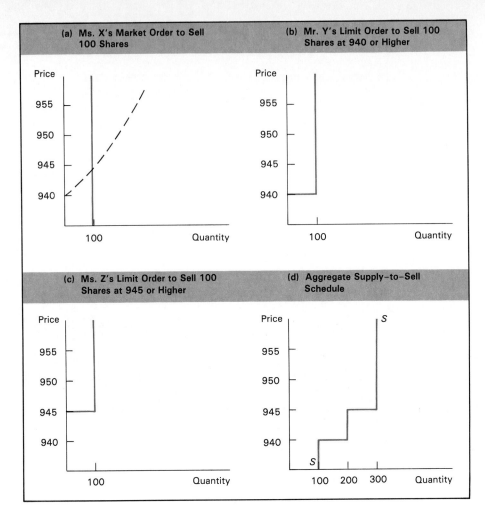

FIGURE 3–2
Individual investors' supply-to-sell
schedules.

aggregate all the orders to sell Michelin (both market and limit orders), it would be possible to determine how many shares would be sold at every possible price. Assuming that only Ms. X, Mr. Y, and Ms. Z have placed sell orders, the resulting aggregate supply-to-sell schedule would look like line SS in Figure 3.2(d). Note that at higher prices more shares would be supplied.

☐ **3.1.3 Interaction of the Schedules**

The aggregate demand and supply schedules are shown on one graph in Figure 3.3. Generally, no one would have enough information to draw the actual schedules. However, this in no way diminishes the usefulness of the

schedules as representations of the underlying forces that are interacting to determine the market-clearing price of Michelin.

What actually happens when all the brokers gather together with their order books in hand? A clerk of the exchange "calls out" a price—for example, 940 francs per share. The brokers then try to complete transactions with one another at that price. Those with orders to buy at that price signify the number of shares they wish to buy. Those with orders to sell do likewise. Some tentative deals will be made, but as Figure 3.3 shows, more shares will be demanded at 940 than will be supplied. In particular, 300 shares will be demanded, but only 200 shares will be supplied. When trading is completed (meaning all possible tentative deals have been made), there will be a number of brokers calling "buy" but nobody will stand ready to sell to them. The price of 940 is too low.

Seeing this, the clerk will cry out a different price—for example, 950. Since the previous trades are all canceled at this point, the brokers will consult their orders books once again and signify the extent to which they are willing to buy or sell shares at this new price. In this case, as Figure 3.3 shows, when trading is completed, there will be a number of brokers calling "sell," but nobody will stand ready to buy from them. In particular, 300 shares will be supplied but there will be a demand for only 200 shares. The price of 950 is too high.

Undaunted, the clerk will try again, and again, if necessary. Only when there are relatively few unsatisfied brokers will the price (and the associated tentative deals) be declared final. As Figure 3.3 shows, 945 is such a price. At 945, customers collectively wish to sell 300 shares. Furthermore, there is a collective demand for 300 shares at this price. Thus, quantity demanded equals quantity supplied. The price is "just right."

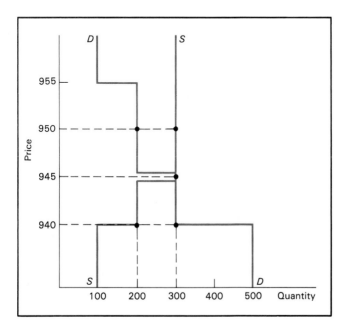

FIGURE 3–3
Determining a security's price by the interaction of the demand-to-buy and supply-to-sell schedules.

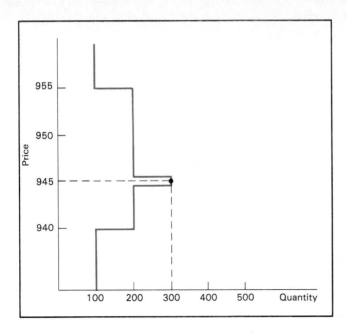

FIGURE 3–4
Aggregate quantity traded.

Another way to view this process is to focus on the quantity that would actually be traded at any given price. For any particular price, this is the smaller of (1) the quantity people are willing to buy and (2) the quantity others are willing to sell, as shown in Figure 3.4. At the price where the quantity that would be traded is maximized, demand will equal supply. As can be seen in the figure, this occurs at a price of 945.

Trading procedures employed in security markets vary from auction markets to dealer markets and from call markets to continuous markets. However, the similarities are more important than the differences. In the United States, for example, specialists at the New York Stock Exchange and dealers in the over-the-counter market provide some of the functions of the clerk at the Paris Bourse, and trades can take place at any time. Nevertheless, the basic principles of security price determination still operate. In general, market price equates quantity demanded with quantity supplied.

3.2 DEMAND-TO-HOLD SECURITIES

For some purposes it is useful to ignore moment-to-moment changes in customers' orders and focus instead on the fundamental forces at work. Instead of asking how many shares an investor wishes to buy or sell at a given price, the number of shares the investor wishes to hold at that price can be determined. There is, of course, a close relationship between the two quantities. If an investor wishes to hold more shares than are currently held, the difference is the investor's demand-to-buy schedule. Conversely, if an investor wishes to hold fewer shares than are currently held, the difference is the investor's supply-to-sell schedule.

□ 3.2.1 The Demand-to-Hold Schedule

In Figure 3.5 one investor's *demand-to-hold schedule* for a security is shown by curve *dd*. This simply plots the number of shares that the investor wishes to hold at each possible price. In general, lower prices are associated with larger numbers of shares. Of course, the entire schedule is predicated on the investor's current feelings about the security's future prospects. If something makes the investor more optimistic about the security, he or she will generally wish to hold more shares at any given price. In that case, the entire schedule may shift to the right, as shown by curve *d'd'*. Alternatively, if something makes the investor more pessimistic about the security, the entire curve may shift to the left, as shown by curve *d"d"*.

A factor that complicates an analysis of this type is the tendency for some investors to regard sudden and substantial price changes in a security as indicators of changes in the future prospects of the issuer. In the absence of further information, an investor may interpret such a change as an indication that "someone knows something that I don't know." While exploring the situation, the investor may at least temporarily revise his or her own assessment of the issuer's prospects and, in doing so, may alter the demand-to-hold schedule. For this reason, few investors place limit orders at prices substantially different from the current price, for fear that such orders would be executed only if prospects changed significantly, giving recognition to the idea that a careful reevaluation would be in order before buying or selling shares under such conditions.

Despite this complication, it is possible to construct an aggregate schedule indicating the total number of shares of a given firm that investors will wish to hold at various prices, assuming no change in their views of the relative prospects of the firm. This overall demand-to-hold schedule, obtained by adding the individual investors' demand-to-hold schedules, would look like curve *DD* in Figure 3.6. In the short run, at least, the available number of shares is fixed—for example, at *Q* in the figure. Only one price will equate the aggregate demand-to-hold with the available number of shares. In Figure

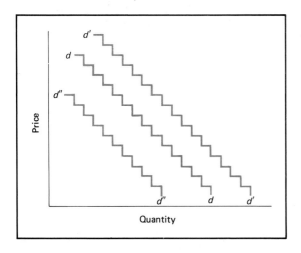

FIGURE 3–5
An individual investors' demand-to-hold schedule.

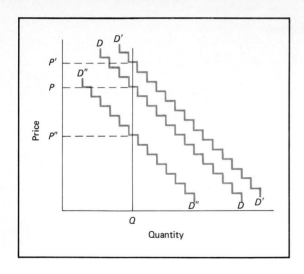

FIGURE 3–6
Aggregate demand-to-hold and available quantity schedules.

3.6, it is P. At any higher price, current holders of the security will collectively wish to hold fewer shares than are outstanding. In their attempts to sell such shares, they will drive the price down until they or others are willing to hold all the shares. Conversely, if the price is below P, investors will collectively wish to hold more shares than are available. In their attempts to buy shares, they will drive the price up until they no longer want additional shares. Ultimately, the price will settle at P, where the aggregate demand equals the available quantity.

☐ 3.2.2 Elasticity of the Schedule

How elastic (that is, flat) will the aggregate demand-to-hold schedule for a security be? The answer depends in part on the extent to which the security is regarded as "unique." Securities are considered more unique when they have few close substitutes. Securities are considered less unique when they have more close substitutes. This means that the aggregate demand schedule will be more elastic (that is, more flat) for less unique securities. Equivalently, the less unique a security is, the greater the increase in the quantity demanded will be for a given fall in price. This is because these shares will produce a smaller increase in the typical portfolio's risk when substituted for other shares.

☐ 3.2.3 Shifts of the Schedule

If one investor becomes more optimistic about the prospects for a security, while at the same time another investor becomes more pessimistic about the same security, they may very likely trade with one another with no effect on the aggregate demand-to-hold schedule. In this situation there will be

no change in the market price for the security. However, if more investors become optimistic rather than pessimistic, the schedule will shift to the right (for example, to $D'D'$ in Figure 3.6), causing an increase in price (to P'). Correspondingly, if more investors become pessimistic than optimistic, the schedule will shift to the left (for example, to $D''D''$ in Figure 3.6), causing a decrease in price (to P'').

3.3 THE EFFECTS OF PROCEDURES FOR SHORT SALES

Thus far, the individual investor's demand-to-hold schedule has been drawn only in the region of positive quantities. But there is more to it: The higher the price, the smaller the quantity the investor will wish to hold. At some price, the desired amount is zero, and at higher prices, the investor may consider short selling the security.

If short sellers received the proceeds from such sales, an individual investor's demand-to-hold schedule for a given security would look like the curve in Figure 3.7(a). This curve can be thought of in either of two ways: as a demand curve (that is, at price A, the investor wishes to hold quantity B) or as a marginal value curve (that is, if quantity B is held, the marginal value of one share more or less will be the amount A).

In fact, however, short sellers do not receive the proceeds of such sales. Instead, these proceeds are held by the short seller's brokerage firm as collateral. In most instances, the short seller does not even receive interest on this money and, furthermore, short sellers must meet initial margin requirements on the face amount of the short-sale proceeds. This changes the situation from that shown in Figure 3.7(a). Selling a security one owns generates cash that can be used for other purposes, but selling a security that one does not own requires an investment of cash. Thus, the decision to go short requires a higher price than it would if the short seller got the full use of the proceeds.[1] The effective demand-to-hold schedule would look like the curve in Figure 3.7(b). To the right of the vertical axis the curve is the same as in Figure 3.7(a), but to the left the curve is higher.

The effect of this is shown in Figure 3.7(c). The solid curve is the effective demand-to-hold schedule. The dashed curve is the portion of the original demand curve in Figure 3.7(a) that is to the left of the vertical axis. If the current price of the security is P^*, this investor will go short only Q_1^* shares, not Q_2^* shares. Thus, his or her pessimism about the security will not have as much impact on the market as it would if short sellers got the full use of the short-sale proceeds. In a sense, the person chooses a holding (Q_1^*) at which he or she considers the marginal value (M^*) to be less than the current market price (P^*).

---

[1] For an argument that this causes securities to be "overpriced," see Edward M. Miller, "Risk, Uncertainty, and Divergence of Opinion," *Journal of Finance* 32, no. 4 (September 1977):1151–68.

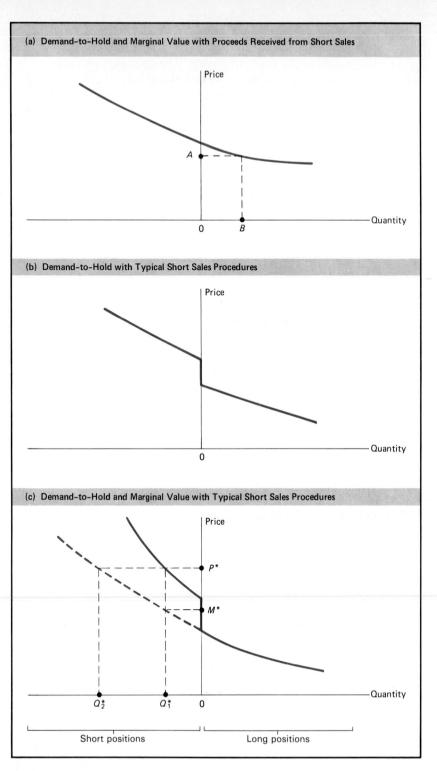

FIGURE 3–7
Demand-to-hold curves.

3.4 PRICE AS A CONSENSUS

However one chooses to analyze security price determination, it is important to remember that a free market price for a security reflects a kind of consensus. This can be seen in Figure 3.8. Assume that the current market price for this particular security is P^*. Some individuals hold the security. For each of them, the situation is like that shown in Figure 3.8(a), where it can be seen that the investor has adjusted his or her portfolio so that the marginal value of a share (M^*) equals its market price.

A few investors may be short sellers. Their situation is like that shown in Figure 3.8(b). Because of the short-sale rule, each short seller will have taken a position at which the marginal value of a share is less than the price. Many investors will choose to hold no shares, and thus their position is neither long nor short. Their situation is shown in Figure 3.8(c). For each of them, the marginal value is equal to or, as in the case shown here, somewhat below the market price.

Were it not for short-selling rules, every investor would adjust his or her portfolio holdings until the marginal value of a security equaled its current market price. Since the market price is the same for everyone, so would be the marginal value for all investors (assuming all investors pay attention to the market). Price would clearly represent a consensus of investor opinion about value.

Short-selling rules change this situation, but only slightly. Since some investors (primarily pessimists) might choose holdings at which marginal value is below the market price, this market price could be slightly higher than an average of investors' marginal values. Accordingly, securities may be slightly "overpriced."

However, short-sale rules are likely to have a small impact on market prices. Even for the short seller, the disparity between market price and marginal value may be small. For those who hold no shares, it would be smaller yet (or even zero). And, for those who hold shares, it will be zero. Moreover, short positions are typically a small fraction of long positions. For practical purposes, price can be reasonably considered to be equal to a consensus opinion of investors concerning marginal value. For it to be seriously in error as an estimate of that value, many investors must be poorly informed or poor analysts. Moreover, there must be either (1) a preponderance of such investors with overly optimistic forecasts or (2) a preponderance of such investors with overly pessimistic forecasts. Otherwise, the actions of such investors will offset each other, making price a good estimate of the present value of the security's future prospects.

3.5 MARKET EFFICIENCY

Imagine a world in which (1) all investors have costless access to currently available information about the future; (2) all investors are good analysts; and (3) all investors pay close attention to market prices and adjust their holdings appropriately. In such a market, a security's price will be a good

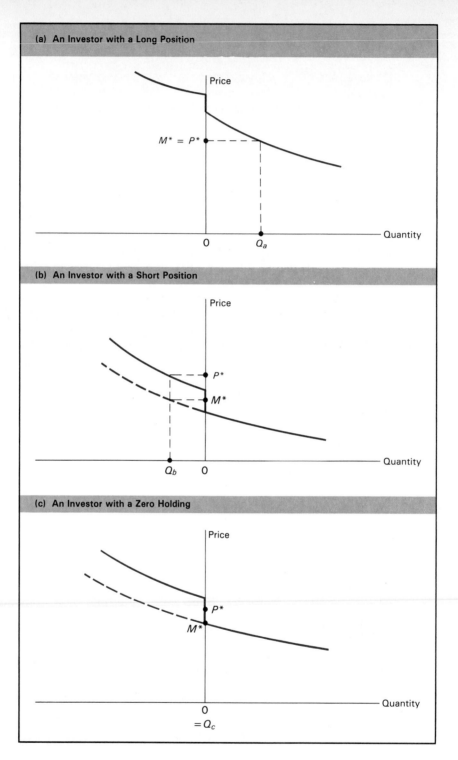

FIGURE 3–8
Price of a security as a consensus.

estimate of its *investment value*, where investment value is the present value of the security's future prospects as estimated by well-informed and capable analysts.

An *efficient market* can now be defined:

> A (perfectly) efficient market is one in which every security's price equals its investment value at all times.

In an efficient market, a set of information is fully and immediately reflected in market prices. But what information? A popular definition is the following:[2]

FORM OF EFFICIENCY	SET OF INFORMATION REFLECTED IN SECURITY PRICES
Weak	Previous prices of securities
Semistrong	All publicly available information
Strong	All information, both public and private

An equivalent definition of an efficient market is the following:

> A market is efficient with respect to a particular set of information if it is impossible to, on the average, make abnormal profits by using this set of information to formulate buying and selling decisions.

For example, a market would be described as having *weak-form efficiency* if it were impossible to make abnormal profits by using past prices to make decisions about when to buy and sell securities. The evidence suggests that major security markets in the United States are weak-form efficient. However, U.S. markets do not conform so well to the definition of *semistrong-form efficiency* (although the lack of a precise meaning for "publicly available" makes this form of efficiency somewhat ambiguous). They conform even less well to the definition of *strong-form efficiency*.[3]

In an efficient market, any new information would be immediately and fully reflected in prices. New information is just that: new, meaning a surprise (anything that is not a surprise is predictable and should have been predicted before the fact). Since happy surprises are about as likely as unhappy ones, price changes in an efficient market are about as likely to be positive as negative. Whereas a security's price might be expected to move upward by an amount that provides a reasonable return on capital (when considered in conjunction with dividend payments), anything above or below this would, in such a market, be unpredictable. In a perfectly efficient market, price changes would be random.[4]

---

[2] Eugene F. Fama, "Efficient Capital Markets: A Review of Theory and Empirical Work," *Journal of Finance* 25, no. 5 (May 1970):383–417.

[3] For an extensive discussion of efficient markets and related evidence, see Chapters 9 and 11 in George Foster, *Financial Statement Analysis* (Englewood Cliffs, N.J.: Prentice Hall, 1986).

[4] In this situation, security prices are said to follow a *random walk*, meaning that security price changes (say, from one day to the next) are independently and identically distributed. That is, the price change from day t to day $t + 1$ is not influenced by the price change from day $t - 1$ to t, and the size of the price change from one day to the next can be viewed as being determined by the spin of the roulette wheel (with the same roulette wheel being used every day).

Now consider a crazy market, in which prices never bear any particular relationship to investment value. In such a world, price changes might also appear to be random. However, major security markets in the United States are certainly not crazy. They may not attain perfect efficiency, but they are certainly much closer to it than to craziness. To understand financial markets, it is important to understand perfectly efficient markets.

As mentioned earlier, in an efficient market, a security's price will be a good estimate of its investment value, where investment value is the present value of the security's future prospects as estimated by well-informed and capable analysts. Any substantial disparity between price and value would reflect market inefficiency. In a well-developed and free market, major inefficiencies are rare. The reason is not hard to find. Major disparities between price and investment value will be noted by alert analysts, who will seek to take advantage of their discoveries. Securities priced below value (known as underpriced or undervalued securities) will be purchased, creating pressure for price increases due to the increased demand to buy. Securities priced above value (known as overpriced or overvalued securities) will be sold, creating pressure for price decreases due to the increased supply to sell. As investors seek to take advantage of opportunities created by temporary inefficiencies, they will cause the inefficiencies to be reduced, denying the less alert and the less informed a chance to obtain large abnormal profits.

In the United States there are thousands of professional security analysts and even more amateurs. Not surprisingly, due to their actions the major U.S. security markets appear to be much closer to efficiency than to craziness.

3.6 SUMMARY

This chapter has discussed how the forces of supply and demand interact in determining a security's market price. This price can be thought of as representing a consensus opinion about the future prospects for the security. Furthermore, in an efficient market, a security's market price will fully reflect all available information that is relevant to the security at that time. This can be attributed to the actions of thousands of security analysts, who—upon identifying mispriced securities—place orders that tend to remove the mispricing.

QUESTIONS AND PROBLEMS

1. What is the difference between call security markets and continuous security markets?
2. How is an investor's demand-to-buy or supply-to-sell schedule for a particular security related to the investor's demand-to-hold schedule for that same security?
3. Using an aggregate demand-to-hold schedule and associated demand-to-buy or supply-to-sell schedules, explain and illustrate the effect of the following events on the equilibrium price and quantity traded of Albany Corporation's stock.

a. Albany officials announce that next year's earnings are expected to be significantly higher than analysts had previously forcasted.

b. A wealthy shareholder initiates a large secondary offering of Albany stock.

c. Another company, quite similar to Albany in all respects except for being privately held, decides to offer its outstanding shares for sale to the public.

4. Short sellers do not receive the proceeds from their short sales, must put up initial margin, and often do not receive interest on these sums held by their brokers. How does this affect the aggregate demand-to-hold schedules for securities?

5. We all know that investors have widely diverse opinions about the future course of the economy and earnings forecasts for various industries and companies. How then is it possible for all these investors to arrive at an equilibrium price for any particular security?

6. Distinguish between the three forms of market efficiency.

7. Is it true that in a perfectly efficient market no investor would consistently be able to earn a profit?

8. While security markets may not be perfectly efficient, what is the rationale for expecting them to be highly efficient?

9. When a corporation announces its earnings for a period, the volume of transactions in its stock may increase, but frequently that increase is not associated with significant moves in the price of its stock. How can this be explained?

10. What are the implications of the three forms of market efficiency for technical and fundamental analysis (discussed in Chapter 1)?

11. The years 1986 and 1987 will probably be long remembered for the insider trading scandals that were exposed.

a. Is successful insider trading consistent with the three forms of market efficiency? Explain.

b. Play the role of devil's advocate and present a case outlining the benefits to financial markets of insider trading.

Chapter 4

THE VALUATION OF RISKLESS SECURITIES

A useful first step in understanding security valuation is to consider those fixed-income securities that are certain of making their promised payments in full and on time. The obvious candidates are the securities representing the debt of the U.S. government. Since the government can print money whenever it chooses, the promised payments for such securities are virtually certain to be made on schedule. However, there is a degree of uncertainty as to the purchasing power of the promised payments. While U.S. government bonds may be riskless in terms of their nominal payments, they may be quite risky in terms of their real (or inflation-adjusted) payments.

Despite this concern with inflation risk, it will be assumed hereafter that there are fixed-income securities whose nominal and real payments are certain. Specifically, to the extent that inflation exists, it will be assumed that its magnitude can be accurately predicted. Such an assumption makes it possible to focus on the impact of time on security valuation. Having accomplished this, the influence of other attributes on security valuation can be considered.

4.1 INVESTMENT

☐ 4.1.1 Deciding How Much to Invest

To begin with the simplest possible case, the plight of Robinson Crusoe will be analyzed. Crusoe has just been shipwrecked on an uninhabited island with little more than 20 bushels of corn. His knowledge of shipping routes leads him to expect to be saved in two years. In the meantime, he must decide how much corn to eat this year and how much to plant (that is, to invest) in order to obtain corn to eat next year. In keeping with the goals of this chapter, it will be assumed that the island is not subject to the uncertainties of nature that plague most farmers; Crusoe can be certain of the results of whatever planting he undertakes.

TABLE 4.1
Productivity of Crusoe's Land.

PLOT NUMBER	BUSHELS OF CORN PLANTED THIS YEAR ON PLOT	YIELD IN BUSHELS OF CORN HARVESTED NEXT YEAR ON PLOT	RETURN ON INVESTMENT ON PLOT	CUMULATIVE YIELD FROM THIS PLUS ALL PREVIOUS PLOTS
1	1	1.36	36%	1.36
2	1	1.34	34	2.70
3	1	1.32	32	4.02
4	1	1.30	30	5.32
5	1	1.28	28	6.60
6	1	1.26	26	7.86
7	1	1.24	24	9.10
8	1	1.22	22	10.32
9	1	1.20	20	11.52
10	1	1.18	18	12.70
11	1	1.16	16	13.86
12	1	1.14	14	15.00
13	1	1.12	12	16.12
14	1	1.10	10	17.22
15	1	1.08	8	18.30
16	1	1.06	6	19.36
17	1	1.04	4	20.40
18	1	1.02	2	21.42
19	1	1.00	0	22.42
20	1	.98	−2	23.40

After carefully surveying the island, Crusoe decides that there are 20 plots of arable land, each capable of taking one bushel of corn. The plots differ in exposure, soil quality, and so on. This is shown in Table 4.1, in which the plots are listed in decreasing order of yield. The best plot offers a return of 36% on an investment (that is, a planting) of 1 bushel of corn, whereas the worst plot offers a return of −2%.

The shaded region in Figure 4.1 shows Crusoe's alternatives. He could, of course, eat all 20 bushels of corn this year, leaving him nothing to eat next year; this strategy is plotted at point A in the figure. If Crusoe chooses instead to invest one of his bushels of corn, reducing the amount eaten to 19 bushels, he can look forward to eating 1.36 bushels next year, since he will use the best plot of land.

If, instead, Crusoe chooses to invest 2 bushels of corn, the incremental investment of one additional bushel of corn today yields only 1.34 bushels of corn next year. Why? Because poorer land must be used. This is simply a special case of the more general *principle of diminishing returns*, where the more invested, the smaller the likely return of each additional unit of investment.

The shaded region in the figure portrays all the investment opportunities shown in Table 4.1 for Crusoe's simple economy. Moving from the origin to the right on the horizontal axis represents increasing the amount of current consumption and decreasing the amount of investment. Consequently, the curved boundary to the investment opportunity set slopes down

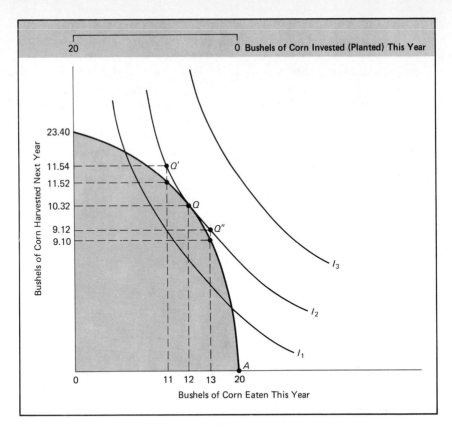

FIGURE 4–1
Making the consumption–investment decision.

and to the right, indicating that more consumption now will lead to less investment and, thus, less consumption next year.

☐ 4.1.2 Using Indifference Curves

How much corn will Crusoe decide to consume now? The answer depends on his feelings about present versus future consumption. These feelings can be shown graphically by a series of indifference curves, each of which displays combinations of current and future consumption that Crusoe finds equally desirable.[1] For example, he considers any combination on curve I_1 to be as desirable as any other on that curve. Similarly, he considers any combination of curve I_2 to be as desirable as any other on that curve. Furthermore, he would prefer a combination on I_2 over one on I_1, since the combinations on I_2 are "northeast" of those on I_1 and, thus, represent a higher level of aggregate consumption. Similarly, Crusoe would prefer a combination on I_3 over one

---

[1] These indifference curves should not be confused with the ones presented in Chapter 6, where the decision facing the individual is between risk and return, not current and future consumption.

on either I_2 or I_1. To keep from cluttering up the figure, only three of Crusoe's indifference curves have been drawn.

What will Crusoe do? From all his available investment opportunities, he will pick the one that is most desirable. Graphically, this is the investment opportunity corresponding to the point where an indifference curve is just tangent to the investment opportunity curve. In the figure, this is shown by point Q: From his initial stock of 20 bushels of corn, Crusoe will choose to eat 12 bushels this year and to invest the remaining 8 bushels. As a result of this investment, he will look forward to harvesting 10.32 bushels, all of which he will eat next year while waiting for his ship to come in.

What is the return on Crusoe's investment when he plants 8 bushels of corn now and harvests 10.32 bushels a year later? The rate of return is $(10.32 - 8)/8 = 29\%$. This is the *average return on investment* in the economy as a whole. His *marginal return on investment* is the return he earned on the last bushel planted, which in this case is the eighth bushel. Looking at Table 4.1, it can be seen that this corresponds to the yield on plot number 8, which is 22%.

4.2 INVESTMENT AND INTEREST

Moving a step closer to reality, assume that Crusoe is not alone. In particular, assume he has been preceded by Friday, who owns all the land on the island outright. However, Crusoe owns all the corn. If no one else were to intrude, the final outcome could depend on some form of cheating or violence. To avoid such an unpleasantry, assume that one of the clerks from the Paris Bourse is scheduled to drop by and "call out" a loan rate at which Crusoe will lend Friday corn today in return for Friday promising to repay a certain amount of corn one year later.

☐ 4.2.1 Demand and Supply of Capital

Given a rate at which Friday can borrow corn, how much will he take? Assume that Crusoe will provide corn now if he is paid an interest rate (in corn, not dollars) of 31%. In other words, for every bushel Friday takes, he must pay back 1.31 bushels next year. Referring to Table 4.1, borrowing 1 bushel clearly makes sense. This is because Friday can take the bushel, plant it in plot 1, and have a yield of 1.36 bushels a year later. Then Friday can pay back Crusoe 1.31 bushels, leaving himself a profit of .05 bushels $(1.36 - 1.31)$. Similarly, borrowing a second bushel will add .03 bushels $(1.34 - 1.31)$ to Friday's profit, and borrowing a third bushel will add .01 bushels $(1.32 - 1.31)$ to his profit. However, any more borrowing would be unprofitable for Friday. At an interest rate of 31%, Friday will take 3 bushels of corn. Figure 4.2 shows this, as well as the amount he will borrow at other interest rates, with the step function labeled *demand for capital* (sometimes referred to as the marginal efficiency of capital). Note that the lower the interest rate, the greater will be the quantity of capital (that is, corn) demanded. Not sur-

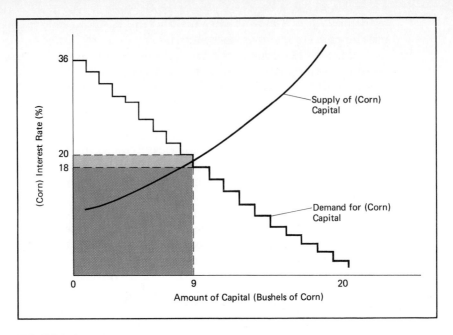

FIGURE 4-2
Demand and supply of capital.

prisingly, this is simply the information from Table 4.1, plotted in a different form.

How much capital (that is, corn) will Crusoe offer at various interest rates? The answer depends on the initial amount he owns and his attitudes toward present versus future consumption. However, the *supply of capital* shown in Figure 4.2 is typical: the higher the interest rate, the greater the amount of present consumption people are willing to forgo in favor of future consumption.

As in Paris, the visiting clerk wants to maximize the amount invested. Since this will be the smaller of (1) the amount Friday will want to borrow and (2) the amount Crusoe will want to lend, the appropriate interest rate, as shown in Figure 4.2, is about 19%. At this rate Crusoe will want to lend 9 bushels of corn in return for 10.71 bushels $[9 + (.19 \times 9)]$ next year. Moreover, at this rate, Friday will want to borrow just 9 bushels, knowing he will obtain a total yield of 11.52 bushels, leaving .81 bushels (11.52 − 10.71) in profit for his undertaking.

In the real world, *interest rates will adjust until the total amount of capital demanded by producers equals the amount that owners of capital are willing to supply.* Fundamentally, demand depends on investment opportunities, whereas supply depends on preferences for present versus future consumption and on the ownership of wealth. Together, they determine the interest rate.

This is often difficult to see, since the day-to-day forces affecting interest rates appear to relate more to government policy, flotations of new securities

by corporations, and so on. Although such activities do have an impact on interest rates, they are usually only ripples on the surface; the underlying forces of investment opportunities and preferences for present versus future consumption are the major determinants.

4.3 NOMINAL VERSUS REAL INTEREST RATES

In real economies there is, of course, more to life than corn. A person can trade present corn for future corn, present wheat for future wheat, present wine for future automobiles, and so on.

Modern economies gain much of their efficiency through the use of money—a generally agreed-upon medium of exchange. Instead of trading present corn for a future Toyota, as in a barter economy, the citizen of a modern economy can trade his or her corn for money (that is, "sell it"), trade the money for future money (that is, "invest it"), and finally trade the future money for a Toyota (that is, "buy it"). The rate at which he or she can trade present money for future money is the nominal (or monetary) interest rate—usually simply called the interest rate.

In periods of changing prices the nominal interest rate may prove a poor guide to the real return obtained by the investor. While there is no completely satisfactory way to summarize the many price changes that take place in such periods, most governments attempt to do so by measuring the cost of a specified bundle of major items. The "overall" price level computed for this representative combination of items is usually called a *cost-of-living index*, or consumer price index.

Whether or not the index is relevant for a given individual depends to a major extent on the similarity of his or her purchases to the bundle of goods and services used to construct the index. Moreover, such indices tend to overstate increases in the cost of living and understate decreases for people who do purchase the chosen bundle of items. There are two reasons for this. First, improvements in quality are seldom taken adequately into account. Perhaps more important, little or no adjustment is made in the bundle as relative prices change. The rational consumer can reduce the cost of attaining a given standard of living as prices change by substituting relatively less expensive goods for those that have become relatively more expensive.

Despite these drawbacks, cost-of-living indices provide at least rough estimates of changes in prices. And such indices can be used to determine an overall real rate of interest. For example, assume that during a year in which the nominal rate of interest is 7%, the cost-of-living index increases from 121 to 124. This means that the bundle of goods and services that cost $100 in some base year cost $121 at the beginning of the year and $124 at the end of the year. The owner of such a bundle could have sold it for $121 at the start of the year, invested the proceeds at 7% to obtain $121 × 1.07 = $129.47 at the end, and then purchased $129.47/$124 = 1.0441 bundles at the end of the year. The real rate of interest was, thus, 1.0441 − 1 = 4.41%.

These calculations can be summarized in the following formula:

$$\frac{C_0(1 + \text{NIR})}{C_1} = 1 + \text{RIR} \qquad (4.1)$$

where:

C_0 = level of the cost-of-living index at the beginning of the year,
C_1 = level of the cost-of-living index at the end of the year,
NIR = the nominal interest rate,
RIR = the real interest rate.

Alternatively, equation (4.1) can be written as:

$$\frac{1 + \text{NIR}}{1 + c} = 1 + \text{RIR} \qquad (4.2)$$

where c = the change in the cost-of-living index, or $(C_1 - C_0)/C_0$. In this case, $c = (124 - 120)/120 = .02479$, so prices increased by about 2.5%.

For quick calculation, the real interest rate can be estimated by simply subtracting the rate of change in the cost-of-living index from the nominal interest rate:

$$\text{RIR} \approx \text{NIR} - c \qquad (4.3)$$

where $\approx$ means "is approximately equal to." In this case, the quick calculation results in an estimate of 7% − 2.5% = 4.5%, which is reasonably close to the true value of 4.41%.

Sad to say, inflation seems to be here to stay, but its precise magnitude is hard to estimate accurately in advance. For this reason, further discussion of real versus nominal interest rates is deferred until Chapter 11. Suffice it to say here that it may be best to view the expected real interest rate as determined by the underlying forces described in earlier sections, with the nominal interest rate approximately equal to this amount plus the expected change in prices.

4.4 YIELD-TO-MATURITY

Robinson Crusoe was faced with a one-time investment decision, since he knew a ship was coming to rescue him after two years on the island. However, most people consider investments that will pay off not only next year but also the following year, and the year after that, and so on. Since interest rates are associated with investments and investments differ in longevity, there are many interest rates, not just one. Furthermore, there are many ways that interest rates can be calculated. One such method results in an interest rate that is known as the yield-to-maturity; another results in an interest rate known as the spot rate, which is discussed in the next section.

In describing yields-to-maturity and spot rates, three hypothetical Treasury securities that are available to the public for investment are considered. Such securities are widely believed to be free from default risk, meaning that investors have no doubts about being paid fully and on time.

Thus, the impact of differing degrees of default risk on yields-to-maturity and spot rates has been removed by considering these securities.

The three Treasury securities to be considered are referred to as bonds A, B, and C. Bond A matures in one year, at which time the investor will receive $1000. Similarly, bond B matures in two years, at which time the investor will receive $1000. Bond C is a coupon bond that pays the investor $50 one year from now and matures two years from now, paying the investor $1050 at that time. The prices at which these bonds are currently being sold in the market are:

> Bond A (the one-year pure-discount bond): $934.58
> Bond B (the two-year pure-discount bond): $857.34
> Bond C (the two-year coupon bond): $946.93

The *yield-to-maturity* on any fixed-income security is the single interest rate (with interest compounded at some specified interval) that, if paid by a bank on the amount invested, would enable the investor to obtain all the payments made by the security in question. It is a simple matter to determine the yield-to-maturity on the one-year security, bond A. Since an investment of $934.58 will pay $1000 one year later, the yield-to-maturity on this bond is the rate r_A that a bank would have to pay on a deposit of $934.58 in order for the account to have a balance of $1000 after one year. Thus, the yield-to-maturity on bond A is the rate r_A that is the solution to the following equation:

$$(1 + r_A) \times \$934.58 = \$1000 \qquad (4.4)$$

which is 7%.

In the case of bond B, assuming annual compounding at a rate r_B, an account with $857.34 invested initially (the cost of B) would grow to $(1 + r_B) \times \$857.34$ in one year. Leaving this total intact, the account would grow to $(1 + r_B) \times [(1 + r_B) \times \$857.34]$ by the end of the second year. The yield-to-maturity is the rate r_B that makes this amount equal to $1000. In other words, the yield-to-maturity on bond B is the rate r_B that is the solution to the following equation:

$$(1 + r_B) \times [(1 + r_B) \times \$857.34] = \$1000 \qquad (4.5)$$

which is 8%.

For bond C, consider investing $946.93 in an account. At the end of one year, the account would grow in value to $(1 + r_C) \times \$946.93$. Then the investor would remove $50, leaving a balance of $\{[(1 + r_C) \times \$946.94] - \$50\}$. At the end of the second year this balance would have grown to an amount equal to $(1 + r_C) \times \{[(1 + r_C) \times \$946.93] - \$50\}$. The yield-to-maturity on bond C is the rate r_C that makes this amount equal to $1050:

$$(1 + r_C) \times \{[(1 + r_C) \times \$946.93] - \$50\} = \$1050 \qquad (4.6)$$

which is 7.975%.

Equivalently, yield-to-maturity is the discount rate that makes the

present value of the promised future cash flows equal to the current market price of the bond.[2] When viewed in this manner, yield-to-maturity is analogous to internal rate of return, a concept used for making capital budgeting decisions that is often described in introductory finance textbooks. This can be seen for bond A by dividing both sides of equation (4.4) by $(1 + r_A)$, resulting in:

$$\$934.58 = \frac{\$1000}{(1 + r_A)}. \tag{4.7}$$

Similarly, for bond B both sides of equation (4.5) can be divided by $(1 + r_B)^2$, resulting in:

$$\$857.34 = \frac{\$1000}{(1 + r_B)^2} \tag{4.8}$$

whereas for bond C both sides of equation (4.6) can be divided by $(1 + r_C)^2$:

$$\$946.93 - \frac{\$50}{(1 + r_C)} = \frac{\$1050}{(1 + r_C)^2}$$

or

$$\$946.93 = \frac{\$50}{(1 + r_C)} + \frac{\$1050}{(1 + r_C)^2}. \tag{4.9}$$

Since equations (4.7), (4.8), and (4.9) are equivalent to equations (4.4), (4.5), and (4.6), respectively, the solutions must be the same as before, with $r_A = 7\%$, $r_B = 8\%$, and $r_C = 7.975\%$.

For coupon-bearing bonds, the procedure for determining yield-to-maturity involves trial and error. In the case of bond C, a discount rate of 10% could be tried initially, resulting in a value of $913.22 for the right-hand side of equation (4.9), a value that is too low. This indicates that the number in the denominator is too high, so a lower discount rate, such as 6%, is used next. In this case, the value on the right-hand side is $981.67, which is too high and indicates that 6% is too low. This means the solution is between 6% and 10%, and the search could continue until the answer, 7.975%, is found.

Fortunately, computers are good at trial-and-error calculations. One can describe a very complex series of cash flows to a computer and get an answer concerning yield-to-maturity in short order. In fact, some hand-held calculators come with built-in programs to find yield-to-maturity, where one simply enters the number of days to maturity, the annual coupon payments, and the current market price and then presses the key that indicates yield-to-maturity. The lights blink as the calculator engages in its trial-and-error procedure; then in a few seconds the answer appears.

Yield-to-maturity is the most commonly used measure of a bond's "interest rate," or "return." It can be computed for any bond and it facilitates

---

[2] This calculation assumes that the bond will not be called prior to maturity. If it is assumed that the bond will be called as soon as possible, then the discount rate that makes the present value of the corresponding cash flows equal to the current market price of the bond is known as the bond's *yield-to-call*.

comparisons among different investments. However, it has some serious drawbacks. In order to understand these drawbacks, the concept of spot rates must be introduced.

4.5 SPOT RATES

A *spot rate* is measured at a given time as the yield-to-maturity on a pure-discount security and can be thought of as the interest rate associated with a spot contract. Such a contract, when signed, involves the immediate loaning of money from one party to another. The loan, along with interest, is to be repaid in its entirety at a specific time in the future. The interest rate that is specified in the contract is the spot rate.

Bonds A and B in the previous example were pure-discount securities, meaning an investor who purchased either one would expect to receive only one cash payment from the issuer. Accordingly, in this example the one-year spot rate is 7% and the two-year spot rate is 8%. In general, the t-year spot rate s_t is the solution to the following equation:

$$P_t = \frac{M_t}{(1 + s_t)^t} \tag{4.10}$$

where P_t is the current market price of a pure-discount bond that matures in t years and has a maturity value of M_t. For example, the values of P_t and M_t for bond B would be $857.34 and $1000, respectively, with $t = 2$.

Spot rates can also be determined in another manner if only coupon-bearing Treasury bonds are available for longer maturities. Generally the one-year spot rate (s_1) will be known, since there generally will be a one-year pure-discount Treasury security available for making this calculation. However, it may be the situation that no two-year pure-discount Treasury security exists. Instead, only a two-year coupon-bearing bond may be available for investment, having a current market price of P_2, a maturity value of M_2, and a coupon payment one year from now equal to C_1. In this situation, the two-year spot rate (s_2) is the solution to the following equation:

$$P_2 = \frac{C_1}{(1 + s_1)^1} + \frac{M_2}{(1 + s_2)^2}. \tag{4.11}$$

For example, assume that only bonds A and C exist. In this situation it is known that the one-year spot rate, s_1, is 7%. Now, equation (4.11) can be used to determine the two-year spot rate, s_2, where $P_2 = \$946.93$, $C_1 = \$50$, and $M_2 = \$1050$:

$$\$946.93 = \frac{\$50}{(1 + .07)^1} + \frac{\$1050}{(1 + s_2)^2}.$$

The solution to this equation is $s_2 = .08 = 8\%$. Thus, the two-year spot rate is determined to be the same in this example regardless of whether it is determined directly by analyzing pure-discount bond B or indirectly by an-

alyzing coupon-bearing bond C in conjunction with bond A. Although this will not always be the case, often the differences are insignificant.

4.6 DISCOUNT FACTORS

Having determined a set of spot rates, it is a straightforward matter to determine the corresponding set of *discount factors*. A discount factor d_t is equivalent to the present value of $1 to be received t years in the future from a Treasury security and is equal to:

$$d_t = \frac{1}{(1 + s_t)^t}.\tag{4.12}$$

The set of these factors is sometimes referred to as the *market discount function* and changes day to day as spot rates change. In the example, d_1 = $1/(1 + .07)^1$ = .9346 and d_2 = $1/(1 + .08)^2$ = .8573.

Once the market discount function has been determined, it is fairly straightforward to find the present value of any Treasury security (or, for that matter, any default-free security). Let C_t denote the cash payment to be made to the investor at year t on the security being evaluated. The multiplication of C_t by d_t is termed *discounting*: converting the given future value into an equivalent present value. The latter is equivalent in the sense that P present dollars can be converted into C_t dollars in year t via available investment instruments, given the currently prevailing spot rates. An investment paying C_t dollars in year t with certainty should sell for $P = d_t C_t$ dollars today. If it sells for more, it is overpriced; if it sells for less, it is underpriced. These statements rest solely on comparisons with equivalent opportunities in the marketplace. Valuation of default-free investments thus requires no assessment of individual preferences, only careful analysis of available opportunities in the marketplace.

The simplest and, in a sense, most fundamental characterization of the structure of the market for default-free bonds is given by the current set of discount factors, referred to earlier as the market discount function. With this set of factors, it is a simple matter to evaluate a default-free bond that provides more than one payment, for it is, in effect, a package of bonds, each of which provides only one payment. Each amount is simply multiplied by the appropriate discount factor, and the resultant present values are summed.

For example, assume that the Treasury is preparing to offer for sale a two-year coupon-bearing security that will pay $70 in one year and $1070 in two years. What is a fair price for such a security? It is simply the present value of $70 and $1070. This can be determined by multiplying $70 and $1070 by the one-year and two-year discount factors, respectively. Doing so results in ($70 × .9346) + ($1070 × .8573), which equals $982.73.

No matter how complex the pattern of payments, this procedure can be used to determine the value of any default-free bond of this type. The general formula for the bond's present value (*PV*) is:

$$PV = \sum_{t=1}^{n} d_t C_t \qquad (4.13)$$

where the bond has promised cash payments C_t for each year t through year n.

At this point, it has been shown how spot rates and, in turn, discount factors can be calculated. However, no link between different spot rates (or different discount factors) has been established. For example, it has yet to be shown how the one-year spot rate of 7% is related to the two-year spot rate of 8%. The concept of forward rates makes the link.

4.7 FORWARD RATES

In the example, the one-year spot rate was determined to be 7%. This means that the market has determined that the present value of $1 to be paid by the Treasury Department in one year is $1/1.07, or $.9346. That is, the relevant discount rate for converting a cash flow one year from now to its present value is 7%. Since it was also noted that the two-year spot rate was 8%, the present value of $1 to be paid by the Treasury Department in two years is $1/1.08^2$, or $.8573.

An alternative view of $1 to be paid in two years is that it can be discounted in two steps. The first step determines its equivalent one-year value. That is, $1 to be received in two years is equivalent to $1/(1 + f_{1,2})$ to be received in one year. The second step determines the present value of this equivalent one-year amount by discounting it at the one-year spot rate of 7%. Thus, its current value is

$$\frac{\$1/(1 + f_{1,2})}{(1 + .07)}.$$

However, this value must be equal to $.8573, since it was mentioned earlier that according to the two-year spot rate, $.8573 is the present value of $1 to be paid in two years. That is,

$$\frac{\$1/(1 + f_{1,2})}{(1 + .07)} = \$.8573 \qquad (4.14)$$

which has a solution for $f_{1,2}$ of 9.01%.

The discount rate $f_{1,2}$ is known as the *forward rate* from year 1 to year 2. That is, it is the discount rate for determining the equivalent value of a dollar one year from now if it is to be received two years from now. In the example, $1 to be received two years from now is equivalent in value to $1/(1.0901) = $.9174 to be received one year from now (in turn, note that the present value of $.9174 is $.9174/1.07 = $.8573).

Symbolically, the link between the one-year spot rate, two-year spot rate, and one-year forward rate is:

$$\frac{\$1/(1 + f_{1,2})}{(1 + s_1)} = \frac{\$1}{(1 + s_2)^2} \qquad (4.15)$$

which can be rewritten as:

$$(1 + f_{1,2}) = \frac{(1 + s_2)^2}{(1 + s_1)} \qquad (4.16)$$

or

$$(1 + s_1)(1 + f_{1,2}) = (1 + s_2)(1 + s_2) \qquad (4.17)$$

More generally, for year $t - 1$ and year t spot rates, the link to the forward rate between years $t - 1$ and t is:

$$(1 + f_{t-1,t}) = \frac{(1 + s_t)^t}{(1 + s_{t-1})^{t-1}}, \qquad (4.18)$$

or

$$(1 + s_{t-1})^{t-1} \times (1 + f_{t-1,t}) = (1 + s_t)^t. \qquad (4.19)$$

There is another interpretation that can be given to forward rates. Consider a contract made now, in which money will be loaned a year from now and paid back two years from now. Such a contract is known as a *forward contract*; the interest rate on the one-year loan that is specified in it (note that the interest will be paid when the loan matures in two years) is known as the forward rate.

It is important to distinguish this rate from the rate for one-year loans that will prevail for deals made a year from now (the spot rate at that time). A forward rate applies to contracts made now but relating to a period "forward" in time. By the nature of the contract, the terms are certain now, even though the actual transaction will occur later. If instead one were to wait until next year and sign a contract to borrow money in the spot market at that time, the terms might turn out to be better or worse than today's forward rate, since the future spot rate is not perfectly predictable.

In the example, the marketplace has priced Treasury securities such that a representative investor making a two-year loan to the government would demand an interest rate equal to the two-year spot rate, 8%. Equivalently, the investor would be willing simultaneously to (1) make a one-year loan to the government at an interest rate equal to the one-year spot rate, 7%, and (2) sign a forward contract with the government to loan the government money one year from now, being repaid two years from now, where the interest rate to be paid is the forward rate, 9.01%.

When viewed in this manner, forward contracts are implicit. However, forward contracts are sometimes made explicitly. For example, a contractor might obtain a commitment from a bank for a one-year construction loan a year hence at a fixed rate of interest. Financial futures markets (discussed in Chapter 19) provide standardized forward contracts of this type. For example, in April 1987 one could contract to pay $984.70 in September 1987 to purchase a 90-day Treasury bill that would pay $1000 in December 1987.

4.8 FORWARD RATES AND DISCOUNT FACTORS

In equation (4.12) it was shown that a discount factor for t years could be calculated by adding 1 to the spot rate for t years, raising this sum to the power t, and then taking the reciprocal of the result. For example, it was shown that the two-year discount factor associated with the two-year spot rate of 8% was equal to $1/(1 + .08)^2 = .8573$.

Equation (4.17) suggests an equivalent method for calculating discount factors. In the case of the two-year factor, this method involves multiplying the one-year spot rate by the forward rate and taking the reciprocal of the result:

$$d_2 = \frac{1}{(1 + s_1) \times (1 + f_{1,2})} \tag{4.20}$$

which in the example is

$$d_2 = \frac{1}{(1 + .07) \times (1 + .0901)}$$

$$= .8573.$$

More generally, the discount factor for year t that is shown in equation (4.12) can be restated as follows:

$$d_t = \frac{1}{(1 + s_{t-1})^{t-1} \times (1 + f_{t-1,t})}. \tag{4.21}$$

Thus, given a set of spot rates, it is possible to determine the market discount function in either of two ways, both of which will provide the same figures. First, the spot rates can be used in equation (4.12) to arrive at a set of discount factors. Alternatively, the spot rates can be used to determine a set of forward rates and then the spot rates and forward rates can be used in equation (4.21) to arrive at a set of discount factors.

4.9 DURATION

Most bonds provide periodic coupon payments ("interest" payments) in addition to a final ("par") payment at maturity. Depending on the relative magnitudes of these payments, a bond may be more or less like others with the same maturity date. A measure of the average time prior to the receipt of payment is obtained by calculating the bond's *duration*. This is simply a weighted average of the lengths of time prior to the payments, using the relative present values of the payments as weights.

The two-year coupon bond analyzed earlier provides an illustration. Recall that this bond had a payment of $70 one year hence and that the present value of this payment was $70 \times .9346 = 65.42. Its final payment of $1070, to be made two years hence, had a present value of $1070 \times .8573$

TABLE 4.2
Calculating the Duration of a Bond.

TIME UNTIL RECEIVE OF PAYMENT (1)	PRESENT VALUE OF PAYMENT (2)	PRESENT VALUE OF PAYMENT AS A PROPORTION OF THE PRESENT VALUE OF THE BOND (3)	(1) × (3) = (4)
1	$ 65.42	$ 65.42/$982.73 = .0666	.0666
2	917.31	$917.31/$982.73 = .9334	1.8668
	$982.73	1.0000	1.9334

= $917.31. In total, the present value of the bond was $65.42 + $917.31 = $982.73. As shown in Table 4.2, this bond had a duration of 1.9334 years.

Bonds of similar duration are more likely to react in similar ways to changes in interest rates than are bonds of similar term-to-maturity but different durations. This should not be surprising. Term-to-maturity measures only the time until the last payment is due; it takes no account of the pattern of any intervening payments. Duration takes both factors into account and thus measures a bond's payment characteristics more accurately.[3]

4.10 COMPOUNDING

Thus far, the discussion has concentrated on annual interest rates by assuming that cash flows are compounded (or discounted) annually. This is often appropriate, but for more precise calculations a shorter period may be more desirable. Moreover, some lenders explicitly compound funds more often than once each year.

Compounding is the payment of interest on interest. At the end of each compounding interval, interest is computed and added to principal. This sum becomes the principal on which interest is computed at the end of the next interval. The process continues until the end of the final compounding interval is reached.

No problem is involved in adapting the previously stated formulas to compounding intervals other than a year. The simplest procedure is to count in units of the chosen interval. For example, yield-to-maturity can be calculated using any chosen compounding interval. If payment of P dollars now will result in the receipt of F dollars ten years from now, the yield-to-maturity can be calculated using annual compounding by finding a value r_a that satisfies the equation

$$P(1 + r_a)^{10} = F \qquad (4.22)$$

since F will be received ten annual periods from now. The result, r_a, is expressed as an annual rate with annual compounding.

---

[3] Duration is discussed more extensively in Chapter 14.

Alternatively, yield-to-maturity can be calculated using semiannual compounding by finding a value r_s that satisfies the equation

$$P(1 + r_s)^{20} = F \qquad (4.23)$$

since F will be received 20 semiannual periods from now. The result, r_s, is expressed as a semiannual rate with semiannual compounding. It can be doubled to give an annual rate with semiannual compounding; alternatively, the annual rate with annual compounding can be computed for a given value of r_s by using the following equation:

$$1 + r_a = (1 + r_s)^2. \qquad (4.24)$$

For example, consider an investment costing $2315.97 that will pay $5000 10 years later. Applying equations (4.22) and (4.23) to this security results in

$$\$2315.97(1 + r_a)^{10} = \$5000$$

and

$$\$2315.97(1 + r_s)^{20} = \$5000$$

respectively, where the solutions are $r_a = 8\%$ and $r_s = 3.923\%$. Thus, this security can be described as having an annual rate with annual compounding of 8%, a semiannual rate with semiannual compounding of 3.923%, and an annual rate with semiannual compounding of $2 \times 3.923\% = 7.846\%$.[4]

To reduce the massive confusion caused by the many different methods that can be used to express interest rates, the Federal Truth-in-Lending Act requires every lender to compute and disclose the *annual percentage rate* (APR) implied by the terms of a loan. This is simply the yield-to-maturity, computed using the most frequent time between payments on the loan as the compounding interval. Although some complications arise when payments are required at irregular intervals, the use of APRs has clearly simplified the task of comparing lenders' terms.

Semiannual compounding is commonly used to determine the yield-to-maturity for bonds, since coupon payments are usually made twice a year. Most preprogrammed calculators and computers use this approach.

4.11   THE BANK DISCOUNT METHOD

Despite the truth-in-lending law, other methods are still used to summarize interest rates. One time-honored procedure is the *bank discount method*. If someone "borrows" $100 from a bank, to be repaid a year later, the bank will discount the interest of, for instance, 8% and give the borrower $92. According to the bank discount method, this is an interest rate of 8%. The borrower only receives $92, for which he or she must pay $8 in interest after one year. The true interest rate (APR) must be based on the money the

---

[4] Note how, using equation (4.24), $r_a = (1.03923)^2 - 1 = 8\%$, a solution that is the same as the one provided by equation (4.22).

borrower actually gets to use. In this case, the rate is 8.70%, since \$8/\$92 = .0870.

It is a simple matter to convert an interest rate quoted on the bank discount method to a true interest rate. If the bank discount rate is BDR, then the true rate is simply $BDR/(1 - BDR)$. The previous example provides an illustration: $.08/(1 - .08) = .0870$.

4.12   CONTINUOUS COMPOUNDING

When computing an investment's return, the compounding interval can make a difference. For example, regulations may limit a savings institution to paying a fixed rate of interest but make no specifications about the compounding interval. This was the situation in early 1975, when the legal limit on interest paid by savings and loan companies on deposits committed from six to ten years was 7.75% per year. Initially, most savings and loans paid simple interest—thus, \$1 deposited at the beginning of the year would grow to \$1.0775 by the end of the year. Later, in an attempt to attract depositors, some enterprising savings and loans announced that they would pay 7.75% per year, compounded semiannually at a rate of 7.75%/2 = 3.3875%. This meant that \$1 deposited at the beginning of the year would grow to \$1.03875 at the end of six months, and this total would then grow to \$1.03875 × 1.03875 = \$1.079 by the end of the year, for an effective annual interest rate of 7.9%. This procedure was considered within the letter, if not the spirit, of the law.

Before long, other competitors offered 7.75% per year compounded quarterly (that is, 7.75%/4 = 1.938% per quarter), giving an effective annual interest rate of 7.978%. Then others offered to compound the 7.75% rate on a monthly basis (at 7.75%/12 = .646% per month), for an effective annual interest rate of 8.031%. The end was reached when one company offered continuous compounding of the 7.75% annual rate. This rather abstract procedure represents the limit as interest is compounded more and more frequently. If r represents the annual rate of interest (in this case, 7.75%) and n is the number of times compounding takes place per year, the effective rate, r_e, is given by:

$$\left(1 + \frac{r}{n}\right)^n = 1 + r_e. \tag{4.25}$$

Thus, with semiannual compounding of 7.75%,

$$\left(1 + \frac{.0775}{2}\right)^2 = (1 + .03875)^2 = 1.079$$

and with quarterly compounding,

$$\left(1 + \frac{.0775}{4}\right)^4 = (1 + .01938)^4 = 1.07978$$

and so on. As the compounding interval grows shorter, the number of times compounding takes place (n) grows larger, as does the effective interest rate, r_e.

Mathematicians can prove that as n grows larger, the quantity $[1 + (r/n)]^n$ becomes increasingly close to e^r, where e stands for the number 2.71828 (rounded to five-place accuracy). In this case, $e^{.0775} = 1.0806$, indicating an effective annual rate of 8.06%.[5]

A more general formula for continuous compounding can also be derived. At an annual rate of r, with continuous compounding P dollars will grow to F_t dollars t years from now, where the relationship between P, r, and F_t is:

$$Pe^{rt} = F_t. \tag{4.26}$$

Similarly, the present value of F_t dollars received t years later at an annual rate of r that is continuously compounded will be

$$P = \frac{F_t}{e^{rt}}. \tag{4.27}$$

Thus, if spot rates are expressed as annual rates with continuous compounding, then the discount factors can be calculated as:

$$d_t = \frac{1}{e^{rt}}. \tag{4.28}$$

These last three formulas can be used for any value of t, including fractional amounts (for example, if F_t is to be received in $2\frac{1}{2}$ years, then $t = 2.5$).

4.13 YIELD CURVES

At any time, treasury securities will be priced approximately in accord with the existing set of spot rates and the associated discount factors. Although there have been times when all the spot rates were roughly equal in size, generally they have different values. Often the one-year spot rate is less than the two-year spot rate, which in turn is less than the three-year spot rate, and so on (that is, s_t increases as t increases). At other times, the one-year spot rate is greater than the two-year spot rate, which in turn is greater than the three-year spot rate, and so on (that is, s_t decreases as t increases). It is wise for the security analyst to know which case currently prevails, as this is a useful starting point in valuing fixed-income securities.

Unfortunately, this is easier said than done. Only the bonds of the U.S. government are clearly free from default risk. However, such bonds differ in tax treatment as well as in callability and other features. Despite these problems, a summary of the approximate relationship between yields-to-maturity on Treasury securities of various terms-to-maturity is presented in each issue of the *Treasury Bulletin*. This summary is given in the form

---

[5] Tables of natural logarithms may be used for such calculations. The natural logarithm of 1.0806 is .0775, and the antilogarithm of .0775 is 1.0806.

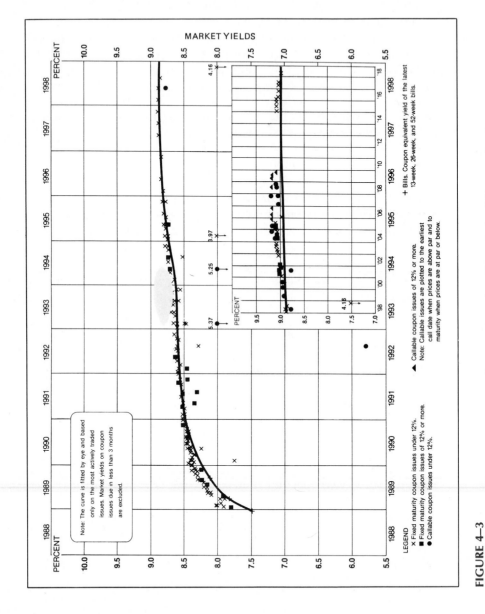

FIGURE 4–3
Yield curve of treasury securities, September 30, 1987 (based on closing bid quotations).

SOURCE: Treasury Bulletin Fall Issue, December 1987, p. 47.

of a graph illustrating the current yield curve. Figure 4.3 provides an example.

A *yield curve* is a graph that shows the yields-to-maturity (on the vertical axis) for Treasury securities of various maturities (on the horizontal axis) as of a particular date. This provides an estimate of the current *term structure* of interest rates and changes daily as yields-to-maturity change.

As Figure 4.3 shows, this relationship between yields and maturities is less than perfect. That is, not all Treasury securities lie exactly on the yield curve. Part of this is due to the previously mentioned differences in tax treatment, callability, and the like. Part is due to the fact that the yield-to-maturity on a coupon-bearing security is not clearly linked to the set of spot rates currently in existence. Since the set of spot rates is a fundamental determinant of the price of any Treasury security, there is no reason to expect yields to lie exactly on the curve. Indeed, a more meaningful graph would be one where spot rates are measured on the vertical axis instead of yields-to-maturity. With this in mind, an interesting question to ponder is, Why are the spot rates of different magnitudes? And why do the differences in these rates change over time, where sometimes long-term spot rates are greater than short-term spot rates and sometimes the opposite occurs? Attempts to answer such questions can be found in various term structure theories.

4.14 TERM STRUCTURE THEORIES

Three theories have been generally used to explain the term structure of interest rates.[6] The focus of the discussion is on the term structure of spot rates, since it is these rates and not yields-to-maturity that are critically important in determining the price of any Treasury security.

☐ 4.14.1 The Unbiased Expectations Theory

The *unbiased expectations theory* holds that the forward rate represents the average opinion of the expected future spot rate for the period in question. Thus, a set of spot rates that is rising can be explained by arguing that the marketplace (that is, the general opinion of investors) believes that spot rates will be rising in the future. Conversely, a set of decreasing spot rates is explained by arguing that the marketplace expects spot rates to be falling in the future.[7]

The marketplace expects spot rates to change because either the real

---

[6] For a thorough review of these theories and the associated empirical evidence, see Chapter 19 of John H. Wood and Norma L. Wood, *Financial Markets* (San Diego, Calif.: Harcourt Brace Jovanovich, 1985) and Chapter 5 of James C. Van Horne, *Financial Market Rates and Flows* (Englewood Cliffs, N.J.: Prentice Hall, 1984).

[7] Recently a "modern" expectations theory has been developed that is economically more logical than the "unbiased" expectations theory. However, it provides approximately the same empirical implications and explanations of the term structure as those given by the unbiased expectations theory. Thus, given the similarities of the two theories, only the unbiased expectations theory is presented. For more on the modern expectations theory, see Wood and Wood, *Financial Markets*, pp. 645–51.

rate or the inflation rate is expected to change. For example, the reason the spot rates are expected to rise could be due to a perception in the marketplace that inflation is going to accelerate in the future. Conversely, spot rates might be expected to decline because of a perception that inflation is going to slow down in the future.

In order to understand this theory more fully, consider the earlier example where the one-year spot rate was 7% and the two-year spot rate was 8%. The basic question is, Why are these two spot rates different? Equivalently, why is the term structure upward-sloping?

Consider an investor with $1 to invest for two years (for ease of exposition, it will be assumed that any amount of money can be invested at the prevailing spot rates). This investor could follow a *maturity strategy*, investing the money now for the full two years at the two-year spot rate of 8%. With this strategy, at the end of two years the dollar will have grown in value to $1(1.08)(1.08) = $1.1664. Alternatively, the investor could invest the dollar now for one year at the one-year spot rate of 7%, so that the investor knows that one year from now he or she will have $1(1.07) = $1.07 to reinvest for one more year.

Although the investor does not know what the one-year spot rate will be one year from now, the investor has an *expectation* about what it will be (this expected future spot rate will hereafter be denoted by $es_{1,2}$). If the investor thinks it will be 10%, then his or her $1 has an expected value two years from now of $1(1.07)(1.10) = $1.177. In this case, the investor would choose a *rollover strategy*, meaning the investor would choose to invest in a one-year security at 7% rather than in the two-year security, since he or she would expect to have more money at the end of two years by doing so (note that $1.177 > $1.1664).

However, an expected future spot rate of 10% cannot represent the general view in the marketplace. If it did, people would not be willing to invest money at the two-year spot rate, since a higher return would be expected from investing money at the one-year rate and using the rollover strategy. Thus, the two-year spot rate would quickly rise, since the supply of funds for two-year loans at 8% would be less than the demand. Conversely, the supply of funds for one year at 7% would be more than the demand, causing the one-year rate to fall quickly. Thus, a one-year spot rate of 7%, a two-year spot rate of 8%, and an expected future spot rate of 10% cannot represent an equilibrium situation.

What if the expected future spot rate is 6% instead of 10%? In this case, according to the rollover strategy, the investor would expect $1 to be worth $1(1.07)(1.06) = $1.1342 at the end of two years. Since this is less than the value the dollar will have if the maturity strategy is followed ($1.1342 < $1.1664), the investor would choose the maturity strategy. Again, however, an expected future spot rate of 6% cannot represent the general view in the marketplace because if it did, people would not be willing to invest money at the one-year spot rate.

Earlier, it was shown that the forward rate in this example was 9.01%. What if the expected future spot rate was of this magnitude? At the end of two years the value of $1 with the rollover strategy would be $1(1.07)(1.0901)

= \$1.1664, the same as the value of \$1 with the maturity strategy. In this case, equilibrium would exist in the marketplace because the general view would be that both strategies have the same expected return. Accordingly, investors with a two-year holding period would not have an incentive to choose one strategy over the other.

Note that an investor with a one-year holding period could follow a maturity strategy by investing \$1 in the one-year security and receiving \$1.07 after one year. Alternatively, a *naive strategy* could be followed, where a two-year security could be purchased now and sold after one year. If so, the expected selling price would be \$1.1664/1.0901 = \$1.07, for a return of 7% (the security would have a maturity value of \$1.1664 = \$1(1.08)(1.08), but since the spot rate is expected to be 9.01% in a year, its expected selling price is just the discounted value of its maturity value). Since the maturity and naive strategies have the same expected return, investors with a one-year holding period would not have an incentive to choose one strategy over the other.

Thus, the unbiased expectations theory asserts that the expected future spot rate is equal in magnitude to the forward rate. In the example, the current one-year spot rate is 7% and, according to this theory, the general opinion is that it will rise to a rate of 9.01% in one year. It is this expected rise in the one-year spot rate that is the reason behind the upward-sloping term structure when the two-year spot rate (8%) is greater than the one-year spot rate (7%).

In equation format, the unbiased expectations theory states that the expected future spot rate is equal to the forward rate:

$$es_{1,2} = f_{1,2}. \tag{4.29}$$

Thus, equation (4.17) can be restated with $es_{1,2}$ substituted for $f_{1,2}$, as follows:

$$(1 + s_2)(1 + s_2) = (1 + s_1)(1 + es_{1,2}) \tag{4.30}$$

which can be conveniently interpreted to mean that the expected return from a maturity strategy must equal the expected return on a rollover strategy.[8]

The previous example dealt with an upward-sloping term structure, where the longer the term, the higher the spot rate. It is a straightforward matter to deal with a downward-sloping term structure, where the longer the term, the lower the spot rate. While the explanation for an upward-sloping term structure was that investors expect spot rates to rise in the future, the reason for the downward-sloping curve is that investors expect spot rates to fall in the future.

An interesting followup question is, Why do investors expect spot rates to change, either rising or falling, in the future? A possible answer to this question can be found by noting that the spot rates that are observed in the marketplace are nominal rates. That is, they are a reflection of the underlying real rate and the expected inflation rate.[9] If either (or both) of these rates

---

[8] Equation (4.29) can be expressed more generally as $es_{t-1,t} = f_{t-1,t}$. Thus, using equation (4.19), the unbiased expectations theory states that, in general, $(1 + s_t)^t = (1 + s_{t-1})^{t-1} \times (1 + es_{t-1,t})$.

[9] See Chapter 11 for a discussion of the nature of the relationship between nominal rates, real rates, and expected inflation rates.

is expected to change in the future, then the spot rate will be expected to change.

For example, assume a constant real rate of 3%. Since the current one-year spot rate is 7%, this means that the general opinion in the marketplace is that the expected rate of inflation over the next year is approximately 4% (the nominal rate is approximately equal to the sum of the real rate and expected inflation rate). Now, according to the unbiased expectations theory, the expected future spot rate is 9.01%, an increase of 2.01% from the current one-year spot rate of 7%. The spot rate is expected to rise by 2.01% because the inflation rate is expected to rise by 2.01%. That is, the expected inflation rate over the next 12 months is approximately 4%, and over the following 12 months it is expected to be higher, at approximately 6.01%.

To recapitulate, the two-year spot rate (8%) is greater than the one-year spot rate (7%) because investors expect the future one-year spot rate to be greater than the current one-year spot rate. They expect it to be greater because of an anticipated rise in the expected rate of inflation, from approximately 4% to approximately 6.01%.

In general, when current economic conditions make short-term spot rates abnormally high (owing, say, to a relatively high current rate of inflation), according to the unbiased expectations theory, the term structure should be downward-sloping. This is because inflation would be expected to abate in the future. Conversely, when current conditions make short-term rates abnormally low (owing say, to a relatively low current rate of inflation), the term structure should be upward-sloping, since inflation would be expected to rise in the future. Examination of historical term structures suggest that this is what has actually happened, since the structure has been upward-sloping in periods of lower interest rates and downward-sloping in periods of higher interest rates.

However, examining historical term structures uncovers a problem. In particular, with this theory, it is logical to expect that over time there will be roughly as many occurrences of upward-sloping term structures as downward-sloping term structures. In reality, upward-sloping structures tend to be more frequent. The liquidity preference theory provides an explanation for this observation.

☐ 4.14.2 The Liquidity Preference Theory

The *liquidity preference theory* (also known as the liquidity premium theory) starts with the notion that investors are primarily interested in purchasing short-term securities. That is, even though some investors may have longer holding periods, there is a tendency for them to prefer short-term securities. This is because these investors realize that they may need their funds earlier than anticipated and recognize that they face less "price risk" (that is, interest rate risk) if they invest in shorter-term securities.

For example, an investor with a two-year holding period would tend to prefer the rollover strategy, since he or she would be certain of having a

given amount of cash at the end of one year, when it may be needed. If a maturity strategy had been followed, then the investor would have to sell the two-year security after one year if cash was needed. However, it is not known now what price the investor would get if he or she were to sell the two-year security in one year. Thus, there is an extra element of risk associated with the maturity strategy that is absent from the rollover strategy.[10]

The upshot is that investors with a two-year holding period will not choose the maturity strategy if it has the same expected return as the rollover strategy, since it is riskier. The only way investors will follow the maturity strategy and buy the two-year securities is if its expected return is higher. That is, borrowers are going to have to pay the investors a risk premium in the form of a greater expected return in order to get them to purchase two-year securities.

Will borrowers be inclined to pay such a premium when issuing two-year securities? Yes, they will be so inclined. First, frequent refinancing may be costly in terms of registration, advertising, paperwork, and so on. These costs can be lessened by issuing relatively long-term securities. Second, some borrowers will realize that relatively long-term bonds are a less risky source of funds than relatively short-term bonds, since they will not have to be as concerned about the possibility of refinancing in the future at higher interest rates. Thus, borrowers may be willing to pay more (via higher expected interest costs) for relatively long-term funds.

In the example, the one-year spot rate was 7% and the two-year spot rate was 8%. As mentioned earlier, according to the liquidity preference theory, the only way investors will agree to follow a maturity strategy is if the expected return from doing so is higher than the expected return from following the rollover strategy. This means that the expected future spot rate must be something *less* than the forward rate of 9.01%—perhaps it is 8.6%. If so, then the value of a $1 investment in two years is expected to be $1(1.07)(1.086) = $1.1620, given the rollover strategy is followed. Since the value of a $1 investment with the maturity strategy is $1(1.08)(1.08) = $1.1664, it can be seen that the rollover strategy has a lower expected return for the two-year period, which can be attributed to its smaller degree of price risk.

The difference between the forward rate and the expected future spot rate is known as the *liquidity premium*. It is the "extra" return given investors in order to entice them to purchase the more risky two-year security. In the example, it is equal to 9.01% − 8.6% = .41%. More generally,

$$f_{1,2} = es_{1,2} + L_{1,2} \qquad (4.31)$$

---

[10] Unfortunately, this risk is often referred to as *liquidity risk*, when it more appropriately should be called *price risk*, since it is the price volatility associated with longer-term securities that is of concern to investors. Partially offsetting this price risk is a risk that is present in the rollover strategy and absent from the maturity strategy—namely, the risk associated with having an uncertain reinvestment rate at the end of the first year when the rollover strategy is chosen. The liquidity preference theory assumes that this risk is of relatively little concern to investors.

where $L_{1,2}$ is the liquidity premium for the period commencing one year from now and ending two years from now.[11]

How does the liquidity preference theory explain the slope of the term structure? In order to answer this question, note that with the rollover strategy, the expected value of a dollar at the end of two years is $1(1 + s_1)(1 + es_{1,2})$. Alternatively, with the maturity strategy the expected value of a dollar at the end of two years is $1(1 + s_2)(1 + s_2)$. As mentioned earlier, according to the liquidity preference theory there is more risk with the maturity strategy, which in turn means that it must have a higher expected return. That is, the following inequality must hold:

$$\$1(1 + s_2)(1 + s_2) > \$1(1 + s_1)(1 + es_{1,2})$$

or
$$(4.32)$$
$$(1 + s_2)(1 + s_2) > (1 + s_1)(1 + es_{1,2}).$$

This inequality is the key to understanding how the liquidity preference theory explains the term structure.[12]

Consider the downward-sloping case first, where $s_1 > s_2$. The preceding inequality will hold in this situation only if the expected future spot rate ($es_{1,2}$) is substantially smaller than the current one-year spot rate (s_1).[13] Thus, a downward-sloping term structure will be observed only when the marketplace believes that interest rates are going to decline substantially.

As an example, assume that the one-year spot rate (s_1) is 7% and the two-year spot rate (s_2) is 6%. Since 7% is greater than 6%, this is a situation where the term structure is downward-sloping. Now, according to the previously given inequality,

$$(1 + .06)(1 + .06) > (1 + .07)(1 + es_{1,2})$$

which can hold only if the expected future spot rate ($es_{1,2}$) is substantially less than 7%. Given the one-year and two-year spot rates, the forward rate ($f_{1,2}$) is equal to 5.01%. Assuming the liquidity premium ($L_{1,2}$) is .41%, then according to equation (4.31), $es_{1,2}$ must be 5.01% − .41% = 4.6%. Thus, the term structure is downward-sloping because the current one-year spot rate of 7% is expected to decline to 4.6% in the future.

In comparison, the unbiased expectations theory would also explain the term structure by saying that the reason it was downward-sloping was because the one-year spot rate was expected to decline in the future. However, the unbiased expectations theory would expect the spot rate to decline only to 5.01%, not 4.6%.

---

[11] It should be noted that while the forward rate can be determined, neither the expected future spot rate nor the liquidity premium can be observed. All that can be done is estimate their respective values.

[12] Equation (4.31) can be expressed more generally as $f_{t-1,t} = es_{t-1,t} + L_{t-1,t}$. Thus, using equation (4.17), the liquidity preference theory states that

$$(1 + s_t)^t = (1 + s_{t-1})^{t-1} \times (1 + es_{t-1,t} + L_{t-1,t}).$$

Since $L_{t-1,t} > 0$, it follows that, in general,

$$(1 + s_t)^t > (1 + s_{t-1})^{t-1} \times (1 + es_{t-1,t}).$$

[13] If $es_{1,2}$ were equal to or greater than s_1, then the inequality would not hold in the correct direction, since it was assumed that $s_1 > s_2$.

Consider next the case of a flat term structure, where $s_1 = s_2$. The preceding inequality will hold in this situation only if $es_{1,2}$ is less than s_1. Thus, a flat term structure will occur only when the marketplace expects interest rates are going to decline. Indeed, if $s_1 = s_2 = 7\%$ and $L_{1,2} = .41\%$, then $f_{1,2} = 7\%$ and, according to equation (4.31), the expected future spot rate is $7\% - .41\% = 6.59\%$, a decline from the current one-year spot rate of 7%. This is in contrast to the unbiased expectations theory, where a flat term structure would be interpreted to mean that the marketplace expected interest rates to remain at the same level.

The last case of an upward-sloping yield curve is one where $s_1 < s_2$. If it is slightly upward-sloping, this can be consistent with an expectation that interest rates are going to decline in the future. For example, if $s_1 = 7\%$ and $s_2 = 7.1\%$, then the forward rate is 7.2%. In turn, if the liquidity premium is .41%, then the expected future spot rate is $6.79\% = 7.2\% - .41\%$, a decline from the current one-year spot rate of 7%. Thus, the reason for the slight upward slope to the term structure is that the marketplace expects only a slight decline in the spot rate. In contrast, the unbiased expectations theory would argue that the reason for the slight upward slope was the expectation of a slight increase in the spot rate.

If the term structure is more steeply sloped, then it is more likely that the marketplace expects interest rates to rise in the future. For example, if $s_1 = 7\%$ and $s_2 = 7.3\%$, then the forward rate is 7.6%. Continuing to assume a liquidity premium of .41%, equation (4.31) indicates that the marketplace expects the one-year spot rate to rise from 7% to $7.6\% - .41\% = 7.19\%$. The unbiased expectations theory would also explain this steep slope by saying that the spot rate was expected to rise in the future but by a larger amount. In particular, the unbiased expectations theory would state that the spot rate was expected to rise to 7.6%, not 7.19%.

In summary, with the liquidity preference theory, downward-sloping term structures are indicative of an expected decline in the spot rate, whereas upward-sloping term structures may indicate either an expected rise or decline, depending on how steep the slope is. Generally, the steeper the slope, the more likely it is that the marketplace expects spot rates to rise. If roughly half the time investors expect spot rates will rise and half the time investors expect spot rates will decline, then the liquidity preference theory suggests that there should be more occurrences of upward-sloping term structures than downward-sloping ones. As mentioned earlier, this is indeed what has happened.

□ 4.14.3 **The Market Segmentation Theory**

A third explanation for the determination of the term structure rests on the assumption that there is *market segmentation*: Various investors and borrowers are asserted to be restricted by law, preference, or custom to certain maturities. Perhaps there is a market for short-term securities, another for intermediate-term securities, and a third for long-term securities. According

to the market segmentation theory, spot rates are determined by supply and demand conditions in each market. Furthermore, in its most restrictive form, investors and borrowers will not leave their market and enter a different one when the current rates suggest to them that there is a substantially higher expected return available by making such a move.

With this theory, an upward-sloping term structure exists when the intersection of the supply and demand curves for shorter-term funds is at a lower interest rate than the intersection for longer-term funds. Conversely, a downward-sloping term structure would exist when the intersection for shorter-term funds was at a higher interest rate than the intersection for longer-term funds.

□ 4.14.4 Empirical Evidence on the Theories

Empirical evidence provides some insight into the determinants of the term structure, but it is difficult to assess the relative importance of these three theories with a high degree of precision.

The market segmentation theory receives relatively slight empirical validation. This is understandable when it is realized that the theory will not hold if there are some investors and borrowers who are flexible enough to be willing to move into whatever segment has the highest expected return. By their actions, these investors and borrowers will give the term structure a continuity that is linked to expectations of future interest rates.

There does appear to be some evidence that the term structure conveys information about expected future spot rates, as hypothesized by both the unbiased expectations and liquidity preference theories. However, the evidence tends to favor the latter theory, since liquidity premiums also appear to exist.[14] In particular, there appear to be liquidity premiums of increasing size associated with Treasury securities of up to roughly one-year in maturity. However, there do not appear to be any additional premiums beyond one-year maturities. That is, investors seem to demand a premium in order to get them to purchase a one-year security instead of, say, a one-month security. However, no additional premiums are needed in order to get them to purchase two-year securities (even though the two-year security has more price risk than a one-year security).

In summary, it appears that expectations about future spot rates are important determinants of the term structure. Liquidity premiums appear to exist but do not increase in size beyond roughly a year, meaning that investment strategies involving securities with maturities of one year or more will have roughly the same expected return.

Examining the term structure of interest rates is important for deter-

---

[14] The empirical evidence is not without dispute. Fama has argued that the evidence is inconsistent with both the unbiased expectations and liquidity preference theories, but McCulloch refutes Fama's findings and argues in favor of the latter theory. See Eugene F. Fama, "Term Premiums in Bond Returns," *Journal of Financial Economics* 13, no. 4 (December 1984):529–46 and J. Huston McCulloch, "The Monotonicity of the Term Premium: A Closer Look," *Journal of Financial Economics* 18, no. 1 (March 1987):185–92 and "An Estimate of the Liquidity Premium, *Journal of Political Economy* 83, no. 1 (February 1975):95–119. See also the sources in footnote 6.

mining the current set of spot rates, which can be used as a basis for valuing any fixed-income security. Such an examination is also important because it provides some information about what the marketplace expects regarding the level of future interest rates.

4.15 SUMMARY

In order to understand how bonds are valued in the marketplace, it is convenient initially to examine those fixed-income securities that are free from default risk. The only securities meeting this requirement are those issued by the Treasury; thus, the focus of this chapter has been on those securities and their interest rates.

In periods of changing prices the nominal interest rate may prove a poor guide to the real return obtained by the investor. Although there is no completely satisfactory way to summarize the many price changes that take place in such periods, most governments attempt to do so by measuring the rate of change in a cost-of-living index. For quick calculation, the real interest rate can be estimated by simply subtracting the rate of change in this index from the nominal interest rate.

Often a bond is described and compared to others in terms of its yield-to-maturity, which is the discount rate that makes the present value of all of the bond's promised future cash flows equal to its current market price. A special kind of yield-to-maturity known as a spot rate is useful for security valuation. It is special in that it is the yield-to-maturity on a pure-discount security—that is, a security that has only one promised future cash flow associated with it. Once several related spot rates (each one associated with a different maturity) have been calculated, they can be used to value coupon-bearing Treasury securities, for example.

A forward rate can be thought of as the interest rate that will be paid on money that is borrowed at some specific time in the future and is to be repaid at an even more distant time in the future. The contract that specifies this rate (and all the other terms of the loan) is known as a forward contract. Such a contract differs from a spot contract in that both contracts can be signed at the same time, but the spot contract loan will take place immediately after the signing, whereas the forward contract loan will take place at a later date.

Most bonds provide periodic coupon payments (interest) in addition to a final (par) payment at maturity. Depending on the relative magnitudes of these payments, a bond may be more or less like others with the same maturity date. A measure of the average time prior to the receipt of payment is obtained by calculating the bond's duration. Bonds of similar duration are more likely to react in similar ways to changes in interest rates than are bonds of similar term-to-maturity but different durations.

At any point in time, Treasury securities will be priced approximately in accord with the existing set of spot rates. Although there have been times when all the spot rates are roughly equal in size, generally they have different values. It is wise for the security analyst to know what the yield curve for

Treasury securities currently looks like, as this is a useful starting point in valuing fixed-income securities. This curve provides an estimate of the current term structure of interest rates and will change daily as yields-to-maturity change.

Forward rates play an important role in two term structure theories, which are theories that offer explanations for why the yield curve is not flat. That is, these theories offer explanations for why current spot rates associated with different maturities are of different sizes. The unbiased expectations theory states that forward rates represent the consensus opinion about what spot rates will be in the future. In comparison, the liquidity preference theory states that forward rates overstate the consensus opinion about what spot rates will be in the future. Both theories agree that changes in people's expectations about the future level of spot rates (perhaps because of a change in the expected rate of inflation) will cause a change in the term structure.

In contrast to these two theories, the market segmentation theory states that different spot rates have different sizes due to the interaction of supply and demand for funds in markets that are separated from each other by maturity.

Which theory seems to be correct? Although a definitive answer has yet to be provided, the evidence seems to favor the liquidity preference theory when explaining why spot rates of one year or less are of different sizes. However, longer-term spot rates seem to be in accord with the unbiased expectations theory. Thus, examining the term structure of interest rates is important because it provides some information about what the marketplace expects regarding the level of interest rates in the future.

QUESTIONS AND PROBLEMS

1. At the end of 1974, Emil Bildilli held a portfolio of long-term U.S. government bonds valued at $14,000. At the end of 1981, Emil's portfolio was worth $16,932. Referring to Table 1.1, calculate the annualized real rate of return on Emil's bond portfolio over this seven-year period

2. Consider two bonds, each with a $1,000 face value and each with three years remaining to maturity.

   a. The first bond is a pure-discount bond that currently sells for $804.96. What is its yield-to-maturity?

   b. The second bond currently sells for $775.40 and makes annual coupon payments at a rate of 6% (that is, it pays $60 in interest per year). The first interest payment is due one year from today. What is this bond's yield-to-maturity?

3. Distinguish between spot rates and forward rates.

4. Assume that the current one-year spot rate is 6% and the forward rates for one year hence and two years hence, are, respectively:

$$f_{1,2} = 7\%$$

$$f_{2,3} = 8\%.$$

What should be the market price of a 6% coupon bond, with a $1,000 face value, maturing three years from today? The first interest payment is due one year from today. Interest is payable annually.

5. Assume the government has issued three bonds. The first, which pays $1,000 one year from today, is now selling for $909.09. The second, which pays $100 one year from today and $1,100 one year later, is now selling for $991.81. The third, which pays $1000 one year from today, $1000 one year later, and $1,100 one year after that, is now selling for $977.18.

   a. What are the current discount factors for dollars paid one, two, and three years from today?

   b. What are the forward rates?

   c. Honus Wagner, a friend, offers to pay you $500 one year from today, $600 two years from today, and $700 three years from today in return for a loan today. Assuming that Honus will not default on the loan, how much should you be willing to loan?

6. Mercury National Bank offers a passbook savings account that pays interest at a stated annual rate of 6%. Calculate the effective annual interest rate paid by Mercury National if it compounds interest:

   a. Semiannually

   b. Daily (365 days in a year)

   c. Continuously

7. Marty Marion is considering placing $30,000 in a three-year, default-free fixed-income investment which promises to provide interest at the rate of 8% during the first year, 10% in the second year, and 12% in the third year.

   a. Assuming semiannual compounding, to what value is Marty's investment expected to grow after three years?

   b. Recalculate your answer to part (a) assuming continuous compounding.

   c. What will be Marty's average annual continuously compounded rate of return over the three years?

8. Using *The Wall Street Journal* as a data source, turn to the table entitled "Treasury Bonds, Notes & Bills." Find the yield-to-maturity for Treasury securities maturing in one month, three months, one year, five years, ten years, and twenty years. With this information, construct the yield curve as of the paper's publication date.

9. Is it true that an observed downward-sloping yield curve is inconsistent with the liquidity preference theory of the term structure of interest rates? Explain.

10. Assume that the current structure of forward interest rates is upward sloping. Which will have a lower yield-to-maturity:

    a. A 15-year zero-coupon bond or a 10-year zero-coupon bond?

    b. A 10-year 5% coupon bond or a 10-year 6% coupon bond?

11. How would your answers to question 10 change if the forward interest rate structure were downward sloping?

12. Three theories explaining the term structure of interest rates are described in the chapter. Which theory do you believe best explains the relationship between spot rates and term-to-maturity? Provide supporting arguments for your answer.

Chapter 5

THE VALUATION OF RISKY

SECURITIES

Payments received from riskless securities can be accurately predicted: Neither their amounts nor their timing is uncertain. But many securities do not meet such high standards. Some or all of their payments are *contingent* on events with respect to amount, timing, or both. A bankrupt corporation may not make its promised bond payments in full or on time. A worker who is laid off may pay his or her bills late (or not at all). A corporation may reduce or eliminate its dividend if its business becomes unprofitable, and so on.

The security analyst must try to evaluate these circumstances affecting a risky investment's payments and enumerate the key events upon which such payments are contingent. For example, an aircraft manufacturer's fortunes may depend on whether or not the firm is awarded a major contract by the government, whether or not its recently introduced commercial aircraft is accepted by the airlines, whether or not there is an upturn in the economy with a concomitant increase in demand for airline travel, and so on. To properly value the stock of such a company the analyst must consider each of these contingencies and estimate the corresponding effect on the firm and its stock.

The identification of important influences and the evaluation of the impact of each one is exceedingly difficult. Among other things, the appropriate level of detail must be determined. The number of potentially relevant events is almost always very large, and the analyst must attempt to focus on the relatively few that appear to be most important. In some cases it may be best to differentiate only a few alternatives (for example, whether the economy will turn up, turn down, or stay the same). In some cases, finer distinctions may be needed (for example, whether the gross national product will be up 1%, 2%, 3%, and so on).

The process of identifying and evaluating key influences is central to security analysis. The *use* of such estimates is of concern in this chapter. After the contingencies have been identified and the corresponding payments estimated, how can the value of the security be determined?

5.1 MARKET VERSUS PERSONAL VALUATION

One approach to the valuation of risky securities focuses on the investor's personal attitudes and circumstances. Given his or her assessment of the likelihood of various contingencies, and feelings about the corresponding risks involved in an investment, an investor might determine the amount he or she would be willing to pay, by some sort of introspection. This would be a "personal" valuation of the security.

Such an approach would be appropriate if there were only one investment in the world. But such is not the case. A security need not and should not be valued without considering available alternatives. Current market values of other securities provide important information, since a security is seldom so unique that nothing else is even comparable. Security valuation should not be done in a vacuum; it should instead be performed in a market context.

Key to this approach is the comparison of one investment or combination of investments with others having comparable characteristics. For example, assume that A and B in Figure 5.1(a) are similar in this respect; then the two should be equal in value.

Now imagine that alternative B includes a security that an investor wishes to value—call it X. Moreover, assume that all other securities included in A and B are regularly traded and that their market values (prices) are widely reported and easily determined. Combination B can be thought to have two components: security X and the rest, which will be represented by C, as in Figure 5.1(b). Combination C might include many securities, only one, or, as a very special case, none at all.

If people are willing to purchase combination A for a present value of PV_A, they should be willing to purchase combination B for the same amount, since the two provide comparable prospects. Thus,

$$PV_A = PV_B.$$

The present value of B will, however, be simply the sum of the present values of its components:

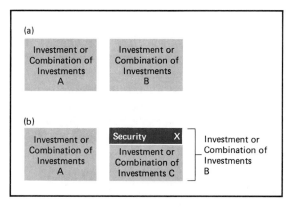

FIGURE 5–1
Comparing combinations of investments.

(a)

Investment or Combination of Investments A

Investment or Combination of Investments B

(b)

Investment or Combination of Investments A

Security X
Investment or Combination of Investments C

Investment or Combination of Investments B

$$PV_B = PV_X + PV_C.$$

This implies that the present value of security X can be determined solely by reference to market values placed on the securities comprising combinations A and C. Since

$$PV_A = PV_X - PV_C$$

then

$$PV_X = PV_A + PV_C.$$

5.2 APPROACHES TO SECURITY VALUATION

It is reasonable enough to say that market prices of "comparable investments" should be used to determine the value of a security. But when are two investments truly comparable?

An obvious case arises when investments provide identical payments in every possible contingency. If an investment's outcome is affected by relatively few events, it may be possible to purchase a set of other investments, each of which pays off in only one of the relevant contingencies. A properly selected mix of such investments may thus be completely comparable to the one to be valued. The next section illustrates this approach with an example drawn from the field of insurance.

A much more common approach to valuation is less detailed but more useful. Two alternatives are considered comparable if they offer similar expected returns and contribute equally to portfolio risk. Central to this view is the need to assess the probabilities of various contingencies. The remainder of this chapter and the next four chapters are devoted to this more widely used *risk-return approach*.

5.3 EXPLICIT VALUATION OF CONTINGENT PAYMENTS

☐ ### 5.3.1 Insurance

Insurance policies are highly explicit examples of contingent payments. One can buy a $100,000 one-year "term" life insurance policy on a reasonably healthy 60-year-old for about $2300. This, of course, can be viewed as an investment (albeit a morbid one): The sum of $100,000 will be paid by the insurance company if the insured dies within a year; otherwise nothing at all will be paid. Involved is the sacrifice of a present certain value ($2300) for a future uncertain value. The only relevant event is the possible death of the insured, and the relationship between that event and the amount to be paid is crystal clear.

Now imagine that a reasonably healthy 60-year-old executive asks you for a one-year loan. The executive would like as much as possible now; in

return he or she promises to pay you $100,000 at the end of the year. Your problem is to determine the present value of that promise—that is, how much to advance now. Put somewhat differently, you must determine an appropriate interest rate for the loan.

To keep the example simple, assume that the only source of uncertainty is the borrower's ability to remain in this position and thus earn the requisite money, and that this depends only on his or her continued presence among the living. In other words, if the borrower lives, the $100,000 will be repaid in full and on time; otherwise, you will receive nothing.

The piece of paper representing the executive's promise to pay $100,000 is your security X. What is it worth? The answer clearly depends in an important way on the available alternatives. And a crucial factor is the current rate of interest.

Assume that the going rate for riskless one-year loans is 8%. If there were no doubt whatever that the executive would repay the loan, it would be reasonable to advance $92,592.59 (since $100,000/$92,592.59 = 1.08). However, the uncertainty connected with the loan makes this inadvisable. The appropriate amount is obviously less. But how much less?

In this case an answer can easily be determined. It would be entirely reasonable to advance at least $90,292.59, making the *promised* interest rate on the loan approximately 10.75% (since 100,000/90,292.59 = 1.1075). The basis for this calculation is quite simple. It relies on the fact that an investor can insure against the relevant risk, obtaining an overall position that is completely riskless.

Table 5.1 provides the details. The relevant event is whether or not the executive survives the year. The loan is thus a risky investment, paying $100,000 only if the executive lives. The life insurance policy is also a risky investment, paying $100,000 only if the executive dies. But a *portfolio* that includes both investments is totally riskless: Its owner will receive $100,000, no matter what happens! By paying $90,292.59 for the loan and $2,300 for the insurance policy, an investor could give up $92,592.59 now for a certain payment of $100,000 a year hence—obtaining a riskless return of 8%, which is the going rate on other riskless ventures.

This is, of course, an application of the general procedure described in the previous section. Figure 5.2 summarizes the details in the format used earlier, for purposes of comparison.

TABLE 5.1
Costs and Payments for a Loan and an Insurance Policy.

ITEM	EVENT		
	Executive Dies	Executive Lives	Cost
Loan	0	$100,000	$90,292.59
Insurance policy	$100,000	0	2,300.00
Total	$100,000	$100,000	$92,592.59

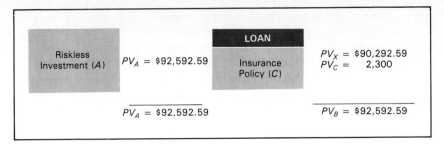

FIGURE 5–2
Comparing two riskless investments.

☐ 5.3.2 Valuation in a Complete Market

Assume, for the present, that market values can be used to estimate the present value of any contingent payment. A market in which such detailed quotations are available is termed *complete*. While no real market conforms to this specification, it is useful to see how valuation would be done in such circumstances.

First, a way to represent the present value of a guaranteed commitment to pay $1 at a specified time if (and only if) a specified event or "state of the world" occurs is needed. The following will suffice:

$$PV(\$1, t, e)$$

where

t = the time at which the dollar is to be paid

e = the event that must occur if the dollar is to be paid.

Armed with this notation, any risky investment can now be analyzed. Every possible contingency could, in theory, be considered separately, giving a (probably very lengthy) list of contingent payments of the following form:

TIME OF PAYMENT	EVENT ON WHICH PAYMENT IS CONTINGENT	AMOUNT OF PAYMENT
t_1	e_1	D_1
t_2	e_2	D_2
.	.	.
.	.	.
.	.	.

Of course, some of the events might be the same, as might some of the times and amounts.

To find the present value of the investment, the present value of each of its contingent payments must be found and then added.

(1) TIME OF PAYMENT	(2) EVENT ON WHICH PAYMENT IS CONTINGENT	(3) AMOUNT OF PAYMENT	(4) DISCOUNT FACTOR	(5) = (3) × (4) PRESENT VALUE
t_1	e_1	D_1	$PV(\$1, t_1, e_1)$	$D_1 \times PV(\$1, t_1, e_1)$
t_2	e_2	D_2	$PV(\$1, t_2, e_2)$	$D_2 \times PV(\$1, t_2, e_2)$
.	.	.	.	.
.	.	.	.	.
.	.	.	.	.

Total value = _____

This method of valuation is commonly termed the *state-preference* approach, since it begins with the assumption that people's preferences are for *state-contingent claims* and concludes that securities will be valued on the basis of their payoffs in different "states of the world."

☐ 5.3.3   The Limitations of Insurance

Some believe that Lloyd's of London will insure almost anything. Perhaps so. This could ease the security analyst's task considerably. He or she would only (!) have to determine the payments $(D_1, D_2, \ldots)$ associated with an investment, the times at which they could be made $(t_1, t_2, \ldots)$, and the events on which they were contingent $(e_1, e_2, \ldots)$. The analyst could then use the premiums specified for the relevant insurance policies as estimates of appropriate discount factors $[PV(\$1, t_1, e_1), (PV(\$1, t_2, e_2), \ldots]$, and perform the required calculations.

But even if Lloyd's will insure anything, the premiums charged for many policies might attract no takers. There are a number of interrelated reasons for this. As a case in point, imagine an aerospace company, the future profits of which depend heavily on whether or not the firm will be awarded a major government contract. Why not buy an appropriate insurance policy from Lloyd's, guaranteed to pay off if the firm loses the contract? Then only Lloyd's and the other firms in the industry would care about the outcome.

The idea is obviously whimsical. If Lloyd's were even willing to issue such a policy, the cost would be more than anyone would be likely to pay. But why?

First, because of differences in *information*. Those familiar with the company or the government or both have better information about the likely outcome and can better assess the likelihood of various alternatives. Lloyd's operates at least partly in the dark. To protect itself, it will charge more than otherwise.

Second, there is the likelihood of *adverse selection*. If a policy of this sort is offered at a price low enough to attract anyone at all, the insurer can expect the firms that are least likely to win the contract to buy insurance,

whereas those most likely to get the contract take their chances. This occurs frequently with life insurance. The less healthy an individual, the more likely he or she is to buy a policy; for this reason, the insured is usually required to pass a medical examination as a condition of sale. An examination of the health of a company's bid to win a government award might be much more difficult or expensive, so an insurance company must set its fees for such a policy on the assumption that it would end up insuring the riskiest client or clients.

Another factor is the thoroughly modern phenomenon described by the term *moral hazard*. The purchase of insurance may affect the likelihood of the event in question. If the manager of a firm is insured against the loss of the contract, he or she may well put less effort into the attempt to win it, increasing the likelihood of its loss and the insurance company's obligation to pay off. This explains the reluctance of an insurance company to insure a house or car for more than its replacement value and the desire of many stockholders to have a corporation's officers own some of the firm's stock and none of its competitors' issues. Here again, the insurance company will account for this effect when setting prices.

Finally, there is the simple matter of *overhead*. Insurance people like to eat, as do investors who provide the capital that insurance companies need. The costs of doing business will, over the long pull, be reflected in the prices charged for that business. No financial service is free, and insurance is no exception.

For all these reasons securities markets do not conform to the specifications of the complete-market state-preference model. Although the approach is helpful for addressing certain theoretical issues, it is less useful for investment purposes than the risk-return (or "mean-variance") approach, to which the discussion now turns.

5.4 PROBABILISTIC FORECASTING

☐ 5.4.1 Assessing Probabilities

Lacking a plethora of widely available and low-cost insurance policies, it is not possible to value an investment without explicitly considering the likelihood of various outcomes. Instead, the analyst must attempt to assess directly the likelihood of each major event that can affect an investment. In short, he or she must engage in *probabilistic forecasting*.

The idea is simple enough, although its implementation is exceedingly difficult. The analyst expresses his or her assessment of the likelihood of every relevant event as a *probability*. If he or she feels that the chances of an event's taking place are 50-50, a probability of .50 is attached to the event. If the chances seem to be 3 out of 4, the probability is $3/4$, or .75 (another way of expressing this is to say that the *odds* are 3 to 1 that the event will take place). If the analyst considers an event to be absolutely *certain*, a probability of 1.0 should be assigned. If he or she feels an event is completely impossible, its probability of occurrence is zero.

It is important, of course, to be consistent in one's estimates. For example, if the events on a list are *mutually exclusive* and *exhaustive* (that is, one of them, but only one, will take place), the probabilities should sum to one.

Probability is, at base, a *subjective* concept. Even simple cases fall under this heading. For example, a gambler may assess the probability of a coin's coming up heads at .5, based on knowledge of coins and observations of the coin in question over the past. But the estimate is still subjective, involving the implicit assumption that the coin really is "fair" and that the past is an appropriate guide to the future. Similar cases arise frequently in security analysis. Relative *frequencies* of various returns in the past are sometimes used as estimates of the *probabilities* of such returns in the future. Clearly this procedure relies on assumptions that require subjective judgment and may in some circumstances be totally inappropriate. Forecasts based on the extrapolation of past relationships are neither wholly objective nor necessarily to be preferred over predictions obtained in more subtle ways.

Probabilistic forecasting entails a decision to confront uncertainty head on, acknowledge its existence, and try to measure its extent. Instead of attempting to answer a question such as "What will General Motors earn next year?" the analyst explicitly considers some of the more likely alternatives and the likelihood of each one. This brings the analysis out in the open, allowing both the estimator and the user or users of such estimates to assess the reasonableness of the values. Insistence on a single number for each estimate, with no measure of associated uncertainty, would suggest naiveté or insecurity on the part of the producer or the consumer of such predictions.

In some organizations analysts engage in explicit probabilistic forecasting, passing on all their detailed assessments to others charged with bringing together the estimates made within the group. In other organizations the analysts make explicit probabilistic forecasts but summarize their evaluations in a relatively few key estimates, sending only the latter to others. In still other organizations analysts do not engage in explicit probabilistic forecasting; instead, they produce estimates that summarize their implicit beliefs about the probabilities of various events. As always, it is not the form but the substance that matters.

☐ 5.4.2 Probability Distributions

It is often convenient to portray probabilistic forecasts graphically. The possible outcomes are represented on the horizontal axis and the associated probabilities on the vertical axis. Figure 5.3 provides an example.

In this case the outcomes are qualitatively different in nature and can be listed only on the horizontal axis; the ordering and spacing are arbitrary.

Figure 5.4 shows a somewhat different case. Here the alternative outcomes differ quantitatively and with regard to only one variable: earnings per share next year. In this instance the analyst has chosen to group together

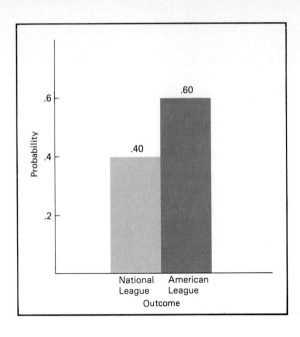

FIGURE 5–3
Probabilities of a National or American League team winning the world series.

all possibilities from $.90 to $.99, assess the probability that the actual amount will fall within that range, and then repeat the process for the range from $1.00 to $1.09, the range from $1.10 to $1.19, and so on.

The analysis could, of course, have been conducted at a more detailed level, with probabilities estimated for outcomes in the ranges from $.90 to $.94, $.95 to $.99, and so on. An even more detailed analysis would assign

FIGURE 5–4
Probabilities of next year's earnings per share (using wide ranges).

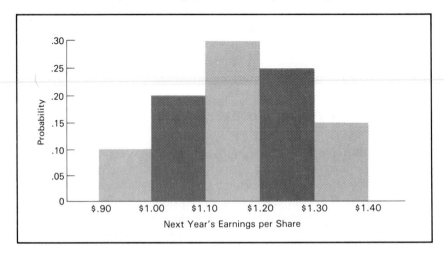

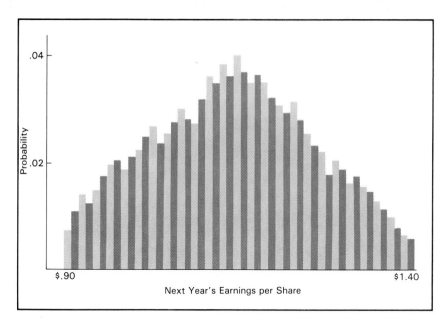

FIGURE 5–5
Probabilities of next year's earnings per share (using narrow ranges).

a probability to every possible outcome. In this case the bars would be numerous, and each would be very thin, as shown in Figure 5.5. Note that the more numerous the number of bars, the smaller the sizes of associated probabilities.

The ultimate in a detailed prediction is represented by a *continuous probability distribution*. Such a curve represents, in effect, the tops of many thin bars. (Technically, the curve represents what happens when there is an infinite number of such bars.) Three examples of curves of this type are shown in Figure 5.6; note that the vertical axis now measures probability density (instead of probability).

If continuous probability distributions are to be used, the analyst can forgo explicitly assessing particular individual outcomes. Instead, the analyst must draw a curve that seems to represent the situation as he or she sees it. The relative likelihood of any single outcome (such as earnings per share of $1.035) is zero. However, the relative likelihood of any range of earnings is found by simply finding the size of the area under the curve but above the horizontal axis. Thus, the likelihood of earnings being between $1.03 and $1.04 could be found by measuring the area under the curve between $1.03 and $1.04, which in this case is approximately .07 (that is, there is a chance of 7 out of 100 that earnings will be between $1.03 and $1.04 next year). With a discrete probability distribution such as those shown in Figures 5.4 and 5.5, it was noted that the sum of the probabilities had to be 1. Now,

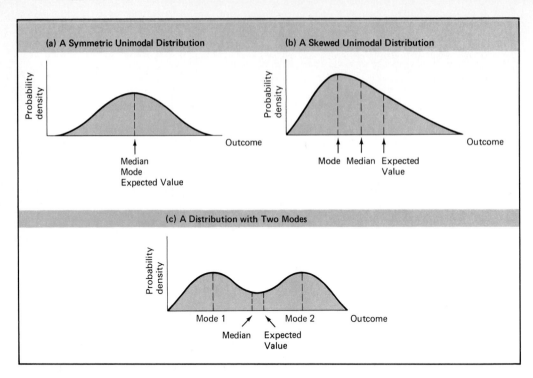

FIGURE 5–6
Continuous probability distributions.

with a continuous probability distribution, the total area under the curve must sum to 1.

☐ 5.4.3 Event Trees

When events follow one another over time or are in any sense dependent on one another, it is often useful to describe the alternative sequences with a tree diagram. Figure 5.7 provides an example.

A borrower has promised to pay $15 one year hence and $8 two years hence, if possible. The analyst feels the odds are only 40-60 that the first payment will in fact be made in full. Otherwise, the analyst feels the borrower will be able to pay only $10 one year hence.

As far as the second year is concerned, the likely situation depends, in this analyst's judgment, on the outcome in the first year. If the borrower manages to pay the full $15 in the first year, the analyst feels the odds are only 1 to 9 that the borrower will be able to meet the $8 commitment at the end of two years. Otherwise, the borrower will pay less: $6. On the other hand, if the borrower pays out $10 in the first year, although there appears to be no chance of recovering the $5 shortfall, the analyst feels the odds are

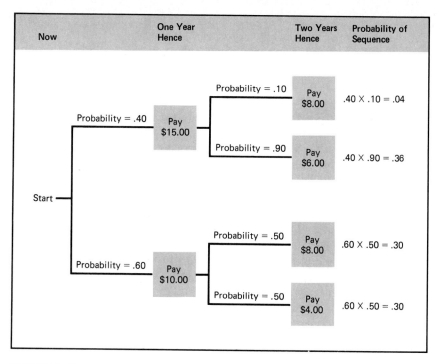

Now	One Year Hence	Two Years Hence	Probability of Sequence
		Probability = .10 Pay $8.00	.40 × .10 = .04
	Probability = .40 Pay $15.00		
		Probability = .90 Pay $6.00	.40 × .90 = .36
Start			
		Probability = .50 Pay $8.00	.60 × .50 = .30
	Probability = .60 Pay $10.00		
		Probability = .50 Pay $4.00	.60 × .50 = .30

FIGURE 5–7
An event tree.

about even that the promised $8 will be paid in the second year. If this does not happen, the analyst feels that $4 will be paid instead.

Figure 5.7 also shows the probability of each of the four possible sequences, or paths, through the tree. For example, the probability that both payments will be made in full is only .04, since there are only 40 chances out of 100 that the first payment will be made, and of those, only 1 out of 10 is expected to be followed by payment in full of the final obligation. This gives 4 out of 100 chances for the sequence: a probability of .04.

☐ 5.4.4   Expected Value

Often an analyst is uncertain about an outcome but wishes (or is required) to summarize the situation with one or two numbers—one indicating the *central tendency* of the distribution of outcomes and one measuring *relevant risk*. Both return and risk are discussed in subsequent chapters; the remainder of this chapter concentrates on the former.

How might a single number intended to summarize a set of possible outcomes be obtained? Obviously no satisfactory way can be found if the alternative outcomes differ qualitatively (for example, the National League versus the American League in winning the World Series). But if the outcomes

differ quantitatively, and especially if they differ in only one dimension, a number of possibilities present themselves.

Perhaps the most common procedure is to adopt the *most likely* value. This is known as the *mode* of the probability distribution (for a continuous probability distribution, the mode is the outcome with the highest probability density). Figure 5.6 shows the mode of each of the distributions. Note that in Figure 5.6(c) there are two modes: In this case, no single number can be used to answer the question in this manner.

Another alternative is to provide a "50-50" number—a value that is as likely to be too low as to be too high. This is called the *median* of the probability distribution. As shown in Figure 5.6, it may differ significantly from the mode(s).

A third alternative is to use an *expected value* (also known as the mean value), a weighted average of all the possible outcomes, using the associated probabilities as weights. It takes into account all the information expressed in the distribution, both the *magnitude* and the *probability* of occurrence of each possible outcome. Almost any change in an investment's prospects or probabilities will affect the expected value of its outcomes (as it should).

In many instances there are no differences among these three measures. If the distribution is symmetric (each half is a mirror image of the other) and unimodal (there is one most likely value), then the median, mode, and expected value coincide, as in the case shown in Figure 5.6(a). Thus an analyst may choose to think in terms of, say, a 50-50 (median) value, even though the number wanted is the expected value. Only if the underlying probability distribution is highly skewed might this procedure lead to difficulties.

In those cases in which the values do differ, there are good reasons to prefer the expected value. As stated earlier, it takes all the estimates into account. But it has another advantage. Estimates about the prospects for securities serve as inputs for the process of portfolio construction or revision. The expected value of the return for a portfolio is related in a straightforward way to the expected values of the returns for its securities, but neither the median nor the mode for a portfolio can, in general, be determined from comparable values for its securities.

Table 5.2 provides an example of the computation of expected values. An analyst is trying to predict the impact on the prices of two securities of a surprise television address scheduled by the president . The analyst has delineated a number of possible announcements, ranging from changes in the situation in the Mideast through a decision concerning the federal deficit. The alternatives represented in the table have been defined to be mutually exclusive and exhaustive (that is, every possible combination is shown in a different row). After much thought and with some trepidation, the analyst has also estimated the probability of each announcement and the resultant effect on the prices of the two securities. Finally, the analyst has computed the associated values of a portfolio containing one share of each stock.

The expected values are shown at the bottom of the table. Each is obtained by multiplying the probability of every announcement by the associated price, then summing. For example, the expected price of security A is determined by computing $[(.10 \times \$40.00) + (.20 \times \$42.00) + \cdots]$;

TABLE 5.2

Analysis of Effects of Announcements on Two Securities and
a Portfolio of Both Securities.

ANNOUNCEMENT	PROBABILITY	PREDICTED PRICE OF SECURITY A	PREDICTED PRICE OF SECURITY B	PREDICTED VALUE OF A PORTFOLIO OF A AND B
a	.10	$40.00	$62.00	$102.00
b	.20	42.00	65.00	107.00
c	.10	40.50	60.00	100.50
d	.25	41.00	61.00	102.00
e	.15	38.00	65.00	103.00
f	.10	40.50	59.00	99.50
g	.05	45.00	58.00	103.00
h	.05	40.50	58.00	98.50
	Expected Values:	$40.73	$61.90	$102.63

that of security B by computing [(.10 × $62.00) + (.20 × $65.00) + · · ·];
and that of the portfolio by computing [(.10 × $102.00) + (.20 × $107.00)
+ · · ·]. Not surprisingly, the expected value of the portfolio equals the sum
of the expected values of its component securities. When the expected values
for the securities are added together, one is, in effect, adding (.10 × $40.00
+ · · ·) to (.10 × $62.00 + · · ·). Clearly this will give the expected value
of the portfolio, which is .10 × ($40.00 + $62.00) + · · ·.

☐ **5.4.5 Expected Versus Promised Yield-to-Maturity**

If payments from a bond are certain, there is no difference between the
expected yield-to-maturity and the promised amount. However, many bonds
fail to meet these standards. Two types of risk may be involved. First, the
issuer may defer some payments. A dollar received farther in the future is,
of course, worth less in present value than a dollar received on schedule;
thus the present value of a bond will be smaller, the greater the likelihood
that this might happen. The second type of risk is potentially more serious.
The borrower may default, in whole or in part, on some of the interest
payments or on the principal at maturity. A firm becomes bankrupt when
it is clearly unable to meet such obligations; the courts then divide the
remaining assets among the various creditors in accordance with provisions
agreed upon when the debts were issued.

To estimate the expected yield-to-maturity for a risky debt instrument,
in principle all possible outcomes and the probability of each one should be
considered. The simple example shown in Figure 5.7 can be used to illustrate
the procedure. Assume the security in question costs $15; that is, the borrower
wants $15 now in return for a commitment to pay $15 one year hence and
$8 two years hence. The promised yield-to-maturity is the interest rate that
makes the present value of these payments equal $15. In this case it is
38.51% per year, a substantial figure indeed.

TABLE 5.3

Promised Versus Expected Yield-to-Maturity.

PAYMENT ONE YEAR HENCE	PAYMENT TWO YEARS HENCE	PROBABILITY	YIELD-TO-MATURITY
$15	$8	.04	38.51%
15	6	.36	30.62
10	8	.30	13.61
10	4	.30	−5.20
		Expected yield-to-maturity =	15.09%

But the analyst feels that the probability of actually receiving this yield-to-maturity is only .04. Table 5.3 shows the possible sequences (paths in the event tree), as well as the probability and the yield-to-maturity for each one. The expected yield-to-maturity is simply the weighted average of these values, using the probabilities as weights (for example, $(.04 \times 38.51\%) + (.36 \times 30.62\%) + (.30 \times 13.61\%) + (.30 \times -5.20\%) = 15.09\%$).

The expected yield-to-maturity is considerably less than the promised amount: 15.09% as opposed to 38.51%. And the former is clearly the more relevant figure for investment analysis.

This is an important point. The yield-to-maturity, as normally calculated, is based on promised payments, made at the promised times. If there is any risk that the borrower's commitments will not be paid fully and on time, the expected yield-to-maturity is less than this figure; and the greater the risk, the greater the disparity. This is illustrated in Table 5.4, which shows the (promised) yield-to-maturity values for four groups of bonds classified by Standard & Poor's, a major rating service, as having different degrees of risk. Although the *levels* of all four yields reflect general interest rates at the time, the *differences* among them are primarily due to differences in risk. If promised yields of all bonds were the same, the expected yields of high-risk bonds would be less than those of low-risk ones—an unlikely situation indeed. Instead, riskier bonds promise higher yields so that their expected yields can be at least as large as those of less risky ones.

TABLE 5.4

Standard & Poor's Composite Bond Yields.

RATING	YIELD-TO-MATURITY
AAA	9.67%
AA	9.94
A	10.28
BBB	10.65

SOURCE: Standard & Poor's *Bond Guide*, July 1988, p. 3.

The nature of most debt obligations would be more obvious if contracts were written somewhat differently. At present, a standard bond with no extra features "guarantees" that the borrower will pay the lender, say, $90 per year for 20 years, then $1000 twenty years hence. A more appropriate statement would indicate that the borrower gurantees to pay *no more than* $90 per year for 20 years, and $1000 twenty years hence.

5.5 EXPECTED HOLDING-PERIOD RETURN

☐ 5.5.1 Calculating Holding-Period Return

Yield-to-maturity calculations do not take into account any changes in the market value of a security prior to maturity. This might be interpreted as implying that the owner has no interest in selling the instrument prior to maturity, no matter what happens to its price or his or her situation. The calculation also fails to treat intermediate payments in a fully satisfactory way. If the owner does not wish to spend interest payments, he or she might choose to buy more of these securities. But the number that can be bought at any time depends on the price at that time, and yield-to-maturity calculations fail to take this into account.

While few dispute the value of yield-to-maturity as at least an indicator of bond's overall return, it should be recognized as no more than this. For some purposes other measures may prove more useful. Moreover, for other types of securities there is no maturity: Common stocks provide the most important example.

A measure that can be used for any investment is *holding-period return*. The idea is to specify a holding period of major interest, and then assume that any payments received during the period are reinvested. Although assumptions may differ from case to case, the usual procedure assumes that any payment received from a security (for example, a dividend from a stock, a coupon payment from a bond) is used to purchase more units of that security at the then current market price. Using this procedure, the performance of a security can be measured by comparing the value obtained in this manner at the end of the holding period with the value at the beginning. This *value-relative* can be converted to a holding-period return by subtracting 1 from it:

$$r_{hp} = \frac{\text{value at the end of the holding period}}{\text{value at the beginning of the holding period}} - 1.$$

Put another way: the *holding-period return is the holding-period value-relative minus 1*.

Holding-period return can be converted to an equivalent return per period. Allowing for the effect of compounding, the appropriate procedure would be to find the value that satisfies the relationship

$$(1 + r_g)^N = 1 + r_{hp}$$

or

$$r_g = (\sqrt[N]{1 + r_{hp}}) - 1$$

where:

N = the number of periods in the holding period,

r_{hp} = the holding-period return,

r_g = the equivalent return per period, compounded every period.

Suppose that a stock sold for $46 per share at the beginning of one year, paid dividends of $1.50 during that year, sold for $50 at the end of the year, paid dividends of $2 during the next year, and sold for $56 at the end of that year. What was the return over the two-year holding period?

To simplify the calculations, assume that all dividend payments are received at year-end. Then the $1.50 received during the first year could have bought $1.50/$50, or .03, shares of the stock at the end of the first year. In practice, of course, this would be feasible only if the money were pooled with other funds similarly invested—for example, in a mutual fund or simply in an investor's own portfolio (for example, the dividends from 100 shares could have been used to buy three additional shares). In any event, for each share originally held, the investor would have obtained $1.03 \times \$2$, or $2.06, in dividends in the second year, and have had stock with value of $1.03 \times \$56$, or $57.68 at the end of the second year. The ending value would thus have been $57.68 + $2.06, giving a value-relative of:

$$\frac{\$59.74}{\$46.00} = 1.2987.$$

The holding-period return was thus 29.87% per two years. This is equivalent to $\sqrt{1.2987} - 1 = .1396$, or 13.96% per year.

An alternative method of computation treats the overall value-relative as the product of value-relatives for the individual periods. For example, if V_0 is the value at the beginning, V_1 the value at the end of the first year, and V_2 the value at the end of the second year:

$$\frac{V_2}{V_0} = \frac{V_2}{V_1} \times \frac{V_1}{V_0}.$$

Moreover, there is no need to carry the expansion in number of shares from period to period, since the factor (1.03 in the example) will simply cancel out in the subsequent periods' value-relatives. Each period can be analyzed in isolation, an appropriate value-relative calculated, and the set of such value-relatives multiplied together.

In our example, during the first year, ownership of a stock with an initial value of $46 led to stock and cash with a value of $50 + $1.50 at the end of the year. Thus,

$$\frac{V_1}{V_0} = \frac{\$51.50}{\$46.00} = 1.1196.$$

During the second year, ownership of stock with an initial value of $50 led to stock and cash with a value of $56 + $2 at year-end. Thus:

$$\frac{V_2}{V_1} = \frac{\$58}{\$50} = 1.16.$$

The two-year holding-period value-relative was therefore:

$$1.1196 \times 1.16 = 1.2987$$

which is exactly equal to the value obtained earlier.

The value-relative for each period can be viewed as 1 plus the return for that period. Thus the return on the stock being analyzed was 11.96% in the first year and 16% in the second. The holding-period value-relative is the product of 1 plus each return. If N periods are involved,

$$\frac{V_N}{V_0} = (1 + r_1)(1 + r_2) \cdots (1 + r_N).$$

To convert the result to a holding-period return stated as an amount per period, with compounding, one can take the *geometric mean* of the periodic returns:

$$1 + r_g = \sqrt[N]{(1 + r_1)(1 + r_2) \cdots (1 + r_N)}.$$

More sophisticated calculations may be employed within this overall framework. Each dividend payment can be used to purchase shares immediately upon receipt, or, alternatively, allowed to earn interest in a savings account until year-end. Brokerage and other costs associated with reinvestment of dividends can also be taken into account, although the magnitude of such costs will undoubtedly depend on the overall size of the holdings in question. The appropriate degree of complexity will, as always, be a function of the use for which the values are obtained.

Unhappily, the most appropriate holding period is often at least as uncertain as the return over any given holding period. Neither an investor's situation nor his or her preferences can usually be predicted with certainty. Moreover, from a strategic view, an investment manager would like to hold a given security only as long as it outperforms available alternatives. Attempts to identify such periods in advance are seldom completely successful, but managers quite naturally continue to try to discover them.

Holding-period return, like yield-to-maturity, provides a useful device for simplifying the complex reality of investment analysis. While no panacea, it allows an analyst to focus on the most relevant horizon in a given instance and offers a good measure of performance over such a period.

☐ 5.5.2 Estimating Expected Holding-Period Return

It is a relatively straightforward matter to calculate holding-period return after the fact. It is quite another thing to estimate it in advance. Any uncertainty surrounding payments by the issuer of a security during the period must be taken into account, but this is usually much simpler than the task of estimating the end-of-period market values, which often constitute a large

portion of overall return. For example, it might seem a simple matter to estimate the return over the next year for a share of Xerox stock. Dividends to be paid are relatively easy to predict. But the price at year-end will depend on investors' attitudes toward the company and its stock at that time. To predict even a one-year holding-period return one must consider a much longer period and assess not only the company's future but also investors' future attitudes about that future—a formidable task indeed.

Quite clearly, estimation of holding-period return must account in some way for uncertainty. If a single estimate is required, it should conform to the principles stated earlier. Explicitly or implicitly, an *expected value* should be provided. The various possibilities should be considered along with their probabilities.

> Expected holding-period return is a weighted average of possible holding-period returns, using probabilities as weights.[1]

☐ 5.5.3 Estimating a Bond's Expected Holding-Period Return

Once the importance of market values is recognized, the presence of a new kind of risk becomes obvious. And the idea of a truly riskless investment becomes a relative matter.

Assume that an investor is interested in a holding period of five years. What sort of investment would be riskless for these purposes? Obviously, one with no default risk, which promises a payment at the end of five years and at no other time. Any other investment will involve some risk. The five-year holding-period return from a bond that provides semiannual coupon payments will depend on the prices at which such payments can be used to purchase additional units of the bond (or some other instrument). The return on a bond with a maturity in excess of five years will depend on the price at which it can be sold at the end of the fifth year. The return on a shorter-maturity bond will depend on the instruments that are available when the proceeds must be reinvested, and their prices at those times.

Since bond prices depend in large part on interest rates, this source of uncertainty is sometimes termed *interest-rate risk* (or price risk). In many cases it is far more important than default risk. Moreover, it makes even U.S. government debt risky, unless there is a perfect correspondence between the investor's desire for cash and the payments promised by the bond in question.

Interest-rate risk should be incorporated in any analysis of expected holding-period return. For U.S. government securities this requires estimates of possible future interest rates and their associated probabilities. For other securities the likely future differentials for various levels of risk must also be taken into account.

---

[1] Expected return is also the *mean* of the probability distribution of holding-period returns—hence the "mean" in the term *mean-variance approach*, which is the cornerstone of modern portfolio theory.

5.6 EXPECTED RETURN AND SECURITY VALUATION

There is a very simple relationship between expected holding-period return, expected end-of-period value, and current value:

$$\text{Expected holding-period return} = \frac{\text{expected end-of-period value}}{\text{current value}} - 1.$$

Thus,

$$\text{Current value} = \frac{\text{expected end-of-period value}}{1 + \text{expected holding-period return}}.$$

In words: To value a security, one needs to estimate the expected value at the end of a holding period and the expected return for the holding period that is appropriate for such a security.

The final phase is crucial. What is the "appropriate" expected return, and on what does it depend? Therein lies the remainder of the theory of valuation.

5.7 SUMMARY

This chapter has discussed methods of valuing securities whose payments to investors are, to varying degrees, uncertain. One method involves valuing investments that provide identical payments in every possible contingency. However, the risk-return approach is more common and useful. With this approach, two securities are viewed as being comparable if they have similar expected returns and contribute similar amounts of risk to a portfolio.

With the risk-return approach, it might seem appropriate to value a security by using the expected return on an investment that is riskless over the period in question. However desirable such a relatively simple procedure might seem, it is clearly inconsistent with the general behavior of investors.

By and large, investors are risk-averse. Other things equal, they prefer less risk to more. However, other things equal, they also prefer more expected return to less. Not surprisingly, this implies that in the process of valuation one should require a higher expected return on a security, the greater the relevant risk involved.

Risk is not a simple concept: It thus requires extended discussion. The next four chapters provide such discussions.

QUESTIONS AND PROBLEMS

1. In March of 1987, a major bookmaker in Las Vegas accepted bets on the baseball teams that would eventually go to the World Series. For example, one could pay $10 at the time to bet that the Minnesota Twins would represent the American League in the World Series. The payoff on such a bet was set at $1,500 if the Twins did go

to the World Series, and zero otherwise. Payoffs for bets on all teams in the American League West were:

Team	Payoff per $1 Bet
California Angels	$ 90
Chicago White Sox	180
Kansas City Royals	60
Minnesota Twins	150
Oakland Athletics	130
Seattle Mariners	250
Texas Rangers	210

   a. What was the present value of $1 contingent on the event (state of the world) "The Twins go to the World Series"?

   b. What was the present value of $1 contingent on the event "The Mariners go to the World Series"?

   c. Why did the answers for (a) and (b) differ?

   d. If someone had offered to pay you $1 if any team in the American League West went to the World Series, how much would you have paid for this bet ("security")? If you had been virtually certain that one of these teams would go to the World Series, would your answer differ? Why?

2. The probability distribution in Figure 5.6(b) is "skewed to the right." Explain why the distribution's expected value is greater than the median, which in turn is greater than the mode.

3. Calculate the expected return, mode, and median for a stock having the following probability distribution:

Return	Probability of Occurrence
−40%	.03
−10	.07
0	.30
15	.10
30	.05
40	.20
50	.25

4. Consider Springfield Company, whose stock currently sells for $10 per share. Dode Paskert, a financial analyst, has estimated the stock's potential year-end prices and associated probabilities over the next two years:

Year 1   The stock has a 30% chance of rising to $20. It has a 60% chance of rising to $12. It has a 10% chance of falling to $8.

Year 2   If the stock rises to $20 in Year 1, it has a 50% chance of rising to $25 and a 50% chance of falling to $15. If the stock rises to $12 in Year 1, it has a 70% chance of rising to $15 and a 30% chance of falling to $10. If it falls to $8 in Year 1, it has a 40% chance of falling to $4 and a 60% chance of rising to $12.

   a. Draw an event tree for Springfield Company stock.

   b. Based on this event tree, calculate the stock's expected price at the end of year 2.

5. Pol Perritt purchased 100 shares of Montgomery Inc. and held the stock for four years. Pol's holding-period returns over these four years were:

Year	Return
1	+20%
2	+30
3	+50
4	−90

   a. What was the value-relative of Pol's investment over the four-year period?

   b. What was Pol's geometric mean return for the four-year period?

6. Distinguish between expected holding-period return and yield-to-maturity.

7. What are the advantages and disadvantages of using past investment results to assess the probabilities of future investment outcomes?

8. The average annualized return on the S&P 500 index of common stocks from 1926 through 1986 was 12.12%. If, on January 1, 1987 you had been required to provide an estimate of the expected return on the S&P 500 over the coming year, would you have chosen 12.12%? Why or why not?

Chapter 6

THE PORTFOLIO SELECTION PROBLEM

In 1952 Harry M. Markowitz published a landmark paper that is generally viewed as the origin of the "modern portfolio theory" approach to investing.[1] Markowitz's approach to investing begins by assuming that an investor has a given sum of money to invest at the present time. This money will be invested for a particular length of time, known as the investor's *holding period*. At the end of the holding period, the investor will sell the securities that were purchased at the beginning of the period and then either spend the proceeds on consumption or reinvest the proceeds in various securities (or do some of both). Thus, Markowitz's approach can be viewed as a single-period approach, where the beginning of the period is denoted by $t = 0$ and the end of the period is denoted by $t = 1$. At $t = 0$, the investor must make a decision on what particular securities to purchase and hold until $t = 1$.[2] Since a portfolio is a collection of securities, this decision is equivalent to selecting an optimal portfolio from a set of possible portfolios and is thus often referred to as the "portfolio selection problem."

In making this decision at $t = 0$, the investor should recognize that security returns (and thus portfolio returns) over the forthcoming holding period are unknown. Nevertheless, the investor could estimate the *expected returns* (or mean returns) on the various securities under consideration and then invest in the one with the highest expected return. (Methods for estimating expected returns are discussed in Chapter 16.) Markowitz notes that this would generally be an unwise decision because the typical investor, while wanting returns to be high, also wants returns to be as certain as possible. This means that the investor, in seeking both to maximize expected return and minimize uncertainty (that is, *risk*), has two conflicting objectives

---

[1] Harry M. Markowitz, "Portfolio Selection," *Journal of Finance* 7, no. 1 (March 1952):77–91. See also his book entitled *Portfolio Selection*, (New Haven, Conn.: Yale University Press, 1959).

[2] Markowitz recognized in Chapter 13 of *Portfolio Selection* that investing was generally a multiperiod activity, where at the end of each period, part of the investor's wealth was consumed and part was reinvested. Nevertheless, his one-period approach can be shown to be optimal under a variety of reasonable circumstances. See Edwin J. Elton and Martin J. Gruber, *Finance as a Dynamic Process*, (Englewood Cliffs, N.J.: Prentice Hall, 1975), particularly Chapter 5.

that must be balanced against each other when making the purchase decision at $t = 0$. The Markowitz approach for how the investor should go about making this decision gives full consideration to both these objectives.

One interesting consequence of having these two conflicting objectives is that the investor should diversify by purchasing not just one security but several. The ensuing discussion of Markowitz's approach to investing begins by defining more specifically what is meant by initial and terminal wealth.

6.1 INITIAL AND TERMINAL WEALTH

In equation (1.1) of Chapter 1 it was noted that the one-period rate of return on a security could be calculated as

$$\text{Return} = \frac{\text{end-of-period wealth} - \text{beginning-of-period wealth}}{\text{beginning-of-period wealth}} \qquad (1.1)$$

where beginning-of-period wealth is the purchase price of one unit of the security at $t = 0$ (for example, one share of a firm's common stock), and end-of-period wealth is the market value of the unit at $t = 1$, along with the value of any cash (and cash equivalents) paid to the owner of the security between $t = 0$ and $t = 1$.

☐ ### 6.1.1 Determining the Rate of Return on a Portfolio

Since a portfolio is a collection of securities, its return r_p can be calculated in a similar manner:

$$r_p = \frac{W_1 - W_0}{W_0}. \qquad (6.1)$$

W_0 denotes the aggregate purchase price at $t = 0$ of the securities contained in the portfolio. W_1 denotes the aggregate market value of these securities at $t = 1$ as well as the aggregate cash (and cash equivalents) received between $t = 0$ and $t = 1$ from owning these securities. Equation (6.1) can be manipulated algebraically, resulting in

$$W_0(1 + r_p) = W_1. \qquad (6.2)$$

From equation (6.2) it can be seen that *initial wealth* (as W_0 is sometimes called), when multiplied by 1 plus the rate of return on the portfolio, is equal to *terminal wealth* (as W_1 is sometimes called).

Earlier, it was noted that the investor must make a decision on what portfolio to purchase at $t = 0$. In doing so, the investor does not know what the value of W_1 will be for most of the various alternative portfolios under consideration, since the investor does not know what the rate of return will be for most of these portfolios.[3] Thus, according to Markowitz, the investor

---

[3] One portfolio that would not have an uncertain rate of return would involve the investor putting all of his or her initial wealth in a government security that matures at $t = 1$. Alternatively, the investor's initial wealth could be put into a passbook savings account at a bank. However, for almost all other portfolios the rate of return would be uncertain.

should view the rate of return associated with any one of these portfolios to be what is known in statistics as a *random variable*. Now, it is known from statistics that a random variable can be "described" by what are known as its *moments*, two of which are its *expected value* (or mean) and *standard deviation*.[4]

Markowitz's approach to investing asserts that the investor, in making a decision on which portfolio to purchase, should evaluate these portfolios on the basis of their expected returns and standard deviations. That is, the investor should estimate the expected return and standard deviation of each portfolio and then choose the "best" one based on the relative magnitudes of these two parameters. The intuition behind this is actually quite straight-forward. Expected return can be viewed as a measure of the potential reward associated with any portfolio, and standard deviation can be viewed as a measure of the risk associated with any portfolio. Thus, once each portfolio has been examined in terms of its potential rewards and risks, the investor is in a position to identify the one portfolio that appears most desirable to him or her.

An Example

As an example, consider the two alternative portfolios denoted by A and B, shown in Table 6.1. Portfolio A has an expected annual return of 8% and portfolio B has an expected annual return of 12%. Assuming the investor has initial wealth of $100,000 and a one-year holding period, this means that the expected levels of terminal wealth associated with A and B are $108,000 and $112,000, respectively. It would appear, then, that B is the more desirable portfolio. However, A and B have annual standard deviations of 10% and 20%, respectively. Table 6.1 shows that this means there is a 2% chance that the investor will end up with terminal wealth of $70,000 or less if he or she purchases B, whereas there is virtually no chance that the investor's terminal wealth will be less than $70,000 if A is purchased. Similarly, B has a 5% chance of being worth less than $80,000, whereas A again has no chance. Continuing, B has a 14% chance of being worth less than $90,000, whereas A has only a 4% chance. Going on, B has a 27% chance of being worth less than $100,000, whereas A has only a 21% chance. Since the investor has initial wealth of $100,000, this last observation means there is a greater probability of having a negative return if B (27%) is purchased instead of A (21%). Overall, it can be seen from Table 6.1 that A is less risky than B, meaning that on this dimension A would be more desirable. The ultimate decision in regard to whether to purchase A or B will depend on this particular investor's attitudes toward risk and return, as is shown next.

---

[4] A random variable's expected value is, in a sense, its "average" value. Thus, the expected value for the return of a portfolio can be thought of as its expected, or average, return. The standard deviation of a random variable is a measure of the dispersion (or spread) of possible values the random variable can take on. Accordingly, the standard deviation of a portfolio is a measure of the dispersion of possible returns that could be earned on the portfolio. Sometimes *variance* is used as a measure of the dispersion instead of standard deviation. However, since the variance of a random variable is simply the squared value of the standard deviation of the random variable, this distinction is not of importance here. Later these concepts are discussed in more detail.

TABLE 6.1

A Comparison of Terminal Wealth Levels
for Two Hypothetical Portfolios.

LEVEL OF TERMINAL WEALTH	PERCENT CHANCE OF BEING BELOW THIS LEVEL OF TERMINAL WEALTH	
	PORTFOLIO A [a]	PORTFOLIO B [b]
$ 70,000	0%	2%
$ 80,000	0%	5%
$ 90,000	4%	14%
$100,000	21%	27%
$110,000	57%	46%
$120,000	88%	66%
$130,000	99%	82%

[a] The expected return and standard deviation of A are 8% and 10%, respectively.
[b] The expected return and standard deviation of B are 12% and 20%, respectively.
Initial wealth is assumed to be $100,000, and both portfolios are assumed to have normally distributed returns.

6.2 INDIFFERENCE CURVES

The method that should be used in selecting the most desirable portfolio involves the use of *indifference curves*. These curves represent an investor's preferences for risk and return and thus can be drawn on a two-dimensional figure, where the horizontal axis indicates risk as measured by standard deviation (denoted by σ_p) and the vertical axis indicates reward as measured by expected return (denoted by $\bar{r}_p$).

Figure 6.1 illustrates a "map" of indifference curves that a hypothetical

FIGURE 6–1
Map of indifference curves for a risk-averse investor.

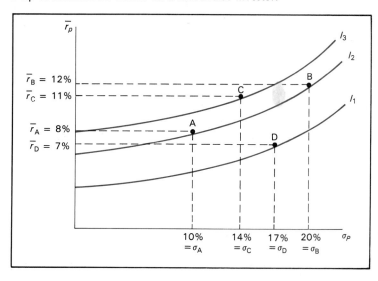

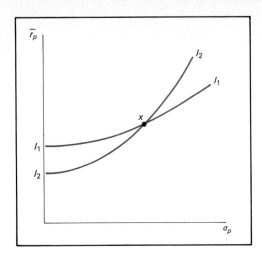

FIGURE 6–2
Interesting indifference curves.

investor might possess. Each curved line indicates one indifference curve for the investor and represents all combinations of portfolios that the investor would find equally desirable. For example, the investor with the indifference curves in Figure 6.1 would find portfolios A and B (the same two portfolios that were shown in Table 6.1) equally desirable, even though they have different expected returns and standard deviations, since they both lie on the same indifference curve, I_2. Portfolio B has a higher standard deviation (20%) than portfolio A (10%) and is therefore less desirable on that dimension. However, exactly offsetting this loss in desirability is the gain in desirability provided by the higher expected return of B (12%) relative to A (8%). This example leads to the first important feature of indifference curves: *All portfolios that lie on a given indifference curve are equally desirable to the investor.*

An implication of this feature is that *indifference curves cannot intersect.* Consider the two intersecting curves that are shown in Figure 6.2. Here the point of intersection is represented by X. Remember that all the portfolios on I_1 are equally desirable. This means they are all as desirable as X, since X is on I_1. Similarly, all the portfolios on I_2 are equally desirable and are as desirable as X, since X is also on I_2. Given X is on both indifference curves, all the portfolios on I_1 must be as desirable as those on I_2. But this presents a contradiction, since I_1 and I_2 are two curves that are supposed to represent different levels of desirability. Thus, in order for there to be no contradiction, these curves cannot intersect.

Although the investor represented in Figure 6.1 would find portfolios A and B equally desirable, he or she would find portfolio C, with an expected return of 11% and a standard deviation of 14%, to be preferable to both of them. This is because portfolio C happens to be on an indifference curve, I_3, that is located to the northwest of I_2. Now, C has a sufficiently larger expected return relative to A to more than offset its higher standard deviation and, on balance, make it more desirable than A. Equivalently, C has a sufficiently smaller standard deviation than B to more than offset its smaller expected return and, on balance, make it more desirable than B. This leads to the

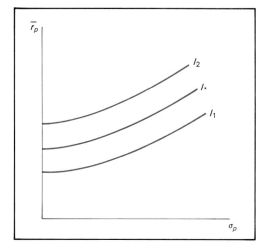

FIGURE 6–3
Plotting a third indifference curve
between two others.

second important feature of indifference curves: *An investor will find any portfolio that is lying on an indifference curve that is "further northwest" to be more desirable than any portfolio lying on an indifference curve that is "less northwest."*

Lastly, it should be noted that *an investor has an infinite number of indifference curves*. This simply means that whenever there are two indifference curves that have been plotted on a graph, it is possible to plot a third indifference curve that lies between them. As can be seen in Figure 6.3, given indifference curves I_1 and I_2, it is possible to graph a third curve I^* lying between them.

A good question to ask at this point is, How does an investor determine what his or her indifference curves look like? After all, each investor has a map of indifference curves that, while having the previously noted features, is nevertheless unique to that individual. It turns out that one method of explicitly determining the shape and location of an investor's indifference curves involves asking that investor a set of questions about gambles.[5]

For example, an investor might be asked which one of two alternatives he or she would find more desirable. The first alternative would simply involve receiving a certain cash payoff of $5000. The second alternative involves the flip of a coin where heads means a payoff of $4000 and tails means a payoff of $10,000. If the investor states that he or she would prefer the coin flip, then the size of the certain payoff is increased to $5500, for example, and the question is repeated. However, if the certain payoff is preferred, then its payoff is lowered to $4500, for example, and the question is repeated. This procedure of changing the size of the certain payoff and repeating the question is continued until a payoff is reached where the investor finds both alternatives equally desirable. At this juncture it is possible to tell something

---

[5] For an example of how this procedure can be utilized, see Ralph O. Swalm, "Utility Theory—Insights into Risk Taking," *Harvard Business Review* 44, no. 6 (November–December 1966):123–36. Also see footnote 6.

about the investor's attitudes towards risk and return. Once the investor is asked about other different-sized gambles, it will be possible to estimate the shape and location of his or her indifference curves.

A second method, shown in Chapter 22, involves presenting the investor with a set of hypothetical portfolios, along with their expected returns and standard deviations. Then he or she is asked to choose the most desirable one. Given the choice that is made, the shape and location of the investor's indifference curves can be estimated. This is because it is presumed that the investor would have acted as if he or she has indifference curves in making this choice, even though indifference curves would not have been explicitly used.

In summary, every investor has an indifference map representing his or her preferences for expected returns and standard deviations.[6] This means the investor should determine the expected return and standard deviation for each potential portfolio, plot them on a graph such as Figure 6.1, and then select the one portfolio that lies on the indifference curve that is furthest northwest. As shown in this example, from the set of the four potential portfolios—A, B, C, and D—the investor should select C.

6.3 NONSATIATION AND RISK AVERSION

☐ 6.3.1 Nonsatiation

Two assumptions are implicit in this discussion of indifference curves. First, it is assumed that investors, when given a choice between two otherwise identical portfolios, will choose the one with the higher level of expected return. More fundamentally, an assumption of *nonsatiation* is made in utilizing the Markowitz approach, meaning that investors are assumed always to prefer higher levels of terminal wealth to lower levels of terminal wealth. This is because higher levels of terminal wealth allow the investor to spend more on consumption at $t = 1$ (or in the more distant future). Thus, given two portfolios with the same standard deviation such as A and E in Figure 6.4, the investor will choose the portfolio with the higher expected return. In this case, it is portfolio A.

However, it is not quite so obvious what the investor will do when having to choose between two portfolios having the same level of expected return but different levels of standard deviation, such as A and F. This is where the second assumption enters the discussion.

---

[6] At some point the reader may wonder why an investor's preferences are based only on expected returns and standard deviations. For example, it may seem logical that the investor's preferences should be based on expected returns, standard deviations, and the probability that a portfolio will lose money. Two reasons are often stated for why an investor's preferences are based on just expected returns and standard deviations. First, if security returns have normal probability distributions, then portfolio returns are completely described by expected returns and standard deviations. Second, if investors have quadratic utility functions, then they will look only at expected returns and standard deviations in evaluating portfolios. See Gordon J. Alexander and Jack Clark Francis, *Portfolio Analysis*, (Englewood Cliffs, N.J.: Prentice Hall, 1986), particularly Chapters 2 and 3, for more details. It should be noted that there is some dispute about the validity of using utility theory to describe people's behavior. The people holding the opposing viewpoints are typically economists and psychologists, and they are often referred to as rationalists and behaviorists, respectively. For a discussion of their views, see the entire second part of the October 1986 issue of the *Journal of Business*.

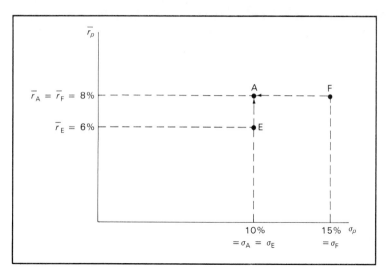

FIGURE 6–4
Nonsatiation, risk aversion, and portfolio choice.

Risk Aversion

Generally, it is assumed that investors are *risk-averse*, which means that the investor will choose the portfolio with the smaller standard deviation, A.[7] What does it mean to say that an investor is risk-averse? It means that the investor, when given the choice, will not want to take fair gambles, where a fair gamble is defined to be one that has an expected payoff of zero with an equal chance of winning or losing. For example, imagine flipping a coin where heads means you win $5 and tails means you lose $5. Since the coin has a 50-50 chance of being heads or tails, the expected payoff is $0 ((.5 × $5) + (.5 × −$5)). Accordingly, the risk-averse investor will choose to avoid this gamble. Intuitively, the investor avoids the gamble because the potential loss represents an amount of "displeasure" that is greater than the amount of "pleasure" associated with the potential gain.

The two assumptions of nonsatiation and risk-aversion are what lead to indifference curves having positive slopes and being convex (convexity means that the slope increases when moving from left to right along the curve).[8] Although it is assumed that all investors are risk-averse, it is not assumed that they have identical degrees of risk aversion. Some investors may be highly risk-averse, and some might be only slightly so. This means that different investors will have different maps of indifference curves. Panels (a), (b), and (c) of Figure 6.5 display maps for investors that are highly risk-

---

[7] Investors that are *risk-seeking* would choose F, and investors that are *risk-neutral* would find A and F to be equally desirable. The appendix to this chapter discusses both risk-neutral and risk-seeking investors.

[8] That is, imagine drawing a straight line connecting any two points on an indifference curve. The curve is convex if the straight line lies entirely above the curve. The underlying rationale for convexity lies in utility theory; see footnote 6.

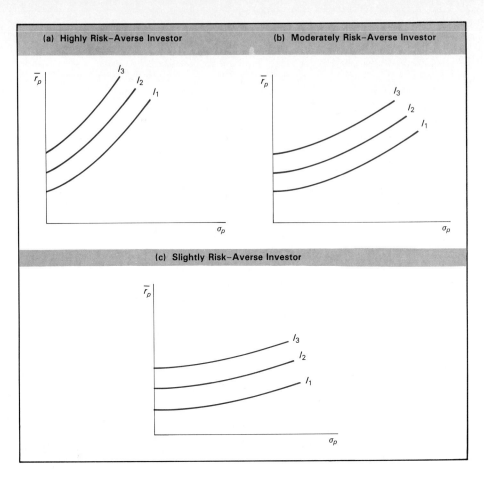

FIGURE 6–5
Indifference curves for different types of risk-averse investors.

averse, moderately risk-averse, and slightly risk-averse, respectively. As can be seen in these figures, a more risk-averse investor has more steeply sloped indifference curves.

6.4   CALCULATING EXPECTED RETURNS AND STANDARD DEVIATIONS FOR PORTFOLIOS

The previous section introduced the portfolio-selection problem that every investor faces. It also introduced the investment approach of Harry Markowitz as a method of solving that problem. With this approach, an investor should evaluate alternative portfolios on the basis of their expected returns and standard deviations by using indifference curves. In the case of a risk-averse investor, the portfolio with the indifference curve that is the furthest northwest would be the one selected for investment.

However, at this point certain questions have been left unanswered. In particular, how does the investor calculate the expected return and standard deviation for a portfolio?

☐ 6.4.1 Expected Returns

With the Markowitz approach to investing, the focus of the investor is on terminal (or end-of-period) wealth, W_1. That is, in deciding which portfolio to purchase with his or her initial (or beginning-of-period) wealth, W_0, the investor should focus on the effect the various portfolios have on W_1. This effect can be measured by the expected return and standard deviation of each portfolio.

As mentioned previously, a portfolio is a collection of securities. Thus, it seems logical that the expected return and standard deviation of a portfolio should depend on the expected return and standard deviation of each security contained in the portfolio. It also seems logical that the amount invested in each security should be important. Indeed, this is the case.

In order to show how the expected return of a portfolio depends on both the expected return of the individual securities and the amount invested in these securities, consider the three-security portfolio shown in Table 6.2(a). Assume that the investor has a one-year holding period and that for this period he or she has estimated the expected returns on Able, Baker, and Charlie stock to be 16.2%, 24.6%, and 22.8%, respectively. This is equivalent to stating that the investor has estimated the expected end-of-period values of these three stocks to be, respectively, $46.48 [since ($46.48 − $40)/$40 = 16.2%], $43.61 [since ($43.61 − $35)/$35 = 24.6%], and $76.14 [since ($76.14 − $62)/$62 = 22.8%].[9] Furthermore, assume that this investor has initial wealth of $17,200.

Using End-of-Period Values

The expected return on this portfolio can be calculated in several ways, all of which give the same answer. Consider the method shown in Table 6.2(b). This method involves calculating the expected end-of-period value of the portfolio and then using the formula for calculating rate of return shown in Chapter 1. That is, first the initial portfolio value (W_0) is subtracted from the expected end-of-period value of the portfolio ($\overline{W}_1$), and then this difference is divided by the initial portfolio value (W_0), the result of which is the portfolio's expected return. Although the example shown in Table 6.2(b) involves three securities, the procedure can be generalized to any number of securities.

Using Security Expected Returns

An alternative method for calculating the expected return on this portfolio is shown in Table 6.2(c). This procedure involves calculating the expected

---

[9] The figures given for the expected end-of-period values include both the expected prices and the expected dividends for the period. For example, Able has an expected end-of-period value of $46.48, which could consist of a hypothetical expected cash dividend of $2 and share price of $44.48. These expected returns and values are estimated by use of security analysis, which is discussed in Chapter 16.

TABLE 6.2

Calculating the Expected Return for a Portfolio.

(a) SECURITY AND PORTFOLIO VALUES.

SECURITY NAME	NUMBER OF SHARES IN PORTFOLIO (1)	INITIAL MARKET PRICE PER SHARE (2)	TOTAL INVESTMENT (3) = (1 × 2)	PROPORTION OF INITIAL MARKET VALUE OF PORTFOLIO (4) = (3)/W_0
Able Co.	100	$40	$4,000	$4,000/$17,200 = .2325
Baker Co.	200	35	7,000	7,000/17,200 = .4070
Charlie Co.	100	62	6,200	6,200/17,200 = .3605

Sum of proportions = 1.0000

(b) CALCULATING THE EXPECTED RETURN FOR A PORTFOLIO USING END-OF-PERIOD VALUES.

SECURITY NAME	NUMBER OF SHARES IN PORTFOLIO (1)	EXPECTED END-OF-PERIOD VALUE PER SHARE (2)	AGGREGATE EXPECTED END-OF-PERIOD VALUE (3) = (1) × (2)
Able Co.	100	$46.48	$46.48 × 100 = $4648
Baker Co.	200	43.61	43.61 × 200 = 8722
Charlie Co.	100	76.14	76.14 × 100 = 7614

Expected end-of-period value of portfolio = $\overline{W}_1$ = $20,984

Portfolio expected return = $\bar{r}_p$ = $\dfrac{\$20,984 - \$17,200}{\$17,200}$ = 22.00%

(c) CALCULATING THE EXPECTED RETURN FOR A PORTFOLIO USING SECURITY EXPECTED RETURNS.

SECURITY NAME	PROPORTION OF INITIAL MARKET VALUE OF PORTFOLIO (1)	SECURITY EXPECTED RETURNS (2)	CONTRIBUTION TO PORTFOLIO EXPECTED RETURN (3) = (1 × 2)
Able Co.	.2325	16.2%	.2325 × 16.2% = 3.77%
Baker Co.	.4070	24.6	.4070 × 24.6 = 10.01
Charlie Co.	.3605	22.8	.3605 × 22.8 = 8.22

Portfolio expected return = $\bar{r}_p$ = 22.00%

return of a portfolio as the weighted average of the expected returns of its component securities. The relative market values of the securities in the portfolio are used as weights. In symbols, the general rule for calculating the expected return of a portfolio consisting of N securities is

$$\bar{r}_p = \sum_{i=1}^{N} X_i \bar{r}_i \qquad \text{(6.3a)}$$

$$= X_1 \bar{r}_1 + X_2 \bar{r}_2 + \cdots + X_N \bar{r}_N \qquad \text{(6.3b)}$$

where:

$\bar{r}_p$ = the expected return of the portfolio,

X_i = the proportion of the portfolio's initial value invested in security i,

$\bar{r}_i$ = the expected return of security i,

N = the number of securities in the portfolio.

Thus, an *expected return vector* can be used to calculate the expected return for any portfolio formed from the N securities. This vector consists of one column of numbers, where the entry in row i contains the expected return of security i. In the previous example, the expected return vector was estimated by the investor to be

$$
\begin{matrix}
\text{Row 1} \\
\text{Row 2} \\
\text{Row 3}
\end{matrix}
\begin{bmatrix}
16.2\% \\
24.6\% \\
22.8\%
\end{bmatrix}
$$

where the entries in rows 1, 2, and 3 denote the expected returns for securities 1, 2, and 3, respectively.

Since the portfolio's expected return is a weighted average of the expected returns of its securities, *the contribution of each security to the portfolio's expected return depends on its expected return and its proportionate share of the initial portfolio's market value*. Nothing else is relevant. It follows from equation (6.3a) that an investor who simply wants the greatest possible expected return should hold one security: the one he or she considers to have the greatest expected return. Very few investors do this, and very few investment advisers would counsel such an extreme policy. Instead, investors should diversify, meaning that their portfolios should include more than one security. This is because diversification can reduce risk, as measured by the standard deviation.

☐ 6.4.2 Standard Deviations

A useful measure of risk should somehow take into account both the probabilities of various possible "bad" outcomes and their associated magnitudes. Instead of measuring the probability of a number of different possible outcomes, the measure of risk should somehow estimate the extent to which the actual outcome is likely to diverge from the expected outcome. Standard deviation is a measure that does this, since it is an estimate of the likely divergence of an *actual* return from an *expected* return.

It may seem that any single measure of risk would provide at best a very crude summary of the "bad" possibilities. But in the more common situation where a portfolio's prospects are being assessed, standard deviation may prove to be a very good measure of the degree of uncertainty. The clearest example arises when the *probability distribution* for a portfolio's returns can be approximated by the familiar bell-shaped curve known as a *normal probability distribution*. This is often considered a plausible assumption for an-

alyzing returns on diversified portfolios when the holding period being studied is relatively short (say a quarter or less).

A question with standard deviation as a measure of risk is, Why count "happy" surprises (those above the expected return) at all in a measure of risk? Why not just consider the deviations *below* the expected return? Measures that do so have merit, but if a distribution is symmetric, such as the normal distribution, the results will be the same. Why? Because the left side of a symmetric distribution is a mirror image of the right side. Thus, a list of portfolios ordered on the basis of "downside risk" will not differ from one ordered on the basis of standard deviation if returns are normally distributed.[10]

Formula for Standard Deviation

For the three-security portfolio consisting of Able, Baker, and Charlie, the formula for the standard deviation is

$$\sigma_p = \left[\sum_{i=1}^{3} \sum_{j=1}^{3} X_i X_j \sigma_{ij} \right]^{1/2} \tag{6.4}$$

where σ_{ij} denotes the *covariance* of the returns between security i and security j. Covariance is a statistical measure of the relationship between two random variables. That is, it is a measure of how two random variables such as the returns on securities i and j "move together." A positive value for covariance indicates that the securities' returns tend to go together—for example, a better-than-expected return for one is likely to occur along with a better-than-expected return for the other. A negative covariance indicates a tendency for the returns to offset one another—for example, a better-than-expected return for one security is likely to occur along with a worse-than-expected return for the other. A relatively small or zero value for the covariance indicates that there is little or no relationship between the returns for the two securities.

Closely related to covariance is the statistical measure known as correlation, since it is known that the covariance between two random variables is equal to the correlation between the two random variables times the product of their standard deviations:

$$\sigma_{ij} = \rho_{ij}\sigma_i\sigma_j \tag{6.5}$$

where ρ_{ij} (the Greek letter rho) denotes the *correlation coefficient* between the return on security i and the return on security j. The correlation coefficient rescales the covariance to facilitate comparison with corresponding values for other pairs of random variables. Correlation coefficients always lie between -1 and $+1$. A value of -1 represents perfect negative correlation, and a value of $+1$ represents perfect positive correlation. Most cases lie between these two extreme values.

---

[10] If returns are not normally distributed, the use of standard deviation can still be justified in an approximate sense provided there are small probabilities of extremely high and low returns. See H. Levy and H. M. Markowitz, "Approximating Expected Utility by a Function of Mean and Variance," *American Economic Review* 69, no. 3 (June 1979):308–17; and Yoram Kroll, Haim Levy, and Harry M. Markowitz, "Mean-Variance versus Direct Utility Maximization," *Journal of Finance* 39, no. 1 (March 1984):47–61.

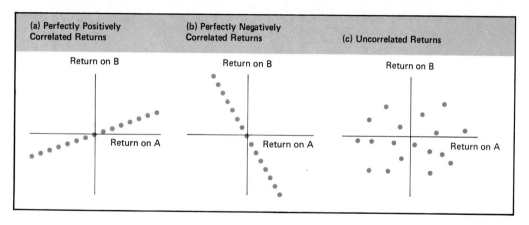

FIGURE 6–6
Returns on two securities.

Figure 6.6(a) presents a scatter diagram for the returns on hypothetical securities A and B when the correlation between these two securities is perfectly positive. Note how all the points lie precisely on a straight upward-sloping line. This means that when one of the two securities has a relatively high return, then so will the other. Similarly, when one of the two securities has a relatively low return, then so will the other.

Alternatively, the returns on the two securities will have a perfectly negative correlation when the scatter diagram indicates that the points lie precisely on a straight downward-sloping line, as shown in Figure 6.6(b). In such a case the returns on the two securities can be seen to move opposite each other. That is, when one security has a relatively high return, then the other will have a relatively low return.

A case of special importance arises when the scatter diagram of security returns shows a pattern that cannot be represented even approximately by an upward-sloping or downward-sloping line. In such an instance, the returns are uncorrelated, meaning the correlation coefficient is zero. Figure 6.6(c) provides an example. In this situation, when one security has a relatively high return, then the other can have either a relatively high, low, or average return.

Given an understanding of covariance and correlation, it is important to understand how the double summation indicated in equation (6.4) is performed. Although there are many ways of performing double summation, all of which lead to the same answer, one way is perhaps more intuitive than the others. It starts with the first summation and sets i at its initial value of 1. Then the second summation is performed for j going from 1 to 3. At this point, i in the first summation is increased by 1, so that now $i = 2$. Again the second summation is performed by letting j go from 1 to 3, except that now $i = 2$. Continuing, i in the first summation is again increased by 1, so that $i = 3$. Then the second summation is again performed by letting j go from 1 to 3. At this point, note that $i = 3$ and $j = 3$, which are the

upper limits for both the first and second summations. This means it is time to stop, as the double summation has been finished. This process can be shown algebraically as follows:

$$\sigma_p = \left[\sum_{j=1}^{3} X_1 X_j \sigma_{1j} + \sum_{j=1}^{3} X_2 X_j \sigma_{2j} + \sum_{j=1}^{3} X_3 X_j \sigma_{3j} \right]^{1/2} \tag{6.6a}$$

$$= [X_1 X_1 \sigma_{11} + X_1 X_2 \sigma_{12} + X_1 X_3 \sigma_{13}$$

$$+ X_2 X_1 \sigma_{21} + X_2 X_2 \sigma_{22} + X_2 X_3 \sigma_{23} \tag{6.6b}$$

$$+ X_3 X_1 \sigma_{31} + X_3 X_2 \sigma_{32} + X_3 X_3 \sigma_{33}]^{1/2}.$$

Each term in the double sum involves the product of the weights for two securities, X_i and X_j, and the covariance between these two securities. Note how there are nine terms to be added together in order to calculate the standard deviation of a portfolio consisting of three securities. It is no coincidence that the number of terms to be added together (9) equals the number of securities squared (3^2).

In general, calculating the standard deviation for a portfolio consisting of N securities involves performing the double sum indicated in equation (6.4) over N securities, thereby involving the addition of N^2 terms:

$$\sigma_p = \left[\sum_{i=1}^{N} \sum_{j=1}^{N} X_i X_j \sigma_{ij} \right]^{1/2}. \tag{6.7}$$

An interesting feature of the double sum occurs when the subscripts i and j refer to the same security. In equation (6.6b) this occurs in the first ($X_1 X_1 \sigma_{11}$), fifth ($X_2 X_2 \sigma_{22}$), and ninth ($X_3 X_3 \sigma_{33}$) terms. What does it mean to have the subscripts for covariance refer to the same security? For example, consider security one (Able) so that $i = j = 1$. Since σ_{11} denotes the covariance of security 1 (Able) with security 1 (Able), equation (6.5) indicates that

$$\sigma_{11} = \rho_{11} \sigma_1 \sigma_1. \tag{6.8}$$

Now the correlation of any security with itself, in this case ρ_{11}, can be shown to be equal to $+1$.[11] This means that equation (6.8) reduces to

$$\sigma_{11} = +1 \times \sigma_1 \times \sigma_1 \tag{6.9}$$

$$= \sigma_1^2$$

which is just the square of the standard deviation of security 1, known as the *variance* of security 1. Thus, the double sum involves both variance and covariance terms.

As an example, consider the following *variance-covariance matrix* for the stocks of Able, Baker, and Charlie:

---

[11] Remember that correlation refers to how two random variables move together. If the two random variables are the same, then they must move exactly together with each other. This can be visualized by graphing the values of the same random variable on both the X-axis and Y-axis. In such a graph, all points would lie on a straight 45° line passing through the origin, thereby implying a correlation of $+1$.

	Column 1	Column 2	Column 3
Row 1	146	187	145
Row 2	187	854	104
Row 3	145	104	289

The entry in cell (i, j) denotes the covariance between security i and security j. For example, the entry in $(1, 3)$ denotes the covariance between the first and third securities, which in this case is 145. Also, the entry in cell (i, i) denotes the variance of security i. For example, the variance of security 2 appears in cell $(2, 2)$, and is equal to 854. Using this variance-covariance matrix along with the formula given in equation (6.6b), the standard deviation of the previously mentioned portfolio that had $X_1 = .2325$, $X_2 = .4070$, and $X_3 = .3605$ can now be calculated:

$$\sigma_p = [X_1 X_1 \sigma_{11} + X_1 X_2 \sigma_{12} + X_1 X_3 \sigma_{13}$$

$$+ X_2 X_1 \sigma_{21} + X_2 X_2 \sigma_{22} + X_2 X_3 \sigma_{23}$$

$$+ X_3 X_1 \sigma_{31} + X_3 X_2 \sigma_{32} + X_3 X_3 \sigma_{33}]^{1/2}$$

$$= [(.2325 \times .2325 \times 146) + (.2325 \times .4070 \times 187) + (.2325 \times .3605 \times 145)$$

$$+ (.4070 \times .2325 \times 187) + (.4070 \times .4070 \times 854) + (.4070 \times .3605 \times 104)$$

$$+ (.3605 \times .2325 \times 145) + (.3605 \times .4070 \times 104) + (.3605 \times .3605 \times 289)]^{1/2}$$

$$= [277.13]^{1/2}$$

$$= 16.65\%.$$

There are several interesting features about variance-covariance matrices that deserve mention. First, such matrices are square, meaning that the number of columns equals the number of rows and that the total number of cells for N securities equals N^2.

Second, the variances of the securities appear on the diagonal of the matrix, which are the cells that lie on a line going from the upper left-hand corner to the lower right-hand corner of the matrix. In the previous example, the variance of security 1 (146) appears in row 1 of column 1. Similarly, the variances of securities 2 and 3 appear in row 2 of column 2 (854) and row 3 of column 3 (289), respectively.

Third, the matrix is symmetric, meaning the number appearing in row i of column j also appears in row j of column i. That is, the elements in the cells above the diagonal also appear in the corresponding cells below the diagonal. In the previous example, note that 187 appears in row 1 of column 2, and also in row 2 of column 1. Similarly, 145 appears in both row 1 of column 3 and row 3 of column 1, and 104 appears in both row 2 of column 3 and row 3 of column 2. The reason for this feature is quite simple—the covariance between two securities does not depend on the order in which the two securities are specified. This means that, for example, the covariance between the first and second securities is the same as the covariance between the second and first securities.

6.5   SUMMARY

Markowitz's approach to investing is based in statistics, inasmuch as it begins with the premise that security returns are random variables. As with random variables, securities (and, in turn, portfolios) can be compared by examining their moments. Markowitz has suggested that the investor should look at two such moments—expected return and standard deviation. That is, when faced with a set of portfolios, the investor should first determine the expected return (also known as the mean return) and standard deviation of return associated with each portfolio. Having done so, the investor is then in the position of making a fully informed decision about which one to purchase. This decision should hinge on the investor's attitudes toward risk and return as exemplified by his or her indifference curves. In particular, the investor should choose the portfolio that lies on the indifference curve that is furthest northwest.

Having said this, it is logical next to consider two questions: How can the investor make a choice on the basis of expected return and standard deviation when facing an infinite number of possible portfolios? And what happens when one of the securities has a certain return and borrowing is allowed? Chapter 7 provides the answers to these questions.

APPENDIX A
RISK-NEUTRAL AND RISK-SEEKING INVESTORS

Earlier it was mentioned that the Markowitz approach assumes investors are risk-averse. Although this is a reasonable assumption to make, it is not necessary to do so. Alternatively, it can be assumed that investors are either risk-neutral or risk-seeking.

Consider the risk-seeking investor first. This investor, when faced with a fair gamble, will want to take the gamble. Furthermore, larger gambles are more desirable than smaller gambles. This is because the pleasure derived from winning is greater than the displeasure derived from losing. Since there is an equal chance of winning or losing, on balance the risk-seeking investor will want to take the gamble. What this means is that when faced with two portfolios that have the same expected return, this type of investor will choose the one with the higher standard deviation.

For example, in choosing between A and F in Figure 6.4, the risk-seeking investor will choose F. This suggests that the risk-seeking investor will have negatively sloped indifference curves.[12] In addition, risk-seeking investors will prefer to be on the indifference curve that is furthest northeast. Figure 6.7 illustrates a map of the indifference curves for a hypothetical risk-seeking

---

[12] It can also be shown that for a risk-seeking investor, these indifference curves will be concave, meaning their slopes decrease when moving from left to right along any particular one. The underlying rationale for concavity lies in utility theory; see footnotes 6 and 8.

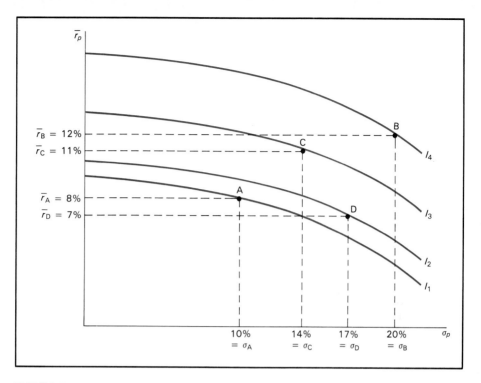

FIGURE 6–7
Map of indifference curves for a risk-seeking investor.

investor. As shown in the figure, when choosing among A, B, C, and D (the same four portfolios shown in Figure 6.1), this investor will choose B.

The risk-neutral case lies between the risk-seeking and risk-averse cases. Whereas the risk-averse investor *does not want* to take fair gambles, and the risk-seeking investor *does want* to take such gambles, the risk-neutral investor *does not care* whether or not the gamble is taken. This means that risk, or, more specifically, standard deviation, is unimportant to the risk-neutral investor in evaluating portfolios. Accordingly, the indifference curves for such investors are horizontal lines as shown in Figure 6.8. These investors prefer to be on the indifference curve that is furthest north. When faced with the choice of A, B, C, and D, such an investor will choose B, since it has the highest expected return.

Although investors can be either risk-seeking or risk-neutral, there is evidence to suggest that they are more accurately characterized as being, in general, risk-averse. One piece of evidence is the observation that riskier securities have historically had higher average returns, suggesting investors have had to be induced with higher rewards in order to get them to make riskier purchases. If investors were not risk-averse, they would not have had to be induced in this manner.

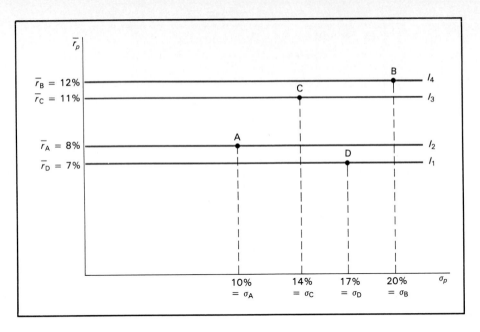

FIGURE 6–8
Map of indifference curves for a risk-neutral investor.

QUESTIONS AND PROBLEMS

1. Listed below are a number of portfolios and expected returns, standard deviation of returns, and the amount of satisfaction (measured in utils) they provide Arky Vaughn. Given this information, graph Arky's identifiable indifference curves.

Portfolio	Expected Return	Standard Deviation	Utility
1	5%	0%	10 utils
2	6	10	10
3	9	20	10
4	14	30	10
5	10	0	20
6	11	10	20
7	14	20	20
8	19	30	20
9	15	0	30
10	16	10	30
11	19	20	30
12	24	30	30

2. Why are the indifference curves of typical investors assumed to slope upward to the right?

3. Why are typical investors assumed to prefer portfolios on indifference curves lying to the northwest?

4. What is meant by the statement that "risk-averse investors exhibit diminishing marginal utility"? Why does diminishing marginal utility cause an investor to refuse to accept a "fair bet"?

5. Why are the indifference curves of more risk-averse investors more steeply sloped than those of investors with less risk aversion?

6. Consider the following two sets of indifference curves for investors Hack Wilson and Kiki Cuyler. Determine whether Hack or Kiki:

   a. Is more risk averse,

   b. Prefers investment A to investment B,

   c. Prefers investment C to investment D.

   Explain the reasons for your answers.

7. Given the following information about four stocks comprising a portfolio, calculate each stock's expected return. Then, using these individual security expected returns, calculate the portfolio's expected return.

Stock	Initial Investment Value	Expected End-of-Period Investment Value	Proportion of Portfolio Initial Market Value
A	$ 500	$ 700	19.2%
B	200	250	7.7
C	1,000	1,100	38.5
D	900	1,350	34.6

8. Both the covariance and the correlation coefficient measure the extent to which the returns on securities move together. What is the relationship between the two statistical measures? Why is the correlation coefficient a more convenient measure?

9. Given the following variance-covariance matrix for three securities, as well as the percentage of the portfolio that each security comprises, calculate the portfolio's standard deviation.

	Security A	Security B	Security C
Security A	459	-211	112
Security B	-211	312	215
Security C	112	215	179
	$X_A = .30$	$X_B = .50$	$X_C = .20$

10. Listed here are estimates of the standard deviations and correlation coefficients for three stocks.

Stock	Standard Deviation	Correlation with Stock: A	B	C
A	12%	1.00	-1.00	0.20
B	15	-1.00	1.00	0.60
C	10	0.20	0.60	1.00

   a. If a portfolio is composed of 30% of stock A and 70% of stock C, what is the portfolio's standard deviation?

   b. If a portfolio is composed of 30% of stock A, 30% of stock B, and 40% of stock C, what is the portfolio's standard deviation?

   c. If you were asked to design a portfolio using stocks A and B, what percentage investment in each stock would produce a zero standard deviation? [*Hint*: Some algebra is necessary to solve this problem. Remember that $X_B = (1 - X_A)$.]

Chapter 7

PORTFOLIO ANALYSIS

The previous chapter introduced the portfolio selection problem that every investor faces. It also introduced the investment approach of Harry Markowitz as a method of solving that problem. With this approach, an investor should evaluate alternative portfolios on the basis of their expected returns and standard deviations by using indifference curves. In the case of a risk-averse investor, the portfolio with the indifference curve that is the "furthest northwest" would be the one selected for investment.

However, the previous chapter left certain questions unanswered. In particular, how can Markowitz's approach be used once it is recognized that there are an infinite number of portfolios available for investment? What happens when the investor considers investing in a set of securities, one of which is riskless? What happens when the investor is allowed to buy securities on margin? This chapter will provide the answers to these questions, beginning with the first one.

7.1 THE EFFICIENT SET THEOREM

As mentioned earlier, an infinite number of portfolios can be formed from a set of N securities. Consider the situation with Able, Baker, and Charlie companies where N is equal to 3. The investor could purchase just shares of Able or just shares of Baker. Alternatively, the investor could purchase a combination of shares of Able and Baker. For example, the investor could put 50% of his or her money in each company, or 25% in one company and 75% in the other, or 33% in one and 67% in the other, or any percent (between 0% and 100%) in one company with the rest going into the other company. Without even considering investing in Charlie, there are already an infinite number of possible portfolios in which to invest.[1]

Does the investor need to evaluate all these portfolios? Fortunately,

---

[1] This can be seen by noting that there are an infinite number of points on the real number line between 0 and 100. If these numbers are thought of as representing the percentage of the investor's funds going into shares of Able, with 100 minus this number going into Baker, it can be seen that there are an infinite number of portfolios that could be formed from just two different securities. In making this assertion, however, it has been assumed that an investor can buy a fraction of a share if he or she so desires. For example, the investor can buy not only one or two or three shares of Able but also 1.1 or 1.01 or 1.001 shares.

the answer to this question is no. The key to why the investor needs to look at only a subset of the available portfolios lies in the *efficient set theorem*, which states that:

> An investor will choose his or her optimal portfolio from the set of portfolios that:
> 1. Offer maximum expected return for varying levels of risk, and
> 2. Offer minimum risk for varying levels of expected return.

The set of portfolios meeting these two conditions is known as the *efficient set*, or *efficient frontier*.

7.1.1 The Feasible Set

Figure 7.1 provides an illustration of the location of the *feasible set*, also known as the opportunity set, from which the efficient set can be located. The feasible set simply represents the set of all portfolios that could be formed from a group of N securities. That is, all possible portfolios that could be formed from the N securities lie either on or within the boundary of the feasible set (the points denoted by G, E, S, and H in the figure are examples of such portfolios). In general, this set will have an umbrella-type shape similar to the one shown by the figure. Depending on the particular securities involved, it may be more to the right or left, higher or lower, or fatter or skinnier than indicated here. The point is that its shape will, except in perverse circumstances, look similar to what appears here.

FIGURE 7–1
Feasible and efficient sets.

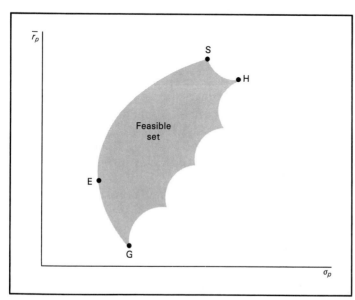

☐ 7.1.2 The Efficient Set Theorem Applied to the Feasible Set

The efficient set can now be located by applying the efficient set theorem to this feasible set. First, the set of portfolios that meet the first condition of the efficient set theorem must be identified. Looking at Figure 7.1, there is no portfolio offering less risk than that of portfolio E. This is because if a vertical line were drawn through E, there would be no point in the feasible set to the left of the line. Also, there is no portfolio offering more risk than that of portfolio H. This is because if a vertical line were drawn through H, there would be no point in the feasible set to the right of the line. Thus, the set of portfolios offering maximum expected return for varying levels of risk is the set of portfolios lying on the "northern" boundary of the feasible set between points E and H.

Considering the second condition next, there is no portfolio offering an expected return greater than portfolio S, since no point in the feasible set lies above a horizontal line going through S. Similarly, there is no portfolio offering a lower expected return than portfolio G, since no point in the feasible set lies below a horizontal line going through G. Thus, the set of portfolios offering minimum risk for varying levels of expected return is the set of portfolios lying on the "western" boundary of the feasible set between points G and S.

Remembering that both conditions have to be met in order to identify the efficient set, it can be seen that only those portfolios lying on the "northwest" boundary between points E and S do so. Accordingly, these portfolios form the efficient set, and it is from this set of *efficient portfolios* that the investor will find his or her optimal one. All other portfolios are "inefficient" and can be safely ignored.

☐ 7.1.3 Selection of the Optimal Portfolio

How will the investor select an *optimal portfolio*? As shown in Figure 7.2, the investor should plot his or her indifference curves on the same figure as the efficient set and then choose the portfolio that is on the indifference curve that is furthest northwest. This portfolio will correspond to the point where an indifference curve is just tangent to the efficient set.[2] As can be seen in the figure, this is portfolio O^* on indifference curve I_2. Although the investor would prefer a portfolio on I_3, no such portfolio exists, and so wanting to be on this indifference curve is just wishful thinking. In regard to I_1, there are several portfolios that the investor could choose (for example, O). However, the figure shows that portfolio O^* dominates these portfolios, since it is on an indifference curve that is further northwest. Figure 7.3 shows how the highly risk-averse investor will choose a portfolio close to E. Figure 7.4 shows

---

[2] Appendix A discusses some of the principles involved in determining the location of Markowitz's efficient set and the composition of the investor's optimal portfolio.

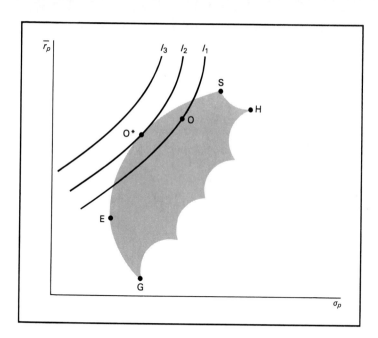

FIGURE 7–2
Selecting an optimal portfolio.

FIGURE 7–3
Portfolio selection for a highly risk-averse investor.

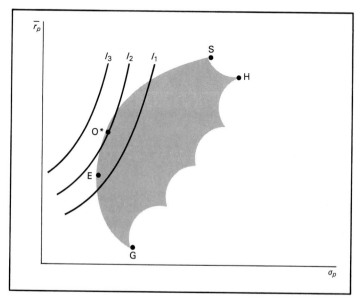

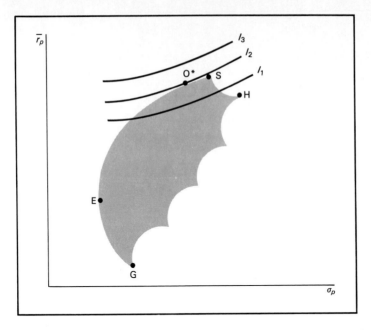

FIGURE 7–4
Portfolio selection for a slightly risk-averse investor.

that the investor who is only slightly risk-averse will choose a portfolio close to S.[3]

Upon reflection, the efficient set theorem is quite rational. In Chapter 6, it was shown that the investor should select the portfolio that put him or her on the indifference curve furthest northwest. The efficient set theorem, stating that the investor need not be concerned with portfolios that do not lie on the northwest boundary of the feasible set, is a logical consequence.

Indifference curves for the risk-averse investor were shown to be positively sloped and convex in Chapter 6. Now it will be shown that the efficient set is generally concave, meaning that if a straight line is drawn between any two points on the efficient set, the straight line will lie below the efficient set. This feature of the efficient set is important because it means that there will be only one tangency point between the investor's indifference curves and the efficient set.

7.2 CONCAVITY OF THE EFFICIENT SET

In order to see why the efficient set is concave, consider the following two-security example. Security 1, the Ark Shipping Company, has an estimated expected return of 5% and standard deviation of 20%. Security 2, the Gold Jewelry Company, has an estimated expected return of 15% and standard

---

[3] The risk-neutral investor will choose portfolio S, whereas the risk-seeking investor will choose either S or H.

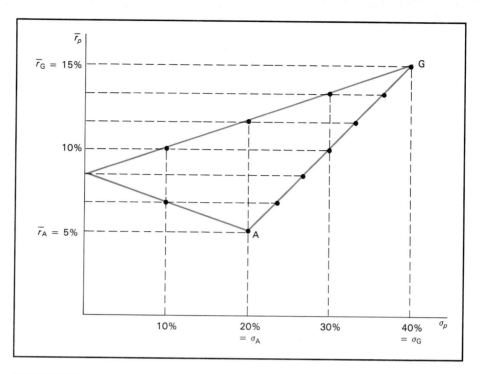

FIGURE 7–5
Upper and lower bounds to combinations of securities *A* and *G*.

deviation of 40%. Their respective locations are indicated by the letters *A* and *G* in Figure 7.5.

Now consider all possible portfolios that an investor could purchase by combining these two securities. Let X_1 denote the proportion of the investor's funds invested in Ark Shipping and $X_2 = 1 - X_1$ denote the proportion invested in Gold Jewelry. Thus, if the investor purchased just Ark Shipping, then $X_1 = 1$ and $X_2 = 0$. Alternatively, if the investor purchased just Gold Jewelry, then $X_1 = 0$ and $X_2 = 1$. A combination of .17 in Ark Shipping and .83 in Gold Jewelry is also possible, as are respective combinations of .33 and .67, and .50 and .50. Although there are many other possibilities, only the following seven portfolios will be considered:

	PORTFOLIO A	PORTFOLIO B	PORTFOLIO C	PORTFOLIO D	PORTFOLIO E	PORTFOLIO F	PORTFOLIO G
X_1	1.00	.83	.67	.50	.33	.17	.00
X_2	.00	.17	.33	.50	.67	.83	1.00

In order to consider these seven portfolios for possible investment, their expected returns and standard deviations must be calculated. All the necessary information to calculate the expected returns for these portfolios is at hand. In doing so, equation (6.3a) must be utilized:

$$\bar{r}_p = \sum_{i=1}^{N} X_i \bar{r}_i$$

$$= \sum_{i=1}^{2} X_i \bar{r}_i \qquad (6.3a)$$

$$= X_1 \bar{r}_1 + X_2 \bar{r}_2$$

$$= (X_1 \times 5\%) + (X_2 \times 15\%).$$

For portfolios A and G, this calculation is trivial, since the investor is purchasing shares of just one company. Thus, their expected returns are 5% and 15%, respectively. For portfolios B, C, D, E, and F, the expected returns are, respectively:

$$\bar{r}_B = (.83 \times 5\%) + (.17 \times 15\%)$$

$$= 6.70\%$$

$$\bar{r}_C = (.67 \times 5\%) + (.33 \times 15\%)$$

$$= 8.30\%$$

$$\bar{r}_D = (.50 \times 5\%) + (.50 \times 15\%)$$

$$= 10\%$$

$$\bar{r}_E = (.33 \times 5\%) + (.67 \times 15\%)$$

$$= 11.70\%$$

$$\bar{r}_F = (.17 \times 5\%) + (.83 \times 15\%)$$

$$= 13.30\%.$$

In calculating the standard deviation of these seven portfolios, equation (6.7) must be utilized:

$$\sigma_p = \left[\sum_{i=1}^{N} \sum_{j=1}^{N} X_i X_j \sigma_{ij} \right]^{1/2}$$

$$= \left[\sum_{i=1}^{2} \sum_{j=1}^{2} X_i X_j \sigma_{ij} \right]^{1/2} \qquad (6.7)$$

$$= [X_1 X_1 \sigma_{11} + X_1 X_2 \sigma_{12} + X_2 X_1 \sigma_{21} + X_2 X_2 \sigma_{22}]^{1/2}$$

$$= [X_1^2 \sigma_1^2 + X_2^2 \sigma_2^2 + 2 X_1 X_2 \sigma_{12}]^{1/2}$$

$$= [(X_1^2 \times 20\%^2) + (X_2^2 \times 40\%^2) + 2 X_1 X_2 \sigma_{12}]^{1/2}.$$

For portfolios A and G, this calculation is trivial, since the investor is purchasing shares of just one company. Thus, their standard deviations are just 20% and 40%, respectively.

For portfolios B, C, D, E, and F, application of equation (6.7) indicates that the standard deviations depend on the magnitude of the covariance

between the two securities. As shown in equation (6.5), this covariance term is equal to the correlation between the two securities multiplied by the product of their standard deviations:

$$\sigma_{12} = \rho_{12} \times \sigma_1 \times \sigma_2$$

$$= \rho_{12} \times 20\% \times 40\%$$

$$= 800\rho_{12}.$$

This means that the standard deviation of any portfolio consisting of Ark Shipping and Gold Jewelry can be expressed as:

$$\sigma_p = [(X_1^2 \times 20\%^2) + (X_2^2 \times 40\%^2) + (2X_1X_2 \times 800\rho_{12})]^{1/2} \quad \textbf{(7.1)}$$

$$= [400X_1^2 + 1600X_2^2 + 1600X_1X_2\rho_{12}]^{1/2}.$$

Consider portfolio D first. The standard deviation of this portfolio will be somewhere between 10% and 30%, the exact value depending upon the size of the correlation coefficient. How were these bounds of 10% and 30% determined? First, note that for portfolio D, equation (7.1) reduces to:

$$\sigma_D = [(400 \times .25) + (1600 \times .25) + (1600 \times .5 \times .5 \times \rho_{12})]^{1/2} \quad \textbf{(7.2)}$$

$$= [500 + 400\rho_{12}]^{1/2}.$$

Inspection of equation (7.2) indicates that σ_D will be at a minimum when the correlation coefficient, ρ_{12}, is at a minimum. Now, remembering that the minimum value for any correlation coefficient is -1, it can be seen that the lower bound on σ_D is:

$$\sigma_D = [500 + (400 \times -1)]^{1/2}$$

$$= [500 - 400]^{1/2}$$

$$= [100]^{1/2}$$

$$= 10\%.$$

Similarly, inspection of equation (7.2) indicates that σ_D will be at a maximum when the correlation coefficient is at a maximum, which is $+1$. Thus, the upper bound on σ_D is:

$$\sigma_D = [500 + (400 \times 1)]^{1/2}$$

$$= (500 + 400)^{1/2}$$

$$= (900)^{1/2}$$

$$= 30\%.$$

In general, it can be seen from equation (7.1) that for any given set of weights X_1 and X_2, the lower and upper bounds will occur when the correlations between the two securities are -1 and $+1$, respectively. Applying the same analysis to the other portfolios reveals that their lower and upper bounds are as follows.

| STANDARD DEVIATION OF PORTFOLIO |||
Portfolio	Lower Bound	Upper Bound
A	20%	20.00%
B	10	23.33
C	00	26.67
D	10	30.00
E	20	33.33
F	30	36.67
G	40	40.00

These values are shown in Figure 7.5.

Interestingly, the upper bounds all lie on a straight line connecting points A and G. This means that any portfolio consisting of these two securities cannot have a standard deviation that plots to the right of a straight line connecting the two securities. Instead, the standard deviation must lie on or to the left of the straight line. This observation suggests a motivation for diversifying a portfolio. Namely, *diversification generally leads to risk reduction*, since the standard deviation of a portfolio will generally be less than a weighted average of the standard deviations of the securities in the portfolio.

Also interesting is the observation that the lower bounds all lie on one of two line segments that go from point A to a point on the vertical axis corresponding to 8.30% and then to point G. This means that any portfolio consisting of these two securities cannot have a standard deviation that plots to the left of either of these two line segments. For example, portfolio B must lie on the horizontal line going through the vertical axis at 6.70% but bounded at the values of 10% and 23.33%.

In sum, any portfolio consisting of these two securities will lie within the triangle shown in Figure 7.5, with its actual location depending on the magnitude of the correlation coefficient between the two securities.

What if the correlation were zero? In this case, equation (7.1) reduces to:

$$\sigma_p = [(400X_1^2) + (1600X_2^2) + (1600X_1X_2 \times 0)]^{1/2}$$

$$= [400X_1^2 + 1600X_2^2]^{1/2}.$$

Applying the appropriate weights for X_1 and X_2, the standard deviation for portfolios B, C, D, E, and F can therefore be calculated as follows:

$$\sigma_B = [(400 \times .83^2) + (1600 \times .17^2)]^{1/2}$$

$$= 17.94\%$$

$$\sigma_C = [(400 \times .67^2) + (1600 \times .33^2)]^{1/2}$$

$$= 18.81\%$$

$$\sigma_D = [(400 \times .50^2) + (1600 \times .50^2)]^{1/2}$$

$$= 22.36\%$$

$$\sigma_E = [(400 \times .33^2) + (1600 \times .67^2)]^{1/2}$$

$$= 27.60\%$$

$$\sigma_F = [(400 \times .17^2) + (1600 \times .83^2)]^{1/2}$$

$$= 33.37\%.$$

Figure 7.6 indicates the location of these portfolios along with the upper and lower bounds that were shown in Figure 7.5. As can be seen, these portfolios—as well as all other possible portfolios consisting of Ark Shipping and Gold Jewelry—lie on a line that is curved or bowed to the left. Although not shown here, if the correlation were less than zero, the line would curve more to the left. If the correlation were greater than zero, it would not curve quite as much to the left. The important point of this figure is that as long as the correlation is less than $+1$ and greater than -1, the line representing the set of portfolios consisting of various combinations of the two securities will have some degree of curvature to the left. Furthermore, the northwest portion will be concave.

Although the previous example used two individual securities, Ark Shipping and Gold Jewelry, and considered all possible portfolios that could be formed by combining them, it is important to recognize that the same principle holds if two portfolios are combined into a third portfolio. That is,

FIGURE 7–6
Portfolios formed by combining securities A and G.

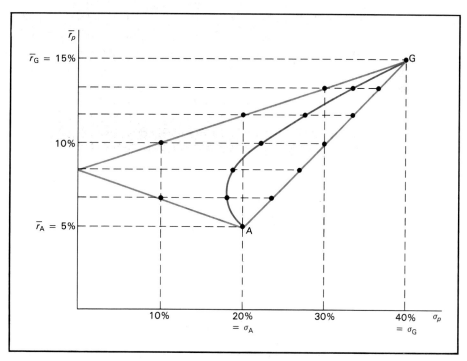

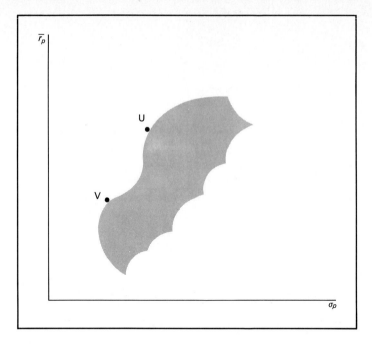

FIGURE 7–7
Concavity of the efficient set.

point A in Figure 7.6 could represent a portfolio of securities with an expected return of 5% and a standard deviation of 20%, and point G could represent another portfolio of securities with an expected return of 15% and a standard deviation of 40%. Combining these two portfolios will result in a third portfolio that has an expected return and standard deviation dependent upon the proportion invested in A and G. Assuming the correlation between A and G is zero, the location of the third portfolio will lie on the curved line connecting A and G.

Recognizing this, it can now be shown why the efficient set is concave.[4] One way to do this is to show that it cannot have any other shape. Consider the efficient set shown in Figure 7.7. Note that there is a "dent" in it between points U and V. That is, there is a region on it where it is not concave. This cannot be a truly efficient set, since an investor could put part of his or her funds in the portfolio located at U and the rest of his or her funds in the portfolio located at V. The resulting portfolio, a combination of U and V, would have to lie to the left of the alleged efficient set. Thus, the new portfolio would be "more efficient" than a portfolio with the same expected return that was on the alleged efficient set between U and V.

For example, consider the portfolio on the alleged efficient set that lies halfway between U and V; it is indicated as point W in Figure 7.8. If it truly

---

[4] This "curvature property" can also be used to explain why the right-hand side of the feasible set has the umbrella shape noted in Figure 7.1.

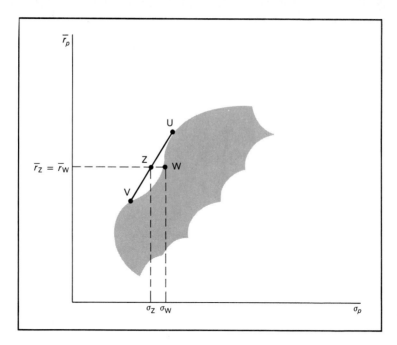

FIGURE 7–8
Removing a "dent" from the efficient set.

is an efficient portfolio, then it would be impossible to form a portfolio with the same expected return as W but with a lower standard deviation. However, by putting 50% of his or her funds in U and 50% in V, the investor would have a portfolio that dominates W, since it would have the same expected return but a lower standard deviation. This lower standard deviation can be explained as follows: If the correlation between U and V were $+1$, this portfolio would lie on the straight line connecting U and V and would thus have a lower standard deviation than W. In Figure 7.8, Z denotes this point. Since the actual correlation is less than $+1$, it would have a standard deviation even lower than Z's standard deviation. This means that the alleged efficient set was constructed in error, since it is easy to find "more efficient" portfolios in the region where it is not concave.

With the Markowitz approach, it is assumed that the assets being considered for investment are individually risky. That is, each one of the N risky assets has an uncertain return over the investor's holding period. Since none of the assets has a perfectly negative correlation with any other asset, all the portfolios also have uncertain returns over the investor's holding period and thus are risky. Furthermore, with the Markowitz approach the investor is not allowed to use borrowed money along with his or her initial wealth to purchase a portfolio of assets. This means that the investor is not allowed to use financial leverage, which in Chapter 2 was referred to as margin.

Next, the Markowitz approach to investing is expanded by first allowing

the investor to consider investing in not only risky assets but also in a risk-free asset. That is, there will now be N assets available for purchase, consisting of $N - 1$ risky assets and one risk-free asset. Second, the investor will be allowed to borrow money but will have to pay a given rate of interest on the loan.[5] The next section considers the effect of adding a risk-free asset to the set of risky assets.

7.3 ALLOWING FOR RISK-FREE INVESTING

□ 7.3.1 Defining the Risk-free Asset

What exactly is a *risk-free asset* in the context of Markowitz's approach? Since this approach involves investing for a single holding period, it means that the return on the risk-free asset is certain. That is, if the investor purchases this asset at the beginning of the holding period, then he or she knows exactly what the value of the asset will be at the end of the holding period. Since there is no uncertainty about the terminal value of the risk-free asset, the standard deviation of the risk-free asset is, by definition, zero.

In turn, this means that the covariance between the rate of return on the risk-free asset and the rate of return on any risky asset is zero. This can be seen by remembering that the covariance between the returns on any two assets i and j is equal to the product of the correlation coefficient between the assets and the standard deviations of the two assets: $\sigma_{ij} = \rho_{ij}\sigma_i\sigma_j$. Given that $\sigma_i = 0$ if i is the risk-free asset, it follows that $\sigma_{ij} = 0$.

Since a risk-free asset has, by definition, a certain return, this type of asset must be some kind of fixed-income security with no possibility of default. Since all corporate securities have some chance of default, the risk-free asset cannot be issued by a corporation. Instead, it must be a security issued by the federal government. However, not just any security issued by the U.S. Treasury qualifies as a risk-free security.

Consider an investor with a three-month holding period who purchases a Treasury security maturing in 20 years. Such a security is risky, since the investor does not know what this security will be worth at the end of his or her holding period. That is, interest rates very likely will have changed in an unpredictable manner during the investor's holding period, meaning that the market price of the security will have changed in an unpredictable manner. Since the presence of such *interest-rate risk* makes the value of the Treasury security uncertain, it cannot qualify as a risk-free asset. Indeed, any Treasury security with a maturity date greater than the investor's holding period cannot qualify as a risk-free asset, regardless of whether it matures one day or $19\frac{3}{4}$ years after the end of the investor's holding period.

Next, consider a Treasury security that matures before the end of the investor's holding period, such as a 30-day Treasury bill in the case of an

---

[5] Credit for extending Markowitz's model to include risk-free borrowing and investing belongs to James Tobin in "Liquidity Preference as Behavior Towards Risk," *Review of Economic Studies* 26, no. 1 (February 1958):65–86; and "The Theory of Portfolio Selection," in *The Theory of Interest Rates*, ed. F. H. Hahn and F. P. R. Brechling (London: Macmillan, 1965).

investor with the three-month holding period. In this situation, the investor does not know at the beginning of the holding period what interest rates will be in 30 days. This means that the investor does not know the interest rate at which the proceeds from the maturing Treasury bill can be reinvested (that is, "rolled over") for the remainder of the holding period. The presence of such *reinvestment-rate risk* in all Treasury securities of shorter maturity than the investor's holding period means that these securities do not qualify as a risk-free asset.

This leaves only one type of Treasury security to qualify as a risk-free asset—a Treasury security with a maturity that matches the length of the investor's holding period. For example, the investor with the three-month holding period would find that a Treasury bill with a three-month maturity date had a certain return. Since this security matures at the end of the investor's holding period, it provides the investor with an amount of money at the end of the holding period that is known for certain at the beginning of the holding period when an investment decision has to be made.[6]

Investing in the risk-free asset is often referred to as *risk-free lending*, since such an investment involves the purchase of Treasury bills, and thus involves a loan by the investor to the federal government.

With the introduction of a risk-free asset, the investor is now able to put part of his or her money in this asset and the remainder in any of the risky portfolios that are in Markowitz's feasible set. Adding these new opportunities expands the feasible set significantly and, more importantly, changes the location of part of Markowitz's efficient set. The nature of these changes needs to be analyzed, since investors are concerned with selecting a portfolio from the efficient set. In doing so, consideration is given initially to determining the expected return and standard deviation for a portfolio that consists of combining an investment in the risk-free asset with an investment in a single risky security.

☐ 7.3.2 **Investing in Both the Risk-free Asset and a Risky Asset**

In Chapter 6, the companies of Able, Baker, and Charlie were assumed to have expected returns, variances, and covariances as indicated in the following expected return vector and variance-covariance matrix:

$$ ER = \begin{bmatrix} 16.2 \\ 24.6 \\ 22.8 \end{bmatrix} \qquad VC = \begin{bmatrix} 146 & 187 & 145 \\ 187 & 854 & 104 \\ 145 & 104 & 289 \end{bmatrix}. $$

Defining the risk-free asset as security number 4, consider all portfolios that involve investing in both the common stock of Able and the risk-free asset.

---

[6] To be truly risk-free, the security must not provide the investor with any coupon payments during the holding period. Instead, it must provide the investor with only one cash inflow, and that inflow must occur at the end of the investor's holding period. Any intervening coupon payments would subject the investor to reinvestment-rate risk, since he or she would not know the rate at which the coupon payments could be invested for the remainder of the holding period. It should also be noted that the discussion has focused on an asset that is risk-free in nominal terms, since the presence of inflation means that virtually all Treasury securities are risky in real terms.

Let X_1 denote the proportion of the investor's funds invested in Able, and $X_4 = 1 - X_1$ denote the proportion invested in the risk-free asset. If the investor put all his or her money in the risk-free asset, then $X_1 = 0$ and $X_4 = 1$. Alternatively, the investor could put all his or her money in just Able, in which case $X_1 = 1$ and $X_4 = 0$. A combination of .25 in Able and .75 in the risk-free asset is also possible, as are respective combinations of .50 and .50, and .75 and .25. Although there are other possibilities, the focus here will be on these five portfolios:

	PORTFOLIO A	PORTFOLIO B	PORTFOLIO C	PORTFOLIO D	PORTFOLIO E
X_1	.00	.25	.50	.75	1.00
X_4	1.00	.75	.50	.25	.00

Assuming that the risk-free asset has a rate of return (often denoted by r_f) of 4%, all the necessary information for calculating the expected returns and standard deviations for these five portfolios is at hand. Equation (6.3a) can be used to calculate the expected returns for these portfolios:

$$\bar{r}_P = \sum_{i=1}^{N} X_i \bar{r}_i$$

(6.3a)

$$= \sum_{i=1}^{4} X_i \bar{r}_i.$$

Now, portfolios A, B, C, D, and E do not involve investing in the second and third securities (that is, Baker and Charlie companies), meaning that $X_2 = 0$ and $X_3 = 0$ in these portfolios. Thus, the previous equation reduces to:

$$\bar{r}_p = X_1 \bar{r}_1 + X_4 \bar{r}_4$$

$$= (X_1 \times 16.2\%) + (X_4 \times 4\%)$$

where the risk-free rate is now denoted $\bar{r}_4$.

For portfolios A and E this calculation is trivial, since all the investor's funds are being placed in just one security. Thus, their expected returns are just 4% and 16.2%, respectively. For portfolios B, C, and D, the expected returns are, respectively,

$$\bar{r}_B = (.25 \times 16.2\%) + (.75 \times 4\%)$$

$$= 7.05\%$$

$$\bar{r}_C = (.50 \times 16.2\%) + (.50 \times 4\%)$$

$$= 10.10\%$$

$$\bar{r}_D = (.75 \times 16.2\%) + (.25 \times 4\%)$$

$$= 13.15\%.$$

The standard deviations of portfolios A and E are simply the standard deviations of the risk-free asset and Able, respectively. Thus, $\sigma_A = .00$ and

$\sigma_E = 12.08\%$. In calculating the standard deviations of portfolios B, C, and D, equation (6.7) must be utilized:

$$\sigma_p = \left[\sum_{i=1}^{N} \sum_{j=1}^{N} X_i X_j \sigma_{ij} \right]^{1/2}$$

$$= \left[\sum_{i=1}^{4} \sum_{j=1}^{4} X_i X_j \sigma_{ij} \right]^{1/2}$$

(6.7)

Remembering that $X_2 = 0$ and $X_3 = 0$ in these portfolios, this equation reduces to

$$\sigma_p = [X_1 X_1 \sigma_{11} + X_1 X_4 \sigma_{14} + X_4 X_1 \sigma_{41} + X_4 X_4 \sigma_{44}]^{1/2}$$

$$= [X_1^2 \sigma_1^2 + X_4^2 \sigma_4^2 + 2 X_1 X_4 \sigma_{14}]^{1/2}.$$

This equation can be reduced even further, since security 4 is the risk-free security that, by definition, has $\sigma_4 = 0$ and $\sigma_{14} = 0$. Accordingly, it reduces to:

$$\sigma_p = [X_1^2 \sigma_1^2]^{1/2}$$

$$= [X_1^2 \times 146]^{1/2}$$

$$= X_1 \times 12.08\%.$$

Thus, the standard deviations of portfolios B, C, and D are:

$$\sigma_B = .25 \times 12.08\%$$

$$= 3.02\%$$

$$\sigma_C = .50 \times 12.08\%$$

$$= 6.04\%$$

$$\sigma_D = .75 \times 12.08\%$$

$$= 9.06\%$$

In summary, the five portfolios have the following expected returns and standard deviations:

PORTFOLIO	X_1	X_4	EXPECTED RETURN	STANDARD DEVIATION
A	.00	1.00	4.00%	0.00%
B	.25	.75	7.05	3.02
C	.50	.50	10.10	6.04
D	.75	.25	13.15	9.06
E	1.00	.00	16.20	12.08

These portfolios are plotted in Figure 7.9. In this figure, it can be seen that the portfolios lie on a straight line connecting the points representing the location of the risk-free asset and Able. Although only five particular combinations of the risk-free asset and Able have been examined here, it can

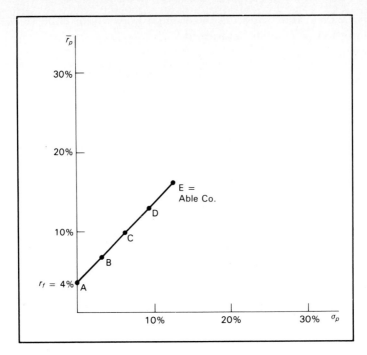

FIGURE 7–9
Combining risk-free investing with investing in a risky asset.

be shown that any combination of the risk-free asset and Able will lie somewhere on the straight line connecting them; the exact location will depend on the relative proportions invested in these two assets. Furthermore, this observation can be generalized to combinations of the risk-free asset and any risky asset. That is, any portfolio that consists of a combination of the risk-free asset and a risky asset will have an expected return and standard deviation such that it plots on a straight line connecting them.

☐ **7.3.3 Investing in Both the Risk-free Asset and a Risky Portfolio**

Next, consider what happens when a portfolio consisting of more than just one risky security is combined with the risk-free asset. For example, consider the risky portfolio that consists of Able and Charlie in proportions of .80 and .20, respectively. Its expected return (denoted by $\bar{r}_{PAC}$) and standard deviation (denoted by σ_{PAC}) are equal to:

$$\bar{r}_{PAC} = (.80 \times 16.2\%) + (.20 \times 22.8\%)$$

$$= 17.52\%$$

$$\sigma_{PAC} = [(.80 \times .80 \times 146) + (.20 \times .20 \times 289) + (2 \times .80 \times .20 \times 145)]^{1/2}$$

$$= 12.30\%.$$

Any portfolio that consists of an investment in both *PAC* and the risk-free asset will have an expected return and standard deviation that can be calculated in a manner identical to what was previously shown for combinations of an individual asset and the risk-free asset. That is, a portfolio that has the proportion X_{PAC} invested in the portfolio *PAC*, and the proportion $X_4 = 1 - X_{PAC}$ in the risk-free asset will have an expected return and standard deviation that are equal to, respectively,

$$\bar{r}_p = (X_{PAC} \times 17.52\%) + (X_4 \times 4\%)$$

$$\sigma_p = X_{PAC} \times 12.30\%.$$

For example, consider investing in a portfolio that consists of *PAC* and the risk-free asset in proportions of .25 and .75, respectively.[7] This portfolio will have an expected return of

$$\bar{r}_p = (.25 \times 17.52\%) + (.75 \times 4\%)$$

$$= 7.38\%$$

and a standard deviation of

$$\sigma_p = (.25 \times 12.30\%)$$

$$= 3.08\%.$$

Figure 7.10 shows that this portfolio lies on a straight line connecting the risk-free asset and *PAC*. In particular, it is indicated by the point *P* on this line. Other portfolios consisting of various combinations of *PAC* and the risk-free asset will also lie on this line, with their exact locations depending on the relative proportions invested in *PAC* and the risk-free asset. For example, a portfolio that involves investing a proportion of .50 in the risk-free asset and a proportion of .50 in *PAC* lies on this line exactly halfway between the two end points.

In summary, combining the risk-free asset with any risky portfolio can be viewed as being no different from combining the risk-free asset with an individual risky security. In both cases, the resulting portfolio has an expected return and standard deviation such that it lies on a straight line connecting the two endpoints.

☐ 7.3.4   The Effect of Risk-free Investing on the Efficient Set

As mentioned earlier, the feasible set is changed significantly as a result of the introduction of risk-free investing. Figure 7.11 shows how it changes the feasible set for the example at hand. Here, all risky assets and portfolios, not just Able and *PAC*, are considered in all possible combinations with the risk-free asset. In particular, note that there are two boundaries that are straight lines emanating from the risk-free asset. The bottom line connects

---

[7] Note that investing the proportion .25 in portfolio *PAC* is equivalent to investing the proportion .20 (.25 × .80) in Able and the proportion .05 (.25 × .20) in Charlie.

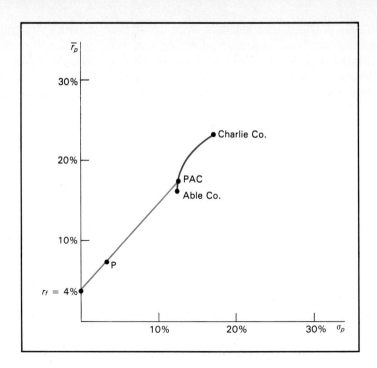

FIGURE 7–10
Combining risk-free investing with investing in a risky portfolio.

FIGURE 7–11
Feasible and efficient sets when risk-free investing is introduced.

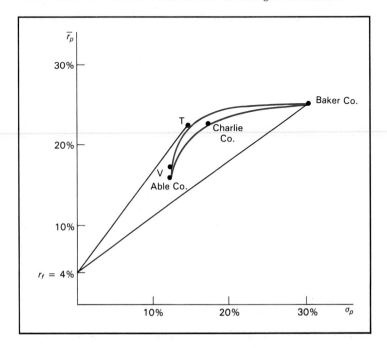

the risk-free asset with Baker. Thus, it represents portfolios formed by combining Baker and the risk-free asset.

The other straight line emanating from the risk-free asset represents combinations of the risk-free asset and a particular risky portfolio on the efficient set of the Markowitz model. It is a line that is just tangent to the efficient set of the Markowitz model, with the tangency point being denoted by T. This tangency point represents a risky portfolio consisting of Able, Baker, and Charlie in proportions equal to, respectively, .12, .19, and .69.[8] Substituting these proportions into equations (6.3a) and (6.7) indicates that the expected return and standard deviation of T are 22.4% and 15.2%, respectively.

Whereas other risky efficient portfolios from the Markowitz model can also be combined with the risk-free asset, portfolio T deserves special attention because there is no other portfolio consisting purely of risky assets that, when connected by a straight line to the risk-free asset, lies northwest of it. In other words, of all the lines that can be drawn emanating from the risk-free asset and connecting with either a risky asset or risky portfolio, none has a greater slope than the line that goes to T.

This is important, since part of the efficient set of the Markowitz model is dominated by this line. In particular, the portfolios on the Markowitz model efficient set going from the minimum risk portfolio, denoted by V, to T are no longer efficient when a risk-free asset is made available for investment. Instead, the efficient set now consists of a straight-line segment and a curved segment. The straight-line segment is the straight line going from the risk-free asset to T and thus consists of portfolios made up of various combinations of the risk-free asset and T. The curved segment consists of those portfolios to the northwest of T on the Markowitz model efficient set.

□ 7.3.5 The Effect of Risk-free Investing on Portfolio Selection

Figure 7.12 shows how an investor would go about selecting an optimal efficient portfolio when there is a risk-free asset available for investment in addition to a number of risky assets. If the investor's indifference curves look like those shown in panel (a), then the investor's optimal portfolio O^* will involve investing part of his or her initial wealth in the risk-free asset and the rest in T because O^* lies on the straight-line segment of the efficient set.[9] Alternatively, if the investor is less risk-averse and has indifference curves that look like those shown in part (b), then the investor's optimal portfolio O^* will not involve any risk-free investing because O^* lies on the curved segment of the efficient set that lies to the northeast of T.

---

[8] Just how these weights are determined is shown in Appendix A.

[9] A more risk-averse investor (meaning an investor whose indifference curves have greater slopes) would choose an optimal portfolio that is closer to the risk-free asset on the line that connects the risk-free asset to T. Ultimately, if the investor is infinitely risk-averse, the optimal portfolio will consist of an investment in just the risk-free asset.

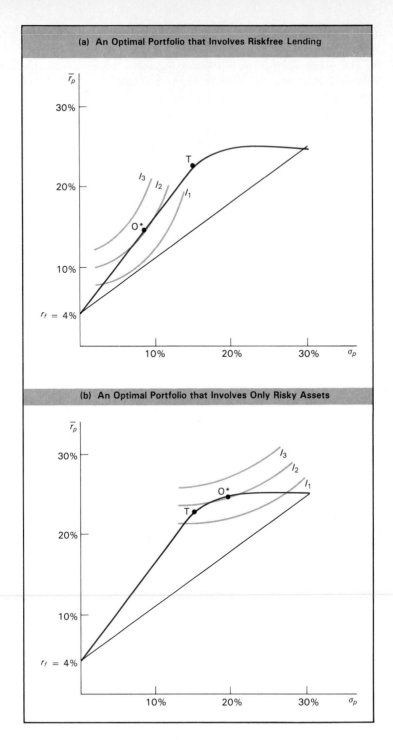

FIGURE 7–12
Portfolio selection with risk-free investing.

7.4 ALLOWING FOR RISK-FREE BORROWING

The analysis presented in the previous section can be expanded by allowing the investor to borrow money. This means that the investor is no longer restricted to his or her initial wealth when it comes time to decide how much money to invest in risky assets.[10] However, if the investor borrows money, then interest must be paid on the loan. Since the interest rate is known and there is no uncertainty about repaying the loan, it is often referred to as *risk-free borrowing*.

It will be assumed that the rate of interest charged on the loan is equal to the rate of interest that could be earned from investing in the risk-free asset.[11] Using the earlier example, this means that the investor now not only has the opportunity to invest in a risk-free asset that earns a rate of return of 4% but also may borrow money, for which the investor must pay a rate of interest equal to 4%.

The effect that the introduction of risk-free borrowing has on the location and shape of the efficient set is as significant as the effect that the introduction of risk-free investing had on it. However, it should be recognized that no investor would want simultaneously to invest in the risk-free asset and incur risk-free borrowing. Doing so would mean that the investor was engaged in two activities when an identical position could have been established with only one activity.

For example, an investor who is considering investing $5000 in the risk-free asset in order to earn 4% while at the same time paying interest at a rate of 4% in order to borrow $9300 could equivalent simply borrow $4300 = $9300 − $5000. Accordingly, the investor can be allowed to invest or borrow at the risk-free rate, but not do both, without any loss of generality in the analysis.

Earlier, the proportion invested in the risk-free asset was denoted by X_4, and this proportion was constrained to be a nonnegative number between 0 and 1. Now, with the opportunity to borrow at the same rate, X_4 will no longer be so constrained. In the earlier example, the investor had initial wealth of $17,200. If the investor borrows money, then he or she will have in excess of $17,200 to invest in the risky securities of Able, Baker, and Charlie.

For example, if the investor borrows $4300, then he or she will have a total of $17,200 + $4300 = $21,500 to invest in these securities. In this situation, X_4 can be viewed as being equal to −$4,300/$17,200 = −.25. However, the sum of the proportions must still equal 1. This means that if the investor has borrowed money, the sum of the proportions invested in risky assets would be greater than 1. For example, borrowing $4300 and

---

[10] Allowing for borrowing can be viewed as giving the investor the opportunity to engage in margin purchases if he or she so desires. That is, with borrowing the investor is allowed to use financial leverage.

[11] Appendix B discusses what happens to the efficient set when the investor is able to borrow but at a rate that is greater than the rate that can be earned by investing in the risk-free asset. Other models based on a variety of different assumptions are presented in Chapter 4 of *Portfolio Analysis* by Gordon J. Alexander and Jack Clark Francis (Englewood Cliffs, N.J.: Prentice Hall, 1986).

investing \$21,500 in Able means that the proportion in Able, X_1, is \$21,500/ \$17,200 = 1.25. Note how in this case $X_1 + X_4 = 1.25 + (-.25) = 1$.

☐ 7.4.1 Borrowing and Investing in a Risky Security

In order to evaluate the effect that the introduction of risk-free borrowing has on the efficient set, the example presented in the previous section will be expanded. In particular, consider portfolios F, G, H, and I, where the investor borrows a proportion of his or her initial wealth equal to .25, .50, .75, and 1.00, respectively. In all four portfolios, the investor will invest all the borrowed funds as well as his or her own funds in Able. Thus, the proportions for these portfolios can be summarized as follows:

	PORTFOLIO F	PORTFOLIO G	PORTFOLIO H	PORTFOLIO I
X_1	1.25	1.50	1.75	2.00
X_4	-.25	-.50	-.75	-1.00

The expected returns of these portfolios are calculated in the same manner shown in the previous section. That is, equation (6.3a) is still used:

$$\bar{r}_p = \sum_{i=1}^{N} X_i \bar{r}_i \qquad \text{(6.3a)}$$

$$= \sum_{i=1}^{4} X_i \bar{r}_i$$

$$= X_1 \bar{r}_1 + X_4 \bar{r}_4$$

$$= (X_1 \times 16.2\%) + (X_4 \times 4\%).$$

Thus, portfolios F, G, H, and I have the following expected returns:

$$\bar{r}_F = (1.25 \times 16.2\%) + (-.25 \times 4\%)$$
$$= 19.25\%$$

$$\bar{r}_G = (1.50 \times 16.2\%) + (-.50 \times 4\%)$$
$$= 22.30\%$$

$$\bar{r}_H = (1.75 \times 16.2\%) + (-.75 \times 4\%)$$
$$= 25.35\%$$

$$\bar{r}_I = (2.00 \times 16.2\%) + (-1.00 \times 4\%)$$
$$= 28.40\%.$$

Similarly, the standard deviations of these portfolios are calculated by using equation (6.7), as in the previous section:

$$\sigma_p = \left[\sum_{i=1}^{N} \sum_{j=1}^{N} X_i X_j \sigma_{ij} \right]^{1/2}$$

$$= \left[\sum_{i=1}^{4} \sum_{j=1}^{4} X_i X_j \sigma_{ij} \right]^{1/2}$$

(6.7)

which was shown to reduce to

$$\sigma_p = X_1 \times 12.08\%.$$

Thus, the standard deviations of the four portfolios are

$$\sigma_F = 1.25 \times 12.08\%$$

$$= 15.10\%$$

$$\sigma_G = 1.50 \times 12.08\%$$

$$= 18.12\%$$

$$\sigma_H = 1.75 \times 12.08\%$$

$$= 21.14\%$$

$$\sigma_I = 2.00 \times 12.08\%$$

$$= 24.16\%.$$

In summary, these four portfolios, as well as the five portfolios that involve risk-free investing, have the following expected returns and standard deviations:

PORTFOLIO	X_1	X_4	EXPECTED RETURN	STANDARD DEVIATION
A	.00	1.00	4.00%	0.00%
B	.25	.75	7.05	3.02
C	.50	.50	10.10	6.04
D	.75	.25	13.15	9.06
E	1.00	.00	16.20	12.08
F	1.25	− .25	19.25	15.10
G	1.50	− .50	22.30	18.12
H	1.75	− .75	25.35	21.14
I	2.00	− 1.00	28.40	24.16

In Figure 7.13, it can be seen that the four portfolios that involve risk-free borrowing (F, G, H, and I) all lie in the same straight line that goes through the five portfolios that involve risk-free investing (A, B, C, D, and E). Furthermore, the larger the amount of borrowing, the further out on the line the portfolio lies (equivalently, the smaller the value of X_4, the further out on the line the portfolio lies).

While only four particular combinations of borrowing and investing in Able have been examined here, it can be shown any combination of borrowing and investing in Able will lie somewhere on this line, with the exact location depending on the amount of borrowing. Furthermore, this observation can be generalized to combinations of risk-free borrowing and an investment in

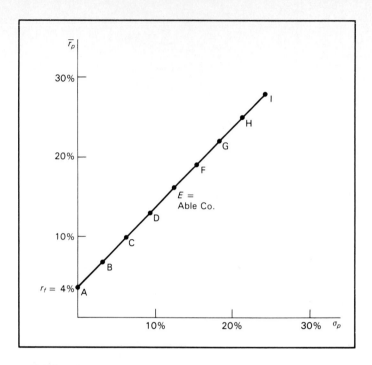

FIGURE 7–13
Combining risk-free borrowing and investing with investing in a risky asset.

any particular risky asset. That is, borrowing at the risk-free rate and investing all the borrowed money and the investor's own money in a risky asset results in a portfolio that has an expected return and standard deviation that lie on the extension of the straight line connecting the risk-free rate and the risky asset.

□ 7.4.2 Borrowing and Investing in a Risky Portfolio

Next, consider what happens when a portfolio of more than one risky asset is purchased with both the investor's own funds and borrowed funds. Earlier it was shown that the portfolio having proportions invested in Able and Charlie equal to .80 and .20, respectively, had an expected return of 17.52% and a standard deviation of 12.30%. This portfolio was referred to as *PAC*. Any portfolio that involves borrowing money at the risk-free rate and then investing these funds and the investor's own funds in *PAC* will have an expected return and standard deviation that can be calculated in a manner identical to the one previously shown when borrowing was incurred and Able was purchased. That is, a portfolio that involves borrowing the proportion X_4 and investing these funds and all the investor's own funds in *PAC* will

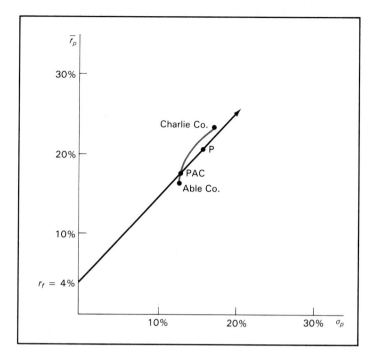

FIGURE 7–14
Combining risk-free borrowing and investing with investing in a
risky portfolio.

have an expected return and standard deviation that are equal to, respectively,

$$\bar{r}_p = (X_{PAC} \times 17.52\%) + (X_4 \times 4\%)$$

$$\sigma_p = X_{PAC} \times 12.30\%.$$

For example, consider borrowing an amount of money equal to 25% of the investor's initial wealth and then investing all the investor's own funds and these borrowed funds in *PAC*. Thus, $X_{PAC} = 1 - X_4 = 1 - (-.25) = 1.25$.[12] This portfolio will have an expected return of

$$\bar{r}_p = (1.25 \times 17.52\%) + (-.25 \times 4\%)$$

$$= 20.90\%$$

and a standard deviation of

$$\sigma_p = (1.25 \times 12.30\%)$$

$$= 15.38\%.$$

In Figure 7.14, it can be seen that this portfolio (denoted by P) lies on the extension of the line that connects the risk-free rate with *PAC*. Other port-

---

[12] Note that investing the proportion 1.25 in portfolio *PAC* is equivalent to investing the proportion 1.00 (1.25 × .80) in Able and the proportion .25 (1.25 × .20) in Charlie.

folios consisting of *PAC* and borrowing at the risk-free rate will also lie on this extension, with their exact locations depending on the amount of the borrowing. Thus, borrowing in order to purchase a risky portfolio is no different than borrowing in order to purchase an individual risky asset. In both cases, the resulting portfolio lies on an extension of the line connecting the risk-free rate with the risky investment.

7.5 ALLOWING FOR BOTH RISK-FREE INVESTING AND BORROWING

☐ 7.5.1 The Effect of Risk-free Investing and Borrowing on the Efficient Set

Figure 7.15 shows how the feasible set is changed when both risk-free investing and borrowing at the risk-free rate are allowed. Here, all risky assets and portfolios, not just Able and *PAC*, are considered. The feasible set is the entire area between the two lines emanating from the risk-free rate that go through the location of Baker and the portfolio denoted by *T*. These two lines extend indefinitely to the right if it is assumed that there is no limit to the amount of borrowing that the investor can incur.

The straight line that goes through the portfolio *T* is of special impor-

FIGURE 7–15
Feasible and efficient sets when risk-free borrowing and investing are introduced.

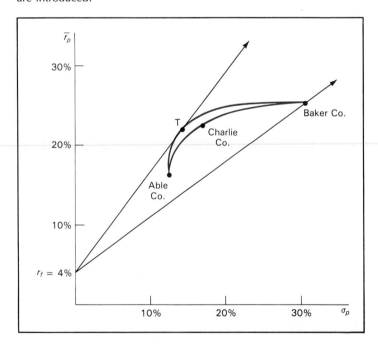

tance, since it represents the efficient set. That is, it represents the set of portfolios that offer the investor the best opportunities, since it represents the set of feasible portfolios lying furthest northwest. Portfolio T, as was mentioned earlier, consists of investments in Able, Baker, and Charlie in proportions of .12, .19, and .69, respectively.

As before, the line going through T is just tangent to the Markowitz model efficient set. None of the portfolios, except for T, that were on the Markowitz model efficient set are efficient when risk-free investing and borrowing are introduced. This can be seen by noting that every portfolio (except T) that lies on the Markowitz model efficient set is dominated by a portfolio on this straight line having the same standard deviation along with a higher expected return.

☐ 7.5.2 The Effect of Risk-free Investing and Borrowing on Portfolio Selection

Given the opportunity to either invest or borrow at the risk-free rate, an investor would identify the optimal portfolio by plotting his or her indifference curves on this graph and noting where one of them is tangent to the linear efficient set. Figure 7.16 shows two alternative situations. If the investor's indifference curves look like the ones in panel (a), then the investor's optimal portfolio $O*$ will consist of an investment in the risk-free asset as well as in T. Alternatively, if the investor is less risk-averse and has indifference curves that look like those in part (b), then the investor's optimal portfolio $O*$ will consist of borrowing at the risk-free rate and investing these funds as well as his or her own funds in T.[13]

7.6 SUMMARY

At this point, the essentials of the Markowitz approach to investing have been presented. There are four stages to this approach. In the first stage the investor, seeking the optimal portfolio to purchase, begins by specifying a set of securities for consideration.

In the second stage, analysis of the prospects of these securities, traditionally known as security analysis, is conducted. This means that the expected returns, variances, and covariances must be estimated for all the securities being considered.

In the third stage, the efficient set is determined. This involves using the previously estimated expected returns, variances, and covariances to determine the composition and location of the efficient portfolios that form the efficient set. If only risky securities are being considered for possible investment, the efficient set will be a curved line that is upward sloping and concave. With the addition of risk-free opportunities, the efficient set becomes

---

[13] The less risk-averse the investor is, the smaller the proportion in the risk-free rate (X_f) and the larger the proportion in T (X_T).

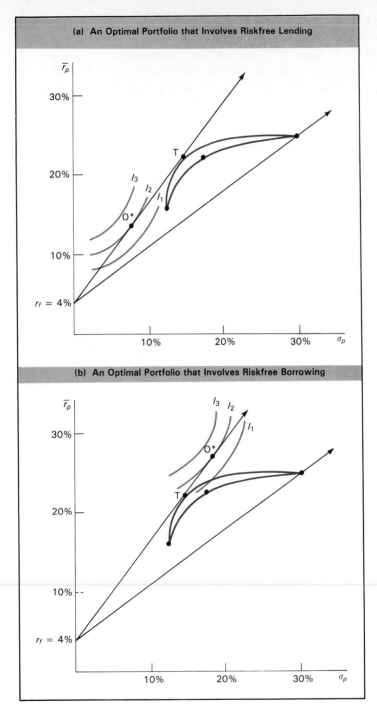

FIGURE 7–16
Portfolio selection with risk-free borrowing and investing.

a straight line lying to the northwest of the previous curved efficient set. All the portfolios on this straight line involve combining one portfolio consisting of just risky assets with either risk-free investing or risk-free borrowing. Indeed, this portfolio consisting of just risky assets is the only portfolio that the curved efficient set and the straight-line efficient set have in common.

The fourth and final stage is to identify the investor's optimal portfolio. This involves noting the portfolio corresponding to the point where one of the investor's indifference curves is tangent to the efficient set.

In implementing the Markowitz approach, these four stages of portfolio selection may be performed by different people. One or more security analysts may be responsible for stage 2, a portfolio manager for stage 3, and an investment counselor (or adviser), plus the investor, for stages 1 and 4.[14] Some investors may perform some (or all) of these functions themselves. Even in organizations with large staffs, there may be some overlap in functions. In summary, it is important to recognize that conceptually different functions are involved and that rather different skills may be required for successful performance at each stage.

Chapter 8 utilizes the model presented here but involves a significant change in focus. So far, the discussion has focused on what economists would call a normative model for investing. That is, a prescriptive model, in which people are told how they should make their investment decisions, has been presented. The realm of positive economics is entered next, wherein the implications that arise if everyone follows this approach to investing is examined. In this examination, it is seen that a descriptive model of how assets are priced can be derived. Logically, this model has been referred to as the capital asset pricing model.

APPENDIX A
DETERMINING THE INVESTOR'S OPTIMAL PORTFOLIO

If the investor is to consider all possible efficient portfolios that can be formed from N securities, there needs to be some way to determine the composition (that is, the security weights) of each one of these portfolios. After this is done, the expected returns and standard deviations of these efficient portfolios can be calculated and then the efficient set can be located on a graph. At this point, the investor can proceed to select the optimal portfolio by plotting his or her indifference curves and note which efficient portfolio corresponds to the tangency point. This appendix describes some of the principles involved in determining the composition of the investor's optimal portfolio. It begins with the curved efficient set of Markowitz.

---

[14] Regarding stage 4, in some situations, a professional adviser could present the investor with at least a rough assessment of the risk-return trade-offs depicted on the efficient set and then ask the investor to choose a preferred portfolio. In other situations, the adviser could attempt to assess the investor's circumstances and attitudes and then make the choice for the investor. In yet other situations, a money-management organization could describe a set of risk-return attitudes that it plans to assume in its management of a portfolio and then invite those individuals with similar attitudes to purchase shares that represent partial ownership of the portfolio.

A.1 THE MARKOWITZ MODEL

☐ A.1.1 Determining the Composition and Location of the Efficient Set

Previously, it was noted that there are an infinite number of possible portfolios available to the investor, but that the investor needs to be concerned with only those portfolios that are on the efficient set. However, Markowitz's efficient set is a curved line, which means that there are an infinite number of points along it. This, in turn, means that there are an infinite number of efficient portfolios! How can Markowitz's approach be used if an investor needs to identify the composition of each one of an infinite number of portfolios? Fortunately, there is no need to despair. Markowitz saw this potential problem and, in a major contribution, presented a method for solving it.[15] It involves the use of a quadratic programming algorithm known as the *critical-line method*.

Although the algorithm is beyond the scope of this book, it is important to recognize what it does. To begin with, the investor must estimate the expected return vector and variance-covariance matrix. For example, consider the three-security example presented earlier in the chapter.[16] The expected return vector, denoted by ER, and the variance-covariance matrix, denoted by VC, were estimated to be

$$ER = \begin{bmatrix} 16.2 \\ 24.6 \\ 22.8 \end{bmatrix} \qquad VC = \begin{bmatrix} 146 & 187 & 145 \\ 187 & 854 & 104 \\ 145 & 104 & 289 \end{bmatrix}.$$

The algorithm then identifies a number of *corner portfolios* that are associated with these securities and completely describe the efficient set. A corner portfolio is an efficient portfolio with the following property: Any combination of two adjacent corner portfolios will result in a portfolio that lies on the efficient set between the two corner portfolios. Just what this means is illustrated in the example.

The algorithm begins by identifying the portfolio with the highest expected return. This portfolio corresponds to point S in Figure 7.1 and is an efficient portfolio. It is composed of just one security—the security with the highest expected return. That is, if the investor wanted to purchase that portfolio, all he or she would have to do is to purchase shares of the company whose stock has the highest expected return. Any other portfolio would have a lower expected return, since at least part of the investor's funds would be placed in shares of other companies that have an expected return lower than S, thereby causing the portfolio to have an expected return lower than S.

In the example, the company whose shares have the highest expected return is the second one, Baker Company. The corresponding efficient port-

---

[15] See Harry Markowitz, "The Optimization of a Quadratic Function Subject to Linear Constraints," *Naval Research Logistics Quarterly* 3, nos. 1–2 (March–June 1956):111–33.

[16] This example is based on one from Markowitz's book entitled *Portfolio Selection* (New Haven, Conn.: Yale University Press, 1959), 176–85.

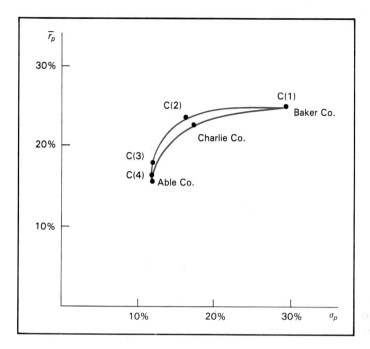

FIGURE 7–17
Corner portfolios.

folio is the first of several corner portfolios that the algorithm will identify. Its composition is given by the following weight vector, denoted by $X(1)$:

$$X(1) = \begin{bmatrix} .00 \\ 1.00 \\ .00 \end{bmatrix}.$$

Its expected return and standard deviation correspond to the expected return and standard deviation of Baker, which are equal to 24.6% and $(854)^{1/2} = 29.22\%$, respectively. In Figure 7.17, this corner portfolio is denoted by $C(1)$.

The algorithm then identifies the second corner portfolio. This portfolio is on the efficient set below the first corner portfolio and has a composition given by the following weight vector, denoted by $X(2)$:

$$X(2) = \begin{bmatrix} .00 \\ .22 \\ .78 \end{bmatrix}.$$

That is, the second corner portfolio is a portfolio where the investor puts 22% of his or her funds into Baker common stock and the remainder, 78%, into Charlie common stock. Applying these weights to equations (6.3a) and (6.7), the expected return and standard deviation of this corner portfolio can be calculated; they are equal to 23.20% and 15.90%, respectively. In Figure 7.17, this corner portfolio is denoted by $C(2)$.

What is important about the first and second corner portfolios is that

they are *adjacent* efficient portfolios, and any efficient portfolio lying on the efficient set between them has a composition that is just a combination of their compositions. For example, the efficient portfolio lying halfway between them has the following composition:

$$[.5 \times X(1)] + [.5 \times X(2)] = .5 \times \begin{bmatrix} .00 \\ 1.00 \\ .00 \end{bmatrix} + .5 \times \begin{bmatrix} .00 \\ .22 \\ .78 \end{bmatrix} = \begin{bmatrix} .00 \\ .61 \\ .39 \end{bmatrix}.$$

That is, the portfolio has weights of .61 in Baker stock and .39 in Charlie stock. Using equations (6.3a) and (6.7), the expected return and standard deviation of this portfolio turn out to be 23.9% and 20.28%, respectively.

Having identified the second corner portfolio, the algorithm then identifies the third one. Its composition is:

$$X(3) = \begin{bmatrix} .84 \\ .00 \\ .16 \end{bmatrix}.$$

These weights can now be used to calculate the expected return and standard deviation of this portfolio, which are 17.26% and 12.22%, respectively. As was noted for the previous two corner portfolios, this corner portfolio is an efficient portfolio and is denoted by $C(3)$ in Figure 7.17.

Since they are adjacent, combinations of the second and third corner portfolios result in efficient portfolios that lie on the efficient set between them. For example, if the investor puts 33% of his or her money in the second corner portfolio and 67% in the third corner portfolio, then the resulting efficient portfolio has the following composition:

$$[.33 \times X(2)] + [.67 \times X(3)] = .33 \times \begin{bmatrix} .00 \\ .22 \\ .78 \end{bmatrix} + .67 \times \begin{bmatrix} .84 \\ .00 \\ .16 \end{bmatrix} = \begin{bmatrix} .56 \\ .07 \\ .36 \end{bmatrix}.$$

Using equations (6.3a) and (6.7), this portfolio can be shown to have an expected return of 19.10% and a standard deviation of 12.88%.

Earlier it was mentioned that only combinations of *adjacent* corner portfolios will be efficient. This means that portfolios formed by combining *nonadjacent* corner portfolios will not lie on the efficient set. For example, the first and third corner portfolios are nonadjacent, which means that any portfolio formed by combining them will not be efficient. For example, if the investor put 50% of his or her funds in the first corner portfolio and 50% in the third corner portfolio, the resulting portfolio would have the following compositions:

$$[.5 \times X(1)] + [.5 \times X(3)] = .5 \times \begin{bmatrix} .00 \\ 1.00 \\ .00 \end{bmatrix} + .5 \times \begin{bmatrix} .84 \\ .00 \\ .16 \end{bmatrix} = \begin{bmatrix} .42 \\ .50 \\ .08 \end{bmatrix}.$$

With these weights, the expected return and standard deviation of this portfolio can be shown to be equal to 20.93% and 18.38%, respectively. However, this is an inefficient portfolio. Since its expected return (20.93%) lies between

TABLE 7.1

Corner Portfolios for a Three Security Example.

Corner Portfolio	WEIGHTS			CORNER PORTFOLIO	
	Able Co.	Baker Co.	Charlie Co.	Expected Return	Standard Deviation
C(1)	.00	1.00	.00	24.60%	29.22%
C(2)	.00	.22	.78	23.20	15.90
C(3)	.84	.00	.16	17.26	12.22
C(4)	.99	.00	.01	16.27	12.08

the expected return of the second (23.20%) and third (17.26%) corner portfolios, by combining these two adjacent corner portfolios the investor will be able to form an efficient portfolio that has the same expected return but lower standard deviation.[17]

Continuing, the algorithm now identifies the composition of the fourth corner portfolio:

$$X(4) = \begin{bmatrix} .99 \\ .00 \\ .01 \end{bmatrix}.$$

Its expected return and standard deviation can be calculated to be 16.27% and 12.08%, respectively. Having identified this portfolio as the one corresponding to point E in Figure 7.1 (and $C(4)$ in Figure 7.17), meaning it is the portfolio that has the least standard deviation of all feasible portfolios, the algorithm stops. The four corner portfolios, summarized in Table 7.1, completely describe the efficient set associated with the stocks of Able, Baker, and Charlie.

It is a simple matter for the computer, using its capability for graphics, now to draw the graph of the efficient set. Perhaps it will find the composition, and in turn the expected return and standard deviation, for each of 20 efficient portfolios that are evenly spaced between the first and second corner portfolios. Then it will "connect the dots," tracing a straight line between each of the twenty successive portfolios. This will give the graph the appearance of a curved line, as shown in Figure 7.17, since these portfolios are located close to each other. Proceeding in a similar fashion, 20 efficient portfolios between the second and third corner portfolios will be located and the corresponding segment of the efficient set traced. Then the same procedure will be followed for the region between the third and fourth corner portfolios, at which point the graph has been completely drawn.

---

[17] In this example, the efficient portfolio having an expected return of 20.93% can be determined by solving the following equation for Y: $(23.20\% \times Y) + [17.26\% \times (1 - Y)] = 20.93\%$. Since this is a linear equation with one unknown, it can easily be solved. The solution, $Y = .62$, indicates that by putting .62 of his or her funds in the second corner portfolio and .38 $(1.00 - .62)$ in the third corner portfolio, the investor will have an efficient portfolio with the same expected return but lower standard deviation (specifically, 14.09%) than the portfolio involving a 50-50 combination of the first and third corner portfolios.

□ A.1.2   Determining the Composition of the Optimal Portfolio

Once the location and composition of Markowitz's efficient set have been determined, the composition of the investor's optimal portfolio can be determined. This portfolio, indicated by O^* in Figure 7.2, corresponds to the tangency point between the efficient set and one of the investor's indifference curves. The procedure for determining its composition starts by the investor noting graphically the level of its expected return. That is, from the graph the investor can note where O^* is located and then calibrate its expected return simply by using a ruler and extending a line from it to the vertical axis (with computers, more precise ways exist for doing this).

Having done so, the investor can now identify the two corner portfolios having expected returns "surrounding" this level. That is, the investor can identify the corner portfolio with the expected return nearest but greater than this level (the surrounding corner portfolio that is "above" O^*) and the corner portfolio with the expected return nearest but less than this level (the surrounding corner portfolio that is "below" O^*).

If the expected return of the optimal portfolio is denoted by $\bar{r}^*$ and the expected returns of these two surrounding portfolios are denoted by $\bar{r}^a$ and $\bar{r}^b$, respectively, then the composition of the optimal portfolio can be determined by solving the following equation for Y:

$$\bar{r}^* = (\bar{r}^a \times Y) + [\bar{r}^b \times (1 - Y)]. \qquad (7.3)$$

The optimal portfolio will consist of a proportion Y of the "above" surrounding corner portfolio and a proportion $1 - Y$ of the "below" surrounding corner portfolio.

In the example, if the optimal portfolio had an expected return of 20%, then it can be noted that the second and third corner portfolios are the above and below surrounding corner portfolios, since they have expected returns of 23.20% and 17.26%, respectively. Equation (7.3) thus looks like:

$$20\% = (23.20\% \times Y) + [17.26\% \times (1 - Y)].$$

Solving this equation for Y results in $Y = .46$, meaning that the optimal portfolio consists of a proportion of .46 in the second corner portfolio and .54 in the third corner portfolio. In terms of the amount of investment in the securities of Able, Baker, and Charlie companies, this translates to:

$$[.46 \times X(2)] + [.54 \times X(3)] = .46 \times \begin{bmatrix} .00 \\ .22 \\ .78 \end{bmatrix} + .54 \times \begin{bmatrix} .84 \\ .00 \\ .16 \end{bmatrix} = \begin{bmatrix} .45 \\ .10 \\ .45 \end{bmatrix}.$$

Thus, the investor should put 45%, 10%, and 45% of his or her funds in shares of Able, Baker, and Charlie, respectively.

More generally, if the weight vectors of the above and below surrounding corner portfolios are denoted by X^a and X^b, respectively, then the weights for the individual securities comprising the optimal portfolio will be equal to $(Y \times X^a) + [(1 - Y) \times X^b]$.

A.2 INTRODUCING RISK-FREE OPPORTUNITIES

☐ A.2.1 Determining the Composition and Location of the Efficient Set

When risk-free opportunities are added to the Markowitz model, the efficient set is a straight line going through the portfolio T. This portfolio is known as the tangency portfolio, since it lies at the point on the curved efficient set of Markowitz that is tangent to a straight line emanating from the risk-free rate.

Determining the composition and location of T involves the same procedures that were presented earlier in this appendix. In the example, portfolio T lies on the curved efficient set of the Markowitz model in Figure 7.15 between the second and third corner portfolios that are shown in Figure 7.17, where they are denoted $C(2)$ and $C(3)$, respectively. Since T lies between these two corner portfolios, its composition is a weighted average of the compositions of $C(2)$ and $C(3)$ that are shown in Table 7.1. These weights (.86 in $C(2)$ and .14 in $C(3)$) can be determined graphically by noting T's expected return. Specifically, a horizontal line can be drawn from T to the vertical axis, where the expected return of T can be measured.

In this case, the expected return is 22.4%. Since T lies between $C(2)$ and $C(3)$, its expected return must be a weighted average of the expected returns of $C(2)$, the above surrounding corner portfolio, and $C(3)$, the below surrounding corner portfolio. Thus, its composition, in terms of $C(2)$ and $C(3)$, can be determined by using equation (7.3) with $\bar{r}^* = 22.4\%$, $\bar{r}^a = 23.20\%$, and $\bar{r}^b = 17.26\%$:

$$22.4\% = (23.20\% \times Y) + [17.26\% \times (1 - Y)].$$

The solution to this equation is $Y = .86$. Thus, T consists of $C(2)$ and $C(3)$ in the proportions of .86 and .14, respectively.

In terms of the amount of investment in Able, Baker, and Charlie, this translates to:

$$[.86 \times X(2)] + [.14 \times X(3)] = .86 \times \begin{bmatrix} .00 \\ .22 \\ .78 \end{bmatrix} + .14 \times \begin{bmatrix} .84 \\ .00 \\ .16 \end{bmatrix} = \begin{bmatrix} .12 \\ .19 \\ .69 \end{bmatrix}.$$

That is, T consists of an investment of 12% in Able, 19% in Baker, and 69% in Charlie.

☐ A.2.2 Determining the Composition of the Optimal Portfolio

Once the location and composition of the tangency portfolio have been determined, the straight-line efficient set can be located. Then the composition of the investor's optimal portfolio can be determined. This portfolio, indicated by O^* in Figure 7.16, corresponds to the tangency point between the efficient set and one of the investor's indifference curves. The procedure for deter-

mining its composition is similar to that described earlier in this appendix for the Markowitz model. It starts by the investor noting graphically the level of its expected return. That is, from the graph the investor can note where O^* is located and then calibrate its expected return by simply using a ruler and extending a line from O^* to the vertical axis.

If the expected return of the optimal portfolio is denoted by $\bar{r}^*$ and the risk-free rate and the expected return of the tangency portfolio are r_f and $\bar{r}_T$, respectively, then the composition of the optimal portfolio can be determined by first solving the following equation for Y:

$$\bar{r}^* = (\bar{r}_T \times Y) + [r_f \times (1 - Y)]. \tag{7.4}$$

The optimal portfolio will consist of a proportion Y of the tangency portfolio and a proportion $1 - Y$ of the risk-free rate. Thus, the proportions to be invested in each risky security can be calculated by taking their proportion in T and multiplying them by Y.

In the example, if the optimal portfolio of the investor corresponds to the one shown in part (a) of Figure 7.16, then $\bar{r}^* = 14\%$. Thus, equation (7.4) would be:

$$14\% = (22.4\% \times Y) + [4\% \times (1 - Y)] \tag{7.5}$$

since $\bar{r}_T = 22.4\%$ and $r_f = 4\%$. The solution to equation (7.5) is $Y = .54$, meaning that the optimal portfolio consists of a proportion of .54 in the tangency portfolio and .46 in the risk-free asset. In terms of the amount of investment in the securities of Able, Baker, and Charlie companies, this translates to:

$$[.54 \times X(T)] = .54 \times \begin{bmatrix} .12 \\ .19 \\ .69 \end{bmatrix} = \begin{bmatrix} .07 \\ .10 \\ .37 \end{bmatrix}.$$

Thus, the investor should invest an amount of money that is equal to 7%, 10%, and 37% of his or her initial wealth in shares of Able, Baker, and Charlie, respectively. Furthermore, 46% of the investor's initial wealth should be used to buy Treasury bills, the risk-free asset.

Alternatively, if the optimal portfolio of the investor corresponds to the one shown in part (b) of Figure 7.16, then $\bar{r}^* = 27\%$. Thus, equation (7.4) would be:

$$27\% = (22.4\% \times Y) + [4\% \times (1 - Y)] \tag{7.6}$$

and the solution would be $Y = 1.25$, meaning that the optimal portfolio consists of borrowing an amount of money equal to 25% of the investor's initial wealth and then investing the borrowed money and the initial wealth in T. In terms of the amount of investment in the securities of Able, Baker, and Charlie companies, this translates to:

$$[1.25 \times X(T)] = 1.25 \times \begin{bmatrix} .12 \\ .19 \\ .69 \end{bmatrix} = \begin{bmatrix} .15 \\ .24 \\ .86 \end{bmatrix}.$$

Thus, the investor should invest an amount of money that is equal to 15%, 24%, and 86% of his or her initial wealth in shares of Able, Baker, and Charlie, respectively.

APPENDIX B
ALLOWING FOR DIFFERENT BORROWING AND LENDING RATES

In this chapter, it was assumed that the investor could borrow funds at the same rate that could be earned on an investment in the risk-free asset. As a result, the feasible set became the area bounded by two straight lines emanating from the risk-free rate. The upper line represented the efficient set and had one portfolio in common with the curved efficient set of the Markowitz model. This portfolio was located where the straight line from the risk-free rate was tangent to the curved efficient set. Now the concern will be with what happens if it is assumed that the investor can borrow but at a rate that is greater than the rate that can be earned by an investment in the risk-free asset. The rate on the risk-free asset will be denoted by r_{fL}, where L indicates lending, since, as was mentioned earlier, an investment in the risk-free asset is equivalent to lending money to the government. Also, the rate at which the investor can borrow money will be denoted by r_{fB} and is of a magnitude such that $r_{fB} > r_{fL}$.

One way to understand the effect on the efficient set of assuming that these two rates are different is as follows. First, consider what the efficient set would look like if risk-free borrowing and lending were possible at the same rate, r_{fL}. The resulting efficient set would be the straight line shown in Figure 7.18 that goes through the points r_{fL} and T_L.

Second, consider what the efficient set would look like if risk-free borrowing and lending were possible at the higher rate, r_{fB}. The resulting efficient set would be the straight line shown in Figure 7.18 that goes through the points r_{fB} and T_B. Note that the portfolio T_B lies on Markowitz's efficient set above the portfolio T_L, since it corresponds to a tangency point associated with a higher risk-free rate.

Third, since the investor cannot borrow at r_{fL}, that part of the line emanating from r_{fL} that extends past T_L is not available to the investor and can thus be removed from consideration.

Fourth, since the investor cannot lend at the risk-free rate r_{fB}, that part of the line emanating from r_{fB} and going through T_B but lying to the left of T_B is not available to the investor and can thus be removed from consideration. The northwest boundary of what is left, shown in Figure 7.19, is the resulting efficient set.

This efficient set consists of three distinct but connected segments. The first segment is the straight line going from r_{fL} to T_L; it represents various amounts of risk-free lending combined with investing in the portfolio of risky assets denoted T_L. The second segment is the curved line going from T_L to T_B, which represents various risky portfolios that were also on Markowitz's curved efficient set. The third segment is the straight line extending outward

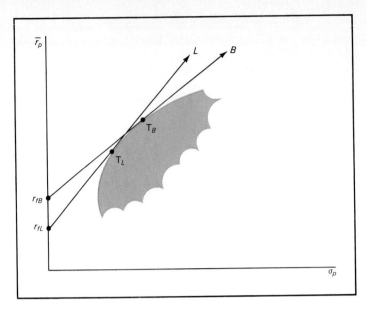

FIGURE 7–18
Evaluating different risk-free rates.

from T_B; it represents various amounts of borrowing combined with an investment in the risky portfolio denoted by T_B.

The optimal portfolio for an investor will be, as before, the portfolio that corresponds to the point where an indifference curve is tangent to the

FIGURE 7–19
Efficient set when the risk-free rates are different.

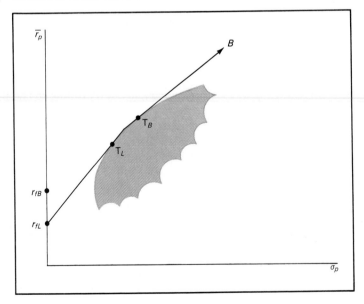

efficient set. Depending on the investor's indifference curves, this tangency point could be on any one of the three segments that comprise the efficient set.

QUESTIONS AND PROBLEMS

1. When is the standard deviation of a portfolio equal to the weighted average of the standard deviations of the component securities? Show this mathematically for a two-security portfolio. (*Hint*: Some algebra is necessary to solve this problem. Remember that $\sigma_{ij} = \rho_{ij}\sigma_i\sigma_j$. Try different values of ρ_{ij}.)

2. In terms of the Markowitz model without risk-free borrowing and lending, explain how an investor goes about identifying his or her optimal portfolio. Use words and graphs. What specific information does the investor need to identify this portfolio?

3. Discuss why the concepts of covariance and diversification are closely related.

4. Briefly explain why the efficient set must be concave.

5. Why is a pure discount government security with no risk of default still risky to an investor whose holding period does not coincide with the maturity date of the security?

6. The covariance between a risk-free asset and a risky asset is zero. Explain why this is the case and demonstrate it mathematically.

7. Why does the efficient set, with the Markowitz model extended to include risk-free borrowing and lending, have only one point in common with the efficient set of the Markowitz model without risk-free borrowing and lending? Why are the other points on the "old" efficient set no longer desirable? Explain with words and graphs.

8. How does the feasible set change when risk-free borrowing and lending are introduced into the Markowitz model? Explain with words and graphs.

9. Given the following expected return vector and variance-covariance matrix for three assets:

$$ER = \begin{bmatrix} 10.1 \\ 7.8 \\ 6.0 \end{bmatrix} \qquad VC = \begin{bmatrix} 210 & 140 & 0 \\ 140 & 90 & 0 \\ 0 & 0 & 0 \end{bmatrix}.$$

and given the fact that Pie Traynor's risky portfolio is split 50-50 between the two risky assets:

a. Which security of the three must be the risk-free asset? Why?

b. Calculate the expected return and standard deviation of Pie's portfolio.

c. If the risk-free asset makes up 25% of Pie's total portfolio, what is the total portfolio's expected return and standard deviation?

10. What will be the effect on total portfolio expected return and risk if you borrow money at the risk-free rate and invest in the optimal risky portfolio.

11. Suppose your level of risk aversion changed as you grew older (and richer) and that you became less risk-averse. In a world of risk-free borrowing and lending, how would your optimal portfolio change? Would the types of risky securities you hold change? Explain with words and graphs.

12. (Appendix Question) What is a corner portfolio? Why are corner portfolios important for identifying the composition of the efficient set?

13. (Appendix Question) How does the efficient set change when the condition of borrowing and lending at the same risk-free rate is changed to borrowing at a rate greater than the rate at which risk-free lending can be conducted? Explain with words and graphs.

Chapter 8

THE CAPITAL ASSET PRICING

MODEL

Chapters 6 and 7 presented a method for identifying an investor's optimal portfolio. With this method, the investor needs to estimate the expected returns and variances for all securities under consideration. Furthermore, all the covariances among these securities need to be estimated and the risk-free rate needs to be determined. Once this is done, the investor can find out the composition of the tangency portfolio as well as its expected return and standard deviation. At this juncture the investor can identify the optimal portfolio by noting where one of his or her indifference curves touch but do not intersect the efficient set. This portfolio will involve investing in the tangency portfolio, along with a certain amount of either risk-free borrowing or lending, since the efficient set is linear (that is, a straight line).

Such an approach to investing can be viewed as an exercise in *normative economics*, where investors are told what they should do. Thus, the approach is prescriptive in nature. In this chapter the realm of *positive economics* is entered, where a descriptive model of how assets are priced is presented. The model assumes, among other things, that all investors use the approach to investing given in Chapters 6 and 7. The major implication of the model is that the expected return of an asset will be related to a measure of risk for the asset that is known as beta. The exact manner in which expected return and beta are related is specified by the *capital asset pricing model* (CAPM).[1]

This model provides the intellectual basis for a number of the current practices in the investment industry. Although many of these practices are actually based on various extensions and modifications of the CAPM, a sound

---

[1] Credit for the initial development of the CAPM is usually given to William F. Sharpe, "Capital Asset Prices: A Theory of Market Equilibrium under Conditions of Risk," *Journal of Finance* 19, no. 3 (September 1964):425–42; John Lintner, "The Valuation of Risk Assets and the Selection of Risky Investments in Stock Portfolios and Capital Budgets," *Review of Economics and Statistics* 47, no. 1 (February 1965):13–37 and "Security Prices, Risk, and Maximal Gains from Diversification," *Journal of Finance* 20, no. 4 (December 1965):587–615; and Jan Mossin, "Equilibrium in a Capital Asset Market," *Econometrica* 34, no. 4 (October 1966):768–83. A major contribution was also made by Eugene F. Fama in "Risk, Return, and Equilibrium: Some Clarifying Comments," *Journal of Finance* 23, no. 1 (March 1968):29–40, where the Sharpe and Lintner papers were reconciled.

understanding of the original version is necessary in order to understand them. Accordingly, this chapter presents the original version of the CAPM.[2]

8.1 ASSUMPTIONS

In order to see how assets are priced, a model (that is, a theory) must be constructed. This requires simplification in that the model builder must abstract from the full complexity of the situation and focus only on the most important elements. The way this is achieved is by making certain *assumptions* about the environment. These assumptions need to be simplistic in order to provide the degree of abstraction that allows for some success in building the model. The "reasonableness" of the assumptions (or lack thereof) is of little concern. Instead, the test of a model is in its ability to help one understand and predict the process being modeled. As Milton Friedman, recipient of the 1976 Nobel Memorial Prize in Economics, has stated in a famous essay:

> ☐ [T]he relevant question to ask about the "assumptions" of a theory is not whether they are descriptively "realistic," for they never are, but whether they are sufficiently good approximations for the purpose in hand. And this question can be answered only by seeing whether the theory works, which means whether it yields sufficiently accurate predictions.[3]

Some of the assumptions behind the CAPM are also behind the normative approach to investing that was described in the previous two chapters. These assumptions are as follows:

1. Investors evaluate portfolios by looking at the expected returns and standard deviations of the portfolios over a one-period horizon.
2. Investors are never satiated, so when given a choice between two otherwise identical portfolios, they will choose the one with the higher expected return.
3. Investors are risk-averse, so when given a choice between two otherwise identical portfolios, they will choose the one with the lower standard deviation.
4. Individual assets are infinitely divisible, meaning that an investor can buy a fraction of a share if he or she so desires.
5. There is a risk-free rate at which an investor may either lend (that is, invest) or borrow money.
6. Taxes and transactions costs are irrelevant.

To these assumptions the following are added:

---

[2] Some extended versions of the CAPM are discussed in Appendix A. For a more extensive treatment, see Chapter 8 of Gordon J. Alexander and Jack Clark Francis, *Portfolio Analysis* (Englewood Cliffs, N.J.: Prentice-Hall, 1986).

[3] Milton Friedman, *Essays in the Theory of Positive Economics* (Chicago: The University of Chicago Press, 1953), 15.

7. All investors have the same one-period horizon.
8. The risk-free rate is the same for all investors.
9. Information is freely and instantly available to all investors.
10. Investors have *homogeneous expectations*, meaning that they have the same perceptions in regard to the expected returns, standard deviations, and covariances of securities.

As can be seen by examining these assumptions, the CAPM reduces the situation to an extreme case. Everyone has the same information and agrees about the future prospects for securities. Implicitly, this means that investors analyze and process information in the same way. The markets for securities are *perfect*, meaning there are no "frictions" to impede investing; potential impediments such as finite divisibility, taxes, transactions costs, and different risk-free borrowing and lending rates have been assumed away. This allows the focus to be changed from how an individual should invest to what would happen to security prices if everyone invested in a similar manner. By examining the collective behavior of all investors in the marketplace, the nature of the resulting equilibrium relationship between each security's risk and return can be developed.

8.2 THE CAPITAL MARKET LINE

□ 8.2.1 The Separation Theorem

Having made these ten assumptions, the resulting implications can now be examined. First, investors would analyze securities and determine the composition of the tangency portfolio. In doing so, *everyone would obtain the same tangency portfolio*. However, this is not surprising, since there is complete agreement among investors on the estimates of the securities' expected returns, variances, and covariances as well as on the size of the risk-free rate. This also means that the linear efficient set (described in Chapter 7) is the same for all investors because it simply involves combinations of the agreed-upon tangency portfolio and risk-free rate.

Since all investors face the same efficient set, the only reason they will choose different portfolios is because they have different indifference curves. Thus, different investors will choose different portfolios from the same efficient set because they have different preferences toward risk and return. For example, as was shown in Figure 7.16, the investor in part (a) will choose a different portfolio than the investor in part (b). However, while the chosen portfolios will be different, *each investor will choose the same combination of risky securities*, denoted by T in Figure 7.16. That is, each investor would spread his or her funds among risky securities in the same relative proportions, adding risk-free borrowing or lending in order to achieve a personally preferred overall combination of risk and return. This feature of the CAPM is often referred to as the *separation theorem*:

> The optimal combination of risky assets for an investor can be determined without any knowledge about the investor's preferences toward risk and return.

In other words, the determination of the optimal combination of risky assets can be made separately from the determination of the shape of an investor's indifference curves.

The reasoning behind the separation theorem involes a property of the linear efficient set that was introduced in Chapter 7. There it was shown that all portfolios located on the linear efficient set involved an investment in a tangency portfolio combined with varying degrees of risk-free borrowing or lending. With the CAPM, each person faces the same linear efficient set, meaning that each person will be investing in the same tangency portfolio (combined with a certain amount of either risk-free borrowing or lending that depends upon that person's indifference curves). It therefore follows that the risky portion of each person's portfolio will be the same.

In the example from Chapter 7, three securities were considered, corresponding to the stock of Able, Baker, and Charlie companies. With a risk-free rate of return of 4%, the tangency portfolio T was shown to consist of investments in Able, Baker, and Charlie in proportions equal to .12, .19, and .69, respectively. If the ten assumptions of the CAPM are made, then the investor shown in part (a) of Figure 7.16 would invest approximately half of his or her money in the risk-free asset and the remainder in T. The investor shown in part (b), on the other hand, would borrow an amount of money equal to approximately half of the value of his or her initial wealth and proceed to invest these borrowed funds as well as his or her own funds in T.[4] Thus, the proportions invested in the three stocks for the investors of parts (a) and (b) would equal: [5]

$$(.5) \times \begin{bmatrix} .12 \\ .19 \\ .69 \end{bmatrix} = \begin{bmatrix} .060 \\ .095 \\ .345 \end{bmatrix} \text{ for the investor in part (a),}$$

$$(1.5) \times \begin{bmatrix} .12 \\ .19 \\ .69 \end{bmatrix} = \begin{bmatrix} .180 \\ .285 \\ 1.035 \end{bmatrix} \text{ for the investor in part (b),}$$

While the proportions to be invested in each of these three risky securities for the panel (a) investor (.060, .095, .345) can be seen to be different in size from their values for the panel (b) investor (.180, .285, 1.035), the relative proportions are the same, being equal to .12, .19, and .69, respectively.

□ 8.2.2   The Market Portfolio

Another important feature of the CAPM is that in equilibrium, each security must have a nonzero proportion in the composition of the tangency portfolio.

---

[4] If the investor had initial wealth of $40,000, this means that he or she would borrow $20,000 and then invest $60,000 ($40,000 + $20,000) in T.

[5] Note how the proportions in these three stocks sum to .5 for the panel (a) investor and 1.5 for the panel (b) investor. Since the respective proportions for the risk-free rate are .5 and −.5, the aggregate proportions for the stocks and risk-free rate sum to 1.0 for each investor.

That is, no security could, in equilibrium, have a proportion in T that was zero. The reasoning behind this feature lies in the previously mentioned separation theorem in which it was asserted that the risky portion of every investor's portfolio would be independent of the investor's risk-return preferences. The justification for the theorem was that the risky portion of each investor's portfolio would simply be an investment in the tangency portfolio. If every investor is purchasing T and T does not involve an investment in each security, then nobody is investing in those securities with zero proportions in T. This means that the prices of these zero-proportion securities must *fall*, thereby causing the expected returns of these securities to *rise* until the resulting tangency portfolio has a nonzero proportion associated with them.

In the previous example, Charlie had a current price of $62 and an expected end-of-period price of $76.14. This meant that the expected return for Charlie was ($76.14 − $62)/$62 = 22.8%. Now imagine that the current price of Charlie is $72, not $62, meaning that its expected return is ($76.14 − $72)/$72 = 5.8%. If this were the case, the tangency portfolio associated with a risk-free rate of 4% would involve just Able and Baker in proportions of .90 and .10, respectively.[6] Since Charlie has a proportion of zero, nobody would want to hold shares of Charlie. Consequently, orders to sell would be received in substantial quantities, with virtually no offsetting orders to buy being received. As a result, Charlie's price would fall, as brokers would try to find someone to buy the shares. However, as Charlie's price falls, its expected return would rise, since the same end-of-period price of $76.14 is forecast for Charlie as before and it would now cost less to buy one share. Eventually, as the price falls, investors would change their minds and want to buy shares of Charlie. Ultimately, at a price of $62, investors will want to hold shares of Charlie so that, in aggregate, the number of shares demanded will equal the number of shares outstanding. Thus, in equilibrium, Charlie will have a nonzero proportion in the tangency portfolio.

Another interesting situation could also arise. What if each investor concludes that the tangency portfolio should involve a proportionate investment in the stock of Baker equal to .40, but at the current price of Baker there are not enough shares outstanding to meet the demand? In this situation orders to buy Baker will flood in, and brokers will raise the price in search of sellers. This will cause the expected return of Baker to fall, making it less attractive and thereby reducing its proportion in the tangency portfolio to a level where the number of shares demanded equals the number of shares outstanding.

Ultimately, everything will balance out. When all the price adjusting stops, the market will have been brought into equilibrium. First, each investor will want to hold a certain amount of each risky security. Second, the current market price of each security will be at a level where the number of shares that are demanded equals the number of shares that are outstand-

---

[6] Although the expected return of Charlie has been changed, all the variances and covariances as well as the expected returns for Able and Baker are assumed to have the same values that were given in Chapter 7. The singular change in the expected return of Charlie alters not only the composition of the tangency portfolio but, more generally, the location and shape of the efficient set.

ing.[7] Third, the risk-free rate will be at a level where the total amount of money borrowed equals the total amount of money lent. As a result, the proportions of the tangency portfolio will correspond to the proportions of what is known as the *market portfolio*, defined as follows:

> The market portfolio is a portfolio consisting of an investment in all securities where the proportion to be invested in each security corresponds to its relative market value. The relative market value of a security is simply equal to the aggregate market value of the security divided by the sum of the aggregate market values of all securities.[8]

The reason the market portfolio plays a central role in the CAPM is because the efficient set consists of an investment in the market portfolio, coupled with a desired amount of either risk-free borrowing or lending. Thus, it is common practice to refer to the tangency portfolio as the market portfolio and to denote it as M instead of T. In theory, M consists of not only common stocks but also such other kinds of investments as bonds, preferred stocks, and real estate. However, in practice many people restrict M just to common stocks.

While the performance of the market portfolio is not reported in the daily press, indices measuring the performance of some of its major components are available. One of the most widely known is Standard & Poor's 500 Stock Price Index (generally referred to as the S&P 500), a value-weighted average of the market prices of 500 large stocks. Since each stock's price is weighted by the relative market value of its outstanding shares and since primarily stocks with large market values are included, this index represents the performance obtained in the stock market segment of the market portfolio reasonably well.

Complete coverage of the stocks listed on the New York Stock Exchange is provided by the NYSE Composite Index, which is like the S&P 500 in that it is a value-weighted index of stock prices but is broader in that it considers more stocks. The American Stock Exchange computes a similar index for the stocks it lists, and the National Association of Security Dealers provides a value-weighted index of the prices of over-the-counter stocks traded on the NASDAQ system. The Wilshire 5000-stock index is the most comprehensive index of common stock prices that is published regularly in the United States and is thus closer than the others to representing the overall performance of American common stocks.[9]

Without question the most widely quoted market index is the Dow Jones Industrial Average (DJIA). Although based on the performance of only 30 stocks and utilizing a less satisfactory averaging procedure, the DJIA pro-

---

[7] In this situation the market for the security is said to have *cleared*.

[8] The aggregate market value for the common stock of a company is equal to the current market price of the stock times the number of shares outstanding.

[9] There are a variety of other indices of common stock prices that are commonly reported in the daily press. Many of these are components of the major indices. For example, *The Wall Street Journal* reports on a daily basis not only the level of the S&P 500 but also the levels of the Standard & Poor's Industrials, Transportations, Utilities, and Financials. These last four indices reflect the performance of particular sectors of the stock market. Their components, 500 stocks in total, make up the S&P 500. See Chapters 21 and 24 for a more thorough discussion of stock market indices.

TABLE 8.1

Stocks in the Dow Jones Industrial Average at Year-End, 1988.

Allied-Signal
Alcoa
American Express
American Telephone & Telegraph
Bethlehem Steel
Boeing
Chevron
Coca-Cola
DuPont
Eastman Kodak
Exxon
General Electric
General Motors
Goodyear Tire
IBM
International Paper
McDonald's
Merck
Minnesota Mining & Manufacturing
Navistar
Philip Morris
Primerica
Proctor & Gamble
Sears Roebuck
Texaco
USX
Union Carbide
United Technologies
Westinghouse
Woolworth

SOURCE: Adapted from *The Wall Street Journal*, Dow Jones & Company, Inc., January 30, 1989, p. C3.

vides at least a fair idea of what is happening to stock values.[10] Table 8.1 provides a listing of the 30 stocks whose prices are reflected in the DJIA.

□ 8.2.3   The Efficient Set

In the world of the CAPM, it is a simple matter to determine the relationship between risk and return for efficient portfolios. Figure 8.1 portrays it graphically. Point M represents the market portfolio and r_f represents the risk-free rate of return. Efficient portfolios plot along the line starting at r_f and going through M and consist of alternative combinations of risk and return obtainable by combining the market portfolio with risk-free borrowing or lending. This linear efficient set of the CAPM is known as the *capital*

---

[10] Charles Dow started this index in 1884 by simply adding the prices of 11 companies and then dividing the sum by 11. In 1928, securities were added to bring the total number up to 30, and since then the composition of these 30 has been changed periodically. Due to things like stock dividends and splits, the divisor is no longer simply equal to the number of stocks in the index.

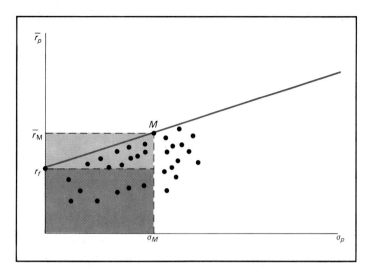

FIGURE 8–1
The capital market line.

market line (CML). All portfolios other than those employing the market portfolio and risk-free borrowing or lending would lie below the CML, although some might plot very close to it.

The slope of the CML is equal to the difference between expected return of the market portfolio and that of the riskless security, $\bar{r}_M - r_f$, divided by the difference in their risks, $\sigma_M - 0$, or $(\bar{r}_M - r_f)/\sigma_M$.[11] Since the vertical intercept of the CML is r_f, the straight line characterizing the CML has the following equation:

$$\bar{r}_p = r_f + \left[\frac{\bar{r}_M - r_f}{\sigma_M}\right] \sigma_p \tag{8.1}$$

where $\bar{r}_p$ and σ_p refer to the expected return and standard deviation of an efficient portfolio.[12] In the previous example, the market portfolio associated with a risk-free rate of 4% consisted of Able, Baker, and Charlie in the proportions of .12, .19, and .69, respectively. Since it was shown in Chapter 7 that the expected return and standard deviation for a portfolio with these proportions was 22.4% and 15.2%, respectively, the equation for the resulting CML is:

$$\bar{r}_p = 4 + \left[\frac{22.4 - 4}{15.2}\right] \sigma_p$$

$$= 4 + 1.21\sigma_p.$$

---

[11] The slope of a straight line can be determined if the location of two points on the line are known. It is determined by rise over run, meaning it is determined by dividing the vertical distance between the two points by the horizontal distance between the two points. In the case of the CML, two points are known, corresponding to the risk-free rate and the market portfolio, so its slope can be determined in this manner.

[12] The equation of a straight line is of the form $y = a + bx$, where a is the vertical intercept and b is the slope. Since the vertical intercept and slope of the CML are known, its equation can be written as shown here by making the appropriate substitutions for a and b.

Equilibrium in the security market can be characterized by two key numbers. The first is the vertical intercept of the CML (that is, the risk-free rate), which is often referred to as the reward for waiting. The second is the slope of the CML, which is often referred to as the reward per unit of risk borne. In essence, the security market provides a place where time and risk can be traded with their prices determined by the forces of supply and demand. Thus, the intercept and slope of the CML can be thought of as the "price of time" and the "price of risk," respectively. In the example, they are equal to 4% and 1.21, respectively.

8.3 THE SECURITY MARKET LINE

☐ 8.3.1 Implications for Individual Risky Assets

The CML represents the equilibrium relationship between the expected return and standard deviation for efficient portfolios. Individual risky securities will always plot below the line, since a single risky security, when held by itself, is an inefficient portfolio. The CAPM does not imply any particular relationship between the expected return and the standard deviation (that is, total risk) of an individual security. To say more about the expected return of an individual security, deeper analysis is necessary.

In Chapter 6 the following equation was given for calculating the standard deviation of any portfolio:

$$\sigma_p = \left[\sum_{i=1}^{N} \sum_{j=1}^{N} X_i X_j \sigma_{ij} \right]^{1/2} \tag{6.7}$$

where X_i and X_j denoted the proportions invested in securities i and j, respectively, and σ_{ij} denoted the covariance of returns between security i and j. Now consider using this equation to calculate the standard deviation of the market portfolio:

$$\sigma_M = \left[\sum_{i=1}^{N} \sum_{j=1}^{N} X_{iM} X_{jM} \sigma_{ij} \right]^{1/2} \tag{8.2}$$

where X_{iM} and X_{jM} denote the proportions invested in securities i and j in the market portfolio, respectively. It can be shown that another way to write equation (8.2) is as follows:

$$\sigma_M = \left[X_{1M} \sum_{j=1}^{N} X_{jM} \sigma_{1j} + X_{2M} \sum_{j=1}^{N} X_{jM} \sigma_{2j} + X_{3M} \sum_{j=1}^{N} X_{jM} \sigma_{3j} \right.$$
$$\left. + \cdots + X_{NM} \sum_{j=1}^{N} X_{jM} \sigma_{Nj} \right]^{1/2}. \tag{8.3}$$

At this point a property of covariance can be used: The covariance of security i with the market portfolio (σ_{iM}) can be expressed as:

$$\sum_{j=1}^{N} X_{jM} \sigma_{ij} = \sigma_{iM}. \tag{8.4}$$

This property, as applied to each one of the N risky securities in the market portfolio, results in the following;

$$\sigma_M = [X_{1M}\sigma_{1M} + X_{2M}\sigma_{2M} + X_{3M}\sigma_{3M} + \cdots + X_{NM}\sigma_{NM}]^{1/2} \quad (8.5)$$

where σ_{1M} denotes the covariance of security 1 with the market portfolio, σ_{2M} denotes the covariance of security 2 with the market portfolio, and so on. Thus, the standard deviation of the market portfolio is equal to the square root of a weighted average of the covariances of all the securities with it, where the weights are equal to the proportions of the respective securities in the market portfolio.

At this juncture an important point can be observed. Under the CAPM each investor holds the market portfolio and is concerned with its standard deviation, since that will influence the magnitude of his or her investment in the market portfolio. The contribution of each security to the standard deviation of the market portfolio can be seen in equation (8.5) to depend on the size of its covariance with the market portfolio. Accordingly, each investor will note that *the relevant measure of risk for a security is its covariance with the market portfolio*, σ_{iM}. This means that securities with larger values of σ_{iM} will be viewed by investors as contributing more to the risk of the market portfolio. It also means that securities with larger standard deviations should not be viewed as being riskier than those securities with smaller standard deviations.

From this analysis it follows that securities with larger values for σ_{iM} will have to provide proportionately larger expected returns in order for investors to be interested in purchasing them. In order to see why, consider what would happen if such securities did not provide investors with proportionately larger levels of expected return. In this situation these securities would contribute to the risk of the market portfolio while not contributing proportionately to the expected return of the market portfolio. This means that deleting such securities from the market portfolio would cause the expected return of the market portfolio, relative to its standard deviation, to rise. Since investors would view this as a favorable change, the market portfolio would no longer be the optimal risky portfolio to hold. Thus, security prices would be out of equilibrium.

The exact form of the equilibrium relationship between risk and return can be written as follows:

$$\bar{r}_i = r_f + \left[\frac{\bar{r}_M - r_f}{\sigma_M^2}\right]\sigma_{iM}. \quad (8.6)$$

As can be seen in part (a) of Figure 8.2, equation (8.6) represents a line having a vertical intercept of r_f and a slope of $[(\bar{r}_M - r_f)/\sigma_M^2]$. Since the slope is positive, the equation indicates that securities with larger covariances (σ_{iM}) will be priced so as to have larger expected returns $(\bar{r}_i)$. This relationship between covariance and expected return is known as the *security market line* (SML).[13]

---

[13] A more rigorous derivation of the SML is provided in Appendix B.

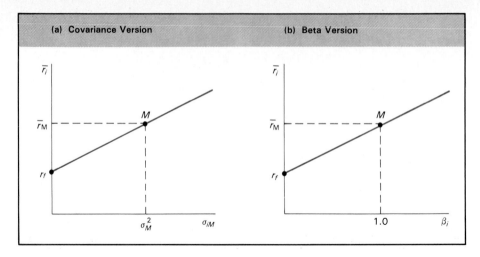

FIGURE 8–2
The security market line.

Interestingly, a risky security with $\sigma_{iM} = 0$ will have an expected return equal to the rate on the risk-free security, r_f. Intuitively, the reason for this is that the risky security, just like the risk-free security, does not contribute to the risk of the market portfolio. This is so even though the risky security has a positive standard deviation, whereas the risk-free security has a standard deviation of zero.[14]

Also of interest is the observation that a risky security with $\sigma_{iM} = \sigma_M^2$ will have an expected return equal to the expected return on the market portfolio, $\bar{r}_M$. This is because such a security contributes an average amount of risk to the market portfolio.

Another way of expressing the SML is as follows:

$$\bar{r}_i = r_f + (\bar{r}_M - r_f)\beta_i \qquad (8.7)$$

where the term β_i is defined as

$$\beta_i = \frac{\sigma_{iM}}{\sigma_M^2}. \qquad (8.8)$$

The term β_i is known as the *beta coefficient* (or simply the *beta*) for security i, and is an alternative way of representing the covariance risk of a security. Equation (8.7) is a different version of the SML, as can be seen in part (b) of Figure 8.2. While having the same intercept as the earlier version shown in equation (8.6), r_f, it has a different slope. The slope of this version is $\bar{r}_M - r_f$, whereas the slope of the earlier version was $(\bar{r}_M - r_f)/\sigma_M^2$.

One property of beta is that *the beta of a portfolio is simply a weighted*

---

[14] It is even possible for some risky securities (meaning securities with positive standard deviations) to have expected returns less than the risk-free rate. According to the CAPM, this will occur if they have $\sigma_{iM} < 0$, thereby contributing a negative amount of risk to the market portfolio (meaning they cause the risk of the market portfolio to be lower than it would be in their absence).

average of the betas of its component securities, where the proportions invested in the securities are the respective weights. That is, the beta of a portfolio can be calculated as

$$\beta_p = \sum_{i=1}^{N} X_i \beta_i. \tag{8.9}$$

Earlier it was shown that the expected return of a portfolio is a weighted average of the expected returns of its component securities, where the proportions invested in the securities are the weights. This means that since every security plots on the SML, so will every portfolio. More broadly:

> Not only every security but also every portfolio must plot on an upward-sloping straight line in a diagram with expected return on the vertical axis and beta on the horizontal axis.

This means that efficient portfolios plot on both the CML and the SML, whereas inefficient portfolios plot only on the SML.

Also of interest is that the SML must go through the point representing the market portfolio itself. Its beta is 1, and its expected return is $\bar{r}_M$, so its coordinates are $(1, \bar{r}_M)$. Since risk-free securities have beta values of 0, the SML will also go through a point with an expected return of r_f and with coordinates of $(0, r_f)$. This means that the SML will have a vertical intercept equal to r_f and a slope equal to the vertical distance between these two points, $\bar{r}_M - r_f$, divided by the horizontal distance between these two points, $1 - 0$, or $(\bar{r}_M - r_f)/(1 - 0) = \bar{r}_M - r_f$. Thus, these two points suffice to fix the location of the SML, indicating the "appropriate" expected returns for securities and portfolios with different beta values.

The equilibrium relationship shown by the SML comes to exist through the combined effects of investors' adjustments in holdings and the resulting pressures on security prices (as shown in Chapter 3). Given a set of security prices, investors calculate expected returns and covariances and then determine their optimal portfolios. If the number of shares of a security collectively desired differs from the number available, there will be upward or downward pressure on its price. Given a new set of prices, investors will reassess their desires for the various securities. The process will continue until the number of shares collectively desired for each security equals the number available.

For the individual investor, security prices and prospects are fixed, whereas the quantities held can be altered. For the market as a whole, however, these quantities are fixed (at least in the short run) and prices are variable. As in any competitive market, equilibrium requires the adjustment of each security's price until there is consistency between the quantity desired and the quantity available.

It may seem logical to examine historical returns on securities in order to determine whether or not securities have been priced in equilibrium as suggested by the CAPM. However, the issue of whether or not such testing of the CAPM can be done in a meaningful manner is controversial. In addition,

Markowitz has suggested that affirmative test results are not necessary in order to make practical use of the CPM.[15]

□ 8.3.2 An Example

In the example that was used earlier, Able, Baker, and Charlie were shown to form the market portfolio in proportions equal to .12, .19, and .69, respectively. Given these proportions, the market portfolio was shown to have an expected return of 22.4% and a standard deviation of 15.2%. The risk-free rate in the example was 4%. Thus, for this example the SML as indicated in equation (8.6) is:

$$\bar{r}_i = r_f + \left[\frac{\bar{r}_M - r_f}{\sigma_M^2}\right]\sigma_{iM} \tag{8.6}$$

$$= 4 + \left[\frac{22.4 - 4}{(15.2)^2}\right]\sigma_{iM}$$

$$= 4 + .08\sigma_{iM}. \tag{8.10}$$

The following expected return vector and variance-covariance matrix were used in the examples shown in Chapters 6 and 7, and are also used here:

$$ER = \begin{bmatrix} 16.2 \\ 24.6 \\ 22.8 \end{bmatrix} \quad VC = \begin{bmatrix} 146 & 187 & 145 \\ 187 & 854 & 104 \\ 145 & 104 & 289 \end{bmatrix}.$$

At this point, the covariances of each security with the market portfolio can be calculated by using equation (8.4). More specifically, the covariances for the market portfolio for Able, Baker, and Charlie are equal to:

$$\sigma_{1M} = \sum_{j=1}^{3} X_{jM}\sigma_{1j}$$

$$= (.12 \times 146) + (.19 \times 187) + (.69 \times 145)$$

$$= 153$$

$$\sigma_{2M} = \sum_{j=1}^{3} X_{jM}\sigma_{2j}$$

$$= (.12 \times 187) + (.19 \times 854) + (.69 \times 104)$$

$$= 257$$

$$\sigma_{3M} = \sum_{j=1}^{3} X_{jM}\sigma_{3j}$$

$$= (.12 \times 145) + (.19 \times 104) + (.69 \times 289)$$

$$= 236.$$

---

[15] See Chapter 10 of Alexander and Francis, *Portfolio Analysis*; and Harry M. Markowitz, "Nonnegative of Not Nonnegative: A Question About CAPMs," *Journal of Finance* 38, no. 2 (May 1983):283–95.

Note how the SML as given in equation (8.10) states that the expected return for Able should be equal to $4 + (.08 \times 153) = 16.2\%$. Similarly, the expected return for Baker should be $4 + (.08 \times 257) = 24.6\%$ and the expected return for Charlie should be $4 + (.08 \times 236) = 22.8\%$. Each one of these expected returns corresponds to the respective value given in the expected return vector.

Alternatively, equation (8.8) can be used to calculate the betas for the three companies. More specifically, the betas for Able, Baker, and Charlie are equal to:

$$\beta_1 = \frac{\sigma_{1M}}{\sigma_M^2}$$

$$= \frac{153}{(15.2)^2}$$

$$= .66$$

$$\beta_2 = \frac{\sigma_{2M}}{\sigma_M^2}$$

$$= \frac{257}{(15.2)^2}$$

$$= 1.11$$

$$\beta_3 = \frac{\sigma_{3M}}{\sigma_M^2}$$

$$= \frac{236}{(15.2)^2}$$

$$= 1.02.$$

Now equation (8.7) indicated that the SML could be expressed in a form where the measure of risk for an asset was its beta. For the example under consideration, this reduces to:

$$\bar{r}_i = r_f + (\bar{r}_M - r_f)\beta_i$$

$$= 4 + (22.4 - 4)\beta_i \tag{8.11}$$

$$= 4 + 18.4\beta_i.$$

Note how the SML as given in this equation states that the expected return for Able should be equal to $4 + (18.4 \times .66) = 16.2\%$. Similarly, the expected return for Baker should be $4 + (18.4 \times 1.11) = 24.6\%$ and the expected return for Charlie should be $4 + (18.4 \times 1.02) = 22.8\%$. Each one of these expected returns corresponds to the respective value given in the expected return vector.

It is important to realize that if any other portfolio is assumed to be the market portfolio, meaning that if any set of proportions other than .12, .19, and .69 is used, then such an equilibrium relationship between expected

returns and betas (or covariances) will not hold. Consider a hypothetical market portfolio with equal proportions (that is, .333) invested in Able, Baker, and Charlie. Since this portfolio has an expected return of 21.2% and a standard deviation of 15.5%, the hypothetical SML would be as follows:

$$\bar{r}_i = r_f + \left[\frac{\bar{r}_M - r_f}{\sigma_M^2}\right] \sigma_{iM}$$

$$= 4 + \left[\frac{21.2 - 4}{(15.5)^2}\right] \sigma_{iM}$$

$$= 4 + .07\sigma_{iM}.$$

Able has a covariance with this portfolio of

$$\sigma_{1M} = \sum_{j=1}^{3} X_{jM}\sigma_{1j}$$

$$= (.333 \times 146) + (.333 \times 187) + (.333 \times 145)$$

$$= 159,$$

which means that Able's expected return according to the hypothetical SML should be equal to $4 + (.07 \times 159) = 15.1\%$. However, since this does not correspond to the 16.2% figure that appears in the expected return vector, a portfolio with equal proportions invested in Able, Baker, and Charlie cannot be the market portfolio.[16]

8.4 MARKET AND UNIQUE RISK

Since beta (or covariance) is the relevant measure of risk for a security according to the CAPM, it is only appropriate to explore the relationship between it and the *total risk* of the security. This relationship is of the following form:

$$\sigma_i = [\beta_i^2 \sigma_M^2 + \sigma_{\epsilon i}^2]^{1/2}. \tag{8.12}$$

Here the total risk of security i, measured by its standard deviation and denoted by σ_i, is shown to be broken down into two components. The first component is the portion related to moves of the market portfolio. It is equal to the product of the square of the beta of the firm and the variance of the market portfolio and is often referred to as the *market* (or systematic) *risk* of the security. The second component is the portion not related to moves of the market portfolio. It is denoted by $\sigma_{\epsilon i}^2$ and is often referred to as the *unique* (or nonmarket or unsystematic) *risk* of the security.

From the earlier example, the betas of Able, Baker, and Charlie were

---

[16] Baker and Charlie have covariances of 382 and 179, respectively, which means that their expected returns should be equal to $30.74\% = 4 + (.07 \times 382)$ and $16.53\% = 4 + (.07 \times 179)$. However, these figures do not correspond to the respective figures (24.6% and 22.8%) appearing in the expected return vector, indicating there are discrepancies for all three securities. While this example has used the covariance version of the SML, the analysis is similar for the beta version of SML shown in equation (8.7).

calculated to be .66, 1.11, and 1.02, respectively. Since the standard deviation of the market portfolio was equal to 15.2%, this means that the market risks of the three firms are equal to $(.66^2 \times 15.2^2) = 100$, $(1.11^2 \times 15.2^2) = 285$, and $(1.02^2 \times 15.2^2) = 240$, respectively.

The unique risk of any security can be calculated by squaring both sides of equation (8.12),

$$\sigma_i^2 = \beta_i^2 \sigma_M^2 + \sigma_{\epsilon i}^2 \qquad (8.13)$$

and then solving for $\sigma_{\epsilon i}^2$:

$$\sigma_i^2 - \beta_i^2 \sigma_M^2 = \sigma_{\epsilon i}^2. \qquad (8.14)$$

Thus, equation (8.14) can be used to calculate the unique risk of Able, Baker, and Charlie, respectively:

$$\sigma_{\epsilon 1}^2 = 146 - 100$$
$$= 46$$
$$\sigma_{\epsilon 2}^2 = 854 - 285$$
$$= 569$$
$$\sigma_{\epsilon 3}^2 = 289 - 240$$
$$= 49.$$

Unique risk is usually expressed as a standard deviation. This is calculated by taking the square root of $\sigma_{\epsilon i}^2$ and equals $\sqrt{46} = 6.8\%$ for Able, $\sqrt{569} = 23.9\%$ for Baker, and $\sqrt{49} = 7\%$ for Charlie.

At this point one may wonder, Why break total risk into two parts? For the investor, it would seem that risk is risk—whatever its source. The answer lies in the domain of expected returns.

Market risk is related to the risk of the market portfolio and to the beta of the security (or portfolio) in question. Securities (or portfolios) with larger betas will have larger amounts of market risk. In the world of the CAPM, securities (or portfolios) with larger betas will have larger expected returns. These two relationships together imply that securities (or portfolios) with larger market risks should have larger expected returns.

Unique risk is not related to beta. This means that there is no reason why securities (or portfolios) with larger amounts of unique risks should have larger expected returns. Thus, according to the CAPM, market risk is rewarded, whereas unique risk is not.

8.5 EXPECTED VERSUS ACTUAL VALUES

Forecasting a security's return is analogous to forecasting tomorrow's high temperature. The meteorologist has some model for estimating what the *expected* high temperature will be. For example, the model may have two

components where the expected high is equal to the sum of (1) .9 times the expected low temperature tonight and (2) 14°.

Based on this model, the actual high temperature that subsequently occurs can be thought of as having three components. Specifically, the actual high temperature can be thought of as being equal to the sum of (1) .9 times the actual low tonight, (2) 14°, and (3) a random error term. This random error term can be thought of as representing the outcome from a spin of a roulette wheel, where the expected outcome from spinning the wheel is zero (perhaps the wheel has degrees from $-5°$ to $+5°$ evenly spaced on it).

Note that there are two related models involved here—one for the *expected* high temperature and one for the *actual* high temperature. The analogy with security returns is that there are again two such models involved—one for expected returns (the SML, which has two components) and one for actual returns (the characteristic line, which has three components). The discussion begins with expected returns.

8.6 EQUILIBRIUM EXPECTED RETURNS

According to the CAPM, asset prices will adjust until equilibrium occurs whereby each and every security plots on the SML. Equivalently, in equilibrium the expected return on security i over the forthcoming holding period will be given by

$$\bar{r}_i^e = r_f + (\bar{r}_M - r_f)\beta_i \qquad (8.15)$$

where:

$\bar{r}_i^e$ denotes the *equilibrium* expected return on security i,

$\bar{r}_f$ denotes the risk-free rate,

$\bar{r}_M$ denotes the expected return on the market portfolio, and

β_i denotes the beta coefficient for security i.

For example, assume the expected return on the market portfolio is 15% and the risk-free rate is 10%. Furthermore, assume securities A and B have betas of 1.2 and .8, respectively. In this situation, the equilibrium expected return on security A is equal to 16% = 10% + [(15% − 10%) × 1.2]. Similarly, the equilibrium expected return on security B is 10% + [(15% − 10%) × .8] = 14%.

Figure 8.3 provides a graphic representation of this example. Since it has been assumed that the expected return on the market portfolio is 15% and the risk-free rate is 10%, the location of the SML has been fixed. This is because it must pass through these two points. As mentioned earlier, the SML indicates that any security with a beta of 1.2 will have an equilibrium expected return of 16%. Similarly, any security with a beta of .8 will have an equilibrium expected return of 14%.

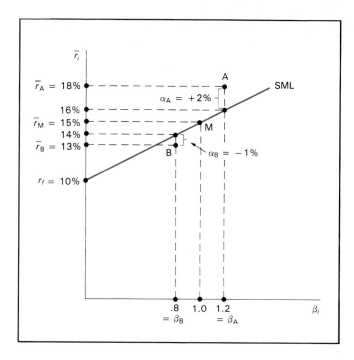

FIGURE 8–3
Equilibrium expected returns for securities.

8.7 RETURN-GENERATING PROCESSES

☐ 8.7.1 The Characteristic Line

Equation (8.15) can be rewritten as

$$\bar{r}^e_i - r_f = (\bar{r}_M - r_f)\beta_i \qquad (8.16)$$

thereby showing that the equilibrium expected *excess return* for a security over the forthcoming holding period is equal to the product of the expected excess return on the market portfolio and the beta of the security.

However, equation (8.16) is not a model for what the actual excess return on a security will be over the forthcoming holding period. For this purpose, a *return-generating process* is used. The *characteristic line* is a type of return-generating process that is based on equation (8.16):

$$r_i - r_f = (r_M - r_f)\beta_i + \epsilon_i \qquad (8.17)$$

where r_i is the actual return on security i that will occur over the forthcoming holding period, r_f is the risk-free rate for this period, and r_M is the actual return on the market portfolio for this period. The term β_i is the beta for security i for this period, whereas the last term, ϵ_i, is known as the security's *random error term.*[17]

---

[17] It is also common practice to use the following equation as the return-generating process for a security: $r_i = a_i + r_M\beta_i + e_i$, where a_i is a constant and e_i is a random error term. This equation is also often referred to as the *market model*.

The random error term for a security is a random variable with an expected value of zero and a standard deviation denoted by $\sigma_{\epsilon i}$. It can be thought of as the outcome that will occur when a roulette wheel is spun. One feature of such a random error term is that its expected outcome is zero.

For example, security A may be thought of as having a random error term corresponding to a roulette wheel with integer values on it that range from -10% to $+10\%$, with the values evenly spaced.[18] This means that there are 21 possible outcomes, each of which has an equal probability of occurring. Given the range of numbers, it also means that the expected outcome of the random error term is zero:

$$[-10 \times \tfrac{1}{21}] + [-9 \times \tfrac{1}{21}] + \cdots + [9 \times \tfrac{1}{21}] + [10 \times \tfrac{1}{21}] = 0.$$

As can be seen, this calculation involves multiplying each outcome by its probability of occurring and then summing up the resulting products. The standard deviation of this random error term can now be shown to be equal to 6.06%:

$$\{[(-10-0)^2 \times \tfrac{1}{21}] + [(-9-0)^2 \times \tfrac{1}{21}] + \cdots \\ + [(9-0)^2 \times \tfrac{1}{21}] + [(10-0)^2 \times \tfrac{1}{21}]\}^{1/2} = 6.06\%.$$

This calculation involves subtracting the expected outcome from each possible outcome, then squaring each one of these differences, multiplying each square by the probability of the corresponding outcome occurring, adding the products, and finally taking the square root of the resulting sum.

Figure 8.4 illustrates the roulette wheel corresponding to this random error term. In general, securities will have random error terms whose corresponding roulette wheels have different ranges and different forms of uneven spacing. Although all will have an expected value of zero, they will typically have different standard deviations. For example, security B may have a random error term whose expected value and standard deviation are equal to 0 and 4.76%, respectively.[19]

□ 8.7.2 Actual Excess Returns

The characteristic line for security i given in equation (8.17) suggests that the actual excess return for this particular security can be thought of as having two components. The first component is equal to the actual excess return on the market portfolio, multiplied by the security's beta coefficient. The second component is equal to the outcome from a spin of the roulette wheel for the security.

---

[18] Since the range refers to the possible outcomes and the spacing refers to the probabilities of the various outcomes occurring, it can be seen that the roulette wheel is just a convenient way of referring to the random error term's probability distribution. Typically, it is assumed that the random error term has a normal probability distribution.

[19] This would be the case if security B had a random error term whose roulette wheel had integers from -9% to $+9\%$ on it, but the spacing for each integer between -5% and $+5\%$ was twice as large as the spacing for each integer from -9% to -6% and $+6\%$ to $+9\%$. This means that the probability of any specific integer between -5% and $+5\%$ occurring is equal to $\tfrac{2}{30}$, whereas the probability of any specific integer from -9% to -6% and $+6\%$ to $+9\%$ occurring is equal to $\tfrac{1}{30}$.

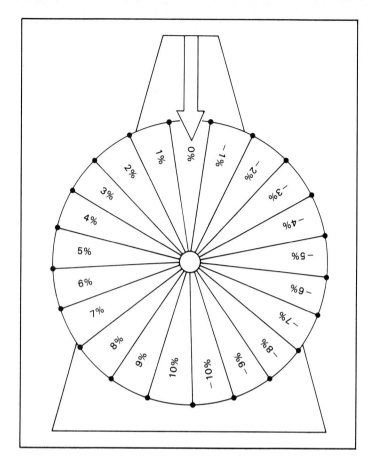

FIGURE 8–4
Security A's random error term.

The characteristic line for security A would look like

$$r_A - r_f = [(r_M - r_f) \times 1.2] + \epsilon_A \qquad \textbf{(8.18)}$$

since the security's beta was determined to be 1.2. Thus, the actual excess return of security A will consist of an excess return on the market portfolio multiplied by 1.2, and a random error term.

Similarly, the characteristic line for security B would look like:

$$r_B - r_f = [(r_M - r_f) \times .8] + \epsilon_B \qquad \textbf{(8.19)}$$

since the security's beta was determined to be equal to .8.

The solid line in part (a) of Figure 8.5 provides a graph of the characteristic line for security A. This line corresponds to the characteristic line given by equation (8.18) but without the random error term. Accordingly, the graph for the characteristic line of security A corresponds to the following equation:

$$r_A - r_f = [(r_M - r_f) \times 1.2].$$

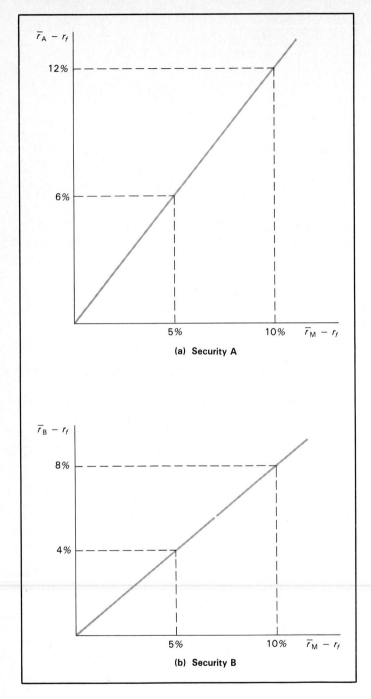

(a) Security A

(b) Security B

FIGURE 8–5
Characteristic lines.

Here the vertical axis measures the excess return on security A, $r_A - r_f$, whereas the horizontal axis measures the excess return on the market portfolio, $r_M - r_f$. The line goes through two points. First, the line goes through the origin, since the intercept is zero. Second, the line goes through the point corresponding to the equilibrium expected excess return on the security (16% − 10% = 6%) and on the market portfolio (15% − 10% = 5%). It should be noted that this line will have a slope equal to the beta of the security, 1.2.[20]

Part (b) of Figure 8.5 presents the graph of the characteristic line for security B:

$$r_B - r_f = [(r_M - r_f) \times .8].$$

This line also goes through the origin and a point corresponding to the equilibrium expected excess return on the security (14% − 10% = 4%) and on the market portfolio (15% − 10% = 5%). Note that its slope is equal to the beta of the security, .8.

At this point it can be seen that since the slope of a security's characteristic line is equal to the security's beta, *a security's beta measures the sensitivity of the security's returns to the market portfolio's returns*. Both lines in Figure 8.5 have positive slopes, indicating that the higher the returns on the market portfolio, the higher the returns on the two securities. However, the two securities have different slopes; hence they have different sensitivities to returns on the market portfolio. Specifically, security A has a higher beta than security B; thus, the characteristic line of A has a greater slope than the characteristic line of B, indicating that the returns on A are more sensitive than the returns on B to the returns on the market portfolio.

For example, if the market portfolio has a return that is 20%, it will have returned 5% more than expected (its expected return was 15%) and 10% more than the riskfree rate. Part (a) of Figure 8.5 indicates that security A should have an excess return that is 12%, which is 6% ([(20% − 10%) × 1.2] − 6%) more than initially expected in this situation. Similarly, part (b) indicates that security B should have an excess return that is 8%, which is 4% ([(20% − 10%) × .8] − 4%) more than initially expected in this situation. The reason for the 2% (6% − 4%) difference is because security A has a higher beta than security B—that is, A is more sensitive than B to returns on the market portfolio.

The random error term suggests that for a given return on the market portfolio, the actual return on a security will lie off the line shown by its graph.[21] If the actual excess returns on securities A and B subsequently turn out to be 9% and 11%, respectively, and the market portfolio's actual excess return turns out to be 10%, then the actual excess return on A and B could be viewed as having the following two components:

---

[20] This can be seen by remembering that the slope of a line connecting two points is equal to the vertical distance between the two points divided by the horizontal distance between the two points. In this example, such a calculation results in (6% − 0%)/(5% − 0%) = 1.2, the beta of security A.

[21] To be completely accurate, if the random error term takes on a value of zero, then the security will lie *on* the line. However, the probability of this occurring is very small for most securities.

	SECURITY A	SECURITY B
Actual excess return on the market portfolio × beta	12% = 10% × 1.2	8% = 10% × .8
Random error outcome	−3% = 9% − 12%	3% = 11% − 8%
Actual excess return	9%	11%

In this case, the roulette wheels for A and B can be thought of as having been "spun," resulting in values (that is, random error outcomes) of -3% for A and $+3\%$ for B. These values can be viewed as being equal to the distance by which each security's actual return ended up being above or below its characteristic line.

8.8 DIVERSIFICATION

In equation (8.12) the total risk of any security i, measured by its standard deviation and denoted by σ_i, was shown to consist of two parts: (1) market (or systematic) risk, denoted by $\beta_i^2 \sigma_M^2$, and (2) unique (or nonmarket or unsystematic) risk, denoted by $\sigma_{\epsilon i}^2$.

The characteristic line provides a convenient interpretation for the term $\sigma_{\epsilon i}^2$ in this equation. This term is the variance of the random error term ϵ_i appearing in equation (8.17).

☐ 8.8.1 Portfolio Total Risk

When the return on every risky *security* is related to the return on the market portfolio as specified in equation (8.17), what can be said about the total risk of a *portfolio*? If the proportion of funds invested in security i for a given portfolio p is denoted by X_i, then the actual excess return on this portfolio will be:

$$r_p - r_f = \left(\sum_{i=1}^{N} X_i r_i \right) - r_f$$

$$(8.20)$$

$$= \sum_{i=1}^{N} X_i (r_i - r_f).$$

Substituting the right-hand side of equation (8.17) for $r_i - r_f$ in equation (8.20) results in the following characteristic line for the portfolio:

$$r_p - r_f = \sum_{i=1}^{N} X_i[(r_M - r_f)\beta_i + \epsilon_i]$$

$$= \left(\sum_{i=1}^{N} X_i \beta_i \right)(r_M - r_f) + \sum_{i=1}^{N} X_i \epsilon_i$$

$$(8.21)$$

$$= (r_M - r_f)\beta_p + \epsilon_p$$

where

$$\beta_p = \sum_{i=1}^{N} X_i \beta_i \qquad \text{(8.22a)}$$

$$\epsilon_p = \sum_{i=1}^{N} X_i \epsilon_i. \qquad \text{(8.22b)}$$

In equation (8.22a) the portfolio's beta (β_p) is shown to be a weighted average of the betas of the securities (β_i), using their relative proportions in the portfolio as weights. Similarly, in equation (8.22b) the portfolio's random error term (ϵ_p) is a weighted average of the random error terms of the securities, again using their respective proportions in the portfolio as weights. Thus, the portfolio's characteristic line is a straightforward extension of the characteristic line for individual securities given in equation (8.17).

From equation (8.21), it follows that the total risk of a portfolio, measured by the standard deviation of the portfolio's returns and denoted by σ_p, will be

$$\sigma_p = [\beta_p^2 \sigma_M^2 + \sigma_{\epsilon p}^2]^{1/2} \qquad \text{(8.23)}$$

where

$$\beta_p^2 = \left(\sum_{i=1}^{N} X_i \beta_i \right)^2 \qquad \text{(8.24a)}$$

and, assuming the random error components of security returns are uncorrelated,

$$\sigma_{\epsilon p}^2 = \sum_{i=1}^{N} X_i^2 \sigma_{\epsilon i}^2. \qquad \text{(8.24b)}$$

Equation (8.23) shows that the total risk of any portfolio can be viewed as having two components similar to the two components of the total risk of an individual security. These components are again referred to as market risk ($\beta_p^2 \sigma_M^2$) and unique risk ($\sigma_{\epsilon p}^2$).

Next, it will be shown that increased *diversification* can lead to the reduction of a portfolio's total risk. This will occur due to a reduction in the size of the portfolio's unique risk, whereas the portfolio's market risk will remain approximately the same size.

□ 8.8.2 **Portfolio Market Risk**

Generally, the more diversified a portfolio (that is, the larger the number of securities in the portfolio), the smaller each proportion X_i will be. This will not cause β_p to either decrease or increase significantly unless a deliberate attempt is made to do so by adding either low or high beta securities, respectively, to the portfolio. That is, since a portfolio's beta is an average of the betas of its securities, there is no reason to suspect that increasing the amount of diversification will cause the portfolio beta, and thus the market risk of the portfolio, to change in a particular direction. Accordingly,

Diversification leads to *averaging* of market risk.

This makes sense because when prospects for the economy turn sour (or rosy), most securities will fall (or rise) in price. Regardless of the amount of diversification, portfolio returns will always be susceptible to such market-wide influences.

☐ 8.8.3   Portfolio Unique Risk

The situation is entirely different for unique risk. In a portfolio, some securities will go up as a result of unexpected good news specific to the company that issued the securities (such as an unexpected discovery of a new drug by a pharmaceutical company). Other securities will go down as a result of unexpected company-specific bad news (such as an industrial accident by a chemical company). Looking forward, approximately as many companies can be expected to have good news as bad news, leading to little anticipated net impact on the return of a "well-diversified" portfolio. This means that as a portfolio becomes more diversified, the smaller its unique risk, and, in turn, its total risk, will be.

This can be quantified precisely if the random error components of returns are assumed to be uncorrelated, as was done when equation (8.24b) was written. Consider the following situation. If the amount invested in each security is equal, then the proportion X_i will equal $1/N$ and the level of unique risk, as shown in equation (8.24b), will be equal to:

$$\sigma_{\epsilon p}^2 = \sum_{i=1}^{N} \left[\frac{1}{N} \right]^2 \sigma_{\epsilon i}^2$$

$$= \frac{1}{N} \left[\frac{\sigma_{\epsilon 1}^2 + \sigma_{\epsilon 2}^2 + \cdots + \sigma_{\epsilon N}^2}{N} \right].$$

(8.25)

The value inside the square brackets in equation (8.25) is simply the average unique risk for the component securities. But the portfolio's unique risk is only $1/N$ as large as this, since the term $(1/N)$ appears outside the square brackets. Now as the portfolio becomes more diversified, the number of securities in it (that is, N) becomes larger. In turn, this means that $1/N$ becomes smaller, resulting in the portfolio having less unique risk.[22] That is,

Diversification can substantially *reduce* unique risk.

Roughly speaking, a portfolio that has 20 or more securities in it will have a negligible amount of unique risk. This means that its total risk will be approximately equal to the amount of market risk that is present.[23] Thus, such portfolios are "well diversified."

---

[22] Actually, all that is necessary for this reduction in unique risk to occur is for the maximum amount invested in any one security to continually decrease as N increases.

[23] See John L. Evans and Stephen Archer, "Diversification and the Reduction of Dispersion: An Empirical Analysis," *Journal of Finance* 23, no. 5 (December 1968):761–67.

□ 8.8.4 An Example

Consider the two securities, A and B, that were referred to earlier. These two securities had betas of 1.2 and .8, respectively, and the standard deviations of their random error terms were, respectively, 6.06% and 4.76%. Thus, given that $\sigma_{\epsilon A} = 6.06\%$ and $\sigma_{\epsilon B} = 4.76\%$, it follows that $\sigma_{\epsilon A}^2 = .0606^2 = .0037$ and $\sigma_{\epsilon B}^2 = .0476^2 = .0023$. Now, assume that the standard deviation of the market portfolio, σ_M, is 8%, which implies that the variance of the market portfolio is $.08^2 = .0064$. Using equation (8.12), this means that the standard deviation of securities A and B are, respectively, as follows:

$$\sigma_A = [(1.2^2 \times .0064) + .0037]^{1/2}$$

$$= (.0129)^{1/2}$$

$$= 11.36\%$$

$$\sigma_B = [(.8^2 \times .0064) + .0023]^{1/2}$$

$$= (.0064)^{1/2}$$

$$= 8.00\%.$$

A Two-Security Portfolio

Consider combining securities A and B into a portfolio, with an equal amount of the investor's money going into each security. That is, consider a portfolio that has $X_A = .5$ and $X_B = .5$. Since $\beta_A = 1.2$ and $\beta_B = .8$, the beta of this portfolio can be calculated using equation (8.22a):

$$\beta_p = X_A \beta_A + X_B \beta_B$$

$$= (1.5 \times 1.2) + (.5 \times .8)$$

$$= 1.0.$$

Using equation (8.24b), the variance of the portfolio's random error term, $\sigma_{\epsilon p}^2$, will be equal to

$$\sigma_{\epsilon p} = (.5^2 \times .0037) + (.5^2 \times .0023)$$

$$= .0015.$$

In turn, this indicates that the standard deviation of the portfolio's random error term, $\sigma_{\epsilon p}$, is equal to:

$$\sigma_{\epsilon p} = \sqrt{.0015}$$

$$= 3.87\%.$$

From equation (8.23), it can be seen that this portfolio will have the following standard deviation:

$$\sigma_p = [(1.0^2 \times .0064) + .0015]^{1/2}$$

$$= [.0079]^{1/2}$$

$$= 8.89\%.$$

This represents the total risk of the two-security portfolio.

A Three-Security Portfolio

Consider what would happen if a third security (C) was combined with the other two to form a three-security portfolio having $X_A = X_B = X_C = .33$. This third security has a beta of 1.0 and a random error term whose standard deviation $(\sigma_{\epsilon C})$ is 5.50%. Thus, the variance of the random error term is $\sigma_{\epsilon C}^2 = .055^2 = .0030$, and the security's standard deviation is

$$\sigma_C = [(1.0^2 \times .0064) + .0030]^{1/2}$$

$$= [.0094]^{1/2}$$

$$= 9.70\%.$$

First of all, note that the three-security portfolio has the same amount of market risk as the two-security portfolio, since both portfolios have a beta of 1.0:

$$\beta_p = X_A \beta_A + X_B \beta_B + X_C \beta_C$$

$$= (.33 \times 1.2) + (.33 \times .8) + (.33 \times 1.0)$$

$$= 1.0.$$

Thus, increased diversification has not lead to a change in the level of market risk. Instead, it has led to an averaging of market risk.

Using equation (8.24b), the variance of the portfolio's random error term will be equal to

$$\sigma_{\epsilon p}^2 = (.33^2 \times .0037) + (.33^2 \times .0023) + (.33^2 \times .0030)$$

$$= .0010.$$

In turn, this indicates that the standard deviation of the portfolio's random error term is equal to

$$\sigma_{\epsilon p} = \sqrt{.0010}$$

$$= 3.13\%.$$

Note that the standard deviation of this three-security portfolio's random error term is less than the standard deviation of the two-security portfolio's random error term (that is, $3.13\% < 3.87\%$). In turn, the standard deviation of the two-security portfolio's random error term is less than the standard deviation of either one of the securities' random error terms (that is, $3.87\% < 6.06\%$ and $3.87\% < 4.76\%$). Thus, in this example increased diversification has indeed reduced unique risk.

From equation (8.23), it can be seen that this three-security portfolio will have the following standard deviation:

$$\sigma_p = [(1.0^2 \times .0064) + .0010]^{1/2}$$

$$= [.0074]^{1/2}$$

$$= 8.60\%.$$

This represents the total risk of the portfolio and is less than the total risk of the two-security portfolio (8.60% < 8.89%). Thus, diversification has led to a reduction in total risk.

8.9 DISEQUILIBRIUM

Many investors spend a great deal of time searching for securities that appear to be *mispriced*. There are two types of mispriced securities:

A security is *underpriced* (or undervalued) if its expected return is greater than the appropriate expected return for securities with comparable relevant attributes.

A security is *overpriced* (or overvalued) if its expected return is less than the appropriate expected return for securities with comparable relevant attributes.

What attributes are relevant? And what is the appropriate expected return for a given set of attributes? The answer depends on which equilibrium theory of asset pricing is used. For the CAPM, only one attribute is relevant (beta), and the appropriate expected return is that shown by the SML, as given in equation (8.15).

Security prices and expected returns either conform to a given equilibrium theory of asset pricing or they do not. If at least some securities do not conform to this theory, then according to *that theory there is disequilibrium* in their prices and expected returns. However, it is more likely that this particular theory is not valid and some other (perhaps unknown) equilibrium theory is valid. Instead of attempting to discover this theory, an incredibly difficult if not impossible task, many investors assume that *most* securities are priced to give equilibrium expected returns according to some theory, with certain other ones being mispriced and in disequilibrium.

It is important to note that investors will typically disagree on which securities are mispriced. Some investors may feel that a given security is underpriced, others may feel it is overpriced, and still others may feel it is priced correctly. One implication is that a security may not be mispriced when an investor believes it is mispriced. Keep in mind that the discussion that follows is from the perspective of one investor whose opinions may not be shared by anyone else.

□ 8.9.1 Alpha

The extent to which an investor believes a security is mispriced can be measured by its *alpha*. The idea here is to compare the expected return on a security, denoted by $\bar{r}_i$, with the *equilibrium expected return* for the security, denoted by $\bar{r}_i^e$ in equation (8.15). The equilibrium expected return for a security is what the expected return "should be" if the security were priced correctly.

Specifically, a security's alpha is the *difference between its expected return and an appropriate (equilibrium) expected return*:

$$\alpha_i = \bar{r}_i - \bar{r}_i^e. \tag{8.26}$$

Thus, a security will be mispriced and in disequilibrium if, in the opinion of the investor, it has a nonzero alpha, since then its expected return $\bar{r}_i$ will not be equal to its equilibrium expected return $\bar{r}_i^e$. (How an investor can go about estimating a security's alpha is discussed in Chapter 16).

Equation (8.15) gives the value of the equilibrium expected return for any security based on the CAPM. Thus, equation (8.26) can be rewritten by substituting the right-hand side of equation (8.17) for $\bar{r}_i^e$ in equation (8.26), resulting in

$$\alpha_i = \bar{r}_i - [r_f + (\bar{r}_M - r_f)\beta_i]. \tag{8.27}$$

Equation (8.27) shows that an investor will view a security as being mispriced relative to the CAPM if he or she believes it has a nonzero alpha. This situation will occur if the investor has estimated the security's expected return $\bar{r}_i$ and found it to be different from $r_f + (\bar{r}_M - r_f)\beta_i$.

Continuing with the earlier example, imagine a certain investor has examined the two securities that were referred to as A and B and, as before, estimates their betas to be equal to 1.2 and .8, respectively. However, this investor has estimated the expected return for security A over the forthcoming holding period to be equal to 18%. According to equation (8.27), he or she believes the security is mispriced, since it has a nonzero alpha equal to $+2\% = 18\% - 16\%$. (Remember that earlier it was shown that any security with a beta of 1.2 has an equilibrium expected return of 16%).

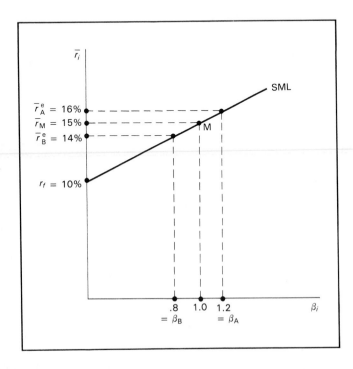

FIGURE 8–6
Alphas for securities.

In regard to security B, this investor has estimated its expected return to be equal to 13%. Noting it has a nonzero alpha of $-1\% = 13\% - 14\%$, he or she believes that security B is also mispriced.

Figure 8.6 provides a graphical illustration of this example. Since the expected return on the market portfolio has been assumed to be 15% and the risk-free rate has been assumed to be 10%, the location of the SML is the same as in Figure 8.3. As mentioned earlier, the SML indicates that any security with a beta of 1.2 that is priced correctly will have an expected return of 16%. Similarly, any security with a beta of .8 that is priced correctly will have an expected return of 14%.

It can be seen in Figure 8.6 that with the CAPM, a security's alpha is equal to the vertical distance by which it lies above or below the SML. Thus, a security with a positive estimated alpha (such as A) will lie above the SML and be viewed as underpriced. A security with a negative estimated alpha (such as B) will lie below the SML and be viewed as overpriced. Securities that are felt to be priced correctly will have estimated alphas of zero and lie on the SML.

☐ 8.9.2   The Return-Generating Process

Equation (8.27) can be rewritten as

$$\bar{r}_i - r_f = \alpha_i + (\bar{r}_M - r_f)\beta_i \qquad (8.28)$$

thereby showing that the expected excess return for a security over the forthcoming holding period has two components, being equal to the sum of (1) the alpha of the security and (2) the product of the expected excess return on the market portfolio and the beta of the security.

However, equation (8.28) is not a model for what the actual excess return on a security will be over the forthcoming holding period. For this purpose a return-generating process that is based on equation (8.28) is used:

$$r_i - r_f = \alpha_i + (r_M - r_f)\beta_i + \epsilon_i. \qquad (8.29)$$

It can be seen that, with the exception of alpha (α_i), this return-generating process is identical to the one in equation (8.17). Thus, in cases where alpha is zero, the two are identical. Accordingly, equation (8.29) is known as the *characteristic line* for a security, with the one given in equation (8.17) being a special case where alpha is zero.

The characteristic line for security i that is given in equation (8.29) suggests that the actual excess return for this particular security can be thought of as having three components. The first component is equal to the alpha of the security. The second component is equal to the actual excess return on the market portfolio, multiplied by the security's beta coefficient. The third component is equal to the random error term's outcome.

In the case of the investor who has estimated security's A's alpha and beta to be equal to 2% and 1.2, respectively, the characteristic line for this security would look like:

$$r_A - r_f = 2\% + [(r_M - r_f) \times 1.2] + \epsilon_A. \qquad (8.30a)$$

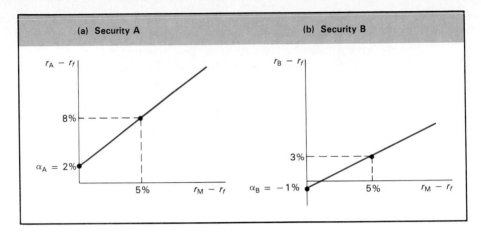

FIGURE 8–7
Characteristic lines (with disequilibrium).

Thus, the actual excess return of security A will consist of an alpha of 2%, the excess return on the market portfolio multiplied by 1.2, and a random error term.

Similarly, the characteristic line for security B would look like

$$r_B - r_f = -1\% + [(r_M - r_f) \times .8] + \epsilon_B \qquad (8.30b)$$

since its alpha and beta were estimated to be equal to -1% and .8, respectively.

□ 8.9.3 Graphing Characteristic Lines

The solid line in panel (a) of Figure 8.7 provides a graph of the characteristic line for security A. This line corresponds to the return-generating process given in equation (8.30a) but without the random error term. Accordingly, the graph of the characteristic line for security A corresponds to the following equation:

$$r_A - r_f = 2\% + [(r_M - r_f) \times 1.2].$$

Here the vertical axis measures the expected excess return on the particular security $(r_A - r_f)$, and the horizontal axis measures the expected excess return on the market portfolio $(r_M - r_f)$. The line goes through two points. First, the line goes through the point on the vertical axis corresponding to the value of alpha, which in this case is 2%. Second, the line goes through the point corresponding to the forecasted expected excess return on the security $(18\% - 10\% = 8\%)$ and on the market portfolio $(15\% - 10\% = 5\%)$. It should be noted that this line will have a slope equal to the beta of the security, which is 1.2 in this example.[24]

Part (b) of Figure 8.7 presents the graph of the characteristic line for security B:

$$r_B - r_f = -1\% + [(r_M - r_f) \times .8].$$

---

[24] The slope is equal to $(8\% - 2\%)/(5\% - 0\%) = 1.2$, which is the beta of security A.

This line goes through the point on the vertical axis corresponding to the value of security's B's alpha, -1%. It also goes through the point corresponding to the forcasted expected excess return on the security (13% − $10\% = 3\%$) and on the market portfolio ($15\% - 10\% = 5\%$) and has a slope equal to the beta of security B, which is .8 in this example.

These two characteristic lines are similar to those shown earlier in Figure 8.5. Both sets of characteristic lines have the same respective slopes, since these slopes correspond to the securities' betas, and these betas are the same regardless of whether or not the securities are mispriced. The only difference in the characteristic lines is in the location of the vertical intercepts. In Figure 8.5, both securities were assumed to be fairly priced and thus had alphas of zero. This resulted in the lines passing through the origin. However, if the securities are believed to be mispriced, then they will have nonzero alphas and their characteristic lines will have a nonzero vertical intercept that corresponds to their alphas as shown in Figure 8.7. Thus, the characteristic lines in Figure 8.7 are parallel to those shown in Figure 8.5.

As in Figure 8.5, the random error term indicates that for a given return on the market portfolio, the actual return on a security will lie off its characteristic line. For example, imagine as before that the actual excess returns on securities A and B subsequently turn out to be 9% and 11%, while the market portfolio's actual excess return turns out to be 10%. In this situation the actual excess returns on A and B would have the following three components, according to the investor who felt these two securities were initially mispriced:

	SECURITY A	SECURITY B
Alpha	2%	−1%
Actual excess return on the market portfolio times beta	12% = 10% × 1.2	8% = 10% × .8
Random error outcome	−5% = 9% − (2% + 12%)	4% = 11% − (−1% + 8%)
Actual excess return	9%	11%

In this case, the roulette wheels for A and B can be thought of as having been spun, resulting in values (that is, random error outcomes) of −5% for A and +4% for B. These values can be viewed as being equal to the distance each security's actual return ended up being above or below its characteristic line after the holding period had elapsed. Note how these random error outcomes differ from those shown earlier for an investor who felt the securities were fairly priced. Specifically, they differ by the amount of alpha, since fairly priced securities have zero alphas.

8.10 DETERMINING THE EFFICIENT SET

In Chapter 7, the tangency portfolio was shown to correspond to the point where a ray originating from the risk-free rate was tangent to the curved efficient set of risky securities. However, in order to determine the location and composition of the tangency portfolio, the investor must estimate the

expected returns for all the securities under consideration as well as all the variances and pairwise covariances. This will enable the investor to construct the curved efficient set of Markowitz. Adding the risk-free rate will subsequently allow the tangency portfolio to be identified, thereby allowing the construction of the linear (that is, straight-line) efficient set. At this point, the optimal portfolio can be identified by noting where one of the investor's indifference curves is tangent to the linear efficient set.

Considerable effort is needed to construct this linear efficient set. First, the expected return for each security must be estimated. Given there are N risky securities, this means that N parameters must be estimated. Second, the variance for each one of these securities must be estimated. Again, since there are N risky securities, this means that another N parameters must be estimated. Third, the covariance between each pair of risky securities must be estimated. There are $(N^2 - N)/2$ of these parameters to be estimated.[25] Lastly, the risk-free rate must be determined. This means that in total the number of parameters that need to be estimated is equal to $(N^2 + 3N + 2)/2$, determined as follows:

Expected returns	N
Variances	N
Covariances	$\dfrac{N^2 - N}{2}$
Risk-free rate	1
Total	$\dfrac{N^2 + 3N + 2}{2}$

For example, if there were 100 risky securities under consideration, then $[100^2 + (3 \times 100) + 2]/2 = 5151$ parameters would need to be estimated, consisting of 100 expected returns, 100 variances, 4950 covariances, and the risk-free rate. These parameters can be estimated one by one, a task that will be quite time-consuming if not, practically speaking, impossible. Alternatively, an approximate approach based on the characteristic line can be used.[26]

With the "characteristic line approach," the risk-free rate and expected return on the market portfolio must be estimated initially. Then the alpha and beta for each security must be estimated. At this point, $(2 + 2N)$ parameters have been estimated (2 for r_f and $\bar{r}_M$; $2N$ for the alpha and beta

---

[25] This number was arrived at in the following manner. The variance-covariance matrix has N rows and N columns, meaning that there are N^2 cells in it whose corresponding parameters need to be estimated. The cells on the diagonal contain the N variances mentioned earlier, leaving $(N^2 - N)$ parameters to be estimated. Since the variance-covariance matrix is symmetric, only those covariances below the diagonal need be estimated (this is because they also appear in corresponding locations above the diagonal), leaving a total of $(N^2 - N)/2$ parameters to be estimated.

[26] It is an approximate approach because it makes a number of assumptions, some of which are questionable. For example, this approach assumes that the random error terms for any two securities are uncorrelated (an assumption that was needed in deriving equation (8.24b). This means that the outcome from a spin of the roulette wheel for one security (such as Mobil) has no bearing on the outcome from a spin of the roulette wheel of any other security (such as Exxon). It can be argued that this is not true for securities within certain industries. See Benjamin F. King, "Market and Industry Factors in Stock Price Behavior," *Journal of Business* 39, no. 1 (January 1966):139–70; and James L. Farrell, Jr., "Analyzing Covariation of Returns to Determine Homogeneous Stock Groupings," *Journal of Business* 47, no. 2 (April 1974):186–207.

for each of N risky securities). In turn, these figures can be used to estimate the expected return for each security using equation (8.28), restated as follows:

$$\bar{r}_i = \alpha_i + [r_f + (\bar{r}_M - r_f)\beta_i].\qquad(8.31)$$

Earlier, the risk-free rate was determined to be 10% and the expected return on the market portfolio was estimated to be 15%. Given these figures, the expected return for security A was estimated to be 18%, since the alpha and beta of this security were estimated to be 2% and 1.2, respectively:

$$\bar{r}_A = 2\% + \{10\% + [(15\% - 10\%) \times 1.2]\}$$

$$= 18\%.$$

Similarly, the expected return for security B was estimated to be 13%, since its alpha and beta were estimated to be -1% and .8%, respectively:

$$r_B = -1\% + \{10\% + [(15\% - 10\%) \times .8]\}$$

$$= 13\%.$$

Using the characteristic line approach, the variance for any security i can be estimated by multiplying the squared value of the security's beta by the variance of the market portfolio and then adding the variance of the random error term to the product. The equation for doing this is as follows:

$$\sigma_i^2 = \beta_i^2 \sigma_M^2 + \sigma_{\epsilon i}^2 \qquad(8.32)$$

where σ_M^2 denotes the variance on the market portfolio and $\sigma_{\epsilon i}^2$ denotes the variance of the random error term for security i.

Assuming the variance on the market portfolio is 49, the variances of security A and B can be estimated as follows:

$$\sigma_A^2 = (1.2^2 \times 49) + 6.06^2$$

$$= 107.28$$

$$\sigma_B^2 = (.8^2 \times 49) + 4.76^2$$

$$= 54.02$$

respectively. This means that the standard deviations of these securities are estimated to be equal to 10.38% = $\sqrt{107.28}$ and 7.35% = $\sqrt{54.02}$, respectively.

Lastly, the covariance between any two securities i and j can be estimated by the product of three numbers: the beta of security i, the beta of security j, and the variance of the market portfolio. That is, the following formula can be used:

$$\sigma_{ij} = \beta_i \beta_j \sigma_M^2.\qquad(8.33)$$

Thus, for securities A and B, their estimated covariance would be:

$$\sigma_{AB} = 1.2 \times .8 \times 49$$

$$= 47.04.$$

In summary, if the characteristic line approach is used to estimate expected returns, variances, and covariances, then the following parameters must first be estimated:

Risk-free rate	1
Expected return on the market portfolio	1
Variance of the market portfolio	1
Alpha for each security	N
Beta for each security	N
Variance of random error term for each security	N
Total	3N + 3

Thus, for 100 risky securities, $(3 \times 100) + 3 = 303$ parameters need to be estimated when the characteristic line approach is used to determine the efficient set and tangency portfolio. With this approach, once these 303 parameters have been estimated, then it is a simple matter to use equations (8.31), (8.32), and (8.33) to estimate the expected returns, variances, and covariances, in turn, for the risky securities. Alternatively, the expected returns, variances, and covariances could have been estimated one by one, as noted earlier, in which case 5151 parameters would need to be estimated. As can be seen with this example, the characteristic line approach results in a notable reduction in the number of parameters that need to be estimated.

With the characteristic line approach (or the one-by-one approach), after the expected returns, variances, and covariances have been estimated, a computer can be given these values along with the risk-free rate. Then, using a "quadratic programming algorithm" (such as the one described in Appendix A to Chapter 7), the computer can identify the composition and location of the tangency portfolio. Once this is done, the location of the linear efficient set can be determined by simply drawing a line between the risk-free rate and the tangency portfolio. At this juncture, the investor's optimal portfolio can be determined by noting where one of the indifference curves touches (but does not intersect) the linear efficient set.

8.11 SUMMARY

The capital asset pricing model is an economic model that describes how securities are priced in the marketplace. It has its roots in the normative mean-variance approach to investing that was first developed by Markowitz. That is, if certain assumptions are made, one of which is that all investors follow Markowitz's approach, then it can be shown that the expected return on a security will be positively and linearly related to the level of its beta. Simply put, the higher a security's beta, the higher its expected return. The beta of a security is, therefore, the relevant measure of the security's risk. Conversely, the standard deviation (or variance) of a security is not the relevant measure of the security's risk.

The intuitive reasoning behind the CAPM is that each investor is concerned with the standard deviation of the portfolio that he or she holds.

Since each investor holds the market portfolio, usually in conjunction with either borrowing or lending at the risk-free rate, this means that investors are concerned with the standard deviation of the market portfolio. Accordingly, individual securities are evaluated in terms of their contribution to the standard deviation of this portfolio. Since this contribution can be measured by the beta of the security, it follows that the relevant measure of the risk of a security is its beta.

This means that investors will consider holding a security with a higher beta only if it has a higher expected return. In a sense, investors have to be enticed to hold riskier securities, and the enticement that they demand is to have such securities carry higher levels of expected return.

An analogy can be made between forecasting the return on a given security and forecasting tomorrow's high temperature at a given location. In order to make the temperature forecast, the meteorologist needs some model for estimating what the expected high temperature will be. Similarly, the investor needs a model for estimating what a security's expected return will be. The version of the SML given in equation (8.28) is such a model. Here the term alpha was introduced as a measure of the amount of a security's mispricing. Positive alphas are indications of underpricing; negative alphas are indications of overpricing. In equilibrium, all securities will be fairly priced and will thus have alphas equal to zero.

A model for the actual high temperature that will occur tomorrow can be thought of as being similar to the expected high temperature model except that it involves actual outcomes and a random error term. A return-generating process known as the characteristic line, given in equation (8.29), provides a similar way of thinking about the actual return that will occur for a given security over the forthcoming holding period. Thus, there are two models for both the meteorologist and the investor. For the meteorologist, there is one for the expected high temperature and one for the actual high temperature. For the investor, there is one for expected returns (such as a version of the SML) and one for actual returns (such as the characteristic line).

Assuming the characteristic line is a reasonably accurate return-generating process for securities, it can be shown that the total risk of a portfolio has two components—market risk and unique risk. Increased diversification will typically lead to a reduction in the total risk of a portfolio until the portfolio contains roughly 20 securities. This can be attributed to a reduction in the amount of unique risk present in the portfolio, since increased diversification leads to an averaging of market risk. However, once the portfolio has roughly 20 securities in it, most of the unique risk will have disappeared, and further diversification will not have a noticeable impact on the total risk of the portfolio.

If securities are priced according to the CAPM, then the investor's optimal portfolio consists of purchasing the market portfolio and engaging in either risk-free lending or risk-free borrowing. If disequilibrium is introduced where an investor believes some securities have nonzero alphas, then the identification of the investor's optimal portfolio becomes more complicated. As shown in this chapter, one approach that is based on the CAPM

involves the use of the concept of the characteristic line. This approach simplifies what needs to be forecast in order to determine the composition and location of the tangency portfolio, a portfolio that should be purchased (at least in part) by the investor.

APPENDIX A
SOME EXTENDED VERSIONS OF THE CAPM

The original capital asset pricing model makes strong assumptions and gives strong implications. In the years since it was developed, more complex models have been proposed. These models generally involve relaxing some of the assumptions associated with the original CAPM, and are often referred to as *extended versions of the CAPM* (or extended capital asset pricing models). Some of them are described in this appendix, and others are described in Chapter 9.

A.1 EFFICIENT INVESTMENT POLICIES WHEN BORROWING IS RESTRICTED OR EXPENSIVE

☐ **A.1.1 The Capital Market Line**

The original CAPM assumes that investors can lend or borrow at the same risk-free rate of interest. In reality, such borrowing is likely to be either unavailable or restricted in amount. What impact might the relaxation of this risk-free borrowing assumption have on the CAPM?

A useful way to answer the question makes the following alternative assumptions: (1) investors can lend money risklessly—that is, they can purchase assets that provide a risk-free return of r_{fL}; or (2) investors can borrow money without limit at a higher rate of interest, r_{fB}. These risk-free rates are shown on the vertical axis of Figure 8.8; the "umbrella area" represents risk-return combinations available from investment solely in risky assets.[27]

If there are no opportunities to borrow or lend at the risk-free rate, the efficient set would be the curve WT_LT_BY, and many combinations of risky securities would be efficient. However, the availability of risk-free lending at the rate r_{fL} makes the risky portfolios between W and T_L inefficient, since combinations of risk-free lending and the portfolio plotting at T_L provide more return for the same risk.

Similarly, the ability to borrow money at rate r_{fB} makes another portfolio, denoted by T_B, of special interest. Risky portfolios between T_B and Y are now inefficient, since levered holdings of T_B dominate them by providing more return for the same risk.

Investors with attitudes toward risk that suggest neither borrowing nor lending should hold efficient combinations of risky securities plotting

---

[27] A more rigorous development of this figure is presented in Appendix B of Chapter 7.

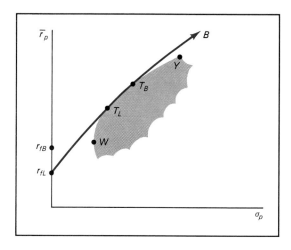

FIGURE 8–8
Efficient set when the risk-free rates are different.

along curve $T_L T_B$. Accordingly, their holdings should be tailored to be consistent with differences in their degrees of aversion to risk.

In this situation the CML is now two lines and a curve, corresponding to the line going from r_{fL} to T_L, then the curve from T_L to T_B, and then the line from T_B on out to the northeast in Figure 8.8.

□ A.1.2   The Security Market Line

What becomes of the Security Market Line when the risk-free borrowing rate exceeds the risk-free lending rate? The answer depends on whether or not the market portfolio is in fact one of the efficient combinations of risky securities along the boundary between T_L and T_B in Figure 8.8.[28] If it is not, little more can be said. If it is, a great deal can be said.

Figure 8.9 shows a case in which the market portfolio (shown by point M) is efficient. In part (a) a line has been drawn that is tangent to the efficient set at point M. When this line is extended to the vertical axis, the resulting intercept is denoted $\bar{r}_z$. In part (b) only this tangency line is shown.

A striking characteristic of Figure 8.9(b) is this: It is precisely the same picture that would be produced in a market in which investors could borrow and lend without limit at a hypothetical risk-free rate equal in value to $\bar{r}_z$. Whereas only point M along the line emanating from $\bar{r}_z$ would be attainable, the expected returns of risky securities would be the same as they would be in a hypothetical market with borrowing and lending at $\bar{r}_z$. That is, all risky securities (and portfolios consisting of these securities) would plot along an SML going through point $\bar{r}_z$, as shown in Figure 8.10.

The vertical intercept of the SML indicates the expected return on a security or portfolio with a beta of zero. Accordingly, this extension of the CAPM is termed the *zero-beta capital asset pricing model*. This version of

---

[28] If investors could obtain the proceeds from short sales and there were no restrictions on such sales, then the maket portfolio would definitely plot on the efficient set between T_L and T_B.

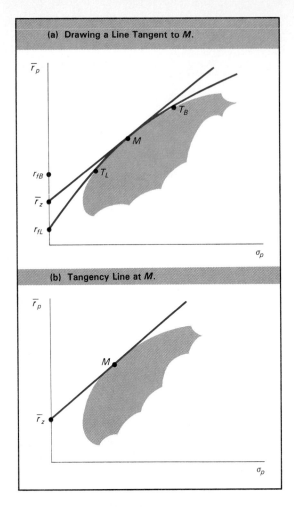

(a) Drawing a Line Tangent to M.

(b) Tangency Line at M.

FIGURE 8–9
Risk and return when the market portfolio is efficient.

the CAPM implies that the SML will be flatter than implied by the original version, since $\bar{r}_z$ will be above r_{fL}. As a practical matter, it means that $\bar{r}_z$ must be inferred from the prices of risky securities, since it cannot simply be found in the quotations of current prices on, for example, Treasury bills. Many organizations that estimate the SML generally find that it conforms more the zero-beta CAPM than to the original CAPM.

Cases in which borrowing is either impossible or costs more as one borrows larger amounts lead to only minor modifications in the conclusions. As long as the market portfolio is efficient, all securities will plot along an SML, but the "zero-beta return" will exceed the risk-free rate at which funds can be invested.

A.2 HETEROGENEOUS EXPECTATIONS

A number of researchers have examined the implications of assuming that different investors have different perceptions about expected returns, standard deviations, and covariances. More specifically, the assumption of ho-

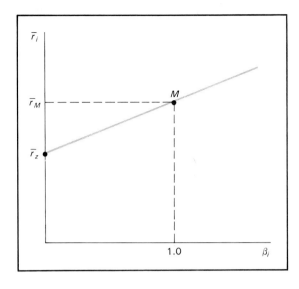

FIGURE 8–10
The "zero-beta" security market line.

mogeneous expectations has been replaced by these researchers with an assumption of *heterogeneous expectations*.

In one such study, it was noted that each investor would face an efficient set that was unique to him or her.[29] This means that the tangency portfolio (denoted by T in Chapter 7) is unique to each investor, since the optimal combination of risky assets for an investor depends on that investor's perceptions about expected returns, standard deviations, and covariances. Furthermore, an investor will likely determine that his or her tangency portfolio does not involve an investment in some securities (that is, certain securities may have zero proportions in the tangency portfolio). Nevertheless, the SML will still exist. This was shown by aggregating the holdings of all investors, and remembering that in equilibrium each security's price has to be at a level where the amount of the security demanded equals the supply of the security. Now, however, the equilibrium expected return for each security will be a complex weighted aveage of all investors' perceptions of its expected return. That is, from the viewpoint of a representative, or average, investor, each security will be priced fairly, so its expected return (as perceived by this investor) will be linearly and positively related to its beta.

A.3   LIQUIDITY

The original CAPM assumes that investors are concerned only with risk and return. However, other characteristics may also be important to investors. For example, *liquidity* may be important. Here, liquidity refers to the cost of selling or buying a security "in a hurry." For example, a house is regarded

---

[29] John Lintner, "The Aggregation of Investor's Diverse Judgements and Preferences in Purely Competitive Security Markets," *Journal of Financial and Quantitative Analysis* 4, no. 4 (December 1969):347–400. For a discussion of the work of other researchers in this area (as well as other extensions of the CAPM), see Chapter 8 of Alexander and Francis, *Portfolio Analysis*.

as a relatively illiquid investment, since usually a "fair" price for it cannot be obtained quickly. In terms of securities, liquidity may be measured by the size of the spread between the bid and ask prices, with smaller spreads suggesting greater liquidity. Furthermore, it is reasonable to assume that many investors would find more liquid portfolios to be more attractive, keeping everything else the same. However, investors undoubtedly differ in their attitudes toward liquidity. For some it is very important; for others, somewhat important; and for yet others, of little importance.

Under these conditions, security prices would adjust until, overall, investors would be content to hold the outstanding securities. The expected return of a security would be based on two characteristics of the security:

1. The marginal contribution of the security to the risk of an efficient portfolio. This would be measured by the familiar beta (β_i) of the security.
2. The marginal contribution of the security to the liquidity of an efficient portfolio. This would be measured by the liquidity (L_i) of the security.

Now, other things equal, investors dislike large values of β_i but like large values of L_i. This means that two securities with the same beta but different liquidities would not have the same level of expected return. To understand why they would have different levels of expected return, consider what would happen if they had the same level of expected return. In such a situation investors would buy the security with the greater liquidity and sell the one with the lesser liquidity. This would push the price of the first security up and the second one down. Ultimately, in equilibrium the quantity demanded would equal the quantity supplied and the security with the greater liquidity would have a relatively lower expected return. Similarly, two securities with the same liquidity but different betas would not have the same level of expected return. Instead, the security with the higher beta would have a higher expected return.

Figure 8.11 shows the equilibrium relationship one might expect among $\bar{r}_i$, β_i, and L_i. For a given level of β_i, more liquid securities have lower expected returns. And for a given level of L_i, more risky securities have higher expected returns as in the original CAPM. Lastly, there are securities with various levels of β_i and L_i that provide the same level of $\bar{r}_i$. The figure is three-dimensional, since now expected returns are related to two characteristics of securities. Accordingly, it is sometimes referred to as a *Security Market Plane*.[30]

If expected returns are based on beta, liquidity, and a third characteristic, then a four-dimensional CAPM would be necessary to describe the

---

[30] The term Security Market Plane is a trademark of Wells Fargo Bank. For more on the relationship between liquidity and stock returns, see Yakov Amihud and Haim Mendelson, "Liquidity and Stock Returns," *Financial Analysts Journal* 42, no. 3 (May/June 1986):43–48, and "Asset Pricing and the Bid-Ask Spread," *Journal of Financial Economics* 17, no. 2 (December 1986):223–49.

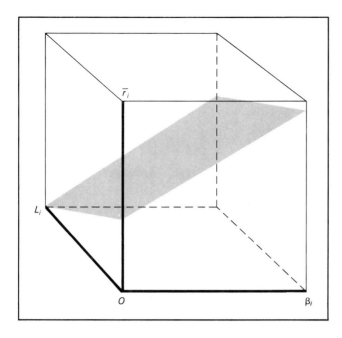

FIGURE 8–11
Security market plane.

corresponding equilibrium.[31] Although a diagram cannot be drawn for this type of extended CAPM, an equation can be written for it. Such an equation, by analogy to the three-dimensional plane, is termed a *hyperplane*.

> In equilibrium, all securities will plot on a *Security Market Hyperplane*, where each axis measures the contribution of a security to a characteristic of efficient portfolios that matter (on average) to investors.

The relationship between the expected return of a security and its contribution to a particular characteristic of efficient portfolios depends on the attitudes of investors to the characteristic:

> If, on the average, a characteristic (such as liquidity) is liked by investors, then those securities that contribute more to that characteristic will, other things equal, offer lower expected returns. Conversely, if a characteristic (such as beta) is disliked by investors, then those securities that contribute more to that characteristic will offer higher expected returns.

In a capital market with many relevant characteristics, the task of tailoring a portfolio for a specific investor is more complicated, since only

---

[31] Taxes were thought to be such a characteristic before the Tax Reform Act of 1986, when the tax rate on income from capital gains was less than the tax rate on dividend income. In considering such taxes, one study found that the before-tax expected return of a security was a positive linear function of its beta and its dividend yield. That is, the higher a security's beta or dividend yield, the higher its before-tax expected return. The reason securities with higher dividend yields would have had higher before-tax expected returns was because they would be taxed more heavily. See M. J. Brennan. "Taxes, Market Valuation and Corporate Financial Policy," *National Tax Journal* 23, no. 4 (December 1970):417–27. The issue of whether or not dividends influence before-tax expected returns has been contentious; it is discussed in Chapters 15 and 16 of Thomas E. Copeland and J. Fred Weston, *Financial Theory and Corporate Policy*, (Reading, Mass.: Addison-Wesley, 1988).

an investor with average attitudes and circumstances should hold the market portfolio. In general:

> If an investor likes a characteristic more (or dislikes it less) than the average investor, he or she should generally hold a portfolio with relatively more of that characteristic than is provided by holding the market portfolio. Conversely, if an investor likes a characteristic less (or dislikes it more) than the average investor, he or she should generally hold a portfolio with relatively less of that characteristic than is provided by holding the market portfolio.

For example, consider an investor who likes having a relatively liquid portfolio. Such an investor should hold a portfolio consisting of relatively liquid securities. Conversely, an investor who has relatively little need for liquidity should hold a portfolio of relatively illiquid securities.

The right combination of "tilt" away from market proportions will depend on the extent of the differences between the investor's attitudes and those of the average investor and on the added risk involved in such a strategy. A complex capital market requires all the tools of modern portfolio theory for managing the money of any investor who is significantly different from the "average investor." On the other hand, in such a world, investment management should be relatively passive: After the selection of an initial portfolio, there should be minor and infrequent changes.

APPENDIX B
A DERIVATION OF THE SECURITY MARKET LINE

Figure 8.12 shows the location of the feasible set of the Markowitz model, along with the risk-free rate and the associated efficient set that represents the capital market line. Within the feasible set of the Markowitz model lies every individual risky security. An arbitrarily chosen risky security, denoted by i, has been selected for analysis and is shown on the figure.

Consider any portfolio, denoted by p, that consists of the proportion X_i invested in security i and the proportion $1 - X_i$ invested in the market portfolio M. Such a portfolio will have an expected return equal to

$$\bar{r}_p = X_i\bar{r}_i + (1 - X_i)\bar{r}_M \tag{8.34}$$

and a standard deviation equal to

$$\sigma_p = [X_i^2\sigma_i^2 + (1 - X_i)^2\sigma_M^2 + 2X_i(1 - X_i)\sigma_{iM}]^{1/2}. \tag{8.35}$$

All such portfolios will lie on a curved line connecting i and M, such as the one shown in Figure 8.12.

Of concern is the slope of this curved line. Since it is a curved line, its slope is not a constant. However, its slope can be determined with the use of calculus. First, using equation (8.34), the derivative of $\bar{r}_p$ with respect to X_i is taken:

$$\frac{d\bar{r}_p}{dX_i} = \bar{r}_i - \bar{r}_M. \tag{8.36}$$

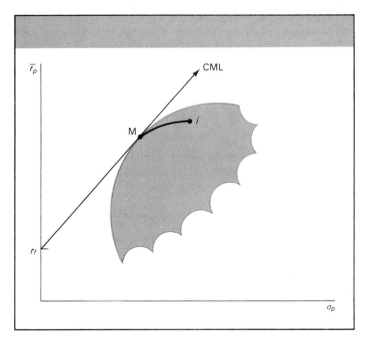

FIGURE 8–12
Deriving the security market line.

Second, using equation (8.35), the derivative of σ_p with respect to X_i is taken:

$$\frac{d\sigma_p}{dX_i} = \frac{X_i\sigma_i^2 - \sigma_M^2 + X_i\sigma_M^2 + \sigma_{iM} - 2X_i\sigma_{iM}}{[X_i^2\sigma_i^2 + (1 - X_i)^2\sigma_M^2 + 2X_i(1 - X_i)\sigma_{iM}]^{1/2}}. \qquad (8.37)$$

Third, it can be noted the slope of the curved line iM, $d\bar{r}_p/d\sigma_p$, can be written as:

$$\frac{d\bar{r}_p}{d\sigma_p} = \frac{d\bar{r}_p/dX_i}{d\sigma_p/dX_i} \qquad (8.38)$$

Finally, the slope of iM can be calculated by substituting equations (8.36) and (8.37) into the numerator and denominator of equation (8.38), respectively:

$$\frac{d\bar{r}_p}{d\sigma_p} = \frac{[\bar{r}_i - \bar{r}_M][X_i^2\sigma_i^2 + (1 - X_i)^2\sigma_M^2 + 2X_i(1 - X_i)\sigma_{iM}]^{1/2}}{X_i\sigma_i^2 - \sigma_M^2 + X_i\sigma_M^2 + \sigma_{iM} - 2X_i\sigma_{iM}}. \qquad (8.39)$$

Of interest is the slope of the curved line iM at the endpoint M. Since the proportion X_i is zero at this point, the slope of iM can be calculated by substituting zero for X_i in equation (8.39). After doing so, many terms drop out, leaving:

$$\frac{d\bar{r}_p}{d\sigma_p} = \frac{[\bar{r}_i - \bar{r}_M][\sigma_M]}{\sigma_{iM} - \sigma_M^2}. \qquad (8.40)$$

At M the slope of the CML, $(\bar{r}_M - r_f)/\sigma_M$, must equal the slope of the curved line iM. This is because the slope of the curved line iM increases when moving from the endpoint i, converging to the slope of the CML at the endpoint M. Accordingly, the slope of the curve iM at M, as shown on the right-hand side of equation (8.40), is set equal to the slope of the CML:

$$\frac{[\bar{r}_i - \bar{r}_M][\sigma_M]}{\sigma_{iM} - \sigma_M^2} = \frac{\bar{r}_M - r_f}{\sigma_M}. \tag{8.41}$$

Solving equation (8.41) for r_i results in the covariance version of the SML:

$$\bar{r}_i = r_f + \left[\frac{\bar{r}_M - r_f}{\sigma_M^2}\right]\sigma_{iM}. \tag{8.6}$$

The beta version of the SML is derived by substituting β_i for σ_{iM}/σ_M^2 in equation (8.6).

QUESTIONS AND PROBLEMS

1. Will an investor who owns the market portfolio have to buy and sell units of the component securities every time the relative prices of those securities change? Why?
2. Explain the significance of the slope of the SML. How might the slope of the SML change over time?
3. The risk of an efficient portfolio to an investor is measured by the standard deviation of the portfolio's returns. Why shouldn't the risk of an individual security be calculated in the same manner?
4. It is true that a security with a high standard deviation of returns is not necessarily highly risky to an investor? Why might you suspect that securities with above-average standard deviations of returns tend to have above-average betas?
5. You are given the following information on two securities, the market portfolio, and the risk-free rate:

	Expected Return	Correlation with Market Portfolio	Standard Deviation
Security 1	15.5%	0.90	20.0%
Security 2	9.2	0.80	9.0
Market Portfolio	12.0	1.00	12.0
Risk-free Rate	5.0	0.00	0.0

a. Draw the SML.
b. What are the betas of the two securities?
c. Plot the two securities on the SML.
6. Is an investor who owns any portfolio of risky assets other than the market portfolio exposed to some unique risk?
7. Consider the following information:

Security	Beta	Equilibrium Expected Return	Expected Return
A	1.75	21.0%	16.7%
B	1.20	16.6	24.0
C	1.30	17.4	17.4
D	0.75	13.0	16.0

The risk-free interest rate is 7% and the market portfolio's expected return is 15%.

a. Calculate the securities' expected alphas.

b. Plot the SML and the securities' expected returns and equilibrium expected returns.

c. What should be your investment action with respect to each of these securities?

8. With respect to the return-generating process, how is the standard deviation of the random error term related to the characteristic line?

9. In the following table you are presented with ten years of excess return data for Hartford Inc. and the market portfolio. Plot these excess returns on a graph, with the market portfolio's excess returns on the horizontal axis and Hartford's excess returns on the vertical axis. Draw your best guess of the characteristic line through these points. From this graph only, compute an estimate of the beta of Hartford's stock.

Year	Hartford Inc.	Market Portfolio
1	8.1%	8.0%
2	3.0	0.0
3	5.3	14.9
4	1.0	5.0
5	-3.1	-4.1
6	-3.0	-8.9
7	5.0	10.1
8	3.2	5.0
9	1.2	1.5
10	1.3	2.4

10. Consider the stocks of two companies, Atlanta Corp. and Birmingham Associates.

a. If you are told that the slope of Atlanta Corp.'s characteristic line is 1.20 and the slope of Birmingham Associates' characteristic line is 1.00, which stock is more risky? Why?

b. If you are now also told that the standard deviation of the random error term for Atlanta stock is 10.0%, while it is 21.5% for Birmingham stock, how is your answer changed? Explain.

11. You are given the following information on three stocks that make up your portfolio. In addition, you know that the market portfolio has an expected return of 13% and a standard deviation of 18%. The risk-free rate is 5%.

Stock	Beta	Standard Deviation of Random Error Term	Weight in Portfolio
A	1.10	7.0%	29%
B	0.80	2.3	50
C	1.00	1.0	30

a. What is the portfolio's equilibrium expected return?

b. What is the portfolio's standard deviation?

12. Why is the characteristic line approach a considerably more practical technique than the original Markowitz approach for constructing the efficient set?

Chapter 9

FACTOR MODELS AND ARBITRAGE
PRICING THEORY

The objective of modern portfolio theory is to provide a means by which the investor can identify his or her optimal portfolio when there are an infinite number of possibilities. Using a framework involving expected returns and standard deviations, it was shown that the investor needs to estimate the expected return and standard deviation for each security under consideration for inclusion in the portfolio, along with all the covariances. With these estimates, the investor can derive the curved efficient set of Markowitz. Then, for a given risk-free rate, the investor can identify the tangency portfolio and determine the location of the linear efficient set. Finally, the investor can invest in the tangency portfolio and borrow or lend at the risk-free rate, with the amount of borrowing or lending depending on the investor's risk-return preferences.

Chapter 8 presented a type of return-generating process known as the characteristic line. However, there are many other types of return-generating processes for securities. These types of processes are often called *factor models* (or index models) because they assert that the return on a security is sensitive to the movements of various *factors* (or indices). In attempting to accurately estimate expected returns, variances, and covariances for securities, these models are potentially more useful than the characteristic line. They have this potential because it appears that actual security returns are sensitive to more than movements in the market portfolio.[1] That is, within the economy there seems to be more than one pervasive factor that affects security returns. Given the belief that there is more than one factor, a goal of security analysis is to identify these factors in the economy and the sensitivities of security returns to movements in these factors. A formal statement of such a relationship is termed a *factor model of security returns*. The discussion begins with the simplest form of such a model, a *single-factor model*.

---

[1] For example, see William F. Sharpe, "Factors in NYSE Security Returns, 1931–1979," *Journal of Portfolio Management* 8, no. 4 (Summer 1982):5–19. Other studies are cited in William F. Sharpe, "Factor Models, CAPMs, and the ABT (sic)," *Journal of Portfolio Management* 11, no. 1 (Fall 1984):21–25.

9.1 SINGLE-FACTOR MODELS

Some investors argue that the return-generating process for securities involves a single factor. Some examples of such a single factor include the growth rate in gross national product (GNP) and the growth rate in industrial production. In general, a single-factor model can be represented in equation form as follows:

$$r_i = a_i + b_i F + e_i \tag{9.1}$$

where F is the value of the factor and b_i is the *sensitivity* of security i to this factor (sometimes b_i is referred to as the factor loading or attribute of the security). If the value of the factor were zero, the return on the security would equal $a_i + e_i$. Here e_i is a random error term just like the random error term that was discussed in Chapter 8. That is, it is a random variable with an expected value of zero and a given standard deviation σ_{ei}, and it can be thought of as the outcome occurring from a spin of a roulette wheel. This means that the expected return on security i, according to the single-factor model, can be written as:

$$\bar{r}_i = a_i + b_i \overline{F}. \tag{9.2}$$

Thus, the term a_i can be seen to represent the expected return on security i if the expected value of the factor was zero.

With the single-factor model, it can also be shown that the variance of any security i is equal to

$$\sigma_i^2 = b_i^2 \sigma_F^2 + \sigma_{ei}^2 \tag{9.3}$$

where σ_F^2 is the variance of the factor F and σ_{ei}^2 is the variance of the random error term e_i. Furthermore, the covariance between any two securities i and j can be shown to equal

$$\sigma_{ij} = b_i b_j \sigma_F^2. \tag{9.4}$$

Equations (9.3) and (9.4) are based on two critical assumptions. The first assumption is that the random error term and the factor are uncorrelated, meaning that the outcome of the factor has no bearing on the outcome of the random error term. The second assumption is that the random error terms of any two securities are uncorrelated, meaning that the outcome of the random error term of one security has no bearing on the outcome of the random error term of any other security. In other words, the returns of two securities will be correlated (that is, move together) only through common reactions to the factor. If either of these two assumptions is invalid, then the model is an approximation and a different factor model (perhaps one with more factors) will theoretically be a more accurate model of the return-generating process.

The characteristic line can now be shown to be an example of a single-factor model where the factor is the return on the market portfolio. In Chapter 8, the characteristic line appeared as

$$r_i - r_f = \alpha_i + (r_M - r_f)\beta_i + \epsilon_i \tag{8.29}$$

where α_i and β_i are the alpha and beta of the security, respectively, and ϵ_i is a random error term with an expected value of zero and a standard deviation of $\sigma_{\epsilon i}$. However, this equation can be rewriten as:

$$r_i = r_f + \alpha_i + (r_M - r_f)\beta_i + \epsilon_i \qquad (9.5)$$
$$= [\alpha_i + r_f(1 - \beta_i)] + \beta_i r_M + \epsilon_i.$$

Comparing equation (9.5) with the general form of the single-factor model given in equation (9.1), it can be seen that the characteristic line is an example of a single-factor model where the factor is the return on the market portfolio (that is, $F = r_M$). Furthermore, the terms a_i and b_i of the single-factor model can be interpreted to be equal to $[\alpha_i + r_f(1 - \beta_i)]$ and β_i, respectively.

As an illustration, assume security i has $\alpha_i = +3\%$ and $\beta_i = .9$. Given a risk-free rate of 10%, the characteristic line of this security is

$$r_i - 10\% = 3\% + [(r_M - 10\%) \times .9] + \epsilon_i \qquad (9.6)$$

which can be rewritten as follows:

$$r_i = 10\% + 3\% + [(r_M - 10\%) \times .9)] + \epsilon_i \qquad (9.7)$$
$$= 4\% + .9 r_M + \epsilon_i.$$

Note how the characteristic line for security i, when rewritten as in equation (9.7), is similar to the single-factor model of equation (9.1), where the factor is the return on the market portfolio (that is, $F = r_M$) and $a_i = 4\%$, $b_i = .9$, and $e_i = \epsilon_i$.

However, as mentioned earlier, there are other examples of single-factor models. An investor may believe that it is more accurate to view security returns as being related to one common factor such as the growth rate in GNP. For this investor, F is the growth rate in GNP, b_i is the sensitivity of security i to the growth rate in GNP, and a_i is the expected return of security i if there is zero growth in GNP.

□ 9.1.1 Two Important Features of Single-Factor Models

There are two features of single-factor models that are of interest. First, in order to determine the composition of the tangency portfolio, the investor needs to estimate all the expected returns, variances, and covariances. This can be done with a single-factor model by estimating a_i, b_i, and σ_{ei} for each of the N risky securities. Also needed are the expected value of the factor, F, and its standard deviation, σ_F. With these estimates, equations (9.2), (9.3), and (9.4) can subsequently be used to calculate the expected returns, variances, and covariances for the securities. Using these values, the curved efficient set of Markowitz can then be derived, from which the tangency portfolio can be determined for a given risk-free rate.[2]

The second interesting feature of single-factor models has to do with

---

[2] In the case of the characteristic line, this means that the investor needs to estimate α_i, β_i, and σ_{ei} for each of the N risky securities; also needed are the expected return on the market portfolio, $\bar{r}_M$, and its standard deviation, σ_M, along with the risk-free rate, r_f. See Chapter 8 for more details.

diversification. Earlier it was shown that diversification leads to averaging of market risk and a reduction in unique risk. This feature is also true for any single-factor model, except now instead of market and unique risk, the words factor and nonfactor risk are used. That is, in equation (9.3) the first term on the right-hand side is known as the *factor risk* of the security, and the second term is known as the *nonfactor* (or idiosyncratic) *risk* of the security.

With a single-factor model, the standard deviation of a portfolio is equal to

$$\sigma_p = \left[\left(\sum_{i=1}^{N} X_i b_i \right)^2 \sigma_F^2 + \sum_{i=1}^{N} X_i^2 \sigma_{ei}^2 \right]^{1/2}$$

$$= (b_p^2 \sigma_F^2 + \sigma_{ep}^2)^{1/2}$$

(9.8a)

where:

$$b_p = \sum_{i=1}^{N} X_i b_i$$

(9.8b)

$$\sigma_{ep}^2 = \sum_{i=1}^{N} X_i^2 \sigma_{ei}^2.$$

(9.8c)

Equation (9.8a) shows that the total risk of any portfolio can be viewed as having two components similar to the two components of the total risk of an individual security shown in equation (9.3). In particular, the first and second terms on the right-hand side of equation (9.8a) are the factor risk and nonfactor risk of the portfolio, respectively.

As a portfolio becomes more diversified, meaning the number of securities in it becomes larger, each proportion X_i will become smaller. However, this will not cause b_p either to decrease or to increase significantly unless a deliberate attempt is made to do so by having securities with values of b_i that are either low or high, respectively. This is because, as equation (9.8b) shows, b_p is simply a weighted average of the sensitivities of the securities, b_i, with the values of X_i serving as weights. Thus, *diversification leads to an averaging of factor risk.*

However, it can be shown that as a portfolio becomes more diversified, there is reason to expect σ_{ep}^2, the nonfactor risk, to decrease. This can be shown by examining equation (9.8c). Assuming the amount invested in each security is equal, then this equation can be rewritten by substituting $1/N$ for X_i:

$$\sigma_{ep}^2 = \sum_{i=1}^{N} \left[\frac{1}{N} \right]^2 \sigma_{ei}^2$$

$$= \frac{1}{N} \left[\frac{(\sigma_{e1}^2 + \sigma_{e2}^2 + \cdots + \sigma_{eN}^2)}{N} \right].$$

The value inside the brackets is the average nonfactor risk for the component securities. But the portfolio's nonfactor risk is only $1/N$ as large as this, since the term $1/N$ also appears outside the brackets. Thus, as the portfolio becomes

more diversified, the number of securities N in it becomes larger. This means that $1/N$ becomes smaller, which in turn reduces the nonfactor risk of the portfolio. Simply stated, *diversification reduces nonfactor risk*.[3]

9.2 MULTIPLE-FACTOR MODELS

The health of the economy affects most firms, and thus changes in expectations concerning the future of the economy can be expected to have profound effects on the returns of most securities. However, the economy is not a simple, monolithic entity. Several common influences with pervasive effects might be identified:

1. Expectations about the growth rate of real GNP
2. Expectations about real interest rates
3. Expectations about levels of inflation
4. Expectations about future oil prices

Instead of a single-factor model, a multiple-factor model for security returns that considers these various influences may be more accurate. As an example of a multiple-factor model, consider a two-factor model. That is, assume the return-generating process contains two factors.

☐ 9.2.1 Two-Factor Models

In equation form, the two-factor model is as follows:

$$r_i = a_i + b_{i1}F_1 + b_{i2}F_2 + e_i \tag{9.9}$$

where F_1 and F_2 are the two factors that are pervasive influences on security returns (for example, F_1 could be the growth rate in GNP and F_2 could be the rate of inflation); and b_{i1} and b_{i2} are the sensitivities of security i to these two factors. As with the single-factor model, e_i is a random error term and a_i is the expected return on security i if each factor has a value of zero.

Four parameters need to be estimated for each security with the two-factor model. They are a_i, b_{i1}, b_{i2}, and the standard deviation of the random error term, denoted by σ_{ei}. For each of the factors, two parameters need to be estimated. These parameters are the expected value of each factor ($\overline{F}_1$ and $\overline{F}_2$) and the standard deviation of each factor (σ_{F1} and σ_{F2}).

With these estimates, the expected return for any security i can be determined by using the following formula:

$$\bar{r}_i = a_i + b_{i1}\overline{F}_1 + b_{i2}\overline{F}_2. \tag{9.10}$$

If the factors are uncorrelated, then the variance for any security i will be

$$\sigma_i^2 = b_{i1}^2\sigma_{F1}^2 + b_{i2}^2\sigma_{F2}^2 + \sigma_{ei}^2 \tag{9.11}$$

---

[3] Actually, all that is necessary for this reduction in nonfactor risk to occur is for the maximum amount invested in any one security to continually decrease as N increases.

and the covariance between any two securities i and j can be determined by

$$\sigma_{ij} = b_{i1}b_{j1}\sigma_{F1}^2 + b_{i2}b_{j2}\sigma_{F2}^2. \tag{9.12}$$

If the factors are correlated, then more complex equations are needed to determine variances and covariances.[4]

As with the single-factor model, once the expected returns, variances, and covariances have been determined using these equations, the investor can derive the curved efficient set of Markowitz. Then, for a given risk-free rate, the tangency portfolio can be identified, after which the investor can determine his or her optimal portfolio.

Everything said earlier regarding single-factor models and the effects of diversification apply here as well:

1. Diversification leads to averaging of factor risk.
2. Diversification can substantially reduce nonfactor risk.
3. For a "well-diversified portfolio," nonfactor risk will be insignificant.

As with a single-factor model, the sensitivity of a portfolio to a particular factor in a multiple-factor model is a weighted average of the sensitivities of the securities, where the weights are equal to the proportion invested in each security. This can be seen by noting that the return on a portfolio is a weighted average of the returns of its component securities:

$$r_p = \sum_{i=1}^{N} X_i r_i. \tag{9.13}$$

Substituting the right-hand side of equation (9.9) for r_i on the right-hand side of equation (9.13) results in

$$r_p = \sum_{i=1}^{N} X_i (a_i + b_{i1}F_1 + b_{i2}F_2 + e_i)$$

$$= \left(\sum_{i=1}^{N} X_i a_i \right) + \left(\sum_{i=1}^{N} X_i b_{i1}F_1 \right) + \left(\sum_{i=1}^{N} X_i b_{i2}F_2 \right) + \left(\sum_{i=1}^{N} X_i e_i \right) \tag{9.14}$$

$$= a_p + b_{p1}F_1 + b_{p2}F_2 + e_p$$

where:

$$a_p = \sum_{i=1}^{N} X_i a_i$$

$$b_{p1} = \sum_{i=1}^{N} X_i b_{i1}$$

---

[4] If the factors are correlated, then equation (9.11) would need to have the term $2b_{i1}b_{i2}\text{COV}(F_1, F_2)$ added to its right-hand side, and equation (9.12) would need to have the term $(b_{i1}b_{j2} + b_{i2}b_{j1})\text{COV}(F_1, F_2)$ added to its right-hand side. Here $\text{COV}(F_1, F_2)$ denotes the covariance between the two factors and is equal to the correlation between them times the product of their standard deviations, σ_{F1} and σ_{F2}. Other assumptions are also necessary; for example, the random error terms must be uncorrelated with each other and with each factor.

$$b_{p2} = \sum_{i=1}^{N} X_i b_{i2}$$

$$e_p = \sum_{i=1}^{N} X_i e_i.$$

Note how the portfolio sensitivities, b_{p1} and b_{p2}, are weighted averages of the respective individual security sensitivities, b_{i1} and b_{i2}.

☐ 9.2.2 Sector-Factor Models

Securities in the same industry or "economic sector" often move together, responding similarly to changes in prospects for that sector. Some investors acknowledge this by using a special kind of multiple-factor model referred to as a *sector-factor model*. In order to use a sector-factor model, each security must be classified as belonging to a sector. For a two-sector-factor model, each security must be classified as belonging to one of two economic sectors.

For example, let sector 1 consist of all industrial companies and sector 2 consist of all nonindustrial companies (such as utility, transportation, and financial companies). It should be kept in mind, however, that both the number of sectors and what each sector consists of is an open matter that is left to the investor to decide.

With this two-sector-factor model, the return-generating process for securities is of the same general form as the two-factor model given in equation (9.9). However, with the two-sector-factor model, F_1 and F_2 now denote sector-factor 1 and 2, respectively. Furthermore, any particular security belongs to either sector-factor 1 or 2 but not both. By definition this means that, depending on the sector-factor to which the security belongs, the value of either b_{i1} or b_{i2} equals 1; the other one will correspond to the sector-factor to which the security does not belong and will be set equal to 0.

As an illustration, consider General Motors (GM) and Delta Air Lines (DAL). The two-sector-factor model for GM would be:

$$r_{GM} = a_{GM} + b_{GM1}F_1 + b_{GM2}F_2 + e_{GM}. \tag{9.15}$$

However, since GM belongs to sector-factor 1 (the industrial sector), the coefficients b_{GM1} and b_{GM2} are assigned values of 1 and 0, respectively. Having made this assignment, equation (9.15) reduces to:

$$r_{GM} = a_{GM} + F_1 + e_{GM}. \tag{9.16}$$

Thus, only the values of a_{GM} and σ_{eGM} need to be estimated for GM with the two-sector-factor model, whereas with a two-factor model the values of a_{GM}, b_{GM1}, b_{GM2}, and σ_{eGM} need to be estimated.

Similarly, since DAL belongs to the nonindustrial sector, it would have the following two-sector-factor model:

$$r_{DAL} = a_{DAL} + b_{DAL1}F_1 + b_{DAL2}F_2 + e_{DAL} \tag{9.17}$$

which would reduce to:

$$r_{DAL} = a_{DAL} + F_2 + e_{DAL} \tag{9.18}$$

since b_{DAL1} and b_{DAL2} would be assigned values of 0 and 1, respectively. Thus, only the values of a_{DAL} and σ_{eDAL} need to be estimated for DAL with the two-sector-factor model.

In general, whereas four parameters need to be estimated for each security with the two-factor model (a_i, b_{i1}, b_{i2}, and σ_{ei}), only two parameters need to be estimated with the two-sector-factor model (a_i and σ_{ei}), since two parameters have been assigned values of either zero or one. With these estimates of the individual security parameters, along with estimates of $\overline{F}_1$, $\overline{F}_2$, σ_{F1}^2, and σ_{F2}^2, the investor can use equations (9.10), (9.11), and (9.12) to calculate expected returns, variances, and covariances, respectively. This will then enable the investor to derive the curved efficient set of Markowitz, from which the tangency portfolio can be determined for a given risk-free rate.

☐ 9.2.3 General Factor Models

As mentioned earlier, factor models are sometimes called index models. A number of investment firms have used single-index (that is, single-factor) models for portfolio management. Increasingly, however, multiple-index (that is, multiple-factor) models are being employed. Frequently, these models contain both *common factors* that affect all securities to a greater or lesser extent (for example, the growth rate in GNP) and *sector factors* that affect only particular subgroup of securities (for example, industries).[5]

In an important sense, a major task of investment analysis is to determine an appropriate factor model. This means determining how many factors there are and what they represent. Such a task is not easy, and definitive proof that a correct answer has been obtained is extremely unlikely. Differences of opinion concerning the relative usefulness of alternative factor models will persist, providing the investor with a wide range of choice. Once this choice is made, the investor can focus on estimating the appropriate parameters, thereby allowing expected returns, variances, and covariances to be calculated. With these as inputs, the curved efficient set of Markowitz can be derived. From this set the tangency portfolio associated with a given risk-free rate can be determined. At this point, the investor will be able to identify his or her optimal portfolio by finding the combination of the tangency portfolio and risk-free rate that provides the most desirable trade-off of risk and return.

☐ 9.2.4 Factor Models and Equilibrium

It should be kept in mind that a factor model is *not* an equilibrium model of asset pricing. However, if equilibrium exists, then there will be certain

---

[5] See Sharpe, "Factors in NYSE Security Returns." The factor model discussed in this article is subsequently used in Blake R. Grossman and William F. Sharpe, "Financial Implications of South African Divestment," *Financial Analysts Journal* 42, no. 4 (July/August 1986):15–29. To see how factor models can be used to evaluate the performance of portfolio managers, see the Appendix to Chapter 23. For more on multiple-index models, see Gordon J. Alexander and Jack Clark Francis, *Portfolio Analysis* (Englewood Cliffs, N.J.: Prentice Hall, 1986), 83–92.

relationships between the parameters of the factor model and those of the equilibrium asset pricing model.

For example, if actual returns can be viewed as being generated by a single-factor model where the factor is r_M, then according to equation (9.2), expected returns will be equal to $a_i + b_i \bar{r}_M$, since $\bar{F} = \bar{r}_M$. But if equilibrium exists according to the CAPM, then equation (8.7) can be used to show that expected returns will also be equal to $r_f + (\bar{r}_M - r_f)\beta_i$, which can be rewritten as:

$$
\begin{aligned}
\bar{r}_i &= r_f + (\bar{r}_M - r_f)\beta_i \\
&= r_f - r_f\beta_i + \bar{r}_M\beta_i \\
&= (1 - \beta_i)r_f + \bar{r}_M\beta_i.
\end{aligned} \tag{8.7}
$$

This means that the parameters of the single-factor model and CAPM must have the following relationships:

$$
a_i = (1 - \beta_i)r_f
$$

$$
b_i = \beta_i.
$$

That is, if expected returns are determined according to the CAPM and actual returns are generated by a single-factor model, then a_i and b_i must be equal to $(1 - \beta_i)r_f$ and β_i, respectively.

9.3 ARBITRAGE PRICING THEORY

Arbitrage pricing theory (APT), like the CAPM, is an equilibrium model of asset pricing.[6] Unlike the CAPM, APT assumes that returns are generated by a factor model. Furthermore, although the CAPM made certain strong assumptions about investor preferences (for example, investors were assumed to be risk-averse), APT makes no such strong assumptions. That is, APT is not based on the idea that investors look at portfolios in terms of expected returns and standard deviations. Instead, APT requires only that investors prefer higher levels of wealth to lower levels of wealth.

☐ 9.3.1 Factor Portfolios

As mentioned previously, APT assumes returns are generated by a factor model. It does not specify how many factors there are or what they represent. For ease of exposition, assume there are two factors, F_1 and F_2, which means that security returns are generated according to equation (9.9). It is also

---

[6] For the initial development of APT, see Stephen A. Ross, "The Arbitrage Theory of Capital Asset Pricing," *Journal of Economic Theory* 13, no. 3 (December 1976):341–60; and "Risk, Return, and Arbitrage," sec. 9 in *Risk and Return in Finance*, vol. I, ed. Irwin Friend and James L. Bicksler (Cambridge, Mass.: Ballinger Publishing Company, 1977).

necessary to assume that there are "very many" securities and that the sensitivities to the two factors differ substantially among securities.[7]

In such a world, a number of investment strategies exist. Particularly interesting is the strategy involving portfolios that represent *pure factor plays*. Given enough securities with different characteristics, it should be possible to construct a portfolio that has unit sensitivity (that is, a sensitivity of size 1) to one factor, no sensitivity to the other factor, and zero nonfactor risk. The trick in forming such a portfolio is to combine positions in the securities to "hedge out" (that is, remove) the sensitivity of the portfolio to all but one factor. Furthermore, a large number of securities should be held so that the number of securities that will experience "good" nonfactor returns can be expected to be roughly the same as the number of securities that will experience "bad" nonfactor returns. This will result in the portfolio having nearly zero nonfactor risk.

For example, assume that securities A, B, and C have the following sensitivities:

SECURITY	b_{i1}	b_{i2}
A	$-.40$	1.75
B	1.60	$-.75$
C	.67	$-.25$

If an investor has \$1000 to invest and puts \$300 in security A, \$700 in security B, and nothing in security C, then the proportions invested will be $X_A = .3$, $X_B = .7$, and $X_C = .0$. The sensitivity of this portfolio to factors 1 and 2 will be 1 and 0, respectively:

$$b_{p1} = (-.40 \times .3) + (1.60 \times .7) + (.67 \times .0)$$

$$= -.12 + 1.12 + 0$$

$$= 1.0$$

$$b_{p2} = (1.75 \times .3) + (-.75 \times .7) + (-.25 \times .0)$$

$$= .525 - .525 - .000$$

$$= 0.$$

If it were possible to invest in a great many securities like these, it would be possible to create a portfolio with very little nonfactor risk, meaning that $e_p = 0$. Thus, by choosing the proportions appropriately, the investor could create a portfolio (call it pI) that is sensitive only to factor 1:

$$r_{pI} = a_{pI} + F_1 \tag{9.19}$$

---

[7] For a discussion of these assumptions and why the resulting asset pricing equation is not exact but approximate, see Philip H. Dybvig, "An Explicit Bound on Individual Assets' Deviations from APT Pricing in a Finite Economy," *Journal of Financial Economics* 12, no. 4 (December 1983):483–96; and Mark Grinblatt and Sheridan Titman, "Factor Pricing in a Finite Economy," *Journal of Financial Economics* 12, no. 4 (December 1983):497–507. Since the approximation errors are arguably small, the presentation that follows ignores them.

Since $b_{pI1} = 1$, $b_{pI2} = 0$, and $e_{pI} = 0$. This would be a *pure factor* 1 portfolio. By design, its return moves with the first factor on a one-for-one basis.

An alternative strategy could create a *pure factor* 2 portfolio. If the investor with $1000 decided to invest $625 in securities like A and $375 in securities like C, the sensitivities of the resulting portfolio would be:

$$b_{p1} = (-.40 \times .625) + (1.60 \times .0) + (.67 \times .375)$$

$$= -.25 + .00 + .25$$

$$= .00$$

$$b_{p2} = (1.75 \times .625) + (-.75 \times .0) + (-.25 \times .375)$$

$$= 1.09 + .00 - .09$$

$$= 1.00.$$

If this could be done over many securities, then it would have very little nonfactor risk; the result would be a portfolio (call it pII) sensitive only to factor 2:

$$r_{pII} = a_{pII} + F_2. \tag{9.20}$$

In a market with many securities of diverse characteristics, it would be theoretically possible to create "pure factor" portfolios that are sensitive to only one factor and have insignificant nonfactor risk. In practice, the required conditions are not met completely, meaning it is only possible to create "impure factor" portfolios that are sensitive primarily (but not exclusively) to one factor with relatively little nonfactor risk. Although APT assumes that pure factor portfolios can be created, it should be kept in mind that the reasonableness of the assumption is not of concern. Instead, it is the accuracy of the predictions of APT that are of importance.

□ 9.3.2 Expected Returns on Factor Portfolios

The expected return from a pure factor portfolio will depend on the expected value of the relevant factor. It is convenient to break this expected return into two parts: (1) the risk-free rate of interest and (2) the rest, which is typically indicated by the Greek letter *lambda*, λ, and may be regarded as the *expected return premium per unit of sensitivity to the factor*. Thus, the expected return on a pure factor 1 portfolio is:

$$\bar{r}_{pI} = r_f + \lambda_1. \tag{9.21}$$

Similarly, the expected return on a pure factor 2 portfolio is:

$$\bar{r}_{pII} = r_f + \lambda_2. \tag{9.22}$$

As an example, if the risk-free rate is 7% and $\bar{r}_{pI}$ is 16.6%, then λ_1 will be $16.6\% - 7\% = 9.6\%$. And if $\bar{r}_{pII}$ is 13.4%, then λ_2 will be $13.4\% - 7\% = 6.4\%$. This means that the expected return premiums per unit of sensitivity to factors 1 and 2 are 9.6% and 6.4%, respectively.

It is possible that many alternative combinations of securities could be used to construct a pure factor 1 portfolio. Will each such combination have the same expected return? Under the theory, yes. Whereas pure factor portfolios may not be unique in their composition, their expected returns should be.

Imagine a situation in which two pure factor 1 portfolios had different expected returns. This could only be due to differences in their a-values (a_{pI} in equation (9.19)). Now, consider selling short the portfolio with the lower expected return and purchasing the portfolio with the greater expected return. In this situation, the investor stands to make an abnormal return *no matter what happens to factor* 1. This clearly will not persist, because two identical assets (in this case, the two pure factor 1 portfolios) must, in equilibrium, be priced to provide the same expected return.

Opportunities where they are not so priced will cause certain investors, known as *arbitrageurs*, to spring into action. They will purchase the securities in the portfolio with the higher expected return and sell those in the portfolio with the lower expected return. In turn, this will drive up the prices of the former, driving down the expected return of the corresponding portfolio. It will also drive down the prices of the latter, driving up the expected return of the corresponding portfolio. This would continue until the two portfolios have the same expected return.

As a result of prices moving in this fashion, the investor would make an abnormal return and, before long, such an opportunity to get "something for nothing" would have disappeared. That is, *arbitrage* will ensure that all pure factor 1 portfolios will have the same expected return, $r_f + \lambda_1$.[8]

The presence of a risk-free rate is a natural part of APT. With a great many diverse securities, it will be possible to construct a portfolio that has zero sensitivity to every factor and is sufficiently diversified to have insignificant nonfactor risk. Its expected return, which will be virtually risk-free, can be used as a base from which other expected returns are measured.

☐ 9.3.3 Expected Returns on Securities

By splitting funds among (1) a risk-free portfolio and (2) pure factor portfolios, it is possible for the investor to form a portfolio with almost any sensitivity to each factor. Moreover, such portfolios can be constructed to have insignificant nonfactor risks.

For example, assume that the return on security k is related to factors 1 and 2 as follows:

$$r_k = a_k + .8F_1 + 1.5F_2 + e_k. \tag{9.23a}$$

Thus, if an investor had $1000 to invest, he or she could put it all in security k and have an expected return of

---

[8] In general, arbitrage takes place when the same security sells for two different prices in two different markets. It involves the purchase of the security in the market where the lower price exists and the near simultaneous sale of the same security in the market with the higher price. One result of doing this is the riskless earning of abnormal profits; another result is that the price discrepancy will disappear quickly.

$$\bar{r}_k = a_k + .8\overline{F}_1 + 1.5\overline{F}_2. \qquad (9.23b)$$

Now, consider an alternative strategy in which $1300 is borrowed at the risk-free rate to supplement the investor's $1000. This means that the proportion invested in the risk-free asset is $(-\$1300/\$1000) = -1.3 = X_f$. Of the resulting $2300, $800 is invested in a pure factor 1 portfolio and the remaining $1500 is invested in a pure factor 2 portfolio. This means that the proportions invested in these two portfolios are $(\$800/\$1000) = .8 = X_I$ and $(\$1500/\$1000) = 1.5 = X_{II}$, respectively. The expected return on the resulting portfolio, denoted by K, can be calculated as a weighted average of its three components:

$$\bar{r}_K = (X_f \times r_f) + (X_I \times \bar{r}_{pI}) + (X_{II} \times \bar{r}_{pII})$$

$$= (-1.3 \times r_f) + (.8 \times \bar{r}_{pI}) + (1.5 \times \bar{r}_{pII})$$

$$= (-1.3 \times r_f) + [.8 \times (r_f + \lambda_1)] + [1.5 \times (r_f + \lambda_2)] \qquad (9.24)$$

$$= -1.3r_f + .8r_f + .8\lambda_1 + 1.5r_f + 1.5\lambda_2$$

$$= r_f + .8\lambda_1 + 1.5\lambda_2.$$

Note how the expected return of the two pure factor portfolios given in equations (9.21) and (9.22) have been substituted for $\bar{r}_{pI}$ and $\bar{r}_{pII}$, respectively, in equation (9.24).

Now, compare portfolio K with security k. Each has a sensitivity of .8 to factor 1 and a sensitivity of 1.5 to factor 2. Security k is subject to additional risk due to uncertainty about its nonfactor return, e_k. Portfolio K has virtually no risk of this type. What if the expected return from security k were less than that of portfolio K? Clearly, the portfolio would dominate the security, since the portfolio would provide a greater expected return with less risk than the security. A clever arbitrageur could sell security k short and purchase portfolio K, expecting to profit from the difference in their expected returns. The situation would not be totally riskless, since the nonfactor return of security k could swamp the difference in expected returns. However, if there were many securities like k, this source of risk could be removed through diversification.

What if the expected return from security k were more than that of portfolio K? In this case, there is no obvious dominance. However, a clever arbitrageur could sell the portfolio short and purchase the security, expecting to profit from the difference in expected returns. Here too, the situation would not be totally riskless, since the nonfactor return could swamp the difference in expected returns. However, if there were many securities like k, this source of risk could be removed through diversification.

The conclusion is that the expected return of security k would be equal to the expected return of portfolio K in equilibrium. That is, arbitrage would ensure that the expected return of security k would be

$$\bar{r}_k = r_f + .8\lambda_1 + 1.5\lambda_2. \qquad (9.25)$$

More generally, for any security i:

$$\bar{r}_i = r_f + b_{i1}\lambda_1 + b_{i2}\lambda_2. \qquad (9.26)$$

Equation (9.26) is the asset pricing equation of APT.[9] In words, it states that:

> The expected return of a security will be related to its sensitivity to each pervasive factor. Moreover, the relationship will be linear, with a common intercept term that is equal to the risk-free rate.

Like the equation obtained from the CAPM, APT equation (9.26) asserts that there is a linear relationship between (1) expected returns and (2) the various relevant attributes of securities. In the case of the CAPM, the relevant security attribute was beta (β_i), whereas in the case of APT, the relevant security attributes are sensitivities to major factors (b_{i1} and b_{i2}). However, as mentioned earlier, APT is silent about how many of these factors exist and what they represent. In turn, this means that APT is silent about the lambda values, such as λ_1 and λ_2 in equation (9.26). They can be positive, negative, or zero. Identification of the factors and the associated lambda values involves both empirical work and judgment.

Equation (9.26) refers to equilibrium expected returns for securities. However, disequilibrium can be represented with this equation in a manner similar to the CAPM. In particular, an alpha term can be added to the right-hand side of the equation to indicate the amount of mispricing. An overpriced security would have a negative alpha. This would mean that its expected return would be less than its equilibrium expected return of $r_f + b_{i1}\lambda_1 + b_{i2}\lambda_2$. In turn, this suggests that the security is not an attractive one to purchase (or to hold onto if it is already owned). Similarly, an underpriced security would have a positive alpha, meaning its expected return would be greater than its equilibrium return and that it is an attractive security to purchase.

9.4 A SYNTHESIS OF APT AND THE CAPM

Unlike APT, the CAPM does not assume that returns are generated by a factor model. However, this does not mean that the CAPM is inconsistent with a world in which returns are generated by a factor model. Indeed, it is possible to have a world where returns are generated by a factor model, where the remaining assumptions of APT hold and where all the assumptions of the CAPM hold. This situation will now be examined.

☐ 9.4.1 Beta Coefficients and Factor Sensitivities

If security returns are generated by a factor model, it is possible to relate the beta coefficient of any particular security to its sensitivities to the factors. Assuming returns are generated by a two-factor model, it can be shown that

---

[9] Equation (9.26) is based on there being two factors in the economy. If there are more factors, the equation is extended in a straightforward manner. For example, if there were three factors, then equation (9.26) would have the term $b_{i3}\lambda_3$ added onto the right-hand side.

the covariance of the return on security i with the return of the market portfolio M will be:

$$COV(r_i, r_M) = [COV(F_1, r_M) \times b_{i1}] \\ + [COV(F_2, r_M) \times b_{i2}] + COV(e_i, r_M) \quad \text{(9.27)}$$

where COV denotes covariance of the two variables inside the following parentheses.

In Chapter 8, it was shown that the beta coefficient for a security could be obtained by dividing $COV(r_i, r_M)$ by the variance of the market portfolio, σ_M^2:[10]

$$\beta_i = \frac{COV(r_i, r_M)}{\sigma_M^2}. \quad \text{(9.28)}$$

Thus, when both sides of equation (9.27) are divided by σ_M^2, the result is:

$$\beta_i = \left[\frac{COV(F_1, r_M)}{\sigma_M^2} \times b_{i1} \right] + \left[\frac{COV(F_2, r_M)}{\sigma_M^2} \times b_{i2} \right] + \frac{COV(e_i, r_M)}{\sigma_M^2}. \quad \text{(9.29)}$$

As a practical matter, the term $COV(e_i, r_M)/\sigma_M^2$ will be very small, so little is lost by ignoring it. Each of the other two terms involves the ratio of a factor's covariance with the market portfolio to the variance of the market portfolio. These ratios can be viewed as the *factor betas*. This is because each ratio is identical to the right-hand side of equation (9.28) except that the value of the factor appears in the place of the return on the security:

$$\beta_{F1} = \frac{COV(F_1, r_M)}{\sigma_M^2} \quad \text{(9.30)}$$

$$\beta_{F2} = \frac{COV(F_2, r_M)}{\sigma_M^2}. \quad \text{(9.31)}$$

This leads to the conclusion that

$$\beta_i = \beta_{F1} b_{i1} + \beta_{F2} b_{i2}. \quad \text{(9.32)}$$

Since β_{F1} and β_{F2} are constants and do not vary from one security to another, equation (9.32) shows that the beta coefficient of a security is a function of its sensitivities to the pervasive factors. Accordingly, the reason securities have different betas is because they have different sensitivities.

As an example, assume that the factor beta for GNP, β_{F1}, is equal to 1.2, and that the factor beta for inflation, β_{F2}, is .8. Given the sensitivities of securities A, B, and C that were shown earlier, equation (9.32) can be used to determine their beta coefficients:

$$\beta_A = (1.2 \times -.40) + (.8 \times 1.75) = .92$$

$$\beta_B = (1.2 \times 1.60) + (.8 \times -.75) = 1.32$$

$$\beta_C = (1.2 \times .67) + (.8 \times -.25) = .60.$$

---

[10] See equation (8.6), where σ_{iM} was used instead of $COV(r_i, r_M)$ to denote the covariance of the return on security i with the return of the market portfolio M.

☐ 9.4.2 Expected Returns, Factor Betas, and Security Sensitivities

As a result of making the assumptions necessary for the CAPM, the expected return of security i was shown in Chapter 8 to be related to its beta coefficient:

$$\bar{r}_i = r_f + [(\bar{r}_M - r_f)\beta_i]. \tag{8.7}$$

If returns are generated by a two-factor model, the beta coefficient of a security will be related to its sensitivities to the factors and the factor betas, as shown in equation (9.32). Substituting the right-hand side of equation (9.32) for β_i in equation (8.7) results in

$$\bar{r}_i = r_f + [(\bar{r}_M - r_f) \times (\beta_{F1}b_{i1} + \beta_{F2}b_{i2})] \tag{9.33}$$

$$= r_f + [(\bar{r}_M - r_f)\beta_{F1}]b_{i1} + [(\bar{r}_M - r_f)\beta_{F2}]b_{i2}.$$

Comparing equation (9.33) to APT asset pricing equation (9.26), it can be seen that if the assumptions of both APT and the CAPM hold, then the lambda terms must have the following values:

$$\lambda_1 = (\bar{r}_M - r_f)\beta_{F1} \tag{9.34}$$

$$\lambda_2 = (\bar{r}_M - r_f)\beta_{F2}. \tag{9.35}$$

Substituting the right-hand side of these two equations into the right-hand side of equation (9.33) results in

$$\bar{r}_i = r_f + \lambda_1 b_{i1} + \lambda_2 b_{i2}. \tag{9.36}$$

By itself, APT says nothing about the sizes or the magnitudes of the factor expected return premiums, λ_1 and λ_2. However, if the CAPM also holds, it can provide some guidance. This guidance is given in equations (9.34) and (9.35), which have been shown to exist if the assumptions of both APT and the CAPM hold.

Imagine that factor 1 moves with the market portfolio, meaning that it is positively correlated with the market portfolio and that $COV(F_1, r_M)$ is positive.[11] In turn, β_{F1} must be positive because it equals $COV(F_1, r_M)$, a positive number, divided by σ_M^2, another positive number. Since $\bar{r}_M$ is greater than r_f, $(\bar{r}_M - r_f)$ will be positive, and thus $(\bar{r}_M - r_f)\beta_{F1}$ will be positive. It follows from equation (9.34) that λ_1 will be positive.[12] Furthermore, since λ_1 is positive, it can be seen in equation (9.36) that the higher the value of b_{i1}, the higher will be the expected return of the security. To generalize, if a factor is positively correlated with the market portfolio, then a security's expected return will be a positive linear function of the security's sensitivity to that factor.

With a similar kind of argument, it can be shown that if factor 2 moves

---

[11] $COV(F_1, r_M)$ will be positive if the correlation is positive, since it is equal to the product of the correlation and the standard deviations of F_1 and r_M.

[12] The greater the extent to which factor 1 moves with the market portfolio, meaning the higher the correlation between F_1 and r_M, the greater will be the associated expected return premium, λ_1. For a discussion of the implications of factor 1 being the market portfolio, see K. C. John Wei, "An Asset-Pricing Theory Unifying the CAPM and APT," *Journal of Finance* 43, no. 4 (September 1988):881–92; and Stephen A. Ross and Randolph W. Westerfield, *Corporate Finance* (St. Louis, Mo.: Times Mirror, 1988), 181–95.

against the market portfolio, meaning F_2 is negatively correlated with r_M, then (1) β_{F2} will be negative; (2) $(\bar{r}_M - r_f)\beta_{F2}$ will be negative; and (3) λ_2 will be negative. Thus, from equation (9.36), it follows that the higher the value of b_{i2}, the lower will be the expected return of the security. Again generalizing, if a factor is negatively correlated with the market portfolio, then a security's expected return will be a negative linear function of the security's sensitivity to that factor.

Using the earlier example, where $\beta_{F1} = 1.2$ and $\beta_{F2} = .8$, and assuming that $r_f = 7\%$ and $\bar{r}_M = 15\%$, equation (9.33) will be as follows:

$$\bar{r}_i = r_f + [(\bar{r}_M - r_f)\beta_{F1}]b_{i1} + [(\bar{r}_M - r_f)\beta_{F2}]b_{i2}$$

$$= 7 + [(15 - 7) \times 1.2]b_{i1} + [(15 - 7) \times .8]b_{i2}$$

$$= 7 + 9.6b_{i1} + 6.4b_{i2}.$$

Note that both λ_1 and λ_2 are positive, being equal to 9.6 and 6.4, respectively. Thus, the larger b_{i1} is, the larger $\bar{r}_i$ will be. Furthermore, the larger b_{i2} is, the larger $\bar{r}_i$ will be.

If β_{F2} had been equal to $-.8$ instead of $+.8$, then $\lambda_2 = (15 - 7) \times -.8 = -6.4$, and the preceding equation would have been

$$r_i = 7 + 9.6b_{i1} - 6.4b_{i2}.$$

Thus, a negative value for β_{F2} would have led to a negative value for λ_2. In such a situation, the larger b_{i2} is, the smaller $\bar{r}_i$ will be. Accordingly, the sign of each lambda determines whether a security's expected return is a positive or negative function of its sensitivity to that lambda.

9.5 SUMMARY

It seems reasonable to assume that a set of factors generates security returns. It is also reasonable to assume that most investors like higher levels of expected return and dislike higher levels of risk. Thus, it is not unreasonable to argue that the conditions necessary for both APT and the CAPM to hold are in existence.

In such a setting, it can be argued that the two theories combined are more powerful (that is, make stronger predictions) than either one alone and can therefore provide considerably more guidance for investment decisions. While it is interesting to wonder if historical data support either theory (or both), Markowitz has noted that affirmative test results are not necessary in order to make sensible practical use of these asset pricing models.[13] Since one of the more contentious issues currently being debated in finance is whether or not either asset pricing model can be meaningfully

---

[13] Harry M. Markowitz, "Nonnegative or Not Nonnegative: A Question About CAPMs," *Journal of Finance* 38, no. 2 (May 1983):283–95.

tested with historical data, there would appear to be wide latitude for the practical use of such models.[14]

Due to their complex statistical nature, actual usage of these models has generally been confined to professional money managers. These investors have the resources necessary to implement such models in the management of multimillion dollar portfolios. While there are many variations on how these models have been used, undoubtedly more variations will appear in the future as investors gain more experience with the models.[15] Nevertheless, it is unlikely that any one model will ever be shown conclusively to be superior to any other, since the models involve "unobservables" such as expected returns, betas, and sensitivities. These unobservables can only be estimated, which means that substantial errors can occur in doing so. As a result, investors will have to decide for themselves what models they favor and how they will use them. Ultimately, the value of any model to the investor will depend on the accuracy of its predictions.

APPENDIX A
TESTING EQUILIBRIUM THEORIES OF ASSET PRICING

Equilibrium theories such as the capital asset pricing model and arbitrage pricing theory imply that in the consensus opinion of well-informed investors, securities with certain attributes will, other things being equal, have large expected returns, whereas those with other attributes will have small expected returns. Such concepts are based on opinions held *ex ante* (Latin for "before the fact") about possible returns and their relative probabilities. *Ex post* (Latin for "after the fact"), only one outcome will be recorded for each stock. Investors will then form new and possibly different opinions, another set of stock returns will subsequently be recorded, and so on.

This makes it extremely difficult to test whether security attributes and expected returns do in fact go together in the manner implied by either the CAPM or APT. Moreover, such theories are relatively silent concerning simple ways in which a security's *future* attributes and expected return might be estimated by processing *historical* data.

To bridge this gap, a number of investigators have used historical security returns as surrogates for expected returns. This requires an assumption that relevant predictions do not change from period to period and that sufficient information is available to determine what such expectations

---

[14] For an argument that the CAPM cannot be tested, see Richard Roll, "A Critique of the Asset Pricing Theory's Tests; Part I. On Past and Potential Testability of the Theory," *Journal of Financial Economics* 4, no. 2 (March 1977):129–76. For an argument that APT cannot be tested, see Jay Shanken, "The Arbitrage Pricing Theory: Is It Testable?" *Journal of Finance* 37, no. 5 (December 1982):1129–40. A discussion of certain tests of the CAPM and APT, along with Roll and Shanken's arguments, is presented in the appendix. For a more extensive discussion, see Chapters 10 and 14 of Alexander and Francis, *Portfolio Analysis*.

[15] As an example, consider Wells Fargo. In managing common stock portfolios, they have used at one time or another variations of the CAPM that include a liquidity adjustment and a dividend yield adjustment. For a description of how they were used, see George Foster, *Financial Statement Analysis* (Englewood Cliffs, N.J.: Prentice Hall, 1986), 428–30.

actually were. Thus, average historical returns are used as estimates of expected returns. Two obvious objections may be made. First, expectations almost certainly change from time to time (nothing in theory suggests this cannot happen). Second, even if expectations did not change over time, an extremely long historical record might be required to obtain reasonably accurate estimates of their magnitudes. Despite these and other problems, it is potentially worthwhile examining historical data.

Any test of an equilibrium theory based on historical data is a *joint* test of (1) certain assumptions such as the one just mentioned concerning the stability of predictions and (2) a particular theory of equilibrium. If such a test fails, it may indicate that the equilibrium theory is in error. Alternatively, one or more of the other assumptions may be inappropriate. As a practical matter, such tests cannot *reject* an equilibrium theory. They can, however, provide suggestive evidence.

A.1   TESTS OF THE CAPITAL ASSET PRICING MODEL

Both the original and extended versions of the capital asset pricing model suggest that, other things being equal, securities with relatively large *ex ante* betas will have relatively large expected returns. This does not mean that they will necessarily have, *ex post*, larger actual returns. If the market goes up substantially, actual returns can be expected to be higher for high-beta securities. However, these are expectations, and ignore the unsystematic element of a security's return, which can cause a security with a relatively large beta to have a relatively small return when the market goes up substantially. Thus, even if the CAPM is valid, actual returns may bear little if any relationship to expectations and, hence, to *ex ante* betas.

An additional problem concerns the measurement of beta. Beta should measure a security's sensitivity to a widely diversified market portfolio that includes all types of stocks, bonds, real estate, and so on. Many empirical studies have instead used a broad-based index of widely traded stocks, since adequate data on other types of securities has been difficult or impossible to obtain. Clearly, a security's beta measured relative to, say, a market portfolio consisting of all stocks listed on the New York Stock Exchange could differ significantly from one measured relative to a market portfolio consisting of all stocks in the United States, let alone a market portfolio consisting of all stocks in the world.

Despite all these problems it is instructive to see how well common stocks with different historical betas have done over time.

Risk-Return Classes

The development of a computerized file of monthly returns for all stocks listed on the NYSE from 1926 to the present has facilitated extensive investigation of risk and return for such securities.[16] Using this file, the re-

---

[16] Performed at the Center for Research in Security Prices (CRSP) at the University of Chicago, and sponsored by Merrill Lynch, Pierce, Fenner and Smith, Inc. Currently, a computerized file with daily returns is also available.

lationship between risk and return can be examined by measuring each security's beta relative to an index of the returns on all NYSE stocks over some historical period (such as five years).[17] Once this has been done, portfolios can be formed that are designed to include many stocks but also to differ as much as possible in regard to the size of their betas. For example, on January 1, 1931, all securities could be listed in order of the size of their historical betas. Then equal dollar amounts of the top 10% of all securities might be placed hypothetically in one portfolio, equal dollar amounts of the next 10% in another portfolio, and so on. On January 1, 1932, the process was repeated by using updated estimates of each security's beta and rebalancing each portfolio to again contain equal dollar proportions of the stocks in the appropriate part of the listing. Thus, the approach is based on one-year holding periods. It defines several *risk-return classes* of stocks with similar historical betas and thus, it is hoped, similar future betas and expected returns.

Figure 9.1 shows some of the results. In part (a), each bar indicates the arithmetic average annual return from 1931 through 1967 for a risk-return class. Part (b) shows the *ex post* beta values, and part (c) provides a plot of the average returns and *ex post* beta values for all ten classes, along with the best-fit regression line.[18] Despite the potential problems with such analyses, the results are substantially consistent with the theoretical CAPM relationship between expected returns and beta values.

Figure 9.2 shows the results from a study concerned with longer holding periods. In this case, eight five-year nonoverlapping periods from mid-1928 through mid-1968 were analyzed and the percentage change in value determined for an account that remained fully invested during each period (all dividends received during the five years were reinvested; portfolios were rebalanced monthly). The results are roughly consistent with a positive relationship between beta values and medium-term returns.

Historic beta values cannot be counted on to predict returns precisely, even relative to market moves, over every period. Figure 9.3 plots the average monthly returns over four different 105-month periods for ten risk-return classes based on historical beta values. In each case, the market return (indicated by a square) exceeded the risk-free rate of interest. Three of the lines of best fit are upward-sloping as expected, but one is not.

Historical Beta Factor

Many factor models include a security's historical beta as an attribute. The corresponding *historical beta factor* provides a measure of the difference in returns between high-historical beta stocks and low-historical beta stocks, keeping other attributes equal. If historical betas are useful for predicting future betas, the beta factor should be positive in most periods when the

---

[17] Individual security betas can be estimated by using a statistical procedure known as simple regression or ordinary least squares (OLS); for a discussion, see Chapter 15.

[18] The equation of the line is $ar_p = 5.54 + 12.75\beta_p$, where ar_p and β_p denote the average return and *ex post* beta for portfolio p; the correlation between ar_p and β_p is .97.

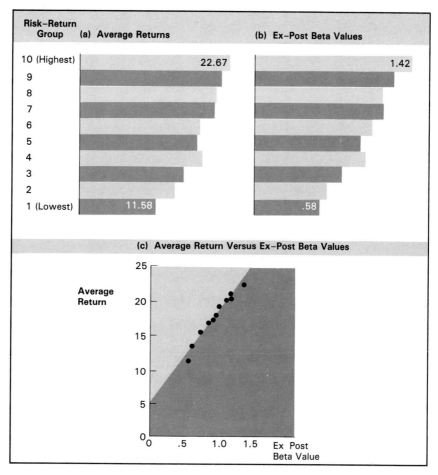

FIGURE 9–1
Performance of ten risk-return classes for one-year holding periods, 1931–1967.

SOURCE: William F. Sharpe and Guy M. Cooper, "Risk-Return Classes of New York Stock Exchange Common Stocks, 1931–1967," Financial Analysis Journal 28, no. 2 (March–April 1972): 51.

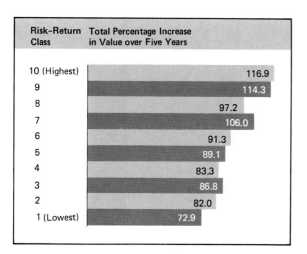

FIGURE 9–2
Average performance of ten risk-return classes over eight five-year holding periods, 1928–1968.

SOURCE: Marshall E. Blume and Irwin Friend, "Risk, Investment Strategy and the Long-run Rates of Return," *Review of Economics and Statistics* 56, no. 3 (August 1974): 263.

261

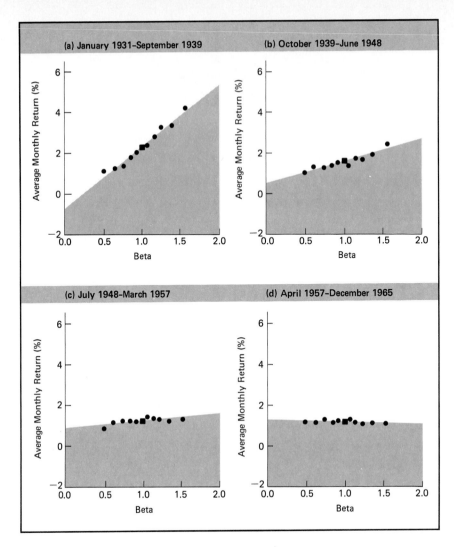

FIGURE 9–3
Performance of ten risk-return classes, four 105-month periods, 1931–1965.

SOURCE: Fischer Black, Michael C. Jensen, and Myron Scholes, "The Capital Asset Pricing Model: Some Empirical Tests," in Michael C. Jensen (ed.), *Studies in the Theory of Capital Markets* (New York: Praeger Publishers, Inc. 1972): 105–6.

return on stocks exceeds the risk-free rate of interest and negative in most periods when the return on stocks is less than the risk-free rate.

Figure 9.4 shows that this has in fact been the case. In months in which the excess return on the New York Stock Exchange (that is, the market return minus the Treasury bill rate) was positive, the beta factor was generally positive—stocks with high-historical betas tended to outperform those with low-historical betas. In months in which the excess return on stocks was negative, the beta factor was generally negative—stocks with high-

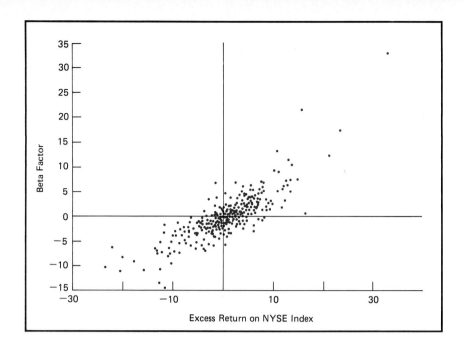

FIGURE 9–4
Beta factor values and NYSE returns, 1928–1982.

SOURCE: Blake Grossman and William F. Sharpe, "Factors in Security Returns," paper presented at the Center for the Study of Banking and Financial Markets, University of Washington, March 1984.

historical betas tended to underperform those with low-historical betas. The relationship is highly significant statistically (for example, the *t*-statistic of 41.7 is significant at the 99% confidence level).

Although most of the points in Figure 9.4 are in the upper-right and lower-left quadrants, some are not. In such cases the actual relationship between return and beta differed from what might be expected according to the CAPM.

Tests of the Zero-Beta CAPM

In a detailed test of the original and zero-beta CAPM, portfolio classes were used to examine the relationship between average returns and historical betas. The classes were also tested to see if average returns were related in a nonlinear manner to betas and if average returns were related to unique risks.

Figure 9.5 contrasts the actual relationship for the period from 1938 through mid-1968 with the original CAPM. The vertical intercept, which corresponds to the zero-beta return, is .61% per month (equivalent to approximately 7.32% per year), while the average Treasury bill return, which corresponds to the risk-free rate of interest, was only .13% per month (equivalent to approximately 1.56% per year). The difference was substantial and statistically significant. Assuming that betas measured relative to a stock

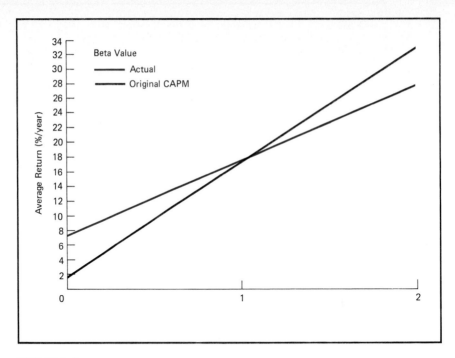

FIGURE 9–5
Average return and beta.

SOURCE: Adapted from Eugene F. Fama and James D. MacBeth, "Risk, Return and Equilibrium: Empirical Tests," *Journal of Political Economy* 81, no. 3 (May 1973): 622.

index are adequate surrogates for "true" betas measured relative to the overall market portfolio, such results provide more support for the zero-beta version of the CAPM than for the original version.

Similar tests have been performed using returns from securities in other countries, with mixed but not dissimilar results.[19]

A.2   TESTS OF THE ARBITRAGE PRICING THEORY

Since the arbitrage pricing theory assumes a factor model of security returns, any test of its predictions must incorporate such a factor model and be, in effect, a joint test of the equilibrium theory and the appropriateness of the selected factor model. Moreover, the APT makes relatively weak predictions. It does imply that when all pervasive factors are taken into account, the remaining portion of return on a typical security should be expected to equal the risk-free interest rate. Testing this implication is possible in principle but difficult in practice. For example, when a model such as that shown in

---

[19] For a comprehensive summary of studies using European data, see Gabriel Hawawini, *European Equity Markets: Price Behavior and Efficiency*, Monograph Series in Finance and Economics 1984–4/5, Salomon Brothers Center for the Study of Financial Institutions, Graduate School of Business Administration, New York University.

equation (9.9) is fit to data for stock returns, the "zero factor" will include elements of a "stock factor." Analyses using both bonds and stocks can include corresponding factors explicitly, reducing the possibility that the zero factor does, in fact, include elements of pervasive sources of risk. However, it may never be possible to find a set of securities so diverse that consistency of the zero factor with risk-free interest rates can be used as a test of the APT.

A more promising test concerns the prediction that security expected returns will be related only to sensitivities to pervasive factors. In particular, there should be no relationship between expected returns and securities' nonfactor risks. Since the total risk of a security includes nonfactor risk as well as factor risk, its inclusion in an analysis of expected returns should not help explain differences in expected returns.

One study used data from 1962 through 1972, computing average returns, sensitivities to each of five factors (obtained via factor analysis), and the total standard deviation of returns for 1260 securities.[20] Given the computational demands of the factor analysis method utilized, much of the analysis had to be perfomed on groups of 30 stocks rather than on the full set of securities. For each of the resulting 42 groups, regression analysis was performed with average return as the dependent variable and sensitivities to the five factors and total standard deviation as independent variables. In the majority of groups there was a statistically significant relationship between average return and sensitivity to at least one factor; it was also determined that it is unlikely that there are more than five important factors.[21] Furthermore, average returns in the majority of groups were not significantly related to total standard deviation. The results, while not definitive, are consistent with the theory.

QUESTIONS AND PROBLEMS

1. In what significant ways does APT differ from the CAPM?
2. Is it true that if one believes APT is a correct theory of asset pricing, then the risk-return relationship derived from the CAPM is necessarily incorrect? Why?
3. If security returns are generated by a multiple-factor model and the CAPM does not exist, is the basic process of constructing the efficient set and determining the investor's optimal portfolio materially altered? Explain.

---

[20] Richard Roll and Stephen A. Ross, "An Empirical Investigation of the Arbitrage Pricing Theory," *Journal of Finance* 35, no. 5 (December, 1980):1073–1103. For two recent empirical papers that suggest the APT prices most securities with little error and is better than the CAPM, see Bruce N. Lehmann and David M. Modest, "The Empirical Foundations of the Arbitrage Pricing Theory," *Journal of Financial Economics* 21, no. 2 (September 1988):213–54; and Gregory Connor and Robert A. Korajczyk, "Risk and Return in an Equilibrium APT: Application of a New Test Methodology," *Journal of Financial Economics* 21, no. 2 (September 1988):255–89.

[21] A later study found that there were four factors, corresponding to (1) expected and unexpected inflation, (2) industrial production, (3) the yield spread between high-grade and low-grade corporate bonds, and (4) the yield spread between long-term and short-term government bond returns. See Nai-Fu Chen, Richard Roll, and Stephen A. Ross, "Economic Forces and the Stock Market," *Journal of Business* 59, no. 3 (July 1986):383–403.

4. Included among the factors that might be expected to be pervasive are growth in real GNP, real interest rates, unexpected inflation, and oil prices. For each factor, provide an example of an industry that is expected to have a high (either positive or negative) sensitivity to the factor.

5. What is meant by the term "arbitrage profit?"

6. Assume that returns on securities are generated by three factors according to the following relationship:

$$r_i = r_f + b_{i1}F_1 + b_{i2}F_2 + b_{i3}F_3 + e_i.$$

Given two securities, X and Y, if:

$r_f = 4\%$	$b_{X1} = 0.07$	$\sigma_{F1} = 12\%$
$F_1 = 5\%$	$b_{X2} = 1.30$	$\sigma_{F2} = 14\%$
$F_2 = 7\%$	$b_{X3} = 1.10$	$\sigma_{F3} = 8\%$
$F_3 = 8\%$	$b_{Y1} = 0.80$	$\sigma_{eX} = 20\%$
	$b_{Y2} = 0.90$	$\sigma_{eY} = 30\%$
	$b_{Y3} = 1.20$	

a. What is the expected return for stocks X and Y?

b. What is the standard deviation of stocks X and Y?

7. What is a "pure factor" portfolio? How are such portfolios constructed?

8. Assume that security returns are generated by a factor model in which two factors are pervasive. The sensitivities of two securities and of the risk-free asset to each of the two factors is shown below, along with the expected return on each security.

SECURITY	b_{i1}	b_{i2}	EXPECTED RETURN
A	0.50	0.80	16.2%
B	1.50	1.40	21.6
r_f	0.00	0.00	10.0

a. If Dots Miller has $100 to invest and sells short $50 of security B and purchases $150 of security A, what is the sensitivity of Dots' portfolio to the two factors? (Ignore margin requirements.)

b. If Dots now borrows $100 at the risk-free rate and invests the proceeds of the loan along with the original $100 in securities A and B in the same proportions as described in part (a), what is the sensitivity of this portfolio to the two factors?

c. What is the expected return on the portfolio created in part (b)?

d. What is the expected return premium of factor 2?

9. Assume that the CAPM holds and that returns on securities are generated by the following factor model:

$$r_i = r_f + b_{i1}F_1 + b_{i2}F_2 + e_i.$$

You are also given the following information:

$\sigma_M^2 = 324$	$b_{A1} = 0.80$	$b_{B1} = 1.00$
$COV(F_1, r_M) = 156$	$b_{A2} = 1.10$	$b_{B2} = 0.70$
$COV(F_2, r_M) = 500$		

a. Calculate the beta coefficients of securities A and B.

b. If the risk-free rate is 6% and the expected return on the market portfolio is 12%, what is the expected return on securities A and B?

10. Benny Kauff has asserted that, "The CAPM does not *assume* that returns are generated by a factor model. However, it does *imply* that returns are generated by a factor model." Explain what Benny means.

11. (Appendix Question) Some people have argued that the market portfolio can never be measured and that the CAPM, therefore, is untestable. Others have argued that the APT specifies neither the number of factors nor their identity and, hence, is also untestable. If these views are correct, does this mean the theories are of no value? Explain.

Chapter 10

TAXES

A well-worn saying holds that nothing is certain but death and taxes. Unfortunately, governments are sometimes responsible for the former, and they are virtually always the source of the latter. Moreover, governmental activities normally play a central role in determining changes in the overall price level of an economy. Occasionally, such changes are in the downward direction—that is, there is deflation. The more common experience, however, is that of rising prices, or inflation.

Neither taxation nor inflation should be regarded as an unmitigated evil. Each provides benefits to some individuals that may outweigh the associated costs that others have to bear. Regardless of whether or not the benefits outweigh the costs, both taxes and inflation have an impact on investment decisions and investment results. And, they are sufficiently important in present-day societies to warrant considerable discussion. While the next chapter deals with inflation, this chapter provides an overview of some of the more important aspects of taxation from the viewpoint of the investor.

Federal and state tax laws play a major role in the way securities are priced in the marketplace, since investors are understandably concerned with after-tax returns, not before-tax returns. Accordingly, the investor should determine the tax rate applicable to him or her before making any investment decision. This tax rate is not the same for all securities for a given individual investor: It can be as low as 0% in the case of certain tax-exempt securities issued by states and municipalities and in excess of 35% for corporate bonds, when both federal and state taxes are considered. After determining the applicable tax rate, the investor can estimate a security's expected after-tax return and risk. Upon doing so, an investment decision can be made wisely.

10.1 TAXES IN THE UNITED STATES

Since the United States contains the world's largest capital market, this chapter focuses on taxes levied on U.S. citizens and corporations. Many other countries, however, impose taxes similar to those of the United States, so that much of this discussion is at least partly relevant for non–U.S. citizens.

Many of the specific tax rates and provisions in this chapter were enacted with the Tax Reform Act of 1986. Changes do occur from year to year, and current regulations should, of course, be consulted when preparing tax returns or considering major investment decisions. However, the material given here can be considered broadly representative of current taxation (primarily federal) in the United States.

Generally speaking, the most important taxes for investment decision making are personal and corporate income taxes. The essential elements of each will be described, and the manner in which they influence the pricing of securities will be considered.[1]

10.2 CORPORATE INCOME TAXES

There are three forms of business organizations in the United States and in most other countries—corporations, partnerships, and single proprietorships. The corporate form of organization is the largest in terms of the dollar value of assets owned, even though there are more firms organized as partnerships or single proprietorships. Legally, a corporation is regarded as a separate entity, whereas a proprietorship or partnership is considered an extension of its owner or owners. Income earned by proprietorships and partnerships is taxed primarily through the personal income tax levied on their owners. Income earned by a corporation may be taxed twice—once when it is earned, via the corporate income tax, and again when it is received as dividends by holders of the firm's securities, via the personal income tax.[2]

This double taxation of corporate income may at first seem inefficient, if not unfair. It also raises questions about the efficiency of the corporate form of organization. Suffice it to say that limited liability and the ability to subdivide ownership and to transfer shares of that ownership appear to be of sufficient value to more than offset the tax law disadvantages. Moreover, without the corporate income tax, personal tax rates would have to be increased if the level of government expenditures were to remain constant without increasing the national debt.

☐ 10.2.1 Corporate Tax Rates

The corporate income tax is relatively simple in one respect. Usually there are only a few basic rates. For example, in 1988 a tax rate of 15% was applicable to the first $50,000 of taxable annual income, a rate of 25% to the next $25,000, a rate of 34% to the next $25,000, a rate of 39% to the next $235,000, and a rate of 34% to all additional income. Figure 10.1 illustrates what are known as the *marginal tax rate* and *average tax rate* schedules for corporations. A corporation's marginal tax rate is the tax rate

---

[1] The appendix briefly discusses gift and estate taxes.

[2] Certain corporations with 35 or fewer shareholders may elect to be treated as partnerships for tax purposes. Such firms, often called "Subchapter S corporations" (after the enabling provision of the Internal Revenue Code), constitute an exception to the general rule.

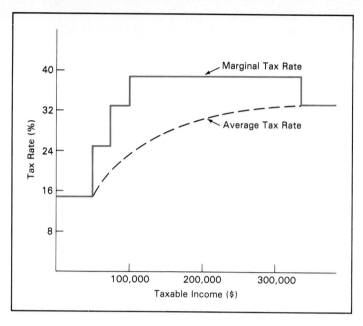

FIGURE 10–1
Marginal and average corporate tax rate, 1988.

it would pay on an additional dollar of income. For example, a corporation earning $85,000 would pay $17,150 in income taxes:

$$0.15 \times \$50,000 = \$\ 7,500$$
$$0.25 \times\ \ \ 25,000 = \ \ \ 6,250$$
$$0.34 \times\ \ \ 10,000 = \underline{\ \ \ 3,400}$$

$$\text{Total income tax} = \$17,150.$$

For this corporation, the marginal tax rate is 34%, since an additional dollar of income would be taxed at this rate. In other words, if this firm had income of $85,001 instead of $85,000, its tax bill would have been $17,150.34 instead of $17,150. Thus $.34 ($17,150.34 − $17,150.00) more in taxes would be paid as a result of earning $1 ($85,001 − $85,000) more in income.

The average tax rate is equal to the total amount of taxes paid divided by the total income subject to tax. The average tax rate for the previous example would thus be $17,150/$85,000 = 20.18%. That is, 20.18% of this firm's total income would be taken by the government in the form of corporate income taxes. As can be seen in Figure 10.1, the average rate is equal to the marginal rate for incomes below $50,000 and above $335,000. For incomes between these two figures, the average rate is below the marginal rate.

The average rate measures the overall impact of taxes, but the marginal rate is more relevant for most decisions. For example, if a corporation were considering an investment that would increase its income from $85,000 to

$90,000 each year, the increase in income after taxes would be $(1 - .34) \times \$5000 = \$3300$, not $(1 - .2018) \times \$5000 = \$3991$.

As shown in Figure 10.1, the larger a corporation's taxable income, the closer its average tax rate comes to the marginal tax rate, until the rates are equal for incomes above \$335,000. Most corporations with publicly traded shares have incomes of at least this size, meaning that most corporations pay taxes on their reported income at an average rate that is equal to the marginal rate of 34%.

☐ 10.2.2 Defining Income

Corporate income is partly a philosophic concept, partly an artifact of legal requirements, partly a result of accounting conventions, partly an indication of the hopes of the firm's management, and sometimes only incidentally related to underlying economic factors.

For tax purposes, corporate income is defined as revenues minus expenses. However, a problem arises in measuring these two elements. Simply put, this problem involves determining when to recognize revenues and expenses as having occurred. If a company sells an airplane this year but payment is to be made in installments over the next 5 years, when is the sales price to be considered taxable revenue? If a new plant is to be built and paid for this year but is to be used to produce goods for the next 20 years, when is the outlay to be considered as an expense? Accountants have a set of procedures, known as generally accepted accounting principles (GAAP), that can be utilized to handle these and many more subtle cases. However, there is extremely wide latitude within these principles.

The government has prescribed certain limits on the procedures that can be used to calculate income when determining a corporation's income tax liability. In some cases, the firm is required to use the same procedures when reporting its income to its stockholders; in other cases it can (and often does) use different procedures, sometimes resulting in a noticeably different income figure.[3]

☐ 10.2.3 Depreciation

The determination of the annual amount of depreciation of an asset that is used in a business provides a dramatic example of the effect that alternative accounting procedures can have on income. If a corporation buys a computer for \$1 million, it is entitled to charge off this cost as a deductible expense when computing taxable income. Each dollar deducted will reduce such income by a dollar and, hence, taxes paid by \$.34, assuming the marginal corporate income tax rate is 34%. Thus, the \$1 million outlay will produce tax savings of \$340,000. However, the present value of these tax savings depends on the years in which they are obtained. The sooner the cost can

---

[3] Differences of this sort are usually described in the firm's annual report.

be written off, the greater the benefit to the firm. The best of all possible worlds for the corporation and its owners would be to deduct the entire cost of the computer as an expense in the year in which it is incurred. Barring this, the firm would like to allocate the cost against income as soon as possible.

Congress, in making tax laws, and the Internal Revenue Service (IRS), in administering them, look at the situation in different ways. Whereas the taxpayer would like to maximize the present value of tax savings, the tax collector would like to minimize it. Thus, Congress and, in turn, the IRS, set limits on the manner in which outlays for fixed assets may be deducted as expenses. For example, the cost of land may not be deducted at all, since it is not normally considered to be a depreciating asset, although the cost of improvements to land (for example, sidewalks and buildings) can generally be deducted over a period of years. The cost of fixed assets that are regarded as having a limited useful life may also be deducted over a period of years.

For purposes of reporting corporate income to stockholders, a manager might want to allocate the cost of a fixed asset over the period during which it is expected to contribute to revenue. This is usually called the asset's *estimated useful life*. For tax purposes, as long as the firm is profitable, it is generally advantageous to underestimate the useful life in order to write off the cost as rapidly as possible. To control this urge, the IRS has come up with a standard set of procedures for allocating the costs of fixed assets to years subsequent to their purchase.

When reporting to shareholders, many firms depreciate the costs of fixed assets using the *straight-line method*. With this method, the same proportion of the cost of a particular asset is written off in each year of the asset's useful life. However, for assets placed in service after 1980 (modified for assets placed in service after 1986), a potentially more advantageous procedure may be used for calculating taxable income. The *accelerated cost-recovery system* (ACRS) prescribes specific methods of depreciation for various types of assets. For this purpose, assets are divided into eight broad classes based on their estimated useful life. Table 10.1 lists the classes and the allowable method of depreciation.

As the name implies, with ACRS the write-off is rapid (accelerated).[4] Although the total amount written off will be the same under both methods of depreciation, the present value will generally be more (and thus, the present value of taxes paid will be less) if the ACRS method were to be adopted instead of the straight-line method. That is, with straight-line depreciation, equal percentages of the cost of the property can be deducted each year, whereas with ACRS, larger percentages can be deducted in the earlier years (offset by smaller percentages in the later years). Accordingly, the firm will pay lower income taxes in the earlier years and higher income taxes in the later years if it uses ACRS relative to straight line. Since the total amount of taxes paid over the entire lifetime of the asset is the same with both methods and since postponing taxes is beneficial due to the time value of money, firms usually find it advantageous to use ACRS.

There are many reasons why corporate income reported to stockholders

---

[4] The last two classes of assets are an exception, since they allow only straight-line depreciation.

TABLE 10.1

Accelerated Cost Recovery System Classes.[a]

CLASS	EXAMPLES OF TYPES OF ASSETS	DEPRECIATION METHOD[b]
3-year	Certain tools	200% Double-declining-balance
5-year	Automobiles, light trucks, computers	200% Double-declining-balance
7-year	Heavy trucks, office furniture	200% Double-declining-balance
10-year	Water transport vehicles (e.g., barges)	200% Double-declining-balance
15-year	Land improvements (e.g., sidewalks)	150% Double-declining-balance
20-year	Railroad structures	150% Double-declining-balance
27.5-year	Residential real property	Straight line
31.5-year	Nonresidential real property	Straight line

[a] For property placed in service after 1986.
[b] Annual depreciation with the double-declining-balance method is calculated by first dividing the cost of the asset by its life; then this figure is multiplied by 2 if the method is 200% (or 1.5 if the method is 150%) to arrive at the first year's depreciation. The second year takes the cost less the previous amount of depreciation and divides it by the original life; the resulting figure is then multiplied by 2 (or 1.5) to arrive at the second year's depreciation. Future calculations are made similarly.

may differ from that used for tax purposes, but different depreciation assumptions are often a major factor. If the tax paid by a large profitable corporation diverges significantly from 34% of the apparent taxable income, as reported to stockholders, examination of the depreciation procedures may prove illuminating.

☐ 10.2.4 Inventory Valuation

Another vexing problem associated with the measurement of corporate income concerns the cost of inventory sold during the year. This problem arises when prices are changing and a firm holds inventory for long periods. To take a fairly simple case, imagine a retailer of sailboats. At the start of the year the retailer has 100 boats in stock, all purchased for $10,000 each. During the year the retailer takes delivery of 100 more but must pay $11,000 each. During the year 110 boats are sold, which means the retailer ends the year with 90 in stock. What was the cost of the 110 boats that were sold during the year?

The retailer may have sold all the 100 "old" boats first and then sold 10 of the "new" boats, or the retailer may have sold all the 100 new boats first and then sold 10 of the old boats. Alternatively, some other mixture of old and new boats might have been sold. However, specific identification of the boats sold is rarely taken into account in the calculation of revenue. An accountant may assume any of the above combinations, without regard for the actual facts of the situation.

The impact of different assumptions is shown in Table 10.2. In the first column, all the old boats are assumed to have been sold first—this is the *first-in, first-out (FIFO) method*. In the second column, all the new boats are assumed to have been sold first—this is the *last-in, first-out (LIFO) method*. In the third column, equal numbers of both old and new boats are assumed to have been sold—this is the *average-cost method*.

TABLE 10.2

The Impact of Different Inventory Valuation Methods.

REVENUE: 110 BOATS AT $15,000 = $1,650,000		
Cost by FIFO Method	Cost by LIFO Method	Cost by Average-Cost Method
100 at $10,000 = $1,000,000	100 at $11,000 = $1,100,000	55 at $10,000 = $ 550,000
10 at 11,000 = 110,000	10 at 10,000 = 100,000	55 at 11,000 = 605,000
$1,110,000	$1,200,000	$1,155,000
Income $ 540,000	$ 450,000	$ 495,000
Tax − 183,600	− 153,000	− 168,300
Income after tax $ 356,400	$ 297,000	$ 326,700
Cost of remaining inventory:		45 at $10,000 +
90 at $11,000 = $ 990,000	90 at $10,000 = $ 900,000	45 at $11,000 = $ 945,000

When prices have been rising, the LIFO method will permit a corporation to charge a larger amount to cost of goods sold now, with a smaller amount being charged in the future. This will lower current taxes and raise them in the future. The net result is a fall in the present value of taxes paid, which is beneficial to the owners of the firm. Since rising prices are so much a phenomenon of modern society, one would expect firms to adopt the LIFO method for tax purposes, just as one would expect firms to adopt accelerated depreciation for tax purposes. However, there is a difference between the two situations. The Internal Revenue Code requires a firm using the LIFO method for tax purposes to also use it for computing income reported to shareholders. Thus, the firm can either report a high income and pay high taxes with FIFO or report a low income and pay low taxes with LIFO. This can be seen in Table 10.2.

Before 1970, many firms used the FIFO method, suggesting that in times of moderate inflation, many managers were willing to sacrifice some real benefits to improve the appearance of their firm's financial statements. However, as the pace of inflation increased, usage of the LIFO method became much more common.

☐ 10.2.5 Amortization and Depletion

Allocation of the cost of a fixed asset over its estimated useful life is termed depreciation. A comparable procedure applied to a natural resource, such as an oil reserve, is known as *depletion*. When applied to certain intangible assets, the procedure is known as *amortization*. Amortization is often handled with procedures similar to those used for the depreciation of tangible assets. But depletion is another matter.

Depletion is utilized to allocate the cost of finding or purchasing a so-called wasting asset to the units of the asset removed and sold. For example, the cost of "bringing in" an oil well may be divided by the estimated number

of barrels of oil that can be pumped out of the well and the resulting amount written off as an expense for each barrel sold. If the initial estimate of the number of barrels of oil in the well proves to have been in error, adjustments can be made so that the entire cost of bringing in the well, but no more, is deducted. This is the *cost method* of depletion; it differs only in detail from the procedure used for the depreciation of fixed assets.

More controversial is the *percentage depletion method*. This method allows a stated percentage of the gross income from the property (before any costs) to be deducted as an expense. In 1987, the percentage ranged from 5% to 22%, depending on the particular natural resource. An upper limit is generally placed on the amount deducted in this manner. In 1987, the upper limit was 50% of the net taxable income (after nondepletion deductions) from the property. Note that with this method, the amount deducted as an expense need bear no relationship to the actual cost. Apparently, Congress approved this method in order to encourage the discovery, development, and use of certain domestic natural resources (although skeptics would argue that it was approved in order to provide political support for elected officials in those states that contain a significant amount of natural resources).

☐ 10.2.6 Deductibility of Interest Payments

One of the major attributes of both corporate and personal income taxes in the United States is the deductibility of interest payments. Interest is regarded as an expense and can therefore be deducted from revenue when calculating taxable income. For example, consider two firms, each with revenues of $25,000 and noninterest expenses of $15,000. Firm A is financed by both debt and equity and pays $5000 in interest to its creditors. As shown in Table 10.3, its net income after taxes is $4250, which is available to be paid as dividends, if desired. Thus, a total amount of $9250 ($5,000 + $4,250) can be paid to those who provided the firm's capital.

The other part of the table shows the results for firm B, which differs only with respect to financing. All its capital was provided by common stock financing. Thus, the entire $10,000 of income is subject to tax, leaving only $8500 for distribution to those who provided the firm's capital.

TABLE 10.3
The Effect of Deducting Interest Payments.

	FIRM A	FIRM B
Revenue	$25,000	$25,000
Cost of goods sold	15,000	15,000
Revenue minus expense	10,000	10,000
Interest paid	5,000	0
Taxable income	5,000	10,000
Tax (at 15%)	750	1,500
Available for dividends	$ 4,250	$ 8,500

The deductibility of interest payments provides an apparent tax advantage for the use of debt over equity funds. For this reason, it may seem surprising that firms do not choose to obtain more of their capital by issuing bonds. Indeed, the dramatic difference in tax treatment raises substantial questions about the definition of debt and interest, on the one hand, and stocks and dividend payments, on the other. The IRS pays considerable attention to any arrangement designed to provide the tax characteristics of debt with the financial characteristics of equity. To qualify as debt, there must be a definite lender, a definite borrower, a definite ascertainable obligation (a specific amount), and a time of maturity (date when the debt must be repaid). That is, debt should be represented by an instrument (a legal document such as a contract) that contains an unconditional legal obligation to pay a certain sum either on demand or on a specific date, with interest. Payments made under any other arrangement are not likely to be deductible for purposes of income taxation.

Failure to make interest payments may have serious consequences for the firm and its management. In many cases bankruptcy results, with mandatory and costly corporate reorganization. The greater the magnitude of interest payments in relation to dividend payments, the greater the probability of this type of unfortunate event. This risk of bankruptcy, along with the associated costs of bankruptcy, provides a potential brake on the use of debt financing, despite its obvious tax advantage.

☐ 10.2.7 Corporate Income from Dividends, Interest, and Capital Gains

Congress has provided that 80% of the dividends *received* by a corporation can be excluded from income when calculating the corporation's income tax liability. The effective tax rate on an additional dollar of dividends received by a corporation with an income in the 34% range is thus $(1 - .80) \times .34 = .068$, or 6.8%. The reason for this special treatment of dividends is to avoid the triple taxation of income. Consider how dividends would be taxed if this 80% exclusion did not exist. Corporation A is taxed on its income and then pays dividends to one of its stockholders, corporation B. Corporation B then pays taxes on its income, which includes the dividends received from A. Finally, the stockholders of B pay income taxes on the dividends received from B. Thus, a dollar of income earned by A would be taxed three times (a tax on A, then a tax on B, then a tax on the stockholders of B) if the dividend exclusion did not exist. With the dividend exclusion, a dollar of income earned by A is taxed, for all practical purposes, only twice.

No deduction is allowed for interest received by a corporation; it is simply added to income and taxed at the regular rates. This means that the effective tax rate on interest received from bonds is 34%, an amount substantially greater than the 6.8% effective tax rate on common and preferred stocks. This differential tax treatment has an effect on the relative prices that corporate investors are willing to pay for these securities, since their concern is with relative after-tax yields. That is, since preferred stocks are

generally viewed as being riskier than bonds, the after-tax yield on preferred stocks needs to be higher in order for investors to be interested in purchasing them. Given the favorable tax treatment on preferred stocks for corporate investors, it is possible for preferred stocks to have a lower before-tax yield than bonds while still enabling the corporate investor who buys the more risky preferred stock to be rewarded by earning, relative to bonds, a higher after-tax yield. Since noncorporate investors face the same marginal tax rate for both dividend income from preferred stocks and interest income from bonds, preferred stocks will provide such investors with a relatively lower after-tax return. It follows that preferred stocks are relatively unattractive investments for noncorporate investors.

Table 10.4 provides an example that illustrates the before-tax and after-tax yields for both a corporate investor with a marginal tax rate of 34% and an individual investor with a marginal personal tax rate of 28%. It can be shown that the individual investor will be better off purchasing the bond, whereas the corporate investor will be better off purchasing the preferred stock. Careful scrutiny will reveal this to be true for any other marginal tax rate for the individual investor.

☐ 10.2.8   Tax-Exempt Organizations

Many organizations are wholly or partly exempt from federal income taxes. Nonprofit religious, charitable, or educational foundations generally qualify. A small tax (2% in 1987) is levied on the net investment income of such a foundation. In addition, the foundation should pay out either all income received by the end of the year following receipt or a minimum percentage of its assets (5% in 1987), whichever is higher, since failure to do so can result in a confiscatory tax on the difference.

TABLE 10.4

Comparison of Yields of Preferred Stocks and Corporate Bonds.

	INVESTMENT	
	Preferred Stock	Corporate Bond
A. Features		
Price	$10 per share	$1000 per bond
Annual dollar yield	$.70 per share	$80 per bond
Aggregate investment	100 shares	1 bond
Cost of aggregate investment	$1,000	$1000
Aggregate annual dollar yield	$70	$80
Before-tax percentage yield	7% = $70/$1000	8% = $80/$1000
B. Corporate Investor[a]		
After-tax dollar yield	$65.24 = $70[1 − (.20 × .34)]	$52.80 = $80(1 − .34)
After-tax percentage yield	6.524% = $65.24/$1000	5.28% = $52.80/$1000
C. Individual Investor[b]		
After-tax dollar yield	$50.40 = $70(1 − .28)	$57.60 = $80(1 − .28)
After-tax percentage yield	5.04% = $50.40/$1000	5.76% = $57.60/$1000

[a] Assuming a marginal corporate income tax rate of 34%.
[b] Assuming a marginal individual income tax rate of 28%.

Investment companies, often called mutual funds, may elect to be treated as regulated investment companies for tax purposes. This privilege is granted if certain conditions are met. For example, the funds of the investment company must be invested primarily in securities, without undue concentration in any one. Thus, its income takes the form of dividends and interest received on its investments, as well as capital gains from price appreciation realized when investments are sold at a price that is higher than their purchase price. A regulated investment company pays income tax only on income and capital gains not distributed to its shareholders. As a result of this tax treatment, such companies distribute substantially all income and gains and, in doing so, end up not having to pay any taxes.

Employee pension, profit-sharing, and stock-bonus plans may also qualify for tax-exempt status. Such a plan may entrust its assets, which are usually securities, to a *fiduciary* (for example, a bank). The fiduciary receives new contributions, makes required payments, and manages the investments owned by the plan. A fiduciary under a qualified plan (that is, a plan that meets all the requirements of applicable legislation) pays no taxes on either income or capital gains.

Another example of a tax-exempt entity is the personal trust. Here, funds are provided for the benefit of one or more individuals by another individual or individuals with a fiduciary serving as a trustee. Some trusts are created by wills, others by a contract among living persons. Whatever the origin, trusts generally pay taxes only on income that is not distributed to the designated beneficiaries.

Income and capital gains earned by investment companies, pension funds, and personal trusts do not go untaxed forever. Payments made to investment company shareholders, pension fund beneficiaries, and the beneficiaries of personal trusts are subject to applicable personal income tax rules. The exemptions apply only to taxes that might otherwise be levied at the previous stage.

10.3 PERSONAL INCOME TAXES

Although the corporate income tax is an important feature of the investment scene, its impact on most individuals is indirect. This is not so for the personal income tax. Few investors can avoid dealing with it in detail, at both an economic and an emotional level. Its provisions have major and direct impacts on investment behavior.

☐ 10.3.1 Personal Tax Rates

Taxes must be paid on an individual's income, defined as "all wealth which flows to the taxpayer other than as a mere return of capital. It includes gains and profits from any source, including gains from the sale or other disposition

TABLE 10.5

Personal Income Tax Rates, 1988.

TAXABLE INCOME		AMOUNT OF TAXES
At Least	But Not More Than	
Single Taxpayers:		
$ 0	$ 17,850	$ 0 + 15% of income over $ 0
17,850	43,150	2,678 + 28 of income over 17,850
43,150	89,560	9,762 + 33 of income over 43,150
89,560	. . .	25,077 + 28 of income over 89,560
Married Taxpayers Filing Jointly:		
$ 0	$ 29,750	$ 0 + 15% of income over $ 0
29,750	71,900	4,463 + 28 of income over 29,750
71,900	149,250	16,265 + 33 of income over 71,900
149,250	. . .	41,790 + 28 of income over 149,250

of capital assets."[5] Certain items are excluded from the definition of income; others are deducted from it before computing the tax due. Moreover, capital gains and losses are subject to special procedures which are described in a later section. Deductions and exclusions of special importance for investment purposes are described in this section as well as in later sections.

Two figures are relevant for tax purposes. Adjusted gross income is obtained by subtracting certain allowed deductions (for example, business expenses and contributions to certain retirement funds) from gross income. This amount, less a number of personal expense deductions, equals taxable income, the figure on which tax liability is based. The amount of tax calculated on this basis must be paid unless the taxpayer is able to claim tax credits, which may be subtracted directly from the tax liability to obtain a final amount due the government.

While the Tax Reform Act of 1986 brought sweeping changes aimed at simplification, many people are still of the opinion that almost nothing about personal income taxes in the United States is simple.[6] Two different schedules of tax rates are currently in effect, the appropriate one depending on whether the particular taxpayer is single or married and filing a joint return with his or her spouse. Table 10.5 shows the tax rates in effect in 1988 for both of these types of taxpayers. The rates are plotted in Figures 10.2(a) and 10.2(b).

The top line in each figure shows the marginal tax rate, which was defined earlier when corporate income taxes were being discussed. A similar definition applies here. That is, it is the tax rate an individual would pay on an additional dollar of taxable income. While this rate is constant over certain ranges of income, it increases as the taxpayer moves to higher taxable income brackets except for the last bracket, when it decreases from 33% to 28%.

The lower line in both Figure 10.2(a) and (b) shows the average tax

---

[5] *1988 Federal Tax Course* (Englewood Cliffs, N.J.: Prentice Hall, 1987), 89.

[6] The act itself is over 900 pages long.

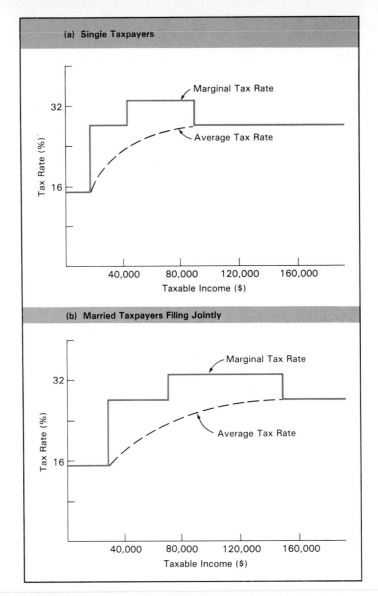

FIGURE 10–2
Marginal and average personal tax rates, 1988.

rate, which was also defined earlier when corporate income taxes were being discussed. Again, a similar definition applied here. That is, the average tax rate is the ratio of total tax paid to total taxable income and is generally smaller than the marginal tax rate.[7]

Earlier, it was mentioned that for corporations, the marginal tax rate

---

[7] The exceptions are for taxpayers in the lowest and highest income brackets, where the average and marginal tax rates are equal.

is generally more relevant than the average tax rate in making certain kinds of decisions. This observation is also true for individuals and married couples. For example, consider a married couple with taxable income of $60,000 who are evaluating an investment opportunity that is expected to increase their taxable income by $3000. Using the figures in Table 10.5, the impact this opportunity will have on their taxes is as follows:

	BEFORE INCREASE	AFTER INCREASE	DIFFERENCE
Taxable income	$60,000	$63,000	$3000
Tax	12,933[a]	13,773[b]	840
Spendable income	$47,067	$49,227	$2160

Marginal tax rate = ($13,773 − $12,933)/$3000 = $840/$3000 = 28.00%

[a] $12,933 = $4,463 + [.28 × ($60,000 − $29,750)].
[b] $13,773 = $12,933 + (.28 × $3000).

As shown in this table, the increase of $3000 in taxable income will result in an increase of $840 in taxes, leaving a net increase in spendable income of $2160. The calculations for this particular example are simple because the change in taxable income left the taxpayer in the same bracket. Thus, 28% of the additional income will be taxed away, leaving 72% to be spent. The fact that the average tax rate is 21.56% ($12,933/$60,000) before the increase and 21.86% ($13,773/$63,000) after the increase is irrelevant to this couple in deciding whether or not to make the investment.

When a decision moves income into a higher bracket, the computations are more complex. For example, assume the opportunity in question would increase income by $20,000. Again using the figures in Table 10.5, the impact on taxes would be:

	BEFORE INCREASE	AFTER INCREASE	DIFFERENCE
Taxable income	$60,000	$80,000	$20,000
Tax	12,933[a]	18,938[b]	6,005
Spendable income	$47,067	$61,062	$13,995

Marginal tax rate = ($18,938 − $12,933)/$20,000 = $6,005/$20,000 = 30.03%

[a] $12,933 = $4,463 + [.28 × ($60,000 − $29,750)].
[b] $18,938 = $16,265 + [.33 × ($80,000 − $71,900)].

As shown in this table, an increase of $20,000 in taxable income will result in an increase of $6005 in taxes, leaving a net increase in spendable income of $13,995. Thus, 30.03% of the additional income will be taxed away, an amount greater than the 28% figure that was applicable to the previous example. As before, the average tax rate of 21.56% ($12,933/$60,000) before the increase and 23.67% ($18,938/$80,000) after the increase is irrelevant to the couple in making their decision.

□ 10.3.2   Tax-Exempt Bonds

A major consideration for investors with large taxable incomes is the possibility of obtaining tax-exempt income. The simplest way to accomplish this is to purchase *tax-exempt bonds*. These securities exist because the notion of federalism has been interpreted to imply that the federal government should tax neither states and municipalities nor the income produced from their bonds.[8] While the legal basis is complex, the facts are simple. Interest income from most bonds issued by states, municipalities, and their agencies need not be included in taxable income in determining the amount of federal taxes that are owed. The benefit for a high-bracket taxpayer is notable.

Consider again the couple in the previous example. Assume that for the same cost, they can obtain an increase in taxable income of either $20,000 per year by investing in corporate bonds or $15,000 per year by purchasing tax-exempt bonds. As shown earlier, their effective tax rate on an increase of $20,000 in taxable income would be 30.03%, leaving 69.97%, or $13,995, to be spent. But $15,000 in tax-exempt income could all be spent—clearly a preferable investment opportunity.

This relationship is no secret. Not surprisingly, tax-exempt bonds offer lower pretax rates of interest than others. Thus, they are not attractive for investors with low marginal tax rates. For example, if the couple had a marginal tax rate of 15% instead of 30.03%, they would prefer the corporate bonds. This is because their after-tax return would be $17,000 [$20,000 × (1 − .15)], an amount greater than the $15,000 provided by the tax-exempt bonds.

If couples with a marginal tax rate of 30.03% find the tax-exempt bonds more attractive and couples with a marginal tax rate of 15% find the corporate bonds more attractive, then there should be a marginal tax rate in between these two rates that makes couples in that bracket indifferent between the two types of bonds. In this example, if the couple had a marginal tax rate of 25%, they would be indifferent between the corporate bonds and the tax-exempt bonds, since both would provide an after-tax return of $15,000. However, a 25% marginal tax rate does not currently exist. What this means is that couples with rates equal to or greater than the next highest tax rate (28%) would prefer the tax-exempt bonds; couples with rates equal to or less than the next lowest tax rate (15%) would prefer the corporate bonds.

The 25% marginal tax rate figure was determined by solving the following equation for t:

$$\$20,000 \times (1 - t) = \$15,000.$$

More generally, the marginal tax rate can be arrived at by solving the following equation for t:

$$\text{Taxable bond yield} \times (1 - t) = \text{tax-exempt bond yield}$$

---

[8] Chapter 12 describes various types of bonds that are available for investment and gives a more detailed discussion of how they are taxed.

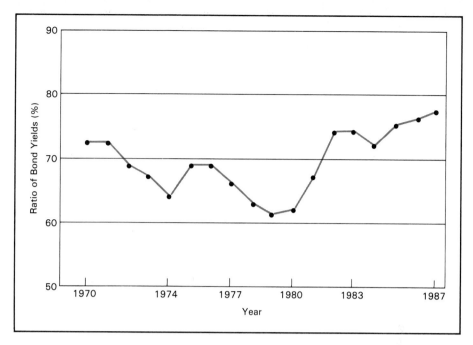

FIGURE 10–3
Ratio of prime long-term municipal bond yield to new Aa long-term public utility bond yield, 1970–1987.

SOURCE: Adapted from *Analytical Record of Yields and Yield Spreads*, Salomon Brothers, Inc. (New York: June 1988), Part III, Table 4.

or

$$1 - t = \text{tax-exempt bond yield/taxable bond yield}$$

or

$$t = 1 - \text{ratio of tax-exempt to taxable bond yields.}$$

Figure 10.3 shows the ratio, over time, of the yield-to-maturity for a group of tax-exempt bonds issued by municipalities to that of a group of taxable bonds issued by public utilities.[9] On this basis, tax-exempt bonds appear to be competitive with taxable bonds for investors subject to marginal tax rates between 20% (when the ratio of bond yields is 80%) and 40% (when the ratio of bond yields is 60%). For those fortunate enough to be considering investments that provide income in the higher ranges, tax-exempt bonds are well worth investigation. Less fortunate investors are likely to find them unattractive.

□ **10.3.3 Alternative Minimum Tax**

Disturbed by reports that some wealthy individuals were using tax shelters to pay only a small percentage of their income in taxes, Congress has added

---

[9] These yields are compared in Chapter 12 (see, in particular, Figure 12.7).

an *alternative minimum tax* (of great complexity) to the Internal Revenue Code.

Taxpayers with substantial *tax preference items* must compute an *alternative minimum taxable income*, which, in effect, involves adding back some of the deductions for such items to the (regular) taxable income.[10] From this, an exemption amounting to $40,000 for married taxpayers filing joint returns and $30,000 for single taxpayers is subtracted.[11] The alternative minimum tax is 21% of the result. If this is smaller than the "standard" tax liability, no additional taxes need be paid. Otherwise, the alternative minimum tax must be paid (instead of the standard tax).

☐ 10.3.4 Deductible Expenses

Certain interest payments may be deducted from an individual's income to determine taxable income (although, in general, the total amount deducted in any year for interest on funds borrowed to finance investments may not exceed net investment income). This deduction significantly lowers the effective cost of financing an investment by borrowing. Since property taxes are also deductible, the after-tax cost of home ownership is likely to be considerably lower than the before-tax cost, the magnitude of the difference depending on the relevant marginal tax rates for the taxpayer involved. Since the "income" associated with home ownership is taken in kind (by living in the home), such an investment is likely to prove attractive to many taxpayers. This is the intent of Congress, and the high degree of ownership of homes (including condominiums) in the United States is at least partly due to such incentives to own rather than rent.

Many expenses associated with investing may be deducted from income. In order to be deductible, they must be ordinary and necessary and in line with reasonable expectations of a profitable return. Thus, the fees of investment advisers and subscriptions to financial publications may be deducted. However, investments that habitually produce financial losses but nonfinancial pleasure may be considered hobbies. Accordingly, the Internal Revenue Service may deny some or all of the associated deductions. This possibility should concern the racehorse owner, for example, but not the serious investor.

☐ 10.3.5 Capital Gains and Losses

The provisions of the personal income tax laws that deal with the treatment of capital gains and losses have had a great impact on investor behavior. Only the basic elements of these provisions can be described here. Complete

---

[10] *Tax preference items* are such things as accelerated depreciation on fixed assets as well as previously excluded interest income and gains on stock option plans provided to executives.

[11] This exemption becomes smaller if the amount of the alternative minimum taxable income exceeds a certain level.

understanding of the details would require an effort sufficient to keep many lawyers, tax accountants, and investment advisers busy.

Realization

A change in the market value of a capital asset is not relevant for tax purposes until it is *realized* as a capital gain (or loss) by sale or exchange. If a security purchased for $50 appreciates to a value of $100 in a year, no tax is due on the *unrealized capital gain*. But if it is sold for $120 two years after purchase, the difference of $70 must be declared as capital gains realized at the time of sale and tax paid at the rate applicable to it.

This rule makes the end of the year an interesting time for stockbrokers. Depending on their situations, taxpayers may be either anxious or reluctant to realize capital gains or losses before a new tax year begins.

Consider, for example, a taxpayer who earlier in the year had sold 1000 shares of stock A for $50 per share, having purchased A three years ago for $20 per share. This investor has a capital gain of $30,000 (= 1,000 × ($50 − $20)) and will have to pay taxes on this gain if nothing is done. However, it is now December and the investor currently owns 1000 shares of stock B, which is selling for $65 per share. Having purchased it four years ago for $95 per share, the investor has an unrealized loss of $30,000 (1,000 × ($65 − $95)) on the investment in B. Nevertheless, the investor believes that stock B will rebound in the near future and, hence, wants to continue owning it. It might seem at first glance that the investor should sell B on December 31 and then buy it back January 1, thereby establishing a capital loss of $30,000 on B to offset the capital gain on A. This would remove the tax liability that the investor had on the gain on A, while essentially maintaining his or her position in B. However, the same stock cannot be bought and sold simultaneously in such tax exchanges. This is because the tax laws preclude a deduction associated with a loss on a *wash sale* where a security is sold and a "substantially identical" one is bought within 30 days.

Brokerage firms publish lists pairing similar stocks for those investors who wish to sell a particular stock for tax purposes; by selling a stock and simultaneously purchasing the matching stock, the investor will continually be able to maintain a portfolio with similar investment characteristics. In the previous example, a brokerage firm may have stocks B and C matched together. These two stocks have different issuers but may be in the same industry and, in the opinion of the brokerage firm, be poised for a similar rebound next year. Accordingly, the investor might sell B and purchase C.

End-of-year sales and purchases motivated by tax considerations are fairly common. At this time, securities that experienced substantial price changes during the year tend to have large numbers of trades as holders sell to realize gains or losses. If buyers recognize that the sellers are motivated by knowledge of the tax laws and not some previously unrecognized bad news affecting the company in question, such "selling pressure" should not seriously depress the company's stock price.

Capital gains and losses are, of course, those realized on *capital assets*, but the regulations define capital assets rather narrowly. Capital assets include all kinds of property except that held in conjunction with the tax-

payer's trade or business (for example, inventories). Gains or losses on property that is an integral part of a taxpayer's business are considered regular income. Gains on the sale of one's personal residence are capital gains, but, owing to special provisions in the tax law, some gains on property held only to rent to others may be considered income. Pro rata appreciation of a fixed-income security issued at a significant discount (for example, a 90-day Treasury bill) may also be considered income, as it is more like interest than capital gains.

The capital gain or loss realized when an asset is sold or exchanged is the difference between the value received and the asset's *adjusted basis*. For an asset purchased outright, the (initial) basis is equal to the actual cost of the asset. For an asset received as a gift or inheritance, the recipient's basis may be the donor's adjusted basis or the value at the time of receipt, depending on the relationship between the two and the value at the time of the sale.

While an asset is held, improvements may be made and their costs added to the basis. On the other hand, any return of capital must be deducted from the basis, as must depreciation. The basis is adjusted to account for such changes. The accounting required can become rather complicated. For example, if an investor buys 100 shares at $40 each, then buys another 100 at $50, and later sells 100 shares at $60, what is the realized capital gain? If the two round lots are kept separate and only shares costing the higher amount were sold, the gain is $10 per share. This is the preferred alternative, since it minimizes current tax outlays. If, however, adequate identification of the lots is not possible, regulations require FIFO accounting, which would place the basis of $40 per share and the gain at $20 per share.

The ability to control the realization of capital gains and losses has a number of obvious advantages. Most important, tax can be paid at the most opportune time. The clearest case involves the realization of capital gains around the time of retirement. Shortly before retirement is usually a time when the taxpayer's income is relatively high, which in turn means that the taxpayer's marginal tax rate is relatively high. After retirement the taxpayer's income and, in turn, marginal tax rate are usually substantially lower. Accordingly, it is generally advantageous for the taxpayer who is near retirement to wait until after retirement to realize any capital gains.

Treatment

With the passage of the Tax Reform Act of 1986, the treatment of capital gains and losses for tax purposes became much simpler. Now, all capital gains and losses must be brought together to obtain a net capital gain or net capital loss figure. Having made this calculation, the taxpayer will fall into one of the following two categories and be taxed as indicated:

1. Net capital gain. This is taxed as ordinary income.
2. Net capital loss. If the loss is less than or equal to $3000, the entire amount may be deducted from the taxpayer's ordinary income. Any excess over $3,000 can be deducted from ordinary income in future years.

Special provisions apply to capital gains realized from the sale of an individual's main residence. If a new residence is purchased within two years, no tax need be paid, provided the price of a new home exceeds the proceeds realized from the sale of the old one. In this case, the untaxed gain on the old home will be added to any gain from the new one when it is sold later. Thus, the upwardly-mobile individual or couple who would never think of buying a less-expensive home can look forward to a life that is free from the payment of capital gains taxes on increases in property values.

An additional provision softens the blow if cheaper housing is desired later in life. A person 55 or older can elect to make a once-in-a-lifetime exclusion of the first $125,000 of realized gain on the sale of a residence if he or she has lived there for three of the preceding five years.

☐ 10.3.6   State Income Taxes

Most states levy personal income taxes, following a format similar to that of the federal government. Although lower, state taxes are also likely to be progressive. The impact of these taxes is not quite as large as might first appear, since income taxes paid to state governments may be deducted from income before computing federal income tax. For example, consider an investor whose marginal rates for state and federal income taxes are 10% and 28%, respectively. Assume in this example that federal taxes are not deductible in computing state taxes. An additional $100 of income will result in $10 of state tax. This leaves $90 subject to federal income tax, thereby increasing the investor's federal income taxes by $25.20. Overall, $35.20 will be taxed away, giving an effective combined marginal rate of 35.2%. More generally, the combined marginal tax rate equals $s + [(1 - s)f]$, where s and f denote the marginal state and federal tax rates, respectively.

The situation becomes a bit more complicated if the state allows the taxpayer to deduct the amount of federal taxes paid in determining the amount of taxable income. In this situation there is *cross-deductibility*, since state taxes are deductible for federal tax purposes and federal taxes are deductible for state tax purposes. Now, using the previous $100 example, $100 \times [.1 - (.1 \times .28)]/[1 - (.1 \times .28)] = $7.41 will be paid in state income taxes and $100 \times [.28 - (.1 \times .28)]/[1 - (.1 \times .28)] = $25.93 will be paid in federal income taxes, for a combined total of $33.34. Thus, the effective combined marginal tax rate is 33.34%. More generally, the amount of state tax paid per additional dollar earned equals $[s - (s \times f)]/[1 - (s \times f)]$, and the corresponding amount of federal tax paid equals $[f - (s \times f)]/[1 - (s \times f)]$. The combined marginal tax rate is therefore $[s + f - (2 \times s \times f)]/[1 - (s \times f)]$.

Another interesting feature of state taxation is that the interest income from bonds issued by municipalities within a state may be exempt from that state's income tax. Some states extend this exemption to include dividends from certain corporations domiciled within the state. Furthermore, cities that levy personal income taxes typically exempt from taxation the interest income on any municipal bonds they have issued. In this situation, the

resident of the city that purchases such a bond escapes taxation on three levels—federal, state, and local.

10.4 TAX SHELTERS

Many advertisements implore high tax-bracket investors to put their money in cattle, oil drilling, real estate, and other investments with purportedly attractive tax characteristics. Such "tax shelters" are devised to take advantage of tax provisions allowing large deductions to create a "tax loss" in the present, followed later by a profit, generally in the form of a capital gain. Since their attractiveness is greater the higher the taxpayer's marginal tax rate, presumably only those in the highest brackets should find such investments interesting. Such enterprises are generally formed as limited partnerships. A promoter, or general partner, puts together the operation, with individual investors as limited partners. The hoped-for results are tidy profits for the promoter and the investors, at the expense of the tax collector.

A little thought should call into question the likely results for such an investment. First of all, many of the key provisions of the tax law have been changed recently, and it is not unrealistic to expect more changes in the future. Second, even if loopholes remain unplugged, economic forces may diminish any opportunities for abnormally high profits. If large gains can be made, why should the promoter share them to any major extent with the investors? But one can go even further. If large profits remain for promoters, why won't more promoters enter the business? The answer is that they will, potentially until the risk and return available from promoting tax shelters is competitive with that in other occupations. Anomalies in the tax laws are more likely to bring abnormally large amounts of investment into cattle-feeding programs, oil drilling, and so on, than to provide well-lighted roads to untold riches for high-tax-bracket investors.

This is not to deny that advantages can be gained from the early discovery of some scheme for tax-sheltered investment. Often investors in such deals reduce their taxes, as advertised, but only by taking real and permanent losses. Occasionally, the arrangements appear more like con games in which the professional swindler profits at the expense of the amateur investor, leaving the Internal Revenue Service unscathed.

10.5 SUMMARY

In spite of the attempts of various elected governmental officials to provide "tax simplification," the federal government has established a set of tax laws that not only are incredibly complex but are also frequently changing. Further complicating the situation is the existence of state tax laws. This chapter has attempted to provide a brief overview of the major provisions of income tax laws, since they have a major impact on the pricing of securities in the marketplace and a direct bearing on what securities different investors should purchase.

APPENDIX A
FEDERAL ESTATE AND GIFT TAXES

A.1 ESTATE TAXES

A person may escape taxes by dying, but his or her heirs may not. State governments usually impose "death taxes," and the federal government requires payment of an estate tax. Double taxation is offset to an extent, however, as some of the state tax may be credited against the federal estate tax liability.

The federal estate tax (formally, the Unified Estate and Gift Tax) is progressive, as reflected in Table 10.6. This table reflects the rates in effect in 1988. The actual tax that must be paid on an estate will equal an amount calculated using this table, less a tax credit (amounting to $192,800 in 1988, this credit can alternatively be applied to gift taxes).

Not all of an estate is subject to taxation. An unlimited marital deduction makes it possible for property that is transferred to a surviving spouse to be deducted from the total value of the estate in determining the size of the taxable estate. Property transferred to certain charitable nonprofit organizations may also be deducted. Furthermore, any debts, funeral expenses, and costs of administering the estate are deductible.

For example, consider a decedent that has an estate of $3,000,000 and has left $1,500,000 to a spouse and $200,000 to various charities and has funeral and estate-related expenses of $50,000; the remainder is left to other individuals. In this case, the taxable estate would be $1,250,000. Using Table 10.6, estate taxes of $448,300 would be levied by the IRS. These would be

TABLE 10.6

Federal Estate and Gift Tax Schedule, 1988.

TAXABLE ESTATE		AMOUNT OF TAXES			
At Least	But Not More Than				
$ 0	$ 10,000	$ 0 + 18%	of estate over	$ 0
10,000	20,000	1,800 + 20	of estate over	10,000
20,000	40,000	3,800 + 22	of estate over	20,000
40,000	60,000	8,200 + 24	of estate over	40,000
60,000	80,000	13,000 + 26	of estate over	60,000
80,000	100,000	18,200 + 28	of estate over	80,000
100,000	150,000	23,800 + 30	of estate over	100,000
150,000	250,000	38,800 + 32	of estate over	150,000
250,000	500,000	70,800 + 34	of estate over	250,000
500,000	750,000	155,800 + 37	of estate over	500,000
750,000	1,000,000	248,300 + 39	of estate over	750,000
1,000,000	1,250,000	345,800 + 41	of estate over	1,000,000
1,250,000	1,500,000	448,300 + 43	of estate over	1,250,000
1,500,000	2,000,000	555,800 + 45	of estate over	1,500,000
2,000,000	2,500,000	780,800 + 49	of estate over	2,000,000
2,500,000	. . .	1,025,800 + 50	of estate over	2,500,000

reduced by the $192,800 tax credit, resulting in a tax bill of $448,300 − $192,800 = $255,500.

A.2 GIFT TAXES

Partly to foil attempts to evade or reduce estate and income taxes, the federal government levies taxes on large gifts. Any transfer of property without adequate compensation by the recipient may make the donor subject to the gift tax.

A number of provisions make the gift tax of little or no consequence for many people. Gifts up to $10,000 may be made tax-free by a donor ($20,000 for a couple) to an individual every year, with no restrictions on the number of individuals to whom such gifts are made.[12] Thus, a person can give away hundreds of thousands of dollars without incurring any gift tax liability, as long as each recipient receives no more than $10,000 per year. Moreover, gifts to nonprofit organizations are exempt. Since financial assets may be given as gifts (real assets, such as artwork or real estate, may also be given), it is possible for a wealthy person to give appreciated securities to his or her alma mater, thereby escaping both capital gains and gift taxes; the donor also benefits because both the original cost and part of the appreciation can be treated as a charitable contribution in determining personal income taxes (thus, it is not surprising that gifts rise during the bull market).

As suggested earlier, the federal gift tax is integrated with the estate tax; together they form a aggregate tax on life and death transfers. Consider an individual who gives $1,010,000 to a daughter one year and $1,010,000 to a son the next year. The tax the first year would be based on $1,000,000 ($1,010,000 less the $10,000 deduction), and would result in the donor facing a gift tax of $345,800 (from Table 10.6). The donor could use the $192,800 tax credit on gifts and estates to reduce the gift tax to $153,000. The tax the second year would be based on $2,000,000, resulting from the $1,000,000 taxable gift the year before and the $1,000,000 taxable gift during the current year. From Table 10.6, the gift tax would amount to $780,800, reduced by the tax credit of $192,800 and the tax paid the previous year of $153,000 so that the final amount of tax due in the second year would be $780,800 − (192,800 + $153,000) = $435,000. Since the entire tax credit of $192,800 has been used up to offset gift taxes, it cannot be used later when the donor dies and estate taxes are being calculated.

Upon death, taxable gifts (such as the $2,000,000 given in the example) are added to the donor's estate and the tax liability on the total amount computed. Gift taxes paid (such as the corresponding $780,800) are subtracted from this liability to determine the tax actually due. It should be kept in mind that, as with other types of federal taxes, there are exceptions and special provisions that can complicate these calculations.

---

[12] A donor may give unlimited gifts to a spouse without incurring any gift tax.

QUESTIONS AND PROBLEMS

1. Why is the marginal tax rate more relevant to investment decision-making than the average tax rate?

2. Given the following income tax schedule, draw a graph illustrating the marginal and average tax rates as a function of income level.

Income	Tax Rate
$0 – $10,000	10%
$10,001 – $20,000	13
$20,001 – $30,000	15
$30,001 – $50,000	20
$50,001 and above	25

3. Why would a corporation report one annual income figure to their shareholders and another to the tax authorities?

4. What is the ACRS? Why does it produce tax advantages to those corporations that can use it?

5. Given that interest payments are tax deductible for a corporation while dividend payments are not, why don't corporations finance all of their operations with debt?

6. Preferred stocks have several fixed-income characteristics, yet generally provide lower after-tax yields to individual investors than do straight-debt securities. However, corporations seem to find preferred stock investments particularly attractive. Why?

7. Heine Groh expects consumer prices to rise at a 7% rate next year, and has negotiated a 9.5% pay increase. Given a 35% marginal income tax bracket, will this pay increase cause Heine's real income (that is, purchasing power) to grow? Explain.

8. Is the following statement by Pinky Higgins true or false? Because tax-exempt municipal bonds provide investors with interest income that is exempt from federal (and possibly state and local) taxes, all investors should therefore prefer tax-exempt municipal bonds to other similar risk debt investments. Explain your answer.

9. A corporate bond is selling for $950. It matures in a year, at which time the holder will receive $1000. In addition, the bond will pay $50 in interest during the year. What would be the after-tax return on the bond to an investor in the 50% marginal income tax bracket? (Assume that capital gains do not receive preferential tax treatment.) What would be the after-tax return if the bond had been a tax-free municipal bond?

10. Consider a tax-exempt municipal bond yielding 6%. To an investor in the following marginal tax brackets, what is the equivalent before-tax yield on a taxable bond?
    a. 10%
    b. 28%
    c. 33%

11. What is a wash sale? Why does the IRS prohibit such transactions for tax calculation purposes?

12. Jean Dubuc lives in a state where the tax schedule lists an 8% marginal tax rate. The federal tax schedule lists a 25% marginal tax rate. Accounting for cross-deductibility:
    a. What is Jean's effective state marginal tax rate?
    b. What is Jean's effective federal marginal tax rate?
    c. What is Jean's effective combined marginal tax rate?

Chapter 11

INFLATION

The story is told of the modern-day Rip Van Winkle, who awoke in the year 2010 and immediately called his broker. (Fortunately, pay phones at the time permitted a call of up to three minutes without charge.) He first asked what had happened to the $10,000 he had instructed the broker to put in short-term Treasury bills, continually reinvesting the proceeds. The broker promptly informed him that due to high interest rates and the power of compounding, his initial $10,000 investment had grown to be worth over $1 million. Stunned, Mr. Van Winkle inquired about his stocks, which were also worth about $10,000 when he dozed off. The broker told him that he was in for an even more pleasant surprise: They were now worth $2.5 million. "In short, Mr. Van Winkle," said the broker, "you are a millionaire 3.5 times over."

At this point an operator cut in: "Your three minutes are over, please deposit $100 for an additional three minutes." While this clearly overstates the case, there is no doubt that inflation is a major concern for investors. By and large, people have come to fear significant inflation, particularly when it is unpredictable.

This chapter discusses the benefits and costs of inflation, along with who gains and who loses when it is present. The impact that inflation has on investment decisions and results is also discussed.

11.1 INFLATION IN THE UNITED STATES

☐ 11.1.1 Measuring Inflation

There is no completely satisfactory way to summarize the price changes that have occurred over a given time period for the large number of goods and services available in the United States. Nevertheless, the federal government has attempted to do so by measuring the cost of a specific mix of major items (a "basket of goods") at various points in time. The "overall" price level computed for this representative combination of items is termed a *cost-of-living index*. The percentage change in this index over a given time period can then be viewed as a measure of the inflation (or deflation) that took place from the beginning of the period to the end of the period.

Whether or not this measure of inflation is relevant for a given individual depends to a major extent on the similarity of his or her purchases to the mix of items used to construct the index. Even if an individual finds the mix to be appropriate at the beginning of a period, the rate of increase in the mix over the time period is likely to overstate the increase in the cost of living for the individual. There are two reasons for this. First, improvements in the quality of the items in the mix are seldom taken adequately into account. This means the end-of-period price for a good is not comparable to the beginning-of-period price, since the good is different. For example, a new Toyota may have a 5% higher sticker price than a similar model had the previous year, but the newer model may have better tires on it than the older model. Hence, it would be inaccurate to conclude that the price of this particular model rose by 5% over the year.

Second and perhaps more important, little or no adjustment is made in the mix as relative prices change. The rational customer can reduce the cost of attaining a given standard of living as prices change by substituting relatively less expensive goods for those that have become relatively more expensive. For example, if the price of beef rises 20% over a given year while the price of chicken rises only 10% over the same year, then the customer may start to eat more chicken and less beef. Failure to take into account this change in the mix will result in an overstatement in the rate of inflation. Despite these two drawbacks, cost-of-living indices provide at least rough estimates of changes in prices.

In Chapter 1, Table 1.1 provided some historical perspective on the rate of inflation in the United States. It showed the annual rate of increase in the *Consumer Price Index* (CPI) from 1926 through 1986.[1] As an aid to interpretation, these rates are plotted on a graph shown in Figure 11.1(a). As can be seen in the figure, the CPI did not grow at a constant rate over the period of 1926 to 1986. Following the substantial deflation from 1926 to 1933, prices increased in almost every year. Generally speaking, there were four subperiods with different rates of inflation: fairly rapid (but uneven) inflation from 1934 to 1952, mild inflation from 1953 to 1965, and again fairly rapid (but uneven) inflation from 1966 to 1981, followed again by mild inflation for 1982 to 1986.

Table 11.1 shows the average annual rate of growth of the CPI for each of these subperiods, measured by what is known as the *geometric mean* growth rate of the CPI. This growth rate, when compounded over the subperiod and applied to the beginning index value, results in the ending index value. For example, at the end of 1965, the CPI was 95.5 and at the end of 1981, it was at 281.5 (here the CPI was adjusted so that its value in 1967 was 100). Thus, the geometric mean growth rate was 7.0%, since 95.5, when compounded at this rate over 16 years, equals 281.5:

$$281.5 = 95.5 \times (1 + .070)^{16}.$$

---

[1] The Consumer Price Index is based on the retail prices for a basket of some 400 different goods and services. It is calculated monthly by the Bureau of Labor Statistics of the U.S. Department of Commerce.

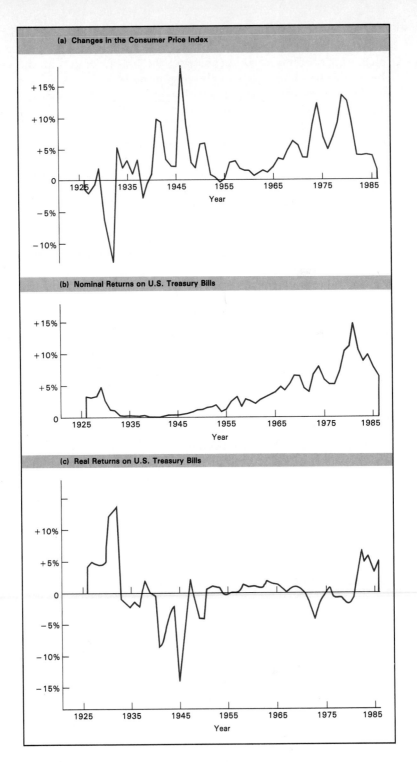

FIGURE 11–1
Nominal and real returns on short-term default-free investments, 12-month periods
ending December 1926–December 1986.

*SOURCE:*Ibbotson Associates, *1987 Yearbook* (Chicago: 1987).

TABLE 11.1

Growth Rates of the U.S. Consumer Price Index.

FROM	TO	RATE OF GROWTH (% PER YEAR)
1926	1933	−3.8%
1934	1952	3.8
1953	1965	1.4
1966	1981	7.0
1982	1986	3.3

More generally, the geometric mean (g) can be calculated by solving the following equation for g:

$$C_e = C_b(1 + g)^y \qquad (11.1)$$

which results in

$$g = \left(\frac{C_e}{C_b}\right)^{1/y} - 1 \qquad (11.2)$$

where y denotes the number of years and C_e and C_b denote the ending and beginning CPI values, respectively.

11.2 PRICE INDICES

As mentioned earlier, no price index can prove totally satisfactory as an indicator of the cost of living for all consumers. Most indices are likely to overstate the extent to which the cost of attaining a given level of satisfaction actually increases during any inflationary period, even for the people whose purchases the index was intended to reflect. Although this is fairly well understood and most governments compute a number of alternative indices to provide a wider choice for analysis, many people tend to focus on one index as an indicator of the price level.

In the United States the CPI often fills this role, despite some attempts by government officials to discourage such widespread use.[2] Recognizing its importance, the composition of the market basket of goods used to make up the CPI has been changed from time to time in order to provide a more representative basket of goods. Furthermore, the process by which the relevant data are gathered and verified has periodically been improved.

11.3 NOMINAL AND REAL RETURNS

☐ 11.3.1 Nominal Returns

Modern economies gain much of their efficiency through the use of money— a generally agreed-upon medium of exchange. Instead of trading corn for a

---

[2] A number of authorities prefer "deflators" derived from gross national product figures, but such indices have not received the publicity accorded the CPI.

stereo to be delivered in one year, as in a barter economy, the citizen of a modern economy can trade his or her corn for money and then trade this "current" money for "future" money by investing it. Later, the "future" money can be used to buy a stereo. The rate at which the citizen can trade current money for future money depends on the investment he or she makes and is known as the *nominal return* (also known as the nominal rate).

□ 11.3.2 Real Returns

In times of changing prices, the nominal return on an investment may be a poor indicator of the *real return* (also known as the real rate) obtained by the investor.[3] This is because part of the additional dollars received from the investment may be needed to recoup the citizen's lost purchasing power due to inflation that has occurred over the investment period. As a result, adjustments to the nominal return are needed to remove the effect of inflation in order to determine the real return. Frequently, the CPI is used for this purpose.

For example, assume that at the start of a given year the CPI is at a level of 121 and that at the end of the year it is at a level of 124. This means that it costs $124 at the end of the year to buy the same amount of the CPI market basket of goods that at the start of the year could have been purchased for $121. Assuming the nominal return is 8% for this year, the citizen who started the year with $121 and invested it would have $121 × 1.08 = $130.68 at year-end. At this point, the citizen could purchase ($130.68/$124) − 1 = .0539 = 5.39% more of the CPI market basket of goods than at the beginning of the year. Thus, the real return for this investment was 5.39%, after allowing for inflation.

These calculations can be summarized in the following formula:

$$\left(C_0 \times \frac{1 + NR}{C_1} \right) - 1 = RR \qquad (11.3)$$

where:

C_0 = CPI at the beginning of the year,
C_1 = CPI at the end of the year,
NR = the nominal return,
RR = the real return.

Alternatively, the citizen could note that an increase in the CPI from 121 to 124 can be translated into an inflation rate of (124/121) − 1 = .0248, or 2.48%. Denoting this inflation rate as I, the real return can be calculated using the following formula:

$$\left(\frac{1 + NR}{1 + I} \right) - 1 = RR. \qquad (11.4)$$

---

[3] Here, real return refers to the increase in purchasing power that the citizen has received as a result of making a particular investment.

Note that for the example, RR = (1.08/1.0248) − 1 = .0539, or 5.39%.

For quick calculation, the real return can be estimated by simply subtracting the inflation rate from the nominal return:

$$\text{NR} - I \cong \text{RR} \qquad (11.5)$$

where ≅ means "is approximately equal to." In this example, the quick method results in an estimate of the real return of .08 − .0248 = .0552, or 5.52%. Thus, the error resulting from use of this method is .0552 − .0539 = .0013, or .13%.[4]

☐ **11.3.3 The Effect of Investor Expectations**

The simplest view of investors' attitudes toward inflation is that they are concerned with real returns, not nominal returns, and that a single price index is adequate to characterize the difference. Looking to the future, investors do not know what the rate of inflation will be, nor do they know what the nominal return on an investment will be. However, in both cases they have expectations about what these figures will be, which are denoted as EI (expected rate of inflation) and ENR (expected nominal return), respectively. Thus, the expected real return on an investment can be approximated by:

$$\text{ERR} = \text{ENR} - \text{EI}. \qquad (11.6)$$

If a security is to provide a given expected real return, the expected nominal return must be larger by the expected rate of inflation for the relevant holding period. This can be seen by rearranging equation (11.6):

$$\text{ENR} = \text{ERR} + \text{EI}. \qquad (11.7)$$

For example, if the expected rate of inflation is 4% and a given security is to provide investors with an expected real return of 6%, then the security must be priced in the marketplace so that its expected nominal return is 10%. In summary, if investors are concerned with real returns, all securities will be priced by the actions of the marketplace so that expected nominal returns incorporate the expected rate of inflation.

11.4 INTEREST RATES AND INFLATION

At the start of a given investment holding period, nominal interest rates for securities having no risk of default should cover both a requisite expected real return and the expected rate of inflation for the period in question. At the end of the period, the real return actually received will be the difference between the nominal return and the rate of inflation actually experienced.

---

[4] This error will be larger for higher rates of inflation. Thus, in those countries with "hyperinflation," the quick method will have a substantial amount of error associated with it. For example, if the nominal return is 110% and the inflation rate is 100%, then the true real return is 5%, but the quick method will indicate it is twice as large, 10%.

Only when actual inflation equals expected inflation will the actual real return equal the expected real return on such securities.

As mentioned earlier, Figure 11.1(a) indicates the annual rate of inflation, as measured by changes in the CPI, over the 61-year time period of 1926–1986. Part (b) shows how short-term nominal interest rates varied over this time period; Treasury bill rates, taken from Table 1.1, are used for this purpose. Part (c), gotten by subtracting part (a) from part (b), represents real returns.

One cannot help being struck by the fact that those who invested in short-term securities over this period frequently ended up with less purchasing power than they started with, since the real return was negative in 25 of the 61 years. Perhaps even more surprising, the average real return over the period was close to zero.

Although expected real returns may vary from year to year, this variation may be relatively small. If so, investors may have been willing to invest in short-term highly liquid securities even though they expected to earn nothing at all in real terms. If they are currently willing to do so, such securities will be priced to give an expected real return of approximately zero.[5]

If this assumption is made, the "market's" predicted rate of inflation over the near future can be estimated by simply looking at the nominal interest rate (also known as the yield) on short-term government securities, namely, Treasury bills. In a sense, this Treasury bill rate represents a consensus prediction of inflation—a prediction that an "average" investor in this market would make and one that is likely to be more accurate than the predictions of any single forecaster.

11.5 THE EFFECT OF INFLATION ON BORROWERS AND LENDERS

Although deviations of actual inflation from expected inflation may have relatively little effect on the real return on investments in general, they may have a significant effect on specific investments. In fact, one would expect a direct impact on the real returns associated with investments whose payments are fixed in terms of dollars to be received.

A simple example will illustrate the relationship. Assume that everyone currently expects the rate of inflation to be 5% over the next year and that a lender has agreed to make loans at a nominal rate of 5% (that is, the lender is content with having an expected real return of zero). Thus, one can borrow $100 now and, one year later, pay back $100 × 1.05 = $105 for a one-year loan. That is, if actual inflation equals expected inflation, a one-year loan would require a payment equivalent to $100 in constant (current) dollars a year hence. In this case, the real rate of interest would turn out to be zero.

---

[5] However, there apparently are periods of time when such securities have an expected real return that is positive. For example, in the 1980–1986 period, Treasury bill returns actually exceeded the rate of change in the CPI by over 4%. This suggests that investors probably expected a positive real return over the latter part of the period.

Now, imagine that an individual takes advantage of the lender's offer, borrowing $100 for one year. How will the borrower and lender be affected if actual rate of inflation differs from the expected rate of inflation?

Assume that in the first year, prices rise by 9% instead of the expected 5%, meaning that unexpected inflation is 4% = 9% − 5%. In this situation, the short-term borrower gains at the expense of the lender because the borrower still must repay $105, but in terms of constant dollars, this is only $105/1.09 = $96.33, a figure that is less than the amount of the loan. As a result, the lender receives a real rate of interest of ($96.33 − $100)/$100 = −3.67%, instead of the anticipated rate of 0%.

What if first-year prices had risen by only 3%, meaning that unexpected inflation is −2% = 3% − 5%? In this situation, the short-term lender gains at the expense of the borrower. Although the borrower must repay $105, in terms of constant dollars this amounts to $105/1.03 = $101.94, a figure that is greater than the amount of the loan. As a result, the lender receives a real rate of interest of ($101.94 − $100)/$100 = 1.94% instead of the anticipated rate of 0%.

These results can be generalized: When the actual rate of inflation exceeds the expected rate of inflation, those with commitments to make payments that are fixed in nominal terms (debtors) gain in real terms at the expense of those to whom payments are to be made (creditors). Conversely, when actual inflation is less than expected inflation, creditors gain and debtors lose.[6] This uncertainty in the real return on fixed-income securities that is due to uncertain inflation is frequently referred to as *purchasing power risk*.

11.6 INDEXATION

The previous section suggests that in a world of uncertain inflation, even default-free bonds are subject to purchasing power risk. Contractual nominal interest rates can cover expected inflation, but the subsequent real return from any investment with fixed nominal payments will depend on the actual amount of inflation. As long as the two differ, the expected real return will be uncertain. However, there is a way to design a bond so that its expected real return is certain. This involves the use of *indexation*.

If a specified price index can adequately measure purchasing power, there is no reason why a contract cannot be written with specified real payments instead of specified nominal payments. Thus, if the CPI currently stands at C_0 and will be C_1 one year later, C_2 two years later, and so on, in return for a ten-year loan of $100 a borrower might promise to pay $10 × C_1 one year later, $10 × C_2 two years later, . . . , and $110 × C_{10} ten years

---

[6] More specifically, it can be shown that long-term borrowers are likely to gain somewhat more than short-term borrowers when actual inflation exceeds expected inflation and lose somewhat more when actual inflation falls below expectations. Similarly, long-term lenders are likely to lose somewhat more than short-term lenders when actual inflation exceeds expectations and gain somewhat more when actual inflation falls below expectations.

later. To convert these payments to constant real dollars, each one must be divided by the corresponding price level:

TIME	AMOUNT IN NOMINAL DOLLARS	PRICE LEVEL (CPI)	AMOUNT IN REAL DOLLARS
1	$10 \times C_1$	C_1	10
2	$10 \times C_2$	C_2	10
.	.	.	.
.	.	.	.
.	.	.	.
10	$110 \times C_{10}$	C_{10}	110

The real value of each payment is the amount shown in the final column, regardless of what happens to prices (that is, regardless of the actual values of C_1, C_2, and so on). Thus, the loan is said to be fully indexed, since all amounts are tied to a stated price index on a one-for-one basis. This means that when the price index goes up by 10%, for example, all the subsequent payments go up by 10%.

In some countries, a great many contracts are tied to standard price indices (two notable examples are Israel and Brazil). Government bonds, returns on savings accounts, wage contracts, pension plans, insurance contracts—all have been indexed at various times and places. In the United States, social security payments are indexed, as are the wages and pension plans of many employees. Some of these are fully indexed, while others are only partially indexed, meaning that, for example, payments might be increased by 7% when the price index increases by 10%.

The key advantage of indexation is its role in reducing or eliminating purchasing power risk. Typically, higher expected inflation is accompanied by increased uncertainty about the actual rate of inflation. This increased uncertainty means that the potential gains and losses to both nonindexed borrowers and nonindexed lenders are larger. Since both borrowers and lenders dislike the prospect of losses more than they like the prospect of gains, there will be increased pressure for indexation by both borrowers and lenders when a country moves into periods of high inflationary expectations.

Thus, when uncertainty about inflation is substantial, one would expect indexation to become widespread. However, laws regulating interest rates frequently prevent the issuance of fully indexed debt, since these laws usually place a ceiling on the nominal rate but not the real rate. This leads to predictable inefficiencies when expected inflation increases, since rationing of credit that is subject to such ceilings would be required. Rationing would be necessary because a ceiling on the nominal rate means that the real rate declines as inflationary expectations increase, which in turn makes this type of credit attractive to borrowers.[7]

A notable example occurred in the 1970s in the United States. At that time, ceilings placed on nominal rates paid by savings and loan companies, coupled with increased inflationary expectations, caused a substantial out-

---

[7] Actually, rationing might not occur, since lenders may simply refuse to make those kinds of loans that are subject to ceilings when inflationary expectations are high.

flow of funds from such companies and a corresponding reduction in the amount of money made available by them for home mortgages. On the other side were those issuers of securities that were not subject to rate ceilings and who offered an appropriate nominal rate and, thus, had little difficulty in attracting funds. The term *disintermediation* was invented to describe this pattern of funds' flow.

Since inflation is generally harder to predict for longer time periods relative to shorter time periods, uncertainty about inflation often leads to a reduction in the average term-to-maturity of newly issued fixed-income securities. Here term-to-maturity refers to the length of time from the date of issuance of the security until the date that last payment is to be made. For example, the average term-to-maturity of fixed-coupon debt issued in periods of great inflationary uncertainty is usually shorter than in more stable times.

Alternatively, debt with long maturities can be written with *variable rates* (also known as floating rates) of interest. Such instruments provide long-term debt at short-term rates. Interest payments are allowed to vary, with each one determined by adding a fixed number of percentage points (say, 2%) to a specified base rate that changes periodically. Two base rates frequently used are the prime rate and the yield on 90-day Treasury bills. If short-term interest rates anticipate inflation reasonably well, such a variable rate security is a kind of substitute for a fully indexed bond.

11.7 REPLACEMENT COST ACCOUNTING

One definition of earnings (that is, profits) holds that if a firm paid out the entire amount of earnings each year, it would neither increase nor decrease in size, measured by the real value of its productive capacity. This notion is often summarized by the term *sustainable earnings*. A firm that pays out more than the total amount of such earnings can be expected to decline, whereas one that pays out less can be expected to grow.

Although there may be some objections to the principle of this definition of earnings, there are more problems associated with its implementation. And, these problems are seriously aggravated in an inflationary environment.

Consider a firm that purchases ten units of some semifinished good at the beginning of each year, hires labor to work on it, and then sells the finished product at the end of the year. For simplicity, assume that labor is paid from the proceeds of sales. In the absence of inflation, the firm's operations might be summarized as follows:

Receipt from sales (10 units at $200 each)		$2000
Less cost of goods sold:		
Purchase of semifinished goods (10 units at $100 each)	$1000	
Labor wages	800	
Total cost		1800
Net earnings		$ 200
Net cash received at year-end ($2000 − $800)		1200

Thus, the firm invests $1000 at the beginning of the year to purchase semifinished goods in order to obtain $1200 a year later, giving the firm a

rate of return of 20%. Viewed somewhat differently, after an initial investment of $1000, earnings of $200 can be paid out each year, assuming no inflation. This $200 is the magnitude of sustainable earnings.

Now, assume that after purchasing the semifinished goods, all prices and wages increase by 10%. The results would then be as follows.

Receipt from sales (10 units at $220 each)		$2200
Less cost of goods sold:		
Purchase of semifinished goods (10 units at $100 each)	$1000	
Labor wages	880	
Total cost		1880
Net earnings		$ 320
Net cash received at year-end ($2200 − $880)		1320

Thus, an investment of $1000 produces a net cash inflow of $1320 one year later, for a return of 32% and earnings of $320. However, this is not the amount of sustainable earnings. Assuming no further inflation, $1100 will be required to replace the inventory of 10 units at the beginning of the next year. This means that only $1320 − $1100 = $220 can be paid out if the firm is to avoid a decline in real productive capacity. Put somewhat differently, the total "earnings" of $320 resulted from an increase in the value of the firm's inventory of $100 plus "adjusted" earnings from normal operations of $220.

To make this distinction, a number of authorities recommend *replacement cost accounting*. In essence, this involves the use of estimated replacement costs (future costs) instead of historic costs (past costs) when calculating profits. In this case such a procedure would give:

Receipt from sales (10 units at $220 each)		$2200
Less cost of goods sold:		
Purchase of semifinished goods (10 units at $110 each)	$1100	
Labor wages	880	
Total cost		1980
Net adjusted earnings		$ 220
Net cash received at year-end ($2200 − $880)		1320

An equivalent procedure would be to subtract an *inventory valuation adjustment* from reported profit. This adjustment would represent the excess of replacement cost over the reported cost:

Receipt from sales (10 units at $220 each)		$2200
Less cost of goods sold:		
Purchase of semifinished goods (10 units at $100 each)	$1000	
Labor wages	880	
Total cost		1880
Net earnings		$ 320
Less inventory valuation adjustment:		
Replacement cost (10 units at $110 each)	$1100	
Reported cost (10 units at $100 each)	1000	
Amount of adjustment		100
Net adjusted earnings		$ 220

Even after the adjustment, profit is stated in current (that is, year-end) dollars. To compare this amount with that of a previous year, the value must be adjusted for price-level changes. In this case, the amount in current dollars is $220, whereas the amount in constant dollars is $220/1.10 = $200 (which is the amount that would have been earned in the absence of inflation).

The size of the appropriate inventory valuation adjustment depends on the length of time inventory is held, the extent of the rise in its replacement cost, and the method used to account for such costs when calculating reported earnings. As discussed in Chapter 10, the LIFO method comes closest to replacement costs, and the FIFO method lies at the other end of the spectrum.

A similar situation arises with capital assets. Using various depreciation formulas, their historic costs are charged to operations over their assumed productive lives. As discussed in Chapter 10, accelerated depreciation is generally used for tax purposes, but more gradual procedures may be used for reporting earnings to stockholders. However, assets "used up" in the production process are generally valued at historic, not replacement, costs. Other things being equal, this will cause an understatement of cost and an overstatement of sustainable earnings.

At the beginning of each year, a firm will own certain capital assets. During the year the replacement costs of these assets may change, resulting in associated gains or losses, although such changes may not be realized at that time. The portion of these assets used up in production (and thus depreciated) should be valued at replacement cost in order to estimate sustainable earnings from operations. If historic costs are used instead, the resulting amount should be adjusted to account for the difference between replacement and historic costs.

The U.S. Department of Commerce in its *Survey of Current Business*

TABLE 11.2

Earnings Before and After Inventory Valuation and Capital Consumption Adjustments; U.S. Nonfinancial Corporations, 1976–1986.

YEAR	EARNINGS BEFORE TAXES ($ BILLIONS) (1)	EARNINGS BEFORE TAXES AFTER ADJUSTMENTS ($ BILLIONS) (2)	PERCENTAGE DIFFERENCE (3)	PERCENTAGE CHANGE IN THE CONSUMER PRICE INDEX (4)
76	135.0	107.3	20.5%	4.8%
77	153.5	126.3	17.7	6.8
78	174.3	137.6	21.1	9.0
79	193.4	136.7	29.3	13.3
80	177.8	120.2	32.4	12.4
81	177.3	147.4	16.9	8.9
82	123.5	118.1	4.4	3.9
83	148.8	171.0	−14.9	3.8
84	186.3	221.2	−18.7	4.0
85	175.9	227.8	−29.5	3.8
86	174.6	225.7	−29.3	1.1

SOURCE: U.S. Department of Commerce, *Survey of Current Business*, various issues.

reports the estimated percentage of corporate earnings attributable to inventory valuation increases. The estimated difference between aggregate depreciation based on historic cost (*capital consumption*) and that based on replacement cost (*economic capital consumption*) is also reported. Columns 1 and 2 in Table 11.2 show how earnings are altered in inflationary times when the *inventory valuation adjustment* and *capital consumption adjustment* are taken into account. Not surprisingly, as a comparison of columns 3 and 4 shows, the adjustment to earnings is generally of greater magnitude when the rate of inflation is higher, with the adjustment being negative during recent years when inflation has been low.

Thus, it is not surprising that the Financial Accounting Standards Board's *Statement of Accounting Standards Number 33* requires firms with either total assets of more than \$1 billion or with inventories, property, plant, and equipment with a gross value of more than \$125 million to provide supplementary inflation-adjusted financial statements to their stockholders. This allows the stockholders to estimate more accurately the level of the firm's sustainable earnings.

11.8 TAXATION, INFLATION, AND THE RETURN ON CAPITAL

Certain general features of the U.S. tax system lead to movements of wealth from the private sector to the federal government that increase with the rate of inflation. Thus, one of the potential beneficiaries of inflation in the U.S. is the federal government.[8]

Consider a one-year security with an expected real pretax return of 7% that is held by someone in a 30% marginal tax bracket. In the absence of inflation, the investor would expect to receive a real return of $(1 - .3) \times 7\% = 4.9\%$. Now, assume that expected rate of inflation is 2%, so that the expected pretax nominal return on the security is $[(1.07 \times 1.02) - 1] = 9.14\%$. In this case, the investor's expected after-tax nominal return is $(1 - .3) \times 9.14\% = 6.40\%$, but in real terms this is $[(1.0640/1.02) - 1] = 4.31\%$. Similarly, if expected inflation is 4%, then the expected pretax nominal return will be 11.28%, the investor's expected after-tax nominal return will be 7.90%, and his or her expected after-tax real return will be 3.75%.

Since it is reasonable to assume that, over time, actual inflation rates will approximately equal expected inflation rates, it can be seen that the higher the actual inflation rate, the lower the actual real after-tax return. In this example, the after-tax real return decreased from 4.9% with no inflation to 4.31% with 2% inflation and to 3.75% with 4% inflation. Thus, taxation of interest income can be viewed as being equivalent to having an effective tax rate on real returns that increases with inflation; that is, the higher the inflation rate, the larger the portion of the real pretax return that is being allocated to the government. This phenomenon could be avoided by levying taxes on real returns instead of nominal returns.

---

[8] The federal government also benefits from unexpected inflation because it is the largest borrower of funds in the economy and, as shown earlier, borrowers in general benefit when inflation turns out to be higher than expected.

For the expected after-tax real return of a fixed-income security to be the same with a high expected rate of inflation as with a low expected rate of inflation, its current price must be sufficiently lower with the high inflation rate. This will result in the expected pretax nominal return being sufficiently higher in order to compensate for both the higher inflation rate and the larger effective tax rate. In the previous example, the expected pretax nominal return would have to rise to 10.0% if the expected rate of inflation were 2% and to 13.0% if it were 4%. If this asset were a bond that pays the investor $1000 one year later, its current price would have to be $934.58 with no expected inflation, $909.09 with 2% expected inflation, and $884.96 with 4% expected inflation:

Expected rate of inflation	0.0%	2.0%	4.0%
Expected pretax nominal rate of return	7.0%	10.0%	13.0%
Expected after-tax nominal return = (1 − .3) × pretax nominal return	4.9%	7.0%	9.1%
Expected after-tax real return = [(1 + after-tax nominal return) ÷ (1 + rate of inflation)] − 1	4.9%	4.9%	4.9%
Current price of a bond paying $1000 in one year = $1000/(1 + expected pretax nominal rate of return)	$934.58	$909.09	$884.96

Unfortunately, this is not the way bond prices and expected pretax nominal returns react to changes in the expected rate of inflation, as is shown next.

11.9   SECURITIES AS HEDGES AGAINST INFLATION

It is reasonable to assume that investors are more concerned with real returns than with nominal returns, since real returns reflect how much better off they are after adjusting for inflation. Accordingly, securities that provide a hedge against inflation should be considered more attractive, other things being equal, than those that do not. But what does it mean to say that a security is a "hedge" against inflation? And what does empirical research suggest about the abilities of various types of investments to act as such hedges?

For a tax-exempt investor, a security would be a perfect inflation hedge if its actual nominal rate of return moved one-for-one with the actual rate of inflation, since its real return would then be the same no matter what the rate of inflation. However, as shown in the previous section, for a tax-paying investor, the relationship would have to be more than one-for-one in order for the security to be a perfect hedge against inflation.

Determining a Security's Sensitivity to Inflation

The ability of a security to hedge against inflation is indicated by the term h_i in the following equation:

$$NR_{it} = a_i + h_i AI_t + w_{it} \tag{11.8}$$

where:

NR_{it} = the actual nominal return on security i in period t,

a_i = a constant,

h_i = a constant representing the sensitivity of security i's return to the rate of inflation,

AI_t = the actual rate of inflation in period t, and

w_{it} = the uncertain portion of the nominal return of security i that is not related to the rate of inflation in period t.

Now, remember from earlier that the actual rate of inflation in any period can be viewed as having two components:

$$AI_t = EI_t + UI_t \qquad (11.9)$$

where:

EI_t = the expected rate of inflation for period t, and

UI_t = the unexpected rate of inflation for period t.

Thus, if at the beginning of the period the expected rate of inflation is 5%, but it subsequently turns out actually to be 6%, then the unexpected rate of inflation for the period is $+1\%$.

Equation (11.8) omits the separation in the actual rate of inflation that is shown in equation (11.9). However, such a separation should be made, since a security might serve as a hedge against expected inflation and not against unexpected inflation, or vice versa. Thus, to consider these two components of inflation separately, equation (11.8) can be modified as follows:

$$NR_{it} = a_i + h_i^e EI_t + h_i^u UI_t + w_{it} \qquad (11.10)$$

where:

h_i^e = a constant representing the sensitivity of security i's nominal return to the expected rate of inflation,

h_i^u = a constant representing the sensitivity of security i's nominal return to the unexpected rate of inflation.

The other terms are as defined earlier. Note that at the beginning of period t, both UI_t and w_{it} are uncertain and are as likely to end up being positive as negative at the end of the period. Note also that a security with $h_i^e = 1$ would be regarded as being a perfect hedge against expected inflation, a security with $h_i^u = 1$ would be regarded as being a perfect hedge against unexpected inflation, and a security with both h_i^e and h_i^u equal to 1 would be regarded as being a perfect hedge against actual inflation.

As indicated earlier, a rough estimate of the expected rate of inflation over a short-term period is provided by the return on Treasury bills that mature at the end of the period and are bought at the beginning of the period. For example, the return available today on six-month Treasury bills can be viewed as a consensus estimate of inflation over the forthcoming six months and is therefore representative of the *expected rate of inflation* (EI_t). Once the six months have passed, the actual rate of inflation (AI_t) will be known.

TABLE 11.3

Sensitivities of Assets to Expected and Unexpected Inflation,
Six-Month Holding Periods, July 1959–July 1971.

ASSET	SENSITIVITY TO EXPECTED INFLATION (h_i^e)	SENSITIVITY TO UNEXPECTED INFLATION (h_i^u)
1–2 year U.S. government bonds	1.08	−1.15
2–3 year U.S. government bonds	1.03	−1.75
3–4 year U.S. government bonds	.88	−2.37
4–5 year U.S. government bonds	.79	−2.75
Private residential real estate	1.27	1.14
Common stocks[a]	−4.26	−2.09

[a] Value-weighted average of all stocks listed on New York Stock Exchange.
SOURCE: Eugene F. Fama and G. William Schwort, "Asset Returns and Inflation," *Journal of Financial Economics* 5, no. 2 (November 1977):130–1. By permission of North-Holland Publishing Co., Amsterdam.

At that time, equation (11.9) can be used to estimate the *unexpected rate of inflation* (UI_t) by calculating the difference between the actual rate of inflation and the Treasury bill return.

To determine the sensitivity of any particular security to both expected and unexpected inflation, more than one six-month time period needs to be used. In one study, 24 six-month time periods—from July 1959 through July 1971—were used.[9] This means that 24 estimates of both expected and unexpected inflation were calculated. Furthermore, the actual rates of return were calculated for the same 24 six-month periods for a number of different securities. Then, by comparing the returns on these various securities with the estimates of expected and unexpected inflation over a number of periods, the historical sensitivities of the securities (h_i^e and h_i^u) were estimated.[10]

Table 11.3 provides the estimates derived in this manner for several types of securities. U.S. government bonds appear to have provided hedges against expected inflation on approximately a one-for-one basis, since their sensitivities to expected inflation are all in the vicinity of a value of 1. However, since all these bonds had negative values of h_i^u, they all failed to serve as hedges against unexpected inflation.[11] Furthermore, the values of h_i^u were more negative when the life of the bond was longer. This relationship is not surprising in light of the way investors revise expectations based on recent experience, as shown in the following example.

Assume that inflation is expected to run at the semiannual rate of 5% (that is, 10% per year) throughout the future. At the beginning of the year, a 10% one-year government bond is priced to return 5% per six months (that is, it is selling for par of $1000, provides $50 coupon payments every six months, and is expected to sell for $1000 at midyear, right after a coupon

---

[9] Eugene F. Fama and G. William Schwert, "Asset Returns and Inflation," *Journal of Financial Economics* 5, no. 2 (November 1977):115–46.

[10] The procedure used to estimate these sensitivities is known as multiple regression.

[11] This was also observed for long-term corporate bonds in a later study. See Kenneth R. French, Richard S. Ruback, and G. William Schwert, "Effects of Nominal Contracting on Stock Returns," *Journal of Political Economy* 91, no. 1 (February 1983):70–96.

payment is made). Now, assume that during the first half of the year inflation runs at the semiannual rate of 6% (that is, 12% per year). Investors are likely to revise their estimate of inflation upward for the second half of the year—say from 5% to 5.5%. But, if the one-year bond is to return 5.5% over the second half of the year, its price at midyear must be lower than it would have been if it were to provide a return of 5% over the second half of the year. In particular, its price would have to be $995.26, not the expected $1000. This means that investors who held it during the first half of the year would not obtain a return of 5%, but instead would obtain a lesser return of 4.53%, since they would receive a lower-than-expected selling price at the end of the first six months.

As a result, higher-than-expected inflation (6% > 5%) caused them to obtain a lower-than-expected return (4.53% < 5%). Similarly, lower-than-expected inflation would cause investors to obtain a higher-than-expected return. This means that the six-month return on a one-year government bond would have a negative relationship with unexpected inflation, as was observed in Table 11.3.

Next, consider the price impact on a 10% two-year government bond that is also initially priced to have a semiannual return of 5% (that is, it is

---

A. 10% One-year U.S. government bond with semiannual $50 coupon payments:

Assume it is currently priced at $1000 so as to provide the investor with a 5% semiannual return.

Price at the end of six months in order to provide an investor with a return of 5% over the last six months of the bond's life:

$$($1050/1.05) = $1000.$$

Expected return over first six months:

$$[($1000 - $1000) + $50]/$1000 = 5\%.$$

Price at the end of six months in order to provide an investor with a return of 5.5% over the last six months of the bond's life:

$$($1050/1.055) = $995.26.$$

Actual return realized over the first six months:

$$[($995.26 - $1000) + $50]/$1000 = 4.53\%.$$

B. 10% Two-year U.S. government bond with semiannual $50 coupon payments:

Assume it is currently priced at $1000 so as to provide the investor with a 5% semiannual return.

Price at the end of six months in order to provide an investor with a 5% semiannual return over the last 18 months of the bond's life:

$$($1050/1.05^3) + ($50/1.05^2) + ($50/1.05^1) = $1000.$$

Expected return over first six months:

$$[($1000 - $1000) + $50]/$1000 = 5\%.$$

Price at the end of six months in order to provide an investor with a semiannual return of 5.5% over the last 18 months of the bond's life:

$$($1050/1.055^3) + ($50/1.055^2) + ($50/1.055^1) = $986.51.$$

Actual return realized over the first six months:

$$[($986.51 - $1000) + $50]/$1000 = 3.65\%.$$

---

selling for par of $1000 and provides $50 coupon payments every six months for the next two years). Again, assume inflation over the first six months turns out to be 6%, whereupon investors revise their expectations of the future semiannual rate of inflation to be 5.5%. Now, if the two-year bond is to have a semiannual return of 5.5% over the remaining 18 months of its life, its price will have to drop by even more than the drop in the price of the one-year bond. In particular, its price would have to drop to $986.50, which is less than the $995.26 price of the one-year bond.

As a result, higher-than-expected inflation (6%) would cause the two-year bonds to have a lower-than-expected six-month return (3.65%). Furthermore, this return is even lower than the six-month return on the one-year bonds (4.53%). Conversely, lower-than-expected inflation would cause the two-year bonds to have a higher-than-expected six-month return. Furthermore, this return is even higher than the six-month return on the one-year bonds. Consequently, the six-month return on a two-year government bond would have an even more negative relationship with unexpected inflation than the one-year government bond, and indeed this is what was observed in Table 11.3. Also, this analysis implies that the negative relationship between returns and unexpected inflation will, in general, be more negative the longer the life of the government bond. Again, this is what is observed in Table 11.3.

Residential real estate provides a bright spot in an otherwise gloomy record of the relationship between security returns and unexpected inflation. As shown in Table 11.3, it alone had positive estimates with values near one for both h_i^e and h_i^u. Thus, it appears that residential real estate has historically served as a hedge against both expected and unexpected inflation.

The record of common stocks as an inflation hedge is depressing, to say the least. With negative values for both h_i^e and h_i^u, historically they have not served as hedges against either expected or unexpected inflation.[12] Quite the contrary—stock returns have tended to be lower when the rate of either expected or unexpected inflation is greater.[13] In turn, this implies that stock returns have tended to be lower when the actual rate of inflation is greater.

However, this does not imply that stocks cannot provide returns greater than the rate of inflation. Indeed, there is every reason to expect stocks to provide positive real returns over the long term. After all, in Chapter 1 it was observed that over the time period of 1926 to 1986, the average annual rate of inflation was 3.14%, whereas the average annual return on common stocks was 12.12%. Thus, over this time period, common stocks had a positive real return of approximately 8.98% = 12.12% − 3.14%.

---

[12] These observations appear to be the result of a positive relationship between stock returns and real activity in the economy, and a negative relationship between real activity, and inflation. See Eugene F. Fama, "Stock Returns, Real Activity, Inflation, and Money," *American Economic Review* 71, no. 4 (September 1981): 545–64; and Stephen A. Buser and Patrick J. Hess, "Stock Returns, Inflation, and Treasury Yields," unpublished paper, University of Minnesota, September, 1988.

[13] A subsequent study of common stocks found that unexpected inflation did not benefit firms with relatively high levels of nominal liabilities (such as accounts payable and long-term debt). This was surprising, since it was thought that these firms would gain from unexpected inflation due to an unexpected decline in the real value of their nominal liabilities (more simply, unexpected inflation should benefit debtors at the expense of creditors). See French, Ruback, and Schwert, "Effects of Nominal Contracting."

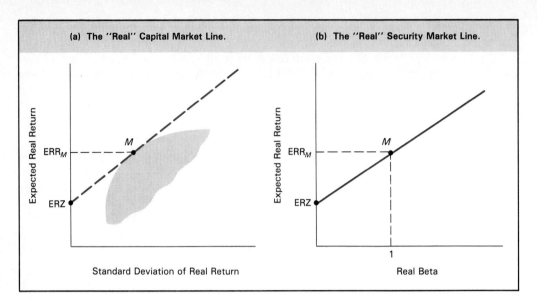

FIGURE 11–2
The capital asset pricing model in real terms.

11.10 INFLATION HEDGING AND EXPECTED RETURN

The original capital asset pricing model deals with nominal returns. If the rate of inflation is reasonably predictable, this causes no problem, for inflation will add little to the uncertainty concerning the return of any asset. But if there is considerable uncertainty about the rate of inflation, the situation is different. First, the real return of a default-free investment such as a U.S. Treasury bill will not be certain. Second, the risk associated with the real return of the market portfolio may differ considerably from the risk associated with its nominal return. Third, the beta of a security relative to the market portfolio may change when both the security's returns and market portfolio's returns are expressed in real terms instead of nominal returns.

If investors think in terms of real returns, the relationship between risk and return may look like that shown in Figure 11.2. The shaded area in part (a) indicates the "real" capital market line, which represents all available risk-return combinations in terms of real returns (note that there is no risk-free alternative). Point M represents the market portfolio, which is assumed to be an efficient investment. The situation is thus formally equivalent to the *zero-beta* model. As part (b) shows, securities will be priced as if it were possible to borrow or lend without limit at a risk-free rate of ERZ. Thus, all securities and portfolios will plot along a straight line such as that shown in part (b), relating expected real return to "real beta." The equation of this "real" security market line is

$$\text{ERR}_i = \text{ERZ} + (\text{ERR}_M - \text{ERZ})\beta_i^r \qquad (11.11)$$

where:

> ERR_i = the expected real return on security i,
>
> ERZ = the expected real return of a security or portfolio with a real beta of zero,
>
> ERR_M = the expected real return on the market portfolio, and
>
> β_i^r = security i's real beta (that is, $cov(RR_i, RR_M)/var(RR_M)$).

Equation (11.11) provides a succinct statement of the effect of uncertain inflation on security expected returns. But what does it imply about the relationship among expected nominal returns, nominal betas, and sensitivities of nominal returns to inflation? As shown in the appendix, in such a world, securities will also plot on a security market plane with these three attributes on the axes. The equation of such a plane is

$$ENR_i = Z_1 + Z_2\beta_i^n - Z_3h_i^u \qquad (11.12)$$

where:

> ENR_i = the expected nominal return on security i,
>
> Z_1 = the expected nominal return on a security or portfolio with both β_i^n and h_i^u equal to zero,
>
> β_i^n = security i's nominal (that is, traditional) beta (that is, $cov(NR_i,NR_M)/var(NR_M)$),
>
> h_i^u = security i's sensitivity to unexpected inflation (that is, $cov(NR_i,UI)/var(UI)$),
>
> UI = unexpected inflation,
>
> Z_2 = a positive constant, and
>
> Z_3 = a positive constant.

In a world of uncertain inflation, the third term ($Z_3h_i^u$) indicates:

Securities will be priced to give lower expected nominal returns, other things equal, the greater their ability to hedge against unexpected inflation.

The value of Z_3 indicates the reduction in expected nominal return per unit increase in inflation sensitivity. Not surprisingly, the greater the uncertainty about inflation, the greater will be the magnitude of this reduction. However, since uncertainty concerning the market portfolio's nominal return is typically much greater than that concerning inflation, the effect of differences in β_i^n on ENR_i—indicated by the magnitude of Z_2—will generally be considerably greater.

Stocks of firms with large net monetary debtor positions should be better hedges against unexpected inflation than those of firms with large net monetary creditor positions. However, differences in inflation sensitivities among stocks may be relatively small and difficult to predict in advance (this is apparently true in the United States; see footnote 12). If so, the inclusion of inflation sensitivity in a security market plane or hyperplane may add only slightly to the explanation of differences in expected returns under

normal circumstances. But when uncertainty about inflation is considerable, differences in hedging abilities—especially among different classes of assets—are likely to be accompanied by substantial differences in expected returns.

As is typical in an efficient market, bad news tends to accompany good news. For example, the good news might be that real estate is a good hedge against inflation; the bad news is that its expected return is less than that of assets that entail similar risk in other regards but that are poorer hedges against inflation.

11.11 SUMMARY

Like taxes, inflation seems to be continually present in the postwar economy of the United States. It is of importance to investors because of its effect on both the pricing of securities and the subsequent level of nominal and real returns. In particular, the expected rate of inflation has an impact on how various securities are priced in the marketplace. For example, Treasury bills appear to be priced so as to reflect the consensus opinion about what inflation will be over their lifetime.

Having purchased a security, the subsequent actual rate of inflation will determine the investor's real return. Real returns are important to the investor because they represent how much an investor's purchasing power has increased (or decreased) and thus indicate how much better (or worse) off the investor is.

In general, when inflation turns out to be greater than expected, borrowers gain and lenders lose. That is, the actual real return paid by borrowers and received by lenders is less than what they initially expected. Conversely, when inflation turns out to be less than expected, borrowers lose and lenders gain. One method of removing such risks from fixed-income securities involves indexation, whereby security payments are adjusted to reflect the rate of inflation that has actually occurred. However, such indexing is rarely seen in the United States.

It makes sense for investors to want to hold securities that provide protection against both expected and unexpected inflation. Unfortunately, with the exception of real estate, the historical record suggests that most securities do not provide such protection. Fixed-income securities appear to be priced to protect the investor against expected inflation, but provide little protection against unexpected inflation. More surprising is the observation that common stocks do not appear to offer protection against either expected or unexpected inflation. Nevertheless, over the long term, common stocks do appear to have positive real returns of approximately 9%.

APPENDIX A
EXPECTED RETURNS, BETAS, AND INFLATION HEDGING

In a world of uncertain inflation where investors are concerned with real returns, security prices could adjust until all securities and portfolios plotted

on the "real" security market line given in equation (11.11). To see how this relates to more traditional concepts, equation (11.5) can be used to show that

$$RR_i = NR_i - I \tag{11.13}$$

$$RR_M = NR_M - I \tag{11.14}$$

where I is the rate of inflation and the other terms are as defined earlier in the chapter. Equations (11.13) and (11.14) can be used to show that

$$ERR_i = ENR_i - EI \tag{11.15}$$

$$ERR_M = ENR_M - EI \tag{11.16}$$

where EI is the expected rate of inflation.

Substituting the right-hand sides of equations (11.15) and (11.16) into equation (11.11) results in

$$ENR_i - EI = ERZ + (ENR_M - EI - ERZ)\beta_i^r \tag{11.17}$$

where, by definition:

$$\beta_i^r = \frac{\text{cov}(RR_i, RR_M)}{\text{var}(RR_M)}. \tag{11.18}$$

Using equations (11.13) and (11.14), equation (11.18) can be rewritten as

$$\beta_i^r = \frac{\text{cov}(NR_i, NR_M)}{\text{var}(RR_M)} - \frac{\text{cov}(NR_i, I)}{\text{var}(RR_M)} - \frac{\text{cov}(NR_M, I)}{\text{var}(RR_M)} + \frac{\text{var}(I)}{\text{var}(RR_M)} \tag{11.19}$$

which can be shown to be equivalent to:

$$\beta_i^r = \frac{\text{var}(NR_M)}{\text{var}(RR_M)} \beta_i^n - \frac{\text{var}(I)}{\text{var}(RR_M)} h_i^u + \frac{\text{var}(I) - \text{cov}(NR_M, I)}{\text{var}(RR_M)}. \tag{11.20}$$

Substituting the right-hand side of equation (11.20) for β_i^r in equation (11.17) results in:

$$ENR_i = \left\{ EI + ERZ + (ENR_M - EI - ERZ) \left[\frac{\text{var}(I) - \text{cov}(NR_M, I)}{\text{var}(RR_M)} \right] \right\}$$
$$+ \left\{ (ENR_M - EI - ERZ) \left[\frac{\text{var}(NR_M)}{\text{var}(RR_M)} \right] \right\} \beta_i^n \tag{11.21}$$
$$- \left\{ (ENR_M - EI - ERZ) \left[\frac{\text{var}(I)}{\text{var}(RR_M)} \right] \right\} h_i^u$$

which reduces to the equation shown earlier in the chapter:

$$ENR_i = Z_1 + Z_2 \beta_i^n - Z_3 h_i^u. \tag{11.12}$$

In examining equation (11.12), first note that

$$\frac{Z_2}{Z_3} = \frac{\text{var}(NR_M)}{\text{var}(I)}$$

and, since the variance of NR_M is large (for example, $400 = 20^2$) relative to that of I (for example, $25 = 5^2$), Z_2 is likely to be considerably greater than Z_3. This means that the effect of β_i^n on ENR_i is likely to be considerably greater than the effect of h_i^u on ENR_i. Second, note that if $var(I) = 0$, then equation (11.12) simplifies to the zero-beta version of the capital asset pricing model.

QUESTIONS AND PROBLEMS

1. Given the following beginning and ending values for a particular price index, and the respective number of years between the measurement of the two values, calculate the annual compounded (geometric mean) inflation rate.

	Price Index Beginning Value	Price Index Ending Value	Years Covered
a.	100	115	1
b.	115	170	3
c.	170	150	2

2. Why do cost of living indices frequently overstate the true economic impact of inflation on typical consumers?

3. Distinguish between the nominal and the real rate of return on an investment.

4. Kirby Higbe started 1989 with investments valued at $10,500. At the end of 1989 those same investments were worth $12,000. During the same time period the price index rose from 210 to 230. What was Kirby's real rate of return during 1989?

5. Why is it reasonable to assume that rational investors will build in an expected inflation premium into the returns they require from their investments?

6. In the late 1970s and early 1980s, a period of unexpectedly high inflation, Happy Felsch referred to long-term bonds issued by U.S. corporations and the Treasury as "certificates of confiscation." Why would Happy make such a comment?

7. Also in the late 1970s and early 1980s, there was considerable discussion concerning the "quality" of corporate earnings. Straight-line depreciation and the FIFO inventory valuation methods were often cited as the causes of "poor quality" earnings. Further, it was argued that these accounting methods effectively resulted in tax overpayments. Discuss the reasons for both contentions.

8. Why is it often argued that the federal government is the greatest beneficiary of inflation?

9. Many economists contend that during periods of inflation, taxes on investment income reflect, in part, a tax on the return of capital and, hence, are inequitable. Explain the reasoning behind this argument.

10. Explain why the returns on bonds are found to be negatively correlated with unexpected inflation. Why does this relationship become progressively more negative as one considers longer lived bonds?

11. Sherry Magee bought a two-year 12% coupon U.S. Treasury note at the beginning of 1989. The bond was bought at its face value of $10,000. Over the first year, inflation ran at a semiannual rate of 8%. Investors' inflation expectations at the end of 1989 rose to a 7% semiannual rate.

   a. At the beginning of 1990, at what price would the bond have to sell at in order to offer investors a 7% semiannual return over the last year of the bond's life?

   b. If the bond were priced at the figure calculated in part (a), what return would Sherry have earned over the year 1989?

12. Common stocks, somewhat surprisingly, do not appear to be effective hedges against either expected or unexpected inflation. Explain why the stocks of some companies might be better hedges against inflation than others.

13. Assume that the current relationship between expected nominal returns, beta values, and inflation sensitivities has been estimated to be:

$$\text{ENR}_i = 6.0 + (4.0 * \beta_i) - (.20 * h_i)$$

Stock A has a beta of 1.00 and provides no hedge against inflation. What should be its expected return? Stock B has a beta of 1.10. How sensitive to inflation would its return have to be to make its appropriate expected nominal return equal to that of stock A?

Chapter 12

FIXED-INCOME SECURITIES

This chapter surveys the major types of fixed-income securities, with an emphasis on those currently popular in the United States. Such a survey cannot be exhaustive. A security is, after all, a contract giving the investor certain rights to the future prospects of the issuer. Because the rights given the investor can differ from one security to another and because the future prospects of issuers can differ substantially, the number of different types of fixed-income securities is quite large, making a complete survey virtually impossible.

The term *fixed-income* is commonly used to cover the types of securities discussed in this chapter, but it is a bit misleading. Typically, these securities promise the investor that he or she will receive certain specified cash flows at certain specified times in the future. It may be one cash flow, in which case the security is known as a *pure-discount security*. Alternatively, it may involve multiple cash flows. If all these cash flows (except for the last one) are of the same size, they are generally referred to as *coupon payments*. The specified date beyond which the investor will no longer receive cash flows is known as the *maturity date*. On this date, the investor receives the *principal* (also known as the par value or face value) associated with the security, along with the last coupon payment. However, all the cash flows are promised and thus may not be received. That is, in many cases there is at least some risk that a promised payment will not be made in full and on time.

12.1 SAVINGS DEPOSITS

Perhaps the most familiar type of fixed-income investment is the personal savings account at a bank, savings and loan company, or credit union. Such an account provides substantial (if not complete) safety of principal, low probability of failure to receive interest, high liquidity, and a relatively low return.

☐ 12.1.1 Commercial Banks

Many people maintain a checking account in a commercial bank. Formally, these accounts are termed *demand deposits*, since money can be withdrawn

on demand by the depositors. While the bookkeeping required to keep track of withdrawals and deposits is costly to the bank, the balance in such an account is available to support interest-earning loans made by the bank. Within bounds set by regulations, banks offer terms for checking accounts that reflect these aspects. Customers with small balances who write many checks pay the bank, whereas those with large balances who write few checks are paid by the bank. Often, the two elements are identified separately, with service charges assessed for check writing and interest paid on average balances. In some cases the amount of interest paid increases substantially if a larger minimum balance is maintained.

An alternative to a checking account is a standard savings account. Although a written request for a withdrawal may be required up to 30 days in advance, in practice, requests for withdrawals are almost always honored immediately. Almost any amount may be invested in a savings account. No security is issued; instead, the current balance plus interest earned is posted to the bank's records and (if desired) to the depositor's passbook.

Many banks also offer money market accounts and negotiable order of withdrawal (NOW) accounts, which pay interest and on which checks may be written. Credit unions offer services similar to these accounts, via share draft accounts, and many investment companies (described in Chapter 20) provide at least limited check-writing services.

The standard (passbook) savings account is only one of many types of *time deposits*. A single-maturity deposit may be withdrawn at a stated maturity date (for example, one year after the initial deposit). A multiple-maturity deposit may be withdrawn at a stated date or left for one or more periods of equal length (thus, a 90-day multiple-maturity deposit can be withdrawn roughly every three months after the date of the initial deposit). In practice, most single-maturity and multiple-maturity deposits can be withdrawn at any time. However, a penalty must be paid when this is done prior to maturity. Often, the penalty takes the form of recomputing the interest earned using a lower rate. Sometimes, an additional penalty may be deducted from the recomputed account balance.

Some types of time deposits may be made in almost any amount, whereas others may be made only in units of, for example, $1000 each. The latter may be represented by *certificates of deposit* (CDs), which clearly qualify as securities. Large-denomination CDs (generally $100,000 or more and known as jumbo CDs) may be negotiable—that is, the original depositor may sell the certificate to someone else before maturity. In most cases all interest is paid, along with the principal, at maturity. The top part of Figure 12.1 shows average yields of CDs with various maturities, issued by major banks in certain big states, as published each Friday in *The Wall Street Journal*.

Most bank accounts in the United States are insured by the Federal Deposit Insurance Corporation (FDIC), a government agency that guarantees the payment of principal on any account up to a stated limit ($100,000 in 1988) if the bank is closed and liquidated. The FDIC, created in 1933, levies insurance premiums on its member banks and is authorized to borrow funds from the U.S. Treasury, if needed, although it has never done so. By opening

BANXQUOTE® MONEY MARKETS

Survey ended Thursday, December 8, 1988
AVERAGE YIELDS OF MAJOR BANKS

	MMI*	One Month	Two Months	Three Months	Six Months	One Year	Two Years	Five Years
NEW YORK								
Savings	7.25%	6.93%	z	7.94%	8.36%	8.67%	8.59%	8.97%
Jumbos	7.25%	8.70%	8.62%	8.62%	8.67%	8.77%	9.00%	9.38%
CALIFORNIA								
Savings	5.73%	5.70%	5.70%	6.53%	7.45%	7.70%	7.88%	8.07%
Jumbos	6.13%	7.15%	7.37%	7.77%	8.15%	8.23%	8.33%	8.43%
PENNSYLVANIA								
Savings	5.97%	5.65%	z	7.60%	8.12%	8.44%	8.53%	8.76%
Jumbos	7.05%	8.07%	8.15%	8.13%	8.22%	8.43%	8.62%	8.98%
ILLINOIS								
Savings	6.41%	5.94%	z	7.46%	7.86%	8.12%	8.32%	8.84%
Jumbos	6.68%	7.80%	8.68%	8.32%	8.44%	8.59%	9.10%	9.03%
TEXAS								
Savings	6.92%	7.22%	7.29%	7.38%	7.67%	8.41%	8.55%	8.83%
Jumbos	6.92%	8.30%	8.30%	8.30%	8.30%	8.95%	9.07%	9.12%
FLORIDA								
Savings	5.93%	6.70%	6.70%	7.55%	8.15%	8.32%	8.42%	8.57%
Jumbos	5.93%	7.30%	8.05%	8.05%	8.33%	8.53%	8.91%	9.06%
NATIONAL AVERAGE								
Savings	6.37%	6.59%	6.83%	7.45%	7.93%	8.28%	8.38%	8.67%
Jumbos	6.66%	7.92%	8.17%	8.20%	8.35%	8.58%	8.77%	8.92%
WEEKLY CHANGE (in percentage point)								
Savings	+0.02	+0.05	+0.05	+0.02	+0.08	+0.11	+0.11	+0.06
Jumbos	+0.04	+0.28	+0.04	+0.04	+0.05	+0.05	+0.14	+0.10

SAVINGS CD YIELDS OFFERED THROUGH LEADING BROKERS

	Three Months	Six Months	One Year	Two Years	Five Years
NATIONAL AVERAGE	8.65%	8.71%	9.01%	9.16%	9.23%
WEEKLY CHANGE	−0.03	−0.03	+0.14	+0.12	−0.10

*Money Market Investments.   z-Unavailable.

Each depositor is insured by the Federal Deposit Insurance Corp. (FDIC) or Federal Savings and Loan Insurance Corp. (FSLIC) up to $100,000 per issuing institution.
COMPOUND METHODS: c-Continuously. d-Daily. w-Weekly. m-Monthly. q-Quarterly. s-Semi-annually. a-Annually. si-Simple Interest.

YIELD BASIS: A-365/365. B-360/360. C-365/360.

The information included in this table has been obtained directly from broker-dealers, banks and savings institutions, but the accuracy and validity cannot be guaranteed. Rates are subject to change. Yields, terms and creditworthiness should be verified before investing.

HIGH YIELD SAVINGS

Small minimum balance, generally $500 to $10,000

Money Market Investments	Rate		Yield
Eastern Svgs, Baltimore Md	8.54%	dA	8.91%
Alamo Svgs, San Antonio Tx	8.45%	mA	8.79%
International Svgs, San Diego	8.15%	dA	8.49%
Peoples Svgs, Llano Texas	8.05%	mC	8.35%
New South FSB, Birmingham Al	8.05%	mA	8.35%

One Month CDs	Rate		Yield
Bank Audi, New York	8.75%	siC	8.87%
Republic National, New York	8.05%	dA	8.38%
Merchants Bank, Kansas City Mo	8.04%	dA	8.37%
Seasons Svgs, Richmond Va	8.25%	siC	8.36%
North American, San Antonio Tx	8.25%	siA	8.25%

Six Months CDs	Rate		Yield
Capitol Bank, Boston	9.00%	mA	9.38%
First Service, Fitchburg Ma	9.19%	siA	9.19%
Empire of America, Buffalo NY	8.76%	dA	9.15%
Safra Nat'l Bank, New York	8.67%	dA	9.06%
Seasons Svgs, Richmond Va	8.75%	qC	9.04%

One Year CDs	Rate		Yield
Capitol Bank, Boston	9.00%	mA	9.38%
Bayview Fedl, Corpus Christi Tx	9.00%	qA	9.31%
Seasons Svgs, Richmond Va	9.00%	qC	9.31%
Empire of America, Buffalo NY	8.85%	dA	9.25%
Columbia Svgs, Newport Bch CA	9.00%	sA	9.20%

HIGH YIELD JUMBOS

Large minimum balance, generally $95,000 to $100,000

Money Market Investments	Rate		Yield
Peoples Svgs, Llano Texas	8.80%	mC	9.16%
Eastern Svgs, Baltimore Md	8.54%	dA	8.91%
Chevy Chase, Laurel Md	8.50%	mA	8.84%
Alamo Svgs, San Antonio Tx	8.45%	mA	8.79%
Barclays Bank, New York	8.35%	dA	8.71%

One Month Jumbo CDs	Rate		Yield
Boston Safe, Boston	9.20%	siC	9.33%
Commodore Svgs, Dallas	9.20%	siA	9.20%
National Bank, Detroit	9.00%	siC	9.13%
First Network, Los Angeles	9.00%	siA	9.00%
First Deposit, Tilton NH	9.00%	siA	9.00%

Six Months Jumbo CDs	Rate		Yield
Peoples Svgs, Llano Texas	9.38%	siC	9.51%
First Network, Los Angeles	9.38%	siA	9.38%
North American, San Antonio Tx	9.38%	siA	9.38%
New Braunfels, New Braunfels Tx	9.38%	siA	9.38%
Hallmark Svgs, Plano Texas	9.38%	siA	9.38%

One Year Jumbo CDs	Rate		Yield
Peoples Svgs, Llano Texas	9.63%	siC	9.76%
First Network, Los Angeles	9.50%	siA	9.50%
Sun Svgs, Parker Co	9.50%	siA	9.50%
Jefferson Svgs, Beaumont Texas	9.50%	siA	9.50%
Commodore Svgs, Dallas	9.50%	siA	9.50%

certain kinds of multiple accounts, each under the limit, an investor can have a considerable amount covered by deposit insurance.

12.1.2 Savings and Loan Companies and Mutual Savings Banks

Savings and loan companies and mutual savings banks accept relatively short-term deposits, then use the money primarily to make relatively long-term loans, often for home mortgages. All mutual savings banks and mutual savings and loan companies are nominally owned by their members, whereas stock savings and loan companies are owned by stockholders (like commercial banks), who may or may not deposit funds or obtain loans there.

Mutual savings and loan companies and mutual savings banks pay *dividends* instead of interest. The distinction is more semantic than real, however. The Internal Revenue Service treats such payments as interest for tax purposes.

In the United States, most accounts in savings companies are insured by a government agency—either the FDIC or the Federal Savings and Loan Insurance Corporation (FSLIC). The principal of each account is insured up to the same limit used for bank accounts but here, too, judicious use of multiple accounts makes it possible to have even more covered by deposit insurance.

The terms for deposits offered by institutions of this type are generally similar to those offered by commercial banks. The bottom part of Figure 12.1 presents the highest yields on CDs of various maturities that are issued by federally insured "thrift institutions," as reported weekly in *The Wall Street Journal*.

12.1.3 Credit Unions

A credit union accepts deposits from members of the credit union (membership is limited to individuals sharing some kind of common bond, often a common employer) and then loans these funds to other members. Typically, loans are relatively small and relatively short-term (for example, to finance the purchase of an automobile). Excess funds are invested in highly liquid short-term assets.

Each credit union is owned by its members, who elect a board of directors. Deposits are generally similar to passbook accounts in a bank or savings and loan company and also earn dividends instead of interest. Many credit unions also offer CDs and checking accounts to their members.

Deposits in all federally chartered credit unions are insured by the National Credit Union Administration (NCUA), a U.S. government agency

FIGURE 12–1
Yields on certificates of deposits.

SOURCE: Reprinted by the permission of *The Wall Street Journal*, © Dow Jones & Company, Inc. (December 6, 1988): p. C 21.

that serves the same function as the FDIC and the FSLIC. The amount and type of insurance coverage provided by all these agencies is essentially identical.

☐ 12.1.4 Other Types of Personal Savings Accounts

A number of institutions similar to those just described can be found. For example, there are companies chartered to accept deposits and use the proceeds to make consumer loans. In some countries, the government-run post office accepts savings deposits. Certain kinds of life insurance policies include a savings component, since payments often exceed the amount strictly required to pay for just the insurance involved. The cash value of such a policy may be obtained by cancellation; alternatively, some or all of it may be borrowed without canceling the policy. The implicit rate of return on the cash value of an insurance policy is typically quite low, reflecting the extremely low risk to the policyholder and the length of the insurance company's commitment.

12.2 MONEY MARKET INSTRUMENTS

Certain types of short-term (meaning, arbitrarily, one year or less), highly marketable loans play a major role in the investment and borrowing activities of operating corporations and financial intermediaries. Individual investors with substantial funds may invest in such *money market instruments* directly but most do so indirectly via money market accounts at various financial institutions.[1]

Some money market instruments are negotiable and are traded in active secondary dealer markets; others are not. Some may be purchased by anyone with adequate funds, others only by particular types of institutions. Many are sold on a discount basis—for example, a 90-day note with a face value of $100,000 might be sold for $98,000, where the face value of $100,000 is to be paid to the investor at maturity and the difference of $2000 represents interest income.

Interest rates on such money market instruments are often reported on a *bank discount basis* (this basis was discussed in Chapter 4). In the example, this means that the note will be described in the media as having a discount of 2% per quarter, or 8% per year. However, the discount does not represent the true interest rate on the note. In such a situation, the true interest rate is higher—in this case, it equals $2000/\$98,000 = 2.04\%$ per quarter, or the equivalent of 8.16% per year (with quarterly compounding, it would be $1.0204^4 - 1 = 8.41\%$).

---

[1] Short-term obligations of the U.S. government and its agencies are also considered money market instruments; they are described in the next section. A concise summary description of the various types of money market instruments is contained in *Instruments of the Money Market*, ed. Timothy Q. Cook and Timothy D. Rowe, Federal Reserve Bank of Richmond, 1986; and Marcia Stigum and Frank J. Fabozzi, *The Dow Jones–Irwin Guide to Bond and Money Market Instruments* (Homewood, Ill.: Dow Jones–Irwin, Inc., 1987).

MONEY RATES

Monday, December 5, 1988

The key U.S. and foreign annual interest rates below are a guide to general levels but don't always represent actual transactions.

PRIME RATE: 10½%. The base rate on corporate loans at large U.S. money center commercial banks.

FEDERAL FUNDS: 8⅝% high, 8 9/16% low, 8½% near closing bid, 8⅝% offered. Reserves traded among commercial banks for overnight use in amounts of $1 million or more. Source: Fulton Prebon (U.S.A.) Inc.

DISCOUNT RATE: 6½%. The charge on loans to depository institutions by the New York Federal Reserve Bank.

CALL MONEY: 9½% to 9¾%. The charge on loans to brokers on stock exchange collateral.

COMMERCIAL PAPER placed directly by General Motors Acceptance Corp.:9.20% 30 to 44 days;9% 45 to 59 days;8.70% 60 to 89 days;8.625% 90 to 119 days;8½% 120 to 179 days; 8.35% 180 to 270 days.

COMMERCIAL PAPER: High-grade unsecured notes sold through dealers by major corporations in multiples of $1,000: 9.32% 30 days; 9.22% 60 days; 9.15% 90 days.

CERTIFICATES OF DEPOSIT: 8.55% one month; 8.50% two months; 8.51% three months; 8.59% six months; 8.68% one year. Average of top rates paid by major New York banks on primary new issues of negotiable C.D.s, usually on amounts of $1 million and more. The minimum unit is $100,-000. Typical rates in the secondary market: 9.35% one month; 9.25% three months; 9.25% six months.

BANKERS ACCEPTANCES: 9.22% 30 days; 9.02% 60 days; 8.98% 90 days; 8.95% 120 days; 8.90% 150 days; 8.83% 180 days. Negotiable, bank-backed business credit instruments typically financing an import order.

LONDON LATE EURODOLLARS: 9 11/16% to 9 9/16% one month; 9½% to 9⅜% two months; 9 7/16% to 9 5/16% three months; 9 7/16% to 9 5/16% four months; 9 7/16% to 9 5/16% five months; 9 7/16% to 9 5/16% six months.

LONDON INTERBANK OFFERED RATES (LIBOR): 9 11/16% one month; 9 7/16% three months; 9 7/16% six months; 9 9/16% one year. The average of interbank offered rates for dollar deposits in the London market based on quotations at five major banks.

FOREIGN PRIME RATES: Canada 11.75%; Germany 6%; Japan 3.375%; Switzerland 5.25%; Britain 13%. These rate indications aren't directly comparable; lending practices vary widely by location.

TREASURY BILLS: Results of the Monday, December 5, 1988, auction of short-term U.S. government bills, sold at a discount from face value in units of $10,000 to $1 million: 8.04%, 13 weeks; 8.25%, 26 weeks.

FEDERAL HOME LOAN MORTGAGE CORP. (Freddie Mac): Posted yields on 30-year mortgage commitments for delivery within 30 days. 10.45%, standard conventional fixed-rate mortgages; 8.50%, 2% rate capped one-year adjustable rate mortgages. Source: Telerate Systems Inc.

FEDERAL NATIONAL MORTGAGE ASSOCIATION (Fannie Mae): Posted yields on 30 year mortgage commitments for delivery within 30 days (priced at par). 10.39%, standard conventional fixed rate-mortgages; 9.80%, 6/2 rate capped one-year adjustable rate mortgages. Source: Telerate Systems Inc.

MERRILL LYNCH READY ASSETS TRUST: 7.50%. Annualized average rate of return after expenses for the past 30 days; not a forecast of future returns.

FIGURE 12–2

Interest rates on money market instruments.

SOURCE: Reprinted by permission of The Wall Street Journal, © Dow Jones & Company, Inc. (December 6, 1988): p. C 21.

The Wall Street Journal publishes, on a daily basis, a list of the current interest rates on a number of money market instruments. Figure 12.2 presents such a list. Some of the types of money market instruments mentioned on this list are described next.

☐ 12.2.1 Commercial Paper

Commercial paper is an unsecured short-term promissory note issued by both financial and nonfinancial companies. The dollar amount of commercial

paper outstanding exceeds the amount of any other type of money market instrument except for Treasury bills, with the majority being issued by financial companies such as bank holding companies as well as companies involved in sales and personal finance, insurance, and leasing. Such notes are often issued by large firms that have unused lines of credit at banks, making it highly likely that the loan will be paid off when it becomes due. As a result, the interest rates on commercial paper reflect this, being relatively low in comparison with other corporate fixed-income securities.

Commercial paper is usually issued in denominations of $1000 or more, with maturities of up to 270 days (the maximum allowed by the Securities and Exchange Commission without registration). Such paper is generally not negotiable, but the issuer may be willing to prepay the note (perhaps by issuing another) if necessary.

□ 12.2.2   Certificates of Deposit

Certificates of deposit are certificates representing time deposits at commercial banks or savings and loan associations that were mentioned earlier. Large-denomination (or jumbo) CDs are issued in amounts of $100,000 or more, have a specified maturity, and generally are negotiable, meaning they can be sold by one investor to another. Such certificates are insured by the FDIC, FSLIC, or NCUA but only for $100,000 (in 1988).

Interestingly, foreign banks that have branches in the United States also offer dollar-denominated CDs to investors. Such CDs have been dubbed Yankee CDs by the media.

□ 12.2.3   Bankers' Acceptances

Historically, *bankers' acceptances* were created to finance goods in transit; currently they are generally used to finance foreign trade. For example, the buyer of the goods may issue a promise in writing to the seller to pay a given sum within a short period of time (for example, 180 days or less). A bank then "accepts" this promise, obligating itself to pay the amount when requested, and obtains in return a claim on the goods as collateral. The written promise, known as a bankers' acceptance, becomes a liability of both the bank and the buyer of the goods.

The seller of the goods, having received the written promise from the buyer that the bank has accepted, need not wait until the promise is due in order to receive payment. Instead, the acceptance can be sold to someone else at a price that is less than the amount of the promised payment to be made in the future. Thus, such instruments are pure-discount securities.

□ 12.2.4   Eurodollars

In the world of international finance, large short-term CDs denominated in dollars and made in banks outside the United States (most often in London)

are known as *Eurodollar CDs* (or simply Euro CDs). Also available for investment are dollar-denominated time deposits in banks outside the United States, known as *Eurodollar deposits*. A key distinction between Euro CDs and Eurodollar deposits is that Euro CDs are negotiable, meaning they can be traded, whereas Eurodollar deposits are nonnegotiable, meaning they cannot be traded.

The demand and supply conditions for such instruments may differ from the conditions for other U.S. money market instruments, owing to restrictions imposed (or likely to be imposed) by the United States and other governments. However, enough commonality exists to keep interest rates from diverging too much from those available on domestic alternatives. One difference from CDs issued by U.S. banks is that the Euro CDs do not have federal deposit insurance.

□ 12.2.5 Repurchase Agreements

Often one investor (often a financial institution) will sell another investor (often another financial institution) a money market instrument and agree to repurchase it for an agreed-upon price at a later date. For example, investor A might sell investor B, for a price of $10 million, a number of Treasury bills that mature in 180 days. As part of the sale, investor A signs a *repurchase agreement* with investor B. This agreement specifies that after 30 days, investor A will repurchase these Treasury bills for $10.1 million. Thus, investor A will have paid investor B $100,000 in interest for 30 days use of $10 million, meaning that investor B has, in essence, purchased a money market instrument that matures in 30 days.

12.3 U.S. GOVERNMENT SECURITIES

It should come as no surprise that the U.S. government relies heavily on debt financing. Revenues seldom cover expenses, and the difference is financed primarily by issuing debt instruments. Moreover, new debt must be issued in order to get the necessary funds to pay off old debt that comes due. Such *debt refunding* sometimes allows the holders of the maturing debt to exchange it directly for new debt and, in the process, receive beneficial treatment for tax purposes.

Some idea of the magnitude and the ownership of U.S. government debt issued by the Treasury Department can be gained by examining column 1 in Table 12.1. Through various trust funds, the federal government itself is a large holder, as is the Federal Reserve System. However, a large amount is held by state and local governments as well as private investors of one sort or another. For example, these securities are a major factor in the portfolios of commercial banks and other financial institutions. To a lesser extent, business corporations also invest in them, primarily as outlets for relatively short-term excess working capital. The amount held by individual households is also substantial, with over half of their investment in U.S.

TABLE 12.1

Ownership of Outstanding Federal Debt, December 1987[a].

HELD BY	TREASURY DEBT (1)	FEDERAL AGENCY DEBT (2)	TOTAL FEDERAL DEBT (3)
Thrift institutions	$ 41.1	$245.2	$ 286.3
Life insurance companies	73.7	72.3	146.0
Property and liability insurance companies	62.5	39.8	102.3
Public and private noninsured pension funds	176.2	118.4	294.6
Money market funds	16.7	15.7	32.4
Open-end taxable investment funds	166.8	64.8	231.6
Security brokers and dealers	0.0	14.1	14.1
Commercial banks	215.0	159.9	374.9
Business corporations	81.7	1.3	83.0
State and local governments	185.0	94.1	279.1
Foreign investors	297.6	25.2	322.8
Residual: Households direct	366.1	94.3	460.4
Total of privately held federal debt	$1682.4	$945.1	$2627.5
Trust fund holdings	473.4	0.0	473.4
Federal agency holdings	13.1	0.2	13.3
Federal Reserve holdings	244.3	10.5	254.8
Total federal debt	$1983.2	$955.8	$2939.0

[a] Dollar amount expressed in billions.
SOURCE: Adapted from Salomon Brothers Inc., *Prospects for Financial Markets in 1988*, 1987.

government securities being in savings bonds and notes. Lastly, foreign holdings have become quite large in recent years.

Over two-thirds of the public debt is marketable, meaning it is represented by securities that can be sold at any time by the original purchaser through government security dealers. The major nonmarketable issues are held by U.S. government agencies, foreign governments, and individuals (the latter in the form of U.S. savings bonds). Marketable issues include Treasury bills, notes, and bonds. Table 12.2 shows the amounts in each category in September 1988.

The relative maturity dates for U.S. government debt are influenced by a number of factors. As time passes, of course, the term-to-maturity (that is, the remaining time until maturity) of an outstanding issue will decrease. Moreover, the Treasury has considerable latitude in selecting maturities for new issues and can also engage in refunding operations. From time to time, congressional limits on amounts issued or interest paid on certain types of instruments may force reliance on other types of instruments. Debt operations may also be employed as a conscious instrument of governmental economic policy in an attempt to influence the current interest rates for securities of various maturities.

Table 12.3 shows the maturity structure of marketable, interest-bearing debt in September 1988. More than 30% was short-term debt, maturing in less than one year, and about 70% had a maturity date within five years.

Many types of debt have been issued by the U.S. government as well as by U.S. government agencies and organizations sponsored by the federal

TABLE 12.2

Interest-Bearing U.S. Public Debt, September 1988.

CATEGORY		AMOUNT (IN BILLIONS)
Nonmarketable:		
Government account series	$ 536.5	
U.S. savings bonds	106.2	
Foreign series	6.3	
Other	148.0	
Total Nonmarketable Debt		$ 797.0
Marketable:		
Bills	$ 398.4	
Notes	1089.6	
Bonds	299.9	
Other	15.0	
Total Marketable Debt		1802.9
Total Debt		$2599.9

SOURCE: *Treasury Bulletin*, Fall Issue, December 1988, p. 33.

government. Figure 12.3 shows a typical list of price quotations for certain types of debt securities that have been issued by the U.S. government. These securities are discussed next.

☐ 12.3.1 U.S. Treasury Bills

Treasury bills are issued on a discount basis, with maturities of up to 52 weeks and in denominations of $10,000 or more (although at times denominations as small as $1000 have been offered). All are issued in *book-entry form*, where the buyer receives a receipt at time of purchase and the bill's face value at maturity. Although Treasury bills are sold at discount, their

TABLE 12.3

Maturity Structure of Marketable Interest-Bearing U.S. Public Debt Held by Private Investors, September 1988.

MATURITY	AMOUNT (IN BILLIONS)	PERCENT OF TOTAL AMOUNT
Within 1 year	$ 524.2	33.7%
1–5 years	553.0	35.6
5–10 years	232.4	14.9
10–20 years	74.2	4.8
20 years and over	171.4	11.0
Total	$1555.2	100.0%

SOURCE: *Treasury Bulletin*, Fall Issue, December 1988.

TREASURY BONDS, NOTES & BILLS

Thursday, December 8, 1988

Representative Over-the-Counter quotations based on transactions of $1 million or more as of 4 p.m. Eastern time.

Hyphens in bid-and-asked and bid changes represent 32nds; 101-01 means 101 1/32. a-Plus 1/64. b-Yield to call date. d-Minus 1/64. k-Nonresident aliens exempt from withholding taxes. n-Treasury notes. p-Treasury note; nonresident aliens exempt from withholding taxes.

Source: Bloomberg Financial Markets

Treasury Bonds and Notes

Rate	Mat. Date		Bid	Asked	Bid Chg.	Yld.
10⅝	1988	Dec p	99-31	100-03		8.64
6¼	1988	Dec p	99-24	99-28		8.13
6⅛	1989	Jan p	99-19	99-23		7.93
14⅝	1989	Jan n	100-15	100-19	01	8.19
8	1989	Feb p	99-26	99-30	+01	8.14
6¼	1989	Feb p	99-14	99-18		8.10
11⅜	1989	Feb n	100-13	100-17	-01	8.16
11¼	1989	Mar p	100-23	100-27	01	8.26
6⅜	1989	Mar p	99-09	99-13	+01	8.25
7⅛	1989	Apr p	99-10	99-14	-01	8.54
14⅜	1989	Apr n	101-27	101-31	-01	8.39
6⅞	1989	May p	99-05	99-09		8.55
9¼	1989	May n	100-04	100-10	-01	8.45
8	1989	May p	99-19	99-23		8.60
11¾	1989	May n	101-06	101-10	-01	8.55
7⅜	1989	Jun p	99-06	99-10		8.64
9⅝	1989	Jun p	100-12	100-16	-01	8.67
7⅝	1989	Jul p	99-06	99-10	-01	8.72
14½	1989	Jul n	103-07	103-11	-02	8.62
7¾	1989	Aug p	99-05	99-09	-01	8.77
6⅝	1989	Aug p	98-15	98-19	01	8.76
13⅞	1989	Aug n	103-05	103-09	02	8.78
8½	1989	Sep k	99-18	99-22	02	8.88
9⅜	1989	Sep p	100-08	100-12		8.85
11⅞	1989	Oct n	102-08	102-12	-03	8.88
7⅞	1989	Oct p	99-01	99-05	01	8.86
6⅜	1989	Nov p	97-22	97-26	-01	8.86
10¾	1989	Nov n	101-16	101-20	-03	8.88
12¾	1989	Nov p	103-14	103-18	-02	8.68
7¾	1989	Nov p	98-27	98-31	01	8.87
7⅞	1989	Dec p	98-25	98-29	-02	8.97
8⅜	1989	Dec p	99-12	99-16	-01	8.87
7⅜	1990	Jan k	98-07	98-11	-01	8.91
10½	1990	Jan n	101-14	101-18	-03	8.96
3½	1990	Feb	94-15	95-01		7.97
6½	1990	Feb k	97-06	97-10	-05	8.93
7⅛	1990	Feb k	97-26	97-30	-02	8.92
11	1990	Feb p	102-04	102-08	-01	8.93
7¼	1990	Mar p	97-26	97-30	-02	8.94
7⅜	1990	Mar p	98-01	98-05	02	8.88
10½	1990	Apr n	101-26	101-30	-01	8.92
7⅝	1990	Apr p	98-05	98-09	-02	8.95
7⅞	1990	May k	98-14	98-18	-02	8.96
8¼	1990	May	99-06	99-12	-01	8.72
8⅛	1990	May p	98-24	98-28	-02	8.95
11⅜	1990	May p	103-02	103-06	-03	8.95
7¼	1990	Jun p	97-16	97-20		8.91
8	1990	Jun p	98-14	98-18	-02	9.00
10¾	1990	Jul n	102-14	102-18		8.98
8⅜	1990	Jul p	98-31	99-03	-02	8.97
7⅞	1990	Aug k	98-05	98-09	-03	8.98
9⅞	1990	Aug p	101-07	101-11	02	8.98
8⅞	1990	Nov p	99-24	99-28	-03	8.94
6⅝	1990	Dec p	95-17	95-21	-03	8.98
11¾	1991	Jan n	105-02	105-06	-05	8.97
7⅜	1991	Feb p	96-25	96-29	-04	8.96
9⅛	1991	Feb k	100-05	100-09	-03	8.97
6¾	1991	Mar p	95-09	95-13	03	8.99
12⅜	1991	Apr n	106-29	107-01	-03	8.97
8⅛	1991	May p	98-02	98-06	-02	8.97
14½	1991	May n	112-14	112-18	03	8.66
7⅞	1991	Jun n	97-12	97-16	-04	8.99
13¾	1991	Jul n	110-23	110-27	04	8.97
7½	1991	Aug p	96-12	96-16	-03	8.99
8¾	1991	Aug p	99-09	99-13	-02	8.99
14⅞	1991	Aug n	114-14	114-18	04	8.66
9⅛	1991	Sep k	100-04	100-08	04	9.01
12¼	1991	Oct p	107-29	108-01	05	8.98
6½	1991	Nov p	93-20	93-24	02	8.97
8½	1991	Nov p	98-20	98-24	-04	8.99
14¼	1991	Nov n	113-29	114-01	-02	8.72
8¼	1991	Dec k	97-29	98-01	04	9.00
11⅝	1992	Jan p	106-25	106-29	-01	9.01
6⅝	1992	Feb p	93-12	93-16	-02	9.01
14⅝	1992	Feb n	115-18	115-22	-05	8.85
7⅞	1992	Mar p	96-21	96-25	-05	9.01
11¾	1992	Apr	107-19	107-23	09	9.02
6⅝	1992	May k	93-01	93-05	-04	8.98
13¾	1992	May n	113-19	113-23	-07	9.01
8¼	1992	Jun p	97-18	97-22	05	9.02
10⅜	1992	Jul p	103-29	104-01	-06	9.03
4¼	1987-92	Aug	94-16	95-02	+01	5.75
7¼	1992	Aug	94-19	94-29	-07	8.90
8¼	1992	Aug p	97-16	97-20	-05	9.01
8¾	1992	Sep p	99-03	99-07	-05	8.99
9¾	1992	Oct p	102-08	102-12	-04	9.00
8⅜	1992	Nov p	97-26	97-30	-05	9.01
10½	1992	Nov n	104-21	104-25	-07	9.03
8¾	1993	Jan p	99	99-04	-07	9.01
4	1988-93	Feb	94-16	95-02	+01	5.33
6¾	1993	Feb	92-10	92-28	-07	8.82
7⅞	1993	Feb	96-09	96-14	-04	8.91
8¼	1993	Feb p	97-10	97-14	-05	8.99
10⅞	1993	Feb n	106-08	106-12	-07	9.00
7⅜	1993	Apr p	94-02	94-06	-07	9.02
7⅝	1993	May	94-30	95-02	06	9.00
10⅛	1993	May n	103-25	103-29	-07	9.03
7¼	1993	Jul p	93-12	93-16	-06	9.00
7½	1988-93	Aug	94 06	94 12	06	8.99
8⅝	1993	Aug	98-16	98-24	06	8.95
8¾	1993	Aug p	98-29	99-01	-06	8.99
11⅞	1993	Aug n	110-19	110-23	-05	9.01
9½	1994	Oct k	101-28	102	-08	9.05
10⅛	1994	Nov	104-31	105-03	-07	9.00
11⅝	1994	Nov	111-17	111-21	08	9.04
8⅝	1995	Jan p	97-31	98-03	-06	9.03
3	1995	Feb	94-16	95-02	+02	3.91
10½	1995	Feb	106-23	106-27	-07	9.03
11¼	1995	Feb p	110-03	110-07	-07	9.05
8⅜	1995	Apr p	96-22	96-26	-08	9.04
10⅜	1995	May	106-11	106-15	-07	9.02
11¼	1995	May p	110-13	110-17	-07	9.05
12⅝	1995	May	117-13	117-17	-07	8.98
8⅞	1995	Jul p	99-04	99-08	-07	9.03
10½	1995	Aug p	107-01	107-05	-06	9.04
8⅝	1995	Oct p	97-27	97-31	-07	9.03
9½	1995	Nov p	102-05	102-09	08	9.05
11½	1995	Nov	112-12	112-16	-07	9.03
8⅞	1996	Feb p	98-29	99-01	-09	9.06
7⅜	1996	May p	90-29	91-01	-08	9.06
7¼	1996	Nov p	89-25	89-29	-06	9.06
8⅝	1997	Aug k	97-11	97-15	-05	9.05
8½	1997	May k	96-24	96-28	02	9.04
8⅞	1997	Nov p	98-24	98-28	-07	9.06
8⅛	1998	Feb p	94-06	94-10	05	9.05
9	1998	May p	99-19	99-23	05	9.04
9¼	1998	Aug p	101-07	101-11	-03	9.04
7	1993-98	May	87-22	87-26	04	8.94
3½	1998	Nov	94-19	95-05	+04	4.10
8⅞	1998	Nov p	98-31	99-03	-04	9.01
8½	1994-99	May	96-02	96-06	-04	9.07
7⅞	1995-00	Feb	91-20	91-24	04	9.06
8⅜	1995-00	Aug	94-26	94-30	04	9.08
11¾	2001	Feb	119-17	119-23	-08	9.04
13⅛	2001	May	130-01	130-07	13	9.03
8	1996-01	Aug	93-03	93-09	+06	8.89
13⅜	2001	Aug	132-13	132-19	-04	9.01
15¾	2001	Nov	151-06	151-12	-04	8.96
14¼	2002	Feb	139-16	139-22	-04	9.03
11⅝	2002	Nov	120-09	120-15	+06	9.01
10¾	2003	Feb	113-14	113-20	+05	9.02
10¾	2003	May	113-13	113-19	+02	9.04
11⅛	2003	Aug	116-20	116-26	+06	9.03
11⅞	2003	Nov	122-25	122-31	+06	9.04
12⅜	2004	May	127-02	127-08	+05	9.06
13¾	2004	Aug	139-02	139-08	+05	9.02
11⅝	2004	Nov k	121-14	121-20	+07	9.04
8¼	2000-05	May	93-08	93-14	+04	9.02
12	2005	May k	124-22	124-28	+04	9.06
10¾	2005	Aug k	114-04	114-10	+04	9.07

U.S. Treas. Bills

Mat. date	Bid (Discount)	Asked (Discount)	Yield
-1988-			
12-15	3.26	2.24	2.27
12-22	7.81	7.74	7.87
12-29	6.76	6.49	6.60
-1989-			
1- 5	6.86	6.74	6.87
1-12	6.35	6.23	6.35
1-19	7.31	7.24	7.40
1-26	7.57	7.50	7.68
2- 2	7.71	7.67	7.87
2- 9	7.74	7.70	7.91
2-16	7.90	7.86	8.09
2-23	7.80	7.76	8.00
3- 2	7.92	7.88	8.14
3- 9	7.97	7.93	8.20
3-16	8.00	7.96	8.25
3-23	7.97	7.93	8.23
3-30	7.97	7.93	8.24
4- 6	8.02	7.98	8.31
4-13	8.06	8.02	8.36
4-20	8.18	8.14	8.51
4-27	8.04	8.00	8.37
5- 4	8.15	8.11	8.50
5-11	8.16	8.12	8.53
5-18	8.16	8.12	8.54
5-25	8.18	8.14	8.58
6- 1	8.19	8.15	8.60
6- 8	8.20	8.16	8.63
7 6	8.21	8.17	8.65
8- 3	8.22	8.18	8.68
8-31	8.24	8.20	8.73
9-28	8.28	8.24	8.81
10-26	8.27	8.23	8.84
11-24	8.24	8.20	8.85

FIGURE 12–3
Price quotations for U.S. Treasury securities.

SOURCE: Reprinted by the permission of *The Wall Street Journal*, © Dow Jones & Company, Inc. (December 9, 1988): p. C 17.

dollar yield (that is, the difference between the purchase price and face value if the bill is held to maturity) is treated as interest income for tax purposes.

Offerings of 13-week and 26-week bills are usually made once each week; 52-week bills are usually offered every fourth week. All are sold by auction. Bids may be entered on either a competitive or noncompetitive basis. With a competitive bid, the investor states a price he or she is willing to pay (which can be converted to the interest rate that would be earned if the bid is accepted). For example, an investor might enter a bid for a stated number of 13-week bills at a price of 98.512. If the bid is accepted, the investor will pay $9851.20 for each $10,000 of face value, meaning that an investment of $9851.20 will generate a receipt of $10,000 if held to maturity 13 weeks later. With a noncompetitive bid, the investor agrees to pay the average price of all bids that will be accepted by the Treasury.

Before each auction, the Treasury announces the total face value and the maturities of all bills that it plans to issue. At the auction itself, having received the bids, the Treasury accepts all noncompetitive bids. For example, if $6 billion of 13-week bills are to be issued, perhaps $2 billion of noncompetitive bids will have been received by the time of the auction. Since all these bids will be accepted, the Treasury will accept only $4 billion of competitive bids, taking the highest prices offered by competitive-bidding investors. The average price on the accepted competitive bids will be the price charged to the noncompetitive bidders.

Each Tuesday *The Wall Street Journal* publishes the results of the auction that took place on the previous day. Figure 12.4 presents the results of the auction that took place on December 5, 1988.

Individuals may purchase new issues of Treasury bills directly from one of the 12 Federal Reserve banks or indirectly via a bank or broker. Government security dealers maintain an active secondary market in bills, and it is a simple matter to buy or sell one prior to maturity (especially if the original purchase was through a bank or broker). Terms offered by government security dealers are reported daily in the financial press, stated on a bank discount basis. To determine the actual dollar prices, an investor needs to "undo" the bank discount computation.

For example, a bill with 120 days left to maturity might be listed as "7.48% bid, 7.19% ask." Both of these discounts were obtained by multiplying the actual discount by 360/120 (the inverse of the portion of a 360-day year

FIGURE 12–4

Treasury bill auction results for December 5, 1988.

SOURCE: Reprinted by the permission of *The Wall Street Journal,* © Dow Jones & Company, Inc. (December 6, 1988): p. C 21.

Rates are determined by the difference between the purchase price and face value. Thus, higher bidding narrows the investor's return while lower bidding widens it. The percentage rates are calculated on a 360-day year, while the coupon equivalent yield is based on a 365-day year.

	13-Week	26-Week
Applications	$29,137,460,000	$26,122,055,000
Accepted bids	$7,202,615,000	$7,206,855,000
Accepted at low price	97%	15%
Accepted noncompet'ly	$1,269,800,000	$1,082,880,000
Average price (Rate)	97.968 (8.04%)	95.829 (8.25%)
High price (Rate)	97.973 (8.02%)	95.839 (8.23%)
Low price (Rate)	97.968 (8.04%)	95.824 (8.26%)
Coupon equivalent	8.32%	8.73%

Both issues are dated Dec. 8. The 13-week bills mature March 9, 1989, and the 26-week bills mature June 8, 1989.

involved). Thus, to find the actual discount associated with the 7.48% bid, multiply 7.48% by 120/360, resulting in a figure of 2.493%. This means that the dealer is bidding 100% − 2.493% = 97.507% of face value, meaning the dealer is willing to pay $9750.70 for this $10,000 Treasury bill.

Similarly, the dealer is offering to sell such a bill at a discount of 100% − [7.19% × (120/360)] = 2.397%, meaning the dealer is willing to sell such a bill for $10,000 × (100% − 2.397%) = $9760.30. The difference between the prices—$9.60 = $9760.30 − $9750.70—is known as the *dealer's spread* and serves as compensation for carrying inventories of bills, taking associated risks, and bearing the clerical and other costs associated with being a market-maker.

In addition to the bid and asked discounts, *The Wall Street Journal* and other media provide an *equivalent yield* that is based on the asked price. In the example, the equivalent yield would be calculated by determining the dollar yield on the security ($10,000 − $9760.30 = $239.70) and then dividing this figure by the purchase price ($239.70/$9760.30 = 2.455%) in order to arrive at the rate of return associated with purchasing the security. Then, this rate of return is annualized by multiplying it by 365 and then dividing the product by the number of days until maturity. The resulting figure is the equivalent yield. In the example, the equivalent yield is 2.455% × (365/120) = 7.47%.

☐ 12.3.2 U.S. Treasury Notes

Treasury notes are issued with maturities from one to ten years and generally make coupon payments semiannually. Some, issued prior to 1983, are in *bearer* form, with coupons attached; the owner simply submits each coupon on its specified date to receive payment for the stated amount. Beginning in 1983, the Treasury ceased the issuance of bearer notes (and bonds). All issues since then are in *registered* form; the current owner is registered with the Treasury, which sends him or her each coupon payment when due and the principal value at maturity. When a registered note is sold, the new owner's name and address are substituted for those of the old owner on the Treasury's books.

Treasury notes are issued in denominations of $1000 or more. Coupon payments are set at an amount so the notes will initially sell close to par value. In most cases an auction is held, with both competitive and noncompetitive bids being submitted.

Treasury notes are traded in an active secondary market made by dealers in U.S. government securities. For example, as shown in Figure 12.3, *The Wall Street Journal* carried the following quotation:

RATE	MAT. DATE	BID	ASKED	BID CHG.	YIELD
10½	1992 Nov n	104-21	104-25	-07	9.03

This indicated that a note (n), maturing in November 1992, carried a coupon rate of 10½%. It could be sold to a dealer for $104^{21}/_{32}\%$ of par value, which

is equivalent to $1046.5625 per $1000 of par value. Alternatively, it could be purchased from a dealer for $104^{25}/_{32}\%$ of par value, which is equivalent to $1047.8125 per $1000 of par value (thus, the dealer's spread was equal to $1047.8125 − $1046.5625 = $1.25). On that day, the bid price was $^{7}/_{32}$ less than it had been on the previous trading day, resulting in a reported "Bid Chg." of -07 (note how numbers to the right of the hyphen are expressed in 32nds, reflecting an old tradition). The effective yield-to-maturity at the time, based on the asked price, was approximately 9.03% per year.[2]

In practice, the situation facing a potential buyer (or seller) is a little more complicated. The buyer is generally expected to pay the dealer not only the stated price ($1047.8125) but also any *accrued interest*. For example, if 122 days have elapsed since the last coupon payment and 61 days remain, then an amount equal to 122/(122 + 61) = $^{2}/_{3}$ of the semiannual coupon ($^{2}/_{3}$ × $52.50 = $35) is added to the stated purchase price to determine the total amount required (in this case, $35 + $1047.8125 = $1082.8125). Similarly, if an investor were to sell a note to the dealer, the dealer would pay the investor the stated bid price plus accrued interest (in this case, $1046.5625 + $35 = $1081.5625). This procedure is commonly followed with both government and corporate bonds.[3]

□ 12.3.3 **U.S. Treasury Bonds**

Treasury bonds have maturities greater than ten years at the time of issuance. Those issued prior to 1983 may be in either bearer or registered form; more recent issues will be in registered form. Denominations range from $1000 upward. Unlike Treasury notes, some Treasury bond issues have *call provisions* that allow them to be "called" during a specified period (usually the period begins five to ten years prior to maturity and ends at the maturity date). This means that at any scheduled coupon payment date during this period, the Treasury has the right to force the investor to sell the bonds back to the government at par value.

Callable issues can be identified in Figure 12.3 by noting which issues have a range of years given as the maturity date (this range of years indicates the call period). For example, the "4 1988–93" mature in 1993 but may be called beginning in 1988 (the "4" indicates the bonds have a coupon rate of 4%, paid semiannually).

For callable issues, the yield-to-maturity is calculated using the asked price. If this price is greater than par, then the yield-to-maturity is based on an assumption that the bond will be called at the earliest allowable date.

---

[2] As mentioned in Chapter 4, the yield-to-maturity on a bond is the discount rate that makes the present value of the future coupon payments and par value equal to its current market price (which in this case is the asked price).

[3] The procedure for calculating accrued interest on corporate bonds is different in that it is based on an assumption that there are 30 days in each month and 180 days in each semiannual period. Specifically, (1) the number of complete months left until the next coupon payment is determined and multiplied by 30; (2) the number of days left in the current month is determined and added to the previous figure; (3) the resulting figure is subtracted from 180, thereby giving the number of days that have elapsed since the last coupon payment; (4) this figure is divided by 180, giving the fraction of the period that has elapsed; and (5) this fraction is multiplied by the semiannual coupon, resulting in the amount of accrued interest.

Otherwise, Treasury bonds are comparable to Treasury notes, with dealers' bid and asked quotations being stated in the same form.

☐ 12.3.4 U.S. Savings Bonds

Nonmarketable U.S. savings bonds are offered only to individuals and selected organizations. No more than a specified amount (for example, $15,000 of issue price) may be purchased by any person in a single year. Two types are available. Series EE bonds are essentially pure-discount bonds, meaning that no interest is paid on them prior to maturity. The term-to-maturity at the date of issuance has varied from time to time; for bonds issued in 1988, it was 12 years. Series HH bonds mature in 10 years and pay interest semiannually. Both types are registered. Series EE bonds are available in small denominations (the smallest one has an issue price of $25) and may be purchased from commercial banks and many other financial institutions. Some employers even allow employees to obtain them through payroll savings plans. Series HH bonds are available only in exchange for eligible Series EE bonds (that is, a Series EE bond must be purchased first and then held for the minimum time period of six months before it can be exchanged) and can only be obtained from the Treasury Department or one of the 12 Federal Reserve banks.

Series EE bonds issued in 1988 utilize a floating rate with a minimum floor. If a bond is held for five or more years, interest is paid at a rate equal to (1) 85% of the average market return on Treasury bonds and notes with five years remaining to maturity or (2) 6% per year, whichever is larger. The applicable rate is computed and compounded every six months (in May and November). Should the bond be held for less than five years, a lower rate is used to determine the redemption value of the bond. Series HH bonds issued in 1988 provide a fixed anual rate of 6% and can be redeemed at any time for par value.

Unlike most other discount bonds, no taxes are paid on the interest as it accumulates semiannually on the Series EE bonds. Only when these bonds are redeemed is the interest subject to tax. Thus, a $15,000 investment that grows to $30,000 in 12 years will create a tax obligation only at the end of the twelfth year. Furthermore, should a Series EE bond be exchanged for a Series HH bond, this tax obligation on the interest earned on the Series EE bond can be deferred until the Series HH bond is redeemed.

The terms on which savings bonds are offered have been revised from time to time. In some cases, improved terms have been offered to holders of outstanding bonds. Terms have sometimes been inferior to those available on less well-known or less accessible instruments with similar characteristics. At such times, the Treasury Department sells savings bonds by appealing more to patriotism than to the desire for high return.

☐ 12.3.5 Zero-Coupon Treasury Security Receipts

A noncallable Treasury note or bond is, in effect, a portfolio of pure-discount bonds (or, equivalently, a portfolio of *zero-coupon bonds*). That is, each coupon

payment, as well as the principal, can be viewed as a bond unto itself; the investor who owns the bond can therefore be viewed as holding a number of individual pure-discount bonds. In 1982, a number of brokerage firms began separating these components, using a process known as *coupon stripping*.

With this process, Treasury bonds of a given issue are purchased and placed in trust with a custodian (for example, a bank). Sets of *receipts* are then issued, one set for each coupon date. For example, an August 15, 1997, receipt might entitle its holder to receive $1000 on that date (and nothing on any other date). The amount required to meet the payments on all the August 15, 1997, receipts would exactly equal the total amount received on that date from coupon payments on the Treasury securities held in the trust account.

In addition to issuing a set of receipts corresponding to coupon dates, another set of receipts would be issued that mature on the date the principal of the securities held in trust is due. Thus, holders of these receipts share in the principal payment.[4]

Three early examples were Lehman Brothers' Lehman Investment Opportunity Notes (LIONs), Merrill Lynch's Treasury Investment Growth Receipts (TIGRs), and Salomon Brothers' Certificates of Accrual on Treasury Securities (CATs). Not surprisingly, such securities are known in the trade as "animals."

Noting the favorable market reaction to the offering of these stripped securities, in 1985 the Treasury Department introduced a program for investors called Separate Trading of Registered Interest and Principal Securities (STRIPS). This program allows purchasers of certain coupon-bearing Treasury securities to keep whatever cash payments they want and to sell the rest.

Figure 12.5 shows typical market prices for a set of stripped Treasury securities (such as LIONs, TIGRs, CATs, and STRIPS), where price is expressed as a percent of maturity value. As the figure shows, the longer the investor has to wait until maturity, the lower the price of the security.

The Internal Revenue Service requires that taxes be paid annually on the accrued interest earned on such securities. That is, such securities are treated for tax purposes as *original issue discount securities* (OID securities), which are securities originally sold at a discount from par due to their relatively small coupon payments (such tax treatment is also generally applicable to OID securities issued by corporations).

For example, a TIGR that matures in two years for $1000 might be purchased currently for $900. Thus, the investor would earn $100 in interest over two years, realizing it when the TIGR matures. However, the IRS would make the investor pay taxes on a portion of the $100 each year. The amount to be recognized must be calculated on an "economic accrual" basis. This means that the investor cannot report $50 ($100/2) per year as interest income. Instead, first the yield needs to be calculated, which in this case is

---

[4] If the underlying Treasury security is callable, this set of receipts would provide the holders with all coupon payments received after the date of first call as well as the principal.

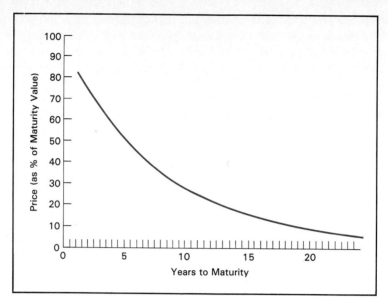

FIGURE 12–5
Typical market prices for a set of stripped Treasury securities.

$(\$1000/\$900)^{1/2} - 1 = 5.4\%$. This means that the implied value of the TIGR at the end of the first year would be $\$900 \times 1.054 = \$948.60$; thus, the amount of interest income to be recognized then is $\$948.60 - \$900 = \$48.60$. The amount of interest income to be recognized in the second year, assuming the TIGR is held to maturity, will be $\$1000 - \$948.60 = \$51.40$ (note that $\$1000 = \$948.60 \times 1.054$). Consequently, the investor has a cash outflow not only when purchasing the TIGR but also every year until it matures; only at that time does the investor experience a cash inflow. As a result, such securities are attractive primarily for tax-exempt investors and for investors in low tax brackets (for example, some people purchase them as investments that are held in the names of their children).

12.4   FEDERAL AGENCY SECURITIES

Although much of the federal government's activity is financed directly, via taxes and debt issued by the Treasury Department, a substantial amount is financed in other ways. In some situations, various government departments provide explicit or implicit backing for the securities of quasi-governmental agencies. In other situations, the federal government has guaranteed both the principal and coupon payments on bonds issued by certain private organizations. In both cases, some of the arrangements are so convoluted that cynics suggest that the original legislative intent was to obscure the nature and extent of governmental backing. In any event, a wide range of bonds with different degrees of government backing has been created in this manner. Many of the bonds are considered second in safety only to the debt obligations of the U.S. government itself.

TABLE 12.4

Debt Outstanding of Federal Agencies and Federally
Sponsored Agencies, December 1987.

DEBT OF FEDERAL AGENCIES	AMOUNT (IN MILLIONS)
Defense Department: Family Housing and Homeowner's Assistance	$ 13
Export-Import Bank	11,978
Federal Housing Administration	183
Government National Mortgage Association	1,615
Postal Service	6,103
Tennessee Valley Authority	18,089
Total	$ 37,981

DEBT OF FEDERALLY SPONSORED AGENCIES	AMOUNT (IN MILLIONS)
Federal Home Loan Banks	$115,725
Federal National Mortgage Association	97,057
Federal Home Loan Mortgage Corporation	17,645
Student Loan Marketing Association	16,503
Farm Credit System	55,275
Financing Corporation	1,200
Total	$303,405

SOURCE: *Federal Reserve Bulletin*, July 1988, p. A33.

Column 2 of Table 12.1 indicates the ownership of these securities. Major investors include thrift institutions, pension funds, and commercial banks. Table 12.4 lists the issuers of these securities and the amounts outstanding in December 1987. A partial list of typical price quotations is shown in Figure 12.6.

☐ 12.4.1 Bonds of Federal Agencies

Bonds issued by federal agencies provide funds for support of things such as housing (either through direct loans or the purchase of existing mortgages); export and import activities (via loans, credit guarantees, and insurance); the postal service; and the activities of the Tennessee Valley Authority. Many issues are guaranteed by the full faith and credit of the U.S. government, but some (for example, those of the Tennessee Valley Authority) are not.

☐ 12.4.2 Bonds of Federally Sponsored Agencies

Federally sponsored agencies are privately owned agencies that issue securities and use the proceeds to support the granting of certain types of loans to farmers, homeowners, and the like. A common procedure involves the creation of a series of governmental "banks," which buy securities issued by private organizations that grant the loans in the first instance. Some or all the initial capital for these banks may be provided by the government, but subsequent amounts typically come from bonds issued by the banks.

GOVERNMENT AGENCY ISSUES

Thursday, December 8, 1988
Mid-afternoon Over-the-Counter quotations usually based on large transactions, sometimes $1 million or more.
Hyphens in bid-and-asked represent 32nds; 101-01 means 101 1/32. a-Plus 1/64. b-Yield to call date. d-Minus 1/64.
Source: Bloomberg Financial Markets

FNMA Issues

Rate	Mat	Bid	Asked	Yld
11.25	12-88	99-31	100-02	3.55
11.75	12-88	99-30	100-02	4.02
11.10	1-89	100-03	100-07	8.17
11.60	2-89	100-11	100-15	8.47
12.10	3-89	100-17	100-25	8.68
7.55	4-89	99-12	99-18	8.78
9.30	6-89	100-04	100-08	8.78
9.50	6-89	100-09	100-12	8.73
8.00	7-89	99-09	99-19	8.70
10.05	8-89	100-15	100-25	8.78
13.13	8-89	102-17	102-25	8.71
12.10	10-89	102-11	102-17	8.86
12.75	10-89	102-29	103-02	8.83
9.85	11-89	100-21	100-27	8.86
11.80	11-89	102-11	102-17	8.85
16.00	11-89	106-11	106-15	8.76
11.30	12-89	101-26	102-04	9.04
6.50	12-89	97-12	97-18	9.09
11.45	1-90	102-05	102-15	9.00
11.05	2-90	102-01	102-08	8.97
8.65	3-90	99-13	99-17	9.03
7.35	4-90	97-23	98-03	8.88
10.30	5-90	101-14	101-20	9.04
11.15	5-90	102-16	102-26	8.98
9.85	7-90	101-02	101-07	9.00
10.00	9-90	101-12	101-18	9.00
10.15	10-90	101-21	101-27	9.02
7.00	11-90	96-09	96-15	9.03
10.90	11-90	102-29	103-07	9.03
8.40	12-90	98-25	98-31	8.97
11.80	12-90	104-23	105-01	9.00
8.75	1-91	99-13	99-19	8.96
8.38	1-91	98-19	98-25	9.02
6.90	2-91	95-17	95-27	9.04
7.65	2-91	97-17	97-23	8.82
12.00	3-91	105-27	106-05	8.91
12.50	3-91	106-27	107-05	8.93
7.20	4-91	96-05	96-11	8.96
8.00	4-91	97-27	98-01	8.94
7.45	5-91	96-07	96-13	9.13
8.55	6-91	98-19	98-29	9.05
7.65	7-91	96-19	96-29	9.01
8.70	8-91	98-29	99-07	9.03
8.40	8-91	98-03	98-13	9.08
7.00	9-91	95-07	95-11	8.94
7.80	10-91	96-29	97-03	8.98
7.38	10-91	95-17	95-27	9.06
9.55	11-91	100-19	100-29	9.18
11.75	12-91	107-01	107-11	8.91
8.50	1-92	98-01	98-11	9.12
7.00	3-92	94-07	94-13	9.02
12.00	4-92	108-17	108-23	8.91
8.45	5-92	98-01	98-07	9.06
8.50	5-92	98-03	98-09	9.09
7.05	6-92	93-31	94-09	8.99
10.13	6-92	102-29	103-07	9.03
8.45	7-92	97-23	98-01	9.10
9.15	9-92	99-27	100-01	9.13
10.60	10-92	104-05	104-15	9.19
9.88	12-92	102-15	102-25	9.03
10.90	1-93	106-01	106-11	9.01
7.95	2-93	95-17	95-27	9.17
7.90	3-93	95-09	95-19	9.17
10.95	3-93	105-31	106-09	9.13
7.55	4-93	94-01	94-07	9.19
10.88	4-93	105-17	105-27	9.20
10.75	5-93	105-03	105-13	9.23

Fed. Home Loan Bank

Rate	Mat	Bid	Asked	Yld
10.70	12-88	99-31	100-03	8.41
7.80	12-88	99-28	99-31	8.14
7.40	1-89	99-23	99-26	8.65
11.38	1-89	100-07	100-11	8.30
6.50	2-89	99-11	99-15	8.84
6.95	2-89	99-16	99-19	8.69
8.30	2-89	99-25	99-28	8.68
10.80	2-89	100-08	100-12	8.77
15.10	2-89	100-26	101-11	8.42
6.90	3-89	99-11	99-14	8.70
7.45	3-89	99-14	99-19	8.71
6.90	4-89	98-31	99-09	8.79
7.35	4-89	99-12	99-15	8.72
7.38	4-89	99-12	99-15	8.75
14.25	4-89	101-22	102	8.63
7.40	5-89	99-06	99-12	8.79
10.20	5-89	100-14	100-20	8.76
7.75	5-89	99-14	99-17	8.78
7.70	6-89	99-10	99-14	8.76
7.75	6-89	99-12	99-15	8.76
7.00	7-89	98-18	98-28	8.86
8.15	7-89	99-17	99-20	8.75
14.13	7-89	103-01	103-07	8.70
8.65	8-89	99-23	99-26	8.89
6.75	9-89	98-01	98-11	8.93
8.55	9-89	99-18	99-21	8.98
12.50	9-89	102-13	102-21	8.92
14.55	9-89	103-30	104-08	8.84
8.50	10-89	99-18	99-22	8.86
9.35	10-89	100-07	100-11	8.91
6.60	11-89	97-21	97-27	8.97
8.80	11-89	99-22	99-26	9.00
11.55	11-89	102-06	102-12	8.92
8.13	11-89	99	99-06	9.02
6.55	12-89	97-11	97-17	9.07
8.25	12-89	99-01	99-08	9.01
11.20	1-90	101-31	102-09	9.01
6.55	1-90	97-08	97-14	8.98
6.70	3-90	97-02	97-07	9.00
7.30	3-90	97-19	97-29	9.03
11.90	3-90	103-03	103-13	9.03
7.05	4-90	97-07	97-13	9.08
7.70	4-90	98-02	98-08	9.07
8.25	5-90	98-22	98-28	9.08
7.75	6-90	97-26	98-04	9.07
9.50	6-90	100-15	100-21	9.03
8.50	7-90	99-02	99-06	9.04
9.75	7-90	100-28	101-06	8.94
7.80	7-90	97-26	98-04	9.05
8.10	8-90	98-14	98-24	8.89
8.95	8-90	99-21	99-25	9.07
8.88	9-90	99-17	99-23	9.03
12.50	9-90	105-13	105-23	8.96
10.30	9-90	101-25	102-03	8.99
7.05	10-90	96-19	96-25	8.94
8.40	11-90	98-25	98-31	8.98
8.90	11-90	99-27	99-31	8.91
13.70	11-90	108-07	108-13	8.93
10.90	12-90	102-27	103-05	9.17

Rate	Mat	Bid	Asked	Yld
10.70	1-93	105-01	105-11	9.11
9.50	1-93	101-01	101-11	9.10
8.05	2-93	95-27	96-05	9.16
8.10	3-93	96-03	96-09	9.16
10.80	3-93	105-23	106-01	9.07
7.55	4-93	93-17	93-27	9.29
8.13	5-93	95-21	95-27	9.28
8.90	5-93	98-15	98-21	9.27
10.75	5-93	105-01	105-11	9.26
7.75	7-93	94-09	94-19	9.21
9.00	7-93	99-05	99-09	9.19
11.70	7-93	109-01	109-07	9.20
7.45	8-93	93-01	93-11	9.22
9.38	8-93	99-31	100-09	9.24
11.95	8-93	109-17	109-27	9.31
7.95	9-93	94-29	95-03	9.23
7.88	10-93	94-19	94-25	9.22
8.80	10-93	98-05	98-09	9.24
7.38	11-93	92-13	92-23	9.24
9.13	11-93	99-15	99-21	9.21
7.38	12-93	92-13	92-19	9.24
12.15	12-93	111-17	111-23	9.19
7.30	1-94	92-02	92-08	9.23
7.45	2-94	92-18	92-24	9.23
12.00	2-94	111-18	111-24	9.11
8.50	4-94	97-07	97-25	9.03
8.88	6-95	97-27	97-31	9.29

Student Loan Marketing

Rate	Mat	Bid	Asked	Yld
8.00	6-89	99-16	99-20	8.68
7.90	7-89	99-13	99-17	8.73
12.85	9-89	102-18	102-24	8.82
13.15	9-90	102-25	102-31	8.80
10.90	2-90	102-01	102-05	8.97
6.95	8-90	96-15	96-25	9.03
7.90	9-90	97-26	98-04	9.05
8.45	12-90	99-29	99-03	8.96

Federal Land Bank

Rate	Mat	Bid	Asked	Yld
8.20	1-90	98-30	99-04	9.02
7.95	4-91	97-15	97-25	9.00
7.95	10-96	92	92-10	9.35
7.35	1-97	88-23	89-01	9.30

GNMA Issues

Rate	Mat	Bid	Asked	Yld (Bond)
8.00		88-14	88-18	9.84
8.50		91-12	91-16	9.90
9.00		94-05	94-09	9.99
9.50		96-31	97-03	10.08
10.00		99-26	99-30	10.16
10.50		102-04	102-08	10.32
11.00		104-07	104-11	10.51
11.50		105-27	105-31	10.76
12.00		107-06	107-10	11.06
12.50		108-16	108-22	11.34
13.00		109-26	110	11.63
13.50		111-18	111-24	11.85

Federal Farm Credit

Rate	Mat	Bid	Asked	Yld
7.75	1-89	99-27	99-30	8.41
8.15	1-89	99-29	100	8.03
8.75	1-89	99-29	100	8.47
11.65	1-89	100-08	100-12	8.19
13.05	1-89	100-14	100-18	8.01
8.20	2-89	99-27	99-30	8.56
8.35	2-89	99-27	99-30	8.53
6.88	3-89	99-14	99-17	8.81
8.60	3-89	99-27	99-30	8.68
8.65	3-89	99-28	100	8.63
8.45	4-89	99-26	99-29	8.62
12.50	4-89	101-06	101-09	8.72
8.30	5-89	99-22	99-26	8.72
7.35	6-89	99-06	99-09	8.90
7.90	6-89	99-15	99-18	8.84
8.85	6-89	99-28	100	8.83
13.70	7-89	102-22	102-30	8.64
8.38	8-89	99-19	99-22	8.85
8.75	9-89	99-24	99-27	8.94

Financial Assistance

Rate	Mat	Bid	Asked	Yld
9.38	7-03	100-27	100-31	9.25
9.45	11-03	100-09	100-13	9.39

Financing Corp

Rate	Mat	Bid	Asked	Yld
10.70	10-17	109-30	110-08	9.64
9.80	11-17	101-10	101-16	9.64
9.40	2-18	97-11	97-21	9.64
9.80	4-18	101-09	101-15	9.65
10.35	8-18	106-21	106-25	9.65
9.65	11-18	100-01	100-05	9.63
9.90	12-18			0.00

World Bank Bonds

Rate	Mat	Bid	Asked	Yld
15.00	12-88	100	100-16	9.27
11.00	10-89	101-12	101-28	9.21
4.50	2-90	95-01	95-17	9.03
5.38	7-91	91-29	92-05	8.94
16.63	11-91	118-15	118-31	9.17
15.13	12-91	115-10	115-26	9.23
5.38	4-92	88-31	89-15	9.28
14.75	6-92	115-15	115-31	9.41
13.63	9-92	112-13	112-29	9.56
10.90	3-93	105-02	105-18	9.43
10.38	5-93	102-16	103	9.66
5.88	9-93	86-19	87-03	9.43
6.50	3-94	89-08	89-24	9.10
6.38	10-94	87-27	88-11	9.10
11.63	12-94	110-06	110-21	9.37
8.63	8-95	97	97-24	9.24
8.13	8-96	93-31	94-23	9.24
9.88	10-97	102-27	103-03	9.39
9.35	12-00	98-23	99-15	9.53
8.85	7-01	94-23	95-02	9.58
8.38	12-01	92-08	92-20	9.42
8.25	5-02	91-06	91-17	9.42
8.35	8-02	91-28	92-07	9.42
12.38	10-02	121-21	122-21	9.52
8.25	9-16	87-15	87-26	9.54
8.63	10-16	91-03	91-15	9.54
9.25	7-17	97-02	97-17	9.55
8.88	3-26	93-07	93-22	9.54

FIGURE 12–6

Price quotations for government agency issues (excerpts).

SOURCE: Reprinted by the permission of The Wall Street Journal, © Dow Jones & Company, Inc. (December 9, 1988): p. C 17.

Although the debts of agencies of this type are usually not guaranteed by the federal government, governmental control is designed to insure that each debt issue is backed by extremely safe assets (for example, mortgages insured by another quasi-governmental agency). Moreover, it is generally presumed that governmental assistance of one sort or another would be provided if there were any danger of default on such debt.

As shown in Table 12.4, there are six federally sponsored agencies. Federal Home Loan Banks make loans to thrift institutions (primarily savings and loan associations). The Federal National Mortgage Association (FNMA, or "Fannie Mae") purchases and sells real estage mortgages—not only those insured by the Federal Housing Administration or guaranteed by the Veterans Administration but also conventional mortgages. The Federal Home Loan Mortgage Corporation ("Freddie Mac") deals only in conventional mortgages. The Student Loan Marketing Association ("Sallie Mae") purchases federally guaranteed loans made to students by other lenders (for example, commercial banks) and may make direct student loans under special circumstances. The Farm Credit System consists of 37 Farm Credit Banks that lend to farmers as well as farm associations and cooperatives. The last type of sponsored agency is the Financing Corporation, established in August 1987 to recapitalize FSLIC.

□ **12.4.3   Participation Certificates**

To support credit for export and import operations as well as home purchases, the government has authorized the issuance of *participation certificates*. A group of assets (for example, mortgages) is placed in a pool, and certificates representing ownership of those assets are issued to pay for them. The holders of the certificates receive the interest and principal payments as they are made, minus a small service charge. The most important certificates of this type are those issued by the *Government National Mortgage Association* (GNMA, or "Ginnie Mae"), known as GNMA modified pass-through securities. These securities are guaranteed by GNMA and backed by the full faith and credit of the U.S. government.

GNMA pass-through securities are created by certain private organizations (such as savings and loans and mortgage bankers) that bundle a package of similar (in terms of maturity date and interest rate) mortgages together. These mortgages must be individually guaranteed by either the Federal Housing Administration or the Veterans Administration (thus making them free from default risk) and have, in aggregate, a principal amount of at least $1 million. Having bundled these mortgages together, an application is made to GNMA for a guarantee on the pass-through securities that each represent $25,000 worth of principal. Once the guarantee is received, the securities are sold to the public through brokers. The interest rate paid on the securities is .5% less than the interest rate paid on the mortgages, with GNMA keeping .1% and the creator .4%.

Unlike most bonds, GNMA pass-through securities pay investors on a monthly basis an amount of money that represents both a pro rata return

of principal and interest on the underlying mortgages. For example, a holder of a $25,000 certificate from a $1 million pool would indirectly "own" 2.5% of each mortgage in the pool. Each month the homeowners make mortgage payments that consist of part principal and part interest. In turn, each month the investor receives 2.5% of the aggregate amount paid by the homeowners. Because the mortgages are free from default risk, there is no default risk on the pass-through securities (if homeowner payments are late, GNMA will borrow money from the Treasury to make sure that the investors are paid in a timely fashion).

There is one particular risk to investors, however, that arises because homeowners are allowed to prepay their mortgages. This prepayment allowance means that the pass-through securities, although initially having a stated life of 30 years, may actually have a much shorter life. This can cause losses if the investor buys an existing pass-through that is selling at a premium, a situation that can happen if interest rates have fallen since the time the pass-through security was created. In such a situation, homeowners may start to prepay their mortgages, meaning that the investor will receive par value on the security shortly after paying a premium for it, thereby causing the investor to incur a loss.

Consider a pass-through security of $25,000, initially issued with a stated interest rate of 14%. Suppose that interest rates subsequently fall so that new pass-throughs carry a stated rate of 12%. At this time, the older pass-through security has $20,000 of principal outstanding, but as a consequence of the fall in interest rates it is selling for a premium, perhaps $22,000. Now suppose that interest rates fall further, to 10%. At this point, many homeowners prepay their mortgages in order to refinance them at the current rate of 10%. As a result, an investor who purchased the older pass-through security for $22,000 ends up shortly thereafter receiving $20,000, thereby losing $2000.

Nevertheless, the interest the public has shown in GNMA pass-through securities has caused a number of similar securities to be created. One, issued in denominations of $100,000 or more, is the "guaranteed mortgage certificate" sold by the Federal Home Loan Mortgage Corporation, a federally sponsored agency that was mentioned earlier. A number of banks have offered similar pass-through mortgage certificates backed by private insurance companies. Some of them have repackaged the cash flows that are paid by the homeowners so that investors can receive something other than a pro rata share of them. Examples include collateralized mortgage obligations (CMOs) and real estate mortgage investment conduits (REMICs).

12.5 STATE AND LOCAL GOVERNMENT SECURITIES

The 1982 Census of Governments showed that there were 82,340 governmental units in the United States in addition to the federal government itself: [5]

---

[5] *1987 Statistical Abstract of the United States*, Table 426, p. 249.

50	states
3,041	counties
19,076	municipalities
16,734	townships
28,588	special districts
14,851	school districts
82,340	total governmental units

A great many of these units borrow money, with their securities called *municipal bonds*, or simply "municipals" (only the securities of the U.S. government are referred to as "governments"). Table 12.5 provides estimates of the amounts of various types of fixed-income securities outstanding at the end of 1987. With approximately $776.3 billion in value, municipals clearly warrant attention.

☐ 12.5.1 Issuing Agencies

Table 12.6 shows the dollar values of municipal bonds issued in 1987 by various issuing agencies, and Table 12.7 shows the purposes for the issuance of such debt. States generally issue debt to finance capital expenditures, primarily for highways, housing, and education.[6] The concept behind the issuance of such debt is that the revenue generated by the resulting facilities will be used to make the required debt payments. In some cases, the link is direct (for example, tolls may be used to pay for a bridge); in other cases somewhat indirect (for example, gasoline taxes may be used to pay for highway construction); or very indirect (for example, state sales taxes or income taxes may be used to pay for the construction of new government buildings).

States cannot be sued without their consent. Thus, bondholders may have no legal recourse in the event of default. This means that state-issued bonds that are dependent on particular revenues from some capital project

TABLE 12.5

Estimated Amounts of Various Fixed-Income Securities Outstanding, December 1987.

TYPE OF SECURITY	AMOUNT (IN BILLIONS)
Privately held federal debt	$2627.5
Corporate and foreign	1101.5
Tax-exempt notes and bonds	776.3
Total	$4505.3

SOURCE: Adapted from Salomon Brothers Inc., *Prospects for Financial Markets in 1988*, 1987.

---

[6] In some cases, no capital expenditure is involved (for example, the proceeds from the debt issue may be used for the payment of a veterans' bonus).

TABLE 12.6

New Security Issues of State and Local Governments in 1987, Classified by Issuer.

ISSUER	AMOUNT (IN BILLIONS)
States	$ 8.4
Special districts and statutory authorities	61.7
Municipalities, counties, and townships	24.9
Total	$95.0

SOURCE: *Federal Reserve Bulletin*, April 1988, p. A34.

may involve considerable risk. However, bonds backed by the "full faith and credit" of a state government are generally considered quite safe in spite of the inability of the bondholders to sue. This is because it is anticipated that state legislatures will do whatever is necessary to see that such bonds are paid off in a timely manner.

Unlike state governments, local governments can be sued against their will, making it possible for bondholders to force officials to collect whatever amount that is needed in order to meet required debt payments. In many cases, only revenues from specific projects can be used (for example, the tolls collected on a particular expressway). In other cases, collections from a particular tax may be used, although possibly only up to some statutory limit.

Some local governments (for example, Cleveland in 1978–1979) have defaulted on their debts and others (for example, New York City in 1975) have "restructured" their debt, giving holders new certificates offering lower or deferred interest and longer maturities in exchange for currently outstanding certificates.

Counties and municipalities are familiar to most people, but other forms of local government also exist. Examples include school districts as well as other districts and authorities that have been created to finance and operate seaports, airports, and the like. All are created by state charter and may be

TABLE 12.7

New Security Issues of State and Local Governments in 1987, Classified by Purpose.

PURPOSE	AMOUNT (IN BILLIONS)
Education	$ 9.2
Transportation	3.6
Utilities and conservation	7.3
Social welfare	9.6
Industrial aid	6.1
Other	17.9
Refunding	41.3
Total	$95.0

SOURCE: *Federal Reserve Bulletin*, April 1988, p. A34.

granted monopoly powers as well as rights to collect certain types of taxes. However, limits are often placed on the amount of taxes collected, the tax rate charged, and the amount (or type) of debt issued.

The primary source of funding for such agencies is the property tax. Since a given property may be liable for taxes levied by several agencies (such as a city, a county, a school district, a port authority, and a sewer district), the risk of an agency's bonds may depend on both the value of property subject to its taxes and the amount of other debt dependent on the same property.

□ 12.5.2 Types of Municipal Bonds

In 1987, new municipal bonds with a par value of $95.0 billion were issued. Of this total, $29.6 billion were general obligation bonds (G.O.s) and $65.4 billion were revenue bonds.[7]

General obligation bonds are backed by the full faith and credit (and thus the full taxing power) of the issuing agency. Most are issued by agencies with unlimited taxing power, although in a minority of cases the issuer is subject to limits on the amount of taxes or the tax rate (or both).

Revenue bonds are backed by revenues from a designated project, authority, or agency or by the proceeds from a specific tax. In many cases, such bonds are issued by agencies that hope to sell their services, pay the required expenses, and have enough left over to meet required payments on outstanding debt. Except for the possible granting of monopoly powers, the authorizing state and local government may provide no further assistance to the issuer. Such bonds are only as creditworthy as the enterprise associated with the issuer.

Many revenue bonds are issued to finance capital expenditures for publicly owned utilities (for example, water, electricity, or gas). Others are issued to finance quasi-utility operations (for example, public transportation). Some are financed by special assessments levied on properties benefiting from the original expenditure (for example, those connected to a new sewer system). *Industrial development bonds* (IDBs) are used to finance the purchase or construction of industrial facilities that are to be leased to firms on a favorable basis. In effect, such bonds provide cheap financing to businesses choosing to locate in the geographical area of the issuer.

Although most municipal financing involves the issuance of long-term securities, there are a number of different types of short-term securities that have been issued in order to meet short-term demands for cash. Traditionally used types include tax anticipation notes (TANs), revenue anticipation notes (RANs), grant anticipation notes (GANs), and tax and revenue anticipation notes (TRANs). In each case, the name of the security refers to the source of repayment. Thus, some can be classified as general obligation securities and others as revenue securities.

More recently, municipalities have started to issue two other kinds of

---

[7] *Federal Reserve Bulletin*, April 1988, p. A34.

short-term securities. *Tax-exempt commercial paper* is similar to corporate commercial paper, having a fixed interest rate and a maturity typically within 270 days. *Variable-rate demand obligations* have an interest rate that changes periodically (perhaps weekly) as some prespecified market interest rate changes. Furthermore, they can be redeemed at the desire of the investor within a prespecified number of days after giving notice to the issuer (for example, seven days after notification of intent).

□ **12.5.3 Tax Treatment**

Through a reciprocal arrangement (actually, it is based on the Constitution) with the federal government, coupon payments on state and local government securities are exempt from federal taxation, and coupon payments on Treasury and agency (except FNMA) securities are exempt from state and local taxation. Similar tax treatment is accorded to short-term and long-term issues that are pure-discount securities.

However, a different tax treatment is generally given to coupon-bearing securities that were issued at par value but were subsequently bought at a discount in the marketplace. Such securities provide the investor with income not only from the coupons but also from the difference between the purchase price and the par value. Unlike the coupons, which are tax-exempt, this difference is treated as taxable interest income. The taxpayer can elect to recognize a portion of the difference as income each year that the security is held (the portion can be either an equal dollar amount each year or an amount based on "economic accrual" that was mentioned earlier in the discussion of stripped securities) and pay ordinary income taxes on that amount. Alternatively, the investor can wait until the security matures and then pay ordinary income taxes on the entire difference (if the security is sold, then the tax would be based on the difference between the selling and purchase price).

Another interesting tax feature of municipals is that if the investor resides in the state of the issuer, then he or she is generally exempt not only from paying federal taxes on the coupon payments but also from paying state taxes. Furthermore, if the investor resides in a city with an income tax and purchases municipals issued by the city, then he or she may also be exempt from paying city taxes on the coupon payments. Thus, a resident of New York City who purchases a municipal security issued by the city (or one of its political subdivisions) will not have to pay federal, state, or city income taxes on the coupon payments. However, if a New York City resident were to purchase a California municipal, then both New York state and New York City income taxes would have to be paid on the coupon payments. Although state and city income taxes are at much lower rates than those of the federal government, this feature nevertheless tends to make local issues more advantageous from an after-tax return viewpoint (an advantage that is offset to a certain degree by the resulting lack of diversification).

The avoidance of federal income tax on interest earned on a municipal bond has made such a security attractive to wealthy individual investors as

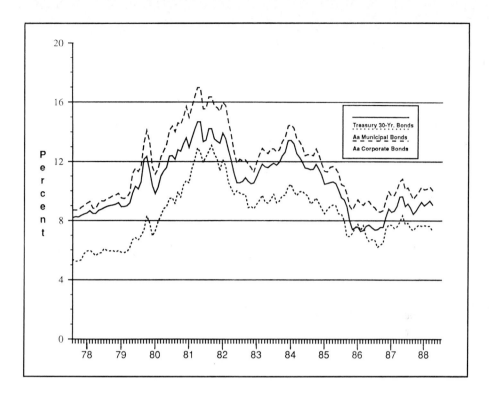

FIGURE 12–7
Average yields of long-term fixed-income securities (monthly averages).

SOURCE: *Treasury Bulletin*, Fall Issue (December 1988): p. 62.

well as corporate investors. As shown in Figure 12.7, this has resulted in municipal securities having yields that are considerably lower than those on taxable securities.[8] Consequently, this has lowered the cost of financing to the municipal issuer and suggests that a federal subsidy has been provided to the issuer.

Over the years, this subsidy has been used to support activities deemed worthy of encouragement (even though the encouragement is somewhat hidden). For example, private universities may issue tax-exempt bonds to finance certain types of improvements and private firms may do so to finance certain pollution-reducing activities. Such bonds are generally backed only by the resources of the issuer, with government involvement limited to the granting of favorable tax treatment. The Tax Reform Act of 1986 has greatly restricted the granting of such tax treatment, leading to the emergence of *taxable municipals* that typically are issued to finance things that are not viewed as essential under the tax law.

---

[8] As noted in Chapter 10 (see Figure 10.3), the yields on municipal bonds have historically been 20% to 40% below the yields of similar taxable bonds.

TABLE 12.8

Estimated Ownership of State and Local Securities,
December 1987.

OWNER	DOLLAR AMOUNT (IN BILLIONS)	PERCENT OF TOTAL AMOUNT
Thrift institutions	$ 3.2	0.4%
Life insurance companies	15.4	2.0
Property and liability insurance companies	98.2	12.6
Public and private noninsured pension funds	0.6	0.1
Investment companies	248.1	32.0
Securities brokers and dealers	0.8	0.1
Commercial banks	172.4	22.2
Nonfinancial corporations	9.6	1.2
Residual: Households direct	228.0	29.4
Total	$776.3	100.0%

SOURCE: Adapted from Salomon Brothers Inc., *Prospects for Financial Markets in 1988*, 1987.

☐ **12.5.4 Ownership of Municipal Securities**

Table 12.8 provides estimates of the ownership of municipal securities at the end of 1987. Since interest on most municipal securities is exempt from income taxes for both individual and corporate investors, such securities are particularly attractive to individual investors, either directly ("households direct") or indirectly ("investment companies") as well as corporate investors, especially commercial banks.

☐ **12.5.5 The Market for Municipal Bonds**

Municipals are usually issued as *serial bonds*, where one prespecified group matures a year after issue, another two years after issue, another three years after, and so on. Alternatively, *term bonds* (that is, bonds that all mature on the same date) or a mixture of serial and term bonds may be issued. The overall package is generally offered by the issuer on a competitive basis to various underwriters. The winning bidder then reoffers the individual bonds, either publicly or via a *private placement*.

Unlike corporate bonds, municipal bonds do not need to be registered with the Securities and Exchange Commission (SEC) before public issuance. Indeed, the federal government leaves most regulation in this market to state and local authorities.

Municipal bonds may be callable at specified dates and prices. Occasionally, the issuing authority is obligated to make designated payments into a *sinking fund*, which is used to buy similar bonds (or perhaps even its own bonds). As the issuing authority's bonds mature, the money for paying them off will come from having the sinking fund sell some of its holdings.

A secondary market in municipal bonds is made by various dealers. However, the relatively small amounts of particular issues and maturities

outstanding limit the size of the market. Many individuals who invest in municipals simply buy new issues and hold them to maturity.

☐ 12.5.6 Municipal Bond Insurance

An investor concerned about possible default of a municipal bond can purchase an insurance policy to cover any losses that would be incurred if coupons or principal are not paid in full and on time.

Some issues are insured at the time of initial offering. Alternatively, an investor can contract with a company to have a specific portfolio of bonds insured. The cost of the insurance will depend on the bonds included and their ratings.

12.6 EUROBONDS

Owing in part to government restrictions on investment in foreign securities, a number of borrowers have found it advantageous to sell securities in other countries. The term *Eurobond* is loosely applied to bonds that are offered outside the country of the borrower and usually outside the country in whose currency the securities are denominated. Thus, a bond issued by a U.S. corporation that is denominated in Japanese yen and sold in Germany and Switzerland would be referred to as a Eurobond.[9]

Since the Eurobond market is neither regulated nor taxed, it offers substantial advantages for many issuers and buyers of bonds. For example, a foreign subsidiary of a U.S. corporation may issue a Eurobond in "bearer" form. No tax is withheld by the corporation, and the tax paid by the purchaser (if any) depends on his or her country of residence. Because of tax reasons, interest rates on Eurobonds tend to be somewhat lower than those of domestic bonds denominated in the same currency.

12.7 CORPORATE BONDS

Corporate bonds are similar to other kinds of fixed-income securities in that they promise to make specified payments at specified times and provide legal remedies in the event of default. Restrictions are often placed on the activities of the issuing corporation in order to provide additional protection for bondholders (for example, there may be restrictions on the amount of additional bonds that can be issued in the future).

Corporate bonds that are pure-discount securities, meaning that they do not provide the investor with coupon payments, generally have the dis-

---

[9] In contrast, a *foreign bond* is a bond that is offered outside the country of the borrower and inside the country in whose currency it is denominated. Thus, a bond issued by a U.S. corporation that is denominated in yen and sold in Japan would be referred to as a foreign bond (in this case, a "samurai bond"). For more on international bond markets (as well as Eurocurrency markets), see J. Orlin Grabbe, *International Financial Markets* (New York: Elsevier Science, 1986).

count taxed as ordinary income by the federal government. The method of taxation is the same as the method for stripped Treasury bonds that was mentioned earlier—namely, a portion of the discount must be recognized as income each year that the security is held, thereby causing the investor to have to pay taxes on that amount.

For corporate bonds carrying coupon payments, the coupon is taxed as income each year. Furthermore, if the bond was originally sold at par but later bought at a discount in the marketplace, then the investor generally has to pay ordinary income taxes on both the coupon payments and the discount. However, the taxes on the discount can be deferred until the bond matures or is sold, if the investor so desires. Otherwise, the investor can recognize a portion of the discount as income each year the bond is held and pay taxes on it. If the investor chooses to do this, then he or she can either take equal portions of the discount each year or take an increasing amount each year (the "economic accrual" method).[10]

From the viewpoint of the issuing corporation, debt differs from equity in two crucial respects. First, principal and interest payments are obligatory. Failure to make any payment in full and on time can expose the issuer to expensive, time-consuming, and potentially disruptive legal actions. Second, unlike dividend payments, interest payments are considered expenses to the corporation, and hence can be deducted from earnings before calculating the corporation's income tax liability. As a result, each dollar paid in interest reduces earnings before taxes by a dollar, thereby reducing corporate taxes by 34¢ for a firm in the 34% marginal tax bracket. This leads to less than a dollar decline in earnings after taxes (in the 34% tax bracket example, the decline in earnings is 66¢).

☐ 12.7.1 The Indenture

An issue of bonds is generally covered by a *bond indenture*, in which the issuing corporation promises a specified *trustee* that it will comply with a number of stated provisions. Chief among these is the timely payment of required coupons and principal on the issue. Other terms are often included to control the sale of pledged property, the issuance of other bonds, and the like.

The trustee for a bond issue, usually a bank or trust company, acts on behalf of the bondholders. Some actions may be required by the indenture, whereas others may be done at the trustee's discretion, such as acting in response to a request from some specific bondholders.

If the corporation defaults on an interest payment, after a relatively short period of time (perhaps one to six months) the entire principal typically becomes due and payable—a procedure designed to enhance the bondholders' status in any forthcoming bankruptcy or related legal proceedings.

---

[10] The taxation of securities in general and bonds in particular is a complex matter, with many exceptions and alternative procedures. Any investor would be well advised to check carefully beforehand to be certain of the method of taxation involved for any security being considered for purchase.

An exhaustive list of the names used to describe bonds would be intolerably long. Different names are often used for the same type of bond, and occasionally the same name will be used for two quite different bonds. A few major types do predominate, however, with relatively standard nomenclature.

Mortgage Bonds. Bonds of this type represent debt that is secured by the pledge of specific property. In the event of default, the bondholders are entitled to obtain the property in question and sell it to satisfy their claims on the firm. In addition to the property itself, the holders of mortgage bonds have an unsecured claim on the corporation.

Mortgage bondholders are usually protected by a number of terms included in the bond indenture. The corporation may be constrained from pledging property for other bonds (or such bonds, if issued, must be "junior," or "second," mortgages, with a claim on the property only after the first mortgage is satisfied). Certain property acquired by the corporation after the bonds were issued may also be pledged to support the bonds.

Collateral Trust Bonds. These bonds are backed by other securities that are usually held by the trustee. A common situation of this sort arises when the securities of a subsidiary firm are pledged as collateral by the parent firm.

Equipment Obligations. Known also as equipment trust certificates, these securities are backed by specific pieces of equipment (for example, railroad cars and commercial aircraft). If necessary, the equipment can be readily sold and delivered to a new owner. The legal arrangements used to facilitate the issuance of such bonds can be very complex. The most popular procedure uses the *Philadelphia plan*, in which the trustee initially holds the equipment and issues obligations and then leases the equipment to a corporation. Money received from the lessee is subsequently used to make interest and principal payments to the holders of the obligations; ultimately, if all payments are made on schedule, the leasing corporation takes title to the equipment.

Debentures. These are general obligations of the issuing corporation and thus represent unsecured credit. To protect the holders of such bonds, the indenture will usually limit the future issuance of secured debt as well as any additional unsecured debt.

Subordinated Debentures. When more than one issue of debentures is outstanding, a hierarchy may be specified. For example, subordinated debentures are junior to unsubordinated debentures, meaning that in the event of bankruptcy, junior claims are to be considered only after senior claims have been fully satisfied.

Other Types of Bonds. *Income bonds* are more like preferred stock (described in a later section) than bonds. Payment of interest in full and on schedule is not absolutely required, and failure to do so need not send the corporation into bankruptcy. Interest on such bonds may or may not qualify as a tax deductible expense for the issuing corporation. This type of bond is rarely used, except in reorganizations of bankrupt railroads.

Guaranteed bonds are issued by one corporation but backed in some way by another (for example, by a parent firm). *Participation bonds* require stated interest payments and provide additional amounts if earnings exceed some stated level. *Voting bonds*, unlike regular bonds, give the holders some voice in management. *Serial bonds*, with different portions of the issue maturing at different dates, are sometimes used by corporations for equipment financing.

Convertible bonds may, at the holder's option, be exchanged for other securities, often common stock. Such bonds, which have become very popular in recent years, are discussed in more detail in Chapter 18.

□ 12.7.3 Call Provisions

Management would like to have the right to pay off the corporation's bonds at par at any time prior to maturity. This would provide desirable flexibility, since debt could be reduced or its maturity could be altered via such refunding. Most important, expensive high-coupon debt that was issued during a time of high interest rates could be replaced with cheaper low-coupon debt if rates decline.

Not surprisingly, investors hold quite a different opinion on the matter. The issuer's ability to redeem an issue at par at any time virtually precludes a rise in price over par and robs the holder of potential gains from price appreciation associated with declining interest rates; moreover, it introduces a new form of uncertainty. A bond with such a feature will almost certainly sell for less than one without it.

Despite the cost of obtaining this sort of flexibility, many corporations include *call provisions* in their bond indentures that give the corporation the option to call some or all of the bonds from their holders at stated prices during specified periods prior to maturity. In a sense, the firm sells a bond and simultaneously buys an option from the holders. The net price of the bond is thus the difference between the value of the bond and the option. (Interestingly, some recent corporate issues have given the investor the option of forcing the issuer to call the security.)

Investors are usually given some *call protection*: During the first few years after being issued, a bond may not be callable. Later, when the bond is callable, a *call premium* may be specified in the call provision. Such a premium indicates that if the issue is called, the issuer must pay the bondholders a *call price* that is a stated amount above par. Often, the amount above par becomes smaller as time passes and the maturity date approaches.

An entire issue may be called, or only specific bonds that are chosen

randomly by the trustee may be called. In either case, *a notice of redemption* will appear in advance in the financial press.

12.7.4 Sinking Funds

A bond indenture will often require the issuing corporation to make annual payments into a *sinking fund*. The idea is to pay part of the principal of the debt (as well as the interest) each year, thereby reducing the amount outstanding at maturity.

Sinking funds operate by having the corporation transmit cash to the trustee, who can then purchase bonds in the open market. Alternatively, the corporation may obtain the bonds itself, by either purchase or call, and deposit them with the trustee. Call prices for sinking fund purchases may differ from those specified for when the entire issue is to be repaid prior to maturity.

Required contributions to a sinking fund may or may not be the same each year. In some cases, the required amount may depend on earnings, output, and so on; in others, the goal is to make the total paid for interest and principal the same each year.

12.7.5 Private Placements

Bonds intended for eventual public sale are usually issued in denominations of $1000 each. Both bearer and registered forms may be utilized. Often, however, a single investor (or a small group of investors) will buy an entire issue. Such *private placements* are typically purchased by large financial institutions.

12.7.6 Bankruptcy

When a corporation fails to make a scheduled coupon or principal payment on a bond, the corporation is said to be in default on that obligation. If the payment is not made within a relatively short period, some sort of litigation almost inevitably follows.

A corporation unable to meet its obligatory debt payments is said to be technically insolvent (or insolvent in the equity sense). If the value of the firm's assets falls below its liabilities, it is said to be insolvent (or insolvent in the bankruptcy sense).

Behind these definitions lie much legislation, many court cases, and varied legal opinions. Although the details differ, the usual situation begins with a default on one or more required coupon payments. If voluntary agreements with creditors cannot be obtained, this usually leads to a filing of bankruptcy—usually "voluntary"—by the corporation itself. Subsequent developments involve courts, court-appointed officials, representatives of the firm's creditors, and the management of the firm, among others.

Liquidation. A question that arises in most cases is whether or not the firm's assets should be liquidated (that is, sold) and the proceeds divided among the creditors. Such an action is taken only if the court feels the resulting value would exceed that likely to be obtained if the firm continued in operation (perhaps after substantial reorganization).

If the firm's assets are liquidated in a *straight bankruptcy*, secured creditors receive either the property pledged for their loans or the proceeds from the sale of the secured property. If this amount falls short of their claims, the difference is considered an unsecured debt of the firm; on the other hand, any excess is made available for other creditors. Next, assets are used to pay the claims of priority creditors to the extent possible. These include claims for such items as administrative expenses, wages (up to a stated limit per person), uninsured pension claims, taxes, and rents. Anything left over is used to pay unsecured creditors in proportion to their claims on the firm.

Reorganization. If the value of a firm's assets, when employed as part of a "going concern," appears to exceed their value in liquidation, a reorganization of the firm and its liabilities may be undertaken. Such proceedings, conducted under the provisions of the Federal Bankruptcy Act, may be voluntary (initiated by the firm) or involuntary (initiated by three or more creditors). A number of parties must concur in the proposed reorganization, including the holders of two-thirds of the value in each general class of creditor that is affected by the reorganization.

Among the goals of reorganization are "fair and equitable" treatment of various classes of securities and the elimination of "burdensome" debt obligations. Typically, creditors are given new claims on the reorganized firm, with the amounts of the new claims intended to be at least equal in value to the amounts that the creditors would have received in liquidation. For example, holders of debentures might receive bonds of longer maturity, holders of subordinated debentures might become stockholders, and stockholders might be left without any claims on the firm.

Arrangements. A third procedure is available to financially distressed corporations. The Federal Bankruptcy Act authorizes *arrangements*, in which debts may be extended (to longer maturities) or reduced.

Some Financial Aspects of Bankruptcy. Although the subject is far too complex for detailed treatment here, two aspects of bankruptcy deserve some discussion. First, the choice between continuation of a firm and liquidation of its assets should be unrelated to considerations of bankruptcy. If an asset can be sold for more than the present value of its future earnings, it should be. Management may have to be taken to court to be forced to do this, but the issue is not really one of solvency or lack thereof.

Second, the definition of insolvency is rather vague. Assume, for the sake of argument, that assets can be adequately valued at the larger of liquidating or going-concern value. A firm is said to be insolvent if this value is less than that of the firm's liabilities. But how should the liabilities be

TABLE 12.9
Estimated Ownership of Corporate and Foreign
Bonds, December 1987.

OWNER	DOLLAR AMOUNT (IN BILLIONS)	PERCENT OF TOTAL AMOUNT
Thrift institutions	$ 13.0	1.2%
Life insurance companies	358.8	32.6
Property and liability insurance companies	54.7	5.0
Public and private noninsured pension funds	294.1	26.7
Investment companies	55.4	5.0
Security brokers and dealers	11.6	1.0
Commercial banks	76.7	7.0
Foreign	155.2	14.1
Residual: Households direct	82.0	7.4
Total	$1101.5	100.0%

SOURCE: Adapted from Salomon Brothers Inc., *Prospects for Financial Markets in 1988*, 1987.

valued? Their current market value will inevitably be less than the value of the assets, whereas their book value can be greater than the value of the assets.

☐ 12.7.7 Ownership of Corporate Bonds

At the end of 1987, investors held a total of $1101.5 billion of corporate and foreign bonds. As can be seen in Table 12.9, the largest investors were life insurance companies and pension funds.

☐ 12.7.8 Trading in Corporate Bonds

Although most of the trading in corporate bonds takes place utilizing dealers in the over-the-counter market, a large number of corporate bonds are listed on the New York Stock Exchange (a notably smaller number are listed on the American Stock Exchange). However, trading in corporate bonds on the NYSE takes place at a location that is different from the location where common stocks are traded. Furthermore, no specialists are involved in the trading of corporate bonds on the NYSE. Instead, orders for "active" issues are traded in a "ring" in the bond room. Here, the member announces a bid or asked price, depending on whether the member is buying or selling. This invites other members to make counteroffers or to accept the announced price.

"Inactive" issues of bonds that are listed on the NYSE are traded through a computer system known as the *automated bond system* (ABS). With this system, members enter their bid or asked prices, along with the quantities, into computer terminals located on the floor of the bond room. Other members can see these orders by looking at display terminals and can respond by entering an order at a terminal.

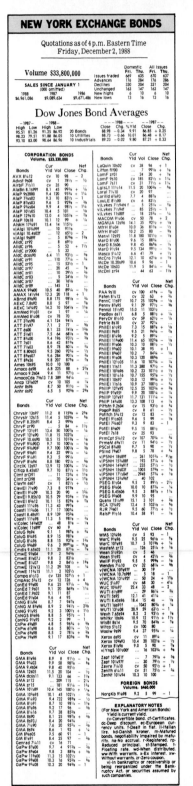

FIGURE 12–8

Price quotations for corporate bonds (excerpts).

SOURCE: Reprinted by the permission of *The Wall Street Journal*, © Dow Jones & Company, Inc. (December 5, 1988): p. C 14.

Since some corporate bonds are traded on the New York Stock Exchange, the prices at which such trades are made can be found in the financial press. Figure 12.8 provides an example. Consider the following entry:

BONDS	CURRENT YIELD	VOLUME	CLOSE	NET CHANGE
ATT 8 5/8s07	9.6	284	90¼	−¾

This entry indicates that American Telephone and Telegraph bonds carrying an $8\frac{5}{8}\%$ coupon (paid semiannually) and maturing in 2007 had a last trade that day at a price of $90\frac{1}{4}$. Since these bonds have a par value of $1000, this means that the last trade was at $902.50. The *current yield*, meaning the annual coupon rate divided by the current closing price, was approximately $86.25/$902.50 = 9.6%. In all, 284 bonds traded hands on the exchange during the day, and the closing price was $\frac{3}{4}$ ($7.50) below that of the previous day.

In a sense, the New York Stock Exchange is the "odd-lot" market for bonds. That is, major trades of bonds are often negotiated elsewhere by dealers and institutional investors, either directly or through brokers. Thus, reported prices on the NYSE may be poor guides to values associated with large transactions.

12.8 PREFERRED STOCK

In some respects, *preferred stock* is like a perpetual bond. A given dollar amount is to be paid each year by the issuer to the investor. This amount may be stated as a percent of the stock's par value (for example, 8% of $100, meaning $8 per year) or directly as a dollar figure (for example, $2.75 per year). Since the security is a stock, such payments are called dividends instead of interest and hence do not qualify as a tax-deductible expense for the issuing corporation. Furthermore, failure to make such payments does not constitute grounds for bankruptcy proceedings.

A recent innovation is adjustable rate preferred stock (ARPS), where the dividend is reset periodically in terms of an applicable rate. For example, the annualized "percent of par" for the dividend might reset every three months to be equal to the largest of the rates on (1) 3-month Treasury bills; (2) 10-year Treasury bonds; and (3) 20-year Treasury bonds. Related to ARPS are dutch auction rate preferred stock (DARPS), where the dividend is reset periodically (more often than for ARPS) at a level that results from bidding by current and potential owners.[11]

Preferred stock is generally "preferred as to dividends." Specified payments must be made on the preferred stock before any dividends may be paid to holders of the firm's common stock. Failure to pay a preferred dividend

---

[11] For a discussion of ARPS and DARPS, see Michael J. Alderson, Keith C. Brown, and Scott L. Lummer, "Dutch Auction Rate Preferred Stock," *Financial Management* 16, no. 2 (Summer 1987):68–73.

in full does not constitute default, but unpaid dividends are usually *cumulative*. This means that all previously unpaid preferred stock dividends must be paid (but seldom with interest) before any dividends may be paid on the common stock.

No indenture is provided with a preferred stock issue. However, various provisions protecting the preferred stockholders against potentially harmful actions may be written into the corporation's charter. For example, one provision may limit the dollar amount of senior securities that can be issued in the future. Although preferred stockholders typically do not have voting rights, there may be another provision that gives them voting rights when the corporation is in arrears on its preferred dividends.

Many issues of preferred stock are callable, often at a premium; such stock is sometimes said to be redeemable at a stated redemption price. Participating preferred stock entitles the holder to receive extra dividends when earnings permit. Convertible preferred stock may, at the option of the holder, be converted into another security (usually the firm's common stock) on stated terms. Some firms issue more than one class of preferred stock, with preference accorded the various classes in a specified order.

In the event of a dissolution of the firm, preferred stock is often preferred as to assets. Generally this means that preferred stockholders are entitled to receive the stock's par value before any payment is made to common stockholders.

Since preferred stock has many features of a bond without the substantial tax advantage that bonds give to the issuer, it is used less often than debt. In 1987, $10.1 billion of such stock was issued, compared with $208.7 billion of publicly offered corporate debt.[12]

As indicated in Chapter 10, interest income from bonds held by a corporate investor is subject to the corporate income tax, but 80% of any dividend income received is exempt from taxation. This makes the effective tax rate on dividends from preferred stock held by a corporate investor approximately 6.8% (.34 × .20), compared to 34% for interest received on bonds that are owned by the corporate investor. For this reason, preferred stocks tend to sell at prices that give lower before-tax returns than long-term bonds, even though the latter may be considerably lower in risk. As a result, preferred stocks are generally unattractive holdings for noncorporate investors, such as individuals and tax-exempt investors.

Many preferred stocks are traded on major exchanges in a manner similar to common stocks. Typically, they are assigned to the same specialist that is responsible for the firm's common stock. Trading prices are reported in the financial press in the same format used for common stocks.

12.9 SUMMARY

There are many types of fixed-income securities that are available for purchase by investors in the United States. In general terms, these securities

---

[12] *Federal Reserve Bulletin*, April 1988, p. A34.

get their name from the fact that they promise to make certain cash payments to their owners at certain times in the future. They can be thought of as belonging to one of several categories—savings deposits, money market instruments, U.S. government securities, federal agency securities, state and local government securities, foreign and Eurobonds, corporate bonds, and preferred stock. Most of these securities are bought and sold through dealers in the over-the-counter market; an exception is preferred stock, which is generally listed on organized exchanges and is assigned to specialists.

QUESTIONS AND PROBLEMS

1. Consider a 13-week Treasury bill, issued today, which is selling for $9,675.00. (Its face value is $10,000.00.)
   a. What is the annual discount based on the selling price of the security?
   b. What is the annual equivalent yield of the security?

2. The U.S. Treasury once issued notes and bonds only in bearer form. Now its notes and bonds are issued only in registered form. Given the characteristics of bearer and registered bonds, speculate as to what reasons might have prompted the Treasury to change the form of issuance.

3. Using *The Wall Street Journal* as a data source, identify a particular Treasury note or bond. What is its coupon rate? What is its maturity date? What is the latest bid-asked spread for the security? What is the security's yield-to-maturity?

4. Describe the standard practice by which sellers of government and corporate bonds are compensated for accrued interest.

5. Why does the IRS treat the difference between the price of a bond purchased at a discount and its face value as ordinary income to the investor, as opposed to treating it as a capital gain?

6. Bonds issued by federal agencies carry an explicit or implicit promise that the federal government will ensure payment of interest and principal. Why then are these securities usually priced by the market to offer yields above Treasury securities?

7. What is a mortgage participation certificate? What is the primary risk that such securities present to investors?

8. Distinguish between a general obligation municipal bond and a revenue bond.

9. Eurobonds have become very popular forms of financing in recent years. What features of the Eurobond market make Eurobonds attractive to issuers and bondholders?

10. A callable bond is sometimes described as a combination of a noncallable bond and an option. Explain why this description is appropriate. Further, explain how these two features impact the price of a callable bond.

11. Consider a $10,000 Treasury bond with a 7.5% coupon interest rate and a 25-year term-to-maturity. The bond has a call provision, effective 15 years from today. The bond has just been sold for $10,020. If the current yield-to-maturity on other Treasury bonds, with the same term-to-maturity and coupon interest rate but callable immediately, is 8%, what dollar value are investors placing on the deferred call provision? Assume that interest payments are made annually.

12. Cozy Dolan is considering purchasing one of two bonds: a corporate bond with a 9% coupon interest rate, selling at par, or a tax-free municipal bond, with a 6% coupon

interest rate, likewise selling at par. Given that Cozy is in the 30% tax bracket, and assuming that all other relevant factors are the same between the two bonds, which bond should Cozy select?

13. Is it true that most corporations that default on their debt eventually enter bankruptcy and see their assets liquidated to repay creditors? Explain.

Chapter 13

BOND ANALYSIS

Consider an investor who believes that the bond market is not semistrong-form efficient. That is, the investor believes that there are situations where public information can be used to identify mispriced bonds. To translate that belief into action about which bonds to buy and sell, an analytical procedure is needed. One procedure involves comparing a bond's yield-to-maturity with a yield-to-maturity that the investor feels is appropriate, based on the characteristics of the bond as well as current market conditions. If the yield-to-maturity is higher than the appropriate yield-to-maturity, then the bond is said to be *underpriced* (or undervalued) and is a candidate for buying. Conversely, if the yield-to-maturity is lower than the appropriate one, then the bond is said to be *overpriced* (or overvalued) and is a candidate for selling (or even short selling).

Alternatively, the investor could estimate the bond's "true," or "intrinsic," value, and compare it with the bond's current market price. Specifically, if the current market price is less than the bond's intrinsic value, then the bond is underpriced, and if it is greater, then the bond is overpriced.

Both procedures for analyzing bonds are based on the capitalization of income method of valuation. The first procedure involving yields is analogous to the internal rate of return method that is discussed in most introductory finance textbooks, whereas the second procedure involving intrinsic value is analogous to the net present value method that also appears in such books. Although the focus in those books is on making an investment decision involving some type of real asset (such as whether or not a new piece of machinery should be purchased), the focus here is on making an investment decision involving a particular type of financial asset—bonds.

13.1 APPLYING THE CAPITALIZATION OF INCOME METHOD TO BONDS

An investor who believes the bond market is efficient would question the ability of other investors to identify mispriced situations. However, if an investor believes such situations exist, then an economically sensible and

logical approach to valuation is needed to identify them. One such approach is the *capitalization of income method of valuation*.[1]

This method of valuation states that the intrinsic value of any asset is based on the discounted value of the cash flows that the investor expects to receive in the future from owning the asset. As mentioned earlier, one way that this method has been applied to bond valuation is to compare the bond's yield-to-maturity (y) with the appropriate one (y^*). Specifically, if $y > y^*$, then the bond is underpriced, and if $y < y^*$, then the bond is overpriced. However, if $y = y^*$, then the bond is said to be fairly priced.

Letting P denote the current market price of a bond with a remaining life of n years and promising cash flows to the investor of C_1 in year 1, C_2 in year 2, and so on, the yield-to-maturity (more specifically, the *promised yield-to-maturity*) of the bond is the value of y that solves the following equation:

$$P = \frac{C_1}{(1 + y)^1} + \frac{C_2}{(1 + y)^2} + \frac{C_3}{(1 + y)^3} + \cdots + \frac{C_n}{(1 + y)^n}.$$

Using summation notation, this equation can be rewritten as:

$$P = \sum_{t=1}^{n} \frac{C_t}{(1 + y)^t}. \qquad (13.1)$$

For example, consider a bond that is currently selling for $900 and has a remaining life of three years. For ease of exposition, assume it makes annual coupon payments amounting to $60 per year and has a par value of $1000. That is, $C_1 = \$60$, $C_2 = \$60$, and $C_3 = \$1060 = \$1000 + \$60$. Using equation (13.1), the yield-to-maturity on this bond is the value of y that solves the following equation:

$$\$900 = \frac{\$60}{(1 + y)^1} + \frac{\$60}{(1 + y)^2} + \frac{\$1060}{(1 + y)^3}$$

which is $y = 10.02\%$. If subsequent analysis indicates that the yield-to-maturity should be 9.00%, then this bond is underpriced, since $y = 10.02\% > y^* = 9.00\%$.

Alternatively, the intrinsic value of a bond can be calculated using the following formula:

$$V = \frac{C_1}{(1 + y^*)^1} + \frac{C_2}{(1 + y^*)^2} + \frac{C_3}{(1 + y^*)^3} + \cdots + \frac{C_n}{(1 + y^*)^n}$$

or, using summation notation,

$$V = \sum_{t=1}^{n} \frac{C_t}{(1 + y^*)^t}. \qquad (13.2)$$

Since the purchase price of the bond is its market price P, the net present value (NPV) to the investor is equal to the difference between the value of the bond and the purchase price:

---

[1] This method is discussed more extensively in Chapter 16.

$$NPV = V - P \qquad\qquad\qquad\text{(13.3)}$$
$$= \left[\sum_{t=1}^{n} \frac{C_t}{(1 + y^*)^t} \right] - P.$$

The NPV of the bond in the previous example is the solution to the following equation:

$$NPV = \left[\frac{\$60}{(1 + .09)^1} + \frac{\$60}{(1 + .09)^2} + \frac{\$1060}{(1 + .09)^3} \right] - \$900$$
$$= \$24.06.$$

Since this bond has a positive NPV, it is underpriced. This will always be the case when a bond has a yield-to-maturity that is more than appropriate (earlier, it was shown that this bond's yield-to-maturity was 10.02%, which is more than 9.00%, the appropriate yield-to-maturity). That is, in general, any bond with $y > y^*$ will always have a positive NPV and vice versa, so that under either method it would be underpriced.[2]

Alternatively, if the investor had determined that y^* was equal to 11.00%, then the bond's NPV would have been $-\$22.19$. This would suggest the bond was overpriced, just as would have been noted when the yield-to-maturity of 10.02% was compared with 11.00%. This will always be the case— a bond with $y < y^*$ will always have a negative NPV and vice versa, so that under either method it would be found to be overpriced.

It should also be pointed out that if the investor had determined that y^* had a value of approximately the same magnitude as the bond's yield-to-maturity of 10%, then the NPV of the bond would be approximately zero. In such a situation, the bond would be viewed as being fairly priced.

Note that in order to use the capitalization of income method of valuation, the values of C_t, P, and y^* must be determined. It is generally quite easy to determine the values for C_t and P, since they are the bond's promised cash flows and current market price, respectively. However, determining the value of y^* is difficult, since the investor must estimate an appropriate value for the bond. Such a decision will depend on the characteristics of the bond, as well as on current market conditions. Given that the key ingredient in bond analysis is determining the appropriate value of y^*, the next section discusses the attributes that should be considered in making such a determination.

13.2 BOND ATTRIBUTES

Six primary attributes of a bond are of significant importance in bond valuation: (1) length of time until maturity; (2) coupon rate; (3) call provisions;

---

[2] A more accurate method of determining a bond's intrinsic value involves the use of spot rates. That is, in determining the NPV of this bond, the investor might have determined that the relevant spot rates for the one-year, two-year, and three-year cash flows are 8.24%, 8.69%, and 9.03%, respectively. Using these values, the bond's intrinsic value would be equal to [$60/(1.0824)] + [$60/(1.0869)^2] + [$1060/(1.0903)^3] = $924.06. Although V is the same in this example when either spot rates or y^* are used in the calculations, this need not always be the case.

(4) tax status; (5) marketability; and (6) likelihood of default. At any time, the structure of market prices for bonds differing in these dimensions can be examined and described in terms of yields-to-maturity. This underlying structure is sometimes referred to as the *yield structure*. Often, attention is confined to differences along a single dimension, holding the other attributes constant. For example, the set of yields of bonds of different maturities constitutes the *term structure* (discussed in Chapter 4), and the set of yields of bonds of different default risk is referred to as the *risk structure*.

Most bond analysts consider the yields-to-maturity for default-free bonds to form the yield structure; "risk differentials" are then added to obtain the relevant yields-to-maturity for bonds of lower quality. While subject to some criticism, this procedure makes it possible to think about a complicated set of relationships sequentially.

The differential between the yields of two bonds is usually called a *yield spread*. Most often, it involves a bond that is under analysis and a comparable default-free bond (that is, a Treasury security of similar maturity and coupon rate). Yield spreads are sometimes measured in *basis points*, where one basis point equals .01%. If the yield-to-maturity for one bond is 11.50% and that of another is 11.90%, the yield spread is 40 basis points.

☐ 13.2.1 Coupon Rate and the Length of Time Until Maturity

These attributes of a bond are important because they determine the size and timing of the cash flows that are promised to the bondholder by the issuer. Given a bond's current market price, these attributes can be used to determine the bond's yield-to-maturity, which will subsequently be compared with what the investor thinks it should be. More specifically, if the market for Treasury securities is viewed as being efficient, then the yield-to-maturity on a Treasury security that is similar to the bond under evaluation can form a starting point in the analysis of the bond.

Consider the previously mentioned bond that is selling for $900 and has promised cash flows over the next three years of $60, $60, and $1060, respectively. In this case, a Treasury security that has a similar cash flow would form the starting point of the analysis. Perhaps a Treasury security with a cash flow over the next three years of $50, $50, and $1050 exists and is selling for $912.89. Since the yield-to-maturity on this security is 8.5%, this forms the starting point in determining what the yield-to-maturity should be on the $900 bond. In this situation, the yield spread between the bond and Treasury security is 1.52% = 10.02% − 8.50%.

☐ 13.2.2 Call Provisions

There are times when, by historical standards, yields-to-maturity are relatively high. Bonds issued during such times may, at first glance, appear to be unusually attractive investments. However, deeper analysis indicates this is not necessarily the case because most corporate bonds have a *call provision*

that enables the issuer to redeem the bonds prior to maturity, usually for a price somewhat above par. This price is known as the *call price*, and the difference between it and the par value of the bond is known as the *call premium*. An issuer will often find it financially advantageous to call the existing bonds if yields drop substantially after the bonds were initially sold, since the issuer will be able to replace them with lower yielding securities that are less costly.[3]

For example, consider a ten-year bond issued at par ($1000) that has a coupon rate of 12% and is callable at $1050 any time after it has been outstanding for five years.[4] If, after five years, yields on similar five-year bonds were 8% (an amount that is substantially less than 12%), the bond would probably be called. This means that an investor who had planned on receiving annual coupon payments of $120 for ten years would instead actually receive the call price of $1050 after five years. At this time, the investor could take the $1050 and reinvest it in the 8% bonds, thereby receiving $84 per year in coupon payments over the last five years (it is assumed here that the investor can purchase a fraction of a bond, so that the full $1050 can be invested in the 8% bonds).

In this example, the investor might have thought that the original bond would remain outstanding for the full ten years, in which case the yield-to-maturity on the initial $1000 investment would have been 12%. However, this apparent yield would not have been earned, since the issuer would have called the bond after five years. In this case, in return for an initial investment of $1000, the investor would receive coupon payments of $120 for each of the first five years, $84 for each of the next five years, and $1050 at the end of the tenth year as a return of principal. Given this pattern of cash flows, the actual yield-to-maturity over the ten years would be 10.96%.

This example suggests that the higher the coupon rate of a callable bond, the greater is the likely divergence between actual and apparent yields. This is borne out by experience. Figure 13.1 plots the coupon rate, set at time of issue, on the horizontal axis. Since most bonds are initially sold at (or very close to) par, the coupon rate is also a measure of the yield-to-maturity that an investor may have thought was obtainable by purchasing one of the newly issued bonds.

The vertical axis in this figure plots the subsequent actual yield-to-maturity obtained up to the original maturity date by an investor, assuming that the payments received in the event of a call were reinvested in non-callable bonds with appropriate maturities. The curve is based on experience for a group of callable bonds issued by utility companies during a period of fluctuating interest rates. As can be seen, the coupon rate and actual yield

---

[3] Many corporate bonds have, in addition to a call provision, a provision for a sinking fund where each year the issuer retires a prespecified portion of the original bond issue. For a further discussion of sinking funds, see James C. Van Horne, *Financial Market Rates and Flows* (Englewood Cliffs, N.J.: Prentice Hall, 1984), 215–18. This book also presents a detailed discussion of the other attributes of bonds that are of importance in valuation.

[4] In this example, the *yield-to-call* (or, to be more specific, the yield-to-first-call) is 12.78%. That is, 12.78% is the discount rate that makes the present value of $120 received after each of the first four years and $1170 ($1050 + $120) at the end of five years equal to the issue price of the bond, $1000. Note how the yield-to-call is greater than the bond's promised yield-to-maturity at the time of issue (12%).

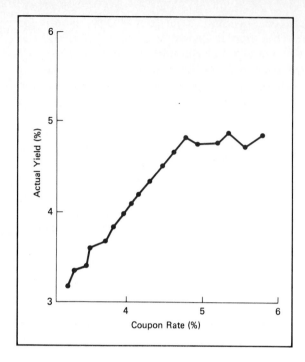

FIGURE 13–1
Promised and actual yields of callable
Aa utility bonds, 1956–1964.

SOURCE: Frank C. Jen and James E. Wert,
"The Effect of Call Risk on Corporate Bond
Yields," *Journal of Finance* 22, no. 4 (December 1967): p. 646.

are quite similar in magnitude until the coupon rate gets near 5%. At this point, higher coupon rates are no longer associated with higher actual yields, since these coupon rates were relatively high during the time period examined; as a consequence, most of the bonds with coupon rates above 5% were ultimately called.

The upshot is that bonds with greater likelihood of being called should have a higher yield-to-maturity. That is, the higher the coupon rate or the lower the call premium, the higher the yield-to-maturity should be. Equivalently, bonds with higher coupon rates or lower call premiums will have lower intrinsic values, keeping everything else equal.

☐ **13.2.3   Tax Status**

In Chapter 10, it was noted that tax-exempt municipal bonds have had yields-to-maturity that were approximately 20% to 40% lower than the yields-to-maturity on similar taxable bonds. Taxation affects bond prices and yields in other ways. For example, any low-coupon bond selling at a discount provides returns in two forms: coupon payments and capital gains. In the United States, both are taxable as ordinary income, but taxes on the latter may be deferred until the bond is either sold or matures. This suggests that such *deep discount bonds* have a tax advantage due to this deferral. As a result, they should have slightly lower before-tax yields than high-coupon bonds, other things equal. That is, such low-coupon bonds will have a slightly higher intrinsic value than high-coupon bonds.

□ 13.2.4 Marketability

Marketability (sometimes also referred to as liquidity) refers to how easily an investor can sell an asset quickly without having to make a substantial price concession. An example of an illiquid asset is a "collectible," such as a piece of artwork. An investor who owns a Van Gogh painting may have to settle for a relatively low price if he or she has to sell it within an hour. If the sale can be postponed for a length of time in order to set up a public auction, undoubtedly a much higher price could be obtained. Alternatively, an investor with $1,000,000 worth of IBM common stock who has to sell these shares within an hour will probably be able to receive a price close to the price previously paid for such assets. Furthermore, it is quite unlikely that waiting would increase the expected selling price of such securities.

Since most bonds are bought and sold in dealer markets, one measure of a bond's marketability is the bid-ask spread that the dealers are quoting on the bonds. Bonds that are being actively traded will tend to have lower bid-ask spreads than bonds that are inactive. This is because the dealer is more exposed to risk when making a market in an inactive security than when making a market in an active security. The source of this risk is the inventory that the dealer holds and the fact that interest rates in general may move in a way that causes the dealer to lose money on his or her inventory. Accordingly, bonds that are actively traded should have a lower yield-to-maturity and a higher intrinsic value than bonds that are inactive, keeping everything else equal.

□ 13.2.5 Likelihood of Default

Currently a number of corporations—the two largest are Standard & Poor's Corporation and Moody's Investors Service, Inc.—provide ratings of the creditworthiness of thousands of corporate and municipal bonds. Such *bond ratings* are often interpreted as an indication of the likelihood of default by the issuer. Figure 13.2 provides details on the ratings assigned by Standard & Poor's, whereas Figure 13.3 provides similar details for Moody's.[5]

A broader set of categories is often employed, with bonds classified as being of either investment grade or speculative grade. Typically, *investment grade bonds* are bonds that have been assigned to one of the top four ratings (AAA through BBB by Standard & Poor's; Aaa through Baa by Moody's). In contrast, *speculative grade bonds* are bonds that have been assigned to one of the lower ratings (BB and below by Standard & Poor's; Ba and below by Moody's). Sometimes these low-rated securities are called, derisively, *junk bonds*.

At times, certain regulated financial institutions (such as banks, savings and loans, and insurance companies) have been prohibited from purchasing

---

[5] Both rating agencies actually use finer gradations than those shown in the figures. Standard & Poor's sometimes places a + or − next to its letter rating if a bond is in a category ranging from AA to CCC. Similarly, Moody's may place a 1, 2, or 3 next to its letter rating if a bond is in a category ranging from Aa down to B.

A Standard & Poor's corporate or municipal debt rating is a current assessment of the creditworthiness of an obligor with respect to a specific obligation. This assessment may take into consideration obligors such as guarantors, insurers, or lessees.

The debt rating is not a recommendation to purchase, sell or hold a security, inasmuch as it does not comment as to market price or suitability for a particular investor.

The ratings are based on current information furnished by the issuer or obtained by Standard & Poor's from other sources it considers reliable. Standard & Poor's does not perform any audit in connection with any rating and may, on occasion, rely on unaudited financial information. The ratings may be changed, suspended or withdrawn as a result of changes in, or unavailability of, such information, or for other circumstances.

The ratings are based, in varying degrees, on the following considerations:

I. Likelihood of default-capacity and willingness of the obligor as to the timely payment of interest and repayment of principal in accordance with the terms of the obligation;

II. Nature of and provisions of the obligation;

III. Protection afforded by, and relative position of, the obligation in the event of bankruptcy, reorganization or other arrangement under the laws of bankruptcy and other laws affecting creditors' rights.

AAA Debt rated AAA has the highest rating assigned by Standard & Poor's. Capacity to pay interest and repay principal is extremely strong.

AA Debt rated AA has a very strong capacity to pay interest and repay principal and differs from the higher rated issues only in small degree.

A Debt rated A has a strong capacity to pay interest and repay principal although it is somewhat more susceptible to the adverse effects of changes in circumstances and economic conditions than debt in higher rated categories.

BBB Debt rated BBB is regarded as having an adequate capacity to pay interest and repay principal. Whereas it normally exhibits adequate protection parameters, adverse economic conditions or changing circumstances are more likely to lead to a weakened capacity to pay interest and repay principal for debt in this category than in higher rated categories.

BB, B, CCC, CC, C Debt rated BB, B, CCC, CC and C is regarded, on balance, as predominantly speculative with respect to capacity to pay interest and repay principal in accordance with the terms of the obligation. BB indicates the lowest degree of speculation and C the highest degree of speculation. While such debt will likely have some quality and protective characteristics, these are outweighed by large uncertainties or major risk exposures to adverse conditions.

Cl The rating Cl is reserved for income bonds on which no interest is being paid.

D Debt rated D is in default, and payment of interest and/or repayment of principal is in arrears.

FIGURE 13–2
Standard & Poor's debt rating definitions.

SOURCE: Standard & Poor's Bond Guide (February 1988): p. 10.

bonds that were not of investment grade. As a consequence, investment grade bonds are sometimes thought to command "superpremium" prices, and hence disproportionately low yields, since an important group of investors is encouraged or forced to purchase them. However, a major disparity in yields could attract a great many new issuers, who would increase the supply of such bonds, thereby causing bond prices to fall and yields to rise. For a significant superpremium to persist, rather substantial market segmentation on both the buying and the selling side would be required. Since there is no clear evidence that segmentation exists, it seems more likely that the differences in yields between investment grade bonds and speculative grade bonds are roughly proportional to differences in default risk.

Aaa

Bonds which are rated **Aaa** are judged to be of the best quality. They carry the smallest degree of investment risk and are generally referred to as "gilt edge." Interest payments are protected by a large or by an exceptionally stable margin and principal is secure. While the various protective elements are likely to change, such changes as can be visualized are most unlikely to impair the fundamentally strong position of such issues.

Aa

Bonds which are rated **Aa** are judged to be of high quality by all standards. Together with the **Aaa** group they comprise what are generally known as high grade bonds. They are rated lower than the best bonds because margins of protection may not be as large as in **Aaa** securities or fluctuation of protective elements may be of greater amplitude or there may be other elements present which make the long term risks appear somewhat larger than in **Aaa** securities.

A

Bonds which are rated **A** possess many favorable investment attributes and are to be considered as upper medium grade obligations. Factors giving security to principal and interest are considered adequate but elements may be present which suggest a susceptibility to impairment sometime in the future.

Baa

Bonds which are rated **Baa** are considered as medium grade obligations, i.e., they are neither highly protected nor poorly secured. Interest payments and principal security appear adequate for the present but certain protective elements may be lacking or may be characteristically unreliable over any great length of time. Such bonds lack outstanding investment characteristics and in fact have speculative characteristics as well.

Ba

Bonds which are rated **Ba** are judged to have speculative elements; their future cannot be considered as well assured. Often the protection of interest and principal payments may be very moderate and thereby not well safeguarded during other good and bad times over the future. Uncertainty of position characterizes bonds in this class.

B

Bonds which are rated **B** generally lack characteristics of the desired investment. Assurance of interest and principal payments or of maintenance of other terms of the contract over any long period of time may be small.

Caa

Bonds which are rated **Caa** are of poor standing. Such issues may be in default or there may be present elements of danger with respect to principal or interest.

Ca

Bonds which are rated **Ca** represent obligations which are speculative in a high degree. Such issues are often in default or have other marked shortcomings.

C

Bonds which are rated **C** are the lowest rated class of bonds and issues so rated can be regarded as having extremely poor prospects of ever attaining any real investment standing.

FIGURE 13–3
Moody's corporate bond ratings.

SOURCE: Moody's Bond Record (January 1988): p. 1.

According to Moody's, ratings are designed to provide "investors with a simple system of gradation by which the relative investment qualities of bonds may be noted." [6] Moreover:

---

[6] *Moody's Bond Record* (New York: Moody's Investors Service, Inc., January 1988):1.

☐ Since ratings involve judgments about the future, on the one hand, and since they are used by investors as a means of protection, on the other, the effort is made when assigning ratings to look at "worst" potentialities in the "visible" future, rather than solely at the past record and the status of the present. Therefore, investors using the ratings should not expect to find in them a reflection of statistical factors alone, since they are an appraisal of long-term risks, including the recognition of many non-statistical factors.[7]

Despite this disclaimer, the influence of "statistical factors" on the ratings is apparently significant. Several studies have investigated the relationship between historical measures of a firm's performance and the ratings assigned its bonds.[8] Many of the differences in the ratings accorded various bonds can, in fact, be attributed to differences in the issuer's situations, measured in traditional ways. For corporate bonds, better ratings are generally associated with lower financial leverage (that is, debt to total assets); smaller past variation in earnings over time; larger asset base (firm size); more profitable operations; and lack of subordination to other debt issues.[9] One use of these findings is in the development of models for predicting the initial ratings that will be given to forthcoming bond issues as well as for predicting changes in the ratings of outstanding bonds.

Default Premiums

Since common stocks do not "promise" any cash flows to the investor, they are not subject to default. To assess the investment prospects for a common stock, all possible holding-period returns might be considered. By multiplying each return by its perceived probability of occurrence and then adding up the products, an estimate of the expected holding period return can be determined.

A similar procedure can be employed with bonds, with the analysis usually focusing on yield-to-maturity. Formally, all possible yields are considered, along with their respective probabilities, and a weighted average is computed to determine the *expected yield-to-maturity*. As long as there is any possibility of default or late payment, the expected yield will fall below the promised yield. In general, the greater the risk of default and the greater the amount of loss in the event of default, the greater will be this disparity.

This is illustrated in Figure 13.4 for a hypothetical risky bond. Its promised yield-to-maturity is 12% but, owing to a high default risk, the expected yield is only 9%. The 3% difference between the promised and

---

[7] *Moody's Bond Record*, p. 1.

[8] For example, see Thomas F. Pogue and Robert M. Soldofsky, "What's in a Bond Rating?" *Journal of Financial and Quantitative Analysis* 4, no. 2 (June 1969):201–28; R. R. West, "An Alternate Approach to Predicting Corporate Bond Ratings," *Journal of Accounting Research* 8, no. 1 (Spring 1970):118–25; George E. Pinches and Kent A. Mingo, "A Multivariate Analysis of Industrial Bond Ratings," *Journal of Finance* 28, no. 1 (March 1973):1–18, and "The Role of Subordination and Industrial Bond Ratings," *Journal of Finance* 30, no. 1 (March 1975):201–6; Robert S. Kaplan and Gabriel Urwitz, "Statistical Models of Bond Ratings: A Methodological Inquiry," *Journal of Business* 52, no. 2 (April 1979):231–61; Ahmed Belkaoui, *Industrial Bonds and the Rating Process* (Westport, Conn.: Quorum Books, 1983).

[9] A summary of previous studies on what factors affect municipal bond ratings (as well as corporate bond ratings) is contained in Chapter 14 of George Foster, *Financial Statement Analysis* (Englewood Cliffs, N.J.: Prentice Hall, 1986). For an interesting look into the rating of municipal bonds, see John E. Petersen, *The Rating Game* (New York: The Twentieth Century Fund, 1974).

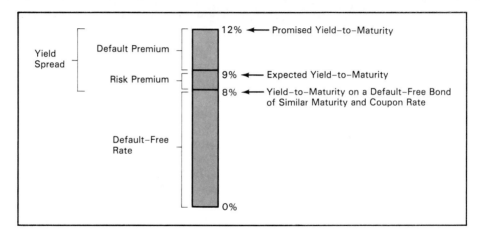

FIGURE 13–4
Yield-to-maturity for a risky bond.

expected yields is the *default premium*. Any bond that has some probability of default should offer such a premium, and it should be greater, the greater the probability of default.

Just how large should a bond's default premium be? According to one model, the answer depends on both the probability of default and the likely financial loss to the bondholder in the event of default.[10] Also important in this model is the level of the bond's expected yield-to-maturity.

Consider a bond that is perceived to be equally likely to default in each year (given it did not default in the previous year), with the probability that it will default in any given year denoted by p_d. Assume that if the bond does default, a payment equal to $(1 - \lambda)$ times its market price a year earlier will be made to the owner of each bond. According to this model, a bond will be fairly priced if its promised yield-to-maturity (y) is

$$y = \frac{\bar{y} + \lambda p_d}{1 - p_d} \tag{13.4}$$

where $\bar{y}$ denotes the bond's expected yield-to-maturity. The difference (d) between a bond's promised yield-to-maturity (y) and its expected yield-to-maturity ($\bar{y}$) was referred to earlier as the bond's default premium. Using equation (13.4), this difference for a fairly priced bond will be equal to

$$d = y - \bar{y}$$
$$= \left[\frac{\bar{y} + \lambda p_d}{1 - p_d} \right] - \bar{y} \tag{13.5}$$

As an example, consider the bond illustrated in Figure 13.4. Assume that this bond has a 6% annual default probability and that it is estimated

[10] The model was developed by Gordon Pye in "Gauging the Default Premium," *Financial Analysts Journal* 30, no. 1 (January/February 1974):49–52.

that if the bond does default, each bondholder will receive an amount equal to 60% of the bond's market price a year earlier (meaning that $1 - \lambda = .60$, which in turn means that $\lambda = .40$). Using equation (13.5), this bond would be fairly priced if its default premium were equal to

$$d = \left[\frac{.09 + (.40 \times .06)}{1 - .06} \right] - .09$$

$$= .0313$$

or 3.13%. Since the actual default premium earlier was estimated to be 3%, it can be seen that the two figures are similar. This suggests the actual default premium is appropriate, according to this model.

What sort of default experience might the long-run bond investor anticipate? And, how is this experience likely to be related to the ratings of the bonds held? In a massive study of all large bond issues and a sample of small bond issues, Hickman attempted to answer these questions.[11] He analyzed investor experience for each bond from 1900 through 1943 to determine the actual yield-to-maturity, measured from the date of issuance to the date on which the bond matured, defaulted, or was called—whichever came first. He then compared this actual yield with the promised yield-to-maturity based on the price at time of issue. Every bond was also classified according to the ratings assigned at time of issue. Part (a) of Table 13.1 shows the major results.

As might be expected, Hickman found that, in general, the riskier the bond, the higher the promised yield at time of issue and the higher the percentage of bonds that subsequently defaulted. However, a surprise was uncovered when the actual yields-to-maturity were compared with promised yields-to-maturity. As the last column on the right of the table shows, in four out of five rating classifications, the actual yield was found to *exceed* the promised yield. Fortunately, a convenient explanation exists for this finding—the period studied by Hickman was one where a substantial drop in interest rates occurred. This is important because the drop made it attractive for issuers to call their outstanding bonds, paying the bondholders a call premium in the process and resulting in an actual yield above the promised yield.

To see what might have happened had this not been the case, Fraine and Mills reanalyzed the data for large investment-grade issues.[12] Their results are shown in part (b) of Table 13.1. The initial columns differ from those in part (a) because smaller issues were excluded. The major difference between the parts appears in the right-hand column, where Fraine and Mills substituted a bond's promised yield for its actual yield whenever the latter was larger, thereby removing the effects of most calls. Unlike Hickman, their results suggest that there was little difference in actual yields within the highest rating classifications.

---

[11] W. Braddock Hickman, *Corporate Bond Quality and Investor Experience* (Princeton, N.J.: Princeton University Press, 1958).

[12] Harold G. Fraine and Robert H. Mills, "The Effect of Defaults and Credit Deterioration on Yields of Corporate Bonds," *Journal of Finance* 16, no. 3 (September 1961):423–34.

TABLE 13.1

Actual and Realized Bond Yields-to-Maturity, 1900–1943.

(a) ALL LARGE AND A SAMPLE OF SMALL ISSUES

Composite Rating	Comparable Moody's Rating	Promised Yield-to-Maturity at Issue	Percent Defaulting Prior to Maturity	Actual-Yield-to-Maturity
I	Aaa	4.5%	5.9%	5.1%
II	Aa	4.6	6.0	5.0
III	A	4.9	13.4	5.0
IV	Baa	5.4	19.1	5.7
V-IX	below Baa	9.5	42.4	8.6

(b) ALL LARGE ISSUES

Composite Rating	Comparable Moody's Rating	Promised Yield-to-Maturity	Actual Yield-to-Maturity	Modified Actual Yield-to-Maturity
I	Aaa	4.5%	5.1%	4.3%
II	Aa	4.5	5.1	4.3
III	A	4.9	5.0	4.3
IV	Baa	5.4	5.8	4.5

SOURCE: (a) W. Braddock Hickman, *Corporate Bond Quality and Investor Experience* (Princeton, N.J.: Princeton University Press, 1953): p. 10. (b) Harold G. Fraine and Robert H. Mills, "The Effect of Defaults and Credit Deterioration on Yields of Corporate Bonds," *Journal of Finance* 16, no. 3 (September 1961):433.

More recently, Altman and Nammacher examined the default experience of corporate bonds over the period of 1970 to 1984.[13] Like Hickman, they also found that bonds with a speculative grade rating at the time of issue subsequently had a much higher default rate than bonds that were initially of investment grade. However, this does not mean that speculative bonds are poor investments. Indeed, after subtracting for losses due to defaults, such low-grade bonds were found to offer attractive returns.

Risk Premiums

It is useful to compare the expected return of a risky security with the certain return of a default-free security. In an efficient market, the difference in these returns will be related to the relevant risk of the security. Consider common stocks, where the investor has a holding period of one year or less. In this situation, the expected return on a share is typically compared with the yield of a Treasury bill having a maturity date corresponding with the end of the holding period (note that the yield on such a Treasury bill is equal to its holding-period return).

Traditionally, a risky bond's expected yield-to-maturity is compared with that of a default-free bond of similar maturity and coupon rate. The

---

[13] Edward I. Altman and Scott A. Nammacher, "The Default Rate Experience on High-Yield Corporate Debt," *Financial Analysts Journal* 41, no. 4 (July–August 1985):25–41.

difference between these yields is known as the bond's *risk premium*. In the example shown in Figure 13.4, default-free bonds of similar maturity and coupon rate offer a certain 8% yield-to-maturity. Since the risky bond's expected yield-to-maturity is 9%, its risk premium is 1% (that is, 100 basis points).

Every bond that might default should offer a default premium. But the risk premium is another matter. Any security's expected return should be related only to its contribution to the risk of a well-diversified portfolio; its total risk is not directly relevant.

For example, if a group of companies all faced the possibility of bankruptcy, but from totally unrelated causes, a portfolio that included all their bonds would subsequently provide an actual return very close to its expected return. This is because the default premiums earned on the bonds that did not default would offset the losses incurred from those bonds that did default. Consequently, there would be little reason for this expected return to differ significantly from that of a default-free bond, since there is little doubt concerning what its actual return will be. Accordingly, each bond should be priced to offer little or no risk premium (but each bond should have a substantive default premium).

However, the risks associated with bonds are not unrelated. Figure 13.5 shows for each year from 1900 to 1965 the ratio of the par value of corporate bonds defaulting during the year to the par value outstanding at the beginning of the year. Not surprisingly, the peaks coincide with periods of economic distress.[14] When business is bad, most firms are affected. The market value of a firm's common stock will decline when an economic downturn is anticipated. If the likelihood of default on its debt also increases, the market value of its outstanding bonds will follow suit. Thus, the holding-

FIGURE 13–5
Default rates 1900–1965.

SOURCE: Adapted from Thomas R. Atkinson and Elizabeth T. Simpson, *Trends in Corporate Bond Quality* (Columbia University Press, 1967): p. 5.

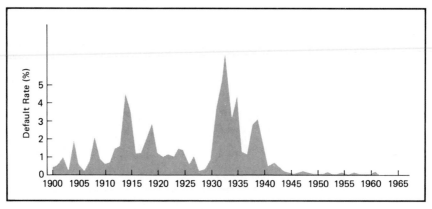

---

[14] A similar observation has been made for municipal bonds. See George H. Hempel, *The Postwar Quality of State and Local Debt* (New York: Columbia University Press, 1971).

TABLE 13.2

Risk and Return, Keystone Bond Funds, 1968–1987.

	FUND B1	FUND B2	FUND B4
	Conservative Bonds	Investment Grade Bonds	Discount Bonds
Average return (% per year)	7.52	8.70	9.05
Standard deviation of return (% per year)	8.69	9.53	10.96
Beta value, relative to S&P 500	.27	.41	.50
Proportion of variance explained by S&P	.26	.50	.55

period return on a bond may be correlated with the returns of other bonds and with those of stocks. Most important, a risky bond's holding-period return is likely to be correlated, to at least some extent, with the return on a widely diversified "market portfolio" that includes both corporate bonds and stocks. This part of the risk of a bond should command a risk premium in the form of a higher expected return, since it is not diversifiable.

The riskier a bond is, the greater its likelihood of default and, in turn, the greater its potential sensitivity to market declines representing lowered assessments of prospects for the economy as a whole. This is illustrated in Table 13.2, which summarizes the investment performance of three portfolios of bonds, known as bond funds, in the Keystone group. All values shown in the table are based on annual returns earned over a 20-year period by each portfolio. As might be anticipated, the most risky bond portfolio (fund B4) had the highest average return and highest standard deviation of return, whereas the least risky bond portfolio (fund B1) had the lowest average return and lowest standard deviation.

To estimate each portfolio's sensitivity to changes in stock prices, each portfolio's returns were compared with those of Standard & Poor's 500. Specifically, a beta was calculated for each portfolio in order to measure the sensitivity of each portfolio to swings in the stock market. As can be seen in the table, the riskier the portfolio, the higher the estimated beta, indicating that riskier bonds moved more with stocks and thus should have had higher average returns.

The final row in the table shows the proportion of the year-to-year variation in bond portfolio returns that were associated with stock market swings. As indicated, relatively more of the risky portfolio's variation was associated with the stock market than was the case with the less risky portfolio. Thus, for less-risky bonds, interest-rate risk appears to have been more important than stock market risk.[15]

---

[15] In a study of preferred stocks, it was found that the price movements of low-rated preferred stocks were related more to the price movements of common stocks than to the price movements of bonds; for high-rated preferred stocks, the findings were just the opposite. See John S. Bildersee, "Some Aspects of the Performance of Non-Convertible Preferred Stocks," *Journal of Finance* 28, no. 5 (December 1973):1187–1201.

The greater a bond's risk of default, the greater its default premium. This alone will cause a bond with a higher default risk to offer a higher promised yield-to-maturity. If it is also true that the greater a bond's risk of default, the greater its risk premium, then the promised yield-to-maturity will have to be even higher. As a result, bonds given lower agency ratings should have higher promised yields-to-maturity if such ratings do reflect the risk of default.

Figure 13.6 shows that this is indeed the case. Each of the curves plots the promised yield-to-maturity for a group of corporate bonds assigned the same ratings by Moody's. Note that the scale is "upside down," so that higher promised yields plot at lower positions on the diagram (such a procedure is often employed for bonds).

Although Figure 13.6 shows that bonds are priced so that higher promised yields go with lower ratings, it also shows that the differences between the yields in the rating categories vary considerably over time. This suggests that agency ratings indicate *relative* levels of risk instead of *absolute* levels of risk.

If an absolute level of risk were indicated by a rating classification, then each classification would be associated with a particular probability of default (or, more accurately, a range of probabilities of default). Consequently, as the economy became more uncertain in terms of things like the near-term level of GNP, bonds would be reclassified as necessary, with most moving to lower ratings. In this situation, yield spreads between classifications would change only slightly, since each classification would still reflect bonds having the same probability of default. However, Figure 13.6 shows that these spreads change a lot over time, an observation that can be interpreted as evidence that the bond market does not believe that the ratings reflect absolute levels of risk.

It is known that rating agencies prefer to avoid making a large number of rating changes as the economy becomes more uncertain. Instead, they prefer to use the classifications to indicate relative levels of risk. This means that an overall increase in economic uncertainty would not result in a significant number of reclassifications. Thus, the probability of default associated with bonds in a given rating classification would be greater at such a time. In turn, the yield spreads between classifications of corporate bonds and the yield spreads between corporate and government bonds would increase. Indeed, there is evidence that the spread between the promised yields of bonds of different rating classifications increases when the degree of uncertainty about the economy increases.

Some models have attempted to take advantage of this observation in order to predict the amount of economic uncertainty. In particular, these models use the size of the yield spread between, say, bonds rated AAA and those rated BBB by Standard & Poor's as an indication of the degree of economic uncertainty. For example, if this spread is widening, then that might be taken as an indication that the near-term future of the economy was becoming more uncertain. It should be noted that there are other models

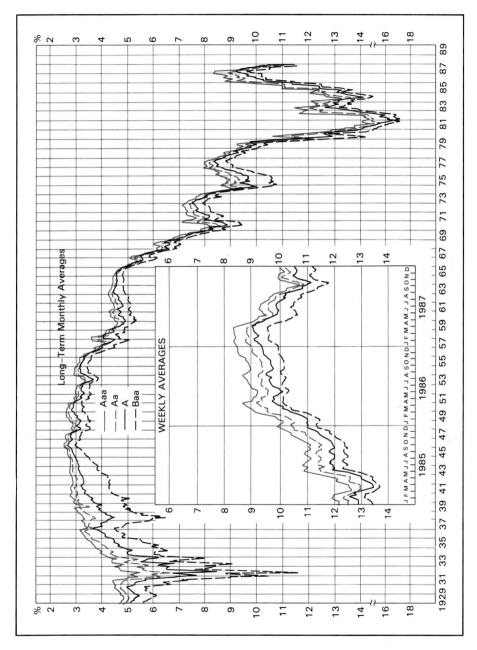

FIGURE 13–6
Corporate bond yields by ratings.

SOURCE: Moody's Bond Record, (January 1988): p. 402.

that do look not at yield spreads but at differences in the holding-period returns of AAA and BBB bonds.

13.4 DETERMINANTS OF YIELD SPREADS

As mentioned previously, when bond analysts refer to a corporate bond's yield spread, they are typically referring to the difference between the corporate bond's promised yield-to-maturity and that of another bond (often a Treasury security) having similar maturity and coupon rate. The greater the risk of default, the greater this spread should be. Moreover, bonds that have more marketability might command an additional "premium" in price and hence offer a lower yield-to-maturity with a corresponding lower spread. Given a large enough sample of bonds, it should be possible to see if these relationships really do exist.

One study of corporate bond prices did just this.[16] Three measures were used to assess the probability of default:

1. The extent to which the firm's net income had varied over the preceding nine years (measured by the coefficient of variation of earnings—that is, the ratio of standard deviation of earnings to average earnings),
2. The length of time that the firm had operated without forcing any of its creditors to take a loss, and
3. The ratio of the market value of the firm's equity to the par value of its debt.

The fourth measure was used to provide an indication of marketability:

4. The market value of the firm's outstanding debt.

First, these measures were calculated, along with the yield spread, for each one of 366 bonds. Second, the logarithm of every yield spread and measure was calculated. Third, statistical methods were used to analyze the relationship between a bond's yield spread and these measures. The one that was found to describe this relationship most accurately was:

$$\begin{aligned} \text{Yield spread} = .987 &+ .307(\text{earnings variability}) \\ &- .253(\text{time without default}) \\ &- .537(\text{equity/debt ratio}) \\ &- .275(\text{market value of debt}). \end{aligned} \quad (13.6)$$

This form of the relationship accounted for roughly 75% of the variation in the bonds' yield spreads.

The advantage of an equation such as this is that the coefficients can be easily interpreted. Since all yield spreads and values had been converted to logarithms, the effect is similar to that of using ratio scales on all axes

---

[16] Lawrence Fisher, "Determinants of Risk Premiums on Corporate Bonds," *Journal of Political Economy* 67, no. 3 (June 1959):217–37.

of a diagram. This means that a 1% increase in a bond's earnings variability can be expected to bring about an increase of .307% in the bond's yield spread, other things being equal. Similarly, a 1% increase in a bond's time without default can be expected to cause a decrease of approximately .253% in the bond's yield spread, and so on. Each coefficient is an elasticity, indicating the percentage change in a bond's yield spread likely to accompany a 1% change in the associated measure. Since every measure was found to be related in the expected direction to the yield spread, the study provides substantial support for the notion that bonds with higher default risk and less marketability have higher yield spreads.[17]

13.5 FINANCIAL RATIOS AS PREDICTORS OF DEFAULT

For years, security analysts have used accounting ratios to indicate the probability that a firm will fail to meet its financial obligations. Specific procedures have been developed to predict default with such ratios. Univariate analysis attempts to find the best single predictor for this purpose, whereas multivariate analysis searches for the best combination of two or more predictors.

☐ **13.5.1 Univariate Methods**

Cash inflows can be viewed as contributions to the firm's cash balance, and cash outflows can be viewed as drains on this balance. When the balance falls below zero, default is likely to occur. This means that the probability of default will be greater for the firm when (1) the existing cash balance is smaller; (2) the expected net cash flow (measured before payments to creditors and stockholders) is smaller; and (3) the net cash flow is more variable.

In an examination of various measures used to assess these factors, it was found that the ratio of net cash flow (income before depreciation, depletion, and amortization charges) to total debt was particularly useful.[18] Figure 13.7(a) shows the mean value of this ratio for a group of firms that defaulted on a promised payment and for a companion group that did not. As early as five years before default the two groups' ratios diverged, and the spread widened as the year of default approached.

This changing spread suggests that the probability of default may not be constant through time. Instead, warning signals may indicate an increase in the probability, which should, in turn, cause a fall in the market price of the firm's bonds along with a fall in the market price of its common stock. Figure 13.7(b) shows that such signals are indeed recognized in the mar-

---

[17] See pp. 510–11 in Foster, *Financial Statement Analysis*, for a discussion of yield spreads of municipal bonds.

[18] William H. Beaver, "Market Prices, Financial Ratios and the Prediction of Failure," *Journal of Accounting Research* 6, no. 2 (Autumn 1968):1979–92. For a more recent study, see James M. Gahlon and Robert L. Vigeland, "Early Warning Signs of Bankruptcy Using Cash Flow Analysis," *Journal of Commercial Bank Lending* 71, no. 4 (December 1988): 4–15.

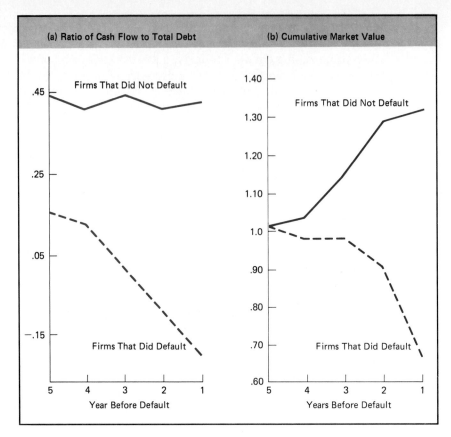

FIGURE 13-7
Financial ratios and market prices for firms that defaulted and those that did not.

SOURCE: William H. Beaver, "Market Prices, Financial Ratios and the Prediction of Failure," *Journal of Accounting Research* 6, no. 2 (Autumn 1968): pp. 182, 185.

ketplace. The median market value of common stock in the firms that did not default went up, while that of the firms that subsequently defaulted went down as the date of default approached.

☐ **13.5.2 Multivariate Methods**

Combinations of certain financial ratios have been considered as possible predictors of default.[19] Statistical analysis has indicated that the most accurate method of predicting default has been to calculate a firm's *Z score* from some of its financial ratios as follows:

$$Z = 1.2X_1 + 1.4X_2 + 3.3X_3 + .6X_4 + .99X_5 \qquad (13.7)$$

---

[19] Edward I. Altman, "Financial Ratios, Discriminant Analysis and the Prediction of Corporate Bankruptcy," *Journal of Finance* 23, no. 4 (September 1968):589–609.

where the following ratios are calculated from information contained in the firm's most recent income statement and balance sheet:

X_1 = (current assets − current liabilities)/total assets
X_2 = retained earnings/total assets
X_3 = earnings before interest and taxes/total assets
X_4 = market value of equity/book value of total debt
X_5 = sales/total assets.

Any firm with a Z-score below 1.8 is considered a likely candidate for default, and the lower the score, the greater the likelihood.[20]

☐ 13.5.3 Investment Implications

The preceding discussion does not mean that securities of firms whose cash-flow-to-total-debt ratio or Z-score had declined should be avoided. It should be remembered that the firms represented by the dashed lines in Figure 13.7 were chosen because they eventually defaulted. Had all firms with declining ratios been selected, corresponding decreases in their market price would undoubtedly have been observed, reflecting the increased probability of future default. However, only some of these firms would have ultimately defaulted, whereas the others would have recovered. Consequently, the gains on the firms that recovered might well have offset the losses on the firms that defaulted. In summary, the net result from purchasing a portfolio of stocks that had declining ratios or Z-scores is that the investor would have received an average return.

What about purchasing bonds of companies that have just had their ratings increased and selling (or avoiding) bonds of companies that have just had their ratings decreased? After all, such changes in ratings should be related to a change in the default risk of the issuer. In a study that looked at the behavior of bond prices around the time of ratings changes, some evidence was found that the bond price adjustment to a rating change occurred in the period from 18 to 7 months *before* the rating change.[21] Little or no evidence of a substantive price change was found either during the month of the rating change or in the period from six months before to six months after the rating change. These findings are consistent with the notion that the bond market is semistrong-form efficient, since bond ratings are predictable from publicly available information.

---

[20] Subsequent refinements to this model have been made, leading to a revised procedure known as *zeta analysis*. See Edward I. Altman, Robert G. Haldeman, and P. Narayanan, "Zeta Analysis: A New Model to Identify Bankruptcy Risk of Corporations," *Journal of Banking and Finance* 1, no. 1 (June 1977):29–54; and J. A. Ohlson, "Financial Ratios and the Probabilistic Prediction of Bankruptcy," *Journal of Accounting Research* 18, no. 1 (Spring 1980):109–31. For a study that suggests the predictive accuracy of both the Z-model and Zeta-model can be improved by adding certain cash flow-based variables, see Abdul Aziz and Gerald H. Lawson, "Cash Flow Reporting and Financial Distress Models: Testing of Hypotheses," *Financial Management* 18, no. 1 (Spring 1989):55–63. A summary of the literature on univariate and multivariate models is contained in Chapter 15 of Foster, *Financial Statement Analysis*.

[21] Mark I. Weinstein, "The Effect of a Rating Change Announcement on Bond Price," *Journal of Financial Economics* 5, no. 3 (December 1977):329–50.

13.6 SUMMARY

Bond analysts are concerned with identifying bonds that are mispriced. In doing so, they often estimate an appropriate yield-to-maturity for a given bond, based on the bond's characteristics and current market conditions. Bond attributes that are important in determining an appropriate yield-to-maturity consist of (1) length of time until maturity; (2) coupon rate; (3) call provisions; (4) tax status; (5) marketability; and (6) likelihood of default.

Determining an appropriate yield-to-maturity on a bond can be related to the use of the capitalization of income method of valuation. This method states that the intrinsic value of any financial asset is simply the present value of the expected future cash flows associated with the asset. In the case of bonds, the cash flows typically consist of coupon payments and par value.

Although the intrinsic value of a bond can be calculated and compared to the bond's market price, it is more common for bond analysts to see whether or not the bond's promised yield-to-maturity is appropriate. If the promised yield is more than appropriate, the bond is underpriced; if the promised yield is less than appropriate, the bond is overpriced.

QUESTIONS AND PROBLEMS

1. Patsy Tebeau is considering investing in a bond currently selling for $8,785.07. The bond has four years to maturity, a $10,000 face value, and an 8% coupon rate. The next interest payment is due one year from today. The appropriate discount rate for investments of similar risk is 10%.

   a. Calculate the intrinsic value of the bond. Based on this calculation, should Patsy purchase the bond?

   b. Calculate the yield-to-maturity of the bond. Based on this calculation, should Patsy purchase the bond?

2. Consider two bonds that both carry coupon rates of 8% and exhibit similar risk characteristics. However, the first bond has five years to maturity while the second has ten years to maturity. The appropriate discount rate for investments of similar risk is 8%. If the discount rate rises by two percentage points, what will be the respective percentage price changes of the two bonds?

3. Why is it convenient to use Treasury securities as a starting point for analyzing bond yields?

4. Burleigh Grimes purchased at par a bond with a face value of $1,000. The bond had five years to maturity and a 10% coupon rate. The bond was called two years later for a price of $1,100, after making its second annual interest payment. Burleigh then reinvested the proceeds in a bond selling at its face value of $1,000, with three years to maturity and a 7% coupon rate. What was Burleigh's actual yield-to-maturity over the five-year period?

5. Nellie Fox acquired at par a bond for $1,000 that offered a 9% coupon rate. At the time of purchase, the bond had four years to maturity. Assuming annual interest payments, calculate Nellie's actual yield-to-maturity if all the interest payments were reinvested in an investment earning 15% per year. What would Nellie's actual yield-to-maturity be if all interest payments were spent immediately upon receipt?

6. Distinguish between yield-to-first call and yield-to-maturity.

7. Based on the default premium model presented in the text, what is the fair value default premium for a bond with an expected yield-to-maturity of 8.5%, a 10% annual default probability, and an expected loss as a percent of market value of 60%?

8. Corporate default appears to be an event specific to an individual company. Yet despite the apparent diversifiable nature of corporate default (meaning that relatively few bonds would default in a well-diversified portfolio), the bond market systematically adds default premiums when valuing corporate bonds. Explain why.

9. Junk bonds are often viewed by investors as having financial characteristics much more akin to common stocks than to high grade corporate bonds. Why?

10. According to Lave Cross, "agency ratings indicate *relative* levels of risk instead of *absolute* levels of risk." Explain the meaning of Lave's statement.

11. Urban Shocker has noted that the spread between the yield-to-maturity on BBB-rated bonds and that on AAA-rated bonds has recently widened considerably. Explain to Urban what this change might indicate.

Chapter 14

BOND PORTFOLIO MANAGEMENT

The methods currently in use for managing bond portfolios can be divided into two general categories—passive and active. Methods in the passive category rest on the basic assumption that bond markets are semistrong-form efficient. That is, current bond prices are viewed as accurately reflecting all publicly available information. Thus, bonds are felt to be priced fairly in the marketplace, providing a return that is commensurate with the risk involved. In addition to believing that individual bonds are not mispriced, passive investors also believe that attempting to predict interest rates is, in general, futile. In summary, passive management rests on the belief that attempts at both security selection (that is, identifying mispriced bonds) and market timing (for example, buying long-term bonds when interest rates are predicted to fall and replacing them with short-term bonds when interest rates are predicted to rise) will be unsuccessful in providing the investor with above-average returns.

Active methods of bond portfolio management are based on the assumption that the bond market is not so efficient, thereby giving some investors the opportunity to earn above-average returns. That is, active management is based on the ability of the portfolio manager either to identify mispriced bonds or to "time" the bond market by accurately predicting interest rates.

This chapter discusses these two general approaches to bond portfolio management. It begins by reviewing some of the findings regarding the efficiency of the bond market.

14.1 BOND MARKET EFFICIENCY

In assessing the efficiency of the bond market, only a few of the major studies are mentioned. The impression obtained from reading them is that bond markets appear to be highly, but not perfectly, semistrong-form efficient. That is, bond prices tend to reflect almost all publicly available information. Not surprisingly, this impression is similar to the one that is obtained from studies of the efficiency of stock markets.

□ 14.1.1 Price Behavior of Treasury Bills

An early study of bond market efficiency focused on the price behavior of Treasury bills. In particular, the prices of Treasury bills were analyzed on a weekly basis from October 1946 through December 1964, a total of 796 weeks. The study found that knowledge of how Treasury bill prices changed in the past was of little use in trying to predict how they would change in the future. Consequently, the results from this study are consistent with the notion that the market for Treasury bills is weak-form efficient.[1]

□ 14.1.2 Experts' Predictions of Interest Rates

Bond market efficiency has also been studied by examining the accuracy of interest rate predictions that have been made by experts. These people use a wide range of techniques and a number of different sources of information. Since it is reasonable to assume their information is publicly available, such studies can be viewed as tests of semistrong-form efficiency.

One way these tests have been conducted involves the building of statistical models that are based on what the experts have said in regard to how interest rates should be predicted. Once these models have been constructed, their predictive accuracy can be evaluated. In one study, six different models were constructed and then their one-month ahead predictions were tested over the two-year period of 1973 to 1974. Consistent with the notion of efficient markets, it was found that a simple model of "no change" was more accurate in predicting interest rates than any of the six statistical models.[2]

Another way these tests have been conducted involves comparing a set of explicit predictions with what subsequently actually occurred. One source of such predictions is the quarterly survey of interest rate expectations that appears in the *Goldsmith-Nagan Bond and Money Market Newsletter*, published by Goldsmith-Nagan, Inc. Specifically, this survey reports the predictions made by a number (roughly 50) of "money market professionals" regarding three-month ahead and six-month ahead levels of 10 different interest rates. In one study, the predictions made from September 1969 through December 1972 (that is, 14 sets of quarterly predictions) were compared with those of a "no-change" model—that is, a model that forecasts no change from the current level of interest rates.[3]

---

[1] For details, see Richard Roll, *The Behavior of Interest Rates* (New York: Basic Books, Inc., 1970). Interestingly, this study also produced evidence rejecting the unbiased expectations theory of the term structure of interest rates.

[2] J. Walter Elliott and Jerome R. Baier, "Econometric Models and Current Interest Rates: How Well Do They Predict Future Rates?" *Journal of Finance* 34, no. 4 (September 1979):975–86. It should be noted that the models used by major economic forecasting firms tend to have similar amounts of accuracy. See Stephen K. McNees, "Forecasting Accuracy of Alternative Techniques: A Comparison of U.S. Macroeconomic Forecasts," *Journal of Business & Economic Statistics* 4, no. 1 (January 1986):5–15, particularly Table 6 where 90-day Treasury bill rate forecasts are evaluated.

[3] Michael J. Prell, "How Well Do the Experts Forecast Interest Rates?" Federal Reserve Bank of Kansas City *Monthly Review* (September–October 1973):3–13.

Interestingly, the professionals seemed to forecast better than the no-change model for short-term interest rates (such as forecasting what the three-month Treasury bill rate will be three months in the future) but did worse than the no-change model for longer-term interest rates (such as forecasting what the intermediate-term Treasury note rate will be three months in the future).

A subsequent study examined the Goldsmith-Nagan predictions of three-month Treasury bill rates six months in the future during the time period from March 1970 through September 1979 (39 predictions).[4] These predictions were compared with those of three "simple" models, the first one being the no-change model. The second simple model was based on the liquidity preference theory of the term structure of interest rates (discussed in Chapter 4). According to this theory, the forward rate implicit in current market rates should be equal to the expected future interest rate plus a liquidity premium. Thus, a forecast of the expected future interest rate can be gotten by subtracting an estimate of the liquidity premium from the forward rate. The third simple model was what statisticians refer to as an autoregressive model. Basically, a forecast of the future Treasury bill rate was formed from the current Treasury bill rate as well as what the Treasury bill rate was one, two, three, and six quarters ago. The study found that the professionals were more accurate than both the no-change model and the liquidity premium model but were less accurate than the autoregressive model.

Another study evaluated the six-month ahead predictions of three-month Treasury bill rates that were made by nine economists and reported semiannually in *The Wall Street Journal*. Evaluating the forecasts published from December 1981 through June 1986, it was found that the no-change model was more accurate.[5]

In summary, it appears from this evidence that the no-change model sometimes provides the most accurate forecasts of future interest rates while at other times the experts are more accurate. On the balance, a reasonable interpretation of these results is that the bond market is nearly semistrong-form efficient. While the bond market may not be perfectly efficient, the evidence clearly suggests that it is hard to be able to consistently forecast interest rates with greater accuracy than a no-change model.[6]

---

[4] Adrian W. Throop, "Interest Rate Forecasts and Market Efficiency," Federal Reserve Bank of San Francisco *Economic Review* (Spring 1981):29–43. This article contains a useful reference list of other studies concerning the prediction of interest rates.

[5] Forecasts implicit in the futures market (discussed in Chapter 19) for Treasury bills were also found to be more accurate than those of the economists but less accurate than those of the no-change model over this time period. For a longer time period, the futures market and no-change model forecasts were of comparable accuracy. See Michael T. Belognia, "Predicting Interest Rates: A Comparison of Professional and Market-Based Forecasts," Federal Reserve Bank of St. Louis *Review* 69, no. 3 (March 1987):9–15.

[6] The reported accuracy of macroeconomic forecasters in regard to Treasury bill rates (see the Early Quarter results for a two-quarter horizon in Table 6 of McNees, "Forecast Accuracy") can be compared to the reported accuracy of the no-change model (see Table 1 of Belognia, "Predicting Interest Rates"). While such a comparison should be done with caution, it does suggest that the no-change model is of similar, and in some cases, superior, accuracy.

☐ 14.1.3   Price Reaction to Bond Rating Changes

A different type of test of market efficiency concerned the reaction of bond prices to rating changes. If ratings are based on public information, then any rating change would follow the release of such information. This suggests that in a semistrong-form efficient market, a bond's price would react to the release of the public information rather than the subsequent announcement of the rating change. Thus, an announcement of a rating change should not trigger a subsequent adjustment in the associated bond's price.

In a study that examined 100 rating changes that took place during the period of 1962 through 1974, no significant changes in bond prices were detected in the period from six months before through six months after the announcement of the change. However, a significant change was observed in the period from 18 months through 7 months before the announcement. Specifically, ratings increases were preceded by price increases, and rating decreases were preceded by price decreases.[7]

☐ 14.1.4   Money Supply Announcements

Every week, generally on Thursday, the Federal Reserve Board announces the current size of the money supply in the economy. Now, it is known that interest rates are related to, among other things, the availability of credit and that the money supply affects this availability. This means that if the money supply figures are surprisingly high or low, then the announcement should trigger adjustments in the levels of various interest rates.[8] Furthermore, such adjustments should take place rapidly in a semistrong-form efficient market. Past studies indicate that such adjustments are indeed rapid, generally taking place within a day after the announcement.[9]

☐ 14.1.5   Summary

In summary, the evidence on the efficiency of the bond market is consistent with the notion that it is highly, but not perfectly, semistrong-form efficient. Statistical tests of past prices of Treasury bills suggest it is efficient. It

---

[7] See Mark I. Weinstein, "The Effect of a Rating Change Announcement on Bond Price," *Journal of Financial Economics* 5, no. 3 (December 1977):329–50. A study of the prices of the common stocks associated with bonds that had rating changes reported similar results—stock prices tended to change several months prior to the announcement dates of the rating changes. See George E. Pinches and J. Clay Singleton, "The Adjustment of Stock Prices to Bond Rating Changes," *Journal of Finance* 33, no. 1 (March 1978):29–44.

[8] For an explanation of this adjustment process, see Richard G. Sheehan, "Weekly Money Announcements: New Information and Its Effects," Federal Reserve Bank of St. Louis *Review* 67, no. 7 (August/September 1985):25–34.

[9] See, for example, Thomas Urich and Paul Wachtel, "Market Response to Weekly Money Supply Announcements in the 1970s," *Journal of Finance* 36, no. 5 (December 1981):1063–72, and "The Effects of Inflation and Money Supply Announcements on Interest Rates," *Journal of Finance* 39, no. 4 (September 1984):1177–88; and Bradford Cornell, "Money Supply Announcements and Interest Rates: Another View," *Journal of Business* 56, no. 1 (January 1983):1–23.

appears that corporate bonds reflect the information leading to a rating change in a timely fashion and that interest rates change rapidly when there is a surprise in the announced size of the money supply, observations that are also consistent with the notion of efficiency.

However, there is some evidence that suggests certain professionals are occasionally able to forecast interest rates in an accurate manner. With this in mind, it is not surprising that some bond managers have opted to follow a passive approach to investing while others have decided to be more active in their approach. These two approaches are presented next, beginning with a discussion of some bond pricing theorems. In turn, these theorems will be related to duration, a concept introduced in Chapter 4, which is the basis for one method of passively managing a bond portfolio.

14.2 BOND-PRICING THEOREMS

Bond-pricing theorems deal with how bond prices move in response to changes in their yields-to-maturity. Before presenting the theorems, a brief review of some terms associated with bonds is given.

The typical bond is characterized by a promise to pay the investor two types of cash flows. The first involves the payment of a fixed dollar amount periodically (usually every six months), with the last payment being on a stated date. The second type of cash flow involves the payment of a lump sum on this stated date. The periodic payments are known as *coupon payments*, and the lump sum payment is known as the bond's principal (or par value or face value). A bond's *coupon rate* is calculated by dividing the dollar amount of the coupon payments a bondholder would receive over the course of a year by the principal of the bond. Lastly, the amount of time left until the last promised payment is made is known as the bond's *term-to-maturity*, whereas the discount rate that makes the present value of all the cash flows equal to the market price of the bond is known as the bond's *yield-to-maturity* (or, simply, yield).

Note that if a bond has a market price that is equal to its par value, then its yield-to-maturity will be equal to its coupon rate. However, if the market price is less than par value (a situation where the bond is said to be selling at a discount), then the bond will have a yield-to-maturity that is greater than the coupon rate. Conversely, if the market price is greater than par value (a situation where the bond is said to be selling at a premium), then the bond will have a yield-to-maturity that is less than the coupon rate.

With this in mind, five theorems that deal with bond pricing have been derived.[10] For ease of exposition, it is assumed that there is one coupon payment per year (that is, coupon payments are made every 12 months). The theorems are as follows:

---

[10] Burton G. Malkiel, "Expectations, Bond Prices, and the Term Structure of Interest Rates," *Quarterly Journal of Economics* 76, no. 2 (May 1962):197–218. Also see Frank J. Fabozzi and T. Dessa Fabozzi, *Bond Markets, Analysis and Strategies* (Englewood Cliffs, N.J.: Prentice Hall, 1989), particularly Chapter 4.

1. *If a bond's market price increases, then its yield must decrease; conversely, if a bond's market price decreases, then its yield must increase.*

   As an example, consider bond A that has a life of five years and a par value of $1000 and pays coupons annually of $80. Its yield is 8%, since it is currently selling for $1000. However, if its price increases to $1100, then its yield will fall to 5.76%. Conversely, if its price falls to $900, then its yield will rise to 10.68%.

2. *If a bond's yield does not change over its life, then the size of its discount or premium will decrease as its life gets shorter.*

   As an example, consider bond B that has a life of five years and a par value of $1000 and pays coupons annually of $60. Its current market price is $883.31, indicating it has a yield of 9%. After one year, if it still has a yield of 9%, it will be selling for $902.81. Thus, its discount has decreased from $1000 − $883.31 = $116.69 to $1000 − $902.81 = $97.19, for a change of $116.69 − $97.19 = $19.50.

   An equivalent interpretation of this theorem is that if two bonds have the same coupon rate, par value, and yield, then the one with the shorter life will sell for a smaller discount or premium. Consider two bonds, one with a life of five years and the other with a life of four years. Both bonds have a par value of $1000, pay annual coupons of $60, and yield 9%. In this situation, the one with a five-year life has a discount of $116.69, whereas the one with a four-year life has a smaller discount of $97.19.

3. *If a bond's yield does not change over its life, then the size of its discount or premium will decrease at an increasing rate as its life gets shorter.*

   As an example, consider bond B again. After two years, if it still has a yield of 9%, it will be selling for $924.06. Thus, its discount has decreased to $1000 − $924.06 = $75.94. Now, the amount of the change in the discount from five years to four years was $116.69 − $97.19 = $19.50, for a percentage change from par of 19.50%. However, the amount of the change from four years to three years is larger, going from $97.19 to $75.94, for a dollar change of $21.25 and a percentage change from par of 21.25%.

4. *A decrease in a bond's yield will raise the bond's price by an amount that is greater in size than the corresponding fall in the bond's price that would occur if there were an equal-sized increase in the bond's yield.*

   As an example, consider bond C that has a life of five years and a coupon rate of 7%. Since it is currently selling at its par value of $1000, its yield is 7%. If its yield rises by 1% to 8%, then it will be selling for $960.07, a change of $39.93. Alternatively, if its yield falls by 1% to 6%, then it will be selling for $1042.12, a change of $42.12, which is of greater magnitude than the $39.93 associated with the 1% rise in the bond's yield.

   This property is sometimes referred to as *convexity*, since a graph representing a bond's price as a function of its yield will be negatively sloped and convex.

5. *The percentage change in a bond's price due to a change in its yield will be smaller if its coupon rate is higher.* (*Note*: This theorem does not apply to bonds with a life of one year or to bonds that have no maturity date, known as consols, or perpetuities.)

As an example, compare bond D with bond C. Bond D has a coupon rate of 9%, which is 2% larger than C's. However, bond D has the same life (five years) and yield (7%) as C. Thus, D's current market price is $1082.00. If the yield on both C and D increase to 8%, then their prices will be $960.07 and $1039.93, respectively. This represents a decrease in the price of C equal to $1000 − $960.07 = $39.93, or 3.993% (*note*: 3.993% = $39.93/$1000). For D, the decrease in price is equal to $1082 − $1039.93 = $42.07, or 3.889% (*note*: 3.889% = $42.07/$1082). Since D has the higher coupon rate, it has the smaller percentage change in price.

It is important for a bond analyst to understand thoroughly these properties of bond prices, since they are valuable in forecasting how bond prices will respond to changes in interest rates. In addition, duration is valuable in understanding how the prices of bonds change in response to a change in interest rates. This concept forms the basis for one method of passively managing a bond portfolio and is discussed next.

14.3 DURATION

One implication of theorem 5 is that bonds having the same maturity date but different coupon sizes may react to a given change in interest rates in a dissimilar manner. That is, the prices of these bonds may adjust by notably different amounts when there is a given change in interest rates. However, bonds with the same duration will react quite similarly.

☐ 14.3.1 Calculation

As mentioned in Chapter 4, *duration* is a measure of the "average maturity" of the stream of payments associated with a bond. More specifically, it is a weighted average of the lengths of time until the remaining payments are made. Consider, for example, a bond with annual coupon payments of $80, a remaining life of three years, and a par value of $1000. Since it has a current market price of $950.25, it has a yield-to-maturity of 10.00%. As shown in Table 14.1, its duration is 2.78 years. Note that this is calculated by taking the present value of each cash flow, multiplying each one by the respective amount of time until it is received, summing the resulting figures up, and then dividing this sum ($2639.17) by the market price of the bond ($950.25).

TABLE 14.1

Calculation of Duration.

TIME UNTIL RECEIPT OF CASH FLOW	AMOUNT OF CASH FLOW	PRESENT VALUE FACTOR	PRESENT VALUE OF CASH FLOW	PRESENT VALUE OF CASH FLOW × TIME
1	$ 80	.9091	$ 72.73	$ 72.73
2	80	.8264	66.12	132.23
3	1,080	.7513	811.40	2434.21
			$950.25	$2639.17

$$\text{Duration} = \frac{\$2639.17}{\$950.25} = 2.78 \text{ years}$$

Specifically, the formula for a bond's duration (D) is

$$D = \frac{\sum_{t=1}^{T} PV(C_t) \times t}{P_0} \tag{14.1}$$

where $PV(C_t)$ denotes the present value of the cash flow to be received at time t, calculated using a discount rate equal to the bond's yield-to-maturity; P_0 denotes the current market price of the bond; and T denotes the bond's remaining life.[11]

Why is duration thought of as the "average maturity of the stream of payments associated with a bond?" This can be seen by realizing that the current market price of the bond, P_0, is equal to the sum of the present values of the cash flows, $PV(C_t)$, where the discount rate is the bond's yield-to-maturity:

$$P_0 = \sum_{t=1}^{T} PV(C_t). \tag{14.2}$$

Thus, there is an equivalent method for calculating a bond's duration that can be seen by rewriting equation (14.1) in a slightly different manner:

$$D = \sum_{t=1}^{T} \left[\frac{PV(C_t)}{P_0} \times t \right]. \tag{14.3}$$

First, the present value of each cash flow $[PV(C_t)]$ is expressed as a proportion of the market price (P_0). Second, these proportions are multiplied by the respective amount of time until the cash flows are received. Third, these figures are added, with the sum being equal to the bond's duration.

---

[11] There are other methods of calculating a bond's duration. For example, instead of using the bond's yield to calculate $PV(C_t)$, the appropriate current spot rate could be used. The concept of duration was initially developed in 1938 by Frederick R. Macauley in *Some Theoretical Problems Suggested by the Movements of Interest Rates, Bond Yields, and Stock Prices in the United States Since 1856* (New York: National Bureau of Economic Research). For an interesting article describing the development of the concept of duration (as well as immunization), see Roman L. Weil, "Macaulay's Duration: An Appreciation," *Journal of Business 46*, no. 4 (October 1973):589–92.

In the example shown in Table 14.1, note that $72.73/$950.25 = .07653 of the bond's market price is to be received in one year. Similarly, $66.12/$950.25 = .06958 is to be received in two years, and $811.40/$950.25 = .85388 is to be received in three years. Note how these proportions sum to one, which means that they can be interpreted as weights in calculating a weighted average. Thus, to calculate the average maturity of the payments associated with a bond, each weight needs to be multiplied by the respective amount of time until the corresponding cash flow is to be received, and then the products need to be summed up: $(1 \times .07653) + (2 \times .06958) + (3 \times .85388) = 2.78$ years.

Note how a zero-coupon bond will have a duration equal to its remaining life, T, since there is only one cash flow associated with such a bond. That is, since $P_0 = PV(C_T)$ for such bonds, equation (14.3) reduces to:

$$D = \frac{PV(C_T)}{P_0} \times T$$

$$= 1 \times T$$

$$= T.$$

For any coupon-bearing bond, its duration will always be less than the amount of time to its maturity date, T. Again, examination of equation (14.3) indicates why this is so. Since the largest value that t can have is T, and each value of t is multiplied by a weight equal to $PV(C_t)/P_0$, it follows that D must be less than T.

☐ 14.3.2 Changes in the Term Structure

As mentioned earlier, when interest rates change, most bond prices also change, but some react more than others. Even bonds with the same maturity date can react quite differently to a given change in interest rates. However, it can be shown that the percentage change in a bond's price is related to its duration in the following fashion:

$$\begin{matrix} \text{Percentage} \\ \text{change in} \\ \text{price} \end{matrix} \cong -D \times \begin{matrix} \text{percentage change} \\ \text{in (one plus the} \\ \text{bond's yield)} \end{matrix} \qquad (14.4)$$

where the symbol $\cong$ means "is approximately equal to." This formula implies that when the yields of two bonds having the same duration change by the same percentage, then the prices of the two bonds will change by approximately equal percentages.

For example, the bond shown in Table 14.1 had a duration of 2.78 and a yield of 10%. If its yield changes to 11%, then the percentage change in (one plus the bond's yield) is $(1.11 - 1.10)/(1.10) = .91\%$. Thus, its price should change by approximately $-2.78 \times .91\% = -2.53\%$. Using a discount rate of 11%, its price can be calculated to equal $926.69, for an actual price change of $950.25 - $926.69 = $23.56 and a percentage change of $23.56/

$950.25 = 2.48\%$. Any other bond having a duration of 2.78 years will experience a similar price change if it has a similar percentage change in its yield.

Consider a bond with a maturity of four years that also has a duration of 2.78 years. When there is a shift in interest rates and the yields on the three- and four-year bonds change by the same amount, then their prices will change similarly. For example, if the yield on the four-year bond goes from 10.8% to 11.81% at the same time the yield on the three-year bond is going from 10% to 11%, then the percentage change in the present value of the four-year bond will be approximately $-2.78 \times [(1.1181 - 1.108)/1.108] = -2.78 \times .91\% = 2.53\%$, which is the same as the percentage change for the three-year bond.

What if the percentage change in one plus the bond's yield is different? Perhaps when the three-year bond goes from a yield of 10% to a yield of 11% (a percentage change of $(1.11 - 1.10)/1.10 = .91\%$), the four-year bond will go from a yield of 10.8% to a yield of 11.5% (a percentage change of $(1.115 - 1.108)/1.108 = .63\%$). In this case, the percentage change in price for the four-year bond will be approximately $-2.78 \times [(1.115 - 1.108)/(1.108)] = -1.75\%$, which is a smaller change than the -2.53% associated with the three-year bond. Accordingly, even though the two bonds have the same duration, it does not automatically follow that their prices will react identically to any change in yields, since these yield changes can be different for two bonds having the same duration.

14.4 IMMUNIZATION

The introduction of the concept of duration has led to the development of the technique of bond portfolio management known as *immunization*.[12] Specifically, this technique allegedly allows a bond portfolio manager to be relatively certain of being able to meet a given promised stream of cash outflows. Thus, once the portfolio has been formed, it is "immunized" from any adverse effects associated with future changes in interest rates.

☐ 14.4.1 How Immunization Is Accomplished

Immunization is accomplished by simply calculating the duration of the promised outflows and then investing in a portfolio of bonds that have an identical duration. In doing so, this technique takes advantage of the observation that the *duration of a portfolio of bonds is equal to the weighted average of the durations of the individual bonds in the portfolio.* For example, if one-third of a portfolio's funds are invested in bonds having a duration of six years and two-thirds of its funds are in bonds having a duration of three

---

[12] For the initial development, see F. M. Redington, "Review of the Principles of Life-Office Valuations," *Journal of the Institute of Actuaries* 78, no. 3 (1952):286–315. A useful book that discusses duration-based investment strategies has been written by Gerald O. Bierwag, entitled *Duration Analysis* (Cambridge, Mass: Ballinger Publishing Company, 1987).

years, then the portfolio itself has a duration of $[(1/3) \times 6] + [(2/3) \times 3] = 4$ years.

Consider a simple situation where a portfolio manager has one and only one cash outflow to make from his or her portfolio—an amount equal to $1,000,000 that is to be paid in two years. Since there is only one cash outflow, its duration is simply two years. Now, the bond portfolio manager is considering investing in two different bond issues. The first bond issue is the one shown in Table 14.1, where the bonds have a maturity of three years. The second bond issue involves a set of bonds that mature in one year, providing the holder of each bond with a single payment of $1070 (consisting of a single coupon payment of $70 and a par value of $1000). Since these bonds are currently selling for $972.73, their yield-to-maturity is 10%.

Consider the choices open to the portfolio manager. All the portfolio's funds could be invested in the one-year bonds, with the notion of reinvesting the proceeds from the maturing bonds one year from now in another one-year issue. However, doing so would entail risks. In particular, if interest rates were to decline over the next year, then the funds from the maturing one-year bonds must be reinvested at a lower rate than the currently available 10%. Thus, the portfolio manager faces reinvestment-rate risk due to the possibility that the funds one year from now can only be reinvested at a lower rate.[13]

A second alternative would be for the portfolio manager to invest all the funds in the three-year issue. However, this also entails risks. In particular, the three-year bonds will have to be sold after two years in order to come up with the $1,000,000. The risk is that interest rates will have risen before then, meaning that bond prices, in general, will have fallen and the bonds will not have a selling price that is equal to or greater than $1,000,000. Thus, the portfolio manager faces interest-rate risk with this strategy.

One proposed solution is to invest part of the portfolio's funds in the one-year bonds and the rest in the three-year bonds. How much should be placed in each issue? If immunization is to be used, the solution can be found by solving simultaneously a set of two equations involving two unknowns:

$$W_1 + W_3 = 1 \qquad \qquad (14.5)$$

$$(W_1 \times 1) + (W_3 \times 2.78) = 2. \qquad \qquad (14.6)$$

Here, W_1 and W_3 denote the weights (or proportions) of the portfolio's funds that are to be invested in the bonds with maturities of one and three years, respectively. Note how equation (14.5) states that the sum of the weights must equal 1, whereas equation (14.6) states that the weighted average of the durations of the bonds in the portfolio must equal the duration of the cash outflow, which is two years.

---

[13] If there were two-year coupon-bearing bonds available for investment, then there would be no reinvestment-rate risk associated with the principal. However, the investor would still face reinvestment-rate risk in terms of the coupon payments received after one year. Although such risk appears to be relatively minor in this example, such risk becomes much more substantial in situations involving promised cash outflows that are more than two years into the future.

The solution to these two equations is easily found. First, equation (14.5) is rewritten as

$$W_1 = 1 - W_3. \tag{14.7}$$

Then, $1 - W_3$ is substituted for W_1 in equation (14.6), resulting in

$$[(1 - W_3) \times 1] + (W_3 \times 2.78) = 2. \tag{14.8}$$

Since this is one equation with one unknown, W_3, it can be easily solved. Doing so results in $W_3 = .5618$. Inserting this value into equation (14.7) indicates that $W_1 = .4382$. Thus, the portfolio manager should put 43.82% of the portfolio's funds in the one-year bonds and 56.18% in the three-year bonds.

In this case, the portfolio manager would need $\$1,000,000/(1.10^2) = \$826,446$ in order to purchase bonds that would create a fully immunized portfolio. With this money, $.4382 \times \$826,446 = \$362,149$ would be used to buy one-year bonds and $.5618 \times \$826,446 = \$464,297$ would be used to buy three-year bonds. Since the current market prices of the one-year and three-year bonds are $\$972.73$ and $\$950.25$, respectively, this means that 372 $(= \$362,149/\$972.73)$ one-year bonds and 489 $(= \$464,297/\$950.25)$ three-year bonds would be purchased.

What does immunization accomplish? According to theory, if yields rise, then the portfolio's losses due to the selling of the three-year bonds at a discount after two years will be exactly offset by the gains from reinvesting the maturing one-year bonds (and first-year coupons on the three-year bonds) at the higher rate. Alternatively, if yields fall, then the loss from being able to reinvest the maturing one-year bonds (and first-year coupons on the three-year bonds) at a lower rate will be exactly offset by being able to sell the

TABLE 14.2

An Example of an Immunized Portfolio.

	YIELD-TO-MATURITY AT THE END OF ONE YEAR		
	9%	10%	11%
Value at $t = 2$ from reinvesting one-year bond proceeds:			
$[\$1070 \times 372.3 \times (1 + y)] =$	$ 434,213	$438,197	$ 442,181
Value at $t = 2$ of three-year bonds: Value from reinvesting coupons received at $t = 1$:			
$[\$80 \times 488.6 \times (1 + y)] =$	42,606	42,997	43,388
Coupons received at $t = 2$:			
$[\$80 \times 488.6] =$	39,088	39,088	39,088
Selling price at $t = 2$:			
$[\$1080 \times 488.6/(1 + y)] =$	484,117	479,716	475,395
Aggregate portfolio value at $t = 2$	$1,000,024	$999,998	$1,000,052

three-year bonds after two years at a premium. Thus, the portfolio is immunized from the effect of any movements in the interest rates in the future.

Table 14.2 shows more explicitly what would happen to the portfolio. The second column shows what the portfolio would be worth at the end of two years if yields remained at 10% over the next two years. As can be seen, the value of the portfolio of one-year and three-year bonds would be approximately equal to the promised cash outflow of $1,000,000. Alternatively, if yields fell to 9% or rose to 11% before one year had passed and remained at the new level, then value of the portfolio would be slightly more than the needed $1,000.000.

☐ 14.4.2 Problems with Immunization

The previous paragraph described what immunization accomplishes in theory. This leaves open the possibility that it might not work quite as well in practice. What can cause it to work less than perfectly? In terms of the example, what can cause the value of the portfolio to be less than $1,000,000 at the end of two years?

Default and Call Risk

To begin with, immunization is based on the belief that all the bonds' promised cash flows will subsequently be paid in full and on time. This means that immunization is based on the assumption that the bond will not default and will not be called before maturity—that is, the bonds are assumed to be free from both call risk and default risk. Consequently, if a bond in the portfolio either enters into default or is called, the portfolio will not be immunized.[14]

Multiple Nonparallel Shifts in a Nonhorizontal Yield Curve

Immunization is also based on the assumption that the yield curve is horizontal and that any shifts in it will be parallel and will occur before any payments are received from the bonds that were purchased. In the example, both the one-year and three-year bonds had the same 10% yield-to-maturity at the start, and the shift of 1% in yields was assumed to be the same for both bond issues. Furthermore, this shift was assumed to occur sometime before one year had passed.

In reality, the yield curve will not be horizontal at the start, and shifts in it are not likely to be either parallel or restricted in when they occur. Perhaps the one-year and three-year bonds will have initial yields of 10% and 10.5%, respectively, with the yields on the one-year and three-year bonds falling by 1% and .8%, respectively, after one year. Indeed, there is evidence

---

[14] For a discussion of how to include nondefault-free callable bonds in an immunized portfolio, see Gordon J. Alexander and Bruce G. Resnick, "Using Linear and Goal Programming to Immunize Bond Portfolios," *Journal of Banking and Finance* 9, no. 1 (March 1985):35–54; and G. O. Bierwag and George G. Kaufman, "Durations of Non-Default-Free Securities," *Financial Analysts Journal* 44, no. 4 (July/August 1988):39–46, 62.

that there is greater volatility in yields of shorter-term securities.[15] If these kinds of shifts were to occur, then it is possible that the portfolio would not be immunized.

If the bond portfolio manager followed a special kind of immunization known as *cash matching*, then frequent nonparallel shifts in a nonhorizontal yield curve would have no adverse effect on the portfolio. This is because cash matching involves the purchase of bonds so that the cash received each period from the bonds is identical in size to the promised cash outflow for that period.

Such a cash-matching portfolio of bonds is often referred to as a *dedicated portfolio*. Note that there is no need to reinvest any cash inflows in the future with a dedicated portfolio, so there is no reinvestment rate risk. Furthermore, since bonds do not have to be sold prior to maturity, there is no interest rate risk either.[16]

In the simplest situation where there is one promised cash outflow, the dedicated portfolio would consist of zero-coupon bonds, where each bond has a life corresponding to the date of the promised cash outflow. In the previous example where there was a promised cash outflow of $1,000,000 after two years, this would be accomplished by purchasing the requisite number of zero-coupon bonds having a maturity of two years.

However, cash matching is often not so easily accomplished. This is because the promised cash outflows may involve an uneven stream of payments for which no zero-coupon bonds exist. Indeed, it can be difficult (if not impossible) and expensive to match cash inflows exactly with promised outflows.

Another potential way around the problem of having nonhorizontal yield curves that have nonparallel shifts is to use one of a variety of more complicated immunization models. These models involve various other assumptions about the current shape of the yield curve and how it will shift in the future. Consequently, the bond portfolio manager must choose the one that is personally viewed as being most accurate. Interestingly, various studies have found that the best performer was the version of immunization that has been described in this chapter, and not the more complicated models. Thus, some researchers argue that the portfolio manager interested in immunization would be well advised to use this version.[17]

An implication is that regardless of the model being used, the bond

[15] See in George G. Kaufman, G. O. Bierwag, and Alden Toevs, eds., *Innovations in Bond Portfolio Management: Duration Analysis and Immunization* (Greenwich, Conn: JAI Press Inc., 1983) the articles by Jeffrey Nelson and Stephen Schaefer, "The Dynamics of the Term Structure and Alternative Portfolio Immunization Strategies," 61–101, and Jonathan E. Ingersoll, Jr., "Is Immunization Feasible? Evidence from the CRSP Data," 163–82.

[16] For more on dedicated portfolios, see Martin L. Leibowitz, "The Dedicated Bond Portfolio in Pension Funds—Part I: Motivations and Basics," *Financial Analysts Journal* 42, no. 1 (January/February 1986):69–75, and "The Dedicated Bond Portfolio in Pension Funds–Part II: Immunization, Horizon Matching and Contingent Procedures," *Financial Analysts Journal* 42, no. 2 (March/April 1986):47–57.

[17] For a summary and set of references, see G. O. Bierwag, George G. Kaufman, Robert Schweitzer, and Alden Toevs, "The Art of Risk Management in Bond Portfolios," *Journal of Portfolio Management* 7, no. 3 (Spring 1981):27–36; G. O. Bierwag, George G. Kaufman, and Alden Toevs, "Duration: Its Development and Use in Bond Portfolio Management," *Financial Analysts Journal* 39, no. 4 (July–August 1983):15–35; and Stephen M. Schaefer, "Immunization and Duration: A Review of Theory, Performance and Applications," *Midland Corporate Finance Journal* 2, no. 3 (Fall 1984):41–58.

portfolio manager must recognize that there is a risk being incurred—the risk that the yield curve will shift in a way that does not correspond with the way assumed by the model. For example, if the model presented here is used, then the bond portfolio is facing risk in that the yield curve will not shift in a parallel manner. Consequently, some people have argued that none of the immunization models are useful.[18] Others have argued that there are ways to use immunization in the presence of such risk, which has been called *stochastic process risk*.[19]

Rebalancing

Another problem with the use of immunization is the affect of the passage of time on the duration of the bonds held and on the duration of the promised cash outflows. As time passes and yields change, these durations can change at different rates so that the portfolio is no longer immunized. This means that the portfolio may need to be *rebalanced* fairly often.

Here, rebalancing refers to selling some bonds currently held and replacing them with others so that afterward, the duration of the portfolio matches the duration of the promised cash outflows. However, since rebalancing causes the portfolio manager to incur transaction costs, the manager might not want to rebalance whenever the durations do not match, since the costs might outweigh the perceived gains from rebalancing. Ultimately, the bond portfolio manager will have to decide how frequently to rebalance the portfolio, taking into consideration the risk of being unbalanced along with the transaction costs associated with rebalancing.

Choosing from Among Many Candidates

Lastly, there are usually many portfolios that have a duration of the requisite length. Which one is the bond portfolio manager to choose? In the example, imagine that in addition to the one-year and three-year bonds, there is a zero-coupon bond having a life of four years (thus, its duration is also four years) that the manager is considering. Now the manager faces a choice of which portfolio to hold, since there are many with the requisite duration of two years. In addition to the one previously described that consisted of just one-year and three-year bonds, there is also one where two-thirds and one-third of the portfolio's funds are invested in one-year bonds and four-year bonds, respectively. (Note how the duration of this portfolio is also two years: $(2/3 \times 1) + (1/3 \times 4) = 2$.) Furthermore, there are many other candidate portfolios.

One possible solution is to choose the portfolio having the highest average yield-to-maturity. Here, the yield of each issue is multiplied by the percentage of the portfolio's funds that are invested in that issue. Another possible solution is to choose the portfolio that most closely resembles a

[18] See N. Bulent Gultekin and Richard J. Rogalski, "Alternative Duration Specifications and the Measurement of Basis Risk," *Journal of Business* 57, no. 2 (April 1984):241–64; for a rebuttal, see G. O. Bierwag, George G. Kaufman, Cynthia M. Latta, and Gordon S. Roberts, "Duration: Response to Critics," *Journal of Portfolio Management* 13, no. 2 (Winter 1987):48–52.

[19] G. O. Bierwag, George G. Kaufman, and Alden Toevs, "Bond Portfolio Immunization and Stochastic Process Risk," *Journal of Bank Research* 13 (Winter 1983):282–91.

"bullet," or "focused," portfolio, since it has been argued that such a portfolio has less stochastic process risk than any other. Such a portfolio is one where the bonds in it have durations (or, alternatively, term-to-maturities) most closely matching the duration of the promised outflows. In the example, the portfolio consisting of just one-year and three-year bonds is more focused than the one consisting of the one-year and four-year bonds.[20]

14.5 ACTIVE MANAGEMENT

As mentioned earlier, active management of a bond portfolio is based on the belief that the bond market is not perfectly efficient. Such management can involve security selection, where attempts are made at identifying mispriced bonds. Alternatively, it can involve market timing, where attempts are made at forecasting general movements in interest rates. It is also possible for an active portfolio manager to be involved in both security selection and market timing. While there are a large number of methods of actively managing a bond portfolio, some general types of active management can be described.

☐ ## 14.5.1 Horizon Analysis

The return on a bond over any given holding period depends on its price at the beginning of the period and its price at the end of the period, as well as its coupon rate. Thus, the return on a bond over a one-year period will depend on the yield structure at the beginning of the year and the yield structure at the end of the year, since the price of the bond at these two points in time will depend on these structures. It follows that possible subsequent changes to the beginning-of-period yield structure must be analyzed in order to analyze possible bond returns over a given holding period. Bond portfolio managers who believe they (or their staffs) are able to identify such changes will want to translate their beliefs into action.

One way of doing this is known as *horizon analysis*, where a single holding period is selected for analysis and possible yield structures at the end of the period (that is, at the "horizon") are considered.[21] The possible returns for two bonds—one currently held and one candidate to replace it—are then analyzed. In doing so, neither bond is assumed to default up to the horizon date. In the process of the analysis, the sensitivities of the returns to changes in key assumptions regarding yields are estimated, allowing at least a rough assessment of some of the relevant risks.

Horizon analysis can be viewed as another way of implementing the capitalization-of-income method of valuation that was discussed in Chapter 13. By focusing on the estimated end-of-period price of a bond, it seeks to determine if the current market price is relatively high or low. That is, for

---

[20] For a discussion of how to select the "best" immunizing portfolio, see Alexander and Resnick, "Using Linear and Goal Programming to Immunize Bond Portfolios."

[21] See Martin L. Leibowitz, "Horizon Analysis for Managed Bond Portfolios," *Journal of Portfolio Management* 1, no. 3 (Spring (1975):23–34, and "An Analytic Approach to the Bond Market," in *Financial Analyst's Handbook*, ed. Sumner N. Levine (Homewood, Ill.: Dow Jones-Irwin, Inc., 1975), 226–77.

a given estimated end-of-period price, a bond will have a relatively high expected return if its current price is relatively low. Conversely, a bond will have a relatively low expected return if its current price is relatively high.

Figure 14.1 represents a page from a standard yield book for bonds with a 4% coupon. As indicated, a 4% bond with ten years remaining to maturity that is currently priced at $67.48 (for ease of exposition, a par of $100 is used here) will have a 9% promised annual yield-to-maturity (or 4.5% semiannually). Five years into the future, such a bond's term-to-maturity will have decreased and the relevant promised yield-to-maturity will probably have changed. Thus, as time passes, the bond might follow a path through the table such as that shown by the dashed line. If so, it would end up at a price of $83.78 at the horizon (five years hence), with an 8% promised annual yield-to-maturity (or 4% semiannually).

Over any holding period, a bond's return typically will be affected by both the passage of time and a change in yields. Horizon analysis breaks this into two parts: one due solely to the passage of time, with no change in yields, and the other due solely to a change in yield, with no passage of time. This is illustrated in Figure 14.1. The total price change from $67.48 to $83.78 (or $16.30) is broken into a change from $67.48 to $80.22 (or $12.74),

FIGURE 14–1

The effect of time and yield change on a 4% coupon bond. *Note:* Y_0 and P_0 denote the bond's yield-to-maturity and price at the beginning of the period; Y_H and P_H denote the bond's yield-to-maturity and price at the horizon (that is, at the end of the period); P_A denotes the bond's price at the horizon if its yield had remained at $Y_0 = 9\%$; yields are compounded semiannually.

SOURCE: William L. Leibowitz, "Horizon Analysis for Managed Bond Portfolios," *Journal of Portfolio Management* 1, no. 3 (Spring 1975): p. 26.

Yield to Maturity (%)	10 Yrs	9 Yrs	...	5 Yrs	...	1 Yrs	0 Yrs
7.00	78.68	80.22		87.53		97.15	100.00
7.50	75.68	77.39		85.63		96.69	100.00
Y_H 8.00	72.82	74.68		83.78 P_H		96.23	100.00
8.50	70.09	72.09		81.98		95.77	100.00
Y_0 9.00 P_0 67.48	67.48	69.60		80.22 P_A		95.32	100.00
9.50	64.99	67.22		78.51		94.87	100.00
10.00	62.61	64.92	...	76.83	...	94.42	100.00
10.50	60.34	62.74		75.21		93.98	100.00
11.00	58.17	60.64		73.62		93.54	100.00

YEARS TO MATURITY

Actual Price Pattern Over Time

Yield Change Effect

Time Effect

followed by an instantaneous change from $80.22 to $83.78 (or $3.56). The intermediate value is the price the bond would command at the horizon if its promised yield-to-maturity had remained unchanged at its initial level of 9%. The actual price is that which it commands at its actual yield-to-maturity of 8%. In summary, the total price change can be broken into two parts, representing the two effects:

$$\text{Price change} = \text{time effect} + \text{yield change effect.} \qquad (14.9)$$

Thus far, no account has been taken of the coupon payments to be received before the horizon date. In principle, one should consider all possible uses of such cash flows or at least analyze possible alternative yield structures during the period to determine likely reinvestment opportunities. In practice, this is rarely done. Instead, a single reinvestment rate is assumed and the future value of all coupon payments at the horizon date is determined by compounding each one using this rate.[22] This takes care of both interest (coupons) and "interest on interest" (that is, interest earned from reinvesting coupon payments), with only the former being accurately predictable at the beginning of the period.

For example, if $2 is received every six months (as in Figure 14.1) with the first payment occurring six months from now and the last one occurring five years from now, and each payment is reinvested at 4.25% per six months, then the value of the end of five years will be approximately $24.29. Of this amount, $20 can be considered interest (coupon payments of $2 for 10 six-month periods) with the remaining $4.29 being interest on interest.

In summary, a bond's overall dollar return has four components—the time effect, the yield change effect, the coupons, and the interest from reinvesting the coupons. In the example, the overall dollar return is:

$$\begin{array}{c} \text{Overall} \\ \text{dollar} \\ \text{return} \end{array} = \begin{array}{c} \text{time} \\ \text{effect} \end{array} + \begin{array}{c} \text{yield} \\ \text{change} \\ \text{effect} \end{array} + \text{coupons} + \begin{array}{c} \text{interest} \\ \text{on} \\ \text{coupons} \end{array}$$

$$= (\$80.22 - \$67.48) + (\$83.78 - \$80.22) + \$20.00 + \$4.29$$

$$= \$12.74 + \$3.56 + \$20.00 + \$4.29$$

$$= \$40.59.$$

This overall dollar return can be converted into an overall rate of return by dividing it by the market price of the bond at the beginning of the period, $67.48. In doing so, it can be seen that a bond's overall rate of return consists of four components:

$$\begin{array}{c} \text{Overall} \\ \text{rate of} \\ \text{return} \end{array} = \frac{\$12.74}{\$67.48} + \frac{\$3.56}{\$67.48} + \frac{\$20.00}{\$67.48} + \frac{\$4.29}{\$67.48}$$

$$= .1888 + .0528 + .2964 + .0635$$
$$= .6015$$

---

[22] The longer the horizon, the greater the importance of the size of the reinvestment rate in determining a bond's return. This means that if the investor's horizon is greater than ten years for example, then alternative reinvestment rates should be considered.

or 60.15%. The first term is the return due to the passage of time, the second term is the return due to yield change, the third term is coupon return, and the fourth term is the return due to the reinvestment of the coupon payments.

Since the second term is uncertain, it is important to analyze it further. In the example, a change in yield from 9.0% to 8.0% will result in a change in the market price from $80.22 to $83.78. Given 8.0% was the expected yield at the horizon, an expected overall rate of return of 60.15% was computed. By using different end-of-period yields, different overall rates of return can be calculated. Then, with estimates of the probabilities of these yields occurring, a feel for the bond's risk can be obtained. Indeed, it can now be seen why bond portfolio managers devote a great deal of attention to making predictions of future yields.

□ **14.5.2   Bond Swaps**

Given a set of predictions about future bond yields, holding-period returns over one or more horizons for one or more bonds can be estimated. The goal of *bond swapping* is to manage a portfolio actively by exchanging bonds to take advantage of any superior ability to predict such yields.[23] In making a swap, the portfolio manager believes that an overpriced bond is being exchanged for an underpriced bond. Some swaps are based on the belief that the market will correct for its mispricing in a short period of time, whereas other types of swaps are based on a belief that corrections will either never take place or will take place over a long period of time.

There are a large number of categories for classifying swaps, and the distinctions between the categories are often blurry. Nevertheless, many bond swaps can be placed in one of four general categories:

Ideally, the *substitution swap* is an exchange of a bond for a perfect substitute, or "twin" bond. The motivation here is temporary price advantage, presumably resulting from a monetary imbalance in the relative supply/demand conditions in the marketplace.

The *intermarket spread swap* is a more general movement out of one market component and into another with the intention of exploiting a currently advantageous yield relationship. The idea here is to trade off of these changing relationships between the two market components. Although such swaps will almost always have some sensitivity to the direction of the overall market, the idealized focus of this type of swap is the spread relationship itself.

The *rate anticipation swap*, on the other hand, is frankly geared toward profiting from an anticipated movement in overall market rates.

---

[23] Bond swaps should not be confused with interest rate swaps, where two issuers of debt keep the respective amounts raised but exchange interest payments. See, for example, Stuart M. Turnbull, "Swaps: A Zero Sum Game?" *Financial Management* 16, no. 1 (Spring 1987):15–21.

The *pure-yield pickup swap* is oriented toward yield improvements over the long term with little heed being paid to interim price movements in either the respective market components or the market as a whole.[24]

Consider a hypothetical portfolio manager who holds some of a 30-year, AA utility bond issue that has a 7% coupon rate. Since these bonds are currently selling at par, their yield-to-maturity is 7%. Now, imagine that there is another 30-year, AA utility bond issue with a 7% coupon rate that is being made available to the manager at a price so that its yield-to-maturity is 7.10%. An example of a substitution swap is where the manager exchanges a given dollar amount of the currently held bonds for an equivalent dollar amount of the second bond issue, thereby picking up 10 basis points in yield.

Alternatively, the manager might note that there is a 10-year, AA utility bond issue outstanding that carries a 6% coupon and is priced at par; thus, its yield is 6%. In this case, there is a 100-basis-point yield spread between the currently held 30-year bonds and the 10-year bonds. If the manager feels this spread is too low, then an intermarket spread swap might be used where some of the 30-year bonds are exchanged for an equivalent dollar amount of the 10-year bonds. Since the manager expects the spread to increase in the future, the yield on the 10-year bonds is expected to fall. This means the price on these bonds is expected to rise by an abnormal amount, resulting in an abnormally high holding-period return.

Another possibility is that the manager feels that yields in general are going to rise. In such a situation, the manager will recognize that the currently held portfolio is very risky because longer-term bonds generally move downward further in price for a given rise in yields than do shorter-term bonds. Accordingly, the manager might use a rate anticipation swap to exchange a given dollar amount of the 30-year bonds for an equivalent amount of some short-term bonds.

Lastly, the manager might not want to make any predictions about future yields or yield spreads. Instead, it might simply be noted that some 30-year, AA industrial bonds are currently priced to yield 8%. In this case, the manager might want to enter a pure-yield pickup swap, where some of the 7% utility bonds are exchanged for an equivalent dollar amount of the 8% industrial bonds, the motivation being to earn the extra 100 basis points in yield from the industrials.

□ 14.5.3 **Contingent Immunization**

One method of bond portfolio management that has both passive and active elements is *contingent immunization*. In the simplest form of contingent immunization, the portfolio is actively managed as long as favorable results are obtained. However, if unfavorable results occur, then the portfolio is immediately immunized.

---

[24] Martin L. Leibowitz, "Horizon Analysis for Managed Bond Portfolios," *Journal of Portfolio Management* 1, no. 3 (Spring 1975):32–33. See also Sidney Homer and Martin L. Leibowitz, *Inside the Yield Book* (Englewood Cliffs, N.J.: Prentice Hall, 1972) and Chapter 16 in Marcia Stigum and Frank J. Fabozzi, *The Dow Jones-Irwin Guide to Bond and Money Market Investments* (Homewood, Ill.: Dow Jones-Irwin, Inc., 1987).

As an illustration, consider the earlier example where the portfolio manager had to come up with $1,000,000 at the end of two years, and the current yield curve was horizontal at 10%. In this situation, it was mentioned that the portfolio manager could immunize the portfolio by investing $826,446 in one-year and three-year bonds. However, it may be that the portfolio manager convinces the client that the portfolio should be contingently immunized with $841,680. This means that the portfolio manager must be certain that the portfolio will be worth at least $1,000,000 at the end of the two years, with any excess going to the client and the manager being compensated accordingly. Equivalently, the portfolio manager must earn a minimum average return of 9% (note that $841,680 $\times$ 1.09^2 = $1,000,000) over the two years. Here, the client is willing to settle for as low a return as 9% but hopes that the portfolio manager will be able to exceed the 10% return that could have been locked in with an immunized portfolio.

In this situation, the manager would proceed to manage the portfolio actively by attempting to engage either in selectivity or timing (or both). Perhaps the arrangement with the client is that the status of the portfolio will be reviewed weekly, and yields that are currently available will be determined.

Consider how the review would be conducted after one year has elapsed and the yield curve is still horizontal but at 11%. First of all, it is noted that $1,000,000/(1.11) = $900,901 would be needed to immunize the portfolio at that point. Second, the market value of the current portfolio is determined to be $930,000. Now, in this example, the arrangement between the client and portfolio manager is that the manager can continue to manage the portfolio actively as long as it is worth at least $10,000 more than the amount needed for immunization. Since it is worth $930,000, an amount greater than $900,901 + $10,000 = $910,901, the portfolio manager can continue being active. However, if the portfolio had been worth less than $910,901, then, according to the agreement, the manager would have immediately immunized the portfolio.[25]

☐ **14.5.4 Riding the Yield Curve**

Riding the yield curve is a method of bond portfolio management sometimes used by people who, having liquidity as a primary objective, invest in short-term fixed-income securities. One way of investing is simply to purchase these securities, hold them until they mature, and then reinvest them. An alternative way is to ride the yield curve, provided certain conditions exist.[26]

One condition is that the yield curve be upward-sloping, indicating that

---

[25] For more on contingent immunization, see the articles by Leibowitz cited in footnote 16 along with Martin L. Leibowitz and Alfred Weinberger, "Contingent Immunization—Part I: Risk Control Procedures," *Financial Analysts Journal* 38, no. 6 (November/December 1982):17–31, and "Contingent Immunization—Part II: Problem Areas," *Financial Analysts Journal* 39, no. 1 (January/February 1983):39–50.

[26] For more on riding the yield curve, see Stigum and Fabozzi, *The Dow Jones-Irwin Guide to Bond and Money Market Investments*, pp. 270–72; Jerome S. Osteryoung, Gordon S. Roberts, and Daniel E. McCarty, "Ride the Yield Curve When Investing Idle Funds in Treasury Bills?" *Financial Executive* 47, no. 4 (April 1979):10–15; and Edward A. Dyl and Michael D. Joehnk, "Riding the Yield Curve: Does It Work?" *Journal of Portfolio Management* 7, no. 3 (Spring 1981):13–17.

longer-term securities have higher yields. Another condition is that the investor believes that the yield curve will remain upward-sloping. Given these two conditions, the investor who is riding the yield curve will purchase securities that have a somewhat longer term-to-maturity than desired and then sell them before they mature, thereby capturing some capital gains.

For example, consider an investor who prefers investing in 90-day Treasury bills. Currently, such bills are selling for $98.25 per $100 of face value, indicating they have a yield of 7.00% (note that $98.25 = $100 − (7.00 × 90/360)). However, 180-day Treasury bills are currently selling for $96.00, indicating they have a higher yield of 8.00% (note that $96 = $100 − (8.00 × 180/360)). Given that this investor believes that the yield curve will remain upward-sloping over the next three months, it can be shown that riding the yield curve will result in a higher return than simply buying and holding the 90-day Treasury bills.

If the investor buys and holds the 90-day Treasury bills, then the resulting annualized rate of return will be

$$\frac{\$100 - \$98.25}{\$98.25} \times \frac{365}{90}$$

which is 7.22%. Alternatively, if the investor buys the 180-day Treasury bills and subsequently sells them after 90 days, then the expected selling price will be $98.25 (note that this is the same as the current price of 90-day bills, since it is assumed that the yield curve will not have changed after 90 days have elapsed). This means that the expected return is

$$\frac{\$98.25 - \$96.00}{\$96.00} \times \frac{365}{90}$$

which is 9.50%. In comparison, the expected return from riding the yield curve is higher. This is because the investor expects to benefit from a decline in yield, a decline that is not due to a shift in the yield curve but is attributable to the shortening of the maturity of the Treasury bills that were initially purchased.

It should be kept in mind that if the yield curve does change, then riding it can be detrimental to the investor's return.[27] That is, riding the yield curve has more risk than simply buying securities that mature at the appropriate time. Similarly, there are two transactions necessary (buying and then selling the security) when riding the yield curve, whereas a maturity strategy has only one transaction (buying the security). Thus, there are going to be larger transactions costs associated with riding the yield curve.

14.6 BONDS VERSUS STOCKS

Bonds and stocks are different kinds of securities, with quite different characteristics. Making an investment decision between them should not be based

---

[27] According to the unbiased expectations theory (discussed in Chapter 4), the yield curve would be expected to shift in such a manner that the expected return of both strategies (in the example, buy and hold the 90-day Treasury bills versus buy and sell the 180-day Treasury bills 90 days later) would be the same.

TABLE 14.3

Historical Relationships Between Bonds and Stocks.

	STOCKS	BONDS	CORRELATION
A. 1926–1985:			
Average quarterly excess return	2.20%	.41%	
Standard deviation	12.39	3.98	
Correlation			.30
B. 1926–1945:			
Average quarterly excess return	2.94%	1.11%	
Standard deviation	18.68	1.99	
Correlation			.45
C. 1946–1985:			
Average quarterly excess return	1.83%	0.06%	
Standard deviation	7.54	4.65	
Correlation			.40

SOURCE: Adapted from Meir Statman and Neal L. Ushman, "Bond Versus Stocks: Another Look," *Journal of Portfolio Management* 13, no. 2 (Winter 1987):33–38.

on some simple one-dimensional comparison. In many cases this decision, known as *asset allocation*, will involve investing in both bonds and stocks.[28]

While historical relationships may not be useful for accurately predicting future relationships, it is instructive to examine the average values, standard deviations, and correlations of past stock and bond returns. These statistics are presented in Table 14.3, based on quarterly excess returns during one time period, 1926–1985, and two subperiods, 1926–1945 and 1946–1985. (The returns were published by Ibbotson Associates; see Figure 1.1 and Table 1.1 in Chapter 1.)

Based on average returns, stocks appear to have a substantial advantage for the investor with a reasonably long horizon. However, there is good reason to believe that the average returns on long-term bonds are not representative of investors' expectations for future returns. The returns show the results obtained by purchasing a long-term bond, holding it for a period of time, and then replacing it with another long-term bond. The total returns include both income and capital gains or losses. During this period, bond price changes were negative more often than positive, averaging roughly −1% per year. A better estimate of investors' expectations might be obtained by assuming that the expected price would be as likely to increase as decrease. Expected future returns on bonds might then have been roughly 1% per year (.25% per quarter) greater than shown in the table.

For an investor concerned with month-to-month variation (such as an investor with a possible need for liquidity or with a short horizon), bonds look relatively more attractive than stocks. This can be seen by examining

---

[28] Chapter 22 presents a discussion of some methods for making the asset allocation decision. For a model on how to measure the interest rate sensitivity of a portfolio consisting of both stocks and bonds, see Martin L. Leibowitz, "Total Portfolio Duration: A New Perspective on Asset Allocation," *Financial Analysts Journal* 42, no. 5 (September/October 1986):18–29.

the standard deviation of returns. In this sense, stocks were riskier than bonds during the period and both subperiods. Note that the increased uncertainty concerning the rate of inflation during the postwar subperiod has increased the variability of bond returns.

The correlation between stock and bond returns has been low, and during various 26-year periods it has even had negative values. This indicates that portfolios combining both stocks and bonds could benefit considerably from the resulting diversification. More recently, however, correlations have been positive (and substantially so), due in part to common reactions to changes in inflationary expectations. Consequently, the gains from diversification have recently been substantially reduced. Nevertheless, from the historical record, it would be reasonable to expect that in the future, bonds will still offer some diversification benefits.

14.7 SUMMARY

This chapter has presented a discussion of bond portfolio management. Various methods exist and can be classified as being either passive or active in nature. Passive methods are based on the assumption that bond markets are efficient, whereas active methods are based on the assumption that bond markets are inefficient. There have been many studies that have attempted to determine the degree of efficiency in the bond market. On balance, these studies indicate that the bond market is highly, but not perfectly, efficient. This means that while it is possible to earn abnormally high returns, it is exceptionally difficult to do so.

One passive method of managing a bond portfolio is based on the concept of duration and is known as immunization. With this strategy, the portfolio manager is attempting to lock in a given return on a portfolio. That is, the manager is attempting to construct a portfolio that will not be adversely affected by future movements in interest rates. This is accomplished by purchasing bonds so that the weighted average of their durations equals the length of the manager's holding period. Although immunization does not work perfectly in practice, a number of people believe it works better than a maturity strategy, where the manager purchases bonds that mature at the end of the holding period.

A number of methods of active management have been discussed in this chapter. They include horizon analysis, swapping, contingent immunization, and riding the yield curve. All these methods seek to provide the portfolio manager with abnormally high returns. Whether they consistently work or not is an unanswered question.

Lastly, bond returns were compared historically with stock returns. It appears that bond returns have had both lower returns and less risk than stocks. Of particular interest is the fact that the correlation of bond and stock returns has typically been low and even negative during some time periods. This suggests that diversification across both stocks and bonds will be worthwhile in the future.

1. Bonds A and B possess coupon rates of 4% and 12%, respectively. Both bonds have ten years to maturity and pay interest annually. If the discount rate on both bonds A and B rises from 8% to 10%, calculate the expected percentage changes in the bonds' prices. Explain why the bonds differ in terms of their percentage price changes.

2. Bonds C and D both possess coupon rates of 10%. However, bond C has four years to maturity, while bond D has ten years to maturity. Assuming a constant discount rate of 8% for both bonds, and assuming that all other relevant factors remain the same, calculate the expected percentage changes in the bonds' prices one year from today. Explain why the bonds differ in terms of their percentage price changes.

3. Consider a bond selling at its par value of $1,000, with three years to maturity and a 6% coupon rate (with annual interest payments). Calculate the bond's duration.

4. Recalculate your answer to question 3 assuming a 10% coupon rate. Why does the bond's duration change?

5. Why must the duration of a coupon-bearing bond always be less than the time to its maturity date?

6. Rank order the following bonds in terms of duration. Explain the rationale behind your rankings. (You do not have to actually calculate the bonds' durations. Simply logical reasoning will suffice.)

BOND	TERM-TO-MATURITY	COUPON INTEREST RATE	YIELD-TO-MATURITY
1	30 years	10.0%	10.0%
2	30	0.0	10.0
3	30	10.0	7.0
4	5	10.0	10.0

7. What impact would you expect the option features of callable bonds and mortgage participation certificates to have on the expected durations of such bonds as opposed to the durations calculated based on the bonds' stated maturity dates?

8. Consider a bond with a 3.5 year duration. If its yield-to-maturity increases from 8.0% to 8.3%, what is the expected percentage change in the price of the bond?

9. Explain why "immunization" permits a bond investor to be confident of meeting a given liability on a predetermined future date.

10. Why can nonparallel shifts in the yield curve cause problems for an investor seeking to construct an immunized bond portfolio?

11. Describe the four components of return on a bond investment over a given holding period.

12. Distinguish between a substitution swap and an intermarket swap.

Chapter 15

COMMON STOCKS

Common stocks are easier to describe than fixed-income securities such as bonds but are harder to analyze. Fixed-income securities almost always have a limited life and an upper dollar limit on cash payments to investors. Common stocks have neither. Although the basic principles of valuation apply to both, the role of uncertainty is larger for common stocks, so much so that it often dominates all other elements in their valuation.

Common stock represents *equity*, or an ownership position, in a corporation. It is a residual claim, in the sense that creditors and preferred stockholders must be paid as scheduled before common stockholders can receive any payments. In bankruptcy, common stockholders are in principle entitled to any value remaining after all other claimants have been satisfied. (However, in practice courts sometimes violate this principle.)

The great advantage of the corporate form of organization is the *limited liability* of its owners. Common stocks are generally "full-paid and nonassessable," meaning common stockholders may lose their investment, but no more. That is, common stockholders have no additional liability if the corporation fails to meet its obligations.

15.1 THE CORPORATE FORM

A corporation exists only when it has been granted a *charter*, or certificate of incorporation, by a state. This document specifies the rights and obligations of stockholders. It may be amended with the approval of the stockholders, perhaps by a majority or two-thirds vote, where each share of stock generally entitles its owner to one vote. Both the initial terms of the charter and the terms of any amendment must also be approved by the state in which the corporation is chartered. The state of Delaware has captured a disproportionate number of corporate charters because it is particularly hospitable in this respect as well as in levying corporate taxes.

☐ 15.1.1 Stock Certificates

The ownership of a firm's stock has typically been represented by a single certificate, with the number of shares held by the particular investor noted

on it. Such a stock certificate is usually registered, with the name, address, and holdings of the investor included on the corporation's books. Dividend payments, voting material, annual and quarterly reports, and other mailings are then sent directly to the investor, taking into account the size of his or her holdings.

Shares of stock held by an investor may be transferred to a new owner with the assistance of either the issuing corporation or, more commonly, its designated *transfer agent*. This agent cancels the old stock certificate and issues a new one in its place, made out to the new owner. Frequently a *registrar* will make sure that this canceling and issuing of certificates has been done properly. Usually banks and trust companies act as transfer agents and registrars. Many stockholders have chosen to avoid these rather cumbersome procedures. Instead, clearing arrangements (discussed in Chapter 2) are used to substitute computerized records for embossed certificates.

☐ 15.1.2 Voting

Since an owner of a share of common stock is one of the owners of a corporation, he or she is entitled to vote on matters brought up at the corporation's annual meeting and to vote for the corporation's directors. Any owner may attend and vote in person, but most choose instead to vote by *proxy*. That is, the incumbent directors and senior management typically solicit all the stockholders, asking each one to sign a proxy statement. Such a statement is a power of attorney authorizing the designated party listed on the statement to cast all of the investor's votes on any matter brought up at the meeting. Occasionally, desired positions on specific issues may be solicited on the proxy statement. However, most of the time the positions held by the incumbents are made known with the proxy solicitation. Since the majority of votes are generally controlled by the incumbents via proxy statements, the actual voting turns out to be perfunctory, leaving little if any controversy or excitement.

Once in a while, however, a *proxy fight* develops. Insurgents from outside the corporation solicit proxies to vote against the incumbents, often in order to effect a takeover of some sort. Stockholders are deluged with literature and appeals for their proxies. The incumbents often win, but the possibility of a loss in such a skirmish tends to curb activities clearly not in the stockholders' best interests.

When proposals are to be voted on, the number of votes given an investor equals the number of shares held. Thus, when a yes or no vote is called for, anyone controlling a majority of the shares will be able to make sure that the outcome he or she favors will receive a majority of the votes. When directors are to be elected, however, there are two types of voting systems that can be used, one of which does not give a majority owner complete control of the outcome. This type of voting system is known as a *cumulative voting system*, whereas the type of voting system that does allow a majority owner to control the outcome completely is known as a *majority voting system*.

Under both systems, the winners of the election are those candidates

who have received the highest vote totals. Thus, if six candidates were running for the three directorships, the three receiving the largest number of votes would be elected.

With both voting systems, a stockholder receives a total number of votes that is equal to the number of directors to be elected times the number of shares owned. However, with the majority voting system, the stockholder may only give any one candidate, as a maximum, a number of votes equal to the number of shares owned. This means that in a situation where three directors are to be elected, a stockholder with 400 shares would have 1200 votes but could give no more than 400 of these votes to any one candidate. Note that if there are a total of 1000 shares outstanding and one stockholder owns (or has proxies for) 501 shares, then he or she can give 501 votes to each of the three candidates he or she favors. In doing so, this stockholder will be certain they are elected, regardless of how the remaining 499 shares are voted. The majority shareholder's candidates would each have 501 votes, whereas the *most* any other candidate could receive is 499 votes. Thus, with a majority voting system, a stockholder owning (or controlling with proxies) one share more than 50% can be certain of electing all the candidates that he or she favors.

The cumulative voting system differs from the majority voting system in that a stockholder can cast his or her votes in any manner. As a result, a minority stockholder can be certain of having some representation on the board of directors, provided the number of shares owned is sufficiently large. In the previous example, the minority owner of the 400 shares could cast all his or her 1200 votes for one candidate. Imagine that this owner wanted director A to be elected, but the majority owner of 501 shares wanted candidates B, C, and D to be elected. In this situation, the minority stockholder could give all 1200 votes to A and be certain that A would be one of the three directors elected, regardless of what the majority stockholder did. If the majority owner held the remaining 600 shares, he or she would have 1800 votes. There is no way that candidate A, favored by the minority stockholder, can come in lower than second place in the vote totals. This is because A will receive 1200 votes, and there is no way that the 1800 votes of the majority stockholder can be cast to give more than one of his or her favored candidates a vote total in excess of 1200. Thus, the minority stockholder can be certain that A will be elected, whereas the majority stockholder can be certain that only 2 of his or her favorites will be elected.

In general, the formula for determining the minimum number of shares a stockholder must own in order to be able to elect a certain number of candidates under a cumulative voting system is

$$n = \left(\frac{ds}{D + 1}\right) + 1 \qquad (15.1)$$

where:

n = the minimum number of shares that must be owned,

d = the number of directors the stockholder wants to be certain of electing,

s = the number of shares outstanding, and

D = the number of directors to be elected.

Thus, the minimum number of shares a stockholder needs in order to be certain of electing one director when three are to be elected and there are 1000 shares outstanding is $[(1 \times 1000)/(3 + 1)] + 1 = 251$. Since in the example the minority stockholder owned 400 shares, it can be seen from the formula that he or she is certain of being able to elect one director. Note that the minimum number of shares that must be owned in order to be certain of electing two directors is $[(2 \times 1000)/(3 + 1)] + 1 = 501$. The minimum number owned to be certain of electing all three directors is $[(3 \times 1000)/(3 + 1)] + 1 = 751$.

In summary, the cumulative voting system gives minority stockholders the right to have some representation on the board of directors, provided the number of shares owned is sufficiently large. In contrast, the majority voting system does not give minority stockholders the right to such representation, even if 49.9% of the shares are owned by the minority stockholder.

The voting system that a corporation decides to use depends not only on the desires of the corporate founders but also the state in which the firm is incorporated. Some states require cumulative voting systems. In Delaware, however, there is no cumulative voting unless it is specifically stated in the corporate charter.

□ 15.1.3 Tender Offers

Periodically, a firm or a wealthy individual who is convinced that the management of a corporation is not fully exploiting its opportunities will attempt a *takeover*. This is frequently done with a *tender offer* being made by a *bidder* to a *target* firm.[1] Before this offer is announced, a small number of the target firm's shares are usually acquired by the bidder in the open market through the use of brokers (once 5% of the stock is so acquired, the bidder has 10 days to report the acquisition to the SEC).

Then, in the bidder's quest to acquire a substantial number of the target's shares, the bid is announced to the public. Advertisements to purchase shares are placed in the financial press, and material describing the bid is mailed to the target's stockholders. The bidder generally offers to buy, at a stated price, some or all shares offered ("tendered") by the current stockholders of the target. This buying offer is usually contingent on the tender of a minimum number of shares by the target's stockholders by a

---

[1] Another form of a takeover is a *merger*. A merger occurs when two firms combine their operations, the result being that only one firm exists. Mergers usually are negotiated by the management of the two firms. Tender offers differ in that the management of the bidder makes a direct appeal to the stockholders of the target firm for their shares. Tender offers also differ in that afterward both firms will still exist, since most tender offers are not for all the shares of the target. For a discussion of the motivations for mergers and tender offers, see Michael C. Jensen and Richard S. Ruback, "The Market for Corporate Control: The Scientific Evidence," *Journal of Financial Economics* 11, nos. 1–4 (April 1983):5–50, and Richard Roll, "The Hubris Hypothesis of Corporate Takeovers," *Journal of Business* 59, no. 1, pt. 2 (April 1986):197–216. A method for acquirers to use in evaluating potential targets is presented in Chapter 9 of Alfred Rappaport, *Creating Shareholder Value* (New York: The Free Press, 1986).

fixed date. When the buying offer is first made, the offered price ("tender price") is generally set considerably above the current market price, although the offer itself usually leads to a subsequent price increase.

Management of the target firm frequently responds to tender offers with advertisements, mailings, and the like, urging its stockholders to reject the bidder's offer. Sometimes a *white knight* will be sought, meaning another firm that is favorably inclined towards current management will be invited to make a better offer to the target's stockholders. Another type of response by management is to pay *greenmail* to the bidder, meaning that any shares held by the bidder will be bought by the target firm at an above-market price. Still another type of response is for management of the target firm to issue a tender offer of its own, known as a *repurchase offer*, where the firm offers to buy back some of its own stock. (Occasionally repurchase offers are made by firms that have not received tender offers from outside bidders.)

Other types of corporate defenses include the *Pac-Man defense*, where the initial target turns around and makes a tender offer for the initial acquirer, the *crown jewel defense*, where the target sells its most attractive assets to make the firm less attractive, and the use of *poison pills*, where the target gives its shareholders certain rights that can be exercised only in the event of a subsequent takeover and that, once exercised, will be extremely onerous to the acquirer.

☐ 15.1.4 Ownership Versus Control

Much has been written about the effects of the separation of ownership and control of the modern corporation.[2] This separation gives rise to what is known as a *principal-agent problem*. In particular, stockholders can be viewed as principals who hire management to act as their agents. The agent is to make decisions that maximize shareholder wealth as reflected in the firm's stock price. No problem would exist if stockholders could *monitor* the managers without cost, since the stockholders would then be capable of determining for certain whether or not management had acted in their best interests. However, monitoring is not costless, and complete monitoring of every decision is, practically speaking, impossible.[3] As a result some, but not complete, monitoring is done. This gives management a certain degree of latitude in making decisions and leaves open the possibility that some decisions will be made that are not in the stockholders' best interests.[4] However, the possibility of a proxy fight or tender offer provides at least some check on such decisions.

---

[2] See, for example, Michael C. Jensen and William H. Meckling, "Theory of the Firm: Managerial Behavior, Agency Costs and Ownership Structure," *Journal of Financial Economics* 3, no. 4 (October 1976):305–60; Eugene F. Fama, "Agency Problems and the Theory of the Firm," *Journal of Political Economy* 88, no. 2 (April 1980):288–307; Eugene F. Fama and Michael C. Jensen, "Separation of Ownership and Control," *Journal of Law and Economics* 26, (June 1983):301–25; Eugene F. Fama and Michael C. Jensen, "Agency Problems and Residual Claims," *Journal of Law and Economics* 26, (June 1983):327–49, and the entire issue of vol. 11 (April 1983) of the *Journal of Financial Economics*.

[3] An example of monitoring is having the firm's financial statements independently audited.

[4] For example, management may decide to have lavishly furnished offices and an executive jet when the conduct of business suggests that these are not merited.

To align the interests of management with their own, stockholders frequently offer certain incentives to management. An example is the use of stock options. These options are given to certain high-level managers and allow them to purchase a specified number of shares at a stated price (often above the market price when the options are initially issued) by a stated date. Thus, they motivate these managers to make decisions that will increase the stock price of the firm as much as possible.

□ **15.1.5 Stockholders' Equity**

Par Value

When a corporation is first chartered, it is authorized to issue up to a stated number of shares of common stock, each of which will often carry a specified *par value*. Legally, a corporation may be precluded from making payments to common stockholders if doing so would reduce the balance sheet value of stockholders' equity below the amount represented by the par value of outstanding stock. For this reason the par value is typically low relative to the price for which the stock is initially sold. Some corporations issue no-par stock (if so, a stated value must be recorded in place of the par value).

When stock is initially sold for more than its par value, the difference may be carried separately on the corporation's books under stockholders' equity. Frequently, the entry is for "capital contributed in excess of par value" or "paid-in capital." The par value of the stock is carried in a separate account, generally simply entitled "common stock," with the amount equal to the number of shares outstanding times the par value per share (for no-par stock, the stated value).

Book Value

With the passage of time, a corporation will generate income, much of which is paid out to creditors (as interest) and stockholders (as dividends). Any remainder is added to the amount shown as cumulative retained earnings on the corporation's books. The sum of the cumulative retained earnings and other entries (such as "common stock" and "capital contributed in excess of par value") under stockholders' equity is the *book value of the equity*. The *book value per share* is obtained by dividing the book value of the equity by the number of shares outstanding.

Reserved and Treasury Stock

Typically, a corporation issues only a part of its authorized stock. Some of the remainder may be specifically reserved for outstanding options, convertible securities, and so on.

When a corporation repurchases some of its own stock, either in the open market through the services of a broker or with a tender offer, the stock may be "held in the treasury." Such *treasury stock* does not carry votes or receive dividends and is equivalent economically (though not legally) to unissued stock.

If a corporation wishes to issue new stock in excess of the amount

originally authorized, the charter must be amended. This requires approval by both the state and the stockholders.

Classified Stock

Some corporations issue two or more classes of common stock. For example, Class A stock might have a preferred position in regard to dividends but might not have any voting rights. In contrast, Class B stock might have full voting rights but a lower position in regard to dividends. Often this is equivalent to an issue of preferred stock, along with a normal issue of common stock.

An interesting example involves the three classes of General Motors common stock. These classes are referred to as $1\frac{2}{3}$ par value, Class E, and Class H stock. Each share has 1, $\frac{1}{4}$, and $\frac{1}{2}$ vote, respectively. In terms of dividends, the Class E and Class H stocks are allowed to receive an amount that does not exceed the "adjusted earnings" of GM's Electronic Data Systems and Hughes Electronics subsidiaries, respectively; the $1\frac{2}{3}$ par value stock is allowed to receive dividends that do not exceed the remainder of GM's earnings.

Another interesting example involves Canadian corporations. Due to the Canada Income Tax Act of 1971, Canadian firms are allowed to have Class A and Class B shares. The only difference between the two classes is that Class A shares receive cash dividends whereas Class B shares receive stock dividends. Furthermore, owners of either class can swap their shares one-for-one for shares of the other class at any time.

Americus Trust Securities

An interesting type of security somewhat like classified stock involves Americus Trust securities. These securities are issued by the Americus Shareowner Service Corporation and are listed on the American Stock Exchange. They can be described most easily with an example.

Americus buys some of the outstanding shares of Exxon and then issues two kinds of trust securities, *Exxon primes* and *Exxon scores*. An investor can subsequently buy either of these securities through a broker and can find each listed on the American Stock Exchange as A-xonpr and A-xonsc, respectively. Note that Exxon itself has nothing to do with either the creation or subsequent trading of the primes and scores.

The owner of an Exxon prime is entitled to all cash dividends that Exxon pays to Americus and any price appreciation in Exxon up to a set limit (the "termination claim") at the expiration of the trust security. The owner of an Exxon score is entitled to all the remaining (if any) price appreciation on Exxon. Given a price limit of $60 and a five-year expiration date, this means that if Exxon is selling for $50 on the expiration date, the prime owner will receive $50 and the score owner will receive nothing. However, if Exxon is selling for $100, then the prime owner will receive $60 and the score owner will receive $40. Currently, there are in excess of 20 companies that have some of their shares divided into primes and scores by Americus.

Letter, or Restricted, Stock

In the United States, security regulations require that most stock be registered with the SEC before it may be sold in a public offering. Under some conditions, unregistered stock may be sold directly to a purchaser, but its subsequent sale is *restricted*, usually by a letter from the buyer stating that the stock is to be held as an investment. Such *letter stock* must be held for at least two years and cannot be sold even at that time unless ample information on the company is available and the amount sold is a relatively small percentage of the total amount outstanding.

15.2 CASH DIVIDENDS

Payments made in cash to stockholders are termed *dividends*. These are typically declared quarterly by the board of directors and paid to the stockholders of record at a date, known as the *date of record*, specified by the board. The dividends may be of almost any size, subject to certain restrictions such as those contained in the charter or in documents given to creditors. Thus, even though this is unusual, dividends may even be larger than the current earnings of the corporation. (If so, they are usually paid out of past earnings.)

Compiling a list of stockholders to receive the dividend is not as simple as it may initially seem, since for many firms the list changes almost constantly as shares are bought and sold. The way of identifying those stockholders who are to receive the dividend is by use of an *ex-dividend date*. Because of the time required to record the transfer of ownership of common stock, major stock exchanges specify an ex-dividend date that is four business days before the date of record. Shares purchased before an ex-dividend date are entitled to receive the dividend in question; those purchased on or after the ex-dividend date are not entitled to the dividend.

For example, a dividend may be declared on April 15 with a date of record of Friday, May 15. In this situation Monday, May 11, is the ex-dividend date. If an investor bought shares on Friday, May 8, he or she would subsequently receive the cash dividend (unless the shares were sold later in the day on the 8th). However, if the shares were bought on Monday, May 11, the investor would not receive the cash dividend. Besides a declaration date (April 15), an ex-dividend date (May 11), and a date-of-record (May 15), there is also a fourth date, the *payment date*. On this date (perhaps May 25) the checks for the cash dividends are put in the mail.

15.3 STOCK DIVIDENDS AND STOCK SPLITS

Occasionally, the board of directors decides to forgo a cash dividend and pays a *stock dividend* instead. For example, if a 5% stock dividend is declared, the owner of 100 shares receives 5 additional shares issued for this occasion. The accounting treatment of a stock dividend is to increase the "common stock" and "capital contributed in excess of par" accounts by an amount equal

to the market value of the stock at the time of the dividend times the number of new shares issued (the "common stock" account would increase by an amount equal to the par value times the number of new shares; the remainder of the increase would go into the "capital contributed in excess of par" account). In order to keep the total book value of stockholders' equity the same, the "retained earnings" account is reduced by a equivalent amount.

A *stock split* is similar to a stock dividend in that the stockholder owns more shares afterward. However, it is different in both magnitude and accounting treatment. With a stock split, all the old shares are destroyed and new ones are issued with a new par value; afterward, the number of new shares outstanding is usually larger than the previous number of old shares by 25% or more, with the exact amount depending on the size of the split. In contrast, a stock dividend usually results in an increase of less than 25%. While a stock dividend results in adjustments to the dollar figures in certain stockholders' equity accounts, no adjustments are made for a split. For example, if a stock with par value $1 is split 2-for-1, the holder of 200 old shares will receive 400 new shares with par value $.50, and none of the dollar figures in stockholders' equity would change.

A *reverse stock split* reduces the number of shares and increases the par value per share. For example, in a reverse 2-for-1 split, the holder of 200 shares with par value $1 would exchange them for 100 shares with par value $2. Again, there would not be any change in the dollar figures in stockholders' equity.

Stock dividends and splits must be taken into account when following the price of a company's shares. For example, a fall in price per share may be due solely to a large stock dividend. To reduce confusion, most financial services provide data adjusted for at least some of these changes. Thus, if a stock split 2-for-1 on January 30, 1988, prices prior to that date might be divided by 2 to facilitate comparison.

□ 15.3.1 Reasons for Stock Dividends and Splits

Why do corporations issue stock dividends and split their stocks? Nothing of importance would appear to be changed, since such actions do not increase revenues or reduce expenses. All that happens is that there is a change in the size of the units in which ownership may be bought and sold. Moreover, since the process involves administrative effort and costs something to execute, one wonders why it is done.

It is sometimes argued that stockholders respond positively to "tangible" evidence of the growth of their corporation. Another view holds that splits and stock dividends, by decreasing the price per share, may bring the stock's price into a more desirable trading range and hence increase the total value of the amount outstanding.

Figure 15.1 presents the average behavior of stock returns for 219 stock splits that occurred between 1945 and 1965. For each split, the stock's "abnormal" return was determined by relating monthly returns on the stock to the corresponding returns in the stock market. This was done month by

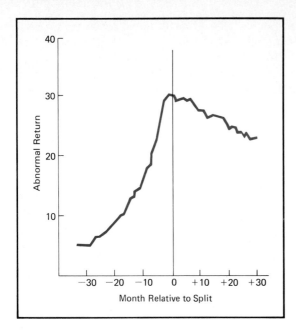

FIGURE 15–1
Abnormal stock returns before and after stock splits.

SOURCE: Sasson Bar-Yosef and Lawrence D. Brown, "A Re-examination of Stock Splits Using Moving Betas," *Journal of Finance* 32, no. 4 (September 1977): p. 1074.

month for the 54-month period immediately prior to the split and the 54-month period immediately following it. These abnormal returns were averaged across firms for each month relative to the firm's split and then cumulated across time.

As the figure shows, the stocks tended to have a positive abnormal return of about 30% during the 54 months prior to splitting. This was probably not due to anticipation of the coming split, since these splits are not announced until roughly two months before the effective date (denoted by 0 in the figure). The causal relationship could well be just the reverse: Stocks split after unusual price increases. That is, unexpected positive developments (such as unexpected large increases in earnings) caused abnormal increases in the stock prices of these firms, after which the firms decided to split their stock. The behavior of the postsplit prices indicates that afterwards investors did not continue to receive positive abnormal returns. In the study shown in Figure 15.1, investors actually lost some ground. Other studies, using different stocks and time periods, found either no abnormal returns or slightly positive abnormal returns after the split.[5]

The evidence also suggests that rather than *decreasing* transaction costs, stock splits actually *increased* them. A study of presplit and postsplit behavior showed that after splits, trading volume rose less than proportionately, and both commission costs and bid-ask spreads, expressed as a percentage of value, increased—hardly reactions that are favorable to stock-

[5] See Eugene F. Fama, Lawrence Fisher, Michael C. Jensen, and Richard Roll, "The Adjustment of Stock Prices to New Information," *International Economic Review* 10, no. 1 (February 1969):1–21; and Guy Charest, "Split Information, Stock Returns and Market Efficiency—I," *Journal of Financial Economics* 6, no. 2/3 (June/September 1978):265–96.

holders.[6] For example, after a 2-for-1 stock split, there will be twice as many shares outstanding, so it is reasonable to expect the daily number of shares that are traded to double and also to expect the commission for buying 200 shares after the split to be the same as the commission for buying 100 shares before the split. Instead, it was found that after the split the number of shares traded daily was less than twice as large and the commission was larger.

15.4 PREEMPTIVE RIGHTS

Under common law (and most state laws), a stockholder has an inherent right to maintain his or her proportionate ownership of the corporation. The existence of these *preemptive rights* means that when new shares are to be sold, the current stockholders must be given the right of first refusal in regard to the purchase of the shares.[7] This is accomplished by issuing a certificate to each stockholder that indicates the number of new shares he or she is authorized to purchase. This number will be proportional to the number of existing shares currently owned by the stockholder. Usually, the new shares will be priced below the current market price of the stock, making such *rights* valuable. The stockholder can exercise the rights by purchasing his or her allotted amount of new shares, thereby maintaining his or her proportional ownership in the firm, but at the cost of providing additional capital. Alternatively, the rights can be sold to someone else.[8]

For example, if a firm needs $10,000,000 for new equipment, it may decide to sell new shares in order to raise the capital. Given that the current market price of the stock is $60 per share, a *rights offering* may be used to raise the capital, in which the *subscription price* is set at $50 per share.[9] Accordingly, $10,000,000/$50 = 200,000 new shares are to be sold. Assuming the firm has 4,000,000 shares outstanding, this means that the owner of one share will receive the right to buy 200,000/4,000,000 = $\frac{1}{20}$ of a new share. Since the number of rights received is equal to the number of shares owned, it can be seen that 20 shares must be owned in order to be able to buy one new share. Thus, if a stockholder owns 100 shares, he or she will receive 100 rights, allowing him or her to buy (1/20) × 100 = 5 new shares. These rights are valuable because the owner of them can buy stock at $50 a share when the market price is significantly higher. The current owner of 100 shares can either use the 100 rights by coming up with cash equal to 5 × $50 = $250 or sell the 100 rights to someone else. But this raises a question: What is a fair price for the rights?

---

[6] See Thomas E. Copeland, "Liquidity Changes Following Stock Splits," *Journal of Finance* 34, no. 1 (March 1979):115–41.

[7] Current stockholders may not be given this right if there is a provision in the charter denying it or if it is denied by the stockholders at the annual meeting.

[8] The investor could simply let the rights expire, causing that investor's proportion in the corporation to decline as others are given ownership in the expanded firm in return for the provision of new capital. Sometimes there is an *oversubscription privilege* given to the subscribing stockholders. This means that those stockholders who have exercised their rights will be given an opportunity to buy the shares that were not purchased.

[9] The subscription price is usually set at roughly 80% of the current market price of the stock.

Rights are distributed in a manner similar to cash dividends. That is, there is a date of record and, four business days earlier, an *ex-rights date*. Before the ex-rights date, the value of a right can be calculated by using the following equation:

$$C_o - (RN + S) = R \qquad (15.2)$$

where:

C_o is the "rights-on" market price of the stock,

R is the value of a right,

N is the number of rights needed to buy one share, and

S is the subscription price.

The equation can be interpreted in the following manner. If an investor purchases one share before the ex-rights date, by definition he or she pays the market price of C_o, shown on the left-hand side of the equation. Alternatively, the investor could purchase the number of rights necessary to buy one share of the new stock at a cost of RN and set aside an amount of money equal to the subscription price S. The total cost of doing this is $RN + S$. The only difference between the two alternatives is that the first one gives the investor not only one share of stock but also one right. Thus, the difference in the cost of the two alternatives, $C_o - (RN + S)$, must equal the value of a right, R, as shown in equation (15.2).

Equation (15.2) can be rewritten as

$$R = \frac{C_o - S}{N + 1}. \qquad (15.3)$$

Thus, in the previous example, the value of a right when the stock is selling for $60 would be equal to approximately ($60 − $50)/(20 + 1) = $.48.

On or after the ex-rights date, the value of a right can be calculated by using the following equation:

$$C_e - (RN + S) = 0 \qquad (15.4)$$

where C_e is the ex-rights market price of the stock. The reasoning behind this equation is similar to the reasoning behind equation (15.2). That is, an investor can purchase one share by either buying it in the open market at a cost of C_e or by purchasing the requisite number of rights and setting aside the subscription price, for a total cost of $RN + S$. Since the purchase of one share ex-rights means the investor does not receive a right, the two alternatives provide the investor with the same item. Thus, the cost of these two alternatives should be equivalent, so the difference in their cost should be zero.

Equation (15.4) can be rewritten as

$$R = \frac{C_e - S}{N}. \qquad (15.5)$$

In the previous example, if the stock is selling for $56 after the ex-rights date, then the value of a right at that time would be approximately ($56 − $50)/20 = $.30.

15.5 STOCK PRICE AND VOLUME QUOTATIONS

Figures 15.2 and 15.3 provide examples of quotations summarizing a day's transactions in stocks traded over the counter and on the major stock exchanges.

Active stocks traded with the aid of the National Association of Securities Dealers' Automated Quotation system (NASDAQ) are summarized in the forms shown in Figure 15.2(a), (b), and (c). Transactions in securities designated National Market Issues are summarized in detail, as shown in Figure 15.2(a). The highest and lowest price recorded in the prior 365 days are shown in the first two columns, followed by the security name and ticker symbol. Next is the annual per share amount of dividends, in dollars, based on the latest declared amount (letters refer to footnotes providing details concerning extra or special dividends; the symbols by the annual high price are also explained in the footnotes). This dollar amount is divided by the

FIGURE 15–2
Summary of active stocks traded with the aid of the NASDAQ system.

SOURCE: Reprinted by permission of *The Wall Street Journal*, © Dow Jones & Company, Inc. (December 5, 1988): pp. C7, C6, and C6 respectively.

(a) National Market Issues

52 Weeks Hi	52 Weeks Lo	Stock	Sym	Div	Yld %	PE	Vol 100s	Hi	Lo	Close	Net Chg
					–A–A–A–						
19¾	8¼	A&W Brands	SODA		...	30	99	18½	18	18½	+ ¾
↓ 16½	4	**ABQ**	**ABQC**		...	53	47	4¾	3¾	4¾	+ ¾
5⅝	1¼	ACC	ACCC		...	20	95	5½	5 5/16	5 5/16	– 1/16
24	10¾	ADC Tel	ADCT		...	9	183	12⅜	11⅞	12⅛	+ ⅛
↓ 23¾	21¾	ADT	ADTLY		...	...	1001	21⅝	21⅜	21⅝	– ⅛
11½	7	AEL Ind A	AELNA		...	...	46	7⅜	7⅜	7⅜	– ⅜
14½	3	AIM Tel	AIMT		...	31	20	4⅜	4¼	4⅜	+ ⅛
6½	3½	AircoaHosp	AIRC	.10j	2.7	31	5	3¾	3¾	3¾	...
3⅜	⅞	ALC Comm	ALCC		...	...	101	2	1 15/16	2	+ 1/16
11¾	6¼	AME	AMEA		...	16	58	10⅛	9⅞	10⅛	...
15¾	6¼	ASK Cptr	ASKI		...	17	1632	15⅛	14⅝	14¾	+ ⅛
17⅜	6⅜	AST Rsrch	ASTA		...	7	2074	8⅝	8⅛	8½	+ ⅜
12½	6½	AaronRents	ARON	.10	1.0	8	2	10	10	10	– ⅛
16¾	8¾	AbeLincSvg	ALFB		...	...	25	16¼	16	16¼	...
2¾	1⅛	AcadInsur	ACIG		...	23	409	1¾	1⅝	1⅝	– 1/16
9⅛	4½	AccelInt	ACLE	t	...	5	17	6¾	6¾	6¾	– ⅛
14½	8½	AcceptIns	ACPT		...	5	132	11¾	11⅜	11⅝	– ⅛
17	10¾	Aceto	ACET	.14b	...	12	57	15½	15	15⅛	+ ⅛
14½	7	Acmat	ACMT		...	...	4	8½	8½	8½	...
11¾	6	Acmat A	ACMTA		...	...	3	7½	7½	7½	...
25¾	12¼	AcmeSteel	ACME	.05e	.2	8	34	22¼	22	22	– ⅛
s 17¾	5⅝	ActnAutRnt	AXXN		...	29	430	17⅜	17	17¼	...
8½	4¼	ActnAutStr	AAST		...	31	4	5¼	5¼	5¼	...
16½	7	Actmedia	ACTM		...	750	1428	7⅞	7½	7½	– ¼
16¾	9¼	Acxiom	ACXM		...	15	24	14¾	14½	14¾	+ ¼
4 3/16	1⅛	AdacLabs	ADAC		...	14	2531	3⅞	3 9/16	3¾	+ ⅛
1 11/16	⅝	**Adage**	**ADGE**		...	...	**3479**	1 5/16	1 3/16	1 9/32	+ 5/32
7¾	4½	Adaptec	ADPT		...	22	208	5⅛	4⅞	4⅞	– ⅛
25¼	13¾	AddintnRes	ADDR		...	9	100	22	21	21	–1
32	12½	AdiaSvcs	ADIA	.14	.6	15	839	22	21½	22	+ ¼
s 49½	20¾	AdobeSys	ADBE		...	30	3054	24¼	22⅜	23¾	+1
5	**2⅜**	**AdvCircuit**	**ADVC**		...	...	**79**	**3¾**	**3½**	**3½**	– ¼
4⅜	1	AdvCptr	ACTP		...	...	15	1¾	1¾	1¾	...
10¾	**4¼**	**AdvMagnet**	**ADMG**		...	**20**	**2**	**6¾**	**6¾**	**6¾**	– ¾
17¾	5¼	AdvMktg	ADMS		...	18	215	15¼	14¾	15¼	+ ⅛
9¼	5⅛	AdvPolymer	APOS		...	...	163	6½	6¼	6½	+ ¼
7⅝	2¼	AdvSemi	ASMIF		...	...	249	5⅞	5⅝	5⅞	+ ⅛
20¼	9¾	AdvTelecom	ATEL		...	...	64	14⅛	13⅞	14⅛	– ⅛
6½	**2½**	**ADVANTA**	**ADVN**		...	...	**379**	**4⅛**	**3¾**	**4⅛**	+ ⅜
5¼	**2¼**	**Advantage**	**ADCO**		...	**41**	**100**	**3¼**	**3¼**	**3¼**	+ ½
7	**3¾**	**AdvoSys**	**ADVO**		...	...	**1220**	**5¼**	**4⅝**	**5⅛**	+ ⅜
4⅜	2	Aequitron	AQTN		...	34	167	3½	3⅛	3⅜	+ ⅛

(b) Other Active Issues

Stock & Div		Sales 100s	Bid	Asked	Net Chg.
AFN		442	13/16	⅞	...
AFP		23	1⅛	1 3/16	...
APAOp		10	7¾	8½	...
ASK Cp		2336	1⅜	1 7/16	+ 5/16
ATC		63	5¾	6	...
Acclaim		1359	4¾	4 13/16	– ½
Acclm wtA		1512	5¼	5⅝	– ⅝
ActnStf		1399	1½	1 9/16	...
Adelph h		6	19¼	20	...
AdNMR		153	4¼	4⅜	...
A NMR wt		65	4	4⅛	...
AdvPr h		30	1 11/16	1 13/16	...
AdPd wtC		84	7/16	19/32	...
Advatex		136	2 9/16	2 11/16	...
AdvCa s		115	1⅞	2	...
AirSen		100	1 5/16	1 7/16	– 1/16
Alcide		761	2⅞	3	...
Alden	.15e	46	4⅝	4⅞	– ⅛
AlexEn		13	13/16	15/16	...
AlfaInt		35	1⅞	2	...
AllATV		30	2⅞	3¼	...
Amribc	.05e	36	18¾	19⅛	...
AAcft s		393	1⅜	1 7/16	...
ABionet		375	15/16	1	...
AmBio		40	2⅛	2¼	...
ABsCpt		174	1⅛	1 3/16	...
AClaim		12	3¼	3⅝	...
ACont pf	3.44	74	12⅝	13	...
AFn pfD	1.00	12	10¼	10½	...
AmInPt		1294	2⅛	2¼	+ 3/32
AmMobl		13	2⅞	3⅛	...
ARecr	.13	38	7⅜	7⅞	...
AmTlc h		847	1½	1⅝	+ 5/16
AmVisn		315	2 7/16	2 9/16	– 3/16
AmAll		2	6¼	6¾	...
An-Con		85	1 1/16	1⅛	...
AnlySur		37	2	2¼	...
AndwGp		100	4	4⅛	...
Angc un		10	2¼	2⅝	...
AngioM		154	2½	2¾	...
AngM wt		44	¼	⅜	...
AngSA	.80e	416	17⅝	17¾	+ ⅝
AngAG	.48e	230	7 5/16	7 7/16	+ 3/16
ApogRb		45	1 13/16	1 15/16	...
ApogeTc		336	7¾	8	+ ¾
Ap DNA		571	1⅜	1 7/16	– 1/16
ApdMicr		3	2½	2¾	...
AquaS h		271	9/16	19/32	...
Aquant		17	15/16	1	...
Arnox		159	⅞	1	+ ⅛
Artagph		450	2⅛	2⅜	...
ArytOp		20	1½	1 13/16	...
Asar wt91		70	11⅛	11⅜	...

(c) Less Active Issues

Stock	Bid	Asked
ACSEn	1 13/32	1½
ACS Ind	3¾	4½
API	⅝	11/16
ASA Int	3/32	5/32
AW A	5/32	5/16
Acap	½	¾
AckCm h	6	7
Acmt a	7½	8¼
ActnPr s	1⅜	2¼
Admar	3/16	¼
AdvDis	5/16	11/32
AdvMf h	1/16	3/16
A NMR un	24¾	28
AdPrd wt	15/32	11/16
AerSyE	2¼	2¾
AirInt	11/16	13/16
AlskAp	½	⅝
Albion	1/16	⅛
Alcd wtB	¼	½
Alfa wt	¼	1
vjAllSea	¾	1
AlphaSo	7/32	9/32
AlsFrm	1	1⅛
AltaEn	⅛	3/16
AltrHlt	¼	9/16
AltrH un	1	1¾
Alubec	1 7/16	1⅝
Amacan	¼	15/32
Amrfrd	3⅛	4½
AmrEco	3/32	⅛
AmCom	1/32	1/16
ACGld	5/16	⅜
AmCrse	¼	5/16
AmDrg	1¼	1 9/32
AmEdu	3/16	¼
AmElc	5/32	7/32
AmEnt	1/16	¼
AEqun h	⅛	3/16
AmFlm	1⅝	1 13/16
AmFl wt	¾	13/16
AmFran	¾	⅞
AGtyF	17/32	9/16
AMdAlt	7/16	9/16
AmAlt wt	1/16	⅛
AMAlt un	½	13/16
AMetl	1¼	1 7/16
APcM s	1⅛	1¾
ASafty	⅜	7/16
AScrn un	5/32	3/16
AmTelmd	⅛	5/32
AToxxic	25/32	13/16
AmerPr	1/16	3/32
Amtch s	2⅜	2½
AndrSt	1	1¾
Angecn	2	2⅛

(a) Stocks Listed on the New York Stock Exchange

	52 Weeks Hi	Lo	Stock	Sym	Div	Yld %	PE	Vol 100s	Hi	Lo	Close	Net Chg
			—A—A—A—									
	27 7/8	14	AAR	AIR	.44	2.0	16	1084	22 7/8	22 1/8	22 1/8	− 7/8
n	10 1/8	8 3/4	ACM OppFd	AOF		...	...	333	9 1/8	8 7/8	9 1/8	+ 1/8
	12 1/8	10 3/4	ACM Gvt Fd	ACG	1.26a	11.5	...	582	11 1/8	10 7/8	11	...
n	10 1/8	10	ACM MgdIncFd	AMF		...	...	30	10 1/8	10	10 1/8	...
n	12 1/8	10 3/8	ACM SecFd	GSF	1.26	12.1	...	911	10 5/8	10 3/8	10 3/8	− 1/4
↓x	10 1/8	8 7/8	ACM SpctmFd	SI	1.01a	11.5	...	x456	8 7/8	8 5/8	8 3/4	...
	5 3/8	2 5/8	AMCA	AIL	.12e	3.7	...	10	3 1/4	3 1/4	3 1/4	...
	6 1/8	3 3/8	AM Int	AM		...	...	408	4 5/8	4 1/2	4 1/2	− 1/8
	23 1/4	18 1/8	AM Int pf		2.00	9.4	...	37	21 3/4	21 1/4	21 1/4	...
	53 1/4	26 3/4	AMR	AMR		...	9	6745	53 1/4	51 7/8	51 7/8	− 3/4
	27	25	ANR pf		2.67	10.5	...	1	25 1/2	25 1/2	25 1/2	...
	9 1/2	5 3/8	ARX	ARX		...	10	373	5 7/8	5 3/4	5 7/8	+ 1/4
	58 3/4	35 1/4	ASA	ASA	3.00a	7.5	...	806	39 7/8	38 1/2	39 7/8	+ 1 1/8
	20 1/4	11	AVX	AVX	.12e	.8	11	290	15 7/8	15 1/4	15 1/4	− 5/8
	52 3/8	42 1/4	AbbotLab	ABT	1.20	2.6	14	2435	46	45 3/8	46	+ 1/4
	21 3/4	15 3/8	Abitibi g	ABY	1.00	...	...	76	16 1/4	16 1/8	16 1/8	− 1/8
	13 7/8	7 1/2	AcmeCleve	AMT	.40	4.8	...	54	8 1/4	7 7/8	8 1/4	+ 1/4
	8 7/8	5 7/8	AcmeElec	ACE	.32b	5.3	26	6	6	5 7/8	6	+ 1/8
	29 1/2	12 3/4	Acuson	ACN		...	23	431	24 1/4	23 1/2	24 1/4	+ 5/8
	17	14 1/2	AdamsExp	ADX	1.82e	12.3	...	89	14 7/8	14 5/8	14 3/4	+ 1/8
	16 7/8	7 1/8	AdvMicro	AMD		...	15	5703	8 1/8	7 7/8	7 7/8	− 1/8
	43 1/2	28 3/4	AdvMicro pf		3.00	10.0	...	63	30	29 1/2	30	+ 1/2
	8 1/2	4 3/4	AdobeRes	ADB		...	...	212	6 3/4	6 5/8	6 3/4	...
	18 1/2	16 1/4	AdobeRes pf		1.84	10.7	...	8	17 1/8	17 1/8	17 1/8	− 1/4
	21 3/4	19 1/4	AdobeRes pf		2.40	11.7	...	6	20 1/2	20 1/2	20 1/2	...
	9 3/4	5 7/8	Advest	ADV	.12	1.8	21	71	6 7/8	6 3/4	6 3/4	− 1/8
	52 1/2	39 1/2	AetnaLife	AET	2.76	5.8	8	1263	47 1/2	46 5/8	47 1/2	+ 1/8
s	**34 1/4**	**20 1/2**	**AffilPub**	**AFP**	**.22**	**.7**	**...**	**1308**	**31 1/2**	**29 5/8**	**31 3/8**	**+ 1 1/2**
	18 5/8	13	Ahmanson	AHM	.88	5.5	9	2797	15 7/8	15 5/8	15 7/8	...
	4 5/8	1 7/8	Aileen	AEE		...	...	39	3 5/8	3 1/2	3 5/8	...
	53 3/8	30 5/8	AirProduct	APD	1.20	3.0	10	1104	39 7/8	39	39 7/8	+ 3/4
	19 3/4	11 1/8	AirbornFrght	ABF	.60	3.2	18	65	18 5/8	18 3/8	18 1/2	− 1/8
	16 3/4	6 3/4	Airgas	ARG		...	16	10	15	14 7/8	14 7/8	− 1/8

(b) Stocks Listed on the American Stock Exchange

	52 Weeks Hi	Lo	Stock	Sym	Div	Yld %	PE	Vol 100s	Hi	Lo	Close	Net Chg
			—A—A—A—									
	8 5/8	3 1/4	ABM Gold	AGO		...	...	126	3 5/8	3 3/8	3 1/2	...
	6	4 1/4	AIFS	AIF		...	...	10	5 1/2	5 1/2	5 1/2	+ 1/8
s	15 7/8	6 1/8	AL Labs	BMD	.12	.9	16	37	12 7/8	12 3/4	12 7/8	− 1/8
s	7 1/2	3 1/2	AMC Entn	AEN	.08j	...	...	3	4	4	4	+ 1/8
	3 3/8	**1**	**AM Int wt**			**...**	**...**	**1**	**1 3/8**	**1 3/8**	**1 3/8**	**− 1/8**
	3 1/2	2 1/2	AOI Coal	AOI	.05e	1.8	69	70	2 3/4	2 3/4	2 3/4	+ 1/8
	3 7/8	1 11/16	ARC Int g	ATV		...	...	86	3 1/8	3	3 1/16	+ 1/16
	11 5/8	5 7/8	AT&E	ATW		...	...	44	10	9 3/4	10	+ 1/8
	2 1/2	**1/2**	**AT&T Crd wt**			**...**	**...**	**60**	**9/16**	**9/16**	**9/16**	**− 1/16**
	10 1/4	2	ATI Med	ATI		...	36	63	4	3 3/4	4	...
	41 3/4	35 1/2	AT&T Fund	ATF	1.97e	4.9	...	81	40 1/4	40	40	− 5/8
	11 1/4	4 3/4	Abiomed	ABD		...	...	5	8 1/8	8 1/8	8 1/8	− 1/8
	6 1/2	3	ActionInd	ACX		...	13	28	3 7/8	3 3/4	3 7/8	...
	17 3/4	12	ActonCp	ATN		...	9	7	12 1/4	12 1/4	12 1/4	...
	2 3/8	1 1/4	AdamsRes	AE		...	5	26	1 1/2	1 3/8	1 3/8	...
	11 1/8	6 3/8	AdamsRusEl	AEI		...	181	68	7 1/4	6 7/8	7 1/4	+ 1/8
	21 3/4	10 1/4	AirExprss	AEX		...	10	119	16 5/8	16 1/8	16 3/8	+ 1/2
	15	8 3/4	AircoaHotel	AHT	2.40	22.9	...	25	10 5/8	10 3/8	10 1/2	...
	3/8	**1/8**	**Alamco**	**AXO**		**...**	**...**	**10**	**3/16**	**3/16**	**3/16**	**− 1/16**
	8 3/8	6	AlbaWaldn	AWS		...	...	8	6 7/8	6 7/8	6 7/8	− 1/4
s	4 1/8	2 1/8	Alfin	AFN		...	10	30	2 1/4	2 1/8	2 1/4	...
n	8 1/2	7/8	AllncBcp	ABK		...	...	8	1	1	1	...
	8 1/2	**3 1/4**	**Allstarlns**	**SAI**	**1.00**	**25.8**	**...**	**175**	**3 7/8**	**3 1/2**	**3 7/8**	**+ 3/8**
	7 1/8	3	Alphalnd	AHA		...	...	148	4 1/8	3 7/8	3 7/8	...
	7 3/4	**4 5/8**	**AlpineGp**	**AGI**		**...**	**...**	**22**	**6 5/8**	**6 1/2**	**6 1/2**	**− 3/8**
	7/16	**1/8**	**Altexlnd**	**AII**		**...**	**...**	**72**	**1/4**	**3/16**	**1/4**	**+ 1/16**
	30 1/8	19 1/2	Alza	AZA		...	47	914	23 7/8	23 1/4	23 5/8	− 3/8
	9/16	**1/8**	**Alza rt**			**...**	**...**	**13277**	**5/16**	**3/16**	**5/16**	**+ 1/8**
	5 5/8	**3 5/8**	**AmBrit**	**ABI**	**.08**	**1.7**	**...**	**35**	**4 3/4**	**4 5/8**	**4 5/8**	**− 1/4**
s	28	12 3/4	Amdahl	AMH	.10	.6	10	7829	18 3/8	17 5/8	17 7/8	...
n↓	19	18	AmFPrepFd2	PF	.14e	.8	...	9	17 3/4	17 3/4	17 3/4	− 1/4
	29 3/8	8	AmBiltrite	ABL	.15	.8	7	25	19	18 7/8	19	+ 1/4

FIGURE 15–3
Summary of activity in stocks traded on major exchanges.

SOURCE: Reprinted by permission of *The Wall Street Journal*, © Dow Jones & Company, Inc. (December 5, 1988): pp. C3 and C9 respectively.

closing price (the price at which the last trade of the day was made) to obtain the figure shown for *dividend yield*. The ratio of the closing price to the last 12 months' earnings per share is given next. The remaining entries summarize the day's transactions. Sales, in hundreds of shares, are indicated, followed by the highest and lowest prices at which trades were completed during the day. The next entry is the closing price, and the final entry shows the difference between the day's closing price and that of the preceding day. If this price change exceeds 5%, then the entire entry for the stock is emboldened; if the volume is relatively large, then the entire entry is underlined.

Information on stocks with somewhat less activity is shown in Figure 15.2(b). Volume traded through NASDAQ during the day is shown (in hundreds of shares), along with the highest bid price and lowest ask price by dealers as of 4 P.M. eastern time. The net change in the bid price from the previous day is also shown. Investors pay the asked price to purchase shares and receive the bid price when they sell shares. In addition, markdowns or markups and commissions may be added by the investor's retail broker.

Information on over-the-counter stocks with relatively little activity is shown in Figure 15.2(c). This information is provided weekly (on Mondays); note that only bid and ask price quotations (as of 4 P.M. eastern time) are given.

Activity in stocks traded on major exchanges is shown in Figure 15.3. Stocks listed on the New York Stock Exchange are shown in the left-hand side of the figure. Those listed on the American Stock Exchange are shown in the right-hand side of the figure. The format is identical to that for NASDAQ National Market Issues.

15.6 INSIDER TRADING

The Securities and Exchange Commission requires the officers and directors of a corporation whose securities are traded on an organized exchange to report any transactions they have made in the firm's shares. Such a report must be filed within ten days following the month in which the transaction takes place. This reporting requirement is also applicable to any stockholder who owns 10% or more of the firm's shares. Such stockholders, officers, and directors are often referred to as *insiders*. The information they provide about their trading is subsequently reported in the Securities and Exchange Commission's monthly *Official Summary of Securities Transactions and Holdings*.[10] For example, the summary of trades made in January (and reported by early February) is published early in March. Thus, up to two months may elapse before knowledge of such trades becomes widespread.

The Securities and Exchange Acts also require corporate insiders to return all short-term profits from security transactions in their own stocks to the corporation. For this purpose, *short term* is defined as less than six months, meaning the shares were both bought and sold within a six-month time period. As a result of this requirement, few insiders buy and sell within a six-month time period. Instead, most prefer to spread their buy and sell orders over a longer time period so they do not have to return their profits.

In the United States, it is illegal for anyone to enter into a security transaction if they have taken advantage of "inside" information about the corporation that is unavailable to other people involved in the transaction. This proscription includes not only insiders but also those to whom they give such secret information (the recipient of such a tip is termed the *tipee*).

Legally, there are two types of nonpublic information: that which is private (that is, legal) and that which is inside (that is, possibly illegal). Unfortunately, the distinction between the two types is highly ambiguous, causing continuing problems for security analysts.

Legal issues aside, two questions of relevance to outside investors may be posed: (1) Do insiders make unusual profits on transactions in their own

---

[10] The *Value Line Investment Survey* (published by Value Line, Inc., New York) reports an "index of insider decisions" for each stock covered in its weekly service. In essence, this is a cumulative index of the net number of purchasers (including those who exercise options) and sellers. The *Weekly Insider Report* (published by Vickers Stock Research Corp., Brookside, N.J.) reports a ratio of total insider buying to total insider selling. For an article about what constitutes insider trading, see Gary L. Tidwell, "Here's a Tip—Know the Rules of Insider Trading," *Sloan Management Review* 28, no. 4 (Summer 1987):93–98.

stocks? (2) If they do, can others profit by following their example as soon as it becomes public knowledge?

Insiders trade their stock for many reasons. For example, some purchases result from the exercise of options and some sales result from the need for cash. Moreover, it is not unusual to find some insiders purchasing a stock during a month in which other insiders are selling it. However, when a major piece of inside information suggests that a stock's value differs significantly from its current market price, it would be reasonable to expect a preponderance of insider trades on one side of the market (that is, either purchases or sales).

One way to search for such situations is to examine the *Official Summary* and count the number of days during a month that each insider traded his or her firm's stock (excluding the exercise of options). If the days on which purchases were made exceeds those on which sales were made, the individual can be counted as a net purchaser during that month; and if the converse holds, the individual is a net seller. Next, the number of net purchasers and sellers for the firm's stock can be considered. If there were at least three more net purchasers than net sellers, for instance, it might be inferred as evidence that, on balance, favorable inside information motivated the insider trades during the month. Conversely, if there are at least three more net sellers than net purchasers, it might be inferred that, on balance, unfavorable insider information motivated the insider trades.

Different cutoff levels could be used in this process to reflect the intensity of insider trading. A cutoff of 1 would require a simple majority of trades of one type, whereas a cutoff of 5 would require a "supermajority" of trades of one type.

Such a procedure was used in a detailed study of insider transactions during the 1950s and 1960s.[11] Table 15.1 summarizes the key results. The two columns on the right-hand side of the table indicate the abnormal returns over an eight-month period on securities that exceeded the cutoff level for insider trading. For example, during the 1960s, if an investor purchased every stock in the sample for which there were three or more net purchasers and sold every stock for which there were three or more more net sellers during a month, more or less coincident with the transactions of the insiders themselves, then the investor would have earned, on average, an abnormal return of 5.07% over the subsequent eight months. If the transactions had been made instead at roughly the time the information was published in the *Official Summary*, an average abnormal return of 4.94% would have been earned over the next eight months.

As the first row in the table shows, a bare majority of insider trades does not appear to isolate possible effects of insider information. But a majority of three, four, or five does seem to do so. The figures shown are gross of any transaction costs, but even so it appears that insiders can and do make money from their special knowledge of their companies. This is not surprising, since if anyone can know the true value of a firm, it should be

---

[11] Jeffrey F. Jaffe, "Special Information and Insider Trading," *Journal of Business* 47, no. 3 (July 1974):410–28. See also Joseph E. Finnerty, "Insiders and Market Efficiency," *Journal of Finance* 31, no. 4 (September 1976):1141–48.

TABLE 15.1

Abnormal Returns Associated with Insider Trading.

SAMPLE			AVERAGE ABNORMAL RETURN OVER EIGHT MONTHS FOLLOWING	
Cut-off (No. of Net Purchasers or Sellers)	No. of Cases	Period	Month of Transaction	Month Information Became Publicly Available
1	362	1960s	1.36%	.70%
3	861	1960s	5.07	4.94
4	293	1950s	5.14	4.12
5	157	1950s	4.48	4.08

SOURCE: Jeffrey F. Jaffe, "Special Information and Insider Trading," *Journal of Business* 47, no. 3 (July 1974):421, 426.

the insiders. Since the information these insiders presumably are using is nonpublic in nature, these findings suggest that markets are not strong-form efficient. (The notion of market efficiency was introduced in Chapter 3).

On the other hand, the abnormal returns associated with transactions that could have been made by outsiders, using only publicly available information on insider trading, are quite surprising. Moreover, those associated with cutoffs of three, four, or five pass statistical tests designed to see if they might be simply due to chance. After transaction costs, trades designed to capitalize on such information would appear still to produce abnormal returns (although not highly so), suggesting that markets are not even semistrong-form efficient. However, more recent studies have found that outsiders cannot use the publicly available information about insider trading to make abnormal profits; these studies thus support the notion that markets are semistrong-form efficient.[12] With such conflicting evidence, it would appear that whether or not insider trading information can be profitably used by outsiders is an open question.

15.7 EX ANTE AND EX POST VALUES

Equilibrium theories such as the capital asset pricing model and arbitrage pricing theory imply that in the opinion of well-informed investors, securities with certain attributes will, other things being equal, have large expected returns, whereas those with other attributes will have small expected returns. Thus, the focus of these theories is on future, or *ex ante*, expected returns. However, only historical, or *ex post*, returns are subsequently observed. These historical returns are undoubtedly different from the expected

---

[12] See Herbert S. Kerr, "The Battle of Insider Trading and Market Efficiency," *Journal of Portfolio Management* 6, no. 4 (Summer 1980):47–58; and Wayne Y. Lee and Michael E. Solt, "Insider Trading: A Poor Guide to Market Timing," *Journal of Portfolio Management* 12, no. 4 (Summer 1986):65–71.

returns, making it extremely difficult to tell whether security attributes and expected returns do, in fact, go together in the manner implied by either the CAPM or APT. Moreover, such theories are relatively silent concerning simple ways in which a security's future, or *ex ante*, attributes and expected return might be estimated by examining historical, or *ex post*, returns.

To bridge this gap, a number of investigators have used the average historical return of a security as an estimate of its expected return. This requires an assumption that the expected return did not change over some arbitrary time period and that this time period contains a sufficient number of historical returns to make a reasonably accurate estimate of the expected return. However, an objection may be made in that expectations almost certainly would have changed over the time period needed to obtain a reasonably useful estimate of the expected return for any given security.[13] Despite this objection, it is worthwhile examining historical returns to see how they can be used to come up with meaningful predictions about the future.[14] The next section explores the prediction of a firm's beta. It begins by discussing the estimation of the firm's historical beta by use of the characteristic line.

15.8 COMMON STOCK BETAS

For purposes of portfolio management, the relevant risk of a security concerns its impact on the risk of a well-diversified portfolio. In the world of the CAPM, such portfolios would be subject primarily to market risk. This suggests the importance of a security's beta, which measures its sensitivity to future market movements. To estimate beta, in principle the possible sources of such movements should be considered. Then, the reaction of the security's price to each of these sources should be estimated, along with the probability of each reaction. In the process, the economics of the relevant industry and firm, the impact of both operating and financial leverage on the firm, and other fundamental factors should be taken into account.

But what about investigating the extent to which the security's price moved with the market in the past? Such an approach ignores the myriad possible differences between the past and the future. However, it is easily done and provides a useful starting point.

As shown in Chapter 8, a security's beta can be regarded as the slope of the security's characteristic line. If this line were constant over time,

---

[13] It has been argued that roughly 300 months (25 years) of historical returns are needed in order for a simple averaging technique to produce reasonably useful estimates of expected returns, provided that the "true" but unobserved expected return is constant during this entire period. See J. D. Jobson and Bob Korkie, "Estimation for Markowitz Efficient Portfolios," *Journal of the American Statistical Association* 75, no. 371 (September 1980):544–54 and "Putting Markowitz Theory to Work," *Journal of Portfolio Management* 7, no. 4 (Summer 1981):70–74.

[14] In doing so, a number of researchers have uncovered certain "empirical regularities" in common stocks; Appendix A discusses a number of them. For a more detailed summary, see Donald B. Keim, "The CAPM and Equity Return Regularities," *Financial Analysts Journal* 42, no. 3 (May/June 1986):19–34; Douglas K. Pearce, "Challenges to the Concept of Market Efficiency," Federal Reserve Bank of Kansas City *Economic Review* 72, no. 8 (September/October 1987):16–33; and Robert A. Haugen and Josef Lakonishok, *The Incredible January Effect*, (Homewood, Ill.: Dow Jones-Irwin, 1988).

meaning it was not changing from period to period, then the *historical beta* for a security could be estimated by examining the historical relationship between the excess returns on the security and on the market portfolio. The statistical procedure used for making such estimates of ex post betas is *simple linear regression*, also known as ordinary least squares (OLS).[15]

As an example, consider estimating the ex post beta for IBM using Standard & Poor's 500 index and the 90-day Treasury bill rate as surrogates for the market portfolio and risk-free rate, respectively. Part (a) of Table 15.2 presents the data necessary to calculate the returns on a quarterly basis over the four-year period from 1982 to 1985 for both IBM and the S&P 500. Part (b) presents the 90-day Treasury bill rate at the beginning of each quarter, the returns on both IBM and the S&P 500, and the excess returns on both IBM and the S&P 500. Part (c) presents the calculations necessary to determine IBM's *ex post* beta and alpha as well as certain other statistical parameters. As can be seen, IBM's beta and alpha were equal to 1.15 and 2.39%, respectively, over this period.[16]

Given these values for alpha and beta, the *ex post* characteristic line for IBM is:

$$r_{IBM} - r_f = 2.39\% + 1.15(r_M - r_f) + \epsilon_{IBM}. \tag{15.6}$$

Figure 15.4 presents a scatter diagram of the excess returns on IBM $(r_{IBM} - r_f)$ and the S&P 500 $(r_M - r_f)$. Also shown in the figure is a graph of the characteristic line, except that the random error term is deleted. That is, the figure has a graph of the following line:

$$r_{IBM} - r_f = 2.39\% + 1.15(r_M - r_f). \tag{15.7}$$

The vertical distance of each point in the scatter diagram from this characteristic line represents an estimate of the size of the random error term for the corresponding quarter. The exact distance can be found by rewriting equation (15.6) as:

$$[r_{IBM} - r_f] - [2.39\% + 1.15(r_M - r_f)] = \epsilon_{IBM} \tag{15.8}$$

For example, looking at part c of Table 15.2, in the third quarter of 1984 the excess return on IBM and the S&P 500 were 14.42% and 6.29%, respectively. The value of ϵ_{IBM} for that quarter can be calculated by using equation (15.8), as follows:

$$[14.42\%] - [2.39\% + 1.15(6.29\%)] = 4.80\%.$$

The values of ϵ_{IBM} can be similarly calculated for the other 15 quarters of the estimation period. The standard deviation of the resulting set of 16

---

[15] For an introduction to regression, see Chapter 10 of James T. McClave and P. George Benson, *Statistics for Business and Economics* (San Francisco: Dellen Publishing Company, 1988).

[16] IBM's beta and alpha would have been equal to 1.17 and 1.94%, respectively, if returns had been used in the calculations instead of *excess* returns. Using returns or excess returns (as well as including or ignoring dividends in calculating returns) appears to make little difference in the estimated size of beta. However, there is a substantive difference in the estimated size of alpha; consequently, it is appropriate to use excess returns when estimating alpha. See William F. Sharpe and Guy M. Cooper, "Risk-Return Classes of New York Stock Exchange Common Stocks, 1931–1967," *Financial Analysts Journal* 28, no. 2 (March/April 1972):46–54.

TABLE 15.2

The Ex Post Characteristic Line for IBM, 1982–1985.

a. QUARTERLY DATA

Quarter		IBM Price at Start	Price at End	Div.	S&P 500 Index at Start	Index at End	Div.
1982	1	$ 58.250	$ 61.000	$ .86	122.74	113.79	$1.76
	2	61.000	60.500	.86	113.79	108.71	1.73
	3	60.500	74.125	.86	108.71	121.97	1.71
	4	74.125	93.000	.86	121.97	138.34	1.71
1983	1	93.000	102.375	.86	138.34	153.02	1.79
	2	102.375	121.000	.95	153.02	168.91	1.79
	3	121.000	128.125	.95	168.91	165.80	1.80
	4	128.125	121.750	.95	165.80	164.04	1.80
1984	1	121.750	112.000	.95	164.04	157.98	1.92
	2	112.000	105.875	.95	157.98	153.20	1.86
	3	105.875	122.625	1.10	153.20	164.62	1.95
	4	122.625	121.000	1.10	164.62	165.37	1.93
1985	1	121.000	128.125	1.10	165.37	181.27	2.00
	2	128.125	124.875	1.10	181.27	192.43	1.96
	3	124.875	126.625	1.10	192.43	185.07	2.01
	4	126.625	152.000	1.10	185.07	209.59	2.05

b. RETURNS

Quarter		90-Day Treasury Bill Return	IBM Return	Excess Return	S&P 500 Return	Excess Return
1982	1	2.97%	6.20%	3.23%	− 5.86%	− 8.83%
	2	3.06	.59	− 2.47	− 2.94	− 6.00
	3	2.85	23.94	21.09	13.77	10.92
	4	1.88	26.62	24.74	14.82	12.94
1983	1	1.90	11.01	9.11	11.91	10.01
	2	2.00	19.12	17.12	11.55	9.55
	3	2.22	6.67	4.45	− .78	− 3.00
	4	2.11	− 4.23	− 6.34	.02	− 2.09
1984	1	2.16	− 7.23	− 9.39	− 2.52	− 4.68
	2	2.34	− 4.62	− 6.96	− 1.85	− 4.19
	3	2.44	16.86	14.42	8.73	6.29
	4	2.40	− .43	− 2.83	1.63	− .77
1985	1	1.89	6.80	4.91	10.82	8.93
	2	1.94	− 1.68	− 3.62	7.24	5.30
	3	1.72	2.28	.56	− 2.78	− 4.50
	4	1.75	20.91	19.16	14.36	12.61

c. CALCULATIONS[a]

Quarter		IBM Excess Returns = Y (1)	S&P 500 Excess Returns = X (2)	Y^2 (3)	X^2 (4)	$Y \times X$ (5)
1982	1	3.23%	− 8.83%	10.42	77.93	− 28.49
	2	− 2.47	− 6.00	6.10	36.05	14.83
	3	21.09	10.92	444.88	119.26	230.34
	4	24.74	12.94	612.26	167.53	320.27
1983	1	9.11	10.01	82.91	100.11	91.10
	2	17.12	9.55	293.13	91.28	163.57

TABLE 15.2 (*Continued*)

The Ex Post Characteristic Line for IBM, 1982–1985.

c. CALCULATIONS[a]

Quarter		IBM Excess Returns = Y (1)	S&P 500 Excess Returns = X (2)	Y² (3)	X² (4)	Y × X (5)
	3	4.45	− 3.00	19.83	8.97	− 13.34
	4	− 6.34	− 2.09	40.25	4.35	13.23
1984	1	− 9.39	− 4.68	88.13	21.94	43.97
	2	− 6.96	− 4.19	48.45	17.54	29.15
	3	14.42	6.29	207.92	39.53	90.66
	4	− 2.83	− .77	8.00	.60	2.18
1985	1	4.91	8.93	24.08	79.82	43.85
	2	− 3.62	5.30	13.09	28.07	− 19.17
	3	.56	− 4.50	.32	20.25	− 2.53
	4	19.16	12.61	367.04	158.93	241.52
Sum (Σ) =		87.18	42.49	2266.81	972.16	1221.14
		= ΣY	= ΣX	= ΣY²	= ΣX²	= ΣXY

1. Beta:

$$\frac{(T \times \Sigma XY) - (\Sigma Y \times \Sigma X)}{(T \times \Sigma X^2) - (\Sigma X)^2} = \frac{(16 \times 1221.14) - (87.18 \times 42.29)}{(16 \times 972.16) - (42.49)^2} = 1.15$$

2. Alpha:

$$\left(\frac{\Sigma Y}{T}\right) - \left(\text{beta} \times \frac{\Sigma X}{T}\right) = \left(\frac{87.18}{16}\right) - \left(1.15 \times \frac{42.29}{16}\right) = 2.39\%$$

3. Standard deviation of random error term:

$$\left[\frac{\Sigma Y^2 - (\text{alpha} \times \Sigma Y) - (\text{beta} \times \Sigma XY)}{T - 2}\right]^{1/2} = \left[\frac{2266.81 - (2.39 \times 87.18) - (1.15 \times 1221.14)}{16 - 2}\right]^{1/2} = 6.836\%$$

4. Standard error of beta:

$$\text{Standard deviation of random error term}/\{\Sigma X^2 - [(\Sigma X)^2/T]\}^{1/2} = \frac{6.836}{\{972.16 - [(42.49)^2/16]\}^{1/2}} = .233$$

5. Standard error of alpha:

$$\text{Standard deviation of random error term}/\{T - [(\Sigma X)^2/\Sigma X^2]\}^{1/2} = \frac{6.836}{\{16 - [(42.49)^2/972.16]\}^{1/2}} = 1.817$$

6. Correlation coefficient:

$$\frac{(T \times \Sigma XY) - (\Sigma Y \times \Sigma X)}{\{[(T \times \Sigma Y^2) - (\Sigma Y)^2] \times [(T \times \Sigma X^2) - (\Sigma X)^2]\}^{1/2}}$$

$$\frac{(16 \times 1221.14) - (87.18 \times 42.29)}{\{[(16 \times 2266.81) - (87.18)^2] \times [(16 \times 972.16) - (42.49)^2]\}^{1/2}} = .798$$

7. Coefficient of determination:

$$(\text{Correlation coefficient})^2 = (.798)^2 = .637$$

8. Coefficient of nondetermination:

$$1 - \text{coefficient of determination} = 1 - .637 = .363$$

[a] All summations are to be carried out over t, where t goes from 1 to T (in this example, t = 1, 2, . . . , 16).

numbers is an estimate of the *standard deviation of the random error term* (or residual standard deviation) and is shown in part c of Table 15.2 to be equal to 6.836%. This number can be viewed as an estimate of the historical unique risk of IBM.

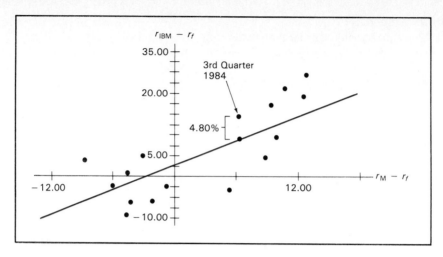

FIGURE 15–4
Ex post characteristic line for IBM.

The characteristic line for IBM shown in Figure 15.4 corresponds to the regression line for the scatter diagram. Recalling that a straight line is defined by its intercept and slope, it can be shown that there are no other values for alpha and beta that will define a straight line fitting the scatter diagram any better than the regression line. This means that there is no line that could be drawn that would result in a smaller standard deviation of the random error term. Thus, the regression line is often referred to as the line of *best fit*.

Equivalently, the line of best fit is the line that has the smallest sum of squared values of the random error terms. That is, the 16 random error terms associated with the regression line can each be squared and then summed. This sum (sum of squared errors) is smaller for the line of best fit than the sum associated with any other line.

For example, if alpha were equal to 1.5% and beta equal to .8 in equation (15.8), then the value of the random error term of ϵ_{IBM} could be calculated for each of the 16 quarters. With these 16 values, the standard deviation of the random error term could be calculated by squaring each value, summing up the squared values, and dividing the sum by $14 = (16 - 2)$; the standard deviation of the random error term would then be the square root of this number. However, it would be larger than 6.836%, which is the standard deviation of the random error term associated with the line of best fit (that is, the line with an alpha of 2.39% and a beta of 1.15).

It should be remembered that a security's "true" historical beta cannot be observed. All that can be done is to estimate its value. Thus, even if a security's true beta remained the same forever, its estimated value, obtained in the manner shown in Table 15.2, would still change from time to time because of errors (known as sampling errors) in estimating it. For example, if the 16 quarters from 1978 to 1981 were examined, the resulting estimated beta for IBM would almost certainly be different from 1.15, the estimated

value for 1982 to 1985. The *standard error of beta* shown in part (c) of Table 15.2 attempts to indicate the extent of such estimation errors. Given a number of necessary assumptions (for example, the true beta did not change during the estimation period of 1982 to 1985), the chances are roughly two out of three that the true beta is within a standard error, plus or minus, of the estimated beta. Thus, IBM's true beta is likely to be between the values of .917 (1.15 − .233) and 1.383 (1.15 + .233). Similarly, the *standard error of alpha* provides an indication of the magnitude of the possible sampling error that has been made in estimating alpha.

The *correlation coefficient* provides an indication of how closely the excess returns on IBM were associated with the excess returns on the S&P 500. Since its range is between − 1 and + 1, the value for IBM of .798 indicates a strong positive relationship between IBM and the S&P 500. That is, larger excess returns for IBM seem to be associated with larger excess returns on the S&P 500.

The *coefficient of determination* represents the proportion of variation in the excess return on IBM that is related to the variation in the excess return on the S&P 500. That is, it shows how much of the movement in IBM's excess returns can be explained by movements in the excess returns on the S&P 500. With a value of .637, it can be seen that the majority of the movement in the excess return on IBM from 1982 to 1985 can be attributed to movement in the excess return on the S&P 500.

Since the *coefficient of nondetermination* is 1 minus the coefficient of determination, it represents the proportion of movement in the excess return on IBM that is not due to movement in the excess return on the S&P 500. Thus, 36.3% of the movement in IBM cannot be attributed to movement in the S&P 500.

Figure 15.5 shows a page from a report prepared by Merrill Lynch, Pierce, Fenner & Smith, Inc. Percentage price changes for many stocks, calculated for each of 60 months (when available), were compared with the corresponding percentage changes in the Standard & Poor's 500 using simple linear regression. Seven of the resulting values from this analysis are of interest for each stock.

The values shown for *Beta* and *Alpha* indicate the slope and intercept, respectively, of the straight line that is the best fit for the scatter diagram of the percentage price changes for the stock and index. For example, during the 60-month period covered, the stock of the Timken Company had a beta and alpha of 1.13 and .65%, respectively.

The value of *R-Sqr*, short for R-squared, is equivalent to the coefficient of determination shown in Table 15.2.[17] Having a value of .40 means that 40% of the variation in Timken's price changes could be attributed to changes in the market index over the 60-month period.

The value for *Resid Std Dev-n* (residual standard deviation) corresponds to the standard deviation of the random error term in Table 15.2. Timken can be seen to have a residual standard deviation of 5.82%.

---

[17] R is used here to denote the correlation coefficient; sometimes the Greek letter rho (ρ) is used instead. Thus, R-squared is equivalent to rho-squared, or the square of the correlation coefficient.

TKR Symb	Security Name	10/79 Close Price	Beta	Alpha	R-Sqr	Resid Std Dev-n	Std.Err of Beta	Std.Err of Alpha	Adjusted Beta	Number of Observ
THRS	THREASHOLD TECKNOLOG	9.750	.85	1.92	.06	12.99	.40	1.69	.90	60
FXN	THREE D DEPTS	4.375	1.71	4.54	.18	17.07	.45	2.21	1.47	60
TDMC	THREE DIMENTIONAL CI	.562	-.63	8.65	.02	41.62	1.46	5.78	-.08	52
TFTA	THRIFTIMART INC A	21.375	.80	1.21	.13	8.49	.26	1.11	.87	60
THRF	THRIFTWAY LEASING CO	.000	1.02	3.84	.02	26.06	.66	3.38	1.01	60
TFD	THRIFTY CORP	11.625	1.92	.87	.46	8.80	.27	1.15	1.61	60
TEXT	TI-CARO	20.500	.94	1.58	.23	7.17	.22	.93	.96	60
TIM	TIDEWATER INC	25.750	.86	.39	.19	7.30	.22	.95	.91	60
TDW	TIDWELL INDS INC	5.750	5.11	4.85	.17	46.73	1.42	6.10	3.73	60
FLY	TIGER INTL INC	19.750	1.63	1.55	.33	9.87	.30	1.29	1.42	60
TI	TIME INC	43.250	1.24	1.39	.36	6.87	.21	.90	1.16	60
TPLX	TIMEPLEX INC	9.125	2.38	5.23	.11	26.83	.82	3.50	1.91	60
PWII	TIMBERLAND INDUSTRIES	6.250	.78	3.18	.06	13.68	.35	1.77	.85	60
TMC	TIMES MIRROR CO	32.500	1.60	1.19	.61	5.41	.16	.71	1.39	60
TKR	TIMKEN CO	51.000	1.13	.65	.40	5.82	.18	.76	1.09	60
TNSL	TINSLEY LABS INC	6.000	.84	1.60	.03	17.49	.48	2.27	.90	60
TLK	TIPPERARY CORP	11.250	.95	2.12	.08	12.86	.39	1.68	.97	60
TIN	TITAN GROUP	1.500	1.53	-1.81	.04	24.91	.85	3.22	1.35	60
TICT	TLL INDUS	3.000	1.61	-.23	.12	17.29	.53	2.26	1.40	60
AIKZ	TOBIAS KOIZIN CO	5.000	1.18	2.44	.07	16.98	.52	2.22	1.12	60
TBN	TOBIN PACKING INC	3.625	1.10	-.41	.09	13.89	.42	1.81	1.06	60
TOCM	TOCOM INC	10.500	1.72	2.98	.19	14.69	.45	1.92	1.48	60
TOD	TODD SHIPYARDS CORP	23.750	.31	3.12	.01	16.88	.51	2.20	.54	60
TOK	TOKHEIM CORP	15.875	2.39	2.46	.39	12.72	.39	1.66	1.92	60
TKM	TOKIO MARINE INS ADR	129.500	.32	1.43	.01	7.57	.23	.99	.55	60
TED	TOLEDO EDISON CO	18.125	.79	-.28	.34	4.60	.14	.60	.86	60
NOHO	TOLEDO TRUSTCORP	27.500	.35	.91	.09	4.35	.13	.57	.57	60
TILLY	TOLLEY INTL CORP	1.000	.21	-2.34	.01	19.46	.59	2.54	.48	60
TLOC	TOMLINSON OIL INC	10.500	1.28	3.68	.07	17.49	.53	2.28	1.19	60
TKA	TONKA CORP	10.875	1.77	.47	.33	10.60	.32	1.38	1.51	60

BASED ON S&P 500 INDEX, USING STRAIGHT REGRESSION

FIGURE 15–5
Sample page from Merrill Lynch, Pierce, Fenner & Smith, Inc., Market Sensitivity Report for November 1979.

SOURCE: Reprinted by permission of Merrill Lynch, Pierce, Fenner, & Smith, Incorporated. Copyright © 1979.

Std. Err. of Beta (standard error of beta) indicates that there is roughly a two-out-of-three chance that the true beta for Timken is between the values of .95 (1.13 − .18) and 1.31 (1.13 + .18). Similarly, the value under *Std. Err. of Alpha* indicates that there is roughly a two-out-of-three chance that the true alpha for Timken lies between −.11 (.65 − .76) and 1.41 (.65 + .76).[18]

The seventh value in Figure 15.5 that is of particular interest is the *Adjusted Beta* value, which is discussed next.

☐ 15.8.1 Adjusting Beta

Without any information at all, it would be reasonable to estimate the beta of a stock to be equal to 1.0, the average size of beta. Given a chance to see how the stock moved relative to the market over some time period, a modification of this prior estimate would seem appropriate. Such a modification would sensibly produce a final estimate of beta that would lie between the value of 1.0 and its estimated value based purely on historical price changes.

Formal procedures for making such modifications have been adopted by most investment firms that estimate betas. The specific adjustments made typically differ from time to time and, in some cases, from stock to stock. In Figure 15.5, the *adjusted beta* values were obtained by giving approximately 66% weight to the historical estimate of beta and approximately 34% weight to the prior value of beta of 1.0 for each stock. Thus, the adjusted beta for Timken is 1.09 = (.66 × 1.13) + (.34 × 1.0). More generally,

$$\beta_a = (.66 \times \beta_h) + (.34 \times 1.0) \tag{15.9}$$

where β_a and β_h are the adjusted and historical betas, respectively.[19] Examination of equation (15.9) indicates that this procedure takes the historical beta for a security and adjusts it by giving it a value closer to 1.0. Thus, historical betas less than 1.0 are made larger but are still less than 1.0, and historical betas greater than 1.0 are made smaller but are still greater than 1.0. The adjustments are in this direction because weights (.66 and .34) are positive and add up to 1.0, indicating the adjustment procedure is an averaging technique.

Table 15.3 shows the extent to which such a procedure anticipates differences between historical and future betas. The second column lists the unadjusted historical betas for eight portfolios of 100 securities each, based on monthly price changes from July 1947 through June 1954 (the portfolios were designed to have significantly different betas during this period). The third column of the table shows the values obtained when an adjustment of the type used by Merrill Lynch was applied. The betas in the fourth column

---

[18] Since the procedure mentioned here does not involve the risk-free rate, the use of the term alpha does not correspond to its use in regard to the characteristic line; instead it is the vertical intercept associated with the market model.

[19] Adjusted betas are also published in the *Value Line Investment Survey*; their adjusted beta is equal to (.67 × β_h) + (.35 × 1.0). Thus, the adjustment procedures of Value Line and Merrill Lynch are quite similar. See Meir Statman, "Betas Compared: Merrill Lynch vs. Value Line," *Journal of Portfolio Management* 7, no. 2 (Winter 1981):41–44.

TABLE 15.3
Ex Ante and Ex Post Beta Values for Portfolios
of 100 Securities Each.

PORTFOLIO (1)	JULY 1947–JUNE 1954		JULY 1954–JUNE 1961 (4)	JULY 1961–JUNE 1968 (5)
	UNADJUSTED (2)	ADJUSTED (3)		
1	.36	.48	.57	.72
2	.61	.68	.71	.79
3	.78	.82	.88	.88
4	.91	.93	.96	.92
5	1.01	1.01	1.03	1.04
6	1.13	1.10	1.13	1.02
7	1.26	1.21	1.24	1.08
8	1.47	1.39	1.32	1.15

SOURCE: Marshall E. Blume, "Betas and Their Regression Tendencies," *Journal of Finance* 30, no. 3 (June 1975):792.

are based on price changes over the subsequent seven years. For a majority of the portfolios, the adjusted betas are closer in magnitude to the subsequent historical betas than are the unadjusted betas. This suggests that the adjusted historical beta is a more accurate estimate of the future beta than the unadjusted historical beta.

The fifth column of Table 15.3 shows the historical betas estimated using data from a third seven-year period. Comparing the unadjusted betas in columns 2, 4, and 5, it can be seen that there is a continuing tendency for betas to shrink toward the mean value of 1.0 over time. Thus, adjustment procedures seem to have some usefulness when it comes to estimating betas for a future time period.

It seems plausible that true betas not only vary over time but have a tendency to move back toward average levels, since extreme values are likely to be moderated over time. A firm whose operations or financing make the risk of its equity considerably different from that of other firms is more likely to move back toward the average than away from it. Such changes in betas are due to real economic phenomena, not simply an artifact of overly simple statistical procedures. There is, however, no reason to expect every stock's true beta to move to the same average in the same manner at the same speed. In this regard, some fundamental analysis of the firm may prove more useful than the adoption of more sophisticated statistical methods for processing past price changes in estimating beta.

At the portfolio level, historical betas can provide useful information about future betas, but historical betas for individual securities are subject to great error and should be treated accordingly. This can be seen by noting the magnitude of the standard errors of the betas shown earlier in Figure 15.5.

Table 15.4 provides another view. Every stock listed on the New York Stock Exchange was assigned to one of ten classes in each year from 1931 through 1967, based on the magnitude of its historical beta calculated using data from the preceding five years. The stocks in the top 10% of each January's

TABLE 15.4

Movement of Stocks Among Beta Classes.

RISK CLASS	PERCENT OF STOCKS IN THE SAME BETA CLASS FIVE YEARS LATER		PERCENT OF STOCKS IN THE SAME BETA CLASS OR WITHIN ONE RISK CLASS FIVE YEARS LATER	
	Actual	Expected if There Were No Relationship	Actual	Expected if There Were No Relationship
10 (highest beta values)	35.2%	10%	69.3%	20%
9	18.4	10	53.7	30
8	16.4	10	45.3	30
7	13.3	10	40.9	30
6	13.9	10	39.3	30
5	13.6	10	41.7	30
4	13.2	10	40.2	30
3	15.9	10	44.6	30
2	21.5	10	60.9	30
1 (lowest beta values)	40.5	10	62.3	20

SOURCE: William F. Sharpe and Guy M. Cooper, "Risk-Return Classes of New York Stock Exchange Common Stocks, 1931–1967," *Financial Analysts Journal* 28, no. 2 (March/April 1972):53.

ranking were assigned to class 10, the next 10% to class 9, and so on. The table shows the percent of the stocks that were in the same class and within one risk class five years later. Also shown are the entries that would be expected if there were no relationship between such past and future beta classes. Examination of the table reveals that individual security betas have some but not a great deal of predictive value.

Figure 15.6 shows that the predictive ability of historical portfolio betas improves with the amount of diversification in a portfolio. The vertical axis

FIGURE 15–6

Percent of differences in beta values attributable to differences in prior year's betas.

SOURCE: Robert A. Levy, "On the Short-term Stationarity of Beta Coefficients," *Financial Analysis Journal* 27, no. 6 (November/December 1971): p. 57.

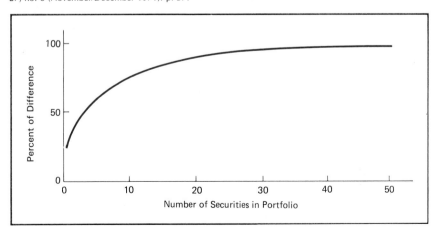

plots the percentage of the differences in (measured) portfolio betas (based on weekly price changes) in one year that can be attributed to differences in their (measured) betas in the prior year. The horizontal axis indicates the number of securities in each portfolio. It can be seen in the figure that the historical betas for portfolios containing roughly 10 to 20 securities or more have a high degree of predictive ability. Thus, individual security betas are worth estimating even though they are rather inaccurate when viewed by themselves. This is because their individual inaccuracies seem to cancel out one another when the beta of a diversified portfolio is calculated, resulting in quite an accurate estimate of the portfolio's beta.

☐ **15.8.2 Industry Beta Values**

The beta of a *firm* depends on both the demand for the firm's products and the firm's operating costs. However, most firms have both debt and equity outstanding. This means that the beta of a firm's *equity* (that is, stock) depends on the beta of the firm and the firm's financial leverage. For example, imagine there are two firms that are identical in every way except that firm A has debt, whereas firm B is free of debt. This means that even though they have the same earnings before interest and taxes (EBIT), they will have different earnings after taxes (EAT) because A, unlike B, has to make interest payments. In this situation, the firm betas for A and B are the same, but the stock beta for A is greater than the stock beta for B. The difference in the debt is the reason for the difference in the stock betas because the debt makes A's earnings available to common stockholders more variable than B's. Thus, the stock beta for A could be viewed as being equal to the stock beta it would have if it had no debt (that is, the beta of B) plus an adjustment for the amount of debt it actually has outstanding.

Firms in industries having highly cyclical demand or large fixed costs might be expected to have higher firm betas than those in industries with more stable demand or greater variable costs, since they will have greater variability in EBIT. Differences in financial leverage could wholly offset such factors, leaving few, if any, differences among the stock betas of firms in different industries. However, this does not seem to be the case. Firms in certain industries do tend to have higher stock betas than those in other industries, and, by and large, the classifications agree with prior expectations.

Table 15.5 shows the average values of beta for stocks in various industry classifications. Stock prices of firms whose products are termed necessities tend to respond less than the stock prices of most other firms when expectations about the future health of the economy are revised. That is, firms in necessities (such as utilities or food) tend to have low betas because they tend to have more stable earnings. On the other hand, stock prices of firms that manufacture luxuries tend to respond more than most others when expectations about the future health of the economy are revised. That is, firms in luxuries (such as travel or electronics) tend to have high betas because they tend to have cyclical earnings.

Information of the type shown in Table 15.5 can be used to adjust

TABLE 15.5

Average Values of Beta for Stocks in Selected Industries,
1966–1974.

INDUSTRY	BETA VALUE	INDUSTRY	BETA VALUE
Air transport	1.80	Chemicals	1.22
Real property	1.70	Energy, raw materials	1.22
Travel, outdoor recreation	1.66	Tires, rubber goods	1.21
Electronics	1.60	Railroads, shipping	1.19
Miscellaneous finance	1.60	Forest product, paper	1.16
Nondurables, entertainment	1.47	Miscellaneous, conglomerate	1.14
Consumer durables	1.44	Drugs, medicine	1.14
Business machines	1.43	Domestic oil	1.12
Retail, general	1.43	Soaps, cosmetics	1.09
Media	1.39	Steel	1.02
Insurance	1.34	Containers	1.01
Trucking, freight	1.31	Nonferrous metals	.99
Producer goods	1.30	Agriculture, food	.99
Aerospace	1.30	Liquor	.89
Business services	1.28	International oil	.85
Apparel	1.27	Banks	.81
Construction	1.27	Tobacco	.80
Motor vehicles	1.27	Telephone	.75
Photographic, optical	1.24	Energy, utilities	.60
		Gold	.36

SOURCE: Barr Rosenberg and James Guy, "Prediction of Beta from Investment Fundamentals," *Financial Analysts Journal* 32, no. 4 (July/August 1976):66.

historical betas. For example, the knowledge that a corporation is in the air transport industry suggests that a reasonable prior estimate of the beta of its stock is 1.8. Thus, it makes more sense to adjust its historical beta toward a value of 1.8 than to 1.0, the average for all stocks, as was suggested in equation (15.9).

☐ 15.8.3 Beta Prediction Equations

The procedure used to adjust historical betas involves an implicit prediction equation for future betas. Equation (15.9) can be written more generally as

$$\beta_a = a + b\beta_h \qquad (15.10)$$

where a and b are constants. However, a stock's historical beta (β_h) is only one of several pieces of information that can be used to predict its future beta (β_a). For example, firms in the airline industry tend to have higher betas than those in the utility industry. This can be incorporated by including industry effects in the equation: [20]

$$\beta_a = a + b\beta_h + (c_1 \times E_1) + (c_2 \times E_2) + \cdots \qquad (15.11)$$

where $a, b, c_1,$ and c_2 are constants. E_1 is the percentage of the firm's earnings that are from industry number 1 (perhaps the airline industry); E_2 is the

---

[20] For a firm whose earnings are entirely in one industry, this is equivalent to adjusting the historical beta of its stock toward an industry average.

TABLE 15.6

A Beta Prediction Equation Derived from a Factor Model.

CONSTANT TERM

Sector	Value
Basic industry	.455
Capital goods	.425
Consumer staple	.307
Consumer cyclical	.443
Credit cyclical	.429
Energy	.394
Finance	.398
Transportation	.255
Utilities	.340

VARIABLE TERMS

Attribute	Coefficient
Beta	.576
Yield	$-.019$
Size	$-.105$

SOURCE: Blake Grossman and William F. Sharpe, "Factors in Security Returns," paper presented at the Center for the Study of Banking and Financial Markets, University of Washington, March 1984.

percentage of the firm's earnings that are from industry number 2 (perhaps the utility industry); and so on.

Other attributes can also be used. For example, stocks with high dividend yields might have lower betas because more of their value is associated with near-term than with far-term dividends. The equation could thus be augmented to

$$\beta_a = a + b\beta_h + (c_1 \times E_1) + (c_2 \times E_2) + \cdots + (d \times Y) \quad (15.12)$$

where d is a constant and Y is the dividend yield of the firm's stock.

Table 15.6 shows a beta prediction equation of this form, using historic data from 1928 through 1982.[21] To estimate the beta of a security using this prediction equation, start with a constant based on the industry (referred to as the *sector*) in which the security is classified. Then add to this constant an amount equal to the security's historical beta times .576 (note that this is similar to the adjustment to historical beta shown in equation (15.9)). Finally, add (1) the security's dividend yield times $-.019$ and (2) the security's "size attribute" times $-.105$.[22] Algebraically, the model is:

---

[21] In this model, both historical and adjusted betas are calculated relative to a value-weighted index of the returns on all stocks listed on the New York Stock Exchange. All attributes were calculated using data available a full month prior to the beginning of the month in which stock returns are measured. This avoids statistical problems and provides results that can be used for actual portfolio management.

[22] The dividend yield is measured in percent per year. The *size attribute* is calculated by taking the logarithm (to the base 10) of the total market value of equity outstanding (that is, price per share times shares outstanding), expressed in billions of dollars.

$$\beta_a = a_s + (.576 \times \beta_h) + (-.019 \times Y) + (-.105 \times S) \quad (15.13)$$

where a_s denotes the constant associated with the sector to which the stock belongs, β_h is the historical beta, Y is the dividend yield, and S is the size of the firm. With this formula, securities having higher yields are predicted to have lower betas, as are those with larger market values of equity outstanding.

An Example

As an example, consider a stock that is classified as belonging to "basic industry." It has a historical beta of 1.2, a dividend yield over the previous 12 months of 4%, and an aggregate market value of $7 billion (that is, the firm has 100 million shares outstanding and the stock is selling for $70 per share). Using equation (15.13), its adjusted beta is

$$\beta_a = .455 + (.576 \times 1.2) + (-.019 \times 4) + [-.105 \times (\log 7)]$$

$$= .455 + .69 - .08 - .09$$

$$= .98.$$

Such prediction equations, based on multifactor models, fit historical data considerably better than those that use only historical betas. One study reported an improvement of 86% over the more simple adjusted beta approach.[23] However, such figures describe only the extent to which the equations fit a given set of data. Since the true test of a prediction equation is its ability to *predict*, only extensive experience with such approaches can, in the final analysis, determine how well various factor models can predict beta values.

☐ **15.8.4 Beta Services**

Services providing betas on a regular basis in published form are available in several countries. Many use only past price changes to form estimates. Some derive their estimates from more general factor models. One service uses weekly data for two years; another, monthly data for five years. One estimates betas for U.S. securities relative to Standard & Poor's 500; another, relative to the New York Stock Exchange Composite Index; and so on. In each case, estimates for individual securities are subject to error. Thus, it is hardly surprising that estimated values for a given security obtained by different services using different procedures are not the same. This does not indicate that some are useless, only that they should be used appropriately and with caution.

---

[23] Barr Rosenberg and Vinay Marathe, "The Prediction of Investment Risk: Systematic and Residual Risk," *Proceedings of the Seminar on the Analysis of Security Prices, University of Chicago*, November 1975. Also see Barr Rosenberg, "Prediction of Common Stock Investment Risk," *Journal of Portfolio Management* 11, no. 1 (Fall 1984):44–53, and "Prediction of Common Stock Betas," *Journal of Portfolio Management* 11, no. 2 (Winter 1985):5–14.

15.9   FACTOR MODELS OF STOCK RETURNS

To operate successfully in the stock market one needs a good model of the relationships among stock returns. Theory provides little guidance concerning the best level of detail for such a model and the specific aspects to be included. The task is thus primarily empirical. Procedures employed for estimating stock factor models typically combine *judgments* concerning important factors with *statistical analysis* of historic data. Both art and science are involved.

☐ 15.9.1   A One-Factor Model

Figure 15.7 provides a (hypothetical) example of the relationship between stock returns in a given time period and one attribute. Each point represents one stock, showing its return during the month of January 19XX (on the vertical axis) and its dividend yield (on the horizontal axis). In this case, securities with higher yields tended to do better (have higher returns) than those with lower yields. To quantify the relationship, a straight line has been fitted to the data points using (simple) regression analysis. Since the points represent different securities and one time period, this is an example of *cross-sectional analysis*.

The equation of the line in Figure 15.7 is

$$\text{Return} = 4.0 + (.5 \times \text{yield}).$$

FIGURE 15–7
A one-factor model.

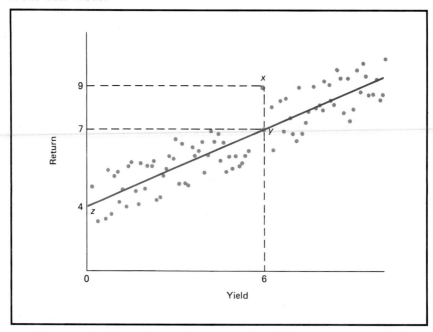

This can be written somewhat more generally as

$$\text{Return} = f_0 + (f_1 \times \text{yield})$$

where:

$f_0 =$ the zero factor

$f_1 =$ factor 1.

The vertical intercept indicates the return on a typical stock with zero yield. Thus, it is termed the *zero factor*. In Figure 15.7, it is 4%. The slope indicates the additional return per unit increase in yield. Since yield is the first (and only) *attribute* in this example, the slope is termed *factor 1*. In Figure 15.7, the yield factor is 0.5 ($=(7 - 4)/6$).

The return on any given security may lie above or below the line. A complete description of the relationship can be written as

$$r_{it} = f_{0t} + b_{i1t}f_{1t} + \epsilon_{it} \qquad (15.14)$$

where:

$r_{it} =$ the return on security i in period t,

$b_{i1t} =$ security i's sensitivity to factor 1 in period t,

$f_{0t} =$ the "zero factor" in period t,

$f_{1t} =$ factor 1 in period t, and

$\epsilon_{it} =$ security i's *nonfactor return* in period t.

Each symbol has been assigned a time-subscript (t) to indicate the particular time period (here, January 19XX). The yield *attribute* has been denoted in the conventional manner, since it is assumed to indicate *sensitivity* to the *yield factor*. The final term indicates the *nonfactor* return of the security during the time period. In Figure 15.7, for example, security x had a nonfactor return of $+2\%$, since it returned 9% while the typical stock with the same yield (such as stock y) returned only 7%.

Empirically determined factors are closely related to the more fundamental factors of a standard factor model but may differ in certain respects. (Appendix B provides the details.) To emphasize the difference between "empirical factors" and "fundamental factors," the former will be denoted by lowercase letters.

In months such as that shown in Figure 15.7, high-yield securities tend to outperform low-yield securities: the yield factor is *positive*. In other months, high-yield securities tend to underperform low-yield securities. The regression line in the corresponding diagram is downward-sloping and the yield factor is *negative*. In still other months there is no relationship between yield and return. The regression line in the corresponding diagram is flat and the yield factor is *zero*.

☐ 15.9.2 A Two-Factor Model

In some months small stocks tend to outperform large stocks. In other months the converse is true. To measure this, one can analyze the relationship

between security returns and size. For this purpose, many models use a "size attribute" computed by taking the logarithm of the total market value of equity outstanding (where the latter is computed by multiplying a security's price per share times the number of shares outstanding). Thus a stock with $1 million of value might be assigned a size attribute of 0, a stock with $10 million a size attribute of 1, a stock with $100 million a size attribute of 2, and so on. This convention is based on the empirical observation that the impact of the "size factor" on a security with a large total value is likely to be twice as great as that on a security with one-tenth the total value. More succinctly: the effect appears to be roughly "linear in the logarithms."

To estimate the "size factor" in a given month, the procedure used in Figure 15.7 to estimate the yield factor could be employed. The size attributes of securities could be plotted on the horizontal axis and their returns plotted (as before) on the vertical axis. The slope of the resultant line would provide an estimate of the size factor for the month.

This procedure has drawbacks, however. Large stocks tend to have high yields. Thus, differences in returns between large and small stocks might be due to some extent to differences in yield, not size. The estimated size factor might be, in part, a reflection of a true yield factor. The problem is, of course, symmetrical. A yield factor estimated as in Figure 15.7 might be, in part, a reflection of a true size factor.

To mitigate this problem, returns can be compared with *both* size and yield attributes, using *multiple* regression. Figure 15.8 provides an illustration. Each security is represented by a point in a three-dimensional graph, with return during the month shown on the vertical axis, its yield attribute

FIGURE 15–8
A two-factor model.

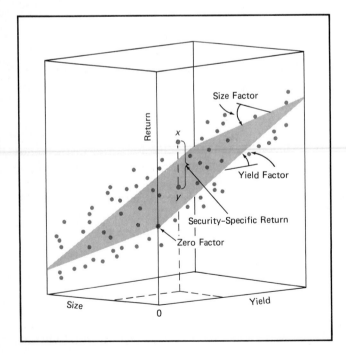

shown on one of the bottom axes, and its size attribute shown on the other. Cross-sectional multiple regression analysis is then used to fit a *plane* to the data.

The relationship in Figure 15.8 can be written as

$$r_{it} = f_{0t} + b_{i1t}f_{1t} + b_{i2t}f_{2t} + \epsilon_{it}. \tag{15.15}$$

In this case, the zero factor indicates the return on a typical stock with zero yield *and* a zero size attribute (for example, a market value of $1 million). Factor 1 is the yield factor—that is, the slope of the plane in the "yield direction." It indicates the additional return per unit of yield *holding other attributes (here, size) constant*. Factor 2 is the size factor: the slope of the plane in the "size direction." It indicates the additional return per unit of size, *holding other attributes (here, yield) constant*. The nonfactor return for a security indicates the difference between its return and that typical of securities with the same attributes (here, securities with the same yield and size).

15.9.3 Multifactor Models

The inclusion of both yield and size, and the use of multiple regression analysis, can help sort out the effects of differences in yield and size on differences in security returns. It cannot deal adequately with influences that are not represented at all, nor can it guarantee that the included attributes are not simply serving as "proxies" for other, more fundamental attributes. Statistical tests can indicate the ability of the variables included in the analysis to explain or predict *past* security returns. But judgment and luck are required to identify variables that can help predict *future* security expected returns, risks, and correlations.

Most factor models of stock returns employ more than two factors (and some use a great many more than two). With M attributes, diagrams must be forsaken, since $M + 1$ dimensions would be required. Cross-sectional multiple regression analysis can be used, however, to obtain a relationship of the form

$$r_{it} = f_{0t} + b_{i1t}f_{1t} + b_{i2t}f_{2t} + \cdots + b_{iMt}f_{Mt} + \epsilon_{it}. \tag{15.16}$$

If a diagram could be drawn, this would plot as a *hyperplane* (the generalization of a plane). In the regression analysis, each security provides one observation, with the return for the month serving as the dependent variable and the selected attributes as the independent variables. The intercept and the slope coefficients from the regression are the factor values, and the residuals' values are the securities' nonfactor returns.

15.9.4 Zero-One Attributes

Attributes such as a security's historic beta, dividend yield, or size are measured with numbers such as .95 or 1.03. But some attributes are represented

more simply, with either 0 or 1. For example, consider a "basic industry attribute." Securities of firms in such industries could be assigned an attribute of 1 (indicating that all their activities are classified in this sector), while securities of firms in other industries could be assigned a basic industry attribute of 0 (indicating that none of their activities is classified in this sector). While a more sophisticated analysis might allow firms to be classified in two or more industries, using values between 0 and 1, most factor models have at least some zero-one attributes of this type.

An extreme model uses only such attributes. M sectors are identified, with

$$b_{ijt} = \begin{cases} 1, & \text{if security } i \text{ is in sector } j \\ 0, & \text{if security } i \text{ is not in sector } j \end{cases}$$

$$f_{jt} = \text{the "sector } j \text{ factor" for period } t.$$

Note that when each security is classified as belonging in one (and only one) sector, no zero factor is used.

A more common approach uses some attributes that are of the zero-one type and some that are not. The factor model used to obtain the beta prediction equation in Table 15.6 was of this type.

15.10 ESTIMATING RISKS AND CORRELATIONS

After fitting a factor model using data for January 19XX, it is a simple matter to fit the same model using data for February 19XX. February returns are used as the dependent variable and security attributes calculated prior to February as independent variables. The resulting coefficients are the February factor values and the residual values are the securities' nonfactor returns for the month.

After five years of this sort of activity, 60 sets of factor values will have been obtained. *If the future is expected to be like the past*, these results can be used to estimate likely factor values for next month. For example, the *average* value of a factor over the last 60 months could be taken as an estimate of the *expected* value of the factor for next month. The *actual* standard deviation of the factor over the past five years could be taken as an estimate of the *uncertainty* concerning its value next month. The *actual* correlation between two factors over the last 60 months could be taken as an estimate of the relevant correlation estimate for next month's values, and so on.

A similar procedure could be applied to the nonfactor returns. After five years, 60 such values will have been obtained for every security. *If the future is expected to be like the past*, the average nonfactor return for security 1 over the last 60 months could be taken as an estimate of its expected value for next month, and the standard deviation of the values could be taken as an estimate of the uncertainty regarding next month's value (that is, the security's *nonfactor risk*). While historic nonfactor returns of some securities may have been correlated with those of other securities or factor values, if the model is "well specified," such correlations should be relatively small and could be assumed to be zero in the future.

Analysis of the behavior of factor values and nonmarket returns from period to period constitutes a final phase when estimating a factor model. After many (for example, 60) cross-sectional analyses, a *time-series analysis* is performed. This may be simple (for example, computing averages, standard deviations, and correlations) or complex (searching for time-dependent patterns in the data, and so on). The goal is to find some way to use *historic* data to make predictions about *future* returns and factor values.

Just as historic data are often used to provide simple estimates of future beta values, so, too, historic factor model results are often used to provide estimates of future *risks* (standard deviations, beta values, and so on) and *correlations*. Empirical evidence suggests that historic data are less valuable for predicting *expected* returns. These are usually estimated more directly, using procedures of the type described in Chapter 16.

15.11 ESTIMATING SENSITIVITIES TO FACTORS

In some factor models, security attributes that serve as sensitivities to factors are selected on "fundamental" grounds. Zero-one variables are based on standard classifications of securities by industry; historic betas are calculated utilizing a selected number of months of prior data; dividend yields, market values of equity outstanding, and other values are computed in standard ways, and so on.

Statistical tests may be used to assess the relevance of such preselected attributes and factors. But such tests cannot measure the usefulness of factors not considered at all.

Some factor models are estimated with a *multiple-phase* approach. In the first phase, historic data are analyzed to obtain promising security attributes. In the second phase, these attributes are used to estimate factor values for various periods. In the final (third) phase, results from the cross-sectional regressions are analyzed (using time-series methods) to estimate risks, correlations, and so on. Statistical procedures can be used to indicate the extent to which the resulting model "fits the data." More relevant are *out-of-sample tests*, which measure the ability of the model to predict risks, returns, correlations, and so on in periods subsequent to those from which the historic data were taken. Such tests can (and should) be the fourth phase of the analysis.

□ 15.11.1 Homogeneous Security Groups

Most stocks move together to some extent when expectations of the future of the economy change and "the market" moves accordingly. But *nonmarket* returns of various securities also move together. A *homogeneous group* is composed of securities that tend to move together, even when there is little or no change in the overall level of the stock market.

Some idea of the ways in which such groups can be identified can be gained from the results of a study that was designed to find possible co-

TABLE 15.7
Influence of Market and Sector Factors
on Security Returns.

Sector	AVERAGE PERCENT OF VARIATION IN MONTHLY RETURN FROM 1961 THROUGH 1969 DUE TO:	
	The Market Factor	The Sector Factor
Growth stocks	31%	15%
Stable stocks	29	12
Cyclical stocks	33	9
Oil stocks	31	31

SOURCE: James L. Farrell, Jr., "Analyzing Covariation of Returns to Determine Homogeneous Stock Groupings," *Journal of Business* 47, no. 2 (April 1974):201.

movement due to neither market nor industry effects. One hundred stocks were selected to cover many different industries in the hope of thwarting any attempt by the computer to group along industry lines. Monthly price changes from 1961 through 1969 were analyzed using a statistical procedure known as *cluster analysis*.

In this case the computer analyzed stock returns and was instructed to stop grouping stocks together when four major clusters remained. With relatively few exceptions, stocks in the first cluster were those considered by most analysts to be *growth stocks*: "companies expected to show an above average rate of secular expansion." [24] The second cluster contained mostly *cyclical stocks*: "those of companies that have an above average exposure to the vagaries of the economic environment." [25] The third group included predominantly *stable stocks*: "those of companies whose earning power is less affected than the average firm by the economic cycle." [26] The final group showed that at least one industry had sufficient homogeneity to stand out despite the attempt to ignore industry effects: during the period studied, the eight oil companies' prices moved together in a manner sufficiently unique to cause the computer to group them in a completely separate cluster.[27]

How much variation in prices could be attributed to these factors? Table 15.7 shows the average values for the stocks in each of the four clusters. Also shown is the size of the market effect (roughly 30%). The results, combined with those of the earlier study, suggest that sector comovement can be as important as industry comovement.

Table 15.8 provides a dramatic indication of the possible results from

[24] James L. Farrell, Jr., "Homogeneous Stock Groupings: Implications for Portfolio Mangement," *Financial Analysts Journal* 31, no. 3 (May/June 1975):50.

[25] Farrell, "Homogeneous Stock Groupings," p. 50.

[26] Farrell, "Homogeneous Stock Groupings," p. 50.

[27] An earlier study found that for the typical stock, approximately 50% of the total price variance from 1927 through 1960 could be attributed to market effects. Roughly an additional 10% could be attributed to industrywide factors. The first figure declined through the period, reaching approximately 30% for the typical stock in the latter part, while the second figure changed little. See Benjamin F. King, "Market and Industry Factors in Stock Price Behavior," *Journal of Business* 39, no. 1 (January 1966):139–70.

TABLE 15.8
Sector Concentration and Portfolio Return.

| | PERCENT INVESTED | | |
Sector	Standard and Poor's 500-Stock Index	Affiliated Fund	T. Rowe Price Fund
Growth	39.8%	10.5%	80.2%
Cyclical	24.0	57.5	8.7
Stable	20.0	18.0	4.1
Oil	16.2	14.0	7.0
Estimated beta	1.00	1.09	1.11
Performance	−29%	−16%	−42%

SOURCE: James L. Farrell, Jr., "Homogeneous Stock Groupings: Implications for Portfolio Management," *Financial Analysts Journal* 31, no. 3 (May/June 1975):58.

concentration in market sectors. The relative proportions in the four sectors are shown for the portfolio represented by Standard & Poor's 500 and for two mutual funds. The two funds had similar market exposures, as indicated by their estimated beta values. During the 19-month period from December 31, 1972, through July 31, 1974, the "market" fell 29%, suggesting that one might have expected the two funds to fall by roughly 32% (since 1.1 × 29% = 31.9%).

In fact, one fund's shares fell much less than the market, and the other's shares fell much more. The portfolio composition figures show why. This was a period when growth stocks did especially poorly. The first fund was well positioned, concentrating more money in cyclical stocks and less in growth stocks than did the market as a whole. The second was poorly positioned, with a heavy concentration in growth stocks, to its investors' detriment. The results could be reversed in a period in which growth stocks do especially well. The point is not that one fund or investment strategy is better than another—rather, that neither fund was in fact as well diversified as a simple check of the number of stocks might suggest.

☐ **15.11.2 Group Factors**

Once homogeneous groups have been identified via cluster analysis or some other method, they may be incorporated into a factor model. The simplest procedure is to assign each security entirely to the group with which it "clusters." The corresponding factor model could include a "market sensitivity" attribute (based, for example, on historic beta) and one zero-one attribute for each of the homogeneous groups. The factors from the cross-section analyses would then represent "the market" and the nonmarket returns of each of the homogeneous groups.

An alternative procedure includes an intermediate step. The nonmarket returns of each security over time are compared with those of the homo-

geneous groups. For each security a time-series regression is performed, and the sensitivities of the security to each of the groups are estimated. These are used as the corresponding attributes in the final phase, instead of zero-one variables.

In a model based on this approach using data from 1968 through 1978 for over 500 stocks, the Boston Company obtained five nonmarket factors, characterized as (1) growth, (2) utility, (3) oil and related, (4) basic industries, and (5) consumer cyclical.[28]

☐ 15.11.3 Composite Attributes

Many models use values such as historic betas, yields, and measures of size as attributes. Each can be considered a *simple attribute*, since it is related to either a single aspect of the security or a ratio of two such aspects.

Some models go farther, combining several aspects of a security into one *composite attribute*, several other aspects into a second composite attribute, and so on. Choices of aspects and formulas for combining them are usually based on econometric analyses of historic data. Table 15.9 shows the fundamental attributes used to compute each of six composite attributes in one widely used model.

☐ 15.11.4 Scenario Approaches

A more fundamental approach is employed by Salomon Brothers—a major institutional brokerage firm:

> ☐ The idea . . . is simple. We build a simple model of corporate profits, specified in terms of a few revenue variables and a few cost variables. One of these simple models is constructed for each company in our data base (about 1500 companies). These are linked to a macro model of the economy. Then the macro model is estimated in several scenarios, a "base case" and a number of alternatives. Each of the alternatives is constructed by altering a single one of the major governing variables that determine the character of the base case. For each scenario, profit models are built for each of about 400 lines of business, a set that includes all the major businesses pursued by the companies in our data base. Finally, the growth rate of profits of each company is modeled in each of the cases, by putting together the appropriate lines of business in the appropriate proportions. From the data thus obtained, we can estimate the sensitivity of the growth rate of a company's expected profits to each of the variables that was used to determine an alternative scenario. These sensitivities are the essential ingredients in the Fundamental Factor Model.[29]

---

[28] Robert D. Arnott, "Cluster Analysis and Stock Price Comovement," *Financial Analysts Journal* 36, no. 6 (November/December 1980):56–62. For an interesting use of cluster analysis, see Jeffery V. Bailey and Robert D. Arnott, "Cluster Analysis and Manager Selection," *Financial Analysts Journal* 42, no. 6 (November/December 1986):20–28.

[29] Source: Tony Estep, Nick Hanson, Michelle Clayman, Cal Johnson, and Jonathan Singer, "The Fundamental Factor Model of Risk and Return in Common Stocks," Salomon Brothers, July 1981. Also see Tony Estep, Nick Hanson, and Cal Johnson, "Sources of Value and Risk in Common Stocks," *Journal of Portfolio Management* 9, no. 4 (Summer 1983):10.

TABLE 15.9

Attributes in the BARRA E1 Factor Model.

1. Index of market variability
   - Historical beta estimate
   - Historical sigma estimate
   - Share turnover, quarterly
   - Share turnover, 12 months
   - Share turnover, five years
   - Trading volume/variance
   - Common stock price (ln)
   - Historical alpha estimate
   - Cumulative range, one year

2. Index of earnings variability
   - Variance of earnings
   - Extraordinary items
   - Variance of cash flow
   - Earnings covariability
   - Earnings/price covariability

3. Index of low valuation and unsuccess
   - Growth in earnings/share
   - Recent earnings change
   - Relative strength
   - Indicator of small earnings/price ratio
   - Book/price ratio
   - Tax/earnings, five years
   - Dividend cuts, five years
   - Return on equity, five years

4. Index of immaturity and smallness
   - Total assets (log)
   - Market capitalization (log)

    Market capitalization
    Net plant/gross plant
    Net plant/common equity
    Inflation adjusted plant/equity
    Trading recency
    Indicator of earnings history

5. Index of growth orientation
   - Payout, last five years
   - Current yield
   - Yield, last five years
   - Indicator of zero yield
   - Growth in total assets
   - Capital structure change
   - Earnings/price ratio
   - Earnings/price, normalized
   - Typical earnings/price ratio, five years

6. Index of financial risk
   - Leverage at book
   - Leverage at market
   - Debt/assets
   - Uncovered fixed charges
   - Cash flow/current liabilities
   - Liquid assets/current liabilities
   - Potential dilution
   - Price-deflated earnings adjustment
   - Tax-adjusted monetary debt

SOURCE: Andrew Rudd and Henry K. Clasing, Jr., *Modern Portfolio Theory: The Principles of Investment Management* (Homewood, Ill.: Dow Jones-Irwin 1982):114.

The factors used in this model consist of (1) inflation, (2) real economic growth, (3) oil prices, (4) defense spending, and (5) real interest rates. For each security, the procedure provides five attributes, representing the sensitivities of the corporation's profits over the next five years to changes in the corresponding variables.

Figure 15.9 shows the relative performance of five "factor play portfolios" over 17 months. Each was constructed to be sensitive to one of the five factors and relatively insensitive to the other four. Changes in the values of such portfolios can be interpreted as representing changes in *expectations* concerning the associated fundamental economic factors.

☐ **15.11.5 Sensitivities to Macroeconomic Variables**

The Salomon Brothers approach uses forward-looking projections of a relatively detailed type to estimate the sensitivities of corporate profits to changes in fundamental economic variables. A simpler approach, based on the assumption that history can provide adequate guidance concerning the

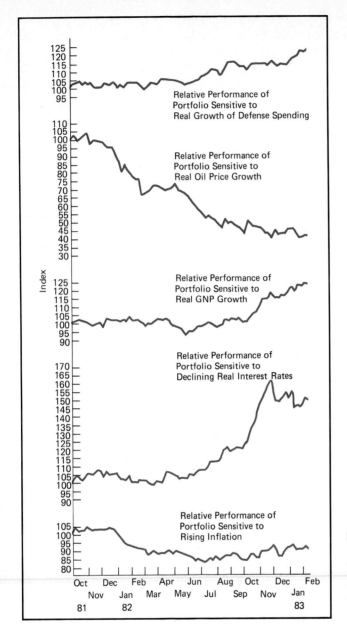

FIGURE 15–9

Relative performance of economic factor portfolios.

SOURCE: Tony Estep, Nick Hanson, and Cal Johnson, "Sources of Value and Risk in Common Stocks," *Journal of Portfolio Management* 9, no. 4 (Summer 1983): p. 11.

future, compares changes in security values with estimates of changes in expectations concerning macroeconomic variables.

In such an analysis, it is important that only changes in *expectations* of such variables be used, since security prices change significantly only in response to *unanticipated* changes in prospects for future profits. Unfortunately, it is often difficult to estimate changes in expectations about future values of key economic variables.

In a study using this approach, four variables were found to be useful:

(1) the growth rate in U.S. industrial production, (2) unanticipated changes in risk premia, measured by the difference between the return on a portfolio of "under Baa bonds" and that of a portfolio of Aaa bonds, (3) twists in the yield curve, measured by the difference between the return on a portfolio of long-term government bonds and that of Treasury bills, and (4) unanticipated inflation, measured by the difference between actual inflation and a prediction derived from Treasury bill rates.[30]

Once values for such unanticipated changes in expectations concerning macrovariables have been obtained, the desired sensitivites of security returns can be estimated. For each security a time-series regression is performed, with each time period providing one observation. In the regression, the security's return is the dependent variable, and the changes in expectations of the macrovariables are the independent variables. The resulting coefficients are estimates of the sensitivities of the security to each of the economic factors. These are then used as the security's attributes when estimating the factor model.

☐ 15.11.6   Factor Analysis

Cluster analysis can be used to estimate zero-one security attributes from historic returns. These attributes can then be used in cross-sectional analyses to derive factor values. The resulting factors may be recognizable as, for example, changes in fundamental economic factors, or they may appear to be simply statistical artifacts. With such a mechanical approach, it may be difficult or impossible to incorporate additional (fundamental) information.

This type of procedure assumes that historic returns contain all the information needed to produce useful estimates of future risks and correlations.

Factor analysis, a more complex procedure, is similar in spirit.[31] Given returns for many securities over many time periods, a computer is used to (1) determine a reasonable number of attributes, (2) compute the corresponding attributes for each security, and (3) derive the corresponding factors for each time period. An early study employing factor analysis suggested that five factors might suffice to represent the "pervasive" underlying determinants of correlation among security returns. Other studies have found more "significant" factors.[32]

There is more information about securities than that reflected in past returns alone, and it is undoubtedly desirable to take it into account when estimating factor models. Factor analysis can provide useful guidance concerning the appropriate number of factors, useful variables, and so on but should not be used as a "black box" into which returns are placed and out

---

[30] Nai-fu Chen, Richard Roll, and Stephen A. Ross, "Economic Forces and the Stock Market," *Journal of Business* 59, no. 3 (July 1986):383–403.

[31] The term *factor analysis* denotes a general approach; there are, in fact, many alternative statistical procedures for performing such an analysis.

[32] Richard Roll and Stephen A. Ross, "An Empirical Investigation of the Arbitrage Pricing Theory," *Journal of Finance* 35, no. 5 (December 1980):1073–1103.

of which come purely mechanical estimates of future prospects, to be used "as is."

15.12   SUMMARY

The corporate form of organization is relatively new. One of the features of this form of organization is that of limited liability, meaning that common stockholders may lose their investment, but no more. Another feature is that common stockholders have a residual claim on the earnings of the corporation, since other securityholders, such as preferred stockholders and bondholders, have priority. A third feature is that common stockholders may vote on issues brought up at the annual meeting and on who will represent them on the board of directors. In regard to electing directors, there are two types of voting systems currently in use, cumulative and majority. The main difference between the two systems has to do with minority representation on the board.

Common stockholders may receive cash dividends or stock dividends from the corporation. In the case of stock dividends, it has been shown that this type of paper transaction does not make stockholders better off. However, this is not surprising, since stock dividends do not result in the corporation being in a healthier financial position. That is, the issuing of stock dividends does not increase sales nor does it decrease expenses. Similarly, common stockholders may experience a stock split but will not be better off as a result.

The relevant measue of the risk of a share of common stock is the impact that the share will have on the risk of a well-diversified portfolio. According to the CAPM, this impact is reflected by the stock's beta. Thus, in measuring a stock's risk over the forthcoming holding period, an investor needs to estimate the stock's *ex ante* beta. One way of doing this is by using past returns to estimate the *ex post* characteristic line for the stock; one of the results of doing this will be the *ex post* beta. Having estimated the *ex post* beta, there are a variety of ways of "adjusting" it to arrive at a more accurate estimate of the *ex ante* beta.

To operate successfully in the stock market, a good model of the relationships among stock returns is needed. Typically, the procedures employed for estimating stock factor models combine judgment with statistical analysis of historical returns. Thus, both art and science are involved.

APPENDIX A
EMPIRICAL REGULARITIES

Recently a number of researchers have uncovered certain *empirical regularities* in common stocks. That is, certain cross-sectional differences among stock returns have been found to occur with regularity. Some regularities should occur according to certain asset pricing models. For example, the CAPM asserts that different stocks should have different returns because different stocks have different betas. What makes the regularities that are

about to be discussed of special interest is that they do not appear to be predicted by any of the asset pricing models. Accordingly, they are sometimes also referred to as *anomalies*.

A.1 THE SIZE EFFECT

One measure of the size of a firm at a particular time is the aggregate market value of its common stock. That is, the size of a firm can be measured by multiplying the market price of its common stock at a particular time by the number of shares it has outstanding.[33] A simple test for seeing if firms that are of smaller size have had higher returns than firms of larger size was conducted by Ibbotson and Sinquefield.[34] All stocks on the New York Stock Exchange were ranked by market value outstanding on December 31, 1925. A portfolio was then formed using the stocks in the bottom quintile (that is, the smallest 20%). Within the portfolio, stocks were purchased in proportion to their market value (that is, the portfolio was value-weighted). This portfolio was "held" for five years. On December 31, 1930, all the stocks on the NYSE were again ranked on size and a new value-weighted portfolio formed from the bottom quintile. This portfolio was "held" for the next five years, when another similar revision was made; such revising continued through 1980.

Returns for the "small-firm portfolio" were then calculated for every month from 1926 through 1983. Table 15.10 contrasts the performance of this portfolio with that of Standard & Poor's 500. Since the S&P 500 consists of stocks with large market capitalizations, this can be viewed as a comparison of small stocks with large ones.

On the average, the small-firm portfolio outperformed the S&P 500 by 0.48% per month, or approximately 5.79% per year. Although the small-firm portfolio outperformed the S&P 500 only 51.7% of the time, the average difference was positive and statistically significant. This does not imply that a small-firm investment strategy dominated investing in the S&P 500. Table 15.10 indicates that the small-firm portfolio's returns varied much more,

---

[33] Some studies have used other measures of size, such as the price-to-earnings ratio (or its inverse, the earnings-to-price ratio) and the ratio of book value of equity per share to market value per share, with similar findings. See S. Basu, "Investment Performance of Common Stocks in Relation to their Price-Earnings Ratios: A Test of the Efficient Market Hypothesis," *Journal of Finance* 32, no. 3 (June 1977):663–82 and "The Relationship Between Earnings' Yield, Market Value and Return for NYSE Common Stocks: Further Evidence," *Journal of Financial Economics* 12, no. 1 (June 1983):129–56; and Barr Rosenberg, Kenneth Reid, and Ronald Lanstein, "Persuasive Evidence of Market Inefficiency," *Journal of Portfolio Management* 11, no. 3 (Spring 1985):9–16. Although the use of price-to-earnings ratios to identify small firms generates results similar to those using market values, there appears to be some question about the ratio's usefulness. See Marc R. Reinganum, "Misspecification of Capital Asset Pricing: Empirical Anomalies Based on Earnings' Yields and Market Values," *Journal of Financial Economics* 9, no. 1 (March 1981):19–46; Rolf W. Banz and William J. Breen, "Sample Dependent Results Using Accounting and Market Data: Some Evidence," *Journal of Finance* 41, no. 4 (September 1986):779–93; Jeffrey Jaffe, Donald B. Kiem, and Randolph Westerfield, "Earnings Yields, Market Values, and Stock Returns, *Journal of Finance* 44, no. 1 (March 1989):135–48.

[34] Roger G. Ibbotson and Rex A. Sinquefield, *Stocks, Bonds, Bills and Inflation: The Past and the Future* (Financial Analysts' Research Foundation, 1982). More elaborate studies of the size effect include Rolf Banz, "The Relationship Between Return and Market Value of Common Stocks," *Journal of Financial Economics* 9, no. 1 (March 1981):3–18; and Marc R. Reinganum, "Misspecification of Capital Asset Pricing."

TABLE 15.10

Small- and Large-Stock Performance, 1926–1983.

	SMALL STOCKS	SP500	SMALL STOCKS – SP500
Average annual return	17.05%	11.26%	5.79%
Annual standard deviation	32.35%	20.62%	18.34%
Number of months with positive values	406	408	360
Percent of months with positive values	58.3%	58.6%	51.7%

SOURCE: Based on data in Roger G. Ibbotson, *Stocks, Bonds, Bills and Inflation 1984 Yearbook* (Chicago: R. G. Ibbotson Associates, Inc., 1984).

having a standard deviation of 32.35%, whereas that of the S&P 500 was 20.62%.

A.2   SEASONALITY IN STOCK RETURNS

The desire of individuals for liquidity may be thought to change from day to day and from month to month. If so, there may be seasonal patterns in stock returns. One might presume that such patterns would be relatively unimportant. Indeed, according to the notion of efficient markets, such patterns should be quite minor (if they exist at all), since they are not suggested by any asset pricing model. However, the evidence indicates that at least two are significant: the "January effect" and the "day-of-the-week effect."

☐ A.2.1   The January Effect

There is no apparent reason to expect stock returns to be higher in certain months than in others. However, in a study that looked at average monthly returns on NYSE-listed common stocks, significant seasonalities were found.[35] In particular, the average return in January was higher than the average return in any other month. Table 15.11 indicates the average stock return in January and the other 11 months for various time periods. Although the difference in returns was minor in the early part of the century, more recently it appears that the average return in January has been approximately 3% higher than the average monthly return in February through December.[36]

---

[35] Michael S. Rozeff and William R. Kinney, Jr., "Capital Market Seasonality: The Case of Stock Returns," *Journal of Financial Economics* 3, no. 4 (October 1976):379–402. For an argument that the market does not have a January Effect, see Jay R. Ritter and Navin Chopra, "Portfolio Rebalancing and the Turn-of-the-Year Effect," *Journal of Finance* 44, no. 1 (March 1989):149–66.

[36] Interestingly, it appears that returns over the first half of any month are significantly higher than the returns over the second half of the month. See Robert A. Ariel, "A Monthly Effect in Stock Returns," *Journal of Financial Economics* 18, no. 1 (March 1987):161–74.

TABLE 15.11

Seasonality in Stock Returns.

TIME PERIOD	AVERAGE STOCK RETURN IN JANUARY	AVERAGE STOCK RETURN IN OTHER MONTHS	DIFFERENCE IN RETURNS
1904–1928	1.30%	.44%	.86%
1929–1940	6.63	−.60	7.23
1941–1974	3.91	.70	3.21
1904–1974	3.48	.42	3.06

SOURCE: Michael S. Rozeff and William R. Kinney, Jr. "Capital Market Seasonality: The Case of Stock Returns," *Journal of Financial Economics* 3, no. 4 (October 1976):388.

☐ A.2.2 The Day-of-the-Week Effect

It has generally been assumed that the expected daily returns on stocks are the same for all days of the week. That is, the expected return on a given stock is the same for Monday as it is for Tuesday, and so on. However, a number of studies have uncovered evidence that refutes this belief. Two early studies looked at the average daily return on NYSE-listed securities and found that the return on Monday was quite different.[37] In particular, the average return on Monday was found to be much lower than the average return on any other day of the week. Furthermore, the average return on Monday was negative, whereas the other days of the week had positive average returns. Table 15.12 displays these findings.

The rate of return on a stock for a given day of the week is typically calculated by subtracting the closing price on the previous trading day from the closing price on that day, adding any dividends for that day to the difference and then dividing the resulting number by the closing price as of the previous trading day:

$$r_t = \frac{(P_t - P_{t-1}) + D_t}{P_{t-1}} \qquad (15.17)$$

where P_t and P_{t-1} are the closing prices on days t and $t - 1$ and D_t is the value of any dividends paid on day t. This means that the return for Monday uses the closing price on Monday as P_t and the closing price on Friday as P_{t-1}. Thus, the change in the price of a stock for Monday $(P_t - P_{t-1})$ actually represents the change in price *over the weekend* as well as during Monday. This observation has caused some people to refer to the "day-of-the-week" effect as the "weekend" effect and has led to further examination of daily returns.

One method for studying the weekend effect is to divide daily returns into two parts. The first part is the return from the close of the previous day to the open of the current day and is referred to as the nontrading-period return. It uses the price of the last trade of the previous day (the *close*) and

---

[37] Kenneth R. French, "Stock Returns and the Weekend Effect," *Journal of Financial Economics* 8, no. 1 (March 1980):55–69; and Michael R. Gibbons and Patrick Hess, "Day of the Week Effects and Asset Returns," *Journal of Business* 54, no. 4 (October 1981):579–96.

TABLE 15.12
Analysis of Daily Returns.

	MONDAY	TUESDAY	WEDNESDAY	THURSDAY	FRIDAY
A. French study					
January 1953–December 1977	−.17%	.02%	.10%	.04%	.09%
B. Gibbons and Hess study					
July 1962–December 1978	−.13%	.00%	.10%	.03%	.08%

SOURCE: Kenneth R. French, "Stock Returns and the Weekend Effect," *Journal of Financial Economics* 8, no. 1 (March 1980):58; and Michael R. Gibbons and Patrick Hess, "Day of the Week Effects and Asset Returns," *Journal of Business* 54, no. 4 (October 1981):582–83.

the price of the first trade of the current day (the *open*) and calculates the return using these prices as the beginning and ending prices, respectively. The second part is the return from the open of the current day to the close of the current day, which is referred to as the trading-period return. It uses the prices of the first and last trades of the current day (the open and close) as the beginning and ending prices, respectively.

For example, the average stock return for Monday involves the change in a stock's price from Friday's close to Monday's close. This change in price can be divided into the change from Friday's close to Monday's open (the nontrading period for Monday) and from Monday's open to Monday's close (the trading period for Monday). Such a division will indicate if the negative return observed for Monday occurred during the weekend or during trading on Monday.

Table 15.13 displays the results of two studies that divided daily returns in this manner.[38] The study by Rogalski examined the set of 500 stocks in the S&P 500, whereas the study by Harris examined all NYSE-listed stocks (a total of 1616 stocks). As shown in Table 15.13, the negative daily return for Monday was observed in both studies. However, the Rogalski study suggests that this negative return occurred over the nontrading period from Friday's close to Monday's open.[39] Consequently, the weekend effect is really a nontrading-weekend effect.

The Harris study, involving a larger sample of stocks but a shorter time period, reached a different conclusion. This study found that the negative daily return for Monday was composed of two roughly equal-sized negative returns during the nontrading period and trading period. Statistical tests indicated that the average nontrading-period return for Monday as well as

---

[38] Richard J. Rogalski, "New Findings Regarding Day-of-the-Week Returns Over Trading and Nontrading Periods: A Note," *Journal of Finance* 39, no. 5 (December 1984):1603–14; Lawrence Harris, "How to Profit from Intradaily Stock Returns," *Journal of Portfolio Management* 12, no. 2 (Winter 1986):61–64, and "A Transaction Data Study of Weekly and Intradaily Patterns in Stock Returns," *Journal of Financial Economics* 16, no. 1 (May 1986):99–117.

[39] Rogalski reported similar findings for the set of 30 stocks in the Dow Jones Industrial Average. His DJIA results were confirmed over the 1974–1983 period by Michael Smirlock and Laura Starks, "Day-of-the-Week and Intraday Effects in Stock Returns," *Journal of Financial Economics* 17, no. 1 (September 1986):197–210. Interestingly, stock prices have been found to be more volatile during trading periods than nontrading peiods; see Kenneth R. French and Richard Roll, "Stock Return Variances: The Arrival of Information and the Reaction of Traders," *Journal of Financial Economics* 17, no. 1 (September 1986), 5–26.

TABLE 15.13
Decomposition of Daily Returns.

	S&P 500[a] JANUARY 1979–APRIL 1984			ALL NYSE[b] DECEMBER 1981–JANUARY 1983		
	Daily	Nontrading	Trading	Daily	Nontrading	Trading
Monday	−.12%	−.13%	.01%	−.18%	−.08%	−.09%
Tuesday	.09	.08	.01	.10	−.01	.11
Wednesday	.13	.05	.08	.15	.05	.10
Thursday	.02	.09	−.07	.17	.02	.15
Friday	.07	.03	.04	.20	.06	.14

SOURCE: [a]Richard J. Rogalski, ''New Findings Regarding Day-of-the-Week Returns over Trading and Non-trading Periods: A Note,'' *Journal of Finance* 39, no. 5 (December 1984):1605; [b]Lawrence Harris, ''How to Profit from Intradaily Stock Returns,'' *Journal of Portfolio Management* 12, no. 2 (Winter 1986):62.

the average trading-period return for Monday were different from the corresponding average returns for the other four days of the week.

These two studies can be reconciled by noting that the Rogalski study involved a sample of large-sized firms, since the S&P 500 consists of such firms, whereas the Harris study involved both small- and large-sized firms. Thus, the behavior of the small firms in the Harris study's sample may have been the source of the discrepancy. With this in mind, Harris looked at the returns of subsamples based on size and indeed found that this was the reason for the discrepancy. That is, the negative average Monday return appears to have occurred during the nontrading period for large-sized firms, whereas for small-sized firms, the negative average Monday return appears to have occurred mostly during the trading period. Since Harris's results in Table 15.13 involved averaging across both large and small firms, it is not surprising that the negative daily return for Monday was composed of two negative returns of roughly equal size during the trading and nontrading periods.

A.3 INTERRELATIONSHIPS

Given the presence of three regularities (the size, January, and day-of-the-week effects), researchers have attempted to see if there are any interrelationships between them. For example, is the January effect more pronounced for small firms? Is the day-of-the-week effect unrelated to the size effect? Is the day-of-the-week effect more dramatic in January than in the other months of the year? A brief discussion of some of the numerous studies that have examined such questions follows.

☐ A.3.1 Size and January Effects

Having observed that small firms have higher returns than large firms and that returns in January are higher than in any other month of the year, it

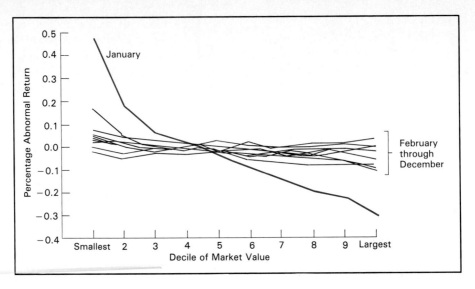

FIGURE 15–10
Interrelationship between the size-effect and the January effect.

SOURCE: Donald B. Keim, "Size-related Anomalies and Stock Return Seasonality: Further Empirical Evidence," *Journal of Financial Economics* 12, no. 1 (June 1983): p. 21.

is interesting to ponder whether or not these two effects are somehow interrelated. One study that examined this issue found that the two effects were strongly interrelated.[40] All NYSE-listed and AMEX-listed stocks over the 17-year period of 1963 to 1979 were examined in this study. At the end of each year, each firm was ranked by the size of the aggregate market value of its equity (that is, the year-end market price per share times the number of shares outstanding). Ten portfolios were then formed based on size with portfolio number 1 containing the smallest 10% of the firms, portfolio number 2 containing the next smallest 10%, and so on.

Abnormal returns were calculated subsequently for each portfolio on a monthly basis over the 17-year period and averaged for each month. Figure 15.10 displays the results.

It can be seen from this figure that the size effect was most pronounced in January, since the line for this month slopes down sharply from left to right. The other 11 months of the year appear to be quite similar to each other. Generally, each one of these months displays a slight downward slope, indicating that the size effect also existed for these months but only to a minor degree. Also of interest is the observation that large firms had a negative abnormal return in January. Thus, the January effect has been due primarily to the behavior of small firms, and the size effect has been concentrated mainly in the month of January.

Further examination of this interrelationship between the size effect and the January effect has revealed that it is concentrated in the first five

---

[40] Donald B. Keim, "Size-related Anomalies and Stock Return Seasonality: Further Empirical Evidence," *Journal of Financial Economics* 12, no. 1 (June 1983):13–32.

trading days of January.[41] In particular, the difference in returns between the smallest-firm portfolio and the largest-firm portfolio over these five days was 8.0%, whereas over the entire year it was 30.4%. Thus, 26.3% (8.0%/30.4%) of the annual size effect occurred during these five days (if the size effect had been spread evenly over the year, then .4% of it would have been attributed to these five days).

Attempts have been made to explain this interrelationship between the January effect and the size effect. One explanation that appears to have some merit has to do with "tax selling." This explanation begins by arguing that stocks that have declined during the year have downward pressure on their prices near year-end as investors sell them to realize capital losses in order to minimize tax payments. After the end of the year, this pressure is removed and the prices jump back to their "fair" values. Note that this argument flies in the face of the notion of efficient markets (the notion of efficient markets would suggest that this cannot be true because if investors sensed that stocks were becoming undervalued at year-end, they would flood the market with buy orders, thereby preventing any substantive undervaluation from occurring). Nevertheless, it does appear to have some merit in that those stocks that declined during the previous year had the largest appreciation in January.[42] However, this association between January returns and previous years' stock price declines does not appear to be attributable to price pressure caused by tax selling. This is because the biggest "losers" during a year appear subsequently to have abnormally high returns for as long as five Januaries thereafter. This contradicts the tax-selling argument, since according to this argument, the abnormal price rebound should occur in only the first subsequent January.[43]

A second possible explanation is that small stocks may be relatively riskier in January than during the rest of the year. If this is true, then they should have a relatively higher average return in January. A study finding that the betas of small stocks tend to increase at the beginning of the year lends support to this explanation.[44]

---

[41] Rogalski ("New Findings") also finds that the anomalous price behavior of stocks in January mostly occurs in the first five trading days. Roll has observed that the largest daily differences in the returns between small firms and large firms occurs over the last trading day of the year and the first four trading days of the year; furthermore, eight of the subsequent ten trading days also have notably large differences in returns. See Richard Roll, "Vas ist das?" *Journal of Portfolio Management* 9, no. 2 (Winter 1983):18–28.

[42] See Roll, "Vas ist das?"; Edward A. Dyl, "Capital Gains Taxation and Year-End Stock Market Behavior," *Journal of Finance* 32, no. 1 (March 1977):165–75; Ben Branch, "A Tax Loss Trading Rule," *Journal of Business* 50, no. 2 (April 1977):198–207; Marc R. Reinganum, "The Anomalous Stock Market Behavior of Small Firms in January: Empirical Tests for Tax-loss Selling Effects," *Journal of Financial Economics* 12, no. 1 (June 1983):89–104; Josef Lakonishok and Seymour Smidt, "Capital Gain Taxation and Volume of Trading," *Journal of Finance* 41, no. 4 (September 1986):951–74.

[43] See K. C. Chan, "Can Tax-Loss Selling Explain the January Seasonal in Stock Returns?" *Journal of Finance* 41, no. 5 (December 1986):1115–28; and Werner F. M. DeBondt and Richard Thaler, "Does the Stock Market Overreact?" *Journal of Finance* 40, no. 3 (July 1985):793–805, and "Further Evidence on Investor Overreaction and Stock Market Seasonality," *Journal of Finance* 42, no. 3 (July 1987):557–81.

[44] Richard J. Rogalski and Seha M. Tinic, "The January Size Effect: Anomaly or Risk Mismeasurement?" *Financial Analysts Journal* 42, no. 6 (November–December 1986):63–70. See also Avner Arbel, "Generic Stocks: An Old Product in a New Package," *Journal of Portfolio Management* 11, no. 4 (Summer 1985):4–13.

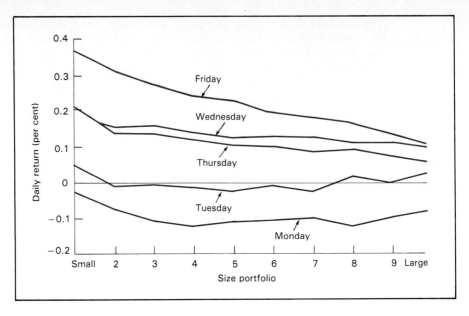

FIGURE 15–11
Interrelationship between the size effect and the day-of-the-week effect.

SOURCE: Donald B. Keim, "The CAPM and Equity Return Regularities," *Financial Analysts Journal* 42, no. 3 (May/June 1986): p. 24.

☐ A.3.2 Size and Day-of-the-Week Effects

A recent study has extended the previously mentioned studies of the day-of-the-week effect back to 1928.[45] That is, daily data from 1928 through 1982 were examined and negative Monday returns were documented over the 55-year period. Furthermore, a similar day-of-the-week effect was observed in a sample of over-the-counter stocks for the period of 1979 to 1982. Then, using all NYSE-listed and AMEX-listed stocks for the period of 1963 to 1979, ten size-based portfolios were formed. Finally, the average return on each day of the week was calculated for each portfolio. As shown in Figure 15.11, negative Monday returns were observed for all sizes of portfolios, and there did not appear to be a systematic relationship between portfolio size and the size of the Monday return. Thus, it appears that the size effect and the day-of-the-week effect have not been related to each other.[46]

Another study examined all the transactions on the NYSE during the period of December 1, 1981, through January 31, 1983, by calculating the

---

[45] Donald B. Keim and Robert F. Stambaugh, "A Further Investigation of the Weekend Effect in Stock Returns," *Journal of Finance* 39, no. 3 (July 1984):819–35.

[46] Interestingly, there did appear to be a relationship between portfolio size and the size of the Friday return. In particular, Friday returns were the largest of the week for all portfolio sizes, and the smaller the portfolio the larger the Friday return. These interrelationships were also documented by Harris, "A Transaction Data Study."

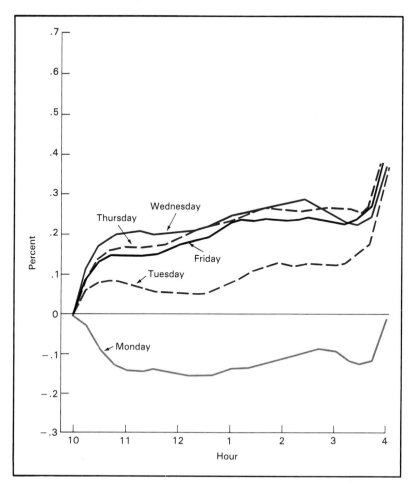

FIGURE 15–12
Cumulated fifteen-minute intraday returns.

SOURCE: Lawrence Harris, "How to Profit from Intradaily Stock Returns," *Journal of Portfolio Management* 12, no. 2 (Winter 1986): p. 63.

rate of return on each stock over 15-minute intervals during trading hours.[47] Figure 15.12 displays the results for all the 1,616 stocks listed on the NYSE during this time period. Several interesting observations can be made. First, the negative returns during trading hours on Monday occurred mostly during the first 45 minutes. After these 45 minutes had elapsed, the behavior of stock prices on Mondays was similar to the other days of the week. Second, on Tuesdays through Fridays, there was a notable upward movement in prices during the first 45 minutes of trading. Third, on all days of the week there was a notable upward price movement at the end of trading hours (further analysis indicated that most of this "end-of-the-day effect" occurred from the next to the last transaction to the last transaction). After forming

---

[47] Harris, "A Transaction Data Study" and "How to Profit."

TABLE 15.14

The January Effect and the Day-of-the-Week Effect.

	MONDAY	TUESDAY	WEDNESDAY	THURSDAY	FRIDAY
a. January returns	.28%	.17%	.14%	.43%	.49%
b. February–December returns	−.15	−.02	.14	.07	.19

SOURCE: Richard J. Rogalski, "New Findings Regarding Day-of-the-Week Returns over Trading and Non-trading Periods: A Note," *Journal of Finance* 39, no. 5 (December 1984):1609–11.

ten portfolios by firm size, these patterns were found to exist for all firm sizes. Thus, both studies that tested to see if there was some relationship between size and the day-of-the-week effect found that none existed.

☐ A.3.3 January and Day-of-the-Week Effects

The results of a study that examined the daily returns on all NYSE-listed and AMEX-listed stocks for the period of 1963 to 1982 are shown in Table 15.14.[48] It can be seen in this table that there has been a striking difference in the day-of-the-week effect between the month of January and the other 11 months of the year. That is, the negative Monday returns that have been widely documented appear to have occurred in the months of February through December but not in January.

Size, January, and Day-of-the-Week Effects

Lastly, interrelations between all three empirical regularities have been examined. The preceding study divided the set of NYSE and AMEX stocks into ten portfolios based on size and then examined the returns for each

TABLE 15.15

Size, January, and Day-of-the-Week Effects.

	PORTFOLIO	MONDAY	TUESDAY	WEDNESDAY	THURSDAY	FRIDAY
a. January returns						
	Smallest = 1	.82%	.58%	.47%	.73%	.92%
	4	.32	.20	.16	.51	.57
	7	.15	.09	.06	.36	.36
	Largest = 10	.02	−.07	−.03	.20	.19
b. February–December returns						
	Smallest = 1	−.07%	−.04%	.15%	.15%	.29%
	4	−.18	−.04	.14	.09	.22
	7	−.16	.00	.14	.06	.15
	Largest = 10	−.13	.04	.12	.03	.09

SOURCE: Richard J. Rogalski, "New Findings Regarding Day-of-the-Week Returns over Trading and Non-trading Periods: A Note," *Journal of Finance* 39, no. 5 (December 1984):1609–11.

---

[48] Rogalski, "New Findings."

portfolio in a manner similar to Table 15.14. The results for the first, fourth, seventh, and tenth portfolios (that is, the smallest, fourth smallest, seventh smallest, and largest portfolios) are shown in Table 15.15.

Several observations can be made. First, the average Monday return in January was positive for all portfolio sizes, whereas during the rest of the year it was negative for all portfolio sizes. Second, the average Monday return in January was related to firm size, with smaller firms having larger returns. Furthermore, this was true for any day during January. Third, during the rest of the year there was a clear relationship between the firm size and the day of the week only on Thursday and Friday, where the smaller the firm the larger the return.

A.4   SUMMARY OF EMPIRICAL REGULARITIES

On balance, what do these regularities suggest the investor should do? First, investors who want to buy stocks should avoid doing so early on Monday. During the other days of the week they should do so as early as possible. Second, investors who want to sell stocks should try to sell late on Friday. If this is not possible, they should wait until at least 45 minutes after the opening except on Monday, when they should try to sell at the opening. Third, if small firms are to be purchased, they should be purchased in late December or somewhat earlier; if small firms are to be sold, they should be sold in mid-January or somewhat later. Fourth, if large firms are to be purchased, they should be purchased in early February or somewhat later; if large firms are to be sold, they should be sold in late December or somewhat earlier.

Several words of caution are in order here. First, it should be noted that there is some question whether or not the first two recommendations are useful during the month of January. Second, none of these empirical regularities is of a sufficient magnitude to suggest that riches are to be made by exploiting them. Indeed, transactions costs would devour most, if not all, of any profits that may be made. All that they suggest is that if, for whatever reason, a buy or sell order is to be placed, there are some times when it may be more advantageous to do so. Third, while these regularities have been found to exist in the past—and in some instances for long periods of time—there is no guarantee that they will continue to exist in the future. It may be the case that as more investors become aware of them and time their trades accordingly, these regularities will cease to exist.

APPENDIX B
EMPIRICAL AND FUNDAMENTAL FACTORS

As indicated in the text, factors determined empirically may differ from fundamental factors. This will be the case even if the relevant attributes are selected and measured without error.

Assume that the underlying factor model is:

$$r_i = a_i + b_{i1}F_1 + \cdots + b_{iM}F_M + e_i. \tag{15.18}$$

From the assumption that the final term has an expected value of zero:

$$\bar{r}_i = a_i + b_{i1}\bar{F}_1 + \cdots + b_{iM}\bar{F}_M \tag{15.19}$$

where:

$$\bar{r}_i = \text{the expected return on security } i$$
$$\bar{F}_1, \ldots, \bar{F}_M = \text{the expected values of factors } 1, \ldots, M.$$

The Arbitrage Pricing Theory implies that:

$$\bar{r}_i = r_f + b_{i1}\lambda_1 + \cdots + b_{iM}\lambda_M \tag{15.20}$$

where:

$$r_f = \text{the riskless rate of interest}$$
$$\lambda_1, \ldots, \lambda_M = \text{the expected return premia for factors } 1, \ldots, M.$$

Since both equations indicate the expected return on the security, the two right-hand sides must equal. This implies that

$$a_i = r_f + b_{i1}(\lambda_1 - \bar{F}_1) + \cdots + b_{iM}(\lambda_M - \bar{F}_M). \tag{15.21}$$

Substituting this value into the equation of the underlying factor model gives

$$r_i = r_f + b_{i1}(\lambda_1 + F_1 - \bar{F}_1) + \cdots + b_{iM}(\lambda_M + F_M - \bar{F}_M) + e_i \tag{15.22}$$

When security returns are regressed on the relevant attributes, the "empirical factors" obtained will equal the parenthesized expressions. Using the notation from the chapter:

$$f_1 = \lambda_1 + (F_1 - \bar{F}_1)$$
$$\vdots$$
$$f_M = \lambda_M + (F_M - \bar{F}_M)$$

where:

$$f_1, \ldots, f_M = \text{empirical factors } 1, \ldots, M.$$

Thus each empirical factor will equal the expected return premium for the corresponding fundamental factor plus the deviation of the fundamental factor from its expected value.

If all relevant attributes are included, the intercept in the cross-section regression should equal the riskless rate of interest. And if historic results are adequate proxies for unchanging expectations, the average values of the empirical factors should equal the expected return premiums. As indicated in the chapter, these are stringent requirements, unlikely to be totally fulfilled in practice.

QUESTIONS AND PROBLEMS

1. Tallahassee Company is conducting the annual election for its five-member board of directors. The firm has 1,600,000 shares of voting common stock outstanding.

a. Under a majority voting system, how many shares must a stockholder own to ensure being able to elect his or her choices to each of the five director seats?

b. Under a cumulative voting system, how many shares must a stockholder own to ensure being able to elect his or her choices to two of the director seats?

c. Arlie Latham holds 20% of Tallahassee's outstanding stock. How many directors can Arlie elect under a cumulative voting system?

2. As takeover and merger activity has increased in recent years, the issue of corporate ownership versus control has become more controversial. Discuss the principal–agent problem as it relates to shareholder–management relations. Specifically, why is there a potential conflict between the two groups? What steps can be taken to mitigate this problem?

3. Why might a corporation wish to issue more than one class of common stock?

4. With respect to the payment of corporate dividends, distinguish between declaration date, ex-dividend date, and date-of-record.

5. Theoretical arguments and empirical research support the case that stock dividends and splits do not enhance shareholder wealth. However, corporations continue to declare stock dividends and splits. Summarize the arguments for and against stock dividends and splits from the perspective of the shareholder.

6. St. Paul Corporation is planning to raise $28,000,000 through the sale of new common stock under a rights offering. The subscription price is $70 per share while the stock currently sells for $80 per share, rights-on. Total outstanding shares equal 10,000,000. Of this amount, Addie Joss owns 100,000 shares.

a. How many shares of stock will each right permit its owner to purchase?

b. What will be the total value of Addie's rights a day before the ex-rights date, assuming the market price of St. Paul stock remains at $80 per share?

c. After the ex-rights date, if the market value of each St. Paul Corp. right equals $.20, what must be the ex-rights market price of St. Paul's stock?

7. From the perspective of efficient market proponents, why is it surprising that trades based on insider trading data found in the SEC's *Official Summary of Securities Transactions and Holdings* appear to produce significant abnormal profits?

8. Shown here are ten quarters of excess return data for Lincoln Associates stock, as well as excess return data over the same period for a broad stock market index. Using this information, calculate the following statistics for Lincoln Associates stock.

a. Beta

b. Alpha

c. Standard deviation of random error term

d. Coefficient of determination

QUARTER	LINCOLN EXCESS RETURN	MARKET EXCESS RETURN
1	3.8%	2.7%
2	5.3	3.1
3	− 7.2	−4.9
4	10.1	9.9
5	1.0	2.7
6	2.5	1.2
7	6.4	3.8
8	4.8	4.0
9	6.0	5.5
10	2.2	2.0

9. Explain the primary differences between multiple-factor models of beta and historical models of beta. In particular, why might you expect that the multiple-factor models would do a better job of forecasting betas than do the historical models?

10. Generally, stocks with a relatively low price per share (roughly $5 per share or less) have higher betas than stocks with a higher price per share. What attributes of low-price stocks might you expect to be correlated with higher beta values?

11. Dizzy Dean owns a portfolio of 50 securities. Having read research that indicates that a well-diversified portfolio can be achieved with 10–20 randomly-selected securities, Dizzy believes almost all nonmarket risk has been eliminated in the 50-security portfolio. Is Dizzy's portfolio truly well diversified if many of its securities happen to be contained in a single homogeneous security group? Explain.

12. (Appendix Question) The empirical regularities cited in this chapter have potentially troubling implications for the Capital Asset Pricing Model and/or the concept of highly efficient markets. Discuss some of these implications.

Chapter 16

THE VALUATION OF COMMON
STOCKS

In Chapter 15, it was noted that one purpose of financial analysis is to identify mispriced securities. Fundamental analysis was mentioned as one approach for conducting a search for such securities. With this approach, the security analyst makes estimates of such things as the firm's future earnings and dividends. If these estimates are substantially different from the average estimates of other analysts but are viewed as being more accurate, then a mispriced security will have been identified. If it is also felt that the market price of the security will adjust to reflect these more accurate estimates, then the analyst will issue either a buy or sell recommendation, depending upon the direction of the anticipated price adjustment. Based upon the capitalization of income method of valuation, dividend discount models have been frequently used by fundamental analysts as a means of identifying mispriced common stocks.

16.1 CAPITALIZATION OF INCOME METHOD OF VALUATION

There are many ways to implement the fundamental analysis approach to identifying mispriced securities. A number of them are either directly or indirectly related to what is sometimes referred to as the *capitalization of income method of valuation*.[1] This method states that the true, or intrinsic, value of any asset is based on the cash flows that the investor expects to receive in the future from owning the asset. Since these cash flows are expected in the future, they are discounted to reflect the time value of money, with the *discount rate* reflecting not only the time value of money but also the riskiness of the cash flows.

Algebraically, the intrinsic value of the asset (V) is equal to the sum of the present values of the expected cash flows:

---

[1] The appendix describes a model used by some fundamental analysts for identifying mispriced common stocks that is not directly related to the capitalization of income method of valuation. For a description of the typical financial characteristics of a stock market "winner," see Marc R. Reinganum, "The Anatomy of a Stock Market Winner," *Financial Analysts Journal* 44, no. 2 (March/April 1988):16–28.

$$V = \frac{C_1}{(1 + k)^1} + \frac{C_2}{(1 + k)^2} + \frac{C_3}{(1 + k)^3} + \cdots$$

$$= \sum_{t=1}^{\infty} \frac{C_t}{(1 + k)^t} \qquad \qquad \textbf{(16.1)}$$

where C_t denotes the expected cash flow associated with the asset at time t and k is the appropriate discount rate for cash flows of this degree risk. In this equation, the discount rate is assumed to be the same for all periods. Since the symbol ∞ above the summation sign in the equation denotes infinity, all expected cash flows, from immediately after making the investment until infinity, are discounted at the same rate in determining V.[2]

☐ **16.1.1   Net Present Value**

For the sake of convenience, let the current moment in time be denoted by zero, or $t = 0$. If the cost of purchasing an asset at $t = 0$ is P, then its *net present value* (NPV) is equal to the difference between its intrinsic value and cost, or

$$\text{NPV} = V - P$$

$$= \left[\sum_{t=1}^{\infty} \frac{C_t}{(1 + k)^t} \right] - P. \qquad \qquad \textbf{(16.2)}$$

The net present value calculation shown here is conceptually the same as the net present value calculation made for capital budgeting decisions that has long been advocated in introductory finance textbooks. Capital budgeting decisions involve deciding whether or not a given investment project should be undertaken (for example, should a new machine be purchased?). In making this decision, the focal point is the NPV of the project. Specifically, an investment project would be viewed favorably if the NPV is positive and unfavorably if its NPV is negative. For a simple project involving a cash outflow now (at $t = 0$) and expected cash inflows in the future, a positive NPV means that the present value of all the expected cash inflows is greater than cost of making the investment. Conversely, a negative NPV means that the present value of all the expected cash inflows is less than the cost of making the investment.

The same views about NPV apply when financial assets (such as a share of common stock), instead of real assets (such as a new machine), are being considered for purchase. That is, a financial asset is viewed favorably and said to be underpriced, or undervalued, if NPV > 0. Conversely, a financial asset is viewed unfavorably and said to be overpriced, or overvalued, if NPV < 0. From equation (16.2), this is equivalent to stating that a financial asset is underpriced if $V > P$:

---

[2] Sometimes the expected cash flows after some time period will be equal to zero, meaning that the summation only needs to be carried out to that point. Even if they are never equal to zero, in many cases the denominator in equation (15.1) will become so large as t gets large (for example, if t is 40 or more for a discount rate of 15%) that the present value of all expected cash flows past an arbitrary time in the future will be roughly zero and can be safely ignored.

$$\sum_{t=1}^{\infty} \frac{C_t}{(1 + k)^t} > P. \qquad (16.3)$$

Conversely, the asset is overvalued if $V < P$:

$$\sum_{t=1}^{\infty} \frac{C_t}{(1 + k)^t} < P. \qquad (16.4)$$

☐ 16.1.2 Internal Rate of Return

Another way of making capital budgeting decisions in a manner that is similar to NPV involves calculating the *internal rate of return* (IRR) associated with the investment project. With IRR, NPV in equation (16.2) is set equal to zero and the discount rate becomes the unknown that must be calculated. That is, the IRR for a given investment is the discount rate that makes the net present value of the investment equal to zero. Algebraically, the procedure involves solving the following equation for the internal rate of return, denoted by k^*:

$$0 = \sum_{t=1}^{\infty} \frac{C_t}{(1 + k^*)^t} - P \qquad (16.5)$$

where k^* is the IRR of the investment. Equivalently, equation (16.5) can be rewritten as

$$P = \sum_{t=1}^{\infty} \frac{C_t}{(1 + k^*)^t}. \qquad (16.6)$$

The decision rule for IRR involves comparing the project's IRR, denoted by k^*, with the required rate of return for an investment of similar risk, denoted by k. Specifically, the investment would be viewed favorably if $k^* > k$ and unfavorably if $k^* < k$. As with NPV, the same decision rule applies if either a real asset or financial asset is being considered for possible investment.

☐ 16.1.3 An Application to Common Stocks

This chapter is concerned with using the capitalization of income method to determine the intrinsic value of common stocks.[3] Since the cash flows associated with an investment in any particular common stock are the dividends that are expected to be paid throughout the future on the shares purchased, the models suggested by this method of valuation are often known as *dividend discount models* (DDMs).[4] Accordingly, D_t will be used instead

---

[3] Chapter 13 discussed how to use this method to value bonds.

[4] Since the focus of DDMs is on predicting dividends, there is a particular situation where using DDMs to value common stocks is exceptionally difficult. This is the situation where the firm has not paid dividends on its stock in the recent past, which results in a complete lack of a historical record on which to base a prediction of dividends. Examples include valuing the stock of a firm being sold to the public for the first time (known as an initial public offering, or ipo) and valuing the stock of a firm that has not paid dividends recently (perhaps the firm has never paid dividends, or perhaps it has suspended paying them). A more extensive discussion of DDMs is contained in the entire November–December 1985 issue of the *Financial Analysts Journal*. For an article that describes some of the current applications of DDMs, see Barbara Donnelly, "The Dividend Discount Model Comes into Its Own," *Institutional Investor* 19, no. 3 (March 1985):77–82.

of C_t to denote the expected cash flow in period t associated with a particular common stock, resulting in the following restatement of equation (16.1):

$$V = \frac{D_1}{(1 + k)^1} + \frac{D_2}{(1 + k)^2} + \frac{D_3}{(1 + k)^3} + \cdots$$

$$= \sum_{t=1}^{\infty} \frac{D_t}{(1 + k)^t}.$$

(16.7)

Usually the focus of DDMs is on determining the true, or intrinsic, value of *one* share of a particular company's common stock, even if larger-size purchases are being contemplated. This is because it is usually believed that larger-size purchases can be made at a cost that is a simple multiple of the cost of one share (for example, the cost of 1000 shares is usually assumed to be 1000 times the cost of one share). Thus, the numerator in DDMs is the cash dividends *per share* that are expected in the future.

However, there is a complication in using equation (16.7) to determine the intrinsic value of a share of common stock. In particular, in order to use this equation the investor must forecast *all* future dividends. Since common stock does not have a fixed lifetime, this suggests that an infinitely long stream of dividends must be forecast. While this may seem to be an impossible task, with the addition of certain assumptions, the equation can be made tractable (that is, usable).

These assumptions center around *dividend growth rates*. That is, the dividend per share at any time t can be viewed as being equal to the dividend per share at time $t - 1$ times a dividend growth rate of g_t:

$$D_t = D_{t-1}(1 + g_t)$$

(16.8)

or, equivalently,

$$\frac{D_t - D_{t-1}}{D_{t-1}} = g_t.$$

(16.9)

For example, if the dividend per share expected at $t = 2$ is $4 and the dividend per share expected at $t = 3$ is $4.20, then $g_3 = (\$4.20 - \$4)/\$4 = 5\%$. The different types of tractable DDMs reflect different sets of assumptions about dividend growth rates and are presented next. The discussion begins with the simplest case, the zero-growth model.

16.2 THE ZERO-GROWTH MODEL

One assumption that could be made about future dividends is that they will remain at a fixed dollar amount. That is, the dollar amount of dividends per share that were paid over the past year (D_0) will also be paid over the next year (D_1), the year after that (D_2), the year after that (D_3), and so on. That is,

$$D_0 = D_1 = D_2 = D_3 = \cdots$$

This is equivalent to assuming that all the dividend growth rates are zero, since if $g_t = 0$, then $D_t = D_{t-1}$ in equation (16.8). Accordingly, this model is often referred to as the *zero-growth* (or no-growth) *model*.

The impact of this assumption on equation (16.7) can be analyzed by noting what happens when D_t is replaced by D_0 in the numerator:

$$V = \sum_{t=1}^{\infty} \frac{D_0}{(1 + k)^t}. \tag{16.10}$$

Fortunately, equation (16.10) can be simplified by noting that D_0 is a fixed dollar amount, which means it can be written outside the summation sign:

$$V = D_0 \left[\sum_{t=1}^{\infty} \frac{1}{(1 + k)^t} \right]. \tag{16.11}$$

The next step involves using a property of infinite series from mathematics. If $k > 0$, then it can be shown that

$$\sum_{t=1}^{\infty} \frac{1}{(1 + k)^t} = \frac{1}{k}. \tag{16.12}$$

Applying this property to equation (16.11) results in the following formula for the zero-growth model:

$$V = \frac{D_0}{k_0} \tag{16.13}$$

Since $D_0 = D_1$, equation (16.13) is sometimes written as

$$V = \frac{D_1}{k}. \tag{16.14}$$

As an example of how this DDM can be used, assume that the Zinc Company is expected to pay cash dividends amounting to $8 per share into the indefinite future and has a required rate of return of 10%. Using either equation (16.13) or equation (16.14), it can be seen that the value of a share of Zinc stock is equal to $8/.10 = $80. With a current stock price of $65 per share, equation (16.2) would suggest that the NPV per share is $80 − $65 = $15. Equivalently, since $V = \$80 > P = \$65$, the stock is underpriced by $15 per share and would be a candidate for purchase.

☐ 16.2.1 **Internal Rate of Return**

Equation (16.13) can be reformulated to solve for the internal rate of return on an investment in a zero growth security. First, the current price of the security is substituted for V; second, k^* is substituted for k. Doing so results in

$$P = \frac{D_0}{k^*}$$

which can be rewritten as

$$k^* = \frac{D_0}{P} \qquad (16.15a)$$

$$= \frac{D_1}{P}. \qquad (16.15b)$$

Applying this formula to the stock of Zinc indicates that $k^* = \$8/\$65 = 12.3\%$. Since the IRR from an investment in Zinc exceeds the required rate of return on Zinc (12.3% > 10%), this method also indicates that Zinc is underpriced.[5]

□ 16.2.2 An Application

The zero-growth model may seem quite restrictive. After all, it does not seem reasonable to assume a given stock will pay a fixed dollar–size dividend forever. While such a criticism has validity for common stock valuation, there is one particular situation where this model is quite useful. Specifically, whenever the intrinsic value of a share of preferred stock is to be determined, this DDM is often appropriate. It is appropriate because most preferred stock is *nonparticipating*, meaning it pays a fixed dollar–size dividend that will not be changed as earnings per share changes. Furthermore, it can be expected to be paid forever, since preferred stock does not have a fixed lifetime.

16.3 THE CONSTANT-GROWTH MODEL

The next type of DDM to be considered is one that assumes dividends grow from period to period at the same rate forever, which is therefore known as the *constant-growth model*. Specifically, the dividends per share that were paid over the previous year (D_0) are expected to grow at a given rate g, so that the dividends expected over the next year (D_1) are expected to be equal to $D_0(1 + g)$. Dividends the year after that are again expected to grow by the rate g, meaning that $D_2 = D_1(1 + g)$. Since $D_1 = D_0(1 + g)$, this is equivalent to assuming that $D_2 = D_0(1 + g)^2$ and, in general,

$$D_t = D_{t-1}(1 + g) \qquad (16.16a)$$

$$= D_0(1 + g)^t. \qquad (16.16b)$$

The impact of this assumption on equation (16.7) can be analyzed by noting what happens when D_t is replaced by $D_0(1 + g)^t$ in the numerator:

$$V = \sum_{t=1}^{\infty} \frac{D_0(1 + g)^t}{(1 + k)^t}. \qquad (16.17)$$

---

[5] A share of common stock has a positive NPV if and only if it has an IRR greater than its required rate of return. Thus, there can never be inconsistent signals given by the two approaches. That is, there will never be a situation where one approach indicates a stock is underpriced and the other approach indicates it is overpriced. This is true not only for the zero-growth model but for all DDMs.

Fortunately, equation (16.17) can be simplified by noting that D_0 is a given dollar amount, which means it can be written outside the summation sign:

$$V = D_0 \left[\sum_{t=1}^{\infty} \frac{(1 + g)^t}{(1 + k)^t} \right] \qquad (16.18)$$

The next step involves using a property of infinite series from mathematics. If $k > g$, then it can be shown that

$$\sum_{t=1}^{\infty} \frac{(1 + g)^t}{(1 + k)^t} = \frac{1 + g}{k - g}. \qquad (16.19)$$

Substituting equation (16.19) into equation (16.18) results in the valuation formula for the constant growth model:

$$V = D_0 \left[\frac{1 + g}{k - g} \right] \qquad (16.20)$$

Sometimes equation (16.20) is rewritten as

$$V = \frac{D_1}{k - g} \qquad (16.21)$$

since $D_1 = D_0(1 + g)$.

As an example of how this DDM can be used, assume that during the past year the Copper Company paid dividends amounting to $1.80 per share. The forecast is that dividends on Copper stock will increase by 5% per year into the indefinite future. Thus, dividends over the next year are expected to equal $1.80(1 + .05) = $1.89. Using equation (16.20) and assuming the required rate of return of 11%, it can be seen that the value of a share of Copper stock is equal to $1.80[(1 + .05)/(.11 − .05)] = $1.89/(.11 − .05) = $31.50. With a current stock price of $40 per share, equation (16.2) would suggest that the NPV per share is $31.50 − $40 = −$8.50. Equivalently, since $V = $31.50 < P = 40, the stock is overpriced by $8.50 per share and would be a candidate for sale if currently owned.

☐ 16.3.1 Internal Rate of Return

Equation (16.20) can be reformulated to solve for the internal rate of return on an investment in a constant growth security. First, the current price of the security is substituted for V and then k^* is substituted for k. Doing so results in

$$P = D_0 \left[\frac{1 + g}{k^* - g} \right] \qquad (16.22)$$

which can be rewritten as

$$k^* = \frac{D_0(1 + g)}{P} + g \qquad (16.23a)$$

$$= \frac{D_1}{P} + g. \qquad (16.23b)$$

Applying this formula to the stock of Copper indicates that $k^* = [\$1.80$ $(1 + .05)/\$40] + .05 = [\$1.89/\$40] + .05 = 9.725\%$. Since the required rate of return on Copper exceeds the IRR from an investment in Copper $(11\% > 9.725\%)$, this method also indicates that Copper is overpriced.

$$12\% = \frac{2.068}{x} + .10 \qquad \frac{1}{x} = \frac{12\% - 10\%}{2.068}$$

☐ 16.3.2 Relationship to the Zero-Growth Model

The zero-growth model of the previous section can be shown to be a special case of the constant-growth model. In particular, if the growth rate g is assumed to be 0, then dividends will be a fixed dollar amount forever, which is the same as saying that there will be zero growth. Letting $g = 0$ in equations (16.20) and (16.23a) results in two equations that are identical to (16.13) and (16.15a), respectively.

While assuming constant growth may seem less restrictive than assuming no growth, it may still be viewed as unrealistic in many cases. However, as will be shown next, the constant-growth model is important because it is embedded in the multiple-growth model.

16.4 THE MULTIPLE-GROWTH MODEL

The most general DDM for valuing common stocks is the *multiple-growth model*. With this model, the focus is on a time in the future after which dividends are expected to grow at a constant rate g. Although the investor is still concerned with forecasting dividends, these dividends do not need to have any specific pattern until this time, after which they will be assumed to have the specific pattern of constant growth. If this time is denoted by T, then dividends $D_1, D_2, D_3, \ldots, D_T$ will be forecast separately by the investor (the investor also forecasts when this time T will occur). Thereafter, dividends are assumed to grow by a constant rate g that the investor must also forecast, meaning that

$$D_{T+1} = D_T(1 + g)$$

$$D_{T+2} = D_{T+1}(1 + g) = D_T(1 + g)^2$$

$$D_{T+3} = D_{T+2}(1 + g) = D_T(1 + g)^3$$

and so on. Figure 16.1 presents a time line of dividends and growth rates associated with the multiple-growth model.

In determining the value of a share of common stock with the multiple growth model, the present value of the forecasted stream of dividends must be determined. This can be done by dividing the stream into two parts, finding the present value of each part, and then adding these two present values together.

The first part consists of finding the present value of all the forecasted dividends up to and including T. Denoting this present value by V_{T-}, it is equal to

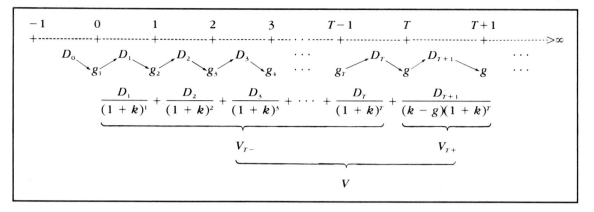

FIGURE 16–1
Time line for multiple growth model.

$$V_{T-} = \sum_{t=1}^{T} \frac{D_t}{(1 + k)^t}. \qquad (16.24)$$

The second part consists of finding the present value of all the forecasted dividends after T and involves the application of the constant growth model. The application begins by imagining that the investor is not at time zero ($t = 0$) but is at time T ($t = T$) and has not changed his or her forecast of dividends for the stock. This means that next period's dividend, D_{T+1}, and all those thereafter are expected to grow at the rate g. Thus, the investor would be viewing the stock as having a constant growth rate, and its value *at time T (V_T)* could be determined with the constant-growth model of equation (16.21):

$$V_T = D_{T+1}\left[\frac{1}{k - g}\right]. \qquad (16.25)$$

One way to view V_T is that it represents a lump sum that is just as desirable as the stream of dividends after T. That is, an investor would find a lump sum of cash equal to V_T, to be received at T, to be equally desirable to the stream of dividends D_{T+1}, D_{T+2}, D_{T+3}, and so on. Now, given that the investor is at time zero ($t = 0$), not at T, the present value at $t = 0$ of the lump sum V_T must be determined. This is done simply by discounting it for T periods at the rate k, resulting in the following formula for finding the present value at time zero for all dividends after T, denoted by V_{T+}:

$$V_{T+} = V_T\left[\frac{1}{(1 + k)^T}\right]$$
$$= \frac{D_{T+1}}{(k - g)(1 + k)^T}. \qquad (16.26)$$

Having found the present value of all dividends up to and including T with equation (16.24) and the present value of all dividends after T with

equation (16.26), the value of the stock can be determined by summing these two amounts:

$$V = V_{T-} + V_{T+}$$

$$= \sum_{t=1}^{T} \frac{D_t}{(1 + k)^t} + \frac{D_{T+1}}{(k - g)(1 + k)^T}. \tag{16.27}$$

Figure 16.1 illustrates the valuation procedure for the multiple growth DDM that is given in equation (16.27).

An Example

As an example of how this DDM can be used, assume that during the past year the Magnesium Company paid dividends amounting to $.75 per share. Over the next year Magnesium is expected to pay dividends of $2 per share. Thus, $g_1 = (D_1 - D_0)/D_0 = (\$2 - \$.75)/\$.75 = 167\%$. The year after that dividends are expected to amount to $3 per share, indicating that $g_2 = (D_2 - D_1)/D_1 = (\$3 - \$2)/\$2 = 50\%$. At this time, the forecast is that dividends will grow by 10% per year into the indefinite future, indicating that $T = 2$ and $g = 10\%$. Consequently, $D_{T+1} = D_3 = \$3(1 + .10) = \$3.30$. Given a required rate of return on Magnesium shares of 15%, the value of V_{T-} and V_{T+} can be calculated, respectively, as follows:

$$V_{T-} = \frac{\$2}{(1 + .15)^1} + \frac{\$3}{(1 + .15)^2}$$

$$= \$4.01$$

$$V_{T+} = \frac{\$3.30}{(.15 - .10)(1 + .15)^2}$$

$$= \$49.91$$

Summing V_{T-} and V_{T+} results in a value for V of $4.01 + $49.91 = $53.92. With a current stock price of $55 per share, Magnesium appears to be fairly priced. That is, since V and P are nearly of equal size, Magnesium is not mispriced.

□ **16.4.1   Internal Rate of Return**

The zero-growth and constant-growth models had equations for V that could be reformulated in order to solve for the internal rate of return on an investment in a stock. Unfortunately, a convenient expression similar to equations (16.15a), (16.15b), (16.23a), and (16.23b) is not available for the multiple-growth model. This can be seen by noting that the expression for IRR is derived by substituting P for V and k^* for k in equation (16.27):

$$P = \sum_{t=1}^{T} \frac{D_t}{(1 + k^*)^t} + \frac{D_{T+1}}{(k^* - g)(1 + k^*)^T}. \tag{16.28}$$

This equation cannot be rewritten with k^* isolated on the left-hand side, meaning that a closed-form expression for IRR does not exist for the multiple growth model.

However, all is not lost. It is still possible to calculate the IRR for an investment in a stock conforming to the multiple growth model by using an "educated" trial-and-error method. That is, after setting up equation (16.28), an estimate for k^* can be tried. If the resulting value on the right-hand side is larger than P, then a larger k^* can be tried. Conversely, if the resulting value is smaller than P, then a smaller k^* can be tried. Continuing this search process, the investor could hone in on the value of k^*.[6]

Applying equation (16.28) to the Magnesium Company results in

$$\$55 = \frac{\$2}{(1 + k^*)^1} + \frac{\$3}{(1 + k^*)^2} + \frac{\$3.30}{(k^* - .10)(1 + k^*)^2}. \tag{16.29}$$

Initially a rate of 14% may be used in attempting to solve this equation for k^*. Inserting 14% for k^* in the right-hand side of equation (16.29) results in a value of $67.54. Earlier 15% was used in determining V and resulted in a value of $53.92. This means that k^* must have a value between 14% and 15%, since $55 is between $67.54 and $53.92. If 14.5% is tried next, the resulting value is $59.97, suggesting a higher rate should be tried. If 14.8% and 14.9% are subsequently tried, the respective resulting values are $56.18 and $55.03. Since $55.03 is the closest to P, the IRR associated with an investment in Magnesium is 14.9%. Given a required return of 15% and an IRR of approximately that amount, the stock of Magnesium appears to be fairly priced.

☐ 16.4.2 Relationship to the Constant-Growth Model

The constant-growth model can be shown to be a special case of the multiple-growth model. In particular, if the time when constant growth is assumed to begin is set equal to zero, then

$$V_{T-} = \sum_{t=1}^{T} \frac{D_t}{(1 + k)^t} = 0$$

and

$$V_{T+} = \frac{D_{T+1}}{(k - g)(1 + k)^T} = \frac{D_1}{k - g}$$

since $T = 0$ and $(1 + k)^0 = 1$. Given that the multiple-growth model states that $V = V_{T-} + V_{T+}$, it can be seen that setting $T = 0$ results in $V = D_1/(k - g)$, a formula that is equivalent to the formula for the constant growth model.

---

[6] It would be a relatively simple matter to program a computer to conduct the search for k^* in equation (16.28).

□ 16.4.3 Two-Phase and Three-Phase Models

Two dividend discount models that are sometimes used are the two-phase and the three-phase models.[7] The two-phase model assumes a constant growth rate (g_1) exists only until some time T, when a different growth rate (g_2) is assumed to begin and continue thereafter. The three-phase model assumes a constant growth rate (g_1) exists only until some time T_1, when a second growth rate is assumed to begin and last until a later time T_2, when a third growth rate is assumed to begin and last thereafter. By letting V_{T+} denote the present value of all dividends after the last growth rate has begun and V_{T-} denote the present value of all the preceding dividends, it can be seen that these models are just special cases of the multiple growth models.

In applying the capitalization of income method of valuation to common stocks, it might seem appropriate to assume that the stock will be sold at some point in the future. In this case, the expected case flows would consist of the dividends up to that point as well as the expected selling price. Since dividends after the selling date would be ignored, the use of a dividend discount model may seem to be improper. However, as is shown next, this is not so.

16.5 VALUATION BASED ON A FINITE HOLDING PERIOD

The capitalization of income method of valuation involves discounting all dividends that are expected throughout the future. Since the simplified models of zero growth, constant growth, and multiple growth are based on this method, they too involve a future stream of dividends. Upon reflection, it may seem that such models are relevant only for an investor who plans to hold a stock forever, since such an investor would expect to receive this stream of future dividends.

But what about an investor who plans to sell the stock in a year?[8] In such a situation, the cash flows that the investor expects to receive from purchasing a share of the stock are equal to the dividend expected one year from now (for ease of exposition, it is assumed that common stocks pay dividends annually) and the expected selling price of the stock. Thus, it would seem appropriate to determine the intrinsic value of the stock to the investor by discounting these two cash flows at the required rate of return as follows:

$$V = \frac{D_1 + P_1}{(1 + k)}$$

$$= \frac{D_1}{1 + k} + \frac{P_1}{1 + k}$$

(16.30)

---

[7] For a discussion of these models, see Russell J. Fuller and Chi-Cheng Hsia, "A Simplified Common Stock Valuation Model," *Financial Analysts Journal* 40, no. 5 (September/October 1984):49–56; and Eric H. Sorensen and David A. Williamson, "Some Evidence on the Value of Dividend Discount Models," *Financial Analysts Journal* 41, no. 6 (November/December 1985):60–69.

[8] The analysis is similar if it is assumed that the investor plans to sell the stock after some other length of time, such as six months or two years.

where D_1 and P_1 are the expected dividend and selling price at $t = 1$, respectively.

In order to use equation (16.30), the expected price of the stock at $t = 1$ must be estimated. The simplest approach assumes that the selling price will be based on the dividends that are expected to be paid after the selling date, $t = 1$. Thus, the expected selling price at $t = 1$ is

$$P_1 = \frac{D_2}{(1 + k)^1} + \frac{D_3}{(1 + k)^2} + \frac{D_4}{(1 + k)^3} + \cdots$$

$$= \sum_{t=2}^{\infty} \frac{D_t}{(1 + k)^{t-1}}.$$

(16.31)

Substituting equation (16.31) for P_1 in the right-hand side of equation (16.30) results in

$$V = \frac{D_1}{1 + k} + \left[\frac{D_2}{(1 + k)^1} + \frac{D_3}{(1 + k)^2} + \frac{D_4}{(1 + k)^3} + \cdots \right] \left[\frac{1}{1 + k} \right]$$

$$= \frac{D_1}{(1 + k)^1} + \frac{D_2}{(1 + k)^2} + \frac{D_3}{(1 + k)^3} + \frac{D_4}{(1 + k)^4} + \cdots$$

$$= \sum_{t=1}^{\infty} \frac{D_t}{(1 + k)^t}$$

which is exactly the same as equation (16.7). Thus, valuing a share of common stock by discounting its dividends up to some point in the future and its expected selling price at that time is equivalent to valuing stock by discounting all future dividends. Simply stated, the two are equivalent because the expected selling price is itself based on dividends to be paid after the selling date. Thus, equation (16.7)—as well as the zero-growth, constant-growth, and multiple-growth models that are based on it—is appropriate for determining the intrinsic value of a share of common stock regardless of the length of the investor's planned holding period.

An Example

As an example, reconsider the common stock of the Copper Company. Over the past year it was noted that Copper paid dividends of $1.80 per share, with the forecast that the dividends would grow by 5% per year forever. This means that dividends over the next two years (D_1 and D_2) are forecast to be $1.80(1 + .05) = $1.89 and $1.89(1 + .05) = $1.985, respectively. If the investor plans to sell the stock after one year, the selling price can be estimated by noting that at $t = 1$, the forecast of dividends for the forthcoming year would be D_2, or $1.985. Thus, the anticipated selling price at $t = 1$, denoted by P_1, would be equal to $1.985/(.11 − .05) = $33.08. Accordingly, the intrinsic value of Copper to such an investor would be equal to the present value of the expected cash flows, which are $D_1 = $1.89 and $P_1 = $33.08. Using equation (16.30) and assuming a required rate of 11%, this value is equal to ($1.89 + $33.08)/(1 + .11) = $31.50. Note that this is the same amount that was calculated earlier when all the dividends from now to

infinity were discounted using the constant growth model: $V = D_1/(k - g) = \$1.89/(.11 - .05) = \$31.50$.

16.6 MODELS BASED ON PRICE-EARNINGS RATIOS

Despite the inherent sensibility of dividend discount models, many security analysts use a much simpler procedure to value common stocks. First, a stock's earnings per share over the forthcoming year (E_1) will be estimated and then the analyst (or someone else) will estimate a "normal" *price-earnings ratio* for the stock. The product of these two numbers gives the estimated future price (P_1). Together with estimated dividends to be paid during the period (D_1) and current price (P), the estimated return on the stock over the period can be determined:

$$\text{Expected return} = \frac{(P_1 - P) + D_1}{P}. \tag{16.32}$$

Some security analysts expand this procedure, estimating earnings per share and price-earnings ratios for optimistic, most likely, and pessimistic scenarios to produce a rudimentary probability distribution of a security's return. Other analysts determine whether a stock is underpriced or overpriced by comparing the stock's actual price-earnings ratio with its normal price-earnings ratio, as is shown next.[9]

In order to make this comparison, equation (16.7) must be rearranged and some new variables must be introduced. To begin, it should be noted that earnings per share (E_t) are related to dividends per share (D_t) by the firm's *payout ratio* (p_t):

$$D_t = p_t E_t. \tag{16.33}$$

Note that if an analyst has forecast earnings per share and payout ratios, then he or she has implicitly forecast dividends.

Equation (16.33) can be used to restate the various DDMs where the focus is on estimating what the stock's price-earnings ratio should be instead of on estimating the intrinsic value of the stock. In order to do so, $p_t E_t$ is substituted for D_t in the right-hand side of equation (16.7), resulting in a general formula for determining a stock's intrinsic value that involves discounting earnings:

$$V = \frac{D_1}{(1 + k)^1} + \frac{D_2}{(1 + k)^2} + \frac{D_3}{(1 + k)^3} + \cdots$$

$$= \frac{p_1 E_1}{(1 + k)^1} + \frac{p_2 E_2}{(1 + k)^2} + \frac{p_3 E_3}{(1 + k)^3} + \cdots \tag{16.34}$$

$$= \sum_{t=1}^{\infty} \frac{p_t E_t}{(1 + k)^t}.$$

----

[9] Alternatively, some analysts focus on the *earnings-price ratio*, which is the reciprocal of the price-earnings ratio. Accordingly, the formulas for a stock's normal earnings-price ratio can be found by simply taking the reciprocal of the forthcoming formulas for determining a stock's normal price-earnings ratio.

Earlier, it was noted that dividends in adjacent time periods could be viewed as being "linked" to each other by a dividend growth rate, g_t. Similarly, earnings per share in any year t can be linked to earnings per share in the previous year $t - 1$ by a growth rate in earnings per share, g_{et}:

$$E_t = E_{t-1}(1 + g_{et}). \qquad (16.35)$$

This implies that

$$E_1 = E_0(1 + g_{e1})$$

$$E_2 = E_1(1 + g_{e2}) = E_0(1 + g_{e1})(1 + g_{e2})$$

$$E_3 = E_2(1 + g_{e3}) = E_0(1 + g_{e1})(1 + g_{e2})(1 + g_{e3})$$

and so on, where E_0 is the actual level of earnings per share over the past year, E_1 is the expected level of earnings per share over the forthcoming year, E_2 is the expected level of earnings per share for the year after E_1, and E_3 is the expected level of earnings per share for the year after E_2.

These equations relating expected future earnings per share to E_0 can be substituted into equation (16.34), resulting in

$$V = \frac{p_1[E_0(1 + g_{e1})]}{(1 + k)^1} + \frac{p_2[E_0(1 + g_{e1})(1 + g_{e2})]}{(1 + k)^2}$$
$$+ \frac{p_3[E_0(1 + g_{e1})(1 + g_{e2})(1 + g_{e3})]}{(1 + k)^3} + \cdots \qquad (16.36)$$

Since V is the intrinsic value of a share of stock, it represents what the stock should be selling for if it were fairly priced. It follows that V/E_0 represents what the price-earnings ratio should be for the stock if it were fairly priced; it is sometimes referred to as the stock's *normal* price-earnings ratio. Dividing both sides of equation (16.36) by E_0 and simplifying results in the formula for determining the normal price-earnings ratio:

$$\frac{V}{E_0} = \frac{p_1(1 + g_{e1})}{(1 + k)^1} + \frac{p_2(1 + g_{e1})(1 + g_{e2})}{(1 + k)^2}$$
$$+ \frac{p_3(1 + g_{e1})(1 + g_{e2})(1 + g_{e3})}{(1 + k)^3} + \cdots \qquad (16.37)$$

This shows that, other things being equal, a stock's normal price-earnings ratio will be *higher*:

The *greater* the expected payout ratios ($p_1, p_2, p_3, \ldots$),
The *greater* the expected growth rates in earnings per share ($g_{e1}, g_{e2}, g_{e3}, \ldots$), and
The *smaller* the required rate of return (k).

The qualifying phrase "other things being equal" should not be overlooked. For example, a firm cannot increase the value of its shares by simply planning on having greater payouts. This will increase $p_1, p_2, p_3, \ldots$ but will decrease the expected growth rates in earnings per share $g_{e1}, g_{e2},$

g_{e3}, ... Assuming the firm's investment policy is not altered, the effects of the reduced growth in earnings per share will just offset the effects of the increased payouts, leaving value per share unchanged.

Earlier, it was noted that a stock was viewed as being underpriced if $V > P$ and overpriced if $V < P$. Since dividing both sides of an inequality by a positive constant will not change the direction of the inequality, such a division can be done here to the two inequalities involving V and P, where the positive constant is E_0. The result is that a stock can be viewed as being underpriced if $V/E_0 > P/E_0$ and overpriced if $V/E_0 < P/E_0$. Thus, a stock will be underpriced if its normal price-earnings ratio is greater than its actual price-earnings ratio and overpriced if its normal price-earnings ratio is less than its actual price-earnings ratio.

Unfortunately, equation (16.37) is intractable, meaning it cannot be used to estimate the normal price-earnings ratio for any stock. However, simplifying assumptions can be made that result in tractable formulas for estimating normal price-earnings ratios. These assumptions, along with the formulas, parallel those made previously regarding dividends and, with one exception, are discussed next.[10]

□ 16.6.1   The Zero-Growth Model

The zero-growth model assumed that dividends per share remained at a fixed dollar amount forever. This is equivalent to assuming that earnings per share remain at a fixed dollar amount forever, with the firm maintaining a 100% payout ratio. It is assumed to be 100% because if a lesser amount were assumed to be paid out, it would mean that the firm was retaining part of its earnings. These retained earnings would be put to some use and would thus be expected to increase future earnings per share. However, future earnings per share have been assumed to be constant, so it would be inconsistent to assume constant earnings and a payout ratio of less than 100%.

Accordingly, the zero-growth model assumes $p_t = 1$ for all time periods and $E_0 = E_1 = E_2 = E_3$ and so on. This means that $D_0 = E_0 = D_1 = E_1 = D_2 = E_2$ and so on, allowing valuation equation (16.13) to be restated as

$$V = \frac{E_0}{k}. \tag{16.38}$$

Dividing equation (16.38) by E_0 results in the formula for the normal price-earnings ratio for a stock having zero growth:

$$\frac{V}{E_0} = \frac{1}{k}. \tag{16.39}$$

---

[10] The exception is the multiple-growth case, which is discussed in Appendix B.

An Example

Earlier, it was assumed that the Zinc Company was a zero-growth firm paying dividends of $8 per share, selling for $65 a share, and having a required rate of return of 10%. Since Zinc is a zero growth company, this means that it has a 100% payout ratio, which, in turn, means that $E_0 = \$8$. At this point, equation (16.38) can be used to note that a normal price-earnings ratio for Zinc is $1/.10 = 10$. Since Zinc has an actual price-earnings ratio of $\$65/\$8 = 8.1$ and since $V/E_0 = 10 > P/E_0 = 8.1$, it can be seen that Zinc stock is underpriced.

□ 16.6.2 The Constant Growth Model

Earlier, it was noted that dividends in adjacent time periods could be viewed as being connected to each other by a dividend growth rate, g_t. Similarly, it was noted that earnings per share can be connected by an earnings growth rate, g_{et}. The constant growth model assumes that the growth rate in dividends per share will be the same throughout the future. An equivalent assumption is that earnings per share will grow at a constant rate (g_e) throughout the future, with the payout ratio remaining at a constant level (p). This means that

$$E_1 = E_0(1 + g_e)$$

$$E_2 = E_1(1 + g_e) = E_0(1 + g_e)(1 + g_e)$$

$$E_3 = E_2(1 + g_e) = E_0(1 + g_e)(1 + g_e)(1 + g_e)$$

and so on. In general, earnings in year t can be connected to E_0 as follows:

$$E_t = E_0(1 + g_e)^t. \tag{16.40}$$

Substituting equation (16.40) into the numerator of equation (16.34) and recognizing that $p_t = p$ results in the following:

$$V = \sum_{t=1}^{\infty} \frac{pE_0(1 + g_e)^t}{(1 + k)^t}$$

$$= pE_0 \left[\sum_{t=1}^{\infty} \frac{(1 + g_e)^t}{(1 + k)^t} \right] \tag{16.41}$$

The same mathematical property of infinite series given in equation (16.19) can be applied to equation (16.41), resulting in

$$V = pE_0 \left[\frac{1 + g_e}{k - g_e} \right] \tag{16.42}$$

It can be noted that the earnings-based constant growth model has a numerator identical to the numerator of the dividend-based constant growth model, since $pE_0 = D_0$. Furthermore, the denominators of the two models are identical if the growth rates in earnings and dividends are the same (that is, if $g_e = g$). Examination of the assumptions of the models reveals

that these growth rates must be equal. This can be seen by recalling that constant earnings growth means

$$E_t = E_{t-1}(1 + g_e).$$

When both sides of this equation are multiplied by the constant payout ratio, the result is

$$pE_t = pE_{t-1}(1 + g_e).$$

Since $pE_t = D_t$ and $pE_{t-1} = D_{t-1}$, this equation reduces to:

$$D_t = D_{t-1}(1 + g_e)$$

which indicates that dividends in any period $t - 1$ will grow by the earnings growth rate, g_e. Since the dividend-based constant growth model assumed dividends in any period $t - 1$ would grow by the dividend growth rate g, it can be seen that the two growth rates must be equal for the two models to be equivalent.

Equation (16.42) can be restated by dividing each side by E_0, resulting in the following formula for determining the normal price-earnings ratio for a stock with constant growth:

$$\frac{V}{E_0} = p\left[\frac{1 + g_e}{k - g_e}\right]. \qquad (16.43)$$

An Example

Earlier, it was assumed that the Copper Company had paid dividends of $1.80 per share over the past year, with a forecast that dividends would grow by 5% per year forever. Furthermore, it was assumed that the required rate of return on Copper was 11%, and the current stock price was $40 per share. Now, assuming E_0 was $2.70, it can be seen that the payout ratio was equal to $1.80/$2.70 = $66\frac{2}{3}$%. This means that the normal price-earnings ratio for Copper, according to equation (16.43), is equal to .6667[(1 + .05)/(.11 − .05)] = 11.67. Since this is less than Copper's actual price-earnings ratio of $40/$2.70 = 14.81, it follows that the stock of Copper Company is overpriced.

16.7 SOURCES OF EARNINGS GROWTH

So far, no explanation has been given as to why earnings or dividends can be expected to grow in the future. One way of providing such an explanation utilizes the constant-growth model. Assuming that no new capital is obtained externally and no shares are repurchased (meaning the number of shares outstanding does not increase or decrease), the portion of earnings not paid to stockholders as dividends will be used to pay for the firm's new investments. Given that p_t denotes the payout ratio in year t, then $(1 - p_t)$ is equal to the portion of earnings not paid out, known as the *retention ratio*. Furthermore, the firm's new investments, stated on a per-share basis and denoted by I_t, will be

$$I_t = (1 - p_t)E_t. \tag{16.44}$$

If these new investments have an average return on equity of r_t in period t and every year thereafter, they will add $r_t I_t$ to earnings per share in year $t + 1$ and every year thereafter. If all previous investments also produce perpetual earnings at a constant rate of return, next year's earnings will equal this year's earnings plus the new earnings resulting from this year's new investments:

$$\begin{aligned} E_{t+1} &= E_t + r_t I_t \\ &= E_t + r_t(1 - p_t)E_t \tag{16.45} \\ &= E_t[1 + r_t(1 - p_t)]. \end{aligned}$$

Since the growth rate in earnings per share, as defined earlier, is

$$E_{t+1} = E_t(1 + g_{et+1}) \tag{16.46}$$

a comparison of equations (16.45) and (16.46) indicates that

$$g_{et+1} = r_t(1 - p_t). \tag{16.47}$$

If the growth rate in earnings per share (g_{et+1}) is to be constant over time, then the average return on equity for new investments (r_t) and payout ratio (p_t) must also be constant over time. In this situation, equation (16.47) can be simplified by removing the time subscripts:

$$g_e = r(1 - p). \tag{16.48a}$$

Since the growth rate in dividends per share (g) is equal to the growth rate in earnings per share (g_e), this equation can be rewritten as

$$g = r(1 - p). \tag{16.48b}$$

From this equation it can be seen that the growth rate g depends on (1) the proportion of earnings that is retained $(1 - p)$ and (2) the average return on equity for the earnings that are retained (r).

The constant-growth valuation formula given in equation (16.20) can be modified by replacing g with the expression on the right-hand side of equation (16.48b), resulting in

$$\begin{aligned} V &= D_0\left(\frac{1 + g}{k - g}\right) \\ &= D_0\left[\frac{1 + r(1 - p)}{k - r(1 - p)}\right] \end{aligned} \tag{16.49}$$

In terms of price-earnings ratios, the formula in equation (16.43) becomes:

$$\begin{aligned} \frac{V}{E_0} &= p\left(\frac{1 + g_e}{k - g_e}\right) \\ &= p\left[\frac{1 + r(1 - p)}{k - r(1 - p)}\right] \end{aligned} \tag{16.50}$$

Under these assumptions, a stock's price-earnings ratio should be greater, the greater its average return on equity for new investments, other things being equal.

☐ 16.7.1 An Example

Continuing with the Copper Company, recall that $E_0 = \$2.70$ and $p = 66\frac{2}{3}\%$. This means that $33\frac{1}{3}\%$ of earnings per share over the past year were retained and reinvested, an amount equal to $.3333 \times \$2.70 = \$.90$. The earnings per share in the forthcoming year (E_1) are expected to be $\$2.70(1 + .05) = \$2.835$, since the growth rate (g) for Copper is 5%. The source of the increase in earnings per share of $\$2.835 - \$2.70 = \$.135$ is the $\$.90$ per share that was reinvested at $t = 0$. The average return on equity for new investments (r) is 15%, since $\$.135/\$.90 = 15\%$. That is, the reinvested earnings of $\$.90$ per share can be viewed as having generated an annual increase in earnings per share of $\$.135$. This increase will occur not only at $t = 1$ but also at $t = 2, t = 3$, and so on. Equivalently, a $\$.90$ investment at $t = 0$ will generate a perpetual annual cash inflow of $\$.135$ beginning at $t = 1$.

Expected dividends at $t = 1$ can be calculated by multiplying the expected payout ratio (p) of $66\frac{2}{3}\%$ times the expected earnings per share (E_1) of $\$2.835$, or $.6667 \times \$2.835 = \$1.89$. It can also be calculated by multiplying 1 plus the growth rate (g) of 5% times the past amount of dividends per share (D_0) of $\$1.80$, or $1.05 \times \$1.80 = \$1.89$. It can be seen that the growth rate in dividends per share of 5% is equal to the product of the retention rate $(33\frac{1}{3}\%)$ and the average return on equity for new investments (15%), an amount equal to $.3333 \times .15 = 5\%$.

Two years from now $(t = 2)$, earnings per share are anticipated to be $\$2.835 \times (1 + .05) = \$2.977$, a further increase of $\$2.977 - \$2.835 = \$.142$ that is due to the retention and reinvestment of $.3333 \times \$2.835 = \$.945$ per share at $t = 1$. This expected increase in earnings per share of $\$.142$ is

FIGURE 16–2
Growth in earnings for Copper Company.

-1		0		1		2	
$+$		$+$		$+$		$+ \longrightarrow >\infty$	
$E_0 = \$2.70$			$\$2.700$		$\$2.700$	$\ldots$	
		$\$.90 \times .15 =$	$.135$		$.135$	$\ldots$	
		$E_1 =$	$\$2.835$	$\$.945 \times .15 =$	$.142$	$\ldots$	
				$E_2 =$	$\$2.977$	$\ldots$	
$I_0 = \$ .90$		$I_1 = \$ .945$		$I_2 = \$ .992$		$\ldots$	
$D_0 = 1.80$		$D_1 = 1.890$		$D_2 = 1.985$		$\ldots$	
$E_0 = \$2.70$		$E_1 = \$2.835$		$E_2 = \$2.977$		$\ldots$	

the result of earning 15% on the reinvested $.945, since .15 × $.945 = $.142. In summary, the expected earnings per share at $t = 2$ have three components. The first is the earnings attributable to the assets held at $t = 0$, an amount equal to $2.70. The second is the earnings attributable to the reinvestment of $.90 at $t = 0$, earning $.135. The third is the earnings attributable to the reinvestment of $.945 at $t = 1$, earning $.142. These three components, when summed, equal $E_2 = \$2.70 + \$.135 + \$.142 = \$2.977$. Dividends at $t = 2$ are expected to be 5% larger than at $t = 1$, or 1.05 × $1.89 = $1.985 per share. This amount corresponds to the amount calculated by multiplying the payout ratio times the expected earnings per share at $t = 2$, or .6667 × $2.977 = $1.985. Figure 16.2 summarizes the example.

16.8 A COMMONLY USED APPROACH

There are many ways that DDMs have been used in the investment community. One commonly used approach is based on the multiple-growth model and a view that companies typically evolve through three stages during their lifetime.[11] These stages are as follows.

Growth Stage. The growth stage is characterized by rapidly expanding sales, high profit margins, and abnormally high growth in earnings per share. Because the expected profitability of new investment opportunities is high, the payout ratio is generally low. The unusually high earnings enjoyed in this stage attracts competitors, leading to a gradual decline in the growth rate.

Transition Stage. In the later years of a company's life, increased product saturation begins to reduce its growth rate, and its profit margin comes under pressure. Since there are fewer new investment opportunities, the company begins to pay out a larger percentage of earnings.

Maturity Stage (or *Steady-State Stage*). Eventually, the company reaches a position where its new investment opportunities offer, on average, slightly attractive returns on equity. At that time, its earnings growth rate, payout ratio, and average return on equity stabilize for the remaining life of the company.[12]

Figure 16.3 portrays the stages. Note that the vertical scale is logarithmic, so that a straight line represents a constant rate of growth.

In applying the multiple-growth DDM, a security analyst must estimate a number of variables for each stock being evaluated. One method involves estimating values for the following variables:

---

[11] This approach is based on the work of Nicholas Molodovsky in "Common Stock Valuation," *Financial Analysts Journal* 20, no. 1 (March/April 1965):104–23. The specific version presented here is based on one that has been used by Merrill Lynch and is described in Carmine J. Grigoli, "Demystifying Dividend Discount Models," Merrill Lynch Quantitative Research, April 1982.

[12] Adapted from Grigoli, "Demystifying Dividend Discount Models."

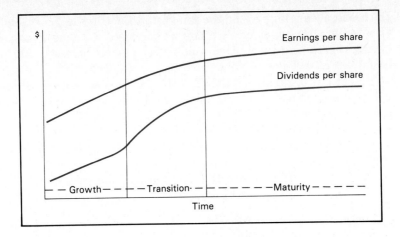

FIGURE 16–3
The three stages of the multiple-growth model.

SOURCE: Adapted from Carmine J. Grigoli, "Demystifying Dividend Discount Models," Merrill Lynch Quantitative Research, April 1982.

1. Expected earnings and dividends for the next five years.
2. The growth rate of earnings and the payout ratio for the start of the transition stage, which is assumed to be in year six.
3. The duration of the transition stage—that is, the number of years until the company reaches the maturity stage.
4. Growth patterns for earnings per share and the payout ratio during the transition stage.
5. The combination of an earnings growth rate and payout ratio that produces the desired average return on equity for new investments during the maturity stage.[13]

The following example shows just how the estimated values for these variables can be used to determine the intrinsic value of a share of stock.

☐ 16.8.1 An Example

Consider using this approach in analyzing the ABC Company on April 30, 1988. Over the past year, ABC has had earnings per share of $1.67 and dividends per share of $.40. After carefully studying ABC, the security analyst has made the following forecasts of earnings per share and dividends per share for the next five years;

$E_1 = \$2.67$ $E_2 = \$4.00$ $E_3 = \$6.00$ $E_4 = \$8.00$ $E_5 = \$10.00$

$D_1 = \$ .60$ $D_2 = \$1.60$ $D_3 = \$2.40$ $D_4 = \$3.20$ $D_5 = \$ 5.00$

---

[13] Adapted from Grigoli, "Demystifying Dividend Discount Models."

These forecasts imply the following payout ratios and earnings-per-share growth rates:

$$p_1 = 22\% \qquad p_2 = 40\% \qquad p_3 = 40\% \qquad p_4 = 40\% \qquad p_5 = 50\%$$

$$g_{e1} = 60\% \qquad g_{e2} = 50\% \qquad g_{e3} = 50\% \qquad g_{e4} = 33\% \qquad g_{e5} = 25\%$$

Furthermore, the analyst believes that ABC will enter the transition stage at the end of the fifth year (that is, the sixth year will be the first year of the transition stage) and that the transition stage will last three years. Earnings per share and the payout ratio for year 6 are forecast to be $E_6 = \$11.90$ and $p_6 = 55\%$ (thus, $g_{e6} = (\$11.90 - \$10.00)/\$10.00 = 19\%$ and $D_6 = .55 \times \$11.90 = \$6.55$).

The maturity stage is forecast to have an earnings per share growth rate of 4% and a payout ratio of 70%. It was shown in equation (16.48b) that with the constant growth model, $g = r(1 - p)$, where r is the average return on equity for new investments and p is the payout ratio. Since the maturity stage has constant growth, this equation can be reformulated and used to determine r:

$$r = \frac{g}{1 - p}. \qquad (16.51)$$

Thus, r for ABC has an implied value of $4\%/(100\% - 70\%) = 13.33\%$, which is assumed to be satisfactory.

At this point, there is only one missing piece of information that is needed to determine the value of ABC—the earnings per share growth rates and the payout ratios for the transition stage. Taking earnings per share first, it has been forecast that $g_{e6} = 19\%$ and that $g_{e9} = 4\%$. One method of determining how 19% will "decay" to 4% is to note that there are three years between the sixth and ninth years and that $19\% - 4\% = 15\%$. A linear decay rate can be determined by noting that $15\%/(3 \text{ years}) = 5\%$ per year. This rate of 5% is deducted from 19% to get g_{e7}, resulting in $19\% - 5\% = 14\%$. Then, it is deducted from 14% to get g_{e8}, resulting in $14\% - 5\% = 9\%$. Lastly, as a check, it can be noted that $9\% - 5\% = 4\%$, the value that was forecast for g_{e9}.

A similar procedure can be used to determine how the payout ratio of 55% in year 6 will grow to 70% in year 9. The linear growth rate is $(70\% - 55\%)/(3 \text{ years}) = 15\%/(3 \text{ years}) = 5\%$ per year, indicating $p_7 = 55\% + 5\% = 60\%$ and $p_8 = 60\% + 5\% = 65\%$. Again, a check indicates that $65\% + 5\% = 70\%$, the value that was forecast for p_9.

With these forecasts of earnings per share growth rates and payout ratios in hand, forecasts of dividends per share can now be made:

$$D_7 = p_7 E_7$$

$$= p_7 E_6 (1 + g_{e7})$$

$$= .60 \times \$11.90 \times (1 + .14)$$

$$= .60 \times \$13.57$$

$$= \$8.14$$

$$D_8 = p_8 E_8$$

$$= p_8 E_6 (1 + g_{e7})(1 + g_{e8})$$

$$= .65 \times \$11.90 \times (1 + .14) \times (1 + .09)$$

$$= .65 \times \$14.79$$

$$= \$9.61$$

$$D_9 = p_9 E_9$$

$$= p_9 E_6 (1 + g_{e7})(1 + g_{e8})(1 + g_{e9})$$

$$= .70 \times \$11.90 \times (1 + .14) \times (1 + .09) \times (1 + .04)$$

$$= .70 \times \$15.38$$

$$= \$10.76.$$

Given a required rate of return on ABC of 12.3%, it can be seen that all the necessary inputs for the multiple growth model have been determined. To begin, it can be seen that $T = 8$, indicating that V_{T-} involves determining the present value of D_1 through D_8:

$$V_{T-} = \frac{\$.60}{(1 + .123)^1} + \frac{\$1.60}{(1 + .123)^2} + \frac{\$2.40}{(1 + .123)^3} + \frac{\$3.20}{(1 + .123)^4}$$

$$+ \frac{\$5.00}{(1 + .123)^5} + \frac{\$6.55}{(1 + .123)^6} + \frac{\$8.14}{(1 + .123)^7} + \frac{\$9.61}{(1 + .123)^8}$$

$$= \$18.99.$$

Then, V_{T+} can be determined using D_9:

$$V_{T+} = \frac{\$10.76}{(.123 - .04)(1 + .123)^8}$$

$$= \$51.25.$$

Combining V_{T-} and V_{T+} results in the intrinsic value of ABC:

$$V = V_{T-} + V_{T+}$$

$$= \$18.99 + \$51.25$$

$$= \$70.24.$$

Given a current market price for ABC of \$50, it can be seen that its stock is underpriced by \$70.24 − \$50 = \$20.24 per share. Equivalently, it can be noted that the actual price-earnings ratio for ABC is \$50/\$1.67 = 29.9 but that a normal price-earnings ratio would be higher, equal to \$70.24/\$1.67 = 42.1, again indicating that ABC is underpriced.

□ 16.8.2 Implied Returns

As shown with the previous example, once the analyst has made certain forecasts, it is relatively straightforward to determine a company's expected dividends for each year up through the first year of the maturity stage. Then, the present value of these predicted dividends can be calculated for a given required rate of return. However, many investment firms use a computerized trial-and-error search procedure to determine the discount rate that equates the present value of the stock's expected dividends with its current price. Sometimes this long-run internal rate of return is referred to as the security's *implied return*. In the case of ABC, its implied return at the end of April 1988 is 14.8%.

□ 16.8.3 The Security Market Line

After implied returns have been estimated for a number of stocks, the associated beta for each stock can be estimated. Then, for all the stocks analyzed, this information can be plotted on a graph that has implied returns on the vertical axis and betas on the horizontal axis.

At this point, there are two methods for estimating the security market line (SML).[14] One method involves determining a line of best fit for this graph by using a statistical procedure known as simple regression. That is, the values of an intercept term and a slope term are determined from the data, thereby indicating the location of the straight line that best describes the relationship between implied returns and betas.

Figure 16.4 provides an example of the estimated SML at the end of April, 1988. In this case, the SML has been determined to have an intercept of 8% and a slope of 4%, indicating that, in general, securities with higher betas are expected to have higher implied returns in the forthcoming period. Depending on the sizes of the implied returns, such lines can have steeper or flatter slopes or even negative slopes.

The second method of estimating the SML involves calculating the implied return for a portfolio of common stocks. This is done by taking a value-weighted average of the implied returns of the stocks in the portfolio, with the resulting return being an estimate of the implied return on the market portfolio. Given this return and a beta of 1, the market portfolio can be plotted on a graph having implied returns on the vertical axis and betas on the horizontal axis. Next, the risk-free rate, having a beta of 0, can be plotted on the same graph. Finally, the SML is determined by simply connecting these two points with a straight line.

Either of these SMLs can be used to determine the required return on a stock. However, they will probably result in different numbers, since the two lines will probably have different intercepts and slopes. For example, note that the first method does not force the SML to go through the risk-

---

[14] There are numerous methods besides those described here. Some of them are based on more complicated versions of the CAPM, whereas others are based on APT (discussed in Chapter 9).

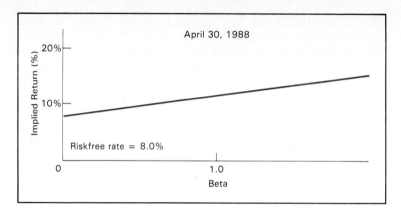

FIGURE 16–4
A security market line estimated from implied returns.

free rate, whereas the second method does. Which one is more accurate can ultimately be determined only by the performance obtained when decisions are based on one method versus that achievable with the other.

☐ 16.8.4 Required Returns and Alphas

Once a security's beta has been estimated, its required return can be determined from the estimated SML. For example, the equation for the SML on April 30, 1988 (shown in Figure 16.4), is:

$$k_i = 8 + 4\beta_i.$$

Thus, if ABC has an estimated beta of 1.1 at the end of April 1988, then it would have a required return equal to $8 + (4 \times 1.1) = 12.4\%$.

Once the required return on a stock has been determined, the difference between the stock's implied return (from the dividend discount model) and this required return can be calculated. This difference can then be viewed as an estimate of the stock's *alpha* and represents ". . . the degree to which a stock is mispriced. Positive alphas indicate undervalued securities and negative alphas indicate overvalued securities."[15] In the case of ABC, its implied and required returns at the end of April 1988 were 14.8% and 12.4%, respectively. Thus, its estimated alpha is $14.8\% - 12.4\% = 2.4\%$. Since this is a positive number, ABC can be viewed as being underpriced.

☐ 16.8.5 The Implied Return on the Stock Market

Another product of this analysis is that the implied return for the portfolio of stocks can be compared with expected returns on bonds. Specifically, the

---

[15] Carmine J. Grigoli, "Common Stock Valuation," Merrill Lynch Quantitative Analysis, May/June 1984. A subsequent procedure divides the estimated alpha by an estimate of the security's unique risk (that is, nonmarket or unsystematic risk) to obtain a *standardized alpha*. Then, based on the magnitude of the standardized alpha, the security is classified into one of ten *standardized alpha deciles*.

difference between the stock and bond returns can be used as an input for recommendations concerning asset allocation between stocks and bonds. That is, it can be used to form recommendations regarding what percentage of an investor's money should go into stocks and what percentage should go into bonds. Typically, the greater the implied return on stocks relative to bonds, the larger the percentage of the investor's money that should be placed in common stocks.

16.9   DIVIDEND DISCOUNT MODELS AND EXPECTED RETURNS

The procedures described here are similar to those employed by a number of brokerage firms and portfolio managers.[16] A security's implied return, obtained from a dividend discount model, is often treated as an expected return, which in turn can be divided into two components—the security's required return and alpha. However, the expected return on a stock over a given holding period may differ from its DDM-based implied rate, k^*. A simple set of examples will indicate why this difference can exist.

Assume that a security analyst predicts that a stock will pay a dividend of $1.10 per year forever. On the other hand, the consensus opinion of "the market" (most other investors) is that the dividend will equal $1.00 per year forever. This suggests that the analyst's prediction is a deviant, or nonconsensus, prediction.

Assume that both the analyst and other investors agree that the required rate of return for a stock of this type is 10%. Using the formula for the zero-growth model, the value of the stock is $D_1/.10 = 10D_1$, meaning the stock should sell for ten times its expected dividend. Since other investors expect to receive $1.00 per year, the stock has a current price (P) of $10 per share. The analyst feels the stock has a value of $1.10/.10 = $11 and thus feels it is underpriced by $11 − $10 = $1 per share.

In this situation, the implied return according to the analyst is $1.10/$10 = 11%. If the analyst buys a share now with a plan to sell it a year later, the rate of return the analyst might expect to earn depends on what assumptions are made regarding (1) the *accuracy of the prediction* and (2) the *rate of convergence of investors' predictions*.

The cases shown in Columns A and B of Table 16.1 assume that the analyst's prediction is correct—at the end of the year the stock does in fact pay the predicted dividend of $1.10. However, in column A, it is assumed that the other investors will regard the higher dividend as a fluke and steadfastly refuse to alter their projections of subsequent dividends from their initial estimate of $1.00. As a result, the security's price at $t = 1$ can be expected to remain at $10 ($1.00/.10). In this case, the analyst's total return is expected to be 11% ($1.10/$10), which is attributed entirely to dividends, since no capital gains are expected.

The 11% expected return can also be viewed as consisting of the required return of 10% plus an alpha of 1% that is equal to the portion of the dividend

---

[16] An example of a similar procedure that has been used by Wells Fargo Investment Advisors is described by George Foster in *Financial Statement Analysis* (Englewood Cliffs, N.J.: Prentice Hall, 1986):428–30.

TABLE 16.1
Predictive Accuracy and Convergence of Predictions.

	A	B	C	D
PREDICTIVE ACCURACY	100%	100%	50%	50%
EXPECTED AMOUNT OF CONVERGENCE	0%	100%	0%	100%
Actual dividend D_1	$ 1.10	$ 1.10	$ 1.05	$ 1.05
Dividend predictions D_2				
Consensus of other investors	1.00	1.10	1.00	1.05
Analyst	1.10	1.10	1.05	1.05
Stock price $P_1{}^a$	10.00	11.00	10.00	10.50
Performance:				
Dividend yield D_1/P	11%	11%	10.5%	10.5%
Capital gain $(P_1 - P)/P$	0	10	0.0	5.0
Total actual return	11%	21%	10.5%	15.5%
Less required return	10	10	10.0	10.0
Actual alpha	1%	11%	0.5%	5.5%

^{a} P_1 is equal to the consensus dividend prediction at $t = 1$ divided by the required return of 10%. The example assumes the current stock price P is $10, and dividends are forecast by the consensus at $t = 0$ to remain constant at $1.00 per share, whereas the analyst forecasts the dividends at $t = 0$ to remain constant at $1.10 per share.

unanticipated by the other investors, $.10/$10. Accordingly, if it is assumed that the analyst's prediction is perfect but there will be no convergence of predictions, then expected return would be set at the implied rate, 11%, and the alpha would be set at 1%.

Column B shows a very different situation. Here, it is assumed that the other investors will see the error of their ways and completely revise their predictions. At the end of the year, it is expected that they too will predict future dividends of $1.10 per year thereafter; thus, the stock is expected to be selling for $11 ($1.10/.10) at $t = 1$. Under these conditions, the analyst can expect to achieve a total return of 21% by selling the stock at the end of the year for $11, obtaining 11% ($1.10/$10) in dividend yield and 10% ($1/$10) in capital gains.

The 10% expected capital gains result directly from the expected repricing of the security due to the complete convergence of predictions. In this case, the fruits of the analyst's superior prediction are expected to be obtained all in one year. Instead of 1% extra per year forever, as in column A, the analyst expects to obtain 1% ($.10/$10) in extra dividend yield plus 10% ($1/$10) in capital gains this year. By continuing to hold the stock in subsequent years, the analyst would expect to earn only the required return of 10% over those years. Accordingly, if it is assumed that the analyst's prediction is perfect and there is complete convergence of predictions, the expected return would be set at 21% and the alpha would be set at 11%.

Unlike the cases in columns A and B, the cases in columns C and D do not assume that the analyst's prediction is perfect. Specifically, it is assumed that actual dividends exceed the consensus forecast of $1.00 by only $.05 instead of by $.10, the amount predicted by the analyst.

In the case shown in Column C, it is assumed that the other investors will regard the first year's dividend of $1.05 as a fluke and refuse to alter their predictions for subsequent years. As a result, the stock price at $t = 1$

will remain at $10, limiting the total actual return to 10.5%. Due to an overly optimistic deviant prediction, the alpha (0.5%) is less than the amount in column A (1%). Accordingly, if it is assumed that the analyst's deviant predictions are halfway accurate but there is no convergence of predictions, the expected return and the alpha would be set at 10.5% and .5%, respectively.

The case in Column D assumes that at year-end, both the analyst and other investors regard the actual dividend of $1.05 as permanent and revise their predictions for subsequent dividends accordingly. Here the two effects operate in different directions. Due to the overly optimistic prediction, the dividend yield will be 10.5%, which is less than the predicted 11%. But since the prediction was in the right direction, capital gains will be realized, as other investors revise their predictions in consideration of the actual results. In this case, the capital gains will more than offset the less-than-expected yield, providing a total return of 15.5% and an alpha of 5.5% that are substantially above the required return and expected alpha of 10% and 1%, respectively. Accordingly, if it is assumed that the analyst's predictions are halfway accurate and there will be complete convergence of predictions, the expected return and alpha would be set at 15.5% and 5.5%, respectively.

In other cases of this sort, the expected return could be more or less than the implied rate. Other things being equal, the expected return will be larger, the greater the assumed degree of predictive accuracy and the faster the assumed rate of convergence of predictions.[17]

Many investors use the implied rate (that is, the internal rate of return, k^*) as a surrogate for a relatively short-term (for example, one-year) expected return, as in column A. This could reflect an assumption of perfect predictive accuracy and no convergence of predictions. More likely, it reflects beliefs that (1) deviant predictions are less than perfectly accurate and (2) other investors will revise their predictions in the corresponding direction by a large-enough amount to provide capital gains that will offset any shortfall from the predicted dividend yield.

An alternative approach does not simply use outputs from a dividend discount model as is but *adjusts* them, based on relationships between previous predictions and actual outcomes. Parts (a) and (b) of Figure 16.5 provide examples.

Each point in Figure 16.5(a) plots a *predicted* return on the stock market (on the horizontal axis) and the subsequent *actual* return for that period (on the vertical axis). The line of best fit (determined by simple regression) through the points indicates the general relationship between prediction and outcome. If the current prediction is 14%, history suggests that an estimate of 15% would be superior.

Each point in Figure 16.5(b) plots a predicted alpha value for a security (on the horizontal axis) and the subsequent abnormal return for that period (on the vertical axis). Such a diagram can be made for all the securities about

---

[17] In a perfectly efficient market (in the semistrong-form sense), the expected degree of predictive accuracy for any analyst using public information would be zero. That is, these analysts would sometimes be right and sometimes be wrong, so that on balance their predictions would be of no value and the average actual alpha would be zero. In such a situation, the expected return for any security would be set at its required return and the expected alpha would be set at zero.

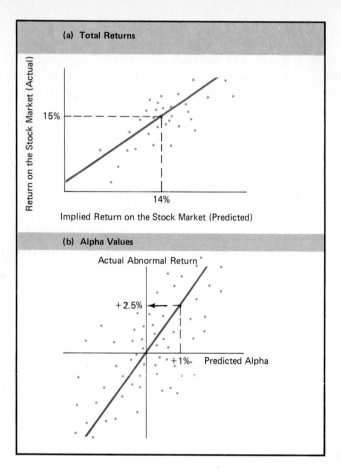

FIGURE 16–5
Adjusting predictions.

which a particular analyst makes predictions, or for all the securities about which the investment firm makes predictions. Again, a line of best fit can be drawn through the points. In this case, if the current prediction of a security's alpha is $+1\%$, this relationship suggests that an adjusted estimate of $+2.5\%$ would be superior.

An important byproduct of this type of analysis is the measure of correlation between predicted and actual outcomes, indicating the nearness of the points to the line. This can serve as a measure of predictive accuracy. If the correlation is too small to be significantly different from zero in a statistical sense, the value of the predictions is subject to considerable question.[18]

---

[18] The correlation coefficient is sometimes referred to as an *information coefficient* (IC). It has been argued that a value of .15 is indicative of good performance with regard to stock forecasting and that several different forecasters have recorded ICs of this magnitude (a value of zero would be expected in a perfectly efficient market). See Keith P. Ambachtsheer, "Profit Potential in an 'Almost Efficient' Market," *Journal of Portfolio Management* 1, no. 1 (Fall 1974):84–87 and "Where Are the Customers' Alphas?" *Journal of Portfolio Management* 4, no. 1 (Fall 1977):52–56; Keith P. Ambachtsheer and James L. Farrell, Jr., "Can Active Management Add Value?" *Financial Analysts Journal* 35, no. 6 (November–December 1979):39–47; and S. D. Hodges and R. A. Brealey, "Portfolio Selection in a Dynamic and Uncertain World," *Financial Analysts Journal* 29, no. 2 (March–April 1973):50–65.

One approach for conducting a search for mispriced securities involves the use of fundamental analysis. In its most basic form, fundamental analysis involves the use of a dividend discount model, where the security analyst forecasts the future stream of dividends on a given stock. After discounting these dividends to get their present value, the analyst is in a position to determine if the stock is mispriced. Specifically, if the current market price of the stock is less than the present value of its forecasted dividends, then the stock is underpriced; if it is more, then the stock is overpriced.

Alternatively, the analyst could determine the discount rate that makes the present value of the forecasted dividends equal to the current market price of the stock. If this rate is more than what is required for stocks of similar risk, then the stock is underpriced; if it is less, then the stock is overpriced.

If these discount rates are taken to be the expected returns on the stocks that have been analyzed, then an equation for the security market line can be estimated. In this situation, the estimated SML is an example of a cross-sectional valuation equation. The use of deviations of individual securities' expected returns from such an equation to identify mispriced securities assumes that deviant predictions have some accuracy. Unfortunately, deviations often persist, indicating that they may be due more to errors in dividend projections or to ignoring relevant factors in the valuation equation than to temporary mispricing. Perhaps more vexing is the fact that both the SML and the betas are likely to change over time. Consequently, the analyst must attempt to shoot at a moving target. That is, the analyst must estimate when and by how much the SML and individual betas will shift, a nearly impossible task.

This does not imply that "bottom-up" analysis of the type described here is useless. Quite the contrary. It provides estimates of the manner in which the market currently values securities, and this is essential information. Even if the deviations of the expected returns of individual securities from the forecasted SML reflect only predictive errors and are thus of no significance, the SML itself could be a good estimate of the current relationship between expected returns and betas and could justify the effort. And if the deviations indicate likely mispricing rather than errors in security analysis, the procedure could be even more valuable.

APPENDIX A
THE GRAHAM-REA MODEL

In 1934, a book that was to become the cornerstone of fundamental analysis was published by Benjamin Graham and David L. Dodd. This book, entitled *Security Analysis*, argued that the *future earnings power* of the firm was the

most important determinant of a stock's value.[19] However, in 1974 Graham himself repudiated the book and the principles contained in it.[20] Instead of following his old approach, Graham, along with James Rea, developed a new approach to identifying underpriced common stocks.[21] The reason for his change in attitude was his belief that the stock market was becoming more and more efficient and that only smaller and smaller pockets of inefficiencies were in existence. Since Graham and Rea believed these inefficiencies tended to be present in the stocks of certain identifiable firms, they developed a set of criteria to spot such stocks.

The Graham-Rea approach can be applied mechanically, since it involves examining the current financial statements of the firm under consideration and relating certain items from these statements to the firm's current stock price and the current yield on triple-A bonds. Ten questions that can be answered with a simple yes or no are involved. Table 16.2 lists them, indicating that the first five questions deal with "rewards" and second five questions deal with "risks." The idea behind these questions is to identify stocks that have the highest reward-to-risk ratio. In order for a stock to be recommended for purchase by Graham and Rea, it need not provide a yes answer to all of the questions.

The simplest way to use the questions is to first remove all stocks that do not provide a yes answer to question 6. Then, of the remaining stocks, remove those that do not provide a yes answer to either question 1, question 3, or question 5. The stocks that are left are candidates for purchase.

In determining when to sell, the Graham-Rea approach says that the investor should sell as soon as the stock has risen 50% or two years have passed since the stock was purchased, whichever occurs first. However, if neither of these two sell signals has occurred and the stock either stops paying dividends or no longer generates the appropriate yes answers to the questions, then it should be sold immediately.

How well has the Graham-Rea approach to investing worked? In a recent study of this approach that focused on New York Stock Exchange and American Stock Exchange securities, three observations were particularly interesting.[22] First, since the approach was publicized it was found that the number of stocks that provided the appropriate yes answers declined dramatically (for example, by 1980 yes answers to questions 1 and 6 occurred

---

[19] Graham and Dodd also argued that each dollar of dividends is worth four times as much as each dollar of retained earnings. Subsequent examination of market data indicates that argument has no support. See J. Ronald Hoffmeister and Edward A. Dyl, "Dividends and Share Value: Graham and Dodd Revisited," *Financial Analysts Journal* 41, no. 3 (May/June 1985):77–78; and Lewis D. Johnson, "Dividends and Share Value: Graham and Dodd Revisited, Again," *Financial Analysts Journal* 41, no. 5 (September/October 1985):79–80. For the most recent edition of the book, see Sidney Cottle, Roger F. Murray, and Frank E. Block, *Graham and Dodd's Security Analysis*, 5th ed. (New York: McGraw-Hill, Inc., 1988). For a brief discussion of their approach to investing, see Roger F. Murray, "Graham and Dodd: A Durable Discipline," *Financial Analysts Journal* 40, no. 5 (September/October 1984):18–23.

[20] See "A Conversation with Benjamin Graham," *Financial Analysts Journal* 32, no. 5 (September/October 1976):20–23.

[21] For a description of this approach, see Paul Blustein, "Ben Graham's Last Will and Testament," *Forbes* 1 August 1977, 43–45; and James B. Rea, "Remembering Benjamin Graham—Teacher and Friend," *Journal of Portfolio Management* 3, no. 4 (Summer 1977):66–72.

[22] Henry R. Oppenheimer, "A Test of Ben Graham's Stock Selection Criteria," *Financial Analysts Journal* 40, no. 5 (September/October 1984):68–74.

TABLE 16.2
Graham–Rea Stock Selection Questions.

A. Rewards:
1. Is the price-earnings ratio less than one-half the reciprocal of the triple-A bond yield? (For example, if the current triple-A rate is 12%, then the reciprocal is $8\frac{1}{3}$, and half of that is $4\frac{1}{6}$. Thus, for a stock to provide a yes answer to this question, its price-earnings ratio must be less than $4\frac{1}{6}$.)
2. Is the price-earnings ratio less than 40% of the highest average price-earnings ratio of the last five years? (Here, the average price-earnings for a stock for a given year is the average stock price for the year divided by the earnings per share for that year.)
3. Is the dividend yield at least two-thirds the triple-A bond yield?
4. Is the stock price below two-thirds of the tangible book value per share? (Here tangible book value per share is simply total assets less total debt, with the difference divided by the number of shares outstanding.)
5. Is the stock price below $\frac{2}{3}$ of the net current asset value per share? (Here net current asset value per share is current assets less total debt, with the difference divided by the number of shares outstanding.)

B. Risks:
6. Is the debt-to-equity ratio less than one? (Here the debt-to-equity ratio is simple total debt divided by total equity as shown on the balance sheet.)
7. Is the current ratio greater than two? (Here the current ratio is current assets divided by current liabilities.)
8. Is total debt less than twice the net current asset value? (Here net current asset value is current assets less total debt.)
9. Has the earnings per share growth rate of the last 10 years averaged at least 7% per year? (If the earnings per share over the last year is denoted by E_0 and the earnings per share over the year ending ten years ago is denoted by E_{-10}, then the growth rate is the value of g that solves the equation $E_0 = E_{-10}(1 + g)^{10}$. To provide a yes answer to this question, g must be least 7%.)
10. Over the time period examined in question 9, have eight or more of the annual growth rates in earnings per share been equal to -5% or more? (Here the ten annual growth rates in earnings per share would be calculated and then examined to see that no more than two of them were less than -5%.)

SOURCE: Adapted from Paul Blustein, "Ben Graham's Last Will and Testament," *Forbes* 1 August 1977, 43–45, and James B. Rea, "Remembering Benjamin Graham—Teacher and Friend," *Journal of Portfolio Management* 3, no. 4 (Summer 1977):66–72.

for only five securities). Second, the historical record suggests that positive abnormal returns would have been earned had this approach been used subsequent to its publication. Third, since many of the firms recommended for purchase were small firms, it is possible that all that this approach does is capture the size effect (that is, the small-firm effect that was discussed in the appendix to Chapter 15). However, the study found that even after adjusting for the size effect, the approach would still have earned positive abnormal returns since its publication.[23]

In closing, it should be noted that a number of professional portfolio managers currently follow the Graham-Rea approach to investing. Examples include the Rea-Graham Fund, LMH Fund, Sequoia Fund, and Pacific Partners Fund.

---

[23] A subsequent study focused on only one of the ten Graham-Rea questions, number 5 in Table 16.2. It found that portfolios consisting of securities that had yes answers to this question would have earned above-market returns. See Henry R. Oppenheimer, "Ben Graham's Net Current Asset Values: A Performance Update," *Financial Analysts Journal* 42, no. 6 (November/December 1986):40–47.

APPENDIX B
THE MULTIPLE-GROWTH MODEL
AND THE PRICE-EARNINGS MODEL

Earlier, it was noted that the most general dividend discount model was the multiple-growth model, where dividends were allowed to grow at varying rates until some point in time denoted T, after which they were assumed to grow at a constant rate. In this situation, the present value of all the dividends was found by adding the present value of all dividends up to and including T, denoted by V_{T-}, and the present value of all dividends after T, denoted by V_{T+}. Specifically, equation (16.27) stated that

$$V = V_{T-} + V_{T+}$$

$$= \sum_{t=1}^{T} \frac{D_t}{(1 + k)^t} + \frac{D_{T+1}}{(k - g)(1 + k)^T}.$$

In general, earnings per share in any period t can be expressed as being equal to E_0 times the product of all the growth rates from the time zero to time t:

$$E_t = E_0(1 + g_{e1})(1 + g_{e2}) \cdots (1 + g_{et}). \qquad (16.52)$$

Since the dividends per share in any period t are equal to the payout ratio times the earnings per share, it follows from equation (16.52) that

$$D_t = p_t E_t \qquad (16.53)$$

$$= p_t E_0(1 + g_{e1})(1 + g_{e2}) \cdots (1 + g_{et})$$

This allows the following expression for V_{T-}:

$$V_{T-} = \frac{p_1 E_0(1 + g_{e1})}{(1 + k)^1} + \frac{p_2 E_0(1 + g_{e1})(1 + g_{e2})}{(1 + k)^2} + \cdots$$

$$+ \frac{p_T E_0(1 + g_{e1})(1 + g_{e2}) \cdots (1 + g_{eT})}{(1 + k)^T}. \qquad (16.54)$$

Similarly, the expression for V_{T+} is

$$V_{T+} = \frac{p E_0(1 + g_{e1})(1 + g_{e2}) \cdots (1 + g_{eT})(1 + g)}{(k - g)(1 + k)^T}. \qquad (16.55)$$

Adding V_{T-} and V_{T+} together and then dividing by E_0 gives the following formula for determining a stock's normal price-earnings ratio with the multiple-growth model:

$$\frac{V}{E_0} = \frac{p_1(1 + g_{e1})}{(1 + k)^1} + \frac{p_2(1 + g_{e1})(1 + g_{e2})}{(1 + k)^2} + \cdots$$

$$+ \frac{p_T(1 + g_{e1})(1 + g_{e2}) \cdots (1 + g_{eT})}{(1 + k)^T} \qquad (16.56)$$

$$+ \frac{p(1 + g_{e1})(1 + g_{e2}) \cdots (1 + g_{eT})(1 + g)}{(k - g)(1 + k)^T}$$

As an example, consider the Magnesium Company again. Its share price is currently $55, and over the past year, earnings per share and dividends per share were $3 and $.75, respectively. For the next two years, forecasted earnings and dividends, along with the earnings growth rates and payout ratios, are as follows:

$$D_1 = \$2.00 \qquad E_1 = \$5.00 \qquad g_{e1} = 67\% \qquad p_1 = 40\%$$

$$D_2 = \$3.00 \qquad E_2 = \$6.00 \qquad g_{e2} = 20\% \qquad p_2 = 50\%.$$

Constant growth in dividends and earnings of 10% is forecast to begin at $T = 2$, meaning that $D_3 = \$3.30$, $E_3 = \$6.60$, $g = 10\%$, and $p = 50\%$.

Given a required return is 15%, equation (16.56) can be used to calculate the normal price-earnings ratio for Magnesium as follows:

$$\frac{V}{E_0} = \frac{.40(1 + .67)}{(1 + .15)^1} + \frac{.50(1 + .67)(1 + .20)}{(1 + .15)^2} + \frac{.50(1 + .67)(1 + .20)(1 + .10)}{(.15 - .10)(1 + .15)^2}$$

$$= .58 + .76 + 16.63$$

$$= 17.97.$$

Since the actual price-earnings ratio of $55/$3 = 18.33 is close to the normal price-earnings ratio of 17.97, the stock of the Magnesium Company can be viewed as fairly valued.[24]

QUESTIONS AND PROBLEMS

1. Sacramento Products currently pays a dividend of $3.00 per share on its common stock.
   a. If Sacramento Products plans to increase its dividend at a rate of 5% per year indefinitely, what will be the dividend per share in 10 years?
   b. If Sacramento Products' dividend per share is expected to be $4.20 per share at the end of five years, at what annual rate is the dividend expected to grow?
2. Jackson Information Services currently pays a dividend of $5.00 per share on its common stock. The dividend is expected to grow at 4% per year forever. Stocks with similar risk currently are priced to provide a 12% expected return. What is the intrinsic value of Jackson stock?
3. Select a stock whose name begins with the first letter of your last name. From the *Value Line Investment Survey* find the average annual compounded growth rate in the stock's dividend over the last five years. Assume that this growth rate will continue indefinitely. Also from the *Value Line Investment Survey* find the beta of the stock. Assuming a riskfree rate of return of 7% and a market expected return of 15%, calculate the SML and the required return on the stock. Finally, using the dividend growth rate and required return, calculate the intrinsic value of the stock. (*Note*: If the data for your stock is incompatible with the constant growth DDM, select another stock.) Compare this intrinsic value to the latest closing price for the stock. Is the

---

[24] Earlier, it was noted that the intrinsic value of Magnesium was $53.92. Since E_0 for Magnesium was $3, it can be verified that the normal price-earnings ratio is 17.97 by noting that $53.92/$3 = 17.97.

stock underpriced or overpriced? What potential problems are involved with this approach to making investment decisions?

4. The constant growth model is an overly simplistic means of valuing most corporations' stocks. However, a number of market analysts believe it is a useful means of estimating a fair value for the stock market as a whole. Why might the constant growth DDM be a more reasonable valuation tool for the market in aggregate as opposed to individual stocks?

5. Salem Air Cleaners Inc. currently pays a dividend on its stock of $6 per share. Next year the dividend is expected to remain constant and then increase to $7 the year after. From that point on, the dividend is expected to grow at $3 per year indefinitely. Stocks with similar risk are currently priced to provide a 10% expected return. What is the intrinsic value of Salem's stock?

6. Chief Medical Inc. is a little known producer of heart pacemakers. The earnings and dividend growth prospects of the company are disputed by analysts. Albert Bender is forecasting 5% growth in dividends indefinitely. However, his brother John is predicting a 20% growth in dividends, but only for the next three years, after which the growth rate is expected to decline to 4% for the indefinite future. Chief dividends per share are currently $3.00. Stocks with similar risk are currently priced to provide a 14% expected return.

   a. What is the intrinsic value of Chief stock according to Albert?

   b. What is the intrinsic value of Chief stock according to John?

   c. Assume that Chief stock now sells for $39¾ per share. If the stock is fairly priced at the present time, what is the implied perpetual dividend growth rate? What is the implied P/E (price-earnings ratio) on next year's earnings, based on this perpetual dividend growth assumption and assuming a 25% payout ratio?

7. Lansing Technologies, a publicly held venture capital investment firm, is currently paying a dividend of $2 per share on earnings of $4 per share. Its stock is selling for $200 per share. Stocks of similar risk are priced to return 15%. What kind of return on equity could explain investors' willingness to pay a price equal to 50 times earnings on this stock?

8. Olympia Corp. is expected to pay out 40% of its earnings and to earn an average of 15% per year on its incremental reinvested earnings forever. Stocks with similar risk are currently priced to provide a 12% expected return. By what percentage can Olympia's earnings be expected to grow each year? What is an appropriate price-earnings multiple for the stock? What portion of the return on Olympia stock is expected to come from capital gains? From dividend yield?

9. A three-stage DDM has become a very popular common stock valuation model. It is used by a number of institutional investors and brokerage firms. What advantages does it offer relative to a simple constant growth DDM? Despite its increased sophistication compared to the constant growth DDM, what disadvantages does it still retain?

10. Fay Thomas, a financial analyst, once remarked: "Even if your dividend estimates and discount rate assumption are correct, dividend discount models identify stocks that will produce positive alphas only if other investors eventually come to agree with the DDM's valuation conclusions." Is this statement correct? Why or why not?

11. Some people assert that a "true" growth company is one whose dividends grow at a rate greater than its required rate of return. Why is the constant growth DDM incapable of valuing such a "true" growth stock?

12. What explanations can you offer for the fact that the Security Market Line shown in Figure 16.4 is so flat?

Chapter 17

EARNINGS

Chapter 16 discussed how the intrinsic value of a share of common stock could be determined by discounting expected dividends per share at a rate of return that was appropriate for a security of similar risk. Alternatively, the implied return on a share of common stock could be determined by finding the discount rate that makes the present value of all the expected dividends equal to the current market price of the stock. In either case, a forecast of dividends per share is necessary. Since dividends per share are equal to earnings per share times a payout ratio, dividends can be forecast by forecasting earnings per share and payout ratios.

Currently, there are numerous methods used by security analysts for forecasting either earnings or dividends. This chapter presents a discussion of some of the important features of dividends and earnings of which the analyst should be aware in making such forecasts. The chapter begins with a discussion of the relationship between earnings, dividends, and investment.

17.1 STOCK VALUATION BASED ON EARNINGS

A continual controversy in the investment community concerns the relevance of dividends versus earnings as the underlying source of value of a share of common stock. Clearly, earnings are important to stockholders because earnings provide the cash flow necessary for paying dividends. However, dividends are also important because dividends are what stockholders actually receive from the firm and are the focus of the dividend discount models discussed in Chapter 16. Indeed, it would seem that if management increased the proportion of earnings per share paid out as dividends, they could make their stockholders wealthier, suggesting that the *dividend decision* (deciding on the amount of dividends to pay) is a very important one.

Ultimately, this controversy was resolved in 1961 when Merton Miller and Franco Modigliani published a seminal paper showing that the underlying source of value of a share of common stock was earnings, not dividends.[1] An implication is that the dividend decision is relatively unimportant to the

---

[1] Merton H. Miller and Franco Modigliani, "Dividend Policy, Growth, and the Valuation of Shares," *Journal of Business* 34, no. 4 (October 1961):411–33.

stockholders, since it will not affect the value of their investment in the firm.

In the course of a year, a firm generates revenues and incurs costs. With cash accounting, the difference between revenues and costs is called cash flow. With accrual accounting, used by almost all firms, both revenues and costs are likely to include estimates made by accountants of the values of noncash items. Items such as depreciation charges are deducted from cash flow to obtain earnings. Moreover, each year some amount is invested in the business. Of the total (gross) investment, a portion is equal in value to the estimated depreciation of various real assets (like machines and buildings); the rest is new (net) investment.

The dollar amount of new investment each year should be based on the investment opportunities available to the firm and should be unaffected by the dollar amount of dividends that has been paid out. In particular, any investment opportunity whose net present value (NPV) is positive should be undertaken. This means that the future prospects of the firm can be described by a stream of expected earnings $(E_1, E_2, E_3, \ldots)$ and the expected net investment required to produce such earnings $(I_1, I_2, I_3, \ldots)$. Taking these two streams as given, it can be shown that management can set the total dollar amount of current dividends (D_0) at any level without making the current stockholders either better or worse off.[2] This is done next, with the focus on earnings and how they can be used to pay for new investments and dividends.

☐ 17.1.1 Earnings, Dividends, and Investment

Figure 17.1(a) shows one way that the firm can use total earnings for the current year (E_0). In this situation, new investment (I_0) is financed out of earnings, and the firm uses the remainder of the earnings to pay dividends (D_0) to its stockholders. For example, if the Plum Company has just earned $5000 and has new investments it would like to make that cost $3000, then Plum could pay for these investments out of earnings and declare a dividend of $2000.

Although earnings are exactly equal to dividends and investment $(E_0 = D_0 + I_0)$, as in Figure 17.1(a), this need not be the case. In the situation shown in Figure 17.1(b), earnings are less than dividends and investment $(E_0 < D_0 + I_0)$. Since the amount of investment has been determined by the number of positive NPV projects that the firm has, this inequality occurs because the firm has decided to pay its current stockholders a higher dividend than was given in Figure 17.1(a). However, in order for higher dividends to be paid, additional funds must be obtained from outside the firm. This is accomplished by a new sale of common stock (it is assumed that the flotation costs associated with a new sale of common stock are negligible).

The funds are obtained through a new sale of common stock instead

---

[2] Here, the quantities of earnings (E_t), new investment (I_t), and dividends (D_t) are measured for the firm on an aggregate basis, not a per-share basis. Note that dividends cannot be set at an arbitrary high value relative to earnings (for example, earnings of $10 million and dividends of $100 million), since the firm would then be unable to get the necessary funds to pay the dividends.

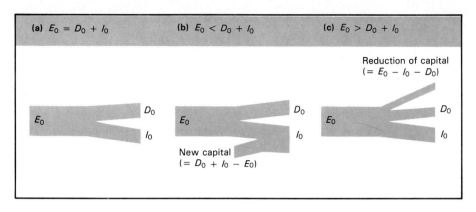

(a) $E_0 = D_0 + I_0$ (b) $E_0 < D_0 + I_0$ (c) $E_0 > D_0 + I_0$

Reduction of capital
$(= E_0 - I_0 - D_0)$

E_0 D_0 I_0 E_0 D_0 I_0 E_0 D_0 I_0

New capital
$(= D_0 + I_0 - E_0)$

FIGURE 17–1
Earnings, dividends, and investment.

of through a new sale of debt because of a desire to avoid the confounding effects of a change in the firm's debt-equity ratio. That is, if debt financing is to be allowed, then two things would be changing at the same time—the amount of the dividend and the debt-equity ratio for the firm. As a result, if stockholders appear to be made better off by a change in the amount of the dividend, their betterment may actually be due to a change in the debt-equity ratio. By prohibiting debt financing, the debt-equity ratio will remain constant and only the amount of the dividend will be allowed to change. Thus, if stockholders appear to be better off, it has to be due to the change in the amount of the dividend, since everything else (specifically, the amount of investment and the debt-equity ratio) has remained fixed.

Note that if investment is financed out of earnings, as in Figure 17.1(a), then it has been financed with equity, obtained internally. In Figure 17.1(b), investment has also been financed with equity, but here the equity has been obtained externally. As a result, the debt-equity ratio for the firm is the same in both situations.

In the case of Plum, instead of paying dividends amounting to $2000, the firm could decide to pay dividends amounting to $3000. Since investment is equal to $3000, Plum will have a cash outflow of $3000 + $3000 = $6000 with earnings amounting to only $5000. This means that Plum will have to sell $6000 − $5000 = $1000 of new common stock.

In Figure 17.1(c), the situation is reversed from 17.1(b), since earnings are now greater than dividends and investment ($E_0 > D_0 + I_0$). Given that the amount of investment has been determined by the number of positive NPV projects that the firm has, this inequality occurs because the firm has decided to pay its stockholders a lower dividend than was given in Figure 16.1(a). In paying this smaller dividend, the firm will be left with excess cash. It is assumed that the firm will use this cash to repurchase some of its outstanding shares in the marketplace (and that the transactions costs associated with such repurchases are negligible).

This last assumption is made due to the desire to keep the situation comparable to the two earlier ones. Allowing the firm to keep the excess

cash would be tantamount to letting the firm invest the cash, an investment decision that was not made in the two earlier cases and, therefore, does not have a positive NPV (remember that I_0 consists of all positive NPV projects). Allowing the firm to keep the excess cash would also mean that the firm has made a decision to lower its debt-equity ratio because retention of the excess cash would increase the amount of equity for the firm, thereby decreasing the amount of debt outstanding relative to the amount of equity.

Continuing with the Plum Company, dividends could be set at $1000 instead of $2000 or $3000. In this case, the firm would have a cash outflow for dividends and investment amounting to $1000 + $3000 = $4000. With earnings of $5000, this means that there will be $5000 − $4000 = $1000 of cash left for the firm to use to repurchase its own stock.

Thus, the firm has a decision to make regarding the size of its current dividends. The amount of current earnings E_0 and the amount of new investment I_0 have been determined. What is left to be decided is the amount of dividends, D_0. They can be set equal to earnings less investment (as in Figure 17.1(a)), greater than this amount (as in Figure 17.1(b)), or less than this amount (as in Figure 17.1(c)). The question that remains to be answered is, Will one of these three levels of dividends make the current stockholders better off than the other two? That is, which level of dividends—$1000, $2000, or $3000—will make the current stockholders better off?

The simplest way to answer this question is to consider a stockholder who presently holds 1% of the common stock of the firm and is determined to maintain this percentage ownership in the future.[3] If the firm follows a dividend policy as shown in Figure 17.1(a), the stockholder's current dividends will equal $.01D_0$, or, equivalently, $.01(E_0 − I_0)$. Similarly, the stockholder's future dividends will equal $.01D_t$, or $.01(E_t − I_t)$.

If the firm follows a dividend policy as shown in Figure 17.1(b), however, the stockholder must invest additional funds in the firm's common stock in order to avoid a diminished proportional ownership position in the firm. This investment is necessary because in this situation the firm must raise funds by selling additional shares in order to pay for the larger cash dividends. Since $E_0 < D_0 + I_0$, the total amount of funds that the firm needs to raise is the amount F_0, such that

$$E_0 + F_0 = D_0 + I_0 \qquad (17.1)$$

or

$$F_0 = D_0 + I_0 − E_0. \qquad (17.2)$$

The amount of the additional investment that the stockholder needs to make in order to maintain a 1% position in the firm is $.01F_0$, which from equation (17.2) is equal to $.01(D_0 + I_0 − E_0)$. Since the stockholder receives 1% of the dividends, the net amount the stockholder receives at time zero is equal to $.01D_0 − .01F_0$, or

$$.01D_0 − .01(D_0 + I_0 − E_0) = .01E_0 − .01I_0. \qquad (17.3)$$

---

[3] The use of such a stockholder is for ease of exposition; the same answer would be obtained if other types of stockholders (such as those who are not interested in maintaining a proportional ownership position in the firm in the future) are considered.

Interestingly, the net amount the stockholder receives, $.01E_0 - .01I_0$, is the same as in the first situation. This is because the amount of the extra cash dividend received is exactly offset by the amount the stockholder needs to spend to maintain his or her position of ownership in the firm.

If the firm follows a dividend policy as shown in Figure 17.1(c), then the firm will be repurchasing shares. Accordingly, the stockholder must sell some shares back to the firm in order to avoid having an increased ownership position in the firm. Since $E_0 > D_0 + I_0$, the total amount of funds that the firm will spend on repurchasing its own shares is the amount R_0, such that

$$E_0 = D_0 + I_0 + R_0 \qquad (17.4)$$

or

$$R_0 = E_0 - D_0 - I_0. \qquad (17.5)$$

The amount of stock that the stockholder needs to sell back to the firm to maintain a 1% position in the firm is $.01R_0$, which from equation (17.5) is equal to $.01(E_0 - D_0 - I_0)$. Since the stockholder receives 1% of the dividends, the total amount the stockholder receives at time zero is equal to $.01D_0 + .01R_0$, or

$$.01D_0 + .01(E_0 - D_0 - I_0) = .01E_0 - .01 I_0. \qquad (17.6)$$

Again, this amount, $.01E_0 - .01I_0$, is the same as in the first situation. That is, in the third situation, the smaller amount of the cash dividend received by the stockholder is exactly made up for by the amount of cash received from the repurchase of shares by the firm.

Thus, no matter what the firm's dividend policy, a stockholder choosing to maintain a constant proportional ownership will be able to spend the same amount of money on consumption at time zero. This amount will be equal to the proportion times the quantity $E_0 - I_0$. Furthermore, this will also be true in the future. That is, in any year t the stockholder will be able to spend on consumption an amount that is equal to the proportion times the quantity $E_t - I_t$.

☐ 17.1.2 Earnings Determine Market Value

In determining the value of 1% of the current shares outstanding, remember that the firm is about to declare and pay current dividends. Regardless of the magnitude of these dividends, the stockholder will be able to spend on consumption an amount equal to only $.01(E_0 - I_0)$. Furthermore, the stockholder will be able to spend on consumption an amount equal to $.01(E_t - I_t)$ in any future year t. Discounting these expected amounts by a (constant) rate k reveals that the value of 1% of the current shares outstanding will be

$$.01V = \frac{.01(E_0 - I_0)}{(1 + k)^0} + \frac{.01(E_1 - I_1)}{(1 + k)^1} + \frac{.01(E_2 - I_2)}{(1 + k)^2} + \cdots .$$

Multiplying both sides of this equation by 100 results in the following expression for the total market value of all shares outstanding:

$$V = \frac{(E_0 - I_0)}{(1 + k)^0} + \frac{(E_1 - I_1)}{(1 + k)^1} + \frac{(E_2 - I_2)}{(1 + k)^2} + \cdots. \qquad (17.7)$$

Equation (17.7) shows that the aggregate market value of equity is equal to the present value of expected earnings net of required investment. Note how the size of the dividends does not enter into the formula. This indicates that the market value of the stock is independent of the dividend decision made by the firm. Instead, the market value of the firm is related to the earnings prospects of the firm, along with the required amounts of new investment needed to produce those earnings.[4]

There is nothing inconsistent between the dividend discount models presented in Chapter 16 and the irrelevance of the dividend decision. The dividend discount models indicated that the value of one share of common stock was equal to the present value of all the dividends expected in the future. The dividend irrelevance argument suggests that if the firm decides to increase its current dividend, then new shares will need to be sold. This, in turn, suggests that future dividends will be smaller, since the aggregate amount of dividends will have to be divided among an increased number of shares outstanding. Ultimately, the current stockholders will be neither better nor worse off, since the increased current dividend will be exactly offset by the decreased future dividends. Conversely, if the firm decides to decrease its current dividend, then shares will be repurchased and future dividends will be increased due to the fewer shares outstanding. Ultimately, the decreased current dividend will be exactly offset by the increased future dividends, again leaving current stockholders neither better nor worse off.

All this can be illustrated with the earlier example of the Plum Company. Since Plum currently has reported earnings of $5000 and investments totaling $3000, if dividends amounting to $2000 were paid, then the stockholder owning 1% of the firm would receive cash amounting to .01 × $2000 = $200.

Alternatively, if dividends amounting to $3000 were paid, then Plum would have to raise $1000 from the sale of new common stock. The stockholder would receive .01 × $3000 = $300 in dividends but would have to pay .01 × $1000 = $100 to purchase 1% of the new stock, thereby maintaining his or her 1% position of ownership. Consequently, the net cash flow to the stockholder would be $300 − $100 = $200, the same amount as in the previous situation.

Lastly, if dividends amounting to $1000 were paid, then Plum would have cash amounting to $1000 to use to repurchase common stock. The

[4] It has been argued that if the tax rate on dividends is greater than the tax rate on capital gains, then stockholders will earn more on an after-tax basis if the firm has a relatively low payout ratio. An additional benefit to stockholders if the firm has a low payout ratio is that capital gains taxes are paid only when the stock is sold and can therefore be deferred. Thus, it appears that stockholders are better off if the firm has a relatively low payout ratio. However, with the Tax Reform Act of 1986, the tax rate on dividends is equal to the tax rate on capital gains, making it largely academic whether or not such an argument is valid. For a more detailed discussion of the issue, along with the relevant citations, see pp. 128–35 of Gordon J. Alexander and Jack Clark Francis, *Portfolio Analysis* (Englewood Cliffs, N.J.: Prentice Hall, 1986).

stockholder, desirous of maintaining a 1% position, would thus sell shares amounting to .01 × $1000 = $100. As a result, the stockholder would have a cash inflow totaling $100 + $100 = $200, again the same amount as in the two previous situations.

Under all three situations, the 1% stockholder would receive the same cash flow at the present time ($200) and have the same claim on the future earnings of Plum. That is, in all three cases, the stockholder would still own 1% of Plum and would therefore receive the same amount of dividends in the future. Accordingly, the 1% stockholder (and all the others) will be neither better nor worse off if Plum pays a dividend amounting to $1000, $2000, or $3000. In summary, the dividend decision is a nonevent—whatever the level of dividends, current stockholders will be neither better nor worse off.

17.2 DETERMINANTS OF DIVIDENDS

Few firms attempt to maintain a constant ratio of dividends to current earnings, since doing so would result in a fluctuating dollar amount of dividends. Dividends would fluctuate because earnings on a year-to-year basis are likely to be quite variable. Instead, firms attempt to maintain a desired ratio of dividends to earnings over some relatively long period, meaning that there is a target payout ratio of dividends to long-run, or sustainable, earnings. As a result, dividends are usually kept at a constant dollar amount and are increased only when management is confident it will be relatively easy to keep paying this increased amount in the future.[5] Nonetheless, larger earnings are likely to be accompanied by some sort of increase in dividends, as Table 17.1 shows.

The first two lines of this table indicate that of the firms examined, 59.3% of the time their earnings rose and the remainder of the time (40.7%

TABLE 17.1

Dividend and Earnings Changes for 392 Major Industrial Firms, 1946–1964.

EARNINGS CHANGES			PERCENT OF CASES IN WHICH FIRMS		
Current Year	Previous Year	Percent of Cases	Increased Dividends	Did Not Change Dividends	Decreased Dividends
+		59.3%	65.8%	13.9%	20.3%
−		40.7	42.8	17.9	39.5
+	+	33.4	74.8	11.4	13.8
+	−	25.9	54.1	17.2	28.7
−	+	24.7	49.7	16.9	33.4
−	−	16.0	31.8	19.4	48.8

SOURCE: Eugene F. Fama and Harvey Babiak, "Dividend Policy: An Empirical Analysis," *Journal of the American Statistical Association* 63, no. 324 (December 1969):1134.

---

[5] In addition to a regular dividend, sometimes a firm will declare a "special," or "extra," dividend, usually at year-end. By calling it a special dividend, the firm is conveying a message to its stockholders that such a dividend is a one-time event.

= 100% − 59.3%) their earnings fell. The majority of the time when current earnings rose, firms increased their current dividends. However, whenever current earnings fell, firms would increase their current dividends as frequently as they would decrease their current dividends (note that, roughly speaking, 42.8% ≈ 39.5%).

The next two lines of the table suggest that firms are more likely to increase current dividends if they have had two consecutive years of rising earnings than if they have had falling and then rising earnings (74.8% > 54.1%). The last two lines of the table suggest that firms are more likely to decrease current dividends if they have had two consecutive years of falling earnings than if they have had rising and then falling earnings (48.8% > 33.4%). Overall, the table shows that firms in general are more likely to increase dividends than to decrease them.

A formal representation of the kind of behavior implied by a constant long-run target payout ratio begins by assuming that the goal of the firm is to pay out p^* (for example, $p^* = 60\%$) of long-run earnings.[6] If this target ratio were maintained every year, total dividends paid in year t would be

$$D_t^* = p^*E_t \qquad (17.8)$$

where D_t^* denotes the target amount for dividends to be paid in year t and E_t is the amount of earnings in year t. The difference between target dividends in year t and the previous year's actual dividends is determined by subtracting D_{t-1} from both sides of equation (17.8), resulting in

$$D_t^* - D_{t-1} = p^*E_t - D_{t-1}. \qquad (17.9)$$

Although firms would like to change their dividends from D_{t-1} to D_t^*, few (if any) firms would actually change their dividends by this amount. Instead, the actual change in dividends is a proportion of the desired change:

$$D_t - D_{t-1} = a(D_t^* - D_{t-1}) \qquad (17.10)$$

where a is a "speed of adjustment" coefficient, a number between 0 and 1.

For example, if a firm has just earned $5 million ($E_t = \$5$ million) and has a target payout ratio of 60%, then it would like to pay dividends amounting to $.6 \times \$5$ million = $3 million. Assuming it paid dividends of $2 million dollars last year, this represents an increase of $3 million − $2 million = $1 million. However, if $a = 50\%$, then the firm will actually increase the dividends by $.5 \times \$1$ million = $500,000. Thus, actual dividends will be equal to $2.5 million = $2 million + $500,000, an amount equal to last year's dividends plus the change in dividends from last year to this year.

This model can be summarized by substituting p^*E_t for D_t^* in equation (17.10) and then solving the resulting expression for D_t:

$$D_t = ap^*E_t + (1 - a)D_{t-1}. \qquad (17.11)$$

---

[6] See John Lintner, "Distribution of Incomes of Corporations Among Dividends, Retained Earnings, and Taxes," *American Economic Review* 46, no. 2 (May 1956):97–113. A similar model that used lagged stock prices instead of contemporaneous accounting earnings was able to perform on a par with Lintner's earnings model. See Terry A. Marsh and Robert C. Merton, "Dividend Behavior for the Aggregate Stock Market," *Journal of Business* 60, no. 1 (January 1987): 1–40.

TABLE 17.2

Target Payout Ratios and Speed of Dividend Adjustment
Factors for 298 Firms, 1946–1968.

SPEED OF ADJUSTMENT COEFFICIENT		TARGET PAYOUT RATIO		PERCENT OF VARIANCE EXPLAINED	
Value	Percent of Firms with Smaller Value	Value	Percent of Firms with Smaller Value	Value	Percent of Firms with Smaller Value
.104	10%	.401	10%	11%	10%
.182	30	.525	30	32	30
.251	50	.584	50	42	50
.339	70	.660	70	54	70
.470	90	.779	90	72	90
average .269		average .591		average 42	

SOURCE: Eugene F. Fama, "The Empirical Relationship Between the Dividend and Investment Decisions of Firms," *American Economic Review* 64, no. 3 (June 1974):310.

Equation (17.11) indicates that the amount of current dividends is based on the amount of current earnings and the amount of the previous year's dividends.[7] In the previous example, $a = 50\%$, $p^* = 60\%$, $E_t = \$5$ million, and $D_{t-1} = \$2$ million. Thus, actual dividends D_t would be equal to $(.5 \times .6 \times \$5 \text{ million}) + [(1 - .5) \times \$2 \text{ million}] = \$2.5$ million.

By subtracting D_{t-1} from both sides of equation (17.11), it can be seen that the change in dividends is equal to:

$$D_t - D_{t-1} = ap^*E_t - aD_{t-1}. \qquad (17.12)$$

When written in this form, the model suggests that the size of the change in dividends will be positively related to the current amount of earnings (since ap^* is a positive number) and negatively related to the amount of the previous period's dividends (since $-aD_{t-1}$ is a negative number). Thus, the larger the current earnings are, the larger the change in dividends, but the larger the previous period's dividends, the smaller the change in dividends.

Statistical analysis has been used to see how well this model describes the way a sample of firms set the amount of their dividends. Table 17.2 summarizes some of the values obtained in one such study. The average firm had a target payout ratio of 59.1% and adjusted dividends by 26.9% of the way toward its target each year. However, most firms' dividends varied substantially from the pattern implied by their targets and adjustment factors. Somewhat less than half (42%) of the annual variance in the typical

---

[7] Looking backward in time, it can be shown that current dividends D_t are a linear function of past earnings E_{t-1}, E_{t-2}, E_{t-3}, and so on. More specifically, it can be shown that:

$$D_t = ap^*[(1 - a)^0E_t + (1 - a)^1E_{t-1} + (1 - a)^2E_{t-2} + (1 - a)^3E_{t-3} + \cdots].$$

Since the quantity $(1 - a)$ is a positive fraction (for example, $\frac{1}{3}$), when it is raised to a power it becomes smaller in value, with larger powers resulting in values closer to zero. Thus, current dividends depend more on recent past earnings than on distant past earnings, and the equation can be approximated by using an arbitrary number of past earnings (the accuracy of the approximation depends on the number used.)

firm's dividends could be explained in this manner. This means that the model, while having explained a portion of the changes in dividends that have occurred, has left a substantial portion unexplained.

17.3 THE INFORMATION CONTENT OF DIVIDENDS

It is reasonable to believe that management has more information about the future earnings of the firm than does the public (which includes its own stockholders). This situation of *asymmetric information* suggests that management will seek to convey their information to the public if they have an incentive to do so. Assuming they have such an incentive, one way of doing so is by announcing a change in the amount of the firm's dividends. When used in this manner, dividend announcements are said to be a *signaling device* that can be used by management to convey information to the public.[8]

A relatively simple view of dividend changes is that an announced increase in dividends is a signal that management has increased its assessment of the future earnings for the firm. The announced increase in dividends is therefore "good news" and will, in turn, cause investors to raise their expectations regarding the future earnings of the firm. Conversely, an announced decrease in dividends is a signal that management has decreased its assessment of the future earnings for the firm. The announced decrease in dividends is therefore "bad news" and will, in turn, cause investors to lower their expectations regarding the future earnings of the firm. An implication is that an announced increase in dividends will cause the firm's stock price to rise, and an announced decrease will cause it to fall.

This simple model of dividend changes can be thought of as a special case of the model given in equation (17.12), where the speed of adjustment a is zero. With this model, the expected change in dividends, $D_t - D_{t-1}$, is zero, suggesting that a simple increase in dividends will be viewed as good news. Conversely, a simple decrease in dividends will be viewed as bad news.

One way of testing to see if dividend changes do indeed convey information to the public is to see how stock prices react to announcements of changes in dividends. However, care must be exercised in conducting such a study, because the firm's announcement of dividends is often made at the same time that the firm announces its earnings. Thus, if such announcements are made at the same time, any price change in the firm's common stock may be attributable to either (or both) announcements. One study attempted to avoid this problem of contamination by looking only at cases where the announcement of earnings was at least 11 trading days apart from the

---

[8] Other signaling devices include changes in the firm's capital structure (for example, announcing an issuance of debt with the proceeds being used to repurchase stock). It has been argued that in order for the signal to be useful to the public, (1) management must have an incentive to send a truthful signal; (2) the signal cannot be imitated by competitors in different financial positions; and (3) there cannot be a cheaper means of conveying the same information. See Stephen A. Ross, "The Determination of Financial Structure: The Incentive-Signalling Approach," *Bell Journal of Economics* 8, no. 1 (Spring 1977):23–40. A summary and list of other important papers in this area is in J. Fred Weston and Thomas E. Copeland, *Managerial Finance* (Chicago: Dryden Press, 1986):661–664.

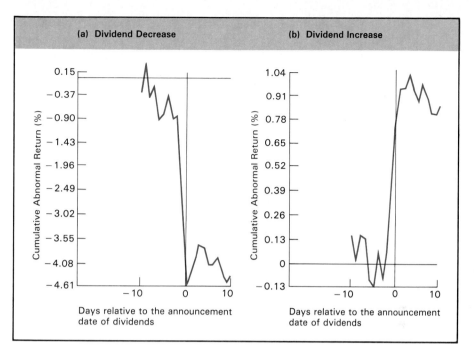

FIGURE 17–2
Cumulative abnormal returns starting ten days before a dividend announcement.

SOURCE: Joseph Aharony and Itzhak Swary, "Quarterly Dividend and Earnings Announcements and Stockholders' Returns: An Empirical Analysis," *Journal of Finance* 35, no. 1 (March 1980): p. 8.

announcement of dividends.[9] Figure 17.2 provides an illustration of the average abnormal return associated with a firm's dividend announcement for those firms that announced their dividends 11 or more days after they announced their earnings (similar results were obtained when the authors examined those cases where dividend announcements preceded earnings announcements).

In those cases where firms announced an increase in their dividends, there is a significant positive reaction in their stock prices. Conversely, in those cases where firms announced a decrease in their dividends, there is a significant negative reaction in their stock prices. These findings strongly support the *information content of dividends hypothesis*, where dividend announcements are asserted to contain inside information about the firm's future prospects.

It should be noted that there is nothing inconsistent with dividends being used as a signal and with the dividend irrelevance argument of Miller

---

[9] Joseph Aharony and Itzhak Swary, "Quarterly Dividend and Earnings Announcements and Stockholders' Returns: An Empirical Analysis," *Journal of Finance* 35, no. 1 (March 1980):1–12. Similar results are reported in Clarence C. Y. Kwan, "Efficient Market Tests of the Informational Content of Dividend Announcements: Critique and Extension," *Journal of Financial and Quantitative Analysis* 16, no. 2 (June 1981):193–206. For a study on the timing of dividend announcements, as well as a listing of studies concerning dividend announcements, see Avner Kalay and Uri Loewenstein, "The Informational Content of the Timing of Dividend Announcements," *Journal of Financial Economics* 16, no. 3 (July 1986):373–88.

and Modigliani that was made earlier. In particular, stockholders will be neither better nor worse off if the *level* of dividends, relative to earnings, is high or low. *Changes* in dividends, however, may be important because they convey information to the public about the future earnings prospects for the firm.

17.4 ACCOUNTING EARNINGS VERSUS ECONOMIC EARNINGS

Since the prediction of earnings is of critical importance in security analysis and investment research, a review of what is known about earnings and the relationship between earnings and prices is essential. At a fundamental level, consideration of the concept of *earnings* itself is needed. Specifically, just what is meant by earnings to those who produce the figures, and how does this meaning affect the valuation process?

☐ 17.4.1 Accounting Earnings

A firm's accountants operate under constraints and guidelines imposed by regulatory authorities and professional organizations such as the Securities and Exchange Commission (SEC) and the Financial Accounting Standards Board (FASB). In cooperation with management, the accountants produce, on a quarterly basis, a set of financial statements for the firm that ends with a figure for the firm's *accounting earnings* (also known as the firm's reported earnings). In a broad sense, such earnings represent the difference between revenues and costs, including the costs associated with nonequity sources of funds (such as debt). This difference, the total earnings available for common stock, is divided by the number of shares outstanding to calculate *earnings per share* (EPS). It may also be divided by the book value per share to calculate the *return on equity* (ROE).

A basic principle of accounting makes the book value of a firm's equity at the end of a period (such as a quarter or year) equal to (1) its value at the end of the previous period plus (2) the portion of accounting earnings for the period that is retained by the firm (here it assumed that there has been no change in the number of shares outstanding during the period). Letting B_t denote the book value of the equity of the firm at the end of period t, E_t^a denote the accounting earnings for period t, and D_t denote the dividends paid during period t, this relationship can be expressed algebraically as

$$B_t = B_{t-1} + E_t^a - D_t \qquad (17.13)$$

From equation (17.13), it can be seen that accounting earnings equals the change in book value of equity plus dividends paid:

$$E_t^a = B_t - B_{t-1} + D_t. \qquad (17.14)$$

☐ 17.4.2   Economic Earnings

Economic earnings (E_t^e) may be defined as the amount that would be obtained in equation (16.14) if the change in the book value of the firm equaled the change in the *economic value of the firm*:

$$E_t^e = V_t - V_{t-1} + D_t. \qquad (17.15)$$

Here the change in the economic value of the firm during period t, $V_t - V_{t-1}$, is defined as the change in the market value of the firm's common stock (assuming there is no change in the market value of the other securities of the firm).[10]

It is easy to show that reported book values and market values (that is, economic values) of stocks are often considerably different. Figure 17.3 shows the ratio of (1) the year-end market price per share for Standard & Poor's Industrial Stock Index to (2) the corresponding year-end book value per share. It can be seen that the ratio is typically greater than 1.0 and has fluctuated considerably from year to year.

Figure 17.4 plots book values (horizontal axis) and market values (vertical axis) for the stocks in the Dow Jones Industrial Average. If investors

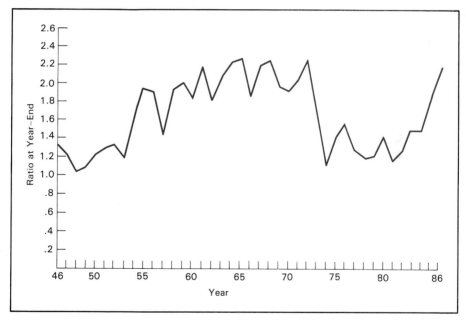

FIGURE 17–3

Ratio of price to book value: Standard & Poor's Industrial Stock Index, 1946–1986.

SOURCE: Standard & Poor's *Statistical Service*, various issues.

---

[10] Sir John R. Hicks, winner of the 1972 Nobel Award in Economics, has defined the weekly economic income of an individual as "the maximum value which he can consume during a week and still be as well off at the end of the week as he was at the beginning" (*Value and Capital*, London: Oxford University Press, 1946, p. 172). The definition of the economic earnings of a firm that is given in equation (17.15) can be viewed as an extension of Hick's definition for an individual.

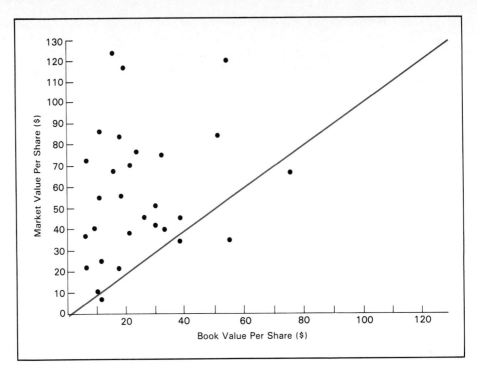

FIGURE 17–4
Market and book values, stocks in Dow Jones Industrial Average, year-end 1986 (except Navistar, which had a negative book value).

viewed market and book values as nearly equivalent, the points would plot along a 45° line (that is, a line with a slope of one) that emanates from the origin. However, as the extensive scatter of the points indicates, market values diverge from book values by different amounts for different stocks.

Both Figure 17.3 and Figure 17.4 indicate that there can be sizable differences between market and book values. Since equations (17.14) and (17.15) show that accounting and economic earnings will be equal only if market and book values are equal, the evidence thus suggests that accounting and economic earnings differ by varying amounts for different firms.

The trouble with accounting earnings is the belief held by certain accountants that investors consider current and recent accounting earnings when estimating the value of a security.[11] This tempts management to try to "manage" such earnings in order to make a firm appear more valuable than it is, thereby fooling investors, at least temporarily. This is permissible since the *generally accepted accounting principles* (GAAP) set by the regulatory authorities (such as FASB) allow a large amount of discretion in how

---

[11] Two assertions that have been made in regard to what investors look at when valuing stocks are known as the mechanistic hypothesis and the myopic hypothesis. The former asserts that investors look only at reported earnings and the latter asserts that investors look only at the short-term future. Both these assertions seem to be invalid when data are analyzed. For an in-depth discussion, see George Foster, *Financial Statement Analysis* (Englewood Cliffs, N.J.: Prentice Hall, 1986), 443–45.

certain items are accounted for (examples include methods for depreciation and inventory valuation). As a result, management may pressure accountants to use those principles that maximize the level of reported earnings, result in a high growth rate of reported earnings, or "smooth" earnings by reducing the year-to-year variability of earnings around a growth rate.[12] Some of these activities can be continued only for a limited number of years; others can go on indefinitely.

To obtain a truly independent estimate of value, analysts must dissect reported earnings. In doing so, they should not be fooled by any accounting illusions, meaning they should not be fooled by any manipulations that may have been made by the accountants at management's request. Anyone who estimates value by applying a formula (no matter how complex) to reported earnings is not producing an estimate that is completely free from all possible manipulations by management. This is not to say that reported earnings are irrelevant for security valuation. Instead, they should be viewed as one source of information about the future prospects of a firm.

17.5 PRICE-EARNINGS RATIOS

Chapter 16 discussed how dividend discount models could be used to determine if stocks were either underpriced or overpriced. One means of making this determination is to compare the actual price-earnings ratio for a firm with what the security analyst had determined it should be. In view of this use of price-earnings ratios, some evidence on the behavior of overall earnings, prices, and price-earnings ratios is now presented.

Part (a) of Figure 17.5 presents a plot of the year-end price-earnings ratios for Standard & Poor's 500. It can be seen from this that the variation in the ratio on a year-to-year basis is considerable, suggesting that investors do not simply apply a standard multiple to earnings in order to determine an appropriate value.

Part (b) of Figure 17.5 presents a plot of earnings per share (the lower jagged line) and price (the upper jagged line) for Standard & Poor's 500.[13] Both lines generally move upward to the right, showing a general trend for both earnings per share and prices to increase over time. However, the two lines are not parallel. This means that earnings per share and prices do not move together in a lockstep manner, an observation that is also apparent in part (a).

☐ 17.5.1 Permanent and Temporary Components of Earnings

When individual common stocks are analyzed, they too show considerable variation in their price-earnings ratios over time. Furthermore, their ratios

---

[12] For a discussion of a number of related issues, see Ross Watts, "Does It Pay to Manipulate EPS?" in *Issues in Corporate Finance* (New York: Stern Stewart Putnam & Macklis, Ltd., 1983).

[13] The vertical axis of this figure actually measures the logarithm of earnings per share and of the price index. In this type of diagram, a given vertical distance represents the same percentage change, no matter where it appears, making it easier to compare relative changes. If, for example, prices changed by the same percentage every year, then the plot in such a diagram would be a straight line sloping upward to the right. If logarithms were not used, the plot would curve upward to the right.

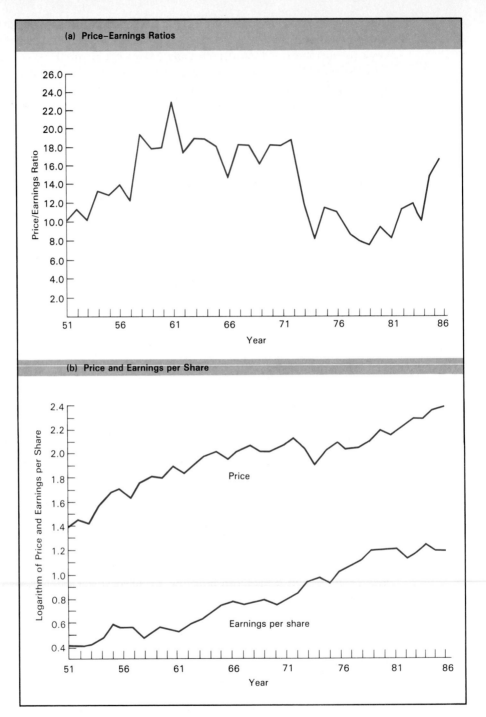

FIGURE 17–5

Price, earnings, and P/E ratios, Standard & Poor's 500, year-end, 1951–1986.

SOURCE: Standard & Poor's *Statistical Service*, various issues.

are quite different from each other at any time. One possible explanation notes that reported earnings can be viewed as having two components. The *permanent* component is the component that is likely to be repeated in the future, whereas the *transitory* component is not likely to be repeated.

Earlier, it was argued that the intrinsic value of a stock depends on the firm's future earnings prospects. This suggests that changes in a stock's intrinsic value and, in turn, its price will be correlated with changes in the permanent component of its earnings but not with changes in the transitory component. If the transitory component is positive, then the price-earnings ratio will be relatively low due to a relatively large number in the denominator. Conversely, if the transitory component is negative, then the price-earnings ratio will be relatively high due to a relatively small number in the denominator.

As an example, consider a firm whose current stock price is $30 per share. Its permanent component of earnings per share over the past year is $4, and its transitory component is $1, resulting in reported earnings of $4 + $1 = $5 and a price-earnings ratio of $30/$5 = 6. Remember that this stock's current price is based on its future prospects, which, in turn, are based on the permanent component of earnings per share over the past year. Thus, if the firm had the same permanent component of $4 but had a transitory component of −$1 instead of $1, the stock would still have a current price of $30 per share. However, its reported earnings would have been $4 − $1 = $3 and its price-earnings ratio would have been $30/$3 = 10.

The permanent component of earnings will change over time, causing investors to revise their forecasts. This will lead to a change in a firm's stock price and, in turn, its price-earnings ratio. However, changes in the transitory component will have an even greater effect on the price-earnings ratio because this component will sometimes be positive and sometimes be negative. As a result, a firm's price-earnings ratio will be variable over time, as was shown in Figure 17.5(a) for the S&P 500. This also means that at any point in time, the transitory component of earnings for a group of firms will have varying sizes, some being positive and some being negative. As a result, at any point in time, firms will have a range of different price-earnings ratios.

If this was a complete explanation for the considerable variation in price-earnings ratios over time and across firms, then most of the variation in a firm's price-earnings ratio would itself be transitory. That is, the ratio would vary over time around some average value. However, the evidence suggests this is not the case. Figure 17.6 shows the behavior over time of such ratios for two groups of stocks. The first group includes stocks with high price-earnings ratios at the beginning of the period (that is, during a portfolio-formation period). The other includes stocks with low price-earnings ratios at the beginning of the period.

Over time, the price-earnings ratios tend to revert to an average ratio for the market as a whole. The changes are substantial in the first two years, owing undoubtedly to the influence of transitory components of earnings. That is, those stocks in the high price-earnings ratio group apparently had, on the average, a negative transitory component in their earnings in the portfolio formation period. (Remember that such a component would tend

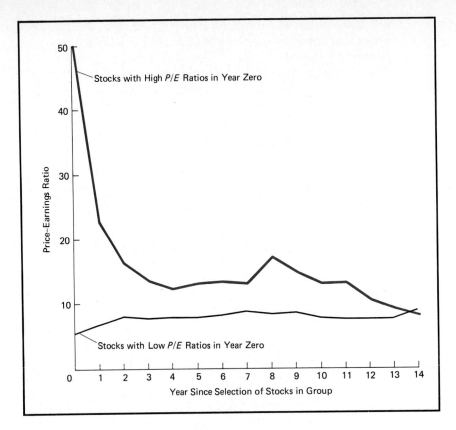

50

Stocks with High *P/E* Ratios in Year Zero

40

30

Price-Earnings Ratio

20

10

Stocks with Low *P/E* Ratios in Year Zero

0   1   2   3   4   5   6   7   8   9   10   11   12   13   14

Year Since Selection of Stocks in Group

FIGURE 17–6
Price-earnings ratios over time for two groups of stocks.

SOURCE: William Beaver and Dale Morse, "What Determines Price-Earnings Ratios?" *Financial Analysts Journal* 34, no. 4 (July–August 1978): 68.

to give a stock a high ratio.) Conversely, those stocks in the low price-earnings ratio group apparently had, on average, a positive transitory component. (Remember that such a component would tend to give a stock a low ratio.) Over future periods, each group of stocks would tend to have an equal number of stocks with positive and negative transitory components, resulting in an average transitory component for each group of roughly zero.

However, Figure 17.6 also shows that the two groups of stocks have different price-earnings ratios for many years after the portfolio formation period. Two explanations can be offered for this persistent difference. First, appropriate discount rates (that is, required returns) differ because of differences in security attributes. This means that there is no reason to expect different firms to have the same ratio. Second, there may be permanent differences between economic and reported earnings due to the use of different accounting methods. As mentioned earlier, there is evidence that the market sees through such differences in reported earnings. Thus, it is not

surprising that the price-earnings ratios of stocks differ and that some of the differences are long lasting.[14]

17.6 RELATIVE GROWTH RATES OF FIRMS' EARNINGS

Since security analysis typically involves forecasting earnings per share, it is useful to examine the historical record to see how earnings per share have changed over time. An interesting question about growth rates in firm earnings over time focuses on *growth stocks*. The very idea of a growth stock suggests that growth in some firms' earnings will exceed the average growth of all firms' earnings in most years, whereas other firms' earnings will grow less than the average.

The results of a study of the earnings' growth rates for 610 industrial companies from 1950 through 1964 are shown in Table 17.3. In every year, each firm's earnings were compared with its earnings in the previous year and the percentage change calculated. The year was counted as "good" for the firm if its percentage change was in the top half of the changes for all firms that year and "bad" if it was in the bottom half. If some firms tend to consistently experience above-average earnings growth rates, then fairly long runs of consistently good years should occur for these firms. Conversely, if some firms tend to consistently experience below-average earnings growth rates, then they should have fairly long runs of consistently bad years.

TABLE 17.3

Earnings Growth Rates, 610 Firms, 1950–1964.

LENGTH OF RUN	ACTUAL NUMBER OF GOOD RUNS	ACTUAL NUMBER OF BAD RUNS	NUMBER OF GOOD OR BAD RUNS EXPECTED IF THE ODDS EACH YEAR WERE 50-50, REGARDLESS OF PAST PERFORMANCE
1	1,152	1,102	1,068
2	562	590	534
3	266	300	267
4	114	120	133
5	55	63	67
6	24	20	33
7	23	12	17
8	5	6	8
9	3	3	4
10	6	0	2
11	2	0	1
12	1	0	1
13	0	0	0
14	0	1	0

SOURCE: Richard A. Brealey, *An Introduction to Risk and Return from Common Stocks* (Cambridge, Mass.: The MIT Press, 1983), 89.

---

[14] For a more thorough discussion of permanent and transitory components of earnings and their relationship to price-earnings ratios, see Chapters 4 and 5 of William H. Beaver, *Financial Reporting: An Accounting Revolution* (Englewood Cliffs, N.J.: Prentice Hall, 1981); William Beaver and Dale Morse, "What Determines Price-Earnings Ratios?" *Financial Analysts Journal* 34, no. 4 (July–August 1978):65–76; and Foster, *Financial Statement Analysis*, 437–42.

The middle two columns of Table 17.3 indicate the actual number of runs of various lengths. The right-hand column shows the number that would be expected if there was a 50-50 chance of either a good year or a bad year. The three columns are remarkably similar. Above-average earnings growth in the past does not appear to indicate above-average growth in the future, and below-average growth in the past does not appear to indicate below-average growth in the future. Flipping a coin seems to be as reliable a predictor of future growth as looking at past growth rates.

A study using longer time periods for measuring growth reached generally similar conclusions.[15] For each of 323 companies with positive earnings in each year from 1946 through 1965, average growth rates were computed for (1) the period from 1946 through 1955 and (2) the period from 1956 through 1965. Differences among firms' earnings growth rates in the first period accounted for less than 1% of the variation in the differences among their earnings growth rates in the second period.

☐ 17.6.1 Annual Earnings

The results of these studies, as well as certain other studies, suggest that *annual* reported earnings follow what is known in statistics as a *random walk model*.[16] That is, annual earnings for the forthcoming year (E_t) can be thought of as being equal to annual earnings over the past year (E_{t-1}) plus a random error term. (Remember that a random error term can be thought of as a roulette wheel where the numbers on the wheel are distributed around zero.) Thus,

$$E_t = E_{t-1} + \epsilon_t \qquad (17.16)$$

where ϵ_t is the random error term. With this model, the estimate of next year's earnings is simply the past year's earnings, E_{t-1}. Another way of viewing a random walk model for earnings is that the change in earnings is independent and identically distributed:

$$E_t - E_{t-1} = \epsilon_t . \qquad (17.17)$$

This means that the change in earnings, $E_t - E_{t-1}$, is unrelated to past changes in earnings and can be thought of as a spin from a roulette wheel that is perhaps unique to the firm but, more importantly, is used year after year. Since the expected outcome from a spin of the roulette wheel is zero, the expected change in earnings is zero. This implies that the expected level of earnings is equal to the past year's earnings, as was suggested earlier.

---

[15] John Lintner and Robert Glauber, "Higgledy Piggledy Growth in America," in James Lorie and Richard Brealey, eds., *Modern Developments in Investment Management* (Hinsdale, Ill.: The Dryden Press, 1978).

[16] For a discussion of these studies, see Chapter 6 of Ross L. Watts and Jerold L. Zimmerman, *Positive Accounting Theory* (Englewood Cliffs, N.J.: Prentice Hall, 1986); and Foster, *Financial Statement Analysis*, Chapter 7 (particularly pp. 238–42).

☐ 17.6.2 Quarterly Earnings

In terms of *quarterly* earnings, consideration must be given to the fact that there is typically a seasonal component to a firm's earnings (for example, many firms have high earnings during the quarter that includes Christmas). As a result, a slightly different model appears to be best for forecasting purposes. This model forecasts the growth in earnings for the forthcoming quarter relative to the same quarter one year ago, a quantity denoted by $QE_t - QE_{t-4}$. It does so by relating this growth to the growth during the most recent quarter relative to the comparable quarter one year before it, $QE_{t-1} - QE_{t-5}$. Formally, the model for the "seasonally differenced series" of quarterly earnings is known as an *autoregressive model of order 1* and is as follows:

$$QE_t - QE_{t-4} = a(QE_{t-1} - QE_{t-5}) + b + e_t \qquad (17.18)$$

where a and b are constants and e_t is a random error term.

Alternatively, the model can be rewritten by moving the term QE_{t-4} to the right-hand side:

$$QE_t = QE_{t-4} + a(QE_{t-1} - QE_{t-5}) + b + e_t. \qquad (17.19)$$

By estimating the constants a and b, this model can be used for forecasting quarterly earnings.[17]

For example, assuming estimates for a and b of .4 and .05, respectively, the forecast of a firm's earnings for the next quarter would be equal to QE_{t-4} + .4($QE_{t-4} - QE_{t-5}$) + .05. Thus, if a firm had earnings per share for the last quarter ($t - 1$) of $3, for four quarters before now ($t - 4$) of $2, and for five quarters before now ($t - 5$) of $2.60, then its forecasted earnings for the forthcoming quarter would be equal to $2 + .4($3 − $2.60) + $.05 = $2.21. Note how the forecast consists of three components—a component equal to last quarter's earnings ($2), a component that considers the year-to-year quarterly growth in earnings (.4($3 − $2.60) = $.16), and a component that is a constant ($.05).[18]

17.7 COMOVEMENT OF EARNINGS

Past changes in security prices are of limited value for the prediction of future changes. And past changes in the overall level of the market are of

---

[17] For a discussion of this model, see George Foster, "Quarterly Accounting Data: Time-Series Properties and Predictive-Ability Results," *Accounting Review* 52, no. 1 (January 1977):1–21. This model can also be used to forecast annual earnings by working forward one quarter at a time and then adding up the forecasts for the forthcoming four quarters. Doing so would result in a forecast of annual earnings (E_t) equal to E_{t-1} + $c(QE_{t-1} - QE_{t-5})$ + $4b$, where $c = a^1 + a^2 + a^3 + a^4$. Note that the random walk model is a special case where a and b are equal to zero. See Watts and Zimmerman, *Positive Accounting Theory*, pp. 152–53, for a discussion of this model and a study that estimated values for a and b. Also see Foster, *Financial Statement Analysis*, 230–45.

[18] It has been argued recently that a slight improvement can be made in this model by replacing the constant term component with what is known as a "moving average" component, which is based on the size of the random error term that occurred four quarters before now (e_{t-4}). See Lawrence D. Brown and Michael S. Rozeff, "Univariate Time-Series Models of Quarterly Accounting Earnings per Share: A Proposed Model," *Journal of Accounting Research* 17, no. 1 (Spring 1979):179–89; and Allen W. Bathke, Jr. and Kenneth S. Lorek, "The Relationship Between Time Series Models and the Security Market's Expectations of Quarterly Earnings," *Accounting Review* 59, no. 2 (April 1984):163–76.

TABLE 17.4

The Proportion of the Variation of a Firm's Earnings
Attributable to Marketwide and Industry Earnings Changes.

| | PROPORTION ATTRIBUTABLE TO: | |
Industry	Marketwide Earnings Changes	Additional Influence of Changes in Industry Earnings
Aircraft	11%	5%
Autos	48	11
Beer	11	7
Cement	6	32
Chemicals	41	8
Cosmetics	5	6
Department stores	30	37
Drugs	14	7
Electricals	24	8
Food	10	10
Machinery	19	16
Nonferrous metals	26	25
Office machinery	14	6
Oil	13	49
Paper	27	28
Rubber	26	48
Steel	32	21
Supermarkets	6	33
Textiles and clothing	25	29
Tobacco	8	19
All firms	21	21

SOURCE: Richard Brealey, "Some Implications of the Comovement of American Company Earnings," *Applied Economics* 3, no. 3 (September 1971):187.

limited help in the prediction of future market moves. However, security price changes are related to concurrent changes in the prices of the market portfolio and, to a lesser extent, an "industry" portfolio.[19] Although the strength of these relationships differs among securities, historical data can generally be utilized to help estimate the relative future strengths of the relationships for different securities. For example, the relationship between a security's returns and market returns has been referred to as the security's beta and can be estimated by examining historical returns. Similarly, the industry that a security belongs to can be determined and a portfolio of stocks in that industry constructed. Then the historical returns on the security can be compared to this portfolio and an industry beta can be estimated.

It has been argued that security prices are determined by economic earnings and that security price movements are related to movements in market and industry prices. Thus, an interesting issue is whether or not movements in the economic earnings of a firm are related to movements in the economic earnings of the market and industry portfolios. Such an issue

---

[19] Although the definition of what constitutes an industry differs from one study to another, various authors have found that security price movements can be attributed not only to market price movements but also to industry price movements. See Alexander and Francis, *Portfolio Analysis*, 195–96, for a description of these studies and the relevant citations.

has been explored by looking at accounting earnings and assuming they are correlated with economic earnings.

Table 17.4 shows that such relationships do exist, at least to some extent. Earnings reported by 217 corporations from 1948 through 1966 were compared first with the earnings for Standard & Poor's 425-stock index (which served as a surrogate for marketwide earnings) and then with the average earnings of all firms in the same industry. The proportion the variation of each firm's earnings that could be attributed to each of these factors was determined. The results shown in the table are the average proportions for all the firms in each industry.

The results differ notably from one industry to another, with the marketwide factor ranging between 5% and 48% and the industry factor ranging from 5% to 49%. The bottom row of the table shows the values obtained by averaging over all 217 corporations. Changes in marketwide earnings accounted for 21% of the variation in the earnings of the typical firm, and changes in the earnings of firms in its industry accounted for another 21%.

Earlier, it was mentioned that a security's beta (sometimes known as its *market beta*) is a measure of how the price of the security will covary with the price of the market portfolio. Similarly, a security's *accounting beta* is a measure of how the accounting earnings of the security will covary with the accounting earnings of the market portfolio. If security prices are related to earnings, then it seems reasonable to expect market betas to be related to accounting betas. Studies that have examined this issue have found that market and accounting betas are significantly correlated, with accounting betas explaining between 20% and 40% of the variation that is observed in market betas.[20]

17.8 EARNINGS ANNOUNCEMENTS AND PRICE CHANGES

A number of studies have shown substantial price changes for stocks of companies that report earnings that differ substantially from consensus expectations. One study looked at three groups of 50 stocks.[21] The first group consisted of the 50 stocks listed on the NYSE that experienced the greatest price rise during 1970. The second group consisted of 50 stocks chosen randomly from all those listed on the NYSE during 1970. The third group consisted of the 50 stocks listed on the NYSE that experienced the greatest price decline during 1970. As shown in Figure 17.7, the median changes in the prices of the stocks in the top, random, and bottom groups were 48.4%, −3.2%, and −56.7%, respectively.

Next, the study looked at the actual change in earnings per share from 1969 to 1970 for each stock in each group. As shown in Figure 17.7, the

---

[20] See, for example, Ray Ball and Philip Brown, "Portfolio Theory and Accounting," *Journal of Accounting Research* 7, no. 2 (Autumn 1969):300–23; and William Beaver and James Manegold, "The Association Between Market-Determined and Accounting-Determined Measures of Systematic Risk: Some Further Evidence," *Journal of Financial and Quantitative Analysis* 10, no. 2 (June 1975):231–84.

[21] Victor Niederhoffer and Patrick J. Regan, "Earnings Changes, Analysts' Forecasts, and Stock Prices," *Financial Analysts Journal* 28, no. 3 (May–June 1972):65–71.

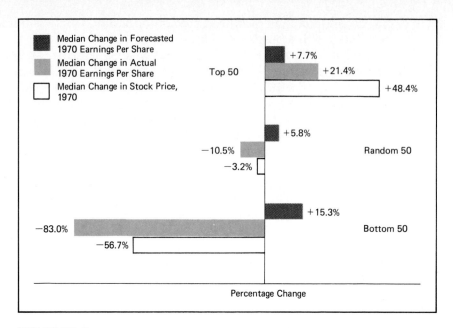

FIGURE 17–7
Earnings and price changes: selected stocks listed on the New York Stock Exchange during 1970.

SOURCE: Victor Niederhoffer and Patrick J. Regan, "Earnings Changes, Analysts' Forecasts, and Stock Prices," *Financial Analysts Journal* 28, no. 3 (May–June 1972): 67.

median changes in earnings per share for the top, random, and bottom groups were 21.4%, −10.5%, and −83.0%, respectively.

Lastly, the study determined the forecasted change in earnings per share at the beginning of 1970 for each stock in each group. This was done by using the predictions contained in Standard & Poor's *Earnings Forecaster*, where estimates made by a number of investment research organizations are reported. The median forecasted changes in earnings per share for the top, random, and bottom groups are shown in Figure 17.7 to be 7.7%, 5.8%, and 15.3%, respectively.

Interestingly, the forecasts of earnings per share hardly correspond to the price movements of the stocks. In fact, the stocks in the bottom group were expected to increase earnings by more than that in the top group (15.3%, compared with +7.7%). However, the prediction for the bottom group was disastrously wrong, with a median earnings per share decline of 83.0%. And, as Figure 17.7 shows, prices definitely followed suit. Overall, it appears that unexpected changes in earnings do indeed affect security prices.

But do earnings surprises affect prices before or after their announcement? In a completely efficient market, such information would be reflected in prices as soon as it had been disseminated to a few major market participants. The reaction of security prices around the time of earnings announcements has been examined by a number of authors and is discussed next.

☐ 17.8.1 Deviations from Time-Series Models of Earnings

A comprehensive study involving 2053 firms from 1974 through 1981 provided evidence concerning the speed of response of security prices to earnings announcements.[22] For each company, an expected earnings figure was computed for each quarter, using the model of the time-series behavior of earnings shown in equation (17.19). With this model, the expected earnings for a firm during period t was equal to $QE_{t-4} + a(QE_{t-1} - QE_{t-5}) + b$. For example, the earnings expected for the firm in the second quarter of 1988 equaled (1) the firm's earnings in the second quarter of 1987 plus (2) the change in earnings from the first quarter of 1987 to the first quarter of 1988 times the parameter a plus (3) the parameter b. The values of a and b were determined by analysis of the behavior of earnings prior to the second quarter of 1988.

Given actual earnings and an estimate of expected earnings, a forecast error (FE_t) can be computed for the firm:

$$FE_t = QE_t - \overline{QE_t} \qquad (17.20)$$

where QE_t is the actual earnings for quarter t and $\overline{QE_t}$ is the expected earnings for quarter t, forecast at time $t - 1$. Simply stated, equation (17.20) indicates that the forecast error for a quarter is the difference between actual earnings for that quarter and the expected earnings.

The forecast error provides a measure of the "surprise" in the quarterly earnings announcement, but it fails to differentiate between stocks for which large forecast errors are routine and those for which they are rare. The important surprises are those associated with forecast errors that are large by historical standards. To account for this, a forecast error can be related to previous errors to obtain a measure of *standardized unexpected earnings* (SUE):

$$SUE_t = \frac{FE_t}{\sigma_{FEt}} \qquad (17.21)$$

where σ_{FEt} is the standard deviation of forecast errors for the 20 quarterly earnings of the firm prior to t. (That is, forecast errors were determined for 20 quarters before t, then the standard deviation for this set of 20 errors was estimated.)

For example, a firm with a forecast of earnings per share of $3 that subsequently reports actual earnings of $5 will have a forecast error of $5 − $3 = $2. That is, the earnings announcement will surprise people by $2. If the standard deviation of past errors is $.80, this surprise will be notable, since SUE = $2/$.80 = 2.50. However, if the standard deviation is $4, then this surprise is minor, since SUE = $2/$4 = .50. Thus, a large positive value for SUE would indicate that the earnings announcement contained significant good news, whereas a large negative SUE would indicate that the earnings announcement contained significant bad news.

---

[22] George Foster, Chris Olsen, and Terry Shevlin, "Earnings Releases, Anomalies and the Behavior of Security Returns," *Accounting Review* 59, no. 4 (October 1984):574–603. For a related paper, see Roger Kormendi and Robert Lipe, "Earnings Innovations, Earnings Persistence, and Stock Returns," *Journal of Business* 60, no. 3 (July 1987): 323–45.

In the study, the SUEs associated with all the earnings announcements for all the firms were ranked from smallest to largest. Then they were divided into ten equal-sized groups based on the ranking. Group 1 consisted of those announcements resulting in the most-negative SUEs, and group 10 consisted of those with the most-positive SUEs. After forming these ten groups, the stock returns for each firm in each group were measured for the period from 60 days before its earnings announcement through 60 days after its announcement. Figure 17.8 shows the *abnormal return* for the average firm in each of the ten groups for three different time periods.

Part (a) shows the average abnormal return for the period from 60 days before the earnings announcement through the day the announcement appeared in the *Wall Street Journal*. This period is denoted by (−60, 0).

Part (b) shows the average abnormal return for the two-day period consisting of the day before the announcement appeared in the *Wall Street Journal* and the day the announcement appeared, a period that is denoted by (−1, 0). Since day 0 is the day the announcement appeared in the *Wall Street Journal*, day −1 is the day the announcement was made to the public. If this announcement was made after trading hours on day −1, investors would not have been able to buy or sell the stock until the next day, day 0. If the announcement was made during trading hours on day −1, then investors could have acted on that day. Due to the inability to pinpoint the hour of the announcement, the return over the two-day period was examined to see the immediate impact of the announcement on the price of the security.

Part (c) shows the average abnormal return for the period from the day after the announcement through 60 days after the announcement, a period that is denoted by (1, 60).

Part (a) shows that prices of firms that announced unexpected high earnings (such as SUE group 10) tended to increase *prior* to the announcement (date 0), suggesting that information relevant to the earnings announcement was becoming available to the market prior to the actual announcement. Conversely, prices of firms that announced unexpectedly low earnings (such as SUE group 1) tended to decrease prior to the announcement, undoubtedly for the same reason. In general, there seems to be a strong positive correspondence between the size of the unexpected earnings and the size of the abnormal return. Note that if an investor knew what the earnings were going to be 60 days before the announcement, then this information could be exploited by either buying the stock if the firm was going to announce unexpected large earnings, or short selling the stock if the firm was going to announce unexpected low earnings. However, since investors generally do not have prior access to earnings, such exploitation is generally impossible. Thus, the existence of abnormal returns prior to the announcement date does not necessarily indicate some sort of market inefficiency.

Part (b) shows that the larger the size of the unexpected earnings, the larger the price movement during the two-day period surrounding the announcement. For example, firms in SUE group 1 had an abnormal return of −1.34%, whereas those in SUE group 10 had an abnormal return of 1.26%. As in part (a), there is a positive relationship between the size of the un-

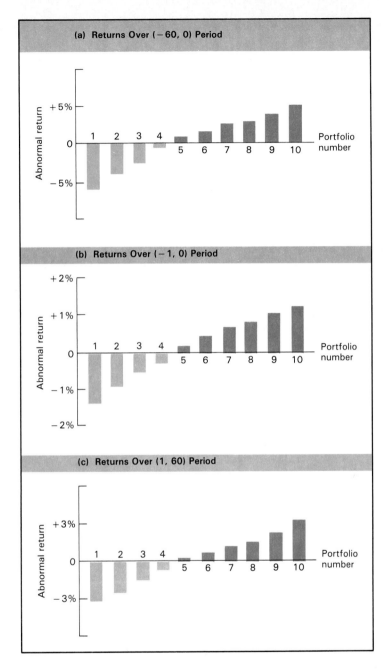

FIGURE 17–8
Security returns in period surrounding earnings announcements.

SOURCE: George Foster, Chris Olsen, and Terry Shevlin, "Earnings Releases, Anomalies, and the Behavior of Security Returns," *Accounting Review* 59, no. 4 (October 1984): 587.

expected earnings and the abnormal stock return.[23] Thus, it appears that the market reacted in a predictable fashion, pushing up the stock prices of those firms announcing good news and pushing down the stock prices of those firms announcing bad news.

As shown in part (c), the changes in stock prices after the announcement dates are quite remarkable in that they appear to suggest an inefficiency exists in the market. Prices of stocks of firms announcing unexpectedly high earnings tended to increase for many days *after* the announcement (the average abnormal return over the 60-day period after the announcement was 3.23% for SUE group 10). Conversely, the prices of firms announcing unexpectedly low earnings tended to decrease for many days after the announcement (the average abnormal return over the 60-day period subsequent to the announcement was -3.08% for SUE group 1).

As was noted, in the two previous parts there seems to be a strong positive correspondence between the size of the unexpected earnings and the size of the abnormal return. This observation suggests that an investor could make abnormal returns by simply looking at quarterly earnings announcements and, based on the magnitude and sign of the unexpected component, act appropriately. That is, if the firm announced earnings that were notably above expectations, the investor should subsequently purchase some of the firm's stock. In contrast, if the announced earnings were notably below expectations, the investor should subsequently sell any holdings and perhaps even short sell the firm's stock. Announcements of earnings that were reasonably close to expectations would not motivate either a buy or sell order.

□ 17.8.2 Security Analysts' Estimates of Future Earnings

In using only the historical record of past earnings to forecast future earnings, it was mentioned earlier that an autoregressive model of order 1, as shown in equation (17.19), seemed to work about as well as any other model. However, security analysts do not restrict themselves just to past earnings when developing their forecasts. Instead, they look at many different pieces of information. This raises several interesting questions. How well can analysts forecast earnings? And do their forecasts incorporate information other than that contained in past earnings? The results of one study that provides some answers to these questions are shown in Table 17.5.[24]

---

[23] Studies have shown that earnings announcements containing good news are often made earlier than expected, whereas those containing bad news are often made later than expected. These studies also show that the *timeliness* (defined as the difference between the actual announcement date and the expected announcement date) affects the size of the abnormal return. Interestingly, around the time of earnings announcements there appears to be both increased trading volume and increased variability in security returns. See Foster, *Financial Statement Analysis*, 377–86; and V. V. Chari, Ravi Jagannathan, and Aharon Ofer, "Seasonalities in Security Returns: The Case of Earnings Announcements," *Journal of Financial Economics* 20, no. 1 (May 1988): 101–21.

[24] Lawrence D. Brown and Michael S. Rozeff, "The Superiority of Analyst Forecasts as Measures of Expectations: Evidence from Earnings," *Journal of Finance* 33, no. 1 (March 1978):1–16. Also see Lawrence D. Brown and Michael S. Rozeff, "Analysts Can Forecast Accurately!" *Journal of Portfolio Management* 6, no. 3 (Spring 1980):31–34; Lawrence D. Brown, Robert L. Hagerman, Paul A. Griffin, and Mark E. Zmijewski, "Security Analyst Superiority Relative to Univariate Time-Series Models in Forecasting Quarterly Earnings," *Journal of Accounting and Economics* 9, no. 1 (April 1987):40–47; and Dan Givoly and Josef Lakonishok,

TABLE 17.5

Accuracy of Mechanical and Judgmental Earnings Forecasts.

EARNINGS FORECAST ERROR AS A PERCENT OF ACTUAL EARNINGS	PERCENT OF FORECASTS WITH A SMALLER ERROR	
	Mechanical Model	Analysts' Forecasts
5%	15.0%	18.0%
10	26.5	32.0
25	54.5	63.5
50	81.0	86.5
75	87.5	90.5
100	89.5	92.0

SOURCE: Lawrence D. Brown and Michael S. Rozeff, "The Superiority of Analyst Forecasts as Measures of Expectations: Evidence from Earnings," *Journal of Finance* 33, no. 1 (March 1978):7–8.

In this study, two sets of forecasts were examined for the quarterly earnings of 50 firms over the period from 1971 through 1975. The first set was obtained by applying sophisticated mechanical models to each firm's previous earnings history (such as the autoregressive model of equation (17.19)). The second set was obtained from the earnings forecasts of security analysts as reported in the *Value Line Investment Survey*.[25] The results suggest that the analysts outperformed the mechanical model.[26] For example, 63.5% of the analysts' forecasts were within 25% of the actual earnings values, whereas only 54.4% of the forecasts made via mechanical models came as close. Analysts appear to base their forecasts on both past earnings and other information, and the latter appears to help.

Often, management itself will make a forecast of next year's earnings for the firm. Generally, the forecasts of security analysts are not as accurate as the forecasts of management when both sets of forecasts are made at about the same time. Since management has private information about the firm, this observation is not surprising.[27]

☐ 17.8.3 Revisions in Security Analysts' Forecasts

When new news about a company becomes available, professional security analysts revise their forecasts of the firm's earnings. As investors respond

---

"The Quality of Analysts' Forecasts of Earnings," *Financial Analysts Journal* 40, no. 5 (September–October 1984):40–47. The citations in the last two papers provide a useful set of references for the reader who is interested in this topic.

[25] Value Line also ranks stocks in terms of their relative attractiveness as investments. For a discussion of the usefulness of the Value Line rankings, see the appendix.

[26] A similar observation was made in a study that examined the forecasts made during the period of 1961 to 1969 by a sample of security analysts working for banks, mutual funds, brokerage houses, investment advisory firms, and pension funds. However, the forecasts were not found to be useful in identifying stocks that subsequently had positive abnormal returns. See John G. Cragg and Burton G. Malkiel, *Expectations and the Structure of Share Prices* (Chicago: The University of Chicago Press, 1982), 85–86 and 165.

[27] See Foster, *Financial Statement Analysis*, 280–85, for a discussion of the properties of management forecasts.

TABLE 17.6

Forecast Revisions and Abnormal Returns, 1976–1980.

REVISION OF CONSENSUS FORECAST FOR:		
Earnings One Year Ahead	Earnings Two Years Ahead	Average Cumulative Abnormal Return for Months +1 through +12 After Date of Revision
Increased		+ .04%
Decreased		− 3.80
Increased	Increased	+ .60
Decreased	Decreased	− 4.57

SOURCE: Philip Brown, George Foster, and Eric Noreen, *Security Analyst Multi-Year Earnings Forecasts and the Capital Market* (Sarasota, Fl.: American Accounting Association, 1985):71, 104.

to such revisions by buying or selling the firm's stock, its price will, in turn, adjust. This raises some interesting questions regarding such revisions. Will this process from revision to stock price adjustment be rapid or somewhat slow? Is the information that caused analysts to revise their earnings estimates valuable to only those who get it early? Should an investor favor stocks whose earnings estimates have been revised upward in the last month? Conversely, should an investor avoid stocks whose earnings estimates have been revised downward?

One study that sought answers to these questions used the earnings forecasts for 2700 companies that are provided to institutional investors by Lynch, Jones and Ryan through their *Institutional Brokers Estimate System* (IBES) database.[28] This study noted that 77.2% of the earnings-per-share forecasts made one year in advance (FY1) were not revised each month and that this percentage increased as the year to be forecast became more distant. Possible explanations are that the security analysts are too busy to revise all their forecasts each month or that only a small number of stocks have new information each month. The study also found that the closer the year whose earnings were being forecast, the more accurate the forecast, an observation that is probably due to the information being of higher quality and quantity as the year gets closer.

To continue, this study also calculated a consensus forecast for a firm's earnings in a particular year by determining the average of the forecasts. Firms were then categorized into those for which these forecasts subsequently were (1) increased or (2) decreased. Returns for securities in each category over the period starting one month after the date of the forecast

---

[28] The forecasts are made by analysts at over 80 brokerage firms. See Philip Brown, George Foster, and Eric Noreen, *Security Analyst Multi-Year Earnings Forecasts and the Capital Market* (Sarasota, Fl.: American Accounting Association, 1985). See also Gary A. Benesh and Pamela P. Peterson, "On the Relation Between Earnings Changes, Analysts' Forecasts and Stock Price Fluctuations," *Financial Analysts Journal* 42, no. 6 (November/December 1986):29–39, 55, along with their list of citations. Another database similar to IBES is *The Icarus Service* provided by Zachs Investment Research, Inc., which provides summaries of forecasts for 2400 companies from 50 U.S. brokerage firms.

revision and continuing for 11 more months were determined and averaged. Table 17.6 shows some of the results.

Stocks whose initial earnings forecasts for one year ahead were subsequently increased did not experience significantly abnormal returns—the abnormal return over the 12-month period was +0.04%. On the other hand, stocks whose initial earnings forecasts were subsequently decreased did have significant abnormal returns of −3.80%.

Stocks whose earnings forecasts for *both* one year ahead and two years ahead changed in the same direction experienced even greater abnormal returns. This finding suggests that capital markets look at more than just current earnings in valuing securities. Furthermore, the results suggest that an inefficiency exists in the stock market in that apparently investors can avoid abnormally poor returns by immediately selling a stock if the stock's forecasted earnings have been revised downwards.

☐ 17.8.4   Sources of Errors in Forecasting

Since security analysts' forecasts are not perfect, it is interesting to consider the major source of their errors. One study examined the IBES database and attempted to break down the forecast errors into three components: (1) errors that could be traced to misjudgments about the economy; (2) errors that could be traced to misjudgments about the firm's particular industry; and (3) errors that were purely due to misjudgments about the firm.[29]

The results indicated the following: Less than 3% of the typical error was due to a misjudgment about the economy; roughly 30% of the typical error was due to a misjudgment about the industry; and more than 65% of the typical error was due to a misjudgment about the firm.

☐ 17.8.5   Unexpected Earnings and Abnormal Returns

One plausible explanation for these results concerns the cost of information transfer. New news must reach a large number of investors before the appropriate new equilibrium price can be completely established. Although large institutional investors can obtain news quickly, it may take some time before it reaches smaller institutional investors and individuals. Thus, after an earnings announcement or forecast revision, there can be a period of abnormal price movement that is related in sign and magnitude to the nature of the announcement.

Alternatively, perhaps the measurement of abnormal returns has been in error. In making such a measurement, a determination of what is a normal return must be made. Such a determination is not straightforward; instead it is fraught with difficulty. This means that the estimated abnormal returns could actually be due to measurement errors, leaving open the possibility

---

[29] Edwin J. Elton, Martin J. Gruber, and Mustafa N. Gultekin, "Professional Expectations: Accuracy and Diagnosis of Errors," *Journal of Financial and Quantitative Analysis* 19, no. 4 (December 1984):351–63.

that a more accurate measure of normal return would have resulted in no significant abnormal returns.

Nevertheless, there appear to be striking differences in subsequent stock returns for firms with different SUEs and different revisions in earnings forecasts. Such differences cannot be explained wholly by different levels of beta. While the magnitudes of the return differences may be too small to warrant extensive trading, they do suggest the consideration of such things as SUE values and forecast revisions when money must be invested or a portion of an existing portfolio liquidated.

17.9 SUMMARY

This chapter has presented some of the important features of dividends and earnings of which a security analyst should be aware when preparing forecasts and making investment recommendations. First of all, it was shown that there is no conflict regarding the underlying source of value for a share of stock. In particular, earnings were shown to be the source of value, not dividends.

Second, a model for explaining the amount of dividends was presented. In this model, the amount of dividends is based on current earnings and the amount of dividends paid in the previous year. However, this model does not work perfectly in explaining dividends. One reason for this failure is that dividends are sometimes used as a signaling device by management to convey information to the public. Consistent with this notion is the observation that an announcement of an unexpected increase in dividends typically results in an upward movement in the firm's stock price, whereas an unexpected decrease results in a downward movement.

Third, it was shown that security analysts should not be fooled by accounting illusions. That is, when analysts are determining the true economic value and earnings of the firm, they should recognize the discretion that accountants have in preparing financial statements. Indeed, the evidence suggests that analysts do see through the veil of accounting illusions, since they appear to be able to estimate earnings more accurately than mechanical models that are based on accounting earnings. In terms of mechanical models, a random walk model seems to be reasonable for describing annual earnings; an autoregressive model of order one is reasonable for describing quarterly earnings.

Fourth, it was shown that one way of explaining why firms have different price-earnings ratios is to recognize that earnings have a permanent and a temporary component. Since prices typically reflect just the permanent component, whereas price-earnings ratios are based on both components, these ratios vary widely.

Fifth, it was shown that there is a positive relationship between accounting betas and market betas. That is, firms whose earnings covary more with marketwide earnings are likely to have higher market betas.

Sixth, it appears that stocks with the highest returns typically have earnings per share that are substantially greater than expected, whereas

those with the lowest returns have earnings per share that are substantially less than expected. Two observations are consistent with this: (1) the greater the amount of unexpected earnings, the greater the stock return before, during, and after the announcement date; and (2) revisions in analysts' forecasts tend to be reflected in stock prices. In summary, the enormous amount of effort devoted to forecasting earnings seems to be justified in that superior ability can result in abnormally high returns.

APPENDIX A
VALUE LINE RANKINGS

It has been observed that investors can use the information contained in either a quarterly earnings announcement or a revision of an earnings forecast by security analysts to make abnormal returns. Another source of information that may be useful to investors is the *Value Line Investment Survey* (published by Value Line, Inc., New York, for $495 per year, which is reputed to be the largest investment advisory service in the United States).

Each week, every one of approximately 1700 stocks is assigned one of five possible ranks by Value Line. By design, the categories include the same number of stocks each week, as follows:

RANK	NUMBER OF STOCKS
1 (highest)	100
2 (above average)	300
3 (average)	900
4 (below average)	300
5 (lowest)	100

Many factors go into the ranking procedure. Not surprisingly, the exact details have not been revealed. However, the key elements are all based on publicly available information: [30]

1. The most recent year's earnings and average stock price, relative to the comparable values for the previous ten years, and the stock's average price over the preceding 10 weeks relative to that of the preceding 52 weeks.
2. A price momentum element that is based on the stock's current price-earnings ratio relative to that of the market, compared with the average of the corresponding figures over the last five years.
3. An earnings momentum element that is based on the most recent quarter's earnings relative to the amount reported four quarters earlier.
4. An earnings surprise element, where the most recent quarter's earnings are compared with the amount forecast by Value Line's security analysts.

---

[30] For details, see Arnold Bernhard, *Investing in Common Stocks with the Aid of the Value Line Rankings and other Criteria of Stock Value* (New York: Arnold Bernhard and Co., Inc., 1975).

TABLE 17.7

Performance of Portfolios Formed on the Basis of Value
Line Rankings.

	RANKING				
	1	2	3	4	5
Actual return over subsequent 26 weeks	7.38%	6.51%	4.10%	2.70%	.37%
Abnormal return over subsequent 26 weeks	.33%	.35%	− .57%	− 1.12%	− 3.05%

SOURCE: Thomas E. Copeland and David Mayers, "The Value Line Enigma (1965–1978): A Case Study of Performance Evaluation Issues," *Journal of Financial Economics* 10, no. 3 (November 1982):298, 301.

A test of the resulting rankings showed them to be of some value.[31] Beginning in November 26, 1965, five portfolios were formed (on paper). The first included all stocks ranked 1 at that time, in equal dollar values; the second included all stocks ranked 2, and so on. After six months each portfolio was altered as necessary to again include equal dollar values of all stocks with the appropriate ranks at that time. The procedure was continued until February 3, 1978, when the last set of portfolios was formed. Then, each portfolio's actual rate of return was measured and adjustments for risk were made to determine abnormal returns. The results, shown in Table 17.7, indicate that both the actual and abnormal returns are perfectly ordered with the rankings of the securities in the portfolios. More in-depth analysis indicated that most of the abnormal returns occurred in the 13-week period subsequent to the formation date. Interestingly, this study shows that the only notable abnormal return is for the securities with a ranking of 5. This suggests that an investor should sell (or even short sell) any securities that have such a ranking.

This study also looked at those securities whose rank had been changed by Value Line. Roughly 70 to 80 securities change ranks each week, evenly split between those being upgraded and those being downgraded. Almost all the changes are of one rank (seldom does a security jump two ranks, for example from 1 to 3, or vice versa). Focusing the analysis around the time of the change in rank, it was determined that, on the average, securities whose rank had been upgraded earned an abnormal return of .77% in the subsequent 13 weeks. Conversely, those securities whose rank had been downgraded earned an abnormal return of − 1.42% in the subsequent 13 weeks. Overall, most of the adjustment in the stock prices of these securities was found to be concentrated in the two-week period subsequent to the publication of the change in rank.[32]

---

[31] Thomas E. Copeland and David Mayers, "The Value Line Enigma (1965–1978): A Case Study of Performance Evaluation Issues," *Journal of Financial Economics* 10, no. 3 (November 1982):289–321.

[32] A later study found that most of the adjustment actually was in the three-day period after the change. The most notable price movement was associated with those stocks being upgraded from 2 to 1. Other notable but less sizable price movements were associated with upgrades from 3 to 2 and downgrades from 1 to 2 and 2 to 3. See Scott E. Stickel, "The Effect of Value Line Investment Survey Rank Changes on Common Stock Prices," *Journal of Financial Economics* 14, no. 1 (March 1985):121–43.

These results do not suggest that Value Line provides a guaranteed formula for outstanding portfolio performance. No transactions costs were charged in the calculations, and turnover was high.[33] But the results do suggest that in choosing among stocks, Value Line rankings may prove useful.[34] It can be conjectured that Value Line rankings "work" primarily because they use quarterly earnings in both the earnings momentum and surprise elements that go into the Value Line ranking procedure.[35] After all, it has been noted that there are abnormal price movements subsequent to the announcement of quarterly earnings.

To summarize, the results suggest there is a two-part puzzle associated with Value Line ranks. First, Value Line appears to have superior forcasting ability that is based on public information. Second, the market takes time to adjust to the Value Line rankings. Both these observations are puzzling because they are inconsistent with the notion of efficient markets.

QUESTIONS AND PROBLEMS

1. For a given level of earnings (E), net new investment (I), and dividends (D), explain why a firm must issue new stock if $E < D + I$ and it desires to maintain a constant debt–equity ratio. Similarly, why must it repurchase shares if $E > D + I$ and it desires to maintain a constant debt-equity ratio?

2. Why is an individual stockholder indifferent between the firm retaining \$1 of earnings or paying out the \$1 of earnings as a dividend, assuming that the stockholder maintains constant proportional ownership in the firm and the firm maintains a constant debt–equity ratio?

3. If the dividend decision is truly irrelevant to the economic value of a corporation, are dividend discount models of any use in estimating the fair price of a corporation's stock? Explain.

4. How are dividends used as a signaling device by corporate management? To the extent that dividends are a signaling device, how are dividend changes related to stock prices?

5. Discuss why there generally does not exist a one-to-one relationship between corporations' book values and their market values.

6. The price per share of Little Rock Company is less than its book value. Does this indicate that those who now hold the firm's shares have lost money in the past? Does it indicate that they are likely to lose money in the future? Does it indicate that Little Rock Company should not undertake any further capital investment? Explain your answers.

---

[33] A discussion of transactions costs is contained in Copeland and Mayers, "The Value Line Enigma," 319–20; and Clark Holloway, "A Note on Testing an Aggressive Investment Strategy Using Value Line Ranks," *Journal of Finance* 36, no. 3 (June 1981):711–19.

[34] Value Line also provides a measure of the risk of individual securities (known as Safety Rank). Interestingly, this rank measure was found to be more highly correlated with subsequent returns than either beta or standard deviation, suggesting it is a useful measure of a security's risk. See Russell J. Fuller and G. Wenchi Wong, "Traditional versus Theoretical Risk Measures," *Financial Analysts Journal* 44, no. 2 (March/April 1988):52–57, 67.

[35] One speculation is that the rankings are simply capturing the size effect by giving higher ranks to smaller firms (the size effect is discussed in Appendix A to Chapter 15). However, tests suggest this is not true. See Gur Huberman and Shmuel Kandel, "Value Line Rank and Firm Size," *Journal of Business* 60, no. 4 (October 1987): 577–89.

7. Why might a steady trend in a firm's reported earnings from year to year suggest that the figures do not represent the firm's economic earnings?

8. Reported earnings typically differ, sometimes considerably, from economic earnings. Nevertheless, it is often argued that reported earnings are intended simply to provide a "source of information" to investors about the value of the firm. If so, might there not be many alternative accounting procedures of equal use to investors? How might one go about evaluating the usefulness of such procedures?

9. Price–earnings ratios for individual companies vary over time and across firms. Discuss some of the possible reasons for this variability.

10. Harlond Clift once wrote in a market newsletter that, "I focus my research on consensus earnings forecasts. Those companies that the consensus believes will produce the largest earnings increases next year are most likely to produce the best returns." Is Harlond's opinion consistent with empirical evidence? Explain why or why not.

11. Why might the price of a stock react only partially to an "earnings surprise" on the first day or two after the earnings announcement?

12. (Appendix Question) The Value Line ranking system has long shown a consistent ability to produce positive risk-adjusted returns. These results have been particularly disconcerting for efficient markets proponents. Why?

Chapter 18

OPTIONS

In the world of investments, an *option* is a type of contract between two people where one person grants the other person the right to buy a specific asset at a specific price within a specific time period. Alternatively, the contract may grant the other person the right to sell a specific asset at a specific price within a specific time period. The person who has received the right and thus has a decision to make is known as the option buyer, since he or she must pay for this right. The person who has sold the right to the buyer and thus must respond to the buyer's decision is known as the option writer.

The variety of contracts containing an option feature is enormous. Even within the domain of publicly traded securities, many types can be found. Traditionally, only certain instruments are referred to as options; the others, though similar in nature, are designated in other ways. This chapter presents an introduction to the institutional features of such contracts, along with some basics regarding how they are valued in the marketplace.

18.1 TYPES OF OPTION CONTRACTS

☐ 18.1.1 Call Options

The most prominent type of option contract is the *call option* for stocks. It gives the buyer the right to buy ("call away") a specific number of shares of a specific company from the option writer at a specific purchase price at any time up to and including a specific date. The contract specifies four items:

1. The company whose shares can be bought
2. The number of shares that can be bought
3. The purchase price for those shares, known as the *exercise price* (or *striking price*)
4. The date when the right to buy expires, known as the *expiration date*

An Example

Consider a simple hypothetical example where investors B and W are thinking about signing a call option contract. This contract will allow B to buy

from W 100 shares of Widget for $50 per share at any time during the next six months. Currently, Widget is selling for $45 per share on an organized exchange. Investor B, the potential option buyer, believes that the price of Widget's common stock will rise substantially over the next six months; investor W, the potential option writer, has a different opinion about Widget, believing its stock price will not rise above $50 over this time period.

Will investor W be willing to sign this contract without receiving something in return from investor B? No, W is running a risk by signing the contract and would demand compensation for doing so. The risk is that Widget's stock price will subsequently rise above $50 per share, in which case W will have to buy the shares at that price and then turn them over to B for only $50 per share. Perhaps the stock will rise to $60, costing W $6000 ($60 × 100 shares) to buy the stock. Then W will give the 100 shares to B and receive in return $5000 ($50 × 100 shares). Consequently, W will lose $1000 ($6000 − $5000).

The point is that the buyer of a call option will have to pay the writer something in order to get the writer to sign the contract. The amount paid is known as the *premium*, although option price is a more appropriate term. In the example, perhaps the premium is $3 per share, meaning that investor B will pay $300 ($3 × 100 shares) to investor W in order to induce W to sign the contract. Since investor B expects Widget's stock price to rise in the future, he or she would expect to make money by purchasing shares of Widget at $45 per share. The attraction of purchasing call options instead of shares is that investor B can apply a high degree of leverage, since only $3 per share needs to be spent in order to purchase the option.

At some point after investors B and W have signed the call option contract, investor W might like to get out of the contract. Breaching the contract is illegal, but getting out is still possible. Investor W could buy the contract back from investor B for a negotiated amount of money and then destroy the document. If Widget rises in one month to $55 per share, perhaps the amount will be $7 per share (or, in total, $700 = $7 × 100 shares). In this case, W will have lost $400 ($300 − $700) and B will have made $400. Alternatively, if Widget falls to $40 per share, perhaps the amount will be $.50 per share (or, in total, $50 = $.50 × 100 shares), in which case W will have made $250 ($300 − $50) and B will have lost $250.

Another way that W can get out of the contract is to find someone else to take his or her position in the contract (the contract has a provision that allows this to be done). For example, if Widget has risen to $55 per share after one month, perhaps investor W will find an investor, denoted by WW, who is willing to become the option writer if W will pay him or her $7 per share (or $700 in total) to do so. Assuming they both agree, the contract will be amended so that WW is now the option writer, with W no longer being a party in the contract.

If investor B subsequently wants to get out of the contract, B could see if someone is willing to pay an agreeable sum of money in order to possess the right to buy Widget stock under the terms of the contract. That is, B could attempt to sell the contract to someone else. In this situation, perhaps investor B will find another investor, denoted by BB, who is willing to pay

B $7 per share (or $700 in total) in return for the right to buy Widget under the terms of the call option contract. Provided B is agreeable, the call option contract will be sold to BB and amended, making BB the option buyer.

In this example, both the original parties, W and B, have "closed out" their positions and are no longer involved in the call option contract. However, the example suggests that the original writer and buyer must meet face to face in order to draw up the terms of the contract. It also suggests that if either the original writer or buyer wants to get out of the contract, then he or she must reach an agreeable price with the other original party or, alternatively, find a third investor to whom the position in the contract can be transferred. Thus, it would appear that there is a great amount of effort involved if an investor wants to deal in options.

Fortunately, this is not the case in the United States due to the introduction of standardized contracts and the maintenance of a marketplace by organized exchanges for listed options.[1] The Options Clearing Corporation (OCC), a company that is jointly owned by several exchanges, greatly facilitates trading in these options. It does so by maintaining a computer system that keeps track of all these options by recording the position of each investor in each one.

Although the mechanics are rather complex, the principles are simple enough. As soon as a buyer and a writer decide to trade a particular option contract and the buyer pays the agreed-upon premium, the OCC steps in, becoming the effective writer as far as the buyer is concerned and the effective buyer as far as the writer is concerned. Thus, at this time all direct links between original buyer and writer are severed. If a buyer chooses to exercise an option, the OCC will randomly choose a writer who has not closed his or her position and assign the exercise notice accordingly. The OCC also guarantees delivery if the writer is unable to come up with the shares.

The OCC makes it possible for buyers and writers to close out (or unwind) their positions at any time. If a buyer subsequently becomes a writer of the same contract, meaning that the buyer later sells the contract to someone else, the OCC computer will note the offsetting positions in this investor's account and will simply cancel both entries. Thus, an investor who buys a contract on Monday and then sells it on Tuesday will be treated as if a contract had been bought on Monday and an identical contract written on Tuesday. The computer will note that the investor's net position is zero and will remove both entries. The second trade is a *closing sale*, since it serves to close out the investor's position from the earlier trade. Closing sales thus allow buyers to sell options rather than exercise them.

A similar procedure allows a writer to pay to be relieved of the potential obligation to deliver stock. Consider an investor who writes a contract on Wednesday and buys an identical one on Thursday. The latter is a *closing purchase* and, analogous to a closing sale, serves to close out the investor's position from the earlier trade.

Call options are *protected* against stock splits and stock dividends on

---

[1] Prior to 1973, options were traded over the counter through the efforts of dealers and brokers. These dealers and brokers brought buyers and writers together, arranged terms, helped with the paperwork, and charged fees for their efforts.

the underlying stock. In the example where the option was on 100 shares of Widget stock with an exercise price of $50, a 2-for-1 stock split would cause the contract to be altered so that it was for 200 shares at $25 per share. The reason for this protection has to do with the effect that stock splits and stock dividends have on the share price of the firm. Since either of these events will cause the share price to fall below what it otherwise would have been, they work to the disadvantage of the call option buyer and to the advantage of the call option writer.

In terms of cash dividends, there is no protection for listed call options.[2] That is, the exercise price and number of shares are unaffected by the payment of cash dividends. For example, the terms of the Widget call option would remain the same if Widget declared a $4 per share cash dividend.

☐ 18.1.2 **Put Options**

A second type of option contract for stocks is the *put option*. It gives the buyer the right to sell ("put away") a specific number of shares of a specific company to the option writer at a specific selling price at any time up to and including a specific date. The contract specifies four items that are analagous to those for call options:

1. The company whose shares can be sold
2. The number of shares that can be sold
3. The selling price for those shares, known as the *exercise price* (or *striking price*)
4. The date when the right to sell expires, known as the *expiration date*

An Example

Consider an example where investors B and W are thinking about signing a put option contract. This contract will allow B to sell to W 100 shares of XYZ Company for $30 per share at any time during the next six months. Currently, XYZ is selling for $35 per share on an organized exchange. Investor B, the potential option buyer, believes that the price of XYZ's common stock will fall substantially over the next six months; investor W, the potential option writer, has a different opinion about XYZ, believing its stock price will not fall below $30 over this time period.

As with the call option on Widget, investor W would be running a risk by signing the contract and would demand compensation for doing so. The risk is that XYZ's stock price will subsequently fall below $30 per share, in which case W will have to buy the shares at $30 per share from B when they are not worth that much in the marketplace. Perhaps XYZ will fall to $20, costing W $3000 ($30 × 100 shares) to buy stock that is only worth $2000 ($20 × 100 shares). Consequently, W would have lost $1000 ($3000 − $2000). In this case, B would make $1000, purchasing XYZ in the marketplace for $2000 and then selling the shares to W for $3000.

---

[2] However, there is protection for any cash dividend that is formally designated a *return of capital*. Furthermore, options that are traded over the counter typically are protected from any type of cash dividend. In both cases, the protection is in the form of a reduction in the exercise price.

As with a call option, the buyer of a put option will have to pay the writer an amount of money known as a *premium* in order to get the writer to sign the contract and assume this risk. Also, as in call options, the buyer and writer may close out (or unwind) their positions at any time by simply entering an offsetting transaction. As with calls, this is easily done for listed put options in the United States, since these contracts are standardized.

Again, the OCC facilitates trading in listed puts, since these options exist only in the memory of its computer system. Just like calls, as soon as a buyer and a writer decide to trade a particular put option contract and the buyer pays the agreed-upon premium, the OCC steps in, becoming the effective writer as far as the buyer is concerned and the effective buyer as far as the writer is concerned. If a buyer chooses to exercise an option, the OCC randomly chooses a writer who has not closed his or her position and assigns the exercise notice accordingly. The OCC also guarantees delivery of the exercise price if the writer is unable to come up with the necessary cash.

Like calls, puts are protected against stock splits and stock dividends on the underlying stock. In the example where the option was on 100 shares of XYZ stock with an exercise price of $30, a 2-for-1 stock split would cause the contract to be altered so that it was for 200 shares at $15 per share. In terms of cash dividends, there is no protection for listed puts.

18.2 OPTION TRADING

Exchanges begin trading in a new set of options on a given stock every three months, where the options have roughly nine months before they expire.[3] For example, options on Widget might be introduced in January, April, July, and October with expiration dates in September, December, March, and June, respectively. Generally, two call options on a stock are introduced at the same time, the two being identical in all aspects except for the exercise price. In terms of the exercise price, if the stock is selling for $100 or less at the time the options are to be introduced, then the two exercise prices will be set at $5 intervals bracketing the stock price.[4] Furthermore, a pair of put option contracts may also be introduced at the same time. For example, if Widget is selling for $43 in January, then two September call options may be introduced that have exercise prices of $40 and $45; similarly, two September put options with exercise prices of $40 and $45 may also be introduced.

After an option has been introduced, new options having the same terms as the existing ones but with different exercise prices may be introduced when the stock price of the company moves up or down so much that it is substantially outside of the initial bracket. In terms of Widget, if its stock

---

[3] For some active stocks, options may be introduced that have only one or two months to expiration. For a detailed description of how options are created and traded, see Chapter 3 of John C. Cox and Mark Rubinstein, *Options Markets* (Englewood Cliffs, N.J.: Prentice Hall, 1985).

[4] If the stock sells for less than $25, then the interval may be $2.50 (for example, at $15 and $17.50 for a stock selling at $16); if the stock sells for more than $100, the interval may be for $10 or even $20. It should be noted that exchange officials have a reasonable amount of latitude in setting the terms of the options.

price rises in the next month to $49, perhaps September put and call options having a $50 exercise price will be introduced.

Once listed, an option remains listed until its expiration date. Specifically, listed options on common stocks generally expire at 10:59 A.M. central time on the Saturday after the third Friday of the specified month.

In recent years, common stock options have been traded on the Chicago Board Options Exchange (CBOE) and on the American, Pacific, Philadelphia, and New York Stock Exchanges. Figure 18.1 shows a portion of the daily listing of the trading activity on the CBOE. The first column shows the name of the company and, indented below it, the closing price on its common stock. The next column shows the exercise price for the option contracts on the company. The next three columns show the premiums on the last trades for call options having expiration dates on the three specified months, and the final three columns show the corresponding premiums for put options.

For example, Boeing common stock closed at $62.75 on December 8, 1988. At the end of that day, Boeing call options with an exercise price of $60 per share that expire on the third Friday of December, January, and February were traded at $3.00, $3.875, and $4.75, respectively. Similarly, Boeing put options with an exercise price of $60 that expire on the third Friday of December, January, and February were traded at $.0625, $.75, and $1.25, respectively.

Some options are not traded during a day and are indicated by the letter r (see, for example, "CBS December 165 calls" in Figure 18.1). Others, although included because of the format of the report, have not been introduced and are therefore unavailable for trading. These contracts are indicated by the letter s (in Figure 18.1 see, for example, "CBS January 180 puts").

At the bottom of all an exchange's listings, the total volume (that is, the number of contracts traded) and open interest (the number of contracts outstanding) for calls and puts are displayed.

Quotations for options are reported in the format shown in Figure 18.1. Additional information is provided every day for the "most active" options on each of several exchanges. Figure 18.2 provides an example of the most active options on the Philadelphia Exchange. After the name of the company and the contract specifications come the sales volume on the contract on that day, the closing price on the contract, the change this represents from the previous day's closing price, and the closing price on the underlying stock.

For example, MCA January 50 calls were traded on the Philadelphia Exchange and were one of the most active issues there on December 8, 1988. On that day, 1262 of these contracts were traded. The premium on the last trade was $1.125 per share (or $112.50 per contract, since a contract is for 100 shares). This represents an increase of $.25 per share (or $25 per contract) from the premium on the previous day. At this time, the closing price on the common stock of MCA was $46.125 per share.

Investors may place the same kinds of orders for options as for stocks—market, limit, stop, and stop-limit orders (these were discussed in Chapter 2). However, the way the orders for options are executed on the exchanges is, in some cases, different from the way that orders for stocks are executed.

LISTED OPTIONS QUOTATIONS

Thursday, December 8, 1988

Options closing prices. Sales unit usually is 100 shares.
Stock close is New York or American exchange final price.

CHICAGO BOARD

Option & NY Close	Strike Price	Calls—Last Dec	Calls—Last Jan	Calls—Last Feb	Puts—Last Dec	Puts—Last Jan	Puts—Last Feb
AlexAl	25	r	r	1	r	r	r
Amdahl	15	r	4	r	r	r	r
18 3/8	17 1/2	1	2	r	1/8	r	r
18 3/8	20	1/8	1/2	1 1/8	r	r	2
AlnGrp	65	2 1/2	3 1/2	r	r	r	r
67	70	r	r	1 3/8	r	r	r
Amoco	70	r	6 1/4	r	r	1/4	r
74 1/4	75	7/8	2	2 5/8	r	1 1/2	2 1/4
74 1/4	80	1/16	r	1/2	r	r	r
A M P	40	3 7/8	r	r	r	r	r
43 3/4	45	r	1 1/16	2	r	r	r
Anadrk	30	r	r	3/4	r	r	r
Baxter	15	r	r	3	r	r	r
17 1/2	17 1/2	3/8	13/16	1 1/4	r	5/8	7/8
17 1/2	20	r	3/16	1/2	r	r	r
17 1/2	22 1/2	s	s	3/16	s	s	r
Blk Dk	20	2 1/4	3 1/8	3 1/4	r	r	r
22 1/8	22 1/2	5/16	1	1 1/4	1/2	r	r
22 1/8	25	1/8	r	7/16	r	r	r
Boeing	60	3	3 7/8	4 3/4	1/16	3/4	1 1/4
62 3/4	65	3/16	1 1/8	1 3/4	2 1/4	2 5/8	3 1/2
Bois C	40	1/2	r	2 1/4	r	r	1 1/2
40 1/4	45	r	r	5/8	r	r	r
C B S	165	r	r	r	r	r	4
168 1/4	170	r	r	6	r	r	r
168 1/4	175	r	r	4 1/4	6 3/4	r	r
168 1/4	180	1/16	s	r	r	s	r
CapCit	350	r	r	r	1 11/16	5 1/2	r
361 3/4	360	5 1/2	9 7/8	r	r	r	r
361 3/4	370	1 1/4	r	9 1/8	r	r	r
Coke	40	r	4 3/8	5	r	r	3/8
44	45	1/4	1 1/8	1 5/8	r	r	r
44	50	r	s	1/4	r	s	r
CocaCE	15	r	3/8	1/2	r	r	r
Colg o	40	s	s	r	s	s	1/4
Colgat	45	r	1 9/16	2 1/4	r	r	r
45 1/2	50	1/16	r	5/8	r	r	r
Cmw Ed	30	2 1/2	r	2 7/8	r	r	r
32 3/8	35	r	r	1/4	r	r	r
C Data	15	r	r	r	r	3/16	r
17 5/8	17 1/2	r	1 1/2	r	r	1 1/8	r
17 5/8	20	3/16	11/16	1 1/8	r	r	r
17 5/8	22 1/2	1/8	s	9/16	r	s	r
17 5/8	25	s	s	3/8	s	s	r
CornGl	60	8 5/8	r	9 1/8	r	r	1/2
68 5/8	65	3 1/2	4 1/4	5	1/8	7/8	1 1/2
68 5/8	70	3/8	1 3/16	2 3/8	r	3 3/8	r
68 5/8	75	r	s	r	r	s	7 3/4
Diebld	35	r	r	r	1/4	r	r
35 3/4	40	r	r	3/4	r	r	r
Edwrds	20	r	5/16	1/2	r	r	r
ForstL	25	r	r	11/16	r	r	r
GnCine	22 1/2	r	r	1 3/4	r	r	r
23	25	1/16	r	5/8	r	r	r
Gn Dyn	50	3/4	1 3/4	2 5/8	1	r	2 1/4
50	55	r	r	r	r	6	r
Gdrich	45	r	r	r	r	r	7/8
50 3/8	50	1	2 3/8	3 1/4	5/8	1 1/4	2 5/8
50 3/8	55	3/16	3/4	1 5/8	4 1/2	4 3/4	4 7/8
50 3/8	60	r	s	5/8	r	s	r
50 3/8	65	s	s	3/8	s	s	r
Harris	25	2 1/2	r	r	r	r	r
27 3/4	30	r	r	13/16	r	r	r
Hewlet	45	4 7/8	6 1/4	6 3/4	r	r	1/2
49 5/8	50	13/16	2 1/16	3 1/8	7/8	1 3/4	2 1/4
49 5/8	55	r	5/8	15/16	4	r	5
49 5/8	60	s	s	1/4	s	s	r
Honwll	55	r	r	r	r	3/4	1
58 1/8	60	5/16	1 1/2	2 1/2	2	2 1/2	r
58 1/8	65	1/16	3/8	7/8	r	r	7
58 1/8	70	r	s	3/8	r	s	11
58 1/8	75	s	s	1/4	s	s	r
58 1/8	80	s	s	1/8	s	s	r
Humana	22 1/2	r	r	3	r	r	r
25	25	r	15/16	1 1/8	r	r	r
25	30	r	r	1/16	r	r	r

FIGURE 18–1
Listed options quotations.

SOURCE: Reprinted by permission of *The Wall Street Journal*, © Dow Jones & Company, Inc. (December 9, 1988): p. C12.

CHICAGO BOARD

		Sales	Last	Chg.	N.Y. Close
CALLS					
SP100	Dec265	18759	$1\frac{7}{8}$	— $\frac{7}{8}$	262.92
SP100	Dec260	11953	5	— $1\frac{1}{4}$	262.92
SP100	Dec270	9848	$\frac{1}{2}$	— 7-16	262.92
Chryslr	Dec25	7584	2	— 1-16	27
RJR Nb	Dec90	7581	1 1-16	— 15-16	$89\frac{7}{8}$
PUTS					
SP100	Dec260	12555	1 9-16	+ $\frac{1}{4}$	262.92
SP100	Dec265	11094	$3\frac{1}{2}$	+ $\frac{1}{2}$	262.92
SP100	Dec255	7304	11-16	+ $\frac{1}{8}$	262.92
SP100	Dec250	4795	5-16	......	262.92
RJR Nb	Dec90	3670	$1\frac{1}{8}$	+ 7-16	$89\frac{7}{8}$

AMERICAN

		Sales	Last	Chg.	N.Y. Close
CALLS					
Ph Mor	Dec90	20525	$8\frac{1}{8}$	+ $\frac{1}{4}$	98
Ph Mor	Dec85	20505	13	+ $\frac{1}{4}$	98
Ph Mor	Dec80	10527	18	......	98
Ph Mor	Dec95	9525	3	+ $\frac{1}{4}$	98
Texaco	Jan55	7857	1	+ 1-16	$50\frac{7}{8}$
PUTS					
PacGE	Dec20	5300	2	......	$18\frac{1}{4}$
MM AM	Dec420	2452	$3\frac{1}{2}$	+ $\frac{3}{8}$	420.99
MM AM	Dec415	2357	$1\frac{3}{4}$	+ 1-16	420.99
Texaco	Jan50	1345	$1\frac{5}{8}$	+ $\frac{1}{4}$	$50\frac{7}{8}$
Texaco	Dec50	1184	$\frac{5}{8}$	— 1-16	$50\frac{7}{8}$

PHILADELPHIA

		Sales	Last	Chg.	N.Y. Close
CALLS					
M C A	Jan50	1262	$1\frac{1}{8}$	+ $\frac{1}{4}$	$46\frac{1}{8}$
UniTel	Jan45	1121	2	+ $\frac{3}{4}$	$45\frac{3}{8}$
TexEst	Jan35	939	11-16	+ $\frac{1}{8}$	$29\frac{7}{8}$
M C A	Feb50	878	$1\frac{7}{8}$	+ $\frac{3}{8}$	$46\frac{1}{8}$
G A F	Jan50	784	7-16	— 1-16	$45\frac{7}{8}$

		Sales	Last	Chg.	N.Y. Close
PUTS					
FarmGp	Dec65	510	1-16	— 1-16	$74\frac{3}{8}$
FarmGp	Dec70	323	$\frac{1}{8}$	— 1-16	$74\frac{3}{8}$
M C A	Jan45	260	$1\frac{1}{2}$	— 3-16	$46\frac{1}{8}$
P P G	Jan35	215	$\frac{1}{4}$	— $\frac{1}{8}$	$38\frac{3}{4}$
LomFn	Dec17½	212	$4\frac{3}{8}$	+ $\frac{1}{4}$	$13\frac{1}{8}$

PACIFIC

		Sales	Last	Chg.	N.Y. Close
CALLS					
SmkB	Dec50	9207	$3\frac{1}{4}$	+ $2\frac{1}{4}$	$51\frac{7}{8}$
SmkB	Jan50	5939	$5\frac{3}{8}$	+ $2\frac{3}{4}$	$51\frac{7}{8}$
SmkB	Dec55	4504	$1\frac{3}{4}$	+ $1\frac{1}{4}$	$51\frac{7}{8}$
SmkB	Dec60	4385	$\frac{7}{8}$	+ $\frac{5}{8}$	$51\frac{7}{8}$
SmkB	Jan55	2822	3	......	$51\frac{7}{8}$
PUTS					
SmkB	Dec50	664	$1\frac{1}{2}$	— $1\frac{5}{8}$	$51\frac{7}{8}$
Unocal	Jan35	548	9-16	— 1-16	$38\frac{1}{8}$
SmkB	Mar45	284	2	— $\frac{5}{8}$	$51\frac{7}{8}$
Compaq	Jan50	276	$\frac{1}{2}$	+ $\frac{1}{8}$	$56\frac{3}{4}$
Gentch	Dec15	267	1-16	......	$16\frac{1}{2}$

NEW YORK

		Sales	Last	Chg.	N.Y. Close
CALLS					
Intrc o	Dec70	1330	11-16	......	
Nynex	Jan65	735	$2\frac{3}{4}$	+ $\frac{1}{2}$	$67\frac{3}{8}$
Maytag	Jan20	519	$\frac{7}{8}$	— $\frac{1}{8}$	$19\frac{7}{8}$
Nynex	Apr65	508	$3\frac{3}{8}$	+ $\frac{3}{8}$	$67\frac{3}{8}$
Intrc o	Dec65	260	$5\frac{1}{8}$	+ $\frac{1}{8}$	
PUTS					
Maytag	Jan20	291	1	— 1-16	$19\frac{7}{8}$
NY Idx	Dec147½	276	1-16	— 1-16	155.37
NY Idx	Dec155	171	1 1-16	— $\frac{1}{8}$	155.37
NY Idx	Dec152½	117	$\frac{3}{8}$	+ 1-16	155.37
NY Idx	Dec150	89	3-16	......	155.37

FIGURE 18–2
Most active options quotations.

SOURCE: Reprinted by permission of *The Wall Street Journal*, © Dow Jones & Company, Inc. (December 9, 1988): p. C12.

As mentioned in Chapter 2, trading on stock exchanges centers around specialists. These people serve two functions, acting as both dealers and brokers. As dealers, they keep an inventory of the stocks that are assigned to them and buy and sell from that inventory at bid and ask prices, respectively. As brokers, they keep the limit order book and execute the orders in it as market prices move up and down. Some option markets, such as the American Stock Exchange, function in a similar manner. These markets have specialists who are assigned specific option contracts, and these specialists act as dealers and brokers in their assigned options. Like the stock exchanges, there may also be *floor traders*, who trade solely for themselves,

hoping to buy low and sell high, and *floor brokers*, who handle orders from the public.

Other option markets, such as the Chicago Board Options Exchange, do not involve specialists. Instead, they involve *market-makers*, who act solely as dealers, and *order book officials* (previously known as board brokers), who keep the limit order book. The market-makers must trade with *floor brokers*, members of the exchange who handle orders from the public. In doing so, the market-makers have an inventory of options and quote bid and ask prices. Although there is one and only one specialist typically assigned to a stock, there usually is more than one market-maker assigned to the options on a given stock. Furthermore, a market-maker is prohibited from handling public orders in his or her assigned options but may handle public orders in other options. That is, market-makers can also act as floor brokers, but only in unassigned options.

The order book official, in keeping the limit order book, is not allowed to engage in any trading. Unlike the specialist, the order book official's limit order book can be shown to other members of the exchange. The order book official stands at the trading post for those options that are his or her responsibility. All orders must be executed by means of an auction at the trading post with "open outcry," meaning that the auction is conducted orally.

Like the organized stock exchanges in the United States, all option exchanges are continuous markets, meaning orders can be executed any time the exchanges are open. However, actual trading in options is, on occasion, far from continuous. In the financial press, it is not unusual to find prices for various options that appear to be out of line with one another or with the price of the underlying stock. It should be remembered that each listed price is that of the last trade of the day and that these trades may have taken place at different times. Apparent price disparities may simply reflect trades that occurred before and after major news, rather than concurrent values at which obviously profitable trades could have been made.

Although a commission must be paid to a stockbroker whenever an option is either written, bought, or sold, the size of the commission has been reduced substantially since options began to be traded on organized exchanges in 1973. Furthermore, this commission is typically smaller than the commission that would be paid if the underlying stock had been purchased instead of the option. However, the investor should be aware that exercising an option will typically result in both the writer and buyer having to pay a commission equivalent to the commission that would be incurred if the stock itself were being bought or sold.

18.3 MARGIN

Any buyer of an option would like some assurance that the writer can deliver as required if the option is exercised. Specifically, the buyer of a call option would like some assurance that the writer is capable of delivering the requisite shares, and the buyer of a put option would like some assurance that the writer is capable of delivering the necessary cash. Since all option con-

tracts are with the Option Clearing Corporation, the OCC is actually the one who is concerned with the ability of the writer to fulfill the terms of the contract.

To relieve the OCC of this concern, margin requirements have been set by the exchanges where the options are traded. However, brokerage firms are allowed to impose even stricter requirements if they so desire, since they are ultimately liable to the OCC for the actions of their investors.

In the case of a call, shares are to be delivered by the writer in return for the exercise price. In the case of a put, cash is to be delivered in return for shares. In either case, the net cost to the option writer is the absolute difference between the exercise price and the stock's market value at the time of exercise. Since the OCC is at risk if the writer is unable to bear this cost, it is not surprising that the OCC has a system in place that protects itself from the actions of the writers. This system is known as *margin*, and it is similar in some ways to the notion of margin associated with stock purchases and short sales that was discussed in Chapter 2.[5]

In a situation known as *covered call writing*, where the writer of a call owns the underlying stock, the writer does not need to come up with any cash. Instead, the premium paid by the buyer is given to the writer but the writer's stock is kept in escrow by the brokerage firm. Thus, if the buyer chooses to exercise the option, the requisite shares are at hand for delivery. If the option expires or if the writer enters a closing purchase, then the writer will have access to the shares.

In a situation known as *naked call writing*, where the writer of a call does not own the underlying stock, the margin requirements are more complicated. Specifically, margin is the higher of two figures. The first figure is equal to the option premium plus 15% of the market value of the underlying stock, less an amount equal to the call's exercise price less than the stock's market price (note that this can be a positive or negative amount). The second figure is equal to the sum of the option premium and 5% of the market price of the underlying stock.

As an example of the margin required for naked call writing, consider an investor who writes a December 60 call and receives a premium of $3 per share. If the underlying stock is selling for $58, then the margin is the higher of two figures calculated as follows:

Method 1: Option premium
        = $3 × 100 shares $ 300
      15% of market value of stock
        = .15 × $58 × 100 shares   870
      Less amount by which call's exercise price
        exceeds stock's market price
        = ($60 − $58) × 100 shares   −200
        Total $ 970

---

[5] It should be noted that a call or put buyer is not allowed to use margin. Instead, the option buyer is required to pay 100% of the option's purchase price. In contrast, the stock buyer could use margin, where part of the cost of purchasing the stock is borrowed.

Method 2: Option premium
　　　　= $3 × 100 shares　　　　　　　　　　　　$　300
　　　　5% of market value of stock
　　　　　　= .05 × $58 × 100 shares　　　　　　　　290
　　　　　　　　　Total　　　　　　　　　　　　$　590

Since the first method results in a higher figure, it is applicable. Thus, in this example the amount of margin required is $970, meaning the writer must deposit $970 in cash with his or her broker. Since the premium can be used for this purpose, the writer needs to come up with only $970 − $300 = $670.

For puts, the margin requirements are similar. If the brokerage account of the writer of a put contains cash (or other securities) amounting to the exercise price of the put, then no margin is required. Furthermore, the writer can remove from the account an amount of cash that is equal to the premium received from the buyer. The reason for this is that the account will still have collateral that is equal in value to the exercise price.

If the brokerage account of a put writer does not contain cash (or securities), then the situation is known as *naked put writing*. The amount of margin required for such a writer is calculated in a manner similar to that for the writer of a naked call option. That is, the put writer must come up with margin equal to the larger of two figures. The first figure is equal to the option premium plus 15% of the market value of the underlying stock, less an amount equal to the stock's market price less than put's exercise price (note that this is the reverse of the amount for a call and can be a positive or negative amount). The second figure is calculated exactly as previously described for calls, being equal to the sum of the option premium and 5% of the market price of the underlying security.

As an example of the margin required for naked put writing, consider an investor who writes a March 40 put and receives a premium of $4 per share. If the underlying stock is selling for $39, then the margin is the higher of two figures calculated as follows:

Method 1: Option premium
　　　　= $4 × 100 shares　　　　　　　　　　　　$　　400
　　　　15% of market value of stock
　　　　　　= .15 × $39 × 100 shares　　　　　　　　585
　　　　Less amount by which stock's market price exceeds
　　　　put's exercise price
　　　　　　= ($39 − $40) × 100 shares　　　　　　−(−100)
　　　　　　　　　Total　　　　　　　　　　　　$1085

Method 2: Option premium
　　　　= $4 × 100 shares　　　　　　　　　　　　$　　400
　　　　5% of market value of stock
　　　　　　= .05 × $39 × 100 shares　　　　　　　　195
　　　　　　　　　Total　　　　　　　　　　　　$　　595

Since the first method results in a higher figure, it is applicable. Thus, in this example the amount of margin required is equal to $1085, meaning the writer must deposit $1085 in cash with his or her broker. Since the premium can be used for this purpose, the writer needs to come up with only $1085 − $400 = $685.

It should be noted that maintenance margin requirements for options are the same as initial margin requirements. Furthermore, the calculation of margin requirements becomes much more complex when the individual is engaged in various investment activities (such as simultaneously buying and writing different put and call options as well as buying some common stocks on margin while short selling others).

18.4 TAXATION OF OPTION PROFITS AND LOSSES

Although income tax regulations can be quite complex, the general approach to the taxation of profits and losses from option trading is reasonably easy to understand. Basically, capital gains and losses are involved, with the net amount being treated as ordinary income if it is a gain and being fully deductible (subject to a $3000 cap) from ordinary income if it is a loss. Commissions paid are added to purchase prices and subtracted from selling prices in determining the amount of the capital gains and losses.

Consider a call option buyer first. If the call is exercised, the buyer is considered to have bought the stock for a total cost equal to the exercise price plus the premium paid for the option itself. When the stock is subsequently sold, the difference between this cost and the selling price is the buyer's capital gain or loss.

If the call buyer later sells the option instead of exercising it, the difference between the buying and selling prices is the amount of the capital gain or loss. However, if the call expires unexercised, the buyer will have a capital loss equal to the premium paid on the option.

Consider the writer of a call option next. If the call is exercised, the writer is considered to have sold the stock for a total value equal to the exercise price plus the premium received for the option. The difference between this value and the price paid when the stock was purchased is the amount of the capital gain or loss incurred by the writer.

If the call writer later buys the option, thereby closing out his or her position, the difference between the premium that was received when the option was written and the premium that was paid to close out the position is the amount of the capital gain or loss. However, if the option expires unexercised, then the writer will have a capital gain equal to the amount of the premium received.

The treatment of puts is quite similar. If the put expires unexercised, then the buyer has a capital loss and the writer has a capital gain that are both equal to the premium on the put. If a closing transaction is entered, then the difference between the buying and selling prices is the amount of the capital gain or loss. If the put is exercised, then the buyer has a capital

gain equal to the exercise price less the amount paid for both the stock and the put. The writer who receives the stock in the situation is treated as having made a stock purchase for an amount equal to the exercise price less the premium received on the put.

These and other rules give rise to a number of strategies that take tax consequences into account. For example, consider an investor who previously bought a stock and has seen its market price rise dramatically. If the investor sells it now, a capital gain will be incurred. However, the investor could buy a January put and hold off selling the stock until the turn of the year. By doing so, the capital gain will be not be realized this year, so no taxes will need to be paid on the stock this year. However, the gain on the stock will have been protected by the use of the put. Once January comes around, the investor can decide to either exercise the put or sell the stock, realizing the gain at that time and thus deferring tax payments for a year.

18.5 VALUATION OF OPTIONS

☐ 18.5.1 Valuation at Expiration

The value of an option is related to the value of the underlying security in a manner that is most easily seen just prior to expiration (which, for simplicity, will be referred to as *at expiration*). Figure 18.3(a) relates the value of a call option with an exercise price of $100 to the price of the underlying stock at expiration. If the stock price is below $100, the option will be worthless when it expires. If the price is above $100, the option can be exercised for $100 to obtain a security with a greater value, resulting in a net gain to the option buyer that will equal the difference between the security's market price and the exercise price. However, there is no need for the option buyer actually to exercise the option. Instead, the option writer can simply pay the

FIGURE 18–3
Values of options at expiration.

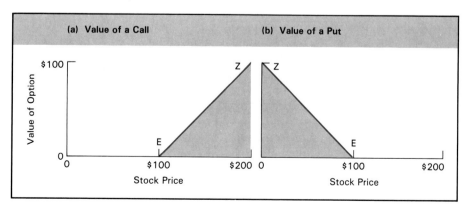

buyer the difference between the security price and the exercise price, thereby allowing both parties to avoid the inconvenience of exercise. This is commonly done for listed options (by using the services of the OCC), although a minority of investors choose to exercise their options, possibly for tax purposes.

Figure 18.3(b) shows the value at expiration of a put option with an exercise price of $100. If the stock price is above $100, the option will be worthless when it expires. If the price is below $100, the option can be exercised to obtain $100 for stock having a lower value, resulting in a net gain to the option buyer that will equal the difference between the exercise price and the stock's market price. As with a call option, neither the put option buyer or writer need actually deal in the stock. Instead, the writer of any put option that is worth exercising at expiration can simply pay the buyer of the option the difference between the stock price and the exercise price.

In both parts of Figure 18.3, the lines indicating the value of a call and a put at expiration can also be interpreted to be the value of a call or put *at the moment the option is exercised*, no matter when that occurs during the life of the option. In particular, for calls the angled line connecting points O, E, and Z is known as the *intrinsic value of the call*. Similarly, for puts the angled line connecting points Z, E, and $200 is known as the *intrinsic value of the put*.

☐ 18.5.2 **Profits and Losses at Expiration**

Figure 18.3 shows the values of call and put options at expiration. However, in order to determine profits and losses from buying or writing these options, the premiums involved must be taken into consideration.[6] Figure 18.4 does this for investors who engage in simple option strategies as well as for investors who engage in some of the more complicated option strategies. Each strategy assumes the underlying stock is selling for $100 at the time an option is initially bought or written. It is also assumed that closing transactions are made just prior to the expiration date for the option being considered. Outcomes are shown for each of five strategies. Since the profit obtained by a buyer is the writer's loss, and vice versa, each diagram in the figure has a corresponding mirror image.

Figure 18.4(a) and (b) shows the profits and losses associated with buying and writing a call, respectively. Similarly, parts (c) and (d) show the profits and losses associated with buying and writing a put, respectively. It can be seen that parts (a) and (c) in Figure 18.4, other than reflecting the premiums paid, are identical to parts (a) and (b) in Figure 18.3.

Parts (e) and (f) in Figure 18.4 illustrate a more complicated options strategy known as a *straddle*. This strategy involves buying (or writing) both a call and a put on the same stock, with the options having the same exercise

---

[6] Since the premium is paid by the buyer to the writer at the time the option is created, it should be compounded to an equivalent value at expiration using an appropriate rate of interest when calculating profits and losses.

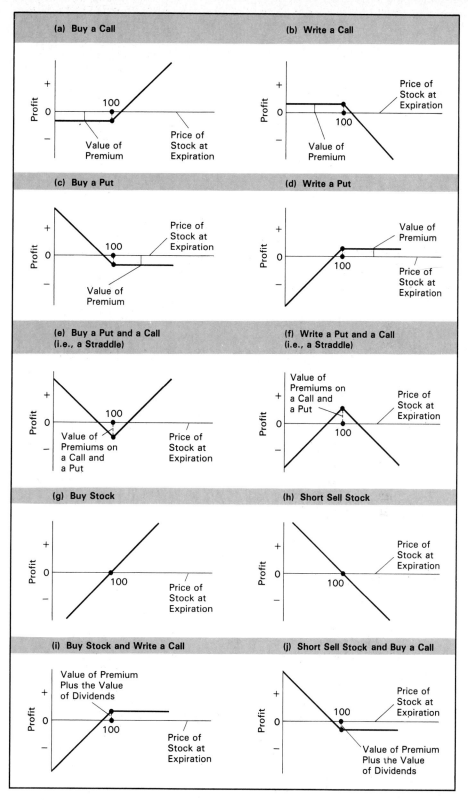

FIGURE 18–4
Profits and losses from various strategies.

price and expiration date.[7] Note how part (e) can be obtained by adding the profits and losses shown in parts (a) and (c), where part (f) can be obtained by adding the profits and losses shown in parts (b) and (d). it can also be seen that parts (e) and (f) are mirror images of each other, again reflecting the fact that the profits to buyers equal the losses to writers, and vice versa.

Part (g) of Figure 18.4 shows the profit or loss made by an investor who avoids options entirely but buys a share of the underlying stock (at $100) at the same time that others buy or write options and sells the stock when the options expire. Assuming no dividends are paid in the interim, the relationship is that shown by the solid line.[8] Similarly, part (h) shows the profit or loss obtained by an investor who short sells the stock at the initial date and then buys it back at the expiration date.

Part (i) of Figure 18.4 shows the results obtained by an investor who buys one share of stock and simultaneously writes a call on it; these results can be obtained by adding the profits and losses shown in parts (b) and (g). As mentioned earlier, such an investor is said to have written a fully covered option. In contrast, the writer who does not hold the underlying stock, depicted in part (b), is said to have written a naked option.

Part (j) of Figure 18.4 shows the results obtained by an investor who short sells one share of stock and simultaneously buys a call option; these results can be obtained by adding the profits and losses in parts (a) and (h). Note that this part is the mirror image of part (i).

Comparison of the diagrams in Figure 18.4 suggests that similar results can be obtained via alternative strategies. Parts (c) and (j) are similar, as are (d) and (i). Neither the premiums involved nor the initial investments required need be equal in every case. Nonetheless, the similarity of the results obtained with different packages of securities suggests that the total market values of the packages will be similar.

☐ 18.5.3   Limits on the Value of a Call Option

Consider three investments. The first is a call option having an exercise price of E and an expiration date, measured in years, of .50 (that is, the expiration date is in six months); the second is the stock on which the option is written; and the third is a riskless investment. With regard to the riskless investment, it is assumed for simplicity that funds can be deposited in a bank at any time during the life of the option and thereafter will earn a fixed periodic risk-free rate.

What is the *most* an investor should pay for this call option? Remembering that the buyer of a call option has the right to purchase a share of

---

[7] *Strips* and *straps* are options strategies similar to a straddle; the former involves combining two puts with one call and the latter involves combining two calls with one put. Another kind of strategy is known as a *spread*, where one call is bought while another is written on the same underlying security. Specifically, a price spread involves two calls having the same expiration date but different exercise prices; a time spread involves two calls having the same exercise price but different expiration dates.

[8] If there are dividends, they should be expressed as a compounded value at the expiration date associated with the options (since they would have been previously received) and added to the line, thereby shifting it upwards.

stock, it is not sensible for an investor to pay more for the right to purchase a share of common stock than the current price of the share itself. That is, investors should be unwilling to pay more for a call option than for the price of the underlying share. This provides an upper limit on the value of the call:

$$P_c \le P_s \qquad (18.1)$$

where P_c denotes the current market price of the call option and P_c denotes the current market price of the underlying stock.

What is the *least* an investor should pay for a call option? Consider the position of an investor who buys one call option and deposits an amount of money into the bank account that pays the risk-free rate. The size of this deposit is equal to the present value of the exercise price, PV(E). It is assumed for simplicity that no dividends will be paid on the common stock at any time up to the expiration date of the option.

Compare this position with a position consisting of the purchase of one share of the underlying common stock. At the expiration of the option, the underlying stock will be selling at a price either above or below the exercise price. If it is above the exercise price, then the investor should use the funds in the bank account to exercise the call option (remember, the deposit of PV(E) will have earned the risk-free rate so that it will now be worth E). Doing so will deplete the bank account while providing the investor with one share of common stock. Thus, if the price of the stock at expiration is above the exercise price, both positions result in the investor owning a share of common stock and are thus of equivalent values.

However, the position of buying a call and making a bank deposit is of superior value if the common stock is selling for a price that is below the exercise price at expiration. In this situation the option is worthless, but the bank account will have a balance equal to the exercise price, E. Thus, part of E can be used to purchase a share of common stock in the secondary market. The remaining balance in the account will represent the amount by which this position ended up being superior.

Since the investor who buys a call and makes the requisite bank deposit ends being better off in some cases and equally well off in other cases, it is logical that the initial cost of taking this position should be greater than the initial cost of buying a share of common stock. Thus, the following inequality should hold:

$$P_c + \text{PV}(E) \ge P_s \qquad (18.2)$$

where the left-hand side shows the cost of buying a call and making the requisite bank deposit and the right-hand side is simply the cost of purchasing a share of the underlying common stock. This inequality can be rearranged, resulting in the following lower limit on the price of a call option:

$$P_c \ge P_s - \text{PV}(E). \qquad (18.3)$$

As an example, consider a call option that has an exercise price of $100 and an expiration date that is nine months in the future. If the risk-free rate is 8% per year, the present value of the exercise price can be calculated as:

$$PV(\$100) = \frac{\$100}{(1 + .08)^{.75}}$$

$$= \$94.39$$

since nine months = .75 of a year. Thus, an investor could buy one call for a price equal to P_c, deposit $94.39 in a bank account that earns 8%, and have a position that is superior to buying one share of common stock at the current price of P_s. The reason for this superiority can be seen by examining the possible market values of the two positions at the expiration date of the call option.

On this date the bank deposit will have grown so that its balance is $100. If the stock at that time is selling for more than $100, the call will be exercised using the entire bank balance. In this case the investor who bought the call and made the bank deposit is no better or worse off than if the stock had been purchased instead. However, if the stock is selling at expiration for less than $100—say, $80—then the call option is worthless but the bank account has $100 in it. Thus, a share of stock could be bought for $80, leaving $20 in the bank account and resulting in the investor being better off than if a share of stock had been initially bought. Accordingly, the cost of buying the call and making the bank deposit must be greater than the cost of buying a share of the underlying stock, as indicated by inequality (18.2).

In addition to inequality (18.2), there is another lower limit to the price of a call option. Specifically, a call option cannot have a negative price. Here a negative price implies that a writer would pay a buyer to take a call option and hold onto it. This is not sensible because the buyer is not under any obligation to exercise the call option. Thus, a writer who pays a buyer to take and hold the option would simply be giving money away. Since this will not happen, there is a second lower limit on the price of a call:

$$P_c \geq 0. \tag{18.4}$$

These three inequalities—(18.1), (18.3), and (18.4)—provide a set of limits on the value of a call option (a set of three limits on the value of a put option is discussed shortly). If the market price of the call were to move outside one of these limits, there would be an opportunity for investors to make abnormal profits via arbitrage. Although transaction costs and taxes might make it unprofitable for some investors to take advantage of such situations, a substantial departure would certainly lead others to act, thereby setting in motion forces that would quickly bring the price of the call back within the limits.

In the example, imagine the option had a price of $7.00 when the stock was selling for $110 and there were nine months until expiration, so that PV($100) = $94.39. In this situation, inequality (18.3) does not hold, since the left-hand side is equal to $7.00, whereas the right-hand side is larger,

being equal to $15.61 = \$110 - \$94.39$. Consequently, an investor should immediately buy the call and make the requisite bank deposit, while simultaneously short selling the common stock. The cost of doing so would be $101.39 ($7.00 + $94.39), assuming that the bank deposit can be used to meet the initial margin requirement on the short sale. Once these transactions have been made, the investor will be certain of making more than the risk-free rate of return.

If at the end of nine months the stock is selling for more than $100, the investor will exercise each call by using the $100 bank balance and then cover the short sale, getting back the short sale proceeds of $110. Thus, the investor's rate of return on the initial investment of $101.39 ($7.00 + $94.39) will be equal to ($110 − $101.39)/$101.39 = 8.49%.

If the stock price is less than $100 at expiration, then each call will be worthless when it expires, and part of the bank balance can be used to cover the short sale. Assuming the stock is selling for $90 per share at expiration, the bank account will have a $10 ($100 − $90) balance after the short sale is covered. Since the investor will then receive the short sale proceeds of $110, the rate of return on the $101.39 initial investment will be equal to ($10 + $110 − $101.39)/$101.39 = 18.39%. Furthermore, the lower the price, the greater the return.[9] Thus, it can be seen that if inequality (18.3) were violated, there would be an opportunity for investors to be certain of making at least 8.49% over nine months, which when annualized is notably greater than the 8% annual risk-free rate of return.

However, the ensuing large number of call purchases will cause the price of the calls ($7) to rise. Conversely, the large amount of short selling will cause the price of the underlying stock ($110) to fall. These prices will quickly adjust (perhaps to $12 and $104, respectively) until inequality (18.3) does hold.

In Figure 18.5 these limits are expressed as equalities. Specifically, inequalities (18.1), (18.3), and (18.4) are given by, respectively,

$$P_c = P_s \qquad\qquad\qquad (18.5)$$

$$P_c = P_s - \text{PV}(E) \qquad\qquad\qquad (18.6)$$

$$P_c = 0. \qquad\qquad\qquad (18.7)$$

Each of these equations represents a straight line that is shown in the figure. These lines serve as boundaries of the shaded region, which indicates where the call option must be priced so that none of the limits are violated.

Figure 18.5 also shows the way the limits change as time passes and the expiration date becomes nearer. Note that the boundary corresponding to equation (18.6) moves to the right as the expiration date approaches, causing the shaded region to become larger. This occurs because the present value of the exercise price rises as the expiration date becomes nearer. That is, PV(E) rises because the length of time E is discounted is smaller. For

---

[9] If the stock is at $100 on the expiration date, then the investor's rate of return will be ($0 + $110 − $101.39)/$101.39 = 8.49%. Stock prices between $100 and $90 will provide the investor with a return between 8.49% and 18.39%.

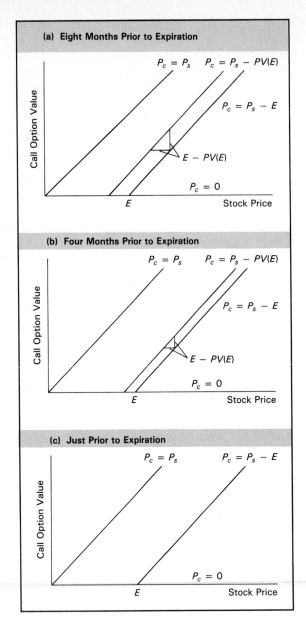

FIGURE 18–5
Limits on the values of a call option.

example, if $E = \$100$, then discounting $100 over four months will result in a larger figure than discounting $100 over eight months. Ultimately, just prior to expiration the effect of discounting will be so negligible that $PV(E) = E$ and the boundary shown by equation (18.6) will simply be

$$P_c = P_s - E. \qquad (18.8)$$

Note how this equation corresponds to the value of a call option moments before it expires, as indicated in Figure 18.3(a).

To make concrete some further principles of option valuation, it will prove helpful to deal with a rather simple kind of stock.[10] Figure 18.6(a) shows the general nature of its behavior. In any given period its price will either jump up to some higher value $(P^+_{s,t+1})$ or down to some lower value $(P^-_{s,t+1})$. Looking forward from time t to time $t + 1$, there are thus two possible states of the world—up $(+)$ and down $(-)$. Associated with each state is a known stock price; the probabilities of the two states $(p^+$ and $p^-)$ have also been estimated.

For every time and stock value there will be some corresponding value for a call option on the stock. These amounts are also indicated in Figure 18.6(a).

The final item in Figure 18.6(a) represents the results obtained by investing some amount of money, X, in the bank. It will grow to $(1 + R)$ times its initial value by the end of the period, and this return is certain. Equivalently, the risk-free rate of interest is fixed at R per period.

All assumptions used previously will be retained. The option under study has an exercise price of $100 and the stock will pay no dividends prior to expiration.

Figure 18.6(b) shows specific numeric values that will be used henceforth. The stock price is assumed to have a 60% chance of increasing 5% each period and a 40% chance of decreasing 5%; its expected return thus equals $(.6 \times + 5) + (.4 \times - 5)$, or 1% per period. The risk-free interest rate is half this, .5% per period (that is, $R = .005$).

Figure 18.6(c) fills in some more values. It covers the situation when the stock price is $100 one period prior to expiration. The time of expiration is denoted by T, one period prior to expiration, $T - 1$, two periods prior, $T - 2$, and so on.

There is a good reason for starting with the period prior to expiration. At expiration, the option value associated with every possible stock price is known: It is $(P_{s,T} - E)$ or zero, whichever is larger. In the situation shown in Figure 18.6(c), the end-of-period option value will be either $5 or $0.

What does this imply for the price of the option at the beginning of the period—that is, how was the box for $P_{c,T-1}$ in Figure 18.6(c) filled in? Not surprisingly, by analogy, as is shown next.

Figure 18.6(d) plots the end-of-period values for the stock and the option. Since there are only two possibilities, all (two) of the points lie on a straight line. The securities' returns are perfectly positively correlated. Whenever this is the case, it is possible to *hedge* one against the other and eliminate all risk.

The difference between the stock prices in the two states is $10; the difference between the option prices is $5. It is possible to hold stock and

---

[10] This "binomial" approach to option valuation was initially presented by William F. Sharpe in the first edition of *Investments* (Englewood Cliffs, N.J.: Prentice Hall, 1978) and has been expanded upon by John C. Cox, Stephen A. Ross, and Mark Rubinstein, "Option Pricing: A Simplified Approach," *Journal of Financial Economics* 7, no. 3 (September 1979):229–63; and Richard J. Rendleman, Jr. and Brit J. Bartter, "Two-State Option Pricing," *Journal of Finance* 34, no. 5 (December 1979):1093–1110.

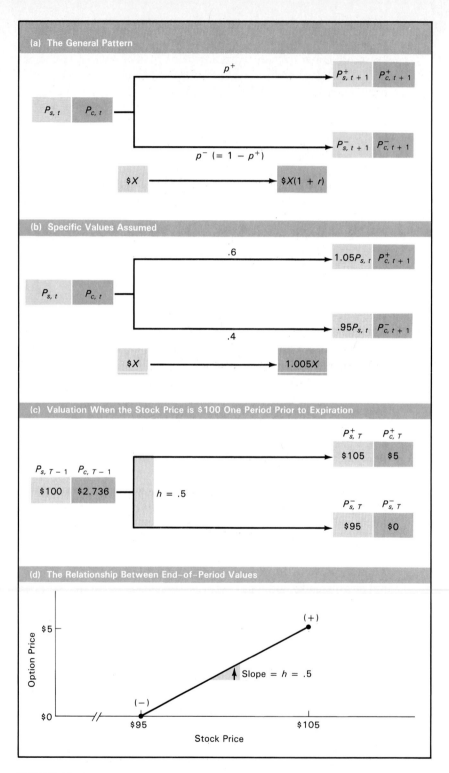

FIGURE 18–6
Stock and option prices.

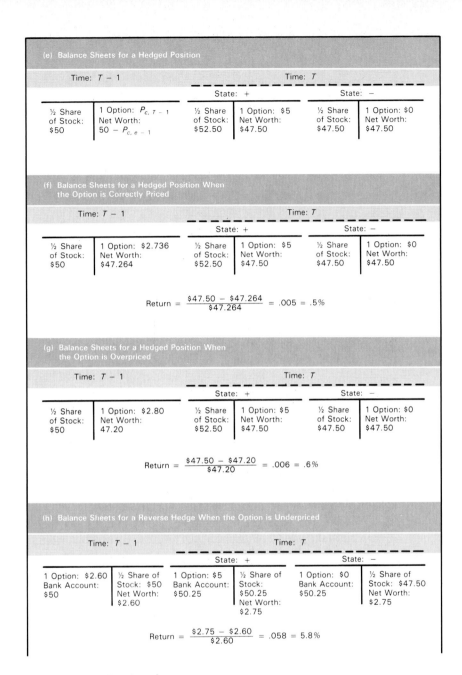

(e) Balance Sheets for a Hedged Position

Time: $T-1$		Time: T			
		State: $+$		State: $-$	
½ Share of Stock: $50	1 Option: $P_{c,\,T-1}$ Net Worth: $50 - P_{c,\,e-1}$	½ Share of Stock: $52.50	1 Option: $5 Net Worth: $47.50	½ Share of Stock: $47.50	1 Option: $0 Net Worth: $47.50

(f) Balance Sheets for a Hedged Position When the Option is Correctly Priced

Time: $T-1$		Time: T			
		State: $+$		State: $-$	
½ Share of Stock: $50	1 Option: $2.736 Net Worth: $47.264	½ Share of Stock: $52.50	1 Option: $5 Net Worth: $47.50	½ Share of Stock: $47.50	1 Option: $0 Net Worth: $47.50

$$\text{Return} = \frac{\$47.50 - \$47.264}{\$47.264} = .005 = .5\%$$

(g) Balance Sheets for a Hedged Position When the Option is Overpriced

Time: $T-1$		Time: T			
		State: $+$		State: $-$	
½ Share of Stock: $50	1 Option: $2.80 Net Worth: $47.20	½ Share of Stock: $52.50	1 Option: $5 Net Worth: $47.50	½ Share of Stock: $47.50	1 Option: $0 Net Worth: $47.50

$$\text{Return} = \frac{\$47.50 - \$47.20}{\$47.20} = .006 = .6\%$$

(h) Balance Sheets for a Reverse Hedge When the Option is Underpriced

Time: $T-1$		Time: T			
		State: $+$		State: $-$	
1 Option: $2.60 Bank Account: $50	½ Share of Stock: $50 Net Worth: $2.60	1 Option: $5 Bank Account: $50.25	½ Share of Stock: $50.25 Net Worth: $2.75	1 Option: $0 Bank Account: $50.25	½ Share of Stock: $47.50 Net Worth: $2.75

$$\text{Return} = \frac{\$2.75 - \$2.60}{\$2.60} = .058 = 5.8\%$$

FIGURE 18–6 (*Continued*)

write a call option and to arrange the proportions so that the differences in payoffs in the two positions are exactly equal. The investor's end-of-period net worth will then be the same in either event. In this case, the appropriate *hedge ratio* is .5; for every option written (sold), one-half a share of stock should be purchased. More generally, the appropriate hedge ratio, denoted

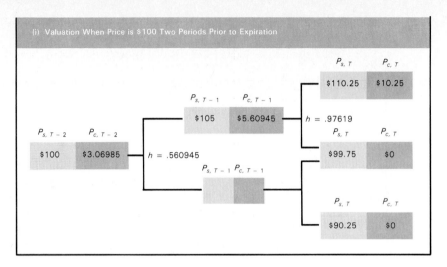

FIGURE 18–6 (*Continued*)

by h, is simply the difference between the end-of-period option values, divided by the difference between the end-of-period stock values:

$$h = \frac{P^+_{c,t+1} - P^-_{c,t+1}}{P^+_{s,t+1} - P^-_{s,t+1}}. \tag{18.9}$$

Figure 18.6(e) shows how this can be employed. An investor buys half a share of stock and sells one call option. The initial investment required is $50 minus the (yet-to-be-determined) price received for writing the option. The value of the "portfolio" at the end of the period will be $47.50, *no matter which state occurs*. The investor has set up a *risk-free hedge* by using the appropriate hedge ratio indicated by equation (18.9).

Now for the analogy where $t + 1 = T$. The rate of interest on a risk-free investment also returns .5% per period. Since the ending value will be $47.50, the required option value is that which satisfies

$$(\$50 - P_{c,T-1})\,1.005 = \$47.50.$$

The solution is

$$P_{c,T-1} = \$2.736.$$

Figure 18.6(f) shows that the hedging strategy will in fact give a certain return equal to the risk-free rate if the option price equals $2.736. Figure 18.6(g) shows that if the option were overpriced, at $2.80, the hedging strategy could give a certain return greater than the risk-free rate. Such a situation would attract attention, bringing out would-be option sellers whose activities would shortly drive the price back down.

What if the option were underpriced, say at $2.60? Then clever investors could *reverse hedge*, buying options and selling stock. Figure 18.6(h) shows

a case in which the stock is sold short and the proceeds placed in an interest-earnings bank account.[11] A certain 5.8% per period is returned on invested funds. Such a situation would attract would-be option buyers, driving the price back up.

Figure 18.6(f) thus portrays the likely situation and an option pricing formula. The option price at time t must satisfy:

$$(hP_{s,t} - P_{c,t})(1 + R) = \begin{Bmatrix} [hP_{s,t+1}^+ - P_{c,t+1}^+] \\ [hP_{s,t+1}^- - P_{c,t+1}^-] \end{Bmatrix} \qquad (18.10)$$

where h is the hedge ratio required to give a risk-free return. The first expression in parentheses on the left represents the funds invested at the beginning of the period. The brackets on the right indicate that either of the two included expressions can be used, for they are both equal to the certain end-of-period value. The formula simply requires the option to be priced so that a portfolio hedged to remove all risk will return the risk-free rate on the funds invested.

Having established the principles summarized in equations (18.9) and (18.10), it is possible to determine the option value for any time and stock price. Figure 18.6(i) does this for the case in which the stock price is $100 two periods prior to expiration. The option price boxes are filled in from right to left. Option values at expiration are simply $(P_s - 100)$ or zero, whichever is larger. This takes care of the option values at time T.

Turning to time $T - 1$, note that if a situation will lead to a worthless option no matter what, the option is already worthless. Thus if the stock price is $95 one period prior to expiration, the option will definitely expire worthless, and the option value is zero. This takes care of another box.

Turning to the situation in which the stock price is $105 one period prior to expiration, equation (18.9) is used to determine the hedge ratio (.97619) and then equation (18.10) applied to determine the option price ($5.60945).

To find the remaining hedge ratio (.560945) and option price ($3.06985), equations (18.9) and (18.10) are applied again using the relevant stock values ($105 and $95) and the previously computed associated option values ($5.60945 and $0).

Figure 18.7 shows some values obtained with this kind of *recursive* calculation. Each curve plots option values associated with various stock prices at a specific time prior to expiration.

One characteristic of the curves in Figure 18.7 is quite general:

If two call options are otherwise identical but one has a longer time remaining before expiration, the longer one will be worth at least as much as the shorter one and generally will be worth more.

---

[11] This is generally not possible in practice, lowering or eliminating the profit from such a hedge and raising the possibility that the option could sell at any price within a band limited by the prices at which hedging or reverse hedging would become profitable.

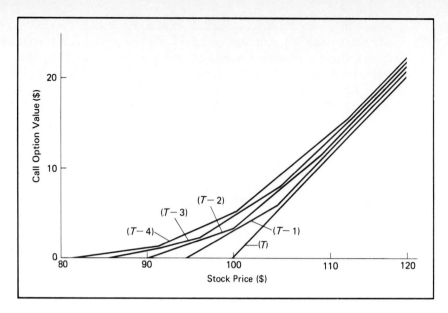

FIGURE 18–7
Option values at various times prior to expiration (based on the numeric example in Figure 18–6).

18.6 THE BLACK-SCHOLES MODEL FOR CALL OPTIONS

In a world not bothered by taxes and transactions costs, an investor could adjust hedge positions almost constantly. The effective length of a period would thus be very small. The smaller the length of each period, the closer the value of a call option calculated in the manner described in the previous section would be to that given by an option valuation formula developed by Black and Scholes.[12] This model can be used to determine the fair (or true) value of a call and was initially developed for calls options on stocks that will not pay any dividends between the time the option is written and the time it expires. Furthermore, the model is applicable only to *European options*, which are options that can be exercised only on their expiration dates.

☐ 18.6.1 Limitations on the Model's Use

At first, this model might seem to have limited use, since almost all options in the United States are known as *American options*, meaning they can be exercised at any time up to their expiration date. Furthermore, most of the common stocks on which they are written do, in fact, pay dividends.

The first drawback of the Black-Scholes model—that it is only applicable to European options—can be dispensed with rather easily when the option

---

[12] Fischer Black and Myron Scholes, "The Pricing of Options and Corporate Liabilities," *Journal of Political Economy* 81, no. 3 (May/June 1973):637–54.

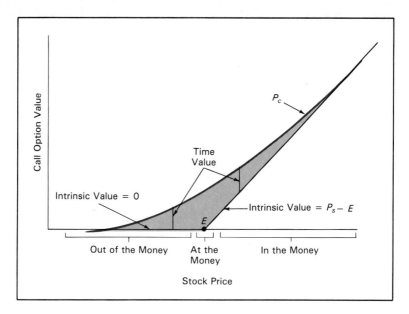

FIGURE 18–8
Option terminology for calls.

is a call and the underlying stock does not pay dividends. This is because it has been shown that it is unwise for an investor holding an American call option on a non-dividend-paying stock to exercise it prior to maturity.[13] Since there is no reason for exercising such an option prior to maturity, the opportunity to do so is worthless. Consequently, there will be no difference in the value of an American and European call option. In turn, this means that the Black-Scholes model can be used to estimate the fair value of American call options on non-dividend-paying stocks.

Figure 18.8 shows why the Black-Scholes model can be used, but first some terminology must be introduced. A call option is said to be *at the money* if the underlying stock has a market price roughly equal to the call's exercise price. If the stock's market price is below the exercise price, the call is said to be *out of the money*, and if the market price is above the exercise price, the call is said to be *in the money*. Occasionally finer gradations are invoked, and one hears of "near the money," "deep in the money," "far out of the money," and so on.

As mentioned earlier, the value of an option if it were exercised immediately is known as its intrinsic value. This value is equal to zero if the option is out of the money. However, it is equal to the difference between the stock price and exercise price if the option is in the money. The excess of the price of the option over its intrinsic value is the option's *time value* (or time premium). As shown in Figure 18.3(a) for call options, at expiration the time value is zero. However, before then the time value is positive. Note

---

[13] See Robert C. Merton, "Theory of Rational Option Pricing," *Bell Journal of Economics and Management Science* 4, no. 1 (Spring 1973):141–83.

that a call option's premium is simply the sum of its intrinsic and time values.

An investor considering exercising a call option on a non-dividend-paying stock prior to its expiration date will always find it cheaper to sell the call option and purchase the stock in the marketplace. This is because exercising the call will result in the investor losing the time value of the option (hence the expression that call options are "worth more alive than dead").

For example, consider a stock that has a current price of $110. If this stock has a call option with an exercise price of $100 that is selling for $14, then the intrinsic and time values of this option are $10 ($110 − $100) and $4 ($14 − $10), respectively. An investor who owns one of these calls could exercise it by spending an additional $100. However, it would be cheaper for the investor to get the share of stock by selling the call option and buying the share of stock in the marketplace, since the additional cost would only be $96 ($110 − $14).

The second drawback of the Black-Scholes model—that it is only applicable to non-dividend-paying stocks—cannot be easily dismissed, since many call options are written on stocks that will pay dividends during the life of the option. In this situation, some procedures have been suggested on how this formula can be amended in order to value call options on such stocks. One of these procedures is presented later.

☐ 18.6.2 The Formula

In a world not bothered by taxes and transactions costs, the fair value of a call option can be estimated by using the valuation formula developed by Black and Scholes. It has been widely used by those who deal with options to search for situations where the market price of an option differs substantially from its fair value. A call option that is found to be selling for substantially less than its Black-Scholes value is a candidate for purchase, whereas one that is found to be selling for substantially more is a candidate for writing. The Black-Scholes formula for estimating the fair value of a call option (V_c) is

$$V_c = P_s N(d_1) - \frac{E}{e^{RT}} N(d_2) \tag{18.11}$$

where:

$$d_1 = \frac{\ln(P_s/E) + (R + .5\sigma^2)T}{\sigma\sqrt{T}} \tag{18.12}$$

$$d_2 = \frac{\ln(P_s/E) + (R - .5\sigma^2)T}{\sigma\sqrt{T}} \tag{18.13a}$$

$$= d_1 - \sigma\sqrt{T} \tag{18.13b}$$

and where:

P_s is the current market price of the underlying stock

E is the exercise price of the option

R is the continuously compounded risk-free rate of return expressed on an annual basis

T is time remaining before expiration expressed as a fraction of a year

σ is the risk of the underlying common stock, measured by the standard deviation of the continuously compounded annual rate of return on the stock.

Mathematically, e is the base of natural logarithms and is approximately equal to 2.71828. This means that E/e^{RT} is the present value of the exercise price when a continuous discount rate is used (it is analagous to $E/(1 + R)^T$, the present value of the exercise price using a discrete discount rate). The quantity $\ln(P_s/E)$ is the natural logarithm of P_s/E. Lastly, $N(d_1)$ and $N(d_2)$ denote the probabilities that deviations of less than d_1 and d_2, respectively, will occur in a normal distribution that has a mean of 0 and a standard deviation of 1.

Table 18.1 provides values of $N(d)$ for various levels of d.[14] This table and a pocket calculator are all that are needed in order to use the Black-Scholes formula for valuing a call option.

For example, consider a call option that expires in three months and has an exercise price of \$40 (thus, $T = .25$ and $E = 40$). Furthermore, the current price and risk of the underlying common stock are \$36 and 50%, respectively, whereas the risk-free rate is 5% (thus, $P_s = 36$, $R = .05$, and $\sigma = .50$). Solving equations (18.12) and (18.13b) provides the following values for d_1 and d_2:

$$d_1 = \frac{\ln(36/40) + [.05 + .5(.50)^2].25}{.50\sqrt{.25}} = -.25$$

$$d_2 = -.25 - .50\sqrt{.25} = -.50.$$

Table 18.1 can be used to find the corresponding values of $N(d_1)$ and $N(d_2)$:

$$N(d_1) = N(-.25) = .4013$$

$$N(d_2) = N(-.50) = .3085.$$

Finally, equation (18.11) can be used to estimate the fair value of this call option:

$$V_c = (36 \times .4013) - \left(\frac{40}{e^{.05 \times .25}} \times .3085\right) = \$2.26.$$

If this call option is currently selling for \$5, the investor should consider writing some of them. This is because they are overpriced (according to the Black-Scholes model), suggesting that their price will fall in the near future. Thus, the writer would receive a premium of \$5 and would expect to be able

---

[14] Table 18.1 is an abbreviated version of a standard cumulative normal distribution table. More detailed versions can be found in most statistics textbooks.

TABLE 18.1

Values of N(d) for Selected Values of d.

d	N(d)	d	N(d)	d	N(d)
		−1.00	.1587	1.00	.8413
−2.95	.0016	−.95	.1711	1.05	.8531
−2.90	.0019	−.90	.1841	1.10	.8643
−2.85	.0022	−.85	.1977	1.15	.8749
−2.80	.0026	−.80	.2119	1.20	.8849
−2.75	.0030	−.75	.2266	1.25	.8944
−2.70	.0035	−.70	.2420	1.30	.9032
−2.65	.0040	−.65	.2578	1.35	.9115
−2.60	.0047	−.60	.2743	1.40	.9192
−2.55	.0054	−.55	.2912	1.45	.9265
−2.50	.0062	−.50	.3085	1.50	.9332
−2.45	.0071	−.45	.3264	1.55	.9394
−2.40	.0082	−.40	.3446	1.60	.9452
−2.35	.0094	−.35	.3632	1.65	.9505
−2.30	.0107	−.30	.3821	1.70	.9554
−2.25	.0122	−.25	.4013	1.75	.9599
−2.20	.0139	−.20	.4207	1.80	.9641
−2.15	.0158	−.15	.4404	1.85	.9678
−2.10	.0179	−.10	.4602	1.90	.9713
−2.05	.0202	−.05	.4801	1.95	.9744
−2.00	.0228	.00	.5000	2.00	.9773
−1.95	.0256	.05	.5199	2.05	.9798
−1.90	.0287	.10	.5398	2.10	.9821
−1.85	.0322	.15	.5596	2.15	.9842
−1.80	.0359	.20	.5793	2.20	.9861
−1.75	.0401	.25	.5987	2.25	.9878
−1.70	.0446	.30	.6179	2.30	.9893
−1.65	.0495	.35	.6368	2.35	.9906
−1.60	.0548	.40	.6554	2.40	.9918
−1.55	.0606	.45	.6736	2.45	.9929
−1.50	.0668	.50	.6915	2.50	.9938
−1.45	.0735	.55	.7088	2.55	.9946
−1.40	.0808	.60	.7257	2.60	.9953
−1.35	.0885	.65	.7422	2.65	.9960
−1.30	.0968	.70	.7580	2.70	.9965
−1.25	.1057	.75	.7734	2.75	.9970
−1.20	.1151	.80	.7881	2.80	.9974
−1.15	.1251	.85	.8023	2.85	.9978
−1.10	.1357	.90	.8159	2.90	.9981
−1.05	.1469	.95	.8289	2.95	.9984

to enter a closing buy order later for a lower price, making a profit on the difference. Conversely, if the call option were selling for $1, the investor should consider buying some of them. This is because they are underpriced and can be expected to rise in value in the future.

☐ **18.6.3 Static Analysis**

Close scrutiny of the Black-Scholes formula reveals some interesting features of European call option pricing. In particular, it can be noticed that the fair value of a call option is dependent on five inputs—the market price of the

common stock (P_s), the exercise price of the option (E), the length of time until the expiration date (T), the risk-free rate (R), and the risk of the common stock (σ). What happens to the fair value of a call option when one of these inputs is changed while the other four remain the same?

1. The higher the price of the underlying stock (P_s), the higher the value of the call option.
2. The higher the exercise price (E), the lower the value of the call option.
3. The longer the time to the expiration date (T), the higher the value of the call option.
4. The higher the risk-free rate (R), the higher the value of the call option.
5. The greater the risk (σ) of the common stock, the higher the value of the call option.

Of these five factors, the first three (P_s, E, and T) are readily determined. The fourth factor, the risk-free rate, is often estimated by using the yield-to-maturity on a Treasury bill having a maturity date close to the expiration date of the option. The fifth factor, the risk of the underlying stock, is not readily observed; consequently, various methods for estimating it have been proposed. Two of these methods are presented next.

☐ 18.6.4   **Estimating a Stock's Risk from Historical Prices**

One method for estimating the risk of the underlying common stock associated with a call option involves analyzing historical prices on the stock. Initially, a set of $n + 1$ market prices on the underlying stock must be obtained from either financial publications like *The Wall Street Journal* or a computer database. These prices are then used to calculate a set of n continuously compounded returns as follows:

$$r_t = \ln\left(\frac{P_{st}}{P_{st-1}}\right) \tag{18.14}$$

where P_{st} and P_{st-1} denote the market price of the underlying stock at times t and $t - 1$, respectively. Here, ln denotes the natural logarithm of the quantity P_{st}/P_{st-1}, which gives a continuously compounded return.

For example, the set of market prices for the stock might consist of the closing price at the end of each of 53 weeks. If the price at the end of one week were \$105 and the price at the end of the next week were \$107, then the return r_t would be equal to $\ln(107/105) = 1.886\%$. Similar calculations will result in a set of 52 returns.

Having calculated a set of n returns on the stock, the next step involves using them to estimate the stock's average return:

$$ar = \frac{1}{n}\sum_{t=1}^{n} r_t. \tag{18.15}$$

The average return is then used in estimating the per-period variance (that is, the square of the per-period standard deviation):

$$s^2 = \frac{1}{n-1} \sum_{t=1}^{n} (r_t - ar)^2. \tag{18.16}$$

This is called the per-period variance because its size is dependent on the length of time over which each return is measured. In the example, weekly returns were calculated and would lead to the estimation of a weekly variance. Alternatively, daily returns could have been used, leading to a daily variance that would be of smaller magnitude than the weekly variance. However, what is needed is not either a weekly or daily variance but an annual variance. This is obtained by multiplying the per-period variance by the number of periods in a year. Thus, an estimated weekly variance would be multiplied by 52 in order to estimate the annual variance, σ^2 (that is, $\sigma^2 = 52s^2$). Alternatively, subjective estimates of the probabilities of possible future prices can be made and then used to estimate the total risk of the stock. Lastly, it is possible to combine these two methods to arrive at an estimate.

For any estimate of future uncertainty, historical data are more likely to prove helpful than definitive. And since recent data may prove more helpful than older data, some analysts study daily price changes over the most recent 6 to 12 months, sometimes giving more weight to later days than to earlier ones. Others take into account the price histories of related stocks and the possibility that a stock whose price has recently decreased may be more risky in the future than it was in the past. Still others make explicit subjective estimates of the future, taking into account changes in uncertainty concerning the economy in general as well as uncertainty in specific industries and in stocks.

In some cases, an analyst's estimate of a stock's risk over the next three months may differ from that for the following three months, leading to the use of different values of σ for call options on the same stock when these options have different expiration dates.

18.6.5 The Market Consensus of a Stock's Risk

Another way to estimate a stock's risk is based on the assumption that a currently outstanding call option is fairly priced in the marketplace. Since this means that $P_c = V_c$, the current market price of the call (P_c) can be entered in place of the fair value of the call (V_c) on the left-hand side of equation (18.11). Next, all the other factors except for σ are entered on the right-hand side, and the resulting equation is solved for σ, the only unknown variable. The solution for σ can be interpreted as representing a consensus opinion in the marketplace on the size of the stock's risk and is sometimes known as the stock's *implicit volatility*.

For example, assume that the risk-free rate is 6% and that a six-month option with an exercise price of $40 sells for $4 when the price of the un-

derlying stock is $36. Different estimates of σ can be substituted into the right-hand side of equation (18.11) until a value of $4 for this side of the equation is obtained. In this example, an estimated value of .40 (that is, 40%) for σ will result in a number for the right-hand side of equation (18.11) that is equal to $4, which is the current market price of the option that is on the left-hand side.

The procedure can be modified by applying it to several call options on the same stock. For example, σ can be estimated for each of several call options on the same stock that have different exercise prices but the same expiration date. Then, the resulting estimates for σ can be averaged and, in turn, used to determine the fair value of another call option on the same stock having yet another exercise price but a similar expiration date.

In the example, σ can be estimated not only for a six-month option having an exercise price of $40 but also for six-month options having exercise prices of $35 and $45. Then, the three estimates of σ can be averaged to produce a "best estimate" of σ, which is used to value a six-month $50 option on the same stock.

Alternatively, the procedure can be modified by averaging the estimates for σ associated with each of several expiration dates. In the example, σ can be estimated not only for a six-month option having an exercise price of $40 but also for three-month and nine-month options that have an exercise price of $40. The three estimates of σ can be averaged to produce a best estimate of σ, which is subsequently used to determine the fair value of a one-month $40 option on the same stock.

There are other ways of using a set of estimates of σ that correspond to different call options on the same stock. Perhaps σ will be estimated for a set of calls having different expiration prices and different exercise prices and then averaged. Perhaps σ will be estimated from historical returns using equation (18.14), with the resulting figure averaged with one or more estimates of the stock's implicit volatility. While it is still too early to tell, it appears that methods based on calculating implicit volatilities are better than methods based on historical returns.[15]

☐ 18.6.6 Hedge Ratios

The slope of the Black-Scholes value curve at any point represents the expected change in the value of the option per dollar change in the price of the underlying common stock. This amount is known as the *hedge ratio* (or delta) of the call option and is equal to $N(d_1)$ in equation (18.11). As can be seen in Figure 18.8 (assuming the market price of the call is equal to its Black-Scholes value), the slope (that is, the hedge ratio) of the curve is always positive. Furthermore, if the stock has a relatively low market price the slope will be near 0; for higher stock prices the slope increases and ultimately approaches a value of 1 for relatively high stock prices.

---

[15] For a further discussion of these methods, see Chapter 6 of Cox and Rubinstein, *Options Markets*; Chapter 9 of Robert A. Jarrow and Andrew Rudd, *Option Pricing* (Homewood, Ill.: Richard D. Irwin, Inc., 1983); and Chapter 10 of Peter Ritchken, *Options* (Glenview, Ill.: Scott, Foresman and Company, 1987).

Because the hedge ratio is typically less than 1, a \$1 increase in the stock price will typically result in an increase in a call option's value of less than \$1. However, the percentage change in the value of the call option will generally be greater than the percentage change in the price of the stock. It is this relationship that leads people to say that options offer high leverage.

The reason for referring to the slope of the Black-Scholes value curve as the hedge ratio is that a "hedge" portfolio, meaning a nearly risk-free portfolio, can be formed by simultaneously writing one call option and purchasing a number of shares equal to the hedge ratio, $N(d_1)$. For example, assume the hedge ratio is .5, indicating that the hedge portfolio consists of writing one call and buying .5 shares of stock. Now, if the stock price rises by \$1, the value of the call option will rise by approximately \$.50. This means that the hedge portfolio would lose approximately \$.50 on the written call option but gain \$.50 from the rise in the stock's price. Conversely, a \$1 decrease in the stock's price would result in a \$.50 gain on the written call option but a loss of \$.50 on the share of stock. Overall, it can be seen that the hedge portfolio will neither gain nor lose value when the price of the underlying common stock changes by a relatively small amount.

Even if the Black-Scholes model is valid and all the inputs have been correctly specified, it should be noted that risk is not permanently eliminated in the hedge portfolio when the portfolio is first formed (or, for that matter, at any time). This is because the hedge ratio will change as the stock price changes and as the life of the option decreases with the passage of time. In order to eliminate risk from the hedge portfolio, the investor will continuously have to alter its composition. Altering it less often will reduce but not completely eliminate risk.

□ 18.6.7   Adjustments for Dividends

Thus far, the issue of dividend payments on the underlying stock during the life of an option has been avoided. Other things being equal, the greater the amount of the dividends to be paid during the life of a call option, the lower the value of the call option. This is because the greater the dividend that a firm declares, the lower will be its stock price. Since options are not "dividend protected," this lower stock price will result in a lower value for the call option.

Moreover, it may pay to exercise an American call option just prior to an ex-dividend date. Earlier, it was mentioned that in the absence of dividends, an American call option would be worth at least as much "alive" (not exercised) as "dead" (exercised). When dividends are involved, however, the situation may be different. This is shown in Figure 18.9.

The call option's value if exercised immediately, referred to in Figure 18.8 as the option's *intrinsic value*, lies along the lower boundary OEZ. If allowed to live, the option's value will lie along the higher Black-Scholes curve as shown in the figure. Imagine that the stock is currently priced at P_{s1} and is about to go ex-dividend for the last time prior to the option's expiration. Afterward, it can be expected to sell for a lower price, P_{s2}. The

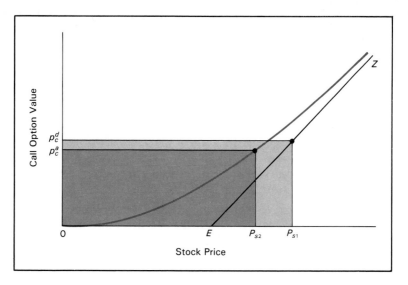

FIGURE 18–9
Option values before and after an ex-dividend date.

Black-Scholes formula can be used to estimate the option's value if it remains alive just after the ex-dividend date. In Figure 18.9, this alive value is P_c^a. If instead the option is exercised just before the ex-dividend date, while the stock price is still P_{s1}, the investor will obtain the dead value (that is, the intrinsic value) of P_c^d. If P_c^d is greater than P_c^a (as is the case in this figure), the option should be exercised now, just before the ex-dividend date; if P_c^d is less than P_c^a, the option should not be exercised.

For a call option on a dividend-paying stock, the possibility of early exercise must be taken into consideration. A number of models have been recommended for doing this, one of which is presented here.[16] This model is known as the *pseudo-American model* and assumes that the dividends to be paid on the common stock over the life of the call option can be predicted with certainty. It should be pointed out that this assumption is not unreasonable, since firms are generally predictable in terms of the timing and size of their quarterly dividends over the next nine months, the maximum life of an option. For ease of exposition, it will be assumed that only one dividend has yet to be paid on the stock and that its ex-dividend date and payment date are the same.

The procedure for using the pseudo-American model for estimating the value of a call option begins by subtracting the present value of the future dividend from the current market price of the common stock. If the dividend, denoted by D, is to be paid time t, then the dividend-adjusted stock price P_s^* is

---

[16] For a more detailed explanation of this model, see pp. 124–32 of Jarrow and Rudd, *Option Pricing*; and pp. 168–69 of Ritchken, *Options*. For a description of other models, see Chapters 9 and 10 of Jarrow and Rudd, *Option Pricing*; pp. 200–203 of Ritchken, *Options*; and Chapters 5 and 6 of Cox and Rubinstein, *Options Markets*.

$$P_s^* = P_s - \frac{D}{e^{Rt}} \qquad\qquad (18.17)$$

where R is the risk-free rate. Then, this dividend-adjusted price is used in place of P_s while all the other inputs (E, R, σ, T) in the Black-Scholes formula given in equation (18.11) are unchanged. Solving the formula for V_c provides an estimate of the value for the call option that is based on the assumption it will be held until expiration.

In the next step, an estimate of the value of the call option is determined based on the assumption that it will be exercised just before the ex-dividend date. As before, the dividend-adjusted price P_s^* is used instead of P_s. However, two additional changes must be made to the inputs. Specifically, the time to the ex-dividend date t is to be used instead of the time to expiration T, and a dividend-adjusted exercise price equal to $E - D$ is to be used instead of the actual exercise price E. The exercise price is adjusted in this manner because the investor will receive the dividend by exercising the option just before the ex-dividend date and thus must come up only with cash equal to $E - D$ in order to exercise the option at that time. The value for V_c that is obtained when P_s^*, t, and $E - D$ (as well as R and σ) are used in the Black-Scholes formula is the value of the call associated with early exercise.

The final estimate of the value for the call option will be the larger of the two estimates for V_c that correspond to holding the option to expiration and exercising it just before the ex-dividend date. Although this method is not exact, it is probably sufficient for many options.[17]

18.7 THE VALUATION OF PUT OPTIONS

As with a call option, a put option is said to be *at the money* if the underlying stock has a market price roughly equal to the put's exercise price. However, the terms *out of the money* and *in the money* have, in one sense, opposite meanings for puts and calls. In particular, a put option is out of the money if the underlying stock has a market price above the exercise price and is in the money if the market price is below the exercise price. Figure 18.10 provides an illustration of how these terms apply to a put option.

As mentioned earlier, the value of either a call or put, if it were exercised immediately, is known as its intrinsic value. This value is equal to zero if the option is out of the money and is equal to the difference between the stock price and exercise price if the stock is in the money. Thus, in another sense, the terms out of the money and in the money have similar meanings for puts and calls.

The excess of the price of a call or put over this intrinsic value is the option's time value (or time premium). As shown for calls and puts in parts (a) and (b) of Figure 18.3, respectively, the time value is zero at expiration.

---

[17] For a comparison of various techniques, see Robert Geske and Kuldeep Shastri, "Valuation by Approximation: A Comparison of Alternative Option Valuation Techniques," *Journal of Financial and Quantitative Analysis* 20, no. 1 (March 1985):45–71; and Chapters 1–4 of Stuart M. Turnbull, *Option Valuation* (Holt, Rinehart & Winston of Canada, Limited, 1987). Turnbull's book comes with floppy disks that contain many computer programs for valuing options.

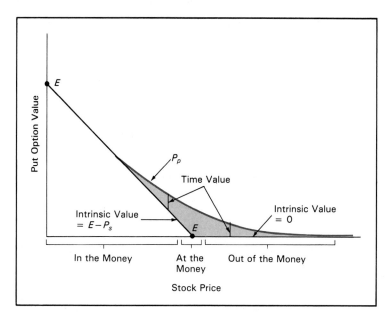

FIGURE 18-10
Option terminology for puts.

However, Figures 18.8 and 18.10 show that the time value is generally positive before expiration. Note that an option's premium is simply the sum of its intrinsic value and time value.

□ 18.7.1 Limits on the Value of a Put Option

Earlier, one upper and two lower limits on the value of a call option were presented. Not surprisingly, put options also have limits on their values. In discussing these limits, it will be assumed that the underlying common stock will not pay any dividends during the life of the put option. Furthermore, it is assumed that the put is a European option, meaning that it can be exercised only on its expiration date.

What is the *most* an investor should pay for a put option? Remembering that the buyer of a European put option has the right to sell a share of common stock on the expiration date for the exercise price E, it is not sensible for an investor to pay more for the put option than will be received if it is exercised. Furthermore, since it cannot be exercised until expiration, an investor should not be willing to pay more than the present value of the exercise price, $PV(E)$. This means that there will be the following upper limit on the value of a put option:

$$P_p \leq PV(E) \tag{18.18}$$

where P_p denotes the current market price of the put option.

There are two lower limits to the value of a put. In order to understand

the first one, consider an investor who deposits an amount of cash equal to the present value of the exercise price in the bank. At the expiration date the investor's deposit will have grown to be equal to the exercise price, E.

Compare this position with a position of buying a put option and one share of the underlying common stock for a total cost of $P_p + P_s$. At the expiration date of the option, the underlying stock will be selling at a price either above or below the exercise price. If it is below the exercise price, then the investor would exercise the put by giving up the share of stock and receiving cash equal to the exercise price E in return. Thus, if the price of the stock at expiration is below the exercise price, both positions result in the investor having cash equal to E.

However, the position of buying a put and a share is of greater value if the common stock is selling for a price that is above the exercise price at expiration. Although the put will be worthless in this situation, the share of common stock with which the investor is left has a value greater than E. Since the investor who buys a put and a share ends up being better off in some cases and equally well off in other cases, it is logical that the initial cost of taking this position should be greater than the initial cost of making the bank deposit. Thus, the following inequality should hold:

$$P_p + P_s \geq \text{PV}(E) \qquad\qquad (18.19)$$

where the left-hand side shows the cost of buying a put and a share and the right-hand side shows the cost of making the bank deposit. This inequality can be rearranged, resulting in the following lower limit on the price of a put:

$$P_p \geq \text{PV}(E) - P_s. \qquad\qquad (18.20)$$

As an example, consider a put option that has an exercise price of $100 and an expiration date that is six months in the future. If the risk-free rate is 10% per year, the present value of the exercise price can be calculated as

$$\text{PV}(\$100) = \frac{\$100}{(1 + .10)^{.50}}$$

$$= \$95.35$$

since six months = .50 year. Thus, an investor could deposit $95.35 in a bank account that earns 10% and have a position that is inferior to buying one put option and one share of the underlying stock for a combined price of $P_p + P_s$. The reason for this inferiority can be seen by examining the possible market values of the two positions at the expiration date of the put option.

On this date the bank deposit will have grown so that its balance is $100. If the stock at that time is selling for less than $100, the put will be exercised, giving the investor an amount of cash equal to the bank balance. In this case the investor who bought the put and share is not better or worse off than if the bank deposit had been made instead. However, if the stock is selling at expiration for more than $100—say, $120—then the put option is worthless but the stock is worth more than the $100 bank balance. Thus,

the investor will be better off if a put and a share of stock had been purchased initially. Accordingly, the cost of buying the put and share must be greater than the cost of making the bank deposit, as indicated by inequality (18.19).

In addition to inequality (18.20), there is another lower limit to the price of a put option. Specifically, a put option cannot have a negative price. Here a negative price would imply that a writer would pay a buyer to take and hold onto a put option. This is not sensible because the buyer is not under any obligation to exercise the put option. Thus, a writer who pays a buyer to take and hold onto the option would simply be giving money away. Since this will not happen, there is a second lower limit on the price of a put:

$$P_p \geq 0. \tag{18.21}$$

These three inequalities—(18.18), (18.20), and (18.21)—provide a set of limits on the value of a put option. If the market price of the put were to move outside one of these limits, there would be an opportunity for investors to make abnormal profits via arbitrage. Although transaction costs and taxes might make it unprofitable for some investors to take advantage of such situations, a substantial departure would certainly lead others to act, thereby setting in motion forces that would quickly bring the price of the put back within the limits.

In the example, imagine the option had a price of $3.00 when the stock was selling for $80 and there were six months until expiration, so that PV($100) = $95.35. In this situation inequality (18.20) does not hold, since the left-hand side is equal to $3.00, whereas the right-hand side is larger, equal to $15.35 = $95.35 − $80.00. Consequently, an investor should immediately buy a put and a share of the stock for a cost of $83 ($3 + $80). In doing so the investor can be certain of making more than the risk-free rate of return.[18]

If at the end of six months the stock is selling for less than $100, the investor will exercise each put by delivering the shares of stock, getting back the exercise price of $100. Thus, the investor's rate of return on the initial investment of $83 ($3 + $80) will be equal to ($100 − $83)/$83 = 20.48%.

If the stock price is greater than $100 at expiration, then each put will be worthless when it expires, and the investor will be left with just the stock. Assuming the stock is selling for $110 per share at expiration, the rate of return on the $83 initial investment will be equal to ($110 − $83)/$83 = 32.53%. Furthermore, the higher the stock price, the greater the return. Thus, it can be seen that if inequality (18.20) was violated, there would be an opportunity for investors to be certain of making at least 20.48% over six months, which when annualized is notably greater than the 10% annual risk-free rate of return.

However, the ensuing large number of put and stock purchases will cause their prices ($3 and $80, respectively) to rise. These prices will quickly

---

[18] If the investor could borrow money, the rate of return from buying puts and the stock would exceed the risk-free return by an even greater amount.

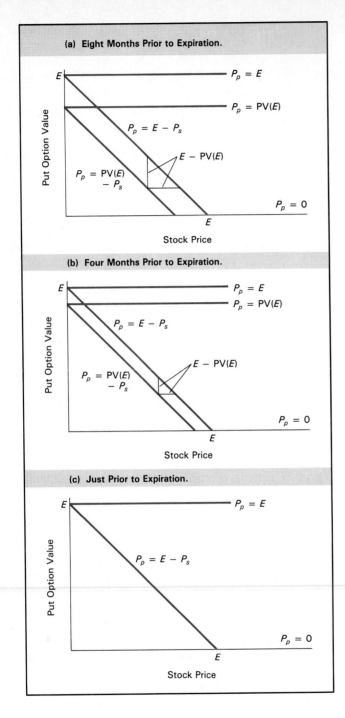

FIGURE 18–11
Limits on the value of a put option.

adjust (perhaps to $10 and $90, respectively) until inequality (18.20) does hold.

In Figure 18.11 these limits are expressed as equalities. Specifically, inequalities (18.18), (18.20), and (18.21) are given by, respectively,

$$P_p = \text{PV}(E) \qquad (18.22)$$

$$P_p = \text{PV}(E) - P_s \qquad (18.23)$$

$$P_p = 0. \qquad (18.24)$$

Each one of these equations represents a straight line shown in the figure. These lines serve as boundaries of the shaded region, which indicates where the put option must be priced so that none of the limits are violated.

Figure 18.11 also shows the way the limits change as time passes and the expiration date becomes nearer. Note that the boundary corresponding to equation (18.22) moves up, whereas the boundary corresponding to equation (18.23) moves to the right as the expiration date approaches. This change occurs because the present value of the exercise price rises as the expiration date becomes nearer. That is, $\text{PV}(E)$ rises because the length of time E is discounted is smaller. For example, if $E = \$100$, then discounting $\$100$ over three months will result in a larger figure than discounting $\$100$ over six months. Ultimately, just prior to expiration the effect of discounting will be so negligible that $\text{PV}(E) = E$ and the boundary shown by equation (18.23) will simply be

$$P_p = E - P_s. \qquad (18.25)$$

Note how this equation corresponds to the value of a put option moments before it expires as indicated earlier in Figure 18.3(b).

18.7.2 Put-Call Parity

Consider a put and a call on the same underlying stock that have the same exercise price and expiration date. Are the market prices of these two options related to each other? If so, just how are they related? Black and Scholes indicated that the market prices should be related, with the nature of the relationship known as *put-call parity*. However, it should be noted that their analysis was done for European options on non-dividend-paying stocks.

Assume that such a call option with an exercise price of E sells for P_c and that a put option on the same stock with the same exercise price and expiration date sells for P_p. Furthermore, assume that it is possible to make a bank deposit today for an amount that is equal to the present value of the exercise price, $\text{PV}(E)$, so that when the options expire the bank balance will be equal to the exercise price E. Lastly, denote the current market price of the underlying stock as P_s.

Consider the following two investment strategies. The first one involves buying a put and a share of stock and costs $P_p + P_s$. The second involves buying a call and making the requisite bank deposit and costs $P_c + \text{PV}(E)$.

The outcomes from these two strategies can be summarized as follows:

	STRATEGY 1	STRATEGY 2
Cost:	$P_p + P_s$	$P_c + \text{PV}(E)$

Value at Expiration:		
Stock price $> E$	Put worthless, so end up owning a share of stock	Bank balance of E used to exercise call, so end up owning a share of stock
Stock price $< E$	Exercise put, so end up with cash equal to E	Call worthless, so end up with bank balance of E

As this table shows, if the stock is selling for more than the exercise price on the expiration date, then both strategies end up with the investor owning a share of stock. Alternatively, if the stock is selling for less than the exercise price on the expiration date, then both strategies end up with the investor owning cash equal to the exercise price E. Thus, regardless of the ending stock price, the investor will end up being exactly as well off with strategy 1 as with strategy 2. Since the two strategies have the same ending value, they should have the same initial cost:

$$P_p + P_s = P_c + \text{PV}(E). \qquad (18.26)$$

This equation is known as the put-call parity theorem; if it is violated, there will be an opportunity for risklessly making abnormal profits (that is, arbitrage). For example, if the left-hand side is greater than the right-hand side, investors would be certain of making more than the risk-free rate by buying a call and making the requisite bank deposit while writing a put and shorting the stock.

Equation (18.26) can be rearranged in the following manner so that it can be used to estimate the value of European put options:

$$P_p = P_c + \text{PV}(E) - P_s. \qquad (18.27)$$

Thus, the value of a put can be estimated by using the Black-Scholes formula to estimate the value of a matching call option, then adding an amount equal to the present value of the exercise price to this estimate, and finally subtracting from this sum an amount that is equal to the current market price of the underlying common stock.

For example, consider a put option that expires in three months and has an exercise price of $40, while the current market price and risk of the underlying common stock are $36 and 50%, respectively. Assuming the risk-free rate is 5%, it was shown earlier that the Black-Scholes estimate of the value for a matching call option was $2.26. Since the 5% risk-free rate is a continuously compounded rate, the present value of the exercise price is equal to $40/($e^{.05 \times .25}$) = $39.50. At this point, having determined that P_c = $2.26, $\text{PV}(E)$ = $39.50, and P_s = $36, equation (18.27) can be used to estimate the value of the put option as being equal to $5.76 = $2.26 + $39.50 − $36.

Alternatively, the Black-Scholes formula for estimating the value of a call given in equation (18.11) can be substituted for P_c in equation (18.27).

After doing so and simplifying, an equation that can be used directly for estimating the value of a put is obtained:

$$P_p = \frac{E}{e^{RT}}N(-d_2) - P_sN(-d_1) \qquad (18.28)$$

where d_1 and d_2 are given in equations (18.12) and (18.13a), respectively.

In the previous example, $d_1 = -.25$ and $d_2 = -.50$; thus $N(-d_1) = N(.25) = .5987$ and $N(-d_2) = N(.50) = .6915$. Applying equation (18.28), the value of this put can be estimated directly:

$$P_p = \left(\frac{40}{e^{.05 \times .25}} \times .6915\right) - (36 \times .5987) = \$5.76,$$

which is the same estimated value as indicated earlier when equation (18.27) was used.

☐ 18.7.3　Static Analysis

Close scrutiny of the put-call parity equation reveals some interesting features of European put option pricing. In particular, it can be noticed that the value of a put option is dependent on the values of the same five inputs used for call valuation—the market price of the common stock (P_s), the exercise price of the option (E), the length of time until the expiration date (T), the risk-free rate (R), and the risk of the common stock (σ). What happens to the value of a put option when one of these inputs is changed while the other four remain the same?

1. The higher the price of the underlying stock (P_s), the lower the value of the put option.
2. The higher the exercise price (E), the higher the value of the put option.
3. Generally, the longer the time to the expiration date (T), the higher the value of the put option.
4. The higher the risk-free rate (R), the lower the value of the put option.
5. The greater the risk (σ) of the common stock, the higher the value of the put option.

The relationships for the underlying stock price (P), exercise price (E), and risk-free rate (R) are in the opposite direction from those shown earlier for call options, whereas the relationships for the time to the expiration date (T) and risk (σ) are in the same direction. It should be noted that exceptions can occur with T when the put is deep in the money. In such a situation, a longer time to expiration could actually decrease the value of the put.

☐ 18.7.4　Early Exercise and Dividends

Equations (18.27) and (18.28) apply to a European put on a stock that will not pay dividends prior to the option's expiration. As with call options, complications arise when it is recognized that most put options are American,

meaning they can be exercised before expiration, and that often dividends on the underlying common stock are paid before the expiration date.

Consider first the ability to exercise a put option at any time up to its expiration date. Earlier, it was shown that if there were no dividends on the underlying stock, then a call option was worth more alive than dead, meaning call options should not be exercised prior to expiration. Such an argument does *not* hold for put options.

Specifically, if a put option is in the money, meaning the market price of the stock is less than the exercise price, then the investor may want to exercise the put option. In doing so, the investor will receive an additional amount of cash equal to $E - P_s$. In turn, this cash can be invested at the risk-free rate to earn money over the remaining life of the option. Since these earnings would not be received by the investor if the put option were held, it would be advantageous in some cases to exercise the put early and thereby receive the earnings.

The possibility of early exercise affects the boundary conditions given in equations (18.18) and (18.20). Specifically, the present value of the exercise price, PV(E), that appears in these two inequalities should be replaced by the exercise price, E. Thus, the set of boundary conditions for an American put option will be:

$$P_p \leq E \tag{18.29}$$

$$P_p \geq E - P_s \tag{18.30}$$

$$P_p \geq 0. \tag{18.31}$$

Consider next the impact of dividends on put valuation. Previously, it was shown that the owner of a call may find it optimal to exercise just *before* an ex-dividend date, since doing so allowed the investor to receive the forthcoming dividends on the stock. With respect to a put, the owner may find it optimal to exercise just *after* the ex-dividend date, since the corresponding drop in the stock price will cause the value of the put to rise.[19]

One approach to valuing an American put on a dividend-paying stock is to use the *pseudo-American model*. As with calls, it is assumed that the size and timing of dividends to be paid on the stock during the life of the put are known with certainty. Consider valuing a put on a stock that will pay one dividend of size D at time t before the expiration date T.

First, the current market price of the underlying stock is reduced by the present value of the dividend as shown earlier in equation (18.17). Second, the put is valued using this dividend-adjusted stock price, along with the other inputs (E, R, σ, T), in equation (18.28); the result will be an estimate of the value of the put, assuming that it will not be exercised until expiration.

Third, the value of the put is estimated by assuming it will be exercised just after the ex-dividend date. This is done by using the time to the ex-dividend date t instead of the time to the expiration date T, along with the

---

[19] See Robert Geske and Kuldeep Shastri, "The Early Exercise of American Puts," *Journal of Banking and Finance* 9, no. 2 (June 1985):207–19.

dividend-adjusted stock price and the other inputs (E, R, σ) in equation (18.28).

Finally, the estimated value of the put is the higher of the two estimates—that is, the estimate based on the assumption that the put will be held to expiration and the estimate based on the assumption that the put will be exercised just after the ex-dividend date. It can be argued that the intrinsic value of the put (that is, the exercise price less the unadjusted stock price) should also be compared with these estimated values, with the highest of the three of them being used as an estimate of the put's fair value.[20]

18.8 OPTIONS ON OTHER KINDS OF ASSETS

Not all options are written on individual issues of common stock. In recent years, many new and somewhat exotic options have been created that have as an underlying asset something other than the stock of a particular company. Some of them are discussed here; the appendix discusses others, and the next chapter discusses what are known as futures options.

☐ 18.8.1 Index Options

A call option on General Motors stock is a relatively simple instrument. Upon exercise, the call buyer literally calls away 100 shares of GM stock. The call writer is expected physically to deliver the shares. In practice, both the buyer and writer may find it advantageous to close their positions in order to avoid the costs associated with the physical transfer of shares. In this event, the buyer may expect a gain (and the seller a loss) approximately equal to the difference between the current market price of the security and the option's exercise price.

It would be entirely feasible to specify that upon expiration, only a "cash settlement" procedure could be used. Here, the writer would be required to pay the buyer an amount equal to the difference between the current price of the security and the call option's exercise price (provided the current price is larger than the exercise price). Similarly, for puts, the writer could be expected to pay the buyer an amount equal to the difference between the option's exercise price and the current market price (provided the exercise price is larger than the current price).

While listed options on individual securities retain the obligation to "deliver," the realization that cash settlement can serve as a subsitute has allowed the creation of index options.

An index option is based on the level of an index of stock prices. Some indices are designed to reflect movements in the stock market, broadly construed. Other, specialized indices are intended to capture changes in the fortunes of particular industries or sectors. Figure 18.12 shows major indices

---

[20] For more exact approaches to valuing American puts, see Chapter 15 in Jarrow and Rudd, *Option Pricing*; Chapters 4 and 5 of Cox and Rubinstein, *Options Markets*; and pp. 169–70 and 203–5 of Ritchken, *Options*.

INDEX TRADING

OPTIONS

Tuesday, December 6, 1988

Chicago Board

S&P 100 INDEX

Strike Price	Calls–Last Dec	Calls–Last Jan	Calls–Last Feb	Puts–Last Dec	Puts–Last Jan	Puts–Last Feb
230	32	33⅝	....	1/16	⅜	15/16
235	....	32	....	1/16	½	1 3/16
240	22¾	27	....	1/16	⅝	1⅝
245	20½	21	....	3/16	15/16	2
250	16¼	17	....	5/16	1½	3¼
255	11¼	14½	15¾	9/16	2 5/16	4
260	6¾	10¼	11⅜	1 5/16	3½	5¼
265	3⅛	6⅞	8⅜	2⅞	5½	9⅛
270	1⅛	4¼	5⅞	6⅛	8¼	11¾
275	5/16	2⅜	3½	11⅛	12⅜	15
280	1/16	1⅛	2¼	....	16¼	19¼
285	1/16	9/16	....	....	....	....

Total call volume 139,648 Total call open int. 354,290
Total put volume 105,080 Total put open int. 395,560
The index: High 264.67; Low 261.11; Close 264.48, +3.05.

S&P 500 INDEX

Strike Price	Calls–Last Dec	Calls–Last Jan	Calls–Last Mar	Puts–Last Dec	Puts–Last Jan	Puts–Last Mar
220	55⅝	....	....	1/16	....	....
230	....	....	48	....	....	⅞
235	41¼	....	....	....	....	1 1/16
240	35¼	36½	....	1/16	5/16	1½
245	....	....	....	1/16	....	....
250	25¼	....	....	⅛	11/16	2⅜
255	20¼	....	28⅛	⅛	....	2½
260	16¼	18⅛	22	3/16	1⅛	3¾
265	14½	16¼	....	5/16	1 13/16	....
270	9¾	12½	16¼	⅝	3⅝	5¾
275	5⅝	6⅞	12½	1 7/16	4⅜	7¼
280	2 7/16	5½	10	3½	6⅛	8⅝
285	11/16	2¾	7¼	7¼	10⅛	10¼
290	3/16	1⅞	....	11¼	14½	....
295	....	....	3¼	....	....	....
300	....	....	1 5/16	21⅝	....	....
315	....	....	....	36⅜	....	....

Total call volume 11,485 Total call open int. 234,609
Total put volume 12,559 Total put open int. 267,000
The index: High 277.89; Low 274.62; Close 277.59, +2.66.

N.Y. Stock Exchange

NYSE INDEX OPTIONS

Strike Price	Calls–Last Dec	Calls–Last Jan	Calls–Last Feb	Puts–Last Dec	Puts–Last Jan	Puts–Last Feb
135	....	....	....	....	⅛	5/16
140	....	....	....	....	5/16	....
145	11⅝	....	....	1/16	9/16	1⅜
147½	....	....	....	⅛	....	....
150	6½	....	....	3/16	1⅝	2 9/16
152½	4⅜	5½	....	5/16	....	....
155	2½	4¾	....	13/16	2⅝	....
157½	1	....	....	....	....	....
160	5/16	2⅛	....	....	4¾	....
165	....	¾	....	....	....	....
170	....	⅛	⅜	....	....	....

Total call volume 1,394. Total call open int. 8,069.
Total put volume 2,017. Total put open int. 9,715.
The index: High 155.88; Low 154.34; Close 155.78, +1.30.

Pacific Exchange

FINANCIAL NEWS COMPOSITE INDEX

Strike Price	Calls–Last Dec	Calls–Last Jan	Calls–Last Mar	Puts–Last Dec	Puts–Last Jan	Puts–Last Mar
160	35	....	....	....	....	....
175	20	23	....	....	....	....
180	16⅝	....	....	....	....	....
185	12½	....	....	....	1⅛	....
190	7⅜	....	....	½	1 11/16	....
195	3¼	5½	....	1⅛	3⅛	5⅞
200	13/16	3	....	3⅝	5¼	....
205	....	....	....	10⅛	....	....
210	....	....	2	13¼	....	....

Total call volume 1,044 Total call open int. 2,639
Total put volume 544 Total put open int. 5,540
The index: High 196.95; Low 194.38; Close 196.60, +2.04

American Exchange

MAJOR MARKET INDEX

Strike Price	Calls–Last Dec	Calls–Last Jan	Calls–Last Feb	Puts–Last Dec	Puts–Last Jan	Puts–Last Feb
375	....	....	....	1/16	....	1⅝
380	....	....	....	⅛	....	....
385	....	....	....	⅛	1⅛	2⅞
390	33⅞	....	....	3/16	⅞	3⅜
395	....	29	31	¼	1¼	3¾
400	25	....	....	⅜	2	....
405	20¼	19½	26¼	½	3⅛	5½
410	16	19¼	....	¾	3⅞	6⅜
415	11¼	16	....	1 7/16	5⅛	7⅝
420	7½	12⅞	14⅝	2 9/16	6⅝	....
425	4⅝	10⅛	12¼	4⅜	9	11¼
430	2 3/16	7	8½	7½	....	....
435	1	4⅝	7½	....	....	....
440	⅜	3¼	....	....	17	....
445	⅛	....	....	....	....	....
450	1/16	....	....	....	....	....

Total call volume 20,549 Total call open int. 40,466
Total put volume 14,734 Total put open int. 40,466
The index: High 423.88; Low 417.67; Close 423.18, +5.47.

COMPUTER TECHNOLOGY INDEX

Strike Price	Calls–Last Dec	Calls–Last Jan	Calls–Last Feb	Puts–Last Dec	Puts–Last Jan	Puts–Last Feb
100	4½	....	....	....	....	....

Total call volume 5 Total call open int. 16
Total put volume 0 Total put open int. 5
The index: High 105.18; Low 103.95; Close 105.04, +0.86.

OIL INDEX

Strike Price	Calls–Last Dec	Calls–Last Jan	Calls–Last Feb	Puts–Last Dec	Puts–Last Jan	Puts–Last Feb
175	4¼	....	....	....	....	....
180	1⅛	....	....	....	....	....
185	....	1 3/16	....	....	....	....

Total call volume 101 Total call open int. 463
Total put volume 0 Total put open int. 544
The index: High 178.52; Low 176.32; Close 178.30, +1.73.

INSTITUTIONAL INDEX

Strike Price	Calls–Last Dec	Calls–Last Jan	Calls–Last Feb	Puts–Last Dec	Puts–Last Jan	Puts–Last Feb
240	....	....	....	....	....	⅞
250	....	....	....	1/16	1½	....
255	....	....	....	1/16	....	....
260	....	....	....	⅛	2 15/16	....
265	13½	....	....	5/16	....	....
270	....	....	....	½	....	....
275	4⅝	....	....	1 5/16	....	....
280	2½	....	7½	3½	....	....
285	¾	....	....	6½	....	....

Total call volume 822 Total call open int. 46,082
Total put volume 4,630 Total put open int. 37,463
The index: High 278.77; Low 274.82; Close 278.49, +3.51.

Philadelphia Exchange

GOLD/SILVER INDEX

Strike Price	Calls–Last Dec	Calls–Last Jan	Calls–Last Feb	Puts–Last Dec	Puts–Last Jan	Puts–Last Feb
90	....	....	....	⅝	2⅛	....
95	¾	....	....	....	....	....

Total call volume 40 Total call open int. 530
Total put volume 14 Total put open int. 267
The index: High 93.13; Low 91.83; Close 92.56, −0.95.

VALUE LINE INDEX OPTIONS

Strike Price	Calls–Last Dec	Calls–Last Jan	Calls–Last Feb	Puts–Last Dec	Puts–Last Jan	Puts–Last Feb
230	....	....	....	....	1¼	....
240	3⅝	....	....	1½	....	....
245	....	....	5¼	3⅝	....	....

Total call volume 61 Total call open int. 651
Total put volume 107 Total put open int. 1,628
The index: High 240.62; Low 239.54; Close 240.61, +0.87.

NATIONAL O-T-C INDEX

Strike Price	Calls–Last Dec	Calls–Last Jan	Calls–Last Feb	Puts–Last Dec	Puts–Last Jan	Puts–Last Feb
255	1¼	....	....	....	....	....

Total call volume 1 Total call open int. 209
Total put volume 0 Total put open int. 21
The index: High 252.76; Low 250.25; Close 252.65, +1.41.

UTILITIES INDEX

Strike Price	Calls–Last Dec	Calls–Last Jan	Calls–Last Feb	Puts–Last Dec	Puts–Last Jan	Puts–Last Feb
180	....	....	....	⅛	1⅛	....

Total call volume 55 Total call open int. 2,829
Total put volume 2,000 Total put open int. 4,291
The index: High 189.27; Low 187.47; Close 189.27 +1.55.

FIGURE 18–12
Index options quotations.

SOURCE: Reprinted by permission of *The Wall Street Journal*, © Dow Jones & Company, Inc. (December 7, 1988): p. C12.

on which options have been offered, along with their quotations. Some of the indices are highly specialized, consisting of only a few stocks. Others are broadly representative of major portions of the stock market. The AMEX Market Value Index covers all the stocks on the American Stock Exchange, and the NYSE Composite Index covers all the stocks on the New York Stock Exchange. The Standard & Poor's 500 Stock Index covers 500 large exchange-listed stocks.

Contracts for index options are not stated in terms of numbers of shares. Instead, the size of a contract is determined by multiplying the level of the index by a multiplier specified by the exchange on which the option is traded. The premium (price) of an index option times the applicable multiplier indicates the total amount paid.

Consider, for example, the S&P 100 index option that is traded on the Chicago Board Options Exchange. Specifically, the call option on this index that has an exercise price of 255 and expires in March has an indicated premium of $14\frac{1}{2}$ on December 8. Since the multiplier for S&P 100 option contracts is 100, this means that an investor would have to pay $1450 ($14\frac{1}{2}$ × 100) for this contract (plus a commission).

After purchasing this contract, the investor could later sell it or exercise it for its cash settlement value. Perhaps in January the S&P 100 will be at 275. In this case, the investor could exercise the call, receiving its intrinsic value of $2000 ((275 − 255) × 100)) for doing so. Alternatively, the investor could simply sell the call on the exchange; in doing so, the amount received would almost certainly be greater than $2000, since it would sell for an amount equal to the sum of its intrinsic and time values (see Figure 18.8).

□ 18.8.2 Interest Rate Options

Call and put options are also traded on debt instruments such as U.S. Treasury bonds and notes. Options on these securities are based on specific issues, with a given dollar amount of face value to be delivered upon exercise. Figure 18.13 shows some of these options that have been offered, along with their quotations.

For example, the CBOE maintains an options market in Treasury bonds where the underlying asset is $100,000 of a specific issue. One such issue carries a 9% coupon rate and matures November of 2018. CBOE calls on this issue having an exercise price of 101 (meaning ($101,000) and expiring in January of 1989 were selling for .24, meaning 24/32% (.75%) of face value, or $750 (.75% × $100,000), on December 6, 1988.

□ 18.8.3 Foreign Currency Options

Call and put options are also traded on foreign currencies such as Swiss francs. These are similar to stock options—when exercised, the underlying asset must be delivered. Since each option involves units of a foreign (non–United States) currency, delivery is made in a bank account in the country

OPTIONS

Tuesday, December 6, 1988
For Notes and Bonds, decimals in closing prices represent 32nds; 1.01 means 1 1/32. For Bills, decimals in closing prices represent basis points; $25 per .01.

Chicago Board Options Exchange
U.S. TREASURY BOND—$100,000 principal value

Underlying Issue	Strike Price	Calls—Last			Puts—Last		
		Dec	Jan	Mar	Dec	Jan	Mar
9⅛% (ybl)	99	....	....	....	0.08	....	....
due 5/2018	99½	....	....	....	0.10	....	....
	100	....	....	....	0.15	....	....
	101½	....	....	....	0.22	....	....
	102	....	....	....	1.01	....	....
9% (ybk)	97½	....	....	....	....	0.18	....
due 11/2018	98	....	....	....	....	0.23	....
	100	....	....	....	....	1.21	....
	101	....	0.24	....	....	....	....
	101½	....	0.25	....	....	....	....
	102	....	....	....	2.12	....	....

Total call vol. 3,605   Call open int. 13,500
Total put vol. 421   Put open int. 9,602
5-YEAR U.S. TREASURY NOTE—$100,000 principal value
Total call vol. 0   Call open int. 50
Total put vol. 0   Put open int. 51
   3 p.m. prices of underlying issues supplied by The Chicago Corp.: T-Bonds 12% 126.10; 8⅞% 98.31; 9% 100.14; 9⅛% 101.14. T-Notes 8¾% 99.09; 8⅞% 99.29; 9% 100.07.

FIGURE 18–13
Interest rate options quotations.

SOURCE: Reprinted by permission of *The Wall Street Journal*, © Dow Jones & Company, Inc. (December 7, 1988): p. C16.

of origin of the currency in question (typically, brokers can readily assist an investor in arranging for this to be done). Figure 18.14 shows some of these options that have been offered along with their quotations.

For example, the Philadelphia Exchange (PHLX) maintains an option market in foreign currencies, one of which is Swiss francs. Specifically, these options involve the delivery of 62,500 Swiss francs. In December 1988, one of the call options on this currency had an exercise price of 70 and an expiration date of March 1989. That is, the dollar amount involved in the exercise of this option was $43,750 (= 62,500 × $.70). The market price (that is, the premium) for this call was 1.17 on December 8, 1988, meaning the cost of purchasing the call was $731.25 ($.0117 × 62,500). Since the exchange rate on that date (68.23, or $.6823 per Swiss franc) was less than the exercise price of this call ($.70), the option was out of the money.

18.9 PORTFOLIO INSURANCE

One use of options is in procuring *portfolio insurance*. Consider an investor who holds a highly diversified portfolio. This investor would like to be able to benefit from any upward movements that may subsequently occur in the

FIGURE 18–14
Foreign currency options quotations.

SOURCE: Reprinted by permission of *The Wall Street Journal*, © Dow Jones & Company, Inc. (December 9, 1988): p. C11.

OPTIONS

Philadelphia Exchange

Thursday, Dec. 8

Option & Underlying	Strike Price	Calls – Last Dec	Jan	Mar	Puts – Last Dec	Jan	Mar
50,000 Australian Dollars-cents per unit.							
ADollr	...81	r	r	r	r	r	0.48
87.32	...83	4.28	r	r	r	r	0.90
87.32	...86	r	r	r	0.37	r	r
87.32	...88	r	r	1.20	r	r	r
87.32	...90	r	r	0.61	r	r	r
50,000 Australian Dollars-European Style.							
87.32	...85	r	2.23	r	r	r	r
31,250 British Pounds-cents per unit.							
BPound	167½	r	r	r	r	r	0.37
185.39	.170	15.00	r	r	r	r	r
185.39	.175	10.00	r	r	r	r	r
185.39	.180	r	r	r	0.13	r	r
185.39	182½	r	r	r	r	1.60	r
185.39	.185	r	r	3.80	1.18	r	r
185.39	187½	0.50	r	r	r	r	r
185.39	192½	r	0.50	r	r	r	r
31,250 British Pounds-European Style.							
185.39	.180	r	r	6.00	r	r	r
50,000 Canadian Dollars-cents per unit.							
CDollr	...82	1.87	r	r	r	r	r
83.83	.82½	1.30	r	r	r	r	r
83.83	...83	0.88	1.05	r	r	0.39	r
83.83	.83½	0.48	r	r	r	0.55	1.02
83.83	...84	0.22	r	0.80	0.40	0.84	r
83.83	.84½	r	r	r	0.68	r	r
83.83	...85	r	0.24	r	r	r	r
50,000 Canadian Dollars-European Style.							
CDollar	..80	3.81	r	r	r	r	r
62,500 West German Marks-cents per unit.							
DMark	..54	r	r	r	r	r	0.25
57.50	...55	2.46	r	r	0.01	0.12	0.36
57.50	...56	1.60	1.84	2.50	0.08	0.23	r
57.50	...57	0.80	1.28	1.86	0.20	0.52	r
57.50	...58	0.23	0.71	r	0.64	0.99	1.43
57.50	...59	r	0.38	0.88	1.72	1.58	r
57.50	...60	0.01	0.18	0.57	r	r	r
6,250,000 Japanese Yen-100ths of a cent per unit.							
JYen	...77	r	r	r	r	r	0.24
81.75	...78	r	r	r	r	r	0.49
81.75	...79	r	r	r	0.07	0.19	0.52
81.75	...80	r	r	r	0.08	0.33	0.79
81.75	...81	1.00	r	r	0.23	0.65	1.15
81.75	...82	0.50	1.15	r	r	1.07	r
81.75	...83	0.16	0.71	1.60	r	1.62	r
81.75	...84	0.05	0.40	r	r	r	r
81.75	...85	r	0.20	r	r	r	3.90
81.75	...86	r	0.12	r	r	r	r
62,500 Swiss Francs-cents per unit.							
SFranc	..60	8.40	r	r	r	r	r
68.23	...64	4.40	r	r	r	r	r
68.23	...66	2.42	r	r	0.03	0.20	r
68.23	...67	1.50	1.78	r	0.15	0.44	r
68.23	...68	0.75	1.22	r	r	0.74	r
68.23	...69	0.32	0.76	1.55	0.90	r	1.74
68.23	...70	r	0.48	1.17	r	r	r
68.23	...71	r	r	0.84	2.75	r	r
68.23	...73	r	r	0.29	r	r	r

Total call vol. 10,553   Call open int. 491,194
Total put vol. 16,286   Put open int. 437,694
r – Not traded. s – No option offered.
Last is premium (purchase price).

stock market but would also like to be protected from any downward movements.[21] There are, in principle, at least three ways this might be accomplished.

---

[21] In an efficient market, investors with "average" attitudes toward risk should not purchase portfolio insurance. Those who are especially averse to "downside risk" (relative to "upside potential") may find it useful to buy insurance. The key is the nature of the investor's attitudes toward risk and return. See Hayne E. Leland, "Who Should Buy Portfolio Insurance?" *Journal of Finance* 35, no. 2 (May 1980):581–94.

Purchasing an Insurance Policy

One alternative would be to sign a contract with an insurance company. For example, assume that a portfolio is currently worth $100,000. The insurance company might agree to cover any loss in value over some specified period, such as over the forthcoming year. At the end of the year, if the portfolio value were $95,000, the insurance company would pay the investor $5000. On the other hand, if the value were $105,000, the insurance company would pay nothing.

Figure 18.15(a) illustrates this situation. The horizontal axis measures the value of the portfolio at year-end. The 45° line *OBC* shows the value of the uninsured portfolio, whereas curve *ABC* shows the value of the insured portfolio. As the figure shows, if the portfolio value at the end of the year is more than $100,000, then the insured portfolio will be worth the same amount as the uninsured portfolio. However, if the portfolio value is less than $100,000, then the insured portfolio is worth more, with the difference be-

FIGURE 18–15
Portfolio insurance.

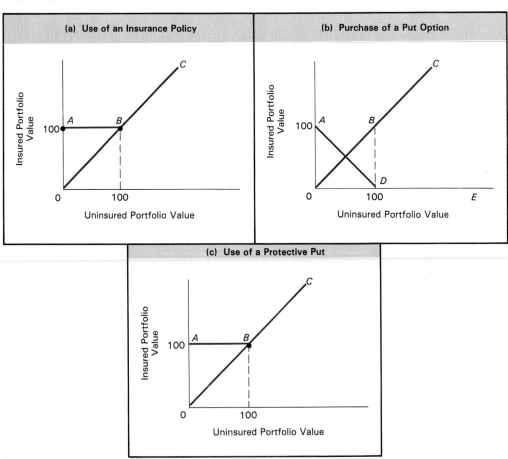

tween the *OB* and *AB* representing the size of the payment made to the investor by the insurance company.

Unfortunately, insurance companies rarely sign contracts of this sort. However, this is not the only alternative. Instead of dealing with an insurance company, the investor could consider purchasing a put option.

☐ 18.9.2 Purchasing a Protective Put

Assume that a put option is available on a stock market index that closely resembles the investor's portfolio. Curve *ADE* in Figure 18.15(b) shows the value to a buyer of such a put at the expiration date, where the put has an exercise price of $100,000 (note how it corresponds to Figure 18.3(b)). Curve *OBC* is the value of the portfolio on the expiration date, assuming the put was not purchased.

What would happen to an investor who (1) held the portfolio and (2) purchased this put? Figure 18.15(c) shows the answer. The value of the portfolio (*ABC*) is simply the combination of the values shown in Figure 18.15(b). Not surprisingly, it is precisely the same as curve ABC in Figure 18.15(a).

In this case, the purchase of a put provides protection against declines in portfolio value. In this role, it is termed a protective put. In practice, stock indices may not closely correspond with an investor's portfolio. Thus, purchase of a put on a stock index may provide only imperfect insurance. In a graph such as that shown in Figure 18.15(c), the resulting curve would be somewhat fuzzy due to the possible divergence of values of the portfolio and index. For example, the portfolio may decline in value by $25,000, while the index is declining by only $10,000. In this case, the portfolio would be insured for only 40% of its decline in value (40% = $10,000/$25,000).

What if neither explicit insurance nor an appropriate put were available? Can something still be done to insure the portfolio's value against market declines? Yes, if the allocation of funds between the portfolio and a riskless security can be altered frequently enough (and at reasonable cost). This type of portfolio insurance involves the creation of a *synthetic put*, and its application involves the use of a dynamic strategy for asset allocation, which is discussed next.

☐ 18.9.3 Creating a Synthetic Put

Insuring a portfolio by creating a synthetic put can most easily be described with an example.[22] Assume that the investor has $100,000 and is considering

---

[22] For an exposition, see Mark Rubinstein and Hayne E. Leland, "Replicating Options with Positions in Stock and Cash," *Financial Analysts Journal* 37, no. 4 (July/August 1981):63–72; Mark Rubinstein, "Alternative Paths to Portfolio Insurance," *Financial Analysts Journal* 41, no. 4 (July/August 1985):42–52; Robert Ferguson, "How To Beat the S&P 500 (without losing sleep)," *Financial Analysts Journal* 42, no. 2 (March/April 1986):37–46; and Thomas J. O'Brien, *How Option Replicating Portfolio Insurance Works: Expanded Details*, Monograph Series in Finance and Economics 1988–4, Salomon Brothers Center for the Study of Financial Institutions, Stern School of Business, New York University.

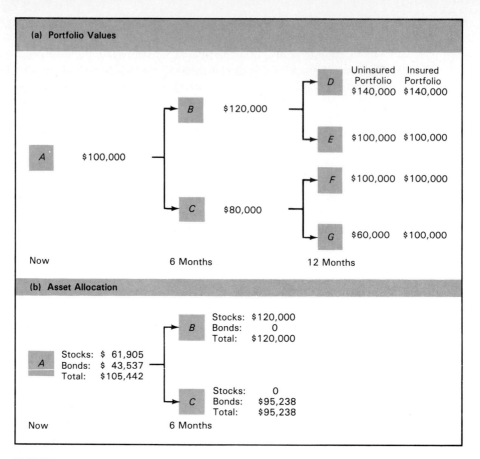

FIGURE 18–16
Creation of a synthetic put.

the purchase of a portfolio of common stocks. It is believed that the market value of this portfolio will either increase to $120,000 or decrease to $80,000 in six months. If it does increase to $120,000, then it will end up being worth either $140,000 or $100,000 after another six months. Alternatively, if it decreases to $80,000, then it will subsequently end up being worth either $100,000 or $60,000. Each one of these possible "states of the world" is indicated by a letter in Figure 18.16(a), with the current state being denoted by state *A*.

Figure 18.16(a) also shows two sets of terminal portfolio values (that is, portfolio values after 12 months) on the assumption that the common stock portfolio is purchased. The first set gives the values of the portfolio if it is uninsured. The second shows the desired portfolio values—that is, the values of an insured portfolio. In this example, the investor wants to be certain that the ending portfolio is worth at least $100,000, while also being

able to earn the returns associated with state D, should that state occur.[23]

What should the investor do initially in order be certain of this? Clearly, the investor cannot simply purchase the portfolio of stocks, since then the portfolio will be worth only $60,000 if state G occurs. However, the investor could consider purchasing portfolio insurance—that is, creating a synthetic put—by investing in both the stock portfolio and risk-free bonds.

The way this is done is to imagine that six months have passed and that state B has occurred. In this situation, how might one be certain to have $140,000 if the final state is D and $100,000 if the state is E? The answer is simple—if state B occurs, make sure the portfolio at that point is worth $120,000. Thus, an initial investment strategy is required that will provide $120,000 if the six-month state turns out to be state B.

It is also possible that after the first six months, state C will occur. In this situation, how might one be certain to have $100,000 regardless of the final state? Assuming that risk-free bonds return 5% per six months, the investor should purchase $95,238 ($100,000/1.05) of these bonds if state C occurs. This means that an initial investment strategy is required that will provide $95,238 if the six-month state turns out to be state C.

Figure 18.16(b) shows the investments and the amounts required in situations B and C. It remains only to determine an appropriate initial set of investments (at point A).

An amount of $1 invested in the common stock portfolio at A will grow to $1.20 after six months if the state at that time is B. More generally, s invested in the common stock portfolio at A will grow to $1.2s$ if the six-month state is B. Similarly, b invested in bonds at A will grow to $1.05b$ after six months. Thus, a set of initial investments that will provide $120,000 if state B occurs can be found by solving the following equation for s and b:

$$1.2s + 1.05b = \$120,000. \tag{18.32}$$

If the six-month state is C, s invested in the common stock portfolio will be worth $.8s$, whereas b invested in bonds will be worth $1.05b$. Thus, a set of initial investments that will provide $95,238 if state C occurs can be found by solving the following equation for s and b:

$$.8s + 1.05b = \$95,238. \tag{18.33}$$

Solutions for s and b that meet *both* equations can now be found, since there are two equations and two unknowns. The solution, shown in Figure 18.16(b), is that the investor should initially put $61,905 in common stocks and $43,537 in bonds (that is, $s = \$61,905$ and $b = \$43,537$), for a total initial investment of $105,442.

Making this initial investment is equivalent to investing $100,000 in the common stock portfolio and buying a protective put option (or an in-

---

[23] In this example, portfolio insurance is sought for a one-year horizon with a floor of 0% (meaning the investor does not want to lose any of the initial investment over the next 12 months). Other horizons and floors, such as a two-year horizon with a floor of -5% (meaning the investor does not want to lose more than 5% of the initial investment over the next 24 months), are possible.

surance policy) for $5442. Indeed, this analysis could be used to determine the appropriate price for such an option or insurance policy. Equivalently, the actions of the investor have resulted in the creation of a synthetic put where the stocks being held are the underlying asset.

By design, this initial investment will provide precisely the desired ending values, but only if the mix is altered as values change. The goal is achieved by using a dynamic strategy in which investments are bought and sold at intermediate points, depending on the returns of the underlying assets.

In the example, if state B occurs, the stocks will be worth $74,286 ($61,905 × 1.2) and the bonds will be worth $45,714 ($43,537 × 1.05), for an aggregate value of $120,000. In this situation, the $45,714 of bonds would be sold and the proceeds used to make an additional investment in the common stock portfolio so that the investor is entirely invested in common stocks for the last six months.

However, if state C occurs, the stocks will be worth $49,524 ($61,905 × .8) and the bonds will be worth $45,714 ($43,537 × 1.05), for an aggregate value of $95,238. In this situation, the $49,524 of stocks would be sold and the proceeds used to make an additional investment in the risk-free bonds for the last six months.

Thus, more money is invested in common stocks if the initial portfolio rises in value, with the money gotten by selling bonds. If the initial portfolio falls in value, more money is invested in bonds, with the money gotten by selling stocks. In this example, the percentage invested in stocks is initially 58.71%. ($61,905/$105,442) and subsequently goes to either 100% (if stocks go up) or 0% (if stocks go down).

More realistic applications involve many time intervals within the one-year period, with smaller stock price movements in each interval. Consequently, there would be more changes in the mix of stocks and bonds after each interval, but the changes would be of smaller magnitude. Nevertheless, the essential nature of the strategy would be the same:

When stock prices rise, sell some bonds and buy more stocks.

When stock prices fall, sell some stocks and buy more bonds.

Often computers are used to monitor stock price movements of investors who have obtained portfolio insurance in this manner. When these movements are of sufficient magnitude, the computer is used to place the requisite buy and sell orders electronically. Since much of this monitoring and ordering is programmed into a computer, portfolio insurance is often referred to as a form of *program trading*.[24]

If there are only two states of the world in each interval, reallocation is possible after every interval, and there are no transaction costs, then the values associated with any desired "insured portfolio" can be replicated exactly with a dynamic strategy. In practice, however, the results are likely to be only approximately equal. First, there are transaction costs associated

---

[24] The next chapter discusses another form of program trading that is known as index arbitrage.

with buying and selling securities for the dynamic strategy.[25] Second, if an interval is defined as a length of time over which only two alternative states may occur, then the amount of time to an interval may be so short that reallocation is impossible after each interval.

In practice, arbitrary rules are applied to avoid frequent revisions and the associated high level of transaction costs, while being reasonably certain of providing the portfolio with the desired level of insurance.[26] Unfortunately, these arbitrary rules did not work very well on Black Monday and Terrible Tuesday (October 19–20, 1987). During these two days, stock prices moved downward so fast that reallocation could not be performed in a timely fashion, resulting in a situation where portfolio insurance did not provide the protection that had been anticipated. As a result, some people believe that dynamic strategies will be used less frequently in the future and that puts will be used more often.[27]

18.10 SUMMARY

This chapter introduced the two main types of option contracts that currently are in existence. Call options allow one person (known as the buyer) to purchase from another person (known as the writer) a specific asset at a specific price at any time up until a stated expiration date. Put options allow one person (known as the buyer) to sell another person (known as the writer) a specific asset at a specific price at any time up until a stated expiration date. Calls and puts typically involve 100 shares of a specific company's stock and have an expiration date of nine months or less.

An investor interested in options can be either a buyer or a writer of an option. However, once a position in an option is assumed, it need not be held for the life of the option. Instead, an offsetting transaction can be made, meaning a buyer can subsequently sell the contract to someone else and a writer can subsequently buy the contract back from someone else. What makes all this possible and relatively easy to do is the fact that the terms of these contracts are standardized, thereby allowing them to be traded on certain organized exchanges at market-determined prices. Thus, a writer who wishes to buy the contract back does not need to deal with the specific investor who bought the contract in the first place. All that is necessary is

---

[25] There is another dynamic strategy for insuring the portfolio that is often preferred because it has smaller transaction costs. Instead of combining stocks with a risk-free bond, it involves combining stocks with a short position in index futures, which are a type of financial contract that is discussed in the next chapter.

[26] For a discussion of transactions costs, see Hayne E. Leland, "Option Pricing and Replication with Transactions Costs," *Journal of Finance* 40, no. 5 (December 1985):1283–1301. For tests of some commonly used arbitrary rules, see Ethan S. Etzioni, "Rebalance Disciplines for Portfolio Insurance," *Journal of Portfolio Management* 13, no. 1 (Fall 1986):59–62; C. B. Garcia and F. J. Gould, "An Empirical Study of Portfolio Insurance," *Financial Analysts Journal* 43, no. 4 (July/August 1987):44–54; and Robert Ferguson, "A Comparison of the Mean-Variance and Long-Term Return Characteristics of 3 Investment Strategies," *Financial Analysts Journal* 43, no. 4 (July/August 1987):55–66.

[27] See Mark Rubinstein, "Portfolio Insurance and the Market Crash," *Financial Analysts Journal* 44, no. 1 (January/February 1988):38–47. For a discussion of various types of dynamic strategies, see Andre F. Perold and William F. Sharpe, "Dynamic Strategies for Asset Allocation," *Financial Analysts Journal* 44, no. 1 (January/February 1988):16–27.

for the writer to buy any contract that has the same terms as the one that was originally written.

The value of an option is bounded by certain market conditions. That is, it can be shown that options have one upper bound and two lower bounds on their values. Should an option have a market price that is outside these bounds, then an opportunity would exist for investors to engage in arbitrage, meaning investors would be able to make abnormal returns with certainty.

Within these bounds, an estimate of the true value of an option can be determined by using a formula developed by Black and Scholes. This formula shows that the value of an option is determined by five factors—the market price of the underlying stock, the exercise price, the life of the option, the risk-free rate, and the risk of the common stock. It can also be shown that a call and put option on the same stock have values that are linked to each other by what is known as the put-call parity theorem, provided the options have the same exercise price and lifespan.

Unfortunately, the Black-Scholes formula and put-call parity theorem are, strictly speaking, applicable only for European options on stocks that will not pay cash dividends over the life of the option. Nevertheless, adjustments can be made so that reasonably accurate estimates of the value of American options on dividend-paying stocks can be obtained.

In addition to put and call options on individual common stocks, options on other kinds of assets exist. Examples include stock indices, debt instruments, and foreign currency. Furthermore, synthetic options can be created by holding the underlying asset and a bond in relative amounts that vary with the market price of the underlying asset. Portfolio insurance, where an investor establishes a floor on the portfolio's return over some specified horizon, involves the creation of a synthetic put.

APPENDIX A
SECURITIES WITH OPTIONLIKE FEATURES

Many securities have features that are similar to stock options, particularly call options. In some cases, the optionlike features are explicit. In other cases, more subtle optionlike features are involved. This appendix discusses some of these securities.

A.1 WARRANTS

A stock purchase warrant (or, more simply, a warrant) is a call option issued by the firm whose stock serves as the underlying security. At the time of issue, a warrant usually has a longer time to expiration (for example, five or more years) than a typical call option. Some perpetual warrants, with no expiration date, have also been issued. Generally, warrants may be exercised

before expiration—that is, they are American call options—but some require an initial waiting period.

The exercise price may be fixed or it may change during the life of the warrant, usually increasing in steps. The initial exercise price is typically set to exceed the market price of the underlying security at the time the warrant is issued, often by a substantial amount.

At the time of issue, one warrant typically entitles the holder to purchase one share of stock for the appropriate exercise price. However, most warrants are protected against stock splits and stock dividends. This means that any warrant with such protection will enable the investor to buy more or less than one share at an altered exercise price if a stock dividend or stock split is declared. For example, a two-for-one stock split would allow the warrantholder to purchase two shares at one-half the original exercise price, whereas a one-for-two reverse stock split would allow the warrantholder to purchase one-half share at twice the original exercise price.

Warrants may be distributed to stockholders in lieu of a stock or cash dividend or sold directly as a new security issue. Alternatively, warrants may be issued in order to "sweeten" an offering of some other kind of security. For example, a bond may be sold by the firm with warrants attached to it. In some cases, the warrants are nondetachable, except upon exercise. This means that if an investor wants to sell one of the bonds, the warrants must either be exercised or sold with the bond. In other cases, the warrants are detachable, meaning that after the initial sale of the bonds an investor may sell either the bonds or the warrants (or both).

Terms associated with a warrant are contained in a warrant agreement, which serves the same function as an indenture for a bond issue. In this agreement, the scope of the warrantholder's protection is defined (for example, the treatment of warrants in the event of a merger); it may also specify certain restrictions on corporate behavior.

Some warrants that are issued with bonds have an additional attribute. Although they may be detached and exercised by paying cash to the corporation, an alternative method of payment is provided. This alternative allows bonds from the initial issue to be used in lieu of cash to pay the exercise price, with the bonds being valued at par for this purpose.

One difference between warrants and call options is the limitation on the amount of warrants that are outstanding. A specific number of warrants of a particular type will be issued; the total cannot easily be increased and typically is reduced as the warrants are exercised. In contrast, a call option can be created whenever two people wish to create one; thus, the number outstanding is not fixed. Exercise of a call option on its stock has no more effect on a corporation than a transaction in its stock on the secondary market. However, the exercise of a warrant does have an effect. In particular, it leaves the corporation with more cash, fewer warrants outstanding, and more stock outstanding.

Warrants are traded on major stock exchanges and on the over-the-counter market. Quotations for those with active markets are provided in the financial press in the sections devoted primarily to stocks.

A.2 RIGHTS

A right is similar to a warrant in that it also is a call option issued by the firm whose stock serves as the underlying security.[28] Rights, also known as subscription warrants, are issued to give existing stockholders their pre-emptive right to subscribe to a new issue of common stock before the general public is given an opportunity. Each share of stock receives one right. A stated number of rights plus cash equal to a specified subscription price are required in order to obtain one new share. To insure the sale of the new stock, the subscription price is usually set below the stock's market price at the time the rights are issued. This does not mean that new subscribers get a bargain, since they must pay old stockholders for the required number of rights, which become valuable as a result.

Rights generally have short lives (from two to ten weeks) and may be freely traded prior to exercise. Up to a specified date, old shares of the stock trade *cum rights*, meaning the buyer of the stock is entitled to receive the rights when issued. Afterward, the stock trades *ex rights* at a correspondingly lower price. Rights for popular issues of stock are sometimes traded on exchanges; others are available in the over-the-counter market. Often trading begins prior to actual availability, with the rights sold for delivery on a *when-issued* basis.

A right is, in effect, a warrant, although one with a rather short time before expiration. It also differs with regard to exercise price, which is typically set above the stock's market price at issuance for a warrant and below it for a right. Because of their short lives, rights need not be protected against stock splits and stock dividends. Otherwise, they have all the attributes of a warrant and should be valued accordingly.

A.3 BOND CALL PROVISIONS

Many firms issue bonds with call provisions that allow the firm to repurchase the bonds before maturity, usually at a price above par value.[29] This amounts to the sale of a straight bond and the simultaneous purchase by the corporation of a call option sold by the purchaser of the bond. The premium is paid by the corporation in the form of a relatively lower selling price for the bond. The writer of the option is the bond purchaser.

Bond call provisions usually can be exercised only after some specified date (for example, five years after issue). Moreover, the exercise price, known as the call premium, may be different for different exercise dates (typically shrinking in size the longer the bond is outstanding). The implicit call option associated with such a bond is thus both longer-lived and more complex than those traded on the listed options markets.

---

[28] Rights are also discussed in Chapter 15.

[29] Bond call provisions are also discussed in Chapter 12 and 13.

A.4 CONVERTIBLE SECURITIES

A particularly popular financial instrument is a security that can be converted into a different security of the same firm under certain conditions. The typical case involves a bond or preferred stock convertible into shares of the firm's common stock, with a stated number of shares received for each bond. Usually, no cash is involved: The old security is simply traded in, and the appropriate number of new securities are issued in return. Convertible preferred stocks are issued from time to time, but tax effects make them, like other preferred stock, attractive primarily to corporate investors. For other investors, many issues of convertible bonds are available.

If a $1000 par value bond can be converted into 20 shares of common stock, the conversion ratio is 20. Alternatively, the conversion price may be said to be $50 ($1000/20), since $50 of the bond's par value must be given up to obtain one common share. Neither the conversion ratio nor the conversion price is affected by changes in a bond's market value.

Conversion ratios are typically set so that conversion will not prove attractive unless the stock price increases substantially from its value at the time the convertible security was first issued. This is similar to the general practice used in setting exercise prices for warrants.

A convertible bond's conversion value, obtained by multiplying the conversion ratio by the stock's current market price, is the value that would be obtained by conversion; it is the bond's current "value as stock." The conversion premium is the amount by which the bond's current market price exceeds its conversion value, expressed as a percent of the latter. A related amount is the convertible's investment value. This value is an estimate, based on the convertible's maturity date, coupon rate, and rating, of the amount for which the bond might sell if it were not convertible. Equivalently, it is the convertible's "value as a straight bond."

Consider a $1000 par value bond convertible into 20 shares of stock. If the market price of the stock is $60 per share, then the conversion value of the bond is $1200 ($60 × 20). If the current market price of the convertible bond is $1300, then its conversion premium is $100 (= $1300 − $1200). Its investment value may be estimated to be $950, meaning that the bond would sell for this much if it did not provide the investor with the option of convertibility.

Convertible securities of great complexity can be found. Some may be converted only after an initial waiting period. Some may be converted up to the bond's maturity date; others only for a stated, shorter period. Some have different conversion ratios for different years. A few can be converted into packages of two or more different securities; others require the additional payment of cash upon conversion.

Convertible bonds are usually protected against stock splits and stock dividends via adjustment in the conversion ratio. For example, a bond with an initial conversion ratio of 20 could be adjusted to have a ratio of 22 following a 10% stock dividend. Protection against cash dividends is not generally provided, but some indentures require that the holders of convertible bonds

be notified prior to payment of cash dividends so they may convert before the resultant fall in the stock's market price.

Convertible securities often contain a call provision, which may be used by the corporation to force conversion when the stock's market price is sufficiently high to make the value of the stock obtained on conversion exceed the call price of the bond. For example, if the conversion value of the bond is $1200 (the bond is convertible into 20 shares of stock that are currently selling for $60 per share) and the call price is $1100, the firm can force conversion by calling the bond. This is because a bondholder faces two choices when the call is received—either convert and receive 20 shares collectively worth $1200 or receive cash of $1100—and should choose the shares since they have the higher value.

A convertible bond is, for practical purposes, a bond with nondetachable warrants plus the restriction that *only* the bond is usable (at par) to pay the exercise price. If the bond were not callable, the value of this package would equal the value of a straight noncallable bond (that is, the estimated investment value) plus that of the warrants. However, most convertible bonds are callable and thus involve a double option: The holder has an option to convert the bond to stock, and the issuing corporation has an option to buy the bond back from the investors.

QUESTIONS AND PROBLEMS

1. Why have organized options exchanges been so important to the growth in options trading?

2. Bid McPhee has just written a call option on Jefferson Computer Services stock. Specifically, Bid sold four June 50 contracts at a premium of $3 per share. Jefferson stock currently sells for $48 per share. How much margin was required?

3. Elizabeth Stroud had only a few hours left to decide whether to exercise a call option on Carson Company stock. The call option has an exercise price of $54. Elizabeth originally purchased the call six months ago for $400 (or $4 per share).

   a. For what range of stock prices should Elizabeth exercise the call on the last day of the call's life?

   b. For what range of stock prices would Elizabeth realize a net loss (including the premium paid for the call)?

   c. If Elizabeth had purchased a put instead of a call, how would your answers to parts (a) and (b) change?

4. On November 18, 1987, three call options on Richmond Associates stock, all expiring in December 1987, sold for the following prices:

EXERCISE PRICE	OPTION PRICE
$50	$7½
60	3
70	1½

Firpo Marberry is considering a "butterfly spread" that involves the following positions:

Buy 1 call at $50 exercise price
Sell (write) 2 calls at $60 exercise price
Buy 1 call at $70 exercise price

   a. What would be the values at expiration of Firpo's spread if Richmond Associates' stock price is below $50? Between $50 and $60? Between $60 and $70? Above $70?

   b. What dollar investment would be required of Firpo to establish the spread?

5. What is the time value of an option? Why does an option's time value decline as the option approaches expiration?

6. Explain why call options on nondividend-paying stocks are "worth more alive than dead."

7. List the variables needed to estimate the value of a call option. Describe how a change in the value of these variables affects the value of a call option.

8. Given the information below, calculate the three-month call option price that is consistent with the Black–Scholes model.

$$P_s = \$47, E = \$45, R = .05, \sigma = .40$$

9. If the premium on a call option has recently declined, does this indicate that the option is a better buy than it was previously? Why or why not?

10. A six-month call option with an exercise price of $40 is selling for $5. The current price of the stock is $41.25. The hedge ratio of the option is .65.

   a. What percentage change in the option's price is likely to accompany a 1% change in the stock's price?

   b. If the beta of the stock is 1.10, what is the beta of the option? (*Hint*: Recall what the beta of a stock implies about the relationship between the stock's price to that of the market.)

11. In February 1988, Gid Gardner sold a September 55 call on Concord Corp. stock for $4.375 per share and simultaneously bought a September 55 put on the same stock for $6 per share. At the time, Treasury bills coming due in September were priced to yield 12.6% and Concord stock sold for $53 per share.

   a. What value would put-call parity suggest was appropriate for the Concord put?

   b. Concord was expected to make three dividend payments between February and September. Could that account for the discrepancy between your answer to part (a) and the actual price of the put? Why or why not?

   c. If Concord stock were to fall to a very low value before September, might it pay for Gid to exercise the put? Why or why not?

12. Distinguish between portfolio insurance implemented through a protective put and through dynamic asset allocation.

13. (Appendix Question) What is the primary advantage to an investor of a warrant compared to a call option?

14. (Appendix Question) Wheeling Corp. has a 10% subordinated convertible debenture outstanding, maturing in 8 years. The bond's face value is $1,000. It currently sells for 99 of par. The bond is convertible into 15 shares of common stock. The company's common stock currently sells for $50 per share.

   a. What is the bond's conversion value?

   b. What is the bond's conversion premium?

   c. What is the bond's investment value?

Chapter 19

FUTURES

Consider a contract that involves the delivery of some specific asset by a seller to a buyer at an agreed-upon future date. Although such a contract also specifies the purchase price, the asset is not to be paid for until the delivery date. However, the buyer and the seller are both requested to make a security deposit at the time the contract is signed. The reason for this deposit is to protect each person from experiencing any losses, should the other person renege on the contract.

These contracts are often referred to as *futures* (short for futures contract), and in the United States they involve assets such as agricultural goods (for example, wheat), natural resources (for example, copper), foreign currencies (for example, Swiss francs), fixed-income securities (for example, Treasury bonds), and market indices (for example, the Standard & Poor's 500).[1] As with options, standardization of the terms in these contracts makes it relatively easy for anyone to create and subsequently trade the contracts.

There are two types of people who deal in futures—speculators and hedgers. *Speculators* buy and sell futures for the sole purpose of making a profit by selling them at a price that is higher (they hope) than their buying price; such people neither produce nor use the asset in the ordinary course of business. In contrast, *hedgers* buy and sell futures to offset an otherwise risky position in the spot market; in the ordinary course of business, they either produce or use the asset.

For example, consider wheat futures. A farmer might note today that the market price for a wheat futures contract with delivery around harvest time is $4 per bushel, a price that is high enough to ensure a profitable year. Although the farmer could sell wheat futures today, alternatively the farmer could wait until harvest and sell the wheat on the spot market at that time.[2] However, waiting until harvest entails risk because the spot price of wheat could fall by then, perhaps to $3 per bushel, which would bring personal ruin to the farmer. In contrast, selling wheat futures today will allow the farmer to lock in a $4-per-bushel selling price. Doing so would remove an

---

[1] The term *commodity futures* is often used to refer to futures on agricultural goods and natural resources.

[2] The *spot market* involves the immediate exchange of an asset for cash; the purchase price of the asset is known as its *spot price*.

element of risk from the primary business of the farmer, growing wheat. Thus, a farmer who sells futures is known as a hedger or, more specifically, a *short hedger*.

Perhaps the buyer of the farmer's futures contract is a baker who uses wheat in making bread. Currently, the baker has enough wheat in inventory to last until harvest season. In anticipation of the need to replenish the inventory at that time, the baker could buy a wheat futures contract today at $4 per bushel. Alternatively, the baker could simply wait until the inventory runs low and then buy wheat in the spot market. However, there is a chance that the spot price will be $5 per bushel at that time. Should this happen, the baker would have to raise the selling price of bread and perhaps lose sales in doing so. Alternatively, by purchasing wheat futures, the baker can lock in a $4-per-bushel purchase price, thereby removing an element of risk from the bread business. Thus, a baker who buys futures is also known as a hedger or, more specifically, a *long hedger*.

The farmer and baker can be compared with a speculator—a person who buys and sells wheat futures, based on the forecast price of wheat, in the pursuit of relatively short-term profits. As mentioned earlier, such a person neither produces nor uses the asset in the ordinary course of business.

A speculator who thinks the price of wheat is going to rise substantially will buy wheat futures. Later, this person will enter a *reversing trade* by selling wheat futures; if the forecast was accurate, a profit is made on an increase in the wheat futures price.

For example, consider a speculator expecting at least a $1 per bushel rise in the spot price of wheat. While this person could buy wheat, store it, and later hope to sell it at the anticipated higher price, it would be easier and more profitable to buy a wheat futures contract today at $4 per bushel. Later, assuming the spot price of wheat rises by $1, the speculator would enter a reversing trade by selling the wheat futures contract for perhaps $5 per bushel (a $1 rise in the spot price of wheat will cause the futures price to rise by about $1). Thus, the speculator will make a profit of $1 per bushel, or $5000 in total, since these contracts are for 5000 bushels. As will be shown later, the speculator might need to make a security deposit of $1000 at the time the wheat futures contract was bought. Since this is returned when the reversing trade is made, the speculator's rate of return is quite high (500%) relative to the percentage rise in the price of wheat (25%).

Alternatively, if a speculator forecasts a substantial price decline, then initially wheat futures would be sold. Later, the person would enter a reversing trade by purchasing wheat futures; assuming the forecast was accurate, a profit is made on the decrease in the wheat futures price.

19.1 THE FUTURES CONTRACT

Futures contracts are standardized in terms of delivery as well as in the type of asset that is permissible for delivery. For example, the Chicago Board of Trade specifies the following requirements for its July wheat contract:

1. The seller agrees to deliver 5000 bushels of either:

   No. 2 sift red wheat
   No. 2 hard red winter wheat
   No. 2 dark northern spring wheat
   No. 1 northern spring wheat

   at the agreed-upon price. Alternatively, a number of other grades can be delivered at specified premiums or discounts from the agreed-upon price. In any case, the seller is allowed to decide which grade shall be delivered.
2. The grain will be delivered by registered warehouse receipts issued by approved warehouses in Chicago or Toledo, Ohio (Toledo deliveries are discounted $.02 per bushel).
3. Delivery will take place during the month of July, with the seller allowed to decide the actual date.
4. Upon delivery of the warehouse receipt from the seller to the buyer, the latter will pay the former the agreed-upon price in cash.

After an organized exchange has set all the terms of a futures contract except for its price, the exchange will authorize trading in the contract.[3] Buyers and sellers (or their representatives) meet at a specific place on the floor of the exchange and try to agree on a price at which to trade. If they succeed, one or more contracts will be created, with all the standard terms plus an additional one—the price involved. Prices are normally stated on a per-unit basis. Thus, if a buyer and seller agree to a price of $4 per bushel for a contract of 5000 bushels of wheat, the amount of money involved is $20,000.

Figure 19.1 shows a set of daily quotations giving the prices at which some commodity futures contracts were traded and the total volume of sales for each type of contract. Such listings of active futures markets are published regularly in the financial press, with each item for delivery (such as corn) having a heading that indicates the number of units per contract (5000 bushels) and the terms on which prices are stated (cents per bushel).

Below the heading for the asset are certain details for each type of contract. Moving from left to right in Figure 19.1, the first column shows the delivery dates for the contracts. For example, there are seven different futures contracts for corn, each one involving the same item but having different delivery dates. Next comes the *open*, denoting the price at which the first transaction was made; the *high* and *low*, representing the highest and lowest prices during the day; and the *settle*, a price that is a representative

---

[3] For a relatively complete description of the terms for many exchange-traded futures contracts, see the *Commodity Trading Manual* (Chicago Board of Trade, 1985); and Robert W. Kolb, *Understanding Futures Markets* (Glenview, Ill.: Scott, Foresman and Company, 1988). These two books also contain descriptions of various futures exchanges.

COMMODITY FUTURES PRICES

Thursday, December 8, 1988

Open Interest Reflects Previous Trading Day.

–GRAINS AND OILSEEDS–

CORN (CBT) 5,000 bu.; cents per bu.

	Open	High	Low	Settle	Change	Lifetime High	Lifetime Low	Open Interest
Dec	256½	260½	255¼	256¾	+ 1½	370	184	4,447
Mr89	269¼	272¼	267¾	269½	+ 1¼	370	193½	124,643
May	273¾	276	272¼	273¾	+ ½	369	207½	39,706
July	276¼	277¾	274¼	275¼	– ¼	360	233	24,968
Sept	260	261½	257¾	258¾	– 1	317¾	245	5,061
Dec	257¼	259	255¼	256	– 1½	295	234	19,283
Mr90	262	262½	261	262	– 1½	270	257½	321

Est vol 31,000; vol Wed 37,050; open int 218,429, –383.

OATS (CBT) 5,000 bu.; cents per bu.

	Open	High	Low	Settle	Change	Lifetime High	Lifetime Low	Open Interest
Dec	203½	204	201	203¾	+ 4¾	389½	162	190
Mr89	209¾	214	209¾	212¼	+ 2¼	367¾	161	5,805
May	211	213¾	211	212¾	+ 1¾	340	187	1,373
July	209	212½	209¼	211½	+ 2	277	201½	1,545
Sept	209½	211½	209	211½	+ 2	231	200	345

Est vol 1,000; vol Wed 1,247; open int 9,258, +119.

SOYBEANS (CBT) 5,000 bu.; cents per bu.

	Open	High	Low	Settle	Change	Lifetime High	Lifetime Low	Open Interest
Jan	773	783	769	773½	+ 5½	1034	553	42,057
Mar	785	796	781½	785½	+ 4½	1023	579	34,252
May	790	801	787	792	+ 5½	1003	647	14,184
July	791	799	785½	788½	+ 3¼	986	685	12,435
Aug	785	786	775½	776	+ 1½	951	725	2,003
Sept	725	731	725	727¼	+ 5¼	835	701	2,975
Nov	693	700	690½	695¼	+ 5½	793	663	10,970
Ja90	704	704¼	701	702½	+ 4½	748	684	427

Est vol 43,000; vol Wed 47,054; open int 119,306, +820.

SOYBEAN MEAL (CBT) 100 tons; $ per ton.

	Open	High	Low	Settle	Change	Lifetime High	Lifetime Low	Open Interest
Dec	248.00	252.00	245.00	245.50	– 1.40	318.70	159.00	2,978
Ja89	249.50	253.00	246.20	246.90	– 1.20	313.00	177.00	23,433
Mar	249.50	253.00	246.00	246.70	– 1.10	308.00	193.50	25,764
May	246.00	248.00	242.00	243.70	– .50	304.00	200.50	8,721
July	239.50	243.00	237.00	238.00	– .70	300.00	221.00	4,918
Aug	231.00	238.00	230.00	230.20	+ 1.20	298.00	217.50	1,292
Sept	221.50	224.50	219.00	220.00	+ .50	290.00	214.00	1,543
Oct	209.50	210.00	209.00	210.00	+ 1.00	237.00	203.00	1,328
Dec	205.00	205.00	204.00	204.00	+ 1.90	270.00	199.50	1,437

Est vol 14,000; vol Wed 15,016; open int 71,414, –231.

–LIVESTOCK & MEAT–

CATTLE–FEEDER (CME) 44,000 lbs.; cents per lb.

	Open	High	Low	Settle	Change	Lifetime High	Lifetime Low	Open Interest
Jan	81.95	82.50	81.75	81.92	– .25	85.05	74.00	5,101
Mr89	81.15	81.55	80.87	81.00	– .35	83.85	74.00	4,728
Apr	80.50	80.70	80.25	80.35	– .35	82.90	74.40	1,314
May	79.20	79.40	79.10	79.17	– .32	81.80	76.00	1,213
Aug	78.20	78.45	78.20	78.30	– .25	80.25	77.50	407

Est vol 2,172; vol Wed 1,221; open int 12,821, –16.

CATTLE–LIVE (CME) 40,000 lbs.; cents per lb.

	Open	High	Low	Settle	Change	Lifetime High	Lifetime Low	Open Interest
Dec	71.10	71.47	70.77	70.87	– .67	75.50	60.25	8,999
Fb89	71.00	71.25	70.55	70.60	– .87	75.60	65.10	32,927
Apr	73.20	73.27	72.65	72.70	– .87	76.47	67.20	20,682

–FOOD & FIBER–

COCOA (CSCE)–10 metric tons; $ per ton.

	Open	High	Low	Settle	Change	Lifetime High	Lifetime Low	Open Interest
Dec	1,410	1,423	1,410	1,411	– 8	2,197	1,103	338
Mr89	1,447	1,477	1,447	1,456	– 10	2,088	1,125	16,173
May	1,450	1,473	1,450	1,462	– 8	2,088	1,152	6,909
July	1,453	1,480	1,453	1,467	– 3	1,985	1,172	3,600
Sept	1,461	1,475	1,461	1,472	– 2	1,850	1,206	1,874
Dec	1,485	1,489	1,480	1,485	– 1	1,735	1,240	4,305
Mr90	....	....	....	1,505	– 3	1,535	1,305	2,614

Est vol 3,266; vol Wed5,003; open int 36,013, –430.

COFFEE (CSCE)–37,500 lbs.; cents per lb.

	Open	High	Low	Settle	Change	Lifetime High	Lifetime Low	Open Interest
Dec	125.50	127.05	125.50	127.00	+ 1.72	150.25	101.00	493
Mr89	124.70	125.85	124.70	125.67	+ 1.33	150.50	112.44	12,458
May	123.30	124.40	123.25	124.27	+ 1.27	150.75	112.13	3,746
July	122.80	123.30	122.80	123.10	+ 1.00	145.00	114.00	1,749
Sept	121.30	122.00	121.30	122.00	+ .79	143.50	114.00	679
Dec	....	....	....	121.34	+ .66	129.25	118.00	104

Est vol 3,200; vol Wed2,389; open int 19,232, –63.

SUGAR–WORLD (CSCE)–112,000 lbs.; cents per lb.

	Open	High	Low	Settle	Change	Lifetime High	Lifetime Low	Open Interest
Jan	11.00	11.00	11.00	9.00	– 1.13	15.00	7.75	90
Mar	11.35	11.55	11.16	11.31	– .16	14.39	7.66	91,697
May	11.05	11.18	10.83	10.97	– .21	13.64	7.87	32,956
July	10.79	10.85	10.60	10.69	– .18	13.40	8.10	7,546
Oct	10.53	10.58	10.32	10.46	– .15	13.30	8.45	12,470
Mr90	10.14	10.27	10.14	10.21	– .13	10.48	8.75	916

Est vol 21,400; vol Wed22,397; open int 145,678, +2,742.

–METALS & PETROLEUM–

COPPER-STANDARD (CMX)–25,000 lbs.; cents per lb.

	Open	High	Low	Settle	Change	Lifetime High	Lifetime Low	Open Interest
Dec	158.80	164.75	158.50	163.25	+ 6.00	164.75	64.70	6,621
Ja89	151.90	157.00	151.90	156.00	+ 6.20	157.00	67.20	131
Mar	138.50	142.00	138.10	140.00	+ 2.70	142.00	66.50	20,028
May	130.00	131.70	129.50	130.00	+ 1.00	131.70	73.15	3,550
July	126.50	126.70	124.30	125.00	+ .20	126.70	76.00	1,922
Sept	122.95	123.00	122.90	121.50	....	123.00	76.00	607
Dec	118.50	119.50	117.50	118.00	....	119.50	77.45	1,088

Est vol 12,000; vol Wed 11,103; open int 33,947, –730.

GOLD (CMX)–100 troy oz.; $ per troy oz.

	Open	High	Low	Settle	Change	Lifetime High	Lifetime Low	Open Interest
Dec	423.20	424.20	422.50	421.80	– 1.00	546.00	395.50	4,538
Fb89	428.50	429.00	426.60	426.70	– 1.00	549.50	401.00	52,258
Apr	434.20	434.50	432.00	432.20	– 1.00	550.00	407.00	16,012
June	439.50	440.10	437.70	437.80	– 1.00	570.00	412.00	22,704
Aug	445.00	445.00	443.60	443.60	– 1.00	575.00	419.30	10,080
Oct	450.80	451.00	450.80	449.30	– 1.10	575.50	423.00	9,943
Dec	456.00	457.00	454.20	455.10	– 1.20	514.50	428.00	14,027
Fb90	....	....	....	461.10	– 1.20	516.00	439.70	4,480
Apr	....	....	....	467.20	– 1.20	525.80	443.00	2,731
June	....	....	....	473.30	– 1.20	497.00	447.00	2,120
Aug	....	....	....	479.60	– 1.20	487.00	453.00	1,136
Oct	....	....	....	486.00	– 1.20	....	....	158

Est vol 42,000; vol Wed 52,209; open int 140,187, –2,526.

PLATINUM (NYM)–50 troy oz.; $ per troy oz.

	Open	High	Low	Settle	Change	Lifetime High	Lifetime Low	Open Interest
Jan	605.00	608.00	597.10	597.80	– 5.60	646.00	459.00	15,736
Apr	597.00	599.00	591.50	591.80	– 4.10	643.50	482.00	7,232
July	599.00	599.00	592.00	590.30	– 4.60	640.00	501.00	1,548

–WOOD–

LUMBER (CME)–150,000 bd. ft.; $ per 1,000 bd. ft.

	Open	High	Low	Settle	Change	Lifetime High	Lifetime Low	Open Interest
Jan	176.60	178.20	176.30	177.40	+ .80	187.60	160.00	2,526
Mr89	179.80	181.20	179.60	180.80	+ 1.00	185.50	171.00	1,439
May	182.90	183.30	182.10	183.00	+ .80	184.90	170.10	513
July	184.40	184.40	183.10	183.10	+ .70	185.30	175.10	488
Sept	184.00	184.40	183.50	184.30	+ .30	184.90	175.10	159

Est vol 726; vol Wed 552; open int 5,179, –40.

–OTHER COMMODITY FUTURES–

Settlement prices of selected contracts. Volume and open interest of all contract months.

Aluminum (CMX) 40,000 lbs.; cents per lb.
Mar 105.00 +.50; Est. vol. 5; Open Int. 158
Cattle-Live (MCE) 20,000 lb. ¢ per lb.
Feb 70.60 –.87; Est. vol. 175; Open Int. 699
Corn (MCE) 1,000 bu.; cents per bu.
Mar 269½ +1¼; Est. vol. 800; Open Int. 8,019
Gold (CBT) 100 troy oz., $ per troy oz.
Feb 426.70 –.80; Est. vol. 1,000; Open Int. 1,339
Gold (MCE) 33.2 fine troy oz.; $ per troy oz.
Jan 424.50 –1.00; Est. vol. 40; Open Int. 206
Gold-Kilo (CBT) 32.15 troy oz.; $ per troy oz.
Feb 426.50 –1.30; Est. vol. 500; Open Int. 838
Hogs-Live (MCE) 15,000 lb.; ¢ per lb.
Feb 43.72 –.45; Est. vol. 70; Open Int. 562
Propane (NYM) 42,000 gal.; ¢ per gal.
Jan 20.75 –.05; Est. vol. 16; Open Int. 749
Rice–Rough (CRCE) 2000 cwt; $ per cwt
Jan 6.800 –.002; Est. vol. 65; Open Int. 1,823
Silver (CBT) 5,000 troy oz., cents per troy oz.
Jan 615.0 –4.0; Est. vol. 20; Open Int. 97
Silver (MCE) 1,000 troy oz.; cents per troy oz.
Jan 616.4 –1.7; Est. vol. 30; Open Int. 678
Soybeans (MCE) 1,000 bu.; cents per bu.
Jan 773½ +5½; Est. vol. 2,500; Open Int. 6,768
Soybean Meal (MCE) 20 tons; $ per ton
Jan 246.90 –1.20; Est. vol. 10; Open Int. 568
Wheat (MCE) 1,000 bu.; cents per bu.
Mar 429¾ +6; Est. vol. 600; Open Int. 6,735

EXCHANGE ABBREVIATIONS
(for commodity futures and futures options)

CBT-Chicago Board of Trade; CME-Chicago Mercantile Exchange; CMX-Commodity Exchange, New York; CRCE-Chicago Rice & Cotton Exchange; CTN-New York Cotton Exchange; CSCE-Coffee, Sugar & Cocoa Exchange, New York; IPEL-International Petroleum Exchange of London; KC-Kansas City Board of Trade; MCE-MidAmerica Commodity Exchange; MPLS-Minneapolis Grain Exchange; NYM-New York Mercantile Exchange; PBOT-Philadelphia Board of Trade; WPG-Winnipeg Commodity Exchange.

FIGURE 19–1
Quotations for future prices.

SOURCE: Reprinted by permission of *The Wall Street Journal*, © Dow Jones & Company, Inc. (December 9, 1988): p. C14.

price (for example, the average of the high and low prices) during the "closing period" designated by the exchange in question (for example, the last two minutes of trading). After the *change* from the previous day's settlement price comes the highest and lowest prices recorded during the lifetime of the contract. The last column on the right shows the *open interest* (the number of outstanding contracts) on the previous day.

For each futures contract, summary figures are given below the figures for the last delivery date (in the case of corn, these summary figures are below the March 1990 delivery date figures) and indicate the total volume (that is, the number of contracts) traded on that day and on the previous trading day as well as the total open interest in such contracts on that day and the change in total open interest from the previous day.

☐ 19.1.1   Futures Markets

The futures contracts shown in Figure 19.1 are traded on various organized exchanges. The Chicago Board of Trade (CBT) was the earliest one, being founded in 1848, and currently is the largest futures exchange in the world. Other futures exchanges are listed in the lower right-hand corner of Figure 19.1.

The method of trading futures on organized exchanges is similar in some ways and different in other ways from the way that stocks and options are traded. Like stocks and options, customers can place market, limit, and stop orders. Furthermore, once an order is transmitted to an exchange floor, it must be taken to a designated spot for execution by a member of the exchange, just as is done for stocks and options. This spot is known as a "pit" because of its shape, which is circular with a set of interior descending steps on which members stand. What transpires in the pit is what distinguishes trading in futures from trading in stocks and options.

First of all, there are no specialists or market-makers on futures exchanges. Instead, members can be floor brokers, meaning they execute customers' orders. In doing so, they (or their phone clerks) each keep a file of any stop or limit orders that cannot be immediately executed. Alternatively, members can be floor traders (those with very short holding periods—less than a day—are known as *locals*, or scalpers), meaning they execute orders for their own personal accounts in an attempt to make profits by buying low and selling high. Floor traders are in some ways similar to market-makers, since a floor trader may have an inventory of futures contracts and may act as a dealer. However, unlike a market-maker, a floor trader is not required to do so.

Second, all futures orders must be announced by "open outcry," meaning that any member wishing to buy or sell any futures contract must verbally announce the order and a price at which the member is willing to trade. By doing so, the order is exposed to everyone in the pit, thereby enabling an auction to take place that will lead to the order being filled at the best possible price.

Each futures exchange has an associated clearinghouse that becomes the "seller's buyer" and the "buyer's seller" as soon as a trade is concluded. The procedure is similar to that used for options, which is not surprising, since the first market in listed options was set up by people associated with a futures exchange (specifically, the Chicago Board Options Exchange was set up by the Chicago Board of Trade).

In order to understand how a clearinghouse operates, consider the futures market for wheat. Assume that on the first day of trading in July wheat, buyer B agrees to purchase 5000 bushels (one contract) from seller S for $4 per bushel (actually, what happens is that a floor broker working for B's brokerage firm and a floor broker working for S's brokerage firm meet in the wheat pit and agree on a price). In this situation, B believes that the price of wheat is going to rise, whereas S believes it is going to fall.

After B and S reach their agreement, the clearinghouse will immediately step in and break the transaction apart. That is, B and S no longer deal directly with each other. Now it is the obligation of the clearinghouse to deliver the wheat to B and to accept delivery from S. At this point, there is an open interest of one contract (5000 bushels) in July wheat, since only one contract exists at this time (technically, there are two, since the clearinghouse has separate contracts with B and S).

It is important to realize that if nothing else is done at this point, the clearinghouse is in a potentially risky position. For example, if the price of wheat rises to $5 per bushel by July, what happens if S does not deliver the wheat? The clearinghouse would have to buy the wheat on the spot market for $25,000 (5000 × $5) and then deliver it to B. Because the clearinghouse will receive the selling price of $20,000 (5000 × $4) from B in return, it will have lost $5000. Although the clearinghouse has a claim on S for the $5000, it faces protracted legal battles in trying to recover this amount and may end up with little or nothing from S.

Alternatively, if the price of wheat falls to $3 per bushel by July, then B will be paying $20,000 for delivery of wheat that is only worth $15,000 (5000 × $3) on the spot market. What happens if B refuses to make payment? In this case, the clearinghouse will not deliver the wheat that it received from S. Instead, it will have to sell the wheat for $15,000 on the spot market. Since the clearinghouse paid $20,000 for the wheat, it has lost $5000. Again, although the clearinghouse has a claim on B for the $5000, it may end up with little or nothing from B.

The procedures that protect the clearinghouse from such potential losses involve having brokers (1) impose initial margin requirements on both buyers and sellers; (2) mark to market the accounts of buyers and sellers every day; and (3) impose daily maintenance margin requirements on both buyers and sellers.

Initial Margin

In order to buy and sell futures, an investor must open a commodity account with a brokerage firm. This type of account must be kept separate from other

accounts (such as a cash account or a margin account) that the investor might have. Whenever a futures contract is signed, both the buyer and seller are required to post initial margin. That is, both the buyer and seller are required to make security deposits that are intended to guarantee that they will in fact be able to fulfill their obligations; accordingly, initial margin is often referred to as *performance margin*. The amount of this margin is roughly 5% to 15% of the total purchase price of the futures contract. However, it is often stated as a given dollar amount regardless of the purchase price.[4]

For example, a July wheat futures contract for 5000 bushels at $4 per bushel would have a total purchase price of $20,000 (5000 × $4). With a 5% initial margin requirement, buyer B and seller S would each have to make a deposit of $1000 (.05 × $20,000). This deposit can be made in the form of cash, cash equivalents (such as Treasury bills), or a bank line of credit and forms the equity in the account on the first day.

Although initial margin provides some protection to the clearinghouse, it does not provide complete protection. As indicated earlier, if the price of wheat rises to $5 per bushel by July, the clearinghouse faces a potential loss of $5000, only $1000 of which can be quickly recovered due to the margin deposit. This is where the use of marking to market, coupled with a maintenance margin requirement, provides the requisite amount of additional protection.

Marking to Market

In order to understand marking to market, the previous example, where B and S were, respectively, a buyer and a seller of a 5000-bushel wheat futures contract at $4 per bushel, is continued. Assume now that on the second day of trading the settle price of July wheat is $4.10 per bushel. In this situation, S has "lost" $500 due to the rise in the price of wheat from $4 to $4.10 per bushel, whereas B has "made" $500. Thus, the equity in the account of S is reduced by $500 and the equity in the account of B is increased by $500. Since the initial equity was equal to the initial margin requirement of $1000, this means that S has equity of $500, and B has equity of $1500. This process of adjusting the equity in an investor's commodity account in order to reflect the change in the settle price of the futures contract is known as *marking to market*. It should also be noted that each day, as part of the marking-to-market process, the clearinghouse replaces each existing futures contract with a new one that has the settle price as reported in the financial press as the purchase price in the new contract.

In general, the equity in either a buyer or seller's commodity account is the sum of (1) the initial margin deposit and (2) the sum of all daily gains, less losses, on open positions in futures. Since the amount of the gains (less losses) changes every day, the amount of equity changes every day.

In the example, if the settle price of the July wheat futures contract had fallen to $3.95 per bushel the day after rising to $4.10, then B would

---

[4] Since Black Monday and Terrible Tuesday (October 19–20, 1987), a number of people have advocated an increase in the size of the performance margin deposit for certain futures contracts (particularly stock index futures, which are discussed later). The level of performance (and maintenance) margin is set by each exchange, with brokers being allowed to set it higher.

have lost $750 (5000 × ($4.10 − $3.95)), whereas S would have made $750 on that day. When their accounts are marked to market at the end of the day, the equity in B's account would have dropped from $1500 to $750, and S's equity would have risen from $500 to $1250.

Maintenance Margin

Another key concept is the requirement of maintenance margin. According to this requirement, the investor must keep the commodity account's equity equal to or greater than a certain percentage of the amount deposited as initial margin. Since this percentage is roughly 75% to 80%, the investor must have equity equal to or greater than 75% to 80% of the initial margin. If this requirement is not met, the investor will receive a margin call from his or her broker. This call is a request for an additional deposit of cash (nothing else can be deposited for this purpose) to bring the equity up to the initial margin level. If the investor does not (or cannot) respond, then the broker will close out the investor's position by entering a reversing trade in the investor's account.

For example, reconsider investors B and S who had, respectively, bought and sold a July wheat futures contract at $4 per bushel; each investor had made a deposit of $1000 in order to meet the initial margin requirement. The next day, the price of the wheat futures contract rose to $4.10 per bushel, or $20,500. Thus, the equity of B had increased to $1500, whereas the equity of S had decreased to $500. If the maintenance margin requirement is 80% of initial margin, both B and S are required to have equity of at least $800 (.80 × $1000) in their accounts every day. Since the actual level of equity for B clearly exceeds this amount, B does not need to do anything. Indeed, B may withdraw an amount of cash equal to the amount by which the equity exceeds the initial margin; in this example, B can withdraw cash of $500.

However, S is undermargined and will be asked to make a cash deposit of at least $500, since this would increase the equity from $500 to $1000, the level of the initial margin. In the event that S refuses to make this deposit, the broker will enter a reversing trade for S by purchasing a July wheat futures contract. The result is that S will simply receive an amount of money approximately equal to the account's equity, $500, and the account will be closed. Since S initially deposited $1000, this represents a personal loss of $500.

Reversing Trades

Suppose that on the next day, B finds that people are paying $4.15 per bushel for July wheat. This represents an additional profit to B of $.05 per bushel, since the price was $4.10 the previous day. If B believes that the price of July wheat will not go any higher, then B might sell a July wheat futures contract for $4.15 to someone else. In this situation, B has made a reversing trade, since B now has offsetting positions with respect to July wheat (equivalently, B is said to have unwound, or closed out, his or her position in July wheat).

At this point, the benefit to B of having a clearinghouse involved can

be seen. Nominally, B is obligated to deliver 5000 bushels of wheat to the clearinghouse in July, which is in turn obligated to deliver it back to B. This situation occurs because B is involved in two July wheat contracts, one as a seller and one as a buyer. However, the clearinghouse will note that B has offsetting positions in July wheat and will immediately cancel both of them. Furthermore, once the reversing trade had been made, B will be able to withdraw the initial margin of $1000 as well as the $750 (5000 × ($4.15 − $4)) profit that has been made.

In effect, a futures contract is replaced every day by (1) adjusting the equity in the investor's commodity account and (2) drawing up a new contract that has a purchase price equal to the current settle price. This daily marking-to-market procedure, coupled with margin requirements, results in the clearinghouse always having a security deposit of sufficient size to protect it from losses due to the actions of the individual investors.[5]

These rather complex arrangements make it possible for futures traders to think in very simple terms. In the example, B bought a contract of July wheat at $4 and sold it two days later for $4.15, making a profit of $.15 per bushel. If S, having initially sold a contract of July wheat at $4, later made a reversing trade for $4.25, then S's position can also be thought of in simple terms—specifically, S sold July wheat for $4 and later bought it back for $4.25, suffering a loss of $.25 per bushel in the process.

19.1.3   Futures Positions

In the previous example, B was the person who initially bought a July wheat futures contract. Accordingly, B now has a long position and is said to be long one contract of July wheat. In contrast, S, having initially sold a July wheat futures contract, has a short position and is said to be short one contract of July wheat.

The process of marking to market every day means that changes in the settle price are realized as soon as they occur. When the settle price *rises*, those with long positions realize *profits* equal to the change and those who are short realize *losses*. When the settle price *falls*, those with long positions realize *losses*, whereas those with short positions realize *profits*. In either event, total profits always equal total losses.

19.1.4   Taxation

Earlier, it was mentioned that there are two types of people who deal in futures—speculators and hedgers. These two types of investors are treated differently by the Internal Revenue Service.

A speculator in futures is considered to have a capital asset for tax purposes, whether he or she is long or short. When the position is closed

---

[5] Actually, only brokerage firms belong to a clearinghouse, and it is *their* accounts that are settled by the clearinghouse at the end of every day. Each brokerage firm acts in turn as a clearinghouse for its own clients. For more information on clearing procedures, see Chapter 4 of the *Commodity Trading Manual*.

out, the resultant profit or loss is treated as a capital gain or loss, and is taxed accordingly. That is, a net gain is taxed at the individual's ordinary income tax rate, and losses are fully deductible (subject to a $3000 cap).

In comparison, since a hedger has dealt in futures as part of a normal business activities, the resulting profit or loss is generally viewed as ordinary income or loss for the business, and is taxed accordingly.

☐ 19.1.5 Open Interest

When trading is first allowed in a contract, there is no open interest, since no contracts are outstanding. Subsequently, as people begin to make transactions, the open interest grows. At any time, open interest equals the amount that those with short positions (the sellers) are currently obligated to deliver. It also equals the amount that those with long positions (the buyers) are obligated to receive.

Open interest figures are typically shown with futures prices in the financial press. For example, Figure 19.1 indicates that on December 8, 1988, a total of 124,643 contracts in March 1989 corn were outstanding on the Chicago Board of Trade. Note the substantial differences in the open interest figures for the other corn contracts on the Chicago Board of Trade on that day. This is quite typical. Figure 19.2 shows why. Open interest in a wheat contract is shown for every month from the preceding January until the contract expired at the end of the delivery month, December. From January until the end of September, more trades were generally made to open new positions than to reverse old ones, and open interest continued to increase. As the delivery month came closer, reversing trades began to outnumber those intended to open new positions, and the open interest began to decline. The amount remaining at the beginning of December was the maximum number of bushels of wheat that could have been delivered against futures contracts at that time, but most of these contracts were also settled by reversing trades instead of delivery.

Relatively few futures positions—less than 3% of the total—end in actual delivery of the asset involved.[6] However, the fact that delivery is a possibility makes a contract's value in the delivery month differ only slightly, if at all, from the spot price (that is, the current market price) of the asset.

If not reversed, most futures contracts require delivery of the corresponding asset. Notable exceptions are market index futures, since they do not require delivery of the set of securities comprising the corresponding index. Instead, an amount equal to the difference between the level of the index and the purchase price is to be paid *in cash* on the delivery date. Nevertheless, as with other types of futures, most positions in market index futures are closed out with reversing trades prior to the date at which delivery (in cash) is required.

---

[6] Merrill Lynch, Pierce, Fenner & Smith, Inc., *Speculating on Inflation: Futures Trading in Interest Rates, Foreign Currencies and Precious Metals*, July 1979.

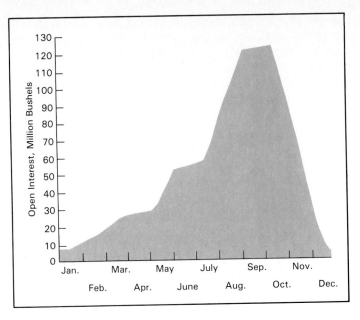

FIGURE 19–2
Open interest, December 1978, Chicago Board of Trade Wheat
Contract: January 3, 1978 through December 28, 1978.

☐ 19.1.6 Price Limits

The *Commodity Futures Trading Commissin* (CFTC), which regulates trading on futures exchanges, places dollar limits on the extent to which futures prices are allowed to vary from day to day. For example, if July wheat closed at $4 on the previous day and the daily price limit is $.20, then on the following day contracts at prices outside the range from $3.80 to $4.20 would not be allowed to be traded on the exchange. If a major piece of news during the day led traders to consider $4.25 a reasonable price for the contract, they would have to either (1) trade privately, foregoing the advantages offered by the exchange; (2) trade on the exchange at the limit price of $4.20; or (3) wait until the next day, when the range of acceptable prices would be from $4 to $4.40.

One result of the "limit move" to $4.20 is that it is entirely possible that no contracts will be traded at all on that day. This is because nobody will want to sell these wheat contracts for a below-market price of $4.20, preferring to wait until the next day when the range of acceptable prices is raised. Indeed, if the news is important enough (such as a massive freeze in Florida, destroying many orange trees and dramatically affecting orange juice futures), there can be limit moves for a number of successive days, with no trading taking place for several days.

The government imposes price limits on futures due to a feeling that traders may overreact to major news and should be protected from voluntarily entering into agreements under such conditions. Interestingly, initial mar-

gins are usually set at an amount that is roughly equal to the price limit times the size of the contract. In the case of wheat having a $.20 price limit and a contract for 5000 bushels, the initial margin is usually about $1000 ($.20 × 5000). Thus, if the price of wheat moves the limit against the investor, no more than the initial margin of $1000 will be lost on the day of the adverse limit move. In a sense, the price limit has protected the investor from losing more than $1000 on that day. However, it is possible that the investor cannot enter a reversing trade as soon as prices have moved the limit, meaning that much larger losses can be incurred later (as in the case of the Florida freeze and orange juice futures).

19.2 BASIS

The difference between the current spot price on an asset (that is, the price of the asset for immediate delivery) and the futures price (that is, the purchase price stated in the futures contract) is known as the *basis* for the futures:

$$\text{Basis} = \text{current spot price} - \text{futures price}. \qquad (19.1)$$

A person with a short position in a futures contract and a long position in the corresponding asset (meaning he or she owns the asset) will profit if the basis is positive and widens (or is negative and narrows). This is because the futures price will be falling or the spot price will be rising (or both); falling futures prices benefits those who are short, and rising spot prices benefits those who own the asset. Using the same type of reasoning, it can be shown that this person will lose if the basis is positive and narrows (or is negative and widens).

Conversely, a person with a long position in a futures contract and a short position in the corresponding asset (meaning he or she has borrowed the asset and sold it and now has an obligation to buy the asset in order to repay the loan) will profit if the basis is positive and narrows (or is negative and widens). However, a loss would be incurred if a positive basis widens (or a negative basis narrows).

The risk of the basis narrowing or widening, causing gains or losses to these people, is known as *basis risk*. The only type of uncertainty they face is about the difference between the spot price of the specific asset and the price of the futures contract. Such a person is said to be *speculating on the basis*.[7]

19.3 SPREADS

It is quite possible to take a long position in a futures contract and a short position in another futures contract in the same asset but with a different delivery date. The person who does this is speculating on changes in the

---

[7] For more on the relationship between spot and futures prices as reflected in the basis, see the *Commodity Trading Manual*, pp. 64–83. It should be noted that sometimes basis is defined as the futures price less the current spot price—the reverse of what is shown in equation (19.1).

difference between the prices of the two contracts, a difference that constitutes the basis for this particular hedge.

Others attempt to profit from temporary imbalances among the prices of futures contracts on different but related assets. For example, one might take a long position in soybeans along with a short position in an item produced from soybeans, such as soybean meal. Another possibility involves a position in wheat with an offsetting position in corn, which serves as a substitute for wheat in many applications.

These people are known as *spreaders* and, like those who speculate on the basis, they reduce or eliminate the risk associated with general price moves. Instead, they take on the risk associated with changes in price differences in the hope that their alleged superior knowledge and ability will enable them to make profits consistently from such changes.

19.4 SPOT PRICES

Most futures exchanges dealing in agricultural commodities provide areas in which buyers and sellers can negotiate cash (or spot) sales. No attempt is made to standardize such agreements; everything, including grade, location, and delivery, is negotiable. For this reason there is no such thing as a standardized spot price. Instead, the price of the futures contract that is closest to delivery is often used as a surrogate for the spot price. In fact, deals in the spot market may even be made in terms of the price of the nearest futures contract—for example, two parties might agree to trade at $.02 per bushel more than the relevant futures price. In essence, such spot trades are conducted in terms of the basis.

The price of any asset is determined by demand and supply. It is in the realm of supply that agricultural commodities such as wheat differ from automobiles, for example. Wheat is a seasonal commodity, generally harvested in the United States from late May through September (although in other countries harvests occur at other times). Seasonality has important implications for price determination for such commodities.

Key is the concept of *carrying costs*. These include all costs associated with holding an inventory of the commodity. The major components are foregone interest on the money invested in the inventory and the cost of storage for the inventory.

If everyone knew that the spot price of a commodity was certain to rise by an amount exceeding its carrying cost, people would start to purchase and store the current supply in order to make a profit from selling it at a later date. As a result, its current spot price would rise, until the predicted future spot price was equal to the current spot price and carrying costs.

For example, if three-month carrying costs amount to $.05 per bushel of wheat, then in a world of certainty the current spot price would, in equilibrium, have to rise by $.05 over the next three months. Consider what anyone would do if the spot price was going to rise by more than this amount. Given a current spot price of $4 and a predicted three-month ahead spot price of $4.15, the investor could buy wheat now at $4 and store it for $.05,

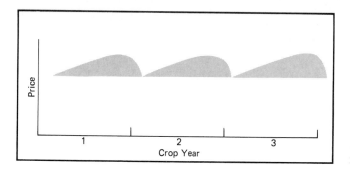

FIGURE 19-3
Spot prices for a seasonal commodity.

while selling a three-month futures contract for $4.15. In doing so, the investor would, without risk, make a profit of $.10 [$4.15 − ($4 + $.05)] per bushel. However, others would also do the same thing until the difference between the current spot price and three-month futures price settled at $.05 per bushel.

In contrast, if everyone knew the spot price of a commodity was certain to rise by an amount less than its carrying cost, people would refrain from purchasing and storing the commodity. That is, the only people buying the wheat would be those who had a current use for it. Consequently, the current spot price would fall until the predicted future spot price was equal to the current spot price and carrying costs.

In practice there is considerable uncertainty about the future price of any commodity. However, the costs associated with storing inventories lead to a typical pattern in which prices of seasonal commodities tend to increase after the main harvest season and fall as each new harvest comes in. Figure 19.3 shows a possible pattern for spot prices over three years when the harvests are of equal size each year. While uncertainty brings relatively random price changes, a pattern roughly similar to this can often be seen in the movements of spot prices.

For natural resources that have futures contracts, such as copper, gold, and silver, there is no "harvest season." Thus, for those items there is no seasonal pattern in spot prices similar to Figure 19.3. Instead, the spot prices are simply a horizontal line. This is also true for foreign currencies, fixed-income securities, and market indices such as Swiss francs, Treasury bonds, and the Standard & Poor's 500.

19.5   FUTURES PRICES

☐ 19.5.1   Certainty

If all spot prices could be predicted with certainty, there would be no reason for anyone to be either a buyer or seller of futures contracts. To understand why, imagine what a futures contract would look like in a world of certainty. First of all, the purchase price in the future contract would simply equal the (perfectly predictable) expected spot price on the delivery date. This

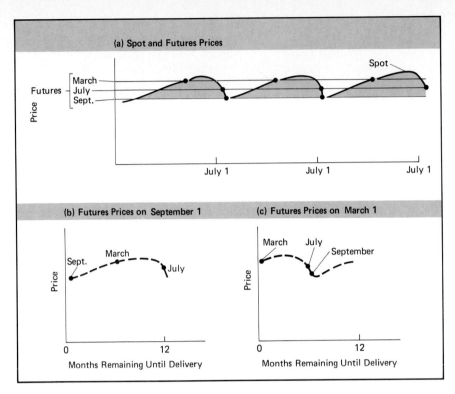

FIGURE 19–4
Commodity prices in a world of certainty.

means that neither buyers nor sellers would be able to make profits from the existence of futures. Second of all, the purchase price would not change as the delivery date got closer. Lastly, no margin would be necessary because there would not be any unexpected "adverse" price movements.

Figure 19.4(a) shows the relationship between the current spot price and the prices of three futures contracts for a seasonal commodity harvested each year in June. The curved line reflects the spot price of the commodity over time. It can be seen that the pattern of the spot price corresponds to the pattern shown in Figure 19.3, rising to a high about May and then declining quickly to a low about October. Three futures contracts are assumed to be traded at any time, offering delivery on the last day of March, July, and September, respectively. Each contract is traded during the 364 days prior to the specified delivery date. Since no uncertainty is involved, there will not be any adverse price movements. Thus, no margin need be posted by either the buyer or seller of the futures contract. Furthermore, the futures price will not change as time elapses. Consequently, the price of the March futures will always be the same, corresponding to a horizontal line in the figure. Similarly, the prices of the July and September futures contracts will remain the same, although at different levels. However, as time passes, the spot price changes, following the cyclical path shown by the curved line in Figure 19.4(a).

Note that during the life of the futures contract the spot price is sometimes above and sometimes below the futures price. Note also that at some times "distant" futures contracts sell for more than "near" ones, and at other times the situation is reversed. This is shown in parts (b) and (c) of Figure 19.4, respectively, which plot the prices of various contracts versus their remaining lives at two times of the year. In this case, if contracts were available for every possible delivery date, their prices would plot along the dashed curves, which reflect the (known) future pattern of spot rates.

☐ 19.5.2 Uncertainty

As a starting point, it is useful to know something about the way in which futures prices and spot prices are related to each other in a world of certainty where forecasting is done with complete accuracy. However, what happens when uncertainty is introduced? Exactly how are futures prices related to expected spot prices? Although there are several possible explanations, no definitive answer has been provided.

Expectations Hypothesis

One possible explanation of the result of uncertainty is given by the *expectations hypothesis*: The current purchase price of a futures contract equals the market consensus expectation of the spot price on the delivery date. In symbols,

$$P_f = \bar{P}_s$$

where P_f is the current purchase price of the futures contract and $\bar{P}_s$ is the expected spot price of the asset on the delivery date. Thus, if a July wheat futures contract is currently selling for $4 per bushel, then it can be inferred that the consensus opinion is that in July the spot price of wheat will be $4.

If the expectations hypothesis is correct, a speculator should not expect either to win or lose from a position in the futures market, be it long or short. Neglecting margin requirements, a speculator who takes a long position in futures agrees to pay P_f at the delivery date for an asset that is expected to be worth $\bar{P}_s$ at that time. Thus, the long speculator's expected profit is equal to $\bar{P}_s - P_f$, which is zero. Conversely, a speculator with a short position will have sold an asset at a price of P_f and will expect to enter a reversing trade at $\bar{P}_s$ on the delivery date. Thus, the short speculator's expected profit is equal to $P_f - \bar{P}_s$, which is zero.

The expectations hypothesis is often defended on the grounds that speculators are indifferent to risk and are thus happy to accommodate hedgers without any compensation in the form of a risk premium. The reason for their indifference has to do with the belief that the impact of a specific futures position on the risk of a diversified portfolio that includes many types of assets will be very small. Thus, speculators holding diversified portfolios may be willing to take over some risk from hedgers with little (if any) compensation in the form of a risk premium.

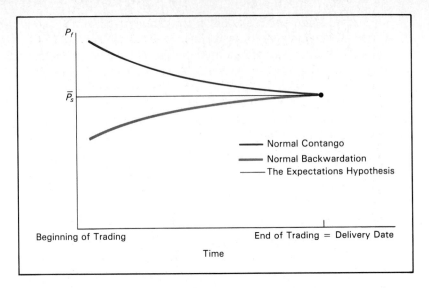

FIGURE 19–5
Price of futures contract through time when the spot price expected at the time of delivery does not change.

Figure 19.5 shows the pattern of futures prices implied by the expectations hypothesis, given the expected spot price $\bar{P}_s$ does not change during the life of the contract.

Normal Backwardation

John Maynard Keynes felt that the expectations hypothesis did not correctly explain futures prices.[8] He argued that, on balance, hedgers will want to be short in futures, and therefore they will have to entice the speculators to be long in futures. Since there are risks associated with being long, Keynes hypothesized that the hedgers would have to entice the speculators by making the expected return from a long position greater than the risk-free rate. This requires the futures price to be less than the expected spot price:

$$P_f < \bar{P}_s.$$

Thus, a speculator who bought a futures contract at a price of P_f would expect to be able to sell it on (or near) the delivery date at a higher price, $\bar{P}_s$. This relationship between the futures and expected spot price has been referred to as *normal backwardation* and implies that the price of a futures contract can be expected to rise during its life, as shown in Figure 19.5.

Normal Contango

A contrary hypothesis holds that, on balance, hedgers will want to be long in futures, and therefore they will have to entice speculators to be short in futures. Since there are risks associated with being short, it can be hypoth-

---

[8] J. M. Keynes, *Treatise on Money*, vol. 2 (London: Macmillan, 1930), 142–44.

esized that the hedgers will have to entice the speculators by making the expected return from a short position greater than the risk-free rate. This requires the futures price to be greater than the expected spot price:

$$P_f > \bar{P}_s.$$

Thus, a speculator who short sold a futures contract at a price of P_f would expect to be able to buy it back on (or near) the delivery date at a lower price, $\bar{P}_s$. This relationship between the futures and expected spot price has been referred to as *normal contango* and implies that the price of a futures contract can be expected to fall during its life, as shown in Figure 19.5.[9]

19.6 RETURNS ON FUTURES

During the period from 1950 through 1976, a portfolio made up of unlevered positions in 23 different futures contracts was compared with a diversified portfolio of common stocks.[10] The average rate of return and risk level of the two portfolios were found to be of similar magnitude:

PORTFOLIO	AVERAGE ANNUAL RETURN	STANDARD DEVIATION
Futures	13.83%	22.43%
Common stocks	13.05	18.95

Given these results, an investor might view the two alternatives as equally desirable. However, during the period 1950 to 1976, a combination of the two portfolios was found to be more desirable than either portfolio by itself. This was due to the fact that the returns of futures and stock portfolios were negatively correlated, suggesting that the return on a combined portfolio would have had considerably less variation than either one separately. Specifically, the correlation coefficient was found to be equal to $-.24$, resulting in the following standard deviations for portfolios with different combinations:

PERCENT IN STOCKS	PERCENT IN FUTURES	STANDARD DEVIATION	AVERAGE ANNUAL RETURN
0%	100%	22.43%	13.83%
20	80	17.43	13.67
40	60	13.77	13.52
60	40	12.68	13.36
80	20	14.74	13.21
100	0	18.95	13.05

---

[9] There are other hypotheses regarding the relationship between futures prices and expected spot prices. See, for example, Paul H. Cootner, "Speculation and Hedging," Stanford University, *Food Research Institute Studies*, Supplement, 1967.

[10] The futures contracts consisted of agricultural goods and natural resources; see Zvi Bodie and Victor Rosansky, "Risk and Return in Commodity Futures," *Financial Analysts Journal* 36, no. 3 (May/June 1980):27–39. Similar conclusions were reached when the period 1978 to 1981 was examined. See Cheng F. Lee, Raymond M. Leuthold, and Jean E. Cordier, "The Stock Market and the Commodity Futures Market: Diversification and Arbitrage Potential," *Financial Analysts Journal* 41, no. 4 (July/August 1985):53–60.

Although there was little difference in the level of the average return for the various portfolios, there was a noticable change in the level of risk. In particular, the portfolio with 60% in stocks and 40% in futures seems to have had much less risk than the others.

Also of interest was the observation that futures have been found to be at least a partial hedge against inflation. During the period 1950 to 1976, the returns on the portfolio of 23 futures were positively correlated with changes in the Consumer Price Index, having a correlation coefficient of .58. In contrast, the returns on the portfolio of common stocks were negatively correlated with changes in the Consumer Price Index, having a correlation coefficient of $-.43$.

19.7 FINANCIAL FUTURES

Futures contracts were limited to those on agricultural goods and natural resources until the 1970s. Since then, financial futures, based on foreign currencies, fixed-income securities, and market indices, have been introduced on major exchanges. Indeed, in terms of trading volume, they are now more important than the traditional futures contracts and the underlying securities. Unlike other types of futures that permit delivery anytime during a given month, most financial futures (the exceptions involve some fixed-income futures) have a specific delivery date.

☐ 19.7.1 Foreign Currency Futures

Anyone who has crossed a national border knows that there is an active spot market for foreign currency and that the rate at which one currency can be exchanged for another varies over time. At any particular point in time, however, all such rates must be in conformance or else a riskless profit-making situation would arise. For example, it is usually possible to exchange U.S. dollars for British pounds, then exchange the British pounds for French francs, and finally, to exchange the French francs for dollars. If all three exchange rates are not in line, an investor might end up with more dollars at the end of this chain of transactions than at the beginning. Such an opportunity would attract large amounts of money, placing pressure on exchange rates and rapidly restoring balance. While transactions costs and certain exchange restrictions might limit the ability of people to exploit such imbalances among exchange rates, they would nevertheless force the rates into being closely lined up.

The familiar market in foreign currency, operated by banks, travel agents, and others, is in effect a spot market, since both the agreement on terms and the actual exchange of currencies occur at the same time. There are also markets for agreements involving the future delivery of foreign currency.

The largest such market is operated by banks and specialized brokers, who maintain close communications with each other throughout the world.

Corporations, institutions, and some individuals deal in this market via large banks. Substantial amounts of money are involved, and every agreement is negotiated separately. Typical rates are quoted daily in the financial press, as shown in Figure 19.6(a). This network of large institutions is generally termed the *market for forward exchange*, since there is no marking to market. Furthermore, since the contracts are not standardized, no organized secondary market for them exists.

However, there is a market that deals in standardized futures contracts for foreign currency.[11] Procedures are similar to those used for commodity futures. For example, one of the currency futures contracts traded on the International Monetary Market (IMM) of the Chicago Mercantile Exchange requires the seller to deliver 12,500,000 Japanese yen to the buyer on a specific date for a number of U.S. dollars agreed upon in advance. Only the price of the transaction (expressed in both dollars per yen and yen per dollar) is negotiated by the parties involved; all other terms are standard. Clearing procedures allow positions to be covered by reversing trades, and few contracts result in the actual delivery of foreign currency. As shown in Figure 19.6(b), prices and volumes for such contracts are quoted daily in the financial press along with those for other futures.

Markets for foreign currency futures attract both hedgers and speculators. Hedgers wish to reduce or possibly eliminate the risk associated with planned future transfers of funds from one country to another.

An Example

For example, an American importer might know on December 8, 1988, that he or she will have to make a payment of 50 million yen to a Japanese exporter in March of 1989. The current exchange rate is $.008178 per yen (or, equivalently, 122.28 yen per dollar), so the anticipated dollar size of the payment is $408,900 ($.008178 × 50,000,000). The risk the importer faces by simply waiting until March to make this payment is that the exchange rate will change in an unfavorable manner—perhaps rising to $.0090 per yen, in which case the dollar cost to the importer will have risen to $450,000 ($.0090 × 50,000,000). The importer can hedge this risk by purchasing a March futures contract for yen. Figure 19.6(b) indicates that the settle price on December 8, 1988, for this contract was $.008287, meaning that the dollar cost of the contract is $414,350 ($.008287 × 50,000,000). Thus, for a cost of $5450 ($414,350 − $408,900), the importer can remove the risk of the yen appreciating against the dollar before the payment date.

Speculators are attracted to the foreign currency futures market when they believe the current price of the futures contract is substantially different from what they expect the spot rate to be on the delivery date.

For example, a speculator might believe the price of the March futures contract for Japanese yen is too high. Perhaps a speculator might believe

---

[11] The prices of foreign currency forward and futures contracts appear to be quite similar. See Bradford Cornell and Marc Reinganum, "Forward and Futures Prices: Evidence from the Foreign Exchange Market," *Journal of Finance* 36, no. 5 (December 1981):1035–45. For an introductory discussion of the pricing relationships between spot, forward, and futures contracts, see Kenneth R. French, "Pricing Financial Futures Contracts: An Introduction," *Journal of Applied Corporate Finance* 2 (1989):59–66; and Darrell Duffie, *Futures Markets* (Englewood Cliffs, N.J.: Prentice Hall, 1989):152–57.

FOREIGN EXCHANGE

Thursday, March 10, 1988

The New York foreign exchange selling rates below apply to trading among banks in amounts of $1 million and more, as quoted at 3 p.m. Eastern time by Bankers Trust Co. Retail transactions provide fewer units of foreign currency per dollar.

Country	U.S. $ equiv. Thurs.	U.S. $ equiv. Wed.	Currency per U.S. $ Thurs.	Currency per U.S. $ Wed.
Argentina (Austral) ...	.2176	.2176	4.595	4.595
Australia (Dollar)	.7295	.7290	1.3708	1.3717
Austria (Schilling)	.08554	.08532	11.69	11.72
Belgium (Franc)				
Commercial rate	.02869	.02867	34.85	34.88
Financial rate	.02865	.02861	34.90	34.95
Brazil (Cruzado)	.009551	.009617	104.70	103.98
Britain (Pound)	1.8470	1.8482	.5414	.5411
30-Day Forward ...	1.8442	1.8453	.5422	.5419
90-Day Forward ...	1.8381	1.8388	.5440	.5438
180-Day Forward ...	1.8291	1.8294	.5467	.5466
Canada (Dollar)	.7957	.7978	1.2568	1.2535
30-Day Forward ...	.7945	.7967	1.2586	1.2552
90-Day Forward ...	.7923	.7945	1.2621	1.2587
180-Day Forward ...	.7891	.7913	1.2673	1.2638
Chile (Official rate) ...	.004090	.004090	244.51	244.51
China (Yuan)	.2687	.2687	3.7220	3.7220
Colombia (Peso)	.003655	.003655	273.60	273.60
Denmark (Krone)	.1568	.1571	6.3765	6.3670
Ecuador (Sucre)				
Official rate	.004090	.004090	244.50	244.50
Floating rate	.002594	.002594	385.50	385.50
Finland (Markka)	.2486	.2488	4.0230	4.0190
France (Franc)	.1765	.1771	5.6645	5.6480
30-Day Forward ...	.1764	.1770	5.6705	5.6510
90-Day Forward ...	.1759	.1766	5.6885	5.6620
180-Day Forward ...	.1753	.1760	5.7055	5.6820
Greece (Drachma) ...	.007491	.007485	133.50	133.60
Hong Kong (Dollar) ...	.1282	.1282	7.8010	7.7995
India (Rupee)	.07710	.07740	12.97	12.92
Indonesia (Rupiah) ...	.0006024	.0006024	1660.00	1660.00
Ireland (Punt)	1.6025	1.6034	.6240	.6237
Israel (Shekel)	.6329	.6329	1.5800	1.5800
Italy (Lira)	.0008091	.0008130	1236.00	1230.00
Japan (Yen)	.007819	.007813	127.90	128.00
30-Day Forward ...	.007835	.007829	127.63	127.73
90-Day Forward ...	.007870	.007865	127.07	127.15
180-Day Forward ...	.007925	.007920	126.19	126.27
Jordan (Dinar)	2.9027	2.9027	.3445	.3445
Kuwait (Dinar)	3.5971	3.5971	.278	.278
Lebanon (Pound)	.002703	.002703	370.00	370.00
Malaysia (Ringgit)	.3916	.3905	2.5538	2.5605
Malta (Lira)	3.0544	3.0544	.3274	.3274
Mexico (Peso)				
Floating rate	.0004405	.0004405	2270.00	2270.00
Netherland(Guilder) .	.5350	.5343	1.8690	1.8715
New Zealand (Dollar)	.6705	.6705	1.4914	1.4914
Norway (Krone)	.1580	.1586	6.3280	6.3050
Pakistan (Rupee)	.05685	.05685	17.59	17.59
Peru (Inti)	.03030	.03030	33.00	33.00
Philippines (Peso)	.04759	.04759	21.01	21.01
Portugal (Escudo) ..	.007326	.007331	136.50	136.40
Saudi Arabia (Riyal) ..	.2666	.2666	3.7505	3.7505
Singapore (Dollar)	.4968	.4968	2.0130	2.0130
South Africa (Rand)				
Commercial rate	.4708	.4674	2.1240	2.1395
Financial rate	.3629	.3702	2.7550	2.7010
South Korea (Won)	.001314	.001314	760.90	760.90
Spain (Peseta)	.008945	.008950	111.80	111.73
Sweden (Krona)	.1688	.1691	5.9235	5.9145
Switzerland (Franc) ..	.7260	.7257	1.3775	1.3780
30-Day Forward	.7291	.7290	1.3715	1.3717
90-Day Forward	.7350	.7352	1.3606	1.3601
180-Day Forward	.7431	.7435	1.3457	1.3450
Taiwan (Dollar)	.03498	.03498	28.59	28.59
Thailand (Baht)	.03959	.03959	25.26	25.26
Turkey (Lira)	.0008449	.0008449	1183.60	1183.60
United Arab(Dirham)	.2722	.2722	3.673	3.673
Uruguay (New Peso)				
Financial	.003289	.003289	304.00	304.00
Venezuela (Bolivar)				
Official rate	.1333	.1333	7.50	7.50
Floating rate	.03401	.03401	29.40	29.40
W. Germany (Mark) ..	.6012	.5999	1.6633	1.6670
30-Day Forward	.6030	.6017	1.6583	1.6620
90-Day Forward	.6066	.6053	1.6486	1.6520
180-Day Forward	.6118	.6106	1.6345	1.6377
SDR	1.37271	1.37360	0.728486	0.728014
ECU	1.24088	1.24237	.....	.....

Special Drawing Rights are based on exchange rates for the U.S., West German, British, French and Japanese currencies. Source: International Monetary Fund.

ECU is based on a basket of community currencies. Source: European Community Commission.

z-Not quoted.

FIGURE 19–6

Quotations for foreign exchange.

SOURCE: Reprinted by permission of *The Wall Street Journal*, © Dow Jones & Company, Inc. (December 9, 1988): p. C11.

that when March comes around, the exchange rate will be $.0075 per yen (or, equivalently, 133.33 yen per dollar). By selling (that is, shorting) a March futures contract for yen, the speculator will be selling yen for $.008287, the settle price on December 8, 1988. At the time delivery has to be made, the speculator believes yen can be bought on the spot market for $.0075, thereby allowing a profit to be made on the difference between the selling and buying prices.[12] Specifically, the speculator expects to be able to make a profit of $9837.50 (($.008287 − $.0075) × 12,500,000) per futures contract.

☐ **19.7.2   Interest Rate Futures**

Futures involving fixed-income securities are often referred to as interest rate futures, since their prices are greatly influenced by the current and forecasted interest rates. More specifically, their pricing can be related to the term structure of interest rates, which in turn is related to the concept of forward rates.[13]

An Example

Just how the pricing of interest rate futures is related to the concept of forward rates can be illustrated with an example. Consider the futures market for 90-day Treasury bills. As Figure 19.7 indicates, on December 8, 1988, any purchaser of a futures contract calling for delivery in June 1989 of $1,000,000 face value of 90-day Treasury bills (maturing in September of 1989) would have paid a settle price of 92.09. More precisely, the seller of the contract was obligated to deliver Treasury bills to the buyer in June 1989 for an amount that would make the interest rate on the T-bills, stated on a discount basis, equal to 7.91% per year. Thus, on December 8, 1988, the forward rate on 90-day Treasury bills to be delivered in June 1989 was 7.91%.

As with commodity futures, neither the buyers nor the sellers of such contracts must maintain their positions until the delivery date. Reversing trades can be made at any time, and relatively few contracts result in actual delivery.

Figure 19.7 shows that on December 8, 1988, the structure of 90-day forward rates was nearly flat, with interest rates ranging from 7.89% for March 1989 delivery to 8.07% for December 1989 delivery. Under the unbiased expectations hypothesis (discussed in Chapter 13), these forward rates can be interpreted to represent what investors, on the average, think spot rates will be in the future. Specifically, the 7.91% forward rate on 90-day

---

[12] Actually, the typical speculator will plan to realize this profit by entering a reversing trade instead of buying yen on the spot market and then making delivery. Similarly, the previously mentioned hedging importer will typically plan to enter a reversing trade.

[13] See Chapter 13 for a discussion of term structure and forward rates. For a discussion of how interest rate futures are related to yield curves, see Chapter 4 of Robert W. Kolb, *Interest Rate Futures* (Richmond, Va.: Robert F. Dame, Inc., 1982); Chapter 5 of Edward W. Schwarz, Joanne M. Hill, and Thomas Schneeweis, *Financial Futures* (Homewood, Ill.: Richard D. Irwin, Inc., 1986); and Martin L. Leibowitz, *The Analysis of Value and Volatility in Financial Futures*, Monograph Series in Finance and Economics 1981–3, Salomon Brothers Center for the Study of Financial Institutions, Graduate School of Business Administration, New York University.

Thursday, December 8, 1988

TREASURY BONDS (CBT)—$100,000; pts. 32nds of 100%

	Open	High	Low	Settle	Chg	Yield Settle	Yield Chg	Open Interest
Dec	89-17	89-23	89-06	89-19	....	9.143	....	105,026
Mr89	89-05	89-12	88-25	89-07	....	9.187	....	267,897
June	88-26	89-00	88-16	88-28	....	9.229	....	40,025
Sept	88-11	88-24	88-07	88-19	....	9.263	....	18,582
Dec	88-01	88-14	87-31	88-10	....	9.297	....	9,786
Mr90	87-26	88-06	87-26	88-03	+ 1	9.324	− .004	7,577
June	....	....	....	87-28	+ 1	9.351	− .004	1,350
Dec	87-05	87-17	87-05	87-15	+ 2	9.401	− .008	239

Est vol 300,000; vol Wed 641,703; op int 450,616, −6,294.

TREASURY BONDS (MCE)—$50,000; pts. 32nds of 100%

	Open	High	Low	Settle	Chg	Yield Settle	Yield Chg	Open Interest
Dec	89-10	89-22	89-08	89-18	+ 1	9.146	− .004	1,129
Mr89	88-30	89-12	88-26	89-06	+ 1	9.191	− .004	5,730

Est vol 6,100; vol Wed 7,921; open int 6,971, −919.

T-BONDS (LIFFE) U.S. $100,000; pts of 100%

	Open	High	Low	Settle	Chg			Open Interest
Dec	89-14	89-17	89-10	89-17	− 0-22	91-15	83-12	3,197
Mr89	88-31	89-07	88-25	89-07	− 0-18	88-20	86-26	5,510

Est vol 7,249; vol Wed 14,343; open int 8,707, +149.

TREASURY NOTES (CBT)—$100,000; pts. 32nds of 100%

	Open	High	Low	Settle	Chg	Yield Settle	Yield Chg	Open Interest
Dec	93-19	93-20	93-12	93-17	− 7	8.994	+ .035	24,685
Mr89	93-19	93-21	93-08	93-14	− 7	9.009	+ .035	54,996
June	93-07	93-12	93-07	93-10	− 6	9.030	+ .031	1,134

Est vol 15,000; vol Wed 50,877; open int 80,879, +1,622.

5 YR TREAS NOTES (CBT) $100,000; pts. 32 of 100%

	Open	High	Low	Settle	Chg	Yield Settle	Yield Chg	Open Interest
Dec	96-05	96-065	95-30	96-01	− 8.0	9.00	+ .06	10,219
Mr89	96-06	96-07	95-295	96-01	− 8.0	9.00	+ .06	22,135
June	....	....	....	96-05	− 7.5	9.01	+ .06	101

Est vol 4,444; vol Wed 8,321; open int 32,455, +646.

5 YR TREAS NOTES (FINEX) $100,000; pts. 32 of 100%

	Open	High	Low	Settle	Chg	Yield Settle	Yield Chg	Open Interest
Dec	....	....	....	95-305	−.075	9.02	+ .06	5,715
Mr89	96-02	96-03	95-27	95-30	−.085	9.03	+ .07	6,653
June	96-01	96-025	95-275	95-29	−.085	9.04	+ .07	2,312

Est vol 2,500; vol Wed 9,158; open int 14,690, +1,377.

TREASURY BILLS (IMM)—$1 mil.; pts. of 100%

	Open	High	Low	Settle	Chg	Discount Settle	Discount Chg	Open Interest
Dec	91.96	91.98	91.95	91.97	− .01	8.03	+ .01	5,993
Mr89	92.11	92.13	92.09	92.11	− .03	7.89	+ .03	18,539
June	92.10	92.12	92.06	92.09	− .06	7.91	+ .06	2,340
Sept	92.04	92.10	92.04	92.08	− .03	7.92	+ .03	458
Dec	....	....	....	91.93	− .01	8.07	+ .01	240

Est vol 4,378; vol Wed 8,633; open int 27,649, +332.

MUNI BOND INDEX(CBT)$1,000; times Bond Buyer MBI

	Open	High	Low	Settle	Chg	High	Low	Open Interest
Dec	89-23	89-28	89-16	89-25	− 3	92-02	80-16	7,836
Mr89	88-07	88-19	88-03	88-16	+ 2	90-31	78-25	9,210
June	86-30	87-12	86-30	87-10	+ 4	90-01	77-06	653
Sept	85-27	86-08	85-27	86-03	+ 4	89-01	78-06	438
Dec	84-23	85-05	84-23	85-02	+ 4	87-25	81-10	276

Est vol 3,500; vol Wed 9,354; open int 18,414, −109.
The index: Close 89-25; Yield 7.99.

EURODOLLAR (IMM)—$1 million; pts of 100%

	Open	High	Low	Settle	Chg	Yield Settle	Yield Chg	Open Interest
Dec	90.66	90.68	90.63	90.66	− .03	9.34	+ .03	108,589
Mr89	90.82	90.83	90.78	90.81	− .04	9.19	+ .04	222,892
June	90.78	90.81	90.76	90.78	− .05	9.22	+ .05	74,781
Sept	90.75	90.76	90.71	90.73	− .04	9.27	+ .04	46,309
Dec	90.57	90.59	90.55	90.57	− .03	9.43	+ .03	27,400
Mr90	90.63	90.64	90.60	90.63	− .02	9.37	+ .02	21,252
June	90.56	90.59	90.54	90.58	− .01	9.42	+ .01	20,421
Sept	90.52	90.55	90.49	90.54	....	9.46	....	15,724
Dec	90.46	90.50	90.44	90.49	+ .01	9.51	− .01	13,228
Mr91	90.49	90.53	90.47	90.52	+ .02	9.48	− .02	9,333
June	90.45	90.51	90.45	90.49	+ .02	9.51	− .02	15,493
Sept	90.44	90.50	90.44	90.48	+ .03	9.52	− .03	9,478

Est vol 83,068; vol Wed 164,800; open int 584,900, +3,706.

EURODOLLAR (LIFFE)—$1 million; pts of 100%

	Open	High	Low	Settle	Change	Lifetime High	Lifetime Low	Open Interest
Dec	90.66	90.68	90.65	90.67	− .08	93.00	89.80	20,249
Mr89	90.81	90.84	90.78	90.81	− .12	92.57	90.15	18,538
June	90.80	90.82	90.77	90.79	− .12	92.10	89.84	5,819
Sept	90.75	90.78	90.75	90.74	− .11	91.83	90.42	3,165
Dec	90.62	90.62	90.62	90.57	− .10	91.67	90.29	717
Mr90	90.61	90.61	90.61	90.62	− .10	91.37	90.38	641
June		....	....	90.56	− .12	90.46	90.46	332
Sept		....	....	90.52	− .12	90.41	90.41	413

Est vol 6,114; vol Wed 11,007; open int 49,874, +15.

STERLING (LIFFE)—£500,000; pts of 100%

	Open	High	Low	Settle	Change	Lifetime High	Lifetime Low	Open Interest
Dec	86.70	86.75	86.67	86.65	− .10	91.15	86.67	24,350
Mr89	87.00	87.02	86.92	86.92	− .14	90.94	86.86	23,993
June	87.64	87.69	87.62	87.62	− .09	90.95	87.51	5,991
Sept	88.16	88.19	88.15	88.16	− .05	90.47	88.07	2,072
Dec	88.52	88.52	88.49	88.50	− .03	90.32	88.44	929
Mr90	88.64	88.64	88.63	88.63	− .03	90.15	88.63	464
June	88.82	88.82	88.82	88.80	− .03	89.80	88.65	325
Sept	88.87	88.87	88.87	88.85	− .03	89.65	88.76	119

LONG GILT (LIFFE)—£50,000; 32nds of 100%

	Open	High	Low	Settle	Change	Lifetime High	Lifetime Low	Open Interest
Dec	94-29	94-26	94-25	94-29	− 0-08	97-80	92-22	5,561
Mr90	95-15	95-19	95-07	95-12	− 0-11	98-08	93-22	25,537
June		....	....	96-30	− 0-11	97-08	97-08	156

Est vol 13,901; vol Wed 22,006; open int 31,254, −2,664.

—OTHER INTEREST RATE FUTURES—

Settlement prices of selected contracts. Volume and open intrest of all contract months.

Treasury Bills (MCE) $500,000; 100.00 yield
Dec 91.97 −1; Est. vol. 20; Open Int. 45
Treasury Notes (MCE) $50,000; pts. 32nds of 100%
Dec 93-17 −7; Est. vol. 5; Open Int. 42

CBT—Chicago Board of Trade. FINEX—Financial Instrument Exchange, a division of the New York Cotton Exchange. IMM—International Monetary Market at Chicago Mercantile Exchange. LIFFE—London International Financial Futures Exchange. MCE—MidAmerica Commodity Exchange.

FIGURE 19–7
Interest rate futures.

SOURCE: Reprinted by permission of *The Wall Street Journal*, © Dow Jones & Company, Inc. (December 9, 1988): p. C16.

Treasury bills to be delivered in June of 1989 can be taken as an indication that on December 8, 1988, investors, on average, expect the interest rate on 90-day Treasury bills to be equal to 7.91% in June of 1989. Since the interest rate that is available on December 8, 1988, on 90-day Treasury bills for immediate delivery is slightly over 8%, it can be seen that investors, on average, expect the interest rate to fall slightly in the near future, and then remain nearly stable.

Actively traded interest rate futures involve underlying securities ranging from short term (such as 90-day Treasury bills) to intermediate term (such as 10-year Treasury notes) to long term (such as 15-year Treasury bonds). Prices are generally stated in terms of percentages of par values for the corresponding securities; yields-to-maturity (or discounts) associated with the settle prices are also shown.[14]

□ 19.7.3 Market Index Futures

Figure 19.8 shows a set of quotations for futures contracts on a variety of market indices. Each of these contracts involves the payment of *cash* on the delivery date of an amount equal to a *multiplier* times the difference between (1) the value of the index at the close of the last trading day of the contract and (2) the purchase price of the futures contract. If the index is above the futures price, those with short positions pay those with long positions. If the index is below the futures price, those with long positions pay those with short positions.

In practice, a clearinghouse is used, and all contracts are marked to market every day. In a sense, the delivery day differs from other days in only one respect—all open positions are marked to market for the last time and then closed.

Cash settlement provides results similar to those associated with delivery of all the securities in the index. It avoids the effort and transaction costs associated with (1) the purchase of securities by people who have taken short futures positions; (2) the delivery of these securities to people who have taken long futures positions; and (3) the subsequent sale of the securities by those who receive them.

Major Contracts

As shown in Figure 19.8, five major market index futures have been available recently. Four of these futures involved stock indices, with the most popular one in terms of both trading volume and open interest being based on the Standard & Poor's 500. This contract is traded on the Index and Option Market Division of the Chicago Mercantile Exchange (CME), whereas the next most popular one, based on the New York Stock Exchange Composite

---

[14] For Treasury bills, the discounts and associated prices are annualized. For some interest rate futures, there is flexibility in just what the seller has to deliver, known as the *quality option*. Sometimes there is also some flexibility regarding when an intention to deliver must be announced, known as the *wild card option*. See, for example, Chapter 3 of Kolb, *Interest Rate Futures*; and Chapters 2 (Appendix) and 14 of Schwarz, Hill, and Schneeweis, *Financial Futures*; and Chapter 9 of Duffie, *Futures Markets*.

```
S&P 500 INDEX (CME) 500 times index
                                          Open
       Open   High   Low  Settle  Chg  High    Low  Interest
Dec   277.50 278.65 277.00 277.60 − .85 285.70 252.20 68,380
Mr89  280.30 281.65 280.00 280.70 − .75 288.50 253.90 67,518
June  283.70 284.50 283.00 283.65 − .80 291.20 263.80    921
   Est vol 51,326; vol Wed 61,467; open int 136,824, −3,341.
   Indx prelim High 278.10; Low 276.55; Close 276.56 −1.55
NYSE COMPOSITE INDEX (NYFE) 500 times index
Dec   155.80 156.65 155.65 156.15 − .25 160.75 137.95  3,823
Mr89  157.45 158.20 157.25 157.65 − .40 162.30 144.25  2,076
June  159.50 159.65 159.15 159.25 − .40 163.35 149.60    991
Sept  160.90 160.90 160.90 160.85 − .40 165.10 153.90    231
   Est vol 5,463; vol Wed; 5,684; open int 7,121, −289.
   The index: High 156.13; Low 155.37; Close 155.37 −.77
MAJOR MKT INDEX (CBT) $250 times index
Dec   422.25 423.90 421.30 422.05 − 1.25 429.60 390.50  4,066
Ja89  425.00 426.25 423.80 424.20 − 1.50 431.00 399.30  2,342
Feb   424.55 426.00 424.20 424.70 − 1.20 427.70 411.30  1,578
Mar   427.00 428.00 425.80 426.20 − 1.30 429.75 404.60    567
   Est vol 3,200; vol Wed 4,860; open int 8,353, +448.
   The index: High 423.88; Low 420.99; Close 420.99 −2.10
KC VALUE LINE INDEX (KC) 500 times index
Dec   241.80 242.10 239.80 240.20 − 1.95 255.40 230.80  1,264
Mr89  245.20 246.00 243.90 244.10 − 1.90 257.80 234.80    329
   Est vol 250; vol Wed 157; open int 1,593, −8.
   The index: High 241.22; Low 240.26; Close 240.28 −.93
CRB INDEX (NYFE) 500 times Index
Dec   244.90 246.20 244.50 244.50 − .05 273.00 231.50    699
Mr89  243.10 244.80 242.50 242.60 − .50 269.00 232.70  1,273
May   243.25 243.25 243.20 241.80 − .50 243.25 232.00    459
   Est vol 685; vol Wed; 224; open int 2,544, −35.
   The index: High 246.52; Low 244.41; Close 244.41 −.69
```

CBT—Chicago Board of Trade. CME—Chicago Mercantile Exchange. KC—Kansas City Board of Trade. NYFE—New York Futures Exchange, a unit of the New York Stock Exchange.

FIGURE 19–8

Index futures.

SOURCE: Reprinted by permission of *The Wall Street Journal*, © Dow Jones & Company, Inc. (December 9, 1988): pp. C12, C15.

Stock Index, is traded at the New York Futures Exchange (NYFE).[15] The two other stock index futures involve the Major Market Index (this index, when multiplied by five, closely resembles the Dow Jones Industrial Average; it is traded on the Chicago Board of Trade); and the Value Line Average Stock Index (traded on the Kansas City Board of Trade).

For all contracts but the Major Market Index Futures, the multiplier is $500; for the Major Market Index, it is $250. Thus, the purchase of an S&P 500 contract when the index is 150 would cost $75,000 ($500 × 150); the subsequent sale of this contract when the index is 155 would result in proceeds of $77,500 ($500 × 155) and a profit of $2500 ($77,500 − $75,000).

Also shown in Figure 19.8 is the CRB Index Futures contract. This contract, traded on the NYFE, is based on an index that is computed daily from the settle prices on a member of commodity futures contracts.

Recently a bond index futures contract has been introduced on the Chicago Board of Trade. It is based on the Municipal Bond Index (MBI), which is an index compiled by *The Bond Buyer* that consists of 40 actively traded tax-exempt bonds, and appears in Figure 19.7.

---

[15] The NYFE is a subsidiary of the New York Stock Exchange.

Trading Volume

The volume of trading in futures contracts is very large. To assess its relative size, the number of contracts can be multiplied by the total dollar value represented by one contract. As shown in Figure 19.8, the estimated volume on December 8, 1988, for S&P 500 futures was 51,326 contracts. At a value of 277.60 for the lowest-priced S&P 500 contract, the total dollar value is in excess of $51,326 \times 277.60 \times \$500 = \$7.1$ billion! In comparison, the average daily dollar value of all trades of shares on the New York Stock Exchange during December 1988 was $4.6 billion per day—a figure that is roughly two-thirds the dollar size of the S&P futures on December 8, 1988.[16] This is not unusual. On many days, the dollar value involved in trades of S&P 500 futures exceeds that of trades of individual stocks.

Hedging

What accounts for the popularity of market index futures in general and the S&P 500 in particular? Simply stated, they provide relatively inexpensive and highly liquid positions similar to those obtained with diversified stock portfolios.

For example, instead of purchasing 500 stocks in anticipation of a market advance, one can invest an equivalent amount of money in Treasury bills and take a long position in S&P 500 futures. Alternatively, instead of trying to take short positions in 500 stocks in anticipation of a market decline, one can take a short position in S&P 500 futures, using Treasury bills as margin.

Another important use of market index futures involves allowing broker-dealers to hedge market risk that is associated with temporary positions they often take in the course of their business.[17] This hedging ultimately benfits investors by providing them with greater liquidity than they would otherwise have.

For example, consider an investor who wants to sell a large block of stock. In this situation, a broker-dealer might agree to purchase the stock immediately at an agreed-upon price and then spend time lining up buyers. In the interim, however, economic news might cause the market to fall, and with it the price of the stock. This would cause the broker-dealer to experience a loss, since the broker-dealer owns the stock during the period between purchasing it from the investor and lining up the ultimate buyers. One traditional way that broker-dealers protect themselves (at least partially) from this risk is to pay the investor a relatively low price for the stock. However, the broker-dealer can now hedge this risk (at least partially) by shorting S&P 500 futures at the time the stock is bought from the investor and reversing this position when the ultimate buyers are found.

---

[16] The monthly total was $96.5 billion; see *Barron's* (New York: Dow Jones & Company, Inc., January 30, 1989), 154.

[17] Similarly, interest rate futures are often used by financial institutions to hedge interest rate risk that they may be exposed to. That is, when a large movement in interest rates would cause a large loss, these institutions will seek protection by either buying or selling interest rate futures.

Conversely, when an investor wants to buy a large block of stock, a broker-dealer might agree to provide it at a certain price and then go about the task of lining up sellers. In the interim, however, economic news might cause the market to rise, and with it the price of the stock. This would cause the broker-dealer to experience a loss, since the price that will have to be paid to the sellers might end up being greater than the price agreed to with the investor. Traditionally, broker-dealers protect themselves from such risk by charging the investor a relatively high price for the stock. However, a broker-dealer can now hedge this risk (at least partially) by going long in S&P 500 futures at the time the investor agrees to buy the stock and then reversing this position when the stock is ultimately bought.

Given competition among broker-dealers, the existence of S&P 500 futures will lead broker-dealers to provide higher bid prices and lower asked prices. This reduced bid-ask spread means that the existence of S&P 500 futures has provided the associated spot market for stocks (that is, the New York Stock Exchange) with greater liquidity.

It should be pointed out that the use of S&P 500 futures in such situations does not remove all risk from the position of the broker-dealer. All it removes is market risk, since these futures contracts involve a broad market index, not an individual stock. Thus, it is possible for the broker-dealer to experience a loss even if an appropriate position has been taken in futures. Specifically, the individual stock with which the broker-dealer is involved may move up or down in price while the S&P 500 is stable, or the S&P 500 may move up or down while the individual stock is stable. In either case, the broker-dealer that has hedged with S&P 500 futures may still experience a loss. The possibility of this happening will be substantial when the broker-dealer has little diversification, with the greatest possibility associated with a one-stock portfolio.

Index Arbitrage

When stock index futures were first proposed, a number of people predicted that at long last there would be an indicator of investor's expectations about the future course of the stock market. It was said that the market price of such a futures contract would indicate the consensus opinion of investors concerning the future level of the associated index. In times of optimism, the futures price might be much higher than the current level of the market, while in times of pessimism, the futures price might be much lower.

Such predictions have since been found to be quite off the mark. This is because the price of a futures contract on an asset will not diverge too much from the spot price of the asset. Should a relatively large divergence occur, clever investors know as "arbitrageurs" can be expected to make trades designed to capture riskless (that is, "arbitrage") profits.

The presence of these arbitrageurs does have an effect on the pricing of stock index futures. Their actions will force the price of a stock index futures contract to stay close to an "appropriate" relationship with the current level of the associated index. To find out just what is meant by appropriate, consider a hypothetical example where today is a day in June when the Standard & Poor's 500 is at 100 and a December Standard & Poor's 500

futures contract is selling for 110. The following investment strategies are compared:

1. Purchase the stocks in the S&P 500, hold them until December and then sell them on the delivery date of the December S&P 500 contract.
2. Purchase a December S&P 500 futures contract along with Treasury bills that mature in December. Hold the futures contract until the delivery date in December.

Strategy 1 would cost $100 (in "index terms") at the outset. In return, it would provide the investor with (1) an amount of money equal to the value of the S&P 500 on the delivery date and (2) dividends on those stocks that went ex-dividend prior to the delivery date. That is, by denoting the level the S&P 500 will have on the delivery date as P_d and assuming the dividend yield over the six-month time period from June to December is 3%, the investor following strategy 1 will receive in December an amount that is equal to P_d + $3 (that is, P_d + (.03 × $100)).

Assume that $100 is invested in Treasury bills in strategy 2. Since Treasury bills can be used as margin on futures, the total cost of strategy 2 is $100, which is the same as the cost of strategy 1. In return, strategy 2 would provide the investor with (1) an amount of money equal to the difference between the value of the S&P 500 and $110 on the delivery date and (2) the face value of the Treasury bills on the delivery date. That is, by assuming that the yield on the Treasury bills is 5%, the investor following strategy 2 will receive in December an amount that is equal to P_d − $5 (that is, ($P_d$ − $110) + (1.05 × $100)).

By design, both strategies require the same initial outlay. Furthermore, both strategies are subject to precisely the same uncertainty, the unknown level of the S&P 500 on the future delivery date, denoted by P_d. However, the inflows are not equal, indicating that an opportunity exists for *index arbitrage*.[18]

In this example, index arbitrage would cause an investor to go long on strategy 1 and short on strategy 2 because strategy 1 has a higher payoff than strategy 2 (note that P_d + $3 > P_d − $5). Going long on strategy 1 means that the investor is to do exactly what was indicated earlier—purchase the stocks in the S&P 500 and hold them until the December delivery date. Going short on strategy 2 means to do exactly the opposite. Specifically, the investor is to short (that is, sell) a December S&P 500 futures contract and sell Treasury bills that mature in December (it is assumed that the investor has these in his or her current portfolio). The net cash outflow of going long on strategy 1 and short on strategy 2 is zero—$100 is spent buying the stocks in going long on strategy 1, which is gotten by selling $100 worth of December

---

[18] Index arbitrage is one of two forms of *program trading*; the other form, known as *portfolio insurance*, is discussed in Chapter 18. For a discussion and example of how futures can be used to procure portfolio insurance, see Stephen R. King and Eli M. Remolona, "The Pricing and Hedging of Market Index Deposits," Federal Reserve Bank of New York *Quarterly Review* 12, no. 2 (Summer 1987):9–20. It should be noted that after Black Monday and Terrible Tuesday (October 19–20, 1987), there has been less use of both portfolio insurance and index arbitrage.

Treasury bills when the investor goes short on strategy 2. The margin necessary for being short on the future contract is met by having purchased the underlying stocks. Thus, no additional cash needs to be committed in order to engage in index arbitrage—all that is necessary is for the investor to own Treasury bills that mature in December.

Having gone long on strategy 1 and short on strategy 2, consider the investor's position on the delivery date in December. First of all, the investor bought the individual stocks in the S&P 500 at $100 and sold them at $110 by being short on the S&P 500 futures contract. Thus, the investor will have made $10 from being long on the individual stocks and short on the futures on the index. Second, the investor will have received dividends totaling $3 (.03 × $100) from owning the stocks from June to December. Third, the investor will have given up $5 (.05 × $100) in interest that would have been earned on the December Treasury bills. This is because the investor sold $100 of these Treasury bills in June in order to get the requisite cash to buy the individual stocks. Overall, the investor would have increased the dollar return that would have been made on the Treasury bills by $8 ($10 + $3 − $5). Furthermore, this increase is certain, meaning it will be received regardless of what happens to the level of the S&P 500. Thus, by going long on strategy 1 and short on strategy 2, the investor will not have increased the risk of his or her portfolio but will have increased the dollar return.

Earlier, it was mentioned that an investor going long on strategy 1 would receive cash of P_d + $3 in December, whereas an investor going long on strategy 2 would receive cash of P_d − $5. It can now be seen that going long on strategy 1 and short on strategy 2 will provide a net dollar return of $8 (that is, $(P_d + \$3) - (P_d - \$5)$), just as was shown in the previous paragraph. However, if enough investors do this, the opportunity for making the $8 riskless profit will disappear. This is because (1) going long on the individual stocks will push the prices of these stocks up, thereby raising the current level of the S&P 500 from 100; and (2) going short on the S&P 500 futures will push the price of the futures down from 110. These two adjustments will continue until it is no longer profitable to go long on strategy 1 and short on strategy 2.

What if the price of the S&P 500 December futures contract were $90 instead of $110? The dollar return from being long on strategy 1 is still equal to P_d + $3. However, the dollar return from being long on strategy 2 will be different. In particular, purchasing Treasury bills and the futures contract will provide the investor with a dollar return in December that is equal to P_d + $15 (that is, $(P_d - \$90) + (1.05 \times \$100)$). Since these two inflows are not equal, again there is an opportunity for index arbitrage. However, it would involve the investor going short on strategy 1 and long on strategy 2. This is because strategy 1 now has a lower payoff than strategy 2 (note that $P_d + \$3 < P_d + \$15$). By doing this, the investor will, without risk, earn $12 (that is, $(P_d + \$15) - (P_d + \$3)$). Furthermore, being short the individual stocks and long the futures will push the current level of the S&P 500 down from 100 and the price of the futures up from 90.

In equilibrium, since these two strategies cost the same to implement, prices will adjust so that their dollar returns are equal. Letting y denote the

dividend yield on the stocks in the index, P_f denote the current price of the futures contract on the index, and P_c denote the current level of the index, the dollar return from strategy 1 is

$$P_d + yP_c.$$

Letting i denote the interest rate on Treasury bills, the dollar return from strategy 2 is

$$(P_d - P_f) + [(1 + i) \times P_c].$$

Setting these two dollar returns equal to each other results in

$$P_d + yP_c = (P_d - P_f) + [(1 + i) \times P_c]. \qquad (19.2)$$

Simplifying this equation results in

$$P_f - P_c = (i - y)P_c. \qquad (19.3)$$

Equation (19.3) indicates that the difference between the price of the futures contract and the current level of the index should depend only on (1) the current level of the index, P_c, and (2) the difference between the interest rate on Treasury bills and the dividend yield on the index, $(i - y)$. As the delivery date nears, the difference between the interest rate and dividend yield diminishes, converging to zero on the delivery date. Thus, as the delivery date approaches, the futures price (P_f) should converge to the current price (P_c).

In the example the interest rate was 5%, the dividend yield was 3%, and the current level of the S&P 500 was 100. This means that the difference between the S&P 500 December futures contract and the current level of the S&P 500 should be $(.05 - .03) \times 100 = 2$. Equivalently, the equilibrium price of the futures contract when the S&P 500 is 100 would be 102. Note that when three of the six months have passed, the interest rate and dividend yield will be 2.5% (5%/2) and 1.5% (3%/2), respectively. Thus, the difference should be about $(.025 - .015) \times 100 = 1$, assuming the S&P 500 is still at 100 at that time.

In practice, the situation is not this simple for a number of reasons. Positions in futures, stocks, and Treasury bills involve transactions costs.[19] This means that arbitrage will not take place unless the difference diverges far enough from the amount shown in equation (19.3) to warrant incurring such costs. The futures price, and hence the difference, can be expected to move within a band around the "theoretical value," with the width of the band determined by the costs of those who can engage in transactions most efficiently.

To add to the complexity, both the dividend yield and relevant interest rate on the Treasury bills are subject to some uncertainty. Neither the amounts of dividends to be declared nor their timing can be specified completely in advance. And, since futures positions must be marked to market daily, the amount of cash required for strategy 2 may have to be varied via

---

[19] People involved in index arbitrage need to be able quickly to make a large number of transactions in individual stocks. In order to do this, they often have their computers send in their orders through the SuperDOT system (this system is discussed in Chapter 2).

additional borrowing (if short on this strategy) or lending (if long on this strategy). Furthermore, on occasion market prices may be reported with a substantial time lag, making the current level and futures price of the index appear to be out of line when they actually are not. Thus, an investor may enter into the transactions necessary for index arbitrage when actual prices are in equilibrium, thereby resulting in a useless incurring of transaction costs.

Stock index futures are used extensively by professional money managers. As a result, prices of such contracts are likely to track their underlying indices very closely, taking into account both dividends and current interest rates. It is unlikely that a private investor will be able to exploit "mispricing" of such a contract by engaging in index arbitrage. Nevertheless, stock index futures can provide inexpensive ways to take positions in the stock market or to hedge portions of the risk associated with other positions. Furthermore, their use can lower transactions costs by reducing the size of the bid-ask spread for investors who may never take direct positions in such contracts.

19.8 FUTURES VERSUS CALL OPTIONS

People occasionally make the mistake of confusing a futures contract with an options contract.[20] With an options contract, there is the possibility that both of the parties involved will have nothing to do at the end of the life of the contract. In particular, if the option is "out of the money" on the expiration date, then the options contract will be worthless and can be thrown away. However, with a futures contract, both parties involved will have something to do at the end of the life of the contract. In particular, the parties are obligated to complete the transaction, either by a reversing trade or by actual delivery.

Figure 19.9 contrasts the situation faced by the buyer and seller of a call option with the situation faced by the buyer and seller of a futures contract. Specifically, terminal values for buyers and sellers are shown at the last possible moment—the expiration date for the option, and the delivery date for the futures contract.

As shown in part (a) of Figure 19.9, no matter what the price of the underlying stock, an option buyer cannot lose and an option seller cannot gain on the expiration date. Option buyers compensate sellers for putting themselves in this position by paying them a premium when the contract is signed.

The situation is quite different with a futures contract. As shown in part (b), the buyer may gain or lose, depending on the price of the asset in the delivery month. Whatever the buyer gains or loses, an exactly offsetting loss or gain will be registered by the seller. The higher the contract price (that is, the price of the futures contract when the buyer purchased it from the seller), the greater the likelihood that the buyer will lose and the seller

---

[20] Adding to the confusion is the existence of a contract known as a *futures option*, which is an option that has a futures contract instead of a stock as its underlying asset. Futures options are discussed in more detail in the appendix to this chapter.

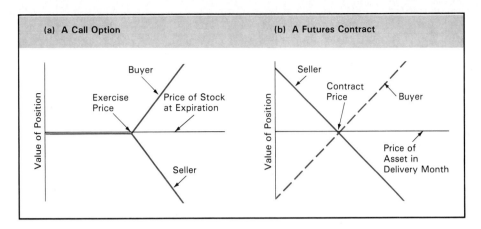

FIGURE 19–9
Terminal values of positions in calls and futures.

will gain. The lower the contract price, the greater the likelihood that the seller will lose and the buyer will gain.

19.9 SYNTHETIC FUTURES

For some assets, futures contracts are unavailable but both put and call options are available. In such cases, an investor can create a *synthetic futures contract*.

The clearest example involves European options on common stocks. As shown in the previous chapter, the purchase of a European call option and the sale of a European put option at the same exercise price and with the same expiration date will provide a value at expiration that will be related, dollar for dollar, to the stock price at that time. This is shown in Figure 19.10.

Part (a) shows the payoffs associated with the purchase of a call at an exercise price of E, whereas part (b) shows the payoff associated with the sale of a put at the same exercise price. The results obtained by taking *both* positions are those shown by the solid line in part (c).

Depending on the prices (that is, premiums) of the call and put, this strategy may initially require either a net outflow of cash or provide a net inflow. For comparability with the purchase of a futures contract, this cash flow may be offset with borrowing or lending as required to bring the net investment to zero. The dashed line in part (c) shows a case in which the call option costs more than is provided by the sale of the put option. The difference is borrowed, requiring the loan repayment shown in the figure. The dashed line thus indicates the net end-of-period payoffs for a strategy requiring no initial outlay. Since these payoffs are equivalent to the payoffs from a futures contract with a contract price equal to F, a "synthetic" futures contract has been created.

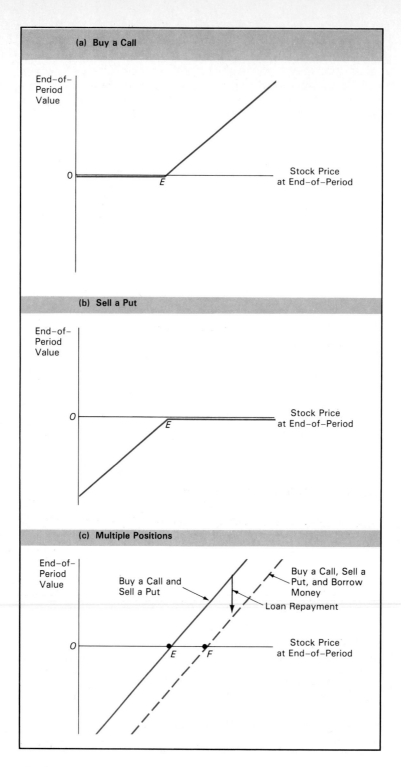

(a) Buy a Call

End-of-Period Value

0

E

Stock Price at End-of-Period

(b) Sell a Put

End-of-Period Value

O

E

Stock Price at End-of-Period

(c) Multiple Positions

End-of-Period Value

Buy a Call and Sell a Put

Buy a Call, Sell a Put, and Borrow Money

Loan Repayment

O

E   F

Stock Price at End-of-Period

FIGURE 19–10
Creating a synthetic futures contract.

In practice, the equivalence is not perfect. Listed options are American, not European, raising the possibility that the buyer of the put will exercise it prior to maturity. Moreover, the synthetic future is not marked to market on a daily basis. Despite these differences, the existence of well-functioning markets for call and put options will enable investors to synthetically create futures on the underlying asset.

19.10 SUMMARY

A futures contract involves the delivery of a specific type of asset at a specific location at a given future point in time. These contracts can be bought and sold at market-based prices on certain organized exchanges due to the fact that the terms of the contract are standardized. In particular, the type of asset, time of delivery, and place of delivery are standardized. Futures contracts currently in existence involve such assets as agricultural goods, natural resources, foreign currencies, fixed-income securities, and market indices.

People who buy and sell such contracts can be classified as either hedgers or speculators. Hedgers are people whose primary motive for buying or selling such contracts is to reduce risk, since these people either produce or use the asset in the ordinary course of their business. Speculators, on the other hand, buy and sell futures in the pursuit of relatively short-term profits. That is, they seek to buy futures contracts at relatively low prices, and hope to sell them at notably higher prices. Interestingly, since 1979 there has been rapid growth in the number of *commodity funds*, which are investment companies that speculate in futures.[21]

Although futures contracts involve the future delivery of an asset, the purchase price of the asset is established when the contract is sold on an exchange. Thus, the purchase price is a market-based one and is related to the anticipated spot price of the asset on the delivery date. Since the anticipated spot price of the asset is, in turn, related to the current spot price of the asset, it is not surprising that the purchase price of the futures contract is related to the current spot price of the asset. Just how these prices are related depends on the asset to be delivered, since some of them are much more costly to store for future delivery than others. Nevertheless, should the price of the futures contract get too far removed from the current spot price of the asset, certain investors, known as arbitrageurs, will immediately enter a larger number of orders in order to make a riskless profit from the perceived price discrepancy. Their actions will cause prices to adjust until the opportunity to make such profits disappears. One prominent example involves index arbitrage, where the futures contract has a stock market index as its asset.

In the previous chapter, it was mentioned that an investor could synthetically create either a put or call option on a stock. Interestingly, futures

---

[21] The performance of these funds has not been attractive. See Edwin J. Elton, Martin J. Gruber, and Joel C. Rentzler, "Professionally Managed, Publicly Traded Commodity Funds," *Journal of Business* 60, no. 2 (April 1987):175–99.

contracts can also be created synthetically. However, in order to do so, an investor must deal in both puts and calls on the asset.

Given sufficient interest, almost anything can be the subject of futures trading, either directly or synthetically. Where there is risk, there will be a demand for ways to reduce it. Futures markets accommodate this demand and facilitate speculation as well. Looking ahead, new futures markets will open and old ones will close, as dictated by the interests of hedgers and speculators.

APPENDIX A
FUTURES OPTIONS

The previous chapter described options, while this chapter has described futures. Interestingly, there are contracts currently in existence that are known as *futures options* (or options on futures). As might be expected, these contracts are, in a sense, combinations of futures and options contracts. In particular, a futures option is an option where the underlying asset is a specific futures contract, with the expiration date on the option being the same as the delivery date on the futures contract.[22] Figure 19.11 provides a set of quotations on some of the more frequently traded ones. As the figure shows, there are both put and call options on futures. Thus, an investor can be either a buyer or a writer of either a put or a call option on a futures contract.[23]

A.1 CALL OPTIONS ON FUTURES CONTRACTS

If a call option on a futures contract is exercised, then the writer must deliver the appropriate futures contract to the buyer. For example, consider the buyer of a call option on July corn where the exercise price is 300 (that is, $3) per bushel. Since the futures contract is for 5000 bushels, the total exercise price is $15,000 (5000 × $3). If the buyer purchased this option at the settle

---

[22] The near-simultaneous quarterly expiration of (1) options on individual stocks and market indices, (2) futures on market indices, and (3) options on market index futures has been referred to as the *triple witching hour*. When it occurs, the stock market is allegedly roiled, particularly in the latter part of the day. See Hans R. Stoll and Robert E. Whaley, "Program Trading and Expiration Day Effects," *Financial Analysts Journal* 43, no. 2 (March/April 1987):16–28; Arnold Kling, "How the Stock Market Can Learn to Live with Index Futures and Options," *Financial Analysts Journal*:43, no. 5 (September/October 1987):33–39; and G. J. Santoni, "Has Programmed Trading Made Stock Prices More Volatile?" Federal Reserve Bank of St. Louis *Review* 69, no. 5 (May 1987):18–29.

[23] For more on futures options, see Chapter 12 of Kolb, *Understanding Futures Markets*; Chapter 17 of Schwarz, Hill, and Schneeweis, *Financial Futures*; Chapters 29 and 34 of Lawrence G. McMillan, *Options as a Strategic Investment* (New York: NYIF Corp., 1986); Chapter 11 of Peter Ritchken, *Options* (Glenview, Ill.: Scott, Foresman and Company, 1987); and Chapter 7 of John C. Cox and Mark Rubinstein, *Options Markets* (Englewood Cliffs, N.J.: Prentice Hall, 1985). For a computer program that can be used to determine the "true" value of these complex contracts, see Chapter 8 of Stuart M. Turnbull, *Option Valuation* (Holt, Rinehart & Winston of Canada, Limited, 1987).

(a) COMMODITY FUTURES OPTIONS

Thursday, December 8, 1988.

– AGRICULTURAL –

CORN (CBT) 5,000 bu.; cents per bu.

Strike Price	Calls – Settle			Puts – Settle		
	Mar-c	May-c	Jly-c	Mar-p	May-p	Jly-p
250	22	26	....	2¼	4¾	8
260	14	20	24½	5	7½	11½
270	8½	14½	20½	9	10¾	16
280	5½	10¾	16¾	15½	17½	21½
290	3½	7¾	13	24	24	27½
300	2½	5¼	10¾	33	32	34½

Est. vol. 6,000, Wed vol. 4,366 calls, 2,684 puts
Open interest Wed 51,078 calls, 32,356 puts

SOYBEANS (CBT) 5,000 bu.; cents per bu.

Strike Price	Calls – Settle			Puts – Settle		
	Jan-c	Mar-c	May-c	Jan-p	Mar-p	May-p
725	49½	71	83½	1	10¾	19
750	28	53	68	4	18½	28
775	12¼	40	55½	13¾	30	39
800	5¼	30½	47	31¾	45	54
825	2	23	37	53½	60	70
850	¾	17	33	77¼	80	....

Est. vol. 11,000, Wed vol. 8,099 calls, 4,765 puts
Open interest Wed 68,998 calls, 30,770 puts

– OIL –

CRUDE OIL (NYM) 1,000 bbls.; $ per bbl.

Strike Price	Calls – Settle			Puts – Settle		
	Jan-c	Feb-c	Mr-c	Jan-p	Feb-p	Mar-p
13	2.43	2.28	2.28	0.01	0.08	0.18
14	1.43	1.38	1.45	0.01	0.18	0.35
15	0.46	0.64	0.77	0.04	0.44	0.67
16	0.02	0.22	0.35	0.60	1.02	1.25
17	0.01	0.06	0.17	1.59	1.86	2.07
18	0.01	0.02	0.07	2.59	2.82	....

Est. vol. 25,432; Wed vol. 13,089 calls; 9,916 puts
Open interest Wed; 90,947 calls; 122,867 puts

HEATING OIL No.2 (NYM) 42,000 gal.; $ per gal.

Strike Price	Calls – Settle			Puts – Settle		
	Jan-c	Feb-c	Mr-c	Jan-p	Feb-p	Mar-p
4400	.0411	.0375	.0285	.0001	.0055	.0190
4600	.0212	.0235	.0200	.0002	.0115	....
4800	.0030	.0140	.0135	.0020	....	....
5000	.0010	.0075	.0075	....	....	....
5200	.0001	.0035	.0025	....	....	....
5400	....	.0020	....	....	....	....

Est. vol. 302; Wed vol. 197 calls; 139 puts
Open interest Wed; 3,893 calls; 2,023 puts

– LIVESTOCK –

CATTLE-FEEDER (CME) 44,000 lbs.; cents per lb.

Strike Price	Calls – Settle			Puts – Settle		
	Jan-c	Mar-c	Apr-c	Jan-p	Mar-p	Apr-p
78	4.12	4.20	....	0.20	1.20	1.60
80	2.47	2.80	2.65	0.55	1.80	2.30
82	1.27	1.80	1.70	1.35	2.80	3.35
84	0.60	1.10	1.15	2.67	4.10	....
86	0.20	0.55	0.70	4.25	5.55	....
88	0.05	0.30	0.40	....	....	....

Est. vol. 205, Wed vol. 90 calls, 156 puts
Open interest Wed; 3,054 calls, 6,359 puts

CATTLE-LIVE (CME) 40,000 lbs.; cents per lb.

Strike Price	Calls – Settle			Puts – Settle		
	Feb-c	Apr-c	Jun-c	Feb-p	Apr-c	Jun-p
66	4.85	....	....	0.25	0.45	0.90
68	3.17	5.32	....	0.57	0.75	1.40
70	1.87	3.85	3.45	1.27	1.22	2.12
72	0.97	2.70	2.50	2.37	2.00	3.02
74	0.47	1.70	1.67	3.87	2.95	4.17
76	0.20	1.02	1.10	5.60	4.25	5.52

Est. vol. 3,651, Wed vol. 1,606 calls, 1,487 puts
Open interest Wed; 30,244 calls, 28,779 puts

– METALS –

COPPER (CMX) 25,000 lbs.; cents per lb.

Strike Price	Calls – Last			Puts – Last		
	Mar-c	May-c	Jly-c	Mar-p	May-p	Jly-p
130	17.40	14.75	14.80	7.55	14.75	19.55
135	14.45	12.75	13.10	9.50	17.60	22.55
140	11.80	11.00	11.50	11.80	20.65	25.75
145	9.75	9.45	10.10	14.65	23.90	29.10
150	7.95	8.05	....	17.75	27.35	....
155	6.45	....	....	21.15	....	....

Est. vol. 2,000, Wed vol. 1,274 calls, 383 puts
Open interest Wed; 10,095 calls, 7,723 puts

GOLD (CMX) 100 troy ounces; dollars per troy ounce

Strike Price	Calls – Last			Puts – Last		
	Feb-c	Apr-c	Jun-c	Feb-p	Apr-p	Jun-p
410	18.60	25.80	32.60	1.90	4.30	6.30
420	10.60	18.50	25.50	3.90	7.10	8.80
430	5.10	12.70	19.70	8.40	10.50	12.50
440	2.20	8.60	14.90	15.50	16.40	17.20
450	1.10	5.30	11.00	24.40	22.70	22.80
460	0.60	3.20	7.90	33.60	30.50	29.20

Est. vol. 3,000, Wed vol. 3,774 calls, 2,739 puts
Open interest Wed; 43,443 calls, 34,696 puts

(b) INTEREST RATE FUTURES OPTIONS

T-BONDS (CBT) $100,000; points and 64ths of 100%

Strike Price	Calls – Last			Puts – Last		
	Mar-c	Jun-c	Sep-c	Mar-p	Jun-p	Sep-p
86	3-51	4-14	....	0-40	1-32	2-08
88	2-23	3-01	3-28	1-11	2-13	2-56
90	1-18	2-02	2-30	2-05	3-10	....
92	0-41	1-23	1-51	3-25	....	....
94	0-19	0-56	1-22	4-63	....	....
96	0-08	0-34	0-59	6-54	....	....

Est. vol. 45,000, Wed vol. 60,015 calls, 64,572 puts
Open interest Wed; 226,599 calls, 243,249 puts

T-NOTES (CBT) $100,000; points and 64ths of 100%

Strike Price	Calls – Last			Puts – Last		
	Mar-c	Jun-c	Sep-c	Mar-p	Jun-p	Sep-p
91	2-56	....	....	0-29	....	....
92	2-08	....	....	0-45	1-19	1-49
93	1-31	1-63	....	1-03	1-44	....
94	0-62	1-31	....	1-32	2-10	....
95	0-39	1-07	....	2-10	....	....
96	0-22	0-51	....	2-57	....	....

Est. vol. 3,000, Wed vol. 3,075 calls, 6,353 puts
Open interest Wed; 15,628 calls, 30,199 puts

MUNICIPAL BOND INDEX (CBT) $100,000; pts. & 64ths of 100%

Strike Price	Calls – Settle			Puts – Settle		
	Dec-c	Mar-c	Jun-c	Dec-p	Mar-p	Jun-p
86	3-50	3-10	....	0-01	0-50	....
88	1-55	1-52	....	0-06	1-27	....
90	0-25	0-54	....	0-45	2-20	....
92	0-02	0-25	....	2-16	3-56	....
94	0-01	....	....	....	....	....
96	....	0-05	....	....	....	....

Est. vol. 452, Wed vol. 5 calls, 2,421 puts
Open interest Wed; 15,093 calls, 23,307 puts

TREASURY BILLS (IMM)-$1 million; pts. of 100%

Strike Price	Calls – Settle			Puts – Settle		
	Mar-c	Jun-c	Sep-c	Mar-p	Jun-p	Sep-p
9150	....	0.60	....	....	0.29	....
9175	....	....	....	....	....	....
9200	0.35	0.45	....	0.24	0.38	....
9225	0.22	0.33	....	0.36	0.50	....
9250	0.13	0.23	....	0.51	0.75	....
9275	0.07	0.15	....	0.70	0.81	....

Est. vol. 0, Wed vol. 0 calls, 0 puts
Open interest Wed; 121 calls, 13 puts

EURODOLLAR (CME) $ million; pts. of 100%

Strike Price	Calls – Settle			Puts – Settle		
	Dec-c	Mar-c	Jun-c	Dec-p	Mar-p	Jun-p
9025	0.42	0.67	0.77	0.01	0.12	0.26
9050	0.20	0.50	0.62	0.04	0.19	0.35
9075	0.05	0.34	0.48	0.14	0.28	0.45
9100	0.01	0.22	0.36	0.35	0.41	0.56
9125	.0004	0.13	0.27	0.59	0.56	0.71
9150	.0004	0.08	0.18	0.84	0.75	0.87

Est. vol. 6,890, Wed vol. 7,524 calls, 12,186 puts
Open interest Wed; 108,334 calls, 119,108 puts

EURODOLLAR (LIFFE) $1 million; pts. of 100%

Strike Price	Calls – Settle			Puts – Settle		
	Dec-c	Mar-c	Jun-c	Dec-p	Mar-p	Jun-p
9025	0.43	0.69	0.82	0.01	0.13	0.28
9050	0.20	0.50	0.65	0.03	0.19	0.36
9075	0.06	0.35	0.51	0.14	0.29	0.47

(c) INDEX FUTURES OPTIONS

S&P 500 STOCK INDEX (CME) $500 times premium

Strike Price	Calls – Settle			Puts – Settle		
	Dec-c	Jan-c	Fb-c	Dec-p	Jan-p	Feb-p
270	8.25	13.35	14.90	0.65	2.70	4.30
275	4.30	9.70	11.45	1.70	4.05	5.75
280	1.65	6.60	8.40	4.05	5.85	7.70
285	0.40	4.15	5.95	7.80	8.35	....
290	0.10	2.40	4.00	12.50	11.55	13.05
295	0.05	1.35	2.55	....	15.40	....

Est. vol. 2,399; Wed vol. 2,870 calls; 2,687 puts
Open interest Wed; 16,344 calls; 22,092 puts

NYSE COMPOSITE INDEX (NYFE) $500 times premium

Strike Price	Calls – Settle			Puts – Settle		
	Dec-c	Jan-c	Feb-c	Dec-p	Jan-p	Feb-p
152	4.25	7.00	7.90	0.30	1.50	2.40
154	2.60	5.60	6.50	0.70	2.00	3.00
156	1.30	4.25	5.25	1.35	2.65	3.70
158	0.55	3.05	4.15	2.60	3.50	4.55
160	0.20	2.10	3.20	4.15	4.55	5.55
162	0.10	1.45	2.40	6.00	5.80	6.75

Est. vol. 77, Wed vol. 29 calls, 71 puts
Open interest Wed; 611 calls, 1,359 puts

CBT–Chicago Board of Trade. CME–Chicago Mercantile Exchange. NYFE–New York Futures Exchange, a unit of the New York Stock Exchange.

FIGURE 19–11
Quotations for futures options.

SOURCE: Reprinted by permission of *The Wall Street Journal*, © Dow Jones & Company, Inc. (December 9, 1988): pp. C14–C16.

price on December 8, 1988 that is given in Figure 19.11, then the buyer would have paid the writer a premium of 10¾ (that is, $.1075) per bushel or $537.50 (5000 × $.1075) in total.

If the buyer subsequently decides to exercise this option, then the writer of this option must deliver a July corn futures contract to the buyer. Furthermore, this futures contract will be fully marked to market at the time it is delivered. In the example, assume that the option is exercised in March when July corn futures are selling for $3.50 per bushel. What happens in March is that the call writer must provide the call buyer with a July corn futures contract that has a delivery price of $3 that has been marked to market. This can be accomplished in two steps. First, the writer must purchase a July corn futures contract and deliver it to the call buyer. Even though the cost of the futures will be $3.50 per bushel (the current market price of July corn futures), this is costless to the call writer. Second, the futures contract that has been delivered must be marked to market, which is done by having the call writer pay the call buyer an amount of cash equal to $.50 ($3.50 − $3) per bushel or $2500 (5000 × $.50) in aggregate. Thus, the call writer has lost $1962.50 ($2500 − $537.50), whereas the call buyer has made an equivalent amount.

This example has shown what happens when the call is exercised, but it should be noted that most futures options are not exercised. Instead, just as with most options and futures, buyers and writers of futures options typically make reversing trades before the expiration date.

A.2   PUT OPTIONS ON FUTURES CONTRACTS

If a put option on a futures contract is exercised, then the writer must accept delivery of the appropriate futures contract from the buyer. For example, consider the buyer of a put option on July corn where the exercise price is 300, meaning $3 per bushel, or $15,000 in total, since the futures contract is for 5000 bushels. If the buyer purchased this put at the settle price on December 8, 1988, that is given in Figure 19.11, then the buyer would have paid the writer a premium of 34½ per bushel, or $1725 (5000 × $.345) in total.

If the buyer subsequently decides to exercise this option, then the writer of this option must accept delivery of a July corn futures contract from the buyer. Furthermore, this futures contract must be fully marked to market at the time it is delivered. In the example, assume that the option is exercised in March when July corn futures are selling for $2.50 per bushel. What happens in March is that the put buyer will become the seller of a July corn futures contract where the purchase price is $2.50 per bushel. Even though this is the current market price of July corn futures, this is costless to the put buyer. However, when this futures contract is marked to market, the put writer must pay the put buyer an amount of cash equal to $.50 ($3.00 − $2.50) per bushel or $2500 (5000 × $.50) in aggregate. Thus, the put

writer has lost \$775 (\$2500 − \$1725), whereas the put buyer has made an equivalent amount.

Again, it should be kept in mind that most put options on futures are not exercised. Instead, these option buyers and writers typically enter reversing trades sometime before the expiration date.

A.3 COMPARISON WITH FUTURES AND OPTIONS

At this point, it is worthwhile thinking about the distinctions between futures and futures options. In doing so, consider an investor who is contemplating *buying* a futures contract. If this contract is purchased, the investor can potentially make or lose a great deal of money. In particular, if the price of the asset rises substantially, then so will the price of the futures, and the investor will have made a sizable profit. In contrast, if the price of the asset drops substantially, then the investor will have lost a sizable amount of money.

In comparison, if the investor had bought a futures call option on the asset, then the investor would also make a sizable profit if the price of the asset rose substantially. Unlike futures, however, if the price of the asset dropped, then the investor need not worry about incurring a sizable loss. Instead, only the premium (the price paid to buy the futures option) would be lost. This does not mean that purchasing a futures call option is better than purchasing a futures contract because the protection on the downside that an investor gets from buying a futures call option is paid for in the form of the premium. This premium would not be present if the investor had bought a futures contract instead.

Consider next an investor who is contemplating *selling* a futures contract. In doing so, the investor can potentially make a great deal of money if the price of the asset declines substantially. However, if the price of the asset rises substantially, then the investor can lose a sizable amount of money.

In comparison, the investor can buy a futures put option on the asset. If this is done, the investor can make a sizable profit if the price of the asset declined substantially. Unlike futures, however, if the price of the asset rose, then the investor need not worry about incurring a sizable loss. Instead, only the premium is lost. Again, this does not mean that purchasing a futures put option is better than selling a futures contract.

QUESTIONS AND PROBLEMS

1. Distinguish between a speculator and a hedger. Give an example of a short hedger and a long hedger.
2. Zack Wheat has just bought four September 5,000-bushel corn futures contracts at \$1.75 per bushel. The initial margin requirement is 3%. The maintenance margin requirement is 80% of the initial margin requirement.

a. How many dollars in initial margin must Zack put up?

b. If the September price of corn rises to $1.85, how much equity is in Zack's commodity account?

c. If the September price of corn falls to $1.60, how much equity is in Zack's commodity account? Will Zack receive a margin call?

3. How does a futures contract differ from a forward contract?

4. Do exchange-imposed price limits protect futures traders from losses that would result in the absence of such limits? Explain.

5. A publication used by farmers such as Mordecai Brown provides diagrams of the typical annual patterns of "cash prices" for a number of seasonal commodities. Should Mordecai expect that the price of a futures contract will follow the same pattern? Why or why not?

6. In the market for a particular agricultural or natural resource commodity, what kind of market forces might lead to normal backwardation or normal contango?

7. Estel Crabtree believes that the spread between long-term and short-term interest rates is going to narrow in the next few months, but does not know which direction interest rates in general will move. What financial futures position would permit Estel to profit from this forecast if it is correct?

8. Why does hedging a common stock portfolio using stock index futures work best if the portfolio being hedged is very similar to the underlying stock index of the futures contract?

9. Assume that the S&P 500 currently has a value of 200 (in "index" terms). The dividend yield on the underlying stocks in the index is expected to be 4% over the next six months. New issue six-month Treasury bills now sell for a six-month yield of 6%.

a. What is the theoretical value of a six-month futures contract on the S&P 500?

b. What potential problems are inherent in this calculation?

10. In December 1989, Granny Hamner bought a January 1990 gold futures contract on the New York Commodity Exchange for $487.50 per ounce. Simultaneously, Granny sold an October 1991 contract for $614.80. At the time, yields on Treasury notes with 1.75 years to maturity were 10.50%. Will this transaction be profitable for Granny? What factors are relevant to making this calculation?

11. In each of the following situations, discuss how Hippo Vaughn might use stock index futures to protect a well-diversified stock portfolio:

a. Hippo expects to receive a sizable bonus check next month and would like to invest in stocks, believing that current stock market prices are extremely attractive (but realizing they may not remain so for long).

b. Hippo expects the stock market to decline dramatically very soon and realizes that quickly selling a stock portfolio would result in a significant transactions costs.

c. Hippo has a large, unrealized gain and for tax purposes would like to defer the gain until the next tax year, which is several weeks away.

12. (Appendix Question) Distinguish between futures contracts and options on futures contracts.

Chapter 20

INVESTMENT COMPANIES

Investment companies are a type of financial intermediary. They obtain money from investors and use it to purchase financial assets such as stocks and bonds. In return, the investors receive certain rights regarding the financial assets the company has bought and any earnings that it may make. In the simplest and most common situation, the investment company has only one type of investor—stockholders. These stockholders directly own the investment company and thus indirectly own the financial assets that the company itself owns.

For an individual, there are two advantages to investing in such companies instead of investing directly in the financial assets these companies own. Specifically, the advantages arise from (1) economies of scale and (2) professional management. In describing these benefits, consider an individual with moderate financial resources who wishes to invest in the stock market.

In terms of economies of scale, the individual could buy stocks in odd lots and thus have a diversified portfolio. However, the brokerage commissions on odd-lot transactions are relatively high. Alternatively, the individual could purchase round lots but would only be able to afford a few different securities. Unfortunately, the individual would then be giving up the benefits of owning a well-diversified portfolio, in which declines in some securities would more likely be offset by gains in others. In order to receive the benefits of diversification and substantially reduced brokerage commissions, the individual could invest in the shares of an investment company. That is, economies of scale make it possible for an investment company to provide diversification at a lower cost per dollar of investment than would be incurred by a small individual investor.

In terms of professional management, the individual investing directly in the stock market would have to go through all the details of investing, including such things as making all buying and selling decisions as well as keeping records of all transactions for tax purposes. In doing so, the individual would have to be continually on the lookout for mispriced securities in an attempt to find undervalued ones for purchase, while selling any that were found to be overvalued. Simultaneously, the individual would have to keep track of the overall risk level of the portfolio so that it did not deviate from some desired level. However, by purchasing shares of an investment com-

pany, the individual can turn over all of these details to a professional money manager.

Many of these managers hope to identify areas of mispricing in the market, exploit them, and share the resultant abnormal gains with investors by charging them for a portion of the gains. However, it appears that they typically cannot find enough mispriced situations so as to recoup more than the additional costs they have incurred, costs that take the form of increased management fees and transaction costs due to the continual buying and selling of securities. Nevertheless, other potential advantages to be gained from investing in an investment company may still outweigh any disadvantages.

Investment companies differ in many ways, and classification is difficult. Common practice is followed here; the term is restricted to those financial intermediaries that do not obtain money from depositors. Thus, the traditional operations of savings and loan companies and banks, for example, are excluded. However, the process of deregulation is rapidly breaking down previous barriers so that the future may very well bring even more competition for traditional investment companies.

20.1 NET ASSET VALUE

An important concept in understanding how investment companies operate is *net asset value* (NAV). Given that an investment company has assets consisting of various securities, it is generally quite easy to determine the market value of all the assets held by the investment company at the end of each business day. For example, an investment company that holds various common stocks traded on the New York Stock Exchange could easily find out what the closing prices were at the end of the day and then simply multiply these prices by the number of shares that they own. After adding up these figures, any liabilities that the investment company had outstanding would be subtracted; dividing the resulting difference by the number of outstanding shares of the investment company produces the NAV for the investment company.

Equivalently, an investment company's NAV at the end of day t (NAV_t) can be determined by using the following equation:

$$NAV_t = \frac{MVA_t - LIAB_t}{NSO_t} \tag{20.1}$$

where MVA_t, $LIAB_t$, and NSO_t denote the market value of the investment company's assets, the dollar amount of the investment company's liabilities, and the number of shares the investment company has outstanding, respectively, as of the end of day t. Thus, an investment company with 4,000,000 shares outstanding whose assets consisted of common stocks with an aggregate market value of $102,000,000 and whose liabilities amounted to $2,000,000 as of November 15, 1988, would report a net asset value on that date of ($102,000,000 − $2,000,000)/4,000,000 = $25 per share.

It should be noted that an investment company's NAV changes each

and every day, since the values of either MVA_t, $LIAB_t$, or NSO_t (or all three) change.

20.2 MAJOR TYPES OF INVESTMENT COMPANIES

The Investment Company Act of 1940 classifies investment companies as follows:[1]

> Unit investment trusts
> Managed investment companies
>> Closed-end investment companies
>> Open-end investment companies

☐ 20.2.1 Unit Investment Trusts

A *unit investment trust* is an investment company that owns a fixed set of securities for the life of the company.[2] That is, the investment company rarely alters the composition of its portfolio over the life of the company.

Formation

To form a unit investment trust, a sponsor (often a brokerage firm) purchases a specific set of securities and deposits them with a trustee (such as a bank). Then, a number of shares known as redeemable trust certificates are sold to the public. These certificates provide their owners with a proportional interest in the securities that were previously deposited with the trustee. All income received by the trustee on these securities is subsequently paid out to the certificate holders, as are any repayments of principal. Changes in the original set of securities (that is, selling some of them and buying different ones) are made only under exceptional circumstances. Since there is no active management of a unit investment trust, the annual fees charged by the sponsor are correspondingly low (perhaps equal to .15% of NAV per year).

Most unit investment trusts hold fixed-income securities and expire after the last one has been paid off (or, possibly, sold). Lifespans range from 6 months for unit investment trusts of money market instruments to over 20 years for trusts of bond market instruments. Some trusts include only federal government bonds, others only corporate bonds, others only municipal bonds, and so on.

Not surprisingly, the sponsor of a unit investment trust will seek compensation for the effort and risk involved in setting up the trust. This is accomplished by setting a selling price for the shares that exceeds the cost of the underlying assets. For example, a brokerage firm might purchase

---

[1] Another classification covers certain companies that issue *face-amount certificates* promising specific payments. This type of company is rare and is not discussed here.

[2] In the United Kingdom, a *unit trust* is an open-end investment company (described in a later section).

$10,000,000 worth of bonds, place them in a unit investment trust, and issue 10,000 shares. Each share might be offered to the public for $1035. When all the shares have been sold, the sponsor would have received $1035 × 10,000 = $10,350,000. This is enough to cover the $10,000,000 cost of the bonds, leaving $350,000 for selling expenses and profit. Markups (or load charges) of this sort range from less than 1% for short-term trusts to 3.5% for long-term trusts.

Secondary Market

Typically, an investor who purchases shares of a unit investment trust is not required to hold the shares for the entire life of the trust. Instead, the shares may usually be sold back to the trust at net asset value, calculated on the basis of bid prices for the assets in the portfolio.[3] That is, the market value of the securities in the portfolio is determined, using dealers' bid quotations. Since unit investment trusts do not have any liabilities, this amount is divided by the number of shares outstanding to obtain the net asset value per share.

When a share is presented for redemption, the trustee may sell one or more securities to raise the required cash. Alternatively, it is possible that a secondary market is maintained by the sponsor of the trust. In this situation, investors can sell their shares back to the sponsor. Furthermore, investors who did not participate in the initial sale can subsequently purchase shares; typically, the sponsor's selling price in the secondary market is equal to the net asset value of the securities in the portfolio (based on the dealers' asked prices) plus a load charge equal to that in effect at the time the trust was created.

☐ 20.2.2 Managed Companies

Whereas a unit investment trust has no board of directors and no portfolio manager, *managed investment companies* have both. Since they are organized as corporations (a few are limited partnerships), a managed investment company has a board of directors that is elected by its shareholders. In turn, the board commonly hires a firm—the "management company"—to manage the company's assets for an annual fee that is typically based (at least in part) on the total market value of the assets. These management companies may be independent firms, investment advisers, firms associated with brokerage firms, or insurance companies. Often the management company is the business entity (for example, a subsidiary of a brokerage firm) that started and promoted the investment company. One management company may have contracts to manage a number of investment companies, each of which is a separate corporation with its own board of directors.

Annual management fees average about .60% (they can range from less

---

[3] Dealers in fixed-income securities generally quote both bid and asked prices. The bid price is the amount the dealer will pay for a security; the asked price is the amount an investor must pay to purchase the security.

than .25% to over 1%) of the market value of the investment company's total assets, with the percentage sliding downward as the assets increase. Some funds provide "incentive compensation," where the better the fund's investment performance, the higher the fee paid to the management company.

In addition to the fee paid by an investment company to its management company, there are administrative and custodial expenses. These services are usually provided by the management company, but the costs are charged to the investment company. For the typical investment company, such annual expenses are roughly .50% of the market value of its total assets. Many investment companies require their management company to cover all expenses over a specified amount, effectively limiting total expenses.[4]

Closed-End Investment Companies

Unlike unit investment trusts, *closed-end investment companies* (or closed-end funds) do not stand ready to purchase their own shares whenever one of their owners decides to sell them. Instead, their shares are traded either on an organized exchange or in the over-the-counter market. Thus, an investor who wants to buy or sell shares of a closed-end fund would simply place an order with a broker, just as if the investor wanted to buy or sell shares of IBM.

Most closed-end funds have unlimited lives. Dividends and interest received by a closed-end fund from the securities in its portfolio are paid out to its shareholders, as are any net realized capital gains. However, most funds allow (and encourage) the reinvestment of such payments. The fund keeps the money and sends the investor additional shares based on the net asset value per share at that time. For example, consider a closed-end fund that has just declared a dividend of $1 per share. If its net asset value were $15 per share, a holder of 30 shares would have a choice of receiving either $30 (30 × $1) or 2 shares ($30/$15).

Being a corporation, closed-end funds can issue new shares not only through reinvestment plans but also with public stock offerings. However, this is done infrequently, and the fund's capital structure is closed most of the time.[5]

Most closed-end funds can repurchase their own shares in the open market, although it is seldom done. Whenever a fund's market price falls substantially below net asset value, a repurchase will increase the fund's net asset value per share. For example, if net asset value were $20 per share at a time when the fund's shares could be purchased in the open market (say, on the New York Stock Exchange) for $16 per share, the managers of

---

[4] Due to a 1980 ruling (Rule 12b-1) by the Securities and Exchange Commission, open-end funds may choose to pay a distribution fee annually. This fee, sometimes being as much as 2% of the market value of total assets, goes for advertising and promoting the fund to prospective purchasers. The alleged benefit to the current owners of the fund is that the subsequent increased size of the portfolio will bring with it certain economies of scale; early indications are that such a benefit is not being realized. See Stephen P. Ferris and Don M. Chance, "The Effect of 12b-1 Plans on Mutual Fund Expense Ratios: A Note," *Journal of Finance* 42, no. 4 (September 1987):1077–82.

[5] Due to restrictions in the Investment Company Act of 1940, few closed-end investment companies have any interest-bearing liabilities outstanding (that is, they typically have only a small amount of current liabilities outstanding).

the fund could sell $20 worth of securities from the fund's portfolio, buy back one of the fund's outstanding shares, and have $4 left over. If the $4 was used to buy securities for the fund, the net asset value per share would increase, with the size of the increase depending on, in addition to the number of shares repurchased and their repurchase price, the number of remaining shares.

The market prices of the shares of closed-end funds are published daily in the financial press, provided the funds are listed on an exchange or traded actively in the over-the-counter market. However, their net asset values are only published weekly, based on closing market prices for securities in their portfolios as of the previous Friday. Figure 20.1 provides an example. Both the net asset value and the last price at which the fund's shares traded on the day in question are shown (if no trade price is available, the last dealer's asked price is indicated). The final column indicates the difference between each fund's stock price and its net asset value. If this difference is positive (meaning the stock price is greater than the NAV), the fund's shares are said to be selling at a premium. Conversely, if this difference is negative (meaning the stock price is less than the NAV), the fund's shares are said to be selling at a discount. For example, Figure 20.1 indicates that the France Fund was selling at a discount while the Korea Fund was selling for a

FIGURE 20–1
Listing of closed-end funds.

Source: Reprinted by permission of *The Wall Street Journal* © Dow Jones & Company, Inc. (December 5, 1988): p. C19 and (December 7, 1988): p. C20.

PUBLICLY TRADED FUNDS

Friday, December 2, 1988

Following is a weekly listing of unaudited net asset values of publicly traded investment fund shares, reported by the companies as of Friday's close. Also shown is the closing listed market price or a dealer-to-dealer asked price of each fund's shares, with the percentage of difference.

Fund Name	Stock Exch.	N.A. Value	Stock Price	% Diff.
Diversified Common Stock Funds				
Adams Express	NYSE	15.86	14¾	– 7.00
Baker Fentress	NYSE	25.14	20⅝	– 17.96
Blue Chip Value	NYSE	7.06	5⅞	– 16.78
Clemente Global Gro	NYSE	b8.77	7	– 20.18
Gemini II Capital	NYSE	17.10	12½	– 26.90
Gemini II Income	NYSE	9.81	12⅞	+ 31.24
General Amer Invest	NYSE	g16.92	14⅛	– 16.52
Global Growth Capital	NYSE	8.60	7¾	– 9.88
Global Growth Incme	NYSE	9.50	9¼	– 2.63
Growth Stock Outlook	NYSE	9.89	9½	– 3.94
Lehman Corp.	NYSE	14.06	11¾	– 16.43
Liberty All-Star Eqty	NYSE	8.27	7⅜	– 10.82
Niagara Share Corp.	NYSE	14.80	11⅞	– 19.76
Nicholas-Applegate	NYSE	8.28	6¾	– 18.48
Quest For Value Cap	NYSE	11.30	8¼	– 26.99
Quest For Value Inco	NYSE	11.78	10⅜	– 11.93
Royce Value Trust	NYSE	9.57	8⅜	– 12.49
Schafer Value Trust	NYSE	8.79	7⅜	– 16.10
Source Capital	NYSE	36.81	36	– 2.20
Tri-Continental Corp.	NYSE	23.16	19¾	– 14.72
Worldwide Value	NYSE	20.18	17	– 15.76
Zweig Fund	NYSE	10.15	10¼	+ 0.99
Closed End Bond Funds				
CIM High Yield Secs	AMEX	9.56	9⅛	– 4.55
Franklin Universal Tr	NYSE	b9.24	9⅜	+ 1.46
Zenith Income Fund	NYSE	8.94	9⅞	+ 10.46

CLOSED-END BOND FUNDS

Tuesday, December 6, 1988

Unaudited net asset values of closed-end bond fund shares, reported by the companies as of Friday, December 2, 1988. Also shown is the closing listed market price or a dealer-to-dealer asked price of each fund's shares, with percentage of difference.

Fund Name	Stock Exch.	N.A. Value	Stock Price	% Diff.
Bond Funds				
ACM Govt Inco Fund	NYSE	10.68	11	+ 3.00
ACM Govt Oppor Fd	NYSE	9.31	9⅛	– 1.99
ACM Govt Securities	NYSE	10.55	10⅜	– 1.66
ACM Govt Spectrum	NYSE	a8.95	8¾	– 2.23
ACM Managed Inco	NYSE	9.13	10⅛	+ 10.90
AMEV Securities	NYSE	10.29	10¼	– 0.39
American Capital Bond	NYSE	b21.11	20⅞	– 1.11
American Capital Inco	NYSE	9.11	9⅛	+ 0.16
American Govt Income	NYSE	a7.01	8	+ 14.12
American Govt Portf	NYSE	a8.96	9⅞	+ 10.21
Blackstone Inco Tr	NYSE	9.12	9⅝	+ 5.54
Blackstone Target Tr	NYSE	9.39	10	+ 6.50
Bunker Hill Income	NYSE	17.79	16¾	– 5.85
CIGNA High Income	NYSE	9.16	9¾	+ 6.44
CNA Income Shares	NYSE	11.39	11⅞	+ 4.26
Circle Income Shares	OTC	12.12	12¾	+ 5.20
Colonial Int High Inco	NYSE	9.19	9⅛	– 0.71
Comstock Ptr Strategy	NYSE	9.68	9⅜	– 3.15
Current Income Shares	NYSE	11.84	11⅛	– 6.04
Dean Witter Govt Inco	NYSE	9.33	9¼	– 0.86
Dreyfus Strt Gov Inco	NYSE	11.30	10⅞	– 3.76
1838 Bond-Deb Trad	NYSE	19.78	18	– 9.00
Excelsior Inco Shares	NYSE	16.92	15¼	– 9.87
First Boston Inco Fd	NYSE	8.61	8½	– 1.28
First Boston Strategic	NYSE	10.93	11¼	+ 2.93

FIGURE 20–1 *(Continued)*

PUBLICLY TRADED FUNDS

	Flexible Portfolio Funds				
America's All Seasn	OTC	5.75	6¾	+	17.39
Zweig Total Return Fd	NYSE	9.23	9⅜	+	1.57
	Specialized Equity and Convertible Funds				
American Capital Conv	NYSE	22.68	21¾	–	4.10
ASA Ltd	NYSE	bc55.83	38¾	–	30.59
Asia Pacific	NYSE	8.64	6½	–	24.77
Bancroft Convertible	AMEX	z	z		z
Bergstrom Capital	AMEX	49.76	47¾	–	4.04
BGR Precious Metals	TOR	be12.12	10	–	17.49
Brazil	NYSE	11.85	8⅜	–	29.32
CNV Holdings Capital	NYSE	8.59	4¼	–	50.52
CNV Holdings Income	NYSE	9.55	11⅜	+	19.11
Castle Convertible	AMEX	21.62	19⅜	–	10.38
Central Fund Canada	AMEX	b5.87	5⅛	–	12.69
Central Securities	AMEX	11.14	9¼	–	16.97
Couns Tandem Secs	NYSE	8.12	5⅞	–	27.65
Cypress Fund	AMEX	9.11	6¾	–	25.91
Duff&Phelps Sel Utils	NYSE	7.72	8	+	3.63
Ellsw Conv Gr&Inc	AMEX	8.26	7⅞	–	4.66
Engex	AMEX	11.75	8¼	–	29.79
Financ'l News Compos	NYSE	16.29	14	–	14.06
1stAustralia	AMEX	10.92	8¾	–	19.87
First Financial Fund	NYSE	8.67	6⅞	–	20.70
First Iberian	AMEX	9.57	7⅞	–	17.71
France Fund	NYSE	b11.64	9½	–	18.38
Gabelli Equity Trust	NYSE	11.21	9¾	–	13.02
Germany Fund	NYSE	8.12	7⅜	–	9.17
H&Q Healthcare Inv	NYSE	7.67	6	–	21.77
Hampton Utils Tr Cap	AMEX	b10.06	8½	–	15.51
Hampton Utils Tr Pref	AMEX	b48.92	46⅜	–	5.20
Helvetia Fund	NYSE	11.18	9⅜	–	16.14
India Growth Fund	NYSE	f12.48	8⅞	–	28.89
Italy Fund	NYSE	b10.28	8⅜	–	18.53
Korea Fund	NYSE	15.72	23⅝	+	50.29
Malaysia Fund	NYSE	9.03	7⅛	–	21.10
Mexico Fund	NYSE	b8.37	5¾	–	31.30
Morgan Grenf SmCap	NYSE	8.45	7¼	–	14.20
Patriot Prem Div Fd	NYSE	z	z		z
Petrol & Resources	NYSE	24.35	22⅜	–	8.11
Pilgrim Regional	NYSE	9.72	7½	–	22.84
Rl Estate Sec Inco Fd	AMEX	8.91	8⅝	–	3.20
Regional Fin Shrs Inv	NYSE	7.82	6¼	–	20.08
Scandinavia Fund	AMEX	8.67	6¼	–	27.91
Scudder New Asia	NYSE	12.20	9⅛	–	25.20
Spain Fund	NYSE	11.50	10¼	–	10.87
Taiwan Fund	AMEX	bh36.30	32⅞	–	9.44
TCW Convertible Secs	NYSE	b8.08	7½	–	7.18
Templeton Em Mkts	AMEX	b9.57	7¾	–	19.02
Templeton Value Fund	NYSE	b9.26	9⅞	+	6.64
Thai Fund	NYSE	10.87	12¾	+	17.30
United Kingdom Fund	NYSE	11.50	9¼	–	19.57
Z-Seven	OTC	d13.18	15½	+	17.60

b-As of Thursday's close. c-Translated at Commercial Rand exchange rate. d-NAV reflects $3.09 per share for taxes. e–In Canadian Dollars.f-As of Wednesday's close.g–11/25/88 Nav:16.51, Mkt:13¾, %diff: –16.72.h–effective 12/1/88 trading on NYSE. z-Not available.

CLOSED-END BOND FUNDS

Ft Dearborn Income	NYSE	14.58	13¾	–	5.69
John Hancock Income	NYSE	15.55	14⅝	–	5.95
John Hancock Invest	NYSE	20.87	20	–	4.17
Hatteras Income Secs	NYSE	16.15	15⅝	–	3.25
High Income Adv Tr	NYSE	9.18	9½	+	3.49
High Income Adv II	NYSE	9.38	9⅜	–	0.05
High Yield Income Fd	NYSE	8.89	8¾	–	1.57
High Yield Plus Fund	NYSE	a9.08	8⅝	–	5.01
INA Investments	NYSE	17.64	17⅜	–	1.50
Independence Sq	OTC	16.57	16¾	+	1.09
Intercapital Income	NYSE	19.14	20⅝	+	7.76
Kemper High Inco Tr	NYSE	10.86	11¾	+	8.20
Kemper Inter Govt Tr	NYSE	9.27	9⅛	–	1.56
Lincoln Natl Dir Place	NYSE	27.62	24¼	–	12.20
Lomas Mtge Sec Fd	NYSE	11.14	12⅛	+	8.84
MFS Gov Mkts Inco	NYSE	9.15	10⅛	+	10.66
MFS Inco & Oppor Tr	NYSE	9.69	9⅞	+	1.91
MFS Intermed Inco Tr	NYSE	9.28	9¼	–	0.32
MFS Multimkt Inco Tr	NYSE	9.08	10⅛	+	11.51
MFS Multimkt Ttl Ret	NYSE	9.33	9	–	3.54
Montgomery Street	NYSE	18.71	18⅜	–	1.79
	Convertible Bond Funds				
Lincoln Natl Convert	NYSE	13.51	11¾	–	13.03
Putnam Hi Inco Conv	NYSE	8.37	7¾	–	7.41
	International Bond Funds				
First Australia Prime	AMEX	11.34	9 15/16	–	12.37
Global Government	NYSE	9.38	9⅜	–	0.05
Global Income Plus	NYSE	9.78	10	+	2.25
Global Yield Fund	NYSE	10.32	10⅛	–	1.89
Kleinwort Benson Aust	NYSE	12.14	11½	–	5.27
Templtn Glbl Gov Inco	NYSE	9.25	10⅛	+	9.46
Templeton Global Inco	NYSE	9.23	9⅜	+	1.57
World Income Fund	AMEX	9.93	9⅞	–	0.55
	Municipal Bond Funds				
Allstate Muni Inco Op	NYSE	9.43	10¼	+	8.70
Allstate Muni Inco Tr	NYSE	10.31	10¼	–	0.58
Allstate Muni Inco II	NYSE	9.68	9⅝	–	0.57
Colonial Muni Inco Tr	NYSE	8.97	9¾	+	8.70
Dreyfus Cal Muni Inco	AMEX	9.13	10¼	+	12.27
Dreyfus Muni Inco	AMEX	9.24	10	+	8.23
Dreyfus NY Muni Inco	AMEX	9.14	10	+	9.41
Dreyfus Strategic Muni	NYSE	9.93	10⅜	+	4.48
Kemper Muni Inco Tr	NYSE	11.14	12	+	7.72
MFS Muni Income Tr	NYSE	9.19	9⅞	+	7.45
Muni Insured Fd Inc	AMEX	9.82	9⅞	+	0.56
MuniVest Fund Inc	AMEX	9.34	10	+	7.07
New York Tax-Exmpt	AMEX	9.89	9⅝	–	2.68
Nuveen CA Muni Inco	NYSE	11.38	11⅜	–	0.04
Nuveen CA Muni Val	NYSE	9.72	9⅞	+	1.59
Nuveen Muni Inco	NYSE	11.26	11¼	–	0.09
Nuveen Muni Value	NYSE	9.74	9¾	+	0.10
Nuveen NY Muni Inco	AMEX	11.28	11½	+	1.95
Nuveen NY Muni Val	NYSE	9.83	10	+	1.73
Nuveen Prem Inco	NYSE	13.92	14½	+	4.17
VanKmpn M CA Muni	AMEX	9.05	9⅞	+	9.12
VanKmpn Mer Muni	NYSE	9.31	10	+	7.41

a-Ex-dividend. b-Fully diluted.
Source: Lipper Analytical Services, Denver Colorado.

premium (these two investment companies are known as "country funds," specializing in French and Korean stocks, respectively).

Open-End Investment Companies

An investment company that stands ready at all times to purchase its own shares at or near their net asset value is termed an *open-end investment*

company (or open-end fund). Most of these companies, commonly known as *mutual funds*, also continuously offer new shares to the public for a price at or near their net asset values.

Some open-end companies, known as *no-load funds*, sell their shares at a price equal to net asset value. Others, known as *load funds*, offer shares through brokers or other selling organizations, which add a percentage *load charge* to the net asset value. The percentage charged is usually smaller, the greater the amount invested, and by law cannot exceed 8.5% of the amount invested. For example, a selling organization receiving $1000 to be invested in a fund might retain as much as $85, leaving $915 to be used to purchase the fund's shares at the current net asset value per share. While this is usually described as a load charge of 8.5%, it is actually equal to 9.3% = $85/$915 of the amount ultimately invested. Load charges of this magnitude are levied by many funds for small purchases.[6]

When mutual fund shareholders want to sell their shares, they usually receive an amount equal to the fund's net asset value times the number of shares sold. However, a few funds charge a *redemption fee* (also known as a back-end load, or exit fee, or contingent deferred sales charge), which may run as high as 6% of the fund's net asset value. Typically, those funds that do charge such a fee will lower the percentage charged if the shareholder owns the shares over a long period. Thus, investors selling their shares within six months of purchase might have to pay a 6% fee, whereas investors selling their shares after owning them for five or more years might not have to pay any fee; for those investors selling between six months and five years, a sliding-scale fee may be applicable.

As is discussed later, the performance of non-load funds as a whole does not differ in any notable way from that of load funds. This is not surprising. The load charge, which goes to the selling organization, represents the cost of education and persuasion. Mail-order firms often sell items for less than stores. Salespersons who work in stores and those who sell mutual funds provide a service and require compensation. Buyers who consider such services worth less than they cost can and should avoid paying for them.

Figure 20.2 shows a portion of the quotations for mutual funds provided in the financial press following each business day.[7] The net asset value, based on closing prices for the fund's securities on the day in question, is shown first. This is followed by the "offer" price—the net asset value plus the load charge applicable to the smallest possible purchase; for no-load funds, this column contains the letters *NL*. The final column indicates the difference (in dollars) between the day's net asset value per share and that computed at the close of the previous trading day.

Figure 20.3 shows the weekly quotations that appear for a special type of mutual fund known as a money market fund. Such funds invest in short-term, fixed-income securities such as Treasury bills, commercial paper, and bank certificates of deposit. Next to the name of such a fund is shown the

---

[6] Funds that have a load charge of 3.5% or less are often referred to as *low-load funds*.

[7] Funds that are listed under a name in boldface type have a common management company that is associated with that name; for example, note all the funds listed under Smith Barney in Figure 20.2.

MUTUAL FUND QUOTATIONS

Wednesday, December 7, 1988

Price ranges for investment companies, as quoted by the National Association of Securities Dealers. NAV stands for net asset value per share; the offering includes net asset value plus maximum sales charge, if any.

FIGURE 20–2

Listing of mutual funds.

Source: Reprinted by permission of *The Wall Street Journal* © Dow Jones & Company, Inc. (December 8, 1988): p. C20.

MONEY MARKET MUTUAL FUNDS

The following quotations, collected by the National Association of Securities Dealers Inc.., represent the average of portfolio maturities and dollar-weighted annualized yields and dollar-weighted portfolio maturities ending Wednesday, December 7, 1988. Yields are based on actual dividends to shareholders.

Fund	Avg. Mat.	7Day Yld.	e7Day Yld.	Assets
AAL MoneyMkt	32	7.91	8.23	73.3
AARP Money	35	7.48	7.76	251.2
ActvAsst GovSc	40	7.74	8.04	251.2
ActvAsst Money	43	8.02	8.34	2691.2
ActvAsst TxFr	32	5.59	5.75	1073.5
AlexBCash Gvt	39	7.83	8.14	234.4
AlexBCash Prm	30	8.03	8.36	954.8
Alliance Capital	41	7.51	7.80	1793.7
AllianceGvt Res	34	7.46	7.74	359.6
AllianceTE Res	45	5.40	5.55	674.4
AllianceTE CA	39	5.32	5.46	92.1
Alliance TE NY	39	4.62	4.73	42.6
AMA PrimePrt	52	7.87	7.39	68.4
AMA TreasPort	37	7.37	7.38	15.9
AmCap Resrv a	24	8.20	8.55	516.8
Amer Natl MM	19	7.69	7.99	13.0
AMEV Money	17	7.50	7.78	75.7
ArchFdMM clA	26	8.07	8.40	299.2
ArchFd TE A	32	5.62	5.78	84.3
ASO Prime	43	8.15	8.47	235.1
ASO US Trs	36	7.99	8.31	68.1
AT Ohio Tax Fr	44	5.40	5.55	260.2
AutomCash Mgt	41	8.15	8.49	965.7
AutomGvt MTr	35	7.89	8.21	2527.1
Axe Hghtn MM	14	7.63	7.93	115.0
Babson Prime	29	7.72	8.02	348.8
BayshreC Rs	55	8.16	8.50	53.6
BayshreUS T	81	7.82	8.13	46.4
Bedf RBB GOB	24	7.62	7.91	45.2
Bedf RBB MM	27	7.79	8.10	48.2
Bedf RBB TFB	42	6.15	6.29	363.4
BenhamCal TF	26	5.43	5.58	84.9
BenhamNatl TF	31	5.61	5.77	15.2
BirrWilson MFd	6	7.41	7.79	327.2
Boston Co Cash	27	7.51	7.87	43.4
BostonCo Gvt	64	7.58	7.87	148.7
BostonCo Mass	55	5.28	5.42	105.7
Bull&Bear DRs	55	7.55	7.84	89.3
CalvrtSocInv a	44	3.98	8.31	794.4
CalvrtTF Rsrv	44	5.95	6.13	
CAM Fund	(z)			
CapCash MgtTr	15	7.82	8.13	3.3
Cap PreservVm	46	7.34	7.61	2325.4
Cap PreservVm 2	1	7.68	7.98	565.0

Fund	Avg. Mat.	7Day Yld.	e7Day Yld.	Assets
FedMaster Trst	44	8.21		2299.6
FedShtUS Gov	29	8.22	8.56	579.9
FedrTaxFree c	59	5.57		2687.2
FFB Govt	37	8.06	8.39	558.2
FFB USGovt	40	7.97	8.29	228.0
FFB TxFrMM	41	5.57	5.72	142.1
FFB USTreas	42	7.88	8.19	134.8
FidelCal TaxFr	48	5.36	5.51	670.9
FidelCash Resv	43	7.95	8.28	10877.0
FidelDivIncm b	32	7.78	8.09	3057.4
FidelDly MM Prt	25	8.01	8.34	587.1
FidDly Tax Ex	37	5.23	5.37	224.0
FidDly US Tr	2	7.86	8.18	434.0
FidUS Govt Res	24	7.68	7.98	1596.6
Fincl Resv	1	8.11	8.45	344.7
FnclTxF Money	27	8.21	8.56	1067.6
FidMM Domstc	20	8.05	8.38	586.9
FidMM Govmmt	34	5.16	5.30	633.1
FidMass TaxFr	39	6.05	6.24	143.0
FidNJ TFMM	67	4.92	5.04	711.1
FidNYTxF MM	40	5.96	6.14	103.6
FidelPA TFMM	37	5.38	5.53	3306.6
FidTaxExmpt c	29	7.89	8.21	353.7
FnclDlvInc Shr	45	8.19	8.53	437.7
FstAm Money	30	5.35	5.50	31.3
FstBstn Money	22	8.09	8.43	123.2
FstBstn CpCsh	77	8.37	8.72	221.3
FirstInstTax Ex	25	5.46	5.60	39.7
FstInvCshMgt f	17	8.03	8.33	212.7
FirstLakeshr Gov	18	7.83	7.83	141.0
FirstLkshr MM	39	7.70	8.00	175.3
FstLkshr TE		5.38	5.52	147.5
FstTrust TaxFr	(z)			
First Variable	23	7.54	7.83	379.1
FlagInTF Cash	41	5.67	5.83	255.1
Flex Fund MM	29	8.38	8.73	211.7
F+ Wash	29	7.72	8.01	64.2
Founders MMk	22	7.72	8.02	57.0
FN NetwkTF	46	5.50	5.69	77.7
Frnk CATEMF	45	5.53	5.69	845.6
Frnk FedMF	1	7.42	7.70	155.7
FrnkIFT Money	31	8.47		141.1
FrnkInInv MM	12	8.66		35.2
FrnkInMnyFd a	26	7.88	8.20	1417.0
Frnk NYTEMF	85	5.01	5.14	54.2
FrnkIn TaxEx c	52	5.25	5.39	213.1
Fund For Tax	53	5.26	5.40	44.1
FundGov Invst	14	7.56	7.68	631.2
FundSource Gv	24	7.68	7.98	109.2
FundSource MT	25	8.12	8.45	145.4
FundSrce Wash	27	7.85	8.16	127.5

Fund	Avg. Mat.	7Day Yld.	e7Day Yld.	Assets
LazardInst Trs	6	7.90	8.21	43.4
Lazard CashM	19	8.02	8.34	421.0
LazardInst Pr	20	8.24	8.58	127.0
Lazard Govt	11	8.02	8.34	467.0
Lazard TxFree	30	5.58	5.74	294.0
LeggMasnCsh	34	7.68	7.98	478.3
LeggMas TE		(z)		
LexGvtScMM	42	7.37	7.65	18.3
LexMoneyMkt a	48	7.34	7.61	193.9
LexTaxFrDiv c	31	4.78	4.90	87.1
LibertyUS Govt	37	7.62	7.91	1331.3
LiquidCapitl Tr	27	8.05	8.37	1210.8
LiquidCashTR f	2	8.59		626.5
LiquidGrn TxFr	53	5.36	5.50	60.3
LiquidGreen Tr	35	7.92	8.24	313.3
LordAbbet Cash	29	7.63	7.93	229.4
LuthBrMon Mkt	27	7.64	7.93	291.6
MacKay Sh MM	36	7.95	8.27	72.3
MAP GovtFund	35	7.64	7.93	30.0
Mariner Cash	47	8.18	8.52	648.4
Mariner Gov	21	7.95	8.27	205.5
Mariner NYTF	95	4.97	5.09	120.1
Mariner TxFree	34	5.75	5.92	78.7
MarinerUS Trs	34	7.84	8.15	98.8
MassCashMgt a	34	7.70	7.65	703.6
MassCshM Trst	30	7.54	7.87	54.0
MassM TE	72	7.72	8.01	44.6
MassM MMFd	53	4.71	5.03	10.1
Mass TE MM	59	7.44	7.72	232.4
McDonald MM	57			
McDonald TxE	73	5.09	5.22	110.2
Meritor MM Fd	(z)			
MerrLGovFd a	(z)			
MerrLInstFd af	(z)			
MerrInst TxEx	(z)			
MerrL RdyAst a	(z)			
MerrL RetRsv a	(z)			
Merrl USA Gr	23	7.70	8.00	75.9
MetLf State St	29	4.68	4.79	90.4
Met NYTF	43	6.43	6.70	134.9
MFS LifeMM	45	5.28	5.42	373.5
MidwstGrp TF	65	6.70		99.3
Midwst Incm Tr	37	7.25	7.51	114.0
MnyMgtP Govt	39	7.41	7.69	21.2
MnyMgtP Pr	32	7.84	8.15	91.5
MnyMgtPl TxF	26	7.88	8.01	83.0
MoneyMktMgt f	42	7.97	8.28	188.6
Money Mkt Trst	38	8.15		1540.5
Monitor Gov	35	7.79	8.10	104.1
Monitor MM	37	8.17	8.51	290.3
Monitor TF	34	5.51	5.66	76.6
MorganKeegn f	8	7.29	7.56	89.4

Fund	Avg. Mat.	7Day Yld.	e7Day Yld.	Assets
TRowePxEx	28	5.49	5.64	1181.0
TRowePUST	24	7.32	7.59	281.0
Safeco MnyMk f	34	8.04	8.34	144.9
Safeco TF MM	34	5.58	5.72	39.3
StClair Prime	26	8.00	8.32	70.1
StClair TxFr	24	5.18	5.31	35.8
SBSF MM Fd	45	8.32	8.67	24.9
ScuddCashInv f	38	7.84	8.15	1462.3
ScuddCaTFM	43	5.33	5.47	58.9
ScuddNYTFM	43	4.98	5.11	34.4
ScuddrGvt Mny	31	7.15	7.17	147.3
ScuddrTaxFr cf	46	5.35	5.32	379.1
ScuddTreas Tr	38	8.12	8.46	59.7
Seagate Prme	55	7.73	8.03	120.0
Seagate Tax Ex	52	5.54	5.69	63.8
Seagate Treas	58	7.24	7.50	143.4
Secur Cash Fd	30	7.76	8.06	52.3
Select Mny Mkt	(z)			
Selig CalTE	4	4.93	5.05	14.4
SelgmnCM Prm	28	7.67	7.97	329.0
SeligmnGov Prt	7	7.47	7.76	26.8
Sentinel Cash	38	7.66	7.65	70.0
Shrsn Cal Div	32	5.51	5.66	302.6
ShrsnDailyDiv f	40	7.88	8.19	11658.6
ShrsnDaily TxF	58	5.50	5.66	3291.9
ShrsnGovt Agen	57	7.51	7.79	3477.4
Shrsn NY Div	57	5.01	5.14	229.8
ShorTerm Govt	57	7.58	7.86	238.6
ShorTerm Asset	15	7.85	8.16	106.3
ShorTerm MM	44	7.84	8.16	743.0
Sigma Moneyfd	11	7.82	8.13	32.5
ShFrmBur Csh	41	7.13	7.38	17.3
SP IFGMuniCA	(z)			
SP IFGMuniFd	(z)			
SP IFGMuniNY	(z)			
S-P IFG FedFd	43	5.71	5.87	1567.1
S-P IFG TFund	23	8.22	8.56	1623.0
S-P IFG TempC	28	8.15	8.48	1866.1
S-P IFG TempCF	31	8.47	8.83	525.3
Standby Reserv	36	7.90	8.21	373.5
StandbyTE Res	36	5.44	5.59	78.2
SteinRoeCsh Rs	35	7.84	8.15	982.5
SteinRoe Govt	37	7.65	7.97	56.5

a-Yield may include capital gains and losses. b-Account size varies yield due to fixed charges. c-Primarily federally tax-exempt securities. e-Effective 7-day yield. f-As of previous day. z-Unavailable.

FIGURE 20-3

Listing of money market mutual funds.

Source: Reprinted by permission of *The Wall Street Journal* © Dow Jones & Company, Inc. (December 8, 1988): p. C21.

average maturity of its holdings, the annual yield based on what was earned over the last seven days, the compounded annual yield based on what was earned over the last seven days, and the aggregate market value of its assets. Not shown, but an important factor in deciding in which money market fund to invest, is the degree of safety (that is, default risk) associated with the assets held by each fund.

A number of institutions that are similar to investment companies exist. The next section describes some of the more important types.

20.3 SIMILAR TYPES OF INVESTMENTS

☐ 20.3.1 Fixed and Variable Annuities

Fixed Annuities

A *fixed annuity* is a contract in which a life insurance company promises to pay the investor a fixed dollar amount on a regular (generally monthly) basis. The size and number of these payments will depend on how much money the investor gives the insurance company and the size of an up-front fee (if any) that is charged. Also important are the investor's age and the annuity option that the investor chooses.

One option the investor may choose is a life annuity, where fixed dollar payments are provided regularly until the investor's death. Another option is a joint and last survivor annuity, where fixed dollar payments of a lesser amount continue on a regular basis until both the investor and spouse have died. A third option is a period certain annuity (or fixed period annuity), where fixed dollar payments are made on a regular basis for a prespecified number of years (perhaps 5, 10, 15, or 20); if the investor dies before then, subsequent payments are made to the investor's beneficiary. A fourth option, known as a life annuity with a period certain, is a combination of the first and third options. With this option, the investor receives regular fixed dollar payments until death. However, if death should occur before some prespecified number of years have elapsed, then payments will continue until that number of years has elapsed.

Variable Annuities

Rather than selecting one of these types of fixed annuities, the investor could select a *variable annuity*. With this kind of annuity, the regular payments are not of a prespecified size but instead are dependent directly on the performance of a portfolio managed by the insurance company.

For example, assume that the present value of a fixed life annuity of $1 per month for a particular individual is $100 (based on an assumed interest rate of 4% and the life expectancy of the individual). In return for giving the insurance company $50,000, the individual can select a fixed life annuity that pays $500 ($50,000/$100) per month (assuming no up-front fee). Alternatively, the $50,000 can be used to buy 125 "annuity units" of a variable annuity, assuming each annuity unit is worth $4 at the time of purchase

(note that 125 = $500/$4). The initial monthly check is still $500, but there-after the amount would be linked to the value of an annuity unit. So, if in a subsequent month the value of a unit rises to $4.10, then that month's check would rise to $512.50 (125 × $4.10); however, if the value of a unit falls to $3.90, then the check would be for $487.50 (125 × $3.90).

The monthly value of an annuity unit is linked to the month-end value of an investment fund in a straightforward manner. The percentage change in the value of the fund—including dividends, interest received, capital gains and losses (realized or not), less expenses (such as an annual fee of around 2%)—is computed. From this, the interest rate assumed in the original fixed annuity valuation (4%) is subtracted. The value of each annuity unit is then increased (or decreased) by the resulting percentage. In effect, the insurance company pays itself a dividend equal to the amount required to cover the interest the company assumed it would receive when the annuities were priced; this dividend is paid no matter what the experience of the fund might have been. Thus, the risk is shifted from the insurance company to the purchasers of the annuities.

In the example, if the fund had a return of +14%, then the value of an annuity unit would go up by $.40 = $4.00 × (14% − 4%) to $4.40 and the investor would receive a check for $5.50 (125 × $4.40). Then, if in the next month the return on the fund were −6%, the value of an annuity unit would go down by $.44 = $4.40 × (−6% − 4%) to $3.96, and the investor would receive a check for $495 (= 125 × $3.96).

In order to sell a variable annuity, the insurance company must set up a separate account, which may be invested directly in a diversified portfolio or simply used to purchase shares in an open-end mutual fund—usually one run by the same company.

Deferred Annuities

The previous discussion described an immediate annuity, where the investor purchases a variable (or fixed) annuity with a single payment. However, the investor has the option of making a series of periodic payments (a deferred annuity), receiving shares in the separate account in return. These shares, known as *accumulation units*, could ultimately be used to purchase either a fixed or variable annuity; the values of the accumulation units for a large number of separate accounts are reported weekly in the financial press (for example, in *Barron's*).

The choice between a variable annuity and a fixed annuity depends on how willing a person is to take on added risk to get a higher expected return. Although professional advisers can help assess the magnitudes of the risk and expected returns that are involved, the final decision must rest with the individual who will bear the risk.

☐ **20.3.2   Commingled Funds**

Banks and insurance companies invest money for individuals and organizations. Banks manage personal trust funds; both banks and insurance companies manage individual retirement funds. Any such fund can be invested

on an individual basis, with specific securities selected and held in a separate account. This is often done for large accounts, but to capture economies of scale, small accounts are often commingled, allowing joint participation in one or more large pools of securities.

The vehicle utilized in this process is the *commingled fund*. In form (but not in law), it is similar to an open-end mutual fund. The securities in the fund are valued periodically, and the total value divided by the current number of units determines a net asset value per unit. On any valuation date, money from an account may be used to purchase units at this value. Alternatively, units purchased at an earlier date may be redeemed at the current net asset value.

A bank or insurance company may offer several commingled funds. One fund may hold only short-term money market instruments, whereas another holds just long-term bonds and yet another holds just common stocks. A commingled fund investing in mortgages may also be offered, as may one investing in real property.[8] When a menu of this sort is available, money from a given trust or retirement account can be invested in two or more commingled funds.

□ 20.3.3 Real Estate Investment Trusts

Real estate investment trusts (REITs), although not classified as investment companies for legal purposes, are similar to closed-end funds in that they serve as a conduit for earnings on certain types of investments, passing them on to their shareholders and avoiding corporate taxation.

REITs must invest primarily in real estate or loans secured by real estate. They can obtain funds by issuing stock, bonds, and even warrants. They can also borrow from banks, issue mortgages on some or all of their property, and issue commercial paper. The stocks of many REITs are listed on major exchanges, and thus price and volume quotations on them are given regularly in the financial press.

Like managed investment companies, REITs hire a management firm for a fee—typically about 1% of the value of assets per year. Most trusts are affiliated with banks, life insurance companies, or mortgage firms, which create them and then serve as their investment managers.

There are two major types of REITs. *Mortgage trusts* invest primarily in mortgages as well as construction and development loans. The latter, which constitute the bulk of the assets of many trusts, are loans made to the builder or developer of a project, with the property serving as collateral. The loans, generally fairly short term, are made on the premise that the property will be finished on time and sold for an amount sufficient to allow the developer to pay off the loan on schedule. *Equity trusts* invest directly in real estate; in effect, they serve as landlords. The property may be financed

---

[8] Due to the illiquidity of the assets, the sponsor of real property commingled funds may reserve the right to limit the redemption of units, either temporarily or until sale of the underlying property. For an analysis of the performance of such funds, see Mike Miles and Arthur Esty, "How Well Do Commingled Real Estate Funds Perform?" *Journal of Portfolio Management* 8, no. 2 (Winter 1982):62–68.

in part by issuing mortgages. A few firms, termed mixed or hybrid trusts, are neither predominantly mortgage nor equity trusts, but combinations of the two types.

Most REITs are highly leveraged. A typical trust might have debt amounting to 70% of its total assets. Consequently, any decline in the value of the property held by such a trust will generally cause a greater percentage decline in the market value of its common stock. Furthermore, adverse changes in the relationship between the interest paid on a trust's short-term debt and that earned on the trust's assets will also result in declines in the market value of the trust's common stock.

In the recession of 1973 to 1974, there were a large number of defaults on construction and development loans and on some long-term mortgages. Many REITs were left with partially finished buildings. Moreover, the short-term interest rates that REITs had to pay on much of their debt were higher than the long-term interest rates that they were receiving on the mortgages they owned. From October 25, 1973, to August 19, 1974, the average stock prices of industrial firms fell by 27%, whereas the average equity and mortgage REIT fell more than 50% and 70%, respectively.[9] Many trusts went bankrupt, including some associated with extremely well-known financial institutions.

The experience of the early 1970s undoubtedly diminished the enthusiasm of those who invested heavily in REITs (especially those who failed to appreciate the fact that leverage increases risk as well as expected return). Nevertheless, REITs are a desirable investment for many individuals due to their unique investment policies and typically high leverage. However, only a portion of an individual's portfolio should usually consist of such securities.[10]

20.4 INVESTMENT POLICIES

Different investment companies follow different investment policies. Some companies are designed as substitutes for their shareholders' entire portfolio; others expect their shareholders to own other securities. Some restrict their domain or selection methods severely; others give their managers wide latitude. Many engage in highly active management, with substantial portfolio changes designed to exploit perceived superior investment predictions. However, others are more passive, concentrating instead on tailoring a portfolio to serve the interests of a particular clientele.

While categorization is difficult, broad classes can be identified. As mentioned earlier, money market funds hold short-term (typically less than one year) fixed-income instruments such as bank certificates of deposit, com-

---

[9] "Real Estate Investment Trusts: A Background Analysis and Recent Industry Developments, 1961–1974," Economic Staff Paper 75, no. 1, Office of Economic Research, U.S. Securities and Exchange Commission (1975).

[10] For empirical evidence, see William L. Burns and Donald R. Epley, "The Performance of Portfolios of REITS + Stocks," *Journal of Portfolio Management* 8, no. 3 (Spring 1982):37–42.

merical paper, and Treasury bills. These open-end funds make it possible for small investors to move in and out of the short-term market. The fund manager will extract an annual fee for this service, usually between .25% and 1% of the average value of total assets. There are usually no load charges, and investors may add or remove money from their accounts at almost any time. Dividends are usually declared daily. Arrangements with a cooperating bank often make it possible to write a check on an account, where the bank obtains the amount involved by redeeming shares in the fund when the check clears.

Bond funds invest in fixed-income securities. Some go farther, specifying that only particular types will be purchased. There are corporate bond funds, U.S. government bond funds, GNMA (or "Ginnie Mae") funds, convertible bond funds, and so on. Some are organized as open-end investment companies, others as closed-end investment companies.

As indicated earlier, the predominant type of unit investment trust in the United States is the bond unit investment trust. Some are based on government issues, others on corporate issues, and still others on specialized types. Municipal bond unit investment trusts, like open-end municipal bond funds, often make it easier for those in high tax brackets to obtain diversification and liquidity, while taking advantage of the exemption of such securities from personal income taxation. Bond unit investment trusts typically hold securities with different coupon payment schedules and pay roughly equal-size dividends every month.

A few open-end investment companies and some unit investment trusts are restricted to holdings of preferred stocks. Others include both bonds and preferred stocks in their portfolios.

Many open-end companies consider themselves managers for the bulk of the investment assets of their clients. Those that hold both equity and fixed-income securities particularly fit this description. Wiesenberger Investment Companies Service's annual *Investment Companies* manual refers to such companies as balanced funds. These funds seek to "minimize investment risks so far as this is possible, without unduly sacrificing possibilities for long-term growth and current income."[11] Somewhat similar to balanced funds are income funds. These funds seek to "provide as liberal a current income from investments as possible."[12] Some of these funds hold relatively constant mixes of bonds, preferred stock, convertible bonds, and equities; others alter the proportions periodically in attempts to "time the market."

A diversified common stock fund invests most of its assets in common stocks, although some short-term money market instruments are often held to accommodate irregular cash flows or to engage in market timing. In 1987, Wiesenberger's manual classified the majority of diversified common stock funds as having one of three types of objectives: (1) capital gain; (2) growth;

---

[11] Wiesenberger Investment Companies Service, *Investment Companies 1987* (New York: Warren, Gorham & Lamont, Inc., 1987), 39.

[12] Wiesenberger, *Investment Companies 1987*, 40. Option-income funds are a type of income fund that invests primarily in high-dividend-paying common stocks, while also writing call options on these stocks. (Call options are discussed in Chapter 18.)

and (3) growth-income.[13] Two factors appear to be involved in this classification: the relative importance of dividend income versus capital gains and the overall level of risk to be taken. The classifications "are arranged in descending order of emphasis on capital appreciation and, consequently, in ascending order of the importance placed on current income and relative price stability."[14] Since high-dividend portfolios are generally less risky than those with low dividends, relatively few major conflicts arise, although two rather different criteria are involved.

Borderline cases remain: "The difference between a Capital Gain Fund and a Growth Fund is a matter of degree, and in some cases little distinction may exist. Similarly, there is no sharp line of demarcation between a Growth Fund and a Growth-Income Fund."[15] Classification is difficult because the official statement of investment objectives in a fund's prospectus is often fuzzy.

The Investment Company Act of 1940 defines a diversified investment company as one that invests at least 75% of its funds in a diversified manner, meaning that within this portion of the portfolio, no single issuer's securities may account for more than 5% of the fund's assets. Furthermore, within this 75% portion, the fund may not own more than 10% of the voting shares of any single issuer (the 25% exemption is designed to encourage funds to invest in small companies). Those not meeting this standard are classified as non-diversified investment companies. Some choose the latter classification simply to maintain flexibility, whereas others do so to specialize in certain types of securities.

Some specialized investment companies concentrate on the securities of firms in a particular *industry* or *sector*. For example, there are chemical funds, aerospace funds, technology funds, and gold funds. Others deal in securities of a particular type; examples include funds that hold restricted (that is, "letter") stock, and funds that invest in over-the-counter stocks. Still others provide a convenient means for holding the securities of firms in a particular *country*, such as the previously mentioned France and Korea funds. There are also investment companies that, by design, invest more widely internationally, purchasing stocks from a variety of different countries (international funds are those investing in non–U.S. securities, while global funds invest in both U.S. and non–U.S. securities).

Although municipal bond unit investment trusts have been available for many years, open-end municipal bond funds were first offered in 1976. Some municipal bond funds hold long-term issues from many states. Others specialize in the long-term issues of governmental units in one state (single-state funds) in order to provide an investment vehicle for residents of that state who wish to avoid paying state taxes (as well as federal taxes) on the

---

[13] Sometimes the capital gain category is referred to as "maximum capital gain," or "aggressive growth." A fourth category ("specialized") consists of funds that, by design, are not highly diversified. One interesting kind of fund (sometimes organized as a limited partnership) is a hedge fund, where the manager will often engage in short selling and margin purchasing of common stocks.

[14] Wiesenberger, *Investment Companies 1987*, 38.

[15] Wiesenberger, *Investment Companies 1987*, 39.

TABLE 20.1

Mutual funds classified by investment objective as of December 31, 1987.

INVESTMENT OBJECTIVE	NUMBER OF FUNDS	TOTAL ASSETS (IN BILLIONS)
Aggressive growth	186	$ 27.3
Growth	308	48.0
Growth-income	188	64.0
Precious metals	22	4.1
International and global	97	19.5
Balanced and flexible	59	13.3
Income	219	38.7
Option-income	19	5.1
U.S. government income	148	88.9
GNMA	55	34.2
Corporate bond	112	33.7
Long-term municipal bond	150	49.2
Long-term single-state municipal bond	218	27.8
Short-term municipal bond	112	54.6
Short-term single-state municipal bond	42	6.9
Money market	389	254.7
Total	2324	$770.0

SOURCE: Adapted from *1988 Mutual Fund Fact Book* (Washington, DC: Investment Company Institute), 20, 29, 87, 88.

income. Still others buy short-term municipal securities, with some specializing in the short-term issues of governmental units in one state.

An index fund attempts to provide results similar or identical to those computed for a specified market index. For example, the *Vanguard Index Trust*, a no-load open-end investment company, provides a vehicle for small investors who wish to obtain results similar to those of Standard & Poor's 500-stock index. Similarly, a number of banks have established commingled index funds, and corporations and other organizations have set up index funds for their own employee retirement trust funds.

Table 20.1 provides an indication of the number of mutual funds having various kinds of investment objectives, along with the amount of assets under their control.

20.5 MUTUAL FUND ACCOUNTS

The United States Internal Revenue Code allows an investment company to avoid corporate income taxation. A unit investment trust, a closed-end investment company, or an open-end investment company can qualify under Subchapter M of the code as a regulated investment company by meeting certain standards concerning diversification and by paying out at least 90%

of its net income, exclusive of capital gains, each year.[16] Net realized capital gains may be distributed or retained. If the company chooses to retain these gains, it must pay a tax calculated at the maximum rate applied to capital gains for personal income taxes. Shareholders are then given credit for having paid tax at this rate on the gains on their shares. However, most companies choose to distribute the gains, making cash payments to the shareholders for their respective portions. Thus, most mutual funds make two kinds of payments to their shareholders—one for income (from dividends and interest that the fund has received) and one for net realized capital gains. However, the shareholders must subsequently pay personal income taxes on these distributions.

☐ 20.5.1   Accumulation Plans

Although an investor can purchase shares in a fund and receive all distributions in cash, this is only one of many possible arrangements. Mutual funds offer plans of several types to satisfy investors' desires for different patterns of contributions and withdrawals over time. Accumulation plans are designed for those who do not want to receive any income or capital gains distributions over some period of time. The simplest procedure involves automatic reinvestment of these distributions, where the shareholder elects to receive additional shares in the fund instead of cash. As with other plans, this often involves fractional shares, but since most accounts are maintained via computerized records, this poses no problem.

Voluntary accumulation plans allow an investor to add to an account as desired, subject only to some minimum amount that must be invested each time. Alternatively, a fixed dollar amount may be invested at periodic intervals—in some cases via automatic bank transfers.

Contractual accumulation plans call for a fixed amount to be contributed at regular intervals (usually monthly) over a relatively long period (often five or more years). Sales charges may or may not be lower than those applicable to a voluntary accumulation plan. The investor is not legally bound to make all the payments, but since a large proportion of early contributions typically goes toward sales charges, commitment to a contractual plan should not be considered if cancellation is at all likely.

The Investment Company Amendments Act of 1970 placed limits on the load charges for contractual plans. Specifically, no more than 50% of the first year's contribution may be allocated to sales charges (that is, at least half must be invested in fund shares). Moreover, if a 50% "front-end" load charge is assessed in the first year, cancellation of the plan within 18 months entitles the investor to a refund reducing the effective charge to 15% of the amount paid in.

A few funds offer insurance with their contractual accumulation plans. This insurance provides the remaining contributions if the investor dies or

---

[16] At least 50% of the company's assets must be diversified, meaning that within this portion (1) no more than 5% of the fund's total assets can be invested in the securities of any one issuer and (2) no more than 10% of the voting share of any one issuer can be held. Moreover, of the remaining portion, no more than 25% of total assets may be invested in the securities of any one company.

is disabled before all the contracted payments have been made. The premium for such insurance is, in effect, added to the sales charge.

□ 20.5.2 Retirement Plans

Accumulation of funds for retirement may be accomplished via an individual retirement account (IRA) or a Keogh plan. In 1987 anyone could contribute up to $2000 of his or her earned income to an IRA, and if the income earner's spouse had no earned income, a total of $2250 could be contributed to two IRAs. No taxes are paid on the earnings of such funds until the investor begins making withdrawals. Furthermore, under certain circumstances the investor can deduct the amount contributed from gross income when personal income taxes are being calculated.[17]

Self-employed individuals can contribute 20% of their net earnings from self-employment (up to a maximum of $30,000 in 1987) to a Keogh plan account, with such contributions also deductible from gross income for tax purposes. Either type of account is maintained by a custodian, often a bank. Contributions and any cash received from investments are invested in accordance with the investor's desires. Funds may be withdrawn beginning at age $59\frac{1}{2}$ and withdrawals must begin by age $70\frac{1}{2}$.

It is increasingly common to find several investment companies operating as a "family of funds." An investor may purchase shares in more than one of the funds under common management and also may switch money from one fund to another. Sales charges for such switching are typically lower than those applicable to similar transactions involving funds managed by different companies; in some cases, transfers within a family may be made without charge. In any event, a single account is usually maintained, with all contributions, withdrawals, and tax information included in one statement.

In this situation, the investor is given the opportunity to make timing decisions, switching money from one fund to another that is believed to be underpriced at that time. For example, consider an investor who owns shares of a gold fund that is in a family which includes a technology fund. If the investor feels that technology stocks are, in general, quite underpriced, then the investor could switch the gold fund shares for technology fund shares.

Many mutual funds offer voluntary withdrawal plans. The investor instructs the fund to pay out either a fixed amount or a specified percentage of the account's value periodically (for example, monthly), decreasing the number of shares that the investor owns in the process.

20.6 MUTUAL FUND PERFORMANCE

Mutual funds need to compute and publicize their net asset values daily. Since their income and capital gain distributions are also publicized, they

---

[17] For example, the contribution will be deductible provided (1) the investor is not covered by an employer-sponsored retirement plan and does not have a Keogh plan; or (2) the investor is single and earns less than $25,000; or (3) the investor is married and the combined incomes are less than $40,000.

are ideal candidates for studies of the performance of professionally managed portfolios. Thus, it is hardly surprising that mutual funds have frequently been the subject of extensive study. In these studies, the rate of return on a mutual fund for period t is calculated by adding the change in net asset value to the amount of income and capital gains distributions made during the period, denoted I_t and G_t, respectively, and dividing this total by the net asset value at the beginning of the period:

$$r_t = \frac{(\text{NAV}_t - \text{NAV}_{t-1}) + I_t + G_t}{\text{NAV}_{t-1}} \qquad (20.2)$$

For example, a mutual fund that had a net asset value of $10 at the beginning of month t and made income and capital gain distributions of, respectively, $.05 and $.04 per share during the month, and then ended the month with a net asset value of $10.03 would have a monthly return of

$$r_t = \frac{(\$10.03 - \$10.00) + \$.05 + \$.04}{\$10.00}$$

$$= 1.20\%.$$

It should be noted that returns calculated in this manner can be used to evaluate the performance of the portfolio manager of a mutual fund, since it indicates the results of the manager's investment decisions. However, it does not necessarily indicate the return earned by the shareholders in the fund, since there may have been a load charge involved. In the example, perhaps the investor paid $10.50 at the beginning of the month for one share of this fund, with $.50 being a front-end load. If this were the case, the investor's return for this month could be calculated using equation (20.2), where NAV_{t-1} would be $10.50, not $10.00:

$$r_t = \frac{(\$10.03 - \$10.50) + \$.05 + \$.04}{\$10.50}$$

$$= -3.62\%.$$

Thus, the return for the investor who bought one share at the beginning of the month and paid a $.50 per share load charge at that time would be -3.62%. However, the portfolio manager was only given $10.00 per share to invest, since the load charge was given to certain people that were responsible for getting the investor to buy the share. Accordingly, the portfolio manager should be evaluated on the basis of the return provided on the $10.00, which in this example was 1.20%.

Recently, data on professionally managed pension funds and bank commingled funds have become available. The performance of the managers of such funds appears to be similar to that of mutual fund managers: They do reasonably well tailoring portfolios to meet clients' objectives, but few seem to be able to consistenly "beat the market." Although the following sections deal only with U.S. mutual funds, many of the results apply to other investment companies, both in the United States and in other countries.[18]

---

[18] For evidence on funds outside the United States see, for example, Jess H. Chua and Richard S. Woodward, "Gains from Market Timing," Monograph Series in Finance and Economics 1986–2, Salomon Brothers Center for the Study of Financial Institutions, Graduate School of Business Administration, New

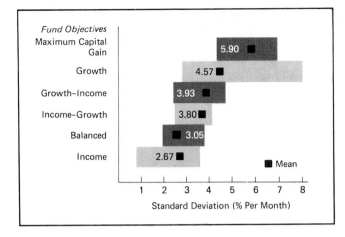

FIGURE 20–4
Risk versus fund objectives: 123 mutual funds, 1960–1969.

Source: John G. McDonald, "Objectives and Performance of Mutual Funds, 1960–1969," *Journal of Financial and Quantitative Analysis* 9, no. 3 (June 1974): p. 316.

☐ **20.6.1 Risk Control**

One of the functions that a mutual fund can perform for its investors is the maintenance of a particular risk posture. Formal statements of objectives provide some idea of a fund's intended posture, but often the wording is vague. Nevertheless, there appears to be a general relationship between portfolio risk and stated objectives.

Figure 20.4 summarizes information on the standard deviations of monthly excess returns over a ten-year period for funds with similar objectives, using classifications assigned by Wiesenberger at the beginning of the period. In particular, the monthly returns for each one of 123 mutual funds were calculated using equation (20.2). Then, using these 120 monthly returns, the standard deviation was calculated for each one of the funds. Each bar in the figure plots the range of values of the standard deviations for funds having the same objective, with the average standard deviation being shown by a square near the middle of the bar. It can be seen that generally, the lower the amount of promised risk, the lower the amount of actual risk (a similar looking figure resulted when beta was used). However, the overlapping of some of the bars indicates that some funds with conservative objectives took on more risk than others with less conservative objectives.

It is quite possible that past risk exposure may be a better guide to future risk exposure than the rather general statements found in a fund's

York University; Andre L. Farber, "Performance of Internationally Diversified Mutual Funds," in *International Capital Markets*, eds. Edwin J. Elton and Martin J. Gruber (Amsterdam: North-Holland Publishing Company, 1975), 298–309; Michael A. Firth, "The Investment Performance of Unit Trusts in the Period 1965–75," *Journal of Money, Credit and Banking* 9, no. 4 (November 1977):597–604; James R. F. Guy, "The Performance of the British Investment Trust Industry," *Journal of Finance* 33, no. 2 (May 1978):443–55, and "An Examination of the Effects of International Diversification from the British Viewpoint on Both Hypothetical and Real Portfolios," *Journal of Finance* 33, no. 5 (December 1978):1425–38; John G. McDonald, "French Mutual Fund Performance: Evaluation of Internationally Diversified Portfolios," *Journal of Finance* 28, no. 5 (December 1973):1161–80; Juan A. Palacios, "The Stock Market in Spain: Tests of Efficiency and Capital Market Theory," in *International Capital Markets*, eds. Edwin J. Elton and Martin J. Gruber (Amsterdam: North-Holland Publishing Company, 1975):114–49; and R. S. Woodward, "The Performance of U.K. Investment Trusts as Internationally Diversified Portfolios Over the Period 1968 to 1977," *Journal of Banking and Finance* 7, no. 3 (September 1983):417–26.

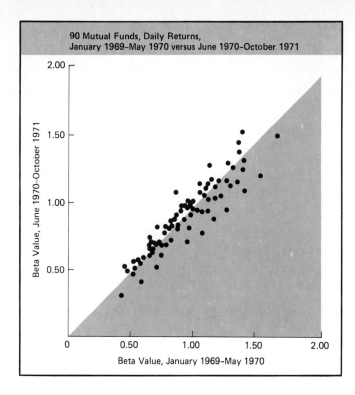

90 Mutual Funds, Daily Returns,
January 1969–May 1970 versus June 1970–October 1971

Beta Value, June 1970–October 1971

Beta Value, January 1969–May 1970

FIGURE 20–5
Past versus future beta values: 90 mutual funds, January 1969–May 1970 versus June 1970–October 1971.

Source: Gerald A. Pogue and Walter Conway, "On the Stability of Mutual Fund Beta Values" (unpublished working paper, MIT Sloan School of Management, June 1972).

prospectus. Figure 20.5 shows that this is often the case. Each point plots the beta for a fund in two different periods (based on daily returns). Even though the points do not plot neatly along a 45° line from the origin that represents equal betas in both periods, there is a clear relationship between "past beta" and "future beta." This suggests that the typical mutual fund keeps it at roughly the same value over time.

☐ 20.6.2 Diversification

An important task for any investment manager is the provision of an appropriate degree of portfolio diversification. The correct amount depends on the proportion of client's funds managed and on the likelihood that superior abnormal returns can be obtained by sacrificing diversification. Since most mutual funds are intended to be a major component of a shareholder's portfolio, it is reasonable to expect them to be substantially diversified.

Figure 20.6 shows that many are. Quarterly excess returns over a five-year period were computed for 100 funds and compared with corresponding values for Standard & Poor's 500-stock index. For each fund a value of R^2, the coefficient of determination, was computed. This indicates the proportion of the variation in a fund's excess returns that can be attributed to variations in excess returns on the index. As the figure shows, approximately 90% of the quarter-by-quarter variation in a typical fund's excess return was as-

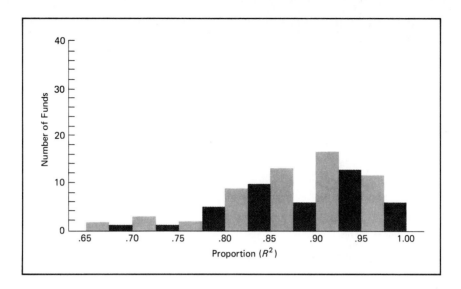

FIGURE 20–6
Proportion of variation in quarterly returns attributable to market fluctuations: 100 mutual funds, 1970–1974.

Source: Merrill Lynch, Pierce, Fenner & Smith, Inc., *Investment Performance Analysis, Comparative Survey, 1970–1974.*

sociated with swings in the value of the S&P 500 during this period, with values ranging from 66% to 98%.

□ 20.6.3 Average Return

Some organizations have established indices based on the net asset values of a sample of mutual funds that have similar stated investment objectives. Thus, one way to evaluate the general performance of mutual funds is to compare their average return as reflected in these indices with the average return of a suitable market index. As shown in Figure 20.7, this is done every week in *Barron's*, where a set of mutual fund indices that have been prepared by Lipper Analytical Services are published. It can be seen in the figure that average returns on the Dow Jones Industrial Average and the S&P 500 are also reported; inexplicably, the time periods covered for the market index returns do not correspond with those for the mutual fund indices. This, an investor would need to calculate the corresponding market index returns in order to evaluate the general performance of various types of mutual funds.

Many studies have compared the performance of investment companies that have invested primarily in common stocks with the performance of a *benchmark portfolio* that consisted of a combination of (1) a market index, such as Standard & Poor's 500-stock index, and (2) a risk-free asset, such

LIPPER MUTUAL FUND PERFORMANCE AVERAGES

Weekly Summary Report
February 9, 1989

Dividends Reinvested Cumulative Performances

Value 12/31/88		3-Months 9/30/88- 12/31/88	Year-to-Date 12/31/87- 12/31/88	5-Years 12/31/83- 12/31/88	10-Years 12/31/78- 12/31/88	15-Years 12/31/73- 12/31/88
2,168.57	Dow Jones Reinvested	+ 3.63%	+ 16.21%	+ 111.35%	+ 341.34%	+ 437.18%
277.72	S&P 500 Reinvested	+ 3.06%	+ 16.55%	+ 103.92%	+ 354.17%	+ 461.66%

Index Value		Weekly 2/02/89- 2/09/89	Year-to-Date 12/31/88- 2/09/89	12-Months 2/11/88- 2/09/89	8/20/87- 2/09/89	12/03/87- 2/09/89
Lipper Indexes NAV (Mil. $)						
403.98	Growth Fund Index	+ 0.09%	+ 6.90%	+ 18.66%	− 5.45%	+ 36.64%
655.96	Growth & Income Index	+ 0.32%	+ 6.03%	+ 19.94%	− 1.48%	+ 36.96%
495.33	Balanced Fund Index	+ 0.02%	+ 4.68%	+ 12.45%	− 4.05%	+ 18.79%
148.07	Gold Fund Index	+ 2.61%	+ 6.55%	+ 8.38%	+ 24.91%	− 12.57%
152.48	Sci & Tech Index	+ 0.10%	+ 6.57%	+ 16.74%	− 12.91%	+ 33.93%
290.66	International Index	+ 2.87%	+ 6.08%	+ 26.86%	− 0.28%	+ 35.82%
General Equity Funds						
17,819.0	Capital Appreciation	+ 0.30%	+ 6.37%	+ 16.97%	− 7.59%	+ 32.17%
52,643.7	Growth Funds	+ 0.23%	+ 6.48%	+ 17.48%	− 6.98%	+ 34.17%
7,847.4	Small Company Growth	+ 0.59%	+ 7.06%	+ 22.34%	− 6.17%	+ 43.08%
62,587.7	Growth and Income	+ 0.12%	+ 5.59%	+ 16.02%	− 2.67%	+ 31.01%
17,628.7	Equity Income	+ 0.35%	+ 4.40%	+ 12.77%	− 1.37%	+ 23.55%
158,526.5	Gen. Equity Funds Avg.	+ 0.26%	+ 6.12%	+ 17.14%	− 5.60%	+ 33.02%
Other Equity Funds						
562.2	Health/Biotechnology	+ 1.16%	+ 7.67%	+ 12.87%	− 11.72%	+ 36.70%
1,762.5	Natural Resources	+ 0.54%	+ 7.75%	+ 19.50%	− 9.79%	+ 31.41%
2,041.3	Science & Technol.	+ 0.17%	+ 6.85%	+ 15.98%	− 13.98%	+ 33.79%
3,511.8	Utility Funds	+ 0.04%	+ 2.38%	+ 10.13%	+ 6.39%	+ 20.53%
2,372.1	Specialty Funds	+ 0.85%	+ 7.01%	+ 20.76%	− 5.64%	+ 35.32%
10,505.6	Global Funds	+ 1.51%	+ 5.32%	+ 19.88%	− 2.57%	+ 29.03%
7,129.5	International Funds	+ 2.39%	+ 5.62%	+ 24.89%	+ 5.41%	+ 32.60%
3,342.1	Gold Oriented Funds	+ 2.22%	+ 5.54%	+ 7.43%	+ 26.96%	− 11.23%
101.5	Option Growth Funds	+ 0.54%	+ 4.21%	+ 7.37%	+ 1.02%	+ 13.26%
4,822.3	Option Income Funds	+ 0.02%	+ 4.41%	+ 15.44%	+ 0.69%	+ 30.02%
194,677.4	All Equity Funds Avg.	+ 0.53%	+ 6.04%	+ 17.35%	− 5.60%	+ 31.45%
Other Funds						
3,310.1	Conv. Sec Funds	+ 0.42%	+ 4.28%	+ 13.57%	− 2.47%	+ 23.60%
11,723.4	Balanced Funds	− 0.03%	+ 3.88%	+ 11.35%	+ 0.76%	+ 21.89%
3,918.0	Income Funds	+ 0.07%	+ 2.79%	+ 9.65%	+ 6.75%	+ 17.70%
3,238.3	World Income Funds	+ 0.35%	− 0.17%	+ 6.74%	+ 15.49%	+ 9.19%
170,444.2	Fixed Income Funds	− 0.21%	+ 1.17%	+ 5.45%	+ 10.15%	+ 10.40%
387,311.4	All Funds Average	+ 0.28%	+ 4.31%	+ 13.30%	− 0.30%	+ 24.18%
	All Funds-Median	+ 0.10%	+ 4.44%	+ 12.55%	+ 0.54%	+ 24.07%
	No. of Funds in Universe	1650	1647	1492	1343	1432

The method of calculating total return data on indices utilizes actual dividends on x-dates accumulated for the quarter and reinvested at quarter end. This calculation is at variance with SEC release 327 of Aug. 8, 1972, which utilizes latest 12-month dividends. The latter method is the one used by Standard & Poor's.

Source: Lipper Analytical Services Inc., Summit, New Jersey 07901

FIGURE 20–7
Mutual fund indices.

Source: Reprinted by permission of *Barron's* © Dow Jones & Company, Inc., (February 13, 1988): p. 173.

as Treasury bills.[19] Each particular combination was chosen so that the benchmark portfolio had a risk level that was equal to that of the investment company. Thus, an investment company that had a beta of .80 would be compared with a benchmark portfolio that had 80% invested in the market index and 20% invested in the risk-free asset.[20]

One way of determining whether or not a mutual fund has beaten the market is to subtract the average return on the benchmark portfolio from the average return of the mutual fund. This amount, when risk is measured by beta, is known as the fund's *ex post alpha*. Figure 20.8(a) shows the distribution of *ex post* alpha values for 70 mutual funds, based on monthly returns beginning in 1955 and going through 1964. The average value was .09% per year, suggesting that the typical fund provided approximately the same return as a market-based passive fund with a constant beta equal to the fund's average beta. Of the 70 funds, 40 had positive *ex post* alphas and 30 had negative *ex post* alphas.

Different time periods give slightly different results. Figure 20.8(b) shows the distribution of *ex post* alphas based on monthly returns for 125 funds beginning in 1960 and going through 1969. The average alpha was .05% per month, or about .60% per year. During this period, the typical fund outperformed a passive fund of similar risk by slightly more than .50% per year, and slightly more than half (53%) of the funds had positive *ex post* alphas.

Figure 20.8(c) provides a third example. It shows returns for 100 funds based on quarterly returns beginning in 1970 and going through 1974. The average *ex post* alpha was −.50% per quarter, or approximately −2.00% per year, and only 20 of the funds had positive alphas.

These results suggest that the average mutual fund has not significantly outperformed an equal-risk passive alternative over any extended period. This is not too surprising. After all, the market's performance is itself an average of the performance of all investors. If, on the average, mutual funds had beaten the market, then some other group of investors would have lost to the market. With the substantial amount of professional management in today's stock market, it is difficult to think of a likely group of victims.

☐ 20.6.4 Consistency of Performance

Despite the rather negative results described thus far, there remains the possibility that a few funds may consistently beat the market due to superior

---

[19] Another useful benchmark portfolio is the relevant Lipper mutual fund index. Performance evaluation for common stock portfolios is discussed in detail in Chapter 23. For a more in-depth summary, see Chapter 13 of Gordon J. Alexander and Jack Clark Francis, *Portfolio Analysis* (Englewood Cliffs, N.J.: Prentice Hall, 1986).

[20] Alternatively, the benchmark portfolio may be based on the investment company's standard deviation relative to that of a market index, such as the S&P 500. For example, if the investment company's standard deviation has been 60% of the index's standard deviation, then the mix should consist of 60% invested in the market index and 40% invested in the risk-free asset. The results from evaluating mutual fund performance when using beta as the measure of risk seems to be very similar to the results when standard deviation is used. See, for example, Hany A. Shawky, "An Update on Mutual Funds: Better Grades," *Journal of Portfolio Management* 8, no. 2 (Winter 1982):29–34.

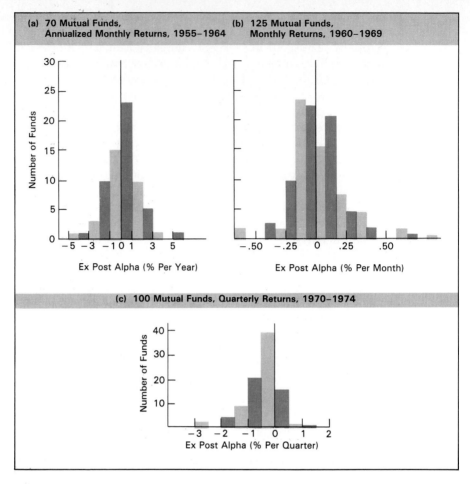

FIGURE 20–8
Mutual fund performance: ex post alpha values.

Source: (a) adapted from Norman E. Mains, "Risk, the Pricing of Capital Assets, and the Evaluation of Investment Portfolios: Comment," *Journal of Business* 50, no. 3 (July 1977): pp. 378–80; (b) United States Securities and Exchange Commission, *Institutional Investor Study Report*, March 10, 1971 (Washington DC: U.S. Governmental Printing Office); (c) Merrill Lynch, Pierce, Fenner & Smith, Inc., *Investment Performance Analysis, Comparative Survey, 1970–1974*.

management. Consider identifying for further analysis those funds that had a run of Y years of superior performance (perhaps $Y = 5$ years). Some (perhaps all) of these funds may simply have had a string of good luck, whereas others may have been managed in a consistently superior fashion. The lucky ones have a 50% chance of above-average performance in the next year (that is, in year $Y + 1$), whereas the skilled ones have better than a 50% chance. This means that if all the managers have simply been lucky, then roughly 50% of the funds will have superior performance in the next year (that is, in year $Y + 1$). However, if some of the managers are indeed skilled, then more than 50% of the managers will have superior performance in the next

year. Furthermore, the greater the number that are skilled, the greater the proportion of funds that will turn in an above-average performance in the next year.

One study examined annual differential returns for 115 funds from 1955 through 1964 and found that of those portfolios that outperformed the market over a three-year period, only 53.4% did so again in the fourth year.[21] Since similar percentages were reported for one-, two-, four-, and five-year periods, it appears that there is little support for the notion that a significant number of mutual fund managers are skilled enough to consistently out-perform a passive portfolio that has equal risk. One possible explanation is that there are skilled mutual fund managers, but they either extract an amount equal to their superior returns in salaries or move from fund to fund often enough to make it difficult to verify their existence.

☐ 20.6.5 Expenses

Funds typically incur two kinds of expenses. Management fees and administrative expenses are direct and generally reported. Transaction costs are only partly measurable in that brokerage commissions are reported, but implicit costs such as bid-ask spreads and the price impacts of trading are usually not even estimated.

By adding management and administrative expenses and explicit transactions costs to a fund's rate of return, it is possible to obtain an estimate of its gross performance (that is, its performance based on the assumption that such expenses were nonexistent). This is done by adding to the numerator of equation (20.2) the per-share values of such expenses. In the example shown earlier, perhaps the fund had paid expenses of this nature totaling $.02 per share during month t. In such a situation, the net return of $.12/$10.00 = 1.20% corresponds to a gross return of ($.12 + $.02)/$10.00 = 1.40%.

Figure 20.9 shows the distribution of *ex post* alphas based on this measure of gross performance for the funds covered in the analysis previously summarized in Figure 20.8(a). While *ex post* alphas based on *net* performance averaged .09% per year, the *ex post* alphas based on *gross* performance averaged 1.07% per year. Moreover, 50 of the 70 funds had positive *ex post* alphas based on gross performance. This suggests portfolio managers have some skill, but not enough to recoup the transaction costs that are incurred in hiring them and carrying out their buy and sell orders.

A study by the Securities and Exchange Commission attempted to estimate the relationship between several factors and portfolio performance.[22] *Ex post* alphas were computed and analyzed for 132 mutual funds using monthly returns from 1965 through 1969. The following observations were made:

---

[21] Michael C. Jensen, "Risk, the Pricing of Capital Assets, and the Evaluation of Investment Portfolios," *Journal of Business* 42, no. 2 (April 1969):167–247. Similar results have been reported for bond portfolios; see Mark Kritzman, "Can Bond Managers Perform Consistently?" *Journal of Portfolio Management* 9, no. 4 (Summer 1983):54–56.

[22] *Institutional Investor Study Report of the Securities and Exchange Commission* (Washington, DC: U.S. Government Printing Office, 1971), vol. 2, pp. 328–32.

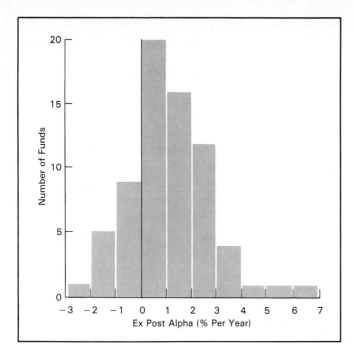

FIGURE 20–9
Mutual fund performance: ex post alpha values based on gross returns.

Source: Adapted from Norman E. Mains, "Risk, the Pricing of Capital Assets, and the Evaluation of Investment Portfolios: Comment," *Journal of Business* 50, no. 3 (July 1977): pp. 378–80.

Larger funds performed no better, other things being equal, than smaller funds, where size is measured by the fund's total assets.

Funds with load charges performed no better, other things being equal, than those with no load charges (consequently, investors in load funds did worse than those in no-load funds).

Funds associated with management companies having larger amounts of assets under their control performed no better, other things being equal, than those with smaller amounts under their control.

However, fund performance was found to be *negatively* related to *portfolio turnover*, which is a periodic measure of how much buying and selling of securities was incurred (technically, it is the ratio of the smaller of purchases or sales during a time period divided by the average total asset value during the period). This suggests that, on the average, the more frequently a mutual fund's portfolio was revised, the lower its subsequent performance.

One possible explanation for this observation is that in an efficient market, more frequent revisions will cause a fund to incur more transaction costs, but without being able to consistently receive gains from the purchase of underpriced securities as an offset. Sometimes revisions in a fund's portfolio may be desirable in order to maintain a desired risk level or dividend yield, but revisions intended to exploit supposed market inefficiencies generally prove undesirable due to the associated transaction costs.

To achieve superior portfolio performance, an investor must either select securities that outperform others of comparable risk or switch from risk class to risk class at appropriate times. The latter strategy is often called *market timing*. The idea is to hold a high-beta portfolio prior to market rises and a low-beta portfolio prior to market declines. An all-equity fund can change its beta by switching among stocks that have different betas. That is, a high-beta portfolio can be achieved by holding high-beta securities, and a low-beta portfolio can be achieved by holding low-beta securities. Although a balanced fund can also do this, it can change its beta in another manner— namely, by altering the relative proportions it has invested in stocks and bonds. Typically, the more a balanced fund has invested in stocks, the higher its beta.

Successful market timing will eventually be reflected in a positive *ex post* alpha that is based on long-term performance. Overall performance may also be separated into one part attributed to security selection and another part attributed to market timing.

In a study of the performance of 57 mutual funds over the period from 1953 through 1962, only one was found with a record suggesting any significant ability to time the market.[23] A later study of the performance of 116 funds from February 1968 through June 1980 found that only three funds had significant timing ability over the entire period, with only one fund having a record indicating significant market timing ability in both the first and the second half of the period.[24]

Such results are not surprising. If many funds were consistently successful at market timing, they would have shown up in the previously mentioned tests for superior overall performance unless they were consistently engaging in inferior security selection that offset their superior timing ability. However, such a situation seems highly improbable. More likely, investment managers find it as difficult to time the market as to select underpriced securities. Such is the lot of an investor in a highly efficient market.

20.7 CLOSED-END FUND PREMIUMS AND DISCOUNTS

Several studies have shown that the performance of diversified closed-end investment company managers in the United States is similar to that of

---

[23] Jack L. Treynor and Kay Mazuy, "Can Mutual Funds Outguess the Market?" *Harvard Business Review* 44, no. 4 (July–August 1966):131–36.

[24] Roy D. Henriksson, "Market Timing and Mutual Fund Performance: An Empirical Investigation," *Journal of Business* 57, no. 1, pt. 1 (January 1984):73–96. Similar results suggesting that mutual fund managers have no special ability to time the market is provided by Stanley J. Kon, "The Market-Timing Performance of Mutual Fund Managers," *Journal of Business* 56, no. 3 (July 1983):323–47; Eric C. Chang and Wilbur G. Lewellen, "Market Timing and Mutual Fund Investment Performance," *Journal of Business* 57, no. 1, pt. 1 (January 1984):57–72; and Chua and Woodward, "Gains from Stock Market Timing."

open-end investment company managers.[25] When returns are measured by changes in net asset values (plus all distributions), closed-end investment companies appear to be neither better nor worse than open-end ones. Again, there is little evidence that portfolio managers can either select underpriced securities or time the market successfully.

However, there is more to be said about closed-end funds. An investor can purchase an open-end fund's shares for their net asset value (plus any required load charge) and sell them later at the subsequent net asset value. Except for any load charges, the performance of the *management* of such a fund, based on net asset values, corresponds exactly to the returns provided to the *shareholders*. This is not the case for closed-end investment companies, since investors buy and sell shares of investment companies at prices determined on the open (secondary) market. Although some companies have share prices that are above their net asset values (such shares are said to sell at a premium), many have share prices below their net asset values (such shares are said to sell at a discount).

The fact that the price of a closed-end investment company differs from its net asset value, with the magnitude of the difference varying from time to time, introduces an added source of risk and potential return to investors. By purchasing shares at a discount, an investor may be able to earn more than just the change in the company's net asset value. Even if the company's discount remains constant, the effective dividend yield will be greater than that of an otherwise similar no-load, open-end investment company, since the purchase price will be less. If the discount is substantial when the shares are purchased, it may subsequently narrow, and the return will be even greater.[26] On the other hand, if the discount increases, the investor's overall return may be less than that of an otherwise comparable open-end investment company.

Some of the risk associated with varying discounts can be reduced by holding a portfolio of shares in several closed-end investment companies. Discounts on different companies move together, but not perfectly. For example, past data suggest that the standard deviation of the percentage change in the ratio of market price to net asset value for a portfolio of 10 to 12 closed-end investment companies is likely to be approximately half that of a typical investment in the shares of a single closed-end investment company.[27]

Explaining the behavior of prices of closed-end investment companies is a challenge for anyone believing that capital markets are perfectly efficient. For anyone not firmly committed to such a view, the purchase of shares of

---

[25] See, for example, William F. Sharpe and Howard B. Sosin, "Closed-End Investment Companies in the United States: Risk and Return," *Proceedings, 1974 Meeting of the European Finance Association*, ed. B. Jacquillat (Amsterdam: North-Holland Publishing Co., 1975); Antonio Vives, "Analysis of Forecasting Ability of Closed-End Fund's Management," (working paper, Carnegie-Mellon University, September 1975) and "Discounts and Premiums on Closed-End Funds: A Theoretical and Empirical Analysis," (Ph.D. diss., Carnegie-Mellon University, 1975).

[26] There is some evidence that discounts narrow during "down markets" and widen during "up markets." See R. Malcolm Richards, Donald R. Fraser, and John C. Groth, "Premiums, Discounts, and the Volatility of Closed-End Mutual Funds," *Financial Review* (Fall 1979):26–33, and "The Attractions of Closed-End Bond Funds," *Journal of Portfolio Management* 8, no. 2 (Winter 1982):56–61.

[27] Sharpe and Sosin, "Closed-End Investment Companies in the United States."

closed-end investment companies at prices sufficiently below net asset values may provide an opportunity for superior returns.[28] One way of realizing superior returns is for the closed-end investment company to convert to an open-end one.[29] By doing so, the discount on the shares would have to disappear, since conversion would result in the investment company offering its shareholders the right to redeem their shares for net asset value.

20.8 SUMMARY

This chapter has described various types of investment companies, along with the advantages associated with investing in them. Unit investment trusts typically make a set of initial investments in fixed-income securities and then hold onto these securities until they mture. Investors in such a trust periodically receive their portion of the interest that the trust itself receives from the securities. Furthermore, the investors receive their portion of the principal on the securities as they mature. Usually, the sponsor of such a trust maintains a secondary market in the certificates that represent ownership in the trust.

Alternatively, investors can decide to purchase shares of managed investment companies, which are continually involved in buying and selling certain kinds of securities. There are two types of managed investment companies—closed-end funds and open-end funds (the latter are more commonly known as mutual funds).

An investor who buys and sells shares of closed-end funds will typically do so by using a broker. The shares of such funds are traded just like the shares of an industrial corporation, with a price determined in the marketplace. Thus, the number of shares outstanding for a closed-end fund is fixed.

In contrast, an investor interested in buying or selling shares of an open-end fund generally deals directly with the fund. The price paid to buy shares is based on the fund's net asset value on the date of purchase, a figure that represents the market value of the assets held by the company on a per share basis. Some open-end funds make the investor pay a commission, known as a load charge, when buying the shares. Others, known as no-load funds, do not impose such a commission. In either case, when an investor subsequently decides to sell shares that were previously purchased, the selling price is based on net asset value at that time.

There are a variety of other types of investments that are similar in nature to the shares of investment companies. Fixed and variable annuities can be purchased by investors, providing them with periodic payments of

---

[28] Burton G. Malkiel advocated such an investment strategy in the 1973, 1975, and 1981 editions of *A Random Walk Down Wall Street* (New York: W. W. Norton & Company, Inc.), but not in the 1985 edition. The basis for his initial advocacy can be found in two studies: Burton Malkiel, "The Valuation of Closed-End Investment Company Shares," *Journal of Finance* 32, no. 3 (June 1977):847–59; and Rex Thompson, "The Information Content of Discounts and Premiums on Closed-End Fund Shares," *Journal of Financial Economics* 6, no. 2/3 (June/September 1978):151–86.

[29] For an analysis of the "open-ending" of closed-end investment companies, see Greggory A. Brauer, " 'Open-Ending' Closed-End Funds," *Journal of Financial Economics* 13, no. 4 (December 1984):491–507.

either a fixed dollar amount or a variable amount that is linked to the performance of a portfolio of common stocks. Individuals can direct banks to invest their money in any one of a number of commingled funds that specialize in making investments in, for example, corporate bonds or common stocks. Individuals can invest indirectly in real estate by either having a bank place their money in a commingled fund that specializes in such investments or by purchasing shares of a real estate investment trust.

Due to data availability, mutual funds have been the subject of many studies of portfolio performance. The results show that, on the average, those mutual funds that indicated they would pursue more risky investment strategies did indeed provide their investors with returns that had higher standard deviations and betas. However, the typical fund was not able to provide its investors with superior rates of return. Furthermore, those few that had been able to provide such returns were generally unable to do so consistently.

More detailed studies indicated that the average fund was not able to engage in selectivity or timing activities in a manner that provided its investors with superior returns. Since fund managers use publicly available information in making their investment decisions, these findings are consistent with the notion of semistrong-form market efficiency. However, this should not be interpreted to mean that individuals should steer clear of mutual funds. Instead, individuals can still look for such funds to provide them with low-cost diversification. Furthermore, such funds will simplify and reduce the amount of the individual's time that is spent on recordkeeping and investing.

QUESTIONS AND PROBLEMS

1. Distinguish between closed-end and open-end investment companies.
2. Based on the evidence presented in the text, how much importance should Lip Pike attach to the past performance of mutual funds if Lip is attempting to select a superior performing fund?
3. What factors should you consider in selecting a mutual fund?
4. Why do some mutual funds have load charges while others do not? Why are investors willing to pay load charges?
5. Why do the stated percentage load charges of mutual funds not fully reflect the percentage costs of these sales fees?
6. Distinguish between a common stock fund and a balanced fund. In particular, compare their expected return and risk characteristics.
7. If most investment managers appear unable to "beat the market" on a risk-adjusted basis, should an investor still consider investing in investment companies? Why or why not?
8. Discuss the advantages and disadvantages of unit investment trusts compared to managed investment companies.
9. Nap Lajoie was attempting to calculate the performance of an investment in the Mercury Fund, an open-end investment company, over the calendar year 1988. Nap took the 1988 year-end net asset value (NAV) of the fund, subtracted the 1987 year-

end NAV, and divided by the 1987 year-end NAV. Was Nap's performance measurement formula correct? Explain.

10. Assuming that certain conditions are satisfied, the income earned by investment companies is exempt from federal taxes. Why?

11. Why do the market prices of closed-end investment company shares represent a "mystery" to proponents of market efficiency?

Chapter 21

FINANCIAL ANALYSIS

In a broad sense, financial analysis involves determining the levels of risk and expected return of individual financial assets as well as groups of financial assets. For example, financial analysis involves both individual common stocks, such as IBM; groups of common stocks, such as the computer industry; or, on an even larger basis, the stock market itself. In this case, financial analysis would result in a decision of how to split the investor's money between the stock and bond markets as well as a decision of whether to buy or sell computer stocks in general and IBM in particular.

An alternative definition of financial analysis is more pragmatic: Financial analysis is what financial analysts do. The *Financial Analyst's Handbook*[1] defines the term *financial analyst* as synonymous with security analyst or investment analyst—"one who analyzes securities and makes recommendations thereon."[2] Using this definition, financial analysis can be viewed as the activity of providing inputs to the portfolio management process. This chapter takes such a view in discussing financial analysis.

21.1 PROFESSIONAL ORGANIZATIONS

In the United States, those who belong to a local society of financial analysts automatically belong to a national organization known as the Financial Analysts Federation. Among other things, membership brings with it a subscription to the *Financial Analysts Journal*, a major source of information on basic research done by other analysts and by members of the academic community. In 1986, there were about 15,000 members in the 56 local societies of the Federation.

In 1962, The Institute of Chartered Financial Analysts was formed by the Financial Analysts Federation to award the professional designation of Chartered Financial Analyst (CFA). During the next 25 years, more than 10,000 analysts were designated CFAs. To become a CFA, one must have

---

[1] Sumner N. Levine, ed., *Financial Analyst's Handbook I* (Homewood, Ill.: Dow Jones-Irwin, 1975).

[2] William C. Norby, "Overview of Financial Analysis," in Levine, *Financial Analyst's Handbook I*, 3.

several years of practical experience and pass a series of three examinations.[3] Figure 21.1, which shows the subjects covered in each of the examinations, provides a good summary of the types of knowledge the successful financial analyst needs.

Societies of financial analysts have been formed around the world. For example, the European Federation of Financial Analysts draws its membership from ten European countries. Other societies are located in countries such as Canada, Australia, Japan, and Brazil.

21.2 REASONS FOR FINANCIAL ANALYSIS

There are two primary reasons for engaging in financial analysis. The first reason is to try to determine certain characteristics of securities; the second reason is to attempt to identify mispriced securities. These reasons are discussed next.

☐ 21.2.1 Determining Security Characteristics

According to modern portfolio theory, a financial analyst will want to estimate a security's future beta and unique risk, since these are needed to determine the risk (measured by standard deviation) of a portfolio. Perhaps the analyst may also want to estimate the dividend yield of a security over the next year in order to determine its suitability for portfolios in which dividend yield is relevant (owing to, for instance, legal restrictions). Careful analysis of such things as a company's dividend policy and likely future cash flows may lead to better estimates than can be obtained by simply extrapolating last year's dividend yield.

In many cases it may be desirable to know something about the sources of a security's risk and return. If a portfolio is being managed for a person who is in the oil business, one might want to minimize the sensitivity of the portfolio's return to changes in oil prices. This is because it is likely that if oil prices are in a decline, then the person's income from the oil business will also be in a decline. If the portfolio were sensitive to oil prices (which would be the case if it contained a substantial investment in oil stocks), then it too would be in a decline in value, thereby reinforcing the deterioration of the person's financial position.[4]

☐ 21.2.2 Attempting to Identify Mispriced Securities

A search for a mispriced security typically involves the use of *fundamental analysis*. In essence, this entails searching for a security in which the financial analyst's estimates of such things as the firm's future earnings and dividends:

---

[3] To obtain more information about becoming a CFA, contact the Institute of Chartered Financial Analysts. Their mailing address is P.O. Box 3668, Charlottesville, VA 22903 and their telephone number is (804)977–6600. A useful annual publication of the Institute is *The CFA Candidate Study and Examination Program Review*.

[4] For a discussion regarding portfolio selection by an investor who has earned income (for example, from wages or from running a business), see Edward M. Miller, "Portfolio Selection in a Fluctuating Economy," *Financial Analysts Journal* 34, no. 3 (May/June 1978):77–83.

1. Differ substantially from consensus (that is, average) estimates of others,

2. Are viewed as being closer to the correct values than the consensus estimates, and

3. Are not currently reflected in the security's market price but eventually will be reflected in its market price.

Two rather different approaches may be taken in the search for mispriced securities using fundamental analysis. The first approach involves valuation, where an attempt is made to determine the appropriate "intrinsic" or "true" value for a security. After making this determination, the intrinsic value is compared with the security's current market price. If the market

FIGURE 21–1
General topic outline, CFA Candidate Study and Examination Program.

Source: The CFA Candidate Study and Examination Program Review (Charlottesville, VA: The Institute of Chartered Financial Analysts, 1987), pp. 2–7.

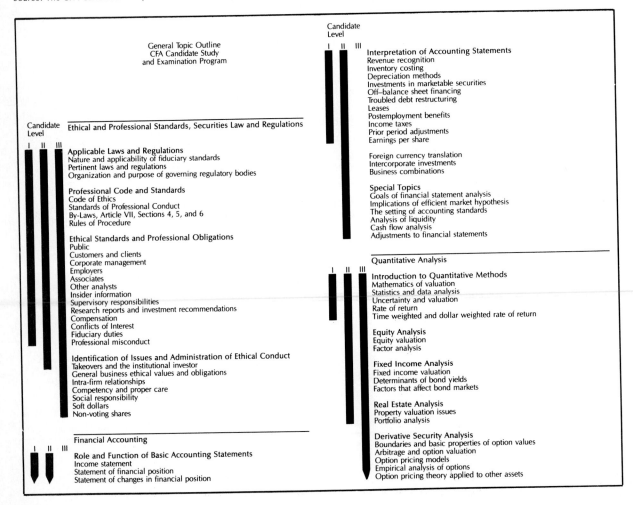

Asset Allocation
Expected return and risk
Estimation issues
The optimal portfolio
Dynamic asset allocation

Performance Measurement
Universe comparisons
Risk adjustment
Benchmark error
Ambiguity between skill and chance
Performance attribution
Normal portfolio
Non-parametric performance measurement
Incentive fees
Gaming performance measurement

Economics

Candidate Level I II III

Focus on Macroeconomics
Concept and measurement of GNP
Business fluctuations and economic forecasting
Inflationary process
Aggregate supply and demand
Macro schools of thought
Forecasting tools and success

Focus on Microeconomics and Analysis
Consumer behavior and business decision making
Costs and supply of goods
Product life cycle
Business structure and regulation

International Economics
Comparative advantage
International payments and exchange

Focus on Analysis, Policy, and Investment Application
Applications to portfolio management
Economic factors of return
Structural change
Current issues

Candidate Level I II III

Techniques of Analysis—Fixed-Income Securities

Types and Characteristics
Taxable, non-taxable
Type of issuer
Maturities
Indenture provisions
Convertible, non-convertible

Mathematical Properties
Interest on interest
Determinants of prices and yields
Duration

Credit Evaluation
Ratings and rating services
Earning power
Asset protection
Terms and covenants

Interest Rates
Term structure
Forecasting

Bond trading
Analysis
Techniques

Risk Management
Futures
Options

New Features
Contingent options and early redemptions
International bond investing

Techniques of Analysis—Equity Securities

Candidate Level I II III

Investment Context
Equity instruments (common stocks, convertible and participating issues, rights, warrants, options and futures)
Development and application of equity instruments
Characteristics of equity markets: indices, economic relationship, comparative risk and return
International instruments, developments, and markets

Candidate Level I II III

Economic Framework
Industry Analysis and Evaluation
Identification of company's business(es)
External factors: political, regulatory, social
Demand analysis: end uses, growth (real and nominal), cyclicality
Supply analysis: degree of concentration, ease of entry, capacity
Profitability: demand/supply balance, pricing and cost
International aspects

Company Analysis and Evaluation
Position within industry
Sales analysis: growth (real and nominal), cyclicality
Earnings analysis: earnings by business segment, consolidated results, components of return on equity
Flow of funds analysis
Balance sheet analysis
Dividends: payout policy and dividend growth
Management appraisal
International equity analysis

Risk Analysis
Qualitative factors: external (political, social, environmental); company business (economic sensitivity, size, growth, financial leverage); stock market (price volatility, share characteristics, market sub-groups)
Quantitative factors: capital asset pricing model (beta, nonsystematic), factor analysis (identification, exposure)

Valuation
Earnings multiples
Dividend discount and other valuation models
Technical analysis
Stock market perceptions

Derivative Securities
Characteristics of options, futures, warrants
Markets for derivative securities
Valuation models
Application of derivative securities

Equity Analysis and the Efficient Markets
Weak, semi-strong and strong forms of efficient market hypothesis
Implications relative to fundamental and technical analysis
Market anomalies

Organization of the Equity Analysis Process
General investment philosophy
Techniques of information collection and processing
Analysts' interaction with other investment professionals
Communication of information inside and outside organizations

Equity Analysis Performance Measurement
Criteria
Techniques
Evaluation process

Objective of Analysis—Portfolio Management

I II III

Principles of Financial Asset Management
Definition of portfolio management, basic concepts—return, risk, diversification, portfolio efficiency
Evolution of portfolio management—traditional and recent developments

Investor Objectives, Constraints and Policies
Liquidity requirement
Return requirement
Risk tolerance
Time horizon
Tax considerations
Regulatory and legal considerations
Unique needs, circumstances and preferences
Determination of portfolio policies

Expectational Factors
Social, political and economic
Capital markets
Individual financial assets

Integration of Portfolio Policies and Expectational Factors
Portfolio construction—asset allocation, active/passive strategies
Monitoring portfolio and responding to change—objectives, constraints and policies, expectational factors
Execution—timing, commission costs, price effects

Portfolio Performance Appraisal
Performance criteria—absolute performance, relative to portfolio objectives and risk level, relative to other portfolios with similar objectives
Measurement of performance—valuation of assets, accounting for income, rates of return and volatility
Evaluation of results—relationship to performance criteria, sources of results

FIGURE 21–1 (Continued)

price is substantially greater than the intrinsic value, the security is said to be overpriced, or overvalued. If the market price is substantially less than the intrinsic value, the security is said to be underpriced, or undervalued. Instead of comparing price with value, the analyst sometimes estimates a security's expected return over a specified period, given its current market price and intrinsic value. This estimate is then compared with the "appropriate" return for securities with similar attributes.[5]

Determining a security's intrinsic value may be done in great detail, using estimates of all major factors (for example, gross national product of the economy, industry sales, firm sales and expenses, and capitalization rates). Alternatively, a shortcut may be taken where, for example, an estimate of earnings per share may be multiplied by a "justified," or "normal," price-earnings ratio to determine the intrinsic value of a share of common stock.[6]

A second approach has the analyst estimate only one or two financial variables and then compare these estimates directly with consensus estimates. For example, next year's earnings per share for a stock may be estimated. If the analyst's estimate substantially exceeds the consensus of other analysts' estimates, the stock may be considered an attractive investment. This is because the analyst expects the actual earnings to provide a happy surprise for the market when announced. In turn, there will be an increase in the stock's price at that time, resulting in the investor receiving a greater-than-normal return. Conversely, when an analyst's estimate of earnings per share is substantially below that of the other analysts, then the analyst expects the market will receive an unhappy surprise. The resulting decrease in the stock's price will lead to a smaller-than-normal return.

At an aggregate level, an analyst may be more optimistic about the economy than the consensus of other analysts. This would suggest that a larger-than-normal investment in stocks be taken, offset perhaps by a smaller-than-normal investment in fixed-income securities. Conversely, a relatively pessimistic view would suggest a smaller-than-normal investment in stocks, offset perhaps by a larger-than-normal investment in fixed-income securities.

Alternatively, the analyst might agree with the consensus view on both the economy and the individual characteristics of specific securities but feel that the consensus view of the prospects for a certain group of securities in a particular industry is in error. In such a case, a larger-than-normal investment may be made in stocks from an industry having prospects about which the analyst feels relatively optimistic. Conversely, a smaller-than-normal investment would be made in stocks from an industry about which the analyst feels relatively pessimistic.

Fundamental analysis of common stocks is discussed in more detail later in this chapter. At that time the method of technical analysis is introduced and compared with fundamental analysis.

---

[5] The capitalization of income method of valuation is often used in the search for mispriced securities. This method was discussed in Chapters 13 and 16, where it was applied to bonds and stocks, respectively.

[6] To avoid complications arising when seeking the intrinsic value of a stock that has negative earnings per share, some analysts estimate sales per share and multiply this figure by a "normal" price–sales ratio.

Many books and articles have been written that allegedly show how financial analysis can be used to beat the market, meaning they purport to show how to make abnormally high returns by investing in the stock market. In order to evaluate such systems, an understanding of what "the market" is and how to measure its performance is in order.

Market Indices

What did the market do yesterday? How much would an unmanaged common stock portfolio have returned last year? Such questions are often answered by examining the performance of a *market index*. Figure 21.2 displays many indices that are commonly discussed. These indices differ from one another with respect to (1) the securities included in the index and (2) the method employed in calculating the value of the index.

In order to understand how some of the most popular indices are computed, consider a simple example where the market index is based on two stocks, referred to as A and B. At the end of day t, their closing prices are, respectively, $10 and $20 per share. Furthermore, at this time A has 1500 shares outstanding and B has 2000 shares outstanding.

There are three weighting methods that are often used in computing a market index. The first method, involving *price weighting*, begins by summing the prices of the stocks that are included in the index and ends by dividing this sum by a constant (the divisor). If the index includes only stocks A and B and was started on day t, the divisor would be equal to the number of stocks in the average, 2. Thus, on day t the index would have a value of $(10 + 20)/2 = 15$. The divisor is adjusted thereafter whenever there is a stock split in order to avoid giving misleading indications of the market's direction.[7]

For example, assume that on day $t + 1$, B splits 2-for-1 and closes at $11 per share, while A closes at $13. In this situation, it is clear that the market has risen, since both stocks have a higher price than on day t after adjusting B for the split. If nothing were done in computing the index, its value on day $t + 1$ would be $(13 + 11)/2 = 12$, a drop of $20\% = (12 - 15)/15$ from day t that falsely suggests the market went down on day $t + 1$. In reality, the market went up to $[13 + (11 \times 2)]/2 = 17.5$, a gain of $16.67\% = (17.5 - 15)/15$.

A stock split is accounted for in a price-weighted index by adjusting the divisor whenever a split takes place. In the example, the divisor is adjusted by examining the index on day $t + 1$, the day of the split. More specifically, the following equation would be solved for the unknown divisor d:

$$\frac{13 + 11}{d} = 17.5. \qquad (21.1)$$

---

[7] The divisor is also adjusted whenever the composition of the stocks in the index changes (meaning whenever one stock is substituted for another).

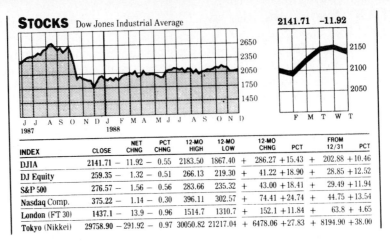

STOCKS Dow Jones Industrial Average

2141.71 −11.92

INDEX	CLOSE	NET CHNG	PCT CHNG	12-MO HIGH	12-MO LOW	12-MO CHNG	PCT	FROM 12/31	PCT
DJIA	2141.71	− 11.92	− 0.55	2183.50	1867.40	+ 286.27	+15.43	+ 202.88	+10.46
DJ Equity	259.35	− 1.32	− 0.51	266.13	219.30	+ 41.22	+18.90	+ 28.85	+12.52
S&P 500	276.57	− 1.56	− 0.56	283.66	235.32	+ 43.00	+18.41	+ 29.49	+11.94
Nasdaq Comp.	375.22	− 1.14	− 0.30	396.11	302.57	+ 74.41	+24.74	+ 44.75	+13.54
London (FT 30)	1437.1	− 13.9	− 0.96	1514.7	1310.7	+ 152.1	+11.84	+ 63.8	+ 4.65
Tokyo (Nikkei)	29758.90	− 291.92	− 0.97	30050.82	21217.04	+ 6478.06	+27.83	+ 8194.90	+38.00

(a)

STOCK MARKET DATA BANK   12/8/88

MAJOR INDEXES

HIGH	LOW (12 MOS)		CLOSE	NET CHG	% CHG	12 MO CHG	% CHG	FROM 12/31	% CHG
DOW JONES AVERAGES									
2183.50	1867.04	30 Industrials	2141.71	− 11.92	− 0.55	+ 286.27	+15.43	+ 202.88	+ 10.46
947.98	699.00	20 Transportation	943.00	− 4.98	− 0.53	+ 250.14	+36.10	+ 194.14	+ 25.92
190.02	167.08	15 Utilities	184.98	− 0.89	− 0.48	+ 10.25	+ 5.87	+ 9.90	+ 5.65
821.36	686.58	65 Composite	812.59	− 4.37	− 0.53	+ 130.67	+19.16	+ 98.32	+ 13.77
266.13	219.30	Equity Mkt. Index	259.35	− 1.32	− 0.51	+ 41.22	+18.90	+ 28.85	+ 12.52
NEW YORK STOCK EXCHANGE									
159.42	131.79	Composite	155.37	− 0.77	− 0.49	+ 24.30	+18.54	+ 17.14	+ 12.40
192.81	158.46	Industrials	187.37	− 1.12	− 0.59	+ 29.88	+18.97	+ 20.33	+ 12.17
75.22	66.41	Utilities	75.02	− 0.09	− 0.12	+ 8.92	+13.49	+ 7.71	+ 11.45
144.14	111.99	Transportation	142.22	− 0.53	− 0.37	+ 31.81	+28.81	+ 23.65	+ 19.95
136.16	107.77	Finance	130.46	− 0.52	− 0.40	+ 22.60	+20.95	+ 15.89	+ 13.87
STANDARD & POOR'S INDEXES									
283.66	235.32	500 Index	276.57	− 1.56	− 0.56	+ 43.00	+18.41	+ 29.49	+ 11.94
326.84	271.27	Industrials	318.46	− 2.08	− 0.65	+ 49.32	+18.33	+ 32.60	+ 11.40
224.83	179.69	Transportation	223.33	− 0.74	− 0.33	+ 46.18	+26.07	+ 33.16	+ 17.44
114.57	100.40	Utilities	113.60	− 0.07	− 0.06	+ 13.84	+13.87	+ 11.48	+ 11.24
26.48	20.43	Financials	25.23	− 0.11	− 0.43	+ 4.81	+23.56	+ 3.60	+ 16.64
NASDAQ									
396.11	302.57	Composite	375.22	− 1.14	− 0.30	+ 74.41	+24.74	+ 44.75	+ 13.54
413.09	304.43	Industrials	369.63	− 1.13	− 0.30	+ 67.50	+22.34	+ 30.69	+ 9.05
435.80	337.96	Insurance	426.59	− 1.02	− 0.24	+ 88.75	+26.27	+ 75.53	+ 21.51
464.91	367.69	Banks	438.72	− 0.96	− 0.22	+ 71.58	+19.50	+ 48.06	+ 12.30
171.39	130.21	Nat. Mkt. Comp.	162.88	− 0.49	− 0.30	+ 33.43	+25.82	+ 20.29	+ 14.23
160.10	117.30	Nat. Mkt. Indus.	143.62	− 0.43	− 0.30	+ 27.19	+23.35	+ 12.51	+ 9.54
OTHERS									
309.59	242.72	Amex	297.38	− 0.39	− 0.13	+ 56.34	+23.37	+ 37.03	+ 14.22
240.97	187.61	Value-Line (geom.)	228.51	− 0.92	− 0.40	+ 41.82	+22.40	+ 26.89	+ 13.34
151.42	109.32	Russell 2000	143.75	− 0.25	− 0.17	+ 35.13	+32.34	+ 23.32	+ 19.36
2794.45	2287.32	Wilshire 5000	2716.52	− 13.46	− 0.49	+ 443.50	+19.51	+ 299.39	+ 12.39

(b)

FIGURE 21–2
Stock market indices published daily in *The Wall Street Journal*.

Source: The Wall Street Journal © Dow Jones & Company, Inc. (December 9, 1988): pp. C1–C2.

The value of d that solves this equation is 1.37. The new divisor will continue in use after day $t + 1$ until there is another split, when it will again be recalculated.

The Dow Jones Industrial Average, one of the most widely followed indices, is calculated in this manner; it involves the prices of 30 stocks that generally represent large-sized firms. Two other Dow Jones averages, one of which uses 20 transportation stocks, the other of which uses 15 utility stocks, are similarly calculated. Levels of these Dow Jones averages are reported in almost every daily newspaper. Historical data on the averages, including quarterly dividends and earnings figures, are published from time to time in *Barron's* and other periodicals.[8]

A second weighting method is known as *value weighting* (or capitalization weighting). With this method, the prices of the stocks in the index are multiplied by their respective numbers of shares outstanding and then added up in order to arrive at a figure equal to the aggregate market value for that day. This figure is then divided by the corresponding figure for the day the index was started, with the resulting value being multiplied by an arbitrarily set beginning index value.

Continuing with the example, assume that the start-up day for the index is day t and that the index is assigned a beginning value of 100. First, note that the aggregate market value on day t is equal to ($\$10 \times 1500$) + ($\$20 \times 2000$) = $\$55,000$. Next, note that the aggregate market value on day $t + 1$ is equal to ($\$13 \times 1500$) + ($\$11 \times 4000$) = $\$63,500$. Dividing $\$63,500$ by $\$55,000$ and then multiplying the result by 100 gives the index value for day $t + 1$ of ($\$63,500/\$55,000$) $\times$ 100 = 115.45. Thus, the market would be reported as having risen by 15.45% = (115.45 − 100)/100 from day t to day $t + 1$.

The Standard & Poor's 500, widely used by institutional investors, is a value-weighted average of 500 large-sized stocks. Standard & Poor's also computes value-weighted indices for industrial, transportation, utility, and financial stocks. Furthermore, a variety of industry indices are also calculated. Values for all indices, along with quarterly data on dividends, earnings, and sales, may be found in Standard & Poor's *Analysts' Handbook* (annual), *Trade and Securities Statistics* (annual), and *Analysts' Handbook Supplement* (monthly).

More comprehensive value-weighted indices for U.S. stocks are computed by others. The New York Stock Exchange publishes a composite index of all stocks listed on that exchange, as well as four subindices (industrials, utilities, transportation, and finance). The American Stock Exchange computes an index of its stocks. The National Association of Securities Dealers (NASD), using its automated quotation service (NASDAQ), computes indices based on the market value of approximately 5000 over-the-counter stocks; in addition to a composite index, NASD calculates indices for six categories

---

[8] Some bond market indices are calculated in this manner. For example, the *Dow Jones 20-Bond Index* is computed by averaging the prices of ten utility and ten industrial bonds. Bond indices are also published by Merrill Lynch, Salomon Brothers, Shearson Lehman Hutton, Standard & Poor's, and others; see Chapter 23 (Figure 23.9) for more on bond indices.

representing industrials, banks, insurance, other finance, transportation, and utilities. NASD also publishes four indices that are based on just those stocks in their National Market System (the previously mentioned NASD indices are based on both NMS and non-NMS stocks). The broadest value-weighted index is calculated by Wilshire Associates. Their index, known as the Wilshire 5000 Equity Index, is based on all stocks listed on the New York and American Stock exchanges plus those "actively traded over-the-counter."[9] Levels of all these indices are published weekly in *Barron's*, with the *Wall Street Journal* providing daily values for several of them.

The third method of weighting is known as *equal weighting*. With this method, equal dollar-size investments are made in the securities in the index. In the case of stocks A and B, on day t the equal-weighted index would involve one share of A and one-half share of B, resulting in a value of $(10 \times 1) + [20 \times (1/2)] = 20$. On day $t + 1$, the index would adjust for the split of B by multiplying its price by 1 (instead of 1/2, as was previously done), resulting in an index value of $(13 \times 1) + (11 \times 1) = 24$, an increase of 20% = $(24 - 20)/20$. An example is the index calculated by the *Indicator Digest*, involving common stocks listed on the New York Stock Exchange.

One popular index that does not involve price weighting, value weighting, or equal weighting is the *Value Line Composite Average*. This index is computed daily by multiplying the previous day's index by the geometric mean of the daily *price relatives* (today's price divided by yesterday's price) of the relevant stocks in the index. For example, the value of the index consisting of stocks A and B on day $t + 1$ would be calculated by first determining the price relatives to be equal to $(13/10) = 1.3$ for A and $(11 \times 2)/20 = 1.1$ for B. Then the geometric mean would be calculated as[10]

$$(1.3 \times 1.1)^{1/2} = 1.1958.$$

If the value of the index on day t was 120, then the value on day $t + 1$ would be reported as $120 \times 1.1958 = 143.496$, an increase of $1.1958 - 1 = 19.58\%$. In the case of the Value Line index, the initial value was set at 100 on June 30, 1961, and has been updated ever since then in this manner.[11]

In summary, four types of indices have been presented; various people use these indices when they refer to how the market has done. However, the indices can give notably different answers. In the example shown here, the market was calculated to have risen by either 16.67%, 15.45%, 20%, or 19.58%, depending on the index used. In practice, most professional money managers investing in NYSE-listed stocks use the S&P 500 as the barometer

---

[9] The Russell 1000, 2000, and 3000 are also broad value-weighted indices, covering roughly the largest 1000 stocks; the next 2000; and the sum of the two. In terms of international indices, *Morgan Stanley Capital International Perspective* publishes value-weighted indices using various combinations of 1371 stocks from 19 different countries, resulting in a "world market index." These and other international indices are discussed in Chapter 24 (see Figure 24.2).

[10] In order to determine the geometric mean for N stocks, multiply their price relatives and then take the Nth root of the resulting product.

[11] Value Line also has indices for industrials, rails, and utilities that are similarly computed and updated.

of the stock market, since it has a fairly wide base and weights larger companies more heavily than smaller companies.

Conveying Advice on Beating the Market

It is interesting to ponder whether or not advice on how to beat the market will remain useful after becoming public. It seems logical that any such prescription that has been in print for long is not likely to allow the investor to beat the market without fail. Even if an approach has worked in the past (just because someone asserts it has worked does not mean that it, in fact, has worked), as more and more investors apply it, prices will be driven to levels at which the approach will not work in the future. Any system designed to beat the market, once known to more than a few people, carries the seeds of its own destruction.

There are two reasons for not including advice on "guaranteed" ways to beat the market in this book. First, to do so would make a successful system public and hence unsuccessful. Second, the authors know of no such system. Some apparent anomalies and possible inefficiencies have been described previously. But any book that purports to open the door to the *certainty* of making abnormally high returns for those who follow its advice should be regarded with the greatest skepticism.

This does not mean that financial analysis is useless. Although individuals should be skeptical when others tell them how to use financial analysis to beat the market, individuals can try to understand the market with the use of financial analysis.

□ 21.2.4 Financial Analysis and Market Efficiency

The concept of an efficient market (discussed in Chapter 3) may appear to be based on a paradox. Financial analysts carefully analyze the prospects for companies, industries, and the economy in the search for mispriced securities. If an undervalued security is found, for example, then it will be purchased. However, the act of purchasing the security will tend to push its price upward toward its intrinsic value, thereby making it no longer undervalued. That is, financial analysis tends to result in security prices that reflect intrinsic values, which is equivalent to saying that financial analysis tends to make markets efficient. But if this is the case, why would anyone perform financial analysis in an attempt to identify mispriced securities?

There are two responses to this question. First, there are costs associated with performing financial analysis. This means that financial analysis may not be conducted on all securities all the time. As a result, the prices of all securities will not reflect intrinsic values all the time. Pockets of opportunity may arise from time to time, thereby opening the possibility for added benefits from financial analysis. This suggests that people should engage in financial analysis only to the point at which the added benefits

cover the added costs.[12] Ultimately, in a highly competitive market, prices would be close enough to intrinsic values to make it worthwhile for only the most skillful analysts to search for mispriced securities. Thus, the market would be nearly, but not perfectly, efficient.[13]

The other response to the question focuses on the first reason given earlier for engaging in financial analysis: to determine certain characteristics of securities. This reason is appropriate even in a perfectly efficient market. Since investors differ in their circumstances (consider the person in the oil business, discussed earlier), portfolios should be "tailored" to accommodate such differences. Successful performance of this task generally requires estimation of certain characteristics of securities, thereby justifying the use of financial analysis.

☐ 21.2.5   **Needed Skills**

To understand and estimate the risk and return of individual securities as well as groups of securities (such as industries), financial markets and the principles of valuation must be understood. Much of the material required for such an understanding can be found in this book. But, as Figure 21.1 indicates, even more is required. Future prospects must be estimated and interrelationships assessed. This requires the skills of an economist and an understanding of industrial organization. To process relevant historical data, some command of quantitative methods is needed, along with an understanding of the nuances of accounting.

This book cannot provide all the material one needs to become a successful financial analyst. Books on accounting, economics, industrial organization, and quantitative methods are required. Instead, some techniques used by financial analysts are discussed, along with some of the pitfalls involved. In addition, sources of investment information are presented.

21.3   EVALUATING INVESTMENT SYSTEMS

Many statements have been made in the past asserting that some mechanical investment system, using only available historical data and a set of objective analytical procedures, can provide results superior to those obtained with a *passive investment system*. (A passive investment system involves simply buying and holding a well-diversified portfolio of stocks over a performance evaluation period; the return on a market index is often used as a substitute for such a portfolio.) Some mechanical systems simply provide predictions of how the market will behave; others prescribe a complete set of instructions

---

[12] If the added benefits exceeded the added costs, then it would be profitable to perform more financial analysis because the incremental benefits from doing so would cover the associated costs. If, on the other hand, the added costs exceeded the added benefits, then it would be profitable to cut back on the amount of financial analysis because costs would be reduced by an amount greater than benefits.

[13] For an interesting argument on why the existence of trading costs results in some investors performing financial analysis in an efficient market, see Bradford Cornell and Richard Roll, "Strategies for Pairwise Competitions in Markets and Organizations," *Bell Journal of Economics* 12, no. 1 (Spring 1981):201–13.

for investing in individual securities. All of them present impressive statistics based on tests using data from some past evaluation period.

Consider as examples the following four statements:

". . . switch from bonds to stocks after the growth rate of the money supply has risen for two months; switch from stocks to bonds after the growth rate of the money supply has been below its most recent peak for 15 months. Historically, such a policy would have produced over twice the return obtained by simply holding stocks."

". . . this simple formula predicted over 95% of the quarterly variation in Standard & Poor's 500-stock index over the period studied."

". . . A portfolio of the 25 stocks with the greatest historical relative strength would have outperformed a portfolio of the 25 stocks with the smallest relative strength in 8 months out of 12."

". . . This completely objective stock selection procedure, which can be performed without error on a microcomputer, would have outperformed 80% of the professionally managed portfolios during the period in question."

Statements such as these four have been made in the past and will undoubtedly continue to be made in the future. Advocates of such mechanical investment systems may sincerely believe they have found the path to instant affluence. However, their proofs often rest on shaky ground. When evaluating any system, it is imperative that several possible errors be avoided.

☐ 21.3.1 Failure to Adjust for Risk

According to the capital asset pricing model, any investment system that results in the selection of high-beta stocks is likely to produce above-average returns in bull markets and below-average returns in bear markets. Since the stock market over the long term has trended upward, on balance such a system will tend to produce above-average returns over the long run. However, an evaluation of the performance of any investment system should involve not only measuring the resulting average return but also determining the amount of risk incurred. Then the average return from a passive investment system of similar risk can be computed for comparison. Techniques for making such comparisons are presented in Chapter 23.

☐ 21.3.2 Failure to Consider Transaction Costs

Systems that rely on constant trading may produce gross returns that exceed those of a passive investment strategy of comparable risk. But this is not an accurate evaluation of a system's performance because transactions costs should be considered in measuring returns. Net returns are calculated by adding transaction costs to the purchase price of an investment and deducting them from the investment's selling price.

For example, if 100 shares of a stock are purchased at $19 per share with a transaction cost of $100, then the cost of the investment is $(100 \times \$19) + \$100 = \$2000$. If the stock is subsequently sold for $23 per share, with another $100 transaction cost, then the proceeds from the sale are $(100 \times \$23) - \$100 = \$2200$. As a result, the net return is

($2200 − $2000)/$2000 = 10%, whereas the gross return is ($2300 − $1900)/$1900 = 21.05%, a substantial difference.

☐ 21.3.3 Failure to Consider Dividends

When the performance of a mechanical system is compared with that of a passive investment system, dividends (and interest payments) are often ignored. This may seriously bias the results. For example, a system may be advocated that, in effect, selects low-yield stocks. The prices of such stocks should increase at a faster rate than those of high-yield stocks with the same amount of risk. This is because a stock's return consists of both dividends and capital appreciation. If two stocks have the same risk, they should have the same return, meaning that the stock with a smaller yield will have a larger capital appreciation. Thus, if just capital appreciation is examined, a system that selects low-yield stocks would tend to show a more rapid rate of capital appreciation than a passive investment strategy involving a well-diversified portfolio consisting of both low-yield and high-yield stocks. Consequently, when yields of systems differ significantly from average yields, it is important to examine returns, not the rate of capital appreciation.

☐ 21.3.4 Nonoperational Systems

Although obvious, it still must be mentioned: To be useful, a system must not require information about the future. For example, many systems require action after some time series of values (such as a stock's price) has reached a peak or trough. But it is rarely apparent until well afterwards that in fact a peak or trough has been reached.

A similar situation arises when an equation is estimated from a set of data. For example, a system might assume that there is a relationship between the money supply at time $t − 1$ and stock prices at time t. The general relationship might be

$$\overline{SP}_t = a + bM_{t-1} \tag{21.2}$$

where $\overline{SP}_t$ is the predicted level of the S&P 500 at time t, M_{t-1} is the level of the money supply at time $t − 1$, and a and b are constants. In this system, the level of the S&P 500 one period from now can be predicted from the current level of the money supply.

To make such a system operational, specific numerical values for a and b are needed. These numbers might be estimated by examining monthly data over a ten-year period from 1978 through 1987, which means that these numbers would be known only after 1987. However, some people might test the predictive ability of the equation over the same ten-year period of 1978 to 1987 using these numbers. In doing so, they fail to realize that the system would not have been operational with these numbers for this test period, since the numbers were determined after the test period. A true test of the predictive ability of this or any system must involve an estimation period that is earlier than the test period. That is, the test period must use *out-of-sample data*, as is discussed shortly.

☐ 21.3.5 Spurious Fits

Using a set of data from a past period, it is not too difficult to discover a system that works quite well when tested on the same data. In spite of the previously mentioned criticism that such a system would not have been operational during the test period, some investors might still be tempted to use it in the future if it worked well enough in retrospect. However, there is another criticism that can be made about such a system.

Imagine that equation (21.2) did not appear to work well. If so, then the following equation could be tried:

$$\overline{SP}_t = a + bM_{t-1} + cM_{t-2} \qquad\qquad \textbf{(21.3)}$$

where M_{t-2} is the level of the money supply at time $t-2$ and c is a constant. If equation (21.3) does not seem to work well, more variables and constants could be tried. Ultimately an equation could be found that appears to work quite well. However, this does not mean that it would be useful to the investor. If 100 seemingly irrelevant systems are tried with a set of data, due to the laws of probability one of them is likely to give results that are "statistically significant at the 1% level." This should not cause undue excitement, since it would not have any notable predictive power in the future.

For example, stock prices in the United States have been shown to be correlated with both sunspot activity and with the length of skirts. Few would associate causal relationships in these instances. Instead, these correlations are likely to have been *spurious*, meaning they probably were coincidental. Without solid reasons to believe that a relationship is due to underlying forces, it would be unwise to predict its continuation in the future.

☐ 21.3.6 Comparisons with Easily Beaten Systems

Often an investment system is said to explain a large part of the variation in some stock index. Figure 21.3 shows the quarterly level of the S&P 500 over a ten-year period (the solid curve) and the levels predicted by a system based on historic levels of the money supply (the dotted curve). The two sets of values appear to be quite similar.

This is actually not very impressive. An extremely simple set of predictions, shown by the dashed curve in Figure 21.3, is even better. This procedure predicts that each quarter's index will equal that of the preceding quarter:

$$\overline{SP}_t = SP_{t-1}. \qquad\qquad \textbf{(21.4)}$$

Any system that is purported to be able to beat the market must predict percentage price changes (or returns), not price levels, because such changes (or returns) determine profits and losses. Thus, a good test is the extent to which predicted changes conform to actual changes. Figure 21.4 shows the percentage price change predicted by the system analyzed in Figure 21.3, along with the corresponding actual change for each quarter. The relationship is, at best, tenuous.

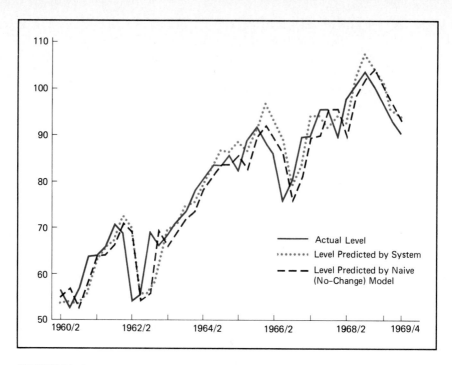

FIGURE 21–3
Actual and predicted levels, Standard & Poor's 500-Stock Index, Second Quarter
1960 through Fourth Quarter 1969.

Source: Kenneth E. Homa and Dwight M. Jaffee, "The Supply of Money and Common Stock Prices,"
Journal of Finance 26, no. 5 (December 1971): p. 1052.

☐ 21.3.7   Reliance on Misleading Visual Comparisons

Occasionally the proponent of a system will produce a graph that plots both
the level of an indicator intended to predict market moves and the levels of
the market itself. Visual comparison of the two curves may suggest that the
indicator does indeed predict changes in the market. However, the eye cannot
easily differentiate between a situation in which changes in a market "predictor" *lead* the market and one in which the changes *lag* behind the market.
This is a crucial distinction because only a leading indicator can bring superior investment performance.

☐ 21.3.8   *Ex Post* Selection Bias

Many studies describe a stock-selection system that outperformed standard
stock market indices. Some of these systems avoid the errors considered
thus far, but another error may be involved. To facilitate computer-based
analysis, a standard set of data might have been employed. For example,
an investigator might use a database prepared in 1988 with stock price data
relating to the period from 1977 through 1987. The stocks included in the
database might have been chosen because they existed and were important
in 1988 (for example, they might have been considered important because

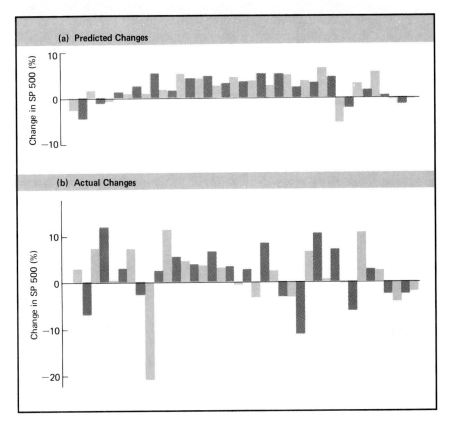

FIGURE 21–4
Predicted and actual quarterly percentage changes, Standard & Poor's 500-Stock Index, Second Quarter 1960 through Fourth Quarter 1969.

Source: Kenneth E. Homa and Dwight M. Jaffee, "The Supply of Money and Common Stock Prices," *Journal of Finance* 26, no. 5 (December 1971): p. 1052.

they were listed on the NYSE in 1988). Discovering a superior investment system from analysis of this database is subject to the criticism of involving *ex post selection bias*. That is, the system discovered in 1988 was based on an analysis of those stocks that were certain to be alive, well, and important in 1988. Accordingly, it should have done well over the period of 1977 to 1987. However, studies of this type implicitly commit an error described earlier —they require some information not available in advance. In particular, they require knowledge before 1988 of which stocks were around in 1988.

☐ 21.3.9   Failure to Use Out-of-Sample Data

Can any evidence concerning a system's ability to beat the market be persuasive? Probably not to those who believe absolutely in market efficiency. But there are appropriate tests that can be undertaken.

The search for a system should be conducted using one set of data, and the test of the system's predictive ability should be performed using an entirely different set of data. The latter set of data is sometimes known as

out-of-sample data (or a holdout sample). To be complete, such a test should involve the (simulated) management of a portfolio and be designed so that each investment decision is based solely on information available at the time the decision is made. Finally, the performance of the system should be measured in the way one would measure the performance of any investment manager (discussed in Chapter 23). This involves, among other things, attempting to determine the probability that the investment results were due to chance rather than skill.

Figure 21.5 shows the performance of one system using out-of-sample data. Values forecast by three predictive systems for quarterly percentage changes in the S&P 500 are shown, along with the subsequent actual changes. Each of the predictive systems worked extremely well with past data. The same cannot be said for their predictions using out-of-sample data.

FIGURE 21–5
Predicted and actual quarterly percentage changes, Standard & Poor's 500-Stock Index, Third Quarter 1970 through Second Quarter 1972.

Source: James E. Pesando, "The Supply of Money and Common Stock Prices: Further Observations on the Econometric Evidence," *Journal of Finance* 29, no. 3 (June 1974): p. 916.

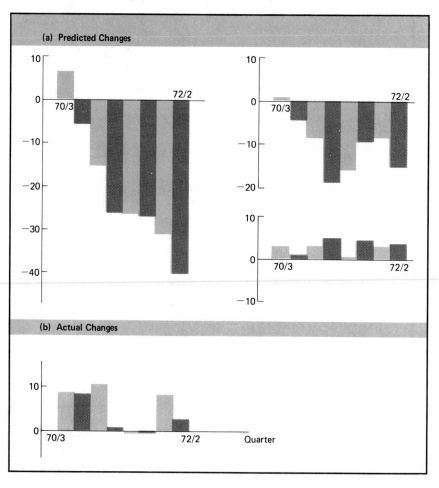

21.4 FUNDAMENTAL VERSUS TECHNICAL ANALYSIS

One of the major divisions in the ranks of financial analysts is between those using fundamental analysis (known as fundamental analysts, or fundamentalists) and those using *technical analysis* (known as technical analysts, or technicians). The fundamentalist tends to look forward; the technician, backward. The fundamentalist is concerned with such things as future earnings and dividends, whereas the technician thinks little (if at all) about such things.

> □ Technical analysis is the study of the internal stock exchange information as such. The word "technical" implies a study of the market itself and not of those external factors which are reflected in the market . . . [A]ll the relevant factors, whatever they may be, can be reduced to the volume of the stock exchange transactions and the level of share prices; or more generally, to the sum of the statistical information produced by the market.[14]

The technician usually attempts to predict short-term price movements and thus makes recommendations concerning the *timing* of purchases and sales of either specific stocks or of groups of stocks (such as industries) or of stocks in general. It is sometimes said that fundamental analysis is designed to answer the question What? and technical analysis to answer the question When?

The concept of technical analysis is completely at odds with the notion of efficient markets:

> □ . . . the methodology of technical analysis . . . rests upon the assumption that history tends to repeat itself in the stock exchange. If a certain pattern of activity has in the past produced certain results nine times out of ten, one can assume a strong likelihood of the same outcome whenever this pattern appears in the future. *It should be emphasized, however, that a large part of the methodology of technical analysis lacks a strictly logical explanation.*[15] [Italics added.]

Thus, technicians assert that the study of past patterns of things such as prices and volumes allows the investor to identify accurately times when certain specific stocks (or groups of stocks, or the market in general) are either overpriced or underpriced.

> □ Like a medical thermometer, [technical analysis] is a signalling device; sometimes a false indication is given when there is no cause for alarm, but when there is cause for alarm, the signal will almost invariably be flashed.[16]

The rest of this chapter is concerned with the principles of fundamental analysis, since such analysis is more prevalent than technical analysis and

---

[14] Felix Rosenfeld, ed., *The Evaluation of Ordinary Shares*, a summary of the proceedings of the Eighth Congress of the European Federation of Financial Analysts Societies (Paris: Dunod, 1975), 297.

[15] Rosenfeld, *The Evaluation of Ordinary Shares*, 297–98.

[16] Robin J. Russo, *Compare—A Technical Timing System* (New York: Dean Witter & Co. Inc., 1976).

is essential if capital markets are to be efficient. Technical analysis is discussed briefly in the first appendix to this chapter, since there is little evidence showing it to be useful in enabling investors to beat the market.[17] Many "proofs" of the ability of technical analysis to beat the market have been offered, but most have committed at least one of the errors described earlier.

□ 21.4.1   Top-Down versus Bottom-Up Forecasting

Fundamental analysts forecast, among other things, future levels of the economy's gross national product, future sales and earnings for a number of industries, and future sales and earnings for an even larger number of firms. Eventually such forecasts are converted to estimates of expected returns of specific stocks and, perhaps, certain industries and the stock market itself. In some cases the conversion is made explicitly. For example, an estimate of next year's earnings per share for a firm may be multiplied by a projected price-earnings ratio in order to estimate the expected price of the firm's stock a year hence, thereby allowing a forecast of the expected return to be made. In other cases the conversion is implicit. For example, stocks with projected earnings exceeding consensus estimates may be placed on an "approved" list.

Some investment organizations that employ financial analysts follow a sequential *top-down approach* to forecasting. With this approach, the financial analysts are first involved in making forecasts for the economy, then for industries, and finally for companies. The industry forecasts are based on the forecasts for the economy and, in turn, the company forecasts are based on the forecasts for both its industry and the economy.

Other investment organizations begin with estimates of the prospects for companies and then build to estimates of the prospects for industries and ultimately the economy. Such a *bottom-up approach* may unknowingly involve inconsistent assumptions. For example, one analyst may use one forecast of foreign exchange rates in projecting the foreign sales of company A, whereas another analyst may use a different forecast in projecting the foreign sales of company B. Top-down systems are less susceptible to this danger, since all the analysts in the organization would use the same forecast of exchange rates.

In practice, a combination of the two approaches is often employed. For example, forecasts are made for the economy in a top-down manner. These forecasts then provide a setting within which financial analysts make bottom-up forecasts for individual companies. The sum of the individual forecasts should be consistent with the original economywide forecast.[18] If not, the process is repeated (perhaps with additional controls) to ensure consistency.

---

[17] See, for example, Robert A. Levy, "The Predictive Significance of Five-Point Chart Patterns," *Journal of Business* 44, no. 3 (July 1971):316–23; and Eugene F. Fama, "Efficient Capital Markets: A Review of Theory and Empirical Work," *Journal of Finance* 25, no. 2 (May 1970):383–417.

[18] Input-output analysis is sometimes used to ensure consistency between various industries and the economy in aggregate. This type of analysis is based on the notion that the output of certain industries (for example, the steel industry) is the input for certain other industries (for example, the household appliance industry).

21.4.2 Probabilistic Forecasting

Explicit probabilistic forecasting often focuses on economywide forecasts, since uncertainty at this level is of the greatest importance in determining the risk and expected return of a well-diversified portfolio. A few alternative economic scenarios may be forecast, along with their respective probability of occurrence. Then accompanying projections are made of the prospects for industries, companies, and stock prices. Such an exercise provides an idea of the likely sensitivities of different stocks to surprises concerning the economy. By assigning probabilities to the different scenarios, risks may also be estimated.

☐ 21.4.3 Econometric Models

An *econometric model* is a statistical model that provides a means of forecasting the levels of certain variables, known as *endogenous variables*. In order to make these forecasts, the model relies on assumptions that have been made in regard to the levels of certain other variables, known as *exogenous variables*. The model may be extremely complex or it may be a simple formula that can be used with a desk calculator. In any event, it should involve a blend of economics and statistics, where economics is used to suggest the forms of relevant relationships and statistical procedures are applied to historical data to estimate the exact nature of the relationships involved.

Some investment organizations utilize large-scale econometric models to translate predictions about such factors as the federal budget, expected consumer spending, and planned business investment into predictions of future levels of gross national product, inflation, and unemployment. Several firms and nonprofit organizations maintain such models, selling either the forecasts or the computer program itself to investment organizations, corporate planners, public agencies, and others.

The developers of large-scale models usually provide several "standard" predictions, based on different sets of assumptions about the exogenous variables; some also assign probabilities to the alternative predictions. In some cases, users can substitute their own sets of assumptions and subsequently examine the resulting predictions.

Large-scale econometric models of this type employ many equations that describe many important relationships. Although estimates of the magnitudes of such relationships are obtained from historical data, these estimates may or may not enable the model to work well in the future. When predictions turn out to be poor, it is sometimes said that there has been *structural changes* in the underlying economic relationships. However, the failure may be due to the influence of factors omitted from the model. In any event, such a situation necessitates changes in either the size of the estimates or the basic form of the econometric model or even both. Rare indeed is the user who does not fine-tune (or completely overhaul) such a model from time to time as further experience is accumulated.

☐ 21.4.4 Financial Statement Analysis

For some, the image of a typical financial analyst is that of a gnome, fully equipped with green eyeshade, poring over financial statements in a back

room. Though the physical description is rarely accurate, it is true that many analysts do study financial statements in an attempt to predict the future.

A company's financial statements can be regarded as the output of a model of the firm—a model designed by management, the company's accountants, and (indirectly) the tax authorities. Different companies use different models, meaning they treat similar events in different ways. One reason this is possible is because generally accepted accounting principles (GAAP), as established by the Financial Accounting Standards Board (FASB), allow a certain degree of latitude in how to account for various events. Examples include the method of depreciating assets (straight-line or accelerated) and the method of valuing inventory (FIFO or LIFO).

To understand a company fully and to compare it with others that use different accounting procedures, the financial analyst must be a financial detective, looking for clues in footnotes and the accompanying text that discuss how the financial statements were prepared. Those who take bottom-line figures such as earnings per share on faith may be more surprised by future developments than those who try to look behind the accounting veil.

The ultimate goal of the fundamental analyst is to determine the values of the outstanding claims on a firm's income (claimants include the firm's bondholders and stockholders). The firm's income must first be projected; then the possible distributions of that income among the claimants must be considered, with relevant probabilities assessed.

In practice, shortcut procedures are often used. Many analysts focus on reported accounting figures, even though such numbers may not adequately reflect true economic values. In addition, simple measures are often used to assess complex relationships. For example, some analysts attempt to estimate the probability that short-term creditors will be paid in full and on time by examining the ratio of liquid assets to the amount of short-term debt. Similarly, the probability that interest will be paid to bondholders in a timely fashion is often estimated by examining the ratio of earnings before interest and taxes to the periodic amount of such interest payments. Often the prospects for a firm's common stock are estimated by examining the ratio of earnings after taxes to the book value of equity.

The use of ratios such as these to facilitate predicting the future is widespread. Some ratios use items from the same financial statement (either a particular balance sheet or income statement), whereas others use items from two different statements. Still other ratios use items from two or more statements of the same type but of different years (for example, this year's balance sheet and last year's balance sheet), or incorporate data on market values.

Ratios may be used in several ways. Some analysts apply absolute standards, on the grounds that a substandard ratio indicates a potential weakness that merits further analysis. Other analysts compare a company's ratios to those of the "average" firm in the same industry in order to detect differences that may need further consideration. Yet others analyze trends in a company's ratios over time, hoping it will help them predict future changes. Still others combine ratios with technical analysis in order to arrive at investment decisions.

One example of how ratios can be used for investing involves the use of price-earnings ratios. This method is partly technical in nature, since it is based on the notion of *contrary opinion*. Specifically, it is based on a belief that stocks with low price-earnings ratios are out of favor in the investment community.[19] Accordingly, this contrarian investment strategy involves simply finding stocks with low price-earnings ratios and then investing in them. Stocks with high price-earnings ratios would be shunned with this strategy, since they would generally represent stocks that are viewed favorably in the investment community. Small firms typically have had higher returns than large firms, even after adjusting for differences in risk; given that small firms typically have had low price-earnings ratios, it is not surprising that such a strategy has been successful in the past.[20] Whether the success will continue in the future is another matter.

Another use of ratios is illustrated in Figure 21.6. In this figure, each ratio is equal to the product of the two ratios on its right-hand side, with one exception. The exception is the turnover ratio (sales/assets), whose reciprocal (assets/sales) equals the sum of the reciprocals of the four ratios on its right-hand side. Given the interrelationships among the ratios, it can be seen that once the future values of these ratios are forecast, then an implied forecast for the price of the firm's stock can be computed. The difficulty with such an approach, however, is in accurately predicting the future values of the ratios.

Ratio analysis can be very sophisticated, but it can also be overly simplistic. Routine extrapolation of a present ratio (or its recent trend) may produce a poor estimate of its future value. (For example, there is no reason for a firm to maintain a constant ratio of inventory to sales). Moreover, a series of simple projections may produce inconsistent financial statements. For example, projections of ratios imply predictions of the levels of various balance sheet items. However, it may be that when these levels are looked at altogether, the resulting balance sheet does not balance.

To project future financial statements, one should build a model that includes the relationships among the items on such statements and outside factors. Traditional ratio analysis does this, but somewhat crudely. A much better procedure uses microcomputers and a type of software known as spreadsheets.[21]

Basically, a spreadsheet is an arrangement of information in rows and columns. Each cell on a traditional (paper) spreadsheet typically contains a number or a label. Some of the numbers (for example, sales) are entered directly; others (for example, earnings before interest and taxes) are computed from the numbers in other cells.

An electronic spreadsheet simulates a traditional spreadsheet on a computer screen. There are, however, notable differences. Most importantly, cells can contain formulas. For example, the cell for earnings before interest and taxes (EBIT) could contain the formula for calculating the value as well

---

[19] David Dremen, *Contrarian Investment Strategy* (New York: Random House, Inc., 1979).

[20] The observation that small firms typically have had abnormally high returns is an empirical regularity known as the size effect; it is discussed in the appendix to Chapter 15.

[21] Lotus Development Corporation has been one of the leading developers of such software. The products Lotus 1-2-3 and Symphony have been top sellers.

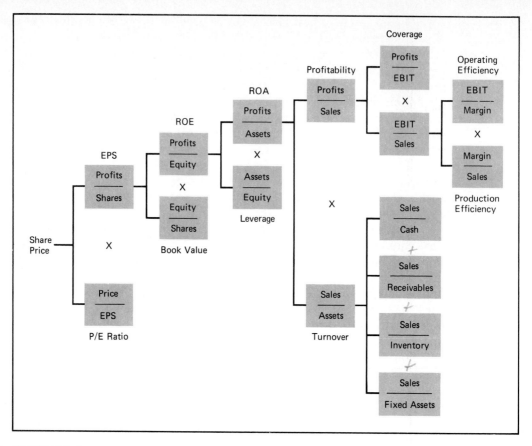

FIGURE 21–6
The use of predicted ratios to compute predicted price.

Source: Samuel E. Stewart, Jr., "Corporate Forecasting," in Sumner N. Levine, ed., *Financial Analyst's Handbook I* (Homewood Il: Dow Jones & Company, Inc., 1975): p. 912.

as the value produced by the formula. Normally, only the value would be displayed, giving an outward appearance similar to that of a traditional spreadsheet. However, any change in the number in the cell for sales would immediately change the value of EBIT, since the formula for EBIT would contain the value for sales as an input. This feature of electronic spreadsheets allows the user to rapidly explore the implications of changes in key assumptions (such as prices, quantities, and costs) on various balance sheet and income statement items. Accordingly, exploration of this sort is often known as sensitivity analysis, or what-if analysis.

In summary, financial statement analysis can help an analyst understand what a company is, where it may be going, what factors affect it, and how these factors affect it. If others are doing such analysis and doing it well, it will be difficult to find mispriced securities in this manner. But it should be possible to more accurately identify firms likely to go bankrupt, firms with higher or lower betas, firms with greater or lesser sensitivities to major factors, and so forth. Increased understanding of such aspects may well provide ample reward for the effort entailed.

21.5 ANALYSTS' RECOMMENDATIONS AND STOCK PRICES

When a security analyst decides that a stock is mispriced and informs certain clients of this, some of the clients may act on the information. As they do so, the price of the security may be afffected. As news of the analyst's recommendation spreads, more investors may act, and the price may react even more. At some point, the analyst's information will be "fully reflected" in the stock price.

FIGURE 21–7
Effect on stock prices of stock recommendations in "Heard on the Street": 1970 and 1971.

Source: Peter Lloyd Davies and Michael Canes, "Stock Prices and the Publication of Second-Hand Information," *Journal of Business* 51, no. 1 (January 1978): p. 52.

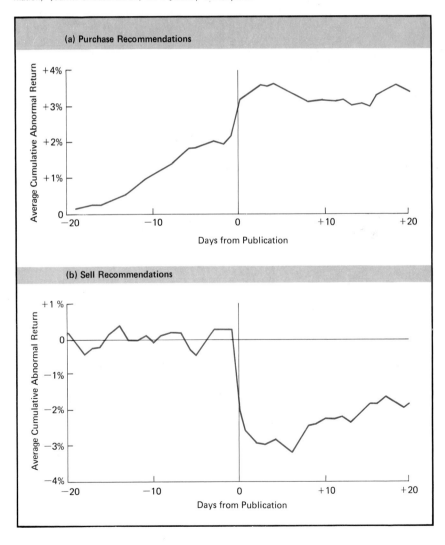

If the analyst decides a stock is underpriced and clients subsequently purchase it, the stock's price will tend to rise. Conversely, if the analyst decides a stock is overpriced and clients subsequently sell it, the stock's price will tend to decline. If the analyst's views were well founded, no subsequent counterreaction in the stock's price would be expected. Otherwise, the price is likely to return to its prerecommendation level at some later time.

An interesting example of the impact of analysts' recommendations is provided by the behavior of prices of stocks mentioned in the "Heard on the Street" column of the *Wall Street Journal*, which periodically summarizes recent stock recommendations. An analyst's opinion is typically published in "Heard on the Street" after it is first given to clients. The analyst's view is thus "somewhat public" for several days before publication, but when the column appears the opinion becomes "very public," since it then reaches a substantially larger audience.

Part (a) of Figure 21.7 summarizes the price reactions of about 597 stocks that received positive opinions in "Heard on the Street" during 1970 and 1971. Part (b) summarizes the reactions of about 188 stocks that received negative opinions during the same time period. In each panel, the vertical axis plots the average cumulative abnormal return—that is, the average return, adjusted for normal reactions to overall market moves. The horizontal axes indicate trading days relative to the date of publication of the recommendation, going from 20 days before to 20 days after publication.

As shown in the two parts, the publication of such a recommendation does typically affect a stock's price.[22] After adjusting for market moves, on the publication date the stocks recommended for purchase rose .923%, whereas the stocks recommended for sale fell 2.374%. Furthermore, after making such adjustments, 70% of the 597 stocks recommended for purchase rose on the date of publication, and 90% of the 188 stocks recommended for sale fell on the date of publication.

The roughly horizontal lines after day 0 in both parts show that both types of recommendations appeared to contain information. This is because the horizontal lines indicate that there was no significant counterreaction in the 20 days after either a buy or sell recommendation was made.

The upward moves in part (a) prior to day 0 suggest prior purchases of the stocks have been made by clients of the analysts. An alternative explanation is that analysts simply recommended purchases of stocks that had recently risen in price. Note, however, that part (b) is quite different: There is no distinct pattern prior to the date of publication of a sell recommendation. This suggests that the analysts did not tend to recommend the sale of securities that had recently fallen in price.

---

[22] Similar observations have been made in regard to the recommendations made by a major brokerage house. See John C. Groth, Wilbur G. Lewellen, Gary G. Schlarbaum, and Ronald C. Lease, "An Analysis of Brokerage House Securities Recommendations," *Financial Analysts Journal*, 35, no. 1 (January/February 1979):32–40. For a comment on this study, see the letter to the editor in the May/June 1980 issue by Clinton M. Bidwell, with a responding letter to the editor in the July/August 1980 issue by Wilbur G. Lewellen. Also see the first footnote in Chapter 22.

21.6 SOURCES OF INVESTMENT INFORMATION

Since information affects the values of investments, the serious financial analyst must be well informed. There is a staggering array of such investment information, some of it published on paper (hard copy) and some of it appearing in computer-readable form.

☐ 21.6.1 Publications

Space precludes a detailed listing of publications relating to various industries here. An excellent bibliography of such sources, compiled by the New York Society of Security Analysts, can be found in the *Financial Analyst's Handbook*.[23] Periodical literature of interest to the financial analyst is indexed by industries, products, and companies in the Predicasts *F&S Index*.

The second appendix to this chapter presents a selected bibliography of general sources of investment information, based on the holdings in the Jackson Library of the Stanford University Graduate School of Business.[24] Nothing can substitute for a careful perusal of these (and other) publications, and no attempt is made here to describe each one. Instead, some of the more essential sources of information are discussed.

Anyone planning to invest in anything should read the *Wall Street Journal*. It provides extensive statistical data, financial news, and even a bit of humor. An alternative is the financial section of the *New York Times*. Most other daily newspapers contain financial information, but much less than the *Journal* or the *Times*. A weekly publication with a wealth of statistical data (particularly in the Market Laboratory section) is *Barron's*.

A useful source of daily stock price and volume figures is the *Daily Stock Price Record*, published by Standard & Poor's Corporation. Each issue covers one calendar quarter, and all values for a given stock are listed in a single column. Standard & Poor's also publishes forecasts of company earnings in the weekly *Earnings Forecaster* and dividend information in the *Dividend Record*. Furthermore, some brokerage houses provide their major clients with copies of Standard & Poor's monthly *Stock Guide* and *Bond Guide*, which are illustrated in Figures 21.8 and 21.9.

Standard & Poor's *Corporation Records* are a major reference source for the financial history and data on individual companies. They consist of six alphabetical volumes and are periodically updated. A second major reference source is provided by Moody's Investor Services, Inc. Their *Manuals* are published annually, with periodic updates, and cover various fields; *Bank & Finance, Industrial, International, Municipal & Government, OTC Industrial, OTC Unlisted, Public Utility*, and *Transportation* are the titles of various volumes. In addition, both Standard & Poor's and Moody's also provide a number of other publications to subscribers.

Historical data and analyses for approximately 1700 stocks and most major industries can be found in the *Value Line Investment Survey*. Adjusted

---

[23] See Levine, *Financial Analyst's Handbook I*, 883–926.

[24] The bibliography was prepared with the assistance of the reference librarians of Jackson Library.

FIGURE 21–8
Standard & Poor's *Stock Guide*, January 1988.

8 A &-Adv

Standard & Poor's Corporation

Index (¶S&P 500, •Options)	Ticker Symbol	Name of Issue (Call Price of Pfd. Stocks)	Market	Com. Rank. & Pfd. Rating	Par Val.	Inst. Hold Cos	Inst. Hold Shs. (000)	Principal Business	Price Range 1971-85 High	1971-85 Low	1986 High	1986 Low	1987 High	1987 Low	Dec. Sales in 100s	December, 1987 Last Sale Or Bid High	Low	Last	%Div. Yield	P-E Ratio
1	SODA	A & W Brands	OTC	NR	1¢	40	3759	Mfr soft drink concentrate	...	...	...	...	16⅝	6¼	3128	11	8¼	10½B	...	d
2	AIR	AAR Corp	NY,M	B+	1	96	9685	Mkts aviation parts/service	11⅞	1¼	17¾	11⅜	25¾	14	12940	19⅞	14	18¾	1.9	17
3	AARN	Aaron Brothers Art	OTC	NR	1¢	11	553	Retail:art supplies,frames	...	...	6¼	5¾	15	5¼	315	9¾	6¼	9B	...	9
4	ARON	Aaron Rents	OTC	B+	1	22	1152	Rents & sells furniture	25¾	10⅜	20	14	17¾	6½	2705	7¼	6½	7B	1.4	9
¶ 5e[1]	ABT	Abbott Laboratories	NY,B,C,M,P,Ph	A+	No	735	112644	Diversified health care prod	36	1⅞	55	31⅞	67	40	95855	48¾	42¼	48¼	2.1	17
6	AB	ABI Amer Businessphones	AS	NR	1¢	1	13	Mkts tel interconnect sys	9	5¾	7½	3⅜	13½	4¼	1515	9⅛	6⅛	8⅞	...	11
7	ABD	Abiomed	AS	NR	1¢	4	85	Medical equip/cardiac sys	...	...	...	...	15¼	4¾	2201	6⅞	4¼	6¾	...	d
8	ABY	Abitibi-Price	NY,To,P	B	No	43	1681	Newsprint,pulp,paper prods	21	2¼	28⅝	15⅛	28	15⅜	2789	21¼	17¾	20½	•3.8	13
9	AGO	ABM Gold Corp Cl'A'	AS	NR	No	17	1573	Explor,dvlp gold properties	...	...	...	...	10⅞	4¾	8269	8⅝	6⅛	6¾	...	75
10	ACAJC	Aca Joe	OTC	C	10¢	11	1241	Operate/license apparel strs	10⅛	⅛	8¼	1⅝	3⅜	¼	35799	½	¼	¼B	...	d
11	ACIG	Academy Insur Gr	OTC	C	10¢	15	2396	Accident,health,life insur	17¼	¼	3¾	2	3⅜	1¾	41892	2¾	2¼	2½B	...	13
12	ACLE	Acceleration Corp	OTC	B--	10¢	15	886	Insurance:credit life/disab	16⅝	2	15½	7⅜	12⅝	4½	5737	8⅛	4½	7⅝B	...	12
13	ACET	Aceto Corp	OTC	B+	1¢	19	1008	Mfrs & dstr chemicals	16¼	½	18¼	14¾	18	10⅛	925	12¼	10⅝	11½B	s1.2	11
14	ACG	ACM Govt Income Fund	NY,M	NR	1¢	3	25	Closed-end investment co	...	...			12	8¾	13164	11⅞	10¾	11¼	10.5	...
¶ 15	AMT	Acme-Cleveland	NY,M	B—	1	68	4130	Mfr automatic mach tools	35⅝	7	14⅞	9	16¾	8½	6012	12⅝	9⅜	12⅛	3.3	17
16	ACE	Acme Electric	NY	B	1	16	1086	Pwr conv eq: transformers	11¼	⅜	8⅞	5⅞	10½	6⅛	763	7¾	6⅞	7¾	s4.1	27
17	ACL	Acme Precision Prod	AS	B—	1	2	60	Mfr precision cutt'g tools	12¼	¾	6⅜	2½	6⅜	1⅝	370	2⅛	1⅜	1¾	...	d
18	ACME	Acme Steel	OTC	NR	1	33	1965	Produce iron&steel products	...	...	10¾	8	17⅞	9⅛	1748	14¾	12¼	14¼B	...	d
19	ACU	Acme United	AS	B	2½	12	1306	Medic eq:shears,scissors	19½	1⅜	12⅛	6⅜	9¼	5⅛	1140	6	5⅛	5½	0.7	d
20	AXXN	Action Auto Rental	OTC	NR	1¢	13	664	Insur replacem't auto rental	...	...	...	...	19½	8	2556	11¼	8½	10½B	...	19
21	ACTA	Action Auto Stores	OTC	NR	No	3	187	Auto parts strs,gas,repairs	...	...	...	...	9¼	3¾	773	6	4¼	5B	...	15
22	ACX	Action Indus	AS,B	B—	10¢	17	1744	Merchandising programs	18¼	½	15⅞	7¾	9⅜	3	2577	4¾	3	4¾	...	d
23	AVSN	Activision Inc	OTC	NR	No	12	1395	Mfr home video game softw	12⅝	⅝	1¾	1	3	¾	12507	1⅜	1	1¼B	...	d
24	ACTM	Actmedia Inc	OTC	NR	1¢	50	4918	Shop'g cart advert'g displays	16¾	6½	21¾	15½	28	11¾	6114	16½	11¾	13½B	...	26
25	ATN	Acton Corp	AS,B,Ph	C	33⅓¢	9	126	Owner,operator CATV systems	94¾	1⅜	16¼	6¼	26½	11¼	525	14¼	12¼	13¾	...	4
26	WS	Wrrt(Pur 0.34524 com at$38.15)	AS	...	...	2		mfr,dstr electronic tel eqp	6½	⅛	⅝	⅛	2⅛	⅛	198	¾	⅝	⅝	...	...
27	ACSN	Acuson Corp	OTC	NR	No	77	6365	Medical ultrasound imaging	...	...	13¼	7½	23¼	10¼	21075	18¾	12¾	18½B	...	29
28	ADAC	ADAC Laboratories	OTC	C	No	15	1652	Nuclear medicine comput sys	27⅜	1	1⅞	½	2⅞	1⅛	12812	1⅞	1⅛	1¾B	...	29
29	ADGE	Adage Inc	OTC	B—	10¢	18	1849	Computer graphics term sys	28⅛	⅛	7¼	1⅞	3¾	⅞	9178	1¼	⅞	1B	...	d
30	ADX	Adams Express	NY,B,M,P	NR	1	24	292	Closed-end investment co	19⅝	7	23⅜	17½	23¼	14⅝	5379	16½	14⅝	14⅞	5.5	..
31	ALL	Adams-Millis	NY,B,M,Ph	A—	No	30	3077	Hosiery & yarn products	11⅜	⅞	16¹¹⁄₁₆	9¹³⁄₁₆	19½	6⅞	3196	10¼	6⅞	9¾	2.5	7
32	AE	Adams Res & Energy	AS,B	C	10¢	4	449	Oil dstr:transp:coal:o&g	35¼	1½	2⅞	1¼	4⅛	1¼	2094	1⅞	1¼	1¼	...	10
33	AAR	Adams-Russell[59]	AS,B,M	↓B	50¢	39	3451	Owns/operates CATV systems	30⅞	⅛	43	18⅜	43¼	20⅞	2556	43¼	41⅞	43	...	..
34	AEI	Adams-Russell Electr	AS	NR	1¢	27	2684	Mfr defense electronic prod	...	...	21½	14	18¾	6⅛	3257	10½	8¾	10⅛	...	51
35	ADPT	Adaptec Inc	OTC	NR	No	41	3247	Mfr computer data flow sys	...	...	13¼	8⅝	20¾	4½	11924	7¾	4½	6½B	...	8
36	ADCT	ADC Telecommunications	OTC	B	20¢	38	5249	Telecommunications equip	10	⅛	14½	8¾	20½	11¾	8599	18¼	13	17⅝B	...	15
37	ADDR	Addington Resources	OTC	NR	No	29	1393	Mining,mkt bituminous coal	...	...	...	...	31¾	14	1555	23	14	22½B	...	13
38	ADSNB	Addison-Wesley Pub[62]	OTC	B+	No	27	847	Pub textbooks, prof, ref books	36½	3¾	42	32½	61¼	36¾	843	44½	37½	42B	2.4	12
39	ADIA	Adia Services	OTC	NR	25¢	37	1452	Temporary personnel service	12⅞	6¼	16¾	10¼	32¼	12½	6523	16	13	15¾B	0.6	15
40	JPAC	ADMAC Inc	OTC	NR	1¢	7	342	Indl/ming cutg,drill sys	13¼	10¼	15¼	2	3⅜	½	5472	1½	½	1⅛B	...	d
41	ADB	Adobe Resources	NY,P	NR	1¢	44	7130	Oil & gas exploration,devel-	12⅜	10⅜	12⅜	5¼	11⅞	4⅜	8257	5⅜	4¼	5¼	...	d
42	Pr A	$1.84cm Cv Pfd([65]21.16)	NY	↕BB—	20	11	487	opment,production	17⅞	14⅝	18⅜	13¾	20½	16¼	225	17½	16⅛	17	10.8	..
43	Pr B	12% cm Pfd([66]21.60)	NY	↑BB—	20	4	251		18	15¼	20¼	16⅜	21⅞	17½	315	20¼	19¼	20B	12.0	..
44	ADBE	Adobe Systems	OTC	NR	No	66	4115	Print,graphic software sys	...	...	13¼	5½	56	12¾	18667	30½	23	29½B	...	35
45	ADVC	Advance Circuits	OTC	↓C	10¢	12	916	Mfr printed circuit boards	11⅝		12¼	2	6¾	2¼	4177	3½	2½	3B	...	d

Uniform Footnote Explanations—See Page 1. Other: [1]Pn:Cycle 2. [51]Fiscal Jul,'84 & prior. [52]©$0.022,'88. [53]□$0.08,'83. [54]□$0.21,'84. [55]1 Beltran Corp wrrt. [56]⊕$2.34,'87. [57]⊕$2.62,'87. [58]Δ$0.28,'83. [59]Cablevision Systems plans acq,$43.075. [60]Dstr of wrrt. [61]Δ$0.51,'83. [62]Cl'B'. [63]Fiscal Nov'85 & prior. [64]13 Mo Dec,'86. [65]Fr 11-1-90,scale to $20 in'97. [66]Fr 11-1-90,scale to $20 in'98.

FIGURE 21–8 (Continued)

Common and Preferred Stocks

A dense financial data table with the following column group headings: Splits, Dividends (Cash Div. Ex. Yr. Since; Latest Payment — Pers, Date; Ex. Div.; Total $ — So Far 1987, Ind. Rate, Paid 1986), Financial Position (Mil-$ — Cash & Equiv., Curr. Assets, Curr. Liab.; Balance Sheet Date), Capitalization (Lg Trm Debt Mil-$, Pfd., Shs. 000 Com.), Earnings $ Per Shr. (Years End; 1983, 1984, 1985, 1986, 1987; Last 12 Mos.), Interim Earnings (Period; $ Per Shr. — 1986, 1987), and Index.

Index	Cash Div. Since	Latest Payment (Pers / Date)	Ex. Div.	Total $ So Far 1987	Ind. Rate	Paid 1986	Mil-$ Cash & Equiv.	Curr. Assets	Curr. Liab.	Balance Sheet Date	Lg Trm Debt Mil-$	Pfd.	Shs. 000 Com.	Yrs End	1983	1984	1985	1986	1987	Last 12 Mos.	Period	1986	1987	Index
1		None Since Public			Nil		9.29	19.3	16.1	9-30-87	68.6	1800	6300	Dc		d0.75	d0.11	pd0.39		d0.25	3 Mo Sep	pNil	0.14	1
2	1973	Q0.09 11-30-87 11-5	0.36	0.34		0.293	5.58	26.9	75.0	8-31-87	17.8		15818	My	0.31	1.13	p0.67	0.85	P1.00	1.13	6 Mo Nov	0.47	0.60	2
3		None Since Public	Nil				3.29	22.3	7.24	10-31-87	6.44		2858	Ja			p0.08	0.85		1.95	6 Mo Oct	0.30	0.50	3
4	1926	S0.05 1-4-88 12-1	0.10	0.10			Equity per shr $7.99		$7.99	9-30-87	29.9		4914	Mr	0.92	1.67	1.04	0.91		1.95	9 Mo Sep	0.59	0.43	4
5	1926	Q0.25 2-15-88 1-11	1.00	0.96		0.80½	4.10	2008	1373	9-30-87	285.		22664	Dc	1.43		2.32		E2.60	2.64	9 Mo Sep	1.62	1.94	5
6		None Since Public	Nil				1.23	12.5	4.54	9-30-87	3.26		1672	Je	0.09	0.56	0.80	0.34		0.81	3 Mo Sep	0.06	0.20	6
7		None Since Public	Nil				14.9	15.8	2.16	9-26-87			4651	Mr	0.03	d0.02	0.10	0.02		0.06	6 Mo Sep	0.03	0.05	7
8	1949	gQ0.25 1-29-88 1-11	1.00	g0.60	g0.60		1.61	967	336	9-30-87	579.	5221	69247	Dc	0.48	1.03	0.06	d1.50		1.62	6 Mo Sep	d1.11	1.23	8
9		None Since	Nil				50.5	53.7	0.64	9-30-87			11300	Dc	0.55	1.03	0.06	d0.15		0.09	9 Mo Sep	d0.13	0.11	9
10		2% Stk 7-27-79 6-25					0.76	9.12	19.2	8-1-87	0.76		18643	Ja	0.60	d0.56	0.07	d0.84		d0.91	9 Mo Nov	d0.20	d0.27	10
11	1985	5% Stk 7-15-85 6-24			Nil		Equity per shr $1.06		$1.06	9-30-87	1.15		70834	Dc	d1.03	d0.79	d2.05	d0.31		0.19	9 Mo Sep	d0.47	0.17	11
12		5% Stk 12-19-86			5% Stk		Equity per shr $0.18		$0.18	9-30-87	18.1	4	pd616	Dc	d0.55	1.22	1.30	0.48		0.48	9 Mo Sep	d0.32	0.47	12
13	1985	*0.067 1-4-88 12-15	0.14	*0.064	0.121		Equity 59.1	12.3	12.3	12-24-87	7.00	260	3450	Dc	0.90		1.32			1.01	3 Mo Sep	d0.13	0.16	13
14	1936	*0.098 1-15-88 12-23	1.13	0.31½			Net Asset Val $11.19		$11.19	6-30-87		161	*4350											14
15	1936	Q0.10 1-13-87 10-26	0.43	0.40		0.40	13.6	86.9	44.9	6-30-87	10.0	161	6279	Sp	d7.39	d2.11	d1.90	d2.04	P*0.71	0.71	3 Mo Sep	d0.13		15
16	1939	Q0.08 12-7-87 11-3	0.32	s0.316	0.32	s0.300	0.35	30.3	8.43	10-2-87	12.3		4261	Je	D0.03	0.54	0.63	0.45	0.16	0.29	3 Mo Sep	0.04	0.17	16
17		Q0.06 12-15-58 11-24			Nil		0.42	10.8	21.0	10-2-87	5.46		984	Sp	d0.25	d0.57	d0.24	d2.97		d2.31	3 Mo Sep	d2.84	d2.64	17
18	1947	0.04 12-10-87 11-6		0.12	0.14	0.32	4.31	24.9	2.05	9-24-87	9.50		5819	Sp	1.03	0.14	0.24	d0.66		d0.16	6 Mo Sep	d1.97	d0.03	18
19		None Paid	Nil				4.23	23.5	2.99	9-26-87	9.80		3173	Sp		0.63	0.08	0.38		0.14	6 Mo Sep	0.10	0.10	19
20		None Since Public	Nil				Equity per shr $2.85		$2.85	6-30-87	42.4		*5473	Sp				0.41		0.54	9 Mo Sep	0.24	0.37	20
21	1966	None Paid	Nil				0.02	18.0	11.9	9-30-87	18.7		2963	Je	d0.09	d0.21	d0.32	0.38	0.34	0.34	3 Mo Sep	0.11	d0.13	21
22	1966	0.06 6-15-87		0.06	Nil	0.12	1.79	91.9	56.4	9-26-87	29.1		5495	Mr	d1.28	d0.44	0.92	1.01	d1.37	d1.35	3 Mo Sep	0.03	d0.05	22
23		None Since Public	Nil				9.93	27.7	9.51	9-26-87	1.83		38500	Dc	0.56	0.32	0.17	0.42		d0.31	6 Mo Sep	d0.08	0.03	23
24		None Since Public	Nil				19.0	46.7	20.7	9-6-87			11744	Dc	d0.15	0.23	0.34	0.40		d0.31	36 Wk Sep	d0.24	0.34	24
25		5% Stk 7-15-82					3.46	5.26	16.1	9-30-87			1183	Sp	d6.35	d6.35	d1.15	d04.70	3.53	3.53	3 Mo Sep	d2.52	d5.71	25
26		** Wrrt 4-1-82 4-2		**			Check terms/trad'g in detail				0.22		641								Wrrts expire 6-1-89			26
27		None Since Public	Nil				32.7	69.0	18.8	9-26-87	2.91	2910	22318	Je	0.36	d0.04	d0.10	d0.40		0.64	9 Mo Sep	*0.25	0.49	27
28		None Since Public	Nil				4.11	25.4	20.9	6-28-87	3.92		21984	Dc	0.51	d3.51	d3.13	d1.77						28
29		None Since Public	Nil				2.02	33.4	5.35	6-26-87			8376	Mr	0.92	0.33	d1.12	d1.32	P*0.08	0.97	6 Mo Sep	0.90	d0.55	29
30	1936	** 0.35 12-21-87 11-17	0.82	**1.10	0.82	0.72	Net Asset Val $16.25		$16.25	12-23-87			24005	Dc	d19.27	d17.96	d20.54	d19.51						30
31	1977	Q0.06 11-30-87 11-10	0.24	0.24	0.24	0.21	6.23	75.0	18.4	9-27-87	42.0		4689	Dc	*0.77	d1.25	d1.15	1.28	1.30	1.30	9 Mo Sep	0.81	0.83	31
32	1977	0.10 8-15-87 5-20			Nil		3.44	5.94	7.21	9-30-87	4.99		6838	Mr	1.59	1.28	d0.73	d0.73	0.13	0.01	9 Mo Sep	d0.09	d0.11	32
33		None Since Public	Nil				3.44	14.4	13.9	6-28-87	57.7	34	6838	Mr	dm1.10		1.26	d0.73		d0.13				33
34		None Since Public	Nil				3.72	70.3	13.9	6-28-87	23.8		6211	Mr		0.04	d1.36	d0.73		0.80				34
35		None Since Public	Nil				17.2	35.5	4.28	9-25-87			7510	Mr	d0.55		d1.41	d0.79		0.79	6 Mo Sep	*0.35	0.35	35
36		None Since Public	Nil				23.5	63.4	18.4	7-31-87	3.22		17865	Dc	d0.33	d0.25	0.61	0.93	P1.18	1.18	9 Mo Sep	p1.35	p1.61	36
37	1956	Q0.40 1-4-88 11-24	1.00	0.92½	0.62½		29.0	59.9	38.6	9-30-87	72.0		5855	Dc	pd0.27	p0.08	d1.31	d1.49	1.75	1.75	9 Mo Sep	1.38	1.51	37
38	1984	Q0.02 W12-18-87 11-30	0.10	0.10	0.08		6.42	89.0	39.1	9-30-87	72.5		12591	Dc	0.33	0.60	0.62	0.16	E3.37	E3.37	9 Mo Sep	3.58	3.84	38
39		None Since Public	Nil				0.98	89.0	8.45	7-31-87	4.07	400	11309	Dc	2.26	0.60	d0.08	0.20	2.85	2.61	6 Mo Oct	d0.75	d0.51	39
40		None Since	Nil				0.98	11.6	8.45	7-31-87	4.07	400	4650	Ap			0.08	0.20						40
41	1986	Q0.46 1-15-88 1-15	1.84	1.84	1.84	1.932	10.7	41.8	30.6	9-30-87	2.17	8055	29833	Dc	pd0.29	pd10.14	d3.03	d3.03	d1.01	d1.01	9 Mo Sep	d1.99	*0.03	41
42	1986	Q0.60 2-15-88 1-15	2.40	2.40	2.40	2.52	Cv into 0.9 com					4159		Dc										42
43		None Since Public	Nil				13.4	18.7	3.68	8-31-87	10.2	4896	1019½	Nv	d0.29	0.01	0.08	d0.36	P0.85	0.85				43
44		None Since Public	Nil				1.23	17.7	10.6	8-29-87	10.2	125	4393	Au	d0.03	0.70	1.16	d0.60	d0.18	0.18				44
45																								45

◆ Stock Splits & Divs By Line Reference Index. *3-for-2, '86, '87. *3-for-2, '83. *2-for-1, '86. *3-for-1, '86, '87. *85;1986 & prior prices in Canadian $. *2-for-1, '83. Adj for 5%, '86.
*4-for-3, '83. 3-for-2, '85; Adj to 4%, '88(ex 87). *10%, '84 Adj to 5%, '87. *4-for-3, '83. *3-for-2, '85. *85;1986 & prior prices in Canadian $. *2-for-1, '83. *Adj for 5%, '85. *11Adj for 5%, '86.
*2-for-1, '86. *2-for-1, '87. Cv into 0.9 com 83:1-for-2, '85, '87. *10%, '83:1-for-2, '85, '87. *3-for-1, '86. *12-for-1, '83. *2-for-2, '83, '85, '87. *13-for-1, '86. *12-for-1, '86. 83:1-for-5 REVERSE, '87. **3-for-1, '86. **3-for-2, '83, '86, '87.

STANDARD & POOR'S CORPORATION

Title-Industry Code & Co. Finances (In Italics) / Individual Issue Statistics Exchange	Ind / Interest Dates	Chgs. 1984 / S&P Quality rating	Eligible	Times Earn. 1985 / Bond Form	Legality Ma	1986 / Legality NH	Yr. End / Legality NY	Cash & Eqv / Redemption Provisions Refund Earliest/Other	Current Assets (Million $) / Call Price For S.F.	Liabs, Date / Call Price Regular	L. Term Debt (Mil $) / Out-st'd'g (Mil $)	Debt % Prop / Underwriter Firm	Year	1972-85 High	1972-85 Low	1986 High	1986 Low	1987 High	1987 Low	Mo. End Price Sale(s) or Bid	Curr Yield	Yield to Mat.
Abbott Laboratories	*21a*	*7.10*		*7.55*		*9.91*	*Dc*	*470*	*2008*	*1373 9-87*	*285*	*17.2*										
• SF Deb 7¾s '96	Ms	AA+	X	R	✓	✓	-	....	100	†101.424	17.1	L4	'71	106	75⅛	100	86	100	92½	96⅜	7.89	8.20
• SF Deb 9.20s '99	aO15	AA+	X	R	✓	✓	-	....	100	†103.22	56.1	G2	'74	111½	58½	103	93⅜	103	95¼	96¾	9.56	9.74
• Nts 11s '93	Fa	AA+	X	R	-	✓	-	....	....	[1]100	100	G2	'83	104	84⅛	112	104½	110½	101	106	10.38	9.48
ACF Indus	*55*	*[2]0.92*		*1.33*		*1.17*	*Dc*	*352*	*447*	*203 9-87*	*1144*	*156*										
Eq Tr Ctf 14⅞s '92	fA	B+	Y	R	-	-	-	....	[3]100	NC	30.0	B1	'82	122	97	122	104¾	105⅞	94½	98	15.18	15.50
Eq Tr Ctf 14½s '96	jD	B+	Y	R	-	-	-	....	100	NC	[4]27.0	B1	'81	114⅞	91⅜	106	99⅞	110	94	94	15.43	15.77
Eq Tr Ctf 11.60s 2000	Mn15	B+	Y	R	-	-	-	....	100	NC	35.0	B1	'80	103½	69⅜	107¾	100	108⅛	91⅛	95⅝	12.13	12.29
SF Deb 15¼s '96	jD15	B	Y	R	-	-	-	....	•[5]100	[6]106.90	460	D8	'84	106	98	109½	101⅛	106⅞	95½	95½	15.97	16.22
Aetna Life & Casual	*35*	*3.86*		*8.83*		*19.08*	*Dc*				*714*											
• Deb 8⅛s 2007	aO15	AAA	X	R	✓	✓	-	....	[7]100	[8]†104.58	220	M8	'77	101½	51¼	98¼	81	100	79¼	87	9.34	9.60
Deb 8s 2017	Jj15	AAA	X	R	-	✓	-	....	[9]100	†104	200	M4	'87	....	....	....	....	97¼	79¼	84⅛	9.48	9.60
Affiliated Bankshrs Colo	*10a*	*2.14*		*1.03*		*0.95*	*Dc*				*69.5*											
Nts 11⅜s '93	Ao	BB+	Y	R	-	-	-	....	....	[10]100	50.0	M8	'83	107⅛	88⅛	112⅛	102⅛	106⅞	98	98	11.86	12.15
AFG Indus	*29*	*4.52*		*3.54*		*6.72*	*Dc*	*162*	*269*	*61.6 9-87*	*193*	*83.9*										
SrSubNts 13⅛s '92	Ao	B+	Y	R	-	-	-	....	z100	[11]†106	70.0	D8	'85	107¼	99½	110¼	105¼	107⅜	95¼	103	13.23	12.68
Air Products & Chemicals	*14b*	*4.84*		*4.93*		*1.01*	*Sp*	*161*	*654*	*366 6-87*	*715*	*37.8*										
• SF Deb 11⅜s 2015	mN	A+	X	R	-	✓	-	[12]105.54	[13]100	†109.97	100	S4	'85	99⅜	99⅜	No Sale		109	109	106⅞	10.64	10.60
Deb 8½s 2006	Ao	A+	X	R	-	✓	-	....	....	[14]100	100	G2	'86	....	....	99⅜	91⅜	96¾	82⅛	87⅜	9.76	10.05
• Nts 12¾s '94	Ao15	A+	X	R	-	✓	-	....	....	[15]100	100	L4	'84	101¼	93½	No Sale		118½	104⅛	112⅛	11.37	10.09
• Nts 11½s '95	Mn	A+	X	R	-	✓	-	....	....	NC	100	G2	'85	105	98⅞	121	113⅜	122⅜	108	110¾	10.38	9.43
Airco, Inc	*14b*	*Subsid of BOC Int'l*																				
SF Deb 9⅝s 2000	aO	A-	X	R	-	✓	-	....	100	†103.47	59.4	D4	'75	106½	59⅛	96	88⅞	104⅛	91¼	95⅜	9.78	9.95
Alabama Bancorporation	*10a*	*Now AmSouth Bancorp, see*																				
• [16]F/R[17]Nts[18] 7s '99	mS	AA-	X	R	-	✓	-	....	....	100	12.9	F2	'74	104½	56	[illegible]	99⅛	101	96	96⅛	7.28	....
Alabama Gas Corp[19]	*73b*	*4.11*		*3.36*		*2.35*	*Sp*	*11.3*	*46.7*	*71.2 6-87*	*51.3*	*30.9*										
1st F [20]8s '94	Fa	A	X	R	-	✓	✓	....	100	102.14	7.25	W6	'69	97⅛	53¼	95¾	87¾	97	86⅛	92⅛	8.68	9.74
1st G [21]9½s '96	Jj	A	X	R	-	✓	✓	....	100	†104.02	12.4	W6	'71	108½	58⅞	104	94¾	105	93	98	9.69	9.86
Deb[22] 8¾s 2012	Mn	A-	X	R	-	✓	-	....	....	[23]105	10.0	E3	'87	....	....	....	....	100	85	89	9.83	9.95
Alabama Power Co.[24]	*72a*	*2.62*		*2.96*		*3.12*	*Dc*	*8.73*	*632*	*656 9-87*	*★2390*	*43.3*										
1st 4⅞s '89	Mn	A	X	CR	-	✓	✓	....	†100.05	†100.19	20.0	M8	'59	87½	48⅛	93½	87	95	92¼	95	5.13	8.94
1st 5s '90	Ao	A	X	CR	-	✓	✓	....	†100.06	†100.37	6.96	H9	'60	84¾	46½	91¼	84⅛	92⅜	89⅝	92	5.43	9.02
1st 4½s '91	Ms	A	X	CR	-	✓	✓	....	†100.37	†100.64	13.0	E1	'61	79⅝	42⅛	87⅛	78⅝	88⅜	84⅝	87½	5.14	9.14
1st 4⅜s '92	Jd	A	X	CR	-	✓	✓	....	100	†100.59	14.4	H9	'62	74	39⅛	82¾	73⅛	84	79¼	82⅝	5.30	9.26
1st 4⅜s '93	Mn	A	X	CR	-	✓	✓	....	100.03	†100.77	13.8	L4	'63	71	38	79¼	70	81	75⅜	79	5.54	9.48
1st 4⅝s '94	Mn	A	X	CR	-	✓	✓	....	†100.45	†101.21	24.1	F2	'64	70⅛	37¾	77¾	68½	79	72¼	76⅛	6.07	9.73
1st 4⅞s '95	mS	A	X	CR	-	✓	✓	....	†100.37	†101.36	33.3	H9	'65	71⅞	37	76¼	67	77⅛	69¾	73⅜	6.62	9.86
1st 6¼s '96	aO	A	X	CR	-	✓	✓	....	†100.69	†102.10	29.4	H9	'66	87	43⅛	83⅛	73¼	84⅛	74⅜	79	7.91	9.89
1st 6½s '97	aO	A	X	CR	-	✓	✓	....	100	†102.02	28.0	L4	'67	89¼	43⅜	83½	73½	84½	74⅛	79	8.23	9.91
1st 7s '98	mN	A	X	CR	-	✓	✓	....	100	†102.42	25.0	L4	'68	94⅞	45⅛	86	75½	87	75⅜	80⅝	8.68	9.96
1st 8⅜s '99	mN	A	X	CR	-	✓	✓	....	†100.56	†103.58	35.0	M8	'69	108	53½	97⅛	86¼	98½	85	90⅜	9.52	9.99
• 1st 9s 2000	mN	A	X	R	-	✓	✓	....	100	†103.73	44.9		'70	111½	52	102	87⅛	102½	87½	92¾	9.70	10.01
• 1st 8½s 2001	jJ	A	X	R	-	✓	✓	....	†100.82	†104.26	85.0	F2	'71	108½	50	99⅛	84⅛	100⅞	83½	88⅝	9.59	10.05
1st 7½s 2002	Jj	A	X	R	-	✓	✓	....	100	†103.37	25.5	L4	'72	100⅞	46	87⅛	76⅛	88¾	75⅛	81⅛	9.24	10.04
• 1st 7⅞s 2002	Ao	A	X	R	-	✓	✓	....	100.22	†103.94	98.0	M8	'72	104½	48	95	80	95⅞	77½	83⅜	9.42	10.06
• 1st 7¾s 2002	mS	A	X	R	-	✓	✓	....	†100.80	†104.23	65.0		'72	104¼	46½	92½	78⅛	94¾	76⅜	82⅞	9.41	10.07
• 1st 8⅞s 2003	fA	A	X	R	-	✓	✓	....	†100.73	†105	100	M8	'73	107	51¾	100½	85¼	102	82	90½	9.81	10.09
• 1st 8¼s 2003	jD	A	X	R	-	✓	✓	....	†100.80	†104.79	75.0	L4	'73	101	49	96¾	81	98⅛	77	84⅝	9.75	10.22
• 1st 9⅝s 2004	Jd	A	X	R	-	✓	✓	....	†100.42	†105.65	100		'74	108⅛	56¼	103¾	92⅛	105⅛	89½	97⅛	10.04	10.11

Uniform Footnote Explanations—See Page 1. Other: [1]Fr 2-1-90. [2]6 Mo Dec'84. [3]Fr 8-1-88. [4]SF call $3M 12-1-87. [5]Fr 12-15-90. [6]Fr 12-15-89. [7]Fr 10-15-88. [8]Fr 10-15-87. [9]Fr 1-15-97. [10]Fr 4-1-90. [11]Fr 4-1-88. [12]Red rest'n(11.41%)to 11-1-95. [13]Fr 11-1-96. [14]Fr 4-1-04. [15]Fr 4-15-91. [16](HRO)On int dates at 100. [17]Int to 2-28-88. [18]Adj aft for T-Bill rates. [19]Subsid of Energen Corp. [20]Incr tr 7 1 4% 8-1-82. [21]Incr tr 8 3/4%,1-1-83. [22](HRO)Ea May 1 fr 1989-Ltd,as defined. [23]Fr 5-1-92. [24]Subsid of Southern Co.

FIGURE 21–9
Standard & Poor's *Bond Guide*, January 1988.

betas are also shown for the individual stocks in the *Survey*. The *Value Line Options* and *Convertibles* manuals, along with the *Survey*, offer estimates of the relative attractiveness of these investments.[25]

Publications of major security analysts' societies include the *Financial Analysts Journal*, (U.S.); *Analyse Financière* (France); and *The Investment Analyst* (United Kingdom). Academic journals that emphasize various aspects of investing include the *Journal of Business*, the *Journal of Finance*, the *Journal of Financial and Quantitative Analysis*, the *Journal of Financial Economics*, and the *Review of Financial Studies*.

Anyone interested in the management of money for institutional or corporate investors (especially pension funds) should read the *Journal of Portfolio Management*, which publishes the views of both practitioners and academicians. A biweekly periodical widely read by institutional investors and money managers is *Pensions and Investment Age*. *Institutional Investor*, a periodical full of "inside information" on the investment industry, is published monthly. Individual investors will find the articles in the monthly issues of the *AAII Journal*, published by the American Association of Individual Investors, to be informative.

Although a company's annual report provides useful information, the annual business and financial report (10-K) filed with the Securities and Exchange Commission usually includes more details.

A source of macroeconomic data such as monetary aggregates (like the money supply) and other monetary items is the *Federal Reserve Bulletin*, a monthly publication by the Board of Governors of the Federal Reserve System. Data on national income and production is published monthly by the U.S. Department of Commerce in the *Survey of Current Business*. The Department of Commerce also publishes on a monthly basis the *Business Conditions Digest*, where various economic indicators can be found. *Leading indicators* have been found to signal future changes in the economy, whereas *lagging indicators* change after the economy has done so; *coincident indicators* change simultaneously with the economy.

☐ **21.6.2   Computer-Readable Data**

The rapid increase in the use of microcomputers by those who invest money for others as well as by those who invest for themselves has led to a major expansion in the availability of computer-readable investment data.

Large amounts of financial and economic data, such as common stock prices and financial statements, are provided on magnetic tapes that are made available to investors for a fee by Standard & Poor's Compustat Services and Value Line, Inc. These databases are also available on a dial-up basis via time-shared computer services and on disks for use in microcomputers.

Dial-up services are also provided by *Compuserve, Dow Jones News/ Retrieval, The Source, Interactive Data Corporation*, and others. Each service is designed so that users of microcomputers can download prices and other data into their own machines easily and inexpensively. Often the data

---

[25] These estimates for common stocks appear to be useful in helping the investor beat the market. See the appendix to Chapter 17.

are in spreadsheet format, readily available for analysis using, for example, Lotus 1-2-3.

Databases containing prices, fundamental information, and predictions made by brokerage houses and others are provided on compact disks by the Lotus Development Corporation and Standard and Poor's Corporation.

21.7 SUMMARY

Financial analysts are people who evaluate securities and then make investment recommendations. These recommendations may be used by professional money managers known as portfolio managers or by certain clients of the analyst. Typically, the financial analyst is trying to determine certain characteristics of securities and to identify mispriced securities. Most methods of performing financial analysis can be categorized as being either fundamental or technical in nature.

Fundamentalists typically forecast future sales, expenses, and earnings for firms. With these forecasts, projections of either future stock prices or returns are made. In contrast, technicians typically focus on charts of stock prices and trading volumes, looking for patterns that are in the early stages of unfolding. Once the beginning of a pattern is identified, then the future can be predicted, since it should turn out to be the ending part of the pattern.

Some financial analysts claim to have some kind of an investment system that will enable them to accurately identify mispriced securities. Furthermore, they often claim their systems have been successful in the past and produce evidence that allegedly supports their assertion. However, just because these analysts claim to have a successful system does not mean that it really has worked in the past and will continue to work in the future. Investors must carefully scrutinize any test results that may be offered, as there often is some kind of error made in assessing the track record of such systems.

APPENDIX A
TECHNICAL ANALYSIS

Most (but not all) technical analysts rely on charts of stock prices and trading volumes. Virtually all employ colorful, and sometimes even mystical, terminology. For example, a significant price rise on relatively large trading volume might be described as an accumulation, where the stock is allegedly moving from "weak hands" to "strong hands." This is because a rising stock price on large trading volume is viewed as a situation where demand is stronger than supply. In contrast, a significant price decline on relatively large trading volume may be described as a distribution, where the stock is allegedly moving from strong hands to weak hands. This is because a declining stock price on large trading volume is viewed as a situation where supply is stronger than demand. In both situations, relatively large trading volume might be considered a sign of a sustainable change in the stock's price, whereas relatively small trading volume indicates a transitory change.

What if there is a period when a stock's price does not move significantly?

If the stock's price movements are within a narrow band, the stock is said to be in a consolidation phase. A price level above which a stock has difficulty rising is known as a resistance level, and a price level below which a stock does not seem to fall is known as a support level.

Such statements may sound meaningful, but they fail to pass the tests of simple logic. First of all, changes in a stock's price occur when the consensus opinion concerning its value changes. This means that large volume associated with a price change reflects only a substantial difference of opinion concerning the impact of new information on the stock's value; small volume reflects smaller differences of opinion. Second, if price or volume data could be used to predict future short-term price moves, investors would rush to exploit such information, moving prices rapidly enough to make the information useless.

A.1 CHARTS

Chartists (technicians who rely on chart formations) nonetheless believe that certain patterns carry great significance, although they often disagree among themselves on the significance of a pattern or even on the existence of a pattern. Before displaying some hypothetical examples of patterns, it should be noted that there are three basic types of charts used. They are known as bar charts, line charts, and point and figure charts.

For a *bar chart* the horizontal axis is a time line, with the vertical axis measuring a particular stock's price. More specifically, corresponding to a given day on the horizontal axis will be a vertical line, the top and bottom of which represent the high and low price for that stock on that day. Somewhere on this vertical line will be a small horizontal line representing the closing price for the day. As an example, consider the following hypothetical stock, whose trading background over the last five days is as follows:

DAY	HIGH PRICE	LOW PRICE	CLOSING PRICE	VOLUME
$t - 5$	11	9	10	200
$t - 4$	12	9	11	300
$t - 3$	13	12	12	400
$t - 2$	11	10	11	200
$t - 1$	14	11	12	500

Part (a) of Figure 21.10 presents a bar chart for this stock, whereas part (b) indicates how such a bar chart of prices can be augmented by adding trading volume at the bottom.

Figure 21.11(a) shows a type of bar chart that is known as "head and shoulders." As time passed, the stock's price initially rose, hit a peak at A, and then fell to a bottom at B. Recovering from this fall, it went up to an even higher peak at C but then fell again to a bottom at D. Next, it rose to a peak at E that was not as high as the previous peak, C, and then started to fall. As soon as the price went down past its previous low, D, immediately a forecast was made that the stock was going to plunge much lower (if the stock had not reached a level equal to D, no such forecast would have been

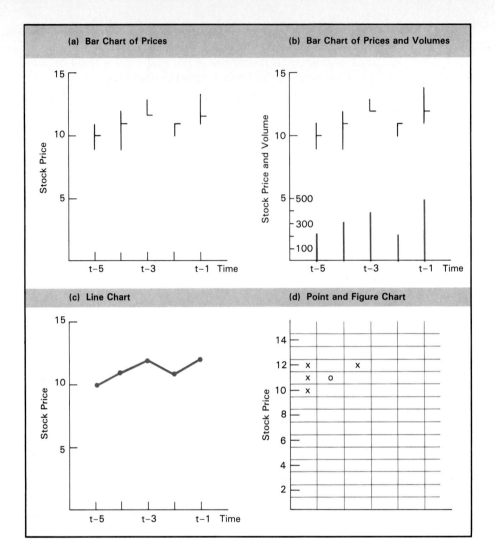

FIGURE 21–10
Types of charts.

made). Figure 21.11(b) shows a type of bar chart know as "inverted head and shoulders," which results in a forecast that the stock is going to rise quickly by a substantial amount.[26]

For a *line chart*, the axes are the same as with a bar chart. However, only closing prices are presented, and they are connected to each other successively with straight lines, as illustrated in part (c) of Figure 21.10.

---

[26] For details on many kinds of patterns, see Alan R. Shaw, "Technical Analysis," in Sumner N. Levine, ed., *Financial Analyst's Handbook I* (Homewood, Ill.: Dow Jones-Irwin, Inc., 1975), 944–88; and Chapter 8 in Jerome B. Cohen, Edward D. Zinbarg, and Arthur Zeikel, *Investment Analysis and Portfolio Management* (Homewood, Ill.: Richard D. Irwin, Inc., 1987).

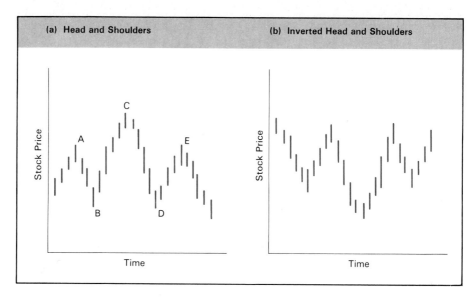

FIGURE 21–11
Bar chart patterns.

While not shown, line charts are also frequently augmented with volume data in a manner identical to bar charts.

Details of construction of *point and figure charts* vary, but the idea is to plot closing prices that form a trend in a single column, moving to the next column only when the trend is reversed. For example, closing prices might be rounded to the nearest dollar and the chart begun by plotting a beginning rounded price on a certain day. As long as the (rounded) price does not change, nothing is done. When a different price is recorded, it is plotted on the chart. A price higher than the initial price is indicated with an X, with any gaps between the prices also marked with an X. A price below the initial price is marked with an O in a similar fashion. Then when a price that is different from the last one is recorded, it is plotted in the same column if it is in the same direction.

For example, if the first different price is above the beginning price, this price is plotted above the original. Then, if a price is recorded that is above the second one, it is plotted in the same column, but if it is below the second one, then it is plotted in a new column to the right of the first column. Continuing, as long as new prices are in the same direction, they are plotted in the same column. Whenever there is a reversal, a new column is started. Part (d) of Figure 21.10 presents a point and figure chart for the same hypothetical stock used in the other panels.

Point and figure enthusiasts look for all sorts of patterns in their charts. As with all chartist techniques, the idea is to recognize a pattern early enough to profit from one's ability to foresee the future course of prices—a neat trick, if one can do it.

A.2   MOVING AVERAGES

Many other procedures are used by technicians. Some construct moving averages to try to detect "intermediate" and long-term" trends. Here a set number of the most recent closing prices on a security are averaged each day. (For example, daily closing prices over the previous 200 days may be used.) This means that each day, the oldest price is replaced with the most recent price in the set of closing prices that will be averaged. Frequently a line chart of these moving averages is plotted along with a line chart of daily closing prices. Each day the charts are updated and then examined for trends to see if there is a buy or sell signal present somewhere.

Alternatively, a long-term moving average may be compared with a short-term moving average (the distinction between the two averages is that the long-term average uses a substantially larger set of closing prices in its calculations than the short-term average). When the short-term average crosses the long-term average, a "signal" is said to have been given. The action recommended will depend on such things as whether the averages have been rising or falling, as well as the direction from which the short-term average crossed the long-term average (it may have been below and now is above, or it may have been above and now is below).

A.3   RELATIVE STRENGTH MEASURES

Another procedure used by technicians involves measuring what they call relative strength. For example, a stock's price may be divided by a price index of its industry each day to indicate the stock's movement relative to its industry. Similarly, an industry index may be divided by a market index to indicate the industry's movement relative to the market, or a stock's price may be divided by a market index to indicate a stock's movement relative to the market. The idea here is to examine changes in these relative strength measures with the hope of finding a pattern that can be used to accurately predict the future.

Some procedures of technical analysts focus on relationships among different indexes. For example, the Dow theory requires that a pattern in the Dow Jones Industrial Average be "confirmed" by a certain movement in the Dow Jones Railroad (now Transportation) Average before action be taken. Another example involves computing the difference between the number of issues advancing and the number declining each day. A chart of the differences cumulated over time, known as the advance-decline line, may then be compared with a market index such as the Dow Jones Industrial Average.

A.4   CONTRARY OPINION

A large number of technical procedures are based on the idea of contrary opinion. The idea here is to determine what the losers are doing and then do the opposite. For example, one might see whether the "odd-lotters" (those

who buy and sell in lots of less than 100 shares each) are buying and then sell any holdings of these stocks. If "the little investor is usually wrong," this will be a procedure that is usually right. However, the basic premise about the little investor has yet to be established.

The widespread availability of personal computers and "dial-up" services with data on stock prices and volumes has made it possible for individual investors to engage in technical analysis in the privacy of their own homes. Producers of software have been quick to provide programs to perform such analysis, complete with multicolored graphs. Nevertheless, the number of individual investors that use fundamental analysis is much larger than the number using technical analysis. Furthermore, fundamental analysis is also the dominant method among those who manage money for a living, the professional money managers.

APPENDIX B
SOURCES OF INVESTMENT INFORMATION

I. GENERAL INFORMATION ON BUSINESS AND FINANCIAL DEVELOPMENTS
  A. Economics Data Handbooks
    1. Economic Statistics Bureau of Washington, D.C. *Handbook of Basic Economic Statistics.*
    2. Standard & Poor's *Statistical Service, Current Statistics.*
    3. U.S. Bureau of the Census. *Statistical Abstracts of the U.S.*
    4. U.S. Office of Business Economics. *Business Statistics.*
  B. Daily Newspapers
    1. *American Banker.*
    2. *Daily Commercial News.*
    3. *Financial Times* (British—London).
    4. *Journal of Commerce.*
    5. *New York Times.*
    6. *Wall Street Journal.*
    7. *Washington Post.*
    8. *Investor's Daily.*
  C. Weekly Newspapers
    1. *Barron's.*
    2. *Commercial and Financial Chronicle.*
    3. *Financial Post* (Canadian).
    4. *Market Chronicle.*
    5. *Vie Francais l'Opinion.*
    6. *Wall Street Transcript.*
    7. *Weekly Bond Buyer.*
    8. *Media General Financial Weekly.*

D. Weekly Periodicals

1. *Business Week* (see especially "Finance" section).
2. *EDP Industry Reports.*
3. *Financial World.*
4. *Investment Dealers' Digest.*
5. *Japan Stock Journal.*
6. *California Business.*
7. *Newsweek* (especially "Business and Finance" section).
8. *San Francisco Business.*
9. *Time* (especially "Business" or "Economy and Business" section).
10. *United States Banker.*
11. *U.S. News & World Report.*
12. *World Business Weekly.*

E. Biweekly Periodicals

1. Chase Manhattan Bank. *International Finance.*
2. *Forbes.*
3. *Fortune.*

F. Monthly Periodicals

1. *Across the Board.*
2. Bank letters: issued by various banks, e.g., Cleveland Trust Company, First National City Bank of New York, Morgan Guaranty, Chase Manhattan, Bank of America, Wells Fargo.
3. *Business Conditions Digest.*
4. *Conference Board Statistical Bulletins.*
5. *Donoghue's Money Fund Report.*
6. *Dun's Business Month.*
7. *Economic Indicators.*
8. Federal Reserve Bank Reviews (regular reviews are issued by all the Federal Reserve Banks).
9. *Federal Reserve Bulletin.*
10. *Federal Reserve Chart Book.*
11. *Financial Executive.*
12. *Finance.*
13. *Going Public* (looseleaf service lists initial public offerings).
14. *institutional Investor.*
15. *Market Value Index.*
16. *Nation's Business.*
17. *OTC Review.*
18. *Stock Market Magazine.*
19. *Survey of Current Business.*
20. *Venture Capital.*
21. *AAII Journal.*

G. Bimonthly Periodicals

1. *Financial Analysts Journal.*
2. *Financial Planner.*
3. *Harvard Business Review.*
4. *Journal of Financial Economics.*

H. Quarterly Periodicals

1. *Business Starts.*
2. *Journal of Business.*
3. *Journal of Finance* (five issues a year).
4. *Journal of Financial and Quantitative Analysis* (five issues a year).
5. *Journal of Money, Credit and Banking.*
6. *Mergers & Acquisitions.*
7. *Journal of Portfolio Management.*
8. *Journal of Banking and Finance.*
9. *Review of Financial Studies.*

I. Annual Economic Reviews
   1. U.S. Bureau of Domestic Commerce. *U.S. Industrial Outlook.*
   2. U.S. Congress. Economic Joint Committee. *The . . . Economic Report of the President; Hearings* (i.e., hearings held to consider the *President's Economic Report*).
   3. U.S. Congress. Economic Joint Committee. *Joint Economic Report* (i.e., the committee's report on their hearings on the *President's Economic Report*).
   4. U.S. Office of Business Economics. *Business Statistics.*
   5. U.S. President. *Economic Report of the President* (together with the annual report of the Council of Economic Advisers).

II. INDUSTRY INFORMATION

   A. Business and Financial Journals and Periodicals (See Section I above)

   B. Government Publications and Documents; see especially:
      1. Annual reports of regulatory commissions such as the F.P.C., F.T.C., I.C.C., and S.E.C.
      2. *Survey of Current Business* (monthly periodical).
      3. *Treasury Bulletin* (monthly periodical).
      4. U.S. Census Bureau. *Census of Manufacturers.*
      5. ————. *Annual Survey of Manufacturers.*
      6. ————. *Census of Retail Trade.*
      7. ————. *Census of Service Industries.*
      8. ————. *Census of Wholesale Trade.*
      9. ————. *Current Industrial Reports.*
      10. ————. *Statistical Abstracts of the U.S.*
      11. U.S. Industry & Trade Administration. *U.S. Industrial Outlook.*
      12. U.S. Mines Bureau. *Minerals Yearbook.*
      13. U.S. Office of Business Economics. *Business Statistics.*

   C. Reports of Investments and Business Services
      1. Value Line, Inc.
         a. *Value Line Investment Survey.*
         b. *Value Line Options.*
         c. *Value Line Convertibles.*
         d. *Value Line OTC Special Situations Service.*
      2. Howard & Company. *Going Public.*
      3. Kidder, Peabody and Co. *Research Service.*
      4 Moody's
         a. *Manuals.*
         b. *Industry Review.*
         c. *Bond Survey.*
         d. *International Bond Review.*
      5. Smith Barney, Harris Upham and Co. *Research Service.*
      6. Standard & Poor's
         a. *Industry Survey.*
         b. *Outlook.*
         c. Statistical Service. *Current Statistics.*
      7. Dun & Bradstreet *Key Business Ratios.*
      8. Robert Morris Associates *Annual Studies.*

   D. Special Bibliographies (indexes to periodicals)
      1. *Business Periodicals Index.*
      2. *DISCLOSURE Journal* (indexes SEC filings of 10-K's, Registrations, etc.).
      3. Predicasts *F&S Index* (U.S., Europe, International—abstracts periodicals by company, product and industry).
      4. ————. *F&S Index of Corporate Change.*
      5. ————. *Forecasts* (abstracts periodicals which contain forecasts for various industries).
      6. ————. *Worldcasts* (forecasts by region).

7. Public Affairs and Information Service. *Bulletin.*
8. *Wall Street Journal Index.*

E. Special Reports of Private Agencies
   1. Audit's Investment Research, Inc.
      a. *Reality Stock Review.*
      b. *Real Estate Disclosure Digest.*
   2. Creative Strategies Inc.
      a. *Industry Analysis Service.*
      b. *Retail Automation Report.*
   3. SRI International *Long Range Planning Service Reports* (includes Index).

F. Acquisitions and Mergers
   1. *Announcements of Mergers and Acquisitions* (monthly publication by The Conference Board).
   2. Financial Stock Guide Service. *Directory of Obsolete Securities.*
   3. Predicasts. *F&S Index of Corporate Change.* Quarterly.
   4. MCR Publishing Company. *Mergers & Acquisitions.*

G. Reports and Brochures of Brokerage and Banking Firms
   1. Bank of America
      a. Daily Quotation Sheets: *U.S. Government Securities, Federal Agencies and Other Securities.*
      b. *Small Business Reporter.*
      c. *Weekly Monetary Summary.*
   2. Bankers Trust. *Current Business Picture.*
   3. Goldman Sachs. *Risk, Return and Equity Valuation* (quarterly).
   4. Kidder Peabody & Co.
      a. *Current Investment Policy and Strategy Implementation.*
      b. *Emerging Growth Stocks.*
      c. *Money and Capital Markets.*
      d. *Monthly Earnings Summary.*
      e. *Monthly Valuation Information.*
      f. *Portfolio Manager's Review.*
   5. Merrill Lynch. *Quantitative Analysis.*
   6. Siegel Trading Company. *Weekly Market Letter.*
   7. Salomon Brothers.
      a. *Analytical Record of Yields and Yield Spreads.*
      b. *Bond Market Roundup.*
      c. *Bond Portfolio Analysis.*
      d. *Comments on Credit.*
      e. *Monthly Stock Review.*
      f. *Preferred Stock Guide.*
      g. *Prospects for Financial Markets.*
      h. *Strategy Systems.*
      i. *Total Rate-of-Return Indexes.*
   8. Smith, Barney, Harris Upham & Co., *Analysts Roundtable.*
   9. Thomson and McKinnon Auchincloss Kohlmeyer
      a. *Commodity Letter.*
      b. *Technical Analysis.*
   10. *Wall Street Transcript* (weekly newspaper, most of whose contents are reprints of brokerage house reports).

H. Trade Association Publications (especially Annual Review Numbers)
   1. *ADP Symbol Guide.*
   2. *Dow Jones Investor's Handbook.*

I. Trade Journals (especially Annual Statistical Numbers)

III. COMPANY INFORMATION

A. Corporation Reports
   1. Annual reports to shareholders.

2. *Disclosure Journal* (indexes annual reports to shareholders, 10-K reports, registration statements).
3. Financial Stock Guide Service. *Directory of Obsolete Securities*.
4. 10-K reports.
5. Prospectuses.
6. Registration statements.

B. Financial and Business Journals (see Section II above; the Predicasts *F&S Index* indexes most of these extensively by S.I.C. code and by company name)

C. Publications of Brokerage and Banking Firms

D. Manuals

1. *Moody's Manuals.* (Bank and Finance; Industrial; International; Municipal & Government; OTC Industrials; OTC Unlisted; Public Utility; Transportation)
2. Standard & Poor's *Standard Corporation Descriptions*.
3. Standard & Poor's *Stock Reports* (American Stock Exchange; New York Stock Exchange; Over-the-Counter and Regional Exchanges).
4. *Walker's Manual of Western Corporations*.

E. Publications of Financial Services

1. Value Line, Inc.,
   a. *Value Line Investment Survey*.
   b. *Value Line Options*
   c. *Value Line Convertibles*
   d. *Value Line OTC Special Situations Service*.
2. *Financial Dynamics* (see also its *Debt Analysis Supplement*).
3. Goldman Sachs. *Risk, Return and Equity Valuation* (quarterly).
4. Hambrecht and Quist Institutional Research
   a. Weekly Report
   b. Monthly Statistical Research Summary
5. Moody's
   a. *Bond Record*.
   b. *Bond Survey*.
   c. *Dividend Record*.
   d. *Handbook of Common Stocks*.
   e. *Industry Review*.
   f. *International Bond Review*.
   g. *Manuals* (see Section IIID above; note especially the semiweekly supplements and the blue sections in the center of annual volumes).
   h. *Stock Survey*.
6. *Quote* (American; New York; Over-the-Counter).
7. *R.H.M. Survey of Warrants, Options & Low-priced Stocks*.
8. Standard & Poor's
   a. *Analysts Handbook* (annual, with monthly supplements).
   b. *Bond Guide*.
   c. *Called Bond Record*.
   d. *Commercial Paper Rating Guide*.
   e. *Corporation Records*.
   f. *Creditweek*.
   g. *Dividend Record*.
   h. *Earnings Forecaster*.
   i. *Industry Surveys*.
   j. *Outlook*.
   k. *Standard Corporation Descriptions* (note especially the daily supplements).
   l. Statistical Service. *Current Statistics*.
   m. *Stock Guide*.
   n. *Stock Reports* (NYSE, ASE, OTC).
9. United Business Service. *United Business & Investment Report*.
10. *Vickers Guide to Investment Company Portfolios*.

IV. SECURITIES MARKET INFORMATION: INVESTMENT ADVICE

   A. Bond and Stock Ratings

      1. Moody's *Manuals.*
      2. Moody's *Bond Record.*
      3. Salomon Brothers. *Preferred Stock Guide.*
      4. Standard & Poor's *Bond Guide.*
      5. Standard & Poor's *Commercial Paper Ratings Guide.*
      6. *Value Line Investment Survey.*
      7. *Value Line Options and Convertibles.*

   B. Beta Factors

      1. Goldman Sachs. *Risk, Return and Equity Evaluation.*
      2. Merrill Lynch. *Quantitative Analysis.*
      3. *Value Line Investment Survey.*

   C. General Market Condition and Outlook

      1. Moody's *Bond Survey.*
      2. Moody's *Stock Survey.*
      3. Publications of brokerage and banking firms (see Section II).
      4. Standard & Poor's *Outlook.*
      5. United Business Service. *United Business and Investment Report.*

   D. Recommendations and Appraisals of Securities

      1. Brokerage and banking house reports and brochures (see Section II).
      2. Goldman Sachs. *Risk, Return and Equity Valuation.*
      3. Merrill Lynch. *Quantitative Analysis.*
      4. Reports of financial reporting agencies and investment services, especially:
         a. Kidder Peabody & Co. *Research Department Service.*
         b. Moody's *Bond Survey.*
         c. Moody's *Stock Survey.*
         d. Standard & Poor's *Creditweek.*
         e. Standard & Poor's *Outlook.*
         f. United Business Service. *United Business & Investment Report.*
         g. *Value Line Investment Survey.*

V. SECURITY PRICE QUOTATIONS

   A. Daily Range and Close

      1. *Commercial and Financial Chronicle* (Monday issue contains high and low, but not the close, for each day of the preceding week).
      2. *New York Times.*
      3. *San Francisco Chronicle.*
      4. Standard & Poor's *Daily Stock Price Record.*
      5. *Wall Street Journal.*

   B. Weekly Range and Close

      1. *Barron's.*
      2. *Financial Post* (Canadian).

   C. Monthly Range

      1. *Bank and Quotation Record.*
      2. *Morgan Stanley Capital International Perspective.*
      3. Standard & Poor's *Daily Stock Price Record* (ASE, NYSE, OTC).

   D. Annual Range

      1. *Bank and Quotation Record* (January issue has range for preceding year; other issues have range for current year to date).
      2. *Barron's* (first issue in January has range for preceding year).
      3. *Commercial and Financial Chronicle* (Monday issue).
      4. Dow Jones *Investor's Handbook* (annual).
      5. Standard & Poor's.
         a. *Bond Guide.*

  b. *Standard Corporation Descriptions.*
  c. *Stock Guide.*
  d. *Stock Reports* (ASE, NYSE, OTC, and regional exchanges).

 E. Other Compendia of Price Quotations
  1. *Daily Stock Price Record* (ASE, NYSE, OTC; each quarterly volume lists range for each stock for each day of the quarter).
  2. National Quotation Bureau. *Monthly Bond Summary.*
  3. National Quotation Bureau. *Monthly Stock Summary.*

VI. SECURITY PRICE INDEXES AND AVERAGES

 A. Daily and Financial Newspapers

 B. Periodicals
  1. *Barron's.*
  2. *Commercial and Financial Chronicle* (Monday issue).
  3. *CPI Detailed Index.*
  4. *Federal Reserve Bulletin.*
  5. *Producer Prices and Price Indexes.*
  6. *Survey of Current Business.*

 C. Special Services
  1. Standard & Poor's
   a. *Outlook.*
   b. Statistical Service. *Current Statistics.*
   c. *Daily Stock Price Index.*
  2. Moody's
   a. *Manuals* (blue section).
   b. *Bond Survey.*
   c. *Stock Survey.*

 D. Other Compendia of Price Indexes and Averages
  1. *Morgan Stanley Capital International Perspective.*
  2. *Dow Jones Averages 1885–1980* (averages for each day since the series began).
  3. L. Fisher and J. H. Lorie, *A Half Century of Returns on Stocks and Bonds.*
  4. Roger G. Ibbotson and Rex A. Sinquefield, *Stocks, Bonds, Bills and Inflation: the Past and the Future*, 1982 edition.
  5. *Wall Street Journal Index* (pages at the back list the Dow Jones averages for each day of the month covered in that volume of the index).

VII. DATA ON MONEY MARKETS

 A. *Weekly Bond Buyer.*

 B. Salomon Brothers
  1. *Analytical Record of Yields and Yield Spreads.*
  2. *Bond Market Roundup* (weekly).
  3. *Bond Portfolio Analysis.*
  4. *Comments on Credit.*
  5. *Prospects for Financial Markets* (annual).
  6. *Total Rate-of-Return Indices.*
 C. *Euromoney* (monthly periodical).

VIII. DATA ON MUTUAL FUNDS

 A. Computer Directions Advisors
  1. *Spectrum 1: Investment Company Stock Holdings Survey.*
  2. *Spectrum 2: Investment Company Portfolios.*

 B. *Donoghue's Money Fund Directory.*

 C. *Donoghue's Money Fund Report.*

QUESTIONS AND PROBLEMS

1. It is often argued that the S&P 500 is a better indicator than the Dow Jones Industrial Average of the performance of the entire U.S. stock market. Explain the reasoning behind this contention.

2. Consider three stocks, X, Y, and Z, with the following closing prices on two particular dates:

STOCK	DATE 1	DATE 2
X	$16	$24
Y	5	4
Z	24	32

On date 1 there are 100 shares of stock X, 200 shares of stock Y, and 100 shares of stock Z outstanding.

a. Construct a price-weighted market index using the three stocks, X, Y, and Z. What is the index's value on date 1?

b. What is the price-weighted index's value on date 2?

c. Assume that on date 2, stock X splits 4-for-1. What is the price-weighted index's value on that date?

d. Construct a value-weighted index using the three stocks. Assign the value-weighted index a value of 100 on date 1. What is the index's value on date 2?

3. According to Ferris Fain, "The success of a stock market index depends on its ability

to measure the performance of stocks not included in the index." Explain what Ferris means.

4. Compare the price reaction to the purchase of stocks that have been identified with a system that previously has been able to "beat the market" with the reactions to (a) the accurate prediction of rainfall, and (b) the accurate prediction of the locations of enemy submarines.

5. If security markets are highly efficient, what role is there for financial analysts?

6. Listed below are several test results from studies of mechanical investment systems. For each test result, identify the primary research error committed and comment as to why the error is applicable to the study.

   a. A portfolio managed using a filter rule (that is, buying a stock after it has appreciated in price by x%, holding the stock until its price has depreciated by x%, then selling the stock) outperforms a broad market index when the filter is very small (that is, when x is small).

   b. An investment system estimated over the 1970 to 1980 time period indicates that the system outperformed a broad market index in the latter half of that period.

   c. A portfolio composed of stocks of highly cyclical industrial companies outperforms a broad market index.

   d. Buying and selling U.S. stocks based on a measure of liberal and conservative voting patterns in Great Britain produces returns that outperform a broad U.S. market index.

   e. The price performance of a portfolio of ipo (that is, initial public offering) high-technology stocks outperforms a broad market index.

7. Bibb Falk, a portfolio manager for a large pension fund, is fond of saying "Buy low, sell high." Why is the system suggested by Bibb not operational?

8. Distinguish between "top-down" and "bottom-up" approaches to financial forecasting. What are the primary advantages and disadvantages of each approach?

9. Is it true that when comparing the reported earnings of corporations, "a dollar is a dollar"?

10. (Appendix Question) Technical analysis is predicated on stock prices moving in repetitive patterns. What would one have to believe about the timing of the receipt of information by financial markets participants in order to believe in the existence of such patterns?

11. (Appendix Question) The closing, high, and low prices for Des Moines Packaging stock over a ten-day interval are shown below. Construct a bar chart for Des Moines Packaging stock over this period of time.

DES MOINES PACKAGING

Day	Closing Price	High	Low
1	20	21	19
2	$20\frac{1}{4}$	$20\frac{1}{4}$	18
3	21	22	$20\frac{1}{2}$
4	$21\frac{1}{8}$	$22\frac{7}{8}$	$21\frac{1}{8}$
5	21	$23\frac{1}{4}$	20
6	$21\frac{3}{4}$	22	$20\frac{3}{4}$
7	22	$23\frac{1}{2}$	$20\frac{1}{8}$
8	$20\frac{1}{8}$	22	$19\frac{1}{4}$
9	$19\frac{1}{8}$	$21\frac{1}{2}$	19
10	$18\frac{1}{4}$	$21\frac{7}{8}$	$17\frac{1}{8}$

12. (Appendix Question) Calculate the relative strength of Des Moines Packaging stock versus the S&P 500 over the ten-day period referred to in problem 11, given the following closing prices for the S&P 500:

	DAY									
	1	2	3	4	5	6	7	8	9	10
S&P 500 Closing Price	300	302	306	310	320	315	330	325	325	330

Chapter 22

INVESTMENT MANAGEMENT

Investment management, also known as portfolio management, is the process by which money is managed. It may be active or passive, may use explicit or implicit procedures, and may be relatively controlled or uncontrolled. The trend is toward highly controlled operations consistent with the notion that capital markets are relatively efficient. However, approaches vary, and many different investment styles can be found. This chapter discusses investment management and in doing so presents various types of investment styles.

22.1 TRADITIONAL INVESTMENT MANAGEMENT ORGANIZATIONS

Few like to be called "traditional." However, many investment management organizations follow procedures that have changed little from those that were popular decades ago and thus deserve the title. Figure 22.1 shows the major characteristics of a typical organization of this type.

Projections concerning the economy, security and money markets, and so on are made (often qualitatively) by economists, technicians, fundamentalists or other market experts within or outside the organization. The projected economic environment is communicated via briefings, reports, and so on—usually in a rather implicit and qualitative manner—to the organization's *security analysts*. Each analyst is responsible for a group of securities, often those in one or more industries (in some organizations, analysts are called industry specialists). Often a group of analysts report to a senior analyst responsible for a sector of the economy or market.

The analysts, often drawing heavily on reports of others (for example, "street analysts" in brokerage houses), make predictions about the securities for which they are responsible. In a sense, such predictions are conditional on the assumed economic and market environments, although the relationship is typically quite loose.

Analysts' predictions seldom specify an expected rate of return or the time over which predicted performance will take place. Instead, an analyst's feelings about a security are often summarized by assigning it one of five codes, where a 1 represents a buy and a 5 represents a sell, as indicated in Figure 22.1. (Some organizations reverse the numbers, so that a 5 is a buy

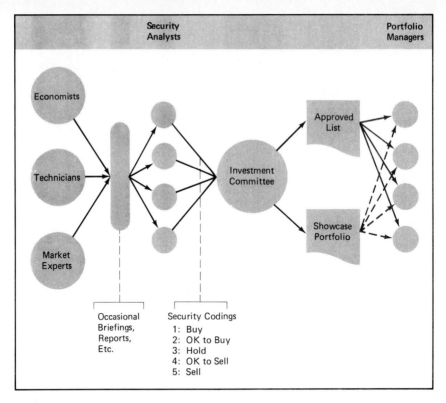

Economists

Technicians

Market
Experts

Investment
Committee

Approved
List

Showcase
Portfolio

Occasional
Briefings,
Reports,
Etc.

Security Codings
1: Buy
2: OK to Buy
3: Hold
4: OK to Sell
5: Sell

FIGURE 22–1
A traditional investment management organization.

and a 1 is a sell; some European organizations favor five codes that are denoted by $+$, $0+$, 0, $0-$, and $-$; some organizations have long-term lists as well as short-term lists.)[1]

These security codings constitute the information formally transmitted to an *investment committee*, which typically includes the senior management of the organization. In addition, analysts occasionally brief the investment committee on their feelings about various securities. The investment committee's major formal output is often an *approved* (or authorized) *list*, which consists of the securities deemed worthy of accumulation in a given portfolio. The rules of the organization typically specify that any security on the list may be bought, while those not on the list should be either held or sold, barring special circumstances.

The presence or absence of a security on the approved list constitutes the major information transmitted explicitly from the investment committee to a *portfolio manager* (or, for example, a trust officer in a bank). In some organizations, senior management supervises a "showcase portfolio" (for

---

[1] One study found that a firm's stock price tended to move upward when analysts upgraded its coding and downward when analysts downgraded its coding. See Edwin J. Elton, Martin J. Gruber, and Seth Grossman, "Discrete Expectational Data and Portfolio Performance," *Journal of Finance* 41, no. 3 (July 1986):699–713; also see footnote 22 in Chapter 21.

example, a bank's major commingled equity fund), the composition of which indicates to portfolio managers the relative intensity of senior management's feelings regarding different securities.

In many ways, this description is a caricature of an investment organization—even one run along traditional lines. But many of these attributes can be observed in practice. Traditional organizations may deal with uncertainty only obliquely, and they may utilize inconsistent estimates. Furthermore, they may fail to fully take into account the relative efficiency of modern capital markets.

22.2 INVESTMENT MANAGEMENT FUNCTIONS

In Chapter 1, a five-step procedure was outlined for making investment decisions. These steps can all be viewed as functions of investment management, and must be undertaken for each client whose money is being managed. They are as follows:

1. *Set investment policy*—determine how much investable wealth the client has, as well as pinpointing his or her investment objectives.
2. *Perform security analysis*—scrutinize individual securities or groups of securities in order to identify mispriced situations.
3. *Construct a portfolio*—identify specific securities to invest in, along with the proportion of investable wealth to be put in each security.
4. *Revise the portfolio*—determine which securities in the current portfolio are to be sold and which securities are to be purchased to replace them.
5. *Evaluate the performance of the portfolio*—determine the actual performance of a portfolio in terms of risk and return, and compare the performance with that of an appropriate "benchmark" portfolio.

The remainder of this chapter deals with how an investment management organization would perform the first four functions; the next chapter deals with the fifth function.

22.3 SETTING INVESTMENT POLICY

One of the key characteristics that differentiates clients from one another concerns their investment objectives. According to modern portfolio theory, these objectives are reflected in the client's attitude toward risk and expected return. As mentioned in Chapter 6, indifference curves are one method of describing these objectives. However, determining a client's indifference curves is not a simple task. In practice, it is often done in an indirect and approximate fashion by estimating the client's level of *risk tolerance*, denoted by τ.[2]

---

[2] The following analysis is discussed in more detail in William F. Sharpe, *Asset Allocation Tools* (Redwood City, Calif.: The Scientific Press, 1987), 34–39; and William F. Sharpe, "Integrated Asset Allocation," *Financial Analysts Journal* 43, no. 5 (September/October 1987):25–32.

☐ 22.3.1 Estimating Risk Tolerance

The starting point in making an estimation of risk tolerance is to provide the client with a set of estimates of the risks and expected returns for different combinations of two hypothetical portfolios. For example, imagine the client is told that the expected return on a stock portfolio is 12%, whereas the return on a risk-free portfolio consisting of Treasury bills is 7.5% (that is, $\bar{r}_S$ = 12% and r_F = 7.5%). Similarly, the client is told that the standard deviation on the stock portfolio is 15%, whereas the standard deviation on the risk-free portfolio is, by definition, 0.0% (that is, σ_S = 15% and σ_F = 0.0%). Additionally, the client is told that all combinations of these two portfolios lie on a straight line that connects them (this is because the covariance between these two portfolios is 0.0, meaning that σ_{SF} = 0.0). Some combinations of these two portfolios are shown in Table 22.1.

Note that the investor is being presented with the efficient set that arises given a set of stocks and risk-free borrowing and lending rates. As shown in Chapter 7, this efficient set is linear, meaning it is a straight line that emanates at the risk-free rate and goes through a tangency portfolio that consists of a certain combination of common stocks.

At this point, the client is asked to identify the combination that appears to be most desirable, in terms of expected return and standard deviation. Note that asking the investor to identify the most desirable combination is equivalent to asking the investor to locate where his or her indifference curves are tangent to the linear efficient set, since this point will represent the most desirable portfolio.[3]

TABLE 22.1

Combinations of Stock and Risk-Free Treasury Bill Portfolios.

PROPORTION IN		EXPECTED RETURN	STANDARD DEVIATION	IMPLIED LEVEL OF RISK TOLERANCE
STOCKS	BONDS			
100%	0%	12.00%	15.0%	100%
90	10	11.55	13.5	90
80	20	11.10	12.0	80
70	30	10.65	10.5	70
60	40	10.20	9.0	60
50	50	9.75	7.5	50
40	60	9.30	6.0	40
30	70	8.85	4.5	30
20	80	8.40	3.0	20
10	90	7.95	1.5	10
0	100	7.50	0.0	00

---

[3] If such a decision is made on behalf of the client (for example, by a trustee for one or more beneficiaries), the task is much more difficult, but a decision is still required.

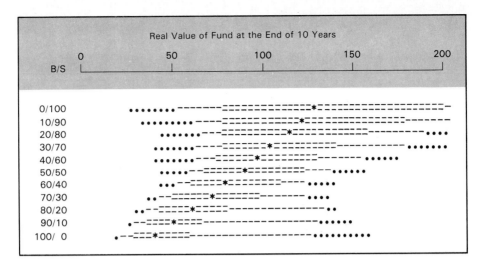

FIGURE 22–2
Effect of the bond/stock mix on the real value of an endowment fund.

☐ 22.3.2 The Trade-off Between Risk and Expected Return

Investment managers and advisory organizations have developed various procedures for helping clients understand the trade-off between risk and expected return so that they can make reasonable decisions in this regard. Figure 22.2 illustrates one of these methods.

An Example

Figure 22.2 is based on a study done for a college. At the time of the study, an amount equal to 6% of the market value of the college's endowment fund was being spent each year. The study assumed that the amount spent in future years would be the same in real dollars. Given this assumption, what might be the real dollar value of the fund at the end of ten years, and how might this be affected by the proportions invested in stocks and bonds?

To answer the question, historical real returns from representative portfolios of bonds and stocks were used. For example, to construct the bar graph at the top of Figure 22.2, a mix of 0% in bonds and 100% in stocks was assumed. The value of the fund was assumed to equal 100 at the beginning of 1926, and year-by-year results were computed for the ten-year period from 1926 through 1935, using the assumed 6% spending rule and the actual real returns in each year. The real value of the fund at the end of 1935 was then determined. The procedure was repeated using returns from 1927 through 1936, 1928 through 1937, and so on, ending with the ten-year period of 1975 through 1984. Thus, 50 periods of ten years each were examined.

The bar graph summarizes the frequency distribution of the resulting 50 end-of-period real values, as follows:

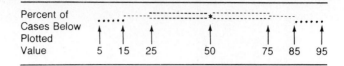

| Percent of Cases Below Plotted Value | 5 | 15 | 25 | 50 | 75 | 85 | 95 |

Note that the asterisk indicates the *median* real dollar value of the fund at the end of ten years for various mixes of stocks and bonds. For the 0/100 mix, the median value of the fund at the end of ten years was approximately 125, or 25% higher than at the start. As can be seen, the lower the proportion in stocks, the lower the median value.

However, attention should also be given to the dispersion of ending values. This can be done by looking at the distance between the left-most and right-most dots. For example, looking at the 60/40 mix, it can be seen that 5% of the time the fund had a value at the end of ten years that was equal to or less than 40 (the left-most dot), and that 5% of the time it had an ending value equal to or greater than 130 (the right-most dot). Thus, 90% of the time (that is, for 45 of the 50 ten-year periods) the ending value was between 40 and 130. In general, it can be seen that the dispersion of possible ending values decreases with a decrease in the proportion invested in stocks until the mix is roughly 60/40, and then the dispersion starts to increase as the proportion in stocks drops further.

In summary, this kind of information is useful in helping the client understand the implications of a portfolio having a higher level of expected return as well as a higher standard deviation. With such information, the client can more easily decide on the stock/bond mix felt to be best.

After the client has selected the best stock/bond mix, what can be said about his or her risk tolerance? One would, of course, like to identify all the indifference curves that represent a client's attitude toward risk and expected return. However, in practice a more modest goal is usually adopted—to obtain a reasonable representation of the shape of such curves in the likely region of risk and expected return within which the client's optimal choices will most likely fall.

The points in Figure 22.3 plot the alternative mixes presented to the client that were given in Table 22.1. Curve *FCS* shows the risk-return characteristics of all possible mixes and point C identifies the attributes of the mix chosen by the client. Note that in this figure, expected return is measured on the vertical axis and variance on the horizontal axis. Although the combinations available to the client plot on a straight line when standard deviation is measured on the horizontal axis, the combinations plot on a concave curve when variance is used (as in this figure).

Assuming that all the possible mixes had been presented to the client and point C had been chosen, it could be inferred that the slope of the client's indifference curve going through C is precisely equal to that of curve *FCS* at this point. As mentioned earlier, this follows from the observation that the portfolio on the efficient set that a client identifies as being the best one corresponds to the one where the client's indifference curves are just tangent to the efficient set.

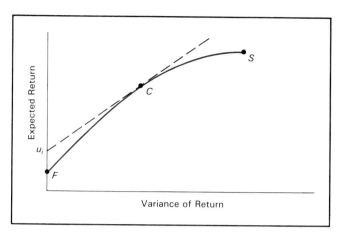

FIGURE 22–3
Inferring client risk tolerance.

☐ 22.3.3 Constant Risk Tolerance

In principle, the choice of a mix provides information about the slope of an indifference curve at only one point. To go beyond this, an assumption must be made about the general shape of the client's indifference curves. An assumption commonly made is that the client has constant risk tolerance over a range of alternative portfolios in the neighborhood of the point originally chosen. Figure 22.4 shows the nature of this assumption. As indicated in part (a), indifference curves in a diagram with variance on the horizontal axis are *linear* when it is assumed that the client has constant risk tolerance. This means that the equation for an indifference curve of such an investor is equivalent to the equation for a straight line, where the variable on the horizontal axis is variance (σ_p^2) and the variable on the vertical axis is expected return ($\bar{r}_p$). Given that the equation of a straight line takes the form of $Y = a + bX$, where a is the vertical intercept and b is the slope, the equation for an indifference curve can be written as

$$\bar{r}_p = a + b\sigma_p^2$$

or

$$\bar{r}_p = u_i + \frac{1}{\tau}\sigma_p^2 \qquad (22.1)$$

where u_i is the vertical intercept for indifference curve i and the slope of the indifference curve is $1/\tau$. Note how any two indifference curves for a client differ from one another by the value of the vertical intercept. This is because the indifference curves are parallel, meaning they have the same slope, $1/\tau$.

Figure 22.4(b) plots the same indifference curves in a more familiar manner—with *standard deviation* on the horizontal axis. Note that the curves have the conventional shape—they indicate that the investor requires more return to compensate for an additional unit of standard deviation as

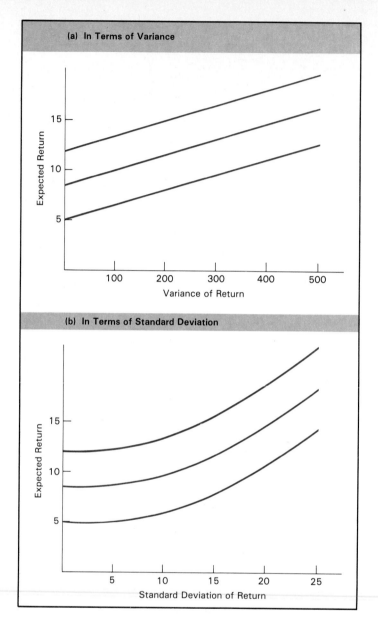

FIGURE 22–4
Constant risk tolerance.

the risk of the portfolio increases. That is, the curves are *convex* when standard deviation is measured on the horizontal axis.

In order to estimate the client's level of risk tolerance, τ, it was mentioned that the slope of the indifference curves, $1/\tau$, would be set equal to the slope of the efficient set at the location of the portfolio that was selected, denoted by portfolio C. Doing so results in the following formula for estimating τ:

$$\tau = \frac{2[(\bar{r}_C - r_F)\sigma_S^2]}{(\bar{r}_S - r_F)^2} \qquad (22.2)$$

where $\bar{r}_C$ denotes the expected return of the portfolio that the client selected, $\bar{r}_S$ and r_F denote the expected return of the stock portfolio and risk-free rate, respectively, and σ_S^2 denotes the variance of the stock portfolios. (A detailed presentation of how this formula was derived is presented in the appendix to this chapter.)

In the example, the client was given a choice between S, F, and various combinations of S and F, where $\bar{r}_S = 12\%$, $r_F = 7.5\%$, and $\sigma_S^2 = (15)^2 = 225$. By using equation (22.2), the level of risk tolerance γ inferred from the choice of portfolio C can be determined to be equal to

$$\tau = \frac{2[(\bar{r}_C - 7.5)225]}{(12 - 7.5)^2} \qquad (22.3)$$
$$= 22.22\bar{r}_C - 166.67.$$

Assuming the choice of a portfolio consisting of a 50% investment in stocks and a 50% investment in risk-free Treasury bills, the client in this example has chosen a portfolio C with an expected return of 9.75%. Accordingly, equation (22.3) can be used to determine the value of τ for this client, resulting in an estimated level of risk tolerance τ equal to $50 = (22.22 \times 9.75) - 166.67$. Thus, the client's indifference curves are estimated to have the form of

$$\bar{r}_p = u_i + \frac{1}{50}\sigma_p^2. \qquad (22.4)$$

Table 22.1 shows the inferred level of risk tolerance τ if a different portfolio had been chosen by the client (these levels were determined by substituting the appropriate values for $\bar{r}_C$ into the right-hand side of equation (22.3) and then solving for τ). First, note that the level of risk tolerance is the same as the percentage invested in the stock portfolio associated with C. That is, equation (22.3) can be rewritten as $\tau = 100X_S$, where X_S is the proportion invested in the stock portfolio associated with C. It can be shown that this will always be the case when $\bar{r}_S - r_F = 4.5\%$ and $\sigma_S = 15\%$, figures that correspond roughly to the postwar experience in the United States.

Second, note how the level of risk tolerance is lower if the selected portfolio is more conservative (that is, when the level of expected return and standard deviation is lower). Thus, more conservative risk-averse clients will have lower levels of risk tolerance than less conservative risk-averse clients.

Having estimated the client's indifference curves, recall from Chapter 6 that the objective of investment management is to identify the portfolio that lies on the indifference curve furthest to the northwest, because such a portfolio will offer the investor the level of expected return and risk that is preferable to all the other portfolios. This is equivalent to identifying the portfolio that lies on the indifference curve that has the highest vertical intercept, u_i. This can be seen graphically in Figure 22.4(a) and (b), where the indifference curves have been extended to the vertical axis.

☐ 22.3.4 Certainty Equivalent Return

The term u_i can be thought of as the *certainty equivalent return* for any portfolio that lies on indifference curve i.[4] Thus, portfolio C in Figure 22.3 is as desirable for this particular client as a portfolio with an expected return of u_i and no risk—that is, one providing a return of u_i with certainty. When viewed in this manner, the job of the portfolio manager is to identify the portfolio with the highest certainty equivalent return.

Equation (22.1) can be rewritten so that the certainty equivalent return u_i appears on the left-hand side. Doing so results in

$$u_i = \bar{r}_p - \frac{1}{\tau}\sigma_p^2. \tag{22.5}$$

This equation shows that the certainty equivalent return can be thought of as a risk-adjusted expected return, since a risk penalty that depends on the portfolio's variance and the client's risk tolerance is subtracted from the portfolio's expected return in determining u_i.

In the example, the investor selected the portfolio with $\bar{r}_p = 9.75\%$ and $\sigma_p^2 = 7.5^2 = 56.25$. Thus, the certainty equivalent return for this portfolio is $9.75 - (56.25/50) = 8.625\%$. Equivalently, the risk penalty for the portfolio that was selected was $56.25/50 = 1.125\%$. If the certainty equivalent return for any other portfolio shown in Table 22.1 is calculated, it will have a lower value (for example, the 80/20 portfolio has a certainty equivalent return of $11.1 - (144/50) = 8.22\%$). Thus, the goal of investment management can be thought of as identifying the portfolio that has the maximum value of $\bar{r}_p - (\sigma_p^2/\tau)$, since it will provide the client with the maximum certainty equivalent return.

22.4 SECURITY ANALYSIS AND PORTFOLIO CONSTRUCTION

☐ 22.4.1 Passive and Active Management

Within the investment industry, a distinction is often made between *passive management*—holding securities for relatively long periods with small and infrequent changes—and *active management*. Passive managers generally act as if the security markets are relatively efficient. Put somewhat differently, their decisions are consistent with the acceptance of consensus estimates of risk and return. The portfolios they hold may be surrogates for the market portfolios that are known as *index funds*, or they may be portfolios that are tailored to suit clients with characteristics that differ from those of the average investor.[5] In either case, passive portfolio managers do not try to beat the market.

---

[4] The term u_i is also known as the expected utility of indifference curve i; it represents the level of satisfaction associated with all portfolios plotting on indifference curve i.

[5] An example of a tailored portfolio would be one consisting of stocks with high dividend yields. Such a portfolio might be purchased for a corporate investor, since 80% of all dividends received by a corporate investor are exempt from corporate income tax.

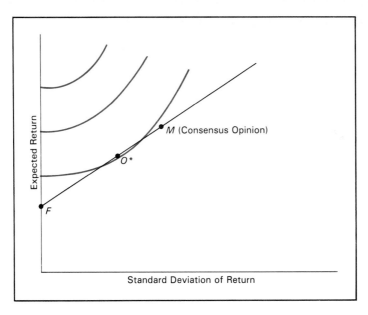

FIGURE 22–5
Passive investment management.

For example, a passive manager might only have to choose the appropriate mixture of Treasury bills and an index fund that is a surrogate for the market portfolio. The best mixture would depend on the shape and location of the client's indifference curves. Figure 22.5 provides an illustration.

Point F plots the risk-free return offered by Treasury bills, and point M plots the risk and expected return of the surrogate market portfolio, using consensus estimates. Mixtures of the two investments plot along line FM. The client's attitude toward risk and return is shown by the set of indifference curves, and the optimal mixture lies at the point O^*, where an indifference curve is tangent to line FM. In this example, the best mixture uses both Treasury bills and the surrogate market portfolio. In other situations, the surrogate market portfolio might be "levered up" by borrowing (that is, money might be borrowed and added to the client's own investable funds, with the total being used to purchase the surrogate market portfolio).

When management is passive, the overall mixture is altered only when (1) the client's preferences change or (2) the consensus opinion about the risk and return of the surrogate market portfolio changes. The manager must continue to assess the latter and keep in touch with the client concerning the former. But no additional activity is required.

Active managers believe that from time to time there are mispriced securities or groups of securities. They do not act as if they believe that security markets are efficient. Put somewhat differently, they use deviant predictions; that is, their estimates of risks and expected returns differ from consensus opinions. While some managers may be more bullish than average

about a security, other managers may be more bearish. The former will hold "more-than-normal" proportions of the security, whereas the latter will hold "less-than-normal" proportions.

Assuming there is no tailoring, it is useful to think of a portfolio as having two components: (1) a market portfolio (actually, a surrogate for it) and (2) deviations designed to take advantage of security mispricing. For example, a portfolio can be broken down as follows:

NAME OF SECURITY (COL. 1)	PROPORTION IN ACTUAL PORTFOLIO (COL. 2)	PROPORTION IN MARKET PORTFOLIO (COL. 3)	ACTIVE POSITION (COL. 4)
S_1	.30	.45	−.15
S_2	.20	.25	−.05
S_3	.50	.30	+.20
	1.00	1.00	.00

The second column shows the actual proportions in the actively managed portfolio. The third column indicates the percentages in a hypothetical surrogate market portfolio—the holdings that might be best for an average client in a perfectly efficient market. The active positions can be represented by the differences between the proportions in the actual and market portfolios. Such differences arise because active managers disagree with the consensus about expected returns or risks. When expressed as differences of this sort, the actual portfolio can be viewed as an investment in the market portfolio with a series of *bets* being placed on certain securities (such as S_3) and against certain other securities (such as S_1 and S_2).

☐ 22.4.2 Security Selection, Asset Allocation, and Market Timing

Security Selection

In principle, the investment manager should make predictions of expected returns, standard deviations, and covariances for all available securities. This will allow an efficient set to be generated, upon which the indifference curves of the client can be plotted. Having done this, the investment manager should invest in those securities that form the optimal portfolio (that is, the portfolio indicated by the point where the indifference curves are tangent to the efficient set) for the client in question. Such a one-stage *security-selection* process is illustrated in Figure 22.6(a).

In practice, this is rarely (if ever) done. Excessive costs would be incurred to obtain detailed predictions of the expected returns, standard deviations, and covariances for all the individual securities under consideration. Instead, the decision of which securities to purchase is made in two or more stages.

Figure 22.6(b) illustrates a two-stage procedure where the investment manager has decided to consider investing in a number of common stocks and corporate bonds for a client. In this case, the expected returns, standard

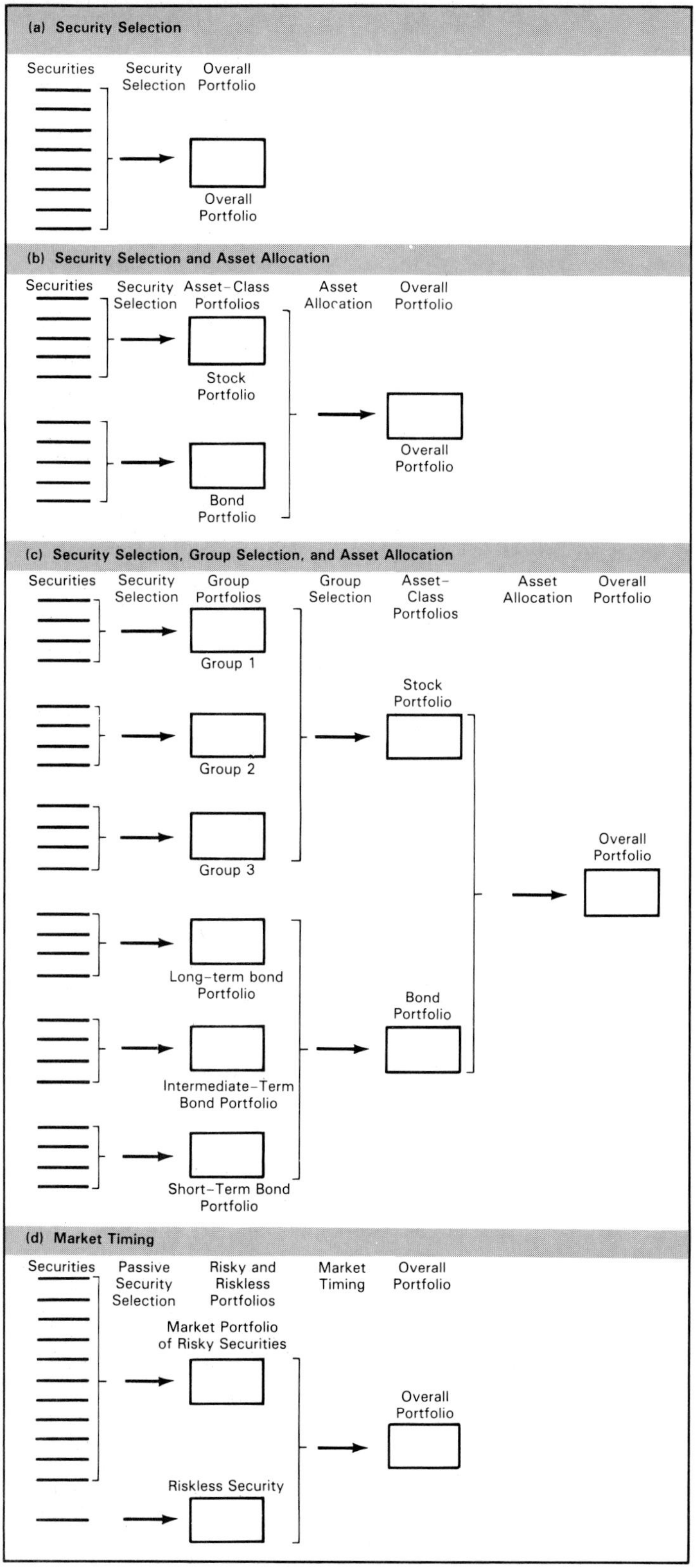

FIGURE 22–6
Investment styles.

deviations, and covariances are estimated for all common stocks under consideration. Then, based on just these common stocks, the efficient set is formed and the optimal stock portfolio is identified. Next, the same analysis is performed for all corporate bonds under consideration, resulting in the identification of the optimal bond portfolio. The security selection process used in each of these two *asset classes* can be described as being myopic. That is, covariances between the individual common stocks and corporate bonds have not been considered in the identification of the two optimal portfolios.

Asset Allocation

The second stage of the process allocates the client's funds among two asset class portfolios and is known as *asset allocation*.[6] In this stage, estimates of the expected return and standard deviation are needed for both the optimal stock portfolio and the optimal band portfolio, along with the covariance between the two portfolios. This will allow the expected return and standard deviation to be determined for all combinations of these two portfolios. Finally, after noting the efficient set from these combinations, the indifference curves of the client can be used to determine which portfolio should be chosen.

For example, the first stage might have indicated the investor should hold the proportions of stocks S_1, S_2, and S_3 given earlier (that is, the optimal stock portfolio has proportions of .30, .20, and .50, respectively). Similarly, the first stage might have indicated that the investor should hold a proportion of .35 in bond B_1 and .65 in bond B_2. Then the second stage might indicate that the client's funds should be split so that 60% goes into stocks and 40% goes into bonds. This translates into individual investments of the following magnitudes:

Stocks:
S_1 .60 × .30 =   .18
S_2 .60 × .20 =   .12
S_3 .60 × .50 =   .30

Bonds:
B_1 .40 × .35 =   .14
B_2 .40 × .65 =   .26
                  1.00

The two-stage process just discussed can be extended by introducing groups. Figure 22.6(c) illustrates a three-stage process. In the first stage, known as security selection, the investment manager exercises discretion in identifying groups of securities in each asset class. Then, having identified a group, the investment manager determines the optimal portfolio associated with it. For example, within the asset class of common stocks, it could be that the investment manager has identified all industrial stocks as the first

---

[6] For more details, see Sharpe, "Integrated Asset Allocation." For evidence suggesting that asset allocation is the most important decision an investor has to make, see Gary P. Brinson, L. Randolph Hood, and Gilbert L. Beebower, "Determinants of Portfolio Performance," *Financial Analysts Journal* 42, no. 4 (July/August 1986):39–44.

group, all utility stocks as the second group, and all transportation stocks as the third group. Within the asset class of bonds, groups of long-term, intermediate-term, and short-term bonds have been identified. Then, the investment manager identifies six optimal portfolios, one for each group of securities.

In the second stage, known as *group selection*, the investment manager determines the appropriate combination of the groups within each asset class. For example, the manager may have decided that the appropriate combination is 70% industrials, 10% utilities, and 20% transportation stocks. Similarly, the manager may have decided that the appropriate combination of bonds is 100% in long-term bonds, with nothing in either intermediate-term or short-term bonds. Thus, at this stage the manager will determine the composition of an optimal stock portfolio and an optimal bond portfolio but will not know how much to allocate to each one.

The third and final stage makes this allocation and is thus referred to as *asset allocation*. It is performed in a manner that is identical to the second stage of the two-stage procedure illustrated in Figure 22.6(b).

Active or passive management may be used in any stage. For example, "active bets" might be placed on individual securities, with funds allocated across security classes based on consensus expected returns for such classes. That is, the investment manager may decide to start every period with 75% in stocks and 25% in bonds. However, the choice of which individual stocks and bonds to invest in will change with time, based on the manager's forecasts.

Alternatively, passive portfolios of individual securities might be constructed, with deviant predictions of asset classes used to allocate funds actively among the classes. For example, the investment manager may decide always to hold common stocks in the same relative proportions they have in the S&P 500, which is often used as a surrogate for the market portfolio. However, the proportion of funds invested in the S&P 500 will change at the start of every period, based on the prognosis for the stock and bond markets. Thus, during one period the manager may have as much as 100% of the client's funds in stocks, on the strong belief that the stock market is going to rise rapidly in the near future. Conversely, during another period the manager may have as much as 100% of the client's funds in bonds, on the strong belief that the stock market will soon crash dramatically.

Market Timing

Figure 22.6(d) portrays a manager following a form of investment style that is known as *market timing*. The only active decision concerns the appropriate allocation of funds between a surrogate market portfolio and a risk-free asset such as Treasury bills. An investment organization following this style changes its mixture of risky and risk-free assets based on its own predictions of the risk and expected return of the market relative to the risk-free rate, even if there is no change in consensus predictions or the client's attitude toward risk and return.

Investment organizations that engage in the type of management where "active bets" are placed on individual securities are said to have a *security-*

selection style. Those that engage in the type of management where active bets are placed on asset classes are said to have an *asset-allocation style*, with market timing being one specific example. Lastly, investment organizations that place active bets on certain groups of securities are said to employ a *group rotation style*. Some organizations use relatively pure *investment styles*, meaning they use basically just one of the three styles previously mentioned. However, others employ various combinations, making it difficult to classify them into neat categories.

Although these styles have been described in terms of modern portfolio theory, it should be pointed out that other procedures could be used to implement them. For example, with modern portfolio theory, an "optimal stock portfolio" (as in Figure 22.6(b)) is to be identified by use of expected returns, standard deviations, and covariances in conjunction with indifference curves. Once the portfolio is identified, the portfolio manager will have determined the appropriate relative investments in individual common stocks. However, such an identification could be made using some other procedure. Often it is done on a much less formal and quantitative basis.

22.5 PORTFOLIO REVISION

With the passage of time, a previously purchased portfolio that is currently held will often be viewed as suboptimal by the investment manager, meaning the portfolio is no longer viewed as the best one for the client. This is because either the client's attitude toward risk and return is thought to have changed or, more likely, the manager's forecasts have changed. In response, the manager could identify a new optimal portfolio and then hope to be able to make the necessary revisions to the current portfolio so that subsequently the new optimal portfolio will be held. However, this is not as straightforward as it might seem at first because transaction costs will have to be paid when any revisions are made.

Such costs were discussed in Chapter 2; they include brokerage commissions and bid-ask spreads. Because of these costs, a security would have to increase in value by a certain amount just to pay these costs and leave the investor neither better nor worse off. This necessary increase in value may exceed 1% for many securities and can range as high as 5% to 10% or more for others.

The existence of transactions costs greatly complicates the life of any investment manager, and the more active the manager, the greater the complications. The hoped-for advantage of any revision must be weighed against the cost of making that revision. That is, a revision can be viewed as bringing certain kinds of benefits—it will either increase the expected return of the portfolio, it will reduce the standard deviation of the portfolio, or it will do both. To be weighed against these benefits are the transactions costs that will be incurred if the revision is made. As a result, some of the revisions in the holdings of individual securities that the manager may initially want to make will be dropped from consideration because of the transaction costs involved. The goal of the manager is to identify the set of

individual revisions that collectively maximize the improvement, after transactions costs, in the risk-return characteristics of the current portfolio.

In order to identify the set of individual revisions, sophisticated procedures (for example, quadratic programming) are required to compare the relevant costs and benefits.[7] Fortunately, improvements in procedures and dramatic decreases in computing costs have made such approaches economically feasible for many investment managers. Asset allocation programs capable of analyzing dozens of asset classes within a minute on an inexpensive microcomputer are widely available within the professional investment community.

22.6 MANAGER-CLIENT RELATIONS

The larger the amount of money managed, the more communication there is likely to be between investment manager and client. Not surprisingly, corporate, union, and government officials responsible for pension funds spend a great deal of time with those who manage their money. Such officials also concern themselves with a number of prior questions: Who should manage the money, how should it be managed, and how should the managers be instructed and constrained?

Many of the aspects of manager-client relations can be characterized as responses to a difference of opinion concerning the manager's abilities to make "good bets." Often, clients will divide their funds among two or more managers. This type of *split-funding* is used by most pension funds. Two reasons are given. First, it allows the employment of managers with different skills or different styles. Second, the impact of erroneous "bets" can be reduced by diversifying across different managers, since the managers are the bettors. However, as more investment managers are used, the overall portfolio is likely to appear more like the market portfolio. Thus, extensive use of split-funding can give results similar to those obtained with an explicit passive fund, but at considerably greater cost to the client, owing to the expenses associated with transactions costs and fees charged by the investment managers.

Whether or not split-funding is used, a client who feels that a manager is betting too much would simply like to reduce the size of the bets. For example, the client might ask a manager to diverge only half as much as he or she normally would from passive proportions of individual securities. Thus, if the manager decides that the optimal proportion in stock S_1 is 30% and the market proportion is 45%, this would mean that the manager would ultimately only invest a proportion equal to (30% + 45%)/2 = 37.5%. However, there is no simple way to monitor compliance. In the example, the manager could buy 45% of S_1 and state that he or she originally wanted to invest 60% in it but settled for 45%, even though truthfully he or she originally

[7] For a description of portfolio revision procedures, see pp. 221–28 of Gordon J. Alexander and Jack Clark Francis, *Portfolio Analysis* (Englewood Cliffs, N.J.: Prentice Hall, 1986); and pp. 65–68 of Sharpe, *Asset Allocation Tools.*

wanted 45%. Instead, another approach is often employed: Limits are placed on the holdings in any single security.[8]

Institutional investors (for example, pension and endowment funds) typically use more than one investment manager and provide each with a set of objectives and a set of constraints on allowed divergences from such normal positions.[9] Individual investors who employ investment managers tend to give such instructions implicitly, if at all. This may reflect less sophistication, a less formal relationship with the manager, or the fact that the management fee for a small account is not large enough to cover the cost of dealing with a series of objectives and constraints.

22.7 SUMMARY

This chapter discussed a five-step procedure for making investment decisions. The steps are (1) set investment policy, (2) perform security analysis, (3) construct a portfolio, (4) revise the portfolio, and (5) evaluate the performance of the portfolio.

With respect to setting investment policy, a procedure was presented for estimating an investor's indifference curves. This procedure involves asking the investor to identify the most desirable portfolio in a set of portfolios. Once such an identification has been made, the shape of the investor's indifference curves can be determined in a straightforward manner.

In terms of security analysis and portfolio construction, a distinction was made between passive and active management. Passive management rests on a belief that markets are efficient and typically involves investing in an index fund. Active management, on the other hand, involves a belief that mispriced situations occur and can be identified with a reasonable degree of accuracy. There are many forms of active management. They can involve security selection, where individual mispriced securities are sought out, and market timing, where the stock market in aggregate is evaluated to see if it is, in general, mispriced. Variations include looking at various groups of securities in the attempt to identify mispriced ones.

Portfolio revision involves realizing that the currently held portfolio is not optimal. That is, there is another portfolio that the investor would prefer to hold instead of the current one. However, whereas the desired portfolio has superior risk-return characteristics, altering the current portfolio so that it will correspond to the desired one will entail transactions costs. Thus, the investor must balance costs with benefits in making revisions to the currently held portfolio.

The last step, evaluating the performance of a portfolio, was not discussed in this chapter. Due to its importance and complexity, it is the subject of the next chapter.

---

[8] There are other kinds of limits frequently imposed on the manager, such as limits on the holdings of bonds versus stocks or on the amount invested in a single industry.

[9] Sometimes the objectives are stated in terms of target or normal positions.

APPENDIX A
DETERMINING THE RISK TOLERANCE OF AN INVESTOR

The purpose of this appendix is to derive in some detail the formula for determining the risk tolerance τ of an investor. As mentioned earlier, the equation for an indifference curve of an investor having constant risk tolerance is of the form

$$\bar{r}_p = u_i + \frac{1}{\tau}\sigma_p^2 \qquad (22.1)$$

where u_i and $1/\tau$ are the vertical intercept and slope for indifference curve i, where variance is measured on the horizontal axis. As the equation shows, an indifference curve will be a straight line, since u_i and $1/\tau$ are constants (thus, the equation is of the general form $Y = a + bX$ and is a straight line). Furthermore, any two indifference curves for an investor will have the same slope $(1/\tau)$ but will have different vertical intercepts (u_i).

In order to estimate the investor's level of risk tolerance τ, it was mentioned that the slope of the indifference curve, $1/\tau$, would be set equal to the slope of the efficient set at the location of the portfolio that was selected, denoted by portfolio C. This is because the indifference curve is tangent to the efficient set at this point, so the two must have the same slope. Thus, the slope of the efficient set at point C must be determined in order to estimate τ.

Let X_S denote the proportion invested in the stock portfolio S and $(1 - X_S)$ denote the proportion invested in a risk-free Treasury bill portfolio F. Now the expected return of any portfolio consisting of S and F is simply

$$\bar{r}_p = X_S\bar{r}_S + (1 - X_S)r_F \qquad (22.6)$$

where $\bar{r}_S$ and r_F are the expected returns of the stock portfolio and the risk-free rate, respectively. This equation can be solved for X_S, resulting in

$$X_S = \frac{\bar{r}_p - r_F}{\bar{r}_S - r_F}. \qquad (22.7)$$

The equation for the variance of portfolio p is equal to:

$$\sigma_p^2 = X_S^2\sigma_S^2 + (1 - X_S)^2\sigma_F^2 + 2X_S(1 - X_S)\sigma_{SF} \qquad (22.8)$$

where σ_S^2 and σ_F^2 are the variances of the stock and risk-free portfolios, respectively, and σ_{SF} is the covariance between these two portfolios. However, since F is the risk-free portfolio, by definition σ_F^2 and σ_{SF} are equal to zero. Thus, equation (22.8) reduces to

$$\sigma_p^2 = X_S^2\sigma_S^2. \qquad (22.9)$$

Next, the right-hand side of equation (22.7) can be substituted for X_S in equation (22.9), resulting in

$$\sigma_p^2 = \frac{(\bar{r}_p - r_F)^2}{(\bar{r}_S - r_F)^2}\sigma_S^2. \qquad (22.10)$$

This equation can be viewed as describing the functional relationship between the expected return and variance of any portfolio p that can be formed by combining the stock portfolio S and the risk-free portfolio F. That is, for a particular S and F, it gives the variance for a portfolio consisting of S and F with expected return $\bar{r}_p$. Equivalently, it represents the slope of the curved line in Figure 22.3 that connects S and F.

Using calculus, the slope of this line can be shown to be equal to [10]

$$\text{Slope} = \frac{(\bar{r}_S - r_F)^2}{2[(\bar{r}_p - r_F)\sigma_S^2]}. \tag{22.11}$$

The next step in estimating the slope of the client's indifference curves is to note that the portfolio on the curve connecting S and F that is of concern is the tangency portfolio C. Thus, the slope of the curve at C is determined by substituting $\bar{r}_C$ for $\bar{r}_p$ in equation (22.11) and equating this value with the slope of the indifference curves, $1/\tau$. Doing this results in the following equation:

$$\frac{1}{\tau} = \frac{(\bar{r}_S - r_F)^2}{2[(\bar{r}_C - r_F)\sigma_S^2]}. \tag{22.12}$$

Finally, equation (22.12) can be solved for τ:

$$\tau = \frac{2[(\bar{r}_C - r_F)\sigma_S^2]}{(\bar{r}_S - r_F)^2}. \tag{22.13}$$

Note that this is the same formula that was given earlier in equation (22.2) for estimating τ, given the client's choice of portfolio C.[11]

At point C equation (22.7) can be rewritten as

$$(\bar{r}_S - r_F)X_S = \bar{r}_C - r_F. \tag{22.14}$$

Thus, $(\bar{r}_S - r_F)X_S$ can be substituted for $\bar{r}_C - r_F$ in the numerator of equation (22.13). Doing so and simplifying results in

$$\tau = \frac{2(X_S\sigma_S^2)}{\bar{r}_S - r_F}. \tag{22.15}$$

In the example given earlier in the chapter, $\sigma_S = 15\%$ and $\bar{r}_S - r_F = 4.5\%$. Substituting these values into equation (22.15) and simplifying results in

$$\tau = \frac{2[X_S \times 15^2]}{4.5} \tag{22.16}$$

$$= 100X_S$$

as was previously mentioned and illustrated in Table 22.1.

---

[10] Note that the slope of this line, $d\bar{r}_p/d\sigma_p^2$, is equal to $1/[d\sigma_p^2/d\bar{r}_p]$. Thus, the slope can be determined by taking the derivative of σ_p^2 with respect to $\bar{r}_p$ in equation (22.10) and then inverting the resulting expression.

[11] Risk tolerance, along with a computer program for estimating the value of τ, is presented in Sharpe, *Asset Allocation Tools*, 33–39.

QUESTIONS AND PROBLEMS

1. Technological changes have decreased the cost and increased the speed of information dissemination in security markets. Why might one suspect that firms following a "traditional" approach to investment management would find it increasingly difficult to generate "positive alphas" (that is, to identify underpriced securities) in this environment?

2. Why is it difficult to specify the risk-return preferences of investment management clients? Why are these problems particularly acute in the case of institutional clients (for example, pension and endowment funds)?

3. Explain the meaning of the slope of an investor's indifference curve at any particular point. For a "typical" risk-averse investor, describe how the investor's risk-return trade-off changes at different points along one of his or her indifference curves.

4. Buzz Arlett, a portfolio manager for an investment management firm, has estimated the following risk-return characteristics for the stock and bond markets.

	EXPECTED RETURN	STANDARD DEVIATION
Stocks	18.0%	22.0%
Bonds	10.0	5.0

Using these estimates, Buzz ran a number of simulations, tracing out the implications of different bond/stock mixes for the financial situation of Zinn Beck, a client. After much thought, Zinn indicated that of the mixes considered, the most desirable was the allocation of 60% to stocks and 40% to bonds. Given this information, calculate Zinn's risk tolerance. [*Hint*: To solve this problem algebraically, write Eq. (22.5) using the 60/40 stock/bond allocation. Do the same for a 61/39 allocation. Finally, set these two formulas equal to each other and solve for the risk tolerance.] Is this answer likely to represent Zinn's risk tolerance over all possible stock/bond allocations?

5. Should an "overpriced" stock definitely be excluded from an investor's portfolio? Why or why not?

6. Studies that simulate the value of an investment portfolio under alternative mixes of stocks and bonds invariably demonstrate that higher stock allocations produce higher returns, particularly as the holding period increases. If you as an investor have a time horizon that is reasonably long, say over ten years, and you have no current income needs, how could you justify holding any bonds in your portfolio?

7. The portfolio manager's job can be defined as identifying the portfolio with the highest certainty equivalent return. Explain.

8. Despite its obvious simplicity and potential benefits, common stock passive management is a relatively "new" investment tool. Yet in the last twenty years, assets under passive management have grown from essentially zero to over $100 billion. What are several possible reasons for the tremendous growth in passive management?

9. It is often argued (especially by active managers) that passive management implies settling for "mediocre" performance. Is this statement necessarily true? Why or why not?

10. Why is the "one-stage" approach to security selection theoretically superior to the "two-stage" approach? Why is the "two-stage" approach preferred by most investment managers?

11. A typical money management firm, particularly one specializing in stocks or bonds, invests in essentially the same portfolio for all of its clients, regardless of the clients' individual risk-return preferences. Speculate as to why money managers often operate in this manner. What can clients do to ensure that their portfolios reflect their own specific risk-return preferences?

12. Many investment management clients split their assets among a number of managers. The rationale for this approach has been described as "diversification of judgment" and "diversification of style." Explain the meaning of these two terms.

Chapter 23

PORTFOLIO PERFORMANCE EVALUATION

An investor who has been paying someone actively to manage his or her portfolio has every right to insist on knowing what sort of performance was obtained. Such information can be used to alter either the constraints placed on the manager, the investment objectives given to the manager, or the amount of money allocated to the manager. Perhaps more importantly, by evaluating performance in specified ways, a client can forcefully communicate his or her interests to the investment manager and, in all likelihood, affect the way in which his or her portfolio is managed. Moreover, an investment manager, by evaluating his or her own performance, can identify sources of strength or weakness. Thus, although the previous chapter indicated portfolio performance evaluation was the last stage of the investment management process, it can also be viewed as simply part of a continuing operation.

Superior performance in the past may have been due to good luck, in which case such performance should not be expected to continue in the future. On the other hand, superior performance in the past may have been due to the actions of a highly skilled investment manager (and support staff). Conversely, inferior performance in the past may have been the result of bad luck, but it may also have been due to excessive turnover, high management fees, or other costs associated with an unskilled investment manager. This suggests that the first task in performance evaluation is to try to determine whether past performance was superior or inferior. Once this task is done, the second task is to try to determine whether such performance was due to skill or luck. Unfortunately, there are difficulties associated with carrying out both of these tasks. Accordingly, this chapter presents not only certain methods that have been advocated and used for evaluating portfolio performance but also a discussion of the difficulties encountered with their use.

23.1 MEASURES OF RETURN

Frequently portfolio performance is evaluated over a time interval of at least four years, with returns measured for a number of periods within the interval—typically monthly or quarterly. This provides a fairly adequate sam-

733

ple size for statistical evaluation (for example, if returns are measured quarterly for four years, there will be 16 observations). Sometimes, however, a shorter time interval must be used in order to avoid examining returns earned under a different investment manager (or the support staff).

In the simplest situation, where the client neither deposits nor withdraws money from the portfolio during a time period, calculation of the portfolio's return is straightforward. All that is required is that the market value of the portfolio be known at two points in time—the beginning and the end of the period.

In general, the market value of a portfolio at a point in time is determined by adding the market values of all the securities held at that particular time. For example, the value of a common stock portfolio at the beginning of a period is calculated by (1) noting the market price per share of each stock held in the portfolio at that time, (2) multiplying each of these stock prices by the corresponding number of shares held, and (3) adding the resulting products. This sum will equal the market value of the portfolio at the beginning of the period.

With the beginning and ending portfolio values in hand, the return on the portfolio can be calculated by subtracting the beginning value (V_b) from the ending value (V_e) and then dividing the difference by the beginning value:

$$r_p = \frac{V_e - V_b}{V_b} \qquad (23.1)$$

For example, if a portfolio has a market value of $40 million at the beginning of a quarter and a market value of $46 million at the end of the quarter, then the return on this portfolio for the quarter is ($46 million − $40 million)/ $40 million = 15%.

Measurement of portfolio returns is complicated by the fact that the client may either add or withdraw money from the portfolio. This means that the percentage change in the market value of the portfolio during a period may not be an accurate measurement of the portfolio's return during that period.

For example, consider a portfolio that at the beginning of a quarter has a market value of $100 million. Just before the end of the quarter the client deposits $5 million with the investment manager, and, subsequently, at the end of the quarter the market value of the portfolio is $103 million. If the quarterly return was measured without consideration of the $5 million deposit, the reported return would be ($103 million − $100 million)/$100 million = 3%. However, this would be incorrect, since $5 million of the ending $103 million market value was not due to the investment actions of the manager. Consideration of the deposit would suggest that a more accurate measure of the quarterly return would be [($103 million − $5 million) − $100 million]/ $100 million = −2%.

Identification of exactly *when* any deposits or withdrawals occur is important in accurately measuring portfolio returns. If a deposit or withdrawal occurs just *before* the end of the period, then the return on the portfolio should be calculated by adjusting the ending market value of the portfolio.

In the case of a deposit, the ending value should be reduced by the dollar amount (as was done in the previous example); in the case of a withdrawal, the ending value should be increased by the dollar amount.

If a deposit or withdrawal occurs just *after* the start of the period, then the return on the portfolio should be calculated by adjusting the beginning market value of the portfolio. In the case of a deposit, the beginning value should be increased by the dollar amount; in the case of a withdrawal, the beginning value should be decreased by the dollar amount. For example, if the $5 million deposit in the earlier example had been received just after the start of the quarter, the return for the quarter should be calculated as [$103 million − ($100 million + $5 million)]/($100 million + $5 million) = −1.90%.

23.1.1 Dollar-Weighted Returns

Difficulties are encountered when deposits or withdrawals occur sometime *between* the beginning and end of the period. One method that has been used for calculating a portfolio's return in this situation results in the portfolio's *dollar-weighted return* (or internal rate of return).

For example, if the $5 million deposit in the earlier example was made in the middle of the quarter, the dollar-weighted return would be calculated by solving the following equation for r:

$$\$100 \text{ million} = \frac{-\$5 \text{ million}}{(1 + r)} + \frac{\$103 \text{ million}}{(1 + r)^2}. \tag{23.2}$$

The solution to this equation, $r = -.98\%$, is a semiquarterly rate of return. It can be converted into a quarterly rate of return by adding 1 to it, squaring this value, and then subtracting 1 from the square, resulting in a quarterly return of $[1 + (-.0098)]^2 - 1 = -1.95\%$.[1]

23.1.2 Time-Weighted Returns

Alternatively, the *time-weighted return* on a portfolio can be calculated when there are cash flows occurring between the beginning and end of the period. This method involves using the market value of the portfolio just before each cash flow occurs. In the earlier example, assume that in the middle of the quarter the portfolio had a market value of $96 million, so that right after the $5 million deposit the market value was $96 million + $5 million = $101 million. In this case, the return for the first half of the quarter would be ($96 million − $100 million)/$100 million = − 4%; the return for the second half of the quarter would be ($103 million − $101 million)/$101 million = 1.98%.

---

[1] This procedure provides a quarterly return with "quarterly compounding." Alternatively, the semiquarterly return could be doubled, resulting in a quarterly return with "semiquarterly compounding" of −.98% × 2 = −1.96%.

Next, these two semiquarterly returns can be combined to give a quarterly return by adding 1 to each return, multiplying the sums, and then subtracting 1 from the product. In the example, this procedure results in a quarterly return of $[(1 - .04)(1 + .0198)] - 1 = -2.1\%$.

☐ 23.1.3 Comparing Dollar-Weighted and Time-Weighted Returns

Which method is preferable for calculating the return on a portfolio? In the example given here, the dollar-weighted return was -1.95%, whereas the time-weighted return was -2.1%, suggesting the difference between the two methods may not be very important. Although this may be true in certain situations, examples can be given to show that such differences can be quite large and that the time-weighted return method is preferable.

Consider a hypothetical portfolio that starts a quarter with a market value of $50 million. In the middle of the quarter, it has fallen to a market value of $25 million, at which point the client deposits $25 million with the investment manager. At the end of the quarter the portfolio has a market value of $100 million. The semiquarterly dollar-weighted return for this portfolio is equal to the value of r in the following equation:

$$\$50 \text{ million} = \frac{-\$25 \text{ million}}{(1 + r)} + \frac{\$100 \text{ million}}{(1 + r)^2}$$

Solving this equation for r results in a value of 18.6%, which in turn equals a quarterly dollar-weighted return of $(1.186)^2 - 1 = 40.66\%$. However, its quarterly time-weighted return is 0%, since its return for the first half of the quarter was -50% and its return for the second half of the quarter was 100% (note that $(1 - .5)(1 + 1) - 1 = 0\%$).

Comparing these two returns—40.66% and 0%—indicates a sizable difference exists. However, the time-weighted return figure of 0% is more meaningful for performance evaluation than the dollar-weighted return figure of 40.66%. The reason for this can be seen by considering the return over the entire quarter on each dollar that was in the portfolio at the start of the quarter. Each dollar lost half of its value over the first half of the quarter, but then the remaining half-dollar doubled its value over the second half. Consequently, a dollar at the beginning was worth a dollar at the end, suggesting a return of 0% on the portfolio is a more accurate measure of the investment manager's performance than the 40.66% figure.

In general, the dollar-weighted return method of measuring a portfolio's return for purposes of evaluation is regarded as inappropriate. The reason behind this view is that the return is strongly influenced by the size and timing of the cash flows (namely, deposits and withdrawals) over which the investment manager has no control. In the example, the dollar-weighted return was 40.66% because the client fortuitously made a big deposit just before the portfolio appreciated rapidly in value. Thus, the 40.66% return figure is due at least partly to the actions of the client, not the manager.

☐ 23.1.4 Annualizing Returns

The previous discussion has focused on calculating quarterly returns. Such returns may be added or multiplied to obtain an annual measure of return. For example, if the return in the first, second, third, and fourth quarters of a given year are denoted by r_1, r_2, r_3, and r_4, respectively, then the annual return could be calculated by adding the four figures:

$$\text{Annual return} = r_1 + r_2 + r_3 + r_4. \tag{23.3}$$

Alternatively, the annual return could be calculated by adding 1 to each quarterly return, then multiplying the four figures, and finally subtracting 1 from the resulting product:

$$\text{Annual return} = [(1 + r_1)(1 + r_2)(1 + r_3)(1 + r_4)] - 1. \tag{23.4}$$

This return is more accurate because it reflects the value that $1 would have at the end of the year if it were invested at the beginning of the year and grew *with compounding* at the rate of r_1 for the first quarter, r_2 for the second quarter, r_3 for the third quarter, and r_4 for the fourth quarter. That is, it assumes reinvestment of both the dollar and any earnings at the end of each quarter.

23.2 MAKING RELEVANT COMPARISONS

The essential idea behind performance evaluation is to compare the returns obtained by the investment manager through active management with the returns that could have been obtained for the client if one or more appropriate alternative portfolios had been chosen for investment. The reason for this comparison is straightforward—performance should be evaluated on a relative basis, not on an absolute basis.

As an example, consider a client who is told that his or her portfolio, invested in common stocks and of average risk, had a return of 20% last year. Does this suggest superior or inferior performance? If the stock market went up by 10% last year, then it suggests superior performance and is good news. However, if the stock market went up by 30% last year, then it suggests inferior performance and is bad news. In order to infer whether the manager's performance is superior or inferior, the returns on similar portfolios that are either actively or passively managed are needed for comparison.

Such comparison portfolios are often referred to as *benchmark portfolios*. In selecting them, the client should be certain they are relevant and feasible, meaning they should represent alternative portfolios that could have been chosen for investment instead of the portfolio being evaluated. *Return* is a key aspect of performance, of course, but some way must be found to account for the portfolio's exposure to *risk*. The choice of benchmark portfolios may be restricted to portfolios perceived to have similar levels of risk, thereby permitting a direct comparison of returns.

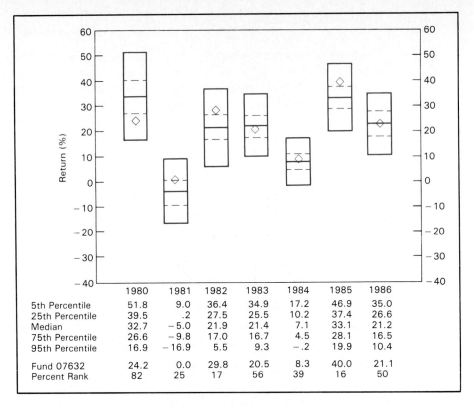

	1980	1981	1982	1983	1984	1985	1986
5th Percentile	51.8	9.0	36.4	34.9	17.2	46.9	35.0
25th Percentile	39.5	.2	27.5	25.5	10.2	37.4	26.6
Median	32.7	−5.0	21.9	21.4	7.1	33.1	21.2
75th Percentile	26.6	−9.8	17.0	16.7	4.5	28.1	16.5
95th Percentile	16.9	−16.9	5.5	9.3	−.2	19.9	10.4
Fund 07632	24.2	0.0	29.8	20.5	8.3	40.0	21.1
Percent Rank	82	25	17	56	39	16	50

FIGURE 23–1
Comparing returns of equity portfolios.

SOURCE: Adapted from SEI, *Funds Evaluation Service*.

Figure 23.1 illustrates such a comparison for a hypothetical common stock (or "equity") portfolio referred to as Fund 07632. In this figure, Fund 07632's performance for each year is represented by a diamond. The hypothetical comparison portfolios are a set of other common stock portfolios that are represented by the box surrounding the diamond. The top and bottom lines of the box indicate the returns of the 5th and 95th percentile comparison portfolios, respectively. Similarly, the top and bottom dashed lines represent the 25th and 75th percentiles. The solid line in the middle represents the median (50th percentile) portfolio.

Alternatively, risk may be explicitly measured so that a single measure of performance taking both return and risk into account can be employed. This will allow benchmark portfolios of varying degrees of risk to be compared with the portfolio being evaluated.

The following discussion of risk-adjusted measures of performance concerns equity (common stock) portfolios; bond portfolios are presented later in the chapter.

23.3 RISK-ADJUSTED MEASURES OF PERFORMANCE FOR EQUITY PORTFOLIOS

Having measured the periodic returns for a portfolio during an evaluation interval (for example, quarterly returns for a four-year evaluation interval), the next step is to determine if these returns represent superior or inferior performance. In order to do this, an estimate of the portfolio's risk level during the evaluation interval is needed. For equity portfolios, two kinds of risk can be estimated—the portfolio's market (or systematic) risk, measured by its beta, and the portfolio's total risk, measured by its standard deviation.

It is important to analyze risk appropriately. The key issue here is determining the impact of the portfolio on the client's overall level of risk. If the client has many other assets, then the market risk of the portfolio provides the relevant measure of the portfolio's impact on the client's overall level of risk. If, however, the portfolio provides the client's sole support, then its total risk is the relevant measure of risk. Risk-adjusted performance evaluation is generally based on one of these two viewpoints, taking either market risk or total risk into consideration.

Assume there are T time periods in the evaluation interval (for example, $T = 16$ when there are four years of quarterly data) and let r_{pt} denote the return on the portfolio during period t. The *average return* on the portfolio, denoted by ar_p, is simply:

$$ar_p = \frac{\sum_{t=1}^{T} r_{pt}}{T}. \tag{23.5}$$

Having calculated ar_p, the *ex post standard deviation* can be calculated as

$$\sigma_p = \left[\frac{\sum_{t=1}^{T} (r_{pt} - ar_p)^2}{T - 1} \right]^{1/2}. \tag{23.6}$$

This estimate of the portfolio's standard deviation can be used as an indication of the amount of total risk that the portfolio had during the evaluation interval.[2] It can be compared directly with the standard deviations of other portfolios, as illustrated in Figure 23.2. (This figure is to be interpreted in the same manner as Figure 23.1.)

The returns of a portfolio may also be compared with those of a substitute for the market portfolio, such as Standard & Poor's 500, in order to determine the portfolio's *ex post beta* during the evaluation interval. Denoting

---

[2] Sometimes the excess return for a portfolio, which is equal to its return minus the risk-free rate $(r_{pt} - r_{ft})$, is used instead of r_{pt} in equation (23.5) to determine the average excess return (denoted by aer_p). Then, the summation in the numerator of equation (23.6) is carried out using $[(r_{pt} - r_{ft}) - aer_p]^2$ instead of $(r_{pt} - ar_p)^2$. The resulting number is the standard deviation of excess returns, which is sometimes used as an estimate of the total risk of the portfolio. Typically, the two standard deviations are quite similar in numerical value.

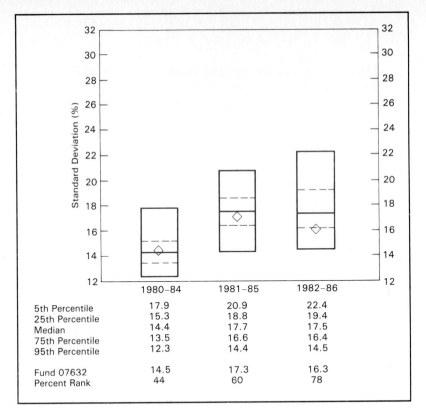

	1980–84	1981–85	1982–86
5th Percentile	17.9	20.9	22.4
25th Percentile	15.3	18.8	19.4
Median	14.4	17.7	17.5
75th Percentile	13.5	16.6	16.4
95th Percentile	12.3	14.4	14.5
Fund 07632	14.5	17.3	16.3
Percent Rank	44	60	78

FIGURE 23–2
Comparing standard deviations of equity portfolios.

SOURCE: Adapted from SEI, *Funds Evaluation Service*.

the excess return on the portfolio during period t by $er_{pt} = r_{pt} - r_{ft}$, the return on the S&P 500 (or some other market substitute) during period t by r_{Mt}, and the excess return on the S&P 500 during period t by $er_{Mt} = r_{Mt} - r_{ft}$, this beta can be estimated as follows:

$$\beta_p = \frac{\left(T \sum_{t=1}^{T} er_{Mt} er_{pt} \right) - \left(\sum_{t=1}^{T} er_{pt} \sum_{t=1}^{T} er_{Mt} \right)}{\left(T \sum_{t=1}^{T} er_{Mt}^2 \right) - \left(\sum_{t=1}^{T} er_{Mt} \right)^2}. \tag{23.7}$$

This estimate of the portfolio's beta can be used as an indication of the amount of market risk that the portfolio had during the evaluation interval.[3] It can

---

[3] Equation (23.7) corresponds to the formula for estimating the slope term in a simple regression model where the independent variable is er_{Mt} and the dependent variable is er_{pt}. Sometimes returns are used in equation (23.7), where er_{Mt} is replaced by r_{Mt} and er_{pt} is replaced by r_{pt}. In this situation, the beta corresponds to the slope term in the *market model* for the portfolio. Typically, the two betas are quite similar in numerical value.

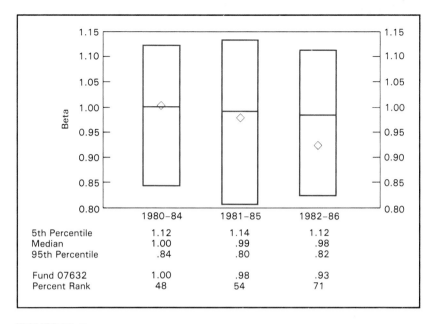

	1980–84	1981–85	1982–86
5th Percentile	1.12	1.14	1.12
Median	1.00	.99	.98
95th Percentile	.84	.80	.82
Fund 07632	1.00	.98	.93
Percent Rank	48	54	71

FIGURE 23–3
Comparing betas of equity portfolios.

SOURCE: Adapted from SEI, *Funds Evaluation Service.*

be compared directly with the betas of other portfolios, as illustrated in Figure 23.3 (this figure is to be interpreted in the same manner as Figure 23.1).

Although a portfolio's return and a measure of its risk can be compared individually with those of other portfolios, as in Figures 23.1 through 23.3, it is often not clear how the portfolio performed on a risk-adjusted basis relative to these other portfolios. For the fund shown in the figures, the average percent rank for the portfolio's return over the five years ending in 1986 is (17 + 56 + 39 + 16 + 50)/5 = 36%. Over the same period, its standard deviation put it in the 78th percent rank.

Assuming the client is concerned with total risk, how does he or she interpret these percent ranks? In the case of the return, the portfolio was slightly above average; in terms of standard deviation, it was less risky than approximately three-fourths of the other portfolios. Overall, this suggests that the portfolio did better on a risk-adjusted basis than the others, but it does not give the client a clear and precise sense of how much better.

Such a sense can be conveyed by certain CAPM-based measures of portfolio performance. Each one of these measures provides an estimate of a portfolio's risk-adjusted performance, thereby allowing the client to see how the portfolio performed relative to other portfolios as well as the market. They are presented next.

☐ 23.3.1 *Ex Post* Characteristic Lines

Over an evaluation interval, an *ex post security market line* (SML) can be estimated by determining the average risk-free rate and market return:

$$ar_f = \frac{\sum\limits_{t=1}^{T} r_{ft}}{T} \tag{23.8}$$

$$ar_M = \frac{\sum\limits_{t=1}^{T} r_{Mt}}{T}. \tag{23.9}$$

Once these averages have been calculated, the ex post SML is simply the equation of the line going through the points $(0, ar_f)$ and $(1, ar_M)$:

$$ar_p^e = ar_f + (ar_M - ar_f)\beta_p. \tag{23.10}$$

Equivalently, the equilibrium average return during this interval of time for a portfolio with a beta of β_p would simply be equal to $ar_f + (ar_M - ar_f)\beta_p$. Accordingly, ar_p^e can be used as the benchmark return for a portfolio with a beta of β_p.

Part A of Table 23.1 presents an example by using the quarterly returns for the S&P 500 over the interval 1982 to 1985, along with corresponding returns on 90-day Treasury bills. Using equations (23.8) and (23.9), the average risk-free return and market return were, respectively, 2.23% and 4.88%. Inserting these values into equation (23.10), the ex post SML for this time interval was:

$$ar_p^e = 2.23\% + (4.88\% - 2.23\%)\beta_p \tag{23.11}$$
$$= 2.23\% + 2.65\%\beta_p.$$

Thus, after estimating a portfolio's ex post beta and entering this value on the right-hand side of equation (23.11), a benchmark return for the portfolio can be determined. For example, a portfolio with a beta of .8 during 1982 to 1985 would have a benchmark return of $2.23\% + (2.65\% \times .8) = 4.35\%$. Figure 23.4 presents a graph of the ex post SML given by equation (23.11).

If the average return on a portfolio was ar_p, calculated as shown in equation (23.5), then one measure of its risk-adjusted performance would be the difference between its average return and its corresponding equilibrium or benchmark return. This difference is generally referred to as the portfolio's *ex post alpha* (or differential return) and is denoted by α_p:

$$\alpha_p = ar_p - ar_p^e. \tag{23.12}$$

A positive value of α_p for a portfolio would indicate that the portfolio had an average return greater than the benchmark return, suggesting its performance was superior. On the other hand, a negative value of α_p would

TABLE 23.1

The *Ex Post* Characteristic Line for the First Fund, 1982–1985.

a. RETURN DATA.

Quarter		Treasury Bill Return	First Fund Return	First Fund Excess Return	S&P 500 Return	S&P 500 Excess Return
1982	1	2.97%	− 8.77%	−11.74%	− 5.86%	− 8.83%
	2	3.06	− 6.03	− 9.09	− 2.94	− 6.00
	3	2.85	14.14	11.29	13.77	10.92
	4	1.88	24.96	23.08	14.82	12.94
1983	1	1.90	3.71	1.81	11.91	10.01
	2	2.00	10.65	8.65	11.55	9.55
	3	2.22	− .22	− 2.44	− .78	− 3.00
	4	2.11	.27	− 1.84	.02	− 2.09
1984	1	2.16	− 3.08	− 5.24	− 2.52	− 4.68
	2	2.34	− 6.72	− 9.06	− 1.85	− 4.19
	3	2.44	8.58	6.29	8.73	6.29
	4	2.40	1.15	− 1.25	1.63	− .77
1985	1	1.89	7.87	5.98	10.82	8.93
	2	1.94	5.92	3.98	7.24	5.30
	3	1.72	− 3.10	− 4.82	− 2.78	− 4.50
	4	1.75	13.61	11.86	14.36	12.61

b. CALCULATIONS[a].

Quarter		First Fund Excess Returns = Y (1)	S&P 500 Excess Returns = X (2)	Y^2 (3)	X^2 (4)	$Y \times X$ (5)
1982	1	− 11.74%	− 8.83%	137.83	77.93	103.66
	2	− 9.09	− 6.00	82.63	36.05	54.54
	3	11.29	10.92	127.46	119.26	123.29
	4	23.08	12.94	532.69	167.53	298.66
1983	1	1.81	10.01	3.28	100.11	18.12
	2	8.65	9.55	74.82	91.28	82.61
	3	− 2.44	− 3.00	5.95	8.97	7.32
	4	− 1.84	− 2.09	3.39	4.35	3.85
1984	1	− 5.24	− 4.68	27.46	21.94	24.52
	2	− 9.06	− 4.19	82.08	17.54	37.96
	3	6.14	6.29	37.70	39.53	38.62
	4	− 1.25	− .77	1.56	.60	.96
1985	1	5.98	8.93	35.76	79.82	53.40
	2	3.98	5.30	15.84	28.07	21.09
	3	− 4.82	− 4.50	23.23	20.25	21.69
	4	11.86	12.61	140.66	158.93	149.56
		$\Sigma Y = 27.31$	$\Sigma X = 42.49$	$\Sigma Y^2 = 1332.34$	$\Sigma X^2 = 972.16$	$\Sigma XY = 1039.85$

1. Beta:

$$\frac{(T \times \Sigma XY) - (\Sigma Y \times \Sigma X)}{(T \times \Sigma X^2) - (\Sigma X)^2} = \frac{(16 \times 1039.85) - (27.31 \times 42.49)}{(16 \times 972.16) - (42.49)^2} = 1.13$$

2. Alpha:

$$\frac{\Sigma Y}{T} - \left(\text{Beta} \times \frac{\Sigma X}{T} \right) = \frac{27.31}{16} - \left(1.13 \times \frac{42.49}{16} \right) = -1.29\%$$

TABLE 23.1 (*Continued*)

3. Standard deviation of random error term:

$$\left[\frac{\Sigma Y^2 - (alpha \times \Sigma Y) - (Beta \times \Sigma XY)}{T - 2}\right]^{1/2}$$

$$= \left[\frac{1332.34 - (-1.29 \times 42.49) - (1.13 \times 1039.85)}{16 - 2}\right]^{1/2} = 3.75\%$$

4. Standard error of beta:

$$\frac{\text{Standard deviation of random error term}}{[\Sigma X^2 - (\Sigma X)^2/T]^{1/2}} = \frac{3.75}{[972.16 - (42.49)^2/16]^{1/2}} = .13$$

5. Standard error of alpha:

$$\frac{\text{Standard deviation of random error term}}{[T - (\Sigma X)^2/\Sigma X^2]^{1/2}} = \frac{3.75}{[16 - (42.49)^2/972.16]^{1/2}} = 1.00$$

6. Correlation coefficient:

$$\frac{(T \times \Sigma XY) - (\Sigma Y \times \Sigma X)}{\{[(T \times \Sigma Y^2) - (\Sigma Y)^2] \times [(T \times \Sigma X^2) - (\Sigma X)^2]\}^{1/2}}$$

$$= \frac{(16 \times 1039.85) - (27.31 \times 42.49)}{\{[(16 \times 1332.34) - (27.31)^2] \times [(16 \times 972.16) - (42.49)^2]\}^{1/2}} = .92$$

7. Coefficient of determination:

$$(\text{Correlation coefficient})^2 = (.92)^2 = .85$$

8. Coefficient of nondetermination:

$$1 - \text{coefficient of determination} = 1 - .85 = .15$$

---

[a] All summations are to be carried out over t, where t goes from 1 to T (in this example, $t = 1, \ldots, 16$).

indicate that the portfolio had an average return less than the benchmark return, suggesting its performance was inferior.[4]

By substituting the right-hand side of equation (23.10) for ar_p^e in equation (23.12), it can be seen that a portfolio's ex post alpha is equal to

$$\alpha_p = ar_p - [ar_f + (ar_M - ar_f)\beta_p]. \qquad (23.13)$$

After determining the values for α_p and β_p for a portfolio, the *ex post characteristic line* for the portfolio can be written as

$$r_p - r_f = \alpha_p + \beta_p(r_M - r_f). \qquad (23.14)$$

Graphically, this is the equation of a straight line, where $r_M - r_f$ is measured on the horizontal axis and $r_p - r_f$ is measured on the vertical axis. Furthermore, the line has a vertical intercept of α_p and a slope of β_p.

As an example, consider the performance of the hypothetical portfolio "First Fund," indicated in part A of Table 23.1 for the evaluation interval of 1982 to 1985. During this interval, the First Fund had an average quarterly

---

[4] This measure of performance is sometimes known as the *Jensen coefficient* because it was developed by Michael C. Jensen in "The Performance of Mutual Funds in the Period 1945–1964," *Journal of Finance* 23, no. 2 (May 1968):389–416.

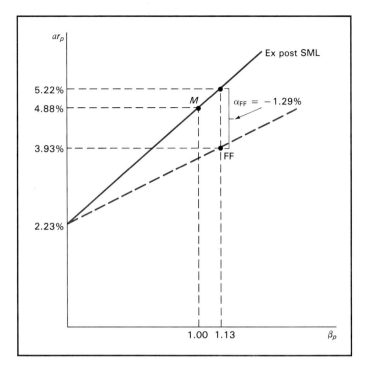

FIGURE 23-4
Performance evaluation using the ex post SML.

return of 3.93%. Using equation (23.7), it can be shown that First Fund had a beta of 1.13. Having an average beta over the 16 quarters that is greater than the market portfolio's beta of 1 indicates that First Fund was aggressive (if it were less than 1, it would have been defensive).

Given these values for its beta and average return, the location of First Fund in Figure 23.4 is represented by the point having coordinates of (1.13, 3.93%), denoted by *FF*. The exact vertical distance from *FF* to the ex post SML can be calculated by using equation (23.13):

$$\alpha_p = ar_p - [ar_f + (ar_M - ar_f)\beta_p]$$

$$= 3.93\% - [2.23\% + (4.88\% - 2.23\%)1.13]$$

$$= -1.29\%.$$

Since *FF* lies below the ex post SML, its ex post alpha is negative, and its performance would be viewed as inferior.[5] Using equation (23.14), the *ex post* characteristic line for First Fund would be

---

[5] Alternatively, if *FF*'s average return had been 6%, then its coordinates would have been (1.13, 6.00%), placing it above the ex post SML. In this situation, *FF*'s ex post alpha would have been .78%, and its performance would have been viewed as superior.

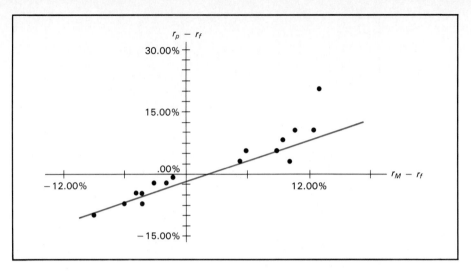

FIGURE 23–5
Ex post characteristic line for first fund.

$$r_p - r_f = -1.29\% + 1.13(r_M - r_f).$$

Figure 23.5 provides an illustration of this line.[6]

The method for determining a portfolio's ex post alpha, beta, and characteristic line suggests the use of a four-step procedure. First, having gathered the necessary return data, the average market return and risk-free rate can be determined with equations (23.8) and (23.9). Second, the portfolio's ex post beta can be determined by using the formula given in equation (23.7). Third, the portfolio's ex post alpha can be determined by using the formula given in equation (23.13). Fourth, these values for alpha and beta can be inserted in equation (23.14) in order to determine the portfolio's ex post characteristic line. However, there is a simpler method for determining a portfolio's ex post alpha, beta, and characteristic line that also provides a number of other pieces of information relating to the portfolio's performance. This method involves the use of simple linear regression and corresponds to the method presented in Chapter 15 for estimating the ex post characteristic line for an individual security.

With this method, the excess return on portfolio p in a given period t is viewed as having three components. The first component is the portfolio's alpha, the second component is a risk premium equal to the excess return on the market times the portfolio's beta, and the third component is a random

---

[6] An alternative measure of performance involves dividing the *ex post* alpha by an estimate of the ex post unique (or unsystematic) risk of the portfolio. This measure, known as the *appraisal ratio*, would be equal to $-1.29\%/3.75\% = -.34$ for First Fund. Comparisons can be made with the value of the appraisal ratio for the market portfolio (its value is defined to be 0) and other portfolios. Note that a positive value indicates superior performance and that the larger the value, the better the performance. See Jack L. Treynor and Fischer Black, "How to Use Security Analysis to Improve Portfolio Selection," *Journal of Business* 46, no. 1 (January 1973):66–86.

error term.[7] These three components can be seen on the right-hand side of the following equation:

$$r_{pt} - r_{ft} = \alpha_p + \beta_p(r_{Mt} - r_{ft}) + \epsilon_{pt}. \qquad (23.15)$$

Since α_p and β_p are assumed to be constant during the evaluation interval, equation (23.15) can be viewed as a regression equation. Accordingly, there are certain standard formulas for estimating α_p, β_p, and a number of other statistical parameters associated with the regression equation.

Part (b) of Table 23.1 presents these formulas, with First Fund being used as an example. As can be seen, the formulas indicate that First Fund's ex post alpha and beta were equal to -1.29% and 1.13, respectively, over the time interval 1982 to 1985. These values are the same as those arising when equations (23.7) and (23.13) were used earlier. Indeed, they will always result in the same values.

Figure 23.5 presents a scatter diagram of the excess returns on First Fund and the S&P 500. Based on equation (23.15), the regression equation for First Fund is

$$r_{FF} - r_f = -1.29\% + 1.13(r_M - r_f) + \epsilon_{FF} \qquad (23.16)$$

where -1.29% and 1.13 are the estimated ex post alpha and beta for First Fund over the 1982 to 1985 time interval. As mentioned earlier, also shown in the figure is the ex post characteristic line for First Fund, a line that is derived by the use of simple linear regression:

$$r_{FF} - r_f = -1.29\% + 1.13(r_M - r_f). \qquad (23.17)$$

The vertical distance between each point in the scatter diagram and the regression line represents an estimate of the size of the random error term for the corresponding quarter. The exact distance can be found by rewriting equation (23.16) as

$$\epsilon_{FF} = (r_{FF} - r_f) - [-1.29\% + 1.13(r_M - r_f)]. \qquad (23.18)$$

For example, in the third quarter of 1984 the excess return on First Fund and the S&P 500 were 6.14% and 6.29%, respectively. The value of ϵ_{FF} for that quarter can be calculated by using equation (23.18) as follows:

$$\epsilon_{FF} = (6.14\%) - [-1.29\% + 1.13(6.29\%)]$$

$$= .32\%.$$

The values of ϵ_{FF} can be calculated similarly for the other 15 quarters of the evaluation interval. The standard deviation of the resulting set of 16 numbers is an estimate of the standard deviation of the random error term (also known as the residual standard deviation), and is shown in part (b) of Table 23.1 to be equal to 3.75%. This number can be viewed as an estimate of the *ex post unique* (or unsystematic or nonmarket) *risk* of First Fund.

The regression line for First Fund that is shown in Figure 23.5 is the

---

[7] The random error term can be viewed as a number that arises from a spin of a roulette wheel, where the numbers on the wheel are symmetrically distributed around zero. That is, the expected outcome from a spin of the roulette wheel is zero; the standard deviation associated with the wheel is denoted by $\sigma_{\epsilon p}$.

line of best fit for the scatter diagram. Given that a straight line is defined by its intercept and slope, there are no other values for alpha and beta that will define a straight line that fits the scatter diagram any better than this one. In simple regression, *best fit* means that there is no line that could be drawn such that the resulting standard deviation of the random error term is smaller than the one of best fit.

It should be pointed out that a portfolio's "true" ex post beta cannot be observed. All that can be done is to estimate its value. Thus, even if a portfolio's true beta remained the same forever, its estimated value, obtained in the manner illustrated in Table 23.1 and Figure 23.5, would still change from time to time because of errors (known as sampling errors) in estimating it. For example, if the 16 quarters for 1983 to 1986 were examined, the resulting estimated beta for First Fund would almost certainly be different than 1.13, the estimated value for 1982 to 1985.

The *standard error of beta* shown in Table 23.1 attempts to indicate the extent of such estimation errors. Given a number of necessary assumptions (for example, the true beta did not change during the estimation period of 1982 to 1985), the chances are roughly two out of three that the true beta is within one standard error, plus or minus, of the estimated beta. Thus, First Fund's true beta is likely to be between the values of 1.13 − .13 = 1.00 and 1.13 + .13 = 1.26. Similarly, the value for *standard error of alpha* provides an indication of the magnitude of the possible sampling error that has been made in estimating it.

The value for the *correlation coefficient* provides an indication of how closely the excess returns on First Fund were associated with the excess returns on the S&P 500. Since its range is between −1 and +1, the value for First Fund of .92 indicates a strong positive relationship between First Fund and the S&P 500. That is, larger excess returns for First Fund seem to have been closely associated with larger excess returns on the S&P 500.

The *coefficient of determination* represents the proportion of variation in the excess return on First Fund that is related to the variation in the excess return on the S&P 500. That is, it shows how much of the movement in First Fund's excess returns can be explained by movements in the excess returns on the S&P 500. With a value of .85, it can be seen that 85% of the movement in the excess return on First Fund over 1982 to 1985 can be attributed to movement in the excess return on the S&P 500.

Since the *coefficient of nondetermination* is 1 minus the coefficient of determination, it represents the proportion of movement in the excess return on First Fund that is not due to movement in the excess return on the S&P 500. Thus, 15% of the movement in First Fund cannot be attributed to movement in the S&P 500.

Although Table 23.1 shows the formulas for calculating all these values, it should be pointed out that there are many different software packages that can carry out all these calculations in a fraction of a second. The only substantive effort involves gathering all the return data shown in part (a) of Table 23.1 and then entering the information into a computer.

☐ 23.3.2   The Reward-to-Volatility Ratio

Closely related to the differential return measure of portfolio performance is a measure known as the *reward-to-volatility ratio*.[8] This measure, denoted by $RVOL_p$, also uses the ex post security market line to form a benchmark for performance evaluation. The calculation of the reward-to-volatility ratio for a portfolio involves dividing its average excess return by its market risk:

$$RVOL_p = \frac{ar_p - ar_f}{\beta_p}. \tag{23.19}$$

Here, the beta of the portfolio can be determined using the formula in equation (23.7).

Continuing with the example of First Fund, it was noted earlier that its average return for the evaluation interval of 1982 to 1985 was 3.93%. Furthermore, it had been noted that the average Treasury bill rate was 2.23%. Thus, the average excess return for First Fund was 3.93% − 2.23% = 1.70% and, given a beta of 1.13, its reward-to-volatility ratio was 1.70%/1.13 = 1.50%.

The reward-to-volatility ratio corresponds to the slope of a line originating at the average risk-free rate and going through the point (β_p, ar_p). This can be seen by noting that the slope of a line is easily determined if two points on the line are known—it is simply the vertical distance between the two points (rise) divided by the horizontal distance between the two points (run). In this case, the vertical distance is $ar_p - ar_f$ and the horizontal distance is $\beta_p - 0 = \beta_p$, so the slope is $(ar_p - ar_f)/\beta_p$; this corresponds to the formula for $RVOL_p$ given in equation (23.19). Note that the value being measured on the horizontal axis is β_p and the value being measured on the vertical axis is ar_p, suggesting that the line can be drawn on the same diagram as the ex post SML.

In the First Fund example, remember that the ex post SML for 1982 to 1985 was shown by the solid line in Figure 23.4. Also appearing in this figure was the point denoted by *FF*, corresponding to $(\beta_p, ar_p) = (1.13, 3.93\%)$ for First Fund. The line in this figure with dots and dashes originates from the point $(0, ar_f) = (0, 2.23\%)$, goes through *FF*, and has a slope of (3.93% − 2.23%)/1.13 = 1.50%, which corresponds to the value noted earlier for $RVOL_p$.

The benchmark for comparison with this measure of performance is the slope of the ex post SML. Since this line goes through the points $(0, ar_f)$ and $(1, ar_M)$, its slope is simply $(ar_M - ar_f)/(1 - 0) = (ar_M - ar_f)$. If $RVOL_p$ is greater than this value, the portfolio lies above the ex post SML, indicating it has outperformed the market. Alternatively, if $RVOL_p$ is less than this value, the portfolio lies below the ex post SML, indicating it has not performed as well as the market.

---

[8] This measure of performance is sometimes known as the *Treynor ratio* because it was developed by Jack L. Treynor in "How to Rate Management of Investment Funds," *Harvard Business Review* 43, no. 1 (January–February 1965):63–75.

In the case of First Fund, the benchmark is $(ar_M - ar_f) = (4.88\% - 2.23\%) = 2.65\%$. Since $RVOL_p$ for First Fund is less than the benchmark $(1.50\% < 2.65\%)$, according to this measure of portfolio performance, First Fund did not perform as well as the market.

In comparing the two measures of performance that are based on the ex post SML, α_p and $RVOL_p$, it should be noted that they *always* give the same assessment of a portfolio's performance relative to the market portfolio. That is, if one measure indicates the portfolio outperformed the market, so will the other. Similarly, if one measure indicates the portfolio did not perform as well as the market, the other measure will show the same thing. This can be seen by noting that any portfolio with a positive ex post alpha (an indication of superior performance) lies *above* the ex post SML and thus must have a slope *greater* than the slope of the ex post SML (also an indication of superior performance). Similarly, any portfolio with a negative ex post alpha (an indication of inferior performance) lies *below* the ex post SML and thus must have a slope *less* than the slope of the ex post SML (also an indication of inferior performance).

However, it should be noted that it is possible for the two measures to *rank* portfolios differently on the basis of performance simply because the calculations are different. For example, if Second Fund had a beta of 1.5 and an average return of 4.86%, its ex post alpha would be $4.86\% - [2.23\% + (4.88\% - 2.23\%)1.5] = -1.34\%$. Thus, its performance appears to be worse than First Fund, since it has a smaller ex post alpha $(-1.34\% < -1.29\%)$. However, its reward-to-volatility ratio of $1.75\% = (4.86\% - 2.23\%)/1.5$ is larger than the reward-to-volatility of 1.50% for First Fund, suggesting its performance was better than the First Fund.

☐ 23.3.3   The Reward-to-Variability Ratio

Both measures of risk-adjusted performance described so far, ex post alpha (that is, differential return) and the reward-to-volatility ratio, use benchmarks that are based on the ex post SML. Accordingly, they measure returns relative to the market risk of the portfolio. In contrast, the *reward-to-variability ratio* is a measure of risk-adjusted performance that uses a benchmark based on the ex post *capital market line* (CML).[9] This means that it measures returns relative to the total risk of the portfolio, where total risk is the standard deviation of portfolio returns.

In order to use the reward-to-variability ratio ($RVAR_p$), the location of the ex post CML must be determined. This line goes through two points on a graph where average return is measured on the vertical axis and standard deviation is measured on the horizontal axis. The first point is the vertical intercept of the line and corresponds to the average risk-free rate during the evaluation interval. The second point corresponds to the location of the market portfolio, meaning its coordinates are the average return and stand-

---

[9] This measure of performance is sometimes known as the *Sharpe ratio* because it was developed by William F. Sharpe in "Mutual Fund Performance," *Journal of Business* 39, no. 1 (January 1966):119–38.

ard deviation of return for the market portfolio during the evaluation interval, or (σ_M, ar_M). Since the ex post CML goes through these two points, its slope can readily be calculated as the vertical distance between the two points divided by the horizontal distance between the two points, or $(ar_M - ar_f)/(\sigma_M - 0) = (ar_M - ar_f)/\sigma_M$. Given a vertical intercept of ar_f, the equation of this line is

$$ar_p^e = ar_f + \frac{ar_M - ar_f}{\sigma_M}\sigma_p. \qquad (23.20)$$

In the example shown in Table 23.1, the average return and standard deviation for the S&P 500, calculated using equations (23.5) and (23.6), were 4.88% and 7.39%, respectively. Since the average return on Treasury bills was 2.23%, the ex post CML for 1982 to 1985 was

$$\begin{aligned} ar_p^e &= 2.23\% + \frac{4.88\% - 2.23\%}{7.39\%}\sigma_p \\ &= 2.23\% + .36\sigma_p. \end{aligned} \qquad (23.21)$$

Figure 23.6 presents a graph of this line.

Having determined the location of the ex post CML, the average return and standard deviation of the portfolio being evaluated can be determined next by using equations (23.5) and (23.6). With these values in hand, the

FIGURE 23–6
Performance evaluation using the ex post CML.

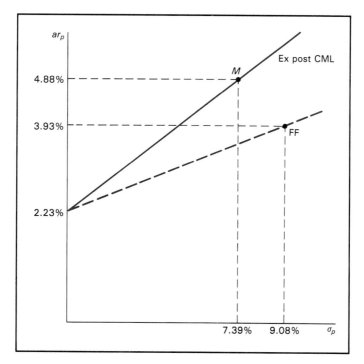

portfolio can be located on the same graph as the ex post CML. In the case of First Fund, its average return and standard deviation were 3.93% and 9.08%, respectively. Thus, in Figure 23.6 its location corresponds to the point having coordinates (9.08%, 3.93%), which is denoted by *FF*.

The calculation of the reward-to-variability ratio ($RVAR_p$) is analogous to the calculation of the reward-to-volatility ratio ($RVOL_p$) described earlier. Specifically, $RVOL_p$ involves dividing the portfolio's average excess return by its beta, whereas $RVAR_p$ involves dividing the portfolio's average excess return by its standard deviation:

$$RVAR_p = \frac{ar_p - ar_f}{\sigma_p} \qquad (23.22)$$

Note that $RVAR_p$ corresponds to the slope of a line originating at the average risk-free rate and going through a point having coordinates of (σ_p, ar_p). This can be seen by noting that the slope of this line is simply the vertical distance between the two points divided by the horizontal distance between the two points, or $(ar_p - ar_f)/(\sigma_p - 0) = (ar_p - ar_f)/\sigma_p$, which corresponds to the formula for $RVAR_p$ given in equation (23.22). Since the value being measured on the horizontal axis is σ_p and the value being measured on the vertical axis is ar_p, the line can be drawn on the same diagram as the ex post CML.

In the First Fund example, recall that the ex post CML for 1982 to 1985 was shown by the solid line in Figure 23.6. Also appearing in this figure was the point denoted by *FF*, corresponding to $(\sigma_p, ar_p) = (9.08\%, 3.93\%)$ for First Fund. The line in this figure with dots and dashes originates from the point $(0, ar_f) = (0, 2.23\%)$ and goes through *FF*; the slope of this line is simply $(3.93\% - 2.23\%)/9.08\% = .19$.

Since the ex post CML represents various combinations of risk-free lending or borrowing with investing in the market portfolio, it can be used to provide a benchmark for the reward-to-variability ratio in a manner similar to the SML-based benchmark for the reward-to-volatility ratio. As noted earlier, the slope of the ex post CML is $(ar_M - ar_f)/\sigma_M$. If $RVAR_p$ is greater than this value, the portfolio lies above the ex post CML, indicating it has outperformed the market. Alternatively, if $RVAR_p$ is less than this value, the portfolio lies below the ex post CML, indicating it has not performed as well as the market.[10]

In the case of First Fund, the benchmark is $(4.88\% - 2.23\%)/7.39\% = .36$. Since $RVAR_p$ is less than the benchmark ($.19 < .36$), First Fund did not perform as well as the market, according to this risk-adjusted measure of portfolio performance.

---

[10] There is a second measure of portfolio performance that is based on the ex post CML. This measure, called the *ex post total risk alpha*, is simply the vertical distance the portfolio lies above or below the ex post CML. It is similar to the measure referred to earlier as ex post alpha (or differential return), except that it is based on a different risk measure (total risk instead of market risk) and uses a different benchmark (the ex post CML instead of the ex post SML).

Comparing the Risk-Adjusted Measures of Performance

The measures of performance that are based on the ex post SML, α_p and $RVOL_p$, can be compared with the measure of performance that is based on the ex post CML, $RVAR_p$. Focusing on $RVOL_p$ (the comparison also applies to α_p), it should be noted that in certain situations, $RVOL_p$ and $RVAR_p$ can give different assessments of a portfolio's performance relative to the market portfolio.

In particular, if $RVOL_p$ indicates the portfolio outperformed the market, it is possible for $RVAR_p$ to indicate the portfolio did not perform as well as the market. The reason for this is that the portfolio may have a relatively large amount of *unique* risk. Such risk would not be a factor in determining the value of $RVOL_p$ for the portfolio, since only *market risk* is in the denominator. However, such risk would be included in the denominator of $RVAR_p$ for the portfolio, since this measure is based on *total risk* (that is, both market and unique risk). Thus, a portfolio with a low amount of market risk could have a high amount of total risk, resulting in a relatively high $RVOL_p$ (due to the low amount of market risk) and a low $RVAR_p$ (due to the high amount of total risk). Accordingly, $RVOL_p$ could indicate the portfolio outperformed the market, while at the same time $RVAR_p$ indicates it did not perform as well as the market.[11]

As an example, consider Third Fund, which had an average return of 4.5%, a beta of .8, and a standard deviation of 18%. Accordingly, $RVOL_{TF} = (4.5\% - 2.23\%)/.8 = 2.71\%$, indicating that Third Fund outperformed the market portfolio, since the benchmark is $(4.88\% - 2.23\%)/1.0 = 2.65\%$. However, $RVAR_{TF} = (4.5\% - 2.23\%)/18\% = .12$, indicating that Third Fund did not perform as well as the market portfolio, since the benchmark is $(4.88\% - 2.23\%)/7.39\% = .36$. The reason for the difference can be seen by noting Third Fund's low beta relative to the market (.8 < 1.0) but high standard deviation relative to the market (18% > 7.39%). This suggests that Third Fund had a relatively high level of unique risk.

It also follows that it is possible for $RVOL_p$ and $RVAR_p$ to rank two or more portfolios differently on the basis of their performance. This is because these two measures of risk-adjusted performance utilize different types of risk.

Continuing with the example, recall that earlier it was shown that First Fund had an average return of 3.93%, a beta of 1.13, and a standard deviation of 9.08%. Thus, $RVOL_{FF} = (3.93\% - 2.23\%)/1.13 = 1.50\%$, which is less than $RVOL_{TF} = 2.65\%$, thereby indicating that First Fund ranked lower than Third Fund. However, $RVAR_{FF} = (3.93\% - 2.23\%)/9.08\% = .13$, which is greater than $RVAR_{TF} = .12$, thereby indicating that First Fund ranked higher than Third Fund.

---

[11] Since the market portfolio does not have any unique risk, it can be shown that if $RVOL_p$ indicates a portfolio did not perform as well as the market, then $RVAR_p$ must also indicate that the portfolio did not perform as well as the market. This is because a portfolio with a relatively high amount of market risk will also have a relatively high amount of total risk.

Did Third Fund do better or worse than the market on a risk-adjusted basis? And did the Third Fund perform better or worse than First Fund? The answer to these two questions lies in identifying the appropriate measure of risk for the client. If the client has many other assets, then beta is the relevant measure of risk, and performance should be based on $RVOL_p$. To such a client, Third Fund should be viewed as a superior performer relative to both the market and First Fund. However, if the client has few other assets, then standard deviation is the relevant measure of risk, and performance should be based on $RVAR_p$. To such a client, Third Fund should be viewed as an inferior performer relative to both the market and First Fund.

23.4 MARKET TIMING

A successful market timer positions a portfolio to have a relatively high beta during a market rise and a relatively low beta during a market decline. This is because, as noted earlier, the expected return on a portfolio is a linear function of its beta:

$$\bar{r}_p = \alpha_p + r_f + (\bar{r}_M - r_f)\beta_p. \qquad (23.23)$$

This means that a high beta portfolio will have a relatively high expected return if a market rise (that is, if $\bar{r}_M > r_f$) is anticipated. Similarly, a low beta portfolio will have a relatively high expected return if a market decline (that is, $\bar{r}_M < r_f$) is anticipated. Accordingly, the portfolio of a successful timer will outperform a benchmark portfolio that has a constant beta equal to the average beta of the timer's portfolio.

For example, if the market timer successfully set the portfolio beta at 0 when $\bar{r}_M < r_f$ and at 2 when $\bar{r}_M > r_f$, the return on the portfolio would be higher than the return on a portfolio having a beta constantly equal to 1. Unfortunately, if the market timer alters the portfolio's beta in ways unrelated to subsequent market moves (for example, sometimes setting the beta equal to zero when $\bar{r}_M > r_f$ and equal to two when $\bar{r}_M < r_f$), then the timer's portfolio will not perform as well as a constant beta portfolio.

To "time the market," either the average beta of the stocks held in the portfolio can be changed or the relative amounts invested in the risk-free asset and stocks can be altered. For example, to increase the beta of a portfolio, low-beta stocks could be sold, with the proceeds used to purchase high-beta stocks. Alternatively, Treasury bills in the portfolio could be sold (or the amount of borrowing increased), with the resulting proceeds invested in stocks.

In Figure 23.7, the excess returns of two hypothetical portfolios are measured on the vertical axis, while those of a market index are on the horizontal axis. Straight lines, fit via standard regression methods, reveal positive ex post alpha values in each case. However, the reasons for this differ. The scatter diagram for the portfolio shown in part (a) seems to indicate that the relationship between the portfolio's excess returns and the market's excess returns was linear, since the points cluster close to the regression

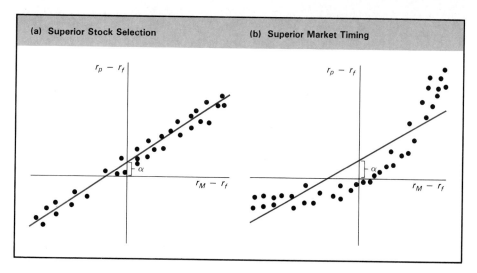

(a) Superior Stock Selection

$r_p - r_f$

α

$r_M - r_f$

(b) Superior Market Timing

$r_p - r_f$

α

$r_M - r_f$

FIGURE 23–7
Superior fund performance.

line. This suggests that the portfolio consisted of securities in a manner such that the beta of the portfolio was roughly the same at all times. Since the ex post alpha was positive, it appears that the investment manager successfully identified and invested in some underpriced securities.

The scatter diagram for the portfolio shown in part (b) seems to indicate the relationship between this portfolio's excess returns and the market's excess returns was not linear, since the points in the middle lie below the regression line and those at the ends lie above the regression line. This suggests that the portfolio consisted of high-beta securities during periods when the market return was high and low-beta securities during periods when the market return was low. Upon examination, it appears that the portfolio has a positive ex post alpha due to successful market timing by the investment manager.

☐ 23.4.1 Quadratic Regression

To measure the ability of an investment manager to time the market successfully, something more complex than a straight line can be fit to scatter diagrams such as those shown in Figure 23.7. One procedure fits a curve, where statistical methods are used to estimate the parameters a, b, and c in the following quadratic regression equation:

$$r_{pt} - r_{ft} = a + b(r_{Mt} - r_{ft}) + c[(r_{Mt} - r_{ft})^2] + \epsilon_{pt} \qquad (23.24)$$

where ϵ_{pt} is the random error term.

The *ex post characteristic curve* shown in Figure 23.8(a) is simply the following quadratic function, where the values of a, b, and c for the portfolio have been estimated by standard regression methods:

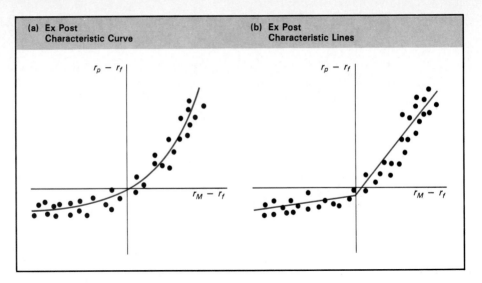

FIGURE 23–8
Ex post characteristic curve and lines.

$$r_{pt} - r_{ft} = a + b(r_{Mt} - r_{ft}) + c[(r_{Mt} - r_{ft})^2]. \qquad (23.25)$$

If the estimated value of c is positive [as it is for the portfolio depicted in Figure 23.8(a)], the curve would become less steep as one moves to the left. This would indicate that the portfolio manager successfully timed the market.[12] Note how this equation corresponds to the equation for the ex post characteristic line if c is equal to zero; in such a situation, a and b would correspond to the portfolio's ex post alpha and beta, respectively.

☐ 23.4.2 Dummy Variable Regression

An alternative procedure fits two ex post characteristic lines to the scatter diagram, as shown in Figure 23.8(b). Periods when risky securities outperform risk-free securities (that is, when $r_{Mt} > r_{ft}$) can be termed *up markets*. Periods when risky securities do not perform as well as risk-free securities (that is, when $r_{Mt} < r_{ft}$) can be termed *down markets*. A successful market timer would select a high up-market beta and a low down-market beta. Graphically, the slope of the ex post characteristic line for positive excess market returns is greater than the slope of the ex post characteristic line for negative excess market returns.

To estimate such a relationship, standard regression methods can be used to estimate the parameters a, b, and c in the following dummy variable regression equation:

---

[12] For details of the method, see Jack L. Treynor and Kay K. Mazuy, "Can Mutual Funds Outguess the Market?", *Harvard Business Review* 44, no. 4 (July–August 1966):131–36; and Anat R. Admati, Sudipto Bhattacharya, Paul Pfleiderer, and Stephen A. Ross, "On Timing and Selectivity," *Journal of Finance* 41, no. 3 (July 1986):715–30.

$$r_{pt} - r_{ft} = a + b(r_{Mt} - r_{ft}) + c[D_t(r_{Mt} - r_{ft})] + \epsilon_{pt}. \qquad (23.26)$$

Here, ϵ_{pt} is the random error term and D_t is a dummy variable that is assigned a value of 0 for any time period t when $r_{Mt} > r_{ft}$ and a value of -1 for any time period t when $r_{Mt} < r_{ft}$. To see how this works, consider the effective equations for different values of $r_{Mt} - r_{ft}$:

VALUE OF $r_{Mt} - r_{ft}$	EQUATION
> 0	$r_{pt} - r_{ft} = a + b(r_{Mt} - r_{ft}) + \epsilon_{pt}$
$= 0$	$r_{pt} - r_{ft} = a + \epsilon_{pt}$
< 0	$r_{pt} - r_{ft} = a + (b - c)(r_{Mt} - r_{ft}) + \epsilon_{pt}$

Note that the parameter b corresponds to the portfolio's up-market beta, whereas $(b - c)$ corresponds to the portfolio's down-market beta. Thus, the parameter c indicates the difference between the two betas and is positive for the successful market timer.

For the portfolio shown in Figure 23.8(b), the ex post characteristic line on the right side of the graph corresponds to the equation

$$r_{pt} - r_{ft} = a + b(r_{Mt} - r_{ft}) \qquad (23.27a)$$

whereas the ex post characteristic line shown on the left side of the graph corresponds to the equation

$$r_{pt} - r_{ft} = a + (b - c)(r_{Mt} - r_{ft}). \qquad (23.27b)$$

In this example, the investment manager has successfully engaged in market timing, since the slope of the line on the right side (that is, b) is greater than the slope of the line on the left side (that is, $b - c$).[13]

In either regression equation (23.24) or (23.26), the value of the parameter a provides an estimate of the investment manager's ability to identify mispriced securities (that is, security selection), and the value of the parameter c provides an estimate of the manager's ability at market timing. The difference between the two equations is that the quadratic equation indicates the portfolio's beta fluctuated over many values, depending on the size of the market's excess returns. This can be seen graphically by noting that the slope of the quadratic curve is continually increasing when moving from left to right in Figure 23.8(a). On the other hand, the dummy variable equation indicates the portfolio's beta fluctuates between just two values, depending on whether r_M is less or greater than r_f. This can be seen graphically by noting that the slope of the equation increases from one value (that is, $b - c$) to a second value (that is, b) when moving from left to right in Figure 23.8(b).

---

[13] For details, see Roy D. Henriksson and Robert C. Merton, "On Market Timing and Investment Performance. II. Statistical Procedures for Evaluating Forecasting Skills," *Journal of Business* 54, no. 4 (October 1981):513–33. Other authors have introduced related methods for distinguishing timing from selectivity; for a brief discussion of them, see pp. 254–59 of Gordon J. Alexander and Jack Clark Francis, *Portfolio Analysis* (Englewood Cliffs, N.J.: Prentice Hall, 1986).

TABLE 23.2
Market Timing Test Results for First Fund.

PARAMETER BEING ESTIMATED[a]	EX POST CHARACTERISTIC LINE	QUADRATIC EQUATION	DUMMY VARIABLE EQUATION
a	−1.29%	−2.12%	−1.33%
	(1.00)	(1.65)	(2.54)
b	1.13	1.03	1.13
	(.13)	(.20)	(.28)
c	—	.02	.02
	—	(.03)	(.78)
Correlation[b]	.92	.91	.91

[a] Standard errors are shown in parentheses below the respective parameters.
[b] The correlation coefficient for the quadratic and dummy variable equations has been adjusted for the number of independent variables.

As an example, consider again the First Fund. Table 23.2 presents the results from applying regression equations (23.24) and (23.26) to this portfolio for the 16 quarters in the interval of 1982 to 1985 along with the ex post characteristic line results. The table does not provide any evidence of either selectivity or market timing ability by the portfolio manager. This can be seen by noting that the parameter a is negative, whereas the parameter c is near zero.[14] Further evidence is provided in regard to the lack of market timing ability by noting that the correlation is higher for the ex post characteristic line than either of the other equations.

☐ **23.4.3   Predictions of Market Direction**

There is another approach to measuring the market timing ability of an investment manager. Unlike the quadratic and dummy variable regression approaches, this one is based on the market return predictions made by the manager. Rather than examining the returns on the portfolio, this approach examines the predicted market returns by comparing them with actual market returns. Accordingly, it assumes that the investment manager alters the composition of the portfolio based on the prediction that has been made.

Consider an investment manager who, prior to each period, makes a prediction about the market's return. Table 23.3 shows four relevant classifications in each part. These classifications are based on (1) the manager's prediction and (2) the corresponding actual outcome. Results from 100 periods are shown, where in 58 of the periods the market was actually up (that is,

---

[14] The size of parameter c (as well as the parameters a and b) should be judged relative to its standard error; in both equations shown here, it is quite small relative to both zero and the respective standard errors. Most standard statistical textbooks have an introductory discussion of the regression procedures that are utilized here. See, for example, chapters 10 to 12 in James T. McClave and P. George Benson, *Statistics for Business and Economics* (San Francisco: Dellen Publishing Company, 1988).

TABLE 23.3

Predictions of Market Direction.

a. MARKET TIMER A

		Actual		
		Up	Down	Total
Prediction:	Up	40	30	70
	Down	18	12	30
	Total	58	42	
Percentage right				52%
Predictive accuracy		69%	29%	98%

b. AN ETERNAL OPTIMIST

		Actual		
		Up	Down	Total
Prediction:	Up	58	42	100
	Down	0	0	0
	Total	58	42	
Percentage right				58%
Predictive accuracy		100%	00%	100%

c. MARKET TIMER B

		Actual		
		Up	Down	Total
Prediction:	Up	34	20	54
	Down	24	22	46
	Total	58	42	
Percentage right				56%
Predictive accuracy		59%	52%	111%

in 58 of the periods, $r_M > r_f$) and in 42 of the periods the market was actually down (that is, in 42 of the periods, $r_M < r_f$).[15]

Part (a) shows the results for an investment manager referred to here as Market Timer A. In 52 of the 100 periods, the prediction of Market Timer A was correct—40 "up" predictions were followed by actual up markets and 12 "down" predictions were followed by actual down markets.

Although it is tempting to consider this record successful, this particular type of analysis does not provide a very useful measure of the predictive ability of the investment manager. The reason can be seen by examining part (b). This part shows the record of the Eternal Optimist, an investment manager who always predicts that stocks will do well. Such a prediction will

---

[15] This conforms to actual experience from 1926 through 1983 when the S&P 500 outperformed Treasury bills 58% of the time.

generally be right more than half the time, since historically there have been more up markets than down markets. In the example shown here, the Eternal Optimist was right 58% of the time. No predictive ability was required to achieve such a record. Instead, the investment manager just had to assume that r_M would be greater than r_f for each period.

The preceding result suggests a measure of the ability of a manager to time the market. As shown in part (a), Market Timer A predicted 40 of the 58 up-market periods correctly. Thus, A's predictive accuracy in up markets equaled 69% (40/58). On the other hand, A predicted only 12 of 42 down markets correctly, for a predictive accuracy of 29% (12/42). As shown in part (b), the Eternal Optimist is perfectly correct (100% = 58/58) in up markets and perfectly incorrect (0% = 0/42) in down markets. A summary measure should take into account the manager's ability to predict accurately both kinds of markets.

One such measure simply adds the two predictive acccuracies. Anyone can achieve a value of 100% for this score by always predicting just one outcome (for example, the Eternal Optimist, who always predicted an up market). A perfect market timer will make a score of 200%, since he or she will be correct 100% of the time in up markets as well as in down markets. Imperfect but valuable market timers will obtain scores between 100% and 200%. The greater the score, the higher the timing ability of the manager.

In the example shown in part (a), Market Timer A fell short of the mark, with an overall score of 98% = 69% + 29%. Part (c) shows the results of a different investment manager, referred to as Market Timer B. This manager was more successful, being right 59% (34/58) of the time in up markets and 52% (22/42) of the time in down markets, for an overall score of 111%. If this reflects skill rather than luck, then B can be expected to enhance the portfolio's rate of return in the future.

23.5 CRITICISMS OF THESE RISK-ADJUSTED PERFORMANCE MEASURES

The previously mentioned risk-adjusted measures of portfolio performance have been criticized on several grounds. Some of the major criticisms are described in this section.

☐ 23.5.1 Use of a Market Surrogate

All the measures other than the reward-to-variability ratio require the identification of a market portfolio. This means that whatever surrogate is used, it can be criticized as being inadequate. Indeed, it has been shown that by making slight changes in the surrogate, the performance rankings of a set of portfolios can be completely reversed (that is, the top-ranked portfolio with one surrogate could be the bottom-ranked portfolio if a slightly different surrogate was used). However, it has been noted that when commonly used NYSE-based surrogates are involved, such as the Dow Jones Industrial Av-

erage, the S&P 500, and an index comparable to the New York Stock Exchange Composite, the performance rankings of common stock portfolios appear to be quite similar.[16]

23.5.2 Distinguishing Skill from Luck

A very long evaluation interval is needed in order to be able to obtain a measure of performance that can distinguish skill from luck on the part of the investment manager. That is, it would be useful to know if an apparently successful manager was skilled or just lucky, since skill can be expected to have a favorable impact on the portfolio's performance in the future, whereas luck cannot be expected to continue. Unfortunately, too many years' worth of experience is generally needed to make such a determination.[17]

23.5.3 Measuring the Risk-Free Rate

The use of Treasury bills for measuring the risk-free rate in determining benchmark portfolios based on either the ex post SML or CML can be criticized. Consider a benchmark portfolio that involves an investment in both Treasury bills and the market portfolio. Such a benchmark portfolio can be criticized for having too low a rate of return, making it easy for a portfolio to show superior performance. This is because Treasury bills may provide excessively low returns to compensate for their high degree of liquidity. If a higher risk-free rate (such as the commercial paper rate) is used, then any benchmark portfolio that lies between this risk-free rate and the market portfolio on either the ex post SML or CML will have a higher rate of return and thus represent a higher but more appropriate standard.

Next, consider a benchmark portfolio that involves levering a positive investment in the market portfolio by borrowing at the risk-free rate. Use of the Treasury bill rate can be criticized because realistic borrowing alternatives typically involve a higher rate and are thus less attractive. Accordingly, benchmarks that involve borrowing at the Treasury bill rate have too high a rate of return, making it difficult for a portfolio to show superior performance. If a higher risk-free borrowing rate (such as the call money rate plus a small premium) is used, then any benchmark portfolio involving risk-free borrowing will have a lower rate of return and thus represent a lower but more appropriate standard.

In summary, measures of portfolio performance based on either the ex post SML or CML and utilizing Treasury bills to determine the risk-free rate

---

[16] See Richard Roll, "Ambiguity When Performance Is Measured by the Security Market Line," *Journal of Finance* 33, no. 4 (September 1978):1051–69; and David Peterson and Michael L. Rice, "A Note on Ambiguity in Portfolio Performance Measures," *Journal of Finance* 35, no. 5 (December 1980):1251–56.

[17] See Dan W. French and Glenn V. Henderson, Jr., "How Well Does Performance Evaluation Perform?" *Journal of Portfolio Management* 11, no. 2 (Winter 1985):15–18.

are alleged to discriminate in favor of conservative portfolios and against aggressive ones.[18]

23.5.4   Validity of the CAPM

The measures of portfolio performance that involve beta (namely, the ex post alpha and reward-to-volatility measures) are based on the CAPM, yet the CAPM may not be the correct asset pricing model. That is, perhaps assets are priced according to some other model. If so, the use of beta-based performance measures will be inappropriate.

Interestingly, a measure analogous to ex post alpha has been shown to be a meaningful guage of performance if the arbitrage pricing theory's (APT) model of asset pricing is believed to be more appropriate.[19] Furthermore, the reward-to-variability ratio is immune to this criticism, since it uses standard deviation as a measure of risk and does not rely on the validity of the CAPM or the identification of a market portfolio.

☐ 23.5.5   Performance Attribution

The previously mentioned risk-adjusted measures of performance concentrate on the question of *how* a portfolio did relative to both a benchmark and a set of other portfolios. The use of quadratic and dummy variable regression is an attempt to evaluate separately the manager's ability at selectivity and timing. However, the client might want to know more about *why* the portfolio had a certain return over a particular time period.[20] *Performance attribution* using a "factor model" is one method that has been used to try to make such a determination; an example is presented in the appendix.

23.6   BOND PORTFOLIO PERFORMANCE EVALUATION

The performance of portfolios consisting of bonds (and other types of fixed-income securities) is often evaluated by comparing their total returns (consisting of coupon payments plus capital gains or losses) with those of an

---

[18] Some people argue that the use of a market surrogate like the S&P 500 will also result in an unfair standard, since investing in a market surrogate is not as simple as it may seem. With the existence of index funds and index futures, this criticism does not appear to have much force.

[19] Under APT (discussed in Chapter 9), there is another measure of portfolio performance that has even more theoretical justification than the APT-based ex post alpha. This measure is analogous to the CAPM-based "appraisal ratio" mentioned in footnote 6 and involves dividing the APT-based ex post alpha by the ex post standard deviation of the APT-based random error term. For details, see Gregory Connor and Robert A. Korajczyk, "Performance Measurement with the Arbitrage Pricing Theory: A New Framework for Analysis," *Journal of Financial Economics* 15, no. 3 (March 1986):373–94; and Bruce N. Lehmann and David M. Modest, "Mutual Fund Performance Evaluation: A Comparison of Benchmarks and Benchmark Comparisons," *Journal of Finance* 42, no. 2 (June 1987):233–65.

[20] For a study that used the CAPM framework to do this, see Eugene F. Fama, "Components of Investment Performance," *Journal of Finance* 27, no. 3 (June 1972):551–67.

index representing a comparable class of securities over some evaluation interval.

☐ 23.6.1 Bond Indices

Bond indices typically represent either the average yield-to-maturity or the average price on a portfolio of bonds that have certain similar characteristics. Figure 23.9 presents various bond indices that are published daily in the *Wall Street Journal*. The indices that are computed by Merrill Lynch are based on average yields, whereas those computed by Dow Jones & Company are based on average bond prices. Perhaps the most prominent bond index that is published in the *Wall Street Journal* is the Shearson Lehman Hutton Treasury Index, which is based on the prices of long-term Treasury bonds. Other frequently used bond indices are calculated by Salomon Brothers (particularly their index that is based on mortgage-backed securities) and *The Bond Buyer* (particularly their municipal bond indices).[21]

☐ 23.6.2 Time Series and Cross-Sectional Comparisons

Figure 23.10 illustrates two ways of comparing the returns on a bond portfolio with those on a bond index over an evaluation interval. In part (a), a time-series comparison is made, where the bond portfolio's quarterly returns over time during the evaluation interval are graphed along with those of the bond index. In part (b), a cross-sectional comparison is made in a manner similar to the equity performance measures that were based on the ex post CML. Here the bond portfolio's average return and standard deviation are graphed and compared with a line that goes through the average risk-free rate and the average return and standard deviation of the bond index (instead of an equity index), based on quarterly returns during the evaluation interval.

☐ 23.6.3 Bond Market Line

A different approach involves the use of a *bond market line*.[22] Assume that the performance of a bond portfolio is to be evaluated over a given quarter (or year, since this approach can be used for a longer period). First, the quarterly return for the portfolio is calculated, along with the portfolio's average duration for the quarter (this could be calculated by averaging the portfolio's duration at the beginning and end of the quarter). The portfolio is then plotted on a graph that measures return on the vertical axis and duration on the horizontal axis. Second, the return and average duration for a broadly representative bond index such as the Salomon Brothers' High-Grade Long-Term Corporate Bond Index are calculated for the same

---

[21] Many of these indices are published weekly in *Barron's*; a discussion of the various methods of preparing market indices is contained in Chapter 21.

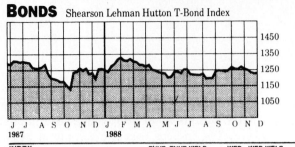

BONDS Shearson Lehman Hutton T-Bond Index

1249.98   −0.12

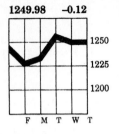

INDEX	THUR	THUR YIELD	WED	WED YIELD	YR AGO	12-MO HIGH	12-MO LOW
Shearson Lehman Hutton treas.	1249.98	9.11%	1250.10	9.11%	1205.05	1329.29	1194.42
DJ 20 Bond	89.34	9.90	89.41	9.84	86.05	91.25	85.78
Salomon mortgage-backed	453.22	10.05	453.93	10.00	405.36	459.10	405.36
Bond Buyer municipal	89-25	7.99	89-24	7.99	85-1	99	82-13
Merrill Lynch corporate	93.19	10.02	93.37	9.98	91.08	96.50	90.73

Dow Jones Bond Averages

	−1987− High Low	−1988− High Low		1988 Close Chg. %Yld	1987 Close Chg.
	95.51 81.26	91.25 86.92	20 Bonds	89.34 −0.07 9.90	86.05 − 0.36
	98.23 79.51	91.88 86.05	10 Utilities	89.38 −0.07 9.92	85.83 − 0.62
	93.10 83.00	90.64 86.96	10 Industrials	89.31 −0.07 9.87	86.26 − 0.10

BOND MARKET DATA BANK   12/8/88

MAJOR INDEXES

HIGH	LOW (12 MOS)		CLOSE	NET CHG	% CHG	12-MO CHG	% CHG	FROM 12/31	% CHG
U.S. TREASURY SECURITIES (Shearson Lehman Hutton indexes)									
1152.47	1099.80	Intermediate	1103.13	− 2.37	− 0.21	− 13.68	− 1.22	− 23.02	− 2.04
1329.29	1194.42	Long-term	1249.98	− 0.12	− 0.01	+ 44.93	+ 3.73	− 0.26	− 0.02
1193.37	1122.99	Composite	1137.02	− 1.84	− 0.16	− 0.24	− 0.02	− 17.86	− 1.55
U.S. CORPORATE DEBT ISSUES (Merrill Lynch: Dec. 31, 1986 = 100)									
96.50	90.73	Corporate Master	93.19	− 0.18	− 0.19	+ 2.11	+ 2.32	+ 0.53	+ 0.57
97.31	93.34	1-10 Yr Maturities	93.99	− 0.18	− 0.19	+ 0.30	+ 0.32	+ 0.65	+ 0.69
96.01	88.66	10+ Yr Maturities	92.89	− 0.11	− 0.12	+ 3.86	+ 4.34	+ 1.67	+ 1.83
95.93	91.77	High Yield	93.82	− 0.08	− 0.09	+ 1.74	+ 1.89	+ 1.07	+ 1.15
96.38	90.57	Yankee Bonds	92.58	− 0.36	− 0.39	+ 1.64	+ 1.80	+ 0.34	+ 0.37
TAX-EXEMPT SECURITIES (Bond Buyer; Merrill Lynch: Dec. 31, 1986 = 100)									
92-14	82-13	Bond Buyer Municipal	89-25	+ -1	+ 0.03	+ 4-24	+ 5.59	+ 2-3	+ 2.42
95.33	89.97	New 10-yr G.O. (AA)	91.23	unch		+ 1.20	+ 1.33	− 2.06	− 2.21
93.42	86.12	New 20-yr G.O. (AA)	89.59	unch		+ 3.47	+ 4.03	+ 0.85	+ 0.96
98.46	85.79	New 30-yr revenue (A)	95.11	unch		+ 9.32	+ 10.86	+ 6.08	+ 6.83
MORTGAGE-BACKED SECURITIES (current coupon; Merrill Lynch: Dec. 31, 1986 = 100)									
97.17	90.70	Ginnie Mae (GNMA)	92.65	− 0.15	− 0.16	+ 1.21	+ 1.32	− 0.04	− 0.04
96.14	90.07	Fannie Mae (FNMA)	91.59	− 0.17	− 0.19	− 1.09	− 1.18	− 2.07	− 2.21
97.33	90.06	Freddie Mac (FHLMC)	91.92	− 0.18	− 0.20	+ 1.35	+ 1.49	+ 0.34	+ 0.37
CONVERTIBLE BONDS (Merrill Lynch: Dec. 31, 1986 = 100)									
93.95	85.90	Investment Grade	91.63	+ 0.26	+ 0.28	+ 5.38	+ 6.24	+ 3.73	+ 4.24
91.29	78.42	High Yield	87.00	+ 0.03	+ 0.03	+ 7.06	+ 8.83	+ 5.62	+ 6.91

quarter, and plotted on the same graph. Third, the 90-day Treasury bill rate at the beginning of the quarter can also be determined and then plotted on the graph (since the Treasury bill is a pure discount security, its duration is the same as its term-to-maturity—90 days, or roughly .25 years). Lastly, the bond market line is constructed by drawing a straight line connecting the Treasury bill and bond index.

The performance of the bond portfolio can now be evaluated with the bond market line being used to serve as a benchmark in evaluating the performance of the bond portfolio. If the bond portfolio lies above the bond market line, such as the one shown in Figure 23.11, it outperformed the benchmark and its performance would be viewed as superior. Conversely, if it lies below the bond market line, it underperformed the benchmark and its performance is viewed as inferior.[23]

Other bond portfolios and indices can also be shown on the graph to give more information on the relative performance of the portfolio being evaluated. In Figure 23.11, one federal government and three corporate bond indices are shown, in addition to the overall corporate bond index published by Merrill Lynch.

23.7 SUMMARY

This chapter has discussed how a portfolio's performance can be evaluated. Doing so is important regardless of whether or not the owner of the portfolio is the one who has been managing the portfolio. If the owner has been the manager, then good performance can be an incentive to continue with existing investment procedures, whereas poor performance can result in changes to these procedures. If the investment manager is someone other than the owner, then good performance can be rewarded, whereas poor performance can result in changing either the constraints placed on the manager, the investment objectives given to the manager, or the size of the portfolio for which the manager is responsible.

In evaluating performance, there are two major tasks. First, it is important to try to determine whether the performance is superior or inferior. This is often done by comparing the performance of the portfolio with the performance of some benchmark portfolio and other actual portfolios. Second,

---

[22] See Wayne H. Wagner and Dennis A Tito, "Definitive New Measures of Bond Performance and Risk," *Pension World* 13, no. 5 (May 1977):10–12, and "Is Your Bond Manager Skillful?" *Pension World* 13, no. 6 (June 1977):9–13. Bond portfolio performance is also discussed in Peter O. Dietz and Jeannette R. Kirschman, "Evaluating Portfolio Performance," Chapter 14 in *Managing Investment Portfolios*, eds. John L. Maginn and Donald L. Tuttle (Boston, Mass.: Warren, Gorham & Lamont, Inc., 1983).

[23] Using the bond market line as a benchmark in this manner is similar to using the SML as a benchmark in evaluating the performance of equity portfolios.

◁

FIGURE 23–9

Bond indices published in *The Wall Street Journal* on Friday, March 11, 1988.

SOURCE: The Wall Street Journal © Dow Jones & Company, Inc. (December 12, 1988):pp. C1, C16, C20.

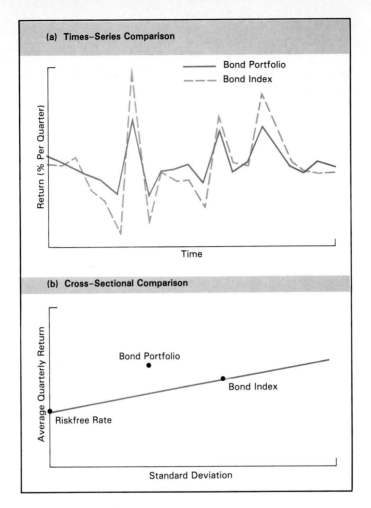

FIGURE 23–10
Bond portfolio performance evaluation.

it is also important to try to determine if a portfolio's performance has been the result of skill or luck. After all, if superior performance was due to skill, then such performance can be expected to continue in the future. Unfortunately, neither of these tasks can be done easily and precisely.

Evaluating performance involves determining the average return and risk of the portfolio over some time interval. For equity portfolios, two measures of risk are often used—beta and standard deviation. Sometimes the average return and risk are looked at separately, and sometimes they are combined into a single risk-adjusted measure of performance. Three such risk-adjusted measures were discussed—ex post alpha, reward-to-volatility ratio, and reward-to-variability ratio. More recently developed measures attempt to see if the investment manager has successfully timed the market.

Performance evaluation of bond portfolio managers also involves cal-

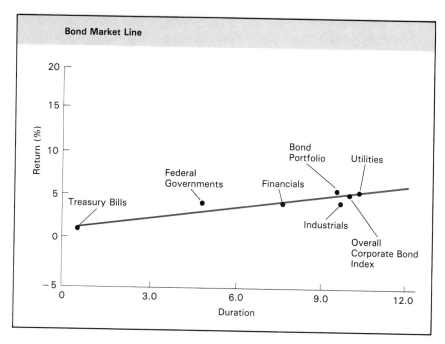

FIGURE 23–11
Bond market line.

SOURCE: Adapted from Wayne H. Wagner and Dennis A. Tito, "Definitive New Measures of Bond Performance and Risk," *Pension World* 13, no. 5 (May 1977), p. 12.

culating the periodic returns on the portfolio over some evaluation interval. Then these periodic returns are compared with those on one or more bond indices. This can be accomplished by either graphing the periodic returns over time, or by comparing the average return and standard deviation (or duration) of the portfolio with those of the bond index.

While these performance measures have been subject to various criticisms, it should be kept in mind that risk should not be ignored in portfolio performance measurement. Instead, such measures should be interpreted with caution, and opinions should be formed with extreme care.

APPENDIX A
PERFORMANCE ATTRIBUTION

With performance attribution, an attempt is made to ascertain why an equity portfolio had a given return over a particular time period. One procedure for making such a determination involves assuming security returns are related to a number of prespecified factors as well as to sector-factors.[24] For example, there may be a beta factor, a size factor, and two sector-factors

---

[24] Factor models are discussed in Chapter 9.

that indicate whether or not a stock is an industrial. With such a model, the returns for a set of stocks during a given time period are related to these factors and sector-factors in the following manner:

$$r_i = \beta_i F_1 + s_i F_2 + c_{i1} SF_1 + c_{i2} SF_2 + \epsilon_i. \tag{23.28}$$

Here each stock has four attributes—β_i, s_i, c_{i1}, and c_{i2}. The attributes β_i and s_i are, respectively, the beta and firm size of stock i in a given time period, and c_{i1} and c_{i2} are sector-factor attributes that have values of 1 and 0, respectively, if stock i is an industrial firm and values of 0 and 1 if stock i is not an industrial firm. (For example, it may be a utility or transportation company such as Northern States Power or Delta Air Lines.)

The factors and sector-factors F_1, F_2, SF_1, and SF_2 are parameters that can be estimated using a statistical technique known as multiple regression. For example, the returns for 500 firms for 1987 could be calculated. Then, the betas for each stock could be estimated using 16 quarters of returns ending with the last quarter of 1986 (by using the characteristic line equation given earlier). The firm size for each stock could be measured by taking the market price per share as of December 31, 1986, multiplying it by the number of shares outstanding at that time, and then taking the logarithm of the product (expressed in billions). Lastly, each firm can be classified as either an industrial or nonindustrial, resulting in a value of 0 or 1 assigned to c_{i1} and c_{i2}. This will give four columns of 500 numbers representing security attributes—one column with the betas for each stock, one column for the firm sizes of each stock, and two columns of 0s and 1s corresponding to whether the firms are industrials or nonindustrials—upon which will be "regressed" the column of returns for the 500 stocks during 1987.

Suppose the resulting regression resulted in estimated values for F_1, F_2, SF_1, and SF_2 of 1.20, −.40, 10.00, and 9.00, respectively. Then, equation (23.28) for 1987 would be

$$r_i = 1.20\beta_i - .40s_i + 10.00c_{i1} + 9.00c_{i2} + \epsilon_i. \tag{23.29}$$

Since the estimated value of F_1 (1.20) is positive, the year of 1987 was one where high beta stocks tended to outperform low beta stocks. Furthermore, since the estimated value of F_2 (−.40) is negative, the year 1987 was one where the stocks of small firms tended to outperform the stocks of large firms. With an estimated value for SF_1 that is greater than the estimated value for SF_2 (10.00 > 9.00), 1987 also appears to have been a year when industrials tended to outperform nonindustrials.

Equation (23.29) can be used to analyze the 1987 return on a stock. Consider, for example, a hypothetical industrial stock that had a return of 12.13%, a beta of .8, and size of 4.00 (its market value was $54.6 billion, so s_i = natural logarithm of 54.6 = ln(54.6) = 4.00). According to equation (23.29), the "normal" return on such a stock is (1.20 × .8) − (.40 × 4.00) + (10.00 × 1) + (9.00 × 0) = 9.36%. Thus, for this stock, its "nonfactor return" (ϵ_i) for 1987 was 12.13% − 9.36% = 2.77%, suggesting this particular stock did relatively well in comparison with other stocks having comparable attributes.

Similar analysis can be conducted on a portfolio's return for 1987. Con-

sider a hypothetical portfolio that had a return of 10.03% in 1987. Upon close examination, it has been determined that this portfolio had an average beta of 1.3 and an average size of 3.2 (that is, the average value of s_i for all the stocks held was 3.2). Furthermore, 67% of the stocks in the portfolio were industrials and 33% were nonindustrials. According to equation (23.29), the normal return on such a portfolio is $(1.20 \times 1.30) - (.40 \times 3.20) + (10.00 \times .67) + (9.00 \times .33) = 9.95\%$. Since the nonfactor return on this portfolio was $10.03\% - 9.95\% = .08\%$, this portfolio shows little evidence of successful security selection.

Such absolute performance evaluation with a factor model is interesting, but in many cases comparative performance is more relevant. A manager may do poorly in a bad market. But if he or she provides a higher return than would have been obtained otherwise, the client is clearly better off. With comparative performance, the overall return of a portfolio is compared with that of one or more other portfolios or market indices in order to determine the *differences* in the returns. Then the *sources* of the differences can be determined with *comparative performance attribution.*

Assume that the i in equation (23.28) refers to the portfolio under evaluation. Letting j refer to the return on a portfolio (or market index) to which it is to be compared, the difference in their returns is simply $r_i - r_j$. Using equation (23.28), this difference can be expressed as

$$r_i - r_j = (\beta_i F_1 + s_i F_2 + c_{i1} SF_1 + c_{i2} SF_2 + \epsilon_i) \\ - (\beta_j F_1 + s_j F_2 + c_{j1} SF_1 + c_{j2} SF_2 + \epsilon_j). \tag{23.30}$$

Gathering similar terms, this equation can be rewritten as

$$r_i - r_j = F_1(\beta_i - \beta_j) + F_2(s_i - s_j) \\ + SF_1(c_{i1} - c_{j1}) + SF_2(c_{i2} - c_{j2}) + (\epsilon_i - \epsilon_j). \tag{23.31}$$

Each of the first four terms represents a differential effect equal to the product of (1) the difference in the attributes of the two portfolios and (2) the actual value of the related factor. The last term in the equation indicates the difference in the nonfactor returns of the two portfolios.

Table 23.4 provides an example where portfolio i is the one mentioned earlier that had a return in 1987 of 10.03%. It is being compared with a portfolio that had a return in 1987 of 11.21%. This comparison portfolio had a beta of 1.50, and the average size of the firms whose stocks it held was 1.40. Furthermore, 80% of the portfolio's funds were invested in industrials, with the remaining 20% being invested in nonindustrials. Using equation (23.29), the normal return on such a portfolio in 1987 was $(1.20 \times 1.50) - (.40 \times 1.40) + (10.00 \times .80) + (9.00 \times .20) = 11.04\%$, indicating the portfolio had a nonfactor return of $11.21\% - 11.04\% = .17\%$.

A direct comparison of the two portfolios reveals a difference in returns of $r_i - r_j = 10.03\% - 11.21\% = -1.18\%$. That is, portfolio i performed worse than portfolio j by 1.18%. Security selection played a small role, since the nonfactor returns were both quite low (.08% for portfolio i and .17% for portfolio j). On balance, sector selection lowered returns for portfolio i relative to portfolio j slightly—the sum of the values in the last column for the two

TABLE 23.4

Comparative Performance Attribution.

	ATTRIBUTE				
	Portfolio i (a)	Portfolio j (b)	Difference (c) = (a) − (b)	Factor (d)	Differential Effect (e) = (c) × (d)
a. Factors:					
Common factors					
Beta	1.30	1.50	−.20	1.20	−.24%
Size	3.20	1.40	1.80	−.40	−.72%
Sector-factors					
Industrials	.67	.80	−.13	10.00	−1.30%
Nonindustrials	.33	.20	.13	9.00	1.17%
					−1.09%

	RETURNS		
	Portfolio i (a)	Portfolio j (b)	Difference (c) = (a) − (b)
b. Returns:			
Factor return	9.95%	11.04%	−1.09%
Nonfactor return	.08%	.17%	−.09%
Total return	10.03%	11.21%	−1.18%

sector-factors was −0.13%. In portfolio i, industrials were underweighted relative to portfolio j, while nonindustrials were overweighted. A successful "sector picker" would have placed bets on (that is, overweighted) the sector with a relatively high factor value (industrials) and placed bets against (that is, underweighted) the sector with a relatively low factor value (nonindustrials), leading to a net positive *sector bet effect*. In 1987, the investment manager for portfolio i was not as successful a sector picker as the investment manager for portfolio j.

The major sources of the relatively lower performance of portfolio i were those associated with common factors. The manager had lower-beta stocks than those in comparison portfolio j during a period when high-beta stocks tended to do better than low-beta stocks. That is, the manager placed a bet against high-beta stocks in favor of low-beta stocks and lost. He or she also had invested in stocks that were larger than those in portfolio j during a period when larger stocks tended to do poorly. That is, the manager placed a bet against smaller firms in favor of larger firms and lost. Both differences lowered returns relative to the comparison portfolio, with the size bet being more detrimental than the beta bet.

QUESTIONS AND PROBLEMS

1. Why do cash inflows and outflows between the beginning and end of a performance evaluation period complicate the measurement of portfolio returns?

2. Ginger Beaumont began the year 1988 with a portfolio valued at $10,000 and made a contribution to and a withdrawal from this portfolio over the next three months. Information regarding amounts and dates of these cash flows and the portfolio's market value at various dates is shown below.

DATE	CONTRIBUTION(+) OR WITHDRAWAL(−)	PORTFOLIO VALUE
12/31/87	$ 0	$10,000
1/31/88	+956	9,000
2/28/88	−659	12,000
3/31/88	0	13,000

   a. Calculate the dollar-weighted return for the three-month period. (*Hint*: Unless you have a suitable calculator, you will have to use trial and error to find the dollar-weighted return. To begin, the monthly dollar-weighted return is less than 10%.)

   b. Calculate the time-weighted return for the three-month period.

   c. Why is the time-weighted return for the quarter less than the dollar-weighted return in this particular problem?

3. Why does performance evaluation require an appropriate benchmark in order to be meaningful? How would you define the term "appropriate" in this context?

4. It is common practice for performance evaluation services to compare the returns on a common stock portfolio to a distribution of returns obtained from a large sample of other common stock portfolios. What potential problems are involved in this sort of analysis?

5. The performance of the Venus Fund, a common stock mutual fund, compared with that of the S&P 500 over a ten-year period, is as follows:

	VENUS FUND	S&P 500
Average quarterly excess return	0.6%	0.5%
Standard deviation of quarterly excess returns	9.9%	6.6%
Beta	1.10	1.00

Dazzy Vance is considering investing in either the Venus Fund or another mutual fund whose objective is to track the performance of the S&P 500. Which fund would you recommend that Dazzy select, assuming that your decision is based solely on past performance? Justify your answer using various measures of risk-adjusted performance.

6. Why is the reward-to-variability ratio a more appropriate measure of performance than the ex post alpha if the portfolio being assessed represents the entire wealth of the portfolio's owner?

7. Can the ex post alpha, the reward-to-volatility ratio, and the reward-to-variability ratio give conflicting answers to the question of whether a particular portfolio has

outperformed the market portfolio on a risk-adjusted basis? If so, which of these measures can conflict with the others, and why can this conflict occur?

8. Does a portfolio's ex post alpha measure gains and losses due to security selection, market timing, or both? Explain.

9. Assume that broad stock market indices, such as the S&P 500, are not good surrogates for the "true" market portfolio. What potential problems does this cause for performance evaluation using the ex post alpha measure?

10. You are given the following historical performance information on the capital markets and the Jupiter Fund, a common stock mutual fund.

YEAR	JUPITER FUND BETA	RETURN ON JUPITER FUND	RETURN ON S&P 500	RETURN ON TREASURY BILLS
1969	0.90	− 2.99%	− 8.50%	6.58%
1970	0.95	0.63	4.01	6.53
1971	0.95	22.01	14.31	4.39
1972	1.00	24.08	18.98	3.84
1973	1.00	− 22.46	− 14.66	6.93
1974	0.90	− 25.12	− 26.47	8.00
1975	0.80	29.72	37.20	5.80
1976	0.75	22.15	23.84	5.08
1977	0.80	0.48	− 7.18	5.12
1978	0.85	6.85	6.56	7.18

a. Compute the Jupiter Fund's average beta over the ten-year period. What investment percentages in the S&P 500 and Treasury bills are required in order to produce a beta equal to the fund's average beta?

b. Compute the year-by-year returns that would have been earned on a portfolio invested in the S&P 500 and Treasury bills in the proportions calculated in part (a).

c. Compute the year-by-year returns that would have been earned on a portfolio invested in the S&P 500 and Treasury bills in the proportions needed to match Jupiter's beta year by year. (*Note*: These proportions will change yearly as the fund's beta changes yearly.)

d. One measure of a fund's *market timing ability* is the average difference between (1) what the fund would have earned annually by investing in the S&P 500 and Treasury bills so that the year-by-year beta equals the fund's actual year-by-year beta, and (2) what the fund would have earned annually by investing in the S&P 500 and Treasury bills so that the year-by-year beta equals the fund's average beta. Given your previous calculations, evaluate Jupiter's market timing ability.

e. One measure of a fund's *security selection ability* is the average difference between (1) the fund's annual return and, (2) what the fund would have earned annually by investing in the S&P 500 and Treasury bills so that the year-by-year beta equals the fund's actual year-by-year beta. Calculate Jupiter's average return and then, using your previous calculations, evaluate Jupiter's security selection ability.

11. Discuss the potential drawbacks of evaluating bond portfolio performance by using a bond market line.

12. (Appendix Question) What is the purpose of performance attribution? What types of problems can hinder performance attribution?

13. (Appendix Question) Assume that security returns are explained by a sector-factor

model. Eugene Stephens has been asked to develop a performance attribution report analyzing the returns on Portfolio A versus those of the market portfolio for the year 1988, and has collected the following information:

	PORTFOLIO A	MARKET PORTFOLIO	SECTOR/FACTOR VALUES
1988 Return	12.50%	5.50%	—
Beta	1.10	1.00	−0.50
Size	1.30	6.00	−0.60
% Industrial	40%	80%	8.00
% Nonindustrial	60%	20%	16.00

Unfortunately, Eugene is confused by the subject of performance attribution. Carry out the analysis for him.

Chapter 24

EXTENDED DIVERSIFICATION

One of the major themes of modern portfolio theory concerns the merits of diversification: In an efficient capital market, sensible investment strategies will include holdings of many different assets. Previous chapters have considered traditional securities, such as stocks and bonds, and some less traditional ones, such as options and futures. However, an investor should also consider holding foreign securities and tangible assets.

This chapter discusses these two aspects of diversification and then turns to a less lofty subject: betting on sporting events. As indicated in previous chapters, active investment management can be considered a form of betting. This rather subtle form of wagering that is handled by security brokers and dealers is compared and contrasted with the more explicit form handled by people at racetracks and by bookmakers.

24.1 INTERNATIONAL INVESTMENT

If the world were under one political jurisdiction, with one currency and complete freedom of trade, then the market portfolio could be thought of as including all securities in the world, each in proportion to its market value. In such a situation, limiting one's investments to securities representing firms located in only one part of the world would most likely result in a relatively low rate of return per unit of risk. After all, few people would advocate that Californians own only securities issued by Californian firms. And in a world without political boundaries, few people would advocate that Americans own only securities issued by American firms.

Unfortunately, there are political boundaries, different currencies, and restrictions on trade and currency exchange. Such unpleasantries diminish, but do not destroy, the advantages to be gained from international investment.

☐ **24.1.1 The World Market Wealth Portfolio**

Figure 24.1 provides a 1984 year-end estimate of the world market wealth portfolio, defined to include those "capital market securities that are most

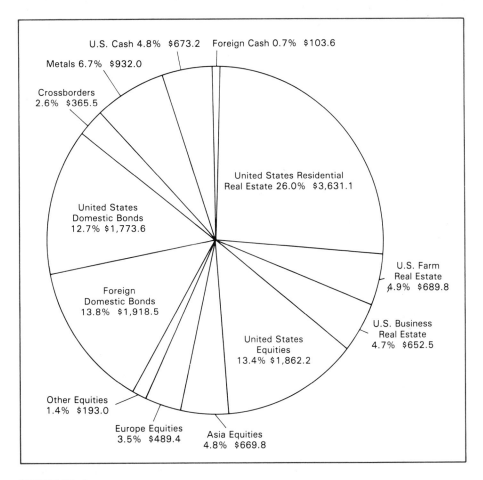

U.S. Cash 4.8% $673.2   Foreign Cash 0.7% $103.6

Metals 6.7% $932.0

Crossborders
2.6% $365.5

United States
Domestic Bonds
12.7% $1,773.6

Foreign
Domestic Bonds
13.8% $1,918.5

Other Equities
1.4% $193.0

Europe Equities
3.5% $489.4

Asia Equities
4.8% $669.8

United States
Equities
13.4% $1,862.2

U.S. Business
Real Estate
4.7% $652.5

U.S. Farm
Real Estate
4.9% $689.8

United States Residential
Real Estate 26.0% $3,631.1

FIGURE 24–1
The World Market Wealth Portfolio, year-end 1984.

SOURCE: Roger G. Ibbotson, Laurence B. Siegel, and Kathryn S. Love, ''World Wealth: Market Values and Returns,'' *Journal of Portfolio Management* 12, no. 1 (Fall 1985), p. 6.

marketable and most readily identifiable. These are the securities that make up the opportunity set faced by most investors.'' [1]

Many problems are encountered in the construction of a world market wealth portfolio. It is almost impossible to represent adequately *all* security markets, as indicated by the authors of the paper from which Figure 24.1 is taken:

☐ We have excluded huge categories of assets from the portfolio, while at the same time we have included categories that are not wealth at all.

. . . the most important omission is human capital, which is probably the largest single component of world wealth. We have also excluded . . . foreign real

---

[1] Roger G. Ibbotson, Laurence B. Siegel, and Kathryn S. Love, "World Wealth: Market Values and Returns," *Journal of Portfolio Management* 12, no. 1 (Fall 1985):5.

estate . . . proprietorships and partnerships . . . many small corporations . . . [and] personal holdings such as automobiles, cash balances, and various consumer capital goods. We have not only omitted a large proportion of wealth, but we also have little idea as to how large the omitted proportion is.

Our inclusions may misrepresent the market even more than our omissions. We have included U.S. and foreign government debt that is almost certainly not backed dollar-for-dollar by government-owned assets such as parks and bridges. More likely, it is backed by claims on a future tax base. Other inclusions in our portfolio also misrepresent wealth. For example, some corporations own parts of other corporations, causing double counting.[2]

Table 24.1 provides a breakdown of the values of equities and bonds that are shown in Figure 24.1.[3] As shown in part (a) of the table, U.S. bonds and stocks made up $3635.8 billion (= $1862.2 + $1773.6) of the $7272.0 billion world equity and bond value at the end of 1984. In percentage terms, this is about half the value of the world total. Part (b) indicates that most of the U.S. equity total is attributable to the equities listed on the New York Stock Exchange, while most of the foreign equity total is attributable to Asian equities.[4] Part (c) indicates that government debt is larger than corporate debt both inside and outside the United States.

☐ 24.1.2 International Equity Indices

In most countries, there are indices of overall stock values and of the values of stocks within various industry or economic sectors. Such indices can be used for assessing "market moves" within the country and, more importantly, for comparative performance measurement. Important indices include the Financial Times-Stock Exchange 100 Index (often referred to as FT-SE, or the "footsie") for the London Stock Exchange; the Nikkei 225 Index for the Tokyo Stock Exchange; and the TSE 300 Composite Index for the Toronto Stock Exchange.[5] As shown in Figure 24.2(a), these and other indices are published daily in the *Wall Street Journal*.

On the international level, the indices produced by *Morgan Stanley Capital International Perspective* are also widely used for such purposes. Monthly values are calculated for the levels of 6 international indices, 19 national indices, and 38 international industry indices. Each index repre-

---

[2] Ibbotson, Siegel, and Love, "World Wealth: Market Values and Returns," 5.

[3] In this table, preferred stocks are arbitrarily listed under corporate debt. Also, a bond is considered to be "crossborder" if the currency of the bond is not the currency of the borrower's home country or the bond is primarily bought by investors outside the borrower's home country.

[4] Since Japanese equities are included in the Asian total, it appears that as of the end of 1984, U.S. equities were of greater market value than Japanese equities. However, data contained in *Morgan Stanley Capital International Perspective*, October 1987 (New York: Morgan Stanley) suggest that Japanese equities have surpassed United States equities in total market value.

[5] Chapter 21 discussed major U.S. stock market indices (see Figure 21.2). For a discussion of European stock markets, see Gabriel Hawawini, *European Equity Markets: Price Behavior and Efficiency*, Monograph Series in Finance and Economics 1984–4/5, Salomon Brothers Center for the Study of Financial Institutions, Graduate School of Business Administration, New York University.

TABLE 24.1

World Equity and Bond Values, Year-End 1984
(in billions of U.S. dollars).

A. SUMMARY		
United States Equities	$1862.2	
Foreign Equities	1352.4	
Total Equities		$3214.4
United States Bonds	$1773.6	
Foreign Bonds	2284.0	
Total Bonds		$4057.6
Total Equities and Bonds		$7272.0

B. MARKET VALUES OF EQUITIES		
United States:		
New York Stock Exchange	$1587.0	
American Stock Exchange	68.2	
Over-the-Counter	207.0	
Total United States		$1862.2
Foreign:		
Europe	$ 489.4	
Asia	669.8	
Other	193.0	
Total Foreign		$1352.4
Total Equities		$3214.4

C. MARKET VALUES OF BONDS			
United States:			
Government			
Notes	$ 720.0		
Bonds	164.8		
Agencies	525.9		
Total Government		$1410.7	
Corporate			
Medium-Term	$ 164.5		
Long-Term	152.9		
Preferred Stock	45.5		
Total Corporate		$ 362.9	
Total United States			$1773.6
Foreign:			
Domestic			
Government	$1288.2		
Corporate	630.3		
Total Domestic		$1918.5	
Crossborders		365.5	
Total Foreign			$2284.0
Total Bonds			$4057.6

SOURCE: Adapted from Roger G. Ibbotson, Laurence B. Siegel, and Kathryn S. Love, "World Wealth: Market Values and Returns," *Journal of Portfolio Management* 12, no. 1 (Fall 1985):7–9.

sents the value of a market-weighted portfolio of stocks (using total shares outstanding). Values for each of the 19 national indices are given in both the local currency and in U.S. dollars based on exchange rates at the time. Values of the other indices are stated only in U.S. dollars. At last count,

(a) Foreign Stock Market Indices

EXCHANGE	12/8/88 CLOSE	NET CHG	PCT CHG
Tokyo Nikkei Average	29758.90	− 291.92	− 0.97
Tokyo Topix Index	2302.60	− 11.60	− 0.50
London FT 30-share	1437.1	− 13.9	− 0.96
London 100-share	1757.9	− 13.8	− 0.78
London Gold Mines	176.7	− 0.9	− 0.51
Frankfurt DAX	1296.53	− 3.04	− 0.23
Zurich Credit Suisse	512.9	nc	
Paris CAC General	393.9	+ 1.0	+ 0.25
Milan Stock Index	1191	closed	
Amsterdam ANP-CBS General	277.5	− 1.4	− 0.50
Stockholm Affarsvarlden	988.3	+ 1.6	+ 0.16
Brussels Stock Index	5373.30	+ 15.77	+ 0.29
Australia All Ordinaries	1476.4	+ 4.7	+ 0.32
Hong Kong Hang Seng	2680.20	− 10.08	− 0.37
Singapore Straits Times	1002.84	+ 3.85	+ 0.39
Johannesburg J'burg Gold	1382	− 10	− 0.72
Toronto 300 Composite	307.21	− 16.86	− 0.51
Euro, Aust, Far East MSCI-p	953.4	− 1.8	− 0.19

p-Preliminary
nc-No change

(b) Morgan Stanley Indices

	Dec 7	Dec 6	% This Year
U.S.	256.6	256.0	+ 11.9
Britain	538.9	537.6	+ 4.5
Canada	359.1	358.1	+ 2.4
Japan	1389.5	1378.1	+ 35.9
France	417.8	415.1	+ 44.8
Germany	202.6	201.0	+ 29.4
Hong Kong	2022.3	2015.6	+ 23.0
Switzerland	168.5	167.9	+ 19.8
Australia	286.8	283.5	+ 10.6
World index	493.0	493.8	+ 20.8

FIGURE 24–2
International equity indices on March 11, 1988.

SOURCE: The Wall Street Journal © Dow Jones & Company, Inc. (December 9, 1988): p. C10.

1371 stocks were included, representing approximately 60% of the aggregate market value listed on the 19 covered stock exchanges.[6]

All 1371 stocks are used to compute the "World" index. The "Europe" index includes 526 companies representing 12 European countries. The "Europe, Australia, Far East" (EAFE) index, representing a portfolio of 911 stocks from 17 countries, is widely used by U.S. investors as a benchmark when evaluating the performance of international portfolio managers. Several of the Morgan Stanley indices are published daily in the *Wall Street Journal*, as shown in part (b) Figure 24.2; the EAFE index appears at the bottom of part (a).

□ 24.1.3 Risk and Return from Foreign Investing

Investing in a foreign security involves all the risks associated with investing in a domestic security, plus additional risks that are encountered because the investor expects to receive cash flows in the future from the foreign security. However, these cash flows will be in a foreign currency and thus will be of relatively little use to the investor if they cannot be converted into the investor's domestic currency. The additional risks associated with foreign

[6] *Morgan Stanley Capital International Perspective*, October 1987 (New York: Morgan Stanley). For more on these and other indices, see Chapter 5 in Bruno Solnik, *International Investments* (Reading, Mass.: Addison-Wesley Publishing Company, Inc., 1986).

investing are due to uncertainties associated with converting these foreign cash flows into domestic currency. They are known as *political risk* and *exchange* (or currency) *risk*.[7]

Political risk refers to uncertainty about the *ability* of an investor to convert the foreign currency into domestic currency. Specifically, a foreign government might restrict, tax, or completely prohibit the exchange of one currency for another. Since such policies change from time to time, the ability of an investor to repatriate foreign cash flows may be subject to some uncertainty. There may even be a possibility of complete expropriation, making political risk very large.

Exchange risk refers to uncertainty about the *rate* at which a foreign currency can be exchanged for the investor's domestic currency in the future. That is, at the time a foreign security is bought, the rate at which future foreign cash flows can be converted into domestic currency is uncertain, and it is this uncertainty that is known as exchange risk.

Hedging Exchange Risk

To an extent, exchange risk can be reduced by hedging in the forward (or futures) market for foreign currency. In the case of default-free fixed-income securities, it may be possible to completely eliminate such risk in this way. For example, assume that a one-year pure discount bond paying 1000 British pounds at maturity can be purchased for 850 British pounds. Furthermore, assume that a forward contract can be signed where the investor will receive $1300 for delivering 1000 British pounds a year from now. In this situation, the rate of return *in British pounds* on this security is 17.65% ((1000 − 850)/ 850)).

If the current (that is, spot) exchange rate were $1.35 per pound, then the cost of this bond to an American investor would be $1147.50 (850 × $1.35). Thus, the rate of return *in American dollars* on this British security would be 13.29% (($1300 − $1147.50)/$1147.50). Except for political risk, this is a certain return, since exchange risk has been completely removed by hedging with a forward contract.

Unfortunately, it is not possible to hedge completely the exchange risk associated with risky investments. Forward contracts can be made to cover expected cash flows, but if the actual cash flows are larger or smaller than expected, then some of the foreign currency may have to be exchanged at the spot rate prevailing at the time that the cash is received. Since future spot rates usually cannot be predicted with complete certainty, this will affect overall risk. As a practical matter, this "unhedgeable" risk is likely to be small. Nevertheless, the cost of hedging foreign investments may exceed the benefit—perhaps by a large amount.

Foreign and Domestic Returns

Changes in exchange rates can cause major differences between the returns obtained by domestic investors and the returns obtained by unhedged foreign investors.

---

[7] The effect these types of risk have on asset pricing has been considered by a number of people. For a discussion and list of references, see Chapters 1 and 5 in Solnik, *International Investments*.

Consider an American investor and a Swiss investor, both of whom purchase shares of a Swiss company whose stock is traded only in Switzerland. Let the price of the stock in Swiss francs be P_0 at the beginning of a period and P_1 at the end of the period. The *domestic return*, denoted by r_d, is

$$r_d = \frac{P_1 - P_0}{P_0}.$$ (24.1)

For example, if P_0 = 10 Swiss francs and P_1 = 12 Swiss francs, then r_d = (12 − 10)/10 = 20%.

For the Swiss investor, r_d is the stock's return. Not so for the U.S. investor. Assume that at the beginning of the period the price (in dollars) of one Swiss franc is $.50. Denoting this exchange rate (that is, the exchange rate at the beginning of the period) by X_0, the cost of a share to the American investor will be $X_0 P_0$. In the example, this cost will be $.50 × 10 = $5.00.

Now, assume that the exchange rate rises to $.55 per Swiss franc at the end of the period. Denoting this by X_1, the ending value of the stock for the American investor will be $X_1 P_1$. In the example, this value will be $.55 × 12 = $6.60.

The *foreign return* (that is, the return to a foreign investor), denoted by r_f, is:

$$r_f = \frac{X_1 P_1 - X_0 P_0}{X_0 P_0}.$$ (24.2)

In the example, the foreign investor (an American) would have earned a return of r_f = ($6.60 − $5.00)/$5.00 = 32% on an investment in the Swiss firm's stock.

In effect, the American made *two* investments: (1) an investment in a Swiss stock and (2) an investment in the Swiss franc. Accordingly, the overall return to the American can be decomposed into a return on the investment in the Swiss stock and a return on an investment in the Swiss franc. This can be illustrated by considering an American who had purchased a Swiss franc at the beginning of the period. If the American subsequently sold the franc at the end of the period, the return on foreign currency, denoted by r_c, would be

$$r_c = \frac{X_1 - X_0}{X_0}.$$ (24.3)

In the example, r_c = ($.55 − $.50)/$.50 = 10%.

From equations (24.1), (24.2), and (24.3), it can be shown that

$$1 + r_f = (1 + r_d)(1 + r_c)$$ (24.4)

which can be rewritten as

$$r_f = r_d + r_c + r_d r_c.$$ (24.5)

In the example, equation (24.5) reveals that r_f = .20 + .10 + (.20 × .10), which is equal to 32%.

The last term in this equation ($r_d r_c$) will generally be smaller than the two preceding ones, since it equals their product and both are generally less than 1.0. Thus, equation (24.5) can be restated as an approximation

$$r_f \approx r_d + r_c. \tag{24.6}$$

It can now be seen that the return on a foreign security (r_f) can be decomposed into two parts, representing the domestic return on the security (r_d) and the return on foreign currency (r_c). In the example, the precise value for r_f was shown earlier to be 32%; use of the approximation indicates its value to be equal to .20 + .10, or 30%. Thus, the approximation is in error by 2%, a relatively small amount.

Expected Returns

Equation (24.6) leads directly to the proposition that the expected return on a foreign security will approximately equal the expected domestic return plus the expected return on foreign currency:

$$\bar{r}_f \approx \bar{r}_d + \bar{r}_c. \tag{24.7}$$

It might be tempting for an investor to purchase a foreign security that has a high expected return in its host country, $\bar{r}_d$, on the belief that this means the security will have a high expected return to the investor, $\bar{r}_f$. However, equation (24.7) reveals this type of logic to be flawed. Just because a foreign security has a high value for $\bar{r}_d$ does not mean that it has a high value for $\bar{r}_f$, since $\bar{r}_c$ can be negative. This can be shown by considering the case of bonds.

The expected domestic returns of bonds in countries with high expected inflation rates will typically be high. However, a foreign investor in a country with a lower expected inflation rate should expect a *negative* return on foreign currency, as his or her currency can be expected to *appreciate* relative to that of the country with the higher expected inflation rate. In evaluating the expected return on the foreign security, there is thus good news (a high expected domestic return, $\bar{r}_d$) and bad news (a negative expected return on foreign currency, $\bar{r}_c$). On balance, the expected foreign return $\bar{r}_f$ might not be as exceptional as first though when just $\bar{r}_d$ was considered. Indeed, if markets were completely integrated, it would be reasonable to expect the values of $\bar{r}_d$ and $\bar{r}_c$ to sum to an amount $\bar{r}_f$ that is equal to the expected return on an equivalent bond in the investor's own country.

Foreign and Domestic Risks

Having seen in equation (24.7) that the expected return on a foreign security consists of two components, it is appropriate that the risk of the foreign security be evaluated next. As before, consider an American investor and a Swiss investor who have purchased shares of a Swiss company. The domestic variance, denoted by σ_d^2, is the risk that the Swiss investor faces with respect to the Swiss stock. Correspondingly, the foreign variance, denoted by σ_f^2, is the risk that the American investor faces with respect to the Swiss stock. Based on equation (24.6), it can be shown that the foreign variance consists of three components:

$$\sigma_f^2 = \sigma_d^2 + \sigma_c^2 + 2\rho_{dc}\sigma_d\sigma_c \qquad (24.8)$$

where σ_c^2 is the variance associated with the currency return to an American from investing in Swiss francs and later exchanging them for American dollars, and ρ_{dc} is the correlation coefficient between the returns on the Swiss stock and the return on Swiss francs.

For example, assume that the domestic variance is 225 (meaning that the domestic standard deviation, σ_d, is $\sqrt{225} = 15\%$) and the currency variance is 25 (meaning the currency standard deviation, σ_c, is $\sqrt{25} = 5\%$). If $\rho_{dc} = 0$, then equation (24.8) indicates that the foreign variance is $225 + 25 = 250$. Accordingly, the foreign standard deviation is $\sqrt{250} = 15.8\%$, which is only slightly greater than the domestic standard deviation of 15%.

Equation (24.8) reveals that the smaller the correlation between returns on a foreign currency and returns on a foreign investment, the smaller will be the foreign variance. One study that used data from 17 countries over the period from January 1971 through December 1980 found an average correlation of .034, which is effectively, zero.[8] Thus, it appears that the correlation is sufficiently small that the foreign variance typically will be near, but not less than, the sum of the domestic and currency variances.[9]

Table 24.2 provides evidence on the relative magnitudes of the three types of risk. Standard deviations of monthly values over the period from December 1970 through December 1980 are shown for domestic risk (corresponding to σ_d), currency risk (corresponding to σ_c), and foreign risk (corresponding to σ_f), where the latter two types of risk have been measured from the perspective of a U.S. investor. The last column represents the ratio of foreign risk to domestic risk. Thus, a ratio greater than 1 can be taken as an indication that the risk to a U.S. investor is greater than the risk to a domestic investor. Indeed, with the exception of Hong Kong stocks, all the ratios are greater than 1, suggesting that fluctuations in currency exchange rates increased the risk a U.S. investor would have faced in buying foreign securities.

The importance of currency risk can easily be exaggerated. Calculations such as those in Table 24.2 assume that investors purchase only domestic goods and services and thus convert all proceeds from foreign investments into their own currency before engaging in any spending for consumption purposes. But most people buy foreign goods and many buy foreign services as well (for example, as tourists). The cheaper another country's currency relative to one's own, the more attractive purchases of its goods and services will be. Other things being equal, it may make sense to invest more in countries whose products and scenery are admired, for the effective currency risk is likely to be smaller there than elsewhere.

---

[8] Bruno Solnik and Eric Nemeth, "Asset Returns and Currency Fluctuations: A Time Series Analysis," paper presented at the second tagung, Geld Banken und Versicherungen, Universitat Karlsruhe, December 1982.

[9] Since standard deviation is the square root of variance, this means that the foreign standard deviation will typically be substantially less than the sum of the domestic and currency standard deviations.

TABLE 24.2
Risks for Domestic and U.S. Investors Based on Historic
Values, December 1970–December 1980.

	(1) DOMESTIC RISK	(2) CURRENCY RISK	(3) FOREIGN RISK	(4) FOREIGN/ DOMESTIC RISK
Stocks				
Australia	24.62%	9.15%	27.15%	1.10
Belgium	13.28	11.02	18.76	1.41
Canada	18.92	4.16	20.29	1.07
Denmark	15.41	10.28	17.65	1.15
France	22.00	10.24	25.81	1.17
Germany	13.87	11.87	18.39	1.33
Hong Kong	47.95	5.63	45.80	.96
Italy	24.21	8.58	26.15	1.08
Japan	16.39	10.42	19.55	1.19
Netherlands	16.37	10.97	18.91	1.16
Norway	28.61	8.89	29.92	1.05
Singapore	35.82	6.52	36.03	1.01
Spain	16.71	9.10	20.26	1.21
Sweden	15.05	8.89	18.06	1.20
Switzerland	16.80	14.67	21.40	1.27
United Kingdom	28.94	8.84	31.61	1.09
United States	16.00	.00	16.00	1.00
Bonds				
Canada	6.16	4.16	7.93	1.29
France	4.39	10.24	11.80	2.69
Germany	6.91	11.87	14.35	2.08
Japan	6.53	10.42	14.36	2.20
Netherlands	7.16	10.97	13.61	1.90
Switzerland	4.33	14.67	15.33	3.54
United Kingdom	12.30	8.84	16.29	1.32
United States	8.96	.00	8.96	1.00

SOURCE: Adapted from Bruno Solnik and Bernard Noetzlin, "Optimal International Asset Allocation," *Journal of Portfolio Management* 9, no. 1 (Fall 1982):13.

□ **24.1.4 Multinational Firms**

Firms operating in many countries provide international diversification at the corporate level. One might expect that investment in the stocks of such *multinational firms* could serve as a good substitute for investment in stocks of foreign ("national") firms.

A number of studies have shown that this may not be the case. In one, returns on portfolios of stocks of multinational firms headquartered in each of nine countries were calculated for the period from April 1966 through June 1974. Then each portfolio's returns were compared with the returns on the market index for the country of its headquarters. The middle column in Table 24.3 shows the proportion of each portfolio's variance that can be attributed to movements in its corresponding "domestic" market index. Fi-

TABLE 24.3

Proportions of Returns on Stocks on Multinational Firms
Explained by Stock Market Indices.

HEADQUARTERS COUNTRY OF MULTINATIONAL FIRMS	PROPORTION OF VARIANCE IN RETURNS EXPLAINED BY	
	DOMESTIC MARKET INDEX	DOMESTIC AND OTHER MARKET INDICES
Belgium	45%	58%
France	45	62
Germany	65	74
Italy	47	51
Netherlands	50	63
Sweden	42	50
Switzerland	52	75
United Kingdom	44	49
United States	29	31

SOURCE: Adapted from Bertrand Jacquillat and Bruno Solnik, "Multinationals Are Poor Tools for Diversification," *Journal of Portfolio Management* 4, no. 2 (Winter 1978):10.

nally, each portfolio's returns were compared with the returns on market indices in all nine countries. The final column in Table 24.3 shows the proportion of each portfolio's variance that can be attributed to movements in its domestic market index as well as the foreign market indices.

During the period covered in Table 24.3, the returns on multinational firms based in the United States had only 2% (31% − 29%) of their variance that could be attributed to foreign market indices. This suggests that U.S.-headquartered multinationals were a poor substitute for direct investment in foreign stocks by U.S. investors. The situation was somewhat better for non–U.S. multinationals, since the differences in the percentages shown in the two columns were greater than 2%. One possible explanation for this is that non–U.S. multinationals have more extensive foreign operations than U.S. multinationals.

☐ 24.1.5   International Listings

The common stocks of many firms are traded not only on the major stock exchange in their home country but also on an exchange in a foreign country. By doing so, foreign investors no longer have to engage in foreign currency transactions when buying and selling the firm's stock. It is also possible that foreign investors can escape certain taxes and regulations to which the investors would be subject if the security were to be bought in the firm's home country. As mentioned in Chapter 2, there are two ways that such internationally listed foreign securities can be traded in the United States.

The first way foreign securities may be traded in the U.S. is with *Amer-*

ican depository receipts (ADRs). ADRs are financial assets that are issued by U.S. banks and represent indirect ownership of a certain number of shares of a specific foreign firm that are held on deposit in a bank in the firm's home country. The advantage of ADRs over direct ownership is that the investor need not worry about the delivery of the stock certificates or converting dividend payments from a foreign currency into U.S. dollars. The depository bank automatically does the converting for the investor and also forwards all financial reports from the firm; the investor pays the bank a relatively small fee for these services. At the end of 1987, the common stocks of 34 foreign firms were traded as ADRs on the New York Stock Exchange, whereas the stocks of 97 foreign firms were traded as ADRs on the NASDAQ system.[10]

The second way foreign securities may be traded in the United States is for the shares of a firm to be traded directly, just like the shares of a typical U.S. firm. At the end of 1987, the common stocks of 33 foreign firms were traded directly on the New York Stock Exchange, whereas stocks of 175 foreign firms were traded directly on the NASDAQ system. Of these, 22 and 138 were Canadian firms, respectively.

One study that examined the diversification implications of investing in ADRs found that such securities were of notable benefit to U.S. investors.[11] Specifically, a sample of 45 ADRs was examined and compared with a sample of 45 U.S. securities over the period of 1973 to 1983. Using an index based on all NYSE-listed stocks, the betas of the ADRs had an average value of .26, which was much lower than the average beta of 1.01 for the U.S. securities. Furthermore, the correlation of the ADRs' returns with those of the NYSE market portfolio averaged .33, whereas U.S. securities had a notably higher average correlation of .53. Given these two observations, it is not surprising that portfolios formed from U.S. securities and ADRs had much lower standard deviations than portfolios consisting of just U.S. securities. For example, portfolios consisting of 10 U.S. securities had an average standard deviation of 5.50%, whereas a 10-security portfolio split evenly between U.S. securities and ADRs had an average standard deviation of 4.41%. Thus, in contrast to investing in multinationals, it seems that investing in ADRs brings significant benefits in terms of risk reduction.

☐ 24.1.6 **Correlations Between Equity Markets**

If all economies were tied together completely, stock markets in different countries would move together, and little advantage could be gained through international diversification. But this is not the case. Table 24.4 shows the correlations of returns on diversified "market" portfolios of equities in various national stock markets with the returns on an index of equities in all the

---

[10] The London Stock Exchange began trading simultaneously many of these ADRs in August 1987, with prices being quoted in U.S. dollars. See National Association of Security Dealers *NASDAQ 1988 Fact Book*, 30–32; New York Stock Exchange *Fact Book 1988*, 25–26.

[11] Dennis T. Officer and J. Ronald Hoffmeister, "ADRs: A Substitute for the Real Thing?" *Journal of Portfolio Management* 13, no. 2 (Winter 1987):61–65. See also Leonard Rosenthal, "An Empirical Test of the Efficiency of the ADR Market," *Journal of Banking and Finance* 7, no. 1 (March 1983):17–29.

TABLE 24.4

Correlations of Annual U.S. Dollar-Adjusted Total Equity
Returns with World Total Equities, 1960–1980.

COUNTRY	CORRELATION
Australia	.753
Austria	− .042
Belgium	.483
Canada	.716
Denmark	.358
France	.384
Germany	.322
Hong Kong	.848
Italy	.281
Japan	.385
Netherlands	.804
Norway	− .045
Singapore	.700
Spain	− .015
Sweden	.470
Switzerland	.557
United Kingdom	.703
United States	.967

SOURCE: Adapted from Roger G. Ibbotson, Richard C. Carr, and Anthony W. Robinson, "International Equity and Bond Returns," *Financial Analysts Journal* 38, no. 4 (July/August 1982):71.

included countries (that is, the "world" portfolio). The value for the United States is large, owing primarily to the importance of the United States in the world index. However, the striking feature is that many of the figures are very small (and some are even negative), even though each of the national indices represents a well-diversified domestic equity portfolio. These low correlations suggest that there are sizable potential advantages, in terms of risk reduction, from international diversification.[12]

24.2   TANGIBLE ASSETS

In the first half of the 1970s, marketable securities such as stocks and bonds provided returns that were relatively disappointing, especially after adjusting for inflation. And, as shown in Chapter 11, neither bonds nor stocks have served as good hedges against unanticipated inflation in recent years. Overall, tangible assets have been better hedges against inflation. One example, real estate, was shown in Chapter 6 to have been an attractive in-

---

[12] Another study of 349 stocks in 11 countries revealed an average intercountry correlation coefficient of .234 for the period from January 1973 to December 1983. See D. Chinhyung Cho, Cheol S. Eun, and Lemma W. Senbet, "International Arbitrage Pricing Theory: An Empirical Investigation," *Journal of Finance* 41, no. 2 (June 1986):313–29. For a multiperiod approach that indicates the benefits from international diversification, particularly for highly risk-averse investors, see Robert R. Grauer and Nils H. Hakansson, "Gains From International Diversification: 1968–85 Returns on Portfolios of Stocks and Bonds," *Journal of Finance* 42, no. 3 (July 1987):721–39.

flation hedge in recent years.[13] Other examples, such as collectible assets and precious metals (like gold and silver), provide various degrees of protection against inflation.

☐ 24.2.1 Collectible Assets

Not surprisingly, disenchantment with returns on marketable securities has led some investors to examine a host of tangible assets that are normally considered only by collectors. Table 24.5 shows the average returns over three five-year periods for several different kinds of collectible assets (often simply referred to as *collectibles*).

Some of the returns shown in the table are quite high. However, none of the collectible assets provided *consistently* high results over all three periods. This is not surprising because if one (or more) had provided consistently high returns, many investors would have been attracted to it and bid its price up to a level where high returns would no longer have been possible.

In a sense, a collectible asset often provides income to the owner in the form of consumption. For example, an investor can admire a Rembrandt, sit on a Chippendale, play a Stradivarius, and drive a Morgan. Value received in this manner is not subject to income taxation and is thus likely to be especially attractive for those in high tax brackets. However, the value of such consumption depends strongly on one's preferences.

If markets are efficient, collectible assets will be priced so those who enjoy them most will find it desirable to hold them in greater-than-market-value proportions, whereas those who enjoy them least will find it desirable to hold them in less-than-market-value proportions (and, in many cases, not at all).

Institutional funds and investment pools have been organized to hold paintings, stamps, coins, and other collectible assets. Such arrangements

TABLE 24.5
Annual Returns on Collectible Assets, Five-Year Periods
Ending June 1.

	1969–1974	1974–1979	1979–1984
Chinese ceramics	31.1%	−3.1%	15.7%
Coins	9.5	32.4	11.3
Diamonds	11.6	13.6	6.1
Old masters	7.3	17.3	1.5
U.S. stamps	14.1	24.9	9.8

SOURCE: Based on data in R. S. Salomon, Jr., and Mallory J. Lennox, "Financial Assets—A Temporary Setback," *Stock Research Investment Policy*, Salomon Brothers, Inc., June 8, 1984.

---

[13] While not a tangible asset, commodity futures were shown in Chapter 19 to have also been an attractive inflation hedge.

are subject to serious question if they involve locking such objects in vaults where they cannot be seen by those who derive pleasure from this sort of consumption. On the other hand, if the items are rented to others, the only loss may be that associated with the transfer of a portion of the consumption value to the government in the form of a tax on income.

Investors in collectibles should be aware of two types of risk that are especially notable. The first is that the bid-ask spread is often very large. Thus, an investor must see a large price increase just to recoup the spread and break even. The second is that collectibles are subject to fads. For example, Chinese ceramics may be actively sought by many investors today, leading to high prices and big returns for earlier purchasers. However, they may fall out of favor later on and plunge in value. Unlike financial assets, there is no such thing as "fair" value for collectibles that can act as a kind of anchor for the market price.

☐ 24.2.2   Gold

In the United States, private holdings of gold bullion were illegal before the 1970s. In other countries, investment in gold has long been a tradition. According to one estimate, at the end of 1984 gold represented over 6% of the world market wealth portfolio.[14]

Table 24.6 contrasts a U.S. investor's returns from gold with the returns from U.S. equities over the period from 1960 through 1984. Gold is clearly a risky investment, but in this period, at least, it also provided high average returns.

For any single investment, risk and return are only parts of the story: Correlations of an asset's return with the returns on other assets are also relevant. In the period covered in Table 24.6, gold price changes were slightly negatively correlated with stock returns. Similar results have been obtained for other periods. Gold thus appears to be an effective diversifying asset for

TABLE 24.6
Characteristics of Gold and U.S. Equity Returns, 1960–1984.

	AVERAGE ANNUAL RETURN	STANDARD DEVIATION OF ANNUAL RETURNS
U.S. equities	10.20%	16.89%
Gold	12.62	29.87
Correlation:		
Gold and U.S. equities	−.09	
Gold and inflation	.63	

SOURCE: Adapted from Roger G. Ibbotson, Laurence B. Siegel, and Kathryn S. Love, "World Wealth: Market Values and Returns," *Journal of Portfolio Management* 12, no. 1 (Fall 1985):17, 21.

---

[14] Ibbotson, Siegel, and Love, "World Wealth: Market Values and Returns," 9.

an equity investor. Table 24.6 also shows that gold prices were highly correlated with the rate of inflation in the United States as measured by changes in the Consumer Price Index. This is consistent with gold's traditional role as a hedge against inflation, since higher inflation generally brings higher gold prices.

Investors interested in gold need not restrict themselves to bullion. Other possibilities range from stocks of gold mining companies to gold futures to gold coins and commemoratives. Furthermore, there are other types of precious metals, such as silver, that investors may want to consider.

24.3   SPORTS BETTING

Throughout the world, large amounts of money are wagered on the outcomes of sporting events. In the United States, betting on horse races is conducted legally at race tracks in many states and via legal off-track betting establishments in some states. In addition, illegal bookmakers in every state accept bets on horse races. Bets on other events—most notably professional football games—are made legally in Nevada and illegally with bookmakers almost everywhere.

There are some interesting parallels between betting and investing in securities. Both involve an initial outlay of cash and an outcome that, being uncertain, can be thought of as a random variable. For both betting and investing, an individual must have some sort of strategy in deciding where to put his or her money—after all, there are a large number of sporting events as well as securities that are available. Furthermore, these strategies can be thought of as being either fundamental or technical in nature. In the case of fundamental strategies, an investor or bettor looks at the underlying strength of the firm or team or horse that is being evaluated, whereas in the case of a technical strategy, only past performance is of concern. Both of these strategies are typically based on publicly available information; thus, the historical performance of investors and bettors can be examined in order to see if the respective financial markets and "sports markets" are semi-strong-form efficient. To begin the discussion, a parallel will be made between a security dealer and a bookmaker.

A security dealer typically wishes to operate with, on average, a small inventory of securities so as to have relatively little exposure to loss through security price fluctuations. To do this, the dealer usually sets a bid price and an asked price that will bring roughly an equal number of orders for purchases and sales in a given time period (say, a week's time). The bid-ask spread represents the dealer's profit margin and part of the investor's transactions costs.

Similarly, in sports betting the bookmaker acts as dealer and wishes to have relatively little "inventory" (exposure to loss). Two major methods are employed to achieve this: *spread betting* and *odds betting*. The former is used for bets on games such as football and baseball and the latter for bets on contests such as horse races and presidential elections.

☐ 24.3.1 Spread Betting

In order to understand spread betting, consider a hypothetical professional football game between the San Francisco 49ers and the Minnesota Vikings. It is widely felt that the 49ers are likely to win. Thus, the bookmaker establishes a spread, perhaps deciding that the 49ers are "favored by 7 points." This means that the final score will, in effect, be modified by subtracting 7 points from the 49ers score and then paying those who bet on the "winner" using that adjusted score. People who bet on San Francisco believe that the team will "cover the spread"; those who bet on Minnesota believe that Minnesota will "beat the spread." If the final score is 28–20 in favor of San Francisco, then after adjusting for the spread the score is 21–20 in favor of San Francisco, and those betting on San Francisco will have won. However, if the final score is 24–20 in favor of San Francisco, then the adjusted score will be 17–20 in favor of Minnesota, and those betting on Minnesota's beating the spread will have won.[15]

The point spread serves as an equilibrating mechanism. Other things being equal, the greater the spread, the smaller will be the amount bet on San Francisco and the larger the amount bet on Minnesota. At some level the "books will be balanced," meaning an equal amount has been bet on both teams. Given local prejudices, this may be accomplished by San Francisco bookmakers "laying off" excess money bet on the 49ers with Minnesota bookmakers who have excess money bet on the Vikings.

The bookmaker makes a living with a range that corresponds to the security dealer's bid-ask spread. Typically, the bettor puts up $11 for a $10 bet, meaning a winner will receive $10 (plus his or her initial $11 bet, if paid in advance), whereas a loser is out the initial $11 bet. If the books are balanced, the bookmaker will pay out $21 for every $22 taken in. For example, if there is one $11 bet on San Francisco and one $11 bet on Minnesota, the books are balanced. Then, whichever team wins, the bookmaker will pay out $21 of the $22 that has been bet.

While bookmakers generally set point spreads to balance their books, in an efficient market such spreads would provide good estimates of the expected differences in points scored (and, by and large, the evidence is consistent with market efficiency).

☐ 24.3.2 Odds Betting

A goal of many "dealers" in bets is to be reasonably certain that after the contest is over, less money will be paid out than is received. To do this, terms must be set so that bets on underdogs are attractive. Spreads are one way; odds are another.

An example from horse racing illustrates the procedure. Assume that Black Socks is favored to win the sixth race at Golden Gate Fields, while the other seven horses are considered inferior but of roughly equal speed.

---

[15] In the event of a tie in the adjusted score, the money that was bet is returned to both sides.

TABLE 24.7

Odds, Amounts Bet, and Payouts for a Horse Race.

HORSE	AMOUNT BET	ODDS	AMOUNT PAID OUT IF HORSE WINS
# 1 (favorite)	$ 300	5-to-3	$800
2	100	7-to-1	800
3	100	7-to-1	800
4	100	7-to-1	800
5	100	7-to-1	800
6	100	7-to-1	800
7	100	7-to-1	800
8	100	7-to-1	800
Total amount bet =	$1000		

If the payoff per dollar bet were the same for all eight horses, most of the bets would be placed on the favorite. To spread the betting over the contenders, a larger amount must be paid per dollar bet if a long shot is bet on and subsequently wins.

Assume that the odds are set at 7-to-1 for each of the seven slow horses. This means that if $1 is bet on one of them and the horse wins, the bettor will receive $8 (the original $1 that was bet plus $7 in winnings). Assume also that the odds on Black Socks are set at 5-to-3, so that every $3 bet on the favorite will return $8 (the original $3 that was bet plus $5 in winnings) if the horse wins. Now imagine that the amounts bet, given these odds, are as shown in Table 24.7. The total pool, or *handle* (that is, the total amount bet), is $1000, but no matter which horse wins the race, only $800 will be paid out. The remaining $200 is for the track, the government, and the bookmaker and is known as the *take*.

The numbers in Table 24.7 may seem contrived, but they represent the kind of situation achieved automatically by parimutuel betting. In this form of wagering (used at most horse racetracks), the actual odds for a horse are determined *after all betting has finished* by subtracting the take (typically about 20%) and the amount bet on the horse from the handle and then dividing this amount by the amount bet on that horse.[16] For example, in the case of Black Socks (horse number 1), the odds are ($1000 − $200 − $300)/$300 = $500/$300 = 5/3, as shown in the table. It should be noted that the dealer is always assured of receiving a fixed percentage (20%) for transaction costs with this procedure.

Betting on horses is a negative-sum game: Owing to transaction costs, the amount paid out is less than the amount paid in. Consequently, the expected return on the average bet will be negative. Since it is difficult to justify such activity on the basis of hedging, a bettor either (1) erroneously believes that he or she is a superior predictor, (2) is willing to pay in this

---

[16] This applies only to bets that a horse will win the race. More complex procedures are used for place (second or better) and show (third or better) bets. In addition, the actual payoff is usually rounded down to the nearest multiple of $.10 per $2 bet, for instance.

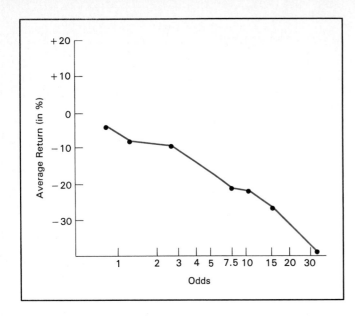

FIGURE 24–3
Average return versus odds in horse race betting.

SOURCE: Wayne W. Snyder, "Horse Racing: Testing the Efficient Markets Model," *Journal of Finance* 33, no. 4 (September 1978):p. 1113.

manner for entertainment, or (3) prefers risk. Undoubtedly, all three aspects play a role in the sports betting market. One attribute that makes betting on sports entertaining is the suspension of the bettor's usual mind-set and the taking of risks with relatively small amounts of money. In such an environment and with limited exposure, even a conservative investor may take pleasure in acting like a riverboat gambler.

Evidence consistent with risk preference of this sort has been found in many analyses of the expected returns from bets on horses with different probabilities of winning races. Figure 24.3 summarizes a number of such studies. The horizontal axis indicates closing odds (on a logarithmic scale). Favorites plot at the left end of the scale and extreme long shots at the right end. The vertical axis indicates average returns. All are negative, but the returns on favorites are considerably better than those on long shots. "Investors" at the track are apparently willing to give up some expected return to get more risk—in this domain they appear to prefer risk.

☐ 24.3.3 **The Efficiency of Horse Race Betting**

Investors in stocks can avail themselves of the results of financial analysis, both fundamental and technical. However, the high degree of efficiency of the stock market diminishes the value of such information for a single investor, since much of it is already reflected in security prices.

A similar situation prevails in the market for horse race betting. Fundamental analyses of such factors as the abilities of horses and trainers and the effects of weather abound, as do technical analyses of trends, reversals, and other changes in "form." If the market is efficient, public information provided by such analysts ("handicappers") will be reflected in prices ("closing odds").

In one test that examined the bets placed at Belmont Race Track in New York State, the odds at the track appeared to reflect the information contained in published "picks" by 14 handicappers. However, this did not seem to be the case in the less "professional" (and higher-transaction-cost) off-track betting market—a fact that may give some solace to those who invest in small and little-followed stocks.[17]

24.4 SUMMARY

As mentioned at the beginning of this chapter, one of the major themes of modern portfolio theory concerns the merits of diversification. Specifically, in an efficient capital market, it is quite sensible for an investor to hold more than one type of asset, since doing so will increase the investor's expected return per unit of risk. Two methods of diversifying that appear to offer such benefits, when added to a common stock portfolio, involve investing in foreign securities and in tangible assets.

Betting on sporting events was discussed because there are some interesting parallels between such betting and investing in securities. For example, both betting and investing involve some form of strategy that can be thought of as being either fundamental or technical in nature. Fundamental strategies would involve examining various types of past data, while technical strategies would involve simply examining past outcomes. After performing such examinations, the investor as well as the bettor would put money on what was perceived to be the favorite, be it a stock, horse, or football team. However, if markets are semistrong-form efficient, then neither the investor nor the bettor that uses publicly available information should be able to consistently "beat the market" or "beat the track."

It is appropriate that this chapter and book be ended on this note. For the financial economist, the relatively efficient nature of security and sports betting markets that has been observed is heartwarming, for it shows once more the effectiveness of competition. For the investor or bettor, such efficiency provides a challenge, to say the least. Accordingly, the next time you place an order with a stockbroker, keep this in mind.

QUESTIONS AND PROBLEMS

1. What types of political risks are relevant only for foreign investors? What types are relevant for both foreign and domestic investors? To what extent and in what manner

---

[17] Stephen Figlewski, "Subjective Information and Market Efficiency in a Betting Market," *Journal of Political Economy* 87, no. 1 (February 1979):75–88. It should be noted that there is some evidence that information is better reflected in the win pool than in the show and place pools. For details of a "system" designed to exploit such discrepancies, see Donald B. Hausch, William T. Ziemba, and Mark Rubenstein, "Efficiency of the Market for Racetrack Betting," *Management Science* 27, no. 12 (December 1981):1435–52; and Peter Asch, Burton G. Malkiel, and Richard E. Quandt, "Market Efficiency in Racetrack Betting," *Journal of Business* 57, no. 2 (April 1984):165–75 and "Market Efficiency in Racetrack Betting: Further Evidence and a Correction," *Journal of Business* 59, no. 1 (January 1986):157–60.

would you expect the current prices of securities in a particular country to reflect these types of political risk?

2. Why would an investor wish to hedge the currency risk in a portfolio of foreign securities? What considerations are relevant to making the decision whether to hedge?

3. How might a U.S. citizen or company use currency futures to hedge against exchange-rate risk?

4. Tris Speaker bought a Japanese stock one year ago when it sold for 280 yen per share and the exchange rate was $0.008 per yen. The stock now sells for 350 yen and the exchange rate is $0.010 per yen. The stock paid no dividends over the year. What was Tris's rate of return on this stock? What would be the rate of return on the stock to a Japanese investor?

5. Why is international diversification attractive to an investor like Jigger Statz who already has a well-diversified domestic portfolio?

6. When a U.S. citizen like Smead Jolly is attempting to estimate the expected return and standard deviation of return for a foreign security, what factors, in addition to those recognized in domestic security analysis, should be considered?

7. Eva Lange wants the diversification benefits of international investments, but does not want to own foreign securities directly. Would investing in domestically head-quartered multinational corporations and ADRs be effective substitutes for Eva? Explain.

8. Is a low correlation between the price movements of two countries' market indices a sufficient condition to ensure that a portfolio containing securities of both countries dominates a portfolio containing only domestic securities?

9. Hal Chase, a neophyte sports gambler, was heard to remark, "The bookmakers took a terrible beating this week because 80% of the underdogs beat the point spread." Does this seem plausible? Why or why not?

10. Picks of handicappers such as Dolph Luque generally do not add directly to the information reflected in the odds given at the track. Does this mean that Dolph and the other handicappers cannot pick winners? Does this mean that their picks are of no value? What aspects of security markets are comparable to the position of track handicappers?

GLOSSARY

Abnormal Return The return earned on a financial asset in excess of that required to compensate for the risk of the asset.

Accelerated Cost Recovery System (ACRS) A method of calculating depreciation, for corporate income tax purposes, that results in a fast write-off of the cost of certain fixed assets over their estimated useful lives.

Account Executive A representative of a brokerage firm whose primary responsibility is servicing the accounts of individual investors.

Accounting Beta A relative measure of the sensitivity of a firm's accounting earnings to changes in the accounting earnings of the market portfolio.

Accounting Earnings (Alternatively, Reported Earnings.) A firm's revenues less its expenses. Equivalently, the change in the firm's book value of the equity plus dividends paid to shareholders.

Accrued Interest Interest earned, but not yet paid.

Active Management A form of investment management which involves buying and selling financial assets with the objective of earning positive risk-adjusted returns.

Active Position The difference between the percentage of an investor's portfolio invested in a particular financial asset and the percentage of a benchmark portfolio invested in that same asset.

Actual Margin The equity in an investor's margin account expressed as a percentage of the account's total market value (for margin purchases) or total debt (for short sales).

Adjusted Beta An estimate of a security's future beta, derived initially from historical data, but modified by the assumption that the security's "true" beta has a tandency over time to move toward the market average of 1.0.

Alpha The difference between a security's expected return and its equilibrium expected return.

Alternative Minimum Tax An Internal Revenue Code requirement that taxpayers with substantial tax-deductible items add back some of the deductions to their regular taxable income. To this income figure, another tax rate is applied. If the resulting tax is higher than the individual's normally-calculated tax, this alternative tax must be paid.

American Depository Receipts (ADRs) Financial assets issued by U.S. banks that represent indirect ownership of a certain number of shares of a specific foreign firm. ADRs are held on deposit in a bank in the firm's home country.

American Option An option that can be exercised any time through its expiration date.

Amortization A means of depreciating certain intangible assets for corporate income tax purposes.

Annual Percentage Rate (APR) With respect to a loan, the APR is the yield-to-maturity of the loan, computed using the most frequent time between payments as the compounding interval.

Anomaly An empirical regularity that is not predicted by any known asset pricing model.

Approved List A list of securities which an investment organization deems worthy of accumulation in a given portfolio. For an organization that uses an approved list, typically any security on the list may be purchased by the organization's portfolio managers without additional authorization.

Arbitrage The simultaneous purchase and sale of the same, or essentially similar, security in two different markets for advantageously different prices.

Arbitrage Pricing Theory An equilibrium model of asset pricing which states that the expected return on a security is a linear function of the security's sensitivity to various common factors.

Arbitrageur A person who engages in arbitrage.

Ask (or Asked) Price The price at which a market-maker is willing to sell a specified quantity of a particular security.

795

Asset Allocation The process of determining the optimal division of an investor's portfolio among available asset classes.

Asset Class A broadly defined generic group of financial assets, such as stocks or bonds.

Asymmetric Information A situation in which one party has more information than another party.

At the Money Option An option whose exercise price is roughly equal to the market price of its underlying asset.

Attribute See Factor Loading.

Automated Bond System (ABS) A computer system established by the New York Stock Exchange to facilitate the trading of inactive bonds.

Average Cost Method A method of valuing inventories that assumes that equal numbers of old and new goods are sold.

Average Return on Investment The total income earned from an investment in an asset, expressed as a percentage of the total investment in the asset.

Average Tax Rate The amount of taxes paid expressed as a percentage of the total income subject to tax.

Back-End Load See Redemption Fee.

Bank Discount Basis A method of calculating the interest rate on a fixed-income security that uses the principal of the security as the security's cost.

Bankers' Acceptance A type of money market instrument. It is a promissory note issued by a business debtor, with a stated maturity date, arising out of a business transaction. A bank, by endorsing the note, assumes the obligation. If this obligation becomes actively traded, it is referred to as a bankers acceptance.

Basis The difference between the spot price of an asset and the futures price of the same asset.

Basis Point 1/100th of 1%.

Basis Risk The risk to a futures investor of the basis widening or narrowing.

Bearer Bond A bond that has attached coupons representing the right to receive interest payments. The owner submits each coupon on its specified date to receive payment. Ownership is transferred simply by the seller endorsing the bond over to the buyer.

Benchmark Portfolio A portfolio against which the investment performance of an investor can be compared for the purpose of determining investment skill. A benchmark portfolio represents a relevant and feasible alternative to the investor's actual portfolio, and in particular, is similar in terms of risk exposure.

Best-Efforts Underwriting A security underwriting in which the members of the investment banking group serve as agents instead of dealers, agreeing only to obtain for the issuer the best price that the market will pay for the security.

Beta Coefficient (Alternatively, Market Beta.) A relative measure of the sensitivity of an asset's return to changes in the return on the market portfolio. Mathematically, the beta coefficient of a security is the security's covariance with the market portfolio divided by the variance of the market portfolio.

Bid-Ask Spread The difference between the price that a market-maker is willing to pay for a security and the price at which the market-maker is willing to sell the same security.

Bidder In the context of a corporate takeover, the firm making a tender offer to the target firm.

Bid Price The price at which a market-maker is willing to purchase a specified quantity of a particular security.

Block House A brokerage firm with the financial capacity and the trading expertise to deal in block trades.

Block Trade A large order (usually 10,000 shares or more) to buy or sell a security.

Bond Ratings An indicator of the creditworthiness of specific bond issues. These ratings are often interpreted as an indication of the likelihood of default on the part of the respective bond issuers.

Bond Swap A form of active bond management which entails the replacement of bonds in a portfolio with other bonds so as to enhance the yield of the portfolio.

Book Value of the Equity The sum of the cumulative retained earnings and other balance sheet entries classified under stockholders' equity such as common stock and capital contributed in excess of par value.

Book Value Per Share A corporation's book value of the equity divided by the number of its common shares outstanding.

Bottom-Up Forecasting A sequential approach to security analysis which entails first making forecasts for individual companies, then for industries, and finally for the economy. Each level of forecasts is conditional on the previous level of forecasts made.

Broker An agent, or middleman, who facilitates the buying and selling of securities for investors.

Call Market A security market in which trading is allowed only at certain specified times. At those times, persons interested in trading a particular security are physically brought together and a market clearing price is established.

Call Money Rate The interest rate paid by brokerage firms to banks on loans used to finance margin purchases by the brokerage firm's customers.

Call Option A contract that gives the buyer the right to buy a specific number of shares of a company from the option writer at a specific purchase price during a specific time period.

Call Premium The difference between the call price of a bond and the par value of the bond.

Call Price The price that an issuer must pay bondholders when an issue is retired prior to its stated maturity date.

Call Provision A provision in some bond indentures that permits an issuer to retire some or all of the bonds in a particular bond issue prior to the bonds' stated maturity date.

Capital Asset Pricing Model (CAPM) An equilibrium model of asset pricing which states that the expected return in a security is a positive linear function of the security's sensitivity to changes in the market portfolio's return.

Capital Consumption Adjustment As calculated by the U.S. Department of Commerce, a measure of the portion of corporate earnings attributable to understated depreciation due to inflation. It is the estimated difference between aggregate depreciation of corporate fixed assets based on historic cost and aggregate depreciation based on replacement cost.

Capital Gain (or Loss) The difference between the current market value of an asset and the original cost of the asset, with the cost adjusted for any improvement or depreciation in the asset.

Capital Market Line The set of portfolios obtainable by combining the market portfolio with riskfree borrowing or lending. Assuming homogeneous expectations and perfect markets, the Capital Market Line represents the efficient set.

Capital Markets Financial markets in which financial assets with a term-to-maturity of typically more than one year are traded.

Capitalization of Income Method of Valuation An approach to valuing financial assets. It is based on the concept that the "true" or intrinsic value of a financial asset is equal to the discounted value of future cash flows generated by that asset.

Capitalization-Weighted Market Index See Value-Weighted Market Index.

Cash Account An account maintained by an investor with a brokerage firm in which deposits (cash and the proceeds from security sales) must fully cover withdrawals (cash and the costs of security purchases).

Cash Matching A form of immunization which involves the purchase of bonds that generate a stream of cash inflows identical in amount and timing to a set of expected cash outflows over a given period of time.

Certainty Equivalent Return For a particular risky investment, the return on a riskfree investment which makes the investor indifferent between the risky and riskfree investments.

Certificate of Deposit A form of time deposit issued by banks and other financial institutions.

Certificate of Incorporation See Charter.

Characteristic Line (Alternatively, Market Model.) A simple linear regression model expressing the relationship between the excess return on a security and the excess return on the market portfolio.

Charter (Alternatively, Certificate of Incorporation.) A document issued by a state to a corporation that specifies the rights and obligations of the corporation's stockholders.

Chartist A technical analyst who primarily relies on stock price and volume charts when evaluating securities.

Clearinghouse A cooperative venture between banks, brokerage firms, and other financial intermediaries, which maintains records of transactions made by member firms during a trading day. At the end of the trading day, the clearinghouse calculates net amounts of securities and cash to be delivered among the members, permitting each member to settle once with the clearinghouse.

Close See Closing price.

Closed-End Investment Company A managed investment company, with an unlimited life, that does not stand ready to purchase its own shares from its owners and rarely issues new shares beyond its initial offering.

Closing Price (Alternatively, Close.) The price at which the last trade of the day took place in a particular stock.

Closing Purchase The purchase of an option contract by an investor that is designed to offset, and thereby cancel, the previous sale of the same option contract by the investor.

Closing Sale The sale of an option contract by an investor that is designed to offset, and thereby cancel, the previous purchase of the same option contract by the investor.

Coefficient of Determination (Alternatively, R-squared.) In the context of a simple linear regression, the proportion of the variation in the dependent variable that is related to variation in (that is, "explained by") the independent variable.

Coefficient of Nondetermination In the context

of a simple linear regression, the proportion of the variation in the dependent variable that is not related to variation in (that is, not "explained by") the independent variable. Equivalently, one minus the coefficient of determination.

Coincident Indicators Economic variables which have been found to change at the same time that the economy is changing.

Collateral Trust Bond A bond that is backed by other financial assets.

Commercial Paper A type of money market instrument. It represents unsecured promissory notes of large, financially sound corporations.

Commingled Fund An investment fund, offered by a bank or insurance company, which is similar to a mutual fund in that investors are permitted to purchase and redeem units that represent ownership in a pool of securities.

Commission The fee an investor pays to a brokerage firm for services rendered in the trading of securities.

Commission Broker A member of an organized security exchange who takes orders that the public has placed with brokerage firms and sees that these orders are executed on the exchange.

Commodity Fund An investment company that speculates in futures.

Commodity Futures Trading Commission (CFTC) A federal agency established by the Commodity Futures Trading Commission Act of 1974 that approves (or disapproves) the creation of new futures contracts and regulates the trading of existing futures contracts.

Common Factor A factor which affects the return on virtually all securities to a certain extent.

Common Stock Legal representation of an equity (or ownership) position in a corporation.

Comparative Performance Attribution Comparing the performance of a portfolio with that of one or more other portfolios (or market indices) in order to determine the sources of the differences in their returns.

Competitive Bidding With respect to selecting an underwriter, the process of an issuer soliciting bids on the underwriting and choosing the underwriter offering the best overall terms.

Competitive Trader See Floor Trader.

Composite Stock Price Tables Price information provided on all stocks traded on the national exchanges, the regional stock exchanges, the NASDAQ system, and the Instinet system.

Compounding The payment of interest on interest.

Consolidated Quotations System A system which lists current bid-ask prices of specialists on the national and regional stock exchanges and of certain over-the-counter dealers.

Consolidated Tape A system which reports trades that occur on the national stock exchanges, the regional stock exchanges, the NASDAQ system, and the Instinet system.

Constant Growth Model A type of dividend discount model in which dividends are assumed to exhibit a constant growth rate.

Consumer Price Index A cost-of-living index which is representative of the goods and services purchased by U.S. consumers.

Contingent Deferred Sales Charge See Redemption Fee.

Contingent Immunization A form of bond management that entails both passive and active elements. Under contingent immunization, as long as "favorable" results are obtained, the bond portfolio is actively managed. However, if "unfavorable" results occur, then the portfolio is immediately immunized.

Continuous Market A security market in which trades may occur at any time during business hours.

Convertible Bond A bond which may, at the holder's option, be exchanged for other securities, often common stock.

Corner Portfolio An efficient portfolio possessing the property that, if combined with any adjacent corner portfolio, the combination will produce another efficient portfolio.

Correlation Coefficient A statistical measure similar to covariance, in that it measures the degree of mutual variation between two random variables. The correlation coefficient rescales covariance to facilitate comparison among pairs of random variables. The correlation coefficient is bounded by the values -1 and $+1$.

Cost-of-Living Index A collection of goods and services, and their associated prices, designed to reflect changes over time in the cost of making normal consumption expenditures.

Cost Method of Depletion A method of depleting natural resources for corporate income tax purposes that takes the total cost of finding or purchasing a "wasting asset" and, for a given time period, expenses an amount based on the proportion of the estimated resource that has been sold during that period.

Coupon Payments The periodic payment of interest on a bond.

Coupon Rate The annual dollar amount of coupon payments made by a bond expressed as a percentage of the bond's par value.

Coupon Stripping The process of separating and selling the individual cash flows of Treasury notes or bonds.

Covariance A statistical measure of the relationship between two random variables. It measures the extent of mutual variation between two random variables.

Covered Call Writing The process of writing a call option on an asset owned by the option writer.

Cross-Deductibility An arrangement among federal and state tax authorities that permits state taxes to be deductible expenses for federal tax purposes, and federal taxes to be deductible expenses for state tax purposes.

Crown Jewel Defense A strategy used by corporations to ward off hostile takeovers. The strategy entails the target company selling off its most attractive assets to make itself less attractive to the acquiring firm.

Cumulative Dividends A common feature of preferred stock which requires that the issuing corporation pay all previously unpaid preferred stock dividends before any common stock dividends may be paid.

Cumulative Voting System In the context of a corporation, a method of voting in which a stockholder is permitted to give any one candidate for the board of directors a maximum number of votes equal to the number of shares owned by that shareholder times the number of directors being elected.

Currency Risk See Exchange Risk.

Current Yield The annual dollar amount of coupon payments made by a bond expressed as a percentage of the bond's current market price.

Date of Record The date, established quarterly by a corporation's board of directors, on which the stockholders of record are determined for the purpose of paying a cash or stock dividend.

Day-of-the-Week Effect (Alternatively, Weekend Effect.) An empirical regularity whereby stock returns appear to be lower on Mondays as opposed to other days of the week.

Day Order A trading order for which the broker will attempt to fill the order only during the day in which it was entered.

Dealer (Alternatively, Market-Maker.) A person who facilitates the trading of financial assets by maintaining an inventory in particular securities. The dealer buys for and sells from this inventory, profiting from the difference in the buying and selling prices.

Dealer's Spread The bid-asked spread quoted by a security dealer.

Debenture A bond that is not secured by specific property.

Debit Balance The dollar amount borrowed from a broker as the result of a margin purchase.

Debt Refunding The issuance of new debt for the purpose of paying off currently maturing debt.

Dedicated Portfolio A portfolio of bonds that provides its owner with cash inflows that are matched against a specific stream of cash outflows.

Deep Discount Bond A bond whose coupon interest rate is considerably below those of other bonds which otherwise possess similar attributes. Hence, these bonds sell at prices significantly below the other bonds.

Default Premium The difference between the promised and expected yield-to-maturity on a bond arising from the possibility that the bond issuer might default on the bond.

Delisting The process of removing a security's eligibility for trading on an organized security exchange.

Delta See Hedge Ratio.

Demand Deposit A checking account at a financial institution.

Demand for Capital (Alternatively, Marginal Efficiency of Capital.) The quantity of capital desired by an investor at varying interest-rate levels.

Demand-to-Buy Schedule A description of the quantities of a security that an investor is prepared to purchase at alternative prices.

Demand-to-Hold Schedule A description of the quantities of a security that an investor desires to maintain in his or her portfolio at alternative prices.

Depletion A means of depreciating certain natural resource assets for corporate income tax purposes.

Depository Trust Company A central computerized depository for securities registered in the names of member firms. Members' security certificates are immobilized and computerized records of ownership are maintained. This permits electronic transfer of the securities from one member to another as trades are conducted between the members' clients.

Depreciation An accounting procedure that allocates the cost of a fixed asset over the estimated useful life of the asset.

Differential Return See Ex Post Alpha.

Discount Broker An organization that offers a limited range of brokerage services and charges fees substantially below those of brokerage firms that provide a full range of services.

Discount Factor The present value of one dollar

to be received from a security in specified number of years.

Discount Rate The interest rate used in calculating the present value of future cash flows. The discount rate reflects not only the time value of money, but also the riskiness of the cash flows.

Discounting The process of calculating the present value of a given stream of cash flows.

Discretionary Order A trading order that permits the broker to set the specifications for the order.

Disintermediation A pattern of funds flow whereby investors withdraw funds from financial intermediaries, such as banks and savings and loans, because market interest rates exceed the maximum interest rates that these organizations are permitted to pay. The investors reinvest their funds in financial assets which pay interest rates not subject to ceilings.

Diversification The process of adding securities to a portfolio in order to reduce the portfolio's unique risk and, thereby, the portfolio's total risk.

Dividend Decision The process of determining the amount of dividends that a corporation will pay its shareholders.

Dividend Discount Model The term used for the capitalization of income method of valuation as applied to common stocks. All variants of dividend discount models assume that the intrinsic value of a share of common stock is equal to the discounted value of the dividends forecast to be paid on the stock.

Dividend Yield The current annualized dividend paid on a share of common stock, expressed as a percentage of the current market price of the corporation's common stock.

Dividends Cash payments made to stockholders by the corporation.

Dollar-Weighted Return A method of measuring the performance of a portfolio over a particular period of time. It is the discount rate which makes the present value of cash flows into and out of the portfolio, as well as the portfolio's ending value, equal to the portfolio's beginning value.

Domestic Return The return on an investment in a foreign financial asset, excluding the impact of exchange rate changes.

Double Auction Bidding among both buyers and sellers for a security that may occur when the specialist's bid-ask spread is large enough to permit sales at one or more prices within the spread.

Duration A measure of the average maturity of the stream of payments generated by a financial asset. Mathematically, duration is the weighted average of the lengths of time until the asset's remaining payments are made. The weights in this calculation are the proportion of the asset's total present value represented by the present value of the respective cash flows.

Earnings Per Share A corporation's accounting earnings divided by the number of its common shares outstanding.

Earnings-Price Ratio The reciprocal of the price-earnings ratio.

Econometric Model A statistical model designed to explain and forecast certain economic phenomena.

Economic Earnings The change in the economic value of the firm plus dividends paid to shareholders.

Economic Value of the Firm The aggregate market value of all securities issued by the firm.

Efficient Market A market for securities in which every security's price equals its investment value at all times, implying that a set of information is fully and immediately reflected in market prices.

Efficient Portfolio A portfolio within the feasible set which offers investors both maximum expected return for varying levels of risk and minimum risk for varying levels of expected return.

Efficient Set (Frontier) The set of efficient portfolios.

Efficient Set Theorem The proposition that investors will choose their portfolios only from the set of efficient portfolios.

Empirical Regularities Differences in returns on securities that occur with regularity from period to period. Of particular interest are empirical regularities not consistent with the Capital Asset Pricing Model.

Endogenous Variable In the context of an econometric model, an economic variable which represents the economic phenomena explained by the model.

Equal-Weighted Market Index A market index in which all the component securities contribute equally to the value of the index, regardless of the various attributes of those securities.

Equilibrium Expected Return The expected return on a security assuming that the security is correctly priced by the market. This "fair" return is determined by an appropriate asset pricing model.

Equipment Obligation (Alternatively, Equipment Trust Certificate.) A bond which is backed by specific pieces of equipment that, if necessary, can be readily sold and delivered to a new owner.

Equipment Trust Certificate See Equipment Obligation.

Equity Trust A type of REIT that makes equity investments in real estate.

Equivalent Yield   The annualized yield-to-maturity on a fixed-income security sold on a discount basis.

Estimated Useful Life   For corporate income tax purposes, the period over which a fixed asset is expected to contribute to the company's revenue.

Eurobond   A bond that is offered outside of the country of the borrower and usually outside of the country in whose currency the security is denominated.

Eurodollar Certificate of Deposit   A certificate of deposit denominated in U.S. dollars and issued by banks domiciled outside of the U.S.

Eurodollar Deposit   A U.S. dollar-denominated time deposit held at a bank domiciled outside of the U.S.

European Option   An option that can only be exercised on its expiration date.

Ex Ante   Before the fact; future.

Ex-Dividend Date   The date on which ownership of stock is determined for purposes of paying dividends. Owners purchasing shares before the ex-dividend date receive the dividend in question. Owners purchasing shares on or after the ex-dividend date are not entitled to the dividend.

Ex Post   After the fact; historical.

Ex Post Alpha   (Alternatively, Differential Return.) A portfolio's alpha calculated on an *ex post* basis. Mathematically, over an evaluation interval, it is the difference between the average return on the portfolio and the equilibrium average return on a portfolio of equal market risk.

Ex Post Selection Bias   In the context of constructing a security valuation model, the use of securities that have performed well and the avoidance of securities that have performed poorly, thus making the model appear more effective than it truly is.

Ex-Rights Date   The date on which ownership of stock is determined for purposes of granting rights to purchase new stock in a rights offering. Owners purchasing shares before the ex-rights date receive the rights in question. Owners purchasing shares on or after the ex-rights date are not entitled to the rights.

Excess Return   The difference between the return on a security and the return on a riskfree asset.

Exchange Distribution or Acquisition   A trade involving a large block of stock on an organized security exchange whereby a brokerage firm attempts to execute the order by finding enough offsetting orders from its customers.

Exchange Risk   (Alternatively, Currency Risk.) The uncertainty in the return on a foreign financial asset due to unpredictability regarding the rate at which the foreign currency can be exchanged into the investor's own currency.

Exercise Price   (Alternatively, Striking Price.) In the case of a call option, the price at which an option buyer may purchase the underlying asset from the option writer. In the case of a put option, the price at which an option buyer may sell the underlying asset to the option writer.

Exit Fee   See Redemption Fee.

Exogenous Variables   In the context of an econometric model, an economic variable taken as given and used in the model to explain the model's endogenous variables.

Expectations Hypothesis   A hypothesis that the futures price of an asset is equal to the expected spot price of the asset on the delivery date of the futures contract.

Expected Rate of Inflation   That portion of inflation experienced over a given period of time that was anticipated by investors.

Expected Return   The return on a security (or portfolio) over a holding period that an investor anticipates receiving.

Expected Return Vector   A column of numbers that correspond to the expected returns for a set of securities.

Expected Value   A measure of central tendency of the probability distribution of a random variable. Equivalently, the mean of the random variable.

Expected Yield-to-Maturity   The yield-to-maturity on a bond calculated as a weighted average of all possible yields that the bond might produce under different scenarios of default or late payments, where the weights are the probabilities of each scenario occurring.

Expiration Date   The date on which the right to buy or sell a security under an option contract ceases.

Face Value   See Principal.

Factor   (Alternatively, Index.) An aspect of the investment environment which influences the returns of financial assets. To the extent that a factor influences a significant number of financial assets, it is termed common or pervasive.

Factor Beta   A relative measure of the mutual variation of a particular common factor with the return on the market portfolio. Mathematically, a factor beta is the covariance of the factor with the market portfolio, divided by the variance of the market portfolio.

Factor Loading   (Alternatively, Attribute or Sensitivity.) A measure of the responsiveness of a security's returns to a particular common factor.

Factor Model   (Alternatively, Index Model.) A re-

turn generating process which attributes the return on a security to the security's sensitivity to the movements of various common factors.

Factor Risk That part of a security's total risk which is related to moves in various common factors and, hence, cannot be diversified away.

Fail to Deliver A situation in which a seller's broker is unable to deliver the traded security to the buyer's broker on or before the required settlement date.

Feasible Set (Alternatively, Opportunity Set.) The set of all portfolios that can be formed from the group of securities being considered by an investor.

Federally Sponsored Agency A privately owned federal agency that issues securities and uses the proceeds to support the granting of various types of special purpose loans.

Fill-or-Kill Order A trading order which is cancelled if the broker is unable to execute it immediately.

Financial Analyst (Alternatively, Security Analyst or Investment Analyst.) An individual who analyzes financial assets in order to determine the investment characteristics of those assets and to identify mispricings among those assets.

Financial Asset See Security.

Financial Institution See Financial Intermediary.

Financial Intermediary (Alternatively, Financial Institution.) An organization that issues financial claims against itself and uses the proceeds of the issuance primarily to purchase financial assets issued by corporations, government entities, and other financial intermediaries.

Financial Investment An investment in financial assets.

Financial Leverage The use of debt to fund a portion of an investment.

Financial Market (Alternatively, Security Market.) A mechanism designed to facilitate the exchange of financial assets by bringing buyers and sellers of securities together.

Firm Commitment An arrangement between underwriters and a security issuer whereby the underwriters agree to purchase, at the offering price, all of the issue not bought by the public.

First-in-First-out Method (FIFO) A method of valuing inventories that assumes that the company's inventory is sold in direct order of accumulation.

Fixed Annuity A series of payments of a fixed and equal amount.

Floating Rate (Alternatively, Variable Rate.) A rate of interest on a financial asset that may vary over the life of the asset, depending on changes in a specified indicator of current market interest rates.

Floor Broker A member of an organized security exchange who assists commission brokers when there are too many orders flowing into the market for the commission brokers to handle alone.

Floor Trader (Alternatively, Competitive Trader or Registered Competitive Market Maker or Registered Trader.) A member of an organized security exchange who trades solely for his or her own account and is prohibited by exchange rules from handling public orders.

Foreign Return The return on an investment in a foreign financial asset, including the impact of exchange rate changes.

Forward Rate The interest rate that links the current spot interest rate over one holding period to the current spot interest rate over a longer holding period. Equivalently, the interest rate agreed to at a point in time where the loan will be made at a future date.

Fourth Market A secondary security market in which investors (typically, financial institutions) trade securities directly with each other, bypassing the brokers and dealers on organized security exchanges and the over-the-counter market.

Fundamental Analysis A form of security analysis which seeks to determine the intrinsic value of securities based on underlying economic factors. These intrinsic values are compared to current market prices to estimate current levels of mispricing.

Futures (Futures Contract) An agreement between two people under which the seller promises to deliver a specific asset on a specific future date to the buyer for a predetermined price to be paid on the delivery date.

Futures Option (Alternatively, Options on Futures.) An option contract for which the deliverable asset is a specific futures contract.

General Obligation Bond A municipal bond that is backed by the full faith and credit of the issuing agency.

Generally Accepted Accounting Principles (GAAP) Accounting rules established by recognized authorities, such as the Financial Accounting Standards Board (FASB).

Geometric Mean Return The compounded per-period average rate of return on a financial asset over a specified time interval.

Good-Till-Cancelled Order See Open Order.

Greenmail An offer by the management of a corporation that is the target of a hostile takeover to repurchase its shares from the hostile bidder at an above-market price.

Group In the context of a specific asset class, a collection of financial assets that have common distinguishing financial characteristics.

Group Selection A component of the security selection process involving the identification of desirable combinations of groups within an asset class.

Guaranteed Bond A bond issued by one corporation but backed by another corporation

Hedge Ratio (Alternatively, Delta.) The expected change in the value of an option per dollar change in the market price of the underlying asset.

Hedger An investor in futures contracts whose primary objective is to offset an otherwise risky position.

Historical Beta An estimate of a security's beta, derived solely from historical returns. Equivalently, the slope of the ex post characteristic line.

Holding Period The length of time over which an investor is assumed to invest a given sum of money.

Holdout Sample See Out-of-Sample Data.

Homogeneous Expectations A situation in which all investors possess the same perceptions with regard to the expected returns, standard deviations, and covariances of securities.

Horizon Analysis A form of active bond management where a single holding period is selected for analysis and possible yield structures at the end of the period are considered. Bonds with the most attractive expected returns under the alternative yield structures are selected for the portfolio.

Hypothecation Agreement A legal arrangement between a brokerage firm and an investor that permits the brokerage firm to pledge the investor's securities as collateral for bank loans, provided the securities were purchased through the investor's margin account.

Idiosyncratic Risk See Nonfactor Risk.

Immunization A bond portfolio management technique that permits an investor to meet a promised stream of cash outflows with a high degree of certainty.

Implicit Volatility The risk of an asset derived from an options valuation model, assuming that an option on the asset is fairly priced by the market.

Implied Return See Internal Rate of Return.

In the Money Option In the case of a call (put) option, an option whose exercise price is less than (greater than) the market price of its underlying asset.

Income Bond A bond for which the size of the interest payments varies, based on the income of the issuer.

Indenture A legal document formally describing the terms of the legal relationship between a bond issuer and bondholders.

Index See Factor.

Index Arbitrage An investment strategy that involves buying a stock index futures contract and selling the individual stocks in the index or selling a stock index futures contract and buying the individual stocks in the index. The strategy is designed to take advantage of a mispricing between the stock index futures contract and the underlying stocks.

Index Fund A passively managed investment in a diversified portfolio of financial assets designed to mimic the investment performance of a specific market index.

Index Model See Factor Model.

Indifference Curve All combinations of portfolios, considered in terms of expected returns and risk, that provide an investor with an equal amount of satisfaction.

Industrial Development Bond (IDB) A form of revenue bond used to finance the purchase or construction of industrial facilities that are leased by the issuing municipality to firms on a favorable basis.

Inefficient Portfolio A portfolio that does not satisfy the criteria of an efficient portfolio and, hence, does not lie on the efficient set.

Inflation The rate of change in a price index over a certain period of time. Equivalently, the percentage change in the purchasing power of a unit of currency over a certain period of time.

Inflation Hedge An asset which preserves the value of its purchasing power over time despite changes in the price level.

Information Content of Dividends Hypothesis The proposition that dividend announcements contain inside information about a corporation's future prospects.

Initial Margin Requirement The minimum percentage of a margin purchase (or short sale) price that must come from the investor's own funds.

Initial Public Offering (IPO) (Alternatively, Unseasoned Offering.) The first offering of the shares of a company to the public.

Initial Wealth The value of an investor's portfolio at the beginning of a holding period.

Insider Narrowly defined, stockholders, officers, and directors of a corporation who own a "significant" proportion of a corporation's stock. More broadly defined, anyone who has access to information that is both "materially" related to the value of a corporation's securities and is unavailable to the general public.

Instinet Acronym for Institutional Network. A

computerized communications system that provides price quotations and order execution for fourth market participants.

Interest Rate Risk   The uncertainty in the return on a fixed-income security caused by unanticipated fluctuations in value of the asset due to changes in interest rates.

Intermarket Spread Swap   A type of bond swap where an investor moves out of one market segment and into another because the investor believes that one segment is significantly underpriced relative to the other.

Intermarket Trading System   An electronic communications network that links the national and regional organized security exchanges and certain over-the-counter dealers. The network provides market-maker price quotes and allows participating brokers and dealers to route orders to market-makers offering the best prices.

Internal Rate of Return   (Alternatively, Implied Return.) The discount rate that equates the present value of future cash flows expected to be received from a particular investment to the cost of that investment.

Intrinsic Value of an Option   The value of an option if it were exercised immediately. Equivalently, the market price of the asset upon which a call option is written less the exercise price of the option (or the exercise price less the market price of the asset in the case of a put option).

Inventory Valuation Adjustment   As calculated by the U.S. Department of Commerce, a measure of the portion of corporate earnings attributable to changes in the value of inventories due to inflation.

Investment   The sacrifice of certain present value for (possibly uncertain) future value.

Investment Advisor   An individual or organization that provides investment advice to investors.

Investment Analyst   See Financial Analyst.

Investment Banker   (Alternatively, Underwriter.) An organization that acts as an intermediary between issuers and the ultimate purchasers of securities in the primary security market.

Investment Banking   The process of analyzing and selecting a means of procuring financing on behalf of an issuer of securities.

Investment Committee   Within a traditional investment organization, a group of senior management responsible for establishing the organization's broad investment strategy.

Investment Company   A type of financial intermediary which obtains money from investors and uses that money to purchase financial assets. In return, the investors receive shares in the investment company, and thus indirectly own a proportion of the financial assets that the company itself owns.

Investment Environment   The financial structure in which investors operate, consisting of the kinds of marketable securities available for purchase or sale and the process by which these securities are bought and sold.

Investment Grade Bonds   Bonds which possess bond ratings that permit them to be purchased by the vast majority of institutional investors, particularly regulated financial institutions. Usually, investment grade bonds have a BBB (Standard & Poor's) or Baa (Moody's) or higher bond rating.

Investment Policy   A component of the investment process that involves determining an investor's objectives and the amount of the funds available to invest.

Investment Process   The set of procedures by which an investor decides what marketable securities to invest in, how extensive those investments should be, and when the investments should be made.

Investment Style   The method an investor uses to take active positions in certain types of securities.

Investment Value   The present value of a security's future prospects as estimated by well-informed market participants.

January Effect   An empirical regularity whereby stock returns appear to be higher in January as opposed to other months of the year.

Junk Bonds   See Speculative Grade Bonds.

Lagging Indicators   Economic variables which have been found to follow movements in the economy.

Lambda   The expected return premium (above the riskfree rate of interest) per unit of sensitivity to a particular common factor.

Last-in-First-out Method (LIFO)   A method of valuing inventories that assumes that the company's inventory is sold in inverse order of accumulation.

Leading Indicators   Economic variables which have been found to signal future changes in the economy.

Letter Stock   (Alternatively, Restricted Stock.) Stock which is unregistered and sold directly to the purchaser, rather than through a public offering. Such stock must be held at least two years and cannot be sold even at that time unless ample information on the company is available and the amount sold is a relatively small percentage of the total shares outstanding.

Limit Order   A trading order which specifies a limit price at which the broker is to execute the order. The trade will be executed only if the broker can meet or better the limit price.

Limit Order Book (Alternatively, Specialist's Book.) The records kept by the specialist identifying the limit, stop, and stop limit orders that brokers want to execute in a particular security.

Limit Price The price specified when a limit order is placed with a broker, defining the maximum purchase price or minimum selling price at which the order can be executed.

Limited Liability An aspect of the corporate form of organization that prevents common stockholders from losing more than their investment if the corporation should default on its obligations.

Liquidity (Alternatively, Marketability.) The ability of investors to convert securities to cash at a price similar to the price of the previous trade in the security, assuming no significant new information has arrived since the previous trade. Equivalently, the ability to sell an asset quickly without having to make a substantial price concession.

Liquidity Preference (Premium) Theory An explanation of the term structure of interest rates. It holds that the term structure is a result of the preference of investors for short-term securities. Investors can only be induced to hold longer-term securities if they expect to receive a higher return.

Liquidity Premium The expected incremental return of longer-term securities over shorter-term securities that compensates investors for the greater interest rate risk entailed in holding longer-term securities.

Listed Security A security that is traded on an organized security exchange.

Load Charge A sales charge levied by a mutual fund when an investor buys its shares.

Load Fund A mutual fund that has a load charge.

Local (Alternatively, Scalper.) A member of an organized futures exchange who trades for his or her own account and has a very short holding period.

Long Hedger A hedger who offsets risk by buying futures contracts.

Low-Load Fund A mutual fund that has a small load charge, usually 3.5% or less.

Maintenance Margin Requirement The minimum actual margin that a brokerage firm will permit investors to keep in their margin accounts.

Majority Voting System (Alternatively, Straight Voting System.) In the context of a corporation, a method of voting in which a stockholder is permitted to give any one candidate for the board of directors a maximum number of votes equal to the number of shares owned by that shareholder.

Managed Investment Company An investment company with a portfolio that may be altered at the discretion of the company's portfolio manager.

Margin Account An account maintained by an investor with a brokerage firm in which securities may be purchased by borrowing a portion of the purchase price from the brokerage firm, or may be sold short by borrowing the securities from the brokerage firm.

Margin Call A demand upon an investor by a brokerage firm to increase the equity in the investor's margin account. The margin call is initiated when the investor's actual margin falls below the maintenance margin requirement.

Margin Purchase The purchase of securities financed by borrowing a portion of the purchase price from a brokerage firm.

Marginal Efficiency of Capital See Demand for Capital.

Marginal Return on Investment The additional income, expressed as a percentage, earned on each additional dollar invested in an asset.

Marginal Tax Rate The amount of taxes, expressed as a percentage, paid on each additional dollar of taxable income received.

Markdown The difference in prices between what an investor's broker receives and what the investor receives for a security sold in the over-the-counter market.

Marked (or Marking) to the Market The process of calculating, on a daily basis, the actual margin in an investor's account. Equivalently, the daily process of adjusting the equity in an investor's account to reflect the daily changes in the market value of the account's assets and liabilities.

Market Beta See Beta Coefficient.

Market Capitalization The aggregate market value of a security, equal to the market price per unit of the security multiplied times the total number of outstanding units of the security.

Market Discount Function The set of discount factors on all default-free bonds across the spectrum of terms-to-maturity.

Market Index A collection of securities whose prices are averaged to reflect the overall investment performance of a particular market for financial assets.

Market-Maker See Dealer.

Market Model See Characteristic Line.

Market Order A trading order which instructs the broker to buy or sell a security immediately at the best obtainable price.

Market Portfolio A portfolio consisting of an investment in all securities. The proportion invested in each security equals the percentage of the total market capitalization represented by the security.

Market Risk (Alternatively, Systematic Risk.) A

part of a security's total risk that is related to moves in the market portfolio and, hence, cannot be diversified away.

Market Segmentation Theory An explanation of the term structure of interest rates. It holds that various investors and borrowers are restricted by law, preference, or custom to certain maturity ranges. Spot rates in each market segment are determined by supply and demand conditions there.

Market Timing A form of active management that entails shifting an investor's funds between a surrogate market portfolio and a riskfree asset, depending on the investor's perception of their near-term prospects.

Marketability See Liquidity.

Markup The difference in prices between what an investor pays and what the investor's broker pays for a security purchased in the over-the-counter market.

Maturity Date The date upon which a bond issuer repays investors the principal of the bond.

May Day The date (May 1, 1975) that the New York Stock Exchange ended its fixed-commission rate requirement and permitted member firms to negotiate commission rates with customers.

Member Corporation See Member Firm.

Member Firm (Alternatively, Member Corporation or Member Organization.) A brokerage firm with one or more memberships in an organized security exchange.

Member Organization See Member Firm.

Merger A form of corporate takeover in which two firms combine their operations and become one firm. Mergers are usually negotiated by the management of the two merging corporations.

Mispriced Security A security that is trading at a price substantially different than its intrinsic value.

Money Market Deposit A short-term fixed income security.

Money Markets Financial markets in which financial assets with a term-to-maturity of typically one year or less are traded.

Mortgage Bond A bond which is secured by the pledge of specific property. In the event of default, bondholders are entitled to obtain the property in question and sell it to satisfy their claims on the issuer.

Mortgage Trust A type of REIT that invests primarily in mortgages as well as construction and development loans.

Multinational Firm A company whose business operations and financial investments extend across a number of countries.

Multiple Growth Model A type of dividend discount model in which dividends are assumed to grow at different rates over specifically defined time periods.

Municipal Bond A bond issued by a state or local unit of government.

Mutual Fund See Open-end Investment Company.

Naked Call Writing The process of writing a call option on a stock that the option writer does not own.

Naked Put Writing The process of writing a put option on a stock when the writer does not have the sufficient cash (or securities) in his or her brokerage account to purchase the stock.

National Association of Securities Dealers (NASD) A self-regulatory agency which establishes rules and regulations and monitors the activities of brokers and dealers in the over-the-counter market.

National Association of Securities Dealers Automated Quotations (NASDAQ) An automated nationwide communications network operated by the NASD which connects dealers and brokers in the over-the-counter market. NASDAQ provides current market-maker bid-ask price quotes to market participants.

National Market System (NASDAQ/NMS) A segment of the over-the-counter market comprised of issues with relatively large trading volumes. More detailed trading information is provided on stocks included in NASDAQ/NMS than on other over-the-counter stocks.

Net Asset Value The market value of an investment company's assets, less any liabilities, divided by the number of shares outstanding.

Net Present Value The present value of future cash flows expected to be received from a particular investment less the cost of that investment.

No Growth Model See Zero Growth Model.

No-Load Fund A mutual fund that does not have a load charge.

Nominal Return The percentage change in the value of an investment in a financial asset, where the beginning and ending values of the asset are not adjusted for inflation over the time of the investment.

Nonfactor Risk (Alternatively, Idiosyncratic Risk or Security Specific Risk.) That part of a security's total risk which is not related to moves in various common factors and, hence, can be diversified away.

Nonmarket Risk See Unique Risk.

Nonsatiation A condition whereby investors are assumed to always prefer higher levels of terminal wealth to lower levels of terminal wealth.

Normal Backwardation An expected relationship between the futures price of an asset and the expected spot price of the asset on the delivery date of the contract. Normal backwardation states that the futures price will be less than the expected spot price.

Normal Contango An expected relationship between the futures price of an asset and the expected spot price of the asset on the delivery date of the contract. Normal contango states that the futures price will be greater than the expected spot price.

Normal Probability Distribution A symmetrical bell-shaped probability distribution, completely described by its mean and standard deviation.

Normative Economics A form of economic analysis which is prescriptive in nature, dealing with what "ought to be."

Odd Lot An amount of stock, generally from 1 to 99 shares.

Open See Opening Price.

Open-End Investment Company (Alternatively, Mutual Fund.) A managed investment company, with an unlimited life, that stands ready at all times to purchase its shares from its owners and usually will continuously offer new shares to the public.

Open Interest The number of a particular futures contract that are outstanding at a particular point in time.

Open Order (Alternatively, Good-Till-Cancelled Order.) A trading order which remains in effect until it is either filled or cancelled by the investor.

Opening Price (Alternatively, Open.) The price at which the first trade of the day took place in a particular stock.

Opportunity Set See Feasible Set.

Optimal Portfolio The feasible portfolio that offers an investor the maximum level of satisfaction. This portfolio represents the tangency between the efficient set and an indifference curve of the investor.

Option A contract between two investors in which one investor grants the other the right to buy (or sell) a specific asset at a specific price within a specific time period.

Options on Futures See Futures Option.

Order Book Officials The people who keep the limit order book in those option markets that involve market-makers instead of specialists.

Order Specification The investor's instructions to a broker regarding the particular characteristics of a trading order, including the name of the security's issuing firm, whether to buy or sell, order size, max-

imum time the order is to be outstanding, and the type of order to be used.

Ordinary Least Squares See Simple Linear Regression.

Organized Exchange A central physical location where trading of securities is done under a set of rules and regulations.

Original Issue Discount Security A security which is issued with a coupon interest rate below prevailing market interest rates on similar securities and, thus, is originally sold at a discount from par value.

Out of the Money Option In the case of a call (put) option, an option whose exercise price is greater than (less than) the market price of its underlying asset.

Out-of-Sample Data (Alternatively, Holdout Sample.) In the context of constructing a security valuation model, information which is obtained from periods different than those used to estimate the valuation model.

Overmargined Account (Alternatively, Unrestricted Account.) A margin account in which the actual margin has risen above the initial margin requirement.

Overpriced Security (Alternatively, Overvalued Security.) A security whose expected return is less than its equilibrium expected return. Equivalently, a security with a negative alpha.

Oversubscription Privilege The opportunity given shareholders who have exercised their rights in a rights offering to buy shares that were not purchased in the offering.

Over-the-Counter Market (OTC Market) A secondary market for securities distinct from an organized security exchange.

Overvalued Security See Overpriced Security.

Pac-Man Defense A strategy used by corporations to ward off hostile takeovers. The targeted company reverses the takeover effort and seeks to acquire the firm making the initial takeover attempt.

Par Value of Bond See Principal.

Par Value of Common Stock The nominal value of shares of common stock as legally carried on the books of a corporation.

Participating Bond A bond that promises to pay a stated rate of interest to its owner, but may also pay additional interest if the issuer's earnings exceed a specified level.

Participation Certificate A bond which represents an ownership interest in a pool of fixed-income securities. The holders of the certificates receive the

interest and principal payments on the pooled securities in proportion to their ownership of the pool.

Passive Investment System (Alternatively, Passive Management.) The process of buying and holding a well-diversified portfolio.

Passive Management See Passive Investment System.

Payout Ratio The percentage of a firm's earnings paid to shareholders in the form of cash dividends.

Pegging The process by which investment bankers attempt to stabilize the price of an underwritten security in the secondary market for a period of time after the initial offering date.

Percentage Depletion Method A method of depleting natural resources for corporate income tax purposes that allows a stated percentage of the gross income from the property (before any costs) to be deducted as an expense during a given time period.

Perfect Markets Security markets in which no impediments to investing exist. These impediments include such things as finite divisibility of securities, taxes, transactions costs, and costly information.

Performance Attribution The identification of sources of returns for a portfolio or security over a particular evaluation interval of time.

Performance Margin The initial margin that must be posted by a futures buyer or seller.

Pink Sheets Written published quotations on over-the-counter stocks that are not listed on NASDAQ.

Poison Pill Defense A strategy used by corporations to ward off hostile takeovers. The targeted company gives its shareholders certain rights that can be exercised only in the event of a hostile takeover, and that, once exercised, will be extremely onerous to the acquirer.

Political Risk The uncertainty in the return on a foreign financial asset due to the possibility that the foreign government might take actions that are detrimental to the investor's financial interests.

Portfolio Construction (Alternatively, Security Selection.) A component of the investment process that involves identifying which assets to invest in and determining the proportion of funds to invest in each of the assets.

Portfolio Insurance An investment strategy designed to guarantee a minimum rate of return while allowing the investor to benefit substantially from the positive returns generated by an investment in a risky portfolio.

Portfolio Manager An individual who utilizes the information provided by financial analysts to construct a portfolio of financial assets.

Portfolio Performance Evaluation A component of the investment process involving periodic analysis of how a portfolio performed in terms of both returns earned and risk incurred.

Portfolio Revision A component of the investment process, involving periodically repeating the processes of setting investment policy, conducting security analysis, and constructing a portfolio.

Portfolio Turnover A measure of how much buying and selling occurs in a portfolio over a given period of time.

Positive Economics A form of economic analysis that is descriptive in nature, dealing with "what is."

Preemptive Rights When a corporation plans an issuance of new common shares, the right of existing shareholders to purchase the new shares in proportion to the number of shares that they currently own.

Preferred Stock A hybrid form of security that has characteristics of both common stocks and bonds.

Premium The price of an option contract.

Price-Earnings Ratio A corporation's current stock price divided by its earnings per share.

Price Impact The effect on the price of a security resulting from a trade in that security. Price impact is the result of several factors: size of the trade, demand for immediate liquidity, and presumed information of the individual or organization placing the order.

Price Relative The price of a security in one period divided by the price of that same security in a previous period.

Price-Weighted Market Index A market index in which the contribution of a security to the value of the index is a function of the security's current market price.

Primary Security Market The market in which securities are sold at the time of their initial issuance.

Principal (Alternatively, Face Value or Par Value of Bond) The nominal value of a bond which is repaid to bondholders at the maturity date.

Principle of Diminishing Returns The proposition that additional investments in a particular asset produce increasingly smaller additional returns.

Private Placement The direct sale of a newly issued security to one or a small number of large institutional investors.

Probabilistic Forecasting A form of security analysis which begins with a series of economic scenarios, along with their respective probabilities of occurrence. Under each of these scenarios, accompanying projections are made as to the prospects for various industries, companies, and stock prices.

Probability Distribution A model describing the

relative frequency of possible values that a random variable can assume.

Professional Money Manager An individual or organization that invests funds on behalf of others.

Program Trading The purchase or sale of a collection of securities as if the collection were one security. Program trades are prominently employed in portfolio insurance and index arbitrage strategies.

Promised Yield-to-Maturity The yield-to-maturity on a bond calculated assuming that all promised cash flows are received on a full and timely basis.

Prospectus The official selling circular that must be given to purchasers of new securities registered with the SEC. The prospectus provides various information about the issuer's business, its financial condition, and the nature of the security being offered.

Proxy The signing by a shareholder of a power of attorney, thereby authorizing a designated party to cast all of the shareholder's votes on any matter brought up at the corporation's annual meeting.

Proxy Fight An attempt by dissident shareholders to solicit proxies to vote against corporate incumbents.

Pseudo-American Model A model for valuing options on stocks that pay dividends over the life of the option. Values for an option are determined by assuming the option is either exercised early (just before each ex-dividend date for calls; just after each ex-dividend date for puts) or at expiration. The highest value obtained is the value of the option.

Purchase Group See Syndicate.

Purchasing-Power Risk The risk experienced by investors in financial assets due to uncertainty concerning the impact of inflation on the real returns produced by those financial assets.

Pure-Discount Security A fixed-income security that promises to make only one payment to its owner.

Pure Factor Play A portfolio which possesses a unit sensitivity to one factor, no sensitivity to any other factor, and has zero nonfactor risk.

Pure Yield Pickup Swap A type of bond swap where an investor exchanges one bond for another to obtain a higher yield over the long term, with little attention paid to the near-term outlook for the bonds' respective market segments or the market as a whole.

Put-Call Parity The relationship between the market price on a put and a call that have the same exercise price, expiration date, and underlying stock.

Put Option A contract that gives the buyer the right to sell a specific number of shares of a company to the writer at a specific price within a specific time period.

R-Squared See Coefficient of Determination.

Random Error Term The difference between the actual value of a random variable and the predicted value based on some model. For a security, the difference between its actual excess return and the excess return calculated from the security's characteristic line.

Random Variable A variable that takes on alternative values according to chance.

Random Walk (or Random Walk Model) In general, it refers to a situation in which changes in the value of a random variable are independent and identically distributed. When applied to common stocks, it refers to a situation in which security price changes are independent and identically distributed, meaning that the size of a security's price change from one period to the next can be viewed as being determined by the spin of a roulette wheel.

Rate Anticipation Swap A type of bond swap where an investor exchanges bonds that are expected to perform relatively poorly for those that are expected to perform relatively well, given an anticipated movement in interest rates.

Rate of Return The percentage change in the value of an investment in a financial asset (or portfolio of financial assets) over a specified time period.

Real Estate Investment Trust (REIT) An investment fund, similar to an investment company, whose investment objective is to hold primarily real-estate-related assets, either through mortgages, construction and development loans, or equity interests.

Real Investment An investment involving some kind of tangible asset, such as land, equipment, or buildings.

Real Return The percentage change in the value of an investment in a financial asset, where the beginning and ending values of the asset are adjusted for inflation over the time of the investment.

Realized Capital Gain (or Loss) A capital gain (or loss) on an asset that is recognized, for tax purposes, through the sale or exchange of the asset.

Red Herring A preliminary prospectus that provides much of the information in the final prospectus, but is not an offer to sell the security, nor does it display an actual offering price.

Redemption Fee (Alternatively, Back-End Load or Contingent Deferred Sales Charge or Exit Fee.) A fee levied by an investment company when an investor sells shares back to the investment company.

Regional Brokerage Firm An organization offering brokerage services that specializes in trading the securities of companies located in a particular region of the country.

Regional Exchange An organized exchange which specializes in trading the securities of companies located in a particular region of the country.

Registered Bond A bond for which the owner is registered with the issuer. The bondholder receives coupon payments directly from the issuer. Ownership changes require notification of the issuer.

Registered Competitive Market Maker See Floor Trader.

Registered Representative See Account Executive.

Registered Trader See Floor Trader.

Registrar A designated agent of a corporation responsible for canceling and issuing shares of stock in the corporation as these shares are issued or traded.

Registration Statement A document filed with the Securities and Exchange Commission prior to initiating a public security offering.

Reinvestment-Rate Risk The uncertainty in the return on a fixed-income asset caused by unanticipated changes in the interest rate at which cash flows from the asset can be reinvested.

Replacement Cost Accounting The use of estimated replacement costs instead of historical book-value costs when calculating corporate earnings.

Reported Earnings See Accounting Earnings.

Repurchase Agreement A type of money market instrument. It involves the sale of a financial asset from one investor to another. The investor selling the asset simultaneously agrees to repurchase it from the purchaser on a stated future date at a predetermined price, which is higher than the original transaction price.

Repurchase Offer An offer by the management of a corporation to buy back some of its own stock.

Residual Standard Deviation See Standard Deviation of the Random Error Term.

Restricted Account A margin account in which the actual margin has fallen below the initial margin requirement, but remains above the maintenance margin requirement.

Restricted Stock See Letter Stock.

Retention Ratio The percentage of a firm's earnings that are not paid to shareholders, but instead are retained by the firm. Equivalently, one minus the payout ratio.

Return Generating Process A statistical model which describes how the returns on a security are produced.

Return on Equity The earnings per share of a firm divided by the firm's book value per share.

Revenue Bond A municipal bond that is backed solely by the revenues from a designated project, authority, or agency, or by the proceeds from a specific tax.

Reverse Stock Split A form of stock split whereby the number of shares is reduced and the par value per share is increased.

Reversing Trade The purchase or sale of a futures (or options) contract designed to offset, and thereby cancel, the previous sale or purchase of the same contract.

Reward-to-Variability Ratio An ex post risk-adjusted measure of portfolio performance where risk is defined as the standard deviation of the portfolio's returns. Mathematically, over an evaluation interval, it is the excess return of a portfolio divided by the standard deviation of the portfolio's returns.

Reward-to-Volatility Ratio An ex post risk-adjusted measure of portfolio performance where risk is defined as the market risk of the portfolio. Mathematically, over an evaluation interval it is the excess return of a portfolio divided by the beta of the portfolio.

Right An option issued to existing shareholders that permits them to buy a specified number of new shares at a designated subscription price. For each shareholder, this number is proportional to the number of existing shares currently owned by the shareholder.

Rights Offering The sale of new stock conducted by first offering the stock to existing shareholders in proportion to the number of shares owned by each shareholder.

Risk The uncertainty associated with the end-of-period value of an investment in an asset or portfolio of assets.

Risk-Adjusted Return The return on an asset or portfolio, modified to explicitly account for the risk to which the asset or portfolio is exposed.

Risk-Averse Investor An investor who prefers an investment with less risk over one with more risk, assuming that both investments offer the same expected return.

Risk-free Asset An asset whose return over a given holding period is certain and known at the beginning of the holding period.

Risk-free Borrowing The act of borrowing funds that are to be repaid with a known rate of interest.

Risk-free Lending (Investing) The act of investing in a risk-free asset.

Risk-Neutral Investor An investor who has no preference between investments with varying levels of risk, assuming that the investments offer the same expected return.

Risk Premium   The difference between the expected yield-to-maturity of a risky bond and the expected yield-to-maturity of a similar default-free bond.

Risk-Seeking Investor   An investor who prefers an investment with more risk over one with less risk, assuming that both investments offer the same expected return.

Risk Structure   The set of yields-to-maturity across bonds that possess different degrees of default risk, but are similar with respect to other attributes.

Risk Tolerance   The trade-off between risk and expected return demanded by a particular investor.

Round Lot   An amount of stock generally equal to 100 shares or a multiple of 100 shares.

Savings   Foregone consumption. The difference between current income and current consumption.

Scalper   See Local.

Seat   The designation of membership in an organized exchange. By holding a seat, the member has the privilege of being able to execute trades using the facilities provided by the exchange.

Secondary Distribution   A means of selling a block of stock where the shares are sold away from an organized exchange after the close of trading in a manner similar to the sale of new issues of common stock.

Secondary Security Market   The market in which securities are traded that have been issued at some previous point in time.

Sector Factor   A factor which affects the return on securities within a particular economic sector.

Securities and Exchange Commission (SEC)   A federal agency established by the Securities Exchange Act of 1934 that regulates the issuance of securities in the primary market and the trading of securities in the secondary market.

Securities Investor Protection Corporation (SIPC)   A quasi-governmental agency that insures the accounts of brokers against loss due to the brokerage firm's failure.

Security   (Alternatively, Financial Asset.) A legal representation of the right to receive prospective future benefits under stated conditions.

Security Analysis   A component of the investment process that involves determining the prospective future benefits of a security, the conditions under which such benefits will be received, and the likelihood of such conditions occurring.

Security Analyst   See Financial Analyst.

Security Market   See Financial Market.

Security Market Line   Derived from the CAPM, a linear relationship between the expected returns on securities and the risk of those securities, with risk expressed as the security's beta (or equivalently, the security's covariance with the market portfolio).

Security Selection   See Portfolio Construction.

Selectivity   An aspect of security analysis which entails forecasting the price movements of individual securities.

Self-Regulation   A method of governmental regulation where the rules and standards of conduct in security markets are set by firms that operate in these markets, subject to the oversight of various federal agencies such as the SEC and CFTC.

Selling Group   A group of investment banking organizations who, as part of a security underwriting are responsible for selling the security.

Semistrong-Form Market Efficiency   A level of market efficiency in which all relevant publicly available information is fully and immediately reflected in security prices.

Sensitivity   See Factor Loading.

Separation Theorem   A feature of the Capital Asset Pricing Model which states that the optimal combination of risky assets for an investor can be determined without any knowledge about the investor's preferences towards risk and return.

Serial Bond   A bond issue with different portions of the issue maturing at different dates.

Settle Price   The representative price for a futures contract determined during the closing period of the futures exchange.

Settlement Date   The date after a security has been traded, on which the buyer must deliver cash to the seller and the seller must deliver the security to the buyer.

Shelf Registration   Under SEC Rule 415, issuers may register securities in advance of their issuance and sell these securities up to a year later.

Short Hedger   A hedger who offsets risk by selling futures contracts.

Short Interest Position   The number of shares of a given company that have been sold short and, as of a given date, the loans remain outstanding.

Short Sale   The sale of a security that is not owned by an investor, but rather is borrowed from a broker. The investor eventually repays the broker in kind by purchasing the same security in a subsequent transaction.

Simple Linear Regression   (Alternatively, Ordinary Least Squares.) A statistical model of the relationship between two random variables in which one variable is hypothesized to be linearly related to the other. This relationship is depicted by a regres-

sion line which is a straight line, "fitted" to pairs of values of the two variables, so that the sum of the squared random error terms is minimized.

Sinking Fund Periodic payments made by a bond issuer to reduce, in an orderly manner, the amount of outstanding principal on a bond issue over the life of the bond.

Size Effect (Alternatively, Small Firm Effect.) An empirical regularity whereby stock returns appear to differ consistently across the spectrum of market capitalization. Over extended priods of time, smaller capitalization stocks have outperformed larger capitalization stocks on a risk-adjusted basis.

Small Firm Effect See Size Effect.

Soft Dollars Brokerage commissions ostensibly paid for having a brokerage firm execute a trade and indirectly designated, in part, as payment for non-trade-related services rendered.

Special Offering A trade involving a large block of stock on an organized security exchange whereby a number of brokerage firms attempt to execute the order by soliciting offsetting orders from their customers.

Specialist A member of an organized exchange who has two primary functions. First, the specialist maintains an orderly market in assigned securities by acting as a dealer: buying and selling from his or her inventory of securities to offset temporary imbalances in the number of buy and sell orders. Second, the specialist facilitates the execution of limit, stop, and stop limit orders by acting as a broker. This is done by maintaining a limit order book and executing these orders as they are triggered.

Specialist Block Purchase or Sale The accommodation of a relatively small block trade by a specialist, who buys or sells from his or her inventory at a price negotiated with the seller or buyer.

Specialist's Book See Limit Order Book.

Speculative Grade Bonds (Alternatively, Junk Bonds.) Bonds which are not investment grade bonds. Usually, speculative bonds have a BB (Standard & Poor's) or Ba (Moody's) or lower rating.

Speculator An investor in future contracts whose primary objective is to make a profit from buying and selling these contracts.

Split-Funding A situation in which an institutional investor divides its funds among two or more professional money managers.

Spot Market The market for an asset which involves the immediate exchange of the asset for cash.

Spot Price The purchase price of an asset in the spot market.

Spot Rate The annual yield-to-maturity on a pure-discount security.

Standard Deviation A measure of the dispersion of possible outcomes around the expected outcome of a random variable.

Standard Deviation of the Random Error Term (Alternatively, Residual Standard Deviation.) In the context of simple linear regression, a measure of the dispersion of possible outcomes of the random error term.

Standard Error of Alpha The standard deviation of a security's estimated alpha, as derived from the ex post characteristic line.

Standard Error of Beta The standard deviation of a security's estimated beta, as derived from the ex post characteristic line.

Standardized Unexpected Earnings The difference between a firm's actual earnings over a given period less an estimate of the firm's expected earnings, with this quantity divided by the standard deviation of the firm's previous earnings forecast errors.

Standby Agreement An arrangement between a security issuer and an underwriter as part of a rights offering. The underwriter agrees to purchase at a fixed price all securities not purchased by current stockholders.

Stochastic Process Risk In the context of immunization, the risk that the yield curve will shift in a way that prevents an immunized bond portfolio from producing its expected cash inflows.

Stock Dividend An accounting transaction that distributes stock to existing shareholders in proportion to the number of shares currently owned by the shareholders. A stock dividend entails a transfer from retained earnings to the capital stock account of a dollar amount that is equal to the market value of the distributed stock.

Stock Split Similar to a stock dividend, an accounting transaction that increases the amount of stock held by existing shareholders in proportion to the number of shares currently owned by the shareholders. A stock split entails a reduction in the par value of the corporation's stock and the simultaneous exchange of a multiple number of new shares for each existing share.

Stop Limit Order A trading order that specifies both a stop price and a limit price. If the security's price reaches or passes the stop price, then a limit order is created at the limit price.

Stop Loss Order See Stop Order.

Stop Order (Alternatively, Stop Loss Order.) A trading order that specifies a stop price. If the security's price reaches or passes the stop price, then a market order is created.

Stop Price The price specified by an investor when a stop order or a stop limit order is placed that defines

the price at which the market order or limit order for the security is to become effective.

Straddle   An options strategy which involves buying (or writing) both a call and a put on the same asset, with the options having the same exercise price and expiration date.

Straight Line Method   A method of calculating depreciation for corporate income tax purposes that allocates the cost of a fixed asset equally over the estimated useful life of the asset.

Straight Voting System   See Majority Voting System.

Street Name   An arrangement between an investor and a brokerage firm where the investor maintains an account in which the investor's securities are registered in the name of the brokerage firm.

Striking Price   See Exercise Price.

Strong-Form Market Efficiency   A level of market efficiency in which all relevant information, both public and private, is fully and immediately reflected in security prices.

Subordinated Debenture   A debenture whose claims, in the event of bankruptcy, are junior to other bonds issued by the firm.

Subscription Price   The price at which holders of rights are permitted to purchase shares of stock in a rights offering.

Substitution Swap   A type of bond swap where an investor exchanges one bond with a lower yield for another with a higher yield, yet both bonds have essentially the same financial characteristics.

Super Designated Order Turnaround (Super DOT)   A set of special procedures established by the New York Stock Exchange to handle routine small trading orders. Through these procedures, participating member firms can route orders directly to the specialist for immediate execution.

Supply of Capital   The quantity of capital offered by investors at varying interest rate levels.

Supply-to-Sell Schedule   A description of the quantities of a security that an investor is prepared to sell at alternative prices.

Sustainable Earnings   The amount of earnings that a firm could pay out each year, with the result that the firm's future earnings neither increase nor decrease.

Syndicate (Alternatively, Purchase Group.)   A group of investment banking organizations that, as part of a security underwriting, are responsible for purchasing the security from the issuer and reselling it to the public.

Synthetic Futures (Synthetic Futures Contract)   The creation of a position equivalent to either the purchase of a futures contract by buying a call option and writing a put option on the asset or to the sale of a futures contract by buying a put option and writing a call option on the asset.

Synthetic Put   A form of portfolio insurance that emulates the investment outcomes of a put option through the use of a dynamic asset allocation strategy.

Systematic Risk   See Market Risk.

Takeover   An action by an individual or firm to acquire controlling interest in a corporation.

Target Firm   A firm that is the subject of a takeover attempt.

Tax-Exempt Bond   A security whose income is not taxable by the federal government.

Taxable Municipal Bond   A municipal bond whose income is fully taxable by the federal government.

Technical Analysis   A form of security analysis which attempts to forecast the movement in the prices of securities based primarily on historical price and volume trends in those securities.

Tender Offer   A form of corporate takeover in which a firm or individual offers to buy some or all of the shares of a target firm at a stated price. This offer is publicly advertised and material describing the bid is mailed to the target's stockholders.

Term Bond   A bond issue where all of the bonds mature on the same date.

Term Structure   The set of yields-to-maturity across bonds that possess different terms-to-maturity, but are similar with respect to other attributes.

Term-to-Maturity   The time remaining until a bond's maturity date.

Terminal Wealth   The value of an investor's portfolio at the end of a holding period. Equivalently, the investor's initial wealth multiplied times one plus the rate of return earned on the investor's portfolio over the holding period.

Third Market   A secondary security market where exchange-listed securities are traded over the counter.

Time Deposit   A savings account at a financial institution.

Time Value (Premium)   The excess of the market price of an option over its intrinsic value.

Time-Weighted Return   A method of measuring the performance of a portfolio over a particular period of time. It is the cumulative compounded rate of return of the portfolio, calculated on each date that a cash flow moves into or out of the portfolio over the performance measurement period.

Timing An aspect of security analysis which entails forecasting the price movements of asset classes relative to one another.

Top-Down Forecasting A sequential approach to security analysis which entails first making forecasts for the economy, then for industries, and finally for individual companies. Each level of forecasts is conditional on the previous level of forecasts made.

Total Risk The standard deviation of the return on a security or portfolio.

Trading Halt A temporary suspension in the trading of a security on an organized exchange.

Trading Post The physical location on the floor of an organized exchange where a specialist in a particular stock is located and where all orders involving the stock must be taken for execution.

Transfer Agent A designated agent of a corporation, usually a bank, which administers the transfer of shares of a corporation's stock between old and new owners.

Treasury Bill A security issued by the U.S. Treasury with a maximum term-to-maturity of one year. Interest and principal are paid only at maturity.

Treasury Bond A security issued by the U.S. Treasury with a term-to-maturity of over seven years. Interest is paid semiannually and principal is returned at maturity.

Treasury Note A security issued by the U.S. Treasury with a term-to-maturity between one and seven years. Interest is paid semiannually and principal is returned at maturity.

Treasury Stock Common stock which has been issued by a corporation and then later purchased by the corporation in the open market or through a tender offer. This stock does not include voting rights or rights to receive dividends and is equivalent economically to unissued stock.

Triple Witching Hour The date when options on individual stocks and market indices, futures on market indices, and options on market index futures expire simultaneously.

Trustee An organization, usually a bank, which serves as the representative of bondholders. The trustee acts to protect the interests of bondholders and facilitates communication between them and the issuer.

Unbiased Expectations Theory An explanation of the term structure of interest rates. It holds that a forward rate represents the average opinion of the expected future spot rate for the time period in question.

Undermargined Account A margin account in which the actual margin has fallen below the maintenance margin requirement.

Underpriced Security (Alternatively, Undervalued Security:) A security whose expected return is greater than its equilibrium expected return. Equivalently; a security with a positive alpha.

Undervalued Security See Underpriced Security:

Underwriter See Investment Banker.

Underwriting The process by which investment bankers bring new securities to the primary security market.

Unexpected Rate of Inflation That portion of inflation experienced over a given period of time that was not anticipated by investors.

Unique Risk (Alternatively, Unsystematic Risk.) That part of a security's total risk which is not related to moves in the market portfolio and, hence, can be diversified away.

Unit Investment Trust An unmanaged investment company with a finite life that raises an initial sum of capital from investors and uses the proceeds to purchase a fixed portfolio of securities (typically bonds).

Unrealized Capital Gain (or Loss) A capital gain (or loss) on an asset that has not yet been recognized for tax purposes through the sale or exchange of the asset.

Unrestricted Account See Overmargined Account.

Unseasoned Offering See Initial Public Offering.

Unsystematic Risk See Unique Risk.

Upstairs Dealer Market An adjunct to organized exchanges, where block houses who are member firms handle large block trades. The block houses act as both agents and principals, lining up trading partners to take the other side of the block orders.

Up-Tick A trade in a security made at a price higher than the price of the previous trade in that same security.

Value-Weighted Market Index (Alternatively, Capitalization-Weighted Market Index.) A market index in which the contribution of a security to the value of the index is a function of the security's market capitalization.

Variable Annuity A series of payments that may vary over time depending on the performance of a specific segment of the financial markets.

Variable Rate See Floating Rate.

Variance The squared value of the standard deviation.

Variance-Covariance Matrix A table which symmetrically arrays the covariances between a number of random variables. Variances of the ran-

dom variables lie on the diagonal of the matrix, while covariances between the random variables lie above and below the diagonal.

Voting Bond A bond that gives its holder a voice in the management of the issuer.

Wash Sale The sale and subsequent purchase of a "substantially identical" security solely for the purpose of generating a tax deductable capital loss.

Weak-Form Market Efficiency A level of market efficiency in which all previous security price data is fully and immediately reflected in current security prices.

Weekend Effect See Day-of-the-Week Effect.

White Knight Another firm, favorably inclined toward a target firm's current management, which during the process of a hostile takeover of that corporation, agrees to make a better offer to the corporation's stockholders.

Yield The yield-to-maturity of a bond.

Yield Curve A visual representation of the term structure of interest rates.

Yield Spread The difference in the promised yields-to-maturity of two bonds.

Yield Structure The set of yields-to-maturity

across bonds differing in terms of a number of attributes. These attributes include term-to-maturity, coupon rate, call provisions, tax status, marketability, and likelihood of default.

Yield-to-Call The yield-to-maturity of a callable bond calculated assuming that the bond is called at the earliest possible time.

Yield-to-Maturity For a particular fixed-income security, the single interest rate (with interest compounded at some specified interval) that, if paid by a bank on the amount invested in the security, would enable the investor to obtain all the payments made by that security. Equivalently, the discount rate that equates the present value of future cash flows from the security to the current market price of the security.

Zero Coupon Bond See Pure-Discount Security.

Zero Growth Model (Alternatively, No Growth Model.) A type of dividend discount model in which dividends are assumed to maintain a constant value in perpetuity.

Zero-Plus Tick A trade in a security made at a price equal to that of the previous trade in that security but higher than that of the last trade made in the security at a different price.

INDEX